Law for Estate Management Students

Law for Estate Management Students

SECOND EDITION

by **RICHARD CARD,** LLM
Professor of Law and Head of Department of Legal Studies, Trent Polytechnic

JOHN MURDOCH, LLB
Lecturer in Law at the University of Reading

and **PETER SCHOFIELD,** BA
Lecturer in Law at the University of Reading

London
Butterworths
1986

United Kingdom	Butterworth & Co (Publishers) Ltd, 88 Kingsway, LONDON WC2B 6AB and 61A North Castle Street, EDINBURGH EH2 3LJ
Australia	Butterworths Pty Ltd, SYDNEY, MELBOURNE, BRISBANE, ADELAIDE PERTH, CANBERRA and HOBART
Canada	Butterworths. A division of Reed Inc, TORONTO and VANCOUVER
New Zealand	Butterworths of New Zealand Ltd, WELLINGTON and AUCKLAND
Singapore	Butterworth & Co (Asia) Pte Ltd, SINGAPORE
South Africa	Butterworth Publishers (Pty) Ltd, DURBAN and PRETORIA
USA	Butterworth Legal Publishers, ST PAUL, Minnesota, SEATTLE, Washington, BOSTON, Massachusetts, AUSTIN, Texas and D & S PUBLISHERS, CLEARWATER, Florida

© Butterworth & Co (Publishers) Ltd 1986

British Library Cataloguing in Publication Data

Card, Richard
  Law for estate management students.—
  2nd ed.
  1. Land use—Law and legislation—
  England 2. Law—England
  I. Title II. Murdoch, J. R. III. Schofield
  P.G.
  344.2′0024333 KD1125

ISBN 0 406 56291 1

Typeset by Latimer Trend & Company Ltd, Plymouth
Printed in Great Britain by Thomson Litho Ltd.
East Kilbride, Scotland

Preface

We were prompted to write the first edition of this book by the belief that there is a need for a comprehensive textbook for estate management students studying courses in basic legal topics, particularly one which treats the subject matter in some depth. The response to the first edition has confirmed our belief.

We have had in mind the syllabuses for examinations in basic legal subjects for degrees in estate management, land management and allied fields, as well as those for the comparable examinations of the Royal Institution of Chartered Surveyors, the Incorporated Society of Valuers and Auctioneers, and other professional bodies. Despite its title, this book should also prove useful for those following similar courses in law for other types of qualification.

This book is divided into four parts. Part I outlines the English legal system, and also describes elements of constitutional law. Parts II, III and IV deal with the law of contract, the law of tort, and land law, respectively. As with the previous edition, in Parts I and II, we have drawn extensively on the companion work, Card and James, *Law for Accountancy Students*. The need to produce a book of a manageable size has meant that we have not dealt with what may be regarded as the more specialist legal subjects studied by estate management students, such as planning law, local government law, or the law of landlord and tenant.

We thank all who have helped us. We owe special debts to Miss Jennifer James, who contributed paras. 1.11 to 1.24, to our wives for their assistance in various ways in the preparation of this book, and to the publishers for compiling the table of cases and statutes and the index.

We have tried to summarise and explain the law as it had been reported on 1 November 1985, although, by amendments at proof stage, we have been able to indicate a few particularly important changes which occurred up to 1 March 1986.

1 March 1986   Richard Card
                                                                 John Murdoch
                                                                 Peter Schofield

Contents

Contents

Contents

Table of statutes

Table of statutes

List of cases

List of cases

List of cases

List of cases

Part I

Outline of the English legal system

Chapter 1
Introduction

1.1 It must be stressed at the beginning that this book is concerned with aspects of *English* law. The laws and legal systems of Scotland and, to a lesser extent, Northern Ireland are distinct from those of England and Wales, and while Scots and Northern Irish law may coincide with English law in certain fields it cannot be assumed that this is always the case.

It is usual to divide English law into categories. These categories are not laid down by any statute but have been devised as aids to exposition. They are by no means hard and fast, and there may be differences of opinion as to the category into which some area of the law falls. For example, the rules relating to vicarious liability, whereby the law regards one person as liable for the torts of another, may be regarded as a distinct category of law, or as falling within the larger categories of employment law or the law of tort.

One set of facts may involve more than one category of law. If A, a taxi-driver, hits a lamp post while driving you to the station, and injures you, the law of contract, the law of tort and criminal law may all be applicable. A has certainly broken his contract to drive you to the station, and if his driving was careless this may occasion not only criminal liability but also tortious liability for any injury occasioned by it. This example illustrates classification of law by reference to the subject matter of the dispute. Common examples of 'subject matter classification' are: the law of contract, the law of tort, criminal law, commercial law, and the law of property.

Law may also be classified by reference to the source of a particular rule.

Classification by reference to the subject matter of a dispute
1.2 When using this method of classification, a major distinction can be drawn between civil and criminal law. It is criminal law which occupies most of the attention of non-lawyers, but lawyers are frequently more concerned with non-criminal, ie civil, law. Civil law can be sub-divided into categories, for example, contract and tort, and these categories of civil law are no less important than criminal law.

1.3 It is surprisingly difficult in theory, though not in practice, to distinguish between civil and criminal law. Criminal cases, which are called prosecutions, are normally initiated by the state, but they may be brought by a private citizen, although this is rare. If a prosecution is successful the accused, or defendant, is liable to punishment. This affords no direct benefit to the victim of the crime since he does not receive fines payable or the fruits of a criminal's labours in prison. The victims of some crimes, such as an attempted theft or blackmail, may have suffered no loss from the commission of the crime anyway. Some crimes can be committed without there being a victim to suffer loss, for example, treason and some offences involving obscene publications. Although punishment does not compensate victims, it is now possible for the criminal courts to order the criminal to make reparation directly to his victim under the Powers of Criminal Courts Act 1973. The victim of a criminal offence cannot prevent a prosecution nor order its discontinuance, however much he may wish to avoid a criminal trial.

In contrast, civil actions are brought by an individual (the plaintiff) who is seeking to obtain compensation for the loss he has suffered or to establish his legal rights. If damages are awarded as the result of a successful civil action, they are payable to the plaintiff and are generally assessed on the basis that they should compensate him and not punish the defendant. In certain restricted circumstances the courts may award punitive damages, which are designed both to compensate the plaintiff and to punish the defendant, but all the damages are payable to the plaintiff and not merely the compensatory element. A plaintiff is not required to commence a civil action and he can discontinue it at any time before judgment.

Facts which disclose a criminal offence may also form the basis of a civil action but the victim cannot have both claims adjudicated by the same court. It is necessary to bring a separate civil action as well as any prosecution which the state may initiate.

1.4   In parts II to IV of this book we concentrate on three of the principal categories of civil law: the law of contract, the law of tort and land law. There are many other generally accepted categories of civil law, some of which involve elements of one or more of those three, such as:

a. *Commercial law* This is concerned with special contractual situations — agency, sale of goods, consumer credit and other matters relating to business transactions.

b. *Employment law* This again involves special and general rules of contract but it also embraces statutory rights and obligations between employer and employee. It includes such topics as health and safety at work (much of which is also covered by the law of tort) and unfair dismissal.

c. *Company law* Companies are legal persons and are subject to special rules both common law and statutory, partly because they are artificial legal persons and partly because of the need to regulate their dealings with shareholders, employees and creditors.

d. *Constitutional law* This is a slightly different category of law in that it is that branch of the law which regulates the principal organs of government and their impact on the individual citizen, as opposed to providing rules which regulate the relationship between one member of society and another.

e. *The law of evidence* This determines how facts are proved in a case, by whom and to what standard. Certain aspects may be relevant to those in the surveying and related professions. Consequently, we consider elements of the law of civil evidence at the end of this chapter.

Classification by reference to the source of the legal rule
1.5 It is also possible to classify law by reference to its source. Common law and legislation are sources of law.

Common law and legislation[1]
1.6 Common law means judge-made law. It is contained in the decisions or judgments made by the judiciary over many centuries. Legislation comprises Acts of Parliament, subordinate legislation (examples of which are byelaws and statutory instruments deriving their authority from Acts of Parliament) and the legislation of the European Communities. Legislation can change the common law, but judges cannot change or ignore legislation, although their interpretation of it may occasionally stultify or modify the wishes of Parliament. Some categories of law, the law of contract and the law of tort for example, are almost entirely based on judicial decisions, and such legislation as amends them is narrow in its scope, whereas much of the law relating to land has a statutory basis. Sometimes, Acts of Parliament seek merely to clarify and codify existing law, but they may create a body of rights and duties where none existed before.[2]

1   Ch 3 below.
2   Many of the provisions of employment law are of this type.

Common law and equity
1.7 The common law can be further sub-divided into common law and equity. If both are branches of the common law and therefore both judge-made law, wherein lies the difference between them? The difference between them is that of their origins. Prior to the Judicature Acts of 1873–1875 there were two systems of courts in England, the common law courts and the Court of Chancery.

1.8 The common law courts had evolved from the centralised system for the administration of justice developed by a powerful monarchy between the eleventh and thirteenth centuries, which had gradually ousted the jurisdiction of the local courts. Therefore, common law is that body of law developed by the common law courts, such as the Court of Exchequer (whose judges were called Barons), the Court of Common Pleas and the Court of King's Bench, prior to the fusion of the administration of justice in 1875, and modifications and extensions effected since 1875. The common law is not static but subject to constant affirmation, revision and development by modern judges.

It is generally accepted that it was only the administration of the law, and not the law itself, which was fused in 1875 and thus it is still possible to speak of common law and equity as distinct bodies of law. Since 1875 a case involving both common law and equitable principles can be heard in one court which can, where necessary, apply both sets of rules. Prior to 1875 the unfortunate litigant might have had to bring two actions—one to establish his common law rights and another before the Court of Chancery to establish his equitable rights. An even more unfortunate party might have succeeded at common law, but have had the efficacy of the court's judgment nullified in equitable proceedings.

1.9 Equity is that body of law developed in the Court of Chancery prior to 1875 and its subsequent amendments and developments. The Court of Chancery developed later than the common law courts because of defects in those courts and in the law which they administered; the common law courts had entangled themselves in an extremely rigid procedure which made it difficult to initiate actions and severely limited the development of the common law, and the remedies available in the common law courts for the successful litigant were inadequate. Thus, the habit arose in the fourteenth and fifteenth centuries of petitioning the King to remedy injustice. After a while, the King delegated the task of determining these petitions to his Chancellor. Initially, the Chancellor decided cases in the name of the King but in 1474 he began to do so in his own name, and this marked the beginning of the Court of Chancery presided over by the Lord Chancellor. Until 1529, the Lord Chancellor was an ecclesiastic whose decisions were supposedly guided by conscience but thereafter he was a lawyer. The procedure in the Court of Chancery was originally less rigid than that of the common law courts; and the basis of decisions was supposed to be the merits of each action and what was just between the parties, with little reference to previous cases. Subsequently, both procedure and substantive law became more rigid; the notion of creating a remedy to fit the particular case before the court disappeared and the Court of Chancery became as much influenced by previous cases as the common law courts. By the nineteenth century the Court of Chancery had a well deserved reputation for tardiness. This was due to the fact that until 1813 all cases were heard by the Lord Chancellor, quite apart from the innate conservatism and caution of some Lord Chancellors.

The rules of equity developed by the Court of Chancery were concerned either with entirely new rights totally unknown to the common law or with remedies (such as rectification and specific performance) designed to counter the inefficacy or injustice of the common law. Equity did not amend the common law but enabled a litigant who had failed to establish a claim at common law, or been disappointed by the remedies available there, to seek an equitable remedy which made good the defects of the common law in a particular case. For example, contracts for the sale of land, if they are to be effective at common law, must comply with the formal requirements of the Law of Property Act 1925, s40, but a sale of land ineffective at common law for failure to comply in this way may be enforced in equity because of its doctrine of part performance.[1] The common law position is not abrogated by the equitable doctrine: it is merely circumvented by equity in appropriate cases.

1   Para 43.18 below.

1.10 Even modern courts, which administer both common law and equity, will tend to consider the common law first and then see if it is affected by equity. This process is reversed where a case is concerned with a body of rules developed almost entirely by equity, for example the law of trusts. If there is a conflict between the rules of the common law and those of equity, the rules of equity prevail.[1] It cannot be emphasised too much that the remedies developed by equity cannot be demanded as of right (unlike common law remedies) but, reflecting the origins of equity in conscience, are discretionary and may or may not be awarded by the court. A litigant who has acted unfairly or inequitably may find that the court will decline to award an equitable remedy and that he must be content with common law remedies. If, for example, a purchaser delays completing the purchase of a house, the vendor has a right to the common law remedy of damages for breach of the contract of sale but no right to have the completion enforced by an order for the equitable remedy of specific performance of the contract (although he may be awarded it at the court's discretion).

1   Now enacted in the Supreme Court Act 1981, s49.

Elements of civil evidence

1.11   When a civil case comes to court,[1] the judge[2] is required to decide what happened in fact and then apply the law to those facts. The rules of law determine what facts are relevant in a particular case (the 'facts in issue'); the rules of evidence determine which party is required to prove (or disprove) those facts, to what standard and also what material can be tendered in evidence.

1   Most legal claims are, in practice, settled out of court.
2   Judges sit without juries in all but a handful of civil cases.

The burden and standard of proof
The burden of proof
1.12   The burden of proof is the requirement placed upon a party to proceedings to prove, to the requisite standard, a fact in issue in those proceedings. Failure by such a party to adduce sufficient evidence on an issue results in it being lost. Hence a party bringing an action for breach of contract must prove the existence of the contract and breach by the defendant. Failure to prove the existence of the contract is fatal to the plaintiff's case for then there can be no issue of breach.

In civil cases the burden of proof generally rests upon the party making a claim: he is alleging that he has a cause of action so he must prove all facts necessary in law to establish that cause of action. Similarly, a party defending an action bears the burden of proving any defence on which he proposes to rely. It must be stressed that this is a general rule and there are exceptions in most areas of civil litigation. Generally, the allocation of the burden of proof on a particular issue is well established by previous cases.

1.13   A party who prima facie bears the burden of proof on an issue may be able to rely upon a presumption of law (an assumption drawn on his behalf by the judges) to satisfy the burden of proof cast upon him. For an illustration of a presumption of law and its operation see paras 20.16 to 20.19 below, in which *res ipsa loquitur* is discussed.

The standard of proof
1.14   A party bearing a burden of proof on an issue in a civil case will be required to prove the existence (or non-existence) of that issue on 'a balance of probabilities'. He is not required to produce absolute proof, nor prove the issue beyond reasonable doubt; instead, he must convince the court that it is more probable than not that the facts he is asserting are true.

7

However the balance of probabilities is a remarkably flexible standard and in some cases, e g when a party to a civil action alleges fraud or some other criminal offence on the part of his opponent,[1] the court takes more convincing than usual before it will hold that the burden of proof is satisfied.

Any single piece of cogent evidence (perhaps the testimony of a single witness or even that of the plaintiff himself) can be sufficient to satisfy the burden of proof cast upon a party. It is rarely a legal requirement that an issue can be won only if there is supporting or corroborative evidence. One good witness may convince a judge and the case be won despite a plethora of witnesses supporting the opposition case if they are less than convincing. Of course, the more credible the evidence that can be gathered by a party the more likely the balance of probabilities will be held to have tipped in his favour.

1   See for example, *R v Milk Marketing Board, ex p Austin* (1983) Times, 21 March: allegation that Austin 'watered' the milk he sold had to be proved beyond reasonable doubt because such a finding affected his livelihood.

Admissibility of evidence

1.15   Material will be considered by a court only if it is both relevant to an issue before the court and admissible as evidence.

Provided that material is admissible as evidence it can be oral, documentary or 'real'. Real evidence consists of material objects, other than documents, open to inspection by the court. Printouts from breath/alcohol testing machines,[1] an automatic radar trace of a ship's course,[2] and even a dog, which was the subject of the action in that it was alleged to be dangerous,[3] have been produced in court (the dog was kept on a chain).

Essentially anyone is a competent witness (ie can choose to give evidence) in a civil case and can be asked questions and be required to answer them on any relevant issue[4] provided that the answers are admissible as evidence.

The two principal cases in which material will not be admitted as evidence are when such material constitutes:

a. an opinion; or

b. hearsay.

1   *Castle v Cross* [1985] 1 All ER 87, [1984] 1 WLR 1372, DC.
2   *The Statue of Liberty* [1968] 2 All ER 195, [1968] 1 WLR 739.
3   *Line v Taylor* (1892) 3 F & F 731.
4   A competent and compellable witness may be permitted to refuse to answer questions about matters which are the subject of a privilege. For example, a lawyer's communications with his client and certain matters affecting the public good are privileged.

Opinion

1.16   A non-expert witness must state facts and not give his opinion on or draw inferences from those facts. The court is the body to decide the significance of evidence and not the witness. However, it is frequently impossible to distinguish fact and opinion absolutely and a witness is allowed to give his opinion as a means of conveying relevant facts. A witness is entitled to say that a vehicle seemed to be travelling very fast, giving reasons for this view, but could not say that the driver was negligent.

1.17 *Expert witnesses* A witness who is an expert on a particular area can state facts *and* give his opinion on those facts, provided that the issue about which the opinion is being given requires expert analysis. A witness is an expert if the judge rules him to be qualified in the relevant area either formally or by appropriate experience.

It must be stressed that merely because a witness is an expert he cannot give his opinions on anything and everything. Expert opinion evidence is admitted only when the issue falls within the area of expertise of the witness (surveyors are experts but not on medical matters) *and* the judge needs assistance in drawing inferences from the facts before the court. In *Alchemy (International) Ltd* v *Tattersalls Ltd*,[1] the judge permitted several experts to testify as to what was, in their opinion, the appropriate procedure to follow in the event of a disputed bit at an auction. Having ruled that this was a case where an auctioneer could not be negligent if he followed sound commercial practice, ie a practice regarded as appropriate by a body of competent professionals, the judge considered the expert opinion evidence on what was sound commercial practice. On the facts he found no negligence on the part of the defendant auctioneers.

1   (1985) 276 Estates Gazette 675.

1.18 An expert witness can give an opinion (where appropriate) on facts before the court even if his view of those facts is necessarily moulded not merely by his own direct knowledge of such matters but also by the expertise of others in his field. Thus an expert called upon to value property can rely not only on his own direct knowledge of property values but also on his general knowledge of property values derived from reports of valuations conducted by others (whether published or unpublished).[1] However, while an expert's opinion may be moulded by reports etc. provided by other experts in the field, he cannot narrate the contents of such reports as *facts* in the case, to do so would be to admit hearsay evidence.[1]

A party wishing to call an expert witness should seek leave to do so from the court and the court can order advance disclosure of any expert's report to the opposing party.

1   *English Exporters (London) Ltd* v *Eldonwall Ltd* [1973] Ch 415, [1973] 1 All ER 726.

Hearsay
1.19 A statement of fact (or opinion) made by a person who is not giving oral evidence in proceedings is hearsay evidence and prima facie inadmissible. An out of court statement of fact (or opinion) made by a witness in proceedings is also inadmissible hearsay if it does not differ from the witness's in-court testimony. Thus, in theory, a witness testifying in an action cannot tell the court what X, who is not a witness, said to him nor what he said out of court to X. However the statutory and common law exceptions to the hearsay rule dramatically reduce the scope of the hearsay rule. Indeed one could almost say that in civil cases the hearsay rule has been abolished by the Civil Evidence Act 1968[1] which we now discuss.

1   This Act does not apply in magistrates' courts but they hear very few civil actions.

1.20 *Civil Evidence Act 1968, s2* Provided that the three following con-

9

ditions are satisfied this section permits the reception of some out of court hearsay statements (oral or documentary).

a. Certain procedures must be complied with (eg notice of intention to rely on the relevant statement must be given to the opposing party). Compliance can be waived by the judge.

b. Leave to admit the statement must be given by the judge.

c. The information contained in the out of court statement must be such that a witness could give that information in evidence directly.

If these conditions are satisfied s2 allows a witness to narrate statements which *he* made out of court and also permits a witness to testify as to out of court statements made *to him* by another person whether or not that other is also giving evidence in the proceedings. A witness can narrate what was said to him by another who is not testifying provided there is good reason for the maker of the statement not giving evidence.[1]

Section 2 would permit a building society which commissioned a property valuation report from a valuer to use that report as evidence in a case if the valuer, if called, could have testified as to the matters detailed in his report.

1 Civil Evidence Act 1968, s8, lists good reasons, eg that the witness cannot, after the exercise of due diligence, be found or is dead or cannot be expected to remember the details of his out of court statement.

1.21 Evidence admissible under s2 (sometimes called first-hand hearsay) can be given such weight as the court thinks appropriate taking into account the circumstances in which the statement was made.[1] Relevant circumstances include whether it was made shortly after the incident detailed in the statement and whether the maker of the statement had an incentive to conceal or misrepresent the facts.

1 Civil Evidence Act, ss6 and 7.

1.22 *Civil Evidence Act 1968, s4* This section permits the reception of 'second-hand hearsay' in limited cases. Second-hand hearsay consists of material compiled by a person who is not a witness from information supplied by yet another person or persons. (Material compiled by a non-witness but from his own observations is admissible under s2.)

An example of second-hand hearsay would be if a manager of a building society, X, purported to relate the contents of a valuation report given him by Y, a partner in a firm of surveyors (who is not giving evidence), that valuation report being based on information supplied by Z, an employee of the partnership.

1.23 Section 4 permits the reception of second-hand hearsay contained in a *document* provided that:

a. the document forms part of a record[1] compiled by a person acting under a duty (eg hospital reports, manufacturers' records, professional reports and certain computer records[2]); and

b. the material contained in that document was compiled by a person who had a duty to make such a compilation from information supplied by a person who had actual knowledge of that information. Such information must have been given to the compiler either directly or via an intermediary who had a duty to pass on the information; and

c. direct oral testimony on the matters contained in the record would have been admissible.

Hence in the example in the previous paragraph the building society manager could narrate the contents of the valuation report.

As with s2, appropriate procedures must be complied with and leave given by the court before evidence is admissible under s4. The court, as with s2, may give such weight to evidence admitted under s4 as it thinks appropriate in the circumstances.

1   This is not defined in the Act.
2   Civil Evidence Act, s5.

1.24   *Two common law exceptions to the hearsay rule*   Not all evidence of a statement by someone else is hearsay; if it is produced merely to prove the fact that the statement was made, as opposed to the truth of what was stated, it is not hearsay evidence and is therefore admissible at common law. For example, if it was an issue in proceedings whether a person had died at or after a particular time a witness could testify that he heard the deceased (who is patently not a witness) speak after that time.

A hearsay statement which constituted an admission on the part of a non-witness can be given in court by a witness who heard that admission. Thus, a workman injured at work and suing his employer in negligence could testify that on reporting his injury to his employer the employer said 'not more trouble with that machine, it injured X only last week'.

Chapter 2

Administration of the law

The courts

2.1 The first thing to be noted in any discussion of the court system is that not every type of court exercises both a civil and a criminal jurisdiction. Moreover, within the sphere of either of these jurisdictions, the particular type of court which will try the case (or hear an appeal) will depend on a number of disparate factors. Opposite is a chart which shows the outline of the court structure and the following paragraphs explain this, beginning at the bottom.

Magistrates' courts[1]

2.2 A magistrates' court is constituted by justices of the peace. The terms 'justice of the peace' and 'magistrate' are synonymous[2] and henceforth to avoid confusion we shall use the word 'magistrate'. Normally a magistrates' court must be composed of at least two magistrates. The most important exception is that one magistrate can conduct committal proceedings in his capacity of examining magistrate.

Magistrates are appointed by the Lord Chancellor (or by the Chancellor of the Duchy of Lancaster) in the name of the Queen as magistrates for a particular area (normally a county). Each county is divided into a number of petty sessional divisions (ie magistrates' courts districts). There are over 20,000 magistrates; all but about 50 of them are 'lay' magistrates. Lay magistrates are unpaid but get an allowance for loss of earnings and for expenses. They are not required to possess any legal qualifications: for legal advice they rely on their clerk, who is a solicitor or a barrister, but even though the clerk to the magistrates is legally qualified an individual court may be served by an unadmitted assistant. In the inner London area, and in some other places, jurisdiction is exercised both by lay magistrates and by stipendiary (ie salaried) magistrates, who are barristers or solicitors of seven years' standing or more. Stipendiary magistrates sit alone and have all the powers of two lay magistrates in a magistrates' court.

The Lord Chancellor can dismiss a magistrate without showing cause. Magistrates are put on the supplemental list at the age of 70, which is *de facto* retirement in that they cease to be entitled to exercise judicial functions. Magistrates may be put on the supplemental list before that age either at their own request or on the ground of 'age, infirmity or other like cause' or neglect of judicial duties.

THE COURT STRUCTURE

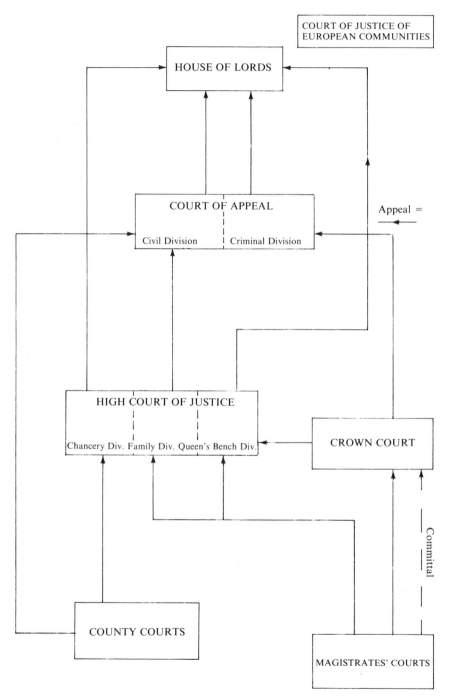

Magistrates' courts have jurisdiction in both criminal and civil matters. Their summary procedure is inexpensive and speedy but their jurisdiction only extends to matters of minor importance compared with that of the other courts of trial in the court system.

1 The principal statute governing the constitution and jurisdiction of magistrates' courts is the Magistrates' Courts Act 1980.
2 Except that 'justice of the peace' includes those on the supplemental list.

Criminal jurisdiction

2.3 There are two methods of trying persons accused of criminal offences. One is by judge and jury in the Crown Court after committal for trial on a written accusation of crime called an indictment; the other is summary trial by a magistrates' court without a jury. Over 96% of criminal cases are tried summarily. Magistrates' courts have two functions:

a. That of a court of summary jurisdiction or petty sessions, which hears and determines cases, subject to appeal. Not only do magistrates' courts deal summarily with those minor offences which are defined in the statute creating them as summary offences (ie offences which only triable in a magistrates' court) but they may also try offences which are 'triable either way' (ie either in a magistrates' court or on indictment in the Crown Court) with the consent of the accused. Magistrates cannot impose a sentence in excess of six months' imprisonment, except that they may impose consecutive sentences up to a total of twelve months' if the accused has been convicted of more than one offence triable either way.

b. That of examining magistrates by whom committal proceedings are held as a necessary preliminary, in almost all cases, to a trial by jury in the Crown Court. The function of examining magistrates is different from that when they sit to hear and determine a case. The question in committal proceedings is whether there is evidence upon which a reasonable jury properly directed could convict. It matters not that the magistrates themselves would not have convicted on the evidence before them. The system acts as a filter so that persons against whom there is no evidence upon which a reasonable jury could convict are spared the anxiety and expense of a trial. If the magistrates decide that there is no prima facie case against the accused, they decline to commit him for trial and discharge him.

2.4 A person convicted by a magistrates' court may appeal to the Crown Court against conviction, or against sentence, or against both, except that if he pleaded guilty he may appeal to the Crown Court against sentence only. An alternative avenue of appeal is to appeal to a divisional court of the Queen's Bench Division. This is open to the prosecution or the defence, or to any other party to a proceeding before a magistrates' court, if aggrieved with the determination of the magistrates are being wrong in law or in excess of jurisdiction. This type of appeal is solely concerned with questions of law or jurisdiction, but is usually the preferable course to adopt when the appeal is founded on such questions alone.

Civil jurisdiction

2.5 This is very varied. It extends over the recovery of certain civil debts, such as income tax, electricity and gas charges, and rates; the grant and renewal of licences; and 'domestic proceedings'.

'Domestic proceedings' are probably the most important aspect of the civil jurisdiction of magistrates' courts. Magistrates' courts have powers in matrimonial proceedings to make maintenance orders for the complainant spouse on proof that the defendant spouse has failed to provide reasonable maintenance, or has behaved in such a way that the complainant cannot reasonably be expected to live with the defendant, or is in desertion. In such proceedings the magistrates may also make orders concerning the separation of the spouses and, whether or not one of the above grounds is proved, concerning the custody and maintenance of any child of the family. Apart from these matrimonial proceedings, magistrates' courts also have powers under a number of statutes to make orders concerning the custody and maintenance of children, and they may also make adoption orders. When hearing domestic proceedings, a magistrates' court must be composed of not more than three magistrates, including, so far as practicable, both a man and a woman. Unless the court otherwise directs, only the officers of the court, and parties to the case and their legal representatives, witnesses, and news reporters may attend. There are strict limitations on the particulars which may be published in a news report of domestic proceedings.

2.6 Appeals in civil proceedings in magistrates' courts generally lie to the Crown Court with a further (or alternative) appeal on a point of law to the Queen's Bench Division of the High Court by case stated, except that in domestic proceedings appeal is to the Family Division and there is no alternative of appeal to the Crown Court.

Juvenile courts
2.7 Generally, someone aged under 17 who is charged with a criminal offence must be tried in a juvenile court.

A juvenile court also hears civil 'care proceedings', in which a variety of orders can be made concerning those under 17 on the ground that they are in need of care and control.

Essentially, a juvenile court is composed in the same way as a magistrates' court hearing domestic proceedings and similar restrictions apply concerning attendance and news reporting. Appeal from a juvenile court lies to the Crown Court with a further (or alternative) appeal by case stated on a point of law to a divisional court of the Queen's Bench Division (criminal proceedings) or to the Family Division (care proceedings).

County courts
2.8 The jurisdiction of county courts is exclusively civil. England and Wales are divided into 285 county court districts, each with its own court house, office and staff, which are grouped into 63 circuits.

Each county court circuit has assigned to it one or more circuit judges. Circuit judges are appointed by the Queen on the recommendation of the Lord Chancellor to serve in the Crown Court[1] and in the county courts, and to carry out such other judicial functions as may be conferred on them. Generally, only circuit judges specifically assigned to a county court circuit sit in the county court. Those qualified to be a circuit judge are barristers of at least ten years' standing or recorders[2] who have held office for three years. They retire at the end of the completed year of service in which they reach 72, although the Lord Chancellor may retain the services of a circuit judge until he is 75. A circuit judge can be dismissed by the Lord Chancellor on grounds of incapacity or misbehaviour.[3]

There are county court registrars, solicitors of seven years' standing appointed and removable by the Lord Chancellor, in each circuit. They supervise the administrative business of the court and also have jurisdiction to try claims not exceeding £500 in value (although normally such a claim will be referred to arbitration, as we show in para 2.13 below). In addition, by leave of the judge of the court and with the consent of the parties, a county court registrar may try any other action. A registrar has the full jurisdiction of the judge where the defendant admits the claim or does not appear at the hearing. He also deals with interlocutory applications which are necessary before an action can be tried and with other ancillary matters. An appeal lies from the registrar to the judge.

1   Paras 2.21–2.23 below.
2   Para 2.21 below.
3   Courts Act 1971, ss16 and 17, as amended. To reduce delay in the administration of justice, the Lord Chancellor can appoint deputy circuit judges on a temporary basis. Deputy circuit judges and recorders can deputise for a circuit judge in a county court.

Jurisdiction

2.9   Under the provisions of the County Courts Act 1984, county courts have jurisdiction over a wide range of civil matters. This jurisdiction, which is subject to financial limits, includes:

a.   Jurisdiction over actions in contract or tort, except defamation, or for money recoverable by statute, where the debt or damages claimed do not exceed £5,000. A county court has jurisdiction over defamation or a claim in excess of £5,000 if the parties agree to accept the jurisdiction of the county court or if the case is remitted to it by the High Court.

b.   Jurisdiction over actions for the recovery of land where the net annual rateable value of the land does not exceed £1,000.

c.   An equity jurisdiction, eg in cases of administration of estates, fore-closure of mortgages and specific performance of contracts for the sale of land, where the amount of the estate, mortgage or purchase price, as the case may be, does not exceed £30,000.

d.   Contentious probate jurisdiction where there is a contested application for the grant or revocation of probate (will) or letters of administration (intestacy), or where there are actions as to the validity of a will, and the net value of the estate is less than £30,000. In practice, this jurisdiction is rarely exercised, trial nearly always being in the Chancery Division of the High Court.

e.   Some county courts have a limited jurisdiction in admiralty matters, eg damage to a ship or its cargo, or pilotage disputes.

2.10   Types of jurisdiction under other statutes include:

a.   (In designated courts) divorce, judicial separation and annulment of marriage cases and proceedings ancillary to them.

b.   Bankruptcy and winding-up of companies.

c.   Matters under the Rent, Landlord and Tenant, Housing and Consumer Credit Acts.

2.11   The procedure in the county courts is simpler, speedier and less costly, than in the High Court. To discourage the conduct of minor litigation in the High Court which could have been brought in a county court, a party, who succeeds in the High Court on a matter falling within county court limits, may in certain circumstances be awarded no costs or only awarded costs on the county court, as opposed to High Court, scale.[1]

1   County Courts Act 1984, s19. This rule only applies to actions in tort or contract.

2.12   Appeal from a county court judge lies to the Court of Appeal (subject to certain conditions), except in bankruptcy where appeals are heard by a single judge of the High Court.

Small claims[1]
2.13   A defended action in the county court must be referred to arbitration if the sum claimed or amount involved is not in excess of £500. If referral to arbitration occurs the hearing takes place before an arbitrator, generally in private, without the formalities associated with a trial. The arbitrator will usually be the registrar, but a party may apply to the registrar for the appointment of any other suitable person. A referral to arbitration of a claim not in excess of £500 may be rescinded by the registrar on the application of a party, if the parties are agreed that the case should be tried in court, or if the case involves a difficult question of law or of fact or an allegation of fraud, or if it would otherwise be unreasonable for the claim to proceed to arbitration.

If the amount in dispute exceeds £500 the matter can still be referred to arbitration if the parties agree to this or one of the parties does not object to the registrar deciding the application for arbitration. If a party does object then the judge can decide whether the case should be dealt with by arbitration. The award of the arbitrator is entered as a judgment in the court proceedings, and is binding as such. The judge has power, on application, to set the award aside.

The advantage of the arbitration procedure is that it is eminently suitable for the litigant in person in small claims cases, which are mainly 'consumer disputes', since it is even more informal and inexpensive than trial in the county court. The arbitration may take place round a table, the oath may not be administered and each party normally bears his own costs. Formality is kept to the minimum necessary to protect the interests of each party.

1   County Courts Act 1984, s64; County Court Rules 1981.

The High Court of Justice
2.14   The High Court is part of the Supreme Court of Judicature, the Crown Court and Court of Appeal being the other two constituent parts. The High Court was established by the Judicature Acts 1873–1875, replacing the separate Courts of Chancery, Queen's Bench, Common Pleas, and Exchequer, and also the Courts of Admiralty, Probate, and Matrimonial Causes.

For historical reasons, the High Court consists of three divisions, each of which, by virtue of the rules of procedure and practice, has a separate jurisdiction. High Court judges are assigned to a particular division but, since they are judges of the High Court, they can exercise any jurisdiction appertaining to a High Court judge, irrespective of the division to which they have been assigned.[1]

High Court judges are appointed by the Queen on the recommendation of the Lord Chancellor. Those qualified for appointment are barristers of at least ten years' standing.[2] A High Court judge has greater security of tenure than a circuit judge since he is only removable on an address presented by both Houses of Parliament to the Queen, except that the Lord Chancellor may, with the concurrence of senior judges, declare vacant the office of a 'superior' judge who is subject to permanent medical incapacity and is unable to tender his resignation. High Court judges must retire on attaining the age of 75.[3]

1 See *Re Hastings* (No 3) [1959] Ch 368, [1959] 1 All ER 698; *Re Kray* [1965] Ch 736, [1965] 1 All ER 710; *Re L* (Infant) [1968] P 119 [1968] 1 All ER 20, CA.
2 Supreme Court Act 1981, s10. To reduce delay, the Lord Chancellor can appoint deputy High Court judges on a temporary basis.
3 Supreme Court Act 1981, s11.

Chancery Division
2.15 The Chancery Division consists of the Lord Chancellor, as its nominal head, although he never sits at first instance, a Vice-Chancellor and, at present, 12 judges. The jurisdiction of the Chancery Division is exercised in London and eight provincial towns.

There are seven masters of the Chancery Division, who are barristers or solicitors of at least ten years' standing appointed by the Lord Chancellor. Applications are made to the masters in chambers in the preliminary stages of litigation, and they make orders thereon in the name of the judge to whom they are assigned. Complicated accounts and inquiries are also referred to them. If a party is not satisfied with the masters' ruling, he may adjourn the matter to the judge.

2.16 The jurisdiction of the Chancery Division is entirely civil and can be split into original and appellate jurisdictions.

a. *Original jurisdiction* By virtue of the Supreme Court Act 1981, s61 and Sch 1, jurisdiction over a number of matters is assigned to the Chancery Division. These include:
i   the administration of estates of deceased persons;
ii   the execution of trusts;
iii the redemption and foreclosure of mortgages;
iv   the rectification and cancellation of deeds;
v   partnership actions;
vi   bankruptcy;
vii the sale, exchange or partition of land, or the raising of charges on land; and
viii all causes and matters under enactments relating to companies.

As can be seen, apart from the absence of financial limits, there is some concurrence between the Chancery Division's original jurisdiction and some of the heads of jurisdiction possessed by the county courts.

b. *Appellate jurisdiction* This is much more limited. Certain statutes empower a single judge to hear appeals of various kinds, eg income tax appeals from the Commissioners of Inland Revenue. A divisional court of the Chancery Division (which normally consists of two judges) hears appeals from county courts in land registration matters.

Queen's Bench Division
2.17 This division is the largest of the three divisions and has the most varied jurisdiction. Its head is the Lord Chief Justice and 49 judges are assigned to it at present. The original civil jurisdiction of this division is exercised in first-tier Crown Court centres,[1] as well as in London.

There are eight masters of the Queen's Bench Division, who must be barristers or solicitors of ten years' standing. These masters supervise the Central Office of the Supreme Court in which official documents are issued and registered. Applications are made to a master in chambers in preliminary stages of litigation in the Queen's Bench Division, appeal lying from his order to a judge.

1 Para 2.21 below.

2.18 The jurisdiction of the Queen's Bench Division can be divided into four heads, the first of which is the busiest:

a. *Original civil jurisdiction* The principal aspects of this are actions in contract and tort. Commercial matters are dealt with by specialist judges in the Commercial Court which sits in London, Liverpool and Manchester and whose procedure is more flexible and speedier than the normal High Court procedure. Similarly, admiralty matters, such as salvage claims, are heard in this division by specialist judges (who often sit with lay assessors in the Admiralty Court). Financial limits apart, there is concurrence between the Division's original civil jurisdiction and some heads of jurisdiction possessed by county courts.

b. *Appellate civil jurisdiction* A single judge (or, if the High Court's decision is final, a divisional court) has jurisdiction to hear appeals from certain tribunals and certain other appeals. In addition, a single judge (or, if the court so directs, a divisional court) hears appeals by way of case stated on a miscellaneous collection of civil matters from magistrates' courts (excluding domestic proceedings and care proceedings), the Crown Court and certain other bodies. A divisional court consists of two or more judges, increasingly two, of whom one will be the Lord Chief Justice or a Lord Justice of Appeal. An appeal by case stated must be on the ground that the determination or decision is wrong in law or is in excess of jurisdiction. The case is not re-heard, the judge or court merely hearing legal argument.

c. *Appellate criminal jurisdiction* A divisional court hears appeals in criminal matters by case stated from magistrates' courts and the Crown Court (in that court's appellate capacity). The appeal must be on the same ground, and is conducted in the same way, as in b. above.

d. *Supervisory jurisdiction* The most important aspects of this are the jurisdiction to issue the writ of habeas corpus and the jurisdiction to make 'prerogative orders' on an application for judicial review against inferior courts (magistrates' courts, county courts and, except in respect of trials on indictment,[1] the Crown Court), tribunals and other decision-making bodies of a public nature, such as local authorities.[2] The prerogative orders are mandamus, prohibition and certiorari. An order of mandamus is used to compel the body to whom it is directed to carry out a definite public duty imposed on it by law. The order cannot be used to compel the body to exercise its discretion in a particular way, but it may be used to compel it to hear and determine a case, or to state a case for the opinion of the High Court.[3] An order of prohibition or certiorari will issue only in relation to an order or decision of a body which is under a public duty to 'act judicially' or 'act fairly' in making that decision, as opposed to purely administratively. This does not mean that prohibition and certiorari issue only to courts or tribunals, for many other bodies, such as local authorities, may sometimes be required to act judicially, and in other cases are required to act fairly. The order of prohibition is used to *prevent* such a body from acting in excess of jurisdiction or otherwise acting improperly. The order of certiorari covers much the same area but *after* such a body has done something and it is desired to review it and, if necessary, quash it on the ground of excess of jurisdiction, denial of natural justice, or error of law on the face of the record. The latter ground is the most common now, partly because the Tribunals and Inquiries Act 1971, s12 requires many tribunals and ministers, after statutory inquiries, to give their reasons for their decisions if requested. We say more about these grounds in para 4.24 below.

Applications for judicial review in civil cases are heard by a single judge unless the court directs a hearing by a divisional court. Applications for judicial review in criminal cases are always heard by a divisional court, as are applications for habeas corpus.

1   Supreme Court Act 1981, s28; *R v Leeds Crown Court, ex p Bradford Chief Constable* [1975] QB 314, [1975] 1 All ER 133, DC; para 2.22 below.
2   In contrast, the supervisory jurisdiction does not extend to arbitrations in pursuance of an agreement out of court, which we discuss in paras 2.39–2.46 below: *Bremer Vulkan Schiffbau Und Maschinenfabrik v South India Shipping Corpn* [1981] AC 909, [1981] 1 All ER 289, HL; Arbitration Act 1979, s1(1).
3   Magistrates' Court Act 1980, s111(6).

Family Division
2.19   The Family Division consists of the President of the Division and, at present, 16 judges. The jurisdiction of this division is entirely civil, and is exercised in London and at first-tier Crown Court centres. It can be divided into original and appellate jurisdictions:

a.   *Original jurisdiction* The Division deals with all aspects of family law; the following are the most important examples:
i   proceedings for divorce, annulment of marriage and judicial separation and ancillary relief (eg financial provision and custody proceedings) connected therewith;
ii   proceedings for the determination of title to property in dispute between spouses;
iii proceedings concerning the occupation of the matrimonial home; and
iv   wardship of court, guardianship and adoption proceedings.

b.   *Appellate jurisdiction* This is principally concerned with appeals from the decisions of magistrates' courts in domestic proceedings and care proceedings.[1] Some such appeals, e g against the making of a maintenance order, must be heard by a divisional court (which must be composed of two or more judges), but others, e g against the making of a care order, will be heard by a single judge unless the court directs a hearing by a divisional court. Appeals of the second type are by case stated.

1 Paras 2.5 and 2.7 above.

2.20 Appeals from the original jurisdiction of any division of the High Court lie to the Court of Appeal (Civil Division), as do appeals from the appellate jurisdiction of any Division,[1] save that appeals from the criminal appellate jurisdiction of a divisional court of the Queen's Bench Division go straight to the House of Lords.

1 But note the 'leap-frogging' exception mentioned at para 2.28b below.

The Crown Court

2.21 The Crown Court in England and Wales is divided into six circuits. In each circuit it sits in a large number of towns, which are divided into first-tier, second-tier and third-tier centres. The first- and second-tier centres are served by High Court and circuit judges and by recorders; the distinction between the two centres is that in the former sittings of the High Court are held for civil cases[1] as well as of the Crown Court for criminal cases. Like the second-tier centres, third-tier centres are limited to Crown Court work but they are only served by circuit judges and recorders with the result that a few very serious offences, such as murder, cannot be tried at them.

The jurisdiction and powers of the Crown Court are exercised by:

a any judge of the High Court;
b any circuit judge;
c any recorder; and
d in some circumstances any judge of the High Court, circuit judge or recorder sitting with lay magistrates.

Recorders are part-time judges of the Crown Court appointed by the Queen on the recommendation of the Lord Chancellor. They must be either barristers or solicitors of at least ten years' standing. A recorder cannot continue in office after the end of the completed year of service in which he reaches 72. His appointment can be terminated by the Lord Chancellor on the grounds of incapacity, misbehaviour or failure to comply with the terms of his appointment.[2]

Lay magistrates cannot act as judges of the Crown Court by themselves but only with a High Court or circuit judge or with a recorder. They must form part of the Crown Court when it hears appeals from magistrates' courts and also when it is sentencing persons who have been committed for sentence by magistrates' courts, but the Lord Chancellor has power to dispense with this requirement. The number of magistrates so sitting must be not less than two nor more than four.[3] Rulings on questions of law are for the judge but decisions on other questions, e g sentence, are the product of all members of the court.[4]

1 Paras 2.17 and 2.19 above.
2 Courts Act 1971, s21.

3   Supreme Court Act 1981, s74.
4   *R v Orpin* [1975] QB 283, [1974] 2 All ER 1121, CA.

Criminal jurisdiction
2.22   The Crown Court has exclusive jurisdiction over all offences tried *by jury* on indictment, an appeal by a convicted person lying to the Court of Appeal.
The Crown Court also has jurisdiction:

a.   to deal with persons committed for sentence by magistrates' courts because their sentencing powers are inadequate; and

b.   to hear appeals from magistrates' courts, including juvenile courts, against conviction or sentence. The appeal takes the form of a full re-hearing of the case, ie the case is tried all over again, witnesses being called, etc. Where the Crown Court has given its decision on such an appeal, either the prosecution or the defence, if dissatisfied with the determination of the Crown Court as being wrong in law or in excess of jurisdiction, may appeal to a divisional court of the Queen's Bench Division by way of case stated.

Juries are not used in *these* cases.

Civil jurisdiction
2.23   The civil jurisdiction of the Crown Court is far less important. It is principally concerned with betting, gaming and liquor licensing appeals, but other appeals within its jurisdiction are appeals from various administrative decisions and from affiliation proceedings in the magistrates' courts.

The Court of Appeal
2.24   The Court of Appeal is composed of the Master of the Rolls, the Lord Chief Justice, the President of the Family Division and, at present, 21 Lords Justices of Appeal (the permitted maximum is 23). Lords Justices are appointed by the Queen on the advice of the Prime Minister. They must have been judges of the High Court or barristers of 15 years' standing.[1] The tenure of their office is the same as for High Court judges.[2] In addition, any High Court judge may be required to sit in the Court of Appeal if this is necessary.[3] The Court of Appeal is divided into a civil and a criminal division. The Master of the Rolls is the President of the Civil Division, and the Lord Chief Justice is the President of the Criminal Division.[4]

1   Supreme Court Act 1981, s10.
2   Para 2.14 above.
3   Supreme Court Act 1981, s9.
4   Ibid, s3.

Court of Appeal (Civil Division)
2.25   This hears appeals from:

a.   The decisions in civil matters of all three divisions of the High Court. An appeal from the determination of an appeal by a divisional court requires leave to be given either by the divisional court or by the Court of Appeal.[1]

b.   The decisions of a county court judge, except in bankruptcy. In actions in contract or tort, and in certain other cases, the leave of the county court judge or of the Court of Appeal is required if the amount of the claim does not exceed one-half of the relevant county court limit (£5,000 in the case of contract or tort).[2]

c. The decisions of the Employment Appeal Tribunal, Restrictive Practices Court, Lands Tribunal and certain other tribunals.[3]

Except in the case of certain appeals from tribunals and appeals from the Restrictive Practices Court (which are by case stated), the method of appeal is by way of re-hearing. This means that the court reviews the whole case from the shorthand notes of the trial and the judge's notes: it does not mean that the witnesses heard in the trial court are re-called, nor that fresh evidence will normally be admitted. Since the Court of Appeal does not have the advantage of seeing the trial witnesses and observing their demeanour, it does not normally upset direct findings of fact (as opposed to inferences from the facts).

Generally, a civil appeal must be heard by three members of the Court of Appeal. However, in certain cases, such as appeals from a county court, an appeal may be heard by two members. A single judge may determine an application for leave to appeal and deal with other matters arising incidentally. The Division may be sitting simultaneously in as many as seven courts. While most appeals are on points of law, an appeal may be against a finding of fact or the exercise of a discretion by the trial judge or against the damages which have been awarded, except in the case of appeals by case stated.

1 Supreme Court Act 1981, s18(1)(e).
2 County Courts Act 1984, s77; County Courts Appeal Order 1981.
3 Paras 2.34, 2.36 and 2.37 below.

Court of Appeal (Criminal Division)
2.26 The Criminal Division hears appeals from persons convicted by the Crown Court on indictment. The prosecution has no right of appeal against an acquittal on indictment.[1] The convicted person may appeal on any of the following grounds:

a. without any leave, against conviction on a question of law alone;

b. with the leave of the Court of Appeal (Criminal Division) or of the trial judge, against conviction:
i on a question of fact alone, or
ii on a question of mixed law and fact;

c. with leave of the Court of Appeal (Criminal Division), against conviction on any other ground which appears to the court to be sufficient; and

d. with leave of the Court of Appeal (Criminal Division), against sentence, unless the sentence is one fixed by law.[2]

In the case of an appeal against conviction, the court will allow the appeal if it thinks that the conviction was under all the circumstances 'unsafe or unsatisfactory', or that there was a wrong decision on any point of law, or that there was a 'material irregularity' in the course of the trial.[3] However, an appeal may be dismissed if the court is of the opinion that 'no miscarriage of justice has occurred' even though the ground of appeal is good.[4] On appeal against sentence, the Court may reduce it or vary it, provided that in the result the appellant is not dealt with more severely than he was in the court below.[5]

This Division normally sits in two courts: one composed of the Lord Chief Justice and two judges of the Queen's Bench Division, and the other of a Lord Justice and two Queen's Bench judges. By way of exception to the general requirement that criminal appeals must be heard by three judges, a two-judge court may hear an appeal against sentence.[6] A single judge may deal with applications for leave to appeal and may perform certain other incidental functions.

1   However, by the Criminal Justice Act 1972, s36, the Attorney General may refer to the Court of Appeal, and ultimately to the House of Lords, a point of law arising at a trial on indictment where the accused was acquitted. The opinion of the court does not affect the acquittal but provides authoritative guidance on the point of law for the future.
2   Criminal Appeal Act 1968, ss1, 9–11.
3   Ibid, s2.
4   Ibid, proviso to s2(1).
5   Ibid, s11(3).
6   Supreme Court Act 1981, s55.

The House of Lords

2.27   While the House of Lords has original jurisdiction over disputed claims to peerages and breaches of privilege, such as contempt of the House or wrongs committed within its precincts, this is of minor importance compared with its appellate jurisdiction. The House of Lords' appellate jurisdiction is discharged by its Appellate Committee. The Appellate Jurisdiction Act 1876 provides that at the hearing of an appeal there must be present at least three of the following—the Lord Chancellor, the Lords of Appeal in Ordinary and such peers who hold or have held high judicial office (eg ex-Lord Chancellors). Normally, five Lords of Appeal in Ordinary hear an appeal and by convention peers other than the above do not attend meetings of the Appellate Committee. Lords of Appeal in Ordinary (commonly called 'Law Lords', and not to be confused with Lords Justices of Appeal[1]) must have held high judicial office for two years or be practising barristers of not less than fifteen years' standing.[2] They are appointed by the Queen on the advice of the Prime Minister and have the same security of tenure and retirement age as High Court judges.[3] At present there are nine Lords of Appeal in Ordinary (the permitted minimum and maximum being seven and eleven). Normally, one or two of the Lords of Appeal are appointed from Scotland. The proceedings of the Appellate Committee are presided over by one or other of two senior Lords of Appeal nominated for this purpose by the Lord Chancellor. The House of Lords has both a civil and a criminal appellate jurisdiction.

1   Para 2.24 above.
2   Appellate Jurisdiction Act 1876, s6.
3   Para 2.14 above.

Civil appellate jurisdiction

2.28   The House of Lords hears:

a.   Appeals from the Court of Appeal (Civil Division), provided that leave has been granted by that Court or by the House.

b.   'Leap-frog' appeals from the High Court. To save cost and delay, the Administration of Justice Act 1969 provides that in most civil cases appeal may be made direct from the High Court to the House of Lords. This procedure may only be used where:
i   the parties agree to it;
ii the High Court judge grants a certificate to sanction it (which he may only do if he is satisfied that a point of law is involved which is of general public importance and which either relates to a matter of construction of an Act — or of a statutory instrument — or else is one in respect of which he considers that he is 'bound' by a decision of the Court of Appeal or of the House of Lords); and
iii the House of Lords gives leave to appeal.

Criminal appellate jurisdiction
2.29   The House of Lords can hear an appeal by either the prosecution or the accused from the determination of an appeal by the Court of Appeal (Criminal Division) or by a divisional court of the Queen's Bench Division provided:

a.   the court below (ie the Court of Appeal or a divisional court) has certified that a point of law of general public importance is involved and that court or the House of Lords is satisfied that the point of law is one which ought to be considered by the House; and

b.   either the court or the House of Lords has granted leave to appeal.[1]

As can be seen, an appeal on a question of fact is not possible to the House of Lords in a criminal case.

1   Criminal Appeal Act 1968, s33.

The Court of Justice of the European Communities (European Court)
2.30   The European Court operates under the Treaties of the European Communities, viz the Treaty of the European Economic Community, the Treaty of the European Coal and Steel Community and the Treaty of the European Atomic Energy Community.[1] The Court consists of thirteen judges and is assisted by six Advocates-General, a type of official unknown to English law. The duty of an Advocate-General is, with complete impartiality and independence, to make reasoned submissions in open court on cases brought before the Court in order to assist in the performance of its functions.
Judges and Advocates-General are appointed for six-year periods by the governments of member states acting in agreement and are eligible for reappointment. They are chosen from those who fulfil the conditions required for the holding of the highest judicial office in their respective countries or who are jurisconsults (ie persons learned in the law) of recognised competence.

1   The relevant provision are Arts 164–188 of the EEC Treaty, Arts 136–160 of the Euratom Treaty and Arts 31–45 of the ECSC Treaty. The provisions of the first two treaties are very similar.

2.31   Before 1973 the House of Lords was the final court of appeal in all cases in this country but the accession of the UK to membership of the

European Communities meant that the European Court became the ultimate court *in matters within its jurisdiction*. Nevertheless, in the great majority of cases arising within the UK the House of Lords remains the ultimate court. The fundamental point that the treaties under which the European Court operates are concerned only with those matters which have a European element must be firmly grasped in order to understand the relationship of the Court to the rest of our legal system.[1]

1 See *H P Bulmer Ltd v J Bollinger SA* [1974] Ch 401, [1974] 2 All ER 1226, CA.

Jurisdiction

2.32 The jurisdiction of the European Court can be divided into the following principal categories:

a.   Matters concerning the conduct of member states or of the institutions of the Communities, such as—

i   the hearing of complaints brought by member states or by the Commission of the European Communities that a member state has failed to fulfil its obligations under the Treaties;

ii   the review of the legality of the regulations, directives and decisions of the Council of Ministers of the European Communities and of the Commission; and

iii the hearing of disputes between member states which relate to the subject matter of the Treaties, provided the states in question agree.

b.   Matters of direct concern to litigants or prospective litigants in this country. Three matters are enumerated—

i   preliminary rulings on the interpretation of the EEC and Euratom Treaties;

ii   preliminary rulings on the validity and interpretation of the regulations, directives, decisions and other acts of the institutions of the Communities; and

iii preliminary rulings on the interpretation of certain statutes of bodies established by an act of the Council.

Where such a question is raised before any court or tribunal of a member state, the court or tribunal *may*, if it considers that a decision on the question is necessary to enable it to give judgment, refer the matter to the European Court for a ruling. However, where any such question is raised in a case pending before a court or tribunal of a member state, against whose decisions there is no judicial remedy under national law (which means the House of Lords in this country), that court or tribunal must generally refer the matter to the European Court for a ruling; in such a case it has no discretion as to whether or not to refer. In terms of the relationship between the European Court and English courts it is important to distinguish between the task of interpreting the Treaties, regulations, etc—to see what they mean—and the task of *applying* them to the case in hand. The English judges have the final say in applying the Treaties, etc: only they are empowered to find the facts and give judgment for one side or the other. However, before they can apply the Treaties, etc they have to see what they mean, and in this task of interpretation English judges are not the final authority: the European Court is.[1]

c. Actions for compensation for wrongful damage caused by Community institutions or their servants in the course of their duties.

d. Disputes between the Communities and their servants (or ex-servants). In these last two cases the Court applies law as well as interpreting it.

1   See *H P Bulmer Ltd v J Bollinger SA* [1974] Ch 401, [1974] 2 All ER 1226, CA.

Specialist courts and tribunals

The Judicial Committee of the Privy Council
2.33   The Judicial Committee of the Privy Council is the final court of appeal from the courts of some Commonwealth countries. It also entertains appeals against 'striking-off' from the disciplinary committees of the medical, dental and related professions, and certain other appeals. The Committee is normally composed of five Lords of Appeal, but other holders or past holders of high judicial office in this country or a Commonwealth country may, and do occasionally, sit.

The Restrictive Practices Court
2.34   This court was established by the Restrictive Trade Practices Act 1956, and is now governed by the Restrictive Practices Court Act 1976. It is a superior court of record, which means that it is not subject to the supervisory jurisdiction of the Queen's Bench Division. The Restrictive Practices Court deals with applications under the Restrictive Trade Practices Act 1976 for the validation of cartel agreements and other restrictive or unfair trade practices.[1] The court consists of three High Court judges (of whom one is president of the court); one judge of the Court of Session in Scotland, one judge of the Supreme Court of Northern Ireland, and not more than ten lay members appointed by the Lord Chancellor. Cases are heard by a presiding judge and at least two other members, except that where only an issue of law is involved a case may be heard by a single member who is a judge.

1   Paras 14.24–14.30 and 14.33–14.35 below.

The Court of Protection
2.35   This court, which is an 'office' of the Supreme Court of Judicature, can assume jurisdiction over the management and administration of the property and affairs of a person who it is satisfied is incapable of managing his property or affairs by reason of mental disorder. Its jurisdiction is conferred by Part VII of the Mental Health Act 1983. Certain orders (e g those authorising proceedings for divorce or the making of a will on the patient's behalf) can only be made by the Lord Chancellor or one of the Chancery judges whom he has nominated to the court. Otherwise, the jurisdiction (including the assumption of responsibility) is, in practice, exercised by the master, deputy master and other officers of the court, subject to appeal to a judge.

The Employment Appeal Tribunal

2.36   This tribunal, a superior court of record established in 1975, is now governed by the Employment Protection (Consolidation) Act 1978. It consists of judges from the High Court and Court of Appeal (one of whom is president) nominated by the Lord Chancellor, at least one judge nominated from the Scots Court of Session and lay members with specialised knowledge of industrial relations. The lay members may be removed by the Lord Chancellor, after consultation with the Secretary of State for Employment, on specified grounds, eg incapacity or misbehaviour. The tribunal has a central office in London but can sit anywhere in Great Britain, in any number of divisions, and is duly constituted when sitting with a judge and two or four lay members (or a judge and one member if the parties consent).

The tribunal's jurisdiction is entirely appellate. It can hear appeals on points of law from industrial tribunals under legislation relating to the following matters: unfair dismissal; redundancy payments; equal pay; sex discrimination; contracts of employment; trade unions and employment protection. In addition, the tribunal can hear appeals on questions of law or fact concerning the certification of a trade union as independent. The tribunal's procedure is designed to be as speedy, informal and simple as possible.

Lands Tribunal

2.37   The Lands Tribunal was established by the Lands Tribunal Act 1949. Its offices are in London but it also sits at various places in the provinces to determine cases. Its membership is composed of lawyers and qualified surveyors appointed by the Lord Chancellor. Its jurisdiction may be exercised by any one or more of its members, the composition of a tribunal in a particular case depending on the nature of the issues involved. The procedure at the hearing is less formal than in court proceedings.

The Lands Tribunal has jurisdiction over the following matters:

a.   appeals from local valuation courts (which are largely composed of local councillors and magistrates and which themselves hear appeals against assessments of the rateable value of land by local valuation officers);

b.   assessment of compensation for the compulsory purchase of land, where this has not been agreed between the acquiring authority and the property owner, or of compensation for certain other matters, such as compensation for planning restrictions restricting new development; and

c.   applications for the variation, modification or discharge of restrictive covenants under the Law of Property Act 1925, s84, as amended,[1] and applications for certificates as to notice under the Rights of Light Act 1959.[2]

1   Paras 39.36–39.38 below.
2   Para 40.40 below.

Other tribunals

2.38   A large number of different tribunals have been created to deal with matters arising under modern legislation, particularly social welfare legislation. These are usually composed of legally qualified chairmen and lay members. Their hallmarks are speed, informality and cheapness. The nature and powers of these tribunals vary but they have the common function of determining the facts of a case and deciding it according to law rather than the dictates of policy. In the case of some 'first instance' tribunals there is a right to appeal to an appellate tribunal or to a minister. In addition, there is generally a right of appeal to the High Court, on a question of law only, from the decision of an appellate tribunal or (if there is not such a tribunal) a 'first instance' tribunal. Whether or not there is the possibility of an appeal, a tribunal's decision may be challenged by applying to the High Court for judicial review (which we mentioned in para 2.18d above, and discuss further in paras 4.23–4.25 below).

In addition, a number of 'domestic tribunals' have been established by private or professional associations to resolve disputes between their own members or to exercise disciplinary powers over them. The jurisdiction of these tribunals is sometimes derived from statute but in other cases rests solely on contract in that, by joining the association, a member contracts to accept the jurisdiction of its domestic tribunal.

Arbitration

2.39   Where it is used as an alternative to proceedings in court or as part of such proceedings, arbitration is a method for the settlement of civil disputes, other than those affecting status (such as divorce and bankruptcy). Arbitration is generally more informal, private, cheaper and quicker than a trial in a court, although, where the main issues are questions of commercial law (as opposed to the facts or commercial practice), trial in the Commercial Court[1] may be cheapest and quickest, and certainly the most appropriate.

A dispute may be referred to arbitration in three ways: by agreement out of court, by statute or by order of the court.

1   Para 2.18a above.

Reference by agreement out of court

2.40   Particularly in commercial and consumer matters, the parties to a dispute may prefer to go straight to arbitration rather than become involved in court proceedings. Hence, they may voluntarily agree before or after the dispute to refer it to arbitration. Many commercial contracts provide for such a reference, as do various codes of practice initiated by trade associations which are incorporated in their standard form contracts. If an arbitration agreement (or 'submission', as it is technically called) is in writing, as is usually the case, it is governed by the Arbitration Acts 1950, 1975 and 1979, and we now proceed to consider the position under those Acts.

Normally, if a party to an arbitration agreement brings court proceedings in respect of a dispute covered by the agreement without referring it to arbitration, the court has jurisdiction to try the case. However, if such proceedings are instituted the other party may, after entering an appearance but before taking any further step in the proceedings, apply to the court for an order staying the proceedings. Where the arbitration agreement is a 'domestic arbitration agreement' the court has a discretion to stay the proceedings (and will normally do so) if there is no sufficient reason why the matter should not be referred to arbitration.[1] In the case of an arbitration agreement which is not a 'domestic' one the court must stay the proceedings, unless satisfied that the arbitration agreement is null and void, inoperative or incapable of being performed, or that there is not in fact any dispute between the parties with regard to the matter agreed to be referred.[2] A 'domestic arbitration agreement' is one which does not provide, expressly or by implication, for arbitration in a foreign state and to which neither:

a.   an individual who is a national of, or habitually resident in, a foreign state, nor

b.   a corporation incorporated in, or centrally managed in, a foreign state, is a party.[3]

The normal position just outlined does not apply if the arbitration agreement contains a '*Scott v Avery*[4] clause', which is an agreement to refer a dispute to arbitration as a condition precedent to an action in the courts. Since no right of action in the courts accrues until the arbitration has taken place non-observance of the clause will afford a complete defence to a court action.

1   Arbitration Act 1950, s4.
2   Arbitration Act 1975, s1.
3   Ibid. The provisions relating to staying court proceedings also apply where the arbitration agreement is made *after* the institution of the court proceedings: *The Tuyuti* [1984] QB 838, [1984] 2 All ER 545, CA.
4   (1856) 5 HL Cas 811, HL; para 14.6 below.

Appointment of arbitrators and umpires

2.41   The parties may name any person whom they wish to act as arbitrator or provide a method for his appointment, as by giving the power of appointment to the president of a relevant professional society. The type of arbitrator chosen depends on the type of case in question. Lawyers are appointed quite frequently, but in some cases a person with the relevant technical expertise, e g an accountant or a surveyor, is appointed.

Normally, arbitration is conducted by a single arbitrator.[1] If specific provision is made for the appointment of two arbitrators, they may appoint an umpire at any time, and must do so forthwith if they cannot agree. It is the umpire's duty to enter on the reference if the arbitrators are unable to agree.[2] The High Court has powers to appoint arbitrators and umpires in default of an appointment by the parties or arbitrators or other person with power of appointment.[3] Where there is a reference to three arbitrators, the award of any two of them is binding (unless the contrary intention is expressed in the arbitration agreement).[4]

A judge of the Commercial Court may, if in all the circumstances he thinks fit, accept appointment as sole arbitrator or umpire in a case of a commercial character, provided the state of business in the High Court permits him to be made available.[5]

1   Arbitration Act 1950, s6.
2   Ibid, s8, as amended by the Arbitration Act 1979, s6.
3   Ibid, s10, as amended by the Arbitration Act 1979, s6.
4   Ibid, s9, as substituted by the Arbitration Act 1979, s6.
5   Administration of Justice Act 1970, s4.

Conduct of the proceedings

2.42 In the absence of contrary terms in the arbitration agreement, an arbitrator or umpire must follow the ordinary rules of English law in reaching his decision, and the normal rules of evidence apply.

2.43 To be valid, the award must decide all the issues submitted to arbitration and not decide other issues. It may provide for the payment of money, direct costs to be paid[1] and order the specific performance of a contract (other than one relating to land or an interest in land),[2] unless the arbitration agreement is to the contrary. The award is final and binding on the parties and persons claiming through them, unless the arbitration agreement otherwise provides,[3] and there is no right of appeal to the courts except on a point of law. However, the High Court has power to remit the case for re-consideration. In addition, it has power to set aside an award where an arbitrator or umpire has misconducted himself or the proceedings, or where the arbitration or award has been improperly procured. Lastly, it has power to remove an arbitrator or umpire who has improperly conducted himself or the proceedings.[4] Examples of misconduct for these purposes are bias, fraud or corruption on the part of an arbitrator, the receipt by him of evidence from one party in the absence of the other, and the failure by him to deal with some of the matters submitted.

1 Arbitration Act 1950, s18.
2 Ibid, s15.
3 Ibid, s16.
4 Ibid, ss22 and 23.

Enforcement of an award

2.44 An award may, by leave of the High Court, be enforced in the same manner as a judgment or order of that court, and, where leave is granted, judgment may be entered in terms of the award.[1] If this is done, the award can be enforced in any way allowed in the case of a judgment. Otherwise, the award is enforced by bringing a court action on the award as a contractual debt.

1 Arbitration Act 1950, s26.

Resort to the courts

2.45 There are two procedures whereby the courts may intervene in arbitration cases:

a. an appeal on a point of law after an award has been made; and

b. an application for the determination of a preliminary point of law in the course of a reference.

Appeal lies to the High Court on any question of law[1] arising out of an award made on an arbitration agreement. Such appeal may be brought by any of the parties to the reference, but unless all the other parties consent the leave of the court must be obtained (and this can only be granted if the court is satisfied that the determination of the question of law could substantially affect the rights of one or more parties to the arbitration agreement). Leave cannot be granted if the parties to the reference in question have effectively agreed to exclude the right of appeal. In *The Nema*,[2] the House of Lords took a restrictive view concerning the exercise by judges of their discretion to grant leave. It held that, generally, leave to appeal should not be granted unless it is shown either that the arbitrator has misdirected himself in point of law or the decision is such that no reasonable person could have reached it. Where the question of law concerns the construction of a contract in standard terms, leave should only be granted if the judge considers that a strong prima facie case has been made out that the arbitrator was wrong in his construction. The test is even stricter where the question of law concerns the construction of a 'one-off' contract or contractual clause (ie one which is not of a standard term nature). Here, leave to appeal should not be granted unless it is apparent to the judge, on a mere perusal of the arbitrator's reasoned award without hearing argument from counsel, that the meaning ascribed to the clause by the arbitrator is obviously wrong. The guidelines laid down in *The Nema* by the House of Lords do not apply where complex questions of EEC law arise; in such a case, the approach of the court to the granting of leave is less strict.[3]

On the determination of an appeal the High Court may confirm, vary or set aside the award, or remit it for re-consideration with its opinion on the question of law which was the subject of the appeal.[4] In order that an appeal, if it takes place, may be effective the court has power to order an arbitrator to give reasons for his decision.[5] An appeal to the Court of Appeal from the High Court's determination of an appeal is possible; but only if (a) the High Court certifies that the question of law to which its decision relates is one of general public importance or is one which for some other special reason should be considered by the Court of Appeal, and (b) the High Court or Court of Appeal gives leave to appeal.[6] A further appeal from the Court of Appeal to the House of Lords is only possible with the leave of that Court or of the House.

The High Court may determine any question of law arising in the course of a reference (a preliminary point of law) on the application of any of the parties to the reference. However, unless all the other parties consent to the application, the court must not entertain it unless it has the consent of the arbitrator or umpire *and* it is satisfied that the determination of the question might substantially reduce the parties' costs and could substantially affect the rights of one or more parties to the arbitration agreement.[7] Notwithstanding any agreement of the parties, the High Court is not bound to entertain the application. Instead, the judge should only entertain it in exceptional circumstances; for example, where the preliminary point of law, if rightly decided, would determine the whole dispute.[8]

Subject to the same restrictions as apply to an appeal from the High Court's determination of an appeal following an award, an appeal to the Court of Appeal lies from a decision of the High Court on a preliminary point of law or from a refusal or grant of an application for such a decision.[9]

1 An appeal cannot be brought on a question of fact. It is normally obvious whether a question is one of fact or of law but it should be noted that a question concerning the construction or frustration of a contract is a question of law: *Tsakiroglou & Co Ltd v Noblee & Thorl GmbH* [1962] AC 93, [1961] 2 All ER 179, HL; *The Nema* [1982] AC 724, [1981] 2 All ER 1030, HL.
2 [1982] AC 724, [1981] 2 All ER 1030, HL.
3 *Bulk Oil (Zug) AG v Sun International Ltd* [1984] 1 All ER 386, [1984] 1 WLR 147, CA.

4 Arbitration Act 1979, s1(2)–(4).
5 Ibid, s1(5) and (6). Also see s1(6A) (added by the Supreme Court Act 1981, s148).
6 Ibid, s1(7).
7 Ibid, s2(1) and (2).
8 *Babanaft International Co SA v Avant Petroleum Inc The Oltonia* [1982] 3 All ER 244, [1982] 1 WLR 871, CA.
9 Arbitration Act 1979, s2(3).

Exclusion agreements

2.46 At common law an agreement, whether contained in the arbitration agreement or made thereafter, which excludes the courts' power to give a final decision on a question of law is void on grounds of public policy and thus of no effect.[1] However, this rule has been severely curtailed by the Arbitration Act 1979, as we now explain. Under that Act, the High Court must not grant leave to appeal to it with respect to a question of law arising out of an award, nor may an application for the determination of a preliminary point of law be made, without the consent of all the parties to the reference, if the parties to the reference in question have made a written agreement excluding the right of appeal or, as the case may be, the right to the determination of a preliminary point of law in the particular case.[2] Such an exclusion agreement may relate to a particular award or be more general in nature, and it is generally irrelevant whether or not it forms part of an arbitration agreement.[3] However, in the case of a 'domestic arbitration agreement' (a term which we defined in para 2.40 above) an exclusion agreement is only operative if it was entered into after the commencement of the relevant arbitration.[4] The same limitation applies where the arbitration relates to an insurance contract or to a 'commodity contract', unless the award or question of law relates to a contract which is expressed to be governed by a law other than English law.[5]

1 *Czarnikow v Roth, Schmidt & Co* [1922] 2 KB 478, CA.
2 Arbitration Act 1979, s3(1).
3 Ibid, s3(2).
4 Ibid, s3(6).
5 Ibid, s4(1). 'Commodity contract' is defined by s4(2) of the Act of 1979 and the Arbitration (Commodity Contracts) Order 1979. The best example is a contract for the sale of goods regularly dealt with on a London commodity market, such as the London Metal Exchange or the London Grain Futures Market.

Reference by statute

2.47 Numerous statutes provide for the reference of certain types of dispute to arbitration. In some cases, eg disputes involving building societies, the parties have an option to refer; in others reference is compulsory, eg disputes involving street works. The provisions of the Arbitration Acts 1950 and 1979 apply to statutory references, with certain exceptions, unless the particular statute otherwise provides. Thus, what we have said above concerning the appointment of arbitrators and umpires, the proceedings, the enforcement of awards and resort to the courts is generally applicable to a statutory reference. However, review by the courts of an award, or of a question of law, in a statutory arbitration cannot be ousted by an exclusion agreement between the parties.[1]

1 Arbitration Act 1979, s3(5).

Reference by order of the court

2.48 The High Court may refer any case within its jurisdiction, or any particular issue in such a case, to be *tried* by an official referee (a circuit judge assigned for such business), a senior officer of the court (such as a master), or, where the issue is of a technical nature requiring specialist knowledge, a special referee.[1] A reference to such an arbitrator can be made even against the wishes of the parties and is particularly likely to be made if:

a.   the prolonged examination of documents, or scientific or local examination, is required; or

b.   the examination of accounts is involved.

The award of the arbitrator is entered as a judgment in the court proceedings, and is binding as such. In certain circumstances an appeal lies to the Court of Appeal (Civil Division).

In addition, the High Court has a similar power to refer to the same persons as above any question in a cause or matter before it for *inquiry and report*. The report may be adopted wholly or partially by the court, and if so adopted is as binding as a judgment to the same effect.[1]

The power of a county court to refer a case to arbitration has been discussed in para 2.13 above. In addition, any question in a case before a county court judge may be referred to the registrar or a referee for inquiry and report.[2]

1   Supreme Court Act 1981, s84; Rules of the Supreme Court, Ord 36.
2   County Courts Act, 1984, s65; County Court Rules 1981.

2.49 References to arbitration by the courts must be distinguished from references to arbitration by agreement or under a statutory provision because they operate in the context of court proceedings rather than as an alternative to them.

The legal profession

Barristers

2.50 Barristers do not form partnerships but instead work together in sets of chambers, sharing rent and other expenses. Their work comprises drafting legal documents and writing opinions on points of law, as well as appearing as advocates. Barristers do not work directly for lay clients but may only accept work from solicitors. Most sets of chambers are in London in the Inns of the Court but there are also chambers in many other major cities. A barrister of more than ten years' standing may apply to be made a Queen's Counsel by the Queen on the Lord Chancellor's advice. The work of a Queen's Counsel is confined to the most important cases and chiefly involves advocacy.

Barristers are members of one of the four Inns of Court (Middle Temple, Inner Temple, Lincoln's Inn and Gray's Inn) but much of the central control of the profession is now vested in the Senate of the Inns of Court and the Bar, and the Bar as a profession is represented by the General Council of the Bar.

Solicitors

2.51 Unlike practising barristers, solicitors are normally members of a partnership or employed by a partnership. Solicitors act as legal advisers on commercial, family and personal matters; they convey land and draft wills, and they prepare cases involving litigation. In addition, solicitors can act as advocates in various tribunals, magistrates' and county courts, and in the Crown Court (when it is hearing appeals from, or sentencing persons committed for sentence by, magistrates' courts). However, they cannot so act in other cases in the Crown Court nor, with some exceptions (such as the Employment Appeal Tribunal and the Patents Court in its appellate capacity), in the High Court or other superior courts. To adopt a medical analogy, a barrister is the 'consultant' and the solicitor the 'general practitioner'.

The Law Society is responsible for the solicitors' branch of the legal profession, the Council of that society being the ultimate authority.

Legal executives

2.52 Legal executives are qualified legal assistants in solicitors' offices who, while working under the control and authority of a solicitor, possess a high degree of expertise in their chosen field. Their professional body is the Institute of Legal Executives which, like the other professional bodies, is responsible for admission to its numbers and holds examinations.

The jury

2.53 The only courts mentioned above in which juries are found are the Crown Court and the High Court (twelve jurors) and the county courts (eight jurors). The use of juries in civil cases is rare and the parties generally have no right to demand a jury; except that a jury must be ordered on the application of either party in cases of defamation, malicious prosecution and false imprisonment, or on the application of a party against whom fraud is charged, unless the case requires a prolonged examination of accounts or documents, or a scientific or local investigation which cannot conveniently be made with a jury.[1] The only civil cases where a jury is common are defamation cases. Provided the accused has pleaded not guilty, a jury is always empanelled in trials on indictment in the Crown Court.

1 Supreme Court Act 1981, s69.

2.54 A person is eligible for jury service if he or she is between the ages of 18 and 65, is included on the electoral register for parliamentary and local government elections, and has been resident in the UK, the Channel Islands or the Isle of Man for five years since the age of thirteen. There are certain exceptions. Some persons are ineligible for jury service, including judges, barristers and solicitors, police officers, clergymen and the mentally ill. Certain ex-prisoners and certain other people who have received non-custodial sentences are disqualified and persons such as peers, soldiers and doctors are excusable as of right.[1]

1 Juries Act 1974, ss1 and 3, and Sch 1 (as amended by the Juries (Disqualification) Act 1984, s1).

2.55   The division of labour between judge and jury is that the judge rules on law, the jury on fact. The judge directs the jury as to the law and they apply it to the facts. Their discussions are in secret, they choose their own foreman and they give no reasons for their decisions. Their verdict in a civil case can be overturned by the Court of Appeal but only if no reasonable jury properly directed could have reached it. In his summing-up the judge may comment on the plausibility of the evidence and may give guidance as to what inferences may be drawn. Generally, the jury must reach a unanimous verdict but a majority of ten (seven in the county courts) may be accepted after the jury have had a reasonable time in all the circumstances for deliberation; there is a minimum time of two hours in the Crown Court.[1] In civil cases the parties can always consent to accept any majority verdict.[2]

1   Juries Act 1974, s17.
2   Recognised in the Juries Act 1974, s17(5).

Chapter 3
Sources of English law

3.1 The direct means by which a law is made or comes into existence constitute legal sources, while a literary source is simply the written material in which a legal source is recorded.

Legislation and judicial precedent are the principal legal sources of English law and the only other source, custom, is now of very little relevance. The courts must consciously look to these sources to determine what the law is and are bound to apply the rules which they create. The literary sources of legislation are the various publications of statutes and statutory instruments. The literary sources of precedent are law reports and, to a lesser extent, certain books of authority.

Legislation

3.2 Unlike many continental countries where, the law having been codified, most legal rules are derived from legislation, our law is predominantly derived from judicial precedent. Leaving aside certain areas which have been codified, such as the law relating to partnership (by the Partnership Act 1890), the body of law concerning private rights is essentially derived from judicial precedent with relatively few alterations made by statute. Normally, the purpose of statutory alteration or revision of this area of the law is to revise a legal rule which has become inappropriate in changing social circumstances and which, because of the operation of the doctrine of judicial precedent, is incapable of adaptation by the courts. The generation of law reform proposals has been greatly assisted since 1965 by the existence of the Law Commission, consisting of full-time Commissioners, assisted by a research staff. Under the Law Commissions Act 1965, it is the duty of the Law Commission to keep under review all the law with a view to its systematic development and reform, including in particular the codification of such law, the elimination of anomalies, the repeal of obsolete and unnecessary enactments, the reduction in the number of separate enactments, and generally the simplification and modernisation of the law. A large number of Law Commission reports and draft Bills have been implemented by Act of Parliament.

Legislation plays a more important part in criminal law, mainly in defining most offences, and in the spheres of company law and family law. Another notable example is legislation concerning the revenue, for instance, the Finance Acts which implement the budget proposals. However, the great majority of modern statutes can be put into the category of 'social legislation'. Such legislation is concerned essentially with regulating the day to day running of the social system rather than with creating criminal offences or rights and duties between individuals. In this area, in particular, much of the flesh is put on the bones of the relevant Act by delegated legislation. Examples of 'social legislation' are the Health and Safety at Work etc Act 1974, the Trade Union and Labour Relations Act 1974, the Landlord and Tenant Acts and the Rent Act 1977.

3.3 Sometimes a statute is described as a consolidating or codifying statute. Where a branch of statute law has evolved piecemeal, a consolidating statute may be passed, for the purpose of clarification, containing substantially the existing law in a consolidated form. An example of a recent consolidation Act is the Income and Corporation Taxes Act 1970. A consolidation Act only consolidates statute law: a codifying Act may codify both case law and statute law, a notable example being the Sale of Goods Act 1893 (which has now been consolidated with subsequent amending statutes in the Sale of Goods Act 1979). However, the object of both consolidation and codification is to simplify and clarify the existing law rather than to effect substantial alterations to it.

3.4 There are essentially three types of legislation: Acts of Parliament; subordinate legislation, which mainly consists of delegated legislation made by government ministers, local authorities and other bodies under powers derived from parliament; and the legislation of the European Communities. Subject to a possible exception which we discuss in para 4.8 below, parliament (which consists of the Queen, House of Lords and House of Commons) is sovereign, which means that it is not subject to any legal limits on its power to create, alter and repeal English law. It also means that an Act of Parliament cannot be questioned in, or by, the courts: it has to be applied by them. In certain cases the validity of subordinate legislation and of most types of legislation of the European Communities can be challenged.

Acts of Parliament

3.5 It is a fundamental common law rule that to be an Act of Parliament a measure requires the assent of the Queen, the House of Lords and the House of Commons. However, this rule has been modified by the Parliament Acts 1911 and 1949 whereby, in the circumstances outlined in para 3.7 below, a measure can be an Act of Parliament without the assent of the House of Lords.

While it is going through the parliamentary process, and before it receives the royal assent, an Act is known as a Bill. Most Bills originate from government departments, having been drafted by parliamentary draftsmen, and are introduced into either House of Parliament by a government minister. By a constitutional convention, Finance Bills (ie Bills authorising taxation) and Consolidated Fund Bills and Appropriation Bills (ie Bills authorising national expenditure) must be introduced in the House of Commons by a government minister. Apart from these types of Bill, a Public Bill may be introduced by an ordinary member of the House of Commons or House of Lords, although the opportunities for doing so are rather limited. Private members' Bills are unlikely to succeed in becoming law because of the limited time available for them, unless they are adopted by the government and accorded extra parliamentary time. A further limitation is that it is a constitutional convention that every Bill whose effect will be to increase taxation or central government expenditure must be supported by a financial resolution moved by a government minister. It follows that if a private member's Bill has such an effect it cannot succeed unless the member can persuade a minister to move a financial resolution. So far we have concentrated on Public Bills, ie Bills which when enacted will be general in their application. In addition, Private Bills—Bills of a local or personal nature—may be presented by local authorities, public corporations, companies, private members or other individuals and are subject to a different parliamentary procedure. A third type of Bill is the Hybrid Bill. A Hybrid Bill is one which is introduced as a Public Bill but which affects the private interests of particular bodies or individuals. Part of the parliamentary procedure for a Hybrid Bill is similar to that for a Private Bill.

The passage of a Bill
3.6 In the case of a Public Bill the normal procedure is as follows, assuming that it is first introduced into the House of Commons.

A Bill is introduced by its sponsor presenting a dummy copy at the table of the House, whereupon it receives a formal First Reading by one of the clerks reading out its title. The Bill is then ordered to be printed and published, and a date is fixed for its Second Reading. At the Second Reading the general principles of the Bill are debated by the House. Amendments to specific clauses may not be moved. Assuming that it is not successfully opposed on Second Reading, the Bill proceeds (after a financial resolution, if one is necessary) to the Committee Stage. This stage involves a clause by clause consideration of the Bill, during which clauses may be amended and new clauses added provided that they are relevant to the subject matter of the Bill. Most routine Bills go to a Standing Committee, a group of around 18 members of parliament reflecting party strength in the House. There are a number of Standing Committees and their sole function is to deal with Bills as and when necessary; a recent innovation is to send some Bills to a 'Special Standing Committee' with the power to question witnesses and request the submission of evidence. However, if a Bill is of constitutional importance, or is straight-forward and uncontroversial, or requires a very rapid passage, it may be considered by a Committee of the Whole House instead of a Standing Committee. The annual Bills authorising public expenditure must be considered by a Committee of the Whole House and the annual Finance Bill is partly considered by such a Committee and partly by a Standing Committee. When the House sits as a Committee the Speaker, who is its normal chairman, vacates the chair, and the Chairman of Ways and Means or his deputy chairs the meeting. The next stage is the Report Stage, which constitutes a detailed review of the Bill as amended in Committee. Further amendments, alteration of amendments made by the Committee, and new clauses, may be made at this stage. The final stage in the House of Commons is the Third Reading, which normally takes place immediately after the Report Stage. This enables the House to take an overall consideration of the Bill, as amended, and to permit it to proceed, or otherwise, as it thinks appropriate. The Third Reading debate is brief and general in nature. Substantive amendments cannot be made at this stage, but minor verbal ones may.

A Bill which has passed all its stages in the Commons then goes to the House of Lords, where it undergoes a similar procedure except that there is never a financial resolution and the Committee Stage is always taken in the Whole House. If the Lords amend the Bill it is returned to the Commons for their consideration. If the Commons agree to the amendments this is the end of the matter, but if they disagree the Bill is returned to the Lords with the Commons' reasons for the disagreement and the Lords consider the matter further. On further consideration in such a case it is most exceptional in modern times for the Lords not to give way. However, in the event of an impasse between the Houses, the Parliament Acts 1911 and 1949 provide that ultimately the wishes of the Commons can prevail. We discuss this matter shortly.

Once a Bill has passed through the above stages it is submitted for royal assent by the Queen, after which it becomes an Act.

The 'official' copies of Acts of Parliament are printed by the Queen's Printer and published by HMSO, which also publishes annual volumes of Public Acts. The Incorporated Council of Law Reporting publishes texts of Acts taken from the Queen's Printer's copies, as do certain commercial publishers who publish annual volumes of Acts of Parliament verbatim, as well as in unbound parts soon after the Act is passed; a leading series is *Halsbury's Statutes of England.*

The procedure for Private Bills does not call for extensive description. Normally, they must have satisfied various strict requirements, such as their purpose being advertised, before they can be laid before parliament and given a First Reading. At the Committee Stage they are examined by small committees of four or five members who, unlike committees dealing with Public Bills, conduct an enquiry into the merits of the Bill. The promoters and opposers of the Bill may appear before the committee and they will usually be represented by counsel; evidence may be called and submissions made. In short, the Committee Stage resembles a judicial inquiry. Otherwise, however, the parliamentary procedure is very similar to that for a Public Bill.

Parliament Acts 1911 and 1949

3.7 At one time the House of Lords had a general power to reject Bills from the House of Commons and thereby prevent them being enacted, but this power has been severely restricted in relation to *Public* Bills by the Parliament Act 1911, as amended by the Parliament Act 1949.

The Parliament Act 1911, s1 provides that any Public Bill which has been passed by the House of Commons and has been certified by the Speaker as a 'Money Bill', ie a Bill whose provisions exclusively relate to central government taxation, expenditure or loans, may be presented for the royal assent even though the House of Lords has failed to pass it without amendment after it has been with that House for one month. This means that the Lords must pass a 'Money Bill' unamended within one month of receiving it, otherwise the royal assent can be given without their assent.

In addition, the Parliament Act 1911, s2, as amended by the Parliament Act 1949, provides that any other Public Bill, with the important exception mentioned below, which has been passed by the House of Commons in two successive sessions and been rejected in each session by the House of Lords, may be presented for the royal assent without the concurrence of the Lords, provided that one year has elapsed between the Second Reading in the Commons in the first session and the Third Reading there in the second session *and* that in both sessions the Bill had been submitted to the Lords at least one month before the end of the session. The result is that the House of Lords may delay a Public Bill, other than a 'Money Bill', for a maximum of one year. Section 2 of the Act of 1911 provides an important exception to the basic rule which it lays down: that rule does not apply to Bills to prolong the maximum duration of a parliament beyond five years. Here the House of Lords retains an unfettered right of veto.

Citation

3.8 Until 1963, statutes were cited by the date of the regnal year or years of the parliamentary session in which the Act was passed, the regnal year being assessed from the monarch's accession, together with a chapter number which denoted the order in which it received the royal assent. Thus, the Law of Property Act 1925 is cited '15 and 16 Geo 5, c20'. Acts passed after 1962 are cited by reference to the calendar year, not the regnal year, in which they were passed. Thus, the Misrepresentation Act 1967 is cited '1967, c7'.

Of course, the more usual way to cite an Act it by its short title.

Commencement and repeal

3.9 An Act of Parliament comes into operation on the date on which it receives the royal assent unless, as frequently occurs, some other date is specified in the Act or is to be appointed either by Order in Council or by a government minister by way of statutory instrument.[1]

An Act of Parliament may be repealed expressly by a subsequent statute, or impliedly by being inconsistent with it (although there is a presumption against implied repeal).[2] Unless the contrary intention appears, repeal does not:

a. revive a previously repealed rule of law; or

b. affect existing rights and liabilities, or legal proceedings, civil or criminal.[3]

No statute becomes obsolete through the passing of time, except for certain Acts usually of an experimental or transitional nature which are expressed to be operative only for a limited period. The most convenient way of finding out whether a statute has been wholly or partly repealed or amended is to look it up in the *Chronological Table of the Statutes* published biennially by the Stationery Office. This covers the period from 1235 to the end of the year preceding publication. Another way is to look at the index to *The Statutes in Force*, which is published annually by the Stationery Office.

1 Interpretation Act 1978, s4.
2 Para 3.25 below.
3 Interpretation Act 1978, ss15 and 16.

Subordinate legislation

3.10 Various institutions, such as the Crown, minister, public corporations and local authorities, have legislative powers. Such legislation is subordinate since it is made by bodies with limited powers and it is always subject to abrogation or amendment by Act of Parliament. Moreover, it may be required to be subject to parliamentary scrutiny and, unlike an Act of Parliament, it may be held invalid in certain cases by the courts. Subordinate legislation can be of two types: delegated legislation and autonomic legislation.

Delegated legislation

3.11 Delegated legislation comprises the great bulk of subordinate legislation. Delegated legislation is legislation made by some executive body under powers delegated to it by Act of Parliament. An Act of Parliament often gives powers to some bodies, such as the Queen in Council (in effect the government), a minister or a local authority or public corporation, to make regulations and prescribe for their breach. Delegated legislation includes sub-delegated legislation which may validly be made where it is authorised by an Act of Parliament, as where an Act provides that the Queen in Council may make regulations empowering a particular minister to make further regulations.

There is a vast amount of delegated legislation—the number of pieces made annually being numbered in thousands, whereas the number of Public and Private Acts of Parliament a year rarely exceeds 150. Recent examples of Acts giving very wide powers of delegated legislation are the European Communities Act 1972[1] and the Consumer Credit Act 1974. Delegated legislation made by the central executive may be required to be made by Order in Council made by the Queen in Council, otherwise it taks the form of regulations, rules or orders made by a minister or government department. Generally, delegated legislation of these types must be made by statutory instrument (formerly Statutory Rules and Orders). Statutory instruments are printed by the Queen's Printer and are available in the same way as Acts of Parliament. They are cited by calendar year and number and by a short title. For instance, the Land Registration (Official Searches) Rules are cited SI 1981 No. 1135. A statutory instrument comes into effect when made unless, as is usual, it specifies a later date.[2] Unlike an Act of Parliament, it is a defence for a person charged with contravening a statutory instrument to prove that it had not been issued by the Stationery Office at the date of the alleged offence, unless it is proved that at that date reasonable steps had been taken to bring the purport of the instrument to the notice of the public, or of persons likely to be affected by it, or of the person charged.[3]

1 Para 3.33 below.
2 *Johnson v Sargant & Sons* [1918] 1 KB 101.
3 Statutory Instruments Act 1946, s3.

3.12 Parliamentary control over statutory instruments is secured to some extent by requirements of 'laying' and of publication. Often the enabling statute will require the instrument to be laid before parliament, in which case it must be so laid before it comes into operation, and in addition an affirmative resolution by parliament may be required to give it effect or it may be made subject to cancellation by a negative resolution of either House within 40 'sitting' days.[1] Closer parliamentary scrutiny of new statutory instruments is provided by the Joint Select Committee on Statutory Instruments, which is composed of members of both Houses and reports to parliament. Its terms of reference include consideration of every statutory instrument laid or laid in draft before parliament, with a view to seeing whether the special attention of parliament should be drawn to the instrument on one of a number of grounds, eg that it is obscurely worded, or appears to impose charges on the subject or on the public revenue, or purports to have a retrospective effect unauthorised by the parent statute. The Select Committee is not concerned with the merits of delegated legislation.

Another type of delegated legislation is the byelaw. Byelaws are made by local authorities, public corporations and certain other bodies authorised by statute. Although general in operation, they are restricted to the locality or undertaking to which they apply. They are not made by statutory instrument.

1 Statutory Instruments Act 1946, ss4 and 5, as clarified by the Laying of Documents before Parliament (Interpretation) Act 1948.

3.13 All forms of delegated legislation are invalid if they are ultra vires. Delegated legislation is ultra vires if it is in excess of the powers conferred by the enabling statute on the rule-making body; or if it is made in breach of a mandatory part of the prescribed procedure concerning their making; or, in the case of byelaws only, if it is unreasonable or excessively uncertain or repugnant to the general law. The invalidity of delegated legislation is either challenged directly before the courts or, more commonly, raised as a defence to an action which concerns the application of the delegated legislation.

3.14 The principal advantages of delegated legislation are:

a. Parliament has insufficient time to deal with details. The availability of delegated legislation enables parliament to limit itself to settling the general policy of a measure, such as the Consumer Credit Act 1974, leaving a minister to supply the detailed provisions in the form of regulations and orders.

b. Delegated legislation is eminently suitable in the case of provisions on technical matters which would be inappropriate for parliamentary discussion.

c. In some cases, the power to make delegated legislation enables a minister to deal speedily with urgent situations, such as an economic crisis or a strike in an essential industry.

d. The power to make delegated legislation is also useful in that, within the terms of the parent Act, it enables the application of an Act to be tailored to deal with contingencies which were not foreseen when the Act was passed.

3.15 On the other hand, delegated legislation is open to the following criticisms:

a. Parliament has neither the time nor the opportunity to supervise all delegated legislation effectively.

b. The detail which delegated legislation provides may be just as important as the general policy of the parent Act, yet parliament cannot discuss its merits.

Autonomic legislation

3.16 Autonomic legislation is legislation made by the Queen by Order in Council, or by autonomous associations within the state, under powers which are not delegated by parliament but which are recognised by the courts. Trade unions and professional associations are examples of auto-nomous associations in this context. The legislation of such autonomous associations is directly binding only on their members, though negatively it binds everyone since interference with it is wrongful; it is invalid if ultra vires. Autonomic legislation made by the Queen in Council is made under the royal prerogative. There is no power under the prerogative to alter the general law of the land[1] but there is a limited prerogative power to legislate for the colonies, the armed forces and the civil service. The prerogative comprises those independent powers left to the Crown by parliament, and legislation outside the prerogative powers of the Crown will be held invalid by the courts.

1 *Case of Proclamations* (1611) 12 Co Rep 74.

Interpretation

3.17 Language being inherently capable of ambiguity and human affairs being capable of great diversity, the courts are often faced with the question whether a particular matter or piece of conduct falls within the wording of a particular legislative provision. The exposition which follows is concerned with the interpretation of Public Acts of Parliament but, essentially, the same rules apply to the interpretation of other Acts of Parliament and of subordinate legislation. In interpreting statutes, the courts are trying to discover parliament's intentions from the words used and may be helped by statutory definitions:

a. The Interpretation Act 1978 provides a number of definitions which apply unless there is a contrary intention, express or implied, in a particular statute, eg 'unless the contrary intention appears, (a) words importing the masculine gender shall include females; and (b) words in the singular shall include the plural and words in the plural shall include the singular'.[1] Again, 'person' includes any body of persons corporate or unincorporate.[2]

b. Many statutes contain an interpretation section towards their end, whose definitions apply throughout the Act unless a contrary intention, express or implied, appears in a particular context.

1 S6.
2 Sch 1.

The literal rule

3.18 The basic rule of statutory interpretation is the literal rule, which states that parliament's intention must be found by interpreting the words used in their ordinary, literal or grammatical sense in their context. If the words can be so interpreted a judge must give effect to that interpretation, unless the statute or the legal context in which the words are used compels him to give the word a special meaning, even though he considers that it produces an undesirable, inexpedient or unjust result or that parliament cannot have intended it.[1] In *IRC v Hinchy*,[2] the House of Lords had to interpret the Income Tax Act 1952, s25(3), which provided that a person who failed to deliver a correct income tax return should forfeit 'the sum of twenty pounds and treble the tax which he ought to be charged under this Act'. The House of Lords held that, in addition to the penalty of £20, a taxpayer who had declared only part of his Post Office interest was liable to pay treble the whole tax chargeable for the year and not merely treble the tax on the undeclared income.

A more recent authority is *Shah v Barnet London Borough Council*,[3] where the House of Lords held that 'ordinarily resident', in the Education Act 1962, s1(1), did not have a special meaning and must be construed according to its natural and ordinary meaning. According to this meaning, it held, a person was 'ordinarily resident' in the UK under the section (and thereby qualified for a student grant) if he habitually and normally resided lawfully in the UK from choice and for a settled purpose (eg education) throughout the prescribed period, apart from temporary or occasional absences.

1 *Duport Steels Ltd v Sirs* [1980] 1 All ER 529, [1980] 1 WLR 142, HL; *Leedale v Lewis* [1982] 3 All ER 808, [1982] 1 WLR 1319, HL.
2 [1960] AC 748, [1960] 1 All ER 505, HL. The actual decision in this case was overruled by the Finance Act 1960, s44, which amended the wording of the provision in question.
3 [1983] 2 AC 309, [1983] 1 All ER 226, HL.

The golden rule

3.19 It may happen that to interpret statutory words according to their ordinary, literal or grammatical sense in their context would give rise to absurdity, repugnancy or inconsistency *with the rest of the statute*. In such a case, the golden rule permits a judge to modify the literal interpretation so as to avoid such a result. The classical exposition of the golden rule was given by Lord Wensleydale in *Grey v Pearson*:[1]

> 'in construing . . . statutes . . ., the grammatical and ordinary sense of the words is to be adhered to, unless that would lead to some absurdity or some repugnance or inconsistency with the rest of the instrument, in which case the grammatical and ordinary sense of the words may be modified so as to avoid that absurdity or inconsistency, but no further.'

1 (1857) 6 HL Cas 61 at 106.

The mischief rule

3.20 The literal rule breaks down, of course, in the face of an ambiguity. In such a case, a judge may apply the mischief rule, which is often called the rule in *Heydon's case* since it was formulated there.[1] The rule is best paraphrased by the statement by Lord Halsbury in *Eastman Photographic Materials Co v Comptroller-General of Patents, Designs and Trade Marks.* 'We are to see what was the law before the Act was passed, and what was the mischief or defect for which the law had not provided, what remedy parliament appointed, and the reason of the remedy'.[2] In applying this rule, the court should so interpret the provision in question as to suppress the mischief and advance the remedy. An example of the application of the mischief rule is *Gorris v Scott*.[3] The plaintiff claimed in respect of the loss of his sheep which were washed overboard and drowned while the defendant was engaged in carrying them by sea. The loss was due to the fact that, in

45

breach of a statutory duty to do so, no pens had been provided. The plaintiff based his claim on the fact that the loss had been caused by the breach of the statutory duty. However, it was held that the purpose of the relevant provision was not to prevent loss overboard but to minimise the spread of contagious diseases, and that therefore the claim did not fall within the 'mischief' of the Act.

1   (1584) 3 Co Rep 7a.
2   [1898] AC 571 at 573.
3   (1874) LR 9 Exch 125.

3.21   It must be clearly understood that the aim of the golden rule and of the mischief is to find out parliament's intention from what parliament has said, not what it meant to say or would have said if it had thought about a newly discovered situation. The rules are limited to giving effect to the words of the statute. They do not extend to reading words into it to rectify an anomaly or absurdity, *unless clear reason is found within the body* of the Act itself:[1] a judge cannot attribute to parliament an intention which parliament never had. For a judge to do so was condemned by Lord Simonds in *Magor and St Mellons RDC v Newport Corpn*,[2] as a 'naked usurpation of the legislative function under the thin disguise of interpretation'. His Lordship added that if a gap is disclosed the remedy lies in an amending Act.

1   *Stock v Frank Jones (Tipton) Ltd* [1978] 1 All ER 948, [1978] 1 WLR 231, HL.
2   [1952] AC 189 at 191, [1951] 2 All ER 839 at 841.

3.22   The following rules and presumptions assist the court in the interpretation of the words in the statute and in the resolution of uncertainties and ambiguities.

Consideration of the whole enactment
3.23   Consideration of the whole enactment, particularly of an interpretation section, assists in resolving apparent ambiguities, inconsistencies or redundancies in a particular provision. In this connection it is of obvious importance to know what parts of an Act may be regarded as intrinsic aids to interpretation.

a.   *Long title and short title* These are part of the Act, but, in practice, the courts do not refer to the short title and only refer to the long title to resolve an ambiguity; in other words the long title is not allowed to restrict the clear meaning of the operative part. In *Re Groos*,[1] it was held that the Wills Act 1861, s3 applied to the will of an alien, even though the long title read: 'An Act to amend the law with respect to wills of personal estates made by British subjects'.

b.   *A preamble* is part of the Act. It appears at the beginning and sets out the background and purpose of the enactment. Modern statutes very rarely contain a preamble and the best known examples appear in earlier statutes. The preamble can only be looked at for guidance if the body of the Act is not clear and unambiguous.[2]

c.   *Punctuation, marginal notes, and headings* to a section or group of sections are inserted into a Bill by the parliamentary draftsmen and can be altered any time up to royal assent. They are not debated by parliament and are therefore not part of the Act (with the result that they may only be looked at to determine the purpose, as opposed to the scope, of the section,[3] although it may be that headings have a wider use).[4] Even in their limited sphere of operation, punctuation and marginal notes in particular carry little weight and cannot oust a meaning indicated by some part of the Act itself.

d. *Schedules,* which are used, for instance, to list repeals and set out transitional or more detailed provisions, are part of the Act, but they cannot affect the interpretation of a word in the body of the Act unless it is ambiguous or uncertain.[5]

1 [1904] P 269.
2 *Powell v Kempton Park Racecourse Co Ltd* [1899] AC 143 at 157.
3 *Director of Public Prosecutions v Schildkamp* [1971] AC 1, [1969] 3 All ER 1640, HL; *R v Kelt* [1977] 3 All ER 1099, [1977] 1 WLR 1365, CA.
4 *Director of Public Prosecutions v Schildkamp* [1971] AC 1 at 28, [1969] 3 All ER 1640 at 1656.
5 *Ellerman Lines Ltd v Murray* [1931] AC 126, HL.

3.24 The rule that the whole enactment must be considered is really part of the principle that words must be taken in their context. A word in itself does not have an absolute meaning: its meaning is relevant to its context (this statement is often described by the Latin tag *noscitur a sociis*). Another important example of this principle is the *ejusdem generis* (of the same class) rule. Enactments often list things forming a class to which a provision is to apply, following the list with some general words implying that some other similar things are intended to fall within the class. Whether something which is not specified in the list of things falls within the general words depends upon whether or not it is *ejusdem generis* as the specified things. In *Powell v Kempton Park Racecourse Co Ltd,*[1] an Act prohibited the keeping of a 'house, office, room or other place' for betting with persons resorting thereto. The House of Lords held that Tattersall's Ring (an uncovered enclosure of a superior sort) at a racecourse was not *ejusdem generis* as the specified things, and was not therefore an 'other place' within the meaning of the Act, since the specific words 'house, office, room' created a *genus* (class) of indoor places. There cannot be a *genus* for the purposes of the present rule unless the 'other' thing is preceded by a list of at least two or more specific things which share the same common characteristics.[2]

1 [1899] AC 143, HL. Also see *Brownsea Haven Properties Ltd v Poole Corpn* [1958] Ch 574, [1958] 1 All ER 205, CA.
2 *Quazi v Quazi* [1980] AC 744, [1979] 3 All ER 897, HL.

Presumptions
3.25 There are a number of presumptions as to the intentions of parliament, which may be rebutted by express words or by necessary implication from the subject matter in the Act itself.

a. *An Act applies to the U K* There is a presumption that an Act applies to the whole of the U K but not elsewhere. Acts frequently reveal a contrary intention by containing a section restricting their operation to one or more of the four home counties, or, in the case of a local Act, to a particular locality: on the other hand, an extension of the application of an Act outside the UK is rarely provided for.

b. *Against retrospective effect of legislation affecting substantive rights* This presumption is not concerned with when a statute comes into operation but with whether it affects factual situations which arose before that date. The presumption applies where the retrospective application of the statute would impair an existing right or obligation.[1] It is particularly strong where the statute creates offences or tax obligations. An example of the rebuttal of the presumption against retrospective effect is provided by an Act of Indemnity, which validates *ex post facto* a thing which was initially invalid or illegal.

c. *Against alteration of the law* Parliament is presumed to know the common law and not to intend to change it, with the result that, unless the words of the statute unmistakably indicate that the common law is changed, they must be interpreted so as not to alter it.[2] As part of the presumption against alteration in the law there are certain more specific presumptions: against the restriction of individual liberty; against compulsory deprivation of property, at least without compensation; and that there should be no criminal liability without fault. The presumption against alteration of the law also applies in relation to statute law. In particular, a consolidating Act is presumed not to introduce a change in the law by a change of words.[3]

d. *Against the Crown being bound* 'It is, of course, a settled rule', said Denning LJ reading the judgment of the Court of Appeal in *Tamlin v Hannaford*, 'that the Crown is not bound by a statute unless there can be gathered from it an intention that the Crown should be bound'.[4] The presumption also extends to employees of the Crown, in the course of their duties, and to Crown property. However, statutes frequently provide that they are to bind the Crown.

Other presumptions made in construing a statute are those against implied repeal of earlier legislation by later, apparently inconsistent, legislation (the earlier only being impliedly repealed if reconciliation is logically impossible); against infringement of international law; and against ousting the jurisdiction of the courts.

1 *Yew Bon Tew v Kenderaan Bas Mara* [1983] 1 AC 553, [1982] 3 All ER 833, PC.
2 *Leach v R* [1912] AC 305, HL.
3 *Beswick v Beswick* [1968] AC 58, [1967] 2 All ER 1197, HL.
4 [1950] 1 KB 18 at 22.

Extrinsic aids
3.26 While a court may look at the enactment as a whole it may not, unlike most continental courts, generally look at material outside the four walls of the Act to find parliament's intention. It cannot, for instance, look at reports of the parliamentary debates on the Bill which became the Act.[1] This may appear to fly in the face of common sense but it must be admitted that it might be difficult to determine a legislative intent from a two, or more, sided parliamentary debate. However, the following extrinsic aids can be looked at for limited purposes:

a. *Dictionaries* can be consulted to ascertain the ordinary and natural meaning, for the purpose of the literal rule, of words which have no particular legal meaning.[2]

b. *Reports of committees* containing proposals for legislation which have been presented to parliament and resulted in the enactment in question can be looked at, for the purpose of the mischief rule, to discover the state of the pre-existing law and the mischief which the enactment was passed to remedy. An example is provided by the House of Lords' decision in *Black-Clawson International Ltd v Papierwerke Waldhof-Aschaffenburg AG*,[3] where their Lordships, in order to interpret the Foreign Judgments (Reciprocal Enforcement) Act 1933, s8, referred to the report of a committee, which had resulted in the passing of the Act, to discover what the pre-existing law was understood to be and what its mischief was. Two of the five Lords of Appeal, Viscount Dilhorne and Lord Simon, went further and stated that it was permissible to look at such a report for a direct statement of what the resulting enactment meant. This minority statement goes further than our courts have been prepared to go in the past and it remains to be seen whether they will now adopt it. Lord Reid and Lord Wilberforce disagreed with it expressly in *Black-Clawson*.

c. *Judicial precedent* The interpretation given by a court to a statutory provision or word may be binding in relation to *that* provision or word in *that* Act, in accordance with the principles of the doctrine of judicial precedent (paras 3.36 to 3.48 below). Moreover, a judicial interpretation of a particular provision in one Act will be a similarly binding precedent in a subsequent one if they both deal with the same subject matter, as where the latter is a consolidating Act.

1 *Assam Railways and Trading Co Ltd v IRC* [1935] AC 445, HL; *Davis v Johnson* [1979] AC 264, [1978] 1 All ER 1132, HL; *Hadmor Productions Ltd v Hamilton* [1983] 1 AC 191, [1982] 1 All ER 1042, HL.
2 *Re Ripon (Highfield) Housing Confirmation Order 1938* [1939] 2 KB 838, [1939] 3 All ER 548, CA.
3 [1975] AC 591, [1975] 1 All ER 810, HL. Also see *Davis v Johnson* [1979] AC 264, [1978] 1 All ER 1132, HL.

Acts giving effect to international conventions
3.27 Increasingly, the purpose of an Act of Parliament is to put into domestic effect an international convention. In such a case recourse may be had to the terms of the convention if a provision of the Act is ambiguous or vague.[1] Sometimes, an Act actually incorporates the convention and in this case there are no limits on recourse to the terms of the convention since they have been made provisions of the Act. Conventions are apt to be more loosely worded than Acts of Parliament, and in *James Buchanan & Co Ltd v Babco Forwarding and Shipping (UK) Ltd*[2] the House of Lords held that a court must interpret the English text of an incorporated convention in a broad and sensible manner, appropriate for the interpretation of a convention, unconstrained by the technical rules of English law. Moreover, the majority of their Lordships held, if there is doubt about the true construction of the English text the court can look at an authorised text in a foreign language to resolve it. In the event of ambiguity or obscurity in the convention, the court can look at material in the public records of the international conference at which it was drafted provided that that material

was intended to clear up the ambiguity or obscurity,[3] a rule which contrasts markedly with the refusal to have recourse to parliamentary debates.

1 *Post Office v Estuary Radio* [1968] 2 QB 740, [1967] 3 All ER 663.
2 [1978] AC 141, [1977] 3 All ER 1048, HL. Also see *Rothmans of Pall Mall (Overseas) Ltd v Saudi Arabian Airlines Corpn* [1981] QB 368, [1980] 3 All ER 359, CA.
3 *Fothergill v Monarch Airlines Ltd* [1981] AC 251, [1980] 2 All ER 696, HL.

General

3.28　The principles of statutory interpretation set out above have come in for a good deal of criticism. To give two examples: there is no rule about which presumption should be applied where two of them conflict, and the restrictions on the extrinsic aids to interpretation are generally regarded as too narrow.

The major criticism, however, relates to the emphasis of the literal approach to statutory interpretation, by which judges are discouraged from seeking to discover (and implement) the policy underlying a statute, as opposed to applying a more liberal 'purposive' approach, whereby a construction is preferred which promotes the general legislative policy and purpose over one which does not and whereby words can be read into a statute to do what parliament would have done if it had the matter in mind. Despite this criticism, the decision of the House of Lords in *Shah v Barnet London Borough Council*[1] constitutes a clear re-affirmation of the literal approach. The only exception was stated by the House of Lords as follows: 'Judges . . . may . . . adopt a purposive interpretation if they can find in the statute read as whole or in material to which they are permitted by law to refer as aids to interpretation an expression of Parliament's policy or purpose'.[2]

1 [1983] 1 All ER 226, HL.
2 Ibid, at 238.

Legislation of the European Communities

3.29　This legislation is to be found in the Treaties of the Communities[1] and in regulations, directives and decisions of their organs. It is largely concerned with economic matters, such as agriculture, free trade, fair competition and transport regulation, but also deals with other matters, such as immigration.

In discussing the types of legislation of the Communities, a fundamental point must be emphasised at the outset: some rules of Community law are 'directly applicable' in the sense that they confer rights and duties on individuals and institutions which are enforceable in the courts of member states without being re-enacted by legislation in those states. This is provided by the Treaties establishing the Communities. However, although the Treaties conclude the matter according to *Community law*, they do not in themselves give the concept of 'direct applicability' legal effect in the *law of the UK*. The reason is that Treaty provisions do not become part of our law unless they have been incorporated into it by legislation. Such incorporation has been achieved by the European Communities Act 1972, s2(1), which provides that those rights and duties which are, as a matter of *Community law*, 'directly applicable' are to have legal effect in the UK.

Section 2(4) of the Act goes on to provide that Acts of Parliament passed or to be passed shall be construed and have effect subject to the directly applicable rules of Community law. We deal with the problem of inconsistency between UK legislation and directly applicable Community law in para 4.8 below.

1   Eg the treaties establishing the European Economic Community, the European Coal and Steel Community and the European Atomic Energy Community, further treaties which merged the main institutions of the Communities, and the Treaty of Accession (including the Act of Accession annexed to it) by which the UK acceded to the Communities.

Regulations

3.30   Certain provisions of the Treaties are directly applicable in the sense described above, but in the main directly applicable rules are contained in 'regulations', which have general application and are made by the Council of Ministers (a political body composed of foreign ministers) or the Commission (a supranational body composed of the highest officials) under the Treaties.

Directives and Decisions

3.31   Directives can be issued or decisions made by the Council or the Commission. Directives are directed to member states, who are obliged to implement them although they have a choice as to the form and methods of implementation. Decisions are addressed either to a member state or to an individual or institution. They are a formal method of enunciating administrative decisions effecting the policy of the Communities and are binding on the addressee.

3.32   While they bind their addressess, directives and decisions are not generally directly applicable in the courts of a member state and require implementation by the government or other parties to be applicable. However, the European Court has held that directives and decisions may be directly applicable without implementation in the member state concerned. An example is provided by *Van Duyn v Home Office*,[1] where the European Court held that a directive was of immediate binding effect so as to confer rights on the plaintiff even though the UK had not implemented that directive. Whether or not a directive or decision is directly applicable depends on an examination of the nature, general scheme and wording of its provisions to see whether they are capable of producing direct effects on their addressees.[2] In practice, very few directives or decisions are likely to be regarded as directly applicable.

1   [1975] Ch 358, [1975] 3 All ER 190, CJEC. Also see *R v Bouchereau* [1978] QB 732, [1981] 2 All ER 924, CJEC.
2   *Franz Grad v Finanzant Traustein* [1971] CMLR 1, CJEC.

3.33   Regulations, directives and decisions are subject to review by the European Court. They can be held invalid on the grounds of lack of competence, or infringement of any essential procedural requirement, or infringement of the Treaties or of any rule of law concerning their application, or misuse of power.[1]

Directives and decisions˙ are implemented in the UK by delegated legislation made under powers given by the European Communities Act 1972, s2(2), which also governs the implementation in further detail of regulations made by the Council or Commission. Orders in Council and departmental regulations made under these powers can include any provision which might be made in an Act of Parliament.[2] This power to make delegated legislation is the widest given to the executive in modern times apart from times of war. The power must be exercised by way of statutory instrument and presumably such an instrument will be ultra vires if it is not related to the affairs of the Communities. There are a number of limits on this power of delegated legislation; for instance, it cannot be used to impose taxation.

1   EEC Treaty, Art 173; Euratom Treaty, Art 146. Also see ECSC Treaty, Art 33.
2   European Communities Act 1972, s2(4). Also see Sch 2.

3.34   The literary source of regulations, directives and the principal decisions is the Official Journal of the European Communities, a huge work. It is usually as effective, and certainly quicker, to consult *Halsbury's Statutes of England* where regulations are set out in full and directives and decisions summarised.

Interpretation of the legislation of the European Communities
3.35   The drafting of the legislation of the Communities is quite unlike that of our legislation but, like the legislation of other European countries, is drafted in terms of broad principle, leaving the courts to supply the detail by giving effect to the general intention of the legislature. As an essential aid to this process, the regulations, directives and decisions mentioned above are required to state the reasons on which they are based and to refer to any proposals or opinions which were required to be obtained pursuant to the Treaties.[1] These are usually incorporated in a preamble.

   The result of this difference in drafting is that the interpretation of the legislation of the Communities, whether by the European Court or by an English court,[2] is not based on a slavish interpretation of the words or the grammatical structure of the sentences but on the purpose or intent of the legislation;[3] in other words, a purposive approach is taken to the interpretation of such legislation.

1   EEC Treaty, Art 190; Euratom Treaty, Art 162.
2   *H P Bulmer Ltd v J Bollinger SA* [1974] Ch 401 at 425–426, [1974] 2 All ER 1226 at 1237–1238.
3   *H P Bulmer Ltd v J Bollinger SA*; Case 41/74: *Van Duyn v Home Office* [1975] Ch 35, [1975] 3 All ER 190, CJEC.

Judicial precedent

3.36   This is the other important legal source and consists of the 'decisions' of courts made in the course of litigation. As will be seen, the 'decisions' of certain courts are more than just authoritative statements of the law since they can be binding (ie must be applied) in subsequent cases where the legally material facts are the same, whether or not the later court considers them to be correct or appropriate. Whether a particular statement of law made by a judge in one case is binding in a subsequent case depends partly on whether the statement formed the ratio decidendi (the reason of the decision) of the case or was merely an obiter dictum (something said by the way), and partly on the relative position of the two courts. Even if it is not binding, a judicial statement of the law has a persuasive effect in subsequent cases, the strength of its persuasiveness being a matter of degree, as we explain in para 3.48 below.

Ratio decidendi and obiter dictum

3.37 Only the ratio decidendi of a case can have binding effect. A judgment usually contains the following elements:

a. A statement of the facts found with an indication, express or implied, of which of them are material facts. In reading the report of a judgment, great care must be taken to ascertain what facts were found to be material.

b. Statements by the judge of the legal principles which apply to the legal issues raised by the material facts and are the reason for his decision. Normally these statements are only made after a review of existing precedents and general legal principles.

c. The actual judgment, decree or order delivered by the judge after application of b. to a., e g that the defendant is liable coupled with an award of damages.

Part c. is binding only on the parties to the case and is not a precedent for the future, nor is part a. in itself. It is part b. of this process which constitutes the ratio decidendi.

3.38 Sometimes the statements of the applicable principles made by the judge may be wider than the material facts warrant. In such a case the ratio of the decision will be limited to that part of it which applies to the material facts and, to the extent that the statement is wider, it will be obiter dictum,[1] to which we now turn. Apart from that just mentioned, there are two other types of obiter dictum.

First, a statement of legal principle is obiter if it relates to facts which were not found to exist in the case or, if found, were not material. Two famous cases provide good examples. In *Central London Property Trust Ltd v High Trees House Ltd*, which we discuss later in this book,[2] Denning J's statement of promissory estoppel was obiter since it applied to a set of facts which were not found to exist in the case. Similarly, in *Rondel v Worsley*,[3] the House of Lords expressed opinions that a barrister who was negligent when acting other than in connection with litigation might be held liable in tort and that a solicitor, when acting as an advocate, might be immune from such liability. Both statements were obiter since the case concerned the tortious liability of a barrister when acting as an advocate.

Second, a statement of legal principle which relates to some or all of the material facts but is not the basis of the court's decision, e g because it is given in a dissenting judgment or because another material fact prevents the principle applying, is also obiter. A leading example is *Hedley Byrne & Co Ltd v Heller & Partners Ltd*.[4] The House of Lords expressed the opinion that the maker of a statement owes a duty of care, in certain circumstances, to persons whom he may expect to rely upon that statement. This opinion was obiter because, although it was based on material facts found to exist in the case, the actual decision—that there was no breach of such a duty—was based on another material fact, that the maker of the statement had made it subject to a disclaimer of responsibility.

1 *Cassidy v Minister of Health* [1951] 2 KB 343, [1951] 1 All ER 574, CA.
2 Para 6.15 below.
3 [1969] 1 AC 191, [1967] 3 All ER 993, HL.
4 [1964] AC 465, [1963] 2 All ER 575, HL.

The hierarchy of the courts and judicial precedent

3.39 We saw in the previous chapter that the system of courts is a hierarchy. Essentially, one court is bound by the ratio decidendi of a case decided by another court if it is lower in the hierarchy than the latter and will not be bound by it if it is higher. Magistrates' courts and county courts are bound by the rationes decidendi in cases decided by High Court judges or the courts above such judges. A High Court judge is bound by the rationes decidendi of cases decided by the Court of Appeal and the House of Lords, and the Court of Appeal is bound by those of the House of Lords. This basic statement will be expanded by taking courts in turn, starting from the top of the hierarchy. For convenience, the word 'decision' will be used to indicate 'ratio decidendi'.

The Court of Justice of the European Communities

3.40 As we said in paras 2.31 and 2.32 above, the European Court is now the ultimate court in the following matters:

a. the interpretation of the EEC and Euratom Treaties;

b. the validity and interpretation of the acts of the institutions of the Communities; and

c. the interpretation of the statutes of bodies established by an act of the Council of the Communities.

Consequently, *in these limited areas of jurisdiction* the decisions of the European Court bind all English courts. Indeed, the European Communities Act 1972, s3(1) provides that any question as to the meaning or effect of any of the Treaties, or as to the validity, meaning or effect of any Community instrument, shall be treated as a question of law (and, if not referred to the European Court, be for determination in accordance with the principles laid down by, and any relevant decision of, the European Court).

The European Court does not observe a doctrine of binding precedent and does not regard itself as bound by its previous decisions,[1] although it leans in favour of consistency with its previous decisions.

1 *Da Costa en Schaake NV v Nederlandse Belastingadministratie* [1963] CMLR 224, CJEC.

The House of Lords

3.41 A decision of the House of Lords binds all courts inferior to it. Until 1966, a decision of the House of Lords also bound that House, a principle which was finally established at the end of the nineteenth century in *London Tramways Co Ltd v LCC*.[1] This meant that a legal principle might become unalterable by the House of Lords, in which case legislation was the only remedy if a change in the law was desired. In 1966, the House of Lords reversed this principle in an extra-judicial statement made by the Lord Chancellor (which has been regarded as having the force of law) declaring that it would not be bound by *its own* decisions where it appeared right to depart from them.[2] The declaration added that in this connection the House would bear in mind the danger of disturbing retrospectively the basis on which contracts, settlements of property and fiscal arrangements have been entered into and also the special need for certainty as to the criminal law. The declaration emphasised that it was not intended to apply elsewhere than in the House of Lords.

So far their Lordships have not made much use of their new-found freedom and have held that it is not enough that they should consider their previous decision was wrong; there must be an additional factor, such as a change of circumstances on which the decision was based or that it is productive of manifest injustice.[3] One of the few cases in which the House of Lords has overruled one of its previous decisions is *Miliangos v George Frank (Textiles) Ltd*,[4] where it overruled its decision in *Re United Railways of Havana and Regla Warehouses Ltd*[5] that judgment must be given in sterling.

1 [1898] AC 375, HL.
2 [1966] 3 All ER 77.
3 *Fitzleet Estates Ltd v Cherry* [1977] 3 All ER 996, [1977] 1 WLR 1345, HL.
4 [1976] AC 443, [1975] 3 All ER 801, HL.
5 [1961] AC 1007, [1960] 2 All ER 332, HL.

The Court of Appeal

3.42   The Civil Division of the Court of Appeal is bound by the previous decisions of the House of Lords. It is also bound by the previous decisions of either division of the Court of Appeal.[1] This was settled by the Court of Appeal in *Young v Bristol Aeroplane Co Ltd*.[2] However, as was recognised in that case, there are three exceptional circumstances where an earlier Court of Appeal decision is not binding on the Civil Division:

a.   Where two of its previous decisions conflict; the decision not followed will be deemed to be overruled.[3]

b.   The Court must refuse to follow a previous decision of its own which, though not expressly overruled, is inconsistent with a later House of Lords decision.

c.   The Court is not bound to follow its previous decision if that decision was given *per incuriam* (ie through lack of care). A decision is given *per incuriam* where some relevant statute or binding precedent, which might have affected the decision, was overlooked by the court in the previous case. Only in very rare instances can a case not strictly within this formulation be held to have been decided *per incuriam*, since such a case must involve a *manifest* slip or error and it must be an exceptional case in some way.[4]

While the *per incuriam* doctrine is also open to the House of Lords as a basis for rejecting one of its own previous decisions, the refusal of the Court of Appeal to follow the House of Lords decision in *Rookes v Barnard*,[5] on the basis that it had been reached *per incuriam* because of two previous House of Lords decisions, was rejected in extremely strong terms by the House of Lords on appeal in *Cassell & Co Ltd v Broome*.[6]

In addition to the exceptions mentioned in *Young v Bristol Aeroplane*, two other exceptions have been indicated by subsequent cases: a decision by a two-judge Court of Appeal hearing an interlocutory appeal does not bind a court of three,[7] and a Court of Appeal decision subsequently disapproved by the Privy Council need not be followed by the Court of Appeal.[8]

1 And those of its predecessors: the Court of Exchequer Chamber and the Court of Appeal in Chancery, but not by the decisions of the now defunct Court of Criminal Appeal.
2 [1944] KB 718, [1944] 2 All ER 293, CA. The rule in *Young v Bristol Aeroplane* was re-affirmed by the House of Lords in *Davis v Johnson* [1979] AC 264, [1978] 1 All ER 1132.
3 As happened in *Fisher v Ruislip-Northwood UDC and Middlesex County Council* [1945] KB 584, [1945] 2 All ER 458, CA.
4 *Williams v Fawcett* [1985] 1 All ER 787, [1985] 1 WLR 501, CA.
5 [1964] AC 1129, [1964] 1 All ER 367, HL.

6 [1972] AC 1027, [1972] 1 All ER 801, HL.
7 *Boys v Chaplin* [1968] 2 QB 1, [1968] 1 All ER 283, CA.
8 *Doughty v Turner Manufacturing Co Ltd* [1964] 1 QB 518, [1964] 1 All ER 98, CA; *Worcester Works Finance Ltd v Cooden Engineering Co Ltd* [1972] 1 QB 210, [1971] 3 All ER 708, CA.

3.43 The Criminal Division of the Court of Appeal is bound not only by the House of Lords and Court of Appeal decisions but also by those of its predecessor, the Court of Criminal Appeal.[1] However, in the case of decisions of the last two named courts there are exceptions:

a. The three exceptions mentioned in *Young v Bristol Aeroplane*.[2]

b. Probably, where the Court of Appeal decision has been disapproved by the Privy Council.

c. The Criminal Division has power to overrule a previous decision of itself or the Court of Criminal Appeal, on the grounds that the law has been 'misapplied or misunderstood',[3] but only if this is necessary in the interests of the appellant.[4]

1 *Hoskyn v Metropolitan Police Comr* (1978) 67 Cr App Rep 88 at 91.
2 *R v Taylor* [1950] 2 KB 368 at 371, [1950] 2 All ER 170, at 172, *R v Ewing* [1983] QB 1039 at 1047.
3 *R v Taylor* [1950] 2 KB 368, [1950] 2 All ER 170; *R v Newsome and Browne* [1970] 2 QB 711, [1970] 3 All ER 455, CA.
4 *R v Spencer; R v Smails* [1985] QB 771, [1985] 1 All ER 673, CA.

Divisional courts
3.44 Divisional courts are bound by decisions of the House of Lords and of the Court of Appeal, except, apparently, a Court of Appeal decision which is *per incuriam*, in that a relevant decision of the House of Lords was not cited.[1] Until recently, a divisional court was bound by its own previous decisions unless the *Young v Bristol Aeroplane* principles applied,[2] or, probably, in criminal cases the law had been misapplied or misunderstood. However, it has now been decided[3] that a divisional court is not bound by a previous decision of a divisional court; it will normally follow such a decision but in rare cases it may depart from a previous divisional court decision if it is convinced that that decision is wrong.[3]

1 *R v Northumberland Compensation Tribunal, ex p Shaw* [1952] 1 KB 338, [1952] 1 All ER 122, CA.
2 *Huddersfield Police Authority v Watson* [1947] KB 842, [1947] 2 All ER 193, DC.
3 *R v Greater Manchester Coroner exp Tel* [1985] QB 67, [1984] 3 All ER 240, DC: *Hornigold v Chief Constable of Lancashire* [1985] Crim LR 792, DC.

High Court judges
3.45 A High Court judge is bound by the decisions of the courts mentioned above (other than a divisional court exercising the supervisory jurisdiction of the High Court), but he is not bound by decisions of another High Court judge although he will treat such a decision as strong persuasive authority and will only refuse to follow it if he is convinced that it is wrong, and with a clear statement of the reason for doing so.[1] Where a High Court judge is faced with two conflicting decisions of other High Court judges, he should normally treat the legal point at issue as settled by the second decision, provided the judge in that case has reached his decision after full consideration of the first decision. The only rare exception is where the

third judge is convinced that the second judge was wrong in not following the first, as, for example, where a binding or persuasive precedent had not been cited in either of the first two cases.[2]

Although, strictly, a High Court judge is not bound by a decision of a divisional court exercising the supervisory jurisdiction of the High Court, it is difficult to imagine him departing from such a decision.[3]

1   *Re Hillas-Drake, National Provincial Bank v Liddell* [1944] Ch 235, [1944] 1 All ER 375.
2   *Colchester Estates (Cardiff) v Carlton Industries plc* [1984] 2 All ER 601, [1984] 3 WLR 693.
3   *R v Greater Manchester Coroner, ex p Tal* [1984] 3 All ER 240 at 248.

Other courts
3.46   County courts, magistrates' courts and other inferior tribunals are bound by the decisions of all the courts mentioned in the previous paragraphs, and by those of High Court judges sitting alone.[1] The decisions of one of these courts are not binding on another mainly because they are not reported.

Although the matter is not free from doubt, it seems that a judge in the Crown Court is similarly bound and that, mainly for the reason just given, a legal ruling by him is never a binding precedent but is merely of persuasive authority.

1   For a limited exception, in the case of a decision by a High Court judge, see *Chief Supplementary Benefit Office v Leary* [1985] 1 All ER 1061, [1985] 1 WLR 84, CA (tribunal exercising jurisdiction formerly vested in a High Court judge not bound by earlier decisions of High Court judges sitting alone).

Application of judicial precedents
3.47   The fact that a judicial precedent may be binding or merely persuasive in a subsequent case has already been touched on. It may also be noticed that a judicial precedent will become devoid of effect if it is overruled by a court competent to do so (normally, one higher in the hierarchy). As opposed to overruling by statute,[1] judicial overruling operates retrospectively, which may have the effect of disturbing financial interests or vested rights generally. For this reason the courts are reluctant to overrule a previous decision unless they consider it is clearly wrong.

Where a precedent is binding on a court, that court must follow it unless that court can distinguish it on the facts. Suppose that the House of Lords has held that if facts A and B exist, principle X applies, and that a case is heard by a High Court judge at first instance where facts A and B exist as well as fact E, which did not exist in the House of Lords' case. The judge may distinguish the House of Lords' case on its material facts and consequently, since that decision will not be binding in relation to the case before him, decide to apply some other principle or to apply principle X by analogy. Since the facts are never identical in any two cases there is wide scope for 'distinguishing'. However, a court inferior to that which gave the previous decision will not normally distinguish it on strained grounds.

1   Para 3.9b above.

3.48   There are various types of persuasive precedents:

a.   Those decisions of courts inferior in the hierarchy to a court which subsequently hears a similar case. Into this category one can also put decisions of the Judicial Committee of the Privy Council on appeals from Commonwealth states, which do not bind English courts or the Privy Council itself. However, the decisions of the Privy Council are particularly persuasive (since the Judicial Committee normally consists of Lords of Appeal in Ordinary), and the Court of Appeal has held that if one of its previous decisions has been disapproved by the Privy Council it is at liberty to depart from it and apply the Privy Council decision.[1]

b.   Where otherwise binding precedent is distinguishable; it will nevertheless have persuasive authority.[2]

c.   Obiter dicta, the persuasiveness of which depends on the seniority of the court or prestige of the judge by whom the words were uttered and the relative position of that court and a subsequent court. One of the most significant examples is the 'neighbour principle' expounded by Lord Atkin in 1932 in *Donoghue v Stevenson*,[3] which was much wider than the actual case required but has become the basis of the modern tort of negligence and has been applied in numerous cases since.

d.   Decisions of Irish, Scottish, Commonwealth and US courts, which decisions are being referred to increasingly by our courts.

1   *Doughty v Turner Manufacturing Co Ltd* [1964] 1 QB 518, [1964] 1 All ER 98, CA; *Worcester Works Finance Ltd v Cooden Engineering Co Ltd* [1972] 1 QB 210, [1971] 3 All ER 708, CA; para 3.42 above.
2   Especially if it is a House of Lords decision: *Re House Property and Investment Co* [1954] Ch 576, [1953] 2 All ER 1525.
3   [1932] AC 562, HL.

General comments
3.49   Essentially, judicial decisions are declaratory of the common law, merely applying existing law to new fact situations. However, where there is no relevant statute or judicial precedent on a particular point, as still happens occasionally, a judge has to decide the case in accordance with general principles and his decision becomes the original source of a new rule since he is making law rather than applying it.

3.50   The advantages of the system of judicial precedent are its precision and detail, and consequent certainty of application, and in these respects it is far superior to a code or statute which cannot hope to anticipate the innumerable factual situations which can arise in a given area of law. It is sometimes said that the system also has the advantage of flexibility in that outmoded or unsound decisions can be overruled or distinguished. Too much should not be made of this since overruling may be difficult, if not impossible, given the relationship of the courts in question. There is also the danger of illogical or over-subtle distinctions being drawn to avoid hardship in a particular case, but increasing the complexity of the law. Moreover, the vast mass of reported cases can make discovering the law an arduous task and cause a precedent to be overlooked.

Literary sources of judicial precedent
3.51   The most important of these are, of course, the law reports. A law report must be differentiated from a court record which simply contains the

name of the parties, the pleadings, the main facts and the decision, decree or order of the court. Apart from containing most of these things, a law report also contains the judgment of the court, which includes the reasoning on which the result was based.

It may appear surprising that there is no official series of law reports. By no means all cases in the superior courts are reported: only those of legal interest. Law reports may be divided roughly into those published from the time of Henry VIII to 1865, and those published subsequently. Before Henry VIII's time there were the Year Books dating from the time of Edward I, which contained notes on the argument, exchanges between bench and bar and rulings on points of law in cases. The publication of law reports began in about 1535. They were usually published under the names of the reporter and, initially, were little more detailed than the Year Books but gradually developed until they came to resemble the modern law report. Altogether there were some hundreds of different series. Most, but not all, of them have been reprinted in a series known as the English Reports. These 'nominate reports', as they are sometimes called, vary a good deal in quality. However, the reports of Coke, often simply referred to as 'The Reports', Dyer, Plowden, Burroughs and certain others are regarded as particularly outstanding and authoritative. The name of the reporters of reports is traditionally cited in abbreviated form in footnote references, e g Co Rep (Coke), Burr (Burroughs), B & Ald (Barnewell and Alderson) and Term Rep (Term Reports).

In 1865, the semi-official 'Law Reports' commenced. One or more volumes is published annually under each of the following titles 'Queen's Bench' ('QB') (covering cases decided in the Queen's Bench Division or by the Court of Appeal on appeals therefrom or from a county court), 'Chancery' ('Ch') (covering cases decided in the Chancery Division or by the Court of Appeal on appeal therefrom), 'Family' ('Fam')[1] (covering cases decided in the Family Division or by the Court of Appeal on appeal therefrom or from a county court in family matters) and 'Appeal Cases' ('AC') (covering decisions of the House of Lords and Privy Council). Since 1952, many cases appearing in the Law Reports have appeared previously, soon after judgment has been given, in the Weekly Law Reports published by the same organisation, the Incorporated Council of Law Reporting, as do some cases not subsequently published in the Law Reports. The difference between the two series is that the Law Reports contain a summary of the arguments of counsel.

Although the Law Reports superseded most of the series of private reports, there are still a number of commercially owned reports. The All England Reports, a weekly publication, are a general series of reports, while others, such as Lloyd's Law Reports, which deal with commercial cases, are more specialised. The All England Reports commenced publication in 1936 and subsequently superseded two other series, the Law Times Reports and the Law Journal Reports. Finally, mention may be made of the Estates Gazette, in which cases of special interest to the landed professions are reported. The citation of law reports is a somewhat complex matter, outside the scope of this book, and the inquiring student is referred to *Where to Look for Your Law*, to Osborn's *Concise Law Dictionary*, or to any volume of *The Digest*, or to Stroud's *Judicial Dictionary*.

Cases decided by the European Court may be found in the Official

Reports of the Court and in the Common Market Law Reports. They are occasionally reported in the series of reports referred to in the last two paragraphs.

A judgment can be cited to a court even though it has not been published in any series of law reports but is merely contained in a transcript. The transcripts of many recent judgments, particularly of the Court of Appeal (Civil Division), are now available on LEXIS, a computerised legal data base. For reasons which are unconvincing, the House of Lords has held that transcripts of unreported judgments of the Court of Appeal (Civil Division) should not be cited on appeals to the House, except with its leave (which will only be given if counsel gives an assurance that the transcript contains a statement of a relevant principle of law whose substance is not to be found in any reported judgment of the Court of Appeal).[2] No doubt, this restrictive approach will be applied by the House to the citation of transcripts of the judgments of other courts, and will be taken by other courts in relation to the citation to them of transcripts.

1   Until 1972 the citation was 'P' since what is now the Family Division was known as the Probate, Divorce and Admiralty Division until its name, and jurisdiction, were changed.
2   *Roberts Petroleum Ltd v Bernard Kenny Ltd* [1983] AC 192, [1983] 1 All ER 564, HL.

3.52 Mention can be conveniently made at this stage of a secondary literary source, certain 'books of authority'. On the Continent the writings of legal authors form an important source of law. In England, in accordance with the traditional approach that the common law is to be found in judicial decisions, the works of writers are of no official effect, except for books of authority. These are books of some antiquity by authors of great eminence which are regarded as being persuasive authority on the common law as it was when they were written and on the present law if it is not shown to have changed. Generally, these do not contain reports of cases but state principles instead. Perhaps the best known books of authority are Coke's *Institutes*, written in the seventeenth century, and Blackstone's *Commentaries* of the eighteenth century. While the works of modern authors are in no way authoritative, the courts are increasingly being referred to them for guidance on the correct interpretation of the law.

Custom

3.53 In Anglo-Saxon times, custom, in the sense of patterns of behaviour recognised and enforced by the courts, was the principal source of law. However, general customs, ie customs universally observed throughout the land, have either fallen into desuetude or become absorbed into judicial precedent or statute.

A process of absorption has also occurred in relation to the general customs of merchants, which were assimilated by our courts in the seventeenth and eighteenth centuries and developed into commercial law as we now know it.

On the other hand, local customs, ie customs operative in a particular locality or among a particular group of people in a particular locality, are even now occasionally recognised by the courts as establishing a local 'law' for the locality in question at variance with the general law of the land, although they must not be contrary to statute or to a fundamental principle of the common law.

Local customs are largely to be found in rights of way and common. Recognition of a local custom depends on a number of conditions being satisfied, the most important of which are that the alleged custom must:

a. Have existed since 'time immemorial', which, theoretically, it will only do if it goes back to 1189 (for reasons of historical accident).

b. Have been continuous. The custom must have been in existence continuously. This means that the right to exercise it must not have been interrupted; but the fact that the right has not actually been exercised for a period of time, even 100 years in one case,[1] does not negative the existence of a local custom (although if the evidence of custom is dubious it will go far to negative any customary right).

c. Not be unreasonable.[2]

d. Be certain, in other words the right claimed must be certain in nature and scope and prove to adhere to a defined locality or group of people.

e. Be recognised as compulsory.[3]

The first condition is not as strict as may appear since the plaintiff will succeed in proving it if he can prove that the practice in question has existed in the locality for a substantial time: the oldest local inhabitant is often called as a witness in this context. If the plaintiff proves this, existence since 1189 will be presumed,[4] provided, of course, that such a practice was possible in 1189. In *Simpson v Wells*,[5] a person who was charged with obstructing a public footway with his refreshment stall pleaded that he did so by virtue of a custom existing at a 'statute sessions', a fair held for hiring servants. His defence failed because statute sessions were first introduced by a fourteenth century statute, so that the custom could not have existed before then.

1 *New Windsor Corpn v Mellor* [1975] Ch 380, [1975] 3 All ER 44, CA.
2 *Wolstanton Ltd and A-G of Duchy of Lancaster v Newcastle-under-Lyme Corpn* [1940] AC 860, [1940] 3 All ER 101, HL.
3 Blackstone's *Commentaries*: 'a custom that all the inhabitants shall be rated towards the maintenance of a bridge will be good, but a custom that every man is to contribute thereto at his own pleasure is idle and absurd, and indeed not custom at all'.
4 *Mercer v Denne* [1905] 2 Ch 538 at 577.
5 (1872) LR 7 QB 214.

Chapter 4
Elements of constitutional law

4.1 It is a well known fact that the UK, unlike most other countries, does not have a written constitution, in the sense of a single document or series of documents containing the fundamental laws of the constitution. Instead, the sources of the constitutional law of the UK are various pieces of legislation and judicial precedent. In addition, the operation of the rules of our constitutional law is affected in certain areas by 'conventions of the constitution' and by parliamentary 'customs'. Although both of these are of great constitutional importance, they are not recognised by the courts and their breach is not attended by legal, as opposed to political, sanctions. It follows that they are not sources of our constitutional law.

Conventions
4.2 Many of the rules which regulate the Queen in her public capacity, the government and parliament and which regulate the relationship between these bodies are conventional rules. Conventions arise from usage or from tacit or express agreement. While they have no legal force, they are observed partly because of political expedience and partly because of respect for tradition.

Examples of constitutional conventions appear throughout this chapter and a few instances will suffice here. Although the office of Prime Minister is referred to in a number of statutes, that office was not established by statute. Instead, it is merely a convention that there is a Prime Minister, and also that there is a Cabinet. Similarly, it is a convention that, with very limited exceptions, the Queen must exercise her official powers only on and in accordance with the advice of her ministers. Another example is that parliament must be summoned annually (although in law it need only meet once every three years). Since these are not rules of law, the only consequences of breach of them are political.

Parliamentary 'custom'
4.3 Many of the rules which govern the internal working of parliament are 'customs' of parliament. Some of these 'customs' are now included in the Standing Orders of the two Houses of Parliament.

Parliament

4.4 The principal function of parliament is the passing of legislation, in which context it is important to remember that it is a common law rule that parliament consists of the Queen, the House of Commons and, unless the Parliament Acts 1911 and 1949 are invoked,[1] the House of Lords. Connected with this function is that of the discussion and sanctioning by parliament of taxation and the expenditure of public money, since both require statutory authority.

Another very important function of both Houses of Parliament is the general supervision of the government and the exercise of control over it. In practice, parliament is seldom able to exercise control over the government directly because, with certain exceptions (such as the Wilson administration of February to October 1974), the government has a majority in the House of Commons and, since the government normally represents a single political party whose members are loath to vote against their own party, the government is usually able to retain its majority in the House of Commons until the next General Election. Of course, if the government party is or becomes a minority in the House of Commons and is in danger of losing a vote of confidence, the amount of control exercisable over the government by parliament is greatly increased since a government which is defeated in the House of Commons on such a vote is required by convention to resign or seek a dissolution of parliament. Even if its opportunities for direct control are limited, parliament may, and does, indirectly control the government since one of the ways in which it exercises its supervisory function is through the daily question time in the House of Commons, during which the policies and operations of the government and its various departments and ministries can be probed.[2] Adverse publicity, following an unsatisfactory answer to such a question, may well lead to a change in government policy. A similar result may also be achieved in consequence of a critical report from one of the Select Committees of the House of Commons, which keep under review various areas of the government's work.

The judicial function of the House of Lords as a court of appeal has already been discussed.[3] Another judicial function possessed by both Houses of Parliament separately is jurisdiction over disputed peerages (Lords) and over disputes concerning a person's eligibility for membership of the House of Commons (Commons). In addition, each House has jurisdiction over breaches of privilege, such as contempt of it or wrongs committed within its precincts.

1 Para 3.7 above.
2 Para 4.17 below.
3 Paras 2.27–2.29 above.

Meetings

4.5 The period between the time when parliament is summoned by Royal Proclamation and its termination by dissolution by the Queen acting on the advice of the Prime Minister, or by lapse of time, is called a parliament. Normally, parliament is dissolved on the advice of the Prime Minister, either because the Prime Minister thinks that a General Election will produce a result favourable to his (or her) party or because he (or she) has been defeated in a confidence vote in the House of Commons. Unless an earlier dissolution is advised, a parliament must end after five years,[1] and a General Election be held, although it is always possible for this period to be extended by a special Act of Parliament, as happened in the Second World War.

Each parliament is divided into sessions, of which there are one or more a year. Parliament is summoned by the Queen at the start of each session and prorogued at its end. Public Bills[2] still in progress when a session is prorogued lapse and have to start afresh if introduced in the next session.

1 Parliament Act 1911, s7.
2 Para 3.5 above.

Composition

4.6 a. *House of Lords* The members of this chamber are the Lords Spiritual and the Lords Temporal. The Lords Spiritual are the Archbishops of Canterbury and York and 24 of the diocesan bishops of the Church of England.

The Lords Temporal comprise:

i   hereditary peers (and peeresses, of whom there are very few) in their own right, other than those of Ireland;
ii persons created life peers under the Life Peerage Act 1958 and thereby entitled to membership of the House of Lords; and
iii Lords of Appeal in Ordinary and ex-Lords of Appeal in Ordinary.[1]

The Lord Chancellor presides at meetings of the House of Lords.

b.   *House of Commons* The Speaker, or one of the Deputy Speakers, presides at meetings of this chamber, which is composed of members of parliament. Members of parliament, of whom there are 650, are the elected representatives, not delegates, of their constituents.

All persons aged 18 or over who are Commonwealth citizens (which in law includes British citizens) or citizens of the Republic of Ireland are entitled to vote at a parliamentary election, except:

i   peers and peeresses in their own right, other than peers of Ireland;
ii persons serving sentences of imprisonment; and
iii persons who have within the previous five years been convicted of a corrupt election practice or (and this only applies to voting in the constituency in question) of an illegal election practice.[2]

Eligible persons may only exercise their right to vote if they are registered in the annual electoral register for the constituency in question. Registration depends on residence in a particular constituency on the qualifying date (10 October).[3] Some people are deemed to be resident on that date. Examples are British citizens living overseas who satisfy certain requirements, servicemen and merchant seamen.

The following are disqualified from membership or continued membership of the House of Commons:

i   persons convicted of corrupt or illegal practices at a parliamentary election, the disqualification being for various periods depending on the facts;[4]
ii persons convicted of an offence and sentenced to prison for more than a year, the disqualification lasting as long as the person concerned is

detained in the British Isles or Republic of Ireland or is unlawfully at large;[5]

iii persons suffering from severe mental illness, although the seat of a member who is detained by reason of such illness is not vacated until he has been detained for six months;[6]

iv peers and peeresses in their own right, other than those of Ireland;

v clergy of the established churches of England and Scotland, Roman Catholic clergymen, and all other episcopally ordained clergymen (other than those of the Church in Wales);[7]

vi members of the Civil Service or of the regular armed forces;

vii full-time judges and full-time members of police forces; and

viii holders of certain other offices of profit under the Crown, although as a special exception no more than 95 holders of specified ministerial offices may sit and vote in the House of Commons at any one time.[8]

A person is disqualified from membership of either House if he is under 21, or bankrupt, or not a Commonwealth citizen or a citizen of the Irish Republic.

1 Appellate Jurisdiction Act 1887; para 2.27 above.
2 Representation of the People Act 1983.
3 Representation of the People Acts 1983 and 1985.
4 Representation of the People Act 1983.
5 Representation of the People Act 1981.
6 Mental Health Act 1983, s141.
7 Eg House of Commons (Clergy Disqualification) Act 1801; Roman Catholic Relief Act 1829.
8 House of Commons Disqualification Act 1975.

Parliamentary sovereignty

4.7 Under this heading we expand upon the legislative function of parliament. Traditionally, parliamentary sovereignty, which some prefer to call parliamentary supremacy, has meant two things:

a. All legislative power in the UK is vested in parliament, or derives its authority from parliament (as is the case with a power to make delegated legislation) and that authority may be removed at any time by parliament, or is exercised at the sufferance of parliament (as is the case with the very limited power to legislate under the royal prerogative for the colonies, the armed forces and the civil service, which is all that remains of the monarchy's pretensions to legislate by proclamation or ordinance). Thus, parliament has no rival in the legislative sphere.

b. Parliament has power by Act of Parliament to enact or abolish any law, and no court in the UK is competent to question the validity or the propriety of any Act of Parliament. In particular, there are no entrenched rights in our constitutional law which cannot be infringed by ordinary legislation and which are safeguarded by a power vested in a supreme court to find such legislation invalid. The sovereignty of parliament in this context is illustrated by the fact that attempts to impugn an Act of Parliament on the gound that it conflicts with the UK's duties under international law have uniformly failed.[1] Thus, under UK law there are no limits to parliament's legislative powers. Nevertheless, there are practical limitations on these powers—a matter dealt with in para 4.11 below; and, although the courts must give effect to a clear intention expressed in a statute however absurd the result, wherever there is a shadow of doubt they do their best to avoid absurd results or to limit the extent of an Act of Parliament by the use of devices such as the golden rule[2] and the various presumptions of interpretation (such as those against retrospective effect or against inconsistency with international law).[3]

1   Eg *Mortensen* v *Peters* 1906 14 SLT 227.
2   Para 3.19 above.
3   Para 3.25 above.

4.8   We discussed the legislative organs of the European Communities and their powers, including the concept of directly applicable legislation, in paras 3.29 to 3.33 above. The legislative organs of the Communities are not subordinate to the U K parliament, and a question which has provoked much controversy concerns the situation where a directly applicable rule of Community law conflicts with an Act of Parliament. In answering this question, the starting point is to recall two things. First, that directly applicable *Community law* is only part of the law of the U K because it has been so incorporated by the European Communities Act 1972, s2(1). Second, that s2(4) of the Act provides that Acts of Parliament passed or to be passed shall be construed and have effect subject to the directly applicable rules of Community law. In consequence, Acts of Parliament already in existence at the time of our accession to the Communities were impliedly repealed to the extent that they were irreconcilably in conflict with existing directly applicable Community law, and the same is true in relation to other Acts of Parliament (including those passed thereafter) if such conflict results from a subsequent piece of directly applicable Community law.

The difficulty surrounds the legal situation where an Act of Parliament is passed which is inconsistent with *pre-existing* directly applicable Community law. *According to Community law*, such an Act could not prevail over the existing Community law, which would take precedence over it,[1] and our courts would have to apply the Community law and ignore the subsequent Act of Parliament.[2] However, this does not seem to be the position *according to the law of the U K*. Admittedly, some writers have suggested that the effect of s2(4) of the 1972 Act is to deny effectiveness to an Act of Parliament which is inconsistent with pre-existing directly applicable Community law, but the better view—which is the view taken so far by our courts, although they have not always expressed themselves very clearly—is that, insofar as it relates to an Act which conflicts with pre-existing Community law, s2(4) merely provides a rule of construction which must give way to a clear contrary intention on the part of parliament in the subsequent Act. More fully, the effect of s2(4) is that, with one exception, U K courts must interpret an Act of Parliament in such a way as to be consistent with pre-existing directly applicable Community law and, if the Act is deficient or inconsistent with that law by some oversight of its draftsman, they must give priority to Community law.[3] The exception is that, if (as is most unlikely) parliament expressed in the Act its intention to enact a provision inconsistent with a directly applicable Community law, the Act of Parliament would prevail in U K law and have to be applied by U K courts,[4] notwithstanding the primacy of Community law under Community law and the consequent breach in that respect of its obligations under Community law by the U K. Thus, the doctrine of the sovereignty of parliament, which is a doctrine of UK law, has not been impaired by the UK's accession to the European Communities.

1 *Costa v ENEL* [1964] CMLR 425 at 455; *Amministrazione delle Finanze dello Stato v Simmenthal SpA* [1978] ECR 629, [1978] 3 CMLR 263, CJEC.
2 *Amministrazione delle Finanze dello Stato v Simmenthal SpA* above.
3 *Shields v E Coomes (Holdings) Ltd* [1979] 1 All ER 456 at 460; *Macarthys Ltd v Smith* [1979] 3 All ER 325, [1979] 1 WLR 1189, CA; *Macarthys Ltd v Smith (No 2)* [1980] IRLR 209, CA.
4 *Macarthys Ltd v Smith* above.

4.9 There can be no doubt that our courts would not accept claims that in some other way parliament can effectively deprive itself of its legislative sovereignty by way of Act of Parliament. This is supported by cases where it has been held that a provision in one Act that legislation inconsistent with it should have no effect does not invalidate an inconsistent provision in a subsequent Act; instead the earlier Act is impliedly repealed to the extent of the inconsistency.[1]

1 *Vauxhall Estates Ltd v Liverpool Corpn* [1932] 1 KB 733; *Ellen Street Estates Ltd v Minister of Health* [1934] 1 KB 590, CA.

4.10 It must be emphasised that what has been said above about parliamentary sovereignty only applies where parliament exercises its legislative function by Act of Parliament. While the courts lack jurisdiction to investigate the parliamentary history of what purports to be an Act of Parliament or to question its validity on the ground that there has been a breach of parliamentary procedure, such as an insufficient number of readings or no readings at all in one of the Houses of Parliament, or that the Act's passage has been procured by fraud,[1] a court could not treat as valid a purported Act of Parliament which on its face had not been passed by parliament. For example, a court could not treat as valid a statute whose initial enacting words indicated (in a case not within the exception provided by the Parliament Acts 1911 and 1949)[2] that the Act had not been passed by the House of Lords, because it would not be an Act of *Parliament*.

1 *British Railways Board v Pickin* [1974] AC 765, [1974] 1 All ER 609, HL.
2 Para 3.7 above.

4.11 In practice, the doctrine of parliamentary sovereignty does not result in absurd legislation nor in legislation which flagrantly violates fundamental liberties or which purports to alter the law of a foreign sovereign state, however possible these and other measures may be in theory. The reason is that, while there are no legal safeguards against such measures, political, economic and social considerations provide effective safeguards.

We have already indicated that parliament will doubtless abstain from passing Acts of Parliament which deliberately conflict with the law of the European Economic Communities; legislation inconsistent with the other international obligations of the UK, whether under a treaty or under general international law, has been and will remain very rare indeed.

Naturally enough, governments are loath to lose office and are unlikely to introduce legislation which will not receive the support of a majority of the House of Commons, lest this should lead to an adverse vote of confidence; and parliament, not wishing to have its credibility impaired, is unlikely to pass legislation which it believes to be unenforceable.

The Executive

The monarchy

4.12 Our monarchy has been a 'constitutional' or 'limited' monarchy since the late eighteenth century. In practice, but not in law, and with the exceptions mentioned shortly, the Queen herself lacks any discretion in the exercise of her wide official powers, including her power to give royal assent to a Bill, since by convention she can only act on and in accordance with the advice of her ministers. The only occasions when the Queen may exercise her powers without ministerial advice, or against it, are:

a. The Queen may dismiss her Prime Minister and other ministers if the government loses its majority, or a confidence vote, in the House of Commons *and* the Prime Minister decides to remain in office instéad of resigning or advising a dissolution of parliament.

b. The Queen may also dismiss her Prime Minister and other ministers if they purport to infringe some basic democratic principle, e g by legislation prolonging the life of a parliament simply in order to avoid defeat at a General Election.

c. The Queen may insist on the dissolution of parliament if deadlock in the House of Commons prevents essential legislation, such as that relating to the levying of taxes and the expenditure of public money, being passed. There is a technical difficulty here since the requisite measures for a dissolution require the co-operation of the Queen's ministers and, if the Prime Minister refuses the Queen's request that she be advised to dissolve parliament, it will first be necessary to dismiss the Prime Minister and appoint one of the Prime Minister's colleagues, if willing, or otherwise the Leader of the Opposition, as Prime Minister so as to take the measures for a dissolution.

d. The Queen may refuse the Prime Minister's advice that parliament be dissolved where she believes that an alternative government, enjoying the confidence of a majority of the existing House of Commons, can be formed *and* that a General Election at that time would clearly be prejudicial to the interests of the country.[1]

It is now a constitutional convention that, in appointing her Prime Minister, the Queen should appoint the leader of the majority party in the House of Commons. However, if no party has an overall majority in that House, the Queen must exercise her discretion in deciding who is best able to command support in the House of Commons. That person, who will normally be the leader of the largest party in the Commons, will then be appointed Prime Minister.

1 For a discussion of these matters, see de Smith, *Constitutional and Administrative Law* (5th edn) pp 123–131.

4.13 Clearly, the Queen's functions are essentially symbolic, but this does not mean that she has no influence over affairs of state outside the limited areas just mentioned. Bagehot, the great writer of the nineteenth century on the constitution, said that she has 'the right to be consulted, the right to encourage, the right to warn'.[1] The fact that most of the monarchs of the last hundred years have reigned for a substantial period has meant that a time has come in those reigns when they have had more experience of the affairs of state than their ministers. Patently, this is a factor which is likely to enhance a monarch's influence. The influence which the Queen may exercise is fostered by the convention by which she receives Cabinet papers and minutes, and other state papers, and by the convention that she is kept adequately informed by the Prime Minister on matters of government policy.

1   *The English Constitution.*

4.14   References to 'the Queen' must be distinguished from 'the Crown', which term refers not just to the Queen but also to her government.

At the start of each reign a Civil List Act is passed; the present one is the Civil List Act 1952, as amended by the Civil List Act 1972. These Acts provide for annual sums to be paid to the Queen and certain other members of the royal family to cover their personal expenses and the expenses of the royal household.

Although the Queen holds private property, what are called 'Crown Lands' belong to the Crown in its public capacity and are not the Queen's private property.

In her private capacity the Queen cannot be sued in tort, but she may consent to be sued for breaches of contract, for the recovery of land or chattels, and in relation to certain other matters, by what is known as Petition of Right procedure. Damages are the only remedy available under this procedure. We deal with actions against the Crown in its public capacity in para 4.22 below.

The Privy Council
4.15   This is the oldest branch of the Executive. Like parliament and the superior courts, its origins can be traced back to the curia regis of early medieval times. Privy Councillors are appointed by the Queen on the advice of the Prime Minister. By convention, members of the Cabinet, appellate judges and the holders of certain other offices are always appointed Privy Councillors. Other people are appointed as a political honour or for public service in the twice-yearly Honours Lists. For most of the 350 or more Privy Councillors their office is a purely honorary one, since the only Privy Councillors who attend the Council's regular meetings are four or five Cabinet ministers, including the Lord President of the Council who conducts the business of the meeting. At meetings of the Privy Council (which are, of course attended by the Queen) legal effect is given by Order in Council, made either under the royal prerogative or under statutory powers, to decisions already taken elsewhere, normally by the government. Thus, the Privy Council itself is essentially a formal body, but it has a number of committees, such as its Judicial Committee,[1] which still have an active decision-making function.

1   Para 2.33 above.

The government
4.16   Once appointed, a Prime Minister forms a government (or administration) by appointing from among his (or her) supporters in parliament Cabinet ministers and other ministers. It is a convention that the Prime

Minister must be a member of the House of Commons and most other ministers are also members of that House, especially those with the important ministries, but some necessarily are members of the House of Lords since the government must have spokesmen in that House.

The government's policies are formulated by the Cabinet, which also takes important governmental decisions. The Cabinet's size varies but it rarely has more than 24 members. Most of the political heads (ie Secretaries of State or ministers) of government departments are in the Cabinet, and so are certain other ministers (such as the Lord President of the Council and the Lord Privy Seal) who do not have departmental responsibilities. A great deal of the work of the Cabinet is done through committees, some of which are 'Cabinet committees' of ministers (which may include ministers outside the Cabinet) while others are committees of senior officials. The Cabinet is assisted in its work by the Cabinet Secretariat, which is composed of civil servants.

An important convention is that of the collective responsibility of the Cabinet to the House of Commons, so that if the government is defeated on a confidence vote in that House it must resign or advise a dissolution of parliament. Another result of collective responsibility is that all members of the Cabinet assume responsibility for Cabinet decisions and actions pursuant to them. Hence, a Cabinet minister must not publicly express his dissent with a Cabinet decision or its implementation; if he feels compelled to do so he must resign first.

Government departments

4.17   These are the executive organs of the government. Each department, eg the Home Office or the Overseas Development Administration, has a political head—ie a minister such as the Home Secretary or the Minister of Overseas Development. These political heads are subject to the doctrine of ministerial responsibility, which comprises two propositions. First, a minister is legally liable for any wrongful executive act done on behalf of the Crown by his department. Second, as a member of parliament a departmental minister is politically responsible to parliament, in that he is deemed to speak and act for the government on all matters within his department's responsibilities, and also in that he must answer to parliament for the acts of his officials.

The work of a government department, including the execution of government policy, is carried out by civil servants. A senior civil servant, called the Permanent Secretary, is the head of each department. One of his tasks is to advise on policy matters.

Executive bodies outside central government

4.18   Some of the areas of responsibility of government departments, eg education, are shared with other bodies such as local authorities, in which case general policy in the particular field and its implementation is the concern of the government department but the day-to-day running and detailed execution of that policy is a matter for the other body. Of course, these other bodies are legally independent of the government but it must not be forgotten that to a greater or lesser extent they are dependent on finance provided by the government.

A number of functions of a governmental character are carried out by public corporations, which are separate corporate bodies. They are often legally independent of the government, in which case they do not act as servants or agents of the Crown. Examples of the range of public corporations are:

a.   commercial undertakings, which are all legally independent, e g the British Railways Board, the National Coal Board and the British Gas Corporation;

b.   non-commercial undertakings, e g Regional Health Authorities;

c.   regulatory bodies, e g the Milk Marketing Board and the White Fish Authority; and

d.   advisory and conciliatory bodies, e g the Equal Opportunities Commission and the Advisory, Conciliation and Arbitration Service.

The commercial undertakings are generally expected to pay their way, but the other public corporations are dependent on finance from the government.

Public corporations are subject to varying degrees of control by the appropriate minister, depending on the terms of their constituent statute. In every case the minister (or the Queen 'on advice') appoints, and can dismiss, the chairman and board members. Public corporations are also subject to parliamentary control; in particular, questions can be asked of the appropriate minister in parliament on matters within the sphere of his responsibility in relation to the corporation. In addition, the reports and accounts of the nationalised industries are investigated by the House of Commons Select Committee on Nationalised Industries.

Powers of the Executive
4.19   The vast majority of the powers of the various branches of the Executive, especially those of local authorities and public corporations, are provided by Act of Parliament or delegated legislation.[1] However, the Crown still possesses a number of powers by virtue of the royal prerogative, a matter which requires further explanation.

Until the revolution of 1688, English monarchs asserted claims to exercise wide powers by virtue of the royal prerogative. Although the revolution had put beyond doubt that for the future parliament's legislative competence was unrivalled and supreme, some of the royal prerogative powers—mainly in the administrative field—continued to be exercised, and some are still exercised. Thus, the prerogative can be defined as the residue of discretionary authority which at any given time is legally left in the hands of the Crown. That is why we said, in para 4.7a above, that the prerogative powers are exercised at the sufferance of parliament. The prerogative powers are exercised either by the Queen, normally acting on the advice of her ministers[2] and through them, or by government ministers, acting on behalf of the Crown. Four examples will serve to indicate the range of the various prerogative powers:

a.   The Queen's powers to summon, dissolve and prorogue parliament are prerogative ones;

b. The Queen retains the prerogative power to legislate, by Order in Council, for the colonies, the armed forces and the civil service;[3]

c. Peerages and other political honours are granted by virtue of the prerogative. In this connection it may be noted that appointments to the Orders of the Garter, of the Thistle and of Merit, and to the Royal Victorian Order, lie in the Queen's personal discretion, ie she does not make these appointments 'on the advice' of her Prime Minister; and

d. Under the prerogative the Crown has exclusive control over the disposition of the armed forces.

1 Paras 3.10–3.15 above.
2 Para 4.12 above
3 Para 3.16 above.

4.20 No attempt can be made here to describe the multifarious powers of the government, local authorities or public corporations, but it should be borne in mind that essentially those powers involve the power to make policy and the power to implement it, which powers may be vested in different bodies. The implementation of policy may involve the power to make subordinate legislation[1] and, in the case of the government, the power to adjudicate on the implementation of a policy in a specific case. The government's powers of adjudication are exercised either by tribunals,[2] permanent bodies which themselves reach a decision on the matter, or by ad hoc inquiries, which inquire into a matter and often simply report their findings and recommendations to a minister who then makes the decision.

1 Paras 3.10–3.16 above.
2 Para 2.38 above.

Review of Executive action

4.21 Executive action may be reviewed by the courts, the Parliamentary Commissioner for Administration and the local 'ombudsmen'; these methods are far more effective than any control which parliament may seek to exercise over a particular action.

4.22 A person aggrieved or injured by the decision, act or omission of a local authority or public corporation may sue for damages in contract or tort, or seek specific performance of a contract, or seek an injunction to restrain a breach of contract or a tort, in the same way as if his action was against any other body. However, while the Crown (ie the government) is generally liable under the Crown Proceedings Act 1947 to pay damages for breach of contract or a tort, neither specific performance nor an injunction can be awarded against the Crown.

It is important to remember that, unless statute expressly provides or a prerogative power exists, no member of any branch of the Executive is above the law. If he does what would otherwise be wrongful he is not allowed to plead that what he did was dictated by administrative policy and cannot be impugned before the courts. Instead, he must justify under the general law any Executive action which affects the Queen's subjects (or aliens resident in her territories).

4.23 Often a person aggrieved by an action or decision by the Executive—

whether a government department, local authority, public corporation or a tribunal—will not have a ground for an action for damages for breach of contract or in tort, or, if he has, will be more concerned to challenge the validity of that action or decision. In such a case he may be able to obtain from the High Court one or more of the following orders:

a. a prerogative order of mandamus, prohibition or certiorari (which orders we described in para 2.18d above);

b. an injunction restraining the taking of an invalid action or decision; or

c. a declaration. A declaration is a judicial declaration of the parties' rights. It is not in itself enforceable, but in practice executive bodies and their officials will normally act in accordance with the terms of the declaration. A declaration is not available in relation to a hypothetical case but only in relation to a concrete case involving a dispute on an issue of law.[1]

The Supreme Court Act 1981, s31(1) requires that an application for an order of mandamus, prohibition or certiorari must be made by an application for judicial review under the Rules of the Supreme Court, Ord 53.

Whenever an application for judicial review under Ord 53 has been made, the High Court has a discretionary power under s31(2) of the Act of 1981 to make a declaration or to grant an injunction. In exercising this discretion, the court must have regard to the nature of the matters in respect of which mandamus, prohibition or certiorari apply; to the nature of the persons and bodies against who these orders may be granted, and to all the circumstances of the case. Although neither s31 of the Act of 1981 nor Ord 53 says so, it has been held by the House of Lords that a person seeking judicial review of the actions or decisions of administrative bodies must apply under Ord 53 if he wishes to obtain a declaration or injunction.[2]

On an application for judicial review, the court may award damages if requested by the applicant, even though it does not make one of the above orders, provided damages could have been awarded if an ordinary action had been brought.[3]

An application for judicial review cannot be made unless leave to apply has been granted. An application for leave is made to a single judge who deals with it without a hearing. An appeal against a refusal of leave is made to a single judge in open court or to a divisional court, and thence to the Court of Appeal from whom there is no appeal to the House of Lords on this matter.[4] If leave is granted, the application is heard by a single judge in civil cases, unless the court otherwise directs a hearing by a divisional court; in criminal cases the application is always heard by a divisional court.

All the orders in a.–c. above are discretionary. With the exception of declarations,[5] they cannot be made against the Crown. However, mandamus, prohibition or certiorari may be granted against a minister or other officer of the Crown in his official capacity. On the other hand, an injunction cannot be granted against a minister or other officer of the Crown if the effect of granting it would be to give relief against the Crown which could not have been obtained in proceedings against the Crown.[6] This precludes injunctions being awarded against ministers and other Crown officers for acts done in the purported exercise of their statutory functions[7] (unless the acts are tortious, in which case an injunction could be awarded against the offending minister or officer in his personal capacity).

1 *Re Barnato* [1949] Ch 258, [1949] 1 All ER 515, CA.
2 *O'Reilly v Mackman* [1983] 2 AC 237, [1982] 3 All ER 1124, HL; *Cocks v Thanet District Council* [1983] 2 AC 286, [1982] 3 All ER 1135, HL.
3 Supreme Court Act 1981, s31(4).
4 *Re Poh* [1983] 1 All ER 287, [1983] 1 WLR 2, HL.
5 Crown Proceedings Act 1947, s21(1).
6 Ibid, s21(2).
7 *Merricks v Heathcoat-Amory and Minister of Agriculture, Fisheries and Food* [1955] Ch 567, [1955] 2 All ER 453, CA.

4.24 A prerogative order, declaration or injunction cannot be granted simply because the court disagrees with the action or decision of the administrative body. Instead, the case must fall within one of the following grounds:

a. *Denial of natural justice* The principles of natural justice must be observed by anybody who is under a public duty to act judicially in reaching a particular decision. There are two principles. First, the *audi alteram partem* principle which requires:
i   that a person be given prior timely and reasonably sufficient notice of the case which he has to meet;[1]
ii that a person be given a fair opportunity to answer the case against him and to put his own case,[2] which does not mean that an oral hearing must be held.[3]
Second, there is the principle against bias which stipulates:
i   that the adjudicator must not have a financial or proprietary interest in the outcome of the proceedings;[4]
ii that there will be a denial of natural justice if, for any other reason, there is a real likelihood of bias in the adjudicator.[5]
Certiorari or a declaration is the appropriate remedy where there has been a denial of natural justice; prohibition or an injunction where it is apprehended.

In a number of cases the courts have held that even where a decision is not of a judicial nature public bodies (and their officials) must act fairly.[6] What 'fairness' requires has not yet been clearly settled, and it may involve a lower standard than natural justice. The same remedies are appropriate for an actual or threatened breach of the requirement of fairness as for a breach of natural justice.

b. *Ultra vires* The action, decision or delegated legislation of an administrative body can be reviewed by the courts if it is substantively or procedurally ultra vires (ie in excess of that body's powers).

An action or decision or delegated legislation will be substantively ultra vires if it is beyond the powers of the body in question, and this includes where the body has made an error of law which led it to believe that the matter was within its powers.[7] In addition, a decision which involves such an unreasonable exercise of a discretion that no reasonable body could have come to it can be impugned by a court[8] (but this does not mean that the court can substitute its own decision on the merits of the decision). On this basis of 'abuse of power' a decision can be impugned, for example, if an administrative body makes it in reliance on irrelevant considerations[9] or for an improper purpose.[10]

An administrative body's action, decision or delegated legislation will be procedurally ultra vires if there has been a breach of the statutory procedure laid down for its making or taking.[11]

As in the case of a decision where there has been a denial of natural justice, an ultra vires action, decision or piece of delegated legislation is a nullity. Where the ultra vires matter has occurred the appropriate remedy is a declaration or (if the matter in question is a decision taken by a body which was under a duty to act judicially or fairly) certiorari. In addition, the ultra vires nature of delegated legislation may be raised as a defence in proceedings based on it. An injunction or (if the matter in question is a decision to be taken by a body which is under a duty to act judicially or fairly) prohibition is the appropriate remedy where the administrative body proposes to do something which will be ultra vires.

c. *Failure to perform a public legal duty,* including a duty to exercise a discretion. Mandamus is the appropriate remedy here.

d. *Error of law on the face of the record*[12] This is relevant to the decisions of bodies which are under a duty to act judicially or fairly. The error must be clear and obvious from the face of the 'record', which includes any documents which the decision makes clear were its basis.[13] It is not enough that the error of law could be discovered by a detailed examination of all the evidence before the adjudicator.[13] Certiorari is the most appropriate remedy here.

1   *Sloan v General Medical Council* [1970] 2 All ER 686, [1970] 1 WLR 1130, PC.
2   *Kanda v Government of the Federation of Malaya* [1962] AC 322, [1962] 2 WLR 1153, PC.
3   *Miller v Minister of Housing and Local Government* [1968] 2 All ER 633, [1968] 1 WLR 992, CA.
4   *Dimes v Grand Junction Canal Proprietors* [1852] 3 HL Cas 759.
5   *R v Camborne JJ, ex p Pearce* [1955] 1 QB 41 at 51.
6   Eg *Re H(K) (An Infant)* [1967] 2 QB 617, [1967] 1 All ER 226.
7   *Anisminic v Foreign Compensation Commission* [1969] 2 AC 147 [1969] 1 All ER 208, HL; *South East Asia Fire Bricks Sdn Bhd v Non-Metallic Mineral Products Manufacturing Employees Union* [1981] AC 363, [1980] 2 All ER 689, PC.
8   *Associated Provincial Picture Houses Ltd v Wednesbury Corpn* [1948] 1 KB 223, [1947] 2 All ER 680, CA; *Secretary of State for Education & Science v Tameside Metropolitan Borough Council* [1977] AC 1014, [1976] 3 All ER 665, HL.
9   *Roberts v Hopwood* [1925] AC 578, HL.
10 *Congreve v Home Office* [1976] QB 629, [1976] 1 All ER 697, CA.
11 *Rayner v Stepney Corpn* [1911] 2 Ch 312.
12 *R v Northumberland Compensation Appeal Tribunal, ex p Shaw* [1952] 1 KB 338, [1952] 1 All ER 122, CA.
13 *Baldwin and Francis Ltd v Patents Appeal Tribunal* [1959] AC 663, [1959] 2 All ER 433, HL.

4.25 Sometimes, statutes purport to confer unchallengeable powers on an administrative body. The courts have given a restrictive interpretation to some of the formulae commonly used for this purpose, with the result that in these cases the exercise of the power will not be unchallengeable or, at least, not wholly unchallengeable. For example, in *Anisminic v Foreign Compensation Commission,*[1] the House of Lords held that a statutory provision that a determination by the Commission was 'not to be questioned in any legal proceedings whatsoever' did not take away the courts' jurisdiction to declare a determination a nullity where it was void ad initio, as it would be if made in breach of natural justice or ultra vires.

It should also be noted that the Tribunals and Inquiries Act 1971, s14(1), provides that a provision in any enactment passed before 1 August 1958, which purports to oust the jurisdiction of the High Court to grant an order of certiorari in relation to a decision, is of no effect. Since 1958, statutes have eschewed such a provision.

1 [1969] 2 AC 147, [1969] 1 All ER 208, HL.

Parliamentary Commissioner for Administration
4.26 The Commissioner is otherwise known as the Ombudsman. His office and terms of reference were established by the Parliamentary Commissioner Act 1967. His function is to provide a safeguard, in cases where there is no judicial remedy, by investigating complaints by members of the public who claim to have suffered injustice in consequence of maladministration in the exercise of administrative functions by those government departments and certain other public bodies, such as the Inland Revenue and the Land Registry, listed in the second Schedule to the Act of 1967. However, even in these cases the Commissioner lacks jurisdiction if the person aggrieved had a right of appeal or review before a court or tribunal, unless the Commissioner considers it was not reasonable to expect him to resort to such a remedy.

The Commissioner does not have jurisdiction over matters listed in the third Schedule of the Act, such as the investigation of crime, foreign affairs or commercial transactions, or over complaints by a person not resident in the UK (unless the act complained of concerns action in relation to him while he was present in the UK).

The essence of the Commissioner's functions is the investigation of 'maladministration': he cannot investigate a decision simply on the ground that it is misguided. 'Maladministration' may take a variety of forms, some involving a positive act and others a failure to act, such as improper discrimination, failing to inform a member of the public of his rights or misleading him, failing to reply to correspondence and unreasonable delay before taking administrative action.

The Commissioner cannot act on his own initiative, nor at the direct request of a member of the public. Instead, a written complaint must be made by the aggrieved person to any member of parliament, and it is for him to decide, with the consent of the person aggrieved, whether to forward it to the Commissioner. If the member addressed decides not to refer the complaint, the person aggrieved can write to member of parliament after member of parliament until he succeeds, if at all, in securing a reference to the Commissioner. On receiving a complaint, the Commissioner has a discretion whether to investigate it. If he decides to do so, he must inform the administrative body concerned. If he decides not to investigate, he must inform the member of parliament who referred the complaint of his reasons.

If the Commissioner decides to proceed, his function is purely investigatory; he has no powers to alter the administrative decision or action if he finds there has been injustice due to maladministration nor to set it aside. Instead, he is limited to making a report on his investigations which he sends to the member of parliament who referred the complaint, to the official concerned and to the head of the latter's department. In addition, if he decides that injustice has been done by maladministration and that, despite his investigation, it remains unremedied (which is rare) he may make a special report to both Houses of Parliament. But even then this may only lead to an official expression of regret. The Commissioner also makes an Annual Report to both Houses on the exercise of his functions. Both types of report are considered by a Select Committee of the House of Commons, and they may be the subject of debate in parliament.

4.27 The Parliamentary Commissioner for Administration has no power to investigate maladministration by local authorities or by most public corporations.

However, the Local Government Act 1972 established Commissioners for Local Administration for England (which at present has three Commissioners) and for Wales (one Commissioner at present). The Commissioners' duty is to investigate complaints of injustice in consequence of maladministration in the execution of administrative functions performed by a local authority, water authority or police authority. Complaints must be written and must be forwarded by a member of the authority concerned, but the Commissioner has power to dispense with this latter requirement if that member refuses the complainant's request to forward it. If the Commissioner decides to investigate the complaint, he must report the result of his investigation to the member who referred the complaint and to the complainant and authority concerned. If the Commissioner has found injustice has been suffered in consequence of maladministration and is not satisfied with the action taken or proposed by the authority to remedy it, he may investigate the matter further and issue a second report, but he has no further powers.

Under the National Health Service Act 1977, there is a Health Service Commissioner for England and one for Wales. At present, both offices are held by the Parliamentary Commissioner for Administration. As Health Service Commissioner he is not limited to the investigation of maladministration but can also investigate a complaint of injustice through failure in a health service. Complaints do not have to be routed to a Health Service Commissioner by way of a member of parliament or other person.

Separation of powers

4.28 Apart from the legislature and the Executive there is a third organ of government in any country, the judiciary, whom we described in ch 2.

Under the constitutions of some countries, such as the US, a very clear distinction is drawn between legislative, executive and judicial powers, so that a member of the legislature cannot simultaneously be a member of the Executive, and so forth, on the ground that individual liberty would be threatened if more than one of these types of powers was given to one person or organ of government. Such a separation does not, and never has, existed in this country, as a few examples drawn from what we have already said demonstrate:

a. the Prime Minister and other ministers are members of the legislature and of the Executive;

b. the Lord Chancellor is chairman of one of the chambers of the legislature, head of the judiciary and a (Cabinet) member of the Executive;

c. judges sometimes exercise functions of an executive nature, eg the determination of applications for licences; and

d. legislative powers are delegated by the legislature to the members of the Executive (such as the Queen in Council, and ministers).

Any risk to individual liberty from the absence of the separation of powers in this country is mitigated by the safeguards, which we have mentioned previously, against the arbitrary exercise of governmental powers.

Part II

The law of contract

Chapter 5
Agreement

5.1 In this part of the book we adopt the following order. In this chapter and the next we outline those basic elements of the law of contract which relate to the existence of a valid and enforceable contract. In the following five chapters (chs 7–11) we deal with contractual obligations, with how they are discharged, and with the remedies available if they are broken. Sometimes what would otherwise be an enforceable contract is invalidated or liable to be set aside because of mistake, misrepresentation, illegality, the incapacity of a party or certain other factors. We deal with these matters in chs 12–15. The last two chapters in this Part are concerned with the law of quasi-contract (otherwise known as the law of restitution), with particular emphasis on its application to contracts, and with the law relating to agency.

5.2 For there to be an enforceable contract:

a. there must be an agreement;

b. the parties must have intended their agreement to be legally binding; and

c. the contract must be supported by consideration or be under seal.

Another point which must be made at the outset is that contracts may be either bilateral or unilateral. A bilateral contract is one in which a party (A) promises to do something if the other party (B) promises to do something in return and B makes that counter-promise. In such a case, the mere exchange of promises normally renders them both enforceable. A unilateral contract, on the other hand, arises where A promises to do something in return for an *act* by B, rather than a counter-promise, as where A promises to pay B a reward if he finds some lost property or where A promises to pay B £10 if he completes a 'sponsored walk'. In such a case B is not bound to do anything at all; only if he does the act, however, will A's promise become enforceable. A less obvious example of a unilateral contract, though one which is of great commercial importance, is the normal type of commission agreement entered into by estate agents, mortgage brokers and the like. According to the decision of the House of Lords in *Luxor (Eastbourne) Ltd v Cooper*,[1] an estate agent instructed to find a purchaser is under no obligation to take any action at all; only when he complies with the client's instructions, however, does the client's promise of commission become enforceable.

Before discussing the basic requirement of any contract, agreement between the parties, something must be said about whether or not an agreement must be in writing in order to be a valid and enforceable contract.

1   [1941] AC 108, [1941] 1 All ER 33, HL.

Form

5.3   With the exceptions mentioned hereafter, English law does not require an agreement to be in writing in order to be a valid and enforceable contract, but there are obvious advantages in reducing it into writing.

Contracts which must be under seal
Leases for three years or more
5.4   These are void at law and pass no legal estate unless made under seal. However, such a lease not made under seal can take effect as a contract to grant a lease, which can be specifically enforced provided it is evidenced in writing or supported by a sufficient act of part performance, and will create the same rights as a lease between the parties for many purposes.[1]

1   See further, paras 33.6 and 43.11–43.19 below.

Contracts in which there is no consideration
5.5   If there is no consideration for the promise made by one party to the other the contract is invalid unless made under seal.[1] A common example of such a contract under seal is a covenant for the gratuitous payment of a sum to a charity over a period of more than three years, whereby the charity is enabled to claim the income tax paid by the donor in addition to the covenanted sum.

1   *Rann v Hughes* (1778) 7 Term Rep 350n.

5.6   A contract under seal is a contract which is made by deed. A deed is a written document which has been signed, sealed (normally by attaching a disc of red adhesive paper to it) and delivered by the person executing it.[1]

A contract under seal is known as a contract of specialty: all other contracts, whether written or not, are known as simple contracts.

1   Para 33.3 below.

Contracts which must be in writing
5.7   Some contracts are invalid or unenforceable unless they are in writing. For example, consumer credit agreements and consumer hire agreements which are not executed in writing in the manner required by the 1974 Consumer Credit Act are enforceable against the debtor or hirer only on an order of the court.[1]

1   Consumer Credit Act 1974, s65.

Contracts which must be evidenced in writing
5.8   Contracts of guarantee[1] and contracts for the sale or other disposition of land or an interest in land[2] do not have to be written but merely be

evidenced in writing before they can be enforced in legal proceedings. We discuss the nature of the required written evidence in the case of the latter type of contracts, and the effects of its absence, in paras 43.11–43.17 below.

1 Statute of Frauds 1677, s4.
2 Law of Property Act 1925, s40. In the case of contracts concerning land or an interest in land, the statement in the text is subject to the doctrine of part performance: paras 43.18 and 43.19 below.

Agreement

5.9 The agreement involved in most contracts can be reduced to an offer by one party which has been accepted by the other. However, not all agreements can easily be so reduced.[1] This is the case, for example, where two parties agree to terms suggested by a third person. It may also be the case where several parties agree independently with X that they will be bound by terms stipulated by him. In such an event the parties may have entered into a contract not merely with X but with each other. In *Clarke v Dunraven*,[2] yachtsmen wrote to the secretary of a yacht club agreeing to be bound by certain rules during a yacht race. The House of Lords held that a contract containing those rules existed between the yachtsmen with the result that a yachtsman whose yacht was damaged was able to recover damages in accordance with the rules. While there was agreement between the yachtsmen to be bound by the rules, it cannot be analysed in terms of offer and acceptance between them.

Since the agreement in most contracts is formed by an offer being made by one party which is accepted by the other, we must now consider what constitutes an offer, what constitutes an acceptance, whether an acceptance must be conveyed to the offeror, and how an offer can be terminated.

1 *Gibson v Manchester City Council* [1979] 1 All ER 972 at 974.
2 [1897] AC 59, HL.

5.10 An offer is made where a person (the offeror) unequivocally expresses to another (the offeree) his willingness to make a binding agreement on the terms specified by him if they are accepted by the offeree. An offer may be made to a specific person, to a group of people, or to the world at large.[1] An offer to a specific person cannot be accepted by anyone else.[2]

The fact that an offer requires an expression of unequivocal willingness to contract means that inquiries and replies to inquiries are not offers, although sometimes they may resemble them. In *Harvey v Facey*,[3] one party inquired as to the lowest acceptable price for certain land, and the other party telegraphed his lowest acceptable price. This was held not to be an offer but merely a reply to the inquiry.

An offer must be distinguished from an 'invitation to treat' (ie an invitation to enter into negotiations which may lead to the making of an offer). In certain situations, what may appear to be an offer by X to Y will be regarded by a court merely as an invitation to treat, unless there is clear evidence that X was willing to be bound as soon as Y indicated his assent or satisfied a particular condition. The following examples of these situations can be given.

1 *Carlill v Carbolic Smoke Ball Co* [1893] 1 QB 256, CA.

2 *Cundy v Lindsay* (1878) 3 App Cas 459, HL.
3 [1893] AC 552, PC.

Invitation to treat

5.11 An invitation to treat is a starting point for contractual negotiations and precedes the making of an offer. In *Fisher v Bell*,[1] a shopkeeper was charged with offering for sale a flick knife which was on display in his shop window.[2] A divisional court held that the display of goods in a shop window was not an offer to sell but an invitation to treat; it was for customers to make the offer. The rationale behind this decision is that a shop is a place for negotiation over the terms of a contract, including the price, and that the shopkeeper invites customers to make him an offer which he can accept or reject as he pleases. This is an unrealistic view of how shops operate today. Circulars sent to potential customers are also invitations to treat for the supply of goods, and not offers.[3]

An area of difficulty which has arisen since the Second World War concerns self-service shops. The display of goods could be regarded as an offer to sell or as an invitation to treat. If it is an invitation to treat it is not immediately obvious when the offer to buy is made. It could be when the goods are picked up, or when they are put in a basket, or when the customer approaches the point of payment, or when they are actually presented for payment. In *Pharmaceutical Society of Great Britain v Boots Cash Chemists (Southern) Ltd*,[4] statute required certain drugs to be sold only under the supervision of a qualified pharmacist. A pharmacist was at the cash desk but, if the sale of drugs had been made before a customer reached it, the statute would have been infringed. The Court of Appeal had no hesitation in finding that the display of goods was only an invitation to treat, and that the contract was concluded at the place of payment, and so Boots were not in breach of the statute. The Court did not determine when the offer was made.

Whether running a bus is an offer or merely an invitation to treat has, surprisingly, never been determined, but obiter dicta would seem to suggest that it is an offer which the passenger accepts on boarding the bus, even though no money has yet been proffered or any destination indicated.[5]

1 [1961] 1 QB 394, [1960] 3 All ER 731, DC.
2 Contrary to the Restrictions of Offensive Weapons Act 1959. The Restriction of Offensive Weapons Act 1961 reverses the actual decision in the case.
3 *Grainger & Son v Gough* [1896] AC 325, HL.
4 [1953] 1 QB 401, [1953] 1 All ER 482, CA.
5 *Wilkie v London Passenger Transport Board* [1947] 1 All ER 258, CA.

Advertisements

5.12 Whether an advertisement is an offer or an invitation to treat depends on the intention with which it is made. Advertisements of rewards and the like are normally offers since the advertiser does not intend any further negotiation to take place. An example is provided by *Carlill v Carbolic Smoke Ball Co*,[1] where the defendants advertised that they would pay £100 to anyone catching influenza after using their product in a specified manner. The Court of Appeal held that, since no further negotiations on the defendants' part were intended, the advertisement constituted an offer made to all the world which would ripen into a contract with anyone who came forward and fulfilled the conditions.

On the other hand, an advertisement of goods for sale is presumptively an invitation to treat and not an offer,[2] because the advertiser intends further negotiations to take place. Similarly, the advertising of an auction is not an offer; instead, those who bid at auction make an offer which the auctioneer is free to accept or reject, and an offer can be withdrawn at any time before the auctioneer accepts.[3] Because the advertisement of an auction is merely a declaration of an intention to hold the auction, potential buyers have no claim against the auctioneers if they fail to hold the auction.[4] Although these rules even apply where an auctioneer advertises an auction as 'without reserve' (ie that the bid of the highest bona fide bidder will be accepted and that the property will not be withdrawn if a reserve price is not reached), so that there is no contract *of sale* if the auctioneer refuses to accept the highest bid and withdraws the property, the auctioneer is liable in such circumstances for breach of a contract *that the sale would be without reserve*. This contract comes into existence as follows: by advertising the sale as without reserve the auctioneer makes an offer to this effect to whoever is the highest bona fide bidder, which is accepted by the person who makes the highest bona fide bid before the property is withdrawn.[5]

1 [1893] 1 QB 256, CA.
2 *Partridge v Crittenden* [1968] 2 All ER 421, [1968] 1 WLR 1204, DC.
3 *Payne v Cave* (1789) 3 Term Rep 148; Sale of Goods Act 1979, s57(2).
4 *Harris v Nickerson* (1873) LR 8 QB 286.
5 *Warlow v Harrison* (1859) 1 E & E 309.

Tenders

5.13 Normally, an announcement that the provision of goods or services (or the purchase of goods or services) is open to tender is not an offer but only an invitation to treat. Consequently, a person who submits a tender normally makes an offer, which may be accepted or rejected by the person seeking tenders.[1] In *Spencer v Harding*,[2] for example, the defendant issued a circular offering by tender the stock in trade of X. This was held not to be an offer. Thus, the defendant was not required to sell the goods to the plaintiff who had submitted the highest tender.

By way of exception, a person who seeks tenders will be held to have made an offer (and to be contractually bound to the highest or lowest tenderer, as the case may be) if it is clear that he intended to be automatically so bound.[3]

1 For acceptance of tenders see para 5.17 below.
2 (1870) LR 5 CP 561.
3 *Harvela Investments Ltd v Royal Trust Co of Canada (CI) Ltd* [1985] 2 All ER 966, [1985] 3 WLR 276, HL.

Acceptance

5.14 To convert an offer into a contract the offeree must make an effective acceptance of the offer and also, usually, communicate this decision to the offeror. A contract may arise during the course of long and complicated negotiations. This may make it difficult for the court to determine the exact moment when the contract arose because, in such cases, no formal statement constituting an offer or acceptance may have been made. If this is so, the conduct of the parties (and all their actions and statements) will be considered by the court to see whether the parties intended to contract and, if there is a contract, when they contracted.

The nature of acceptance

5.15   It should come as no surprise to anyone to learn that one cannot accept an offer of which one is ignorant. This is important in the case where B offers a reward for the performance of a particular action, e g finding his lost dog. If A, who is ignorant of the offer, finds the dog, his action cannot constitute an acceptance of the offer and he cannot claim the reward successfully.[1] Moreover, if someone who knows of the offer performs the specified action for reasons entirely unconnected with that offer, there is no acceptance.[1] But, if his conduct is motivated partly by the offer and partly by other reasons there is a valid acceptance.[2]

A related point is that, if two offers which are identical in terms cross in the post, there can be no contract. The courts will not construe one offer as the offer and the other offer as the acceptance.[3] The practical basis for such a view would seem to be that neither party would know if he was bound, although if the terms of the offers were identical the parties would surely have no objection to being bound.

Another basic rule relating to acceptance is that there must be an unequivocal agreement to the terms proposed in the offer. If an offeree who purports to accept the offer seeks to introduce entirely new terms in his acceptance, this is a counter-offer which may or may not be accepted by the original offeror, and not an acceptance. For example, an offeree cannot agree to accept half the quantity of goods offered by the offeror, even on the same terms as would have applied to the full quantity.[3] A counter-offer puts an end to the offer, so that it cannot subsequently be accepted by the offeree. In *Hyde v Wrench*,[4] for instance, the defendant offered to sell property to the plaintiff for £1,000. The plaintiff 'agreed' to buy the property for £950. This was rejected and the plaintiff then purported to accept the original offer of £1,000. The Master of the Rolls held that the plaintiff's purported acceptance for £950 was a counter-offer which destroyed the original offer, so that it was no longer capable of acceptance when the plaintiff purported to accept it. A counter-offer must be distinguished from an inquiry or request for information by an offeree. Such an inquiry or request, even if answered negatively by the offeror, does not destroy the offer. An example is *Stevenson v MacLean*.[5] The defendant offered to sell iron to the plaintiffs at 40 shillings a ton with immediate delivery. The plaintiffs asked the defendant by telegram if he would sell at the same price if delivery was staggered over two months. On receiving no reply, the plaintiffs accepted the original offer but the defendant failed to deliver and claimed the telegram was a counter-offer. The court rejected the defendant's claim and held that the telegram was a mere request for information, and not a new offer, so that the original offer could still be accepted.

1   *R v Clarke* (1927) 40 CLR 227.
2   *Williams v Carwardine* (1833) 5 C & P 566.
3   *Tinn v Hoffmann & Co* (1873) 29 LT 271.
4   (1840) 3 Beav 334.
5   (1880) 5 QBD 346.

5.16   An acceptance may be express, as where the offeree accepts the offer by a written or oral statement, or it may be manifested by the offeree's conduct. For instance, a cover note issued by an insurance company is an offer to insure which would be accepted by using a car in reliance on it.[1] A more complicated case of acceptance by conduct is that of *Brogden v Metropolitan Rly Co*,[2] in which Brogden was sued for failing to deliver coal. Brogden regularly supplied the company with coal and they decided to draw up a contract for such supply. A draft contract was submitted to Brogden with a blank space for the name of a mutually agreeable arbitrator, and this constituted an offer. Brogden filled in the name of an arbitrator, marked the draft 'approved', and returned it to the agent of the company (who put it in a drawer where it remained). Brogden's action was not an acceptance but a counter-offer,[3] because the company had to consider whether to accept his choice of arbitrator. Nevertheless, the parties bought and sold coal in accordance with the terms of the draft contract. Subsequently, Brogden refused to supply more coal and claimed that there was no binding contract for its supply. The House of Lords inferred from the conduct of the parties, the buying and selling of coal on terms exactly the same as those in the draft contract, that a contract had been concluded on the terms of the final draft, which came into effect with the first order of coal by the company since this manifested the company's acceptance of Brogden's counter-offer. The House of Lords stressed that mere mental acquiescence by the parties that the contract should exist would not have sufficed: it was their actions which completed the contract.

1   *Taylor v Allon* [1966] 1 QB 304, [1965] 1 All ER 557, DC.
2   (1877) 2 App Cas 666, HL.
3   Para 5.15 above.

5.17   The acceptance of tenders illustrates another aspect of acceptance. Tenders can be in two forms.

a.   Where people are invited to tender, for example, by a local authority, for the supply of specified goods or services over a given period, a contract for the supply of those goods or services is constituted when a person's tender (offer) is accepted.

b.   However, if people are invited to tender for the supply of such goods and services as may be required over a given period, a contract is not immediately concluded with the successful tenderer. Instead, his offer is treated as a standing offer and each time an order is placed this constitutes acceptance of the standing offer and there is a contract for the goods or services ordered. Because the person making the successful tender has no definite contract, he can revoke his offer before any particular order is placed, and the person who invited tenders need never place an order.[1]

1   *Great Northern Rly Co v Witham* (1873) LR 9 CP 16.

Communication of acceptance
5.18   If an offer has been made and the offeree has decided to accept, there is normally no completed agreement until he (or his agent) has communicated his acceptance to the offeror (or his agent), by words or conduct which manifest his acceptance.[1] The reason for this is practical: if the offeror is not told that his offer has been accepted he does not know whether he has made a contract or can make offers to others.

Communication of acceptance usually requires actual communication. Consequently, an oral acceptance which is drowned by a passing aeroplane or is inaudible because of interference on the telephone is not effectively communicated.[2] Telex messages sent during office hours are regarded as instantaneous communications and are subject to the same principles as oral acceptances; they take effect when printed out on the offeror's telex machines.[2] However, if an oral or telex acceptance does not reach the offeror and the party accepting does not realise this, there may be a valid communication of acceptance. But this will only be the case where the offeror realises he has missed some of what the offeree is seeking to communicate and does not attempt to discover what he has missed.[3]

1 Para 5.16 above.
2 *Entores v Miles Far East Corpn* [1955] 2 QB 327, [1955] 2 All ER 493, CA; *Brinkibon v Stahag Stahl mbH* [1983] 2 AC 34, [1982] 1 All ER 293, HL. In the latter case, it was held that this rule would not apply where the communication was not instantaneous, as where the telex message is sent out of office hours, and that the time of acceptance in such a case would depend on the parties' intentions and sound business practice, and in some cases on a judgment as to where the risk should lie.
3 *Entores v Miles Far East Corpn* [1955] 2 QB 327 at 333.

5.19 The offeror may dispense, expressly or impliedly, with the need to communicate acceptance by the terms of the offer. In particular, dispensation with the need for communication will normally be implied where the alleged contract is of the unilateral variety. An example is provided by *Carlill v Carbolic Smoke Ball Co*,[1] where the vendors of a product argued that a user of it, who claimed a reward which they had offered to anyone catching influenza after using the product, should have told them of her acceptance of their offer of a reward. The vendors' claim was rejected, since it was clear they had not intended every purchaser of the product to write to them formally accepting the offer of a reward if illness was not avoided.

1 [1893] 1 QB 256, CA.

5.20 While communication of acceptance can be dispensed with by the offeror, he cannot frame his offer in such terms that a contract is presumed to exist unless non-acceptance is communicated: contractual liability cannot be imposed on the offeree in this way; silence is not assent. In *Felthouse v Bindley*,[1] the plaintiff offered to buy X's horse and said that he would presume his offer to be accepted unless he heard to the contrary. X did not reply. The horse was sold by the defendant, an auctioneer, to another. It was held that no contract had been formed: the plaintiff was not entitled to presume acceptance unless he heard to the contrary.

1 (1862) 11 CB NS 869.

5.21 While some offers dispense with the need for communication of acceptance, others require a particular form of acceptance to be employed. The attitude of the courts seems to be that an acceptance made in some other way than that prescribed by the offeror can be effective as long as it is as advantageous to the offeror as the prescribed method;[1] but if it is not, it is ineffective[2] (unless the offeror waives the specified mode).

1 *Tinn v Hoffmann* (1873) 29 LT 271. However, it would seem that there would not be an effective acceptance if the offeror has stated that the acceptance must be made *only* by the specified manner (unless he waives the requirement).
2 *Financings Ltd v Stimson* [1962] 3 All ER 386, [1962] 1 WLR 1184, CA.

5.22 There is another exception to the general rule that acceptance must be actually communicated to be effective. It is that, subject to the qualifications referred to below, a posted acceptance is effective when it is posted, and this is so even if that acceptance is delivered late or is never delivered. This was first established in *Adams v Lindsell*,[1] where a letter of acceptance was posted the day that a postal offer to sell wool was received. The acceptance arrived two days later than expected and, after it had been posted but before it arrived, the offeror sold the wool to another. It was held that a contract had been formed as soon as the letter of acceptance had been posted.

The offeror can exclude the special postal acceptance rule in his offer by specifying that acceptance must be *actually* communicated to him.[2] In addition, the postal acceptance rule will be disregarded, and the general rule prevail, if it is not reasonable to accept by post[3] or if the special rule would give rise to 'manifest inconvenience or absurdity'.[4] For example, it would not be reasonable to accept by post an offer by telex to sell highly perishable goods.

The justification for the special rule for postal acceptances seems to be that the offeror, by expressly or impliedly (eg by making the offer by post) allowing an acceptance to be made by post, must stand the risk of failures of the postal system. However, if a postal acceptance is delayed in the post because of the negligence of the offeree, as where he wrongly addresses the letter, there seems no reason why the court should not decide the acceptance to have been effective at whatever time is least advantageous to the negligent offeree.

1 (1818) 1 B & Ald 681.
2 For an example see *Holwell Securities Ltd v Hughes* [1974] 1 All ER 161, [1974] 1 WLR 155, CA.
3 *Henthorn v Fraser* [1892] 2 Ch 27, 61 LJCh 373, CA.
4 *Holwell Securities Ltd v Hughes* [1974] 1 All ER 161, [1974] 1 WLR 155, CA.

5.23 If an acceptance made by letter is effective when it is posted, then, logically, an attempt to withdraw the acceptance after the letter has been posted should be ineffective since the contract has been concluded. There are no English cases which support this view, although the principle stated is consistent with American cases. On the other hand, the Scottish case of *Countess of Dunmore v Alexander*[1] has been cited as authority for the view that, if a revocation of an acceptance is communicated before a postal acceptance arrives, the revocation is effective. However, the facts of this case are somewhat obscure and it is by no means certain that there had ever been an acceptance of an offer.

1 (1830) 9 Sh (Ct of Sess) 190.

Termination of offers
5.24 An offer may be terminated in several ways: by rejection (including a counter-offer[1]), by revocation, by lapse of time and by death.

1 Para 5.15 above.

Revocation
5.25 At any time until acceptance by the offeree, the offeror can withdraw his offer. The fact that the offeror has given the offeree time to make up his mind does not mean that the offeror is required to keep the offer open for

that length of time. In *Routledge v Grant*,[1] a reply to an offer was required within six weeks; it was held that nevertheless the offer could be withdrawn within that period.

There is an exception to the rule that the offer need not be kept open for a specified period. This is where there is a separate contract whereby the offeror contracts to keep the offer open for a given time. It there is such a contract the offer can be accepted at any time within the specified period. An example of such a contract is the granting of an option.

The revocation of an offer only becomes effective when it is communicated to the offeree. In *Byrne v Van Tienhoven*,[2] the defendants in Cardiff wrote on 1 October to the plaintiffs in New York, offering to sell them goods. The plaintiff received the offer on 11 October and accepted it by telegram on the same day. Meanwhile, on 8 October the defendants had sent a letter to the plaintiffs revoking their offer; this letter reached the plaintiffs on 20 October. It was held that the revocation was ineffective because the plaintiffs' acceptance had taken effect on 11 October (acceptance by telegram being treated in the same way as acceptance by letter) and therefore the defendants' offer was no longer capable of being revoked when their letter of revocation reached the plaintiffs. Consequently, there was a contract between the plaintiffs and defendants for the sale of the goods. There is no parallel rule to that which treats a posted acceptance as a communicated acceptance; a revocation must always be actually communicated.

Communication of revocation may be indirect, in that, if the offeree hears from a reliable source that the offer has been withdrawn (and thereby knows beyond all question of the withdrawal), the courts will regard this as an effective revocation.[3] The difficulty inherent in this is that it is difficult to know what constitutes a reliable source.

1   (1828) 4 Bing 653.
2   (1880) 5 CPD 344.
3   *Dickinson v Dodds* (1876) 2 Ch D 463, CA.

5.26   Special rules apply in the case of unilateral contracts, where A does something (eg returning lost property) in response to B's offer (promise) to do something (eg to pay a reward) if he does it. The general rule is that once the offeree has embarked on the performance of the stipulated act or acts necessary for acceptance, as where B has found lost property and is en route to return it in response to the offer of a reward, the offer cannot be withdrawn.[1] In *Errington v Errington and Woods*,[2] a father purchased a house, partially by means of a mortgage, and allowed his daughter and her husband to live in it. The daughter and her husband paid the mortgage instalments in response to the father's offer that, if they did so, he would give them the house when it was paid for. The Court of Appeal held that this offer could not be revoked once the daughter and her husband had begun performance of the conduct specified in the offer. Of course, in the present type of case the offeror is not bound unless and until the offeree has fully performed the act or acts specified in the offer. This is subject to the important qualification that, if the offeror prevents performance of the necessary act or acts being completed, he cannot rely on the offeree's failure fully to perform as a defence to a breach of contract action by the offeree, because there is an implied obligation on the part of the offeror (which arises as soon as the offeree starts to perform) not to prevent performance by the offeree.[3]

What we have just said will not apply if the terms of the offer, or its surrounding circumstances, indicate that it was not intended to become irrevocable before the offeree had completely performed the envisaged act. A good example is the kind of commission agreement commonly used by estate agents. Although this is a unilateral contract (as we explained in para 5.2 above) it is well settled that the client may revoke his instructions at any time, notwithstanding that the agent may have expended time and money in attempting to find a purchaser.[4] The courts take the view that a change of mind by a client is simply one of the business risks which an estate agent must bear, and his fees for successful negotiations should be at a level sufficient to cover other abortive work.

1   *Offord v Davies* (1862) 12 CB NS 748; *Errington v Errington and Woods* [1952] 1 KB 290, [1952] 1 All ER 149, CA; *Daulia Ltd v Four Millbank Nominees Ltd* [1978] Ch 231 at 239, [1978] 2 All ER 557 at 561.
2   [1952] 1 KB 290, [1952] 1 All ER 149, CA.
3   *Daulia Ltd v Four Millbank Nominees Ltd* [1978] Ch 231 at 239, [1978] 2 All ER 557 at 561.
4   *Luxor (Eastbourne) Ltd v Cooper* [1941] AC 108, [1941] 1 All ER 33, HL.

Lapse of time

5.27   Obviously, an offer which is to remain open for a set time lapses at the end of that time and cannot thereafter be accepted. If no time limit is expressly set for the offer, it will normally lapse after a reasonable period. In *Ramsgate Victoria Hotel v Montefiore*,[1] it was held that an offer to buy shares, which was made in June, could not be accepted in November since the offer had lapsed by then. What is a reasonable period varies, depending on the facts of the case.

1   (1866) LR 1 Ex Ch 109.

Death

5.28   Death after an offer has been accepted cannot affect the validity of a contract.[1] There are, however, cases where either the offeror or the offeree dies before the offer is accepted. If *the offeror* dies the offer does not seem to terminate automatically (except where the offer is clearly of such a type that it must end on death, eg an offer to be cook for X). However, the offeree cannot accept the offer once he knows of the death of the offeror.[2]

The effects of the death of *the offeree* have not been decided conclusively but uncontradicted dicta suggest that the offer lapses. In *Reynolds v Atherton*,[3] it was suggested that an offer, being made to a living person, cannot survive his death and be accepted by someone else. This may be an illustration of the basic rule that an offer made to A cannot be accepted by B. On the other hand, if an offer is made to A or B there seems no reason why the death of B should prevent A accepting it.

1   But it may discharge the contract: see para 10.5 below.
2   *Bradbury v Morgan* (1862) 1 H & C 249; *Coulthart v Clementson* (1879) 5 QBD 42.
3   (1921) 125 LT 690, CA; affd by the House of Lords who did not comment on this point.

Uncertain, inconclusive and conditional agreements

5.29   Here we are concerned with cases where, although there is an agreement, there may not be a legally binding contract because the agreement is uncertain in its terms, or is merely an agreement to agree in the future, or is subject to the operation of a condition.

Uncertainty

5.30 An agreement may be uncertain in that the meaning of particular terms is unclear or in that it lacks some of its vital terms because matters are left open for further negotiation. The latter is an agreement to agree.

Where particular terms are not subject to further negotiation but are vague or unclear, the courts will try to divine the intention of the parties and find a contract, but if such intention cannot be discovered the agreement is not a legally binding contract and cannot be enforced.[1] In *Bushwall Properties Ltd v Vortex Properties Ltd,*[2] for instance, A agreed to buy from B 51½ acres of land for £500,000. Under the terms of the agreement the price was to be paid in three instalments and on each payment a 'proportionate part' of the land was to be conveyed to A. The Court of Appeal held that the agreement was void for uncertainty because it did not provide the machinery for identifying the proportionate part to be conveyed in each phase, nor could a term (based on the parties' presumed intention) be implied as to how each proportionate part was to be identified. Other terms which have been held to be unclear include 'subject to war clause', since there was no universally accepted war clause,[3] and 'purchase on hire-purchase terms', since there was more than one form of hire-purchase terms.[1]

On the other hand, a court can supply the details of an apparently vague term, so that the agreement is a valid contract, if the parties have provided the machinery to ascertain its precise nature, as where there is an agreement for the sale of land at 'market price' (in which case the court can fix that price after making an inquiry),[4] or if the details which the parties must have intended can be implied by reference to the practices and usages of a particular trade or profession to which the parties belong or to the previous dealings of the parties. In *Hillas & Co Ltd v Arcos Ltd,*[5] the parties had entered into an agreement for the sale and purchase of timber in 1930. The agreement contained an option to buy 100,000 standards of timber in 1931 but the size and quality of the timber were not specified. The House of Lords refused to find the agreement unenforceable, clarifying any uncertainties by reference to the previous dealings of the parties and usual practice in the timber trade. The judgment of the House is permeated by the view that the courts ought to strive to give effect to business arrangements and not zealously demand absolute certainty of all terms.

Another case where there can be a valid contract despite the apparent uncertainty of a term is where the parties have provided the machinery for one of them, or for a third party or third parties, to fix the precise nature of that term. This was recognised in *Sudbrook Trading Estate Ltd v Eggleton,*[6] where the House of Lords dealt with the situation where the price of a piece of property was left to be decided by two valuers, one to be appointed by each party. It held that if the task of the valuers, expressly or impliedly, was to fix a fair and reasonable price and that method proved ineffective, either because a party refused to appoint a valuer or because the valuers failed to agree, a court could substitute its own machinery to ascertain the price, eg by appointing its own valuers. On the other hand, it held, if the price was to be fixed by a *named* valuer or valuers it could not be implied that the price was to be a fair and reasonable one because the implication was that the price was to be fixed by a specified means, the use of the named valuer or valuers. In such a case, it held, a court could not substitute its own machinery if for some reason the named valuer or valuers failed to fix the price, and there would not be an enforceable contract for the sale of the property.

There can be a valid contract for the sale of goods or the supply of a service, even though the price is not fixed, or left to be fixed in an agreed manner, and cannot be determined by a course of dealings between the parties. Statute provides that, in such a case, a reasonable price must be paid.[7]

Where an apparently uncertain term can be determined in one of the above ways, the contract is complete on the agreement of the parties even though the precise nature of that term remains to be fixed.[8]

1   *Scammell and Nephew Ltd v Ouston* [1941] AC 251, [1941] 1 All ER 14, HL.
2   [1976] 2 All ER 283, [1976] 1 WLR 591, CA.
3   *Bishop and Baxter Ltd v Anglo-Eastern Trading and Industrial Co Ltd* [1944] KB 12, [1943] 2 All ER 598, CA.
4   *Bushwall Properties Ltd v Vortex Properties Ltd* [1976] 2 All ER 283 at 289.
5   (1932) 147 LT 503, HL.
6   [1983] 1 AC 444, [1982] 3 All ER 1, HL.
7   Sale of Goods Act 1979, s8; Supply of Goods and Services Act 1982, s15.
8   *Sudbrook Trading Estate Ltd v Eggleton* [1983] 1 AC 444 [1982] 3 All ER 1, HL.

5.31 Sometimes it may be possible to ignore uncertainty in an agreement. This can be done, for instance, where the uncertainty relates to what is a meaningless term. In *Nicolene Ltd v Simmonds*,[1] the agreement contained the phrase 'I assume the usual conditions of acceptance apply'. There were no usual conditions of acceptance, but the Court of Appeal said the phrase was meaningless and, since it did not relate to an important term or part of the contract, it could be ignored. A distinction must be drawn between meaningless phrases and phrases which denote that terms are still to be agreed. A phrase is unlikely to be considered meaningless, and thus capable of being ignored, if it concerns an important term of the contract.

1   [1953] QB 543, [1953] 1 All ER 822, CA.

Agreement to agree
5.32 If a vital term of an agreement is open to further negotiation there is no concluded agreement, but merely an agreement to agree. An example is where an agreement for the sale of goods leaves the price to be fixed by agreement between the parties. In *May and Butcher Ltd v R*,[1] the price of surplus tentage which was being sold by a government department to the plaintiffs was such as 'shall be agreed upon from time to time between the government department and the purchasers'. The House of Lords found that, because a vital term was left open for future negotiation, the agreement was not a legally binding contract.

However, if the agreement expressly or impliedly provides a method for resolving the lack of agreement, there will be a valid contract. An example is provided by *Foley v Classique Coaches Ltd*,[2] the Court of Appeal held that an agreement containing the words 'price to be agreed by the parties' was a binding contract. The court felt able to distinguish *May and Butcher Ltd v R*[1] on two grounds. First, on the basis that the parties had acted on the agreement for three years and their implied belief that they had been contractually bound during that period must be given effect, and, second, because the contract provided that in the absence of agreement on price it was to be determined by arbitration. *Beer v Bowden*[3] provides another example. Premises were let for ten years (later extended to 14) at a fixed rent for the first five years, but at a rent 'to be agreed' thereafter. The Court of Appeal implied a term that in the absence of agreement a reasonable rent determined by the court should be paid.

1   [1934] 2 KB 17n, HL.
2   [1934] 2 KB 1, CA.
3   [1981] 1 All ER 1070, [1981] 1 WLR 522n, CA.

Operation of a condition

5.33   An agreement which appears to be a binding contract may never come into operation because it is subject to a condition precedent which is not satisfied.[1] An example is afforded by *Pym v Campbell*.[2] In this case an agreement to purchase a share in an invention was subject to the condition precedent that the invention be approved by X. X failed to approve and thus no binding contract to buy came into existence.[3]

An agreement subject to a condition precedent is not necessarily devoid of all effect. It all depends on the interpretation which the court gives to it.

On its true construction, the effect of an agreement subject to a condition precedent may be that, although the agreement containing it is not binding before the condition is satisfied, neither party can withdraw until it is clear whether or not the condition will be satisfied.[4]

Alternatively, or in addition, the effect of such an agreement may be that one party must do his best to fulfil the condition[5] or, at least, not obstruct its fulfilment.[6] For example, the phrase 'subject to survey' in an agreement for the sale of land has been construed as meaning that the purchaser must proceed with due diligence to obtain a surveyor's report and, having received it, consider it, and must act in good faith. If, in good faith, he is not satisfied with the report he is not obliged to proceed with the purchase, but in the meantime neither party can withdraw.[7]

Lastly, a condition precedent may be construed as imposing no obligation on either party. This is the prima facie[8] construction which has been given to the condition precedent, 'subject to contract', which is usually inserted initially in an agreement to buy land which is for sale by private treaty. Unless there are very exceptional circumstances which oust the prima facie meaning of the phrase,[8] such agreements are simply 'agreements to agree' and are not binding, nor are the parties required to try to ensure that a contract is concluded.[9] Phrases similar to 'subject to contract' have the same effect, except that where an agreement for the sale of land is made 'subject to the purchaser obtaining a mortgage on terms satisfactory *to himself*' a further term is implied that such satisfaction must not be unreasonably withheld.[10]

A condition precedent may be void for uncertainty, in which case the agreement in which it is contained is also void. An example is an agreement for the sale of land 'subject to the purchaser obtaining a satisfactory mortgage', since such a condition is too vague for the courts to enforce.[11]

1   For a different type of condition precedent see para 9.12 below.
2   (1856) 6 E & B 370.
3   In fact, it was held that there was no agreement at all.
4   *Smith v Butler* [1900] 1 QB 694, CA. In *Smallman v Smallman* [1972] Fam 25, [1971] 3 All ER 717, CA, a buyer, who withdrew from an agreement to purchase which was subject to a condition precedent before it was clear whether the condition was satisfied, was unable to recover the deposit he had paid.
5   *Marten v Whale* [1917] 2 KB 480, CA.

6   *Mackay v Dick* (1881) 6 App Cas 251, HL.
7   *Ee v Kakar* (1979) 255 Estates Gazette 879.
8   *Alpenstow Ltd v Regalian Properties plc* [1985] 2 All ER 545.
9   *Winn v Bull* (1877) 7 Ch D 29. See further para 43.2 below.
10 *Janmohamed v Hassam* (1976) Times, 10 June.
11 *Lee-Parker v Izzet (No 2)* [1972] 2 All ER 800, [1972] 1 WLR 775.

5.34 An agreement may also be subject to the operation of a condition subsequent. In such cases an agreement will be a binding contract unless and until the condition occurs. If it does occur, either the contract will automatically cease to bind or one party will have the right to cancel it, depending on the construction of the condition. In *Head v Tattersall*,[1] a contract for the sale of a horse was subject to the condition subsequent that, if the purchaser found within a given time that the horse did not meet its contractual description, the horse could be returned and the contract terminated. During that period, the purchaser found that the horse did not correspond with its description. It was held that he could return it, even though it had been injured in the meanwhile.

1   (1871) LR 7 Exch 7.

Chapter 6
Consideration and privity

6.1 An agreement which complies with the rules specified in the previous chapter will constitute a binding contract, provided it is supported by consideration and the parties intend to enter into a legally binding contract. Alternatively, it will constitute a binding contract if it is made under seal. If a binding contract has been formed only those persons who are parties to the contract can sue or be sued on it. Even where a person has provided consideration, or a contract is expressly intended to confer a benefit or burden on him, he cannot sue or be sued if he is not a party to the contract: this is the doctrine of privity.

Intention to create legal relations
6.2 If an agreement is supported by consideration there is usually an intention to create legal relations, although the parties to an agreement rarely state this intention expressly. If the parties do not wish their agreement to be legally binding, they may expressly state this and the courts will give effect to their intention. In the absence of an express indication of intention, the courts rely on two presumptions in deciding whether there was an intention to create legal relations, both of which can be rebutted expressly or impliedly by the parties:

a. parties to social, domestic and family arrangements do not intend to be legally bound;[1] and

b. parties to business and commercial agreements expect their agreements to be legally binding.

An example of the first type of arrangement is an agreement to give lifts to work, even if it is on an organised basis and involves payment to the car owners for their petrol.[2] While arrangements made within the family or household are presumed not to be intended to be legally binding, the nature of the agreement may clearly indicate that the parties intended a particular arrangement to be binding. In *Simpkins v Pays*,[3] three members of the same household submitted a joint entry to a competition on the basis that they would share any winnings. This arrangement was held to be binding on the parties.

If there is a business arrangement it is extremely difficult to rebut the presumption that the arrangement is to be legally binding, other than by clear words. A case where clear words led to the presumption being rebutted is *Rose and Frank Co v J R Crompton & Bros Ltd*,[4] in which the defendants appointed the plaintiffs their agents to sell their products in America under an agreement which contained an 'honour clause', ie a clause which said the agreement was merely recording the intention of the parties and was binding in honour only and not in law. The plaintiffs sued for alleged breach of contract. The Court of Appeal and the House of Lords held that the honour clause constituted a clearly expressed intention that the agreement was not to be legally binding and that effect had to be given to this intention.

Even where the presumption is rebutted by clear words, this does not prevent the subsequent conduct of the parties to the agreement constituting a binding contract. In *Rose and Frank Co v J R Crompton & Bros Ltd*, the parties to the agency agreement ordered and supplied goods for sale in America. It was held that these orders and acceptances gave rise to binding contracts, even though the agency agreement was not legally binding.

An important statutory exception to the presumption that business and commercial dealings are intended to be legally binding is contained in the Trade Union and Labour Relations Act 1974, s18, which provides that collective agreements between employers and trade unions are presumed not to be legally binding unless they are made in writing and expressly state that the agreement is to be legally binding.

1 *Balfour v Balfour* [1919] 2 KB 571, CA.
2 *Coward v Motor Insurers' Bureau* [1963] 1 QB 259, [1962] 1 All ER 531, CA.
3 [1955] 3 All ER 10, [1955] 1 WLR 975.
4 [1925] AC 445, HL.

Consideration

6.3 Agreements not made under seal[1] mut be supported by consideration if they are to be enforceable, and a person who wishes to enforce a contract must show that he himself provided consideration. It is in the requirement of consideration that English law recognises the idea that a contract is a bargain. If you wish to receive the benefit of the contract you must do something to earn that benefit, either by promising to do something or actually doing something. If a person does something at the request of another, eg finding a lost dog or refraining from smoking in return for the promise of a reward, he thereby not only accepts the offer of a reward but also provides consideration and the contract is known as a unilateral contract. If a party to an agreement promises to do something in response to a promise by the other, as where X promises to pay for goods to be supplied by Y, he thereby provides consideration, and the contract is known as a bilateral contract. In a number of cases, particularly in the nineteenth century,[2] consideration has been defined as follows: that X provides consideration for Y's promise if he confers a benefit on Y, in return for which Y's promise is given, or if he incurs a detriment, in compensation for which Y's promise is given. Certainly if there is either a benefit or a detriment to the appropriate party that is good consideration, but this definition has been criticised and some cases cannot be explained in terms of benefit and detriment. A more modern view of consideration is that each party's action or forbearance, promised or actual, is the price for which the other's is bought, and without that price there would be no bargain.[3]

1 Para 5.6 above.
2 See, for example, *Currie v Misa* (1875) LR 10 Exch 153. For a more recent reference to this type of definition, see *Midland Bank Trust Co Ltd v Green* [1981] AC 513 at 531, [1981] 1 All ER 153 at 159.
3 *Dunlop Pneumatic Tyre Co Ltd v Selfridge & Co Ltd* [1915] AC 847 at 855.

Executed and executory consideration

6.4 Consideration may be 'executed', ie an act done in response to a promise by the other party to the agreement, for example, finding and returning the lost dog for whose return a reward was promised. Alternatively, it may be 'executory', ie a promise of action in response to a promise of the other party, for example, to pay for goods which are to be made by the other party. The concept of executory consideration illustrates the difficulty of the benefit or detriment theory of consideration. When no one has done anything and there are merely promises there is no benefit or detriment to anyone, but it is possible to say that the price of one party's promise was the promise made by the other party. Both executed and executory consideration are good consideration in law, unlike 'past consideration'.

Past consideration

6.5 'Past consideration' is said to have been given by a person when, only *after* he has done something, a promise (e g to reward him) is made in return by another person. 'Past consideration' is an inaccurate expression, since it is not consideration at all and a person who has given it cannot enforce another's promise made in return for it.

The fact that past consideration is not good consideration illustrates the idea that consideration is the price of a promise. In *Re McArdle*,[1] work was done on a family house by X. Her relations then promised to reimburse the cost to her of this work but failed to keep their promise. X sued but failed in her claim for the promised sum because she had provided no consideration for the promise to pay, since the action (doing the work on the house) which she alleged constituted consideration pre-dated the promise by the relatives. The motive for the promise was to reimburse for work done but, since the work was not done at the request of the relatives and was completed before the promise was made, it was past consideration and thus not good consideration.

It would be wrong to think that all actions which are not preceded by an express promise constitute past consideration. If an act is done by X at the request of Y in circumstances where X and Y must have understood that the act was to be remunerated (so that a prior promise of remuneration by Y can be *implied*), the act by X is good consideration.[2] An act done in response to a request accompanied by an implied promise of remuneration may be followed by an express promise to pay a particular sum or confer a particular benefit. If this is so, the promise quantifies the amount due to the party who performed the requested act.[2] If there is no subsequent promise, the amount due is determined on a quantum meruit basis.[3] What transforms apparently past consideration into good consideration is the fact that the action is in response to a request which raises an implied promise of payment. The requested action is the price of the implied promise to pay. In the case of *Re McArdle*[4] there was no prior request or expectation of payment. However, in

Re Casey's Patents, Stewart v Casey,[5] the plaintiffs wrote to Casey saying that 'in consideration of your [past] services as practical manager' they would give him a one-third share in certain patents. This promise was fulfilled but subsequently the plaintiffs sought to recover the patents, claiming that Casey had given no consideration for their promise. The Court of Appeal rejected this argument, saying that Casey's services as manager clearly raised an implication that they would be remunerated and thus Casey had provided consideration, the subsequent express promise merely fixed the amount of that remuneration.

1   [1951] Ch 669, [1951] 1 All ER 905, CA.
2   *Lampleigh v Brathwait* (1615) Hob 105; *Kennedy v Broun* (1863) 13 CB NS 677, 740; *Re Casey's Patents, Stewart v Casey* [1892] 1 Ch 104, CA; *Pao On v Lau Yiu Long* [1980] AC 614, [1979] 3 All ER 65, PC.
3   Para 16.8 below
4   [1951] Ch 669, [1951] 1 All ER 905, CA.
5   [1892] 1 Ch 104, CA.

6.6   In determining whether a contract is supported by consideration, the courts have regard to two factors:

a. consideration must have some value but need not be adequate; and

b. consideration must be real and sufficient, ie what is alleged to be consideration must be an action or promise which the law recognises as capable of being consideration.

Adequacy
6.7   Providing that the alleged consideration has some economic value, the courts will not question its adequacy, even though one party is apparently making a very good bargain and the other is not. In *Mountford v Scott*,[1] £1, paid for an option to purchase a house, was found to be good consideration. Money is always considered to have an economic value and the fact that the amount was small was irrelevant. In *Chappell & Co Ltd v Nestlé Co Ltd*,[2] customers were invited to send for a record, enclosing 1s 6d and three wrappers from the defendant's chocolate bars. The House of Lords found that, while the wrappers might have little intrinsic value (and were indeed thrown away on their receipt), they formed part of the consideration provided by purchasers of the record. There are other examples which illustrate that the courts will not question the adequacy of consideration.

1   [1975] Ch 258, [1975] 1 All ER 198, CA.
2   [1960] AC 87, [1959] 2 All ER 701, HL.

Forbearance to sue
6.8   If a person who could sue another agrees not to pursue his claim, that constitutes good consideration for a promise by the other person. It might be thought that agreeing to abandon an invalid claim[1] cannot be good consideration. However, the abandonment of an invalid claim will be good consideration if the party abandoning it can show that the claim was reasonable in itself, and intended to pursue it, that he genuinely believed the claim had some chance of success and that he was not concealing from the other party facts which would constitute a defence to the claim.[2] The

argument is that abandoning a doubtful claim saves the parties from the uncertainties of litigation and its attendant expense.

The same principles apply where there is no express promise not to sue but the potential plaintiff in fact refrains from pursuing a claim, provided that the forbearance would not have been displayed but for the promise by the potential defendant.[3]

1   For example, in *Poteliakhoff v Teakle* [1938] 2 KB 816, [1938] 3 All ER 686, CA, a creditor's promise not to sue on unenforceable gaming debts was not good consideration for a promise by the debtor because the creditor knew that the claim was invalid.
2   *Horton v Horton* (No. 2) [1961] 1 QB 215, [1960] 3 All ER 649, CA; *Miles v New Zealand Alford Estate Co* (1886) 32 Ch D 266; *Syros Shipping Co SA v Elaghill Trading Co* [1981] 3 All ER 189.
3   *Alliance Bank Ltd v Broom* (1864) 2 Drew & Sm 289.

Gratuitous services
6.9   If a person voluntarily undertakes to do something for another there is no apparent consideration and, if the service is performed defectively, no contractual claim can be maintained. There may, of course, be a claim in tort. However, in some cases, the courts have found consideration, despite its apparent absence, and allowed a contractual claim.

In *Gore v Van Der Lann*,[1] the plaintiff was injured while boarding a bus and sued the conductor in the tort of negligence. The plaintiff was travelling on a free bus pass which contained an exemption clause purporting to exclude the conductor from liability. By statute the clause was invalid if contained in a contract of carriage. The Court of Appeal found that the plaintiff was travelling under such a contract based on the terms of the pass, the consideration which she provided being the acceptance of 'a detriment in return for the advantages gained'.

1   [1967] 2 QB 31, [1967] 1 All ER 360, CA.

Bailment
6.10   Bailment is a transfer of possession of goods on condition that they will eventually be restored to the owner or be otherwise dealt with according to his instructions, e g pawning articles, leaving them in a left luggage office or lending them to a person. The very fact that there is a bailment gives rise to certain duties on the part of the bailee even if there is no consideration given by the owner. If the owner seeks to impose duties above those imposed by law on the bailee he can do so in a contract of bailment. The consideration which the courts require to support a contract of bailment is extremely slight: indeed, in some cases it is difficult to find any consideration.[1]

1   *Bainbridge v Firmstone* (1838) 8 Ad & El 743.

Sufficiency
6.11   The law refuses to recognise certain types of action or promise as capable of constituting consideration, with the result that a person making such an action or promise cannot enforce another's promise given in return for it. Such an action or promise is said not to be sufficient consideration, which is rather confusing since in law it is not consideration at all.

Performance of an existing duty imposed by law

6.12 The law imposes obligations on all people, and it is necessary to discuss whether performing or promising to perform such an obligation can also be good consideration for the contractual promise of another. The basic position was stated in *Collins v Godefroy*,[1] in which the plaintiff gave evidence at the defendant's trial in response to a promise of payment. When he sued for the payment, it was held that he could not succeed because he had provided no consideration since he was obliged by law to give evidence.

But, if the court can discover that the party seeking to show that he provided consideration did more than was required by law, that can constitute good consideration. Since consideration need not be adequate it does not matter that what is done exceeds the legal requirements only slightly. This may be demonstrated by two cases. In *Glasbrook Bros Ltd v Glamorgan County Council*,[2] the company requested greater protection for its mine during a strike than the police thought necessary and offered to pay for the increased police presence. The company later refused to pay, claiming that, since the police were under a legal duty to protect property, they had provided no consideration for the company's promise of payment. The House of Lords held that the company was obliged to pay because, while the police were required to guard the mine, they were free to choose the form of protection, and in this case they had provided more protection than they thought necessary at the request of the company. In *Ward v Byham*,[3] the father of an illegitimate child promised to pay its mother £1 a week for its maintenance if she looked after it, kept it well and happy, and allowed it to choose which parent it wished to live with. When the payments stopped and the mother sued the father, he alleged that since the mother of an illegitimate child is required by statute to maintain it she had provided no consideration for his promise. The Court of Appeal, in line with the increasing judical readiness to find consideration, managed to discover that the mother had done more than her legal duty and thus had provided consideration for the promise, in that as well as maintaining the child she had agreed to keep it well and happy and to allow it to choose with which parent to live.

1 (1831) 1 B & Ad 950.
2 [1925] AC 270, HL.
3 [1956] 2 All ER 318, [1956] 1 WLR 496, CA.

Performance of an existing contractual duty owed to the other party

6.13 If a person is under a contractual duty to do something, a promise to perform it (or performance of it) cannot be good consideration for another promise by the person to whom the contractual duty is already owed. In *Stilk v Myrick*,[1] the crew of a ship were paid a lump sum for a voyage including all normal emergencies. During the voyage two of the crew deserted and the captain promised to pay the wages of the deserters to the rest of the crew if they would continue the voyage short-handed. Once returned to England, the extra wages were not paid and the seamen sued. Their claim failed, the court finding that they had provided no consideration since they were required to cope with normal emergencies by their existing contracts. Desertion or death of fellow crew members was a normal emergency so they had done no more than they had contracted to do. But the court stressed that, if they had promised to do more than they were obliged to do by their existing contracts, they would have provided good consideration. For example, if they had promised to face exceptional hazards that would have been good consideration for their employer's promise.[2]

1 (1809) 2 Camp 317. For a recent affirmation of this rule, see *Syros Shipping Co SA v Elaghill Trading Co* [1981] 3 All ER 189.
2 *Hartley v Ponsonby* (1857) 7 E & B 872; *The Atlantic Baron* [1979] QB 705, [1978] 3 All ER 1170.

6.14 *Debts at common law* Particular difficulty has arisen over debts. If A is under a contractual obligation to pay B and B agrees to forego part of the debt, A has provided no consideration for B's promise and, according to the common law, B can subsequently recover the remainder of the debt. In *Foakes v Beer*,[1] Mrs Beer was owed money under a judgment debt by Dr Foakes. She agreed to accept payment by instalments but the agreement did not refer to the question of interest, which is payable on a judgment debt. Dr. Foakes paid the debt. Mrs Beer then sued for the interest. In reply, Dr Foakes pleaded the agreement between them, in which Mrs Beer had agreed to bring no further action on the judgment. Mrs Beer contended successfully that there was no consideration for her promise and that, therefore, it was not binding. Dr Foakes' payment by instalments of the judgment debts could not be consideration for a promise by her to take no further action. He was merely doing what he was obliged to do. The House of Lords regretted that this decision had to be reached, but considered itself bound by previous cases.

There are exceptions to the rule that part payment of a debt is no consideration for a promise to remit the rest of the debt. In *Pinnel's Case*,[2] for instance, it was said that, provided it was done at the creditor's request, early payment of part of a debt, or part payment at another place than that specified for payment, or payment in kind, even if the value of the goods is less than the debt, is good consideration for a promise by the creditor to forego the remainder of the debt. Thus, if A owes B £100 payable on 1 January 2001 at Reading and, at B's request, A pays £1 on 31 December (or pays £1 at Nottingham on the correct day, or gives B a rose or a scarf on the correct day), then the debt is validly discharged.[3] It used to be thought that a part payment by cheque was good consideration for a promise to remit a debt payable in cash. This has been rejected by the Court of Appeal who decided that nowadays there is no effective difference between cash and a cheque which is honoured.[4]

1 (1884) 9 App Cas 605, HL.
2 (1602) 5 Co Rep 117a.
3 For other exceptions see para 6.20 below.
4 *D and C Builders Ltd v Rees* [1966] 2 QB 617, [1965] 3 All ER 837, CA.

6.15 *Debts in equity* Apart from these exceptions it appeared that a debtor who paid part of a debt, believing that the creditor had agreed to remit the remainder of the debt, had no defence if the creditor sought to recover the amount foregone. However, in 1947 Denning J (as he was then) called upon equity to aid the debtor. In *Central London Property Trust Ltd v High Trees House Ltd*,[1] the plaintiffs let a block of flats to the defendants in 1937 for 99 years at a rent of £2,500 per year. The defendants intended to sub-let the flats but, because of the war, found they had many vacant flats and could not pay the rent out of profits. The plaintiffs agreed to accept a reduced rent of £1,250, which was paid quarterly from 1941 until September 1945, by which time all the flats were let. The plaintiffs demanded full rent from September 1945 and claimed the amount of rent underpaid during the previous quarter. The defendants had provided no consideration for the promise by the plaintiffs to remit the rent, but Denning J found that, while the common law could provide no defence in such a case, equity could. The judge, drawing on two little known cases decided in the nineteenth century, said that where one party gave a promise which he intended to be binding and to be acted on, and which was acted on, that promise could be raised as a defence by the promisee if the promisor sought to enforce his strict legal rights. In this case the plaintiffs had promised to reduce the rent; they intended their promise to be binding, they knew the defendants would act on it and the defendants did so act; therefore the rent underpaid in the past could not be demanded by the plaintiffs since this would be inequitable. However, the judge found that the promise was understood by the parties only to apply under the conditions prevailing at the time it was made, namely, when the flats were only partially let, and that when the flats became fully let, early in 1945, the promise to remit part of the rent ceased to bind the plaintiffs. The judge also suggested that a promise of this type might be terminated by notice. This case illustrates the equitable doctrine known as promissory estoppel,[2] which applies to promises to remit debts (in whole or part) and also to promises not to enforce other contractual rights.

1 [1947] KB 130, [1956] 1 All ER 256n.
2 Estoppel (as opposed to promissory estoppel) is a legal doctrine whereby if a person misrepresents to another an existing fact and intends this misrepresentation to be acted on, and it is acted on by the other who suffers detriment in consequence, he cannot subsequently deny the truth of that fact. The doctrine was inapplicable in the *High Trees* case because the representation was as to the future and not to an existing fact.

Promissory estoppel
6.16 Under the doctrine of promissory estoppel a promise not to enforce a contractual right[1] is given some effect, despite the absence of consideration for it, where it would be inequitable for the promisor simply to go back on his promise and enforce that right. There is recent authority that the doctrine can even apply where the promise is made before the contract is entered into, as where a person who is negotiating to lease property to another promises not to enforce a repairing convenant in the draft lease.[2] This goes beyond the previous authorities, which required or assumed that there must be an existing relationship between promisor and promisee when the promise was made, and its compatibility with certain other rules of the law of contract is as yet unexplained.[3]

The precise scope of promissory estoppel is still not entirely clear; indeed, in *Woodhouse A C Israel Cocoa SA v Nigerian Produce Marketing Co Ltd*,[4] Lord Hailsham LC said that it may need to be reviewed and reduced to a coherent body of doctrine by the courts. Nevertheless, its requirements appear to be as follows:

a. *Unequivocal promise* There must be an unequivocal promise[5] by one party that he will not, at least for the time being, enforce his strict contractual rights against the other. The promise may be either express or implied from conduct.[6] Silence and inaction cannot by themselves give rise to a promissory estoppel because they are by their nature equivocal, since there can be more than one reason why the party concerned is silent and inactive.[7]

b. *Alteration of position* The promisor must have intended that his promise should be acted on by the promisee, and the promisee must have acted on it in the sense of altering his position in reliance on the promise.[8] This requirement was satisfied in *Hughes v Metropolitan Rly Co*,[9] where a tenant, who had been given six months' notice to repair the premises in accordance with a repairing covenant but who had been induced by the landlord soon afterwards to believe that the lease would not be forfeited for failure to repair, failed to repair in reliance on this belief. It is not so easy to discern an alteration of position in the *High Trees* case, but the requirement has been said to be satisfied by the fact that the lessees elected to pay a lesser rent and to continue liable as tenants in reliance on the lessor's promise that a lesser rent would be accepted in satisfaction.[10]

The present requirement means that promissory estoppel cannot arise if the promisee does nothing, by action or inaction, in reliance on the promise but simply does what he was going to do anyway regardless of whether or not the promise was made.[11] This is illustrated by *Fontana NV v Mautner*.[12] T, the tenant of a flat which was not subject to the Rent Act, refused to leave when his tenancy expired, on the grounds that he had been a model tenant for many years and that a move would be disastrous for the health of his chronically-ill wife. At a meeting with a representative of the landlord, T was assured by the representative that he could stay on in the flat as long as he wished, but he subsequently received a notice to quit. In proceedings for possession, Balcombe J rejected T's claim that the assurance gave rise to a promissory estoppel, and made an order for possession. The judge held that this was not a case of promissory estoppel because T had done nothing, by action or inaction, in reliance on the assurance but had simply done what he was going to do *anyway* (and that was to sit tight for as long as he possibly could).

c. *Inequitable for promisor to resile* It must be inequitable for the promisor to go back on his promise.[13] It will only be inequitable for the promisor to resile from his promise if the promisee can show that he has suffered 'detriment', ie some prejudicial effect on his interests. This is judged by looking at the promisee's position *at the moment when the promisor proposes to resile* and seeing whether it would be unjust to allow him to do so, having regard to what was promised, what the promisee has done (or refrained from doing) in reliance on the promise and the position in which he would be if the promisor was allowed immediately to resume his strict rights.[14] 'Detriment', then, is not judged by a comparison of the promisee's position before and after acting on the promise on the assumption that it will be honoured. Normally, the present requirement will be satisfied if the promisee has altered his position in reliance on the promise. However, this will not always be the case, as is shown by *The Post Chaser*,[15] where the promisors resiled from their promise not to enforce their strict rights only two days after making it. It was held that this was not inequitable because, in this short period, the promisees had not suffered any prejudice, despite having relied on the promise.

The present requirement has another aspect; even if it can be said that the promisee has suffered 'detriment', it is not inequitable for the promisor to go back on his promise, and the promisee is therefore not protected by promissory estoppel, if the promise has been procured by improper pressure or fraud on the part of the promisee or an associate (or by other similar conduct which would render it unfair to the promisor to hold him to his promise). In *D and C Builders Ltd v Rees*,[16] the plaintiffs were owed £482 by the defendant who knew that they were in desperate need of money to stave off bankruptcy. The defendant's wife offered the plaintiffs £300 in settlement of the debt, saying in effect that if they refused they would get nothing. The plaintiffs accepted the £300 reluctantly in settlement of the debt but later sued successfully for the balance. Lord Denning MR refused to allow the defendant to rely on promissory estoppel; his wife's conduct had been improper and therefore it was not inequitable for the plaintiffs to go back on their promise and insist on their strict contractual right to payment of the balance.

1   It has been held that the doctrine also applies in the case of other pre-existing legal relationships which could give rise to liabilities and penalties: *Durham Fancy Goods Ltd v Michael Jackson (Fancy Goods) Ltd* [1968] 2 QB 839, [1968] 2 All ER 987. Statements made by Lord Denning MR, e g in *Evenden v Guildford City Association Football Club Ltd* [1975] QB 917, [1973] 3 All ER 269, which deny the need for any legal relationship between the parties are suspect.
2   *Brikom Investments Ltd v Carr* [1979] 2 All ER 753 at 758.
3   Such as the law relating to pre-contractual misrepresentations, Chap. 13.
4   [1972] 2 All ER 271 at 282.
5   *Woodhouse A C Israel Cocoa SA v Nigerian Produce Marketing Co Ltd* [1972] AC 741, [1972] 2 All ER 271, HL; *The Winson* [1981] QB 403, [1980] 3 All ER 556, CA (revsd on other grounds [1982] AC 939, [1981] 3 All ER 688, HL); *The Scaptrade* [1983] QB 529, [1983] 1 All ER 301, CA (affd [1983] 2 AC 694, [1983] 2 All ER 763, HL).
6   *Hughes v Metropolitan Rly Co* (1877) 2 App Cas 439, HL; *B. P. Exploration Co (Libya) Ltd v Hunt No 2)* [1979] 1 WLR 783 at 810.
7   *The Leonidas D* [1985] 2 All ER 796, [1985] 1 WLR 925, CA.
8   *Hughes v Metropolitan Rly Co* (1877) 2 App Cas 439, HL; *Central London Property Trust Ltd v High Trees House Ltd* [1947] KB 130, [1956] 1 All ER 256n; *Tool Metal Manufacturing Co Ltd v Tungsten Electric Co Ltd* [1955] 2 All ER 657, [1955] 1 WLR 761, HL; *Ajayi v R T Briscoe (Nigeria) Ltd* [1964] 3 All ER 556, [1964] 1 WLR 1326, PC. Cf. *Brikom Investments Ltd v Carr* [1979] 2 All ER 753 at 758–759.
9   (1877) 2 App Cas 439, HL.
10 Spencer Bower and Turner *Estoppel by Misrepresentation* (3rd edn) p 393.
11 *Fontana NV v Mautner* (1979) 254 Estates Gazette 199; *The Scaptrade* [1983] QB 529, [1983] 1 All ER 301, CA (affirmed [1983] 2 AC 694, [1983] 2 All ER 763, HL).
12 (1979) 254 Estates Gazette 199.
13 *Birmingham and District Land Co v London and North Western Rly Co* (1888) 40 Ch D 268 at 286; *Tool Metal Manufacturing Co Ltd v Tungsten Electric Co Ld* [1955] 2 All ER 657, [1955] 1 WLR 761, HL; *Ajayi v R T Briscoe (Nigeria) Ltd* [1964] 3 All ER 556, [1964] 1 WLR 1326, PC.
14 *Fontana NV v Mautner* (1979) 254 Estates Gazette 199; *Grundt v Great Boulder Proprietary Gold Mines Ltd* (1937) 59 CLR 641 at 674–675.
15 [1982] 1 All ER 19.
16 [1966] 2 QB 617, [1965] 3 All ER 837, CA.

6.17   *Effect of promissory estoppel* Generally, promissory estoppel only suspends, and does not wholly extinguish, an obligation, so that the promisor may, by giving reasonable notice (which need not be a formal one) to the promisee, revert to his strict contractual rights thereafter.[1] If a promise not to enforce a strict contractual right was clearly intended to be operative only for a certain period, as in the *High Trees* case, the promisor automatically reverts to that right on the expiry of the period, if he has not previously determined his promise by giving reasonable notice.[2]

Where an obligation has been suspended, the effect of the promisor's reversion to the strict contractual position varies. If the obligation is to pay a lump sum or to perform some other act, such as to repair under a repairing covenant in a lease, the effect of a reversion is that the promisee must then perform his strict contractual obligation. An example is provided by *Hughes v Metropolitan Rly Co*,[3] discussed above, where the House of Lords held that the six months' notice to repair which had been suspended ran from the time of the landlord's reversion to his strict contractual rights. On the other hand, where the obligation in question is to make periodic payments (such as the payment of rent) or to make some other performance by instalments, a reversion to the strict contractual position, after a promise to accept part payment (or part performance) in lieu or to waive it entirely, results in the promisee being liable to make future payments (or other performance) in full but (unless the promise otherwise provides) does not render him liable to pay (or perform) what was due, and unpaid (or unperformed), during the currency of the estoppel.[4]

Exceptionally, the effect of promissory estoppel may be to extinguish, and not just suspend, the promisee's obligations because the promisor's promise is irrevocable. It is clear that a promise becomes irrevocable if the promisee cannot revert to his strict contractual position,[5] and it may be that the same is true where the promisor has unequivocally indicated that he intends totally to abandon his right to payment of the debt (or performance of some other obligation), whether or not it is due by instalments.

1 *Tool Metal Manufacturing Co Ltd v Tungsten Electric Co Ltd* [1955] 2 All ER 657, [1955] 1 WLR 761, HL; *Ajayi v R T Briscoe (Nigeria) Ltd* [1964] 3 All ER 556, [1964] 1 WLR 1326, PC. Cf. *D and C Builders Ltd v Rees* [1965] 3 All ER 837 at 841; *Brikom Investments Ltd v Carr* [1979] 2 All ER 753 at 758.
2 *Birmingham and District Land Co Ltd v London and North Western Rly Co* (1888) 40 Ch D 268 at 288.
3 (1877) 2 App Cas 439, HL.
4 *Central London Property Trust Ltd v High Trees House Ltd* [1947] KB 130, [1956] 1 All ER 256n; *Tungsten Electric Co Ltd v Tool Metal Manufacturing Co Ltd* (1950) 69 RPC 108, CA; *Tool Metal Manufacturing Co Ltd v Tungsten Electric Co Ltd* [1955] 2 All ER 657, [1955] 1 WLR 761, HL.
5 *Ajayi v R T Briscoe (Nigeria) Ltd* [1964] 3 All ER 556, [1964] 1 WLR 1326, PC.

6.18 *A shield, not a sword* Promissory estoppel only prevents the promisor from enforcing his strict rights (at least, without reasonable notice) despite the absence of consideration from the promisee for the promise; it cannot be used to found a cause of action. In *Combe v Combe*,[1] an ex-husband promised, informally, to pay his divorced wife maintenance. He failed to pay and she sued him. She had provided no consideration for his promise. Consequently, she alleged that he was estopped from going back on his promise (so that it was binding on him) because she had acted on it by not seeking a court order for maintenance. The Court of Appeal rejected her claim, on the ground that promissory estoppel was a shield and not a sword.

1   [1951] 2 KB 215, [1951] 1 All ER 767, CA. Also see *Argy Trading Development Co Ltd v Lapid Developments Ltd* [1977] 3 All ER 785, [1977] 1 WLR 444; *Syros Shipping Co SA v Elaghill Trading Co* [1981] 3 All ER 189.

6.19   We consider a particular application of the doctrine of promissory estoppel in relation to leases in para 39.8, below.

Promissory estoppel is closely linked with the doctrine of waiver, which we mention in paras. 6.36 and 6.37 below.

Compositions with creditors

6.20   There are two somewhat anomalous areas where partial performance of an existing contractual duty discharges that duty. Both areas concern debts. First, where a debtor makes an arrangement with all his creditors that they will all be paid a given percentage of what they are owed, no creditor who has been paid it can recover more than that given percentage.[1] Second, when a third party pays part of a debt in full settlement, that is a valid discharge of the whole debt, and the creditor cannot recover the balance from the debtor.[2] The reason which has been given is that it would be a fraud on the third party if the creditor could do so.[3]

Neither of these areas can satisfactorily be explained in terms of principle (ie consideration for the creditor's promise) and are best explained on grounds of public policy.

1   *Good v Cheeseman* (1831) 2 B & Ad 328.
2   *Welby v Drake* (1825) 1 C & P 557; *Hirachand Punamchand v Temple* [1911] 2 KB 330, CA.
3   *Hirachand Punamchand v Temple* [1911] 2 KB 330, CA.

Performance of an existing contractual duty owed to a third party

6.21   If a party to a contract with X (the 'third party') is obliged by it to perform some action it might be thought that a subsequent promise by him to perform that action, or his performance of it, cannot be good consideration for a promise by another person. But the cases show that the opposite is true. A number of nineteenth century decisions permitted the discharge of a pre-existing contractual obligation owed to a third party to constitute consideration for a promise. In *Scotson v Pegg*,[1] for example, the plaintiffs had contracted to deliver coal to X, or wherever X ordered it to be delivered. X sold the coal to the defendant and told the plaintiffs to deliver it to him. The defendant then agreed with the plaintiffs that if they delivered the coal he would unload it at a given rate. The defendant failed to unload at this rate and when sued argued that the plaintiffs had provided no consideration for his promise. The court found for the plaintiff but for reasons which are far from clear. In *Chichester v Cobb*,[2] which was decided at a time when engagements were binding contracts, the defendant promised one of the plaintiffs (who were engaged) that, in consideration of their marriage and once all their arrangements were complete, he would pay her £300. The defendant failed to pay the £300 and the plaintiffs sued successfully for the money. The judge held that there was consideration for the defendant's promise without specifying what it was.

In two recent cases, *New Zealand Shipping Co Ltd v A M Satterthwaite Co Ltd*[3] and *Pao On v Lau Yiu Long*,[4] the Privy Council has affirmed that a promise to discharge, or the discharge of, a pre-existing contractual obligation to a third party can be valid consideration for another's promise.

In the former case, consideration for a promise consisted of unloading a ship which the promisee was already bound to unload under a contract with a third party.

1 (1861) 6 H & N 295.
2 (1866) 14 LT 433. See also, *Shadwell v Shadwell* (1860) 9 CBNS 159, where the facts were similar.
3 [1975] AC 154, [1974] 1 All ER 1015, PC.
4 [1980] AC 614, [1979] 3 All ER 65, PC.

Consideration must move from the promisee

6.22 It is not sufficient that there is consideration in the abstract; it is also necessary for a person who wishes to enforce a promise to show that he has provided consideration. This bears a strong resemblance to the doctrine of privity of contract which states that a person who is not party to a contract cannot sue on it. In some early cases claims failed either on the basis that the party seeking to enforce the contract had provided no consideration or because he was not a party to the agreement.[1] But later cases have shown that consideration and privity are two separate requirements and not two facets of the same rule.[2] In many cases it is not necessary to decide on which basis a claim fails but if, as it seems, the rules are separate it is not sufficient to be a party to an agreement to enforce it; consideration must also be provided.

1 *Price v Easton* (1833) 4 B & Ad 433.
2 For example *Dunlop Pneumatic Tyre Co Ltd v Selfridge & Co Ltd* [1915] AC 847, HL.

Privity of contract

6.23 It is a distinct rule of English law that only those persons who are parties to a contract may sue and be sued on that contract, subject to certain recognised exceptions. There are two consequences of the doctrine: a person not a party to a contract is not entitled to enforce the contract, even if it was intended to benefit him and he has provided consideration; and a contract cannot impose obligations on a stranger to it. Suggested reasons for the first consequence are: a. that mere donees should not be able to enforce a contract; and b. that the parties to the contract should not have their freedom to vary it restricted by the existence of third-party rights. There seems more justification for refusing to allow a contract to impose a burden on a third party than for denying the benefit of a contract to a third party whom the contract sought to benefit.

Benefits

Enforcement by the party intended to benefit
6.24 Prior to *Tweddle v Atkinson*,[1] a benefit enforceable by a third person could be conferred on him if there was some family relationship between him and one of the contracting parties. However, in *Tweddle v Atkinson*, a contract between the plaintiff's father and X for the benefit of the plaintiff was regarded as unenforceable by the plaintiff. It may be possible to confer a benefit which he can enforce on someone not really involved in a contract by making him a party to it, even if in name only. Unfortunately, such a

party may be unable to show that he has provided any consideration. The High Court of Australia suggested a circumvention of this difficulty, obiter, in *Coulls v Bagot's Executor and Trustee Co Ltd*,[2] where a contract for the right to quarry a mine made all royalties payable to X, who had granted the right, and his wife jointly. The High Court of Australia held that the wife could have been entitled to the royalties after her husband's death because she was a party to the contract and, even though she had personally provided no consideration for it, the promise to pay her and her husband was supported by consideration furnished by the husband on behalf of himself and his wife.

The fact that, under the doctrine of privity, a third party to a contract is not entitled by virtue of the contract itself to enforce a benefit arising under it does not mean that a contract can never indirectly benefit him. For example, if it is foreseeable that negligent performance of a contract by a party to it will cause loss or injury to a third party, that party may in limited circumstances owe a duty of care to the third party and be liable to him in the tort of negligence if he is in breach of that duty. Thus, in *Junior Books Ltd v Veitchi Co Ltd*,[3] the House of Lords held a building sub-contractor liable for defective workmanship to the owner of the building in question, even though the latter was not a party to the contract for the work (which had been made between a building company, engaged by the owner, and the sub-contractor). Likewise, accountants, surveyors and other professional people may be held liable to people who are not their clients if they cause them foreseeable loss or injury in negligently carrying out a contract made with a client.[4]

1   (1861) 1 B & S 393.
2   [1967] ALR 385.
3   [1983] 1 AC 520, [1982] 3 All ER 201, HL; para 19.25 below.
4   *Ross v Caunters* [1980] Ch 297, [1979] 3 All ER 580; *Yianni v Edwin Evans & Sons* [1982] QB 438, [1981] 3 All ER 593.

Exceptions and qualifications

6.25   There are certain established exceptions and qualifications to the doctrine of privity of contract. If an agent enters into an authorised contract with a third party on behalf of his principal, there is a contract between the principal and the third party.[1] It is possible to assign rights under a contract.[2] A third party can sue on a bill of exchange or cheque.[3] Beneficiaries under certain types of contract of insurance have a statutory right to claim the benefit of the contract even if they are not parties to it. An example is where one spouse has made a life insurance contract which is expressed to be for the benefit of the other.[4]

The requirements of land law have also necessitated some modifications of the strict rules of privity. The benefits of covenants in leases are transferred to successors in title of the landlord and tenant, despite the absence of privity, if the covenants affect the land.[5]

1   Ch 17.
2   See Card and James, *Law for Accountancy Students*, Ch 19.
3   Bills of Exchange Act 1882, s29.
4   Married Women's Property Act 1882, s11.
5   Law of Property Act 1925, ss78, 141 and 142. See paras 39.2–39.7 below.

6.26   The above situations are exceptions or qualifications to the doctrine of privity. It may also be possible to outflank the rule. For example, if a collateral contract can be found, a person not a party to the principal contract can sue on the collateral contract instead. In *Shanklin Pier Ltd v Detel Products Ltd*,[1] the plaintiffs employed contractors to paint their pier and instructed them to buy and use the defendants' paint. The defendants had told the plaintiffs the paint would last for seven to ten years, but it lasted for only three months. It was held that, while the plaintiffs could not sue on the contract of sale of the paint, to which they were not parties, they could sue on a collateral contract between them and the defendants which contained a promise that the paint would last seven to ten years. The plaintiffs had provided consideration for the collateral contract by requiring their contractors to use the defendants' paint. Similarly, in *Andrews v Hopkinson*,[2] the plaintiff entered into a contract of hire purchase with a finance company for a car after the car dealer had misrepresented that she was a 'good little bus'. It was held that the dealer was liable under a collateral contract between himself and the plaintiff.[3]

1 [1951] 2 KB 854, [1951] 2 All ER 471, CA.
2 [1957] 1 QB 229, [1956] 3 All ER 422.
3 See now Consumer Credit Act 1974, ss56 and 75, for a possible claim against the finance company in relation to the dealer's misrepresentation.

6.27 Another method of evasion of the privity doctrine is the use of a trust. The subject matter of a trust is normally tangible property, but when used in this context the subject matter of the trust is the promise given by one party to a contract to the other party that he will benefit a third party. In equity, if a trust of a promise can be discovered, the courts will enforce an agreement for the benefit of the third party; he is regarded as a beneficiary and the party contracting for his benefit as a trustee. In *Lloyd's v Harper*,[1] Lush LJ said that, 'when a contract is made with A for the benefit of B, A can sue on the contract for the benefit of B and recover all that B could have recovered if the contract had been made by B himself'. In this case creditors of a Lloyd's underwriter sought to sue the guarantor of that underwriter on the contract of guarantee. The contract was with Lloyd's, not the creditors, but the Court of Appeal held that Lloyd's could recover on behalf of the creditors, and not merely for their own loss. The difficulty with using the trust concept to defeat the doctrine of privity is that it is not certain when it will apply, and the type of trust recognised by these cases cannot be regarded as the usual type of trust which is subject to strict rules clearly inapplicable here. The decision in *Lloyd's v Harper* allowed the trustee to recover for the third party; it did not give a right to sue to the third party. However, it seems that if the third party wishes to sue he can do so by joining as co-plaintiff the party to the contract who was hoping to benefit him.[2] If the trustee pursues a claim for the beneficiary any damages are payable to the beneficiary. If the trustee refuses to sue either alone or as co-plaintiff, there seems no reason why he should not be joined as co-defendant in an action by the third party beneficiary.

Although no formal words are required, an intention to create a trust, not merely an intention to benefit a third party, must exist, and this is the principal reason why the application of the trust concept is uncertain. In modern times, the courts generally seem reluctant to impute such an intention, in the absence of clear words, and thus to use the trust concept to circumvent the doctrine of privity. In *Re Flavell, Murray v Flavell*,[3] decided in 1883, the terms of a partnership deed (the contract) provided that the executors of a deceased partner should be paid a certain sum for his widow. The executors were held to be trustees for the widow. This can be contrasted with the much more recent case of *Re Schebsman*,[4] where a contract between Schebsman and X Ltd, which provided that in certain circumstances his wife and daughter should be paid a lump sum, was held not to create a trust. The Court of Appeal was influenced by the fact that Schebsman and the company might have wished to vary the agreement, which would have been impossible had the contract created a trust. Finally, in *Green v Russell*,[5] decided in 1959, a contract of insurance between Russell and an insurance company made certain sums payable if any of his employees died. Green, an employee, died; the Court of Appeal found that there was no trust in his favour of the sum due under the contract of insurance.

Beswick v Beswick,[6] the most important recent case on privity of contract, does not discuss trusts and so this attempt to outflank privity seems to have been limited by the courts.

1   (1880) 16 Ch D 290, CA.
2   *Les Affréteurs Réunis SA v Leopold Walford (London) Ltd* [1919] AC 801, HL.
3   (1883) 25 Ch D 89, CA.
4   [1944] Ch 83, [1943] 2 All ER 768, CA.
5   [1959] 2 QB 226, [1959] 2 All ER 525, CA.
6   [1968] AC 58, [1967] 2 All ER 1197, HL.

Enforcement by a party to the contract

6.28   The party who was promised that the benefit would be conferred on the third party may be prepared to sue if the other party to the agreement does not carry out his contractual obligations. Damages, the usual remedy for failure to perform contractual obligations, are available, but, unless the contracting party is suing as agent or trustee for the third party, he cannot recover any damages on behalf of the third party. The reason is that a plaintiff can only recover damages for the loss which he has suffered.[1] If the contract was intended solely to benefit the third party, so that the contracting party has suffered no loss, only nominal damages (usually in the region of £2.00 to £10.00) will be recoverable by the contracting party.[2]

This being so, it is preferable for the contracting party to seek the enforcement of the contract by means of the equitable remedy of specific performance. The advantages of this remedy are illustrated by *Beswick v Beswick*.[3] In this case, in consideration of Peter Beswick transferring his business to his nephew, the nephew agreed to pay his uncle a pension and, after his death, a weekly annuity to his widow. The nephew paid his uncle the pension but only one payment of the annuity was made. The widow, an administratix of her husband's estate, successfully sued her nephew for specific performance of the contract to pay the annuity, although the House of Lords held that she would not have succeeded if she had sued merely as the intended recipient. Thus, if specific performance of a contract can be ordered, a party to a contract or his personal representative can ensure enforcement of the contract for the benefit of a third party. However, the courts will not always order specific performance; it is a discretionary remedy.

1   If the contract is one to provide a contracting party with a benefit which others will also

enjoy, such as a contract for a family holiday or a group coach trip, he is entitled to substantial damages for *his* loss (the family holiday or group coach trip) if that benefit is not provided by the other party: *Jackson v Horizon Holidays Ltd* [1975] 3 All ER 92, [1975] 1 WLR 1468, CA, as explained in *Woodar Investment Development Ltd v Wimpey Construction (UK) Ltd* [1980] 1 All ER 571, [1980] 1 WLR 277, HL. For remedies in general see Chap. 11.
2 *Beswick v Beswick* [1968] AC 58, [1967] 2 All ER 1197, HL.
3 [1968] AC 58, [1967] 2 All ER 1197, HL.

6.29 The converse of specific performance is an injunction whereby an action is required to cease. An injunction may be awarded to restrain a breach of contract adversely affecting a third party at the suit of a contracting party. However, if the breach of contract consists of pursuing a legal claim against the third party, such an action cannot be restrained by injunction, though a stay of the proceedings may be ordered[1] if the contract embodied the promise not to sue the third party *and* the party seeking to stay the proceedings has a sufficient interest in the cesser of the action.[2]

1 Supreme Court Act 1981, s49.
2 *Gore v Van Der Lann* [1967] 2 QB 31, [1967] 1 All ER 360, CA. Also see *Snelling v John G. Snelling Ltd* [1973] QB 87, [1972] 1 All ER 79.

Burdens
6.30 As we have already indicated, the general rule is that only a person who is a party to a contract can be subject to any obligations contained in it; consequently, a third party cannot generally be sued for contravening a provision in a contract made between others.[1]

The exceptions or qualifications to this general rule can be summarised as follows:

a. the burdens of a contract apply to a person on whose behalf the contract was made by an agent;[2]

b. the burdens of covenants in leases are transferred to the successors in title of the landlord and tenant, despite the absence of privity of contract, if the covenants affect the land; we discuss this further in paras 39.2 to 39.7 below;

c. the burdens of negative covenants affecting the use of land, inserted in a contract of sale of land, bind subsequent purchasers of the land, provided certain conditions are satisfied; we discuss this further in paras 39.16 to 39.20 below;

d. in certain cases, the right of a person, by virtue of a contract to which he is party, to make use of a chattel are enforceable against a third party; and

e. in certain cases, a third party can be bound by a provision as to the resale price of goods contained in a contract between others.

The last item in this list merits further explanation at this point.

1 For an authority, see *McGruther v Pitcher* [1904] 2 Ch 306, CA. The actual decision in this case would now be governed by the Resale Prices Act 1976; paras 14.33–14.35 below.
2 Ch 17.

Restrictions on price
6.31 At common law, a contract of sale which fixed the resale price of

goods could not, because of the doctrine of privity, bind a third party who could sell any goods he acquired for whatever price he desired.

The matter is now governed by statute. Under the Resale Prices Act 1976, s26, a supplier who sells goods under a contract which provides a maximum resale price can enforce that price against anyone not party to the contract who acquires the goods for resale with notice of that maximum resale price. Any attempt to fix a *minimum* price is void by virtue of the Resale Prices Act 1976, s9, unless the goods are exempt from the operation of the 1976 Act, in which case s26 of the Act applies and a minimum resale price provision in a contract can be enforced by the supplier against a third party who acquires the goods for resale with notice of the provision.[1]

1   Paras 14.33–14.35 below.

Consideration: discharge and variation

6.32   We have seen that consideration is necessary for the formation of contracts which are not made under seal, and that a promise by the creditor to remit a debt is not binding without the provision of consideration by the debtor. We will now discuss whether consideration is necessary when the parties agree (otherwise than under seal) to discharge (ie end) or to vary their contract before it is completely performed. The discharge of a contract by agreement may be either mutual or unilateral. It will be mutual, subject to the rules discussed later, where both parties still have contractual obligations to perform, ie there is executory consideration on both sides; it will be unilateral, subject to what we say in para 6.34 below, where one party still has contractual obligations to perform but the other party has completed his performance of the contract. Apart from the question of whether consideration is necessary to effect a binding discharge or variation, it is also necessary to discuss whether the agreement which purports to discharge or vary the contract must be made in any particular form.

We discuss other methods of discharge of contracts in later chapters.[1]

1   Discharge by performance, by breach and by frustration: chs 8, 9 and 10.

Mutual discharge

6.33   An agreement to discharge a contract must be supported by consideration. However, if both parties still have contractual obligations to perform, any agreement to discharge the contract relieves both parties from further performance of it. In such a case, both parties have provided consideration, for each party promises not to require further performance of contractual obligations by the other party in return for being absolved himself from further performance.

Unilateral discharge

6.34   A unilateral discharge by agreement is only effective if the party to be absolved has provided consideration for the other's promise to absolve him. In other words, where one party has performed all his contractual obligations prior to the agreement, his promise to release the other party from further performance does not bind him unless that other party provides consideration. Unilateral discharge by agreement is also known as accord (agreement to discharge) and satisfaction (consideration for that agreement).

Accord without satisfaction is ineffective to discharge a contract. Satisfaction usually consists of doing something in return for the promise to discharge, but the satisfaction which is offered may be a promise to do something. If so, it is necessary to decide whether the original contract is discharged from the moment of the accord or only when the promise, which is the alleged satisfaction, has been translated into action. It is a question of construction. If the accord can be construed to mean that the promise to do something was intended to be satisfaction, the original contract is discharged from the making of the accord. However, if, on its true construction, the accord means that *performance* of a promise to do something was intended to be satisfaction, the original contract can only be discharged when the promise is performed. The meaning of the accord is a question of fact in every case. In *Elton Cop Dyeing Co Ltd v Robert Broadbent & Son Ltd*,[1] a buyer of machinery sued the seller for damages. An agreement was made by which the buyer withdrew his claim and the seller agreed to repair the machines partly at his own expense. The buyer then attempted to sue on the original contract of sale but failed, the Court of Appeal finding an accord which on its true construction was supported by satisfaction, viz the promise to repair the machines.

Although the matter has not yet been decided, there is no doubt that promissory estoppel[2] would be available as a defence to a person who has been promised a release from further performance in circumstances where his obligation has not been discharged by accord and satisfaction because he has not provided consideration for the promise.

1 (1919) 89 LJKB 186, CA.
2 Paras 6.16–6.19 above.

Variation and waiver

6.35 If there is an agreement to vary, rather than to discharge, a contract,[1] the agreement must be supported by consideration. Consequently, if the variation of a contract benefits both parties (or could benefit one or other of them[2] depending on the outcome of a contingency) it will have contractual effect, but it will have no effect (because of lack of consideration) if it can only be of benefit to one party. Suppose that a contract between A and B requires A to deliver 100 tons of copper to B in Nottingham on 1 June. If A and B agree that A should, instead, deliver 95 tons on 1 May (or 100 tons on 1 July in Reading) the variation has contractual effect because it benefits both parties; in contrast, a variation whereby B agreed to accept the delivery of 95 tons in Nottingham on 1 June would have no contractual effect because it could only be of benefit to A.[3]

A variation which has no contractual effect because it is unsupported by consideration may have a limited effect as a waiver or by virtue of the doctrine of promissory estoppel, matters to which we shall now turn.

1 For the distinction between agreements to discharge and agreements to vary, see para 6.38 below.
2 As where the variation consists of the alteration of the currency of payment, whose exchange rate against the original currency of payment may go up or down by the time

payment is due: *W J Alan & Co Ltd v El Nasr Export and Import Co* [1972] 2 QB 189, [1972] 2 All ER 127, CA.
3   See, for example, para 6.14 above.

6.36   Because a variation may not be enforceable for lack of consideration or because it has been made in an incorrect form,[1] the common law developed another type of alteration of contract—the waiver. A waiver can take effect even though it is unsupported by consideration from the party seeking to enforce it and even though it is in the incorrect form for a variation. Whether an alteration of a contract is a variation or waiver is said to be a question of intention, but in fact there is no rational distinction between waiver and variation. It is said that a variation alters the terms of the contract while a waiver alters the effect of the original term of the contract; the difficulties of applying such a test are obvious. However, the following effects of a waiver at common law have been revealed by the cases:

a. The waiver binds the party who sought its operation. Therefore, in *Levey & Co v Goldberg*,[2] where a buyer of goods sued for non-delivery by the contractual date, the seller had a defence in that the buyer had himself requested that delivery be postponed until after that date.

b. The waiver binds the party who granted it,[3] at least until he has given reasonable notice that the waiver is withdrawn and that the original contractual term will apply thereafter[4] (unless this is impossible). There is authority that a waiver will be permanently irrevocable if the party who grants it leads the other to believe that he will never enforce the strict contractual right which has been waived.[5]

1   For form see para 6.38 below.
2   [1922] 1 KB 688.
3   *Hartley v Hymans* [1920] 3 KB 475.
4   *Panoutsos v Raymond Hadley Corpn of New York* [1917] 2 KB 473, CA.
5   *Brikom Investments Ltd v Carr* [1979] QB 467, [1979] 2 All ER 753, CA.

6.37   The basis on which the rules on waiver can be justified as an exception to the requirement that promises must be supported by consideration in order to be binding has never been fully explained by the courts. Probably, the rules are based upon some form of estoppel similar to the equitable doctrine of promissory estoppel (which, of course, provides the same solution to the problem of contractual alterations unaccompanied by consideration).[1] However, it appears that there are distinctions between the two sets of rules; one such is that waiver (unlike promissory estoppel) does not require the person who has been promised the forbearance to have altered his position in reliance on that promise[2] (although he will normally have done so), and another that the fact that it is inequitable for the promisor to go back on his promise without reasonable notice is not generally[3] regarded as being a requirement of waiver (as opposed to promissory estoppel).

1   *Charles Rickards Ltd v Oppenheim* [1950] 1 KB 616 at 622, [1950] 1 All ER 420 at 423. For promissory estoppel, see paras 6.16–6.19 above.
2   *Brikom Investments Ltd v Carr* [1979] QB 467, [1979] 2 All ER 753, CA.
3   *Fontana NV v Mautner* (1979) 254 Estates Gazette 199. It may be added as another distinction that the doctrine of waiver only applies to the waiver of contractual obligations; cf para 6.16, n1 above.

Form

6.38 If a contract is *discharged* by an agreement supported by consideration from both parties, the agreement is binding whatever form it is in. For example, a contract by deed can be discharged by deed or in writing or orally.[1]

Variations, on the other hand, are not so straightforward. If the contract which is alleged to have been varied had to be made in writing or evidenced in writing, e g a contract for the disposition of land, the variation must be in writing or evidenced in writing,[2] as the case may be. In the case of such a contract, an oral variation is ineffective (unless the courts can construe the variation as a waiver or equity intervenes) and the validity of the original contract is not affected.[3] However, what the parties choose to call a variation may be regarded by the courts as a discharge of the original contract and the substitution of a new one. If this is the case, the informal 'variation' is effective to discharge the original contract, though whether the new agreement is enforceable or not depends on whether it satisfies the rules for the creation of an enforceable contract.[4]

Whether an alteration is to be regarded as a variation or as a discharge and substitution may be expressly stated by the parties or implied from the nature of the alteration. An alteration will discharge a contract by implication only if it is entirely inconsistent with the original contract. The inconsistency must go to 'the very root of the contract' for there to be an implied discharge.[5] An example of an implied discharge occurred in *Morris v Baron & Co*,[6] where a contract for the sale of blue serge, which at the time had to be evidenced in writing, was effectively discharged by an agreement compromising a dispute about the goods and varying the amount to be sold. Alterations which have been found not to be inconsistent with the original contract are changing the place of delivery of a shipment of tea (this was an alteration of one term out of seven in the contract),[7] and varying the rate of interest of a loan.[8]

1 *Berry v Berry* [1929] 2 KB 316.
2 *Goss v Lord Nugent* (1833) 5 B & Ad 58.
3 *United Dominions Corpn (Jamaica) Ltd v Shoucair* [1969] 1 AC 340, [1968] 2 All ER 904, PC.
4 So that, if the subject matter of the new contract was land, the contract might well have to be in writing or evidenced in writing. See paras 43.11–43.12 below.
5 *British and Benningtons Ltd v North Western Cachar Tea Co Ltd* [1923] AC 48, HL.
6 [1918] AC 1, HL.
7 *British and Benningtons Ltd v North Western Cachar Tea Co Ltd* [1923] AC 48, HL.
8 *United Dominions Corpn (Jamaica) Ltd v Shoucair* [1969] 1 AC 340, [1968] 2 All ER 904, PC.

Chapter 7

Contractual terms

7.1   The terms of a contract may be express or implied.

Express terms

7.2   Clearly, the ascertainment of its express terms is facilitated when the contract has been reduced into writing, particularly because under the 'parol evidence'[1] rule oral or other evidence extrinsic to the document is not admissible generally to add to, vary, or contradict, the terms of the written agreement.[2] However, this rule is not as harsh as might be supposed because in a number of cases extrinsic evidence is admissible, either as an exception to the parol evidence rule or because the circumstances fall outside its bounds. The following can be mentioned as examples.

1 Parol evidence of a written document means extrinsic evidence, whether oral or otherwise: Jowitt's *Dictionary of English Law*.
2 *Jacobs v Batavia and General Plantations Trust Ltd* [1924] 1 Ch 287 at 295.

Implied terms

7.3   The fact that a contract has been reduced into writing does not prevent extrinsic evidence being given to support or rebut the implication of a term into it[1] under rules which are discussed shortly.

1 *Burges v Wickham* (1863) 3 B & S 669; *Gillespie Bros & Co v Cheney, Eggar & Co* [1896] 2 QB 59.

Conditions precedent

7.4   Extrinsic evidence is admissible to show that, although a written contract appears absolute on its face, it was not intended that a binding contract should be created (or that, although there was an immediate binding contract, a party's obligation to perform would not arise) until the occurrence of a particular event, such as a surveyor's report or the availability of finance.[1]

1 *Pym v Campbell* (1856) 6 E & B 370; para 5.33 above.

Invalidating factors

7.5   Extrinsic evidence of a factor, such as mistake or misrepresentation, which invalidates the written contract is, of course, admissible.

Written contract not the whole contract

7.6 While a document which looks like a contract is presumed to include all the terms of the contract, this presumption is rebutted by evidence that the parties did not intend all the terms of their contract to be contained in the document.[1] If the presumption is rebutted, extrinsic evidence is admissible to prove the other terms of the contract. An example is provided by the case of *J. Evans & Son (Portsmouth) Ltd v Andrea Merzario Ltd*, which is discussed in para 7.11 below.

1   *Gillespie Bros & Co v Cheney, Eggar & Co* [1896] 2 QB 59 at 62.

Collateral contracts

7.7 The parol evidence rule will also be circumvented if the court finds that the parties have made two contracts, the main written one and an oral one collateral to it. An example is provided by *Birch v Paramount Estates Ltd*,[1] where the defendants, who were developing a housing estate, offered a house they were then building to the plaintiff, stating orally that it would be as good as the show house. Subsequently, the plaintiff agreed to buy the house but the written contract of sale made no reference to this statement. The completed house was not as good as the show house. The Court of Appeal held that there was an oral contract, to the effect that the house would be as good as the show house, collateral to the contract of sale and upheld the award of damages for its breach.

In essence, a collateral contract exists where A promises B something in return for B making the main contract. A's promise must have been intended by the parties to be legally binding and to take effect as a collateral contract, and not merely as a term of the main contract, and it must be supported by separate consideration, although this may simply be B's making of the main contract.[2] Provided these requirements are satisfied, a collateral contract will be valid and enforceable even though it conflicts with a term in the main contract. This is shown by *City and Westminster Properties (1934) Ltd v Mudd*.[3] In 1941, the defendant became the tenant of a lock-up shop for three years. He was allowed by the landlords, the plaintiffs, to sleep in the shop. In 1944, a second lease for three years was granted to the defendant. In 1947, during negotiations for a new lease, the plaintiffs inserted in the draft lease a clause restricting the use of the premises to trade purposes only. The defendant objected and was told by the plaintiffs' agent that, if he accepted the new lease as it stood, the plaintiffs would not object to him residing on the premises. In consequence, the defendant signed the lease. Later, the plaintiffs sought to forfeit the lease for breach of the covenant only to use the premises for trade purposes. It was held that the defendant could plead the collateral contract as a defence to a charge of breach of the main contract, the lease.

1   (1956) 168 Estates Gazette 396, CA.
2   *Heilbut, Symons & Co v Buckleton* [1913] AC 30, HL.
3   [1959] Ch 129, [1958] 2 All ER 733.

Contractual terms and mere representations

7.8 Where contractual terms are oral they must be proved by the evidence of the parties and other witnesses in the event of a dispute.

Problems can sometimes arise concerning whether a written or oral statement, which is made in contractual negotiations and not explicitly referred to at the time the contract is made, is nevertheless a term of the contract instead of being a mere representation. The present issue can be exemplified as follows. At the time the contract was made A may simply have said to B: 'I offer you £1,000 for the car' to which B replied 'I accept'. These two sentences will probably be the culmination of previous, and perhaps lengthy, negotiations between the parties during which B will have given A a number of assurances as to the condition of the car, its mileage and so on. Whether these pre-contractual statements are contractual terms or undertakings, or simply mere representations, is of importance for the following reason. Breach of a contractual term results in liability in damages, and certain other remedies for breach of contract may also be available to the 'injured party'. On the other hand, if a mere representation turns out to be false there can be no liability for breach of contract, although it *may* be possible for the misrepresentee to have the contract set aside (rescinded) for misrepresentation; and in certain circumstances he can recover damages for misrepresentation. Generally speaking, the remedies for misrepresentation are inferior to those for breach of contract. We discuss the subjects of breach of contract, remedies for breach and misrepresentation in chs 9, 11 and 13, and for the present we are concerned with the question of how it is ascertained whether a pre-contractual statement has become a contractual term.

7.9　A representation will be a contractual term if the parties intended that the representor was making a binding promise as to it.[1] Whether the parties did so intend can only be deduced from all the evidence. Of course, it is always possible for the parties actually to state that a particular representation is or is not a term of their contract. If they do not, then, if an intelligent bystander would infer from the words and behaviour of the parties that a binding promise was intended, that will suffice.[2] In approaching the question of the parties' intentions, the courts take into account factors such as the following.

1　*Oscar Chess Ltd v Williams* [1957] 1 All ER 325 at 327–328.
2　Ibid. See also *Howard Marine and Dredging Co Ltd v A Ogden & Sons (Excavations) Ltd* [1978] QB 574 at 590, [1978] 2 All ER 1134 at 1140.

Execution of a written contract
7.10　If the representation was followed by a written contract in which it does not appear, it will probably (but not necessarily) be regarded as a mere representation[1] since, because of the parol evidence rule, it can only take effect as a contractual term if the court finds that the parties intended that the contract should not be contained wholly in the written document or that the representation should form part of a collateral contract. An example of a case where a pre-contractual representation was found to be a contractual term despite the subsequent execution of a written contract is *J Evans & Son (Portsmouth) Ltd v Andrea Merzario Ltd*, which is discussed in the next paragraph.

1　*Heilbut, Symons & Co v Buckleton* [1913] AC 30 at 50; *Oscar Chess Ltd v Williams* [1957] 1 All ER 325 at 329.

The importance of the representation

7.11 The more important the subject matter of the representation the more likely it is that the parties intended a binding promise concerning it. In particular, if the representation was so important that without it the representee would not have made the contract, the court is very likely to hold that it is a contractual term. In *J Evans & Son (Portsmouth) Ltd v Andrea Merzario Ltd*,[1] the plaintiffs bought some machines from an Italian company. They had previously employed the defendants to arrange transport, and the machinery had always been packed in crates or trailers and carried under deck. On this occasion the defendants' representative told the plaintiffs' that it was proposed that the machinery should be packed in containers. The plaintiffs' repesentative replied that if containers were used they must be stowed under, and not on, deck in case the machinery rusted. He was assured by the defendants' representative that this would be done but this oral assurance was not included in the written agreement subsequently made between the plaintiffs and the defendants. In fact, the containers were carried on deck and two fell into the sea. In the Court of Appeal, Roskill and Geoffrey Lane LJJ held that the oral assurance had become a term of the contract between the parties, which was not wholly written, and that the plaintiff could recover damages for its breach. Roskill LJ stated that in the light of the totality of the evidence it was clear that the plaintiffs had only agreed to contract with the defendants on the basis that the containers were stowed under deck, and therefore the defendants' assurance concerning this had become a contractual term. Similarly, in *Bannerman v White*,[2] a representation that sulphur had not been used in the treatment of hops was found to have become a term of the subsequent contract. It related to a matter of great importance and the buyer would not have made the contract without it.

1 [1976] 2 All ER 930, [1976] 1 WLR 1078, CA.
2 (1861) 10 CBNS 844.

Invitation to verify

7.12 If a seller invites the buyer to check his representation it is very unlikely to be regarded as a contractual term. In *Ecay v Godfrey*,[1] for instance, the seller of a boat said that it was sound but advised a survey. It was held that this advice negatived any intention that the representation should be a contractual term. Conversely, if the seller assures the buyer that it is not necessary to verify the representation since he can take the seller's word for it, the representation is likely to be found to be intended to be a term of the resulting contract if the buyer contracts in reliance on it. In *Schawel v Reade*,[2] the plaintiff, who required a stallion for stud purposes, went to the defendant's stables to inspect a horse. While he was inspecting it, the defendant said: 'You need not look for anything: the horse is perfectly sound. If there was anything the matter with the horse I would tell you'. The plantiff thereupon ended his inspection and a price was agreed a few days later, the plaintiff relying on the defendant's statement. The House of Lords held that the jury's finding that the defendant's statement was a contractual term was correct.

1 (1947) 80 Ll L Rep 286.
2 [1913] 2 IR 64, HL. Cf. *Hopkins v Tanqueray* (1854) 15 CB 130.

Statements of fact, of opinion or as to the future

7.13 A statement of fact is more likely to be construed as intended to have contractual effect than a statement of opinion or as to future facts (eg a forecast).[1] A promise about something which is, or should be, within the promisor's control is very likely to be construed as a contractual term.[2]

1   *Esso Petroleum Co Ltd v Mardon* [1976] 2 All ER 5 at 20.
2   *Oscar Chess Ltd v Williams* [1957] 1 All ER 325 at 329.

Ability of the parties to ascertain the accuracy of the statement

7.14 If the representor had a special skill or knowledge, or was otherwise in a better position than the representee to ascertain the truth of the representation, this strongly suggests that the representation was intended to be a contractual term, and vice versa. An example is provided by *Dick Bentley (Productions) Ltd v Harold Smith (Motors) Ltd.*[1] The plaintiff purchased a Bentley car from the defendants in reliance on their statement that the car had been fitted with a new engine and gear box and had done only 20,000 miles since then. The representation as to mileage, although honestly made, was untrue. The Court of Appeal held that the representation had become one of the terms of the contract because it had been made by a dealer who was in a position to know or find out the car's history, and it could therefore be inferred that the representation was intended to have contractual effect. The Court distinguished its previous decision in *Oscar Chess Ltd v Williams.*[2] There, Williams, a private person, represented in negotiations for the part-exchange of his Morris car that it was a 1948 model. This representation was based on the logbook which had been falsified by a person unknown. The representation was held not to have become a contractual term on the ground that Williams had no special knowledge as to the car's age, while the other party, who were car dealers, were in at least as good a position to ascertain whether the representation was true.

1   [1965] 2 All ER 65, [1965] 1 WLR 623, CA. Cf. *Gilchester Properties Ltd v Gomm* [1948] 1 All ER 493.
2   [1957] 1 All ER 325, [1957] 1 WLR 370, CA.

7.15 It must be emphasised that the factors mentioned above are only guides, not decisive tests or the only factors, to determining the parties' intentions.[1] Sometimes, they can point in different directions.

On many occasions, judges, having found that the parties intended a pre-contractual representation to have contractual effect, have found that it has taken effect under a collateral contract rather than as a term of the main contract.

1   *Heilbut, Symons & Co v Buckleton* [1913] AC 30, HL.

Implied terms

7.16 In addition to its express terms, the contract may contain certain terms implied by custom or by statute or by the courts.

Terms implied by custom

7.17 Terms may be implied by the custom of a particular locality, as in *Hutton v Warren,*[1] or by the usage of a particular trade, as in *Harley & Co v*

Nagata.[2] Although the terms are often used interchangeably, 'usage' differs from 'custom' in that it need not be ancient, but like custom it must be reasonable and certain in the sense that it is clearly established.[3] In *Hutton v Warren*, where a local custom was proved that a tenant was obliged to farm according to a certain course of husbandry for the whole of his tenancy and, on quitting, was entitled to a fair allowance for seeds and labour on the arable land, it was held that a term to this effect was implied in the lease. In *Harley & Co v Nagata*, it was held that, in the case of a time charterparty, a usage that the commission of a broker who negotiated the charterparty should be paid out of the hire which was earned, and should not be payable unless hire was in fact earned, was an implied term of the charterparty.

A customary term cannot be implied if the express wording of the contract shows that the parties had a contrary intention. This is shown by *Les Affréteurs Réunis SA v Leopold Walford (London) Ltd.*[4] Walford acted as a broker in effecting the time charter of a ship. Before the charterparty could be operated, and therefore before any hire could be earned, the French government requisitioned the ship. The charterparty provided that commission should be payable to Walford 'on signing this charter (ship lost or not lost)'. The House of Lords held that Walford could recover his commission because the commercial usage referred to above (commission payable only in respect of hire earned) could have no application since it was inconsistent with the express terms of the charterparty.

1   (1836) 1 M & W 466. For the requirements of a valid local custom, see para 3.53 above.
2   (1917) 23 Com Cas 121.
3   *Cunliffe-Owen v Teather and Greenwood* [1967] 3 All ER 561 at 572.
4   [1919] AC 801, HL.

Terms implied by statutes
7.18   The best known examples of such terms are those implied into contracts for the sale of goods by the Sale of Goods Act 1979 (which consolidated the Sale of Goods Act 1893 and amendments thereto).

Section 12(1) of the Act of 1979 provides that there is an implied condition on the part of a seller of goods that he has a right to sell them. Section 12(2) provides, inter alia, that there is an implied warranty that the goods are free, and will remain free until the property passes, from any charge or encumbrance not known or disclosed to the buyer before the contract is made. Section 13(1) provides that, where there is a contract for the sale of goods by description, there is an implied condition that the goods will correspond with the description. Section 14(2) provides that, where the seller sells goods in the course of a business, there is generally an implied condition that the goods supplied under the contract are of merchantable quality (ie as fit for the purpose or purposes for which goods of that kind are commonly bought as it is reasonable to expect). Section 14(3) provides that, where the seller sells goods in the course of a business and the buyer expressly or impliedly makes known to him any particular purpose for which the goods are being bought, there is generally an implied condition that the goods supplied are reasonably fit for that purpose, whether or not that is a purpose for which such goods are commonly supplied. Unlike ss12 and 13, sub-ss(2) and (3) of s14 only apply where goods are sold *in the course of a business*. 'Business' is not limited to commercial activities in the ordinary sense because it is defined by s61 to include 'a profession and the activities of any governmental department, or local or public authority'. If a private individual sells goods through an agent, such as an auctioneer, acting in the course of a business, the two subsections apply to the sale, unless the buyer knows that the seller is a private individual or reasonable steps have been taken to bring that fact to the buyer's attention before the contract is made.[1] It follows that it is extremely important that an auctioneer acting on behalf of a private client should notify prospective bidders for the goods of this fact, so as to avoid exposing his client to the risk of liability under the two subsections. Finally, s15 provides that where goods are sold by sample there is an implied condition that the bulk will correspond with the sample in quality, that the buyer will have a reasonable opportunity of comparing the bulk with the sample, and that the goods will be free from any defect, rendering them unmerchantable, which would not be apparent on reasonable examination of the sample.

Terms modelled on those implied into sale of goods contracts are implied:

a. into contracts of hire purchase, by the Supply of Goods (Implied Terms) Act 1973, ss8 to 11;

b. into contracts of hire, by the Supply of Goods and Services Act 1982, ss7 to 10; and

c. into contracts analogous to sale under which a person transfers or agrees to transfer to another the property (ie ownership) in goods, by the Supply of Goods and Services Act 1982, ss2 to 5. One example of a contract analogous to sale is a contract for work and materials, such as a contract for double glazing; another is a contract of exchange or part exchange.

Although the exclusion or restriction by the contract of one of the implied terms referred to in this paragraph, or of liability for its breach, is permissible,[2] there are strict limitations on this under the Unfair Contract Terms Act 1977 (paras 9.41 to 9.53 below).

1 Sale of Goods Act 1979, s14(5).
2 Sale of Goods Act 1979, s55; Supply of Goods and Services Act 1982, s11.

7.19 By way of a further example, it may be noted that in a 'contract for the supply of a service' certain terms are implied by the Supply of Goods and Services Act 1982. Such a contract includes, for example, a contract for dry cleaning or for professional services (but does not include a contract of employment or apprenticeship[1]). The fact that goods are transferred or hired under the contract does not prevent it being a contract for the supply of a service.[2] Consequently, for example, while a contract for work and materials will be subject to the implied terms under ss2 to 5 of the Act of 1982 in relation to the materials element, the work element will be subject to the terms implied into a contract of service by that Act.

The following terms are implied by the Act of 1982 into a contract for the supply of a service (such as a contract between a surveyor and his client):

a. by s13, where the supplier of the service is acting in the course of a business, there is an implied term that he will carry out the service with reasonable care and skill;[3]

b. by ss14 and 15, where the time for the service to be carried out (s14), or the consideration for the service (s15), is not stated by the contract, or left to be determined in a manner agreed by the contract, or determined by the course of dealings between the parties, there is an implied term that the service will be carried out within a reasonable time or, as the case may be, that a reasonable charge will be paid. The implied term as to the time of performance only applies where the contract is for the supply of a service by a supplier acting *in the course of a business.*[4]

Section 16 of the Act of 1982 permits the rights, duties and liabilities which may arise by virtue of ss13 to 15 to be negatived or varied, subject to the relevant provisions of the Unfair Contract Terms Act 1977 (paras 9.41 to 9.53 below).

1 Supply of Goods and Services Act 1982, s12(2).
2 Ibid, s12(3).
3 There are very limited exceptions under the Supply of Services (Exclusion of Implied Terms) Orders 1982, 1983 and 1985, the most notable being that the implied term under s13 does not apply to the services rendered by an advocate in court or before any tribunal, inquiry or arbitrator or in carrying out certain preliminary work, nor to the services rendered by a company director to his company.
4 'Business' includes a profession and the activities of any government department or local or public authority: Supply of Goods and Services Act 1982, s18.

7.20 Under the Landlord and Tenant Act 1985, terms as to fitness for habitation and as to repairs are implied into certain types of leases. We discuss these in para 37.4 below.

Terms implied by the courts
7.21 In *Liverpool City Council v Irwin,*[1] the House of Lords recognised that terms could be implied by the courts in two distinct situations:

a. where the term was a necessary incident of the kind of contract in question, and

b. where it was necessary to give 'business efficacy' to the particular contract.

1 [1977] AC 239, [1976] 2 All ER 39, HL.

Implication of a term which is a necessary incident of the type of contract in question.
7.22 When a court implies this type of term for the first time it lays down a general rule for contracts of the same type, eg employment contracts, so that the term will be implied in subsequent cases concerning that type of contract,[1] subject to the rules of precedent, unless it is inconsistent with the express terms of the contract or the contract validly excludes it.[2] In implying a term of the present type, the court is not trying to put the parties' intentions, actual or presumed, into effect but is imposing an obligation on one party or the other.[3] In deciding whether to make such an implication, the courts take into account the reasonableness of the suggested term and whether it is called for by the nature of the subject matter of the type of contract in question.[4]

1 *Lister v Romford Ice and Cold Storage Co Ltd* [1957] AC 555 at 576; *Liverpool City Council*

v *Irwin* [1976] 2 All ER 39 at 46; *Shell (UK) Ltd v Lostock Garages Ltd* [1977] 1 All ER 481 at 487.
2 *Lynch v Thorne* [1956] 1 All ER 744, [1956] 1 WLR 303, CA.
3 *Shell (UK) Ltd v Lostock Garages Ltd* [1977] 1 All ER 481 at 487; *Tai Hing Cotton Mill Ltd v Liu Chong Hing Bank Ltd* [1985] 2 All ER 947, [1985] 3 WLR 317, PC.
4 *Liverpool City Council v Irwin* [1977] AC 239, [1976] 2 All ER 39, HL.

7.23 It is only possible here to refer to a few of the terms implied into contracts under the present heading. In contracts of employment a number of obligations on the employee are implied, for instance: faithfully to serve his employer;[1] not to act against his employer's interests;[2] to use reasonable care and skill in performing his duties;[3] and to indemnify his employer against any liability incurred by the employer as a result of his wrongful acts.[3] Reciprocal terms are implied in the employee's favour, the employer being obliged, for instance, not to require the employee to do any unlawful act,[4] and to use care to provide safe premises and a safe system of work.[5]

Another example of an implied term of the present type is provided by *Liverpool City Council v Irwin*.[6] In that case, the House of Lords held that, where parts of a building have been let to different tenants (the case concerned a high-rise block of flats) and essential rights of access over parts of the building, such as stairs, retained by the landlord have been granted to the individual tenants, a term could be implied into the tenancy agreements that the landlord would take reasonable care to keep them reasonably safe and reasonably fit for use by tenants, their families and their visitors. In a lease of *furnished* premises there is an implied term that they are fit for human habitation *when* let,[7] but for some obscure reason such a term is not implied by the courts in a contract for the sale of land with a house on it or for the letting of land with unfurnished premises on it[8] (although if the vendor or lessor is the builder he may be liable in tort to the purchaser, lessee, or even a visitor, who is injured as a result of his negligent building[9]). Lastly, where a builder contracts to construct a dwelling there is a term implied by the courts that the dwelling, when completed, will be reasonably fit for human habitation.[10] However, this implication may be rebutted where the contract expressly prescribes the way in which the work is to be done and the work is completed according to that specification.[11]

As one last example, it is an implied term of most types of contract of indefinite duration that the contract is terminable by reasonable notice by either party.[12]

1 *Hivac Ltd v Park Royal Scientific Instruments Ltd* [1946] Ch 169, [1946] 1 All ER 350, CA.
2 *Wessex Dairies Ltd v Smith* [1935] 2 KB 80, CA.
3 *Lister v Romford Ice and Cold Storage Co Ltd* [1957] AC 555, [1957] 1 All ER 125, HL.
4 *Gregory v Ford* [1951] 1 All ER 121.
5 *Lister v Romford Ice and Cold Storage Co Ltd* above.
6 [1977] AC 239, [1976] 2 All ER 39, HL.
7 Para 37.4 below.
8 *Hart v Windsor* (1844) 12 M & W 68. For possible liability for breach of statutory duty see paras 23.27–23.28 below.
9 Para 23.26 below
10 *Miller v Cannon Hill Estates Ltd* [1931] 2 KB 113; *Hancock v B W Brazier (Anerley) Ltd* [1966] 2 All ER 901, [1966] 1 WLR 1317, CA; *Basildon District Council v J E Lesser (Properties) Ltd* [1985] QB 839, [1985] 1 All ER 20. For the implication of such a term by statute, see the Defective Premises Act 1972, s1; para 23.27 below.
11 *Lynch v Thorne* [1956] 1 All ER 744, [1956] 1 WLR, 303, CA.
12 *Staffordshire Area Health Authority v South Staffordshire Waterworks Co* [1978] 3 All ER 769, [1978] 1 WLR 1387, CA.

Implication to give business efficacy

7.24 The implication of a term under this heading is less common and can only be made when it is necessary in the particular circumstances to imply a term to give business efficacy to the contract and make it a workable agreement in such manner as the parties would clearly have done if they had applied their minds to the contingency which has arisen. This power of judicial implication was recognised in *The Moorcock*,[1] which concerned a contract permitting the plaintiff to unload his ship at the defendants' jetty. A warranty on the part of the defendants was implied into the contract that the river bed was, so far as reasonable care could provide, in a condition which would not damage the ship when she grounded at low tide, as both parties realised she would. Bowen LJ stated that, where the parties had not dealt with the burden of a particular peril, a court could imply a term which would give such efficacy to the contract as both parties must have intended it to have.

The test which the courts apply in deciding whether to imply a term to give the contract business efficacy is a strict one. A term cannot be implied unless it is *necessary* to give business efficacy to the contract and can be formulated with a *sufficient degree of precision*; it is not enough that it is reasonable in all the circumstances to imply the term.[2] A classic statement of the test is that of Scrutton LJ in *Reigate v Union Manufacturing Co (Ramsbottom) Ltd*:[3] 'A term can only be implied if it is necessary in the business sense to give efficacy to the contract, ie if it is such a term that it can confidently be said that if at the time the contract was being negotiated someone had said to the parties: "What will happen in such a case?" they would both have replied: "Of course, so and so will happen; we did not trouble to say that; it is too clear".'

1 (1889) 14 PD 64, CA.
2 *Liverpool City Council v Irwin* [1977] AC 239, [1976] 2 All ER 39, HL; *Shell (UK) Ltd v Lostock Garages Ltd* [1977] 1 All ER 481, [1976] 1 WLR 1187, CA.
3 [1918] 1 KB 592 at 605. Also see *Shirlaw v Southern Foundries (1926) Ltd* [1939] 2 KB 206 at 227, [1939] 2 All ER 113 at 124.

7.25 Pursuant to these principles, the courts have, for instance, refused to imply terms in the following cases: where tariff booklets were supplied free to a hotel in consideration of its proprietors undertaking to circulate or display them for a specified period, a term to the effect that the proprietors' obligation should cease if the business was sold was not implied;[1] where a petrol company subsidised two neighbouring filling stations during a price cutting war, a term to the effect that it would not abnormally discriminate against the plaintiff's filling station in favour of competitors was not implied into an contract for the exclusive supply of petrol by the petrol company to the plaintiff;[2] where a variety artiste's clothes were stolen from his dressing room during rehearsals, a term was not implied into the contract between him and the theatrical producer that the latter would take reasonable care to ensure that the artiste's effects were not stolen.[3]

In contrast, the courts have, for example, implied a term: into a contract for a Turkish bath, that the couches for reclining on were free from vermin;[4] into a contractual licence, that the premises were of sound construction and reasonably suitable for the purpose required by the licensees;[5] into a contract of transfer of a footballer, which provided that an additional sum be paid when he had scored 20 goals for the first team, that he was entitled to a reasonable opportunity to score the goals;[6] and into a contract for the sale of land, where the vendor undertook to give the purchaser 'first refusal' of adjacent land, that the vendor should not defeat the purchaser's right of 'first refusal' by disposing of the adjacent land to a third party by way of *gift* without first offering it to the purchaser.[7] In addition, the courts have held that generally a term is necessarily implied in any contract that neither party shall prevent the other from performing it.[8]

Since the implication of a term under *The Moorcock* principle is always dependent on the particular circumstances of the case, the implication of a term under it does not lay down a general rule for the future.

1 *General Publicity Services Ltd v Best's Brewery Co Ltd* [1951] 2 TLR 875, CA.
2 *Shell (UK) Ltd v Lostock Garages Ltd* [1977] 1 All ER 481, [1976] 1 WLR 1187, CA.
3 *Deyong v Shenburn* [1946] KB 227, [1946] 1 All ER 226, CA.
4 *Silverman v Imperial London Hotels Ltd* (1927) 137 LT 57.
5 *Western Electric Ltd v Welsh Development Agency* [1983] QB 796, [1983] 2 All ER 629.
6 *Bournemouth and Boscombe Athletic Football Club Co Ltd v Manchester United Football Club Ltd* (1980) Times, 22 May, CA.
7 *Gardner v Coutts & Co* [1967] 3 All ER 1064, [1968] 1 WLR 173.
8 *William Cory & Son Ltd v London Corpn* [1951] 2 KB 476 at 484, [1951] 2 All ER 85 at 88.

7.26 So far our discussion of the law of contract has concentrated on the formation and enforceability of a contract. In the next three chapters we shall be concerned principally with how a contract is discharged.

A contract can be discharged in four ways:

by agreement (which we discussed in paras 6.32 to 6.38 above);
by performance;
by breach;
by frustration.

Chapter 8
Discharge by performance

8.1 A contract is normally discharged by both parties performing their obligations under it, both parties being released from further liability thereby. If only one party performs his contractual obligations he alone is discharged and he acquires a right of action against the other for breach of contract, a subject which we discuss in the next chapter. Special rules govern the discharge of a party who has unsuccessfully tendered performance or whose obligations are performed for him by another.

Performance
8.2 For a party to be discharged by performance he must have precisely performed all his obligations under the contract. Thus, to decide whether a party is discharged by performance, one must first ascertain and construe the terms of the contract, express and implied, to see what his contractual obligations were, and then look at what has happened to see whether what he has done precisely corresponds with those obligations. The requirement of precise performance is a strict one and, if it is not met, it is irrelevant that the performance effected is commercially no less valuable than that which was promised. In *Arcos Ltd v E A Ronaasen & Son,*[1] the plaintiffs contracted to supply the defendants with a certain quantity of timber which, as they knew, was to be used for constructing cement barrels. The contract specified that the timber should be half an inch thick but when it was delivered the defendants discovered that 95% of it was over half an inch thick, although none of it exceeded three quarters of an inch in thickness. It was still perfectly possible for the defendants to use all the wood, as it had been delivered, for the construction of cement barrels but the House of Lords held that they were entitled to reject the whole consignment since the plaintiffs had not performed a contractual obligation which was a condition of the contract.[2] Lord Atkin stated, obiter, that only if a deviation from the terms of the contract was 'microscopic' could the contract be taken to have been correctly performed. An example of this is provided by *Shipton, Anderson & Co v Weil Bros & Co,*[3] where a contract requiring the delivery of 4,950 tons of wheat was held to have been performed by the seller although he had delivered 4,950 tons 55 lbs.

Generally, no demand for performance is necessary to render an obligation to perform operative.[4] Thus, a debtor is bound to seek out his creditor and pay him.[5]

128

1 [1933] AC 470, HL.
2 The contractual obligation broken was the condition implied by the Sale of Goods Act 1979, s13(1), viz that in a sale of goods by description the goods must correspond with that description. See paras 7.18 above and 9.17–9.19 below.
3 [1912] 1 KB 574.
4 A demand will be necessary if there is an express agreement or trade usage requiring it.
5 *Walton v Mascall* (1844) 13 M & W 452.

Payment

8.3 Where the obligation of one party to the other consists in the payment of a sum of money the contract is discharged by the payment of that sum. Payment should, primarily, be made in legal tender[1] but may, with the consent of the creditor, be made by cheque.

1 Para 8.9b below.

8.4 Where a cheque or other negotiable instrument is given in payment, its effect may be absolutely to discharge or only conditionally to discharge the debtor. The discharge will be *absolute* if the creditor promises expressly or impliedly, in accepting the cheque, to discharge the debtor from his existing obligations. If this occurs the creditor loses his right of action on the original contract but can sue on his rights under the instrument if it is dishonoured.[1] However, the presumption is that the creditor only accepts a cheque as a *conditional* discharge, in which case the debtor is not discharged unless, and until, the instrument is honoured; if it is dishonoured, the debtor may be sued on the original contract or on the dishonoured instrument.[2]

1 *Sard v Rhodes* (1836) 1 M & W 153.
2 *Sayer v Wagstaff* (1844) 5 Beav 415; *Re Romer and Haslam* [1893] 2 QB 286, CA.

8.5 If the creditor requests payment through the post, the payment will be deemed to have been duly made even though it is lost in transit after being posted,[1] unless it was sent in a manner inappropriate to the amount in question (eg sending a substantial sum in cash).[2] A request for postal payment may be express or implied, but the mere fact that remittances have been posted over a number of years without any objection by the creditor does not raise such an implication.[3]

1 *Thairlwall v Great Northern Rly Co* [1910] 2 KB 509, DC.
2 *Mitchell-Henry v Norwich Union Life Insurance Society* [1918] 2 KB 67, CA.
3 *Pennington v Crossley & Son* (1897) 77 LT 43, CA.

Proof of payment

8.6 It is commonly, but mistakenly, believed that payment of a debt can only be proved by producing a written receipt. In fact, payment may be proved by any evidence from which payment may be inferred.[1] In particular, the Cheques Act 1957, s3 provides that an unindorsed cheque which appears to have been paid by the banker on whom it is drawn shall be evidence of the receipt by the payee of the sum payable on the cheque.

A debtor is not entitled to insist on a receipt when paying a debt and if he does obtain a receipt it is only prima facie, not conclusive, evidence that a

129

debt has been paid.[2] Therefore, it is always possible for the person who has given the receipt to show either that he has not received payment or that the receipt was given by mistake,[3] or obtained by fraud,[4] or that it was given on certain terms.[5]

1 *Eyles v Ellis* (1827) 4 Bing 112.
2 *Wilson v Keating* (1859) 27 Beav 121.
3 *Cesarini v Ronzani* (1858) 1 F & F 339.
4 *Skaife v Jackson* (1824) 3 B & C 421.
5 *Re W W Duncan & Co* [1905] 1 Ch 307.

Tender of performance

8.7 If a party makes a valid tender (ie offer) of performance of his contractual obligations and the other party refuses to accept performance, the party making the tender is freed from liability for non-performance of those obligations, provided that the tender is made under such circumstances that the other party has a reasonable opportunity of examining the performance tendered, eg the goods tendered, in order to ascertain that it conforms with the contract.[1]

1 *Startup v Macdonald* (1843) 6 Man & G 593 at 610. Also see Sale of Goods Act 1979, s29.

Tender of payment

8.8 If a party makes a valid tender of payment of money which he owes but the other party refuses to accept it, this does not discharge his debt but there is no obligation to make a further tender. If an action is brought for non-payment against a party who has tendered unsuccessfully, all he has to do is to pay the money into court, whereupon, if he has pleaded and proved a valid tender:

a. the costs of the action must be borne by the other party;[1]

b. a claim for interest on the debt subsequent to the rejection of the tender is barred;[2]

c. a right of lien is generally extinguished;[3] and

d. he is not liable for his non-performance.

Thus, a creditor who refuses a valid tender of payment can eventually obtain nothing but the amount originally tendered to him and a debtor who has validly tendered payment is not prejudiced by a refusal to accept it.

1 *Griffiths v Ystradyfodwg School Board* (1890) 24 QBD 307.
2 *Norton v Ellam* (1837) 2 M & W 461.
3 A lien is a right by which a person is entitled to obtain satisfaction for a debt by retaining property belonging to the person indebted to him.

8.9 A valid tender requires the following:

a. The money must be actually produced:[1] it is not enough for the debtor to offer to pay and simply put his hand in his pocket.[2] The sole exception to the requirement of production is where the creditor expressly or impliedly dispenses with it.[3] The creditor will impliedly dispense with the need for production if, when the debtor tells him that he has come to pay a specified amount, the creditor says it is too late or otherwise indicates that he will not accept the money.[3]

b. The tender must be in legal currency: a creditor is not obliged to accept a cheque or other negotiable instrument or payment in currency which is not legal tender.[4] By the Currency and Bank Notes Act 1954 and the Coinage Act 1971 (as amended by the Currency Act 1983), legal tender is as follows:
i   Bank of England notes, to any amount;
ii   gold coins of the Mint, to any amount;
iii silver and cupro-nickel coins of the Mint of more than 10p, up to £10;
iv   silver and cupro-nickel coins of the Mint of not more than 10p, up to £5;
v   bronze coins, up to 20p.

c. Where the amount tendered is greater than the debt due, the tender is invalid if the creditor is required to give change.[5] However, a tender of an excess payment will be valid if, though change is requested, the creditor refuses the tender for some other reason,[6] or if the debtor is happy for the creditor to keep the excess amount.[7]

d. The tender must not be made on any condition. Thus, in *Finch v Miller*,[8] it was held that a tender, made on condition that a receipt for a full discharge be given, was invalid. On the other hand, a valid tender may be made under protest so as to reserve the right of the debtor to dispute the amount, provided it does not impose conditions on the creditor.[9]

e. Where a debt is expressly made payable on a particular day, a tender made after that date is not strictly a valid tender. However, provided it is made before the commencement of an action for the recovery of the debt, it will generally have the same effect as a valid tender.[10]

f. The tender must be in exact accordance with any other special terms of the contract, e g as to place of payment.

1   *Thomas v Evans* (1808) 10 East 101.
2   *Finch v Brook* (1834) 1 Bing NC 253.
3   *Farquharson v Pearl Insurance Co Ltd* [1937] 3 All ER 124.
4   *Blumberg v Life Interests and Reversionary Securities Corpn* [1897] 1 Ch 171 (upheld on appeal [1898] 1 Ch 27, CA).
5   *Robinson v Cook* (1815) 6 Taunt 336.
6   *Bevans v Rees* (1839) 5 M & W 306.
7   *Wade's Case* (1601) 5 Co Rep 114a.
8   (1848) 5 CB 428.
9   *Greenwood v Sutcliffe* [1892] 1 Ch 1, CA.
10 *Briggs v Calverly* (1800) 8 Term Rep 629.

Tender of acts
8.10 Where a party is obliged to perform some act, other than the payment of something, he will make a valid tender of performance if he attempts to perform the act in precise accordance with the terms of the contract. In the case of a contract for the sale of goods, the tender of them must be made at a reasonable hour.[1]

If a party (A) makes a valid tender of an act, but the other (B) refuses to accept the tendered performance, A is entitled to maintain an action for breach of contract.[2] Moreover, if B's refusal is absolute and unqualified it will constitute a renunciation of the contract, in which case A will also be entitled to treat the renunciation as discharging him from his obligation to perform the contract.[3]

An invalid tender does not as a rule prevent the party who made it from subsequently making a valid tender.[4] However, it may be impossible to make a subsequent, valid tender simply because performance had to be made on a particular day and that day is now past. Again, if the invalid tender amounts to a repudiatory breach of the contract and this is treated by the other party as discharging his obligations under the contract, a subsequent tender cannot be valid.

1 Sale of Goods Act 1979, s29.
2 *Startup v Macdonald* (1843) 6 Man & G 593.
3 Para 9.10 below. In such a case A is said to terminate the contract for repudiatory breach. For the full effects of such termination, see paras 9.4–9.7 below.
4 *Tetley v Shand* (1871) 25 LT 658.

Time for performance

8.11 When a contract does not stipulate a time within which a party's contractual obligations must be performed, they must be performed within a reasonable time;[1] if they are not, damages may be recovered for breach of contract.

1 *Postlethwaite v Freeland* (1880) 5 App Cas 599, HL. The Sale of Goods Act 1979, s29 gives this rule statutory effect in relation to a seller's obligation to send goods to a buyer.

8.12 When a time is stipulated for performance of a party's obligations by the contract, the question arises whether time is 'of the essence of the contract'. If it is, the stipulation as to time will be classified as a condition[1] and a party's failure to perform in the stipulated time will not only constitute a breach of contract entitling the other party to maintain an action for damages but also a repudiatory breach of the contract, which the other party can accept as discharging him from his contractual obligations.[2]

1 Para 9.17 below.
2 See, in particular, *Bunge Corpn v Tradax SA* [1981] 2 All ER 513, HL. Also see paras 9.3–9.8 below.

8.13 Whether time is of the essence of a contract, other than a contract for the sale of an interest in land, depends on the parties' intentions. If they are not expressed in the contract, they must be inferred from the nature of the subject matter of the contract and of the obligation which has not been performed in time. In this context certain presumptions have been established. For instance, broadly speaking, a stipulation as to time in a commercial contract is presumptively of the essence of the contract.[1] However, the Sale of Goods Act 1979, s10 provides that a term as to the time of *payment* for goods is deemed not to be of the essence of the contract, unless the contrary intention appears from the contract.

1 *Reuter, Hufeland & Co v Sala & Co* (1879) 4 CPD 239, CA; *Bunge Corpn v Tradax SA* [1981] 2 All ER 513, HL.

8.14 Before the Judicature Act 1873, common law and equity had different rules about when a stipulation as to the time for completion was of the essence in a contract for the sale of an interest in land, but since that Act the equitable rules prevail.[1] The result is that time is not of the essence in such a contract unless it falls within one of the following three categories where equity treated it as of the essence:

a. Where the contract expressly states that stipulations as to time must be strictly complied with. In *Harold Wood Brick Co Ltd v Ferris*,[2] for instance, a stipulation that the purchase of a brickfield should be completed by 31 August which added that 'the purchase shall in any event be completed not later than 15 September' was held to make time (15 September) of the essence of the contract.

b. Where the contract does not expressly make a time stipulation of the essence of the contract, but the stipulated time has passed by, the party who has been subjected to delay can make time of the essence by invoking a period of notice for completion if one is specified in the contract or, if one is not specified, by giving a notice fixing a reasonable time for completion.[3]

c. Where the subject matter of the contract, or the circumstances surrounding it, makes punctual compliance with a stipulation as to time imperative, time must be taken to be of the essence of the contract. For example, under this heading time has been held to be of the essence of a contract for the sale of business premises as a going concern.[4]

Even if time is not of the essence of a contract for the sale of an interest in land, a party who fails to complete within the stipulated time is, of course, in breach of that term and liable in damages, provided that the failure was not due to some conveyancing difficulty or some difficulty with regard to title.[5] Inability to raise the necessary finance is no defence.[5]

1 Law of Property Act 1925, s41.
2 [1935] 2 KB 198, CA.
3 *Stickney v Keeble* [1915] AC 386, HL.
4 *Lock v Bell* [1931] 1 Ch 35. Also see *Harold Wood Brick Co Ltd v Ferris* [1935] 2 KB 198, CA.
5 *Raineri v Miles* [1980] AC 1050, [1980] 2 All ER 145, HL.

Performance by a third party

8.15 In some cases, performance of a contractual obligation by a third party can discharge it. Different rules apply depending on whether or not the person to whom the obligation is owed agrees to accept performance by a third party.

Performance by a third party with creditor's consent

8.16 Payment of a debt (or, presumably, the performance of any other type of obligation) by a third party with the creditor's consent is not sufficient to discharge it, unless it is made by him as agent for, and on behalf of, the debtor and with the debtor's prior authority or subsequent ratification (which can even be given at the trial of an action to enforce the debt against him).[1] If this test is not satisfied the debt is not discharged and therefore remains enforceable against the debtor. In *Smith v Cox*,[2] S was R's tenant and C, an estate agent, was R's agent to collect the rent. S owed

£260 arrears of rent, but C, knowing that R was old and poor, and largely dependent on the rent of the house, had, as the rent became due, sent her out of his own pocket a sum equivalent to the rent owing, trusting to recoup himself out of the rent when it was paid by S. When he failed to obtain the rent, C distrained and recovered the arrears less a deduction for repairs. S sued C, arguing that the distress was unlawful because R had been paid by C and his (S's) liability had been discharged thereby. He admitted that the payments were made without his knowledge and not at his request. It was held that S had not been discharged, and therefore the distress was lawful, because the payments had not been made by C as agent for, and on behalf of, S.

Provided that the above test is satisfied, the contractual obligation is discharged even though the third party's performance which is accepted by the creditor differs from that required by the contract. In *Hirachand Punamchand v Temple*,[3] for instance, a debt was held to be discharged when the creditor accepted a smaller sum from the debtor's father in full settlement, with the result that the creditor's action against the debtor for the balance was dismissed.

1 *Simpson v Eggington* (1855) 10 Exch 845.
2 [1940] 2 KB 558, [1940] 3 All ER 546.
3 [1911] 2 KB 330, CA.

Performance by a third party without creditor's consent

8.17 Even though the creditor does not consent to performance by a third party, it is permissible for the debtor to get a third party precisely to perform his contractual obligation, and hence secure his discharge, provided it can be properly inferred from the terms of the contract, its subject matter and surrounding circumstances that it is a matter of indifference whether the performance is by the debtor or his nominee. This inference is easily made in the case of a debt since, if full payment is made in cash, it is normally a matter of indifference to the creditor that it is paid by someone other than the debtor. The inference has also been drawn in the case of other types of obligation, as is shown by *British Waggon Co v Lea*.[1] The Parkgate Waggon Co had contracted to let a number of railway wagons to the defendants and to keep them in repair. The Parkgate Waggon Co went into liquidation and assigned both the benefit of, and the liabilities under, the contract to the plaintiffs. The defendants claimed to treat the contract as at an end and refused to accept performance by the plaintiffs. It was held that the contract could be validly performed by the plaintiffs since it was a matter of indifference to the defendants who kept the wagons in repair—it being 'work which any ordinary workman conversant with the business could execute'—so long as the work was done efficiently by someone.

On the other hand, the inference that vicarious performance is permissible will not be drawn where the contract expressly or impliedly provides that it must be performed personally by the debtor. Thus, the performance of a contract without the creditor's consent by a third party will not discharge the debtor's liability if the contract is of such a nature that the creditor was relying on some personal skill or other personal qualification of the debtor. Thus, it has been held that personal care and skill is an ingredient of a contract by a warehouseman to store furniture.[2] Obligations under a contract of employment are particularly likely to be held to be personal to the parties.

1   (1880) 5 QBD 149.
2   *Edwards v Newland & Co* [1950] 2 KB 534, [1950] 1 All ER 1972, CA.

8.18 Where performance by a third party without the creditor's consent is permissible, the debtor nevertheless remains liable on the contract for performance and can be sued for non-performance or defective performance by the third party.[1] The third party is not liable on the contract, but if he performs the contract negligently he may be liable in tort.

1   *Stewart v Reavell's Garage* [1952] 2 QB 545, [1952] 1 All ER 1191.

Chapter 9
Breach

9.1 Breach of contract occurs where a party does not perform one or more of his contractual obligations precisely, in the sense discussed in para 8.2 above, and this failure is without lawful excuse. Thus, a breach will occur where a party without lawful excuse refuses to perform one or more of his contractual obligations, or simply fails to perform them, or incapacitates himself from performing them, or performs them defectively. Consequently, to decide whether a party is in breach of contract, one must first ascertain and construe the terms of the contract, express and implied, to see what his contractual obligations were, and then look at what has happened to see whether he has failed without lawful excuse to perform one or more of them precisely.

A person has a lawful excuse for failing to perform his contractual obligations precisely in the following cases:

a. if the contract has been discharged by frustration, a matter which we discuss in the next chapter;

b. if there is impossibility of performance less than frustration; for instance, a temporary illness preventing an employee working provides a lawful excuse for his failure to work during the period of the illness;[1]

c. if he has validly tendered performance of his obligations in accordance with the rules set out in paras 8.7 to 8.10, but this has been rejected by the other party;

d. if the other party has made it impossible for him to perform his obligations.

Before proceeding further, the reader should note that a party's contractual obligations are otherwise known as his 'primary' obligations.

1 *Poussard v Spiers and Pond* (1876) 1 QBD 410.

9.2 Subject to a valid exemption clause to the contrary, whenever a party to the contract is in breach of contract (ie has broken one or more of his primary obligations under the contract) this gives rise by implication of law to a secondary obligation on his part to pay compensation (ie damages) to the other party (the 'injured party') for the loss sustained by him in consequence of that breach, but unless the breach can be classified as a repudiatory breach the primary obligations of the parties so far as they have not been fully performed remain unchanged.[1] The secondary obligation mentioned above is just as much an obligation arising from the contract as is a primary obligation.[1] The injured party may claim damages for breach either by an action of his own or by way of a counter-claim in an action brought against him by the defaulting party, and even where no actual loss or damage to the injured party can be proved nominal damages will be awarded. Quite apart from damages, the injured party may be entitled, additionally or alternatively, to claim an order of specific performance of the contract or an injunction or to recover an agreed sum. We consider the question of remedies in ch 11.

In the case of certain serious breaches of contract, which are commonly described as repudiatory breaches, the injured party can elect to treat the contract as repudiated by the other, accept the repudiation, and recover damage for breach, both parties being discharged from performance of their primary obligations under the contract which would have been due thereafter. If the injured party does this, he is said to terminate (or rescind[2]) the contract for repudiatory breach.

Before we proceed to discuss the question of termination for repudiatory breach, we wish to point out that a party is also entitled to terminate a contract, but not recover damages, in a case where there would have been a repudiatory breach but for the fact that the other party's failure to perform was due to impossibility less than frustration.[3]

---

1 See especially, *Photo Production Ltd v Securicor Transport Ltd* [1980] AC 827 at 848, [1980] 1 All ER 556 at 566.
2 Termination for repudiatory breach should not be confused with recission for misrepresentation (discussed in ch 13), the effects of which (and the rules concerning which) are different.
3 *Poussard v Spiers and Pond* (1876) 1 QBD 410.

Repudiatory breach

Option to terminate or affirm

9.3 A repudiatory breach does not automatically discharge the contract. Instead, the injured party has an option to terminate the contract or to affirm it.[1] However, in two cases there is no such option and the consequences of the breach are the same as for a non-repudiatory breach.

a. Occasionally, a contractual obligation is mutual, in the sense that it is imposed on both parties and not simply on one of them, each party being obliged to co-operate with the other in taking appropriate steps to fulfil it. If a party fails to take steps to fulfil a mutual obligation (without renouncing it[2]), and that failure would otherwise be a repudiatory breach entitling the other party to terminate the contract, the other party cannot do so if he is also in breach of the mutual obligation.[3] An example of this rule is provided by reference to arbitration agreements. Under such an agreement, the parties are under a mutual obligation to co-operate in taking steps by way of application to the arbitrator to prevent such delay in the course of the arbitration as would give rise to the risk that a fair trial could not be achieved. If both parties simply fail to take these steps, both are in breach of their mutual obligation to each other and neither can rely on the other's breach as giving him a right to terminate the arbitration agreement.[4]

b. The second case where an injured party does not have an option to terminate is discussed in para 9.19 below.

1 *Heyman v Darwins Ltd* [1942] AC 356 at 358, [1942] 1 All ER 337 at 340; *Johnson v Agnew* [1980] AC 367 at 397, [1979] 1 All ER 883 at 893.
2 *André & Cie SA v Marine Transocean Ltd* [1981] QB 694, [1981] 2 All ER 993, CA. For a discussion of renunciation, see para 9.10 below.
3 *Bremer Vulkan Schiffbau und Maschinenfabrik v South India Shipping Corpn* [1981] AC 909, [1981] 1 All ER 289, HL.
4 Ibid; *The Hannah Blumenthal* [1983] 1 AC 854, [1983] 1 All ER 34, HL. In exceptional circumstances, failure by both parties over a long period to take the necessary steps may give rise to an inference that there has been an offer by one party to abandon the reference, which has been accepted by the other (and the arbitration agreement thereby terminated): *André & Cie SA v Marine Transocean Ltd* [1981] QB 694, [1981] 2 All ER 993, CA; *The Hannah Blumenthal* [1983] 1 AC 854, [1983] 1 All ER 34, HL; *The Leonidas D* [1985] 2 All ER 796, [1984] 1 WLR 1, CA.

Termination

9.4 The injured party will terminate the contract if he notifies the defaulting party that he regards himself as discharged by the repudiatory breach. Thus, the contract will be terminated if the injured party refuses to accept defective performance, or refuses to accept further performance, or simply refuses to perform his own contractual obligations.

If the injured party elects to terminate the contract, he is discharged for the future from his primary obligations under the contract which would otherwise have been due or continuing thereafter. One result is that he is not obliged to accept or pay for further performance. Another result is that an injured party who has terminated a contract for breach can resist successfully any action for failing thereafter to observe or perform a continuing obligation or an obligation due thereafter.[1] On the other hand, an injured party who has terminated is not generally discharged from his primary obligations which are already due at the time of termination, since rights and obligations which arise from the partial execution of the contract—as well as causes of action which have accrued from its breach—continue unaffected.[2] However, an injured party who has terminated may be entitled:

a. to refuse to pay for partial or defective performance already received by him (see paras 9.12 and 9.13 below); or

b. to reclaim any money which he has paid to the defaulting party if he can (and does) reject the defective performance or if certain other circumstances exist (see para 16.7b below).

1 *General Billposting Co Ltd v Atkinson* [1909] AC 118, HL.
2 *McDonald v Denys Lascelles Ltd* (1933) 48 CLR 457 at 476–477; *Johnson v Agnew* [1980] AC 367 at 396, [1979] 1 All ER 883 at 892; *The Blankenstein* [1985] 1 All ER 475, [1985] 1 WLR 435, CA.

9.5 After termination by the injured party, the defaulting party's position is as follows:

a. He is not discharged from his primary contractual obligations which are due at the time of the termination and have not been performed (so that, for instance, he is still obliged to pay a sum of money then due[1]); and he is also liable to pay damages to the injured party for loss sustained by him in consequence of the breach of any such obligation, since a secondary obligation under the contract to this effect arises by implication of law just as it does where a non-repudiatory breach has occurred.[2]

b. His primary obligations under the contract, so far as they are due or continuing after the termination, are discharged and there is substituted for them by implication of law a secondary obligation arising from the contract to pay damages to the injured party for the loss sustained by him in consequence of their non-performance in the future.[2]

1 *McDonald v Denys Lascelles Ltd* (1933) 48 CLR 457 at 476–477; *Hyundai Heavy Industries Co Ltd v Papadopoulos* [1980] 2 All ER 29, [1980] 1 WLR 1129, HL.
2 *R V Ward Ltd v Bignall* [1967] 1 QB 534, [1967] 2 All ER 449, CA; *Moschi v Lep Air Services Ltd* [1973] AC 331, [1972] 2 All ER 393, HL; *Photo Production Ltd v Securicor Transport Ltd* [1980] AC 827, [1980] 1 All ER 556, HL.

9.6 It may be added that, if the injured party has started to perform his contractual obligations but is unjustifiably prevented from completing them by the other party, he can bring an action for reasonable remuneration. This is called suing on a quantum meruit.[1]

1 Para 11.24 below.

9.7 Termination for repudiatory breach does not necessarily extinguish the contract completely in relation to primary obligations whose performance is due after the time of the election to terminate, since obligations relating to matters such as arbitration or jurisdiction may continue in existence if it was the intention of the parties, when they made the contract, that this should be so.[1] In addition, terms which validly 'liquidate' damages or which validly exclude or restrict liability remain in force.[2]

1 *Heyman v Darwins Ltd* [1942] AC 356, [1942] 1 All ER 337, HL; *Photo Production Ltd v Securicor Transport Ltd* [1980] 1 All ER 556 at 567.
2 *Photo Production Ltd v Securicor Transport Ltd* [1980] AC 827, [1980] 1 All ER 556, HL; *The New York Star* [1980] 3 All ER 257, [1981] 1 WLR 138, PC. For liquidated damages provisions, see para 11.16 below, and for exemption clauses, see paras 9.24 to 9.53 below. The proposition in the text has been given statutory force in relation to exemption clauses which must satisfy the requirement of reasonableness under the Unfair Contract Terms Act 1977 (see paras 9.42 to 9.50 below) by s9 of that Act.

Affirmation
9.8 The injured party will affirm the contract if, with full knowledge of the facts and of his right to terminate the contract,[1] he decides to treat it as still in existence, as where he decides to keep the defective goods delivered or, if the defaulting party has not completed performance, where he calls on him to perform. The injured party does not affirm a contract simply because he does not immediately terminate the contract but delays while he considers whether or not to terminate it.[2]

If the injured party elects to affirm, the contract remains in force, so that both parties are bound to continue performing any outstanding contractual obligations.[3] Each party retains the right to sue for past or future breaches. Thus, if a seller of goods affirms the contract after a repudiatory breach by the buyer, the seller remains liable to deliver possession of the goods to the buyer and the buyer remains liable to accept delivery of the goods and pay the contract price.[4] Another example is provided by *Bentsen v Taylor, Sons & Co*[5] where a charterparty described the ship as 'now sailed or about to sail' from a port to the UK. In fact, she did not sail for another month. This constituted a repudiatory breach of contract[6] but, instead of electing to terminate the contract, the charterers intimated to the shipowner that he was still bound to send the ship to the port of loading and that they, the charterers, would load her there, thereby affirming the contract. When the ship arrived, the charterers refused to load her. The Court of Appeal held that, since the contract had been affirmed, the shipowner was entitled to payment of freight, subject to a set-off for the charterers for damages for the breach of contract referred to above.

1   *Peyman v Lanjani* [1984] 3 All ER 703, [1985] 2 WLR 154, CA.
2   *Bliss v South East Thames Regional Health Authority* [1985] IRLR 308, CA.
3   By way of exception, an employer who wrongfully dismisses an employee is no longer obliged to pay the employee the wages which would have been earned thereafter, even though the employee affirms the contract; the employee can only claim damages for breach of contract: *Gunton v Richmond-upon-Thames London Borough Council* [1981] Ch 448, [1980] 3 All ER 577, CA.
4   *R V Ward Ltd v Bignall* [1967] 1 QB 534, [1967] 2 All ER 449, CA.
5   [1893] 2 QB 274, CA.
6   Because the term broken was a condition, see paras 9.16–9.18 below.

Is an election irrevocable?

9.9   If the injured party elects to terminate a contract for repudiatory breach he cannot thereafter affirm it, by seeking specific performance or otherwise calling on the other party to perform, since both parties are discharged from further performance by the termination.[1]

An election is also irrevocable where the injured party elects unconditionally to affirm the contract, as where he elects to keep defective goods: in such a case he cannot subsequently elect to terminate for repudiatory breach. However, if his affirmation is conditional on the other party rectifying his breach, and this is not done, the injured party can change his mind and proceed to terminate the contract and claim damages for repudiatory breach. Where the injured party obtains an order of specific performance of the contract his affirmation of the contract is conditional, and, if the order becomes impossible of performance or is otherwise not complied with, he can elect to ask the court to terminate the contract and (if the court accedes) recover damages for repudiatory breach.[2]

1   See, for example, *Johnson v Agnew* [1980] AC 367 at 393, [1979] 1 All ER 883.
2   *Austins of East Ham Ltd v Macey* [1941] Ch 338; *Johnson v Agnew* [1980] AC 367, [1979] 1 All ER 883, HL.

Types of repudiatory breach

Renunciation

9.10   Where one party renounces his contractual obligations the other party is entitled to terminate the contract. A party is said to renounce his contractual obligations if he has evinced an unconditional intention not to perform them or otherwise no longer to be bound by the contract.[1] Such an intention is easily established where there has been an express and unequivocal refusal to perform. Thus, if an employee unqualifiedly refuses to carry out his duties his employer is entitled to dismiss him (ie terminate the contract of employment).[2] However, express refusal is not essential; an intent no longer to be bound by the contract can also be implied by the words or conduct of a party. The actual intention of the party is not the crucial issue in such a case; the test is whether his words and conduct were such as to lead a reasonable person to believe that he did not intend to be bound by the contract.[3]

1 *Mersey Steel and Iron Co v Naylor, Benzon and Co* (1884) 9 App Cas 434, HL; *Woodar Investment Development Ltd v Wimpey Construction (UK) Ltd* [1980] 1 All ER 571, [1980] 1 WLR 277, HL.
2 *Gorse v Durham County Council* [1971] 2 All ER 666, [1971] 1 WLR 775.
3 *Ross T Smyth & Co Ltd v Bailey, Son & Co* [1940] 3 All ER 60 at 72; *André et Cie SA v Marine Transocean Ltd* [1981] QB 694, [1981] 2 All ER 993, CA.

Incapacitation
9.11 Even though he has not evinced an intention not to be bound by the contract, a party who, *by his own act or default*, incapacitates himself from performing his contractual obligations is treated as if he had refused to perform them. As Devlin J said in *Universal Cargo Carriers Corpn v Citati*,[1] 'To say "I would like to but cannot" negatives intent to perform as much as "I will not" '. Where a party has incapacitated himself from performing, it is no defence to show that he might be able to recover the capacity to perform.[2] One example of a case where a party has made performance of his obligations impossible is where A has contracted to sell a specific thing to B but then sells it to C.

1 [1957] 2 QB 401 at 437, [1957] 2 All ER 70.
2 *Omnium D'Enterprises v Sutherland* [1919] 1 KB 618, CA.

Failure to perform an entire obligation
9.12 An entire obligation is one whose complete and precise peformance is a condition precedent[1] (ie a pre-condition) of the performance by the other party of his obligations. A particular obligation may be entire:

a. *By statute* For instance, in contracts for the sale of goods the obligation to deliver the *quantity* specified in the contract is entire.[2]

b. *By express agreement between the parties.*

c. *By implication* This occurs where, on the true construction of the contract, the parties intended that complete and precise performance by a party of a particular obligation should be a pre-condition of performance by the other party of his obligations. The cases show that, if B is to pay a lump sum for A's work *after* it has been completed, A's obligation to do the work is impliedly entire.[3] Because of the harsh consequences of finding an obligation to be entire, the courts lean against construing a contract so as to require complete performance of an obligation before the other party's obligations become operative.[4] Thus, if a lump sum is payable for work, but the contract does not say when it is payable, the court is likely to construe the obligation as not being entire but severable.[5]

If a party does not completely and precisely perform an entire obligation, the injured party can terminate the contract and the defaulting party cannot claim any performance by him. This is exemplified by *Sumpter v*

Hedges,[6] where the plaintiff agreed to build two houses and a stable on the defendant's land for a lump sum of £565. The plaintiff did part of the work to the value of about £333 and then abandoned the contract because of lack of money. It was held that the plaintiff's obligation to build the two houses and a stable was entire and, having failed to do so, he could not recover the contract price nor reasonable remuneration for the work done.

1   The present type of 'condition precedent' must be distinguished from that discussed in para 5.33 above, which arises where the parties make an agreement subject to some contingent future event on the basis that no immediate binding contract shall exist until the contingency occurs. The present type of 'condition precedent' does not negative the immediate existence of a binding contract but suspends the liability of one party to perform his obligations until the other party has performed something which he has promised (and is therefore obliged) to do.
2   Sale of Goods Act 1979, s30. This rule does not apply where the contract provides for delivery by instalments: *Regent O H G Aisenstadt und Barig v Francesco of Jermyn Street* [1981] 3 All ER 327.
3   Eg *H Dakin & Co Ltd v Lee* [1916] 1 KB 566, CA.
4   *Roberts v Havelock* (1832) 3 B & Ad 404.
5   Ibid. Severable obligations are discussed in para 9.15 below.
6   [1898] 1 QB 673, CA.

9.13   There are three exceptions to the rule that a party who has not completely and precisely performed an entire obligation cannot recover in respect of any partial performance:

Acceptance of partial performance of entire obligation   A claim to remuneration may be made by a party who has incompletely performed an entire obligation if the other party has accepted such partial performance *voluntarily*. Such acceptance gives rise to an inference that there is a fresh agreement by the parties that payment of a reasonable sum or pro rata be made for the work already done or the goods supplied under the original contract.[1]

Since the right of recovery depends on the inference of a fresh agreement, it is essential that the party from whom payment is demanded has not just received a benefit but has voluntarily accepted it. He must have had an opportunity, at the time when it became clear that there would not be complete performance of the entire obligation, to accept or reject the partial or defective performance. Thus, in *Sumpter v Hedges*,[2] it was held that the builder could not recover reasonable remuneration for the work done because the defendant had no option but to accept the partial performance, viz. the partly erected buildings.

Unjustifiable prevention of performance   If the party to whom the entire obligation is owed unjustifiably prevents performance of it, eg by stating that he will not accept performance, this will normally constitute a repudiatory breach of contract by him.[3] If the other party elects to terminate the contract, he can recover reasonable remuneration for his partial performance by a quantum meruit claim, or, whether he elects to terminate or not, recover damages for breach of contract.

Frustration   As we show in paras 10.13 to 10.17 below, if the contract is discharged by frustration before an entire obligation has been performed, a party who has partly performed it may be able to recover remuneration.

1 *Christy v Row* (1808) 1 Taunt 300; *Sumpter v Hedges* [1898] 1 QB 673 at 674; Sale of Goods Act 1979, s30.
2 [1898] 1 QB 673, CA.
3 Because the courts are usually ready to imply a term that neither party shall prevent the other from performing his contractual obligations (see para 7.25 above), and this term is regarded as a condition (thereby permitting termination for its breach, para 9.17 below).

9.14 *It is important to retain a sense of proportion about entire obligations because they are the exception rather than the rule, as we now propose to demonstrate*
Although a contract containing an entire obligation is known as an entire contract this is usually something of a misnomer because a contract usually comprises a complex of obligations and, even though one of a party's obligations is entire, the rest may not be. Thus, if A agrees to build a house for B for a lump sum payable on completion, his obligation to build the house is impliedly entire, but his other obligations as to time of perfor-mance, quality of work, etc are not entire, unless, very exceptionally, the contract expressly provides that precise performance of them is a precondi-tion of payment.[1] Similarly, if C agrees to sell goods to D, his obligation to deliver the correct quantity is entire by statute, but his other obligations as to the quality of the goods and so on are not normally entire. It follows that, if A builds the house but does so defectively or if C delivers the goods but they are defective, B and D are not entitled to terminate the contract for breach of an entire obligation, no such obligation having been broken; nor, unless the obligation broken is sufficiently important or the effects of its breach sufficiently serious, can they terminate under the ground which we discuss next (paras 9.16–9.21 below). If the contract cannot be terminated, A and C are entitled to their contractual payment, subject to a set-off or counter-claim in favour of B and D. In *H Dakin & Co Ltd v Lee*,[2] the plaintiff builders agreed to repair the defendant's house for £264, payable on completion, in accordance with a specification. They did the repairs but these were defective in three ways: a. only 2 feet of concrete had been put in in underpinning a wall, whereas 4 feet had been specified; b. 4-inch iron columns had been fitted in a bay window, instead of 5-inch ones; c. certain joists in the bay window had not been bolted together in the manner specified. These defects were relatively unimportant. The Court of Appeal held that the plaintiff builders were entitled to recover the £264, less a reduction in respect of the defective work.

1 *Eshelby v Federated European Bank Ltd* [1932] 1 KB 423, CA.
2 [1916] 1 KB 566, CA. Also see *Hoenig v Isaacs* [1952] 2 All ER 176, CA; cf *Bolton v Mahadeva* [1972] 2 All ER 1322, [1972] 1 WLR 1009, CA.

9.15 *Severable obligations* It would be wrong to think that an obligation to build or do some other thing is always an entire obligation. It is only so if the parties expressly or impliedly agree to the effect that, or statute provides that, complete performance of the obligation is a pre-condition of the other party's obligations becoming operative. Otherwise an obligation to do something is known as a 'severable' obligation, and the contract containing it as a severable contract. A clear example of a severable obligation is where the contract provides that payment is due from time to time as specified instalments of the other party's obligation are rendered. In such a case, the latter's obligation to do the work etc. is severable, and so is it if payment is at a fixed rate per item or instalment even though payment is not due until after performance has been completed.

Partial or defective performance of a severable obligation gives the injured party a right of action in damages but it does not entitle him to terminate the contract unless it amounts to a renunciation or falls within the next ground of termination which we discuss. The defaulting party is entitled to recover payment at the stipulated rate for each item or instalment which he has provided, subject to a set-off or counter-claim for damages for breach. In *Taylor v Laird*,[1] for instance, it was held that a person, who had agreed to skipper a steamer on an exploration and trading voyage up the River Niger at a pay of £50 per month but who abandoned the job before the voyage was completed, was entitled to his salary as each month's service was completed and therefore could recover the month's salary outstanding. Similarly, where a contract provides for the supply of 3,000 tons of coal to be delivered in equal monthly instalments over 12 months at £x per ton, the supplier's obligation to deliver is severable so that, if he abandons the contract after four instalments, he is entitled to payment at the contractual rate for those instalments.[2]

1 (1856) 1 H & N 266.
2 *Jackson v Rotax Motor and Cycle Co* [1910] 2 KB 937.

Failure to fulfil an obligation which is not an entire obligation
9.16   Failure to fulfil an obligation which is not an entire obligation is the most common type of breach of contract. Unless the party in default has a lawful excuse the injured party can, of course, recover damages for breach of contract but, leaving aside termination for renunciation[1] or incapacitation,[2] he can only terminate for failure to perform an obligation which is not an entire obligation in two cases:

where it involves breach of a term of the contract which is a condition;

where it involves breach of an 'intermediate term' and the effect of the breach deprives the injured party of substantially the whole benefit of the contract.

1 Para 9.10 above.
2 Para 9.11 above.

9.17   *Breach of condition*   Some contractual terms can be classified as conditions, others as warranties. A condition is a statement of fact, or a promise, which forms an *essential* term of the contract,[1] or, as it is sometimes put, one which goes to the root of the contract. If the statement is not true, or the promise is not fulfilled, the injured party may[2] terminate the contract for breach of condition, as well as claiming damages.[3] In this context the word 'condition' is used in yet another sense. It does not bear its orthodox meaning, discussed in paras 5.33, 5.34 and 9.12 above, of an event by which an obligation is suspended or cancelled but is used to describe a particular type of contractual term. It is certainly an odd word to use for this purpose.

A warranty is a contractual term concerning a less important or subsidiary statement of fact or promise.[4] If a warranty is broken this does not entitle the other party to terminate. It simply entitles him to sue for damages or make a set-off and the party in breach is entitled to the contractual price less the damages or set-off.[5]

In the case of sales of goods, these distinctions have been given statutory effect, the relevant statute now being the Sale of Goods Act 1979.[6]

1   *Heyworth v Hutchinson* (1867) LR 2 QB 447 at 451.
2   Unless the failure in performance is microscopic, para 8.2 above.
3   In relation to contracts for the sale of goods this rule is given statutory effect by the Sale of Goods Act 1979, s11(3).
4   *Oscar Chess Ltd v Williams* [1957] 1 All ER 325 at 328; Sale of Goods Act 1979, s11(3).
5   *Gilbert-Ash (Northern) Ltd v Modern Engineering (Bristol) Ltd* [1974] AC 689, [1973] 3 All ER 195, HL; Sale of Goods Act 1979, s53(1)(a).
6   Ss11(3) and 61(1).

9.18   The classification of a term depends on the following considerations:

a. Sometimes statute provides that particular terms are conditions or warranties, e g the implied conditions and implied warranties under the Sale of Goods Act 1979.[1]

b. In other cases, a term which has been classified as a condition in judicial decisions will be so classified thereafter.[2]

c. In the absence of classification by statute or case authority, a court has to decide whether the broken term is a condition or warranty (if either) by ascertaining the intention of the parties as at the time the contract was made.[3] The parties' intentions are particularly important and it is open to them to agree that what is a condition according to a previous judicial decision shall be a warranty in their contract, and vice versa. Because of the drastic consequences, the courts lean against construing a term as a condition: in fact, they are increasingly reluctant so to construe a term unless compelled by clear evidence of the parties' intentions.[4]

The approach of the courts is as follows:
First, the court must seek to ascertain the intention of the parties as expressed in the contract. If the wording *clearly* reveals that the parties intended that any breach of the term should give rise to a right to terminate, that term will be regarded as a condition. But if the parties clearly did not so intend, the term will not be regarded as a condition even though it is described as a 'condition' in the contract. This is shown by *Schuler AG v Wickman Machine Tool Sales Ltd.*[5] A four-year distributorship agreement provided that the distributor should visit six named customers every week. The agreement described this provision as a 'condition'. The House of Lords held that the contract could not be terminated simply because of breach of this 'condition'. Its reasoning was that the parties could not have intended a mere failure to make one visit to result in a right to terminate. It thought that more probably 'condition' had been used simply to mean 'term'.

Second, if the wording of the contract does not indicate the parties' intentions, the court must ascertain them by inference from the nature, purpose and circumstances of the contract. If, in the context of the whole contract, it is *clear* that the term was so important that a party would *always* want to terminate if it was broken it will be regarded as a condition. An example is *Behn v Burness*,[6] where one term of a charterparty was that the ship was 'now in the port of Amsterdam': the ship was not then there.

The statement was held to be a condition because of the commercial importance attached to such a statement. On the other hand, a term in a charterparty that a ship is seaworthy has not been construed as a condition because it can be broken in a number of ways, in some of which the parties would clearly not intend that the charterer should be entitled to terminate.[7]

1   Para 7.18 above.
2   *The Mihalis Angelos* [1971] 1 QB 164, [1970] 3 All ER 125, CA.
3   *Bunge Corpn v Tradax SA* [1981] 2 All ER 513, [1981] 1 WLR 711, HL.
4   *The Hansa Nord* [1975] 3 All ER 739 at 755; *Bunge Corpn v Tradax SA* [1981] 2 All ER 513 at 542, 551.
5   [1974] AC 235, [1973] 2 All ER 39, HL.
6   (1862) 3 B & S 751.
7   *Hong Kong Fir Shipping Co Ltd v Kawasaki Kisen Kaisha Ltd* [1962] 2 QB 26, [1962] 1 All ER 474, CA.

9.19   There is a special rule which (where it is applicable) prevents a buyer of goods terminating the contract of sale for breach of a condition of it, even though he has not (unconditionally) affirmed it because he lacks the knowledge of the breach necessary for affirmation. This rule—which only applies to contracts for the sale of goods—is provided by the Sale of Goods Act 1979, s11(4). This states that, where a contract for the sale of goods is not severable and the buyer has accepted the goods or part of them, he can only treat a breach of condition as a breach of warranty, 'and not as a ground for rejecting the goods and treating the contract as repudiated', unless there is a term of the contract, express or implied, to that effect.

Section 11(4) only applies where the contract of sale is not severable, so that it is inapplicable to a contract under which goods are to be delivered by instalments, each of which is to be separately paid for, because this is a severable contract.[1] On the other hand, a contract for a lump sum price payable after the completion of delivery is not severable even though it provides for delivery by instalments or the seller has an option to fulfil his obligations by one delivery or two or more,[2] with the result that if the buyer accepts an instalment he is precluded by s11(4) from rejecting later instalments.

By the Sale of Goods Act 1979, s35, a buyer is deemed to have accepted goods:
a   When he intimates to the seller that he has accepted them; or
b.   When the goods have been delivered to him and he does any act in relation to them which is inconsistent with the ownership of the seller, such as re-selling and despatching the whole or part of them to a sub-buyer.[3] However, this is subject to the provisions of s34 to the effect that where goods are delivered to a buyer, which he has not previously examined, he is not deemed to have accepted the goods unless and until he has had a reasonable opportunity of examining them for the purpose of ascertaining whether they conform to the contract. The result is that if a buyer, who has not had a reasonable opportunity to examine the goods, re-sells and despatches them to a sub-buyer, he is not deemed to have accepted them by s34, whereas if he had had a reasonable opportunity to examine them he would have been deemed by s35 to have accepted them; or
c.   When after the lapse of a reasonable time, he retains the goods without intimating to the seller that he has rejected them. Again, this is subject to

s34 so that a buyer is not deemed to have accepted the goods unless he has had a reasonable chance of examining them.

1 Para 9.15 above.
2 *J Rosenthal & Sons Ltd v Esmail* [1965] 2 All ER 860, [1965] 1 WLR 1117, HL.
3 *Hardy (E) & Co v Hillerns and Fowler* [1923] 2 KB 490, CA.

9.20 *Breach of an intermediate term* If the term broken is not a condition, it must not be assumed that it is a warranty for which the only remedy is damages, unless statute or a judicial decision compels such a classification.[1] Instead, the contract must be construed and, unless the contract makes it clear (either by express provision or by necessary implication from its nature, purpose and circumstances) that the parties intended that no breach of the term should entitle the injured party to terminate the contract, the term will be classified as an intermediate (or innominate) term and not as a warranty. If it is so classified one must then ask whether the nature and effect of its breach is such as to deprive the injured party of substantially the whole benefit which it was intended that he should obtain under the contract.[2] If it is, the injured party is entitled to terminate the contract, as well as claiming damages. In applying this test, account must be taken not only of the actual consequences of the breach but also of those whose occurrence is reasonably foreseeable.[3] Regard must also be had to the quantitative ratio between the breach and the contract as a whole.[4] There is high judicial authority in a number of recent cases that the present doctrine, whereby termination for breach of a term depends on the effects of the breach, is preferable to making termination dependent on whether the term itself is classified as a condition or a warranty, since it is far more likely to ensure that termination is possible when it is appropriate.[5] This is an explanation of the increasing reluctance of the courts to classify a term as a condition or warranty.

A leading authority for the present doctrine is *Hong Kong Fir Shipping Co Ltd v Kawasaki Kisen Kaisha Ltd.*[6] The plaintiffs chartered a ship to the defendants for 24 months. The ship was old and needed to be maintained by an adequate and competent engine room crew but the plaintiffs did not provide such a crew and thereby were in breach of a term of the charterparty to provide a ship 'in every way fitted for ordinary cargo service'. Because of the incompetence and inadequacy of the engine room crew and the age of the engines, the ship was held up for repairs for five weeks on her first voyage, and when she reached her destination it was found that further repairs, which would take 15 weeks, were necessary to make her seaworthy. The defendants purported to terminate the charterparty and the plaintiffs sued for breach of contract on the ground that termination was wrongful. The defendants pleaded that the seaworthiness clause was a condition of the contract, and that therefore they could terminate the contract for breach of it. Having held that the clause was not a condition for the reason set out at the end of para 9.18 above, the Court of Appeal held that the effect of the plaintiffs' breach of the clause was not sufficiently serious to justify the defendants in terminating. One reason which it particularly relied on was the fact that after the repairs the ship was still available for 17 of the original 24 months. The defendants' termination had therefore been wrongful.

The same decision was reached in *The Hansa Nord.*[7] Citrus pulp pellets

147

were sold by a German company to a Dutch company, delivery to be made in Rotterdam. The contract included a term that shipment was to be made in good condition. Some of the pellets arrived damaged. The buyers rejected the whole consignment (ie terminated the contract) and the goods were sold by the order of a Dutch court to a third person. Subsequently, they were re-sold at one-third the original contract price to the original buyers who then used the whole consignment for a purpose (cattle food) similar to that for which they had originally bought it (animal feed)— though at a lower rate of inclusion in the case of the damaged pellets. The Court of Appeal held that the 'shipment in good condition' term was not a condition of the contract because it could not have been intended that any breach of it should entitle the buyers to terminate the contract.[8] The Court then turned to the present doctrine and held that the buyers were not entitled to terminate under it because, particularly in the light of the subsequent events, the effect of the breach was not sufficiently serious to justify termination. Thus, the buyers were only entitled to damages and could not treat themselves as discharged from their obligation to accept the pellets and pay the contract price.

1   *Hong Kong Fir Shipping Co Ltd v Kawasaki Kisen Kaisha Ltd* [1962] 2 QB 26 at 63–64; *Reardon Smith Line Ltd v Hansen-Tangen* [1976] 3 All ER 570 at 573–573.
2   *Hong Kong Fir Shipping Co Ltd v Kawasaki Kisen Kaisha Ltd* [1962] 2 QB 26 at 70.
3   Ibid, at 64.
4   Ibid; *Maple Flock Co Ltd v Universal Furniture Products (Wembley) Ltd* [1934] 1 KB 148, CA.
5   Eg *Reardon Smith Line Ltd v Hansen-Tangen* [1976] 3 All ER 570 at 577.
6   [1962] 2 QB 26, [1962] 1 All ER 474, CA.
7   [1976] QB 44, [1975] 3 All ER 739, CA.
8   The Court also held that there was no breach of the implied condition of merchantable quality under the Sale of Goods Act 1979, s14(2); see para 7.18 above.

9.21   These two cases can be contrasted with *Aerial Advertising Co v Batchelors Peas Ltd (Manchester)*.[1] The plaintiffs agreed to conduct an aerial advertising campaign for the defendants. One term of the contract was that the pilot of the aeroplane should telephone the defendants each day and obtain their approval for what he proposed to do. On Armistice Day 1937, the pilot, in breach of this term, failed to contact the defendants and flew over Salford during the two minutes' silence. The aeroplane was towing a banner saying 'Eat Batchelors Peas'. Of course, the term broken was not a condition since breach of it might well only have had trivial consequences, so that the parties could not have intended that its breach should always entitle the defendants to terminate the contract. However, the effect of the particular breach was disastrous since it aroused public hostility towards the defendants and their products. It was held that the defendants were entitled to terminate the contract and therefore the plaintiffs' claim for payment for advertising already done under the contract was dismissed.

1   [1938] 2 All ER 788.

Anticipatory breach
9.22   So far we have been concerned with actual breaches of contract, ie breaches of contractual obligations whose performance is due at the time of

the breach. An anticipatory breach of contract occurs where a party renounces[1] his contractual obligations, or incapacitates himself[2] from performing them, *before the time fixed for their performance.* If a party commits such an anticipatory breach, the injured party can accept the breach as discharging the contract (ie terminate it) and immediately bring an action for damages for breach of contract or a quantum meruit action: he does not have to wait for the time of performance to become due. A leading authority is *Hochster v De La Tour.*[3] The defendant agreed to employ the plaintiff as a courier from 1 June 1852. On 11 May, the defendant informed the plaintiff that his services would no longer be required. The plaintiff brought an action for damages before 1 June and succeeded. Another example is provided by *Lovelock v Franklyn,*[4] where the defendant agreed to assign his interest in a lease to the plaintiff for £140. Before the agreed date of performance arrived, the defendant assigned his interest to another person. It was held that the plaintiff could bring an action for damages immediately: he did not have to wait for the time of performance to arrive.

An anticipatory breach also occurs where, *before the time fixed for performance of some part of his obligations,* a party manifests an intention to act in a way which will be in breach of that part, although he wishes to fulfil the contract and does not know that his intended conduct will be a breach of it. Here, the injured party can only terminate the contract and bring an action immediately for damages or a quantum meruit award if he would be able to terminate on the actual occurrence of the threatened breach,[5] ie if the threatened breach is of:

a. an entire obligation; or

b. a term which is a condition; or

c. an intermediate term and the foreseeable effect of the threatened breach would be such as substantially to deprive the injured party of the benefit which it was intended that he should obtain under the contract.

If the threatened breach of part of a party's unperformed obligations does not fall within one of these three classes, there is no anticipatory breach and the injured party merely has the remedy of damages for breach of contract if, and when, an actual breach occurs.

If the injured party validly terminates the contract for anticipatory breach, the other party is not permitted to change his mind and seek to perform his contractual obligations,[6] but he may do so at any time before there is a valid termination by the injured party.[7]

1 Para 9.10 above.
2 Para 9.11 above.
3 (1853) 2 E & B 678.
4 (1846) 2 QB 371.
5 *Federal Commerce and Navigation Co Ltd v Molena Alpha Inc* [1979] AC 757, [1979] 1 All ER 307, HL.
6 *Xenos v Danube and Black Sea Rly Co* (1863) 14 CB NS 325.
7 *Norwest Holst Group Administration Ltd v Harrison* [1985] ICR 668, [1985] IRLR 240, CA.

9.23 As in the other situations where a party can terminate a contract for the other's failure to perform, a contract is never automatically discharged by anticipatory breach; instead, the injured party has an election to terminate or affirm the contract. If he refuses to accept the anticipatory breach as discharging the contract and continues to insist on performance, he will affirm it. When a contract is affirmed after anticipatory breach the effects are as follows:

a. The injured party loses his right to bring an action for damages for anticipatory breach.

b. The contract remains in force. Each party remains liable to perform his obligations when they become due and will be liable if he fails to perform then. Thus, the party who committed the anticipatory breach is given an opportunity to perform his obligations, and only if he fails to do so will he be liable. The contract remains in existence at the risk of both parties; consequently, if the party who has affirmed after anticipatory breach subsequently commits a breach of contract he will be liable, and either party can take advantage of any supervening circumstance which would justify him in declining to perform.[1]

c. As opposed to the case where the injured party immediately sues for damages for anticipatory breach, a party who affirms is under no duty to mitigate his loss before performance is due.[2] This may result in the recovery of larger damages in the event of ultimate non-performance by the other.[3]

1   *Frost v Knight* (1872) LR 7 Exch 111 at 112; *Avery v Bowden* (1885) 5 E & B 714.
2   *Tredegar Iron and Coal Co Ltd v Hawthorn Bros & Co* (1902) 18 TLR 716, CA.
3   Paras 11.13–11.14, below.

Exemption clauses

9.24   A contract may contain an exemption clause. An exemption clause may purport to exclude or modify the primary obligations of a party which would normally be implied by law from the legal nature of the contract. Alternatively, it may purport to exclude or restrict one of the parties' liability for breach of contract, or some other liability, such as for the tort of negligence, or both. Because exemption clauses could operate very unfairly in the case of standard form contracts, where one party has no real option but to accept the terms offered by the other, a number of restrictive rules have been applied to exemption clauses by the court and, more important, statutory limitations on the validity of many exemption clauses have been introduced.

9.25   Before a defendant can rely on an exemption clause in his favour he must show that it is a term of the contract and that, as a matter of construction, it covers the damage in question. We will look at these matters, as well as certain general limitations on the application of exemption clauses, before turning to the crucial question of their validity.

Term of the contract

9.26   The determination of whether what purports to be an exemption clause is a term of the contract depends very much on whether the clause is contained in a signed contractual document or not. If it is, it is a contractual term, binding on the person who signed the document, even though he was unaware of it (eg because he had not read it).[1]

1   *L'Estrange v Graucob* [1934] 2 KB 394, CA. For an exception, see para 9.35 below.

9.27   In other cases, eg where the clause is printed on a ticket or a notice, the clause will only be a contractual term if adequate notice of it is given. The following rules apply in this connection.

Notice must be given before or at the time of the contract

9.28 The exemption clause is ineffective unless it was brought to the party's notice before or at the time the contract was made. This is shown by *Olley v Marlborough Court Ltd.*[1] The plaintiff and her husband were accepted as guests at a hotel. They paid for a week in advance and went to their room, on the wall of which was a notice exempting the hotel proprietors from liability for the loss or theft of property. Due to the negligence of the hotel staff, property was stolen from the plaintiff's room. The Court of Appeal held that the hotel was not protected by the exemption clause because the contract had been made before the exemption clause was communicated so that it formed no part of the contract.

There is an exception to the present rule. If there has been a course of dealings between the parties on the basis of documents incorporating similar terms exempting liability, then, provided those dealings have been of a consistent nature,[2] the court may imply the exemption clause into a particular contract where express notice is given too late. In *J Spurling Ltd v Bradshaw*,[3] the defendant had dealt with the plaintiff warehousemen for many years. He delivered barrels of orange juice to them for storage. Later, he received a document from them which acknowledged receipt and referred to clauses on its back, one of which excluded the plaintiffs from any liability for loss or damage occasioned by their negligence. Later, the defendant refused to pay the storage charges because the barrels were empty on collection. He was sued for these charges and counter-claimed for negligence. The Court of Appeal held that the exemption clause was incorporated into the contract, and the defendant was therefore bound by it, because in previous dealings he had received a document containing the clause, although he had never read it. Since incorporation of an exemption clause in this way depends on a previous consistent course of dealings between the parties it is less likely to occur in the case of contracts to which a private individual is a party, because normally he will have had insufficient dealings with the other party to constitute a course of dealings; three or four dealings over a five-year period, for instance, have been held insufficient to constitute a course of dealings.[4]

1   [1949] 1 KB 532, [1949] 1 All ER 127, CA.
2   *McCutcheon v David MacBrayne Ltd* [1964] 1 All ER 430, [1964] 1 WLR 125, HL.
3   [1956] 2 All ER 121, [1956] 1 WLR 461, CA.
4   *Hollier v Rambler Motors (AMC) Ltd* [1972] 2 QB 71, [1972] 1 All ER 399, CA.

The notice must be contained in a contractual document

9.29 An exemption clause is ineffective if it, or notice of it, is contained in a document which a reasonable person would not assume to contain contractual terms. Thus, in *Chapelton v Barry UDC*,[1] it was held that an exemption clause contained in a ticket for a deck chair on a beach was ineffective because no reasonable person would expect the ticket to be more than a receipt: he would not assume it contained contractual terms. The same decision was reached concerning a cheque book cover in *Burnett v Westminster Bank Ltd.*[2]

1   [1940] 1 KB 532, [1940] 1 All ER 356, CA.
2   [1966] 1 QB 742, [1965] 3 All ER 81.

Reasonable notice of the exemption clause must be given
9.30 A leading authority is *Parker v South Eastern Rly Co.*[1] The plaintiff left his bag at a station cloakroom. He received a ticket which said on its face: 'See back'. On the back were a number of terms, one of which limited the railway company's liability to £10 per package. The plaintiff's bag was lost and he claimed its value of £24 10s. It was held that the plaintiff would be bound by the exemption clause, even though he had not read it, if the railway company had given reasonable notice of its existence. Notice can be reasonable even though it involves reference to other documents or to a notice.[2] The test laid down in *Parker v South Eastern Rly Co* is objective, and if reasonable notice has been given, it is irrelevant that the party affected by the exemption clause was blind or illiterate or otherwise unable to comprehend its meaning.[3]

1   (1877) 2 CPD 416, CA.
2   *Watkins v Rymill* (1883) 10 QBD 178; *Thompson v London, Midland and Scottish Rly Co* [1930] 1 KB 41, CA.
3   *Thompson v London, Midland and Scottish Rly Co* [1930] 1 KB 41, CA.

Construction
9.31 If an exemption clause is a term of the contract the next question is whether it applies to the loss or damage in question.

It must be emphasised that there is no rule of law that an exemption clause is eliminated, or deprived of effect, regardless of its terms by a breach of contract, however fundamental that breach may be. The question whether, and to what extent, an exemption clause applies in the event of any breach of contract is answered by construing the contract to see whether the parties intended that the clause should apply to the loss or damage which has occurred in the circumstances in which it has occurred. This was stated by the House of Lords in *Photo Production Ltd v Securicor Transport Ltd*,[1] where obiter dicta by the House in *Suisse Atlantique Societe d'Armement Maritime SA v NV Rotterdamsche Kolen Centrale*[2] were explained and applied, and the previous confusion in the authorities (some of which were overruled) clarified.

In the *Photo Production* case, the plaintiffs employed the defendants to check against burglaries and fires at their factory at night. One night, the defendants' patrolman deliberately started a fire in the factory. It got out of control and a large part of the premises was burnt down. The loss and damage suffered amounted to £615,000. By way of defence to the plaintiffs' action to recover this amount as damages, the defendants relied principally on an exemption clause in their contract with the plaintiffs which purported to exempt the defendants from liability for any injurious act by an employee unless it could have been foreseen and avoided by due diligence on their part. The clause added that the defendants were not to be liable for any loss suffered by the plaintiffs through fire, except insofar as such loss was solely attributable to the negligence of the defendants' employees acting within the scope of their employment. The House of Lords held that, although the defendants would otherwise have been liable to the plaintiffs, on its true construction the exemption clause clearly and unambiguously applied to what had occurred, and protected the defendants from liability.[3]

In case it should be thought that the rule that the application of an exemption clause depends on the construction of the contract is liable to cause injustice in consumer contracts and other contracts based on standard terms, we would point out that exemption clauses in such a contract made nowadays are rendered either totally invalid unless fair and reasonable by the Unfair Contract Terms Act 1977, as we explain in paras 9.41 to 9.53 below, even though on their true construction they were intended to apply to what has occurred. It follows that the construction of an exemption clause is now generally of crucial importance only where the contract has been negotiated between businessmen capable of looking after their own interests and of deciding how the risks inherent in the performance of the contract can most economically be borne, which is usually by one or other party insuring against such risks.

We set out below certain rules of construction which are applied to exemption clauses by the courts and which tend to favour the party affected by such a clause.

1 [1980] AC 827, [1980] 1 All ER 556, HL. See also *George Mitchell (Chesterhall) Ltd v Finney Lock Seeds Ltd* [1983] 2 AC 803, [1983] 2 All ER 737, HL.
2 [1967] 1 AC 361, [1966] 2 All ER 61, HL.
3 The contract in this case was a standard form contract, but, since it was entered into before the Unfair Contract Terms Act 1977, the House of Lords was not concerned with the validity of the exemption clause under that Act.

Liability can only be excluded or restricted by clear words
9.32 The liability in question must be precisely covered by the exemption clause relied on. In *Andrews Bros (Bournemouth) Ltd v Singer & Co Ltd,*[1] the plaintiffs entered into a contract to buy 'new Singer cars' from the defendants. One of the cars delivered by the defendants was not a new car, having run a considerable mileage. A clause in the contract exempted the defendants from liability for breach of all 'conditions, warranties and liabilities *implied* by common law, statute or otherwise' but the Court of Appeal held that this did not protect the defendants against liability for breach of an *express* term. A similar decision was reached in *Wallis, Son and Wells v Pratt and Haynes.*[2] The defendants sold by sample to the plaintiffs seed described as 'common English sainfoin'. The contract stated that the defendants gave 'no *warranty* express or implied' as to any matter concerning the seed. The seed turned out to be the inferior and cheaper 'giant sainfoin'. The House of Lords held that the exemption clause did not apply because there had been a breach of the *condition* implied by the Sale of Goods Act 1979, s13 (that goods sold by description correspond with it) and the clause did not purport to exclude liability for breach of condition.

This rule of construction is applied more rigorously in the case of clauses purporting to exclude liability than in the case of those purporting to restrict it.[3]

1 [1934] 1 KB 17, CA.
2 [1911] AC 394, HL.
3 *Ailsa Craig Fishing Co Ltd v Malvern Fishing Co Ltd* [1983] 1 All ER 101, [1983] 1 WLR 964, HL.

All ambiguities in the exemption clause are construed against the party relying on it
9.33   This is in accordance with the rule normally applied in the construction of contracts.[1]

1   *Houghton v Trafalgar Insurance Co* [1954] 1 QB 247, [1953] 2 All ER 1409, CA.

Exclusion of liability for negligence
9.34   The nature of liability for a breach of contract depends on the term broken. In the case of some terms, liability for their breach is strict (ie a party who does not comply with the term is liable despite the absence of any negligence on his part); in the case of others, liability for their breach only arises if the party in question has been negligent. This distinction depends upon whether the term broken simply imposes an obligation to do something or that something be of a certain standard, or whether it imposes an obligation *to take reasonable care* (or the like) in relation to something. It should also be borne in mind that, where contractual liability for the breach in question is strict, the guilty party may also be liable in tort if he can be proved to have been negligent.

If an exemption clause clearly purports to exclude *all* liability, effect must be given to it[1] (subject to the general rules as to the validity of exemption clauses), but if the clause is not so clearly drafted the law is as follows:

Where contractual liability for the breach in question is strict, the clause is normally construed as being confined to that contractual liability, and not as extending to any tortious liability for negligence, with the result that the guilty party is not protected by it if he is proved to have been negligent.[2] A leading example is *White v John Warwick & Co Ltd*.[3] The plaintiff hired a tricycle from the defendants. While he was riding it the saddle tilted forward and he was injured. The contract of hire stated: 'nothing in this agreement shall render the owners liable for any personal injury'. The Court of Appeal held that the exemption clause would not protect the defendants from liability in tort if they were found to have been negligent. Its reason was that, in the absence of the exemption clause, the defendants could have been liable for breach of contract in supplying a defective tricycle[4] irrespective of negligence and the operation of the clause had to be restricted to that stricter liability.

Where liability can be based on negligence and nothing else, the exemption clause will normally be construed as extending to that head of damage, because if it were not so construed it would lack subject matter.[5] This is shown by *Alderslade v Hendon Laundry Ltd*.[6] The defendants contracted to launder the plaintiff's handkerchiefs, the contract limiting their liability 'for lost or damaged articles' to 20 times the laundering charge. The handkerchiefs were lost through the defendants' negligence. The Court of Appeal held that the only way in which the defendants could be made liable for the loss of the handkerchiefs would be if they could be shown to have been guilty of negligence. It held that the exemption clause applied to limit the defendants' liability for negligence because otherwise the clause would be left without any content at all.

Both these rules are only rules of construction and, although they will normally be adopted, the court is free to construe the clause in another way if, on its wording or other evidence, it considers that the parties had some other intention.[7] The court is more likely to depart from these rules of construction where the clause purports to restrict liability than where it purports to exclude it.[8]

1   *Joseph Travers & Sons Ltd v Cooper* [1915] 1 KB 73.
2   *Alderslade v Hendon Laundry Ltd* [1945] KB 189 at 192.
3   [1953] 2 All ER 1021, [1953] 1 WLR 1285, CA.
4   The term broken would have been an implied term that the tricycle was reasonably fit for the purpose for which it was hired: para 7.18 above.
5   *Alderslade v Hendon Laundry Ltd* [1945] KB 189 at 192; *Hollier v Rambler Motors (AMC) Ltd* [1972] 2 QB 71, [1972] 1 All ER 399, CA.
6   [1945] KB 189, [1945] 1 All ER 244, CA.
7   *J Archdale Ltd v Comservices Ltd* [1954] 1 All ER 210, [1954] 1 WLR 459, CA; *Hollier v Rambler Motors (AMC) Ltd* [1972] 2 QB 71, [1972] 1 All ER 399, CA; *The Golden Leader* [1980] 2 Lloyd's Rep 573.
8   *George Mitchell (Chesterhall) Ltd v Finney Lock Seeds Ltd* [1983] 2 All ER 737 at 741.

General limitations on the application of an exemption clause

Misrepresentation

9.35   If the party favoured by an exemption clause induced the other party to accept it by misrepresenting its contents or effect, the clause is rendered ineffective to the extent that it is wider than the misrepresentation, even though the contract was signed by the other party and even though the misrepresentation was innocent. In *Curtis v Chemical Cleaning and Dyeing Co Ltd*,[1] the plaintiff took a dress to the defendants' shop for cleaning. The dress was trimmed with beads and sequins. The plaintiff was asked to sign a receipt exempting the defendants from all liability for any damage to articles cleaned. The plaintiff asked why her signature was required and was told that the receipt exempted the defendants from liability for damage to the sequins and beads. When the dress was returned it was badly stained. It was held that the defendants were not protected by the clause because through their employee they had innocently induced the plaintiff to believe that the clause only referred to damage to the beads and sequins and therefore the clause only protected them against liability for such damage.

1   [1951] 1 KB 805, [1951] 1 All ER 631, CA.

Inconsistent undertakings

9.36   If, at or before the time the contract was made, the party favoured by an exemption clause gives an undertaking which is inconsistent with it, the exemption clause is rendered ineffective to the extent that it is inconsistent with the undertaking, even though the undertaking does not form part of the contract or of a contract collateral to it. In *Mendelssohn v Normand Ltd*,[1] the plaintiff left his car in the defendants' garage on terms contained in a ticket, one of which was that the defendants would not accept any responsibility for any loss sustained by the vehicle or its contents, however caused. The car contained valuables and the plaintiff wanted to lock it, but the attendant told him that this was not permissible. The plaintiff told the attendant about the valuables and the attendant promised to lock the car after he had moved it. On his return, the plaintiff discovered that the valuables had been stolen. The Court of Appeal held that the defendants were not protected by the exemption clause because their employee had in effect promised to see that the valuables were safe, and this oral undertaking took priority over the exemption clause.

1   [1970] 1 QB 177, [1969] 2 All ER 1215, CA. Also see *J Evans & Son (Portsmouth) Ltd v Andrea Merzario Ltd* [1976] 2 All ER 930, [1976] 1 WLR 1078, CA.

Third party generally not protected by an exemption clause

9.37 As part of the doctrine of privity of contract,[1] a person who is not a party to a contract containing an exemption clause is generally not protected by the clause, even though it purports to have this effect. In *Cosgrove v Horsfall*,[2] the Court of Appeal held that a clause in a free bus pass, exempting the London Passenger Transport Board and its servants from liability for injury, was ineffective to protect the servants from liability in tort for negligence since they were not parties to the contract between the Board and the pass-holder. This decision was approved by the House of Lords in *Scruttons Ltd v Midland Silicones Ltd*,[3] although the clause in that case did not expressly purport to exclude or restrict the liability of the third parties in question. A drum containing chemicals was shipped from New York to London. It was consigned to the plaintiffs under a bill of lading which restricted the carriers' liability to $500 (then about £180). While the drum was being handled by the defendants, who were stevedores employed by the carriers, it was damaged through the defendants' negligence; the damage amounted to £593. The contract between the *carriers* and the defendants stated that the defendants should have the benefit of the exemption clause in the bill of lading, but the majority of the House of Lords held that the defendants could not limit their liability to the plaintiffs for negligence by relying on the exemption clause because they were not parties to the bill of lading. These two decisions show that it will sometimes be possible to circumvent an exemption clause by bringing proceedings against an employee or sub-contractor on the ground of his negligence. This may be desirable in the case of a standard form contract, particularly because the employee will usually be reimbursed by his employer for, and a sub-contractor insured against, any damages awarded. However, the reliance on the technical rule of privity of contract is harder to justify in the case of a freely negotiated contract in which one party has agreed to assume the risk of damage, particularly where the contract purports to exempt an employee or sub-contractor of the other party.

1 Para 6.23 above.
2 (1945) 175 LT 334, CA.
3 [1962] AC 446, [1962] 1 All ER 1, HL.

9.38 The position is different where one of the parties, whom we will call A, contracts with B as agent for the third person. In that case the third person is brought into contractual relations with B on terms of the exemption clause provisions in the main contract and is protected by the clause. This was recognised by the Privy Council in *New Zealand Shipping Co Ltd v A N Satterthwaite & Co Ltd*,[1] which showed that there are four prerequisites for the validity of such an agency contract:

a. the main contract must make it clear that the third person is intended to be protected by the exemption clause;

b. the main contract must make it clear that A, in addition to contracting for the exemption clause on his own behalf, is also contracting as agent for the third person that these provisions should apply to the third person;

c. A must have authority from the third person to do that (or the third person can subsequently ratify the agency contract provided he was identifiable at the time it was made[2]); and

d. the third person must have provided consideration for the promise as to exemption made to him, through A as his agent, by B.

In the *New Zealand Shipping Co* case the Privy Council explained how the third person can provide consideration for B's promise as to exemption. The main contract brings into existence a bargain initially unilateral but capable of becoming mutual, between B and the third person, made through A as agent. This will become a full contract when the third person performs services under the main contract. The performance of these services for the benefit of B is the consideration for the agreement by B that the third person should have the benefit of the exemption clause contained in the main contract.

Nevertheless, the *New Zealand Shipping Co* case is of limited effect because:

a. Consideration can only be furnished if the third person does something after the main contract has been made. If he has already performed his services, there can be no unilateral contract of the above type and he will not have furnished the consideration necessary to make enforceable any promise as to exemption.

b. Presumably, the third person cannot be said to accept the offer of a unilateral contract unless he knows of the main contract.

1 [1975] AC 154, [1974] 1 All ER 1015, PC.
2 Para 17.9 below.

Third party not bound by an exemption clause
9.39 Because of the doctrine of privity of contract a third party cannot be deprived of his right to sue in tort by an exemption clause contained in a contract between others, even though it purports to have that effect. An authority is *Haseldine v CA Daw & Son Ltd.*[1] The owners of a block of flats employed the defendants to repair a lift in the block. The defendants repaired the lift negligently and the plaintiff was injured when the lift fell to the bottom of the lift shaft. The defendants were held liable to the plaintiff, it being irrelevant that the contract between the defendants and the owners of the block purported to exempt the defendants from liability for personal injury.

1 [1941] 2 KB 343, [1941] 3 All ER 156, CA.

9.40 The above rule can be avoided in the following cases:

a. If one of the parties to a contract containing an exemption clause in favour of the other contracted as agent for a third person, that person is bound by the clause.

b. It may be that in the following situation a person is bound by an exemption clause contained in a contract between others. It sometimes happens where T has handed goods to A for repair or cleaning that A sub-contracts the work to B. If the contract between A and B contains an exemption clause in favour of B it will not bind T under the law of contract, as we have just seen, and he will be able to recover damages from B for the tort of negligence should B carry out the sub-contracted work negligently. However, T will not have the right to sue B for the tort of negligence if he can be said to have voluntarily assumed the risk of loss or damage; this is because voluntary assumption of risk is a defence to a charge of negligence. There is persuasive authority that T, in the above situation, would be barred by the defence of voluntary assumption of risk if he had expressly or impliedly consented to A making the sub-contract with B on terms usual in the trade, those terms including the exemption clause in question.[1]

1   *Morris v C W Martin & Sons Ltd* [1966] 1 QB 716 at 728; paras 22.2–22.10 below. But see the Unfair Contract Terms Act 1977, s2(3); para 22.5 below.

Validity
9.41   The Unfair Contract Terms Act 1977, which came into force on 1 February 1978,[1] contains a number of provisions greatly limiting the extent to which it is possible to exclude or restrict 'business liability', which is defined as liability (whether in tort or for breach of contract) which arises *in the course of business or from the occupation of premises used for business purposes of the occupier*.[2] In this Act, 'business' includes a profession and the activities of any government department or public or local authority.[3] Although the Act uses the words 'contract term', we propose generally to use the more familiar expression 'exemption clause'.

1   Unfair Contract Terms Act 1977, s31(2).
2   Ibid, s1(3). See further, para 23.3 below.
3   Ibid, s14.

Avoidance of liability for negligence or breach of contract

9.42   *Liability for negligence*   Section 2(1) of the Act provides that a person cannot, by reference to an exemption clause or notice, exclude or restrict his liability for death or personal injury (including any disease or impairment of physical or mental condition) resulting from negligence.

In the case of other loss or damage, s2(2) provides that a person cannot, by reference to an exemption clause or notice, exclude or restrict his liability for negligence, *except in so far as the clause or notice satisfies the 'requirement of reasonableness'*.

These provisions do not extend to a contract of employment, except in favour of the employee.[1]

'Negligence' in this context means the breach—

a. of any obligation, arising from the express or implied terms of a contract, to take reasonable care or exercise reasonable skill in the performance of the contract; or

b. of any common law duty to take reasonable care or exercise reasonable skill; or

c. of the common duty of care imposed by the Occupiers' Liability Act 1957.[2]

1   Unfair Contract Terms Act 1977, Sch 1.
2   Ibid, s1(1). The duties mentioned in b. and c., above, are discussed in chs 19 and 23 below.

9.43 *Liability arising in contract* Section 3 lays down special rules which apply *as between the contracting parties where one of them deals as consumer or on the other's written standard terms of business.*[1] In the present context, a party to a contract 'deals as consumer' in relation to another party if he neither makes the contract in the course of a business nor holds himself out as doing so, and the other party does make the contract in the course of a business.[2] In the case of contracts for the sale, hire purchase or other supply[3] of goods, there is an additional requirement that the goods are of a type ordinarily supplied for private use or consumption. A buyer at an auction or by competitive tender is never regarded as dealing as consumer.[4] It is for those claiming that a party does not deal as consumer to show that he does not.[5]

Section 3 provides that, *as against the party dealing as consumer or on the other's written standard terms of business,* the other party cannot by reference to any contract term—

a. exclude or restrict his liability for breach of contract; or

b. claim to be entitled—
i to render a contractual performance substantially different from that which was reasonably expected of him, or
ii in respect of the whole or any part of his contractual obligation, to render no performance at all,

except in so far as the contract term satisfies the 'requirement of reasonableness'. This provision is widely drawn; for example, under b.i., a term permitting a holiday company to provide accommodation in a different hotel from that specified in the contract may be held invalid, and so, under b.ii., may a term entitling a theatre company to cancel a performance without a refund.

1 Unfair Contract Terms Act 1977, s3(1).
2 Ibid, s12(1).
3 Ie those described in para 9.49 below.
4 Unfair Contract Terms Act 1977, s12(2).
5 Ibid, s12(3).

9.44 *Unreasonable indemnity clauses* Contracts often contain terms requiring one party to indemnify the other against liability incurred by that other in performing the contract. Section 4(1) makes such an indemnity clause void *as against a consumer* unless reasonable. It states that a person dealing as consumer cannot by reference to any contract term be made to indemnify another person (whether a party to the contract or not) in respect of liability that may be incurred by the other for negligence or breach of contract, *except in so far as the contract term satisfies the 'requirement of reasonableness'.* This provision applies whether the liability in question is that of the person to be indemnified or is incurred by him vicariously, and whether that liability is to the person dealing as consumer or to someone else.[1] 'Person dealing as consumer' has the same meaning as in s3.[2]

1 Unfair Contract Terms Act 1977, s4(2).
2 Ibid, s12.

9.45 *Excepted agreements*[1] Sections 2 to 4 do not extend to—

a. any contract of insurance;

b. any contract *so far as* it relates to the creation, transfer or termination of an interest in land[2] or of any right or interest in any patent, trade mark, copyright or the like;

c. any contract *so far as* it relates—
i to the formation or dissolution of a company (which means any body corporate or unincorporated association and includes a partnership), or
ii to its constitution or the rights or obligations of its corporators or members;

d. any contract *so far as* it relates to the creation or transfer of securities or of any right or interest in securities.

Contracts of insurance are totally excepted from the Act, but the other contracts are only excepted *so far as* they relate to the *specified* matters. Presumably, only those parts of such a contract which relate to the specified matters (such as the transfer of an interest in land) are excepted from ss2 to 4 and the rest of the contract is subject to those sections.

Other exceptions relate to charterparties and the like, and are outside the scope of this book.

1 Unfair Contract Terms Act 1977, Sch 1.
2 A mere contractual licence does not create or transfer an interest in land (see para 38.1 below) and therefore *any* exemption clause contained in it is subject to ss2–4.

9.46 *The 'requirement of reasonableness'* In relation to an exemption clause, the requirement of reasonableness is that the clause shall have been a fair and reasonable one to be included having regard to the circumstances which were, or ought reasonably to have been, known or in the contemplation of the parties when the contract was made.[1]

Where a party seeks to restrict liability to a specified sum in reliance on an exemption clause, then, in determining whether the clause satisfies the requirement of reasonableness, regard must be had in particular to—

a. the resources which that party could expect to be available to him for the purpose of meeting the liability should it arise; and

b. how far it was open to him to cover himself by insurance.[2]

It is for the party claiming that an exemption clause satisfies the requirement of reasonableness to show that it does.[3]

1 Unfair Contract Terms Act 1977, s11(1).
2 Ibid, s11(4).
3 Ibid, s11(5).

9.47 *Avoidance of liability arising from sale or supply of goods* Sections 6 and 7 contain additional provisions dealing with attempts to avoid liability where the ownership or possession of goods has passed.

9.48 *Sale and hire purchase* By s6(1) of the Act of 1977, liability for breach of the obligations arising from—

a. the Sale of Goods Act 1979, s12 (seller's implied undertakings as to title etc);[1]

b. the Supply of Goods (Implied Terms) Act 1973, s8 (the corresponding things in relation to hire purchase),
cannot be excluded or restricted by reference to an exemption clause.

Section 6(2) provides that, *as against a person dealing as consumer*, liability for breach of the obligations arising from—

a. the Sale of Goods Act 1979, ss13, 14 or 15 (seller's implied undertakings as to conformity of goods with description or sample, or as to their quality or fitness for a particular purpose);[2]

b. the Supply of Goods (Implied Terms) Act 1973, ss9, 10 or 11 (the corresponding things in relation to hire purchase),

cannot be excluded or restricted by reference to an exemption clause. It must be emphasised that this provision is limited to the implied terms specified. The validity of a clause excluding or restricting liability for breach of any express term will depend on the application of the principles which we have mentioned in para 9.43 above. Unlike s6(1), s6(2) only vitiates the exemption clause as against a person dealing as consumer. In the present context, a party to a contract 'deals as consumer' in relation to another party if—

a. he neither makes the contract in the course of a business nor holds himself out as doing so; and

b. the other party does make the contract in the course of a business; and

c. the goods passing under or in pursuance of the contract are of a type ordinarily supplied for private use or consumption.[3]

A buyer at an auction or by competitive tender is never regarded as dealing as consumer.[4] It has been held that a company which buys goods of the type mentioned in c. above from a party who makes the contract in the course of a business 'deals as consumer' unless the buying of such goods forms at the very least an integral part of the company's business or is a necessary incidental to it,[5] and the same would be true where the buyer was a partnership. Thus, if a company buys from a dealer a Rolls Royce or a yacht for its Chairman, it will 'deal as consumer' and liability for breach of the implied terms just mentioned cannot be excluded or restricted. It is for those claiming that a party does not deal as consumer to show that he does not.[6] Where a party does not deal as consumer s6(3) is the operative provision.

Section 6(3) provides that, *as against a person dealing otherwise than as consumer*, liability for breach of the obligations arising from the Sale of Goods Act 1979, ss13–15, or the Supply of Goods (Implied Terms) Act 1973, ss9–11, can be excluded or restricted by an exemption clause, but *only in so far as the clause satisfies the 'requirement of reasonableness'*.

The provisions of s6(1) and (3) are exceptional in that they are not limited to liabilities arising in the course of business. Section 6 replaces substantially similar provisions introduced by the Supply of Goods (Implied Terms) Act 1973.

---

1   These terms are described in para 7.18 above.

2 These terms are described in para 7.18 above.
3 Unfair Contract Terms Act 1977, s12(1).
4 Ibid, s 12(2).
5 *Peter Symmons & Co Ltd v Cook* (1981) 131 NLJ 758; cf. *Rasbora Ltd v J C L Ltd* [1977] 1 Lloyd's Rep 645.
6 Unfair Contract Terms Act 1977, s12(3).

9.49 *Miscellaneous contract under which the ownership or possession of goods passes* Section 7 of the Act of 1977 deals with exemption clauses purporting to exclude or restrict liability for breach of obligations implied by law[1] into contracts such as those of hire or exchange or for work and materials. Section 7 applies to these contracts a regime which is broadly similar to that just mentioned in relation to sale of goods and hire purchase.

Section 7(2) provides that, *as against a person dealing as consumer* (in the same sense as in sale of goods and hire purchase), liability in respect of the goods' correspondence with description or sample, or their quality or fitness for any particular purpose, cannot be excluded or restricted by reference to an exemption clause.

On the other hand, *as against a person dealing otherwise than as consumer*, s7(3) provides that such liability can be excluded or restricted by reference to such a clause, but *only in so far as the term satisfies the 'requirement of reasonableness'*.

In relation to an exemption clause purporting to exclude or restrict liability for breach of the various terms as to title which are implied by law, the position is as follows. Section 7(3A) provides that, where the contract is one by which a person transfers or agrees to transfer to another the property (ie ownership) in the goods, liability for breach of these terms cannot be excluded or restricted by reference to an exemption clause.

On the other hand, where the property in the goods is not transferred or to be transferred under the contract, s7(4) provides that such liability can be excluded or restricted by such a clause, but *only in so far as the clause satisfies the 'requirement of reasonableness'*. Thus, a different rule applies where such a clause appears in a contract of hire from that which applies where it appears in a contract for, say, work and materials.

1 Supply of Goods and Services Act 1982, ss2–5 and 7–10; see para 7.18 above.

9.50 *The 'requirement of reasonableness' in relation to ss6 and 7* The provisions which we mentioned in para 9.46 concerning the requirement of reasonableness also apply where that requirement is relevant under ss6 and 7. However, in addition, in determining for the purposes of these two sections whether a contract term satisfies the requirement of reasonableness, regard must be had in particular to the guidelines specified in Sch 2 to the Act,[1] viz:

a. the strength of the bargaining positions of the parties relative to each other;

b. whether the customer received an inducement to agree to the term, or in accepting it had an opportunity of entering into a similar contract with other persons, but without having to accept a similar term;

c. where the term excludes or restricts any relevant liability if some condition is not complied with, whether it was reasonable at the time of the contract to expect that compliance with that condition would be practicable;

d. whether the goods were manufactured, processed or adapted to the special order of the customer;

e. whether the customer knew or ought reasonably to have known of the existence and extent of the term (e g because it was in small print or was unlikely to be read in full by the customer). We saw in para 9.26 above that an exemption clause may be a term of the contract even though the customer was unaware of it, especially if he has signed a contractual document containing it. This provision enables the court to hold an exemption clause which is undoubtedly a term of the contract unreasonable, and therefore invalid, because, for instance, the customer could not reasonably have known of its existence.

1   Unfair Contract Terms Act 1977, s11(2).

General

9.51   *International supply contracts*   The limits mentioned above on the exclusion or restriction of liability by an exemption clause do not apply to liability arising under international supply contracts.[1]

An 'international supply contract' means a contract of sale of goods or a contract under which the possession or ownership of goods passes, which is made by parties whose places of business are in different states, provided:

a. the goods are, at the time of the conclusion of the contract, in the course of carriage, or will be carried, from one state to another; or

b. the acts constituting the offer and acceptance were effected in different states; or

c. the contract provides for the goods to be delivered to a state other than that within whose territory the acts constituting the offer and acceptance were effected.[2]

1   Unfair Contract Terms Act 1977, s26(1) and (2).
2   Ibid, s26(3) and (4).

9.52   *Evasion by means of a secondary contract*   Section 10 makes provision to prevent a possible way of evading the Act's limits on the exclusion or restriction of liability. It deals with the case where X, who has rights under (or in connection with the performance of) a contract with Y, makes another contract with Y (or some other person) containing a term whch prejudices or takes away his rights under the first contract. Section 10 provides that, so far as those rights extend to the enforcement of Y's liability under the first contract which the Act prevents Y from excluding or restricting, X is not bound by that term.

9.53   *Varieties of exemption clauses*   As we have shown, the Act repeatedly refers to the 'exclusion or restriction of liability'. These words are given a wide interpretation by s13(1) which provides that, to the extent that the provisions mentioned prevent the exclusion or restriction of any liability, they also prevent:

a. making the liability or its enforcement subject to restrictive or onerous conditions (eg a term requiring 14 days' notice of loss);

b. excluding or restricting any right or remedy in respect of the liability, or subjecting a person to any prejudice in consequence of his pursuing any such right or remedy;

c. excluding or restricting rules of evidence or procedure (eg a term that failure to complain within 14 days is deemed to be conclusive evidence of proper performance of the contract);

and (to that extent) ss2 and 6 and 7 also prevent excluding or restricting liability by reference to terms (and notices) which exclude or restrict the relevant obligation or duty.

Fair Trading Act 1973

9.54 By Part II of the Act the Secretary of State, a Minister or the Director-General of Fair Trading (hereafter referred to as 'the Director') can refer to the Consumer Protection Advisory Committee the question whether a particular trade practice adversely affects the economic interests of consumers in the UK. A consumer trade practice is a practice carried on in connection with the supply of goods or services to consumers and which relates, inter alia, to the terms or conditions, such as exemption clauses, on which goods or services are supplied and the manner in which those terms or conditions are sought to be communicated. If the Director considers that a consumer trade practice has, or is likely to have, the effect of making the terms or conditions of consumer transactions 'so adverse to consumers as to be inequitable', his reference to the Committee may propose recommendations to the Secretary of State to make an order in respect of that practice. In the light of this report the Secretary of State may make an order by statutory instrument prohibiting the particular consumer trade practice. Breach of such an order is a criminal offence, although a contract containing a prohibited exemption clause or other consumer trade practice is not rendered void or unenforceable thereby. By the Consumer Transactions (Restriction on Statements) Order 1976, as amended, the Secretary of State has prohibited any person, in the course of business, displaying, at any place where consumer transactions are effected, a notice which purports to apply to consumer transactions effected there an exemption clause which is void by virtue of the Unfair Contract Terms Act 1977, s6.[1] The Order also prohibits, in relation to consumer transactions, advertisements or documents purporting to apply such a void exemption clause to a consumer transaction.

Part III of the Fair Trading Act enables the Director to take action against a person carrying on a business who has persisted in a course of conduct which is detrimental to the interests of consumers in the UK and which is 'regarded as unfair to them'. If the Director fails to get a satisfactory written assurance that the conduct will cease, or if an assurance given is broken, he can start proceedings before the Restrictive Practices Court, which can make an order directing the person concerned to refrain from the course of conduct in question. Breach of such an order is punishable as contempt of court. Inter alia, a course of conduct is deemed to be unfair to consumers if it consists of contravention of an enactment imposing prohibitions enforceable by criminal proceedings. The effect of this provision seems to be that exemption clauses, and other consumer trade practices, prohibited under delegated legislation made under the power mentioned in the previous paragraph are subject to the present procedure.

1   Para 9.48 above.

Chapter 10
Discharge by frustration

10.1 Under the doctrine of frustration a contract is automatically discharged 'whenever the law recognises that, without default of either party, a contractual obligation has become incapable of being performed because the circumstances in which performance is called for would render it a thing radically different from that which was undertaken by the contract'.[1] This classic statement has been approved in a substantial number of cases.[2]

1 *Davis Contractors Ltd v Fareham UDC* [1956] AC 696 at 729, [1956] 2 All ER 145.
2 See, for example, *National Carriers Ltd v Panalpina (Northern) Ltd* [1981] AC 675, [1981] 1 All ER 161, HL; *The Nema* [1982] AC 724, [1981] 2 All ER 1030, HL; *The Hannah Blumenthal* [1983] 1 AC 854, [1983] 1 All ER 34, HL.

Scope
10.2 Under this heading, we propose to illustrate the scope of the classic statement we have just quoted by reference to *some* of the circumstances in which a contract may be frustrated. A contract may be frustrated if, for example, *subsequent to its formation*:
  a thing essential to its performance is destroyed or becomes unavailable; or
  a fundamental change of circumstances occurs; or
  a party to a contract of a personal nature dies or is otherwise incapacitated from performing it; or
  performance of it is rendered illegal; or
  a basic assumption on which the parties contracted is destroyed.
The doctrine of frustration does not apply to cases where one of these circumstances existed at the time the contract was made: there the legal position must be answered by reference to the law relating to mistake[1] and illegal contracts.[2] In addition, a contract is not discharged by frustration simply because a subsequent event makes its performance more costly or difficult than envisaged when the contract was made. This is shown by *Davis Contractors Ltd v Fareham UDC*.[3] In 1946, the contractors entered into a contract with the council to build 78 houses for the fixed sum of £94,000. Owing to an unexpected shortage of skilled labour and of certain materials, the contract took 22 months to complete instead of the anticipated eight months and cost £115,000. The contractors contended that the contract had been frustrated by the long delay and that they were entitled to a sum in excess of the contract price on a quantum meruit basis (ie reasonable recompense for the benefit which they had conferred). The

166

House of Lords disagreed, holding that the mere fact that unforeseen circumstances had delayed the performance of the contract and made it more costly to perform did not discharge the contract.

1 Paras 12.2–12.9 below.
2 Paras 14.36–14.53 below.
3 [1956] AC 696, [1956] 2 All ER 145, HL.

Supervening destruction or unavailability

10.3 A contract is discharged by frustration if performance of it is rendered impossible by the subsequent destruction or unavailability of a specific thing contemplated by the contract as essential to its performance. A leading authority is *Taylor v Caldwell*.[1] The defendants agreed to hire a music hall and gardens to the plaintiffs on specified days for the purpose of concerts. Before the first of the specified days, the music hall was destroyed by fire without the fault of either party. The defendants were held not liable for breach of contract because performance of the contract had become impossible through the destruction of the hall and they were not at fault. The contract was therefore frustrated and both parties discharged from their contractual obligations.

The subsequent unavailability of a thing will frustrate a contract if it renders performance of the contract in accordance with its terms impossible. This is shown by *Nickoll and Knight v Ashton, Edridge & Co*.[2] The defendants sold the plaintiffs a cargo of cotton seed to be shipped 'per steamship *Orlando* during the month of January'. Before the time for shipping arrived, the ship was so damaged by stranding as to be unable to load in January. It was held that the contract was discharged by frustration.

In order that a contract be frustrated under the present heading, the thing which has been destroyed or is otherwise unavailable must have been expressly or impliedly required by the contract for its performance. This point is well illustrated by *Tsakiroglou & Co Ltd v Noblee & Thorl GmbH*,[3] which concerned a contract for the sale of groundnuts which were to be shipped from the Sudan to Hamburg during November or December 1956. Both parties contemplated that the ship would proceed via the Suez Canal but this was not stated in the contract. On 2 November 1956, the Canal was closed (and remained so for five months). The House of Lords held that the unavailability of the Canal did not frustrate the contract, one of its reasons being that there was no express provision in the contract for shipping via the Canal, nor could a provision be implied to that effect, because the route was immaterial to the buyers. A fortiori, unavailability of a thing does not frustrate the contract if it merely affects the method of performance contemplated by one of the parties.[4] In *Nickoll and Knight v Ashton, Edridge & Co*, for instance, the contract would not have been frustrated if, instead of the name of the ship on which the cargo was to be loaded being stated in the contract, the defendant sellers had merely intended to load on that ship.

1 (1863) 3 B & S 826.
2 [1901] 2 KB 126.
3 [1962] AC 93, [1961] 2 All ER 179, HL.
4 *Blackburn Bobbin Co v T W Allen & Sons* [1918] 2 KB 467, CA.

Fundamental change of circumstances

10.4 A contract is frustrated if an event occurs of such gravity that,

167

although technically the contract could still be performed, it would be the performance of a radically different contract from that contemplated.

In *Jackson v Union Marine Insurance Co Ltd*,[1] a ship was chartered to sail from Liverpool to Newport and there to load rails and then sail to San Francisco with them. She ran aground en route to Newport on 3 January and was not re-floated until 18 February, repairs not being completed until August. It was held that the charterparty had been discharged by frustration because it was found as a fact that the particular voyage contemplated by the parties had become impossible through the ship's temporary unavailability; that a voyage undertaken after the ship had been repaired would have been a different voyage—a voyage for which the shipowner had not contracted and for which the charterers had not the cargo; a voyage as different as though it had been described as intended to be a spring voyage, while the one after repair would be an autumn voyage. A similar decision was reached in *Metropolitan Water Board v Dick, Kerr & Co Ltd*.[2] The company contracted with the Board to construct a reservoir within six years, subject to a proviso that time could be extended if delay was caused by difficulties, impediments or obstructions. After two years had elapsed the Minister of Munitions, acting under statutory powers, required the company to stop work on the contract and remove and sell their plant. The House of Lords held that the interruption created by the prohibition was of such a nature and duration that the contract, if resumed, would in effect be radically different from that originally made. Therefore it was frustrated.

These cases can be contrasted with *Tsakiroglou & Co Ltd v Noblee & Thorl GmbH*. In that case, the House of Lords held that the contract was not frustrated by the closure of the Suez Canal because of voyage round the Cape of Good Hope would not be commercially or fundamentally different from shipping via the Canal, albeit it was more expensive for the sellers.

1 (1874) LR 10 CP 125.
2 [1918] AC 119, HL.

Death or other personal incapacity
10.5 A contract of employment, or any other contract which can only be performed by a party personally, eg a contract to paint a portrait, is discharged by frustration if that party dies[1] or is otherwise rendered *permanently* incapable of performing it.

If a person becomes *temporarily* incapable of performing such a contract, it may be discharged. Normally, whether or not the temporary incapacity frustrates the contract depends on whether, in the light of the probable duration of the incapacity at its inception, performance after it has ceased would be radically different from what was envisaged by the contract and in effect be the substitution of a new contract. In *Morgan v Manser*,[2] the defendant, a comedian, entered into a contract with the plaintiff in 1938 whereby he engaged the plaintiff's services as manager for ten years. In 1940, the defendant was called up and was not demobilised until 1946. It was held that the contract was discharged by frustration in 1940 since it was then likely that the defendant would have to remain in the forces for a very long time. Similarly, if the duration of an employee's illness is likely to be so lengthy as to make performance of a contract of employment for a specified period radically different from that undertaken by him and accepted by his employer, the contract will be discharged by frustration, and so will a contract to perform at a concert on a specified day by an illness of short duration.[3] Conversely, a contract of a personal nature for a specified duration is not frustrated by the illness of a party where this is likely to last for only a small part of the specified period: further performance after the party becomes available again will not be the performance of a radically different contract.

1 *Stubbs v Holywell Rly Co Ltd* (1867) LR 2 Exch 311.
2 [1948] 1 KB 184, [1947] 2 All ER 666.
3 *Robinson v Davison* (1871) LR 6 Exch 269.

10.6 The situation is more complicated where (as in the majority of cases) employment is carried on under a contract of an indefinite duration terminable by notice. There is a decision of the Employment Appeal Tribunal to the effect that the doctrine of frustration does not apply to such a contract.[1] However, this goes against the weight of authority, and the better view is that the doctrine does apply to such a contract,[2] albeit that the approach is somewhat different to that outlined in the last paragraph. The question of frustration often arises here where an employee who has been ill is not given his job back and when he brings proceedings for unfair dismissal he is met by the defence that his contract of employment has already been terminated by a frustrating event, ie his illness. In this context, recent cases show that the question of frustration is to be judged not in the light of the probable duration of the illness at its inception but on the basis of whether, in the light of the situation before the material time (normally, the time of the alleged dismissal), further performance of the employee's future obligations would be radically different from what was envisaged by the contract. The judges have laid down a number of factors to be considered *cumulatively* in answering this test, such as:

a. the terms of the contract, including provisions as to sick pay. (Where there is a provision for sick pay there is a presumption against frustration if the employee appears likely to return during the period of its payment.);

b. how long the employment was likely to last in the absence of sickness;

c. the nature of the employment (for example, in the case of a 'key worker', the need to engage a replacement);

d. the nature of the illness, and how long it has already continued;

e. the period of past employment;[3]

f. whether the time has arrived when the employer can no longer reasonably be expected to keep the sick employee's job open for him; and

g. the acts or omissions of the employer (for example, where the employer has not thought it right to dismiss the absent employee, his reasons for this are *one* of the relevant *factors*).[4]

1 *Harman v Flexible Lamps* [1980] IRLR 418.
2 Eg the cases cited in footnotes 3 and 4.
3 *Marshall v Harland and Wolff Ltd* [1972] 2 All ER 715, [1972] 1 WLR 899.
4 *Egg Stores (Stamford Hill) Ltd v Leibovici* [1976] IRLR 376, [1977] ICR 260; *Hart v A R Marshall & Son (Bulwell) Ltd* [1978] 2 All ER 413, [1977] 1 WLR 1067.

Supervening illegality
10.7 A change in the law or in the circumstances may make performance

of the contract illegal. If the change is such as to make it impossible to perform the contract legally it is discharged by frustration. In *White and Carter Ltd v Carbis Bay Garage Ltd,*[1] for instance, it was held that a contract made in 1939 to display advertisements for three years was frustrated by wartime Defence Regulations prohibiting advertisements of the type in question. On the other hand, in *Cricklewood Property and Investment Trust Ltd v Leighton's Investment Trust Ltd,*[2] the House of Lords held that a 99-year building lease was not frustrated by Defence Regulations prohibiting building for only a small part of that term: performance had merely been suspended, not made impossible.

1   [1941] 2 All ER 633, CA.
2   [1945] AC 221, [1945] 1 All ER 252, HL.

Supervening destruction of a basic assumption on which the parties contracted

10.8   A contract is discharged by frustration if, although it is physically and legally possible for each party to perform his obligations under the contract, a change of circumstances has destroyed a *basic assumption* on which *the parties* contracted. In *Krell v Henry,*[1] the defendant agreed to hire a flat in Pall Mall from the plaintiff for 26 and 27 June, 1902, on one of which days Edward VII was to be crowned. To the plaintiff's knowledge, the defendant hired the flat in order to view the Coronation processions, but this was not mentioned in their written contract. The processions were postponed because of the King's illness. The Court of Appeal held that a view of the processions was not simply the purpose of the defendant in hiring the flat but the basis of the contract for both parties, and that since the postponement of the processions prevented this being achieved the contract was frustrated.

It is not enough that the purpose of one party in making the contract cannot be fulfilled; the basis on which both parties contracted must have been destroyed. This is shown by *Herne Bay Steamboat Co v Hutton,*[2] which also reveals the difficulty in drawing the distinction. The defendant chartered a ship from the plaintiffs for 28 and 29 June, 1902, for the express purpose of taking fare paying passengers to see the Coronation naval review at Spithead and to cruise round the Fleet. The review was cancelled, but the Fleet remained. The Court of Appeal held that the charterparty was not frustrated because the holding of the review was not the basis on which both parties had contracted and it was irrelevant that the purpose of the defendant was defeated.

1   [1903] 2 KB 740, CA.
2   [1903] 2 KB 683, CA.

Limits

10.9   There are no limits on the *type* of contract to which, as a matter of law, the doctrine of frustration can apply. In relation to most types of contract, the applicability of the doctrine is long-established; but it was only in 1980 in *National Carriers Ltd v Panalpina (Northern) Ltd*[1] that the House of Lords finally decided, with one dissentient, that the doctrine of frustration is applicable to a lease, although on the facts the particular lease was not frustrated. Their Lordships stated that cases where a lease would be frustrated would be extremely rare. In the case of a long lease, and it must be remembered that a lease may often be for 99 years or 999 years, a prime reason is that, if the lessee is only deprived temporarily of the use of the premises, the interruption of use will almost never be for long enough to frustrate the contract. Moreover, in the case of the destruction, or the like, of the premises, the lease will normally expressly provide for that event by covenants as to insurance and rebuilding, and thereby exclude the doctrine of frustration.

A contract for a lease and a contract for the sale of land can, of course, be discharged by frustration.[2] However, it is clear that such a contract will only be frustrated in the most extreme cases, since it has been held, for example, that a contract for the sale of premises is not frustrated simply because, before completion of the contract by conveyance, they are destroyed[3] or made subject to a compulsory purchase order.[4] In these cases, at least, the purchaser will be compensated by the payment of insurance monies or compulsory purchase compensation. Much greater hardship will be suffered by the person who has contracted to lease or buy land for re-development but before completion the buildings on it are listed as being of special architectural interest, so that re-development becomes difficult or impossible and the land loses most of its value. It has been held that the contract is not frustrated in such a case,[5] and consequently the person who has contracted to lease or buy remains bound to go ahead with a venture which is financially disastrous.

1   [1981] AC 675, [1981] 1 All ER 161, HL.
2   Contract for a lease: *Rom Securities Ltd v Rogers (Holdings) Ltd* (1967) 205 Estates Gazette 427; contract for sale of land: assumed in *Amalgamated Investment and Property Co Ltd v John Walker & Sons Ltd* [1976] 3 All ER 509, [1977] 1 WLR 164, CA.
3   *Paine v Meller* (1801) 6 Ves 349.
4   *Hillingdon Estates Co v Stonefield Estates Ltd* [1952] Ch 627, [1952] 1 All ER 853.
5   *Amalgamated Investment and Property Co Ltd v John Walker & Sons Ltd* [1976] 3 All ER 509, [1977] 1 WLR 164, CA.

Express provision for frustrating event
10.10   The doctrine of frustration does not apply if the parties have made provision to deal with the frustrating event which has occurred. There is one exception: a contract is frustrated by supervening illegality despite an express provision to the contrary.[1]

A provision concerned with the effect of a possible future event is narrowly construed and, unless on its true construction it covers the frustrating event in question, the doctrine of frustration is not ousted. This is shown by *Metropolitan Water Board v Dick, Kerr & Co Ltd,*[2] discussed above, where the contract for the reservoir provided that in the event of delays 'however caused' the contractors were to be given an extension of time. The House of Lords held that this provision did not prevent the doctrine of frustration applying because it did not cover the particular event which had occurred. Although the event was literally within the provision, the provision could be construed as limited to temporary difficulties, such as shortage of supplies, and not as extending to events which fundamentally altered the nature of the contract and which could not have been in the parties' contemplation when they made the contract.

1   *Ertel Bieber & Co v Rio Tinto Co Ltd* [1918] AC 260, HL.
2   [1918] AC 119, HL.

Foreseen and foreseeable events

10.11 If, by reason of special knowledge, the risk of the particular frustrating event was foreseen or foreseeable by only *one* party the doctrine of frustration cannot apply. It is up to that party to provide against the risk of that event, and if he fails to do so and cannot perform the contract he is liable for breach.[1]

On the other hand, where the risk of the frustrating event was foreseen or foreseeable by both parties, but they did not make provision to deal with it, the doctrine of frustration can apply.[2] In each case, however, it is a question of construction whether the failure to make provision for the event means that each party took the risk of it rendering contractual performance impossible or whether, in the absence of any such intention, the doctrine of frustration should apply to discharge the contract.[3]

1   *Walton Harvey Ltd v Walker and Homfrays Ltd* [1931] 1 Ch 274, CA.
2   *W J Tatem Ltd v Gamboa* [1939] 1 KB 132, [1938] 3 All ER 135; *The Eugenia* [1964] 2 QB 226, [1964] 1 All ER 161, CA.
3   *Chandler Bros Ltd v Boswell* [1936] 3 All ER 179, CA; *The Eugenia* [1964] 2 QB 226. [1964] 1 All ER 161, CA.

Fault of a party

10.12 The doctrine of frustration can only apply if the frustrating event occurred without any fault on the part of either party. The onus of proving fault is on the party alleging it.[1] A deliberate election to pursue a course of conduct which renders performance of the contract impossible or illegal is clearly established as fault in this context; that conduct may in itself be a breach of contract,[2] but it is not necessary that it should be. In *Maritime National Fish Ltd v Ocean Trawlers Ltd*,[3] the plaintiffs chartered to the defendants a trawler fitted with an otter trawl. Both parties knew that use of an otter trawl without a licence from a minister was illegal. Later, the defendants applied for licences for five trawlers which they were operating, including the plaintiffs'. They were only granted three licences and were asked to specify the three trawlers which they wished to have licensed. The defendants named three trawlers other than the plaintiffs'. They then claimed that they were no longer bound by the charterparty because it had been frustrated. The Privy Council held that the frustration was due to the defendants' deliberate act in not specifying the plaintiffs' trawler for a licence and that therefore the doctrine of frustration did not apply and, the charterparty not having been discharged by frustration, the plaintiffs could recover the hire under it.

It has not yet been decided whether a negligent, as opposed to deliberate, act rendering performance of the contract impossible constitutes sufficient fault to render the doctrine of frustration inapplicable.

1   *The Kingswood* [1942] AC 154, [1941] 2 All ER 165, HL.
2   As in *The Eugenia* [1964] 2 QB 226, [1964] 1 All ER 161, CA. In fact, the deliberate conduct in question may constitute a breach by both parties: *The Hannah Blumenthal* [1983] AC 854, [1983] 1 All ER 34, HL.
3   [1935] AC 524, PC.

Effect

10.13 Frustration does not merely make the contract terminable at the election of a party: the frustrating event *automatically* discharges the contract at the time that it is frustrated[1] (except that provisions intended by the parties to apply in the event of frustration, such as one dealing with its consequences, remain in force).[2] Where a contract is severable,[3] part may be discharged by frustration and part remain in force.[4] Leaving aside the complicated question of the effect of frustration on money paid or payable under the contract, the effect of frustration on other obligations under the contract is governed by the common law and is as follows: the discharge of a contract by frustration releases both parties from further performance of any such obligations due after the frustrating event[5] but not from any such obligations due before that time, which remain enforceable.[5]

Turning to the effect of frustration on money paid or payable under the contract, the position is as follows.

1 *Hirji Mulji v Cheong Yue SS Co Ltd* [1926] AC 497, PC.
2 *Heyman v Darwins Ltd* [1942] AC 356, [1942] 1 All ER 337, HL; *B. P. Exploration Co (Libya) Ltd v Hunt (No 2)* [1983] 2 AC 352, [1982] 1 All ER 925, CA; affd ibid, HL.
3 Para 9.15 above.
4 *Denny, Mott and Dickson Ltd v James B Fraser & Co Ltd* [1944] AC 265 at 278–280; *The Nema* [1982] AC 724, [1981] 2 All ER 1030, HL.
5 *Chandler v Webster* [1904] 1 KB 493, CA.

Money paid or payable under the contract before the occurrence of the frustrating event

10.14 At common law, the original position was that an obligation to pay money due before the frustrating event remained enforceable and money paid under the contract before that event was irrecoverable.[1] However, in 1942, in *Fibrosa Spolka Akcyjna v Fairbairn Lawson Combe Barbour Ltd*,[2] a case where money payable in advance for machinery had been paid but the contract had been frustrated before any of the machinery had been delivered, the House of Lords held that the money could be recovered in quasi-contract on the ground of a total failure of consideration, in the sense that the buyers had got nothing of what they had bargained for.

Nevertheless, the decision in the *Fibrosa* case left the law unjust in two ways:

a. The decision only permitted recovery if there had been a total failure of consideration. This could be unjust to the payer of the money because, if he had received any part, however small, of the contractual performance, he could not recover a penny of what he had paid.

b. The decision could also be unjust to a payee who was ordered to return a pre-payment because he might have incurred expenses in seeking to perform the contract.

1 *Chandler v Webster* [1904] 1 KB 493, CA.
2 [1943] AC 32, [1942] 2 All ER 122, HL.

10.15 These injustices were removed by the Law Reform (Frustrated Contracts) Act 1943. Section 1(2) of the Act provides:

a. All sums *payable* under the contract *before* the frustrating event *cease to be payable* whether or not there has been a total failure of consideration.

b. All sums *paid* under the contract *before* the frustrating event are *recoverable* whether or not there has been a total failure of consideration.

c. The court has a discretionary power to allow the payee to set off against the sums so paid or payable a sum not exceeding the value of the expenses he has incurred before the frustrating event in, or for the purpose of, the performance of the contract.

If the court exercises the power referred to in c., it allows the payee to retain the amount stipulated by it (if he has been paid) or to recover the stipulated amount (if the money was payable but not paid). The stipulated amount, which may include an element in respect of overhead expenses and of any work or services performed personally by the payee,[1] cannot exceed the sums paid or payable to him. The following illustrates the operation of these provisions. X contracts with Y to manufacture and deliver certain machinery by 1 March for £5,000, £1,000 to be paid on 1 January and the balance of £4,000 on delivery. The contract is discharged by frustration on 1 February before the machinery is delivered but after X has incurred expenses of £500 in making the machinery. Pursuant to s1(2), Y need not pay the £1,000 if he has not paid it before 1 February or, if he has, he can recover the £1,000, but the court may order Y to pay X up to £500 for his expenses or may allow X to retain up to £500, as the case may be.

1   Law Reform (Frustrated Contracts) Act 1943, s1(4).

Money payable under the contract after the occurrence of the frustrating event
10.16   Such money is not recoverable by the party to whom it was due, in accordance with the rule that frustration releases both parties from performing any contractual obligation due after the frustrating event. Thus, in *Krell v Henry*,[1] it was held that the owner of the flat could not recover a sum payable for the hire of the flat because it was not due until a time after the processions had been postponed (the frustrating event). Likewise, the balance of £4,000 referred to in the example in the previous paragraph is not recoverable by X because it was not due until after the frustrating event. In further contrast to the rules outlined in para 10.15 above, the courts do not have power to allow a claim in respect of his expenses by a party to whom money was payable only after the frustrating event, because the Act of 1943 does not apply in such a case.

1   [1903] 2 KB 704, CA; para 10.8 above.

Award for valuable benefit obtained
10.17   At common law, a party who had benefited another by partly performing the contract before it was frustrated could not recover any sum of money for this.[1] This rule was particularly harsh where payment was not due to him until after the occurrence of the frustrating event because where money was paid or payable before that time he could retain or recover it, as the case might be.

The Law Reform (Frustrated Contracts) Act 1943, s1(3) now makes a monetary award available to either party for a valuable benefit conferred on the other. It provides that where a party to a frustrated contract has, by reason of anything done by any other party in, or for the purpose of, the performance of the contract, obtained a valuable benefit before the frustrating event (other than the payment of money to which s1(2) applies), that other party may recover from him such sum, if any, as the court considers just, having regard to all the circumstances of the case.

In assessing the amount of an award under s1(3), the court must first identify and value the benefit obtained by the benefited party (whom we will call B). Where services have been performed by the other party to the contract (whom we will call A), B's benefit should normally be identified as the end product of those services, rather than as the services themselves.[2] It follows, for example, that, in the case of a building contract which is frustrated when the building is partially completed, the benefit to be valued is the uncompleted building, not the work put in by the builder. This is important because sometimes a relatively small service performed under a contract may confer a substantial benefit, and vice versa. Generally speaking, valuation of the benefit must be made as at the date of the frustration and not at an earlier time when the benefit was received.[2] In particular, the court must take into account the effect in relation to the benefit of the circumstances giving rise to the frustration,[3] so that if a builder (A) contracts to do building work on B's house and, when he has nearly finished, the house (including A's work) is seriously damaged by fire, and the building contract is thereby frustrated, the valuation of the benefit relates to the value of what remains of A's work as at the date of frustration. From the benefit valued in the above way there must be deducted any expenses incurred by the benefited party (B) before the contract was frustrated, including any sums paid or payable by him to A under the contract and retained or recoverable by A under s1(2).[4]

The value of the benefit assessed by the court under the above principles forms the upper limit of an award under s1(3) but not the award itself. This is because the court, having identified and valued the benefit, must then decide on a 'just sum' within that upper limit to award to A in respect of his *performance*. Here, the court should take into particular account the contract consideration, since in many cases it will be unjust to award more than that consideration or a rateable part of it. The fact that A has broken the contract in some way before the frustration has no bearing on the just sum to be awarded to him, although B's claim to damages for the breach may be the subject of a counter-claim or set-off if not statute-barred.[5]

The operation of the Act of 1943 can be illustrated as follows: A, a jobbing decorator, contracts with B to paint the outside of B's house for £300, £100 to be paid on 1 September and the rest on completion. B pays A the £100 on 1 September. After A has painted most of the house the contract is frustrated, A having been seriously incapacitated in a car crash. Under s1(2), A must return the £100 to B, unless and to the extent that the court exercises its discretion to allow A to retain some or all of it. Suppose his expenses were £50 and the court allows him to retain this—only £50 will be recoverable by B. The obligation as to the further £200 is, of course, discharged by frustration and A cannot claim this from B. However, as A has conferred a valuable benefit on B before the frustrating event, s1(3) comes into play. Suppose that the value of the paintwork completed by A is £175 as at the date of the frustration, the court must then deduct what it has allowed A to retain under s1(2) and the resulting sum (ie £125) will be the upper limit of the 'just sum' awarded by the court under s1(3).

1 *Appleby v Myers* (1867) LR 2 CP 651.
2 *BP Exploration Co (Libya) Ltd v Hunt (No 2)* [1983] 2 AC 352, [1982] 1 All ER 925; affd ibid, HL.

3 Law Reform (Frustrated Contracts) Act 1943, s1(3)(b).
4 Ibid, s1(3)(a).
5 *BP Exploration Co (Libya) Ltd v Hunt (No 2)* [1983] 2 AC 352, [1982] 1 All ER 925; affd ibid, HL.

Scope of the Act of 1943

10.18 Where a contract to which the Act applies is severable, e g a contract to work for a year at £400 a month,[1] and a severable part of it is wholly performed before the frustrating event, or wholly performed except in respect of payment of sums which are or can be ascertained under the contract, that part is to be treated as if it were a separate contract and had not been frustrated, and the Act is only applicable to the remainder of the contract.[2] The result is that, if the employee under the above contract works for two months and two weeks and then dies before any salary has been paid, his executors can recover the two months' salary owing to him (each month being treated as a separate contract) *plus* an award under s1(3) of the Act for any valuable benefit conferred by the deceased on the employer during the remaining two weeks.

Where a contract contains a provision (such as one precluding any recovery of any award under the Act or one limiting such an award) which is intended to have effect in the event of circumstances arising which operate, or would but for the provision operate, to frustrate the contract, or is intended to have effect whether such circumstances arise or not, the court must give effect to that provision and only give effect to s1(2) and (3) of the Act to such extent, if any, as is consistent with that provision.[3]

The Act applies to contracts to which the Crown is a party.[4]

The Act does not apply to the following types of contract:

a. A contract of insurance.[5] Generally, a premium is not returnable once the risk has attached.

b. A contract to which the Sale of Goods Act 1979, s7 applies.[6] Section 7 provides that where there is an agreement to sell specific goods, and subsequently, without any fault on the part of the seller or buyer, the goods *perish before the risk passes to the buyer*, the agreement is thereby avoided. Where a contract is avoided under s7, the principles laid down by the House of Lords in the *Fibrosa* case[7] apply. Under these a buyer who has paid for the goods before they perished can recover his payment only if there has been a total failure of consideration, in which case the seller has no right of set-off for any expenses he may have incurred in seeking to perform the contract before the goods perished.

1 Para 9.15 above.
2 S2(4).
3 S2(3). See further, *BP Exploration Co (Libya) Ltd v Hunt (No 2)* [1983] 2 AC 352, [1982] 1 All ER 925; affd ibid, HL.
4 S2(2).
5 S2(5)(b).
6 S2(5)(c).
7 Para 10.14 above.

Chapter 11
Remedies for breach of contract

11.1 In the event of a breach of contract, the injured party may have one or more of the following remedies:

a. He may, subject to any applicable and effective exemption clause,[1] and to the rules discussed in paras 11.2 to 11.20 below, recover damages for any loss suffered as a result of the breach by bringing an action for damages for breach of contract.

b. However, if a breach consists of the other party's failure to pay a debt, ie the contractually agreed price or other remuneration, which *is* due under the contract, the appropriate course for the injured party is to bring an action for the agreed sum to recover *that* amount, rather than an action for damages. We discuss this further in paras 11.21 to 11.23 below. A person who recovers an agreed sum may also recover damages for any further loss which he has suffered.

c. In the case of a repudiatory breach, he may terminate the contract for breach, ie accept the breach as discharging the contract, thereby discharging himself from any obligation to perform the contract further. If the injured party elects to terminate for repudiatory breach, he may also bring an action for damages for any loss suffered. We have already discussed termination for repudiatory breach in detail in paras 9.3 to 9.23 above.

d. Where he has performed part of his own obligations, he may sue in quasi-contract on a quantum meruit for the value of what he has done *if he terminates the contract for breach*. We discuss this further in para 11.24 below.

e. Where he has paid the contractual price, but the other party has totally failed to perform his side of the contract, the injured party may sue in quasi-contract (a matter which we discuss in ch 16) for the return of the money paid *if he terminates the contract for breach*.[2]

f. In appropriate cases, he may seek a decree of specific performance or an injunction in addition to, instead of, damages. We discuss this further in paras 11.25 to 11.32 below.

1 Paras 9.24–9.53 above.
2 See further para 16.7b below.

Damages
11.2 Damages for breach of contract are not awarded to punish the defendant (with the result that the amount awarded is not affected by the

manner of the breach or the motive behind it[1]) but to compensate the plaintiff for the loss or damage which he has suffered as a result of the breach of contract. This means that where he has not suffered any loss or damage as a result of the breach the damages recoverable by him will be purely nominal (usually in the region of £2.00 to £10.00). However, in one exceptional case, a plaintiff can recover substantial damages for a loss which he has not suffered. This case is where the plaintiff made the contract as agent[2] or trustee[3] for another. If the contract is broken and the plaintiff sues for damages on the other's behalf he can recover substantial damages for the loss suffered by the other as a result of the breach.[4]

1 *Addis v Gramophone Co Ltd* [1909] AC 488, HL.
2 Ch 17 below.
3 Para 6.27 above.
4 *Lloyd's v Harper* (1880) 16 Ch D 290, CA; *Woodar Investment Development Ltd v Wimpey Construction (UK) Ltd* [1980] 1 All ER 571, [1980] 1 WLR 277, HL; see further para 6.27 above.

11.3 The principal function of damages for breach of contract is to put the plaintiff into the same position, so far as money can, *as if the contract had been performed.*[1]

In achieving this, damages are most commonly awarded to compensate the plaintiff for the loss of his bargain or of his expectations under the contract. Such damages can be illustrated as follows. Suppose that X agrees to sell some surveying equipment to a surveyor but fails to deliver it. The surveyor can get damages, subject to the rules discussed later in this chapter, to compensate him for being deprived of, and for losing the opportunity of making profitable use of, the equipment until he can acquire a substitute. Another example of damages for loss of bargain or expectations is where, because of the breach of contract, the thing contracted for is worth less than it would have been if there had been no breach of contract. Assuming that he cannot, or does not, reject the defective thing, the injured party can recover damages for loss of expectations and they will be the difference between the thing's actual value and what it would have been worth if it had been in accordance with the contract. As a last example of damages for loss of bargain or expectations, a negligent surveyor will have to pay his client damages assessed on the basis of the difference between the property's actual value and what it would have been worth if it had been in accordance with the survey, as opposed to the costs of repairing the property.

In some cases, damages are awarded to compensate the plaintiff for expenditure which he has incurred in reliance on the contract and which has been wasted as a result of its breach. Damages of this type are called damages for reliance loss. By way of an extension, damages can even be recovered for expenses incurred prior to, and in anticipation of, the contract and wasted as a result of the breach. In *Lloyd v Stanbury*,[2] for instance, the plaintiff, who had made a contract to buy a farm, which was broken by the defendant's failure to complete, was awarded damages for (inter alia) the following losses incurred before there was a binding contract of sale: legal expenses incurred in carrying out pre-contract searches and drafting the contract, and the cost of moving a caravan to the farm, as a temporary home for the defendant, prior to and in anticipation of the contract.

Because they compensate for expenditure which has been wasted *as a result of the breach of contract*, damages for reliance loss cannot be awarded if this would make the plaintiff better off than if the contract had been performed; the obvious example is where he has made a bad bargain. This is shown by *C and P Haulage v Middleton*,[3] where A was granted by B a contractual licence (on a six-month renewable basis) to occupy premises as a workshop. A spent money in making the premises suitable, although the contract provided that fixtures installed by him were not to be removed. Ten weeks before the end of a six-month term, A was ejected in breach of the contractual licence. As a temporary measure, A was permitted by his local authority to use his own home as a workshop, which he did until well after the six-month term had expired. The Court of Appeal held that A could only recover nominal damages. He could not recover, as reliance loss, his expenditure in equipping the premises, because, it was held, if the contract had been lawfully terminated at the end of the six-month term, there would have been no question of him recovering that expenditure and, therefore, to award him such damages would leave him better off than if the contract had been wholly performed. His ability to use his home as a workshop meant that he suffered no loss in terms of the deprivation of his licence. In order to defeat a plaintiff's claim for wasted expenditure, the onus is on the defendant to prove that the expenditure would not have been recovered if the contract had been performed.[4]

A plaintiff has an unfettered right to frame his claim as one for loss of bargain or expectations or as one for reliance loss. Although a claim for reliance loss is particularly appropriate where a plaintiff cannot prove any loss of expectations or can only prove a small loss of this type, a claim for reliance loss is not limited to such cases.[4]

Damages for loss of bargain or expectations and damages for reliance loss are not mutually exclusive since claims for both can be combined if this does not have the effect of compensating the plaintiff twice over for the same loss.[5]

1 *Wertheim v Chicoutimi Pulp Co* [1911] AC 301, PC.
2 [1971] 2 All ER 267, [1971] 1 WLR 535. Also see *Anglia Television Ltd v Reed* [1972] 1 QB 60, [1971] 3 All ER 690, CA.
3 [1983] 3 All ER 94, [1984] 1 WLR 1461, CA.
4 *C.C.C. Films (London) Ltd v Impact Quadrant Films Ltd* [1985] QB16, [1984] 3 All ER 298.
5 *Cullinane v British 'Rema' Manufacturing Co Ltd* [1954] 1 QB 292, [1953] 2 All ER 1257, CA.

11.4 Subject to the rules of remoteness, a plaintiff can recover not merely for the above types of economic loss resulting from the breach of contract, but also for personal injury, injury to property, inconvenience or discomfort,[1] or disappointment, distress or upset, resulting from the breach. In *Jarvis v Swans Tours Ltd*,[2] for instance, the plaintiff booked a 15-day winter sports holiday with the defendants. He did so on the faith of the defendants' brochure, which described the holiday as a house party and promised a number of entertainments, including excellent skiing, a yodeller evening, a bar, and afternoon tea and cakes. In the first week there were 13 guests; in the second the plaintiff was entirely alone. The entertainments fell far short of the promised standard. The Court of Appeal held that the plaintiff was entitled to damages for mental distress and disappointment due to loss of enjoyment caused by the breach of contract. It is uncertain whether damages for emotional distress brought about by breach of contract can be awarded where the subject matter of the contract did not involve the giving of pleasure or enjoyment, unlike a contract to provide a holiday. In *Perry v Sidney Phillips & Son*,[3] damages for emotional distress were awarded against a surveyor who had negligently failed to draw his client's attention to defects in a house which the client later bought. On the other hand, it is clearly established that damages for emotional distress cannot be awarded where the breach is of an employment contract (eg wrongful dismissal)[4] and in a recent case[5] concerned with an employment contract the Court of Appeal stated that such damages for breach of contract cannot be awarded unless the contract was one to provide peace of mind or freedom from distress.

1 *Hobbs v London and South Western Rly Co* (1875) LR 10 QB 111.
2 [1973] QB 233, [1973] 1 All ER 71, CA.
3 [1982] 3 All ER 705, CA.
4 *Addis v Gramophone Co Ltd* [1909] AC 488, HL.
5 *Bliss v South East Thames Regional Health Authority* [1985] IRLR 308, CA.

Remoteness of damage

11.5 In order to succeed in his action for damages, the plaintiff must, of course, prove that the loss or damage (hereafter simply referred to as 'loss') which he has suffered was caused by the defendant's breach of contract.[1] But such proof is not in itself enough to entitle him to damages for that loss, because a defendant will only be liable for it if it was not too 'remote'. Whether or not loss suffered is too remote is determined by applying the rule in *Hadley v Baxendale*[2] (as explained in *Victoria Laundry (Windsor) Ltd v Newman Industries Ltd*[3] and *The Heron II*[4]).

The rule, as explained, provides that damage is not too remote if one of the two following sub-rules is satisfied:

a. if the loss arises naturally, ie according to the usual course of things, from the breach of contract as the probable result of it; or

b. if the loss could reasonably be supposed to have been in the contemplation of the parties, when they made the contract, as the probable result of the breach of it.

Sub-rule a. deals with 'normal' damage which arises in the ordinary course of events, while sub-rule b. deals with 'abnormal' damage which arises from special circumstances.

1 *Weld-Blundell v Stephens* [1920] AC 956, HL.
2 (1854) 23 LJ Exch 179.
3 [1949] 2 KB 528, [1949] 1 All ER 997, CA.
4 [1969] 1 AC 350, [1967] 3 All ER 686, HL.

11.6 In the light of subsequent cases, a numer of things can be said about both sub-rules.

First, the plaintiff can only recover for such loss as was, *at the time of the contract*, within the reasonable contemplation of the parties as the probable result of its breach, *had they had their attention drawn to the possibility of the breach which has in fact occurred.*[1]

Second, what was within the parties' reasonable contemplation depends on the knowledge 'possessed' by them at that time. For this purpose, knowledge 'possessed' is of two kinds: one imputed, the other actual. Under sub-rule a., everyone is taken to know (ie knowledge is imputed) the 'ordinary course of things' and, consequently, what loss is the probable result of a breach of contract in that ordinary course. In addition, 'knowledge possessed' may, in a particular case, include knowledge which the guilty party (and the other party) actually possess of special circumstances outside the ordinary course of things, of such a kind that the breach in these special circumstances would be liable to cause more loss. Such a case attracts sub-rule b. so as to make the additional loss recoverable.[2]

Third, provided the *type* of loss caused by a breach of contract was within the reasonable contemplation of the parties when the contract was made, the loss is not too remote, and damages can therefore be recovered for it, even though its *extent* was much greater than could have been reasonably contemplated[3] and even though it occurred in a way which could not have been reasonably contemplated.[4] An example is provided by *H. Parsons (Livestock) Ltd v Uttley Ingham & Co Ltd.*[5] The defendants supplied the plaintiffs with a hopper in which to store pig nuts. The hopper was not properly ventilated, and this constituted a breach of contract by the defendants; as a result, the pig nuts became mouldy and many of the plaintiffs' pigs suffered a rare intestinal disease (E coli) from which 254 of them died. The plaintiffs were awarded damages by the Court of Appeal for the loss sustained by the death and sickness of the pigs. The reasoning of the majority of the Court of Appeal was that, if the breach had been brought to the parties' attention and they had asked themselves what was likely to happen as a result, they would have contemplated the serious possibility that the pigs would become ill, and that, since the *type* of loss caused (physical harm) was within the parties' reasonable contemplation, it was irrelevant that its extent and the way in which it occurred were not.

1 *H. Parsons (Livestock) Ltd v Uttley Ingham & Co Ltd* [1978] QB 791, [1978] 1 All ER 525, CA.
2 *Victoria Laundry (Windsor) Ltd v Newman Industries Ltd* [1949] 2 KB 528, [1949] 1 All ER 997, CA.
3 *Wroth v Tyler* [1974] Ch 30, [1973] 1 All ER 897; *H. Parsons (Livestock) Ltd v Uttley Ingham & Co Ltd* [1978] QB 791, [1978] 1 All ER 525, CA.
4 *H. Parsons (Livestock) Ltd v Uttley Ingham & Co Ltd* [1978] QB 791, [1978] 1 All ER 525, CA.
5 [1978] QB 791, [1978] 1 All ER 525, CA.

11.7 The degree of probability which is required to satisfy the test of remoteness is that there must have been a serious possibility that the type of loss in question would occur.[1] Thus, it suffices that the plaintiff's loss is such as may reasonably be supposed to have been in the parties' contemplation as a serious possibility, had their attention been drawn to the possibility of the breach which has in fact occurred. It must be emphasised that the particular breach itself need not have been contemplated. Suppose that the loss had been caused by some defect in the subject matter of the contract which is unknown, or even unknowable, when the contract is made. The court has to assume, even though it is contrary to the facts, that the parties had in mind the breach which has occurred when it considers whether the plaintiff's loss was within their reasonable contemplation.[2]

1 *The Heron II* [1969] 1 AC 350, [1967] 3 All ER 686, HL.
2 *H. Parsons (Livestock) Ltd v Uttley Ingham & Co Ltd* [1978] QB 791, [1978] 1 All ER 525, CA.

11.8 The application of the contractual rule of remoteness can best be illustrated by reference to past decisions. In *Hadley v Baxendale*,[1] the plaintiff's mill at Gloucester was brought to a halt when a crankshaft broke. The shaft had to be sent to its makers in Greenwich as a pattern for a new one. The defendant carriers undertook to deliver it at Greenwich the following day, but in breach of contract delayed its delivery so that the duration of the stoppage at the mill was extended. The plaintiff's claim to recover damages for loss of profits caused by the defendants' delay was unsuccessful since this loss was held to be too remote. The basis of the court's decision was that the defendants only knew that they were transporting a broken shaft owned by the plaintiffs. The court applied the two sub-rules in turn, and held:

a. the plaintiffs might have had a spare shaft or been able to borrow one, and therefore the loss of profits did not arise in the usual course of events from the defendants' breach; and

b. on the facts known to the defendants (they were unaware of the lack of a substitute shaft), the loss of profits could not be supposed to have been within the reasonable contemplation of the parties at the time they made the contract as the probable result of the breach.

1   (1854) 23 LJ Exch 179.

11.9 In *Victoria Laundry (Windsor) Ltd v Newman Industries Ltd*,[1] the defendants agreed to sell to the plaintiffs, who were launderers and dyers, a boiler to be delivered on a certain date. The boiler was damaged in a fall and was not delivered until five months after the agreed delivery date. The plaintiffs claimed damages for loss of profits that would have been earned during the five-month period through the extension of their business, and also for loss of several highly lucrative dyeing contracts which they would have obtained with the Ministry of Supply. The Court of Appeal held that the plaintiffs could recover for the loss of 'normal' profits (ie those which would have been earned through an extension of the business) but not for the loss of 'exceptional' profits (ie loss of the highly lucrative contracts), which it treated as a different type of loss. This decision was based on the following application of the two sub-rules:

a. the defendants knew at the time of the contract that the plaintiffs were laundrymen and dyers and required the boiler for immediate use in their business and, with their technical experience and knowledge of the facts, it could be presumed that loss of 'normal' profits was foreseeable by them, and therefore within both parties' reasonable contemplation, as likely to result from the breach; but

b. in the absence of special knowledge, the defendents could not reasonably foresee the loss of the 'exceptional' profits under the highly lucrative contracts.

The case was, therefore, remitted to an official referee for a decision as to the amount of 'normal' profits which had been lost in the circumstances.

1   [1949] 2 KB 528, [1949] 1 All ER 997, CA.

11.10 In *The Heron II*,[1] the plaintiff sugar merchants chartered a ship from the defendant to carry a cargo of sugar from Constanza to Basrah.

The ship deviated in breach of contract and arrived in Basrah nine days later than expected. Because of a fall in the market price of sugar, the plaintiffs obtained £3,800 less for the cargo than would have been obtained if it had arrived on time. The defendant did not know of the plaintiffs' intention to sell the sugar in Basrah, but he did know that there was a market for sugar at Basrah and that the plaintiffs were sugar merchants. The House of Lords held that the plaintiffs' loss of profits (£3,800) was not too remote under sub-rule a., since knowledge could be imputed to the defendant that the goods might be sold at market price on their arrival in Basrah and that market prices were apt to fluctuate daily, and therefore the loss of profits was within the reasonable contemplation of the parties at the time of the contract as a serious possibility in the event of the breach in question.

1 [1969] 1 AC 350, [1967] 3 All ER 686, HL.

Measure of damages

11.11 Assuming that the loss is not too remote from the breach of contract, the next question which the court has to consider is the measure (ie quantification) of damages for that loss.

Generally, there are no specific rules for the quantification of damages. One exception relates to contracts for the sale of goods, where the Sale of Goods Act 1979 provides a number of rules, such as that where there is an available market for the goods in question a buyer who fails to accept and pay for them is liable, prima facie, to pay the difference between the contract price and the market or current price.[1] However, apart from such specific rules, it is up to the court to quantify adequate compensation for the plaintiff's loss as best it can. The fact that the precise assessment of damages is difficult does not prevent an award being made, as is shown by *Chaplin v Hicks*.[2] The defendant advertised that he would employ, as actresses, 12 women to be selected by him out of 50 chosen as the most beautiful by the readers of various newspapers, in which the candidates' photographs appeared. The plaintiff was one of the 50 chosen by the readers but the defendant made an unreasonable appointment for an interview with her, and selected 12 out of the 49 who were able to keep the appointment. In an action for breach of contract, the defendant contended that only nominal damages were payable, since the plaintiff would only have had a one in four chance of being selected. Nevertheless, the Court of Appeal refused to disturb an award of £100 damages for the loss of her chance of being selected.

Where damages are awarded to compensate the plaintiff for loss of his bargain they are normally assessed as at the date of the breach. However, this is not an absolute rule since, if its observance would give rise to injustice, the court has power to fix such other date as may be appropriate in the circumstances.[3] Thus, for example, where a breach of a contract of sale has occurred and, having reasonably sought an order for specific performance of the contract, the plaintiff elects to claim damages in lieu of specific performance or specific performance becomes impossible (without his default), damages should be assessed as at the date of the election[4] or of specific performance becoming aborted,[5] as the case may be. As another example, where the plaintiff could only reasonably have been expected to mitigate his loss at a point of time after the breach, damages should be assessed as at that point of time, or, if that point of time is not earlier, at the date of the hearing.[6]

In the case of an anticipatory breach of contract, damages for loss of bargain are assessed by reference to the time when performance ought to have been made, and not by reference to the time of the anticipatory breach.[7]

1 Sale of Goods Act 1979, s50(3).
2 [1911] 2 KB 786, CA.
3 *Johnson v Agnew* [1980] AC 367 at 400, [1979] 1 All ER 883 at 896.
4 *Domb v Isoz* [1980] Ch 548, [1980] 1 All ER 942, CA.
5 *Johnson v Agnew* [1980] AC 367, [1979] 1 All ER 883, HL.
6 *Radford v de Froberville* [1978] 1 All ER 33, [1977] 1 WLR 1262; *William Cory & Son Ltd v Wingate Investments (London Colney) Ltd* (1978) 248 Estates Gazette 687. For mitigation of loss, see paras 11.13 and 11.14 below.
7 *Tai Hing Cotton Mill Ltd v Kamsing Knitting Factory* [1979] AC 91, [1978] 1 All ER 515, PC; *Gebruder Metelmann GmbH & Co KG v NBR (London) Ltd* [1984] 1 Lloyd's Rep 614, CA.

Effect of tax liability

11.12   One consequence of the fact that damages are designed to compensate the plaintiff for his actual loss is that, whenever a claim for damages includes a claim for loss of income or profit, the income tax which would have been payable by the plaintiff if he had earned that income or profit may have to be taken into account.[1] Tax liability must certainly be taken into account in quantifying the damages in a contractual claim for wrongful dismissal,[2] but the extent to which it should be taken into account in other cases of breach of contract is uncertain.

Tax liability can only be taken into account if, and to the extent that, the sum awarded as damages is not taxable in the plaintiff's hands. The result is that tax liability is generally excluded in quantifying damages for loss of profits because such damages are normally subject to tax in the plaintiff's hands as part of the profits of his business.[3] In the case of damages for wrongful dismissal from employment, which (subject to mitigation, below) are based on the amount the employee would have earned under the contract, these are subject to tax in the plaintiff's hands, except for the first £25,000.[4] The result is that, in assessing damages of under £25,000 for wrongful dismissal, the court must take into account the plaintiff's tax liability and reduce the award accordingly;[5] but in the case of damages exceeding £25,000 the court must take the plaintiff's tax liability into account to the extent of the first £25,000, and reduce that part of the award accordingly, but not in relation to the excess over that sum.[6] In *Parsons v B.N.M. Laboratories Ltd*,[7] for instance, the plaintiff claimed, as damages for wrongful dismissal, loss of salary and commission amounting to £1,200. The Court of Appeal held that the sum must be reduced by £320, which was the amount of income tax payable on the lost salary and commission.

1 *British Transport Commission v Gourley* [1956] AC 185, [1955] 3 All ER 796, HL.
2 *Beach v Reed Corrugated Cases Ltd* [1956] 2 All ER 652, [1956] 1 WLR 807; *Parsons v B.N.M. Laboratories Ltd* [1964] 1 QB 95, [1963] 2 All ER 658, CA.
3 *Diamond v Campbell-Jones* [1961] Ch 22, [1960] 1 All ER 583.
4 Income and Corporation Taxes Act 1970, ss 187, 188 and Sch 4, as amended.
5 *Parsons v B.N.M. Laboratories Ltd* [1964] 1 QB 95, [1963] 2 All ER 658, CA.

6 *Bold v Brough, Nicholson and Hall Ltd* [1963] 3 All ER 849, [1964] 1 WLR 201; cf *Stewart v Glentaggart* [1963] TR 345, 1963 SC 300; *Shove v Downs Surgical plc* [1984] 1 All ER 7.
7 [1964] 1 QB 95, [1963] 2 All ER 658, CA.

Mitigation

11.13 The plaintiff cannot recover for loss which he could reasonably have avoided. Thus, the seller of goods which have been wrongly rejected by the buyer must not unreasonably refuse another's offer to buy them. Similarly, an employee who has been wrongfully dismissed must not unreasonably refuse an offer of employment from another.[1] If such refusals occur, the plaintiff is said to be in breach of his duty to mitigate his loss and cannot recover his unmitigated loss but only the loss which he would have suffered if the damage had been mitigated. If he would have suffered no loss at all, only nominal damages are recoverable.[1]

A leading case on the duty to mitigate is *Payzu Ltd v Saunders*.[2] A contract for the sale of goods by the defendant to the plaintiffs provided that delivery should be as required over a nine-month period and that payment should be made within one month of delivery. The plaintiffs failed to make prompt payment for the first instalment and the defendant, in breach of contract, refused to deliver any more instalments under the contract. He did, however, offer to deliver goods at the contract price if the plaintiffs would pay cash with each order. The plaintiffs refused to do so and brought an action for breach of contract, claiming the difference between the contract price and the market price (which had risen). The Court of Appeal held that the plaintiffs should have mitigated their loss by accepting the defendant's offer, and therefore the damages which they could recover were to be measured by the loss which they would have suffered if the offer had been accepted, not by the difference between the contract and market prices.

The following points may be noted about the duty to mitigate:

a. The phrase 'duty to mitigate' is somewhat misleading because the plaintiff is not legally obliged to do so. He is free to act as he judges to be in his best interest, but if he does so he cannot recover for loss which he could reasonably have avoided.[3]

b. The duty to mitigate may require the plaintiff to do something positive. In the examples given earlier on this page, the seller and the employee would equally have been in breach of their duty to mitigate if they had not made reasonable efforts to seek other offers to buy the goods or alternative equivalent employment: it would not necessarily excuse them that no one had spontaneously made them an offer. Damages cannot be recovered for any loss which would have been avoided if such reasonable steps had been taken.[4]

c. The duty to mitigate only requires the plaintiff to take reasonable steps to minimise his loss. He is not required to embark on hazardous litigation or to risk his commercial reputation in order to minimise his loss. In *Pilkington v Wood*,[5] for instance, the plaintiff failed to bring an action against a third pary, which, if successful would have reduced the loss suffered by him consequent on the defendant's breach of contract. It was held that since the litigation would have been hazardous the plaintiff's failure to embark on it did not involve a breach of the duty to mitigate: the duty did not extend this far.

d. If the plaintiff has to spend money in an endeavour to mitigate his loss, he can recover it as part of the damages awarded provided the expenditure was reasonable, and he can so recover notwithstanding that those steps subsequently prove to have aggravated the damage.[6]

1 *Brace v Calder* [1895] 2 QB 253, CA.
2 [1919] 2 KB 581, CA.
3 *The Solholt* [1983] 1 Lloyd's Rep 605 at 608.
4 *British Westinghouse Co v Underground Electric Rly Co of London* [1912] AC 673 at 689.
5 [1953] Ch 770, [1953] 2 All ER 810. Also see *London & South of England Building Society v Stone* [1983] 3 All ER 105, [1983] 1 WLR 1242, CA.
6 *Hoffberger v Ascot International Bloodstock Bureau Ltd* (1976) 120 Sol Jo 130, CA.

11.14 In some cases the duty to mitigate does not apply:

a. It does not apply where the buyer of either goods or land has a cause of action in damages for defects in the goods or land or for some other breach of contract and the seller offers to re-purchase the property. A refusal by the buyer, however capricious, will not prevent him recovering substantial damages.[1]

b. As we said in para 9.23 above, where there is an anticipatory breach of contract, the injured party has an option *either* to terminate the contract and sue immediately for damages *or* to affirm the contract and await the time of performance, in which case he can then bring an action for damages if the other party is still in breach. If the injured party elects to terminate he is under a duty to mitigate his loss.[2] On the other hand, the injured party is under no duty to mitigate his loss before performance is due if he affirms the contract.[3]

1 *Strutt v Whitnell* [1975] 2 All ER 510, [1975] 1 WLR 870, CA.
2 *Roth & Co v Taysen, Townsend & Co* (1895) 1 Com Cas 240; *Gebruder Metealmann GmbH & Co KG v NBR (London) Ltd* [1984] 1 Lloyd's Rep 614, CA.
3 Para 9.23c above.

Contributory negligence
11.15 The doctrine of contributory negligence, under which a plaintiff in a tort action may have his damages reduced where he is partly at fault,[1] does not apply to an action for breach of contract.[2] As a result, in an action for breach of contract, the court is faced with a somewhat artificial choice; the plaintiff's loss must be held to have resulted either wholly from his own fault (in which case he can recover nothing[3]) or wholly from the defendant's breach of contract (in which case he recovers in full).

1 Law Reform (Contributory Negligence) Act 1945. See para 22.12 below.
2 *Basildon District Council v J E Lesser Ltd* [1985] QB 839, [1985] 1 All ER 20, *AB Marintrans v Comet Shipping Co Ltd* [1985] 3 All ER 442.
3 Para 11.5 above.

Liquidated damages and penalties
11.16 So far we have been concerned with *unliquidated damages*, ie damages which are assessed by the court and not by the agreement of the parties. It is, however, possible for the parties to agree in their contract that in the event of a breach the damages shall be a fixed sum or be calculated in a specific way. Such damages are called *liquidated damages*. Liquidated damages have the obvious advantage that the amount recoverable as

damages is always certain, whereas in the case of unliquidated damages it is uncertain until the court has decided the matter. Provision for liquidated damages is often found in contracts which have to be completed within a certain time. Thus, contracts for building or civil engineering work normally provide for a specified sum to be paid for every day or week of delay.

If a contract containing a liquidated damages provision is broken, the injured party can recover the specified sum, whether this is greater or less than the actual loss suffered. This rule may benefit a plaintiff who has suffered little or no loss but can be to his disadvantage if the loss suffered greatly exceeds the specified sum. In *Cellulose Acetate Silk Co Ltd v Widnes Foundry (1925) Ltd*,[1] the defendants agreed to build machinery for the plaintiffs in 18 weeks and, in the event of taking longer, to pay 'by way of penalty £20 per working week'. The machinery was completed 30 weeks late and the plaintiffs lost £5,850 in consequence. The House of Lords held that the provision for payment was one for liquidated damages and that the plaintiffs could only recover 30 × £20, ie £600.

1 [1933] AC 20, HL.

11.17 Liquidated damages provisions must be distinguished from two other provisions:

a. *Exemption clauses limiting liability* A liquidated damages clause is not an exemption clause limiting liability because it fixes the sum payable for breach whether the actual loss is greater or less, whereas (assuming it is valid) such an exemption clause merely fixes the maximum sum recoverable and, if the actual loss is less than that sum, only the actual loss can be recovered.

b. *Penalty clauses* Where the sum fixed by the contract is a genuine pre-estimate of the loss which will be caused by its breach, the provision is one for liquidated damages, but if instead the sum is intended to operate as a threat to hold a potential defaulter to his bargain it is a penalty.[1] The distinction between a penalty and liquidated damages is crucial because their effects are different.

1 *Law v Redditch Local Board* [1892] 1 QB 127 at 132.

Penalty
11.18 If the actual loss by a plaintiff is less than the sum specified in a penalty clause, he can only recover his actual loss.[1] Suppose that a broken contract contains a penalty clause providing for a £1,000 penalty but the plaintiff's actual loss is only £100, the plaintiff can only recover £100 (whereas if the clause had been one for liquidated damages the plaintiff could have recovered £1,000). On the other hand, if the penalty is less than the actual loss suffered by the plaintiff, eg because of inflation since the contract was made, he cannot recover more than the penalty if he sues for it, although if he sues instead for (unliquidated) damages he can recover the whole of his loss.[2] This option is not, of course, open in the case of a liquidated damages provision.

1 *Wilbeam v Ashton* (1807) 1 Camp 78.
2 *Wall v Rederiaktiebolaget Luggude* [1915] 3 KB 66.

Parties' intention

11.19 Whether an agreed sum is liquidated damages or a penalty depends on the parties' intention and, as is shown by the *Cellulose Acetate* case,[1] the use of the words 'penalty' or 'liquidated damages' in the contract is not conclusive. The crucial question is whether the parties intended the specified sum to be a genuine pre-estimate of the damage likely to be caused by the breach or to operate as a fine or penalty for breach. This intention is to be gathered from the terms and inherent circumstances of the contract at the time it was made, not at the time of its breach.[2] The determination of the parties' intention is aided by a number of rebuttable presumptions of intention summarised by Lord Dunedin in *Dunlop Pneumatic Tyre Co Ltd v New Garage and Motor Co Ltd*:[3]

a. 'It will be held to be a penalty if the sum stipulated for is extravagant and unconscionable in amount in comparison with the greatest loss that could conceivably be proved to have followed from the breach.'

b. 'It will be held to be a penalty if the breach consists only in not paying a sum of money, and the sum stipulated is a sum greater than the sum which ought to have been paid.' In *Kemble v Farren*,[4] for example, the defendant agreed with the plaintiff to appear at Covent Garden for four seasons at £3 6s 8d a night. The contract provided that if either party refused to fulfil the agreement, or any part of it, he should pay the other £1,000 as 'liquidated damages'. The defendant refused to act during the second season. It was held that the stipulation was a penalty. The obligation to pay £1,000 might have arisen simply on the plaintiff's failure to pay £3 6s 8d and was therefore quite obviously a penalty.

c. 'There is a presumption (but no more) that it is a penalty when a single lump sum is made payable by way of compensation, on the occurrence of one or more or all of several events, some of which may occasion serious and others but trifling damage.' This was a second reason for the decision in *Kemble v Farren*. On the other hand—

d. 'It is no obstacle to the sum stipulated being a genuine pre-estimate of damage, that the consequences of the breach are such as to make precise pre-estimation almost an impossibility.' This is illustrated by the *Dunlop* case itself. The plaintiffs supplied tyres to the defendants subject to an agreement that the defendants would not sell below the list price and would pay £5 by way of liquidated damages for every tyre sold in breach of the agreement. The House of Lords held that the stipulated sum was one for liquidated damages. (The agreement would now be void under the Resale Prices Act 1976.[5]) Clearly, the figure of £5 was, at most, only a rough and ready estimate of the possible loss which the plaintiffs might suffer if their price list was undercut.

1 Para 11.16 above.
2 *Dunlop Pneumatic Tyre Co Ltd v New Garage and Motor Co Ltd* [1915] AC 77 at 86–87.
3 [1915] AC 77 at 86.
4 (1829) 6 Bing 141.
5 Para 14.34 below.

Interest

11.20 The Supreme Court Act 1981, s35A provides that, in proceedings before it for the recovery of a debt or damages, the High Court may include in any sum for which judgment is given simple interest for the whole or any part of the period between the date when the cause of action arose and the date of judgment (or the date of payment, if a debt is paid before judgment). In the case of damages exceeding £200 for personal injury, simple interest must be included in the sum for which judgment is given, unless there are special reasons to the contrary. Interest in respect of a debt cannot be awarded under s35A for any period during which interest on the debt already runs, eg under the contract or under some other statutory provision.

By the County Courts Act 1984, s69 provisions of precisely the same effect as s35A are applied to proceedings in a county court. The Arbitration Act 1950, s19A has the same effect as s35A in relation to arbitration proceedings under an arbitration agreement.

Action for agreed sum
11.21 As we said at the start of this chapter, if a breach consists of a party's failure to pay a debt, ie the contractually agreed price or other remuneration, which *is* due under the contract, the appropriate course for the injured party is to bring an action for the agreed sum to recover that amount.

Limitation: sale of goods contracts
11.22 There is an important limitation on an action for the agreed sum in the case of a contract for the sale of goods. The Sale of Goods Act 1979, s49 provides that, unless the agreed price is payable on a specified date irrespective of delivery, an action for it only lies if the property (ie ownership) in the goods has passed to the buyer.

Limitations: repudiatory breach
11.23 Where a repudiatory breach is committed, the injured party may, of course, recover an agreed sum already due at the time of the breach, whether he terminates or affirms the contract.

The position is more complicated where the agreed sum is not due at the time of the repudiatory breach but may become due subsequently:

a. If the injured party elects to terminate the contract, he cannot claim an agreed sum which might have become due to him subsequently.[1]

b. If the injured party elects to affirm the contract, then, as we have already said,[2] the contract remains in force, so that both parties are bound to perform any outstanding contractual obligations. Consequently, if the injured party affirms the contract, he may be able to recover the agreed sum when it becomes due in the future. Whether or not he will be able to recover that sum depends on the rules discussed in the rest of this paragraph.

It was recognised by the majority of the House of Lords in *White and Carter (Councils) Ltd v McGregor*[3] that, if further performance on the part of the injured party is required in order for the sum to become due, he will be unable to recover the agreed sum if his further performance depends on the co-operation of the other party and it is withheld. It is for this reason that a wrongfully dismissed employee cannot sue for his wages payable thereafter (as opposed to damages for breach of contract), even though he has subsequently indicated his willingness to go on working under the employment contract.[4] The limitation recognised by the majority of the House in *White and Carter (Councils) Ltd v McGregor*[3] will not often be satisfied, although it was in that case. The plaintiffs were advertising contractors. They carried on a business of supplying free litter bins to local authorities, the bins being paid for by businesses which hired advertising space on them. The plaintiffs agreed with the defendant garage proprietor to display advertisements for his garage on bins for three years. On the same day, the defendant renounced the contract and asked the plaintiffs to cancel it. They refused, thereby affirming the contract, and proceeded to prepare advertisement plates which they attached to bins and displayed. When the defendants failed to pay at the appropriate time, the plaintiffs sued for the full contract price. The House of Lords held that they could recover the full contract price despite the fact that they had made no effort to mitigate their loss by getting other advertisers in substitution for the defendant and had increased their loss after the renunciation by performing their side of the contract.

Even if he can perform his side of the contract without the co-operation of the other party, and does so, an injured party cannot recover an agreed sum when it becomes due in the future (as opposed to such damages as would be available) if it is shown that he had no legitimate interest, financial or otherwise, in performing the contract rather than claiming damages. This was stated by one of the Law Lords in the *White and Carter* case,[5] where a lack of a legitimate interest was not shown, and has subsequently been adopted in other cases.[6] What is a 'legitimate interest' in this context remains to be fully determined, although it has been held that a commitment to a third party is such an interest.[7] The term is difficult to define since it is arguable that most injured parties have such an interest in seeing their contract performed. Some judges have stated a corresponding, substitute limitation in terms of whether the injured party's conduct in performing the contract was wholly unreasonable (which would prevent him recovering an agreed sum), as opposed to merely unreasonable (which would not).[8] This test would seem to be easier to apply than that of 'legitimate interest'.

1   Para 9.5 above.
2   Para 9.23 above.
3   [1962] AC 413, [1961] 3 All ER 1178, HL.
4   *Denmark Productions Ltd v Boscobel Productions Ltd* [1969] 1 QB 699, [1968] 3 All ER 513, CA; *Gunton v Richmond-upon-Thames London Borough Council* [1981] Ch 448, [1980] 3 All ER 577, CA.
5   [1962] AC 413 at 431.
6   *The Puerto Buitrago* [1976] 1 Lloyd's Rep 250, CA; *The Odenfeld* [1978] 2 Lloyd's Rep 357; *The Alaskan Trader* [1984] 1 All ER 129, [1983] 2 Lloyd's Rep 645.
7   *The Odenfeld* [1978] 2 Lloyd's Rep 357.
8   *The Puerto Buitrago* [1976] 1 Lloyd's Rep 250 at 255; *The Odenfeld* [1978] 2 Lloyd's Rep 357 at 374; *The Alaskan Trader* [1984] 1 All ER 129 at 136.

Quantum meruit

11.24   In a particular situation, which we shall now outline, a claim on a quantam meruit is available to a plaintiff as an *alternative* to a claim for damages for breach of contract.

If a party to a contract unjustifiably prevents the other party performing his contractual obligations, as where he states that he will not accept performance, or renders performance impossible, his conduct will normally constitute a repudiatory breach of contract and the injured party can recover damages for breach of contract, whether he elects to terminate or to affirm the contract. Alternatively, if the injured party has partly performed his obligations under the contract he can claim on a quantum meruit the reasonable value of the work done, provided he has elected to terminate the contract.[1] These rules apply even though the obligation which has not been wholly performed by the injured party is entire.[2] *Planché v Colburn*[3] is a leading authority. A had agreed to write for 'The Juvenile Library', a series published by B, a book on costume and ancient armour. After A had written part of the book, B abandoned the series. It was held that A could recover 50 guineas as reasonable remuneration on a quantum meruit.

One distinction between these two types of remedy is that, whereas an award of damages depends on the existence of a contract and its breach, the right to claim on a quantum meruit does not arise under the law of contract but by virtue of the law of quasi-contract, which we discuss in ch 16 below. Another distinction relates to the amount recoverable. As we have already stated, damages are compensatory, their object generally being to put the plaintiff into the same position, so far as money can do it, as if the contract had been performed. Thus, if the injured party in a case like *Planché v Colburn* decides to sue for damages, the damages awarded will be equivalent to the sum payable to him on completion of his work, less any savings (eg on labour and materials) made through not completing performance. However, if it is shown that the plaintiff would in any event have been unable to perform his entire obligation, he will at most be entitled to nominal damages.[4] On the other hand, a quantum meruit award is restitutory, its object being to restore the plaintiff to the position in which he would have been if the contract had never been made by awarding him an amount equivalent to the value of the work which he has done. Generally, an award of damages will be more generous than a quantum meruit award, but the converse may be true if the plaintiff originally made a bad bargain or if only nominal damages would be awarded.

1 *Planché v Colburn* (1831) 8 Bing 14 at 16.
2 Paras 9.12–9.14 above.
3 (1831) 8 Bing 14.
4 *The Mihalis Angelos* [1971] 1 QB 164, [1970] 3 All ER 125, CA.

Specific performance

11.25 The court may grant a decree of specific performance to the injured party, instead of, or in addition to, awarding him damages. Such a decree orders the defaulting party to carry out his contractual obligations.

11.26 Specific performance will not be granted in the following cases:

a. *Where damages are an adequate remedy* It is for this reason that specific performance of a contract to sell goods is not normally ordered; the payment of damages enables the plaintiff to go out into the market and buy the equivalent goods.[1] However, in exceptional cases, eg where the contract is for the sale of specific goods of a unique character or of special value or interest, the contract will be specifically enforced.[2] By way of contrast, every plot of land is unique, with the result that contracts for the sale or lease of land are always specifically enforceable. This has produced the rule that, since the contract is specifically enforceable in favour of the purchaser or lessee, a vendor or lessor of land can obtain an order of specific performance even though, in his case, damages would be an adequate remedy.[3]

It is because damages are normally adequate that a contractual obligation to pay money is not normally specifically enforceable. However, in addition to the exception just mentioned, there are other exceptions, for instance:

i   as the House of Lords held in *Beswick v Beswick*,[4] a contract to pay money to a third party is specifically enforceable (because any damages awarded would be nominal);

ii where the contract is for an annuity or other periodical payment it is specifically enforceable (thereby avoiding the need to sue for damages every time a payment is not made).[5]

b. *Where consideration has not been provided* The remedy of specific performance is an equitable one and, since equity does not recognise a seal as an effective substitute for consideration, specific performance cannot be awarded in favour of a person who has not provided consideration ('equity will not assist a volunteer') and he is left to his common law remedy of damages.[6]

c. *Where the court's constant supervision would be necessary to secure compliance with the order* An example is provided by *Ryan v Mutual Tontine Westminster Chambers Association*.[7] In the lease of a flat in a block of flats the lessors agreed to keep a resident porter, who should be in constant attendance and perform specified duties. The person appointed got his duties done by deputies and was absent for hours at a time at another job. The court refused to order specific performance against the lessor of the agreement relating to the porter because such an order would have required its constant supervision. As part of the present principle a contract to build or repair is normally not specifically enforceable, the only exception being where:

i   the work is defined by the contract in a sufficiently definite way for the court to be able to see the exact nature of the work which it is asked specifically to enforce; and

ii the plaintiff has a substantial interest in the work which cannot be compensated by damages; and

iii the defendant has possession of the land on which the work is contracted to be done.[8]

d. *Where the contract is for personal services* The obvious example of such a contract is one of employment. The Trade Union and Labour Relations Act 1974, s16 prohibits an order of specific performance against an *employee* to compel him to do any work or to attend at any place for the doing of any work. It is well established by the cases that contracts for personal services not covered by the Act cannot be specifically enforced either, nor can an order of specific performance be made against an employer (except, possibly, in very exceptional circumstances). Reasons given are that such contracts would require constant supervision and that it is contrary to public policy to force one person to submit to the orders of another.

e. *Lack of mutality* There is a rule that in certain cases a plaintiff cannot obtain specific performance against the defendant if, in the circumstances, it would not be available to the defendant against the plaintiff. In *Flight v Bolland*,[9] for instance, it was held that a minor could not be awarded specific performance of the contract in question because such an order could not be made against him in the circumstances. While there is no doubting the present rule, its extent is uncertain.

1 Apart from its inherent jurisdiction to order specific recovery of goods, the court has power under the Sale of Goods Act 1979 to order the specific performance of contracts for the sale of specific or ascertained goods. This power has not been used more liberally than the inherent power.
2 *Behnke v Bede Shipping Co Ltd* [1927] 1 KB 649; *Phillips v Lamdin* [1949] 2 KB 33, [1949] 1 All ER 770; *Sky Petroleum Ltd v VIP Petroleum Ltd* [1974] 1 All ER 954, [1974] 1 WLR 576. Cf *Cohen v Roche* [1927] 1 KB 169.
3 *Cogent v Gibson* (1864) 33 Beav 557.
4 [1968] AC 58, [1967] 2 All ER 1197, HL; para 6.28 above.
5 *Beswick v Beswick* [1968] AC 58, [1967] 2 All ER 1197, HL.
6 *Cannon v Hartley* [1949] Ch 213, [1949] 1 All ER 50.
7 [1893] 1 Ch 116.
8 *Wolverhampton Corpn v Emmons* [1901] 1 KB 515, CA; *Carpenters Estates Ltd v Davies* [1940] Ch 160, [1940] 1 All ER 13; *Jeune v Queen's Cross Properties Ltd* [1974] Ch 97, [1973] 3 All ER 97.
9 (1828) 4 Russ 298.

11.27 If the case does not fall within one of the above cases, specific performance may be ordered, but it must not be forgotten that, since specific performance is an equitable remedy, its award does not lie as of right (unlike the common law remedy of damages) but lies in the court's discretion. Factors which make it unlikely that the court will exercise its discretion in favour of specific performance include:

a. mistake on the part of the defendant, such that it would be unjust specifically to enforce the contract against him;[1]

b. delay in bringing an action for specific performance which resulted in the defendant so changing his position that it would be unjust specifically to enforce the contract against him;[2]

c. exceptional severity of the hardship to the defendant if the contract is specifically enforced against him;[3]

d. breach by the plaintiff of his contractual obligations in circumstances where the grant of specific performance would be unjust to the defendant.[4]

Lastly, it is clearly established that the court will refuse specific performance of a contract for the sale of land in favour of a plaintiff who is in breach of a contractual stipulation concerning the time of completion where time is of 'the essence of the contract',[5] although it will normally grant it to such a plaintiff (subject to a condition that the plaintiff pays damages for his delay) where time is *not* 'of the essence' since this will not cause injustice to the defendant.

1 Paras 12.8 and 12.17 below.
2 *Stuart v London and North Western Rly Co* (1852) De G M & G 721; *Lazard Bros & Co Ltd v Fairfield Properties Co (Mayfair) Ltd* (1977) Times, 12 October.

3   *Patel v Ali* [1984] 1 All ER 978, [1984] 2 WLR 960.
4   *Walsh v Lonsdale* (1882) 21 Ch D 9.
5   *Stickney v Keeble* [1915] AC 386 at 415–416.

Injunction

11.28   An injunction is a court order restraining a party to a contract from acting in breach of a negative stipulation contained in it. By way of comparison, specific performance is concerned with the enforcement of positive contractual stipulations.

11.29   While it is correct to say that injunctions are concerned with restraining breaches of negative contractual stipulations, it would be erroneous to assume that only an express negative stipulation can be remedied by an injunction. Generally, a breach of a positive stipulation can be enjoined if the stipulation can properly be construed as impliedly being a negative stipulation. Thus, in *Manchester Ship Canal Co v Manchester Racecourse Co*,[1] a stipulation for the grant of a 'first refusal' was construed as a stipulation, enforceable by injunction, *not* to sell to anyone else in breach of the stipulation. Similarly, in *Metropolitan Electric Supply Co Ltd v Ginder*,[2] where the defendant had undertaken to take all the electricity required for his premises from the plaintiffs, it was held that this was impliedly an undertaking *not* to take electricity from any other person, which could be enforced by an injunction.

1   [1901] 2 Ch 37.
2   [1901] 2 Ch 799.

11.30   Although the courts are prepared to enforce negative stipulations in a contract for personal services, consistency with the rule that such a contract cannot normally be the subject of a decree of specific performance means that an injunction will not be issued to restrain an employee or the like from breaking a promise not to work for any other person, if this would indirectly amount to compelling him to perform his contract with his employer.[1] This is given statutory force in relation to contracts of employment by the Trade Union and Labour Relations Act 1974, s16, which provides that no court may, by an injunction restraining a breach or threatened breach of a contract of employment, compel an employee to do any work or to attend at any place of work.

On the other hand, a negative promise by an employee or the like will be enforced against him by injunction if it does not indirectly force him to work for his employer. For example, in *Lumley v Wagner*,[2] the defendant, an opera star, agreed to sing at the plaintiff's theatre for three months and in no other theatre during that time. An injunction was granted restraining her from singing for another theatre during the three-month period. *Warner Bros Pictures Inc v Nelson*[3] is a similar case. The defendant, whose stage name was Bette Davis, agreed with the plaintiff company not to work in a film or stage production for any other company for a year nor to be engaged in any other occupation. During the year she contracted to work for another film company. Branson J stated that, while an injunction enforcing all the negative stipulations in the contract could not be granted (because it would force Bette Davis either to be idle or to perform her contract with the plaintiff company), the injunction requested would be granted because it was limited to prohibiting her from working in a film or stage production for anyone other than the plaintiff company; she would still be free to earn her living in some other less remunerative way.

1 *Rely-a-Bell Burglar and Fire Alarm Co Ltd v Eisler* [1926] Ch 609.
2 (1852) 1 De GM & G 604.
3 [1937] 1 KB 209, [1936] 3 All ER 160.

11.31 The law is similar where an employee seeks to enforce a negative stipulation against his employer. Thus, generally, an injunction will not be issued if its effect is to compel the employer to continue employment. But an injunction may be granted in certain exceptional cases where employer and employee retain their mutual confidence. In *Page One Records Ltd v Britton*,[1] The Troggs, a pop group, appointed the plaintiff as their manager for five years, agreeing not to let anyone else act as their manager during that time. After a year, The Troggs dismissed the plaintiff, who sought an injunction restraining them from appointing anyone else as their manager. It was held that an injunction would indirectly compel The Troggs to continue to employ the plaintiff because pop groups could not operate successfully without a manager, and it would be bad to pressure The Troggs into continuing to employ a person in whom they had lost confidence. Therefore the injunction sought was not granted. In comparison, one may note the exceptional case of *Hill v C A Parsons & Co Ltd*.[2] The defendant employers were forced by union pressure to dismiss the plaintiff in breach of contract. An injunction was granted to restrain this breach, even though its effect was to compel the reinstatement of the plaintiff. As the Court of Appeal pointed out, the circumstances were special, in particular because the parties retained their mutual confidence. Despite the general reluctance of the courts to grant specific performance or an injunction in respect of a contract of employment, there are increasing signs that, in cases where the employee's contract requires a specified procedure to be followed before dismissal can take place, the courts will grant an injunction at least to restrain a proposed dismissal in breach of that procedure.[3]

1 [1967] 3 All ER 822, [1968] 1 WLR 157.
2 [1972] Ch 305, [1971] 3 All ER 1345, CA.
3 *Irani v Southampton and South West Hampshire Health Authority* [1985] ICR 590, [1985] IRLR 203; *R v BBC, ex p Lavelle* [1983] 1 All ER 241, [1982] IRLR 404; *Jones v Lee* [1980] ICR 310, [1980] IRLR 67, CA.

11.32 An injunction is like specific performance in that:

a. it may be granted with or without an order for damages;

b. where it is applicable, the grant of an injunction is discretionary (since it is an equitable remedy) and is likely to be refused where, for example, the plaintiff is guilty of delay or is in breach of his own obligations under the contract. In particular, an injunction will normally be refused if damages would be an adequate remedy.

On the other hand, an injunction is a much wider remedy than specific performance, partly because it can be ordered in many situations other than contractual situations, and partly because it can be ordered in contractual situations where specific performance could not, eg where enforcement of the contract would require the court's constant superintendence or where the contract is one for personal services.

Limitation of actions
11.33 An action will be barred if it is not brought within the relevant limitation period. The rules relating to these periods are statutory, the relevant Act being the Limitation Act 1980. If an action is statute-barred this does not extinguish the plaintiff's substantive right but simply bars the procedural remedies available to him. Two consequences of this are that if a debtor pays a statute-barred debt, he cannot recover the money as money not due,[1] and that if a debtor who owes a creditor two or more debts, one of which is statute-barred, pays money to the creditor without appropriating it to a debt which is not statute-barred, the creditor is entitled to appropriate it to the statue-barred debt.[2]

1   *Bize v Dickason* (1786) 1 Term Rep 285 at 287.
2   *Mills v Fowkes* (1839) 5 Bing NC 455.

Limitation periods
11.34 Under the Limitation Act 1980:

a. Actions founded on a simple contract (ie one not under seal) cannot be brought after the expiration of six years from the date on which the cause of action accrued, which is normally when the breach of contract occurs and never when the damage is suffered.[1] However, if the damages claimed consist of or include damages for personal injuries caused by a breach of contract, the time limit is reduced to three years,[2] although this period may be extended in certain circumstances.[3]

b. Actions founded on a contract under seal cannot be brought after the expiration of 12 years from the date on which the cause of action accrued.[4] The special rules mentioned above concerning personal injuries claims also apply here.

1   Limitation Act 1980, s5. For a special rule in relation to actions on certain contracts of loan, see Limitation Act 1980, s6. If the plaintiff can establish a cause of action in tort for negligence, that cause of action accrues (and time runs from) when the damage is suffered: *Pirelli General Cable Works Ltd v Oscar Faber & Partners* [1983] 2 AC 1, [1983] 1 All ER 65, HL. See, further, para 31.21 below.
2   Limitation Act 1980, s11(4).
3   Para 31.22c below.
4   Limitation Act 1980, s8.

Minors and the mentally ill
11.35 If a plaintiff is a minor or mentally unsound when the cause of action accrues, the action may be brought within six years of the removal of the disability or of his death, whichever event happens first.[1] On the other hand, if the limitation period has begun to run, the fact that the plaintiff subsequently becomes of unsound mind does not suspend the running of time, and, if a person is under a disability when his cause of action accrues but dies and is succeeded by someone who also is under a disability, there is no extension of time by reason of the latter's disability.[2]

1   Limitation Act 1980, ss28 and 38(2). The period is three years if damages for personal injuries are claimed: Limitation Act 1980, s28(6).
2   Limitation Act 1980, s28(3).

Fraud, concealment or mistake
11.36 Generally, the fact that the plaintiff is unaware that he has a cause

of action does not prevent the limitation period starting to run, even if the plaintiff does not know that he has a cause of action until after the limitation period has expired. However, the Limitation Act 1980, s32(1) provides that if—

a. the action is based on the fraud of the defendant or someone for whom he is responsible; or

b. any fact relevant to the plaintiff's right of action has been deliberately concealed from him by such a person; or

c. the action is for relief from the consequences of a mistake,

the limitation period does not begin to run until the plaintiff has discovered the fraud, concealment or mistake (as the case may be) or could with reasonable diligence have discovered it. Section 32(2) goes on to provide that a deliberate breach of duty in circumstances in which it is unlikely to be discovered for some time amounts to deliberate concealment of the facts involved in breach of that duty.

Section 32(3) protects the position of third parties. It provides that nothing in s32 shall enable any action to recover the value of, or set aside a transaction affecting, any property to be brought against the purchaser of the property, or any person claiming through him, in any case where the property has been purchased for valuable consideration by an innocent party since the fraud or concealment or (as the case may be) the transaction in which the mistake was made took place. A purchaser is an innocent third party in this context if he neither knew nor had reason to believe that the fraud, concealment or mistake (as the case may be) had occurred *and* (in the case of fraud or concealment only) was not a party to it.[1]

1   Limitation Act 1980, s 32(4).

Extending the limitation period

11.37   An acknowledgment or part payment of a debt or other liquidated pecuniary claim may start time running again, provided that the right of action has not previously become statute-barred (ie the acknowledgment or part payment must be made during the currency of the relevant limitation period).[1] The basic provision is the Limitation Act 1980, s29(5), which provides that where any right of action has accrued to recover any debt or other liquidated pecuniary claim and the person (or his agent) liable or accountable therefor acknowledges the claim or makes any payment in respect thereof, the right of action is deemed to have accrued on the date of the acknowledgment or the payment. Such an extension of a current limitation period may be continually repeated by further acknowledgments or payments.[1]

It must be emphasised that an extension of a limitation period under s29(5) is only possible in the case of a debt or other liquidated sum and that, in the case of an acknowledgment, the claim must be acknowledged as existing (since an acknowledgment that there might be a claim is not enough),[2] but it is not essential that an acknowledgment should quantify the amount due since it suffices if that amount can be assessed by extrinsic evidence without further agreement of the parties.[3] A cause of action for unliquidated damages cannot be extended by an acknowledgment or part payment.

1 Limitation Act 1980, s29(7).
2 *Good v Parry* [1963] 2 QB 418, [1963] 2 All ER 59, CA; *Kamouh v Associated Electrical Industries Ltd* [1980] QB 199, [1979] 2 WLR 795.
3 *Dungate v Dungate* [1965] 3 All ER 818, [1965] 1 WLR 1477.

Acknowledgment

11.38   The acknowledgment must be in writing and signed by the person making it (or his agent), and must be made to the person (or his agent) whose claim is acknowledged.[1] An acknowledgment is only sufficient to start time running again if it amounts to an admission of legal liability to pay the debt in question,[2] but it is not necessary that a promise to pay should be implied. An acknowledgment by one debtor does not bind a joint debtor,[3] unless the acknowledgor can be regarded as an agent for himself and the joint debtor, which will happen, for instance, if they are partners.

1 Limitation Act 1980, s30.
2 *Surrendra Overseas Ltd v Government of Sri Lanka* [1977] 2 All ER 481, [1977] 1 WLR 565.
3 Limitation Act 1980, s31(6).

Part payment

11.39   In order to start time running again, part payment must be clearly referable to the debt. Part payment must be made to the person or (his agent) in respect of whose claim the payment is made. If part payment is made by a joint debtor time starts running again against all the joint debtors.[1]

1 Limitation Act 1980, s31(7).

Equitable relief

11.40   The provisions of the Limitation Act do not apply to claims for equitable relief.[1] However, in cases where, before the Judicature Act 1873, the claim for relief could have been entertained in either the common law courts or in the Court of Chancery, the limitation periods under the Limitation Act 1980 are applied to equitable claims by analogy.[2] The position is different in the case of purely equitable claims, ie claims which could only have been entertained by the Court of Chancery before the Act of 1873, such as claims for specific performance or an injunction. Here, the claim may fail under the equitable doctrine of laches (delay). Traditionally, the rule has been that the plaintiff must show himself to be 'ready, desirous, prompt and eager' to assert his rights,[3] otherwise he may be barred from claiming the equitable relief. But there is authority that, at least where the claim is for specific performance, even gross delay will not bar the claim for equitable relief if it has done the defendant no harm at all.[4] The avoidance of fixed limitation periods in this area is obviously more appropriate to the discretionary nature of equitable remedies.

1 Limitation Act 1980, s36(1).
2 Ibid; *Knox v Gye* (1872) LR 5 HL 656 at 674.
3 *Millward v Earl of Thanet* (1801) 5 Ves 720n.
4 *Lazard Bros & Co Ltd v Fairfield Properties Co (Mayfair) Ltd* (1977) Times, 12 October.

Chapter 12
Mistake

12.1 In certain cases a contract[1] which is made in circumstances where one or both parties are labouring under a mistake is void. If a contract is void for mistake it has no legal effect; consequently, it is unenforceable by either party, and title to property cannot pass under it. A party who has received goods under a void contract will be liable to the transferor in tort if he wrongfully interferes with them, and so will a third party who has bought them from him.

Because of the serious consequences of finding a contract void for mistake, the law defines the situations in which a mistake will render a contract void very narrowly. It follows from this that many mistakes made by a party in concluding a contract are legally irrelevant. Even mistakes which are induced by the other contracting party may not render the contract void, although there may be a remedy for misrepresentation (which we discuss in the next chapter).

A contract *may* be void for mistake:

a. if the parties have reached an agreement, but have done so on the basis of some fundamental mistake which they share; or

b. if, because of a mistake which the parties do not share, they are fundamentally at cross-purposes.

As a preliminary point, it should be noted that a mistake of law will generally be held to be legally irrelevant.[2]

1 It is traditional, although perhaps inaccurate, to describe agreements void for mistake as contracts.
2 *Solle v Butcher* [1950] 1 KB 671, [1949] 2 All ER 1107, CA.

Shared mistake

Common law
12.2 If the parties have reached an agreement on the basis of a misapprehension as to the facts, which is shared by both of them, the contract may be void for mistake. Whether the rules relating to mistake come into play is a matter of construction of the contract. If the contract provides that the risk as to the particular fact or event falls on one party, the law gives effect to the express intention of the parties. If the contract does so provide, then the contract is not void but enforceable. The terms of the contract may not expressly state on whom the risk falls, but the court may be able to

determine an intention that one of the parties should bear it from the terms of the contract. In either case, the position is as follows: if, to take as an example the case of a contract for the sale of specific goods which it turns out have never existed, the buyer assumed the risk of the goods' existence, he must pay the contractual price; but if the seller assumed that risk he will be liable in damages for breach of contract. In the Australian case of *McRae v Commonwealth Disposals Commission*,[1] the Commission sold to McRae the right to salvage a tanker which was, they claimed, lying on a specified reef. There was no reef of that name at the map reference given, nor was there any tanker. The court found as a matter of construction that the Commission had impliedly undertaken that the tanker existed and thus McRae could claim damages for breach of this undertaking. The case can be contrasted with *Clark v Lindsay*,[2] which shows that a contract may also provide a solution, other than placing the risk on one of the parties, should a jointly assumed fact not exist. In *Clark v Lindsay*, A had agreed with B to hire a room along the route of Edward VII's coronation procession. When they made the contract both parties were unaware that the coronation had been postponed because of the King's illness, but the contract expressly provided that, if the procession was postponed, A should have the use of the room on any later day on which it took place. Consequently, it was held that the contract was not void for mistake and both parties were bound to perform their obligations on the re-arranged day.

The approach of construing the contract to see whether it allocates the risk in, or otherwise provides a solution for, the matter about which the parties shared a mistake was adopted also by the House of Lords in *Couturier v Hastie*.[3] Here, a cargo of grain being shipped to the UK was sold after, unknown to the parties, it had 'perished' in the legal sense, in that it had deteriorated and had already been sold by the ship's captain. The seller demanded payment for the cargo. The House of Lords found that on a true construction of the contract the risk that the cargo did not exist had not been placed on the buyer and therefore he did not have to pay for the goods. It was not necessary for the House to decide whether the risk was placed on the seller, who could thus have been sued for non-delivery, or whether the contract was void.

1   (1950) 84 CLR 377.
2   (1903) 88 LT 198.
3   (1856) 5 HL Cas 673, HL.

12.3   If, on its true construction, the contract does not allocate the risk in, or otherwise provide a solution for, the matter concerning which the parties shared a mistake, the rules relating to mistake must be looked at. Under them, not every shared mistake renders a contract void: the mistake must be fundamental. If it is not fundamental the contract is enforceable at common law. One example of a fundamental mistake in this context is a shared mistake as to the existence of the subject matter of the contract. In *Galloway v Galloway*,[1] for instance, a separation agreement based on a marriage which, unknown to the parties, was invalid (and therefore non-existent) was held void. Clearly, in such a case, the separation agreement would not attempt to throw the risk of the marriage being invalid on either party and so it is not surprising that the court did not first consider the question of construction.

Similarly, a contract is void if it is made under a shared mistaken belief that it is possible to perform it, unless on the true construction of the contract one party or the other has agreed to run the risk of impossibility of performance (or the contract provides some other solution to deal with the problem). Thus, it was held in *Cooper v Phibbs*[2] that a contract, whereby X agrees to lease land to Y, which Y already owns, is void at common law, and so is a contract whereby X agrees with Y to cut and process a certain tonnage of a particular crop on land, when there is not that tonnage to be cropped.[3] It would be different, however, if X had warranted (as a seller normally does) that he had title to the land or had guaranteed the yield (in that case, X would be liable for breach of contract) or if Y had agreed to run the risk (ie to pay in any event).

Another example is provided by *Griffiths v Brymer*.[4] As in *Clark v Lindsay*, this case concerned an agreement for the hire of a room along the route of Edward VII's coronation procession, which had been made by the parties in ignorance of the postponement of the procession. The court did not specifically deal with the construction of the contract, but presumably the contract had not allocated the risk of the postponement. It held that the contract was void for mistake and that the plaintiff could recover money he had paid under it.

1 (1914) 30 TLR 531, DC.
2 *Cooper v Phibbs* (1867) LR 2 HL 149, HL.
3 *Sheikh Bros v Ochsner* [1957] AC 136, [1957] 2 WLR 254, PC.
4 (1903) 19 TLR 434.

12.4 If the facts in *Couturier v Hastie* occurred today, the basis of the decision would almost certainly be different (although the buyer would still not be liable) because there is now a special statutory provision dealing with the *perishing* of *specific* goods unknown to the seller before a contract for their sale is made. The Sale of Goods Act 1979, s6 provides that in such a case the contract is void. Presumably, this provision can be displaced if the contract expressly places the risk as to the goods' continued existence on one of the parties. Section 6 does not apply to specific goods which have never existed. In such cases, the contract is first construed and if the risk is placed on either party, expressly or impliedly, the contract governs; but if the risk is not allocated, the contract is void.

12.5 A vexed question is whether a shared mistake as to the *quality* (as opposed to the *existence*) of the subject matter of the contract can ever be sufficiently fundamental to render it void. Frequently, of course, the risk that the goods, etc lack that quality is borne by the seller because the supposed quality of the goods is a term, express or implied, of the contract. If this occurs, the law of mistake is irrelevant because the contract provides that the seller shall be liable for breach of contract if the quality is absent. But if the contract does not allocate the risk that the quality is lacking, is the contract *ever* void for mistake? Dicta in *Bell v Lever Bros Ltd*[1] suggest that in some cases a contract can be void for a shared mistake as to quality. In that case, Bell was employed by Lever Bros under a contract of employment for five years at £8,000 per annum. Lever Bros agreed to pay Bell £30,000 to relinquish this contract. Subsequently, they discovered that they could have terminated the contract without compensation because of breaches of it by Bell. Bell had forgotten about these breaches and he and Lever Bros were treated as being under a shared mistake as to the *quality* of the contract of employment, in that they had believed it was only determinable with Bell's agreement when in truth it was immediately determinable by Lever Bros without his agreement. Lever Bros' claim to recover back the compensation paid, as money paid under a void contract, failed before the House of Lords, who held the contract of compensation valid despite the shared mistake, although three of their Lordships stated that a sufficiently fundamental mistake as to quality might render a contract void. The reader may think that, if the mistake as to quality in this case was not sufficiently fundamental, it is hard to imagine when a mistake as to quality will be.

No case has actually been decided on the basis that a contract was void because of a fundamental mistake as to quality, although it was held, obiter, in *Nicholson and Venn v Smith-Marriott*,[2] that the contract in issue could have been held void for mistake. In that case, a set of linen napkins and table cloths was put up for sale, described as dating from the seventeenth century. Unknown to both the buyers and the sellers, it was in fact Georgian, and the buyers were able to recover for breach of contract since the sellers were in breach of the implied condition under the Sale of Goods Act 1979, s13(1) that the goods corresponded with their description. Strangely, the judge added that, had the buyers sought to recover the whole of the price paid as money paid under a void contract,[3] he would have been diposed to hold the contract void for mistake as to quality.

1   [1932] AC 161, HL.
2   (1947) 177 LT 189.
3   Para 16.7a below.

12.6   The dicta in support of the proposition that a contract can be void for a fundamental mistake as to quality can be contrasted with the actual decisions in a number of cases. In *Solle v Butcher*,[1] the fact that both parties to a lease mistakenly believed that the premises were free from rent control did not render the contract void. Similarly, in *Maggee v Pennine Insurance Co Ltd*,[2] a compromise of a claim under an insurance policy which both parties mistakenly believed to be valid, when in fact the policy was voidable, was held not to be void for mistake. Again, we are prompted to ask, if these mistakes were not fundamental, what sort of mistake would have been? Another example of a mistake as to quality which was not legally relevant occurred in *Harrison and Jones Ltd v Bunten and Lancaster Ltd*.[3] In this case, the parties bought and sold 'Sree brand' kapok. Both parties believed 'Sree brand' to be pure kapok, when in fact it contained other substances. The judge admitted that the purchasers considered it vital that the kapok was pure but refused to hold that the contract was void for mistake.

1   [1950] 1 KB 671, [1949] 2 All ER 1107, CA. Also see *Grist v Bailey*, para 12.9 below.
2   [1969] 2 QB 507, [1969] 2 All ER 891, CA.
3   [1953] 1 QB 646, [1953] 1 All ER 903.

12.7   Our conclusion is that at law a contract can never be void because of a mistake as to quality, however fundamental.

Equity
12.8   If a contract is void at law for mistake, it is of no legal effect and no damages can be awarded for non-performance or faulty performance. Further, equity, following the law, will not grant specific performance.

Moreover, to put the matter beyond doubt, the equitable remedy of rescission (ie setting aside) of the contract can be obtained. Since the contract is void this is not necessary, but it is a useful remedy where there is a formal contractual document, such as a lease. The void lease in *Cooper v Phibbs*[1] was rescinded, for example.

Even though the shared mistake in question does not make the contract void at common law, equitable relief may be available. This relief, which lies in the court's discretion, may take the form of refusing specific performance (which will not affect liability in damages), or of awarding specific performance on terms which do justice, or of rescinding the contract for *mistake*.

1   (1867) LR 2 HL 149, HL.

12.9   Where a contract which is not void for mistake is rescinded, the rescission sets aside a contract which previously existed, and the parties are restored to their former positions. In addition, the court may impose terms on the parties in the interests of justice and equity. Thus, if a contract of sale of goods is rescinded for mistake, this may be done on terms that the buyer is compensated for any improvements which he has made to the goods.

It is not certain what mistakes are sufficient to enable a contract to be rescinded under the equitable power. Certainly, all mistakes which the law considers sufficient will suffice in equity and so will other types of mistake, although the limits are not clearly established.

Two examples of where equity has set aside a contract are *Solle v Butcher*[1] and *Grist v Bailey*,[2] both of which involved mistakes of quality.

In *Solle v Butcher*, a lease was granted at a specified rent in the shared mistaken belief that the nature of the flat had been so changed as not to be a rent-controlled property. As we have said, the Court of Appeal refused to find the contract void but it set it aside in equity. At the time there was a housing shortage and rescission was ordered on terms that the tenant should have an option either to surrender the lease or to stay in the premises under a new lease at the maximum rent which the landlord could charge under the statutory provisions then in force.

In *Grist v Bailey*, the plaintiff agreed to buy a house from the defendant at approximately one-third of its value because the house was sold subject to an existing tenancy which both parties mistakenly believed was protected by the Rent Acts (which would have given the tenant a right to remain in the property indefinitely). On discovering that the tenancy was not protected, the plaintiff sought specific performance and the defendant sought to have the agreement set aside because of the mistake. The contract was not void at law but the mistake was a sufficient mistake as to quality to allow equitable intervention. The action for specific performance was dismissed and the agreement to sell set aside, but only on the term that the defendant should give the plaintiff a chance to enter into a new contract of sale at the full value of the property.

The rescission of a contract for shared mistake is subject to similar bars to those which apply to rescission for misrepresentation and which we outline in para 13.16 below.

1   [1950] 1 KB 671, [1949] 2 All ER 1107, CA.
2   [1967] Ch 532, [1966] 2 All ER 875. For another example, see *Magee v Pennine Insurance Co Ltd* [1969] 2 QB 507, [1969] 2 All ER 891, CA.

Mistake not shared by the parties

Common law

12.10 The fact that a party entered into an apparent contract under a mistake does not normally render the contract void, and the same is true if both parties were labouring under *different* mistaken beliefs. However, a contract will be void if a mistake which is not shared by the parties relates to:

a. the identity of the other party; or

b. a fundamental matter relating to the subject matter of the contract; or

c. whether a particular matter is a term of the contract,

and the mistake is an operative mistake in the sense discussed in para 12.16 below.

Mistake as to identity

12.11 A mistake as to identity can make an apparent contract void; a mistake which merely relates to an attribute, e g credit-worthiness, of the other party can never do so.

In *Cundy v Lindsay*,[1] a rogue, Blenkarn, who had hired premises at 37 Wood Street, wrote to the plaintiffs, offering to buy some goods. Blenkarn deliberately signed his letter 'A Blenkarn & Co' in such a way that the signature appeared to be that of A. Blenkiron & Co. A. Blenkiron & Co were a well-known firm which had traded for many years at 123 Wood Street. The plaintiffs accepted the offer and sent their letter of acceptance to 'Messrs Blenkiron, 37 Wood Street'. Later, goods were delivered under the contract to the same address. The House of Lords held that the plaintiffs had purported to accept an offer made by Blenkiron and had never intended to contract with Blenkarn at all. In consequence, the apparent contract with Blenkarn was void and the innocent party to whom Blenkarn had resold the goods was held liable to the plaintiffs for the tort of conversion. The plaintiffs could, of course, have sued Blenkarn for the torts of conversion and deceit[2] if they could have traced him. In *Cundy v Lindsay*, the plaintiffs were able to establish that they meant to deal only with Blenkiron and not with the writer of the letter; there was thus a mistake as to identity. On the other hand, in *King's Norton Metal Co Ltd v Edridge, Merrett & Co Ltd*,[3] the mistake made by the plaintiffs who sold goods to a rogue who resold them to the defendants was one as to attribute, not identity. In this case, a rogue, one Wallis, offered to buy goods in a letter written on paper headed Hallam & Co and embellished with references to depots and a picture of a factory. The plaintiffs mistakenly believed Hallam & Co to be a respectable firm but they did not think that they were dealing with someone other than the writer of the letter. Their mistake was as to the credit and reliability of the writer of the letter, and not as to the identity of the other party. Thus, they had intended to contract with the writer of the letter and they were bound by the contract.

1 (1878) 3 App Cas 459, HL.
2 Paras 13.20 and 29.3–29.15 below.
3 (1897) 14 TLR 98.

12.12 When the parties contract face to face, it is much more difficult to establish that a mistake relates to the identity, as opposed to attributes, of the other party, and it can normally be presumed that a party intended to deal with the person in front of him. However, every case turns on its facts and it may be possible to establish a mistake as to identity if the identity of one party was of vital importance to the other.

In *Phillips v Brooks Ltd*,[1] a rogue, named North, entered the plaintiff's shop and selected some jewellery, including a ring. He then wrote out a cheque for the full amount. As he did so, he announced that he was Sir George Bullough of St James' Square. The plaintiff had heard of Sir George Bullough; he consulted a directory and found that Sir George Bullough did live at the address given. He therefore allowed North to take away the ring without first having the cheque cleared. North pledged the ring with the defendant, who was wholly innocent. The cheque was dishonoured and the plaintiff sued the defendant in tort for the conversion of the ring. He could only succeed if the contract was void for mistake. The judge held that it was not; his reason was that he found that the plaintiff had intended to contract with the person in the shop. The plaintiff's mistaken belief related to an attribute of the customer (his credit-worthiness), not his identity. It would have been different if the plaintiff had established that the identity of his customer was of particular importance to him. He had, it is true, consulted a directory to see whether there was a Sir George Bullough of St James' Square, but this was not sufficient to rebut the presumption that he intended to deal with the customer before him, whoever he was.

A similar case is that of *Lewis v Averay*,[2] where a rogue, claiming to be Richard Greene, a well-known actor, bought from the plaintiff a car which he then sold to the defendant, who was innocent. The plaintiff sued the defendant for the conversion of his car but failed to establish that he had made a mistake as to the identity of the other party to the agreement. He had to be presumed to intend to deal with the person in front of him, said the Court of Appeal, unless he could establish that the identity of the buyer was of vital importance to him. In this case, the only attempt to check whether the rogue was Richard Greene was the perusal of a Pinewood Studio pass in the name of Richard Green, which was produced by the rogue, and this was insufficient to establish that he intended to deal only with Richard Greene, the actor.

1   [1919] 2 KB 243.
2   [1972] 1 QB 198, [1971] 3 All ER 907, CA.

12.13   Two cases where the plaintiff was able to establish a mistake as to the identity of the other party are *Ingram v Little*[1] and *Sowler v Potter*.[2] In *Ingram v Little*, the plaintiffs, two elderly sisters, were confronted by a rogue who called himself Hutchinson. They agreed to sell him their car, but refused to continue the sale when the rogue proposed to pay by cheque. He then announced himself to be P.G.M. Hutchinson of Stanstead House, Caterham. One sister slipped out to the Post Office, consulted the telephone directory and found that there was a P.G.M. Hutchinson of Stanstead House, while the other sister plied the rogue with conversation. They accepted the cheque, which was dishonoured, and the rogue sold the car to the defendant, whom the sisters sued in conversion. The Court of Appeal found that on the facts of the case the plaintiffs had done sufficient to establish that they intended to deal only with P.G.M. Hutchinson of Stanstead House, and not with the person in front of them. This decision has been greatly criticised but, since all cases turn on their own facts, it may have been correctly decided.

In *Sowler v Potter*,[2] the lease of a café was granted to Potter, who had previously been convicted of keeping a disorderly café under another name, Robinson. Tucker J held that the lease was void because of the lessor's mistaken belief that Potter was not Robinson. The judge found that the lessor's agent, who had concluded the contract, only intended to deal with the person in front of him if that person was not Robinson, a convicted criminal. This case has also been doubted and, since the contract could have been rescinded for misrepresentation, its authority on the law of mistake is limited.

1   [1961] 1 QB 31, [1960] 3 All ER 332, CA.
2   [1940] 1 KB 271, [1939] 4 All ER 478.

Fundamental mistake as to subject matter

12.14   A fundamental mistake as to the subject matter of a contract may render it void. An example of a sufficiently fundamental mistake would be where A agrees to buy a computer from B, mistakenly believing that it is a Sinclair computer when, in fact, it is an Acorn computer. In such a case, there would be no genuine agreement, for the parties are at cross-purposes. Similarly, if X agrees to buy a consignment of wheat from Y, thinking that it is a consignment of oats, his mistake is sufficiently fundamental.[1]

On the other hand, a mistake which simply relates to a quality, but not the essential nature of the thing, is not sufficiently fundamental to render the contract void. Thus, if X agrees to buy oats from Y, mistakenly believing that they are old oats, the contract cannot be void for mistake.[2]

1   *Scriven & Co v Hindley & Co* [1913] 3 KB 564; *Raffles v Wichelhaus* (1864) 2 H & C 906.
2   *Smith v Hughes* (1871) LR 6 QB 597.

Mistake as to the terms of the contract

12.15   A contract may be void if a party mistakenly believes that a particular matter is a term of the contract, even though the mistake does not relate to the identity of the other party or the essence of the subject matter. Thus, if X mistakenly believes that Y warrants that the oats which he is selling him are old oats, the contract may be void for mistake.[1]

In *Hartog v Colin and Shields*,[2] the sellers mistakenly offered to sell goods at a given price per pound when they had intended to offer to sell at that given price per piece, there being about three pieces to the pound. The buyer accepted the offer. The contract was apparently held void because of the sellers' mistake as to the price (a term of the contract). All the preliminary negotiations had been on the basis of price per piece and trade custom also related to price per piece. The effect of this was that the court found that the buyer must have realised that the sellers had made a mistake and could not rush in and accept what would have been a most advantageous offer.

1   *Smith v Hughes* (1871) LR 6 QB 597.
2   [1939] 3 All ER 566.

Operative mistake

12.16   It is not enough that a party was mistaken as to the identity of the other party, or as to the essence of the subject matter, or as to a term of the contract. Such a mistake must be operative to render the contract void and it will only be so if:

a. The other party knew of the mistake, as in *Cundy v Lindsay, Ingram v Little, Sowler v Potter* and *Hartog v Colin & Shields*; or

b. The circumstances are so ambiguous that a reasonable person could not say whether the contract meant what one party thought it meant or what the other party thought it meant. It is only in exceptional cases that the circumstances are so ambiguous. The approach taken by the courts is that if, whatever A's real intention may be, he so conducts himself that a reasonable person would believe that he was assenting to the contract proposed by the other party (B), and B contracts with A in that belief, there is a contract with the meaning and terms understood by B.[1] In *Wood v Scarth*,[2] the defendant wrote to the plaintiff, offering to let him a public house at £63 a year. After an interview with the defendant's clerk, the plaintiff accepted the offer by letter. The defendant had intended also to take a premium for the tenancy and thought that the clerk had made it clear to the plaintiff that this was a term of the contract. The plaintiff accepted the offer, thinking that his only financial obligation was to pay the rent. It was held that there was a contract in the sense understood by the plaintiff.

Wood v Scarth can be contrasted with *Scriven v Hindley*,[3] where the defendants successfully bid at an auction sale for a lot which consisted of tow, thinking that they were bidding for hemp, an infinitely superior product. Both tow and hemp were sold at the auction and samples of each were on display, although the defendants had not inspected them because they had already seen samples of hemp at the plaintiff's showroom. However, the lot in question was misleadingly described in the auctioneer's catalogue and the samples were confusingly marked. It was held that the contract was void. Clearly, in the special circumstances a reasonable person could not say whether there was a contract for the sale of hemp or for the sale of tow.

1   *Smith v Hughes* (1871) LR 6 QB 597 at 607; *Centrovincial Estates plc v Merchant Investors Assurance Co Ltd* (1983) Times, 8 March, CA.
2   (1858) 1 F & F 293.
3   [1913] 3 KB 564.

Equity
12.17   Where a contract is void at common law because of an operative mistake not shared by the parties, equity follows the law and will not grant specific performance[1] of the contract and may, to put the matter beyond doubt, rescind the contract.

In addition, the equitable remedy of specific performance may be refused if justice so demands, and it is reasonable to do so, even though the contract is not void for mistake at common law. It was refused, for instance, in *Wood v Scarth*,[2] although the plaintiff was able to obtain the common law remedy of damages. On the other hand, in *Tamplin v James*,[3] where the defendant had successfully bid for a property under the mistaken belief as to its extent, specific performance was ordered: the defendant's mistake was his own fault since he had failed to check the plans to which the auctioneer had drawn attention.

1 *Webster v Cecil* (1861) 30 Beav 62.
2 (1855) 2 K & J 33, (1858) 1 F & F 293; para 12.16, above.
3 (1880) 15 Ch D 215.

Mistake and documents

Rectification

12.18 We are concerned here with the case where the parties have made a perfectly valid oral agreement but it is later embodied in a document which *records their agreement inaccurately*. In such a case, the equitable remedy of rectification is available. This enables a court to rectify the document so that it embodies the agreement of the parties accurately. Oral evidence is admissible to show that the written document does not represent the agreement of the parties even if the contract at issue is one which must be made or evidenced in writing.

Rectification will normally only be ordered if the document does not represent the intentions of *both* parties. However, provided that there has been a common intention on the part of both parties, rectification can be ordered if: a. one party (A) mistakenly believed that a particular term was (or was not) included in the document to give effect to that intention; and b. the other party (B) *knew* of that mistake but nevertheless failed to draw the mistake to A's notice and allowed the document to be executed: and c. the mistake would benefit B or be detrimental to A.[1] On the other hand, if the document simply fails to mention an obligation which one party, but not the other, had intended to be a term of the contract rectification cannot be ordered.[2]

A document may be rectified to accord with the previously expressed intentions of the parties provided there was a *concluded antecedent agreement*, whether or not it was a binding contract. In *Joscelyne v Nissen*,[3] which finally determined the point, the plaintiff proposed that his daughter-in-law, the defendant, who shared the same house, should take over his car-hire business. It was clearly agreed that, if the defendant took over the business, she would pay many of the household bills relating to the plaintiff's part of the house. However, the subsequent written contract did not impose any obligation to pay the relevant household bills on the defendant and, though taking the profits of the car-hire business, she failed to pay these household bills after a while. The Court of Appeal permitted the written contract to be rectified so as to accord with the oral agreement, even though the latter was not binding.

There is no right to rectification; it will only be ordered where it is just and equitable to do so. For example, the existence of third-party rights dependent on the written contract will bar rectification unless the third party knows of the mistake. Lapse of time may also prevent rectification, and certain written documents cannot be rectified.[4]

1 *A. Roberts & Co v Leicestershire County Council* [1961] Ch 555, [1961] 2 All ER 545; *Thomas Bates & Son Ltd v Wyndham (Lingerie) Ltd* [1981] 1 All ER 1077, [1981] 1 WLR 505, CA.
2 *Riverlate Properties Ltd v Paul* [1974] Ch 133, [1974] 2 All ER 656, CA.
3 [1970] 2 QB 86, [1970] 1 All ER 1213, CA.
4 For example, the articles of association of a company, although the company may alter the articles under the Companies Act 1985.

Documents mistakenly signed

12.19 It is accepted that where a person signs a document which contains a contract he is bound by that contract. This is so even if it is not the contract which he expected and whether or not he has read or understood the document. An exception to this has been established; it is the plea of non est factum (it is not my deed), which, if proved, renders the contract void and permits the signatory of a written contract to deny liability under it.

To succeed in his plea of non est factum, the signatory must prove:

a. that the signed document was radically different in effect from that which he thought he was signing; and

b. that he was not careless in signing the document.

The leading case is the House of Lords' decision in *Saunders v Anglia Building Society*.[1] Mrs Gallie, an elderly widow, occupied a house under a lease. Her nephew, Parkin wished to raise money using the house as security. Mrs Gallie was happy for this to happen, provided she could live in the house rent-free until her death.[2] Because Parkin did not want to pay maintenance to his estranged wife, he adopted a circuitous method of raising money so as to appear not to have any funds. The scheme was to induce Mrs Gallie to assign the property by way of sale to a friend of Parkin, Lee, who would mortgage it and pay the money to Parkin. A document which assigned the property by way of sale was drawn up and Mrs Gallie signed it without reading it; she had, in fact, broken her glasses. She thought the document was a deed of gift transferring the house to Parkin so that he could mortgage it. Lee mortgaged the property to the Building Society but paid Parkin nothing. Mrs Gallie, pleading non est factum, subsequently sought a declaration that the assignment to Lee was void, so that the Building Society could not enforce the mortgage.

The House of Lords rejected Mrs Gallie's plea of non est factum. They found that the document she had signed was not radically different in effect from what she had intended to sign. Legally, there may be a great difference between an assignment by way of sale and a deed of gift, but the effect in this case was the same—to enable Parkin to raise money on the security of the house. Even if the signed document had been radically different from what was intended, Mrs Gallie had failed to establish that she had not been careless. She had not read the document nor asked for it to be read to her; she had consulted no professional advisers and she had not acted sensibly.

In deciding whether a party has established that he was not careless, the standard of the reasonable man applies to those of full age and understanding. On the other hand, the House of Lords' decision suggests that, if the party is illiterate or is mentally handicapped or is blind that characteristic should be taken into account in deciding whether it has been established that he was not careless. On this basis, a court dealing with a case involving an 'incapable' signatory would have to consider whether he used such care as a reasonable man with his incapacity would have used. If a blind man is proposing to sign a document, he should ask for it to be read to him by a trustworthy person, and, if he fails to do so, he cannot rely on non est factum.

1   [1971] AC 1004, [1970] 3 All ER 961, HL.

2 Mrs Gallie died before the case was heard by the House of Lords. Saunders was her executrix.

12.20 In *United Dominions Trust Ltd v Western*,[1] the defendant agreed to buy a car on hire purchase. He signed a document which was in fact a loan agreement with the plaintiffs and which did not specify the price of the car or the deposit paid. Incorrect figures were subsequently inserted by the sellers of the car, as the defendant later learnt. He failed to pay any instalments under the loan agreement and was sued. The Court of Appeal refused to allow the defendant to rely on the doctrine of non est factum because neither of its two requirements had been proved by him. First, the document signed was not radically different from that which he thought he was signing, and, second, since the same legal principles as to carelessness applied to documents signed in blank as they applied to other cases of erroneously signed documents, the defendant had not proved that he had exercised due care in signing in blank.

1 [1976] QB 513, [1975] 3 All ER 1017, CA.

12.21 Since *Saunders v Anglia Building Society*,[1] it seems unlikely that non est factum will be pleaded successfully in more than a few cases.

1 [1971] AC 1004, [1970] 3 All ER 961, HL.

Chapter 13

Misrepresentation, duress and undue influence

Misrepresentation

13.1 A misrepresentation is a false or misleading statement. Where a person makes a contract under a mistake induced by the misrepresentation of the other party, his legal position may be resolved by the application of the law relating to misrepresentation. It should be noted that, unless, as rarely happens, a mistake induced by a misrepresentation is such as to render the contract void under the rules discussed above, it is the rules which follow which govern the situation. These rules are somewhat involved, and different rules apply depending on whether there has been an active misrepresentation or a misrepresentation through non-disclosure.

Active misrepresentation

13.2 When one is faced with a situation involving an 'active misrepresentation' one must first ask whether the representation has become a term of the contract or not, applying the rules set out in paras 7.8 to 7.15 above. The division between active misrepresentations which have remained pre-contractual representations (mere representations) and those which have become terms of a resulting contract is fundamental since the remedies are different.

Active misrepresentations which have remained mere representations

13.3 If the misrepresentation has not become a contractual term, and provided certain requirements are satisfied, two remedies may be available to the misrepresentation: rescission of the contract (unless this is barred) and (in many cases) damages. The requirements mentioned above are that:

the misrepresentation must be one of fact;

it must have been addressed to the person misled; and

it must have induced the contract.

Misrepresentation of fact
13.4 There must be a misrepresentation by words or conduct of a past or

existing fact. It follows that there are many misrepresentations for which no relief is available. The following must be distinguished from misrepresentation of fact.

13.5 *Mere puffs* A representation which is mere vague sales talk is not regarded as a representation of fact, as is shown by *Dimmock v Hallett*.[1] At a sale of land by auction, it was said to be 'fertile and improvable'; in fact it was partly abandoned and useless. The representation was held to be a 'mere flourishing description by an auctioneer' affording no ground for relief. It is a question of fact whether a particular statement is merely vague sales talk or the assertion of some verifiable fact.

1   (1866) 2 Ch App 21.

13.6 *Statements of opinion* A statement which merely expresses an opinion or belief does not give grounds for relief if the opinion or belief turns out to be wrong. In *Bisset v Wilkinson*,[1] the vendor of a farm which had never been used as a sheep farm, told a prospective purchaser that in his judgment the land would support 2,000 sheep. It was held that, this being an honest statement of the vendor's opinion of the farm's capacity, no relief was available. It would have been different if there had been a misrepresentation of its actual capacity since this would have been a misrepresentation of fact.

What has been said in the last paragraph must be qualified by pointing out that in two cases statements of opinion can involve an implied misrepresentation of fact and so give rise to relief:

a. Where a person represents an opinion which he does not honestly hold he will at the same time make a misrepresentation of fact, the fact that he does not honestly hold the opinion.[2]

b. Where a person represents an opinion for which he does not have reasonable grounds, he will at the same time make a misrepresentation of fact if he impliedly represents that he has reasonable grounds for his opinion. A classic example is *Smith v Land and House Property Corpn*.[3] The vendor of a hotel described it as let to 'Mr Frederick Fleck (a most desirable tenant) . . . for an unexpired term of $27\frac{1}{2}$ years, thus offering a first-class investment'. Fleck had not paid the last quarter's rent and had paid the previous one by instalments and under pressure. The Court of Appeal held that the above statement was not merely of opinion but also involved a misrepresentation of fact because the vendor impliedly stated that he had reasonable grounds for his opinion. Too much should not be read into this decision because the court will only find such an implied representation where the facts on which the opinion is based are particularly within the knowledge of the person stating the opinion, and not when the facts are equally known to both parties.[4]

1   [1927] AC 177, PC
2   *Brown v Raphael* [1958] Ch 636 at 641, [1958] 2 All ER 79 at 81.
3   (1884) 28 Ch D 7, CA.
4   *Smith v Land and House Property Corpn* (1884) 28 Ch D 7 at 15.

13.7 *Statements as to the future* Such statements, the best of example of which is a statement of intention, are obviously not statements of fact in themselves and no remedy is available if the future event does not occur. However, a statement as to the future will involve a misrepresentation of fact if its maker does not honestly believe in its truth. In the case of a misrepresentation of intention this rule is well summarised by the statement of Bowen LJ in *Edgington v Fitzmaurice*,[1] that the state of a man's mind is as much a fact as the state of his digestion. In this case the plaintiff was induced to lend money to a company by representations made in a prospectus by the directors that the money would be used to improve the company's buildings and to expand its business. The directors' true intention was to use the money to pay off the company's debts. They were held liable in deceit (fraudulent misrepresentation) on the basis that their misrepresentation of present intentions was a misrepresentation of fact.

1 (1885) 29 Ch D 459, CA.

13.8 *Statements of law* A person who is induced to contract by a misrepresentation of law has no remedy.[1] The only exceptions are:

a. where, as in the case of a statement of opinion or intention, the representor wilfully misrepresents the fact that he does not believe his statement of the law;[2] and

b. where the misrepresentation relates to the existence or meaning of a foreign law, since such a misrepresentation is regarded by our courts as one of fact.[3]

A difficulty in this area is distinguishing a statement of law from a statement of fact. Clearly, a representation as to the *meaning* of a statute is one of law. However, in *West London Commercial Bank v Kitson*,[4] it was held that a misrepresentation of the *contents* of a Private Act was one of fact. The directors of a company represented that the company had power to accept bills and that they had authority to accept on its behalf. There was a misrepresentation since, under the Private Act which incorporated it, the company had no power to accept bills or authorise anyone to do so. It was held that the misrepresentation was one of fact since it related to the contents of a Private Act. It is doubtful whether this decision would be extended to a misrepresentation as to the contents of a Public Act because such a misrepresentation seems clearly to be one as to the general law.

A misrepresentation as to the contents or meaning of a document is one of fact. One authority is *Wauton v Coppard*.[5] The plaintiff contracted to buy a house from the defendant for use as a preparatory school. He made the contract after the defendant's agent had told him that there was nothing in the deed of restrictive covenants to prevent the running of a school. When the plaintiff received the deed he discovered that it prohibited any business or occupation whereby disagreeable noise or nuisance might be caused and he sought to rescind the contract. Romer J held that the misrepresentation made by the defendant's agent was one of fact, and that the contract would be set aside, because it concerned the contents of the deed. Likewise, in *Horry v Tate & Lyle Refineries Ltd*,[6] it was held that a misrepresentation as to the nature and effect of a contract for the settlement of a claim for compensation for personal injuries was one of fact.

1 *Beattie v Lord Ebury* (1872) 7 Ch App 777.
2 The point has not yet been decided by a court. It was left open for future decision in *West London Commercial Bank v Kitson* (1884) 13 QBD 360 at 362–363.
3 *André & Cie SA v Ets Michel Blanc & Fils* [1979] 2 Lloyd's Rep 427, CA.
4 (1884) 13 QBD 360, CA.

5   [1899] 1 Ch 92.
6   [1982] 2 Lloyd's Rep 416.

13.9   *Silence* Not surprisingly, silence cannot generally constitute an active misrepresentation.[1] However, there are two exceptions:

a.   Where silence distorts a positive assertion of fact there will be an active misrepresentation of fact. Thus, in *Dimmock v Hallet*,[2] it was said that if a vendor of land states that farms on it are let, but omits to say that the tenants have given notice to quit, his statement will be a misrepresentation of fact.

b.   Where a representation of fact is falsified by later events, before the conclusion of the contract, there will be an active misrepresentation if the representor fails to notify the other of the change. This is shown by *With v O'Flanagan*.[3] Negotiations for the sale of a medical practice were begun in January 1934. The defendant vendor represented to the plaintiff that the practice was producing £2,000 per annum, which was then true. Between January and May, the defendant was seriously ill and the practice was looked after by a number of locum tenentes with the result that the receipts had fallen to £5 per week by 1 May 1934. On 1 May 1934, the plaintiff, who had not been informed of the change of circumstances, signed a contract to purchase the practice. The Court of Appeal rescinded the contract on the ground that the defendant ought to have communicated the change of circumstances to the plaintiff. It said that the representation made to induce the contract must be treated as continuing until the contract was signed and what was initially a true representation had turned into a misrepresentation.

1   See further paras 13.34 and 13.35 below.
2   (1866) 2 Ch App 21.
3   [1936] Ch 575, [1936] 1 All ER 727, CA.

The misrepresentation must have been addressed by the misrepresentor to the person misled
13.10   A leading authority for this requirement is *Peek v Gurney*.[1] The appellant purchased shares on the faith of misrepresentations contained in a prospectus issued by the promoters of a company. The appellant was not a person to whom shares had been allotted on the first formation of the company but had merely purchased shares from such allottees. The House of Lords held that the appellant could not succeed in his suit against the promoters because the prospectus was only addressed to the first applicants for shares and could not be supposed to extend to others.

The present requirement is not as stringent as may appear at first sight because:

a.   It is possible for a representation to be made to the public in general, as in the case of an advertisement.

b.   A representation need not be made directly to the person misled, or his agent, in order to satisfy the present requirement. It suffices that the representor knew that the person to whom he made the misrepresentation would pass it on to the plaintiff. This is shown by *Pilmore v Hood*.[2] The defendant wished to sell a public house to X and fraudulently misrepresented that the annual takings were £180. X was unable to buy and with the defendant's knowledge persuaded the plaintiff to buy by repeating the defendant's misrepresentation. The defendant was held liable in damages to the plaintiff for his fraudulent misrepresentation. An important limit on the rule in *Pilmore v Hood* is that, if the person (A) to whom the misrepresentation is originally made by the defendant (D) contracts with D as a result, the misrepresentation is deemed to be exhausted. Thus, if A then contracts to sell the property to B, repeating D's misrepresentation, as D knew he would, B has no redress against D because D's misrepresentation, being exhausted, is not regarded as addressed to B.[3] Of course, in such a case B is not remediless because he can pursue the normal remedies for misrepresentation against A who passed on the misrepresentation.

1 (1873) LR 6 HL 377, HL.
2 (1838) 5 Bing NC 97. Also see *Yianni v Edwin Evans & Sons* [1982] QB 438, [1981] 3 All ER 592.
3 *Gross v Lewis Hillman Ltd* [1970] Ch 445, [1969] 3 All ER 1476, CA.

The misrepresentation must have induced the misrepresentee to make the contract

13.11 The question of inducement is one of fact but, if the misrepresentor made a statement of a nature likely to induce a person to contract and with a view to inducing this, it will normally be inferred that it did induce the misrepresentee to contract. However, this inference is rebuttable and will, for example, be rebutted in the following three cases:

a. If the misrepresentee actually knew the truth.[1]

b. If the misrepresentee was ignorant of the misrepresentation when the contract was made. In *Re Northumberland and Durham District Banking Co, ex p Bigge*,[2] the plaintiff, who had bought some shares in a company, sought to have the purchase rescinded on the ground that the company had published false reports of its financial state. He failed; one of the reasons was because he was unable to prove that he had read any of the reports or that anyone had told him of their contents.

c. If the misrepresentee did not allow the representation to affect his judgment. Thus, if the misrepresentee investigates the truth of the representation (as where a prospective purchaser has a house surveyed) and relies on his investigation, rather than the representation, in making the contract the inference of inducement is rebutted, except in the case of fraud. In *Attwood v Small*,[3] the appellant offered to sell a mine, making exaggerated representations as to its earning capacity. The respondent agreed to buy if the appellant could verify his representations and appointed agents to investigate the matter. The agents, who were experienced, visited the mine and were given every facility. They reported that the representations were true and the contract was made. The House of Lords held that the contract could not be rescinded for misrepresentation because the respondents had not relied on the misrepresentations but on their own independent investigations. By way of contrast, the inference of inducement is not rebutted where the misrepresentee could have investigated and discovered the falsity of the representation but chose not to do so.[4]

1 *Begbie v Phosphate Sewage Co* (1875) LR 10 QB 491; *Redgrave v Hurd* (1881) 20 Ch D 1, CA.
2 (1858) 28 LJ Ch 50.
3 (1838) 6 Cl & Fin 232, HL.

4   *Redgrave v Hurd* (1881) 20 Ch D 1, CA; *Laurence v Lexcourt Holdings Ltd* [1978] 2 All ER 810, [1978] 1 WLR 1128.

13.12   Before leaving the requirement of inducement a general point must be noted. Provided that it was one of the inducements, the misrepresentation need not be the sole inducement. This is shown by *Edgington v Fitzmaurice*,[1] where the plaintiff was induced to take debentures in a company partly by a misrepresentation in the prospectus and partly by his own mistaken belief that debenture holders would have a charge on the company's property. He was held entitled to rescission.

1   (1885) 29 Ch D 459, CA.

Remedies for active misrepresentations which have remained mere representations

13.13   Provided the above requirements are satisfied one or more of the remedies set out below is or are available to the misrepresentee. Alternatively, the misrepresentee can refuse to carry out the contract and, provided (generally) that he returns what he obtained under it, successfully resist any claim for damages or specific performance.

Rescission

13.14   The effect of a misrepresentation is to make the contract voidable — not void, so that it remains valid unless and until the misrepresentee elects to rescind it on discovering the misrepresentation. Rescission entails setting the contract aside as if it had never been made, the misrepresentee recovering what he transferred under the contract but having to restore what he obtained under it. The effect of misrepresentation is important in relation to the rights of third parties. If A sells a car to B under a contract which is voidable for B's misrepresentation, a voidable title passes to B and, if C (an innocent purchaser) buys the car from B before A has decided to rescind, A loses the right to rescind and C obtains a valid title.[1] This must be distinguished from the situation where the contract is void for mistake. There, title to the goods never passes and they can always be recovered, or damages obtained in lieu, from the other party or a third person to whom they have been transferred.[2]

1   *White v Garden* (1851) 10 CB 919.
2   *Cundy v Lindsay* (1878) 3 App Cas 459, HL.

13.15   Rescission can be effected in two ways. First, by bringing legal proceedings for an order for rescission. This may be necessary where a formal document or transaction, such as a lease, has to be set aside by a court order. In other cases a court order is not essential but may be advantageous if the misrepresentor is likely to prove unwilling to return what he has obtained under the contract.

Second, rescission can be effected by the misrepresentee making it clear that he refuses to be bound by the contract. Normally, communication of this decision to the misrepresentor is required, but there is an exception. If a fraudulent misrepresentor absconds, it suffices that the misrepresentee records his intention to rescind the contract by some overt act that is reasonable in the circumstances. This was decided by the Court of Appeal in *Car and Universal Finance Co Ltd v Caldwell*.[1] The defendant sold his car to N in return for a cheque which was dishonoured when he presented it the next day.[2] The defendant immediately informed the police and the Automobile Association of the fraudulent transaction. Subsequently, N sold the car to X who sold it to Y who sold it to Z who sold it to the plaintiffs who bought it in good faith. It was held that in the circumstances the defendant had done enough to rescind the contract before the plaintiffs bought the car, title had therefore re-vested in him and the plaintiffs had not got title.

1 [1965] 1 QB 525, [1964] 1 All ER 290, CA.
2 By his conduct in drawing the cheque, N had fraudulently misrepresented that the existing state of facts was such that in the ordinary course of events the cheque would be honoured: *R v Hazelton* (1874) LR 2 CCR 134 at 140.

13.16 There are five bars to the right to rescind:

a. *Affirmation of contract by misrepresentee* This occurs if, after discovering that the misrepresentation is untrue, the misrepresentee declares his intention to waive his right to rescission or acts in a way that such an intention can be inferred. This inference was drawn in *Long v Lloyd*.[1] The plaintiff bought a lorry as the result of the defendant's misrepresentation that it was in excellent condition. On the plaintiff's first business journey the dynamo broke and he noticed several other serious defects. On the next business journey the lorry broke down and the plaintiff, realising that it was in a very bad condition, sought to rescind the contract. The Court of Appeal held that the second journey constituted an affirmation because the plaintiff knew by then that the representation was untrue. Similarly, if a person, who has applied for, and been allotted, shares in reliance on a misrepresentation, subsequently discovers the falsity but nevertheless attempts to sell them, or retains dividends paid on them, or neglects to have his name removed from the register of shareholders, an intention to affirm will be inferred.[2] Once the election to rescind or affirm has been made it is irrevocable.[3]

b. *Lapse of time* This can provide evidence of affirmation where the misrepresentee fails to rescind for a considerable time after discovering the falsity.[4] In addition, lapse of time can operate as a separate bar to rescission in cases where the misrepresentee has not delayed after discovering the falsity. This is shown by *Leaf v International Galleries*,[5] where the plaintiff bought from the defendant a picture of Salisbury Cathedral which the latter had innocently represented to be by Constable. Five years later, the plaintiff discovered that this was a misrepresentation and immediately sought to rescind the contract. The Court of Appeal held that his right to rescind had been lost through lapse of a reasonable time to discover the falsity. This bar probably does not apply in the case of a fraudulent misrepresentation.

c. *Inability to restore* The main objects of rescission are to restore the parties to their former position and to prevent unjust enrichment.[6] Thus, if either party has so changed or otherwise dealt with what he has obtained under the contract that he cannot restore it, rescission is barred.[7] So, for example, the purchaser of a cake cannot rescind the contract if he has eaten it.[7]

There are three qualifications on the present bar:

i A fraudulent misrepresentor cannot rely on his own dealings with what he has obtained as a bar to rescission by the misrepresentee.[8]

ii The fact that a seller has spent the money which he has received does not make restitution impossible since one bank note is as good as another and the seller can restore what he obtained under the contract by handing over other notes.

iii Precise restitution is not required for rescission. Provided the property obtained under the contract can substantially be restored, rescission can be enforced even though the property has deteriorated, declined in value or otherwise changed. For example, in *Armstrong v Jackson*,[9] a broker fraudulently sold shares to the plaintiff. Later, when the shares had fallen to one-twelfth of their value at the time of sale, the plaintiff claimed rescission. It was held that, since the plaintiff could return the actual shares, rescission would be ordered, subject to the defendant's repayment of the purchase price being credited with the dividends received by the plaintiff. However, where the deterioration or loss of value results from the voluntary dealings with it by the person who obtained it under the contract, he must not only account for any profits derived from it but also pay compensation for such deterioration or loss of value.[10] If both parties have benefited from the property obtained by them, the court, in ordering rescission, can set off the benefits received by one party against those received by the other.[11]

d. *Bona fide purchaser for value* As has been indicated in para 13.14, above, if, before the misrepresentee elects to rescind, a third party has innocently purchased the property, or an interest in it, for value from the misrepresentor, his rights are valid against the misrepresentee who loses the chance to rescind. This is illustrated by *White v Garden*,[12] where a rogue bought 50 tons of iron from Garden by persuading him to take in payment a fraudulent bill of exchange. The rogue then sold the iron for value to White who acted in good faith (ie was unaware of the rogue's fraudulent misrepresentation) and Garden delivered the iron to White. The bill of exchange was subsequently dishonoured and Garden seized and removed some of the iron. Garden was held liable for what is now the tort of conversion; he had purported to rescind the contract with the rogue too late, the rogue's voidable title having been made unavoidable when White innocently bought the iron from him. In *Car and Universal Finance Co Ltd v Caldwell*,[13] on the other hand, rescission was not barred because it occurred before the intervention of a bona fide purchaser for value.

e. *The wound-up company* Under the rule in *Oakes v Turquand*,[14] if a shareholder wishes to rescind his contract to take up shares in a company on the ground of misrepresentation he must do so before a winding-up of the company commences.

1 [1958] 2 All ER 402, [1958] 1 WLR 753, CA.
2 *Re Scottish Petroleum Co Ltd* (1883) 23 Ch D 413 at 434.
3 *Re Hop and Malt Exchange and Warehouse Co, ex p Briggs* (1866) LR 1 Eq 483; *Re Scottish Petroleum* (1883) 23 Ch D 413, CA.
4 *Clough v London and North Western Rly Co* (1871) LR 7 Exch 26 at 35.
5 [1950] 2 KB 86, [1950] 1 All ER 693, CA.
6 *Spence v Crawford* [1939] 3 All ER 271 at 288–289.

7   *Clarke v Dickson* (1858) EB & E 148; *Mackenzie v Royal Bank of Canada* [1934] AC 468,
    PC.
8   *Spence v Crawford* [1939] 3 All ER 271 at 280–282.
9   [1917] 2 KB 822.
10 *Erlanger v New Sombrero Phosphate Co* (1878) 3 App Cas 1218 at 1278–1279.
11 *Hulton v Hulton* [1917] 1 KB 813, CA.
12 (1851) 10 CB 919.
13 Para 13.15 above.
14 (1867) LR 2 HL 325, HL.

13.17   Before leaving the bars to rescission it should be noted that the courts have power, in the case of non-fraudulent misrepresentations, to refuse rescission, or to refuse to recognise a purported rescission, and to award damages in lieu. This power is discussed in para 13.24 below.

Damages
13.18   It must be emphasised at the outset that we are concerned here with damages for misrepresentation and not with damages for breach of contract, which we have discussed in ch 11 and which are a different species. Sometimes damages for misrepresentation can be recovered under the common law rules of tort: sometimes under the Misrepresentation Act 1967. Rescission and damages are alternative remedies in many cases, but if the victim of a fraudulent or negligent misrepresentation has suffered consequential loss he may rescind *and* sue for damages.

13.19   The discussion of the rules of assessment of damages for misrepresentation requires the division of the relevant law into five classes:

13.20   *Fraudulent misrepresentation* Fraudulent misrepresentation gives rise to an action for damages for the tort of deceit. The classic definition of fraud in this context was given by Lord Herschell in *Derry v Peek*.[1] Lord Herschell stated that fraud is proved where it is shown that a misrepresentation has been made (i) knowingly, or (ii) without belief in its truth, or (iii) recklessly, careless whether it be true or false. A misrepresentation would not be fraudulent if there was an honest belief in its truth when it was made, even though there were no reasonable grounds for that belief. Motive was irrelevant: an intention to cheat or injure was not required.
   Where they compensate for fraudulent misrepresentation as to the subject matter of the contract, damages for deceit are assessed according to the 'out of pocket rule', ie an amount is awarded which puts the injured party into the position in which he would have been had the fraudulent misrepresentation never been made. Where the misrepresentee has been induced by the fraudulent misrepresentation to agree to purchase a particular thing, this is achieved by awarding the misrepresentee the difference between what he paid for the thing in question and its actual value at that time. An illustration is provided by *McConnel v Wright*,[2] where a person who had been induced to buy shares by a fraudulent misrepresentation in a prospectus recovered the difference between the purchase price and the actual value of the shares, assessed as at the time of the contract.
   The 'out of pocket rule' should be contrasted with the measure of damages for breach of contract. Here the 'loss of the bargain' rule normally applies, as has been explained in para 11.3 above, and the injured party recovers an amount (the difference between the 'represented value' at the

time of the contract and the actual value) which puts him into the position in which he would have been if the representation had been true. This distinction can be demonstrated by the following example. E, a numismatist, is induced to buy a coin by F who deceives him as to its rarity. E pays £100 for the coin which in fact was worth £50. If F's representation had been true the coin would have been worth £200. F's representation does not become a term of the contract and therefore E's only claim for damages is for damages for fraudulent misrepresentation (deceit). These amount to £50 under the 'out of pocket rule'. If the misrepresentation had become a contractual term E could have chosen to sue instead for damages for breach of contract, which would have amounted to £150 under the 'loss of the bargain rule'. It is, of course, possible to envisage situations where the 'out of pocket' rule would afford a more generous measure than the 'loss of the bargain rule', as where if F's representation had been true the coin would have been worth £95.

A person who has been induced into a contract by a fraudulent misrepresentation may also recover damages for any consequential loss or damage, such as expenses, personal injury, damage to his property or distress or disappointment,[3] which he may have suffered, provided it is not too remote. In the tort of deceit the rule of remoteness of damage appears to be that the defendant is liable for all actual damage or loss directly flowing from the deceit,[4] a more liberal rule than that which applies in other torts, and also more liberal than the rule of remoteness which applies in the case of damages for breach of contract, where damages are limited to compensation for consequential loss which was within the parties' reasonable contemplation, when the contract was made, as the probable result of its breach.[5]

1 (1889) 14 App Cas 337, HL.
2 [1903] 1 Ch 546, CA.
3 *Archer v Brown* [1985] QB 401 [1984] 2 All ER 267.
4 *Doyle v Olby (Ironmongers) Ltd* [1969] 2 QB 158, [1969] 2 All ER 119, CA. Contrast *Archer v Brown* [1984] 2 All ER 267 at 277, where the judge accepted that the test was the normal test of reasonable foreseeability.
5 See paras 21.17–21.20 below (other torts), and para 11.5 above (breach of contract).

13.21 *Negligent misrepresentation under the Misrepresentation Act 1967* Section 2(1) of the Act of 1967 provides that where a person has entered into a contract after a misrepresentation has been made to him by another party thereto and as a result of it has suffered loss, then, if the misrepresentor would be liable to damages for misrepresentation if it had been made fraudulently, he is to be so liable notwithstanding that the misrepresentation was not made fraudulently, unless he proves that he had reasonable grounds to believe and did believe up to the time the contract was made that the facts represented were true. In other words, the misrepresentor is deemed negligent, and liable to pay damages, unless he proves in the stated way that he was not negligent. Whether the misrepresentor can prove this will depend, for instance, on whether he was an expert or not, the length of the negotiations and whether he himself had been misled by another. The representor's burden of proof is a difficult one to discharge. This is shown by *Howard Marine and Dredging Co Ltd v A Ogden & Sons (Excavations) Ltd*.[1] During negotiations for the hire of two barges, Howard's agent misrepresented their capacity in reliance on an error in Lloyd's Register. The Court of Appeal held that the burden of proof had not been discharged, since a file in Howard's possession disclosed the real capacity.

Section 2(1) applies where the misrepresentation was made on behalf of a party to the subsequent contract by his agent,[2] but in such a case the misrepresentee only has an action under s2(1) against that party and not against his agent.[3]

Section 2(1) does not state how damages are to be assessed in cases falling within it. Although the matter is not free from doubt, it appears that, where they compensate for misrepresentation as to the subject matter of the contract, damages are assessed according to the 'out of pocket' rule, rather than the 'loss of the bargain' rule which applies in the case of damages for breach of contract;[4] the cases[5] which indicate, or suggest, the contrary are open to doubt. The misrepresentee can only recover for consequential loss if it is not too remote and, in this context, the same rule of remoteness applies as in fraudulent misrepresentation, that of direct consequences.[6]

1 [1978] QB 574, [1978] 2 All ER 1134, CA.
2 *Gosling v Anderson* (1972) 223 Estates Gazette 1743.
3 *Resolute Maritime Inc v Nippon Kaiji Kyokai* [1983] 2 All ER 1; an agent may be liable for a fraudulent misrepresentation or for negligent misrepresentation at common law.
4 *F and B Entertainments Ltd v Leisure Enterprises Ltd* (1976) 240 Estates Gazette 455; *André & Cie SA v Ets Michel Blanc & Fils* [1977] 2 Lloyd's Rep 166 at 177 (this point was not dealt with on appeal: [1979] Lloyd's Rep 427, CA); *Chesneau v Interhome Ltd* (1983) Times, 9 June; *Sharneyford Supplies Ltd v Edge* [1985] 1 All ER 976.
5 *Jarvis v Swan Tours Ltd* [1973] QB 233, [1973] 1 All ER 71, CA; *Davis & Co (Wines) Ltd v Afa-Minerva (EMI) Ltd* [1974] 2 Lloyd's Rep 27; *Watts v Spence* [1976] Ch 165, [1975] 2 All ER 528; *South London Tyre and Battery Centre v Bonar* (1983) 134 NLJ 603, CA.
6 *Davis etc. v Afa-Minerva; F and B Entertainments Ltd v Leisure Enterprises Ltd* (1976) 240 Estates Gazette 455; *McNally v Welltrade International* [1978] IRLR 497.

13.22 *Negligent misrepresentation at common law* The victim of a negligent misrepresentation may be able to sue the misrepresentor under the principles in *Hedley Byrne & Co Ltd v Heller & Partners Ltd*,[1] which we discuss fully in paras 19.13 to 19.16 below. If the misrepresentee chooses to do so, he must prove (i) that the misrepresentor owed him a duty to take reasonable care in making representation, which duty only arises if there is a 'special relationship'; (ii) that the misrepresentor was in breach of that duty, and (iii) that damage resulted from that breach. A 'special relationship' is only established where the misrepresentor has some special knowledge or skill relevant to the advice or information contained in his representation, knows (or it is reasonably foreseeable) that the misrepresentee will rely on that advice or information, and (generally) the misrepresentee has asked for that advice or information (as opposed to the misrepresentor volunteering it).

The *Hedley Byrne* principles were applied to a representation made in pre-contractual negotiations by the Court of Appeal in *Esso Petroleum Co Ltd v Mardon*.[2] In negotiations in 1963 for the tenancy of a filling station, Esso negligently told Mr Mardon that the station had an estimated annual throughput of 200,000 gallons. Mr Mardon was induced to take the tenancy but the actual annual throughput never exceeded 86,000 gallons and Mr Mardon was awarded damages against Esso. One reason for its decision given by the Court of Appeal was that Esso, having special knowledge and skill in estimating petrol throughput, were under the duty of care imposed by *Hedley Byrne*—which applied to pre-contractual statements—and were in breach of that duty. In this case, Mr Mardon could not have relied on the Misrepresentation Act 1967, s2(1) because the misrepresentation had occurred before the Act came into force.

In practice, it is normally better to rely on s2(1) in the case of a negligent misrepresentation because the onus of disproving negligence is placed on the defendant under that section, whereas if he relies on the *Hedley Byrne* principles the plaintiff must prove that they are satisfied. In addition, no special relationship need be proved under s2(1). However, the *Hedley Byrne* principles are still important in cases of pre-contractual misrepresentation in two situations: where the misrepresentation is made by a third party to the contract; and where the contractual negotiations do not result in a contract between the defendant and the plaintiff but the plaintiff nevertheless suffers loss in reliance on the misrepresentation. In both cases, assuming their requirements are satisfied, there can be tortious liability under the principles in *Hedley Byrne*, although there can be no rescission for misrepresentation nor damages under the Act of 1967.

The measure of damages under *Hedley Byrne* is governed by the 'out of pocket rule'[3] and questions of remoteness of damage by the test of reasonable foreseeability at the time of the breach of duty.[4]

1 [1964] AC 465, [1963] 2 All ER 575, HL.
2 [1976] QB 801, [1976] 2 All ER 5, CA.
3 See, for example, *JEB Fasteners Ltd v Marks Bloom & Co Ltd* [1983] 1 All ER 583 at 587.
4 Paras 21.17–21.20 below.

13.23 *Innocent misrepresentation* Subject to what is said in para 13.24 below, damages cannot be awarded for a misrepresentation which is not fraudulent or negligent, as defined above. However, an indemnity—which is different from damages—may be awarded.

13.24 *Damages in lieu of rescission* The Misrepresentation Act 1967, s2(2) provides that, where a person has entered into a contract after a non-fraudulent misrepresentation has been made to him which would entitle him to rescind the contract, then, if it is claimed in proceedings arising out of the contract that the contract ought to be or has been rescinded, the court or arbitrator may declare the contract subsisting and award damages in lieu of rescission, if of the opinion that it would be equitable to do so. The rationale for this power is that rescission may be too drastic in some cases, eg where the misrepresentation was trifling. In exercising his discretion, a judge or arbitrator is required by s2(2) to have regard to the nature of the misrepresentation and the loss that would be caused by it if the contract was upheld, as well as the loss that rescission would cause to the other party.

It must be emphasised that this power to award damages in lieu of rescission can only be exercised if rescission has not been barred, eg by affirmation of the contract, and cannot be exercised in the case of a fraudulent misrepresentation. The assessment of damages under s2(2) is uncertain. Probably, the misrepresentor is liable to pay the difference between the price he received and the actual value of the property and, in the case of consequential loss, compensation for those items for which an indemnity could have been awarded if rescission had been granted. Where a person has been held liable to pay damages under s2(1) of the Act of 1967, the judge or arbitrator, in assessing damages thereunder, must take into account any damages in lieu of rescission under s2(2).[1]

1 Misrepresentation Act 1967, s2(2).

Indemnity

13.25 It has already been noted that the object of rescission is to restore the contracting parties to their former position as if the contract had never been made. As part of this restoration the misrepresentee can claim an indemnity against any *obligations necessarily created by the contract*.[1] The italicised words must be emphasised since they indicate that an indemnity is far less extensive than damages, as was recognised by the Court of Appeal in *Newbigging v Adam*.[2] A classic example of this distinction is provided by *Whittington v Seale-Hayne*.[3] The plaintiffs, breeders of prize poultry, were induced to take a lease of the defendant's premises by his innocent misrepresentation that the premises were in a thoroughly sanitary condition. Under the lease, the plaintiffs covenanted to execute all works required by any local or public authority. Owing to the insanitary condition of the premises the water supply was poisoned, the plaintiffs' manager and his family became very ill, and the poultry became valueless for breeding purposes or died. In addition, the local authority required the drains to be renewed. The plaintiffs sought an indemnity for the following losses: the value of the stock lost; loss of profit on sales; loss of breeding season; rent, and medical expenses on behalf of the manager. Farwell J rescinded the lease and held that the plaintiffs could recover an indemnity for what they had spent on rent, rates and repairs under the covenants in the lease, because these expenses arose necessarily out of the occupation of the premises or were incurred under the covenants in the lease and were thus obligations necessarily created by the contract. However, Farwell J refused to award an indemnity for the loss of stock, loss of profits, loss of breeding season or the medical expenses, since to do so would be to award damages, not an indemnity, there being no obligation created by the contract to carry on a poultry farm on the premises or to employ a manager, etc.

1 *Whittington v Seale-Hayne* (1900) 82 LT 49, adopting the view of Bowen LJ in *Newbigging v Adam* (1886) 34 Ch D 582, CA.
2 (1886) 34 Ch D 582, CA.
3 (1900) 82 LT 49.

13.26 Two further points may be made concerning the award of an indemnity:

a. Being ancillary to rescission, an indemnity cannot be awarded if rescission is barred.

b. The remedy of an indemnity is redundant where the court can, and does, award damages for misrepresentation. However, where there has merely been an innocent misrepresentation and the court decides not to award damages in lieu of rescission, the availability of an award of an indemnity is very important.

Active misrepresentations which have become contractual terms
13.27 Whether a misrepresentation made during pre-contractual negotiations has become a term of the resulting contract, or of a contract collateral

to it, is determined in accordance with the rules set out in paras 7.8 to 7.15 above.

If the misrepresentation has become a contractual term the misrepresentee has a choice between two courses of action.

Breach of contract

13.28 As in the case of the breach of any other contractual term, the misrepresentee can sue for breach of contract. If he does so, he can recover damages for breach of contract (as opposed to damages for misrepresentation). Where the misrepresentation relates to the subject matter of the contract, damages will be assessed according to the normal contractual rule, the 'loss of the bargain' rule, and recovery can also be had for all consequential loss within the parties' reasonable contemplation, at the time the contract was made, as a probable result of the breach. The relevant law has already been discussed in detail in ch 11. In addition, if the misrepresentation has become a condition of the contract, or an 'intermediate term' and there has been a sufficiently serious breach of it, the misrepresentee can also terminate the contract for *breach*, a matter which we discussed in paras 9.3 to 9.21 above.

Misrepresentation Act 1967, s1(a)

13.29 The misrepresentee's alternative course of action is to make use of the Misrepresentation Act 1967, s1(a). Under this provision a person who is induced to enter into a contract by a misrepresentation of fact, which has become a term of the contract, can elect to rescind the contract for *misrepresentation* subject to the bars to rescission mentioned in para 13.16 above. However, if he does so rescind he cannot recover damages for breach of contract since rescission for misrepresentation sets the contract aside for all purposes, including his right to claim damages for its breach, although he may be able to claim damages for misrepresentation, depending on the circumstances, in accordance with the rules set out in paras 13.18 to 13.24 above.

13.30 The choice of a particular course of action will depend very much on whether greater damages will be obtained for breach of contract or for misrepresentation and on whether the plaintiff wishes, and is able, to rescind for misrepresentation.

Avoidance of provision excluding or limiting liability for misrepresentation
13.31 The Misrepresentation Act 1967, s3[1] provides that if a contract contains a term which would exclude or restrict—

a. any liability to which a party to a contract may be subject by reason of any misrepresentation made by him before the contract was made; or

b. any remedy available to another party to the contract by reason of such a misrepresentation,

that term is of no effect, except in so far as it satisfies the requirement of reasonableness; and it is for the person claiming that it satisfies that requirement to show that it does. The requirement of reasonableness is that the term must have been a fair and reasonable one to be included having regard to the circumstances which were, or ought reasonably to have been, known to or in the contemplation of the parties when the contract was made.[2]

1 As substituted by the Unfair Contract Terms Act 1977, s8.
2 Unfair Contract Terms Act 1977, s11(1).

13.32 Section 3 is of great importance in relation to the purported exclusion or restriction of liability for misrepresentations made by estate agents. We must start by reminding the reader that, where an estate agent makes a misrepresentation in respect of a property which he has been instructed to sell and thereby induces another to enter into a contract to buy it, it is his client who becomes liable for misrepresentation to the other party;[1] although, of course, the client may seek to recover an indemnity for his loss from the agent[2] and the agent himself may be held liable to the other party in tort if deceit or negligence can be proved. Not surprisingly, in an attempt to exclude or restrict a client's liability for a misrepresentation made by his estate agent, auction conditions, conditions of sale by tender and the like often contain a contract term (exemption clause) purporting to so exclude or restrict. Such a term is caught by the Misrepresentation Act, s3 and is of no effect except in so far as it satisfies the requirement of reasonableness. In this context, a 'contract term' is not limited to one which expressly excludes or restricts liability, since it has been held that it also includes a term of the contract purporting to nullify any representation altogether so as to bring about a situation in law as if there was no representation, such as a term that 'although the particulars are believed to be correct their accuracy is not guaranteed and any intending purchaser must satisfy himself by inspection or otherwise as to their correctness'.[3] Similarly, it seems that s3 applies to a contract term which states that, notwithstanding any statement of fact included in the particulars, the vendor shall conclusively be presumed to have made no representation.[4] On the other hand, a contract term which denies that an estate agent has any authority at all to make representations is not caught by s3 and may therefore prevent the client from incurring liability for a misrepresentation by the estate agent.[5]

It must be emphasised that s3 is solely concerned with 'contract terms' (ie exemption clauses contained in a contract), and has no application to non-contractual clauses of the type commonly found in estate agents' particulars. Although it has been held that such a non-contractual clause denying that an estate agent has any authority to make representations is effective to prevent the client incurring liability for a misrepresentation by the estate agent,[6] it has been suggested that other non-contractual clauses purporting to exclude or restrict the client's liability for misrepresentation are ineffective to do so.[7]

1 Para 17.30 below.
2 Para 17.16 below.
3 *Cremdean Properties Ltd v Nash* (1977) 244 Estates Gazette 547, CA; *Walker v Boyle* [1982] 1 All ER 634 [1982] 1 WLR 495; *South Western General Property Co Ltd v Marton* (1982) 263 Estates Gazette 1090.
4 *Cremdean Properties Ltd v Nash* (1977) 244 Estates Gazette 547 at 551.
5 *Overbrooke Estates Ltd v Glencombe Properties Ltd* [1974] 3 All ER 511, [1974] 1 WLR 1335.
6 *Collins v Howell-Jones* (1980) 259 Estates Gazette 331, CA.
7 *Cremdean Properties Ltd v Nash* (1977) 244 Estates Gazette 547 at 551.

13.33 Section 3 not only applies where the relevant misrepresentation has remained a mere representation but also where it has become a contractual term—at least, as far as rescission for misrepresentation and damages for misrepresentation are concerned, although it is uncertain whether it applies if the misrepresentee elects to treat it as a breach of contract.

Misrepresentation through non-disclosure

13.34 Generally, mere silence as to a material fact or tacit acquiescence in another's erroneous belief concerning such a fact does not constitute a misrepresentation. Thus, in *Turner v Green*,[1] where two solicitors arranged a compromise of certain legal proceedings, the failure of the plaintiff's solicitor to inform the defendant's of a material fact was held not to be a ground for relief, even though the defendant would not have made the compromise if he had known of that fact.

1   [1895] 2 Ch 205.

13.35 However, in certain situations there is a duty to disclose material facts, breach of which gives rise to relief. Two of these situations have been referred to already: where silence distorts a positive assertion and where a positive assertion is falsified by later events (see para 13.9 above). In these cases silence is deemed to be an active misrepresentation. In addition, in the case of contracts uberrimae fidei—of the utmost good faith—a duty to disclose fully all material facts is imposed, breach of which is regarded as a misrepresentation through non-disclosure for which relief is available.

Contracts uberrimae fidei can be divided into three types:

a. insurance contracts;

b. contracts preliminary to family arrangements; and

c. contracts where one party is in a fiduciary relationship with the other.

Insurance contracts

13.36 An intending assured is under a duty to disclose all material facts known to him.[1] In the case of marine insurance, this duty of disclosure is now imposed by the Marine Insurance Act 1906, s18(1) but otherwise it rests on the common law. A material fact in this context is one which would influence the mind of a prudent insurer in fixing the premium or determining whether he will take the risk.[2] In marine insurance the assured is deemed by s18(1) of the Act of 1906 to know every fact which ought to be known to him, but otherwise the duty of disclosure only extends to those material facts which are actually known to him.[3] However, there is nothing to stop the contract imposing a more stringent duty to disclose all facts whether material or not, and whether known or not, by providing that the accuracy of the information given by the assured is a condition of the validity of the policy. This is a regrettable common practice.

1   An early authority is *Carter v Boehm* (1766) 3 Burr 1905.
2   *London Assurance v Mansel* (1879) 11 Ch D 363; *Lambert v Co-Operative Insurance Society* [1975] 2 Lloyd's Rep 485, CA; *Woolcott v Sun Alliance and London Insurance Ltd* [1978] 1 All ER 1253, [1978] 1 WLR 493; Marine Insurance Act 1906, s18(2). Under the

Rehabilitation of Offenders Act 1974, there is an exception to the duty of disclosure, in that failure to disclose a 'spent' conviction does not amount to breach of that duty. A conviction which has resulted in a sentence of imprisonment for life or for a term of more than two and a half years can never become 'spent' but for other sentences convictions become 'spent' after a prescribed period (which, in the case of imprisonment for more than six months but less than two and a half years, is ten years).

3   *Joel v Law Union and Crown Insurance Co* [1908] 2 KB 863, CA.

Contracts preliminary to 'family arrangements'

13.37   Examples of 'family arrangements' are the settlement, or resettlement, of land between members of a family and the surrender by one member of a family of some proprietary right to another member. Persons making contracts for such purposes are under a duty imposed by equity to make a full disclosure of all material facts known to them.[1]

1   *Gordon v Gordon* (1821) 3 Swan 400.

Contracts where one party is in a fiduciary relationship with the other

13.38   Where one prospective contracting party stands in a fiduciary relationship with the other, he is under a duty imposed by equity to disclose any material fact known to him which might be considered likely to affect the contract between them. Examples of such relationships are: solicitor or accountant and client; trustee and beneficiary; principal and agent; partner and partner; parent and child; and doctor and patient. In such cases, the first named party is deemed to have such influence over the other that the contract will be rescinded unless he proves that he has fulfilled his duty of disclosure, and that the contract is advantageous to the other. Thus, in *Armstrong v Jackson*,[1] where a stockbroker, who was employed to buy shares for his client, sold the client his own shares without disclosing this fact, it was held that the contract could be rescinded because of his breach of his duty of disclosure.

Although the relationship between an employer and an employee is in a sense 'fiduciary', it does not impose on an employee an obligation to disclose a previous breach of his contract of employment when negotiating its termination.[2] On the other hand, in certain circumstances an employee may be under a duty to report to his employer a breach of contract on the part of his co-employees.[3]

1   [1917] 2 KB 822.
2   *Bell v Lever Bros Ltd* [1932] AC 161, HL.
3   *Sybron Corpn v Rochem Ltd* [1983] 2 All ER 707, [1983] 3 WLR 713, CA.

13.39   The effect of a breach of the duty of disclosure in contracts uberrimae fidei is that the person to whom the duty was owed can have the contract rescinded, in which case an indemnity can be awarded where appropriate. The same bars to rescission apply as described above. Alternatively, the person to whom the duty was owed can refuse to carry out the contract and, provided (generally) that he returns what he obtained under it, successfully resist any claim for damages or specific performance. The Misrepresentation Act 1967 does not apply to misrepresentation through non-disclosure in contracts uberrimae fidei.

Duress and undue influence

13.40 We are concerned here with certain situations where a contract can be avoided on the ground that it has been procured by illegitimate pressure or that improper pressure may be presumed. The first case is governed by the common law of duress, and the second by the equitable doctrine of undue influence (and also by what can be called the 'unconscionable bargains principle'). We conclude the discussion by referring to two types of statutory protection against oppressive or unfair bargaining in particular transactions.

Duress

13.41 At one time, only actual or threatened personal violence or imprisonment sufficed for duress at common law,[1] but in recent cases it has been held that this is not so and that any other threat, e g a threat to goods or to a person's business or a threat to break a contract, can constitute duress at common law.[2]

To constitute duress at common law, the pressure must be 'illegitimate', either because what is threatened is unlawful (ie a tort or a crime)[3] or because of the nature of the pressure and of the demand to which it relates. Consequently, a threat to assault someone can amount to duress (because what is threatened is unlawful) and so can a threat to report criminal conduct to the police unless a demand is complied with (because of the nature of the pressure).[4] On the other hand, legitimate commercial pressure cannot constitute duress.[5]

If duress is proved, it is irrelevant that it was not the sole or predominant cause inducing the contract, provided that it was a reason (which it will be presumed to have been unless the contrary is proved).[6]

It appears that duress renders a contract voidable, so that it is valid unless and until it is rescinded by the coerced party (assuming rescission is not barred),[7] not void.

1 Co Litt 253b; *Cumming v Ince* (1847) 11 QB 112 at 120.
2 *The Siboen and The Sibotre* [1976] 1 Lloyd's Rep 293; *The Atlantic Baron* [1979] QB 705, [1978] 3 All ER 1170; *Pao On v Lau Yiu Long* [1980] AC 614, [1979] 3 All ER 65, PC; *The Universe Sentinel* [1983] 1 AC 366, [1982] 2 All ER 67, HL.
3 *Barton v Armstrong* [1976] AC 104 at 121.
4 *The Universe Sentinel* [1983] 1 AC 366, [1982] 2 All ER 67, HL.
5 *The Siboen and The Sibotre* [1976] 1 Lloyd's Rep 293; *Pao On v Lau Yiu Long* [1980] AC 614, [1979] 3 All ER 65, PC.
6 *Barton v Armstrong* [1976] AC 104, [1975] 2 All ER 465, PC.
7 *Pao On v Lau Yiu Long* [1980] AC 614 at 634, [1979] 3 All ER 65; *The Universe Sentinel* [1982] 2 All ER 67 at 75, 88.

Undue influence

13.42 A contract which falls within the equitable doctrine of undue influence is voidable at the instance of the party influenced. There are no precise limits to the doctrine, but the following can confidently be stated.

Under the doctrine of undue influence, equity has given relief where a contract has been procured by duress. Until recently, the equitable rules relating to duress were wider than those at common law, but the recent development of the common law rules means that this is no longer the case and that the doctrine of undue influence is most unlikely to be invoked to deal with the cases of duress.

On the other hand, the doctrine of undue influence remains of great importance where:

a. there is a confidential relationship between the parties to a contract; *and*

Provided that both these requirements are satisfied, a presumption of undue influence by the dominant party arises and, unless it is rebutted, the contract can be set aside at the instance of the weaker party.

Henceforth, we shall limit our discussion of the doctrine of undue influence to an examination of this aspect of it.

Confidential relationship

13.43 What is required here is a special relationship in which one party places confidence in the other who thereby has the opportunity to exercise overt or subtle influence over him; the law will not presume undue influence where the parties are in an ordinary, everyday business relationship.

13.44 In the case of some relationships, the courts have held that it is presumed that the relationship is a confidential one. Examples are the relationships of: parent and child;[1] doctor and patient;[2] solicitor or accountant and client;[3] religious adviser and disciple;[4] and trustee and beneficiary,[5] in each of which the first-named party is presumed to be in a position to influence the other. While the list of relationships which can be presumed to be confidential is not closed, it has been held that the relationships between husband and wife,[6] landlord and tenant,[7] and employer and employee,[7] are not presumed to be confidential.

1 *Bainbrigge v Browne* (1881) 18 Ch D 188, 50 LJ Ch 522.
2 *Mitchell v Homfray* (1881) 8 QBD 587, 50 LJQB 460, CA.
3 *Wright v Carter* [1903] 1 Ch 27, 72 LJ Ch 138, CA.
4 *Allcard v Skinner* (1887) 36 Ch D 145, 56 LJ Ch 1052, CA.
5 *Beningfield v Baxter* (1886) 12 App Cas 167, 56 LJ PC 13, PC.
6 *Howes v Bishop* [1909] 2 KB 390, 78 LJKB 796, CA; *Kings North Trust Ltd v Bell* [1986] 1 All ER 423, CA.
7 *Matthew v Bobbins* (1980) 256 Estates Gazette 603, CA.

13.45 Where a confidential relationship cannot be presumed, the doctrine of undue influence can nevertheless apply if it is positively proved that one party actually had a position of personal ascendancy and influence over the other at the material time. For example, although normally the relationships of banker and client and of creditor and guarantor are not confidential,[1] they will be held to be so if special facts exist which justify such a finding, as is shown by *Lloyds Bank v Bundy*.[2] The defendant was an elderly farmer. A company which was run by his son got into difficulties and the defendant guaranteed its overdraft with the plaintiff Bank, mortgaging his farmhouse, which was his home and only asset, to the Bank as security for the guarantee. In relation to this transaction he had placed himself entirely in the hands of the assistant bank manager who not only explained the legal effects of the transaction *but also went further and advised on more general matters germane to the wisdom of the transaction.* In the light of this special fact it is not surprising that the Court of Appeal held that there was a confidential relationship between the Bank and the defendant and that not only could the mortgage not be enforced but it, and the guarantee, should be set aside.

1 *National Westminster Bank plc v Morgan* [1985] AC 686, [1985] 1 All ER 821, HL.
2 [1975] QB 326, [1974] 3 All ER 757, CA. For another example, see *Horry v Tate & Lyle Refineries Ltd* [1982] 2 Lloyd's Rep 416.

Manifestly disadvantageous contract

13.46 Even if a confidential relationship is presumed or proved, this is not in itself enough to give rise to the presumption that the dominant party took the opportunity to exercise influence over the other. That presumption can only be drawn if the contract between them is manifestly disadvantageous to the weaker party.

This was held by the House of Lords in *National Westminster Bank plc v Morgan*.[1] Mr and Mrs M got into difficulties with the repayments to a building society of the mortgage on their house. Consequently, Mr M sought a bank rescue operation, asking the Bank to refinance the building society loan. The Bank agreed and Mr M executed a legal charge in favour of the Bank to secure a loan from it sufficient to redeem the building society mortgage. Because the house was in joint names, the Bank required Mrs M's signature to the legal charge, and the bank manager called on Mrs M to obtain it. She told him that she did not wish the legal charge to extend to her husband's business activities. The bank manager assured her in good faith, but incorrectly, that the charge did not extend to those liabilities. Without taking any independent legal advice, Mrs M signed the legal charge. Subsequently, Mr and Mrs M fell into arrears with their repayments to the Bank, which obtained a possession order on the house. Mr M died soon afterwards without any business debts owing to the Bank. Mrs M appealed against the possession order, contending that she had signed the legal charge because of undue influence from the bank manager.

The House of Lords rejected this. It held that the case was not one in which there was a presumption of undue influence, not only because the relationship between the parties was merely the relationship of banker and customer and not a confidential relationship, but also because the legal charge was not manifestly disadvantageous to Mr and Mrs M; in fact, it provided a desperately urgent rescue of the house from the building society.

1 [1985] AC 686, [1985] 1 All ER 821, HL.

Rebutting the presumption

13.47 The presumption that undue influence has been exercised can only be rebutted by proof that the party presumed to have been influenced has been placed in such a position as will enable him to form an entirely free and unfettered judgment, independent altogether of any sort of control.[1] The onus of proving this is on the party presumed to have exercised undue influence. The best, but not the only,[2] way of doing so is by proving that the other party received independent and informed advice, particularly legal advice, before making the contract.

1 *Archer v Hudson* (1844) 7 Beav 551 at 560.
2 *Inche Noriah v Shaik Allie Bin Omar* [1929] AC 127, PC.

Unconscionable bargains

13.48 Acting under equitable principles, a court will rescind a contract on the basis that unfair advantage has been taken of a party who was poor, ignorant or weak-minded, or otherwise in need of *special* protection, by the other.[1]

The law on unconscionable bargains has the same basis as the other areas of equitable intervention which have just been mentioned: inequality of bargaining power. Although there are dicta in some cases that this 'common thread' permits the courts to intervene in contractual situations other than those involving pressure or influence, or the taking of an unfair advantage of a poor, ignorant or weak-minded party or one otherwise in need of special protection, recent decisions have rejected the argument that inequality of bargaining power is in itself a ground for rescinding a contract.[2]

1 *Evans v Llewellin* (1787) 1 Cox Eq Cas 333 is an example.
2 *Pao On v Lau Yiu Long* [1980] AC 614, [1979] 3 All ER 65, PC; *Alec Lobb (Garages) Ltd v Total Oil G B Ltd* [1985] 1 All ER 303, [1985] 1 WLR 173, CA.

Bars to rescission[1]

13.49 Where a contract is voidable for duress or undue influence, or because it is an unconsionable bargain, it is valid unless and until it is rescinded. Rescission will be barred in two cases.

1 These bars also apply to gifts made in similar circumstances.

Affirmation

13.50 Rescission is barred if, after the pressure or influence, or fiduciary relationship giving rise to a presumption of undue influence, has ceased, the party influenced expressly or impliedly affirms the contract.[1] An unreasonable lapse of time after removal of the influence before seeking rescission of the contract is a particularly important evidential factor suggesting affirmation,[2] and so is the fact that the party influenced performs obligations under the contract without protest.[3] A secret mental reservation not to affirm in such cases is irrelevant.[3] A person can be held to have affirmed even though he has not had independent advice after the removal of the influence[4] and did not know that he could have the contract rescinded, provided he was aware that he might have rights and deliberately refrained from finding out.[5]

1 *Allcard v Skinner* (1887) 36 Ch D 145, CA; *Fry v Lane* (1888) 40 Ch D 312.
2 *Allcard v Skinner* above.
3 *The Atlantic Baron* [1979] QB 705, [1978] 3 All ER 1170.
4 *Mitchell v Homfray* (1881) 8 QBD 587, CA.
5 *Allcard v Skinner* (1887) 36 Ch D 145 at 192.

Purchasers without notice

13.51 The right to rescission is lost if a third party acquires an interest for value in the property transferred by the party influenced, without notice of the pressure or influence, or fiduciary relationship giving rise to a presumption of undue influence, in question.[1] Rescission is, of course, not barred if the third party does not provide consideration or has notice of the facts.[2]

1 *Bainbrigge v Browne* (1881) 18 Ch D 188.
2 *Lancashire Loans Ltd v Black* [1934] 1 KB 380, CA.

Statutory protection

13.52   Two modern statutes provide some protection against certain types of oppressive or unfair bargaining in particular transactions.

Consumer Credit Act 1974

13.53   Sections 137 to 139 of this Act empower the court to re-open 'extortionate credit bargains' and 'do justice between the parties'. A credit bargain (agreement) is extortionate if the payments to be made under it are 'grossly exorbitant' or if it 'otherwise grossly contravenes the ordinary principles of fair dealing'. In re-opening such an agreement, the court has a number of powers to relieve the debtor (or a surety) from payment of any sum in excess of that fairly due and reasonable. For instance, it may order the setting aside of the whole or part of any obligation imposed on the debtor (or a surety) by the credit bargain or any related agreement, or order the creditor to repay the whole or part of any sum paid under the credit bargain or a related agreement.[1]

1   Para 41.20 below.

Fair Trading Act 1973

13.54   Part II of the Act, which was discussed in para 9.54 above, provides a procedure for making statutory instruments to control, inter alia, consumer trade practices which have, or are likely to have, the effect of subjecting consumers to undue pressure to enter into consumer transactions or of causing the terms or conditions on which consumers enter into them to be so adverse to them as to be inequitable.

If they are detrimental to consumers, the two types of consumer trade practice in issue here may also result in a reference to the Restrictive Practices Court under Part III of the Act for an order restraining the objectionable course of conduct. This procedure was discussed in para 9.54 above.

Chapter 14

Void and illegal contracts

14.1 A contract which would otherwise be valid may be invalid on the ground that it is void or illegal. For convenience, such contracts will be discussed in the following order:

Wagering and gaming contracts.

Other contracts void on grounds of public policy.

Illegal contracts.

Wagering and gaming contracts

14.2 Under the Gaming Act 1845, all wagering and gaming contracts are void[1] and, therefore, unenforceable by either party. A fresh promise, supported by fresh consideration, to pay an unsuccessful bet is also unenforceable.[2] No more need be said about contracts of this type, but the other two types of contract mentioned in the previous paragraph require a more detailed discussion.

1 Gaming Act 1845, s18.
2 Ibid; *Hill v William Hill (Park Lane) Ltd* [1949] AC 530, [1949] 2 All ER 452, HL.

Other contracts void on grounds of public policy

14.3 The following matters must be discussed—

The types of contracts void on grounds of public policy.

The legal effects of such contracts.

14.4 Contracts which are void on grounds of public policy can be divided into three types:

Contracts prejudicial to the married state or to parental obligations.

Contracts ousting the jurisdiction of the courts.

Contracts in restraint of trade.

Contracts prejudicial to the married state or to parental obligations

14.5 An example of such a contract is one to procure a marriage with a particular person, but a contract to introduce a number of persons with a view to promoting a marriage with one or other of them also falls within this category and is therefore void.[1] This is of obvious importance to marriage bureaux.

One other example will suffice: contracts under which parental rights or duties are surrendered are generally void.[2]

1 *Hermann v Charlesworth* [1905] 2 KB 123, CA.
2 Guardianship Act 1973, s1; Children Act 1975, s85(2).

Contracts purporting to oust the jurisdiction of the courts
Agreements relating to arbitration[1]

14.6 An agreement to refer a dispute to arbitration for settlement as a condition precedent to an action in the courts is perfectly valid. This was held in *Scott v Avery*.[2] An insurance policy provided that if there was a dispute relating to the policy the assured could not bring any action in the courts in relation to it until the dispute had been referred to arbitrators and the arbitrators had reached a decision. The House of Lords held that the clause was valid since it did not purport to oust the jurisdiction of the courts but simply laid down a condition which had to be satisfied before the courts might exercise jurisdiction. On the other hand, an agreement, whether contained in an arbitration agreement or made thereafter, which excludes the courts' power to give a final decision on a question of law, may be void on grounds of public policy. We discussed this matter in para 2.46 above. A clause which simply makes the arbitrator the final arbiter on questions of fact is always valid.[3]

1 Also see paras 2.40–2.46 above.
2 (1856) 5 HL Cas 811, HL.
3 *Lee v Showmen's Guild of Great Britain* [1952] 2 QB 329 at 342, [1952] 1 All ER 1175 at 1181.

Maintenance agreements

14.7 If a maintenance agreement between spouses contains a promise by one of them not to apply to the courts for a financial provision order in return for a promise of maintenance by the other, the former spouse's promise is void and unenforceable.[1] In the case of written agreements, this is now provided by the Matrimonial Causes Act 1973, s34, which goes on to state, however, that any other financial arrangements in a written maintenance agreement are valid and binding (unless they are void or unenforceable for any other reason).

1 *Hyman v Hyman* [1929] AC 601, HL.

Contracts in restraint of trade

14.8 These contracts give rise to more complications than other contracts which are void on grounds of public policy. Contracts in restraint of trade may be void at common law or, in some cases (which we deal with in paras 14.24 to 14.35 below), by statute.

Contracts in restraint to trade which are void at common law can be divided into six principal categories:

a. agreements restricting the subsequent occupation of an employee;

b. agreements restricting the subsequent occupation of a partner;

c. agreements between employers regulating labour;

d. agreements between the vendor and purchaser of the goodwill of a business restricting competition by the vendor;

e. exclusive dealing agreements; and

f. cartel agreements.

It must be emphasised that this list is not exclusive and that other types of agreement in restraint of trade are, or may be, void unless they satisfy the tests mentioned in the next paragraph.[1] On the other hand, some agreements which restrain trade are not covered by the present doctrine. Two examples of these appear in paras 14.14 and 14.17 below. Meanwhile, it may be noted that the purposes of a trade union or employers' association do not, by reason of the fact they are in restraint of trade, make void any agreement.[2]

1   *Esso Petroleum Co Ltd v Harper's Garage (Stourport) Ltd* [1968] AC 269, [1967] 1 All ER 699, HL.
2   Trade Union and Labour Relations Act 1974, ss2(5) and 3(5).

14.9   The general tests of validity applicable to contracts falling within the restraint of trade doctrine are as follows:
   A contract in restraint of trade is prima facie void. But—
   Such a contract will be valid and enforceable if—
      first, the person seeking to enforce it shows that the restraint is reasonable between the parties to the contract; *and*, second, the other party does not show that the restraint is unreasonable in the public interest.[1]
The tests of reasonableness must be applied as at the date the contract was made and in the light of the then existing facts and of what might possibly happen in the future. Anything else which has occurred subsequently must be ignored.[2] The application of these tests can be demonstrated by reference to the six categories of agreement mentioned above.

1   These tests have their foundation in *Nordenfeldt's* case [1894] AC 535, HL and *Herbert Morris Ltd v Saxelby* [1916] 1 AC 688, HL.
2   *Putsman v Taylor* [1927] 1 KB 637 at 643; *Gledhow Autoparts Ltd v Delaney* [1965] 3 All ER 288 at 295.

Agreements restricting the subsequent occupation of an employee
14.10   A contract between employer and employee, normally the contract of employment, may contain a covenant (promise) by the employee that he will not be employed in, or conduct, a business competing with his employer's after leaving his employment. This restriction will normally be limited in duration and area. Such a restriction, being in restraint of trade, is prima facie void and will only be valid and enforceable if the tests of reasonableness referred to above are satisfied. The precise nature of these tests in the present context will now be examined.

a. *Reasonable between the parties* Two things must be proved to satisfy this test:
i   The restriction must protect a legally recognised interest of the employer. Only two interests are so recognised:

   a. *Protection of trade secrets and secret processes* An example is provided by *Forster & Sons Ltd v Suggett*.[1] The defendant was the plaintiff company's works manager. He was instructed in secret methods relating to the production of glass which the plaintiff company produced. He agreed that, during the five years after the end of his employment with the plaintiff company, he would not carry on in the UK, or be interested in, glass bottle manufacturing or any other business connected with glass making as carried on by the company. It was held that this restriction was reasonable to protect the plaintiff company's trade secrets and an injunction was ordered to restrain breach of it.

b. Protection of business connections An employer is entitled to prevent an employee misusing influence which he has obtained over the employer's customers and thereby enticing them away.[2] Thus, in *Fitch v Dewes*,[3] where the contract provided that a Tamworth solicitor's managing clerk (who was himself a solicitor) should never practice within seven miles of Tamworth Town Hall, the House of Lords held that the restriction was valid because it constituted a reasonable protection of the employer's business connections against an employee who could gain influence over his clients.

It is not enough merely to show that the restriction purports to protect trade secrets or connections: it must also be shown that they require protection against the particular employee. Thus, the restriction will be invalid if the employee did not know enough about a trade secret to be able to use it or was insufficiently acquainted with customers to be able to influence them. This is shown, for example, by *S W Strange Ltd v Mann*,[4] where a restriction imposed on a bookmaker's manager was held to be void because the business was mostly conducted by telephone and the manager had no chance to get to know his employer's customers or to influence them.

No other interests can be protected validly by the present type of restriction;[5] consequently, a restriction whose object is simply to protect the employer against competition or to protect, for instance, a special method of organisation of a business is invalid.[5]

ii Reasonableness. To be reasonable between the parties, the restriction must be no wider than is reasonably necessary to protect the employer's trade secrets or business connections. Reasonableness is a matter of degree: the terms of the restriction must be measured against the degree of knowledge or influence which the employee has gained in his employment. A fortiori, a restriction will be void if it relates to a wider range of occupations than is reasonably necessary to protect the relevant interests. Two other factors which are particularly important are the duration and area of restriction.

a Duration In *M and S Drapers v Reynolds*,[6] a collector-salesman of a credit drapery firm covenanted not to canvass his employers' customers for a period of five years after leaving their employment. The restriction was held to be void: in view of the lowly position of a collector-salesman it was for a longer period than was reasonably necessary to protect the employers' business connections. On the other hand, the restriction in *Fitch v Dewes* was upheld, even though it was to last for life, because of the degree of influence which the solicitor's clerk would gain over his employer's clients.

b Area In *Mason v Provident Clothing and Supply Co Ltd*,[7] a canvasser in the plaintiff company's Islington branch district covenanted not to work in any similar business for three years within 25 miles of London. The restriction was held to be void because it extended further than was reasonably necessary to protect the plaintiff company's business connections. On the other hand, a covenant by a sales representative employed by a small company that, for two years after leaving his employment, he would not canvass (in the same goods) people *who had been customers of his employer during his employment*, was upheld in *G W Plowman & Son v Ash*,[8] even though it was unlimited in area.

b. *Reasonable in the public interest* The operation of this test is demonstrated by *Wyatt v Kreglinger and Fernau*.[9] The employers of a wool broker promised to pay him a pension on his retirement provided he did not re-enter the wool trade and did nothing to their detriment (fair competition excepted). The broker subsequently sued for arrears of pension but the Court of Appeal held that he could not succeed since the contract was void for two reasons: i. the restriction was unreasonable as between the parties; ii. the contract was unreasonable in the public interest because the permanent restriction on the broker working anywhere in the wool trade deprived the community of services from which it might benefit.

Provided the restriction is reasonable between the parties, employer-employee restrictions will rarely be invalidated on the ground that they are unreasonable in the public interest. However, where the employee has a special skill of particular value to the community, the restriction may well be found unreasonable in the public interest even though it affords reasonable protection for the employer's trade secrets or connections.[10]

It may be noted in passing that, even in the absence of an express restraint, where an employee uses or discloses an employer's trade secrets or confidential information concerning his employer's affairs, or an employee solicits an employer's customers, the employer can obtain an injunction to restrain this.[11] An employer can also obtain an injunction, even in the absence of an express restraint, to restrain an ex-employee disclosing a trade secret of the employer.[12]

1 (1918) 35 TLR 87.
2 *Herbert Morris Ltd v Saxelby* [1916] 1 AC 688 at 709.
3 [1921] 2 AC 158, HL.
4 [1965] 1 All ER 1069, [1965] 1 WLR 629.
5 *Herbert Morris Ltd v Saxelby* [1916] 1 AC 688 at 710.
6 [1956] 3 All ER 814, [1957] 1 WLR 9, CA.
7 [1913] AC 724, HL. Also see *Marley Tile Co Ltd v Johnson* [1982] IRLR 75, CA.
8 [1964] 2 All ER 10, [1964] 1 WLR 568.
9 [1933] 1 KB 793, CA.
10 *Bull v Pitney-Bowes Ltd* [1966] 3 All ER 384, [1967] 1 WLR 273.
11 *Wessex Dairies Ltd v Smith* [1935] 2 KB 80; *Faccenda Chicken Ltd v Fowler* [1986] 1 All ER 617, CA.
12 *Printers and Finishers Ltd v Holloway* [1964] 3 All ER 731, [1965] 1 WLR 1; *Faccenda Chicken Ltd v Fowler* [1986] 1 All ER 617, CA.

Agreements restricting the subsequent occupation of a partner
14.11 Partnership agreements commonly provide that a partner who ceases to be a partner shall not, for a specified period, act or deal with any client of the firm in the professional capacity in which he was a partner. Such a restraint is valid and enforceable only if it is reasonable as between the parties to protect some legitimate interest of the firm and is not

unreasonable in the public interest.[1] What is a legitimate interest of the firm depends largely on the nature of its business and on the ex-partner's position in the firm, but an example of such an interest is a firm's connections with its client. This was held in *Bridge v Deacons*,[2] which was concerned with a covenant in a Hong Kong solicitors' partnership agreement whereby a partner who ceased to be a partner was restricted for five years thereafter from acting as a solicitor in Hong Kong for anyone who had been a client of the firm when he ceased to be a partner or during the preceding three years. The Privy Council held that the covenant, which applied to all the partners, was reasonable as between the parties, since it went no further in extent or time than was reasonable to protect the firm's connections with its clients, and was not unreasonable in the public interest; the covenant was therefore held enforceable against an ex-partner.

1   *Bridge v Deacons* [1984] AC 705, [1984] 2 All ER 19, PC; *Edwards v Worboys* [1984] AC 724, [1984] 2 WLR 850, CA.
2   [1984] AC 705, [1984] 2 All ER 19, PC.

Agreements between employers regulating labour
14.12 The same principles apply to agreements between employers attempting to regulate their labour and imposing mutual restrictions on the re-employment of each other's former employees. This is illustrated by *Kores Manufacturing Co Ltd v Kolok Manufacturing Co Ltd.*[1] The plaintiff and defendant companies were manufacturers of carbon paper and typewriter ribbons. They agreed that neither would employ at any time any person who had been employed by the other during the then past five years. The defendant company broke this agreement. The Court of Appeal held that the agreement was void because it covered all employees, whether or not they knew of the parties' trade secrets, and was also excessive in duration. It was therefore unreasonable as between the parties since it imposed on them a restriction grossly in excess of what was necessary to protect their trade secrets.

A question which is not finally resolved is whether agreements of the present type can ever be valid if their purpose is not to protect the employer's trade secrets or connections but to protect the adequacy and stability of labour forces or some other interest. In the *Kores* case, the Court of Appeal took the view that such an agreement could not be valid. However, in *Eastham v Newcastle United Football Club Ltd,*[2] Wilberforce J was prepared to accept that the proper organisation of football was an interest which could be protected by an agreement between football clubs, although he found that the 'retain and transfer' system (the agreement between these employers) was invalid because it went further than was reasonably necessary to protect that interest. Unless the protectable interests in agreements between employers are legally limited to trade secrets and connections, employers will be able to circumvent the restrictions on employer-employee restraint of trade agreements by making agreements between themselves protecting interests other than their trade secrets or connections.

As the *Eastham* case shows, an employee affected by the present type of contract can challenge it by seeking a declaration that it is void. If he is successful, the declaration will not set the contract aside but it has strong persuasive force on the parties' future conduct.

1   [1959] Ch 108, [1958] 2 All ER 65, CA.

2   [1964] Ch 613, [1963] 3 All ER 139. See also *Greig v Insole* [1978] 3 All ER 449, [1978] 1 WLR 302.

Agreements between the vendor and purchaser of the goodwill of a business restricting competition by the vendor

14.13   Such an agreement is prima facie void for restraint of trade but will be valid and enforceable if it is reasonable between the parties and not unreasonable in the public interest. The following can be said concerning the requirement of reasonableness between the parties:

a. *The restriction must protect the business sold*   An agreement whereby one business surrenders to another its liberty to trade in a particular field is void since mere competition is not a protectable interest.[1] The restriction must relate to an actual business which has been sold. Thus, even though it is contained in what purports to be a contract for the sale of a business, a restriction will be void if there is no actual business to protect. This is shown by *Vancouver Malt and Sake Brewing Co Ltd v Vancouver Breweries Ltd*.[2] The appellants held a licence to brew beer and other liquors but the only trade actually carried on by them under the licence was brewing sake. They purported to sell the goodwill of their licence, so far as it related to brewing beer, to the respondents and covenanted not to brew beer for 15 years thereafter. The Privy Council held that the covenant was void because, if there was a sale, it was merely a sale of the appellants' liberty to brew beer since there was no goodwill of a beer brewing business to be transferred and the covenant was simply a bare restriction on competition.

Other aspects of the rule that the covenant must protect the business actually sold are demonstrated by *British Reinforced Concrete Engineering Co Ltd v Schelff*.[3] The defendant, who ran a small business for the *sale* of 'Loop' road reinforcements, sold it to the plaintiff company, a large company which manufactured and sold 'B.R.C.' road reinforcements. In the contract of sale the defendant covenanted that, for three years after the end of the First World War, he would not 'either alone or jointly or in partnership with any other person or persons whomsoever and either directly or indirectly carry on or manage or be concerned or interested in or act as servant of any person concerned or interested in the business of the manufacture or sale of road reinforcements in any part of the UK'. It was held that this covenant was too wide because it extended to the manufacture of road reinforcements as well as their sale, and thus sought to protect more than the actual business sold (the *sale* of road reinforcements).

b. *The restriction must go no further than is reasonably necessary to protect the business sold*   As was pointed out in the *Schelff* case, the reasonableness of the restriction must be judged by reference to the extent and circumstances of the business sold, and not by the extent and range of any business already run by the purchaser. Reasonableness is judged from the standpoint of both parties. For example, in the *Schelff* case it was held that the 'servant clause' was unreasonable because it would preclude the defendant from becoming the servant of a trust company which, as part of its investments, held shares in a company manufacturing or selling road reinforcements.

The amount of the consideration for the agreement is a relevant factor in assessing the reasonableness of the restriction.[4] In addition, the duration and area of the restriction are particularly important factors to be taken into account in assessing its reasonableness. The approach of the courts is more liberal here than in the case of employer-employee restrictions because buyers and sellers of businesses are more obviously equal bargaining partners. A good example of this liberality is provided by *Nordenfeldt v Maxim Nordenfeldt Guns and Ammunition Co Ltd.*[5] The appellant, who had obtained patents for improving quick-firing guns, carried on, among other things, business as a maker of such guns and of ammunition. He sold the goodwill and assets of the business to a company, entering into a covenant which restricted his future activities. The company later merged with another to become the respondent company and the appellant's earlier covenant was substantially repeated with it. This covenant provided that for 25 years the appellant would not engage, except on behalf of the company, directly or indirectly in the trade or business of a manufacturer of guns, gun mountings or carriages, gunpowder, explosives or ammunition, or in any business competing or liable to compete in any way with that for the time being carried on by the respondent company. The first part of the covenant, relating to engaging in a business manufacturing guns, etc was held by the House of Lords to provide reasonable protection for the business acquired by the company, even though the restriction was worldwide and was to last 25 years, and was therefore valid. It was recognised, however, that the second part of the covenant, relating to engaging in any business competing with that carried on by the company, was void because it went further than was reasonable to protect the business acquired by the company. Similarly, the restriction in the *Schelff* case, even in so far as it related to the management, etc of a business selling reinforcements, was held void because it applied to the whole of the UK, which was regarded as a wider area than was necessary to protect the actual business sold.

1   *Vancouver Malt and Sake Brewing Co Ltd v Vancouver Breweries Ltd* [1934] AC 181, PC.
2   [1934] AC 181, PC.
3   [1921] 2 Ch 563.
4   *Nordenfeldt v Maxim Nordenfeldt Guns and Ammunition Co Ltd* [1894] AC 535 at 565.
5   [1894] AC 535, HL.

Exclusive dealing agreement
14.14   One type of agreement under this heading is a 'solus agreement' whereby A agrees to buy all his requirements of a particular commodity from C. In *Esso Petroleum Co Ltd v Harper's Garage (Stourport) Ltd,*[1] the House of Lords held that such exclusive purchasing agreements were subject to the restraint of trade doctrine and were prima facie void. However, as their Lordships recognised, there are exceptions. The House of Lords held that where a person acquires land by conveyance or lease, and an exclusive dealing agreement relating to the land is inserted into the conveyance or lease, it is not subject to the restraint of trade doctrine. Thus, if an oil company sells or leases a filling station to X, inserting a covenant into the conveyance or lease that X shall only buy petrol supplies from the company, the covenant falls outside the restraint of trade doctrine and is valid. Lord Reid said that the reason for this was that the restraint of trade doctrine only applied where a person gave up a freedom which he would otherwise have enjoyed, and a person buying or leasing land had no previous right to trade there and thus gave up no previous held freedom. The courts will not allow this exception to be used as a device to evade the

restraint of trade doctrine, as is shown by the decision of the Court of Appeal in *Alec Lobb (Garages) Ltd v Total Oil GB Ltd*.[2] In that case, L Ltd (whose proprietors were Mr and Mrs L) owned the freehold of land on which it carried on a garage and filling station business. L Ltd leased the land to T Ltd to raise capital; the lease was followed immediately by a lease-back (which contained a tie provision) by T Ltd to Mr and Mrs L at an annual rent. The Court of Appeal held that it could pierce the corporate veil, recognise a continued identity of occupation and hold that T Ltd could be in no better position with regard to the restraint of trade doctrine by granting the lease-back to the proprietors than if it had granted the lease-back to L Ltd.

1   [1968] AC 269, [1967] 1 All ER 699, HL.
2   [1985] 1 All ER 303, [1985] 1 WLR 173, CA.

14.15   Where the restraint of trade doctrine applies to an exclusive purchasing agreement, the restraint is, of course, valid only if it is reasonable between the parties and is not shown to be unreasonable in the public interest. It appears that, as opposed to the heads of agreements in restraint of trade already mentioned, an exclusive purchasing agreement can be valid even though its object is simply to protect a party against competition (and this is true of the other types of exclusive dealing agreements). The operation of the restraint of trade doctrine to exclusive purchasing agreements is demonstrated by *Esso Petroleum Co Ltd v Harper's Garage (Stourport) Ltd*. Harper's agreed to buy all their petrol requirements from Esso. They also agreed to operate their two garages in accordance with the 'Esso co-operation plan', under which they had to keep the garages open at all reasonable hours and not sell them without getting the purchaser to enter into a similar agreement with Esso. In return, Harper's got a $1\frac{1}{4}$d rebate per gallon off the list price of petrol. In the case of one garage, the agreement was to last for four years five months. The agreement relating to the other garage was to last for 21 years, being contained in a mortgage[1] of the garage to Esso for 21 years which was not redeemable before that time had expired. The House of Lords held that both agreements were prima facie void since neither fell within an exception to the restraint of trade doctrine, even though one was contained in a mortgage. The question was therefore whether the restrictions in the two agreements were reasonable:

a.   The House of Lords held that the agreement for four years five months was reasonable between the parties. It was reasonably required to protect Esso's legitimate interest in securing continuity of their sales outlets, their system of distribution and the stability of their sales. In return, Harper's not only got a rebate on the price of the petrol which they purchased but could also rely on the financial backing of a big company if they were short of funds. The agreement was also reasonable in the public interest.

b.   The House held that the agreement for 21 years was unreasonable between the parties, because its duration was longer than necessary to protect Esso's interests, and therefore void.

The public interest in this context refers to the interest of the public that a person should not be subjected to unreasonable restrictions on his freedom to work or trade, and not to any ultimate economic or social or other advantage to the public at large.[2]

Too much should not be read into the *Esso Petroleum* decision because, as the Court of Appeal held in *Alec Lobb (Garages) Ltd v Total Oil GB Ltd*,[3] every case turns on its facts; the court also pointed out that the adequacy of the consideration received by the party restrained is relevant to the question of the reasonableness of the restraint. In the *Lobb* case, L Ltd, which was insolvent and seriously under-capitalised, leased its garage and filling station for 51 years in consideration of a premium of £35,000 to T Ltd. T Ltd then leased back the premises to Mr and Mrs L (the proprietors of L Ltd) for a period of 21 years, with a right of either party to terminate the lease-back after 7 or 14 years, at an initial rent of £2,250 pa with upwards only rent reviews after 8 and 15 years. The lease-back also contained a tie provision requiring Mr and Mrs L to take all supplies of petrol from T Ltd exclusively.

The Court of Appeal upheld the tie provision as being in reasonable restraint of trade. It took into account, in particular:

a. that the consideration (£35,000) for the lease, and thus the consideration by T Ltd for the tie (since the lease-back was part of the same transaction as the lease), was the market value of the lease, whereas the initial rent under the lease-back was nominal;

b. that under the lease-back Mr and Mrs L were not locked into trading with T Ltd's products from the property for 21 years since they were free to exercise the break-clause in the lease-back after 7 or 14 years; and

c. that L Ltd were insolvent and the sum of £35,000 was designed to enable it to pay its debts and continue in business, and to save Mr and Mrs L from personal bankruptcy, and that the rescue operation had been undertaken reluctantly by T Ltd to preserve the site as an outlet for its petrol.

In the light of these factors, the Court of Appeal held that the tie did not go further than reasonably necessary to provide adequate protection for T Ltd and was reasonable in the interests of Mr and Mrs L because of the benefits which they derived in return. Moreover, the Court held, the tie was not unreasonable in the public interest.

1 Para 41.19 below.
2 *Texaco Ltd v Mulberry Filling Station Ltd* [1972] 1 All ER 513, [1972] 1 WLR 814.
3 [1985] 1 All ER 303, [1985] 1 WLR 173, CA.

14.16 Another type of agreement which may be said to fall under the heading of exclusive dealing agreements is an agreement whereby A agrees to provide his services solely to B for a period. Normally, such a contract does not fall within the restraint of trade doctrine, even though it necessarily involves the restriction of one of the party's right to exercise any lawful activity he chooses, but if the contractual restriction appears to be unnecessary or to be reasonably capable of enforcement in an oppressive manner it is prima facie void and its validity depends upon the twin tests of reasonableness.[1] An example of an exclusive services contract which fell within the restraint of trade doctrine for the reasons just given is *Schroeder Music Publishing Co Ltd v Macaulay*.[2] M, a young and unknown song writer, entered into a contract with S Ltd, who were music publishers, whereby they engaged his exclusive services for five years. Under the contract M assigned to S Ltd full copyright for the whole world in anything composed by him during the period of the contract or before it. If M's royalties exceeded £5,000 during the five-year period the contract was to be automatically extended for another five years. S Ltd reserved the right to terminate the contract with one month's notice, but M had no such rights. S Ltd were not obliged by the contract to publish anything composed by M. The House of Lords held that the contract fell within the restraint of trade doctrine and was void, the main reason for its decision being that the agreement was unreasonable between the parties because, while S Ltd were given the sole right to publish M's songs, they were not bound to do so and could simply leave them lying in a drawer.

1 *Schroeder Music Publishing Co Ltd v Macaulay* [1974] 3 All ER 616, [1974] 1 WLR 1308, HL; *Clifford Davis Management Ltd v W E A Records Ltd* [1975] 1 All ER 237, [1975] 1 WLR 61, CA; *O'Sullivan v Management Agency and Music Ltd* [1984] 3 WLR 448, CA.
2 [1974] 3 All ER 616, [1974] 1 WLR 1308, HL.

14.17 Before leaving exclusive dealing agreements it should be noted that 'sole agency agreements', ie agreements giving a person the sole right to supply a manufacturer's goods, are exempt from the restraint of trade doctrine because they have gained general commercial acceptance.[1]

1 *Esso Petroleum Co Ltd v Harper's Garage (Stourport) Ltd* [1968] AC 269 at 336, [1967] 1 All ER 699 at 731.

Cartel agreements
14.18 These are agreements in which manufacturers or traders undertake to restrict their output, supply or purchase of goods or services, or to restrict competition between them or maintain prices. At common law, a cartel agreement, like any other agreement governed by the restraint of trade doctrine, is prima facie void; to be enforceable it must be justified as reasonable between the parties and not be shown to be unreasonable in the public interest.

We show in paras 14.24 to 14.35 below, how the common law rules concerning cartel agreements have been rendered almost completely obsolete by statute.

Effects
Enforcement of the contract
14.19 Provided that the part of the contract which is void on grounds of public policy can be severed from the rest of the contract, the latter, as opposed to the void part, is enforceable. However, if the void part cannot be severed the whole contract is void and unenforceable. Severance can operate in two ways.

14.20 *Severance of the whole of an objectionable promise* If this can be done the rest of the contract is valid and enforceable. Severance of a whole promise is not possible if it is the whole or the main part (ie substantially the whole) of the consideration furnished by the party who wishes to enforce the contract. Thus, in *Wyatt v Kreglinger and Fernau*, which we discussed in para 14.10b above, it was held that the ex-employee could not enforce the promise to pay him a pension since he had given no valid consideration for it, his only promise—not to compete—being void under the restraint of trade doctrine. The present rule can be demonstrated by contrasting *Bennett v Bennett*[1] with *Goodinson v Goodinson*.[2] In the former case, Mrs Bennett petitioned for divorce and sought maintenance for herself and her son in the petition. Before the decree nisi was granted, she entered into a deed with her husband, in which she promised to withdraw her existing application and not apply to the courts for maintenance for herself or her children, to maintain the son and to indemnify the husband against any legal expenses arising out of the deed. In return, the husband covenanted to pay the wife and son an annuity and to convey certain property. He failed to make the promised payments and the wife sued him on the deed. The Court of Appeal held that the wife's promise not to apply to the courts was void on the ground that it purported to oust the jurisdiction of the courts and that it could not be severed from the rest of the promises because it formed the main consideration from her for the contract. The whole contract was therefore void and unenforceable.

On the other hand, in *Goodinson v Goodinson*,[2] the void promise was held to be severable. A husband and wife who were separated made an agreement whereby the husband promised to pay the wife a weekly sum if she would indemnify him against any debts incurred by her, not pledge his credit for necessaries and not bring maintenance proceedings against him. The husband fell into arrears under the agreement and the wife sued to recover them. The Court of Appeal held that the wife's last promise was void for the same reason as in *Bennett v Bennett* but that it could be severed from the other promises, leaving the rest of the contract valid and enforceable. *Bennett v Bennett* was distinguished because the other promises made by Mrs Goodinson were substantial and the promise not to take the husband to court did not form the main consideration provided by her.

It must be noted that, while these two cases provide the best available illustrations of severance of a whole promise, *Bennett v Bennett* would be decided differently now because, by a subsequent statute, a written maintenance agreement can be enforced even though a party has provided no consideration other than a void promise not to apply to the courts for financial provision.[3]

1 [1952] 1 KB 249, [1952] 1 All ER 413, CA.
2 [1954] 2 QB 118, [1954] 2 All ER 255, CA. Also see *Alec Lobb (Garages) Ltd v Total Oil GB Ltd* [1985] 1 All ER 303 at 311 and 316.
3 Para 14.7 above.

14.21 *Severance of the objectionable part of a promise* This is particularly relevant in restraint of trade contracts. If severance is possible of part of a promise, the rest of the contract, including the unsevered part of the promise, can be enforced. Severance of this type is only possible if two tests are satisfied:

a. The 'blue pencil' test. This test is only satisfied if the objectionable words can be struck out of the promise *as it stands*. This was possible in relation to the offending part of the promise in the *Nordenfeldt* case, which has been discussed in para 14.13b above. Another example is provided by *Goldsoll v Goldman*.[1] The defendant sold his imitation jewellery business in Old Bond Street to the plaintiff, another jeweller. The defendant covenanted that for two years he would not 'either solely or jointly with or as agent or employee for any person or company . . . carry on or be interested in the business of a vendor of or dealer in real or imitation jewellery in the county of London, England, Scotland, Ireland, Wales or any part of the UK and the Isle of Man or in France, the USA, Russia or Spain, or within 25 miles of Potsdamerstrasse, Berlin, or St. Stephan's Kirche, Vienna'. The defendant joined a rival jeweller's in New Bond Street within two years and the plaintiff sought an injunction to restrain breach of the covenant. The Court of Appeal held that the covenant was unreasonably wide in respect of subject matter (for the defendant had not dealt in real jewellery) and also in respect of area (because the defendant had not traded abroad) but that the references to foreign places and real jewellery could be severed because it was possible to delete them from the covenants *as it stood*. After severance, the covenant merely prohibited dealing in imitation jewellery in the UK and the Isle of Man, and an injunction was granted to prevent such dealing.

A more recent example is provided by *Anscombe & Ringland v Butchoff*.[2] A & R, a firm of estate agents carrying on business in London, employed B under a contract containing a clause that, for one year after the termination of the contract, B would not undertake 'either alone or in partnership or as a member of a company nor be interested directly or indirectly in the business of an auctioneer, valuer, surveyor or estate agent within a radius of one mile of the firm's office'. B left the firm and soon afterwards set up in business as an estate agent only 150 yards away from A & R's office. It was held:

i. that the clause was unreasonable in so far as it forbade B to be interested in the business of a surveyor or valuer, for he had never been a surveyor or valuer, and that part of the clause would be severed; but

ii. that part of the clause relating to the carrying on of business as an estate agent within the specified area was reasonable and would be enforced.

If the unreasonable part of the promise cannot be deleted from the promise as it stands, severance of it is not possible. The court cannot rewrite the promise by adding or altering even one word so as to make it reasonable. Thus, in *Mason v Provident Clothing and Supply Co Ltd*,[3] which has already been referred to,[4] where the contract in question contained a promise that the employee would not work within 25 miles of London after leaving his employment, the House of Lords held that the promise was too wide in area, and therefore unreasonable, and refused to re-draft the clause so that it would be reasonable and enforceable. The whole promise was therefore held void and unenforceable.

b. Severance of the objectionable part must not alter the nature (as opposed to the extent) of the original contract. This means that severance of part of a promise is impossible unless it can be construed as being divisible into a number of separate and independent parts. This rule is sensible—otherwise the mechanical deletion of the objectionable part of the promise could radically change the whole contract—but difficult to apply.

The application of this test can be illustrated by two cases. In *Attwood v Lamont*,[5] the plaintiffs owned a general outfitter's business in Kidderminster. The business was divided into a number of departments. The defendant was the head of the tailoring department but had no concern with any other department. In his contract of employment the defendant had undertaken that, after the termination of his employment, he would not 'be concerned in any of the following trades or businesses, that is to say, the trade or business of a tailor, dressmaker, general draper, milliner, hatter, haber-dasher, gentlemen's, ladies' or children's outfitter' within ten miles of Kidderminster. Later the plaintiffs sought to enforce this covenant. They admitted that it was too wide in terms of the trades covered but argued that the references to aspects of the business other than tailoring could be severed, leaving the tailoring restraint enforceable. The Court of Appeal rejected this course because such severance would have altered the whole nature of the covenant: the covenant as it stood was one indivisible covenant (or promise) for the protection of the whole of the plaintiffs' business, not several covenants for the protection of the plaintiffs' several departments, and to alter it would be to alter its nature.

This case can be contrasted with *Putsman v Taylor*.[6] The plaintiff carried on business as a tailor at three places in Birmingham: Snow Hill, Bristol Road and Aston Cross. He employed the defendant at his Snow Hill branch, although under the defendant's contract of employment he could have been directed to work at any of the three branches. The defendant covenanted that for five years after leaving the plaintiff's employment he would 'not carry on any business similar to that of the employer ... or be employed in any capacity by any person ... carrying on a business similar to that of the employer in Snow Hill ... or within half-a-mile radius of Aston Cross ... or Bristol Road'. The Divisional Court held that the Aston Cross and Bristol Road restrictions were unreasonable to protect the plaintiff's business connections but could be severed from the Snow Hill part of the covenant which, presumably, was held to be divisible in substance into several covenants.

1 [1915] 1 Ch 292, CA.
2 (1984) 134 NLJ 37.
3 [1913] AC 724, HL.
4 Para 14.10a above.
5 [1920] 3 KB 571, CA.
6 [1927] 1 KB 637, DC.

Other effects

14.22 In *Hermann v Charlesworth*,[1] a woman who had paid a fee to a 'marriage broker' was held to be entitled to recover it despite the fact that he had introduced her to a number of men. Probably, money or property transferred under other contracts which are wholly void on grounds of public policy, or under a severable part of a contract which is void on such grounds, is recoverable, even though the contract has been performed.

1 [1905] 2 KB 123, CA; para 14.5 above.

14.23 A collateral or subsequent transaction founded on a contract which is wholly void on grounds of public policy, or on a severable void part of a contract, is itself void.

Statute and restraint of trade

Restrictive Trade Practices Act 1976
14.24 The narrow common law rules concerning cartel agreements referred to in para 14.18 above, which reflect a laissez-faire attitude towards economic matters, were rendered almost completely obsolete with the

passing of the Restrictive Trade Practices Act 1956, most of which, together with subsequent amendments, has been consolidated in the Restrictive Trade Practices Act 1976 (which has been amended slightly by the Restrictive Trade Practices Act 1977 and the Competition Act 1980). Under this Act, many cartel agreements (whether or not intended to be legally enforceable) are made subject to registration and judicial investigation.

14.25 The agreements which are subject to this procedure are:

a. *Restrictive agreements as to goods* These are defined as any agreement or arrangement, between two or more persons carrying on business in the UK in the production, supply or processing of goods, by which restrictions are accepted by two or more parties as to:
i   the prices to be charged, made, quoted or paid for goods; or
ii the price to be recommended in respect of the resale of goods supplied; (agreements for the *collective enforcement* of conditions as to resale prices are absolutely prohibited and illegal[1]); or
iii the conditions on which goods are to be supplied, acquired or processed; or
iv the quantities or descriptions of goods to be produced, supplied or acquired; or
v   the processes of manufacture to be applied to any goods; or
vi the persons to or from whom, or the areas or places in or from which, goods are to be supplied or acquired.[2]

b. *Restrictive agreements as to services* These are defined as any agreement or arrangement, between two or more persons carrying on business in the UK in the supply of services of a class designated by the Secretary of State, whereby restrictions are accepted by two or more parties as to:
i   the charges to be made, quoted or paid for designated services; or
ii the conditions on which designated services are to be supplied or obtained; or
iii the extent to which, or the form in which, designated services are to be made available, supplied or obtained; or
iv the persons or classes of persons for whom or from whom, or the areas or places in or from which, designated services are to be made available or supplied or are to be obtained.[3]
The Act excludes from these provisions certain professional services, including the services of surveyors and architects as such. Apart from these, all services have been made designated services by the Secretary of State. However, particular agreements relating to certain types of designated services have been exempted from the requirements of the Act by the Secretary of State. One example is agreements between building societies under which the sole restriction relates to the raising of funds or making of loans, or to the interest rates to be charged for loans or paid to depositors.[4]

c. *Information agreements as to goods or services* The Secretary of State has power to extend the requirement of registration to any class of 'information agreement' as to goods or services.[5] An information agreement is defined as an agreement, between two or more persons carrying on a business of the types referred to above, which provides for the furnishing by two or more parties to each other, or to others, of information relating to certain matters which may be specified in the Secretary of State's order. These matters are the prices or charges to be asked for goods or services, or the conditions on which they are provided, and other matters corresponding to the restrictions mentioned in relation to restrictive agreements as to goods or services.[6]

1 Resale Prices Act 1976, s1; para 14.38 below.
2 Restrictive Trade Practices Act 1976, s6.
3 Ibid, s11.
4 Restrictive Trade Practices (Services) Order 1976; Restrictive Trade Practices Act 1976, Sch 1.
5 Restrictive Trade Practices Act 1976, ss7 and 12; so far only information agreements as to the price and conditions of supply of goods have been made registrable: Restrictive Trade Practices (Information Agreements) Order 1969.
6 Restrictive Trade Practices Act 1976, ss7 and 12.

14.26 *Exempt agreements* Certain agreements, such as 'solus agreements' and 'know how' agreements are excluded from the provisions of the Act,[1] and certain agreements of importance to the national economy or for holding down prices may be exempted by the Secretary of State.[2]

In addition, the Restrictive Trade Practices (Stock Exchange) Act 1984 provides that the Act of 1976 does not apply to certain restrictive agreements between members of the Stock Exchange.

1 Restrictive Trade Practices Act 1976, s28 and Sch 3.
2 Ibid, ss29–31.

14.27 *Registration* Registrable agreements must be registered with the Director-General of Fair Trading before they take effect or within three months of being made, whichever is the earlier.[1] Failure to do so renders the agreement void in respect of all restrictions or information provisions therein and it is unlawful for a party to give effect to them. In addition, a third party injured by such provisions in an unregistered agreement can sue for damages for breach of statutory duty, and the Director can obtain an injunction to stop the parties enforcing or carrying out the restriction or information provisions.[2]

1 Restrictive Trade Practices Act 1976, ss1 and 24.
2 Ibid, s35.

14.28 *Judicial investigation* Once an agreement has been registered the Director must generally refer it to the Restrictive Practices Court which has to determine whether or not the restriction or information provisions in the agreement are 'contrary to the public interest'. If the Court finds that they are, the agreement is rendered void in respect of the offending provisions and the parties can be restrained from enforcing or carrying them out and from making a similar agreement.[1]

A restriction or information provision is presumed to be contrary to the public interest unless it is shown:

a. to be beneficial in one of the eight ways specified in the Act; *and*

b. to be not unreasonable having regard to the balance between those circumstances and any detriment to the public or to persons not parties to the agreement (such as purchasers, consumers, users or sellers of goods, and users or suppliers of services) resulting or likely to result from the operation of the restriction.[2]

1   Restrictive Trade Practices Act 1976, s2.
2   Ibid, ss10 and 19; Competition Act 1980, s28.

14.29   *Trade and service supply associations*   The above provisions concerning registration and investigation also apply to specific recommendations made by such associations to their members if they concern the action to be taken (or not to be taken) in relation to any particular class of good, process of manufacture or service in respect of a matter which, if contained in an agreement, would make the agreement registrable.[1]

1   Restrictive Trade Practices Act 1976, ss8 and 16. Also see the Competition Act 1980, s27.

14.30   The result of these statutory provisions is that the common law rules concerning cartel agreements are now only of practical relevance in relation to the rare cartel agreement which is not registrable under the Act or which satisfies the criteria in the Act but is unreasonable between the parties. The statutory system outlined above has two important advantages over the common law provisions:

a. At common law the validity of a cartel agreement can only come before the courts if a party breaks it or wishes to challenge it. Now, agreements covered by the Act of 1976 must be registered and investigated by the Restrictive Practices Court.

b. The Act provides tests of validity more in accord with modern economic attitudes.

EEC Treaty, Art 85
14.31   Cartel agreements and exclusive dealing agreements[1] may also be void on the ground that they conflict with Art 85 of the Treaty establishing the European Economic Community. Article 85(1) prohibits:
'all agreements between undertakings, decisions by associations of undertakings and concerted practices which may affect trade between Member States [of the European Economic Community] and which have as their object or effect the prevention, restriction or distortion of competition within the common market, and in particular those which:
a. directly or indirectly fix purchase or selling prices or any other trading conditions;
b. limit or control production, markets, technical developments, or investments;
c. share markets or sources of supply;
d. apply dissimilar conditions to equivalent transactions with other trading parties, thereby placing them at a competitive disadvantage;
e. make the conclusion of contracts subject to acceptance by the other parties of supplementary obligations which, by their nature or according to commercial usage, have no connection with the subject of such contracts.'
The following comments must be made concerning Art 85. First, Art 85 only applies to agreements etc. affecting trade between two member states of the European Community. Of course, an agreement between two undertakings in one state may have this effect, as where two companies in this country agree to divide up their European export markets.

Second, infringement of Art 85(1) makes the prohibited agreement automatically void[2] and unenforceable in English law. The EEC Commission also has power to impose a fine or order the discontinuance of the agreement. However, under Community regulations an agreement can be notified to the EEC Commission for an individual exemption or for a declaration that the agreement does not fall within Art 85.[3] Despite the use of the phrase 'automatically void' an agreement is regarded as 'provisionally valid' if it has been notified to the Commission for exemption.[4]

The Restrictive Trade Practices Act 1976 deals with the situation which arises where an agreement is or may be void under both the Act and Art 85. In particular, the Director-General of Fair Trading is given a discretion not to refer an agreement to the Restrictive Practices Court, and the Court has power to decline or postpone the exercise of its jurisdiction having regard to Art 85 and to the effect of any exemption granted thereunder.[5]

1 Subject to the restrictions in Regulations 1983/83 and 1984/83.
2 EEC Treaty, Art 85(2).
3 Ibid, Art 85(3); reg 17/62.
4 Case 13/61: *Bosch v De Geus* [1962] CMLR 1, CJEC.
5 Restrictive Trade Practices Act 1976, ss5 and 21.

14.32 The provisions of Art 85(1) and the rules of the common law restraint of trade doctrines are cumulative; consequently, a cartel agreement (or an exclusive dealing agreement to which Art 85(1) applies) will be invalid in English law unless it is valid under both sets of rules.

Resale Prices Act 1976
14.33 This Act, a consolidation Act, replaces the Resale Prices Act 1964 whose object was to abolish resale price maintenance in the UK, except where it could be shown to be in the public interest. The Act is not concerned with arrangements imposing maximum prices, which remain perfectly valid.

14.34 The Act of 1976 provides that, except in the case of classes of goods exempted by the Restrictive Practices Court, a term or condition of a contract for, or relating to, the sale of goods by a manufacturer or other supplier to a dealer which provides a minimum resale price is void, although this does not affect the enforceability of the rest of the contract.[1] In addition, it is unlawful for any supplier of goods to include, or require the inclusion of, any minimum resale price provision in any such contract, or to notify to dealers or otherwise to publish minimum resale prices (although publication of a recommended price is permitted).[1]

The Act also prohibits the indirect enforcement of such minimum price provisions. It does so by providing that it is unlawful to withhold supplies from dealers who have undercut the stipulated price or who have supplied third parties who have done so, or who are likely so to undercut or to supply third parties who are likely to undercut. For the purpose of this prohibition, a person is treated as withholding supplies of goods if he refuses or fails to supply those goods to the order of the dealer; or if he refuses to supply them to the dealer except at prices or on terms as to credit or other matters which are significantly less favourable than those at or on which he normally supplies those goods to other similar dealers; or if, although he contracts to supply the goods to the dealer, he treats him significantly less favourably than he normally treats other such dealers in respect of delivery or other matters arising in the execution of the contract. However, a supplier is not to be treated as withholding supplies of goods if, in addition to the ground of actual or apprehended price-cutting, he has other grounds which, standing alone, would have led him to withhold those supplies.[2] Moreover, the withholding of supplies of any goods from a dealer is not unlawful if the supplier has reasonable cause to believe that within the previous 12 months the dealer, or another dealer supplied by him, has been using as loss-leaders any goods of the same or a similar description.[3]

The unlawful practices mentioned above can result in civil actions for an injunction 'or other appropriate relief' brought by the Crown, and for breach of statutory duty brought by any person affected by the contravention.[4]

1   Resale Prices Act 1976, s9.
2   Ibid, ss11 and 12.
3   Ibid, s13.
4   Ibid, s25.

14.35   The Act of 1964 empowers the Restrictive Practices Court to make orders exempting a particular class of goods from the above rules. Only two exemption orders have been made: in respect of books and related goods, and of medicaments and related goods. These are, therefore, the only goods in respect of which minimum resale price maintenance is now permissible.

Illegal contracts
14.36   A contract may be illegal in one of three ways, in that:

its formation is prohibited by statute; or

it is performed in a manner which is prohibited by statute; or

it involves an element which is unlawful, immoral or prejudicial to the interests of the state.

These three types of illegality, with their effects on the enforcement of a contract, will be discussed in turn, followed by a discussion of the question of the recovery of money or property transferred under an illegal contract.

Contracts whose formation is prohibited by statute
14.37   A contract is illegal in itself if a statute expressly or impliedly prohibits its making.

14.38   An example of a contract which was *expressly* so prohibited is provided by *Re Mahmoud and Ispahani*.[1] Under wartime delegated legislation it was forbidden to buy or sell linseed oil without a licence. A agreed to sell and deliver some linseed oil to B but B subsequently refused to accept delivery because, unknown to A, he did not have a licence to buy linseed oil. The Court of Appeal held that, there being a clear statutory prohibition of the making of such a contract without a licence, it was illegal and unenforceable by A.

A modern example of a statute expressly prohibiting the formation of a contract is provided by the Resale Prices Act 1976, s1. We mentioned in paras 14.24 to 14.29 above, that cartel agreements may be *void* under the Restrictive Trade Practices Act 1976 but the Resale Prices Act 1976, s1 makes *illegal* agreements for the *collective* enforcement of price maintenance conditions. Section 1 strikes at such agreements between suppliers and between dealers. Any agreement, or even any arrangement, between two or more persons carrying on business in the U K as suppliers of goods is illegal if it provides:

a. that goods shall be withheld from dealers who have infringed a condition as to the prices at which those goods may be sold (this includes putting a dealer's name on a stop-list); or

b. that goods shall not be supplied to such dealers except on terms which are less favourable than those applicable to similar dealers (e.g. by cancellation of a trade discount); or

c. that goods will only be supplied to persons who undertake to withhold or refuse supplies of goods in the above two ways.

In addition, agreements or arrangements authorising the recovery of penalties from offending dealers are illegal.

There are similar provisions relating to agreements between dealers in goods which provide for the like sanctions against suppliers who fail to observe or enforce resale price conditions.

The consequences of a contract which is illegal under s1 are not simply that it is unenforceable. In addition, the Crown may obtain an injunction 'or other appropriate relief', and a person affected by the agreement can bring an action for damages for breach of statutory duty.

1 [1921] 2 KB 716, CA.

14.39 The question whether a statute *impliedly* prohibits the making of a particular contract is productive of uncertainty since its answer depends on judicial interpretation of the statute to ascertain whether parliament intended to forbid the making of the particular contract. Because of the harsh consequences of such a finding, a contract will not be held to be prohibited unless there is a clear implication that this was parliament's intention.[1] One factor which is particularly relevant is whether the object of the statute is to protect the public or a class of persons, eg to protect the public against unqualified persons or to protect licensed persons from competition.[1] If so, this suggests that parliament intended a contract made in breach of the statute to be prohibited. In *Cope v Rowlands*,[2] for instance, a statute provided that anyone who acted as a broker in the City of London without a licence should pay a penalty for each offence. The plaintiff, who was unlicensed, acted as a broker for the defendant whom he later sued for the work which he had done for him. Parke B dismissed the action because, although the statute did not expressly prohibit the contract in question, parliament had intended to protect the public in stockbroking transactions. The statute therefore had to be taken as impliedly prohibiting the making of stockbroking contracts by unlicensed persons.

On the other hand, the fact that the statute's object is sufficiently served by the imposition of the statutory penalty suggests that parliament did not intend a contract made in breach of the statute to be prohibited. In *Smith v Mawhood*,[3] the plaintiff, a tobacconist, sued the defendant for the price of tobacco which he had delivered to him. The defendant pleaded that the contract was illegal because the plaintiff did not have a licence to sell tobacco, nor was his name painted on his premises, as required by statute. It was held that, although the plaintiff had committed a statutory offence, the contract was not illegal because the object of the statute was the imposition of a penalty for revenue purposes, and not the prohibition of contracts of sale by unlicensed dealers.

Another factor to which regard may be had is the inconvenience and injury which would be caused by holding the contract to be illegal.[4]

The approach of the courts is well demonstrated by the decision of the Court of Appeal in *Archbolds (Freightage) Ltd v S Spanglett Ltd*.[5] The defendants contracted with the plaintiffs to carry whisky from Leeds to London. The whisky was stolen en route through the negligence of the defendants' driver and the plaintiffs claimed damages for its loss. The defendants raised the defence that, under the Road and Rail Traffic Act 1933, it was illegal for a person to use a vehicle to carry goods for another for reward unless the vehicle held an 'A' licence, that the vehicle used did not hold an 'A' licence (in fact none of their vehicles held an 'A' licence), and that therefore the contract was illegal and unenforceable. The trial judge dismissed this defence and awarded the plaintiffs damages. The Court of Appeal dismissed the defendants' appeal. It held that if, as had been found, the contract merely provided for the carriage of whisky from Leeds to London, the *formation* of that contract could not be illegal because, even had both parties contemplated that an unlicensed vehicle would be used, this would not be a contractual term. Moreover, the Court continued, even if the contract was to carry goods in a vehicle which did not in fact have an 'A' licence, the contract would still not be illegal in its formation. This was because the Act of 1933 did not expressly prohibit the formation of such a contract; nor did it impliedly prohibit it, since its object was not to interfere with the owner of goods or his facilities for transport but to control competition between transport firms and improve efficiency, and that object was sufficiently served by the penalties prescribed for the transport undertaking using the unlicensed vehicle.

1   *St John Shipping Corpn v Joseph Rank Ltd* [1957] 1 QB 267, [1956] 3 All ER 683.
2   (1836) 2 M & W 149.
3   (1845) 14 M & W 452.
4   *St John Shipping Corpn v Joseph Rank Ltd* [1957] 1 QB 267, [1956] 3 All ER 683.
5   [1961] 1 QB 374, [1961] 1 All ER 417, CA.

Enforcement

14.40   Where a contract is statutorily illegal as formed neither party can enforce it, subject to the exceptions mentioned below, even though he was unaware of the facts constituting the illegality. Thus, in *Re Mahmoud and Ispahani*,[1] the seller could not sue the buyer for refusing to take delivery of the linseed oil; this was so despite the facts that he was unaware that the buyer did not have the necessary licence and that, between the contract and the attempted delivery, he had been assured by the buyer that he had a licence.

A contract which is statutorily illegal as formed can be enforced in part if the illegal portions are severable. The rule is that where a party makes a number of promises one of which is illegal and the rest legal, the illegal promise can be severed and the rest of the agreement enforced provided that:

a. the illegal promise does not constitute the main or only consideration given by that party for the other's promises; and

b. the illegal promise and the legal ones are not inseparable from and dependent upon one another; and

c. the nature of the illegality is not such as to preclude on grounds of public policy the enforcement of the rest of the agreement.[2]

If the statute under which a contract is illegal as formed is a 'class protecting statute', a party to the contract who is a member of the protected class can enforce it.[3] A 'class protecting statute' is one which has been passed to protect a particular class of persons, rather than simply to impose a penalty and prohibit the contract.[4]

1   [1921] 2 KB 716, CA; para 14.38 above.
2   *Kearney v Whitehaven Colliery Co* [1893] 1 QB 700, CA; *Carney v Herbert* [1985] 1 All ER 438, [1984] 3 WLR 1303, PC.
3   *Nash v Halifax Building Society* [1979] Ch 584, [1979] 2 All ER 19.
4   *Green v Portsmouth Stadium Ltd* [1953] 2 QB 190, [1953] 2 All ER 102, CA.

14.41   Although a party to an illegally formed contract cannot recover damages for its breach, subject to the exceptions just mentioned, he may be able to recover damages for misrepresentation if he has been induced to contract by a misrepresentation of fact (which may be of a fact affecting the legality of the contract).[1] Recovery of such damages is certainly possible if the misrepresentation was *fraudulent* and he was ignorant of the illegality;[2] it has not yet been decided whether damages may be recovered for negligent misrepresentation or where the misrepresentee was aware of the illegality.

1   Para 13.4 above.
2   *Shelley v Paddock* [1980] QB 348, [1980] 1 All ER 1009, CA.

Contracts which become illegal because they are performed in a manner which constitutes a statutory offence
14.42   The fact that an offence is committed in performing an initially lawful contract does not necessarily make the contract illegal,[1] and generally it does not have that effect. Thus, for reasons which will become apparent shortly, the fact that an employee of a road haulage company exceeds the speed limit while delivering goods does not render the contract of carriage made by the company illegal.

1   *St John Shipping Corpn v Joseph Rank Ltd* [1957] 1 QB 267, [1956] 3 All ER 683.

14.43   Some statutes expressly state whether breach of their provisions does or does not invalidate a contract. However, generally, it depends on interpretation of the statute to see whether parliament intended that the particular type of contract in question should be prohibited if performed in contravention of the statute. The approach here is the same as that to the question whether a contract is impliedly illegal as formed. Breach of a statute in performing a contract will only be held to invalidate it if there is a clear implication that parliament so intended. A statute whose object is the protection of the public or a class of persons is likely to give rise to such an implication, as will a statute which says that the type of contract in question can only be performed in one way. In *Anderson Ltd v Daniel*,[1] for instance, the statute made it an offence for a person to sell artificial fertilisers without giving the buyer an invoice stating the percentage of certain chemicals. The plaintiffs sold ten tons of artificial fertiliser to the defendants but did not provide the necessary invoice. It was held that, since the statute had specified the only way in which the contract could be performed, and since this had not been done, the contract was rendered illegal and the plaintiffs could not recover the price of the fertiliser. On the other hand, if the purposes of the statute are sufficiently served by the prescribed penalties the statute is unlikely to be construed as prohibiting a contract performed in breach of it. Another factor to be taken into account is the inconvenience or injury to a party which would result from a finding that the contract is prohibited.

These factors were taken into account by Devlin J in *St John Shipping Corpn v Joseph Rank Ltd*.[2] By statute it is an offence to load a ship to such an extent that the load line is below water. The plaintiffs chartered their ship to X to carry grain from the United States to England. The plaintiffs overloaded the ship so that the load line was submerged. The defendants, who were consignees of part of the cargo, withheld part of the freight charge (the equivalent of the amount due on the excess cargo), contending that the plaintiffs could not enforce on the contract because they had performed it unlawfully. Devlin J held that the plaintiffs could recover the amount due. He held that the illegal performance of the contract of carriage did not render it illegal, because the Act merely punished infringements of the load line rules and was not intended to prohibit a contract of carriage performed in breach of them.

1 [1924] 1 KB 138, CA
2 [1957] 1 QB 267, [1956] 3 All ER 683.

Enforcement

14.44 Where a contract has become illegal through performance in breach of a statute, the party who has so performed it cannot enforce the contract, as is shown by *Anderson Ltd v Daniel*,[1] where the plaintiffs' claim for the price of the fertiliser which they had delivered was dismissed because of their illegal performance. A limited exception was recognised in *Frank W Clifford Ltd v Garth*,[2] namely that, if the performance was initially legal but became illegal and the legal and illegal parts of the performance can be precisely valued, the illegal part can be severed and the party who has illegally performed the contract can recover the amount of the contractual price which is attributable to the legal performance. In this case, the defendant engaged the plaintiffs to convert premises into a coffee bar for her. At the time in question, it was illegal to do more than £1,000 worth of such work on any single property in any year without a licence. The defendant had already had £146 worth of work done that year by another contractor. Her contract with the plaintiffs was not for a fixed figure but on a 'cost-plus' basis, and because of various difficulties the plaintiffs' bill was far in excess of £1,000. The Court of Appeal held that, although the plaintiffs could not recover the full amount claimed, they could recover £854 because, until the work in the particular year exceeded £1,000 in value, it was perfectly lawful and only became unlawful in relation to the excess.

Thus, the plaintiffs could recover the amount which fell within the free limit.

1 [1924] 1 KB 138, CA.
2 [1956] 2 All ER 323, [1956] 1 WLR 570, CA.

14.45 The other party to a contract which is illegal as performed can sue on it, unless he knew of the mode of performance adopted (although he need not have known that it was illegal[1]) and allowed the performance to proceed. It is for him to establish his innocence. In *Marles v Philip Trant & Sons Ltd (No. 2)*,[2] for instance, the Court of Appeal held that although a contract for the sale of wheat was illegal, because the seller had not given the buyer certain written details as required by statute, the buyer could nevertheless sue the seller for breach of contract (the wheat having been misdescribed as 'spring wheat') because of his innocence. Similarly, in the *Archbolds (Freightage)* case,[3] the Court of Appeal did not find it necessary to pursue the question whether the hauliers' unlawful performance of the contract rendered it illegal, because the plaintiffs had been ignorant that it was to be so performed and could have sued on the contract of carriage anyway. On the other hand, the plaintiffs failed to recover damages for breach of contract in *Ashmore, Benson, Pease & Co Ltd v A V Dawson Ltd*,[4] where a contract of carriage performed by the defendants in breach of maximum load regulations was held to be illegal, because their transport manager had watched the lorries being overloaded and, by allowing it, had participated in the illegal performance of the contract.

1 *Archbolds (Freightage) Ltd v S Spanglett Ltd* [1961] 1 QB 374, [1961] 1 All ER 417, CA.
2 [1954] 1 QB 29, [1953] 1 All ER 651, CA.
3 [1961] 1 QB 374, [1961] 1 All ER 417, CA. The facts are set out in para 14.39 above.
4 [1973] 2 All ER 856, [1973] 1 WLR 828, CA.

14.46 If a party, who cannot sue on the illegal contract because he has illegally performed it, can prove that a collateral contract existed whereby the other party assumed responsibility for ensuring that the performance would be lawful, as by obtaining a necessary licence, he can recover damages for breach of that collateral contract.[1]

1 *Strongman (1945) Ltd v Sincock* [1955] 2 QB 525, [1955] 3 All ER 90, CA. Alternatively, he may be able to recover damages for misrepresentation.

Contracts involving an element which is unlawful, immoral or prejudicial to the interests of the state
14.47 Sometimes, a contract will be overtly for an unlawful, immoral or state-prejudicial purpose: at other times, an overtly proper contract, or its subject matter, will be intended by one or both of the parties, when the contract is made, to be exploited for such a purpose. Both types of contract are illegal ab initio but their consequences differ.

14.48 Any agreement to commit a crime or tort falls within this head, so that an agreement to assault X is illegal,[1] as is an agreement to publish a libel about X.[2] The width of the present head may be demonstrated by reference to *Miller v Karlinski*[3] and *Alexander v Rayson*.[4] In the former, the terms of an employment contract were that the employee should be paid

£10 a week plus travelling expenses. The contract also provided that he could recover the amount of income tax payable on the £10 by claiming it as travel expenses. The employee later claimed ten weeks' arrears of salary plus 'expenses', most of which related to what was payable in income tax. It was held that since the contract was overtly for an illegal purpose—to defraud the Revenue—it could not be enforced by the employee and his action was dismissed. In contrast, the contract in *Alexander v Rayson*, which was not overtly for an unlawful purpose, was held to be illegal because it was intended to be exploited for such a purpose. The plaintiff let a flat to the defendant at £1,200 pa. The transaction was effected by two documents: a lease of the flat at £450 pa, which provided for certain services to be rendered by the plaintiff, and an agreement that in consideration of £750 pa the plaintiff would render certain services, which were substantially the same as in the lease. Subsequently, the defendant refused to pay an instalment due under the documents. When sued for this, the defendant raised the defence that the object of the two documents was that only the lease was to be disclosed to the local authority to deceive them into reducing the rateable value of the property. The Court of Appeal held that if the documents were intended to be used for an unlawful purpose the plaintiff could not enforce either the lease or the service agreement.

1   *Allen v Rescous* (1676) 2 Lev 174.
2   *Apthorp v Neville & Co* (1907) 23 TLR 575.
3   (1945) 62 TLR 85. See also *Corby v Morrison* [1980] ICR 564.
4   [1936] 1 KB 169, CA.

14.49   Turning to agreements involving immorality, a contract to pay a woman in return for her agreeing to become a mistress is an obvious example of a contract which is illegal on the ground that its purpose is overtly immoral.[1] Likewise, a contract of employment will be held illegal if one of its terms is that the employee should procure prostitutes for his employer's clients, because its purpose is overtly immoral.[2] A contract to hire to a prostitute a car which is intended for use in her profession will be held illegal because the subject matter of the contract is intended to be used for an immoral purpose.[3]

1   *Walker v Perkins* (1764) 1 Wm Bl 517.
2   *Coral Leisure Group Ltd v Barnett* [1981] ICR 503 at 508.
3   *Pearce v Brooks* (1866) LR 1 Ex ch 213.

14.50   Agreements which involve an element prejudicial to the interests of the state include agreements which are hostile to a friendly foreign state,[1] agreements which tend to injure the public service (under which heading an agreement to assign a salary earned in a public office is illegal)[2] and agreements prejudicial to the administration of justice. An example of the last type of agreement is one to suppress, or not to prosecute, a criminal prosecution,[3] but this is limited to crimes of a public nature, e g riot or rape, so that the compromise of a prosecution for a trade marks offence or a domestic assault is not illegal.[4] An agreement not to appear at the public examination of a bankrupt, nor to oppose his discharge, is another example of an agreement which has been held illegal as prejudicial to the administration of justice.

Two other types of agreement which are prejudicial to the administration of justice are those tainted by maintenance or champerty. Maintenance occurs if a person without just cause or excuse supports litigation in a court of law by another in a case in which he has no legitimate interest. Champerty is maintenance plus a further agreement that the person giving such support shall have a share in anything recovered as a result of the litigation. In this context, it may be noted that an agreement, whereby a firm of surveyors is to be paid a fee equivalent to a year's savings on its client's rates if a reduction in the rateable value of the client's premises is secured by its endeavours, is not champertous but perfectly legal. The reason is that, even if the agreement contemplates recourse to the local valuation court, this does not involve a process of litigation in a court of law because a valuation court is not a court of law.[5]

1 *Foster v Driscoll* [1929] 1 KB 470.
2 *Re Mirams* [1891] 1 QB 594.
3 *Keir v Leeman* (1846) 9 QB 371.
4 *Fisher & Co v Appollinaris & Co* (1875) 10 Ch App 297; *McGregor v McGregor* (1888) 21 QBD 424, CA.
5 *Pickering v Sogex Services (UK) Ltd* (1982) 262 Estates Gazette 770.

Enforcement
14.51 The enforceability of a contract which is illegal because it involves an element which is unlawful, immoral or prejudicial to the interests of the state depends on whether or not it overtly involves such an element. If it does, neither party can enforce it however innocent he may be.[1] On the other hand, where the contract is not overtly for one of the above purposes but is intended to be, or its subject matter is intended to be, exploited for such a purpose the situation is as follows:

a. the contract cannot be enforced by a party who intended to exploit it unlawfully, immorally or 'prejudicially';[2] nor

b. can it be enforced by a party who knew the other had such an intention;[3] but

c. it can be enforced by a party who did not know of the other's unlawful, immoral or 'prejudicial' intentions before he performed or tendered performance of his contractual obligations.[4]

Thus, in *Cowan v Milbourn*,[5] where the defendant, who had agreed to let a room to the plaintiff but later refused to fulfil the agreement on learning that the plaintiff intended to use the room for an unlawful purpose (a blasphemous lecture), was sued for breach of contract, it was held that the plaintiff's action failed because of his unlawful intention in relation to the subject matter of the contract. Bramwell B added that the defendant could have sued the plaintiff for the hire charge if he had let him into possession not knowing of his unlawful intentions, but not if he had previously learnt of them. In the *Archbolds (Freightage)* case,[6] the Court of Appeal held that the fact that the hauliers had intended ab initio to carry out the contract of carriage in an unlawful way did not prevent the other party to the contract suing on it because they were ignorant of that intention. A party will have sufficient knowledge in the present context if he has full knowledge of what the other party intends to do; he need not know that it is unlawful.[7]

In contracts involving an element of unlawfulness, immorality or prejudice to the interests of the state it is not possible to sever the illegal part and enforce the rest of the contract.[8]

A party to the present type of contract who cannot enforce it may nevertheless be able to recover damages for misrepresentation if he has been induced to contract by a misrepresentation of fact.[9] Recovery of such damages is certainly possible if the misrepresentation was *fraudulent* and he was unaware of the illegality;[10] it has not yet been decided whether damages may be recovered for negligent misrepresentation or where the misrepresentee was aware of the illegality.

1 *Miller v Karlinski* (1945) 62 TLR 85; *Keir v Leeman* (1846) 9 QB 371; *Corby v Morrison* [1980] ICR 564.
2 *Alexander v Rayson* [1936] 1 KB 169, CA; *Corby v Morrison* [1980] ICR 564.
3 *Pearce v Brooks* (1866) LR 1 Exch 213; *Corby v Morrison* [1980] ICR 564.
4 *Cowan v Milbourn* (1867) LR 2 Exch 230.
5 (1867) LR 2 Exch 230.
6 [1961] 1 QB 374, [1961] 1 All ER 417, CA; the facts are set out in para 14.39 above.
7 *J. M. Allan (Merchandising) Ltd v Cloke* [1963] 2 QB 340, [1963] 2 All ER 258, CA; cf *Waugh v Morris* (1873) LR 8 QB 202.
8 *Bennett v Bennett* [1952] 1 KB 249 at 252–254, [1952] 1 All ER 413; *Miller v Karlinski* (1945) 62 TLR 85; *Kuenigl v Donnersmark* [1955] 1 QB 515, [1955] 1 All ER 46; *Corby v Morrison* [1980] ICR 564. Cf. *Fielding and Platt Ltd v Najjar* [1969] 2 All ER 150 at 153.
9 Para 13.4 above.
10 *Shelley v Paddock* [1980] QB 348, [1980] 1 All ER 1009, CA.

Recovery of money or property transferred under an illegal contract

14.52 The general rule is that a person cannot recover back money or property which he has transferred under an illegal contract, even if the other party has completely failed or refused to perform his contractual obligations. This rule is particularly harsh where a party to such a contract is not permitted to enforce it, since not only are damages for its breach irrecoverable by him but also he cannot successfully claim back what he has transferred under it instead. An authority is *Parkinson v College of Ambulance Ltd.*[1] The secretary of the defendant charity promised the plaintiff that, if he would make a certain donation to the charity, he would procure a knighthood for him. The knighthood did not materialise and the plaintiff sought to recover the £3,000 he had paid. It was held that the contract was illegal (as tending to injure the public service) and that the plaintiff's action, being based on it, must fail. This general rule is normally described by the Latin maxim *in pari delicto potior est conditio defendentis* (where the parties are equally guilty the defendant is in a more favourable position).

1 [1925] 2 KB 1.

14.53 In the following exceptional cases a party to an illegal contract can recover back from the other what he has transferred under it.

a. *Fraudulent misrepresentation by the other party that the contract was lawful* Instead of suing for damages for deceit,[1] the party deceived can recover back what he has transferred under the contract. This is shown by *Hughes v Liverpool Victoria Legal Friendly Society*,[2] where a woman, who had been induced to take out an insurance policy by a fraudulent misrepresentation that it was valid, was held able to recover the premiums which she had paid. The present exception does not apply where the misrepresentation as to the legality of the contract was not fraudulent.[3] However, where a person has been induced to enter into an illegal contract by a misrepresentation of *fact*, he can *rescind the contract for misrepresentation* and recover back what he transferred under it, *provided rescission is not barred*, even though the misrepresentation was innocent.[4]

b. *Contract procured through oppression by the other party* In *Atkinson v Denby*,[5] for example, the plaintiff, a debtor, offered his creditors five shillings in the pound. The defendant, who was one of the creditors, told the plaintiff that he would only accept this dividend if the plaintiff first paid him £50 and gave him a certain bill of exchange. The plaintiff agreed and did so. The contract was illegal because of the fraud on the other creditors, but it was held that the plaintiff could recover the £50 because the contract to defraud had been procured by oppression, since the other creditors would not have accepted the composition if the defendant had not. The basis of this exception, like the previous one, is that the parties are not *in pari delicto*.

c. *No reliance on the illegal contract* A party to an illegal contract can recover back what he has transferred under it if he can establish his right to it without relying on the terms of the illegal contract or its illegality. This exception is of limited application, partly because the ownership of property can pass under an illegal contract (in accordance with the ordinary rules concerning the passing of ownership)[6] if the parties so intend;[7] and where this occurs, as in the case of goods sold under an illegal contract of sale, the transferor cannot recover the property back.

However, where an owner of property has merely transferred some limited interest to another under an illegal contract, as by pledging goods with him or hiring them to him, any rights which he may have independent of his illegal contract will be recognised and enforced. Thus, if A hires goods to B under an illegal contract he can recover them back, or recover damages in lieu, when B's right to possess them has ended. This is because A's right to immediate possession will have revived thereby and consequently he will be entitled to sue B in tort for conversion of the goods without having to base his claim in any way on the terms of the illegal contract or its illegality.[8] On the other hand, if E deposits property with F to secure payment of charges under an illegal contract the property is irrecoverable, unless the charges have been paid, because, once F has pleaded that the property has been pledged with him, E can only base his claim to possession by showing that the pledge was invalid because of the illegality of the contract.[9]

d. *Unlawful purpose not yet carried into effect* This exception is relevant to contracts which are illegal because their purpose is unlawful. A party can recover back what he has transferred under an illegal contract if he genuinely repents (which he will not do if his change of mind is brought about by other's failure to perform the contract or because the illegality has been discovered by the authorities)[10] and withdraws from the contract before the unlawful purpose is partially performed in a substantial way.[11]

e. *Class protecting statutes* If a statute which makes a particular type of contract illegal as formed was passed to protect a particular class of persons, rather than simply to impose a penalty and prohibit the contract,[12] a member of that class who is a party to such a contract can recover back money or property which he has transferred under it, even though the contract has been completely performed.[13] The basis of this exception is that the parties are not *in pari delicto*.[13] Some class protecting statutes which make particular contracts illegal expressly provide for recovery by a member of the protected class of what he has transferred under them. For example, the Rent Act 1977, s125 provides that where an unlawful premium has been paid under any agreement it is recoverable back by the person who paid it (eg the tenant).

1 Para 13.20 above.
2 [1916] 2 KB 482, CA.
3 *Harse v Pearl Life Assurance Co* [1904] 1 KB 558, CA.
4 *Edler v Auerbach* [1950] 1 KB 359, [1949] 2 All ER 692. For these bars see para 13.16 above.
5 (1862) 7 H & N 934.
6 See Card and James *Law for Accountancy Students* (3rd edn) paras 24.11–24.22.
7 *Sajan Singh v Sardara Ali* [1960] AC 167, [1960] 1 All ER 269, PC; *Belvoir Finance Co Ltd v Stapleton* [1971] 1 QB 210, [1970] 3 All ER 664, CA.
8 *Bowmakers Ltd v Barnet Instruments Ltd* [1945] KB 65, [1944] 2 All ER 579, CA.
9 *Taylor v Chester* (1869) LR 4 QB 309.
10 *Bigos v Bousted* [1951] 1 All ER 92; *Alexander v Rayson* [1936] 1 KB 169 at 190.
11 *Kearley v Thomson* (1890) 24 QBD 742, CA; cf *Taylor v Bowers* (1876) 1 QBD 291, CA.
12 *Green v Portsmouth Stadium Ltd* [1953] 2 QB 190, [1953] 2 All ER 102, CA.
13 *Browning v Morris* (1778) 2 Cowp 790; *Kiriri Cotton Co Ltd v Dewani* [1960] AC 192, [1960] 1 All ER 177, PC.

Chapter 15
Capacity to contract

Minors
15.1   The age of majority was reduced from 21 to 18 by the Family Law Reform Act, 1969, s1. Persons under that age are known as minors or infants. The rules relating to the contractual capacity of minors are based on the common law but they were amended extensively by the Infants Relief Act 1874. Minors' contracts can be divided into four types:

valid contracts;

voidable contracts;

contracts absolutely void under the Infants Relief Act 1874, s1;

other invalid contracts.

It should be noticed at the outset that a parent or guardian is never liable for a minor's contract unless the minor acts as his agent, nor can a minor's invalid contract be validated by subsequent parental ratification.

Valid contracts
15.2   Three types of contract made by a minor fall within this heading: contracts for necessary goods for the minor; contracts for necessary services for the minor, and contracts of employment or apprenticeship (and analogous contracts) which are beneficial to the minor. These contracts were not affected by the Infants Relief Act 1874.[1]

1   Paras 15.12–15.15 below.

Contracts for necessary goods for the minor
15.3   Proof that goods were necessaries requires two conditions to be satisfied:

a. *The goods must be suitable to the minor's position in life* Necessaries are not limited to the necessities of life but they do not extend to mere luxuries.[1] They can include anything fit to maintain the minor in his station in life.[2]

b. *The goods must be necessaries according to the minor's actual requirements at the time of delivery* In *Nash v Inman*,[3] the defendant was an undergraduate at Cambridge. The plaintiff, a tailor, supplied him with clothes, including 11 waistcoats. The plaintiff's action for the price of the clothes failed because, the evidence showing that the defendant was amply provided already with clothes suitable to his position, there was no proof of the present condition.

1 *Peters v Fleming* (1840) 6 M & W 42.
2 *Bryant v Richardson* (1866) 14 LT 24 at 26; *Ryder v Wombwell* (1868) LR 3 Exch 90 at 96.
3 [1908] 2 KB 1, CA.

Contracts for necessary services for the minor
15.4 These must satisfy the same tests as contracts for necessary goods. In *Chapple v Cooper*,[1] the following examples of necessary services were given: education, training for a trade, and medical advice. Of course, as was emphasised in that case, whether services are necessaries in a particular case depends on the state and condition of the minor. In *Chapple v Cooper*, funeral expenses for the minor's husband, who had died leaving no estate to defray them, were held to be necessaries; it was stated that necessaries for a minor included necessaries for the minor's spouse or child so that a contract for such necessaries is also valid.

1 (1844) 13 M & W 252.

General points concerning contracts for necessaries
15.5 a. A contract which would otherwise be enforceable against the minor as a contract for necessaries cannot be so enforced if it contains terms which are harsh or onerous on him.[1]

b. A question of some importance is whether a contract for necessaries can be enforced against a minor if it is still executory. In other words, can a minor be sued if he repudiates the contract before the necessary goods have been delivered or the necessary services performed? The answer depends on whether the minor's liability arises because he has made the contract or because the necessaries have been supplied or performed. If liability arises because a contract has been made the minor is liable under the contract and can be sued for breach if he repudiates the contract while it is still executory. If liability arises because the necessaries have been supplied or performed the minor is liable only under the law of quasi-contract; he is liable not because he agreed but because the necessary was supplied or performed.

Although the matter is not entirely free from doubt, it seems that, in the case of contracts for necessary goods, a minor is only liable if the goods have actually been delivered and cannot be sued if he repudiates the contract before delivery.[2] In this context it may also be noted that the Sale of Goods Act 1979, s3 provides that, where necessary goods are sold and delivered to a minor, he must pay a reasonable price for them, which is not necessarily the contract price.

Unlike a contract for necessary goods, a contract for necessary services is enforceable against a minor even though it is executory when the minor repudiates it. The authority is *Roberts v Gray*.[3] Roberts was a famous billiards player. He agreed to take Gray, a minor, on a world billiards tour and to pay his expenses. This was a contract for necessary services, a contract for education and instruction, because its object was to instruct Gray in the profession of a billiards player. Roberts spent time and trouble and incurred liabilities in making preparations for the tour, but before the tour began Gray repudiated the contract. The Court of Appeal held that Roberts could recover damages, even though Gray had not received any instruction from him.

1   *Fawcett v Smethurst* (1914) 84 LJKB 473.
2   *Nash v Inman* [1908] 2 KB 1 at 8 (contrast p 12); *Pontypridd Union v Drew* [1927] 1 KB 214 at 220.
3   [1913] 1 KB 520, CA.

Contracts of employment or apprenticeship and analogous contracts

15.6   Such a contract is valid and enforceable against the minor even though executory, provided that, on the whole, it is beneficial to him. In *Clements v London and North Western Rly Co*,[1] a minor entered into a contract of employment as a porter with the railway company, promising to accept the terms of an insurance scheme to which the company contributed and to forego any claims he might have against the company under the Employers' Liability Act 1880. The terms of the scheme were in some ways more beneficial to him, and in other ways less beneficial, than those of the Act. It was held that the contract, taken as a whole, was for his benefit and that he was bound by it. This case can be contrasted with *De Francesco v Barnum*.[2] An apprenticeship deed was made between a minor, aged fourteen, and the plaintiff. The minor bound herself apprentice to the plaintiff for seven years to learn dancing. In the deed she agreed not to take any professional engagement without the plaintiff's consent, nor to marry. She was to be paid for any performance she might give, but there was no provision for other pay, nor did the plaintiff undertake to find her other work. The minor accepted a professional engagement with the defendant without the consent of the plaintiff, who then sued the defendant for inducing a breach of the apprenticeship deed. The plaintiff's success depended on whether the deed was enforceable against the minor. Fry J held that the deed was unenforceable because, on the whole, it was not beneficial to the minor, being unreasonably harsh and oppressive.

1   [1894] 2 QB 482, CA.
2   (1889) 43 Ch D 165, CA.

15.7   'Analogous contracts' in this context includes contracts whereby a minor earns a fee in his profession or occupation, or obtains a licence to follow his profession or occupation, or becomes a member of a professional body. An example of a case involving an 'analogous contract' is *Chaplin v Leslie Frewin (Publishers) Ltd*.[1] The plaintiff, a minor and a son of Charlie Chaplin, contracted in return for an advance on royalties to give the defendant publishers the exclusive rights to publish his autobiography, entitled 'I couldn't smoke the grass on my father's lawn'. Later he alleged that the completed work, written by ghost writers with his assistance, showed him to be a depraved creature and he sought to repudiate the contract. By a majority, the Court of Appeal held that he could not do so. The contract was binding on him since it was, on the whole, beneficial to him: it would enable him to start as an author and to earn money to keep himself and his wife and child.

1   [1966] Ch 71, [1965] 3 All ER 764, CA.

15.8   For no apparent reason, a minor's trading contract does not fall within the present heading and is not enforceable against him however beneficial to him it may be. For instance, in *Cowern v Nield*,[1] it was held that a contract to deliver hay could not be enforced against a hay and straw dealer who was a minor.

1   [1912] 2 KB 419, DC.

Voidable contracts

15.9   A person who makes one of these voidable contracts while he is a minor is bound by it, unless and until he expressly repudiates it during minority or within a reasonable time of attaining his majority. An adult party to such a contract cannot repudiate it[1] but, of course, he will no longer be bound by the contract if the person who contracted as a minor makes a valid repudiation. There are five types of voidable contract:

a. A contract by a minor to buy or sell land.[2]

b. A purported lease by or to a minor.[3]

c. A contract by a minor to buy shares.[4]

d. A contract to bring property into a marriage settlement.[5]

e. A partnership agreement. A minor who makes a partnership agreement is in a special position compared with the other type of voidable contract. Although he is entitled to share in the profits resulting from the partnership, he is not liable for partnership debts while he is still a minor; but once he attains majority he can be sued for subsequent partnership debts, unless he has repudiated the partnership agreement before the debt in question was incurred and given adequate notice of repudiation to people dealing with the partnership.[6]

Apart from the present types of contract and the valid contracts mentioned above, a contract made by a minor is invalid. The present types of contract are said to be voidable because under them the minor acquires an interest in property of a fairly permanent nature to which continuous rights and duties attach. It would be unjust, the argument continues, to let the minor retain the benefits without fulfilling the obligations and this is prevented by making the contract voidable. This explanation is open to the objection that it could equally apply to other contracts made by a minor which are void in law. Moreover, it is possible to envisage a voidable contract of the present type which does not involve continuous rights and duties thereunder, as in the case of the purchase of freehold land for a lump sum.

1   *Clayton v Ashdown* (1714) 2 Eq Cas Abr 516.
2   *Whittington v Murdy* (1889) 60 LT 956.
3   *Davies v Beynon-Harris* (1931) 47 TLR 424.
4   *North Western Rly Co v M'Michael* (1850) 5 Exch 114.
5   *Edwards v Carter* [1893] AC 360, HL.
6   *Goode v Harrison* (1821) 5 B & Ald 147.

The time of repudiation

15.10   A voidable contract can be repudiated during minority or within a reasonable time of reaching majority. A repudiation during minority is not conclusive and can be withdrawn within a reasonable time of majority.[1] It depends on the facts of each case whether a repudiation after majority was within a reasonable time of reaching that age, and in determining this matter it is irrelevant that for most of the material period the ex-minor was ignorant of this right to repudiate or was unable to decide whether to do so.[2]

1   *North Western Rly Co v M'Michael* (1850) 5 Exch 114 at 127.
2   *Edwards v Carter* [1893] AC 360, HL.

Effect of repudiation

15.11   Repudiation relieves the minor or former minor from contractual liabilities accruing after his repudiation[1] but, in the light of conflicting dicta, it is uncertain whether repudiation relieves him from liabilities which have accrued before repudiation.[2]

A person who exercises the right to repudiate the voidable contract cannot recover back money paid under it unless there has been a total failure of consideration, which will not occur unless he has received nothing of what he has bargained for.[3] This is demonstrated by *Steinberg v Scala*.[4] The plaintiff, a minor, applied for, and was allotted, shares in a company. She paid the amounts due on application and allotment, and also on the first call. She received no dividends and after 18 months claimed to repudiate the allotment and recover back the money she had paid. The Court of Appeal held that, while she could repudiate the contract and thereby avoid liability for further calls, she could not recover back what she had already paid because she had got the shares she bargained for and it was immaterial that she had not received any real benefit by way of dividends: there had been no total failure of consideration.

1   *Steinberg v Scala (Leeds) Ltd* [1923] 2 Ch 452, CA.
2   Contrast *North Western Rly Co v M'Michael* (1850) 5 Exch 114 at 125 (repudiation relieves from accrued liabilities) with *Blake v Concannon* (1870) Ir 4 CL 323 (repudiation does not so relieve). There are dicta in support of both views in the Court of Appeal decision in *Steinberg v Scala (Leeds) Ltd.*
3   *Corpe v Overton* (1833) 10 Bing 252.
4   [1923] 2 Ch 452, CA.

Contracts governed by the Infants Relief Act 1874, s1

15.12   At common law, all contracts made by a minor, other than those previously described, were *negatively* voidable in that they did not bind the minor unless he ratified them within a reasonable time of reaching the age of majority. Negative voidability must be sharply distinguished from the positive voidability of the contracts just mentioned, which bind the minor from the beginning and continue to do so unless and until he repudiates before, or within a reasonable time after, attaining majority. The negatively voidable type of minor's contract was abolished by the Infants Relief Act 1874.

15.13   The Infants Relief Act 1874, s1 provides that the following contracts are 'absolutely void', whether made under seal or not:

a. Contracts for the repayment of money lent or to be lent to a minor Thus, any loan of money to a minor is irrecoverable, even if the money was lent to buy necessaries. However, if money is lent for this purpose and is actually spent on it by the minor, the lender is subrogated to (ie acquires) the rights

266

of the seller and has the same right of recovery of the purchase price that the seller would have had if not paid.[1]

b. *Contracts for goods (other than necessary goods) supplied or to be supplied to a minor* This head covers contracts of exchange,[2] of hire and of hire purchase,[3] as well as contracts of sale.

c. *Accounts stated* An account stated is merely the acknowledgment by a debtor that he owes a sum certain to his creditor. Nowadays it is merely prima facie evidence of this debt, and this evidence may be rebutted by proof that there is no debt, or no valid debt, owing at all.[4] Thus, the inclusion of account stated in the list of 'absolutely void' contracts appears unnecessary.

1   *Re National Permanent Benefit Building Society* (1869) 5 Ch App 309 at 313.
2   *Pearce v Brain* [1929] 2 KB 310, DC.
3   *Yeoman Credit Ltd v Latter* [1961] 2 All ER 294 at 296.
4   *Siqueira v Noronha* [1934] AC 332 at 337.

The effects of s1 on the three types of contract

15.14   The use of the words 'absolutely void' suggests that these contracts are complete nullities and of no legal effect, but this suggestion is not totally correct. The effects of these absolutely void contracts are as follows:

a. The contract cannot be enforced against the minor. Moreover, a ratification of a debt under such a contract, or a fresh promise to pay, made after attaining majority does not, by virtue of s2 of the Act of 1874, make the debt enforceable.

b. In the absence of authority, it would seem that the words 'absolutely void' render the contract unenforceable by the minor.

c. With one exception, the contract is of no legal effect for other purposes. In *R v Wilson*,[1] it was held that a minor could not be made bankrupt in respect of debts which were void under s1. Similarly, it was held in *Coutts & Co v Brown-Lecky*[2] that a guarantee by an adult of a minor's overdraft with a bank was itself void and unenforceable since, the loan by way of overdraft being void, there was no 'debt' to be guaranteed. It should be noted, however, that lenders of money to minors are not completely unprotected: if they get an indemnity against loss from an adult this can be enforced against him. This is shown by *Yeoman Credit Ltd v Latter*.[3] The plaintiff company lent a minor money and got the second defendant, an adult, to indemnify them. The indemnity was held enforceable by the Court of Appeal on the ground that its object was to protect the plaintiff company against loss rather than to make good the minor's legally non-existent debt. As Harman LJ pointed out, the distinction between a guarantee and an indemnity raises 'hair-splitting distinctions of exactly that kind which brings the law into hatred, ridicule and contempt by the public'. In cases of doubt the court will lean in favour of construing a contract between the creditor and adult as being intended to be one of indemnity, rather than of guarantee of the minor's debt.[4]

The exceptional case where the present type of contract does have legal effect is that the property (ie ownership) passes in goods delivered to the minor under a void contract.[5] This rule has the merit of protecting those who purchase the goods from the minor but it may be contrasted with the rule that property does not pass on delivery under a contract void for mistake.[6]

d. Money paid, or property transferred, under the void contract by the minor is only recoverable by him if there has been a total failure of consideration, which will only occur if the minor received nothing of what he bargained for. In *Pearce v Brain*,[7] a minor exchanged his motor cycle for the defendant's car. The car broke down after 70 miles. The contract, being for the supply of non-necessary goods, was void under s1 but it was held that the minor could not recover the motor cycle because he had got what he bargained for (the car) and there was therefore no total failure of consideration.

1   (1879) 5 QBD 28.
2   [1947] KB 104, [1946] 2 All ER 207, DC.
3   [1961] 2 All ER 294, [1961] 1 WLR 828, CA.
4   *Yeoman Credit Ltd v Latter*.
5   *Stocks v Wilson* [1913] 2 KB 235 at 246.
6   Para 12.1 above.
7   [1929] 2 KB 310; relying on *Valentini v Canali* (1889) 24 QBD 166, DC.

Other invalid contracts
15.15   This head covers all contracts made by a minor which are neither for necessaries or of beneficial employment, nor positively voidable by him, nor absolutely void under the Infants Relief Act 1874, s1. Contracts covered by this heading therefore include contracts for the supply of goods, or the loan of money, *by* a minor, contracts to render non-necessary services to a minor and contracts of employment made by a minor which are not beneficial to him. These contracts are governed by common law rules, as amended by s2 of the Act of 1874, and their effect is:

a. They do not bind the minor.

b. They bind the adult party[1] but, while the minor may recover damages, the minor cannot obtain specific performance of the contract.[2]

c. It appears that a minor can only recover money paid, or property transferred, under the contract if there has been a total failure of consideration.

d. In certain cases, such a contract made by a minor becomes binding on him if he makes a fresh promise to perform after reaching majority.

At common law, these contracts were of the *negatively* voidable type referred to in para 15.12 above, so that they became binding on the minor if he *ratified* them within a reasonable time of reaching majority. This rule was amended by the Infants Relief Act, s2, which applies to all contracts which had previously been negatively voidable. Section 2 provides that a debt contracted during minority cannot be rendered enforceable against the minor by a promise to pay (or by ratification of the debt) made after majority, nor is the promise to pay in itself enforceable.[3] In the case of contracts other than those giving rise to a debt on the part of the minor, such as a contract by a minor to supply goods, s2 provides that they can no longer be made enforceable against him by virtue of his ratification after majority. However, if the former minor makes a fresh promise to perform after reaching majority the promise is enforceable. Whether there has been mere ratification or a fresh promise is a difficult question of fact, depending on the former minor's intentions. It is unlikely that a court will infer a fresh promise unless new terms supplementing or varying the original contract are introduced after majority.[4]

1   *Bruce v Warwick* (1815) 6 Taunt 118.
2   *Flight v Bolland* (1828) 4 Russ 298.
3   *Smith v King* [1892] 2 QB 543.
4   *Ditcham v Worrall* (1880) 5 CPD 410; *Brown v Harper* (1893) 68 LT 488.

Liability for torts connected with contracts

15.16   Generally, a minor is liable for his torts, but he is not so liable if he commits a tort in performing or procuring a contract which is not binding on him, otherwise such a contract could be indirectly enforced by means of a tortious action. Thus, in *Jennings v Rundall*,[1] a minor who had hired a mare and injured her by excessive and improper riding was held not liable in tort, and, in *R Leslie Ltd v Sheill*,[2] it was held that a minor who obtained a loan of money by a fraudulent misrepresentation as to his age was not liable in the tort of deceit.

The only exception to the rule, that a tortious action cannot be brought for a tort connected with a contract which is not binding on the minor, is where the minor does something, which is not simply a wrongful performance of something authorised or contemplated by the contract, but is the performance of something prohibited by the contract or not contemplated by it. An example is *Burnard v Haggis*.[3] A minor hired a mare for riding and was given strict instructions 'not to jump or lark with her'. He lent her to a friend who jumped her, causing fatal injuries. The minor was held liable in tort because the jumping was a prohibited act, *Jennings v Rundall* being distinguished on the ground that the minor there had not done a prohibited act but merely an authorised act (riding) improperly. A more modern case is *Ballett v Mingay*,[4] where the plaintiff lent the defendant, a minor, a microphone and amplifier at a weekly rent. The defendant delivered these improperly to X. The Court of Appeal held that the defendant was liable in tort because parting with possession of the goods fell outside the purview of the contract.

1   (1799) 8 Term Rep 335.
2   [1914] 3 KB 607, CA.
3   (1863) 14 CB NS 45.
4   [1943] KB 281, [1943] 1 All ER 143, CA.

Restitution for fraud by the minor

15.17   The most common fraudulent misrepresentation in this context is that the minor is over the age of majority. A minor who, by fraud, induces a contract which is *not otherwise binding on him* is not only not liable in tort,[1] but is also not liable on the contract or in quasi-contract.[2] However, as a matter of equitable intervention, it may be possible to order the restitution of what the minor obtained under such a contract, since equity requires a minor who has obtained an advantage by fraud to restore his ill-gotten gains.[3] Restitution for fraud is best discussed by distinguishing these three types of case:

a. Where the minor obtains goods by fraud and remains in possession of them an order for restitution can clearly be made.[4]

b. Where the minor obtains a loan of money by fraud restitution cannot be ordered, unless, as is unlikely, he still possesses the actual notes or coins and they can be identified. The leading authority is *R Leslie Ltd v Sheill*,[5] where registered moneylenders lent a minor £400 after he had represented he was of full age. The minor spent the £400 and the moneylenders' claim for the restitution of the money was dismissed by the Court of Appeal on the ground that to compel the minor to refund the money would be an indirect enforcement of the void contract of loan, not a restoration of ill-gotten gains.

c. Where the minor obtains goods by fraud, but ceases to possess them because he has sold or exchanged them, it would seem in principle that it should not be possible to order him to restore their proceeds because this would be equivalent to enforcing the contract. However restoration was ordered in such circumstances in *Stocks v Wilson*,[6] where the minor was ordered to account for the proceeds of sale. Lush J's decision in this case is hard to reconcile with that of the Court of Appeal in *R Leslie Ltd v Sheill*, since an order for account is in effect enforcing the contract rather than restoring ill-gotten gains. The decision in *Stocks v Wilson* was criticised, but not overruled, in *Sheill's* case.

1   Para 15.16 above.
2   *Levene v Brougham* (1909) 25 TLR 265, CA; *R Leslie Ltd v Sheill* [1914] 3 KB 607, CA.
3   *R Leslie Ltd v Sheill* [1914] 3 KB 607 at 618.
4   *Clarke v Cobley* (1789) 2 Cox Eq Cas 173.
5   [1914] 3 KB 607, CA.
6   [1913] 2 KB 235.

15.18   The law concerning the contractual capacity of minors is less important now that the age of majority has been reduced to 18. The rules discussed above are not only unduly complex but they are also unsatisfactory in that the balance between the protection of the adult and minor parties to a contract is unduly weighted in favour of the minor. There is good reason for making certain contracts unenforceable against the minor but it seems wrong that, subject to restitution for fraud, he should be able to retain what he has received under such a contract while refusing to perform his side of the bargain.

Mentally disordered and intoxicated persons

15.19   If the Court of Protection[1] has assumed jurisdiction to manage the property and affairs of a person suffering from mental disorder, its powers include making contracts for the benefit of that person and carrying out contracts already made by him.[2] It is possible that such a person is absolutely incapable of entering into a contract which binds him; certainly, he cannot make one purporting to dispose of property since this would interfere with the Court's jurisdiction.[3] Apart from this, mentally disordered persons generally have full contractual capacity, although their contracts may be voidable in the circumstances outlined next.

If a person proves that, because of mental disorder or intoxication, he was incapable, at the time of making the contract, of understanding its nature *and* that the other party knew of this, the contract is voidable at his option.[4] This option can only be exercised when the person is of sane and sober understanding, and if he decides to affirm the contract rather than avoid it he is bound by it.[5]

1 Para 2.35 above.
2 Mental Health Act 1983, s96.
3 *Re Walker* [1905] 1 Ch 160, CA; *Re Marshall* [1920] 1 Ch 284.
4 *Imperial Loan Co v Stone* [1892] 1 QB 599, CA.
5 *Matthews v Baxter* (1873) LR 8 Exch 132.

15.20 A person who is not contractually liable under the above rules is nevertheless liable to pay a reasonable price for necessary goods sold *and delivered* to him since the Sale of Goods Act 1979, s3, which has already been mentioned in relation to minors' contracts,[1] also applies to persons who are incompetent to contract 'by reason of mental incapacity or drunkenness'.

1 Para 15.5b above.

Companies

Legal status
15.21 Under British law, a company (which is an artificial legal person) may be formed in any one of three ways:

a. by registration under the Companies Act 1985; or

b. by Private Act of Parliament (statutory companies); or

c. by Royal Charter (chartered companies).

It is extremely rare (as well as difficult and expensive) to form a company other than under the Companies Act. The Companies Act permits the formation of private companies and public companies (only public companies can apply for listing on the Stock Exchange or the Unlisted Securities Market) and while company law usually applies equally to both types of registered company there are important differences. One important distinction concerns formation. A public limited company must reveal its status and its name, by using the words 'public limited company' (plc), or their Welsh equivalent, and must have a specified minimum amount of capital on its formation. A private limited company must use the word 'limited' (ltd) in its name (or the Welsh equivalent) and need not have capital exceeding two pence on its formation. Both types of registered company are easy to form and the costs of formation are modest.

Companies may be formed for any purpose which their progenitors or promoters choose but trading bodies will usually be in registered form. Statutory companies are often specialised trading bodies, for example, building societies, friendly societies and insurance companies. Chartered companies are typically charitable or quasi-charitable associations or non-trading bodies, such as the Royal Institution of Chartered Surveyors. However, in the past some famous trading companies have been incorporated by Royal Charter, for example, the East India Co and the Hudson Bay Co.

15.22 Other associations of people may pursue some common purpose—trade unions, clubs and partnerships are examples—but companies can be distinguished from other associations in that the company is itself a legal person totally distinct from its shareholders (who are also called members) and employees. Companies are artificial legal persons and when a statute refers to a person then prima facie it means human beings and companies. Even if a company is totally dominated by one shareholder, the company and that shareholder are distinct legal persons.[1] An example is provided by *Lee v Lee's Air Farming Ltd*,[2] where Lee, who was founder, principal shareholder, managing director, and chief pilot of a company, had been killed while engaged on the business of the company. The Privy Council held that, because Lee and the company were distinct legal persons, Lee could enter into a contract of employment with the company and his widow could therefore claim compensation under a government scheme. Had there been no contract of employment her claim would have failed.

Two consequences of the separate legal identities of a company and its members are:

a. A company can sue and be sued in its own name.

b. A company can make contracts on its own behalf (and its members cannot claim the benefit nor be subject to the burden of such contracts[3]).

1 *Salomon v Salomon & Co Ltd* [1897] AC 22, HL.
2 [1961] AC 12, [1960] 3 All ER 420, PC.
3 This is merely the effect of the doctrine of privity, paras 6.23–6.31 above.

Contractual capacity

15.23 Although a company is a legal person, it does not—except in the case of a chartered company[1]—have the contractual capacity of a natural person. The contractual capacity of registered and statutory companies is limited by the memorandum of association and the creating statute respectively.

1 *Sutton's Hospital Case* (1612) 10 Co Rep 23a; *Pharmaceutical Society of Great Britain v Dickinson* [1970] AC 403, [1968] 2 All ER 686, HL.

15.24 When a registered company is created, the people forming the company are required to lodge two documents with the Registrar of Companies at Companies House in Cardiff: the memorandum of association and the articles of association. These documents are available for public inspection.[1] The memorandum of association must state certain specific things including the objects of the company[2] (ie the purposes for which the company was formed and the aims and business it intends to pursue). This provision in the memorandum, the objects clause, defines exclusively what a company may do and for what purposes it can make contracts. If a company enters into a contract which is not authorised, expressly or impliedly, by the objects clause such contract is ultra vires (beyond the powers of the company) and, subject to what we say in para 15.26 below, unenforceable. If a company is formed to manufacture railway rolling stock, it cannot build railways; and, if it attempts to do so, any contracts entered into to promote or carry out the building of railways are beyond the powers of the company and unenforceable by or against the company.[3] A company has the power to make contracts expressly authorised by its objects clause but contracts impliedly authorised by the objects clause will also be enforceable. A company has an implied power to engage in activities which are reasonably incidental to the express objects of the company if they are for the benefit of the company. In *Deuchar v Gas, Light and Coke Co*,[4] a company, which had an express power to transform into a marketable state residuals remaining after the manufacture of its principal product, had implied power to manufacture the reagent required to effect the transformation. It would also have had an implied power to buy the reagent, so that a contract for the purchase of the reagent would have been impliedly authorised and therefore enforceable.

Because an objects clause is contained in a document open to public inspection, everyone is deemed to have notice of it. Since very few people actually consult the objects clause of a company with which they intend to contract, it is extremely easy to enter unknowingly into an ultra vires contract. This can work injustice. In *Ashbury Railway Carriage and Iron Co v Riche*,[5] Riche sued the company for breach of a contract of employment. The contract employed Riche to supervise the building of a railway in Belgium. The company was not authorised to build railways and abandoned the project. The House of Lords rejected Riche's claim, saying that the company had no power to make contracts relating to the pursuance of an unauthorised purpose. The contract was ultra vires, as Riche should have known, because he was deemed to have knowledge of the objects clause of the company, and the contract could not be rendered enforceable by ratification by the shareholders. Therefore, if a person intends to enter into a contract with a company he should check whether the contract is within the contractual capacity of the company as enunciated in the objects clause; such a procedure is clearly impractical.

1 Companies Act 1985, ss1, 7 and 10.
2 Ibid, s2.
3 *Ashbury Railway Carriage and Iron Co Ltd v Riche* (1875) LR 7 HL 653, HL.
4 [1925] AC 691, HL.
5 (1875) LR 7 HL 653, HL.

15.25 Attempts to mitigate the effects of the doctrine of ultra vires have been made by the courts, by companies themselves and most recently by statute. First, the courts have held that if a contract is apparently authorised by the objects clause, but is in fact ultra vires because of the use which the company intends to make of the contract, the company cannot enforce the contract but the other contracting party can. However, the other contracting party can only enforce the contract if he does not know of the intended ultra vires use of the contract.[1] For example, if a company, which is authorised to borrow money to develop its business, borrows money, this does not appear, so far as the lender can tell, to be an ultra vires contract. However, if the company intends to use this money for an ultra vires purpose, it cannot enforce the contract of loan though the lender can[2] (ie he can recover principal and interest) unless he had actual knowledge of the misapplication of the money.

Companies sought to mitigate the effects of the doctrine of ultra vires by drafting objects clauses of immense length which contained many clauses and stated that every clause was an object, hoping thereby to authorise every conceivable purpose and contract they undertook. Lengthy objects clauses received reluctant approval from the House of Lords in *Cotman v*

Brougham,[3] but the effectiveness of stating that all sub-clauses of the objects clause are to be regarded as independent objects was doubted in *Re Introductions Ltd*.[4] In the *Introductions* case, the Court of Appeal distinguished between objects and mere powers by holding that mere powers could only be validly exercised in pursuance of an object. In this case, the company had borrowed money, not to expand its authorised business of showing visitors around Great Britain but to set up a pig farm. The loan was held ultra vires despite a sub-clause in the objects clause permitting the company to borrow money and another sub-clause saying that all sub-clauses of the objects clause were independent objects. The Court of Appeal considered that borrowing money was a mere power and could only authorise borrowings designed to promote the true objects of the company.

A device which has been approved in *Bell Houses Ltd v City Wall Properties Ltd*[5] is that of including a sub-clause in the objects clause authorising the company to make any contract which, in the honest opinion of the directors, would benefit the company. This is probably limited, however, to situations where the company wishes to make a beneficial contract not expressly or impliedly authorised by the objects clause without abandoning their usual authorised business. This decision of the Court of Appeal in *Bell Houses Ltd v City Wall Properties Ltd* seems a useful way of evading the doctrine of ultra vires, at least where the company can show it is still pursuing its authorised business as well.

1   *Re Jon Beauforte (London)* [1953] Ch 131, [1953] 1 All ER 634.
2   *Re Introductions Ltd* [1970] Ch 199, [1969] 1 All ER 887, CA. In this case the lender *knew* of the ultra vires purpose and was unable to enforce its contract, even though it did not realise that the use made of the money by the company was ultra vires.
3   [1918] AC 514, HL.
4   [1970] Ch 199, [1969] 1 All ER 887, CA, approved by the Court of Appeal in *Rolled Steel (Holdings) Ltd v British Steel Corpn* [1984] BCLC 466.
5   [1966] 2 QB 656, [1966] 2 All ER, 674, CA. This device was applied by the House of Lords in *Newstead v Frost* [1980] 1 All ER 363, [1980] 1 WLR 135.

15.26   The most important attack on the rigours of the doctrine of ultra vires is contained in the Companies Act 1985, s35. This section is of immense importance for those dealing with the contractual capacity of companies but its drafting is far from ideal. The section provides that an ultra vires contract shall be enforceable *against* the company by the other party to that contract if certain conditions are satisfied. These conditions are:

a. That the party seeking to enforce the contract acted in good faith; this will be presumed unless the company can prove lack of good faith. Knowing that the company lacked the capacity to make the contract would probably be a lack of good faith, although the section makes it clear that there is no duty to inquire as to whether the company possessed capacity; and

b. That he was 'dealing' with the company. Therefore, non-trading contracts may not be enforceable; and

c. That the transaction which it is sought to enforce has been 'decided on by the directors'. It is not clear whether this means 'decided on' by all, or by a majority of, the directors, nor whether the decision must have been taken at a formal board meeting. Nor is it certain if the particular contract has to have been decided on by the directors or if it is enough for a change of policy, which the contract seeks to implement, to be decided on by the directors. In *International Sales and Agencies Ltd v Marcus*,[1] the judge suggested, obiter, that a decision taken by the only director who was active in the management of the company (there were two others) could be regarded as 'decided on by the directors' but this suggestion is open to doubt.

Despite these problems, s35 will render enforceable against the company many ultra vires contracts.

1   [1982] 3 All ER 551.

15.27   If section 35 does not apply in a particular case there are other remedies which a party to an ultra vires contract may seek to pursue.

a. *Tracing* If the company still has assets which were transferred under an ultra vires contract, the person who supplied the goods can recover them (though he could not sue for their price) even, sometimes, where they have been mixed with similar assets from other sources.[1]

b. *Subrogation* Insofar as money borrowed under an ultra vires contract is used to discharge valid, enforceable debts of the company, the lender can be subrogated to, i e put in the position of, the discharged creditor. However, a lender who is so subrogated does not acquire any preferential rights to repayment which the discharged creditor may have had.[2]

c. *Quasi-contract*[3] A party who provided services for a company under an ultra vires contract may be able to sue on a quantum meruit.[4] An action for money had and received can also be sustained.[5]

1   *Sinclair v Brougham* [1914] AC 398, HL.
2   *Re Wrexham, Mold and Connah's Quay Rly Co* [1899] 1 Ch 440, CA.
3   For quasi-contract generally, see ch 16.
4   *Craven-Ellis v Canons Ltd* [1936] 2 KB 403, [1936] 2 All ER 1066.
5   *Brougham v Dwyer* (1913) 108 LT 504, DC; para 16.7 below.

Partnerships

15.28   A partnership will usually be governed by the rules laid down in the Partnership Act 1890, but it is possible to create limited partnerships and they are governed by the Limited Partnership Act 1907. The limited partnership, which is a partnership with some of the characteristics of a limited liability company, is not very popular in the U K, though much used in continental Europe.

The Partnership Act 1890, s1 defines a partnership as 'the relation existing between two or more persons carrying on a business in common with a view to profit'. Because the partners and the partnership are not separate legal entities, unlike the shareholders and the company in which they hold shares, a partner is liable for the debts and liabilities of the partnership.[1] Conversely, the partners do have a legal interest in the assets of the partnership.[2] Shares in a company may be bought and sold: shares in a partnership are not transferable.[3] The death of shareholders leaves the company unaffected: the death of a partner technically terminates the partnership, though the remaining partners may agree to carry on the partnership.[4] A partnership can usually sue and be sued in its own name.[5]

The maximum number of partners permissible for a partnership engaged in business is 20, except that some types of partnership of professional men may exceed this number.[6] For example, a partnership formed to carry on one or more of the following activities, viz surveying, auctioneering, valuing, estate agency, land agency, or estate management, is permitted to have more than 20 partners, provided that not less than three-quarters of them are members of the Royal Institution of Chartered Surveyors or of the Incorporated Society of Valuers and Auctioneers.[7]

A limited partnership is a partnership where one or more partners has only a limited liability for the debts of the partnership. Every limited partnership must have at least one general partner[8] (ie with full liability for debts) and any limited partner who is active in the affairs of the partnership becomes a general partner.[9] The limited partnership is only suitable for those who wish to invest money in a partnership but take no part in its running; their lack of popularity seems hardly surprising.

It is unusual to find large businesses run as partnerships and, while there are advantages over companies in that there is less publicity for the affairs of the partnership, and perhaps less tax to be paid, these benefits will probably be outweighed by the advantages, of limited liability and tax saving once profits reach a certain size, which are enjoyed by a company.

In making contracts, a partnership has to work through agents, usually the partners, but since the partnership is not a separate legal entity there is no equivalent to the objects clause of a company. In theory, a partnership can make any contract it wishes. Whether a contract entered into by a partner binds his fellow partners depends on the usual rules of agency,[10] with the additional rule that any contract entered into by a partner which would be within the usual practice of the partnership will bind his fellow partners.[11]

1   Partnership Act 1890, s9.
2   Ibid, s20.
3   Ibid, s24.
4   Ibid, s33.
5   Under various rules of the Supreme Court.
6   Companies Act 1985, s716.
7   Partnership (Unrestricted Size) No 1 Regulations 1968.
8   Limited Partnership Act 1907, s4.
9   Ibid, s6.
10   Ch 17.
11   Partnership Act 1890, s5.

Chapter 16
Quasi-contract

16.1 In certain cases, a person is required by law to pay money to another on the ground that he would be unjustly enriched if he was entitled to retain it. For historical reasons, such cases are known as quasi-contracts, which is somewhat misleading because the liability to pay does not arise from any agreement between the parties concerned but is imposed by law. Quasi-contractual obligations only relate to the payment of money: they do not extend to the transfer of other property.

Quasi-contracts can be divided into the following types:

money paid by the plaintiff to the use of the defendant;

money had and received by the defendant to the use of the plaintiff;

quantum meruit;

money had and received by the defendant from a third party to the use of the plaintiff.

Money paid by the plaintiff to the use of the defendant

Payment which relieves the defendant of a legal liability to pay
16.2 This covers two types of case. The first is where P pays money to T and, although P is liable to pay the money to T, the principal liability to pay, as between P and D, was on D. In such a case P can recover from D the money paid, as is shown by *Brook's Wharf and Bull Wharf Ltd v Goodman Bros.*[1] The defendants imported skins from Russia and stored them in the plaintiff's bonded warehouse. The skins were stolen, without any negligence on the plaintiff's part, but they were required to pay the customs duty on them. By statute, the plaintiffs were liable to pay the duty, although the primary liability was on the defendants. It was held that the plaintiffs could recover the amount of duty paid because they had been compelled by law to pay money for which the defendants were primarily liable. Under the present principle, a guarantor who pays the debt of the principal debtor is entitled to be indemnified by him for that amount, and a co-guarantor who has paid more than his due share is entitled to a contribution from the other co-guarantor.

The second type of case is where P discharges D's legal liability to T under compulsion. Thus, if P, a tenant, pays the rent owed by D, his landlord, to T, a superior landlord, to prevent distress by T, D must pay P the amount paid by him.

1   [1937] 1 KB 534, [1936] 3 All ER 696.

Money paid at the request of the defendant
16.3   If P pays money to T at the express or implied request of D, P can recover that sum from D.[1]

1   *Brewer Street Investments Ltd v Barclays Woollen Co Ltd* [1954] 1 QB 428, [1953] 2 All ER 1330, CA.

Money had and received by the defendant to the use of the plaintiff

Money paid under a mistake of fact
16.4   Money paid under a mistaken belief in the truth of a fact which, if true, would have entitled the payee to payment is recoverable by the payer, subject to the exceptions set out later. In *Kelly v Solari*,[1] for example, the plaintiff was the director of a life insurance company which had paid out insurance money to the defendant under her husband's life insurance policy. The policy had, in fact, lapsed because the last premium had not been paid. The company had noted this, but the lapse had been overlooked when the defendant claimed the money. It was held that the plaintiff could recover the money because it had been paid under a mistaken belief in facts which, if true, would have entitled the defendant to payment.

A vexed question is whether, as in *Kelly v Solari*, the mistake must have led the plaintiff to believe a fact which, if true, would have meant that he was *legally* obliged to pay. Although this requirement has been reiterated in a number of cases,[2] the Court of Appeal in *Larner v LCC*[3] held that money paid under a mistake of fact which, if true, would have morally (but not legally) obliged its payment was recoverable. The LCC passed a resolution to make up the pay of their employees who were on war service to the amount of their civil salaries. L was one of their employees and he joined the RAF. Although he had agreed to inform the LCC of any increase in his service wages, he failed to do so and, consequently, was overpaid by the LCC. If the facts had been as supposed, the LCC would only have been morally, not legally,[4] obliged to make the payments, but the mistake was held to be sufficient to entitle the LCC to recover the amount of the overpayment. It may be that the decision in this case can be justified on its special facts and goes no further than holding that a mistake as to moral liability to honour a promise to pay made for reasons of *national policy* (a matter emphasised by the Court of Appeal) is to be equated with mistakes as to legal liability to pay. On this view, the Court of Appeal did not lay down a wider rule that, whenever a person pays money to another under a mistake of fact which causes him to make the payment, he is entitled to recover it as money paid under a mistake of fact. However, in *Barclays Bank Ltd v W J Simms, Son and Cooke (Southern) Ltd*,[5] Goff J stated the law in these broad terms, relying on an impressive list of authorities; but an examination of them suggests that he misinterpreted them, so that his statement of the law must be viewed with suspicion and cannot be regarded with confidence as representing the current state of the law in the light of the authority to the contrary.

Subject to what we have just said, a payment can be recovered from the payee even though the mistake was not shared by the payer and payee,[6] and even though the mistake was induced by a third person.[7]

1 (1841) 9 M & W 54.
2 Eg *Aitken v Short* (1856) 1 H & N 210 at 215; *Maskell v Horner* [1915] 3 KB 106.
3 [1949] 2 KB 683, [1949] 1 All ER 964, CA.
4 Para 6.3 above.
5 [1980] QB 677, [1979] 3 All ER 522.
6 *Barclays Bank Ltd v W J Simms, Son and Cooke (Southern) Ltd* [1980] QB 677, [1979] 3 All ER 522.
7 *R E Jones Ltd v Waring and Gillow Ltd* [1926] AC 670, HL.

16.5 The mistake must be one of fact: money paid under a mistake of law is not recoverable, generally. A mistake as to the construction of a statute,[1] or of regulations,[2] or of a contract,[3] is one of law, but a mistake as to the existence of a private right, such as a person's title to property, is, oddly enough, regarded as a mistake of fact.[4] An exception to the general rule is that if money is paid to an officer of the court, such as a trustee in bankruptcy or a solicitor, under a mistake of law it is recoverable.[5]

The recovery of money paid under a mistake of fact is subject to the following limits:

a. Where the money was paid in connection with a contract between the payer and the payee, there can be no recovery on the ground that it was paid under a mistake of fact, unless the contract itself is void for mistake or is rescinded by the payer.[6]

b. Where the payer intends that the payee should have the money at all events, whether the fact be true or false,[7] or is deemed in law so to intend (which is the case where a bookmaker pays or overpays a betting debt by mistake), he cannot recover it.[8]

c. Where the payer, by words or conduct, makes an unambiguous representation to the payee which leads him to believe he is entitled to treat the money as his own, and the payee in good faith and without notice of the payer's claim does so treat it to his detriment, the payer is estopped (ie prevented) from recovering the money.[9] The payee will act to his detriment merely by spending the money (in whole or *in part*),[10] whether or not this alters the position to his disadvantage.[11] However, estoppel is not available as a defence where the payee was primarily at fault in causing the payment—as, for instance, if the mistake was due to a misrepresentation (even an innocent one) or a breach of duty by the payee.[12] It was for this reason that the payee in *Larner v LCC*,[13] who had spent the money received, could not avail himself of the defence of estoppel; the LCC (the payers) were not at fault, but the payee was because he had not kept them accurately informed of increases in his service pay.

1 *National Pari-Mutuel Association Ltd v R* (1930) 47 TLR 110.
2 *Holt v Markham* [1923] 1 KB 504, CA.
3 *Ord v Ord* [1923] 2 KB 432.
4 *Cooper v Phibbs* (1867) LR 2 HL 149, HL.
5 *Re Condon, ex p James* (1874) 9 Ch App 609, CA.
6 *Norwich Union Fire Insurance Society Ltd v William H Price Ltd* [1934] AC 455, PC; *Barclays Bank Ltd v W J Simms, Son and Cooke (Southern) Ltd* [1979] 3 All ER 522 at 535. For contracts void for mistake, see ch 12, and for rescission, see ch. 13.
7 *Kelly v Solari* (1841) 9 M & W 54 at 58.
8 *Morgan v Ashcroft* [1938] 1 KB 49, [1937] 3 All ER 92, CA, as explained in *Barclays Bank Ltd v W J Simms, Son and Cooke (Southern) Ltd* [1980] QB 677, [1979] 3 All ER 522.

9   *Holt v Markham* [1923] 1 KB 504, CA; *R E Jones Ltd v Waring and Gillow Ltd* [1926] AC 670, HL.
10 *Avon County Council v Howlett* [1983] 1 All ER 1073, [1983] 1 WLR 605, CA.
11 *Skyring v Greenwood* (1825) 4 B & C 281 at 289.
12 *Larner v LCC* [1949] 2 KB 683, [1949] 1 All ER 964, CA.
13 [1949] 2 KB 683 [1949] 1 All ER 964, CA.

Money paid under improper pressure

16.6 Money paid under improper pressure on the part of the payee is recoverable if, quite apart from the pressure, the payer was not legally obliged to pay it.[1]

1   *Maskell v Horner* [1915] 3 KB 106, CA.

Money paid in pursuance of an ineffective contract

16.7 a. *Money paid in pursuance of a void or illegal contract* Money paid in pursuance of a void contract is generally recoverable,[1] except in the case of a gaming contract and in certain other cases.[2]

Money paid under an illegal contract is generally not recoverable but we would remind the reader of the exceptional cases where it is, which we enumerated in para 14.53 above.

b. *Total failure of consideration* Here we are concerned with the case where the plaintiff has deposited or paid money in pursuance of a contract which is perfectly valid but is rendered ineffective by a total failure of consideration on the part of the defendant (ie a total failure to perform his part of the contract). In such a case the plaintiff has an option,[3] either

i   to terminate the contract for breach, in which case he can recover the money which he has paid under quasi-contract,[4] or

ii whether or not he terminates, to seek damages for its breach.

Thus, if P pays D £500 as a deposit on a car but D fails to supply the car, P can terminate the contract and recover the £500 which he paid.

If the failure of consideration is not total but only partial, the quasi-contractual action for the recovery of money paid is not available, so that, whether the contract is terminated or not, the appropriate remedy is an action for damages for breach of contract. There will only be a total failure of consideration if the plaintiff has not got any part of what he bargained for. Thus, if P employs D to build a house for him and pays in advance, and D abandons the work before it is finished, P cannot recover any part of his payment and must claim damages for breach of contract.[5] However, if—

i   the partial performance is such as to entitle the plaintiff to terminate the contract, and he elects to do so, and

ii he is able to restore what he has received under the contract, and does so before he has derived any benefit from it,[6]

he will bring about a total failure of consideration and be entitled to recover any money which he has paid.[7] A common example of this is where the buyer of defective goods rejects them immediately and claims back his payment.

For the sake of completeness, we must add that, in a contract for the sale of goods or of hire purchase, there will be a total failure of consideration if the seller or bailor fails to pass a good title to the goods to the buyer or bailee, even though the buyer or bailee has derived benefit from them before being deprived of them by the true owner. It follows that the buyer or bailee can recover what he has paid for the goods. In *Rowland v Divall*,[8] the plaintiff bought a car from the defendant for £334 and used it for four months. It then transpired that the car had been stolen, although the defendant had dealt with it in good faith, and the plaintiff had to surrender it to the true owner. The Court of Appeal held that the defendant was in breach of the implied condition in the Sale of Goods Act 1979, s12(1), viz that the seller has the right to sell the goods, and the plaintiff was entitled to recover the £334 which he had paid. Its reasoning was that the plaintiff had not received what he had contracted to receive, viz the property (ie ownership) and right to possession of the car, and therefore there was a total failure of consideration entitling him to recover the whole purchase price without any set-off for his use of the car. The decision that there had been a total failure of consideration seems somewhat strained when the buyer had had four months' use of the car before he had to return it to the true owner.

So far we have assumed that the total failure of consideration constitutes a breach of contract. If it does not, e.g. because there is a lawful excuse for the failure, money paid may nevertheless be recovered under the present principle, but the reader is reminded that where the total failure of consideration is due to the frustration of the contract the situation will normally be governed by the Law Reform (Frustrated Contracts) Act 1943.[9]

c. *Money paid by party in breach of contract* If a party who has made an advance payment under the contract then refuses, in breach of contract, to perform it, e g to take delivery of goods which he has agreed to buy, he can recover his payment if it was intended to be a part-payment of the purchase price, unless the contract otherwise provides.[10] On the other hand, if his advance payment was intended as a deposit (ie a guarantee that he would perform his side of the contract) it is not recoverable,[11] unless the contract otherwise provides.[12]

1 See, for instance, paras 14.22 and 16.5 above.
2 *Bridger v Savage* (1885) 15 QBD 363 at 367 (gaming contract). Also see para 15.14d above.
3 Paras 9.3–9.8 above.
4 *Wilkinson v Lloyd* (1845) 7 QB 27.
5 *Whincup v Hughes* (1871) LR 6 CP 78.
6 *Hunt v Silk* (1804) 5 East 449.
7 *Baldry v Marshall* [1925] 1 KB 260.
8 [1923] 2 KB 500, CA. See also *Warman v Southern Counties Car Finance Corpn Ltd* [1949] 2 KB 576, [1949] 1 All ER 711 (a hire-purchase case).
9 Paras 10.15–10.18 above.
10 *Mayson v Clouet* [1924] AC 980.
11 *Harrison v Holland* [1921] 3 KB 297; affd [1922] 1 KB 211, CA.
12 *Palmer v Temple* (1839) 9 Ad & El 508.

Quantum meruit

16.8 A quantum meruit is a claim for reasonable remuneration for services performed or things supplied. Sometimes, the remedy is contractual in that it enables a remuneration to be recovered under a contract which has not fixed a precise sum. We have mentioned examples of this in the relevant parts of this book[1] and confine ourselves here to quasi-contractual quantum meruit claims. These can be made in the following cases:

a. Where the other party to a contract unjustifiably prevents the plaintiff (who has partly performed his contractual obligations) completing them, as where he states that he will not accept performance or renders performance impossible, and the plaintiff has elected to terminate the contract. Here, the remedy of a quantum meruit is an alternative to an action for damages, and may be less generous.[2]

b. Where the plaintiff has performed services in pursuance of a contract which is void. For example, in *Craven-Ellis v Canons Ltd*,[3] the plaintiff was employed as the managing director of a company under a contract which was void because the directors who made it were not qualified to act. It was held by the Court of Appeal that the plaintiff could recover reasonable remuneration on a quantum meruit for services rendered under the contract.

c. Where, in anticipation of concluding a contract with the defendant, the plaintiff has commenced *at the defendant's request* to perform the work which would be required under the contract, but no contract is entered into, the defendant is liable to pay a reasonable sum for the work done pursuant to his request.[4] This is of obvious importance in the type of case where the defendant has given the plaintiff a 'letter of intent' to contract and asked him to start work immediately but never finally concluded a contract.

d. Where necessary goods are supplied to minors, or to mentally disordered or drunken persons, they are liable to pay a reasonable price for them, and the basis of this liability is quasi-contractual.[5]

1 Paras 5.30 above, and 17.19 below, for example.
2 Para 11.24 above.
3 [1936] 2 KB 403, [1936] 3 All ER 1066, CA.
4 *British Steel Corpn v Cleveland Bridge and Engineering Co Ltd* [1984] 1 All ER 504.
5 Paras 15.5b and 15.20 above.

Money had and received by the defendant from a third party to the use of the plaintiff

16.9 The following two situations are among those comprehended by this heading:

a. Where a deposit or other sum of money is paid to a stakeholder pending the determination of the entitlement of two persons to it, the person who becomes entitled to it can recover it.[1]

b. Where D receives money from T, or is otherwise under a monetary obligation (e g a debt) to T, and he is instructed by T to pay the money to P, and he promises P that he will pay him, P may recover the money from D.[2]

1 *Sadler v Smith* (1869) LR 5 QB 40.
2 *Shamia v Joory* [1958] 1 QB 448, [1958] 1 All ER 111.

Chapter 17
Agency

17.1 Agency is the relationship between two legal persons, whereby one person, the principal, appoints another, the agent, to act on his behalf. The relationship is usually, though not necessarily, contractual. The major importance of agency lies in the fact that an authorised agent[1] may affect the legal position of his principal vis-à-vis third parties. In most cases, the agent does this by making a contract on his principal's behalf, or by disposing of property which the principal owns. However, he may also bind his principal in other ways, for example, by signing a document,[2] receiving notice[3] or committing a tort.[4] With certain exceptions, mostly statutory, a principal may do anything through the medium of an agent which he could lawfully do in person.

1 Including one who, though not actually appointed, is given the appearance of authority by his principal: paras 17.32–17.36 below.
2 *LCC v Agricultural Food Products Ltd* [1955] 2 QB 218, [1955] 2 All ER 229, CA.
3 *Proudfoot v Montefiore* (1867) LR 2 QB 511.
4 Paras 30.16–30.18 below.

Three issues
17.2 The three issues with which we are concerned in this chapter are:

a. the relationship of principal and agent (ie the creation of agency, the duties and rights of agents and the termination of agency);

b. the changes in the legal relationship of the principal and third parties which may be effected by an agent; and

c. the legal relationship, if any, between the agent and third parties.

Principal and agent

Creation of agency
17.3 Agency may be created by agreement, express or implied, by ratification or by virtue of necessity. In determining whether a principal (P) has appointed another person to act as his agent (A), it is necessary to decide whether P had the capacity to appoint an agent and whether A had the capacity to act as an agent, before considering how an agent is appointed.

Capacity
17.4 An agent can be appointed to effect any transaction for which the

principal has capacity.[1] A minor can appoint an agent to buy necessaries or make a beneficial contract of service[2] but cannot enter into trading contracts merely by the interpositioning of an adult agent.[3] Companies can only make intra vires contracts (contracts within the powers bestowed on them in the memorandum of association[4]) and cannot extend their contractual capacity by the use of an agent with contractual capacity greater than their own.[5] A mentally disordered person can appoint an agent to purchase or obtain necessaries.[6]

Anyone not suffering from a mental disorder can act as an agent. A minor can act as agent in a transaction which he would not have capacity to effect on his own behalf. For example, a father could appoint his infant son to purchase non-necessary goods on his behalf even though the infant son could not make a binding contract for non-necessary goods on his own behalf. However, an agent who lacks full contractual capacity can only be made personally liable on those contracts which he would have had capacity to make on his own behalf.[7] Further, the agent may well not be liable on the contract of agency itself. Companies, no less than natural legal persons, can be appointed as agents.

1 For the law relating to capacity to contract, see ch 15.
2 *Doyle v White City Stadium Ltd* [1935] 1 KB 110, CA.
3 *G(A) v G(T)* [1970] 2 QB 643, [1970] 3 All ER 546, CA.
4 Para 15.24 above.
5 But see the effect of the Companies Act 1985, s35 on the position of a third party who enters into a contract with a company which the company lacks capacity to make; para 15.26 above.
6 For the contractual capacity of a mentally disordered person see paras 15.19 and 15.20 above.
7 *Smally v Smally* (1700) 1 Eq Cas Abr 6; for when an agent is personally liable on contracts see paras 17.41–17.46 below.

Appointment by express agreement

17.5 An agent may be appointed by express agreement between principal and agent. This agreement is frequently, but not necessarily, a contract. If the appointment is by contract, the usual rules for the formation of contracts must be complied with. Normally, the appointment can be made informally, even if the agent is to transact contracts which must be evidenced in writing. All that is necessary is a desire to appoint A as agent and A's consent to act as such. However, in some cases certain formalities are necessary to create agency. For instance, if an agent has to execute a deed, his appointment must be by deed, and is known as a power of attorney.[1]

The agreement which appoints an agent will usually specify the authority which the principal bestows upon him, though this may be extended by implication.[2] The authority of an agent to bind the principal to a contract with a third party may also be extended by ostensible authority.[3]

1 *Steiglitz v Egginton* (1815) Holt NP 141, and see also the Powers of Attorney Act 1971, ss 1 and 7.
2 Para 17.31 below.
3 Paras 17.32–17.36 below.

Appointment by implied agreement

17.6 If the parties have not expressly agreed to become principal and agent, it may be possible to find an implied agreement based on their conduct or relationship. If the parties have so conducted themselves towards one another that it would be reasonable for them to assume that they have consented to act as principal and agent, then they are principal and agent.[1] For example, the agent of a finance company or of an insurance company may also be held to be the agent of the party seeking finance or insurance if the circumstances warrant an implication of agreement to such an agency relationship.[2] Factors which have been found relevant in determining whether agency has been created by implied agreement are whether one party acts for the other at the other's request and whether commission is payable.

An implied agreement to agency by virtue of the relationship of the parties arises in the case of husband and wife. A wife has authority to pledge her husband's credit for household necessaries even if he has not expressly appointed her his agent.[3]

Since there is no express appointment in the present type of case, the authority which the principal bestows upon the agent is implied authority;[4] but, as with agents expressly appointed, agents impliedly appointed may have the power to bind the principal to contracts with third parties by virtue of ostensible authority.[5]

1   *Ashford Shire Council v Dependable Motors Pty Ltd* [1961] AC 336, [1961] 1 All ER 96, PC.
2   *Newsholme Bros v Road Transport and General Insurance Co Ltd* [1929] 2 KB 356, CA.
3   *Debenham v Mellon* (1880) 6 App Cas 24, HL.
4   Para 17.31 below.
5   Paras 17.32 to 17.36 below.

Ratification

17.7   In certain circumstances, the relationship of principal and agent can be created or extended retrospectively under the doctrine of ratification. What this means is that, if A purports to act as agent for B in a particular transaction (although he is not authorised to do so), B may subsequently 'ratify' or adopt what A has done. In such a case, A is deemed to have been acting as an authorised agent when he effected the transaction.[1] However, ratification only validates past acts of the 'agent' and gives no authority for the future,[2] although frequent acts of ratification by an alleged principal may create agency by implied agreement or confer ostensible authority on the agent.[3]

1   *Bolton Partners v Lambert* (1889) 41 Ch D 295, CA.
2   *Irvine v Union Bank of Australia* (1877) 2 App Cas 366, PC.
3   *Midland Bank Ltd v Reckitt* [1933] AC 1, HL.

17.8   *Effects of ratification*   If a person ratifies a transaction entered into on his behalf he must be taken to have ratified the whole transaction, and not merely those parts which are to his advantage.[1] The effect of ratification is to make the transaction (which is usually a contract) binding on the principal from the moment it was made by the agent.[2] Since the acts of the agent are retrospectively validated, the agent cannot be liable to a third party for breach of warranty of authority, nor to his principal for acting outside the scope of his authority,[3] and can claim commission and an indemnity.[4] Once a contract is ratified, the agent generally ceases to be liable on the contract, but ratification cannot vary rights in property which had vested before ratification.[5] Perhaps the most controversial effect of ratification is that it allows the alleged principal to decide whether to accept a contract or reject it. The third party may wish to repudiate an agreement with the agent because of the agent's lack of authority, but find himself bound by the contract if the alleged principal subsequently ratifies.[6] However, if a contract is made 'subject to ratification' the third party can withdraw prior to ratification and, if he does so, ratification cannot bind him.[7] Because the effects of ratification are at least potentially unfair to third parties, ratification is only possible in some circumstances.

1 *Cornwal v Wilson* (1750) 1 Ves Sen 509.
2 *Bolton Partners v Lambert* (1889) 41 Ch D 295, CA.
3 *Smith v Cologan* (1788) 2 TR 188n. For breach of warranty of authority see para 17.47 below.
4 *Hartas v Ribbons* (1889) 22 QBD 254, CA. For indemnities see para 17.21 below.
5 *Bird v Brown* (1850) 4 Exch 786.
6 *Bolton Partners v Lambert* (1889) 41 Ch D 295, CA.
7 *Warehousing and Forwarding Co of East Africa Ltd v Jafferali & Sons Ltd* [1964] AC 1, [1963] 3 All ER 571, PC.

17.9 *Who can ratify* Only the alleged principal can ratify the actions of his alleged agent and then only if the latter purported to act on his behalf.[1] Therefore, if an agent has not revealed he was acting as an agent, ie he has an undisclosed principal, the undisclosed principal cannot ratify. A leading illustration of this is the case of *Keighley, Maxsted & Co v Durant*.[2] In this case an agent purchased wheat at a price which was higher than he had been authorised to pay. The agent had not revealed that he was acting as an agent when he bought the grain. Because of this the House of Lords found the defendant principal was not liable for breach of contract when he refused to accept delivery of the grain, even though he had purported to ratify the contract of sale. Provided that an agent reveals that he is acting as agent, his principal, even though unnamed, can ratify his unauthorised actions.[3] However, an unnamed principal should be identifiable,[3] unless, perhaps, the third party has shown that he is uninterested in the identity of the principal. Further, there is a strange rule by which unnamed, and possibly unidentifiable, principals can ratify contracts of marine insurance.[4]

A company which is a disclosed principal can only ratify if it is in existence at the time the agent enters into any contract.[5] Even if a company takes the benefit of a pre-incorporation contract it is not liable on it, although it will be liable if it makes a new contract post-incorporation on the same subject matter.[6] Any new contract will not be implied merely because the company takes the benefit of the pre-incorporation contract[7] and any new contract is of course only prospective in effect. An agent who makes a pre-incorporation contract on behalf of a non-existent company is personally liable on it unless personal liability has been excluded 'by contract or otherwise.'[8]

To be able to ratify, the disclosed principal must have had the capacity to make the contract himself at the date when his 'agent' contracted.[9]

1 *Wilson v Tumman* (1843) 6 Man & G 236.
2 [1901] AC 240, HL.
3 *Watson v Swann* [1862] 11 CBNS 756; *Southern Water Authority v Carey* [1985] 2 All ER 1077.
4 *Boston Fruit Co v British and Foreign Marine Insurance Co* [1906] AC 336, HL.
5 *Kelner v Baxter* (1866) LR 2 CP 174.
6 *Howard v Patent Ivory Manufacturing Co* (1888) 38 Ch D 156.
7 *Touche v Metropolitan Railway Warehousing Co* (1871) LR 6 Ch App 671.
8 Companies Act 1985, s36(4).

9   *Boston Deep Sea Fishing and Ice Co Ltd v Farnham (Inspector of Taxes)* [1957] 3 All ER
    204, [1957] 1 WLR 1051.

17.10 *What can be ratified* Apparently any action can be ratified (even
where the purported agent was seeking to benefit himself[1]) except illegal[2] or
void acts. An illustration of a void and thus unratifiable action is an
unauthorised act on behalf of, but ultra vires, a company.[3]
   Considerable difficulty has arisen over forged signatures. Such a forgery
could simply be regarded as a void act and in early cases was so regarded.
However, subsequent interpretation of the leading case, *Brook v Hook*,[4] has
suggested that, while forgeries are generally regarded as unratifiable, it is
for a different reason. Current opinion is that a forged signature by an
agent is unratifiable because in forging a signature the 'agent' was not
purporting to be an agent but to be the person whose signature he forged.

1   *Re Tiedemann and Ledermann Fréres* [1899] 2 QB 66.
2   *Bedford Insurance Co Ltd v Instituto de Resseguros do Brasil* [1985] QB 966, [1984] 3 All ER
    766.
3   *Ashbury Railway Carriage and Iron Co v Riche* (1875) LR 7 HL 653; for a discussion of
    ultra vires see paras 15.23–15.26 above.
4   (1871) LR 6 Exch 89.

17.11 *How to ratify* Ratification may be made by express affirmation of
the unauthorised actions of the agent by the principal.[1] It need not, as a
rule, take any special form, except that, where the agent has without
authority executed a deed, ratification too must be by deed.[2] Ratification
must take place within a reasonable time.[3] What is reasonable is a question
of fact in every case, but if the time for performance of a contract has
passed ratification is impossible.[4]
   Ratification may also be effected by conduct,[5] although mere passive
acceptance of the benefit of a contract may be insufficient,[6] but if the
conduct of the alleged principal amounts to ratification he cannot repudiate
the actions of his agent,[7] Examples of ratification are provided by the
following cases. In *Lyell v Kennedy*,[8] A received rent from property for
many years, although not authorised to do so. When the owner sued him
for an account of the rents, it was held that the owner's action constituted
ratification of A's receipt of the rents. Similarly, in *Cornwal v Wilson*,[9] A
bought some goods in excess of the price authorised by P. P objected to the
purchase but sold some of the goods; it was held that he had ratified the
unauthorised act by selling the goods. An action by the alleged principal
will only be implied ratification if he had a choice of whether or not to act.
If the alleged principal had no real choice, other than to accept the benefit
of the unauthorised actions of his agent, accepting such benefit is not
ratification. For example, if an agent has had unauthorised repairs done on
a ship, merely retaking the ship with these repairs is not ratification by the
alleged principal. This is because if he wished to recover his property he had
to have it with the unauthorised repairs.[10]
   Ratification will, generally, only be implied if the alleged principal has
acted with full knowledge of the facts.[11] But, if the alleged principal is
prepared to take the risk of what his agent has done, he can choose to ratify
without full knowledge. For instance, in *Fitzmaurice v Bayley*,[12] an agent
entered into an unauthorised contract for the purchase of property. The
alleged principal wrote a letter saying he did not know what his agent had
done but would stand by all that he had done. This was an express

ratification by him; he had agreed to bear the risk of being bound by the unauthorised acts of his agent, whatever they were.

1   *Soames v Spencer* (1822) 1 Dow & Ry KB 32.
2   *Hunter v Parker* (1840) 7 M & W 322.
3   *Re Portuguese Consolidated Copper Mines Ltd* (1890) 45 Ch D 16, CA.
4   *Metropolitan Asylums Board of Managers v Kingham & Sons* (1890) 6 TLR 217.
5   *Lyell v Kennedy* (1889) 14 App Cas 437, HL.
6   *Hughes v Hughes* (1971) 221 Estates Gazette 145, CA.
7   *Cornwal v Wilson* (1750) 1 Ves Sen 509.
8   (1889) 14 App Cas 437, HL.
9   (1750) 1 Ves Sen 509.
10   *Foreman & Co Pty Ltd v The Liddesdale* [1900] AC 190, PC.
11   *The Bonita, The Charlotte* (1861) 1 Lush 252.
12   (1856) 6 E & B 868.

Agency of necessity
17.12   Agency of necessity is a limited exception to the concept that agency is based on a consensual relationship between the parties. When certain emergencies occur, immediate action may be necessary and the courts may be prepared to find that the person taking such action was thereby acting as an agent of necessity. A common example of agency of necessity is that masters of ships faced with an emergency are agents of the shipowner, and have authority to enter into contracts with third parties on behalf of him.[1] Frequently, agency of necessity will merely extend the authority of existing agents but in other cases it may create agency where none existed previously—for example, between masters of ships and cargo owners. In other cases, if a person claims to be an agent of necessity, such agency will only affect the relationship of the alleged principal and agent, and will confer no power on the 'agent' to deal with third parties on behalf of the 'principal'. This type of agency of necessity is more likely than the former if the parties were not already principal and agent; for example, someone who salvages a ship cannot make contracts on behalf of the shipowner.
    Agency of necessity will only arise if the 'agent' has no practical way of communicating with the 'principal',[2] if the action of the 'agent' is reasonably necessary to benefit the 'principal'[3] and if the 'agent' has acted bona fide.

1   *The Gratitudine* (1801) 3 Ch Rob 240.
2   *Springer v Great Western Rly Co* [1921] 1 KB 257, CA.
3   *Prager v Blatspiel, Stamp and Heacock Ltd* [1924] 1 KB 566.

A postscript
17.13   In some cases a person will be held to have authority to affect the legal relationship of an apparent principal and third parties, even if the person whose actions thereby bind the apparent principal is not technically an agent. This is not a method of creating agency between principal and agent but it may result in an alleged principal being unable to deny that his apparent agent was authorised to act on his behalf.[1] The doctrine is sometimes called agency by estoppel.

1   Paras 17.32–17.36 below

Duties of an agent

Duty to act
17.14   A paid agent is under a duty to act and any loss suffered by the

principal because of failure to act is recoverable by the principal.[1] If the agent does not intend to act he should inform his principal of this fact, but the agent cannot be made liable for failure to perform acts which are illegal or void.[2] A gratuitous agent does not appear to be under any positive duty to act, although if he chooses to act and does so negligently he is liable.[3]

1 *Turpin v Bilton* (1843) 5 Man & G 455.
2 *Cohen v Kittell* (1889) 22 QBD 680, DC.
3 *Wilkinson v Coverdale* (1793) 1 Esp 74.

Duty to obey instructions

17.15 The primary obligation imposed on an agent is to act strictly in accordance with the instructions of his principal insofar as they are lawful and reasonable. An agent has no discretion to disobey his instructions, even in what he honestly and reasonably regards to be his principal's best interests.[1] If an agent carries out his instructions he cannot be liable for loss suffered by the principal because the instructions were at fault.[2] If the instructions which an agent receives are not complied with he will be responsible to his principal for any loss thereby suffered, even if the loss is not occasioned by any fault on his part.[3] However, if the instructions received by an agent are ambiguous, he is not in breach of his duty if he makes a reasonable but incorrect interpretation of them.[4] If instructions confer a discretion on the agent, he will not be liable for failure to obey instructions if he exercises the discretion reasonably.[5]

The instructions which an agent should obey may be clarified or extended by virtue of custom or trade usage applying in the trade or profession which the agent follows.

1 *Bertram, Armstrong & Co v Godfray* (1830) 1 Knapp 381.
2 *Overend Gurney and Co v Gibb* (1872) LR 5 HL 480.
3 *Lilley v Doubleday* (1881) 7 QBD 510.
4 *Weigall & Co v Runciman & Co* (1916) 85 LJKB 1187, CA.
5 *Boden v French* (1851) 10 CB 886.

Duty to exercise care and skill

17.16 An agent, whether paid or gratuitous, is required to display reasonable care in carrying out his instructions and also, where appropriate, such skill as may reasonably be expected from a member of his profession.[1] If he fails to do so, the agent will be liable for any loss which his principal suffers thereby.

1 Supply of Goods and Services Act 1982, s13. For examples, see para 20.8 below.

Fiduciary duties

17.17 Every agent owes fiduciary duties, ie duties of good faith, to his principal. These duties are based on the confidential nature of the agency relationship. However, it is important to appreciate that an agent may be in breach of these duties, and liable for the consequences, even where he acts innocently.[1] There are two main fiduciary duties—a duty to disclose any conflict of interest and a duty not to take secret profits or bribes.

a. *Conflict of interest* Wherever an agent's own interests come into conflict with those of his principal, he must make a full disclosure to the principal of all relevant facts, so that the latter may decide whether to continue with the transaction. It is this rule which prevents an agent, in the absence of disclosure, from selling his own property to the principal,[2] purchasing the principal's property for himself[3] or acting as agent for both parties to a transaction.[4] Similarly, an estate agent instructed to sell property must not favour one potential purchaser at the expense of others, in the hope of reward from that purchaser.[5] If the agent is in breach of this duty, the principal may have any resulting transaction set aside, claim any profit accruing to the agent and refuse to pay commission.[6]

b. *Secret profits and bribes* If an agent, in the course of his agency and without his principal's knowledge and consent, makes a profit for himself out of his position, or out of property or information with which he is entrusted, he must account for this property to the principal.[7] Thus, an agent may not accept commission from both parties to a transaction,[8] nor keep for himself the benefit of a trade discount while charging his principal the full price,[9] without the principal's informed consent. It makes no difference that the agent has acted honestly throughout, nor even that his actions have conferred substantial benefit upon the principal.[10] Where the secret profit takes the form of a payment from a third party who is aware that he is dealing with an agent, it is called a 'bribe', even if the payment is not made with any evil motive and even if the principal suffers no loss thereby.[11] The taking of a bribe entitles the principal to dismiss the agent,[12] recover either the amount of the bribe or his actual loss (if greater) from the agent or third party,[13] repudiate any transaction in respect of which the bribe was given[14] and refuse to pay commission.[15]

1   *Keppel v Wheeler* [1927] 1 KB 577, CA.
2   *Gillett v Peppercorne* (1840) 3 Beav 78.
3   *McPherson v Watt* (1877) 3 App Cas 254, HL.
4   *Harrods Ltd v Lemon* [1931] 2 KB 157, CA.
5   *Henry Smith & Son v Muskett* (1977) 246 Estates Gazette 655.
6   Para 17.20 below.
7   *Regal (Hastings) Ltd v Gulliver* [1967] 2 AC 134n, [1942] 1 All ER 378, HL.
8   *Andrews v Ramsay & Co* [1903] 2 KB 635, CA.
9   *Hippisley v Knee Bros* [1905] 1 KB 1.
10 *Boardman v Phipps* [1967] 2 AC 46, [1966] 3 All ER 721, HL.
11 *Industries and General Mortgage Co Ltd v Lewis* [1949] 2 All ER 573.
12 *Boston Deep Sea Fishing and Ice Co v Ansell* (1888) 39 Ch D 339, CA.
13 *Mahesan S/O Thambiah v Malaysia Government Officers' Co-Operative Housing Society Ltd* [1979] AC 374, [1978] 2 All ER 405, PC.
14 *Shipway v Broadwood* [1899] 1 QB 369.
15 Para 17.20 below.

Other duties
17.18   An agent also has a duty not to delegate his responsibilities to a sub-agent without the authority of the principal.[1] An agent must also pay over to the principal any money received for the use of the principal in the course of the agency, even if it is claimed by third parties,[2] and an agent must keep proper accounts.

1   *De Bussche v Alt* (1878) 8 Ch D 286, CA.
2   *Blaustein v Maltz, Mitchell & Co* [1937] 2 KB 142, [1937] 1 All ER 497, CA.

Rights of agents

Remuneration
17.19   Where there is a contract of agency, an agent may be entitled

thereunder to be paid for his services. The right to be paid may be an express term of the contract of agency or, in the absence of such a term, may be implied if it was clearly the intention of the parties that the agent was to be paid.[1] The agent will only be entitled to remuneration where he has performed, precisely and completely, the obligations in the agency agreement—it is an entire contract.[2] If an agent does less than he is contractually required to do he can recover nothing, unless the contract provides for payment for partial services.

If the contract of agency expressly provides the amount of remuneration for a given task, this is the amount payable. If the contract merely provides that the agent is to be paid without specifying an amount, he is entitled to recover a reasonable amount.[3] If the contract mentions remuneration, but on its true construction does not entitle the agent to payment, he can recover nothing. For instance, in *Kofi Sunkersette Obu v Strauss & Co Ltd*,[4] the Privy Council refused to allow an agent to recover any commission in a case where the contract of agency provided that the amount of commission, *if any*, was to be fixed by the principal. If there is an implied term providing for payment, the amount of such payment must be determined by the courts. Usually it will be on the basis of what is reasonable, but it may be possible to imply the fixed scale costs of professional men.[5]

In the absence of a contract of agency, an agent may be entitled to be paid on a quantum meruit basis.[6] However, where an agent is to be paid on the occurrence of a certain event, such as a commission on sale, there can be no claim for a quantum meruit if the event does not occur.[7]

1   *Reeve v Reeve* (1858) 1 F & F 280. See also the Supply of Goods and Services Act 1982, s15.
2   Para 9.12 above.
3   *Way v Latilla* [1937] 3 All ER 759, HL.
4   [1951] AC 243, PC.
5   For when the courts will imply terms into contracts see paras 7.21 to 7.25 above.
6   For quantum meruit generally see para 16.8 above.
7   *Howard Houlder & Partners Ltd v Manx Isles SS Co Ltd* [1923] 1 KB 110.

17.20   The mere occurrence of the transaction which the agent is commissioned to effect does not entitle the agent to remuneration: the occurrence must be brought about by the agent unless the contract provides that he is to be paid however the desired result occurs.[1]

If the principal hinders the earning of commission by the agent, the agent cannot recover any commission thereby lost or sue the principal, unless the latter's action amounts to a breach of contract. The contract of agency may contain a term that the principal will not hinder the agent in his efforts to earn his commission,[2] but if it is not an express term the courts are reluctant to imply such a term into the contract of agency.[3]

Even if an agent complies with his instructions, he cannot recover any commission in respect of a transaction rendered void or illegal by statute.[4] An agent who is in breach of his duties towards his principal normally forfeits his right to commission,[5] unless the breach is a technical one and the agent has acted honestly.[6]

1   *Millar, Son & Co v Radford* (1903) 19 TLR 575, CA.
2   A 'sole agency' is a good example.
3   *Luxor (Eastbourne) Ltd v Cooper* [1941] AC 108, [1941] 1 All ER 33, HL. See also para 17.25 below.
4   Ch 14 above.

5   *Salomons v Pender* (1865) 3 H & C 639.
6   *Keppel v Wheeler* [1927] 1 KB 577, CA.

Indemnity

17.21   An agent who has suffered loss or incurred liabilities in the course of carrying out authorised actions for his principal is entitled to be reimbursed or indemnified by the principal.[1] However, he has no right to reimbursement or an indemnity for losses or liabilities arising because of breaches of duty (eg failing to comply with his instructions) or in carrying out an illegal transaction or a transaction rendered void by statute.[2] In *ex p Mather*,[3] a principal employed an agent to purchase smuggled goods. The agent was not entitled to recover the cost of these goods from the principal even though the principal had obtained possession of them.

1   *Hooper v Treffry* (1847) 1 Exch 17.
2   *Capp v Topham* (1805) 6 East 392; *Gasson v Cole* (1910) 26 TLR 468.
3   (1797) 3 Ves 373.

Sub-agents

17.22   Even where an agent is authorised to appoint a sub-agent to carry out his instructions, it is presumed that the person appointed is merely an agent of the agent; he does not, in the absence of clear evidence, become an agent of the principal.[1] As a result, the sub-agent has no claim against the principal for remuneration or indemnity, nor does he owe the principal any duty to act or to obey instructions. It has further been held, somewhat controversially, that the sub-agent owes the principal no duty of care in tort, unless he is also a bailee of the principal's goods.[2] As regards fiduciary duties the position is unclear, for there are conflicting decisions of the Court of Appeal.[3]

1   *Calico Printers' Association Ltd v Barclays Bank* (1931) 145 LT 51.
2   *Balsamo v Medici* [1984] 2 All ER 304, [1984] 1 WLR 951.
3   *Powell and Thomas v Evan Jones & Co* [1905] 1 KB 11, CA; cf *New Zealand and Australian Land Co v Watson* (1881) 7 QBD 374, CA.

Termination of agency

17.23   A contract of agency may be terminated, like any other contract, by agreement,[1] by performance,[2] by breach[3] or by frustration,[4] although it is important to remember that termination of agency between principal and agent need not terminate the agent's ostensible authority (which we discuss in paras 17.32 to 17.36 below). In addition, there are certain special rules applicable to agency, which we now discuss.

1   Paras 6.32–6.38 above.
2   Ch 8 above
3   Ch 9 above.
4   Ch 10 above.

Act of parties

17.24   A contract of agency will not be specifically enforced, because it is a contract for personal services.[1] As a corollary, either party may terminate the relationship at will. This may amount to a breach of contract, as where the agency was for a fixed period which has not expired, or where a required period of notice has not been given. If so, the innocent party is entitled to damages, but the agency itself is nonetheless determined.[2]

As to whether termination of an agency relationship without notice amounts to a breach of contract, we have already seen[3] that, if an agent accepts a bribe, his contract of agency can be terminated without notice. There are other contracts which on their true construction allow either principal or agent to terminate the agreement without any notice.[4] If an agent is employed on a commission basis, so that he is only entitled to remuneration when he does the act required by the agency agreement, for example, sells a house, then it would seem that such contracts can be terminated without notice.[5] Agency contracts which resemble contracts of employment, in that the agent is paid merely for being an agent, rather than for facilitating a particular transaction, require notice.[6]

There are some cases where the authority of an agent is irrevocable. Under the Powers of Attorney Act 1971, s4, a power of attorney expressed to be irrevocable, and given to secure a proprietary interest of the donee of the power, can be revoked neither by the donor of that power without the consent of the donee nor by the death, insanity or bankruptcy of the donor. This is essentially a restatement of the common law rule that, if the agent is given authority by deed, or for valuable consideration, to effect a security or to protect an interest of the agent, that authority is irrevocable while the security or interest subsists.[7] Again, an authority coupled with an interest is not revoked by the death, insanity or bankruptcy of the donor.

1   *Chinnock v Sainsbury* (1860) 30 LJ Ch 409; para 11.26d above.
2   *Page One Records Ltd v Britton* [1967] 3 All ER 822, [1968] 1 WLR 157.
3   Para 17.17b above.
4   *Atkinson v Cotesworth* (1825) 3 B & C 647.
5   *Motion v Michaud* (1892) 8 TLR 253, affd by the Court of Appeal (1892) 8 TLR 447, CA.
6   *Parker v Ibbetson* (1858) 4 CBNS 346.
7   *Gaussen v Morton* (1830) 10 B & C 731.

17.25   A problem may arise where a principal, without actually revoking his agent's authority, effectively brings the agency to an end, for example, by closing down the business to which it relates. In order to recover damages for loss of earnings, the agent must be able to prove that the principal's action amounts to a breach either of an express term of the contract of agency, or of one necessarily implied to give business efficacy.[1] The courts are slow to imply such terms. In *Rhodes v Forwood*,[2] a colliery owner appointed brokers as sole agents for the sale of his coal in Liverpool for seven years or as long as he did business there. After four years the colliery was sold. It was held that the owner had not contracted, either expressly or impliedly, to keep the brokers supplied with coal for sale, and he was therefore not liable for breach of contract. On the other hand, in *Turner v Goldsmith*,[3] a shirt manufacturer expressly agreed to employ a travelling salesman for five years, but his factory was destroyed by fire after only two years. It was held that the manufacturer was not released from his obligation, so that the agent was entitled to damages.

1   Paras 7.24, 7.25 above.
2   (1876) 1 App Cas 256, HL.
3   [1891] 1 QB 544, CA.

Death
17.26   The death of a principal or of an agent determines the agency.[1] An

agent's right to remuneration ceases with the death of his principal, as does his right of indemnity.[2] Most importantly, the actual authority of an agent (and, probably, his ostensible authority) ceases on the death of his principal and any transactions entered into thereafter bind the agent, but not the principal's estate, even if the agent does not know of the death.[3]

1   *Blades v Free* (1829) 9 B & C 167; *Friend v Young* [1897] 2 Ch 421.
2   *Farrow v Wilson* (1869) LR 4 CP 744; *Pool v Pool* (1889) 58 LJP 67.
3   *Blades v Free* (1829) 9 B & C 167.

Insanity

17.27   If a principal becomes insane the agency is terminated, and the agent can presumably claim no commission in relation to transactions entered into after his actual authority is determined by the insanity. Where the agent has ostensible authority, this survives his principal's insanity, and any contract entered into by him is binding upon the principal, unless the third party knew of the insanity.[1] Somewhat inconsistently, however, it has also been held that, provided that the third party did not know of the insanity, the agent can be liable for breach of warranty of authority even if he did not know of the insanity.[2]

1   *Drew v Nunn* (1879) 4 QBD 661, CA.
2   *Yonge v Toynbee* [1910] 1 KB 215, CA.

Bankruptcy

17.28   The bankruptcy of a principal terminates a contract of agency.[1] On the other hand, the bankruptcy of an agent does not automatically determine the agency, unless it effectively prevents the agent from doing what he was appointed to do.[2]

1   *Elliott v Turquand* (1881) 7 App Cas 79, HL.
2   *McCall v Australian Meat Co Ltd* (1870) 19 WR 188.

Effects of termination

17.29   While the termination of agency cannot deprive the agent of any rights to commission or indemnity which have already accrued,[1] it prevents him from acquiring such rights in the future.[2] Furthermore, an agent who continues to act may become liable to a third party for breach of warranty of authority, even if he is unaware that his actual authority has been determined.[3]

In the absence of ostensible authority, a principal is not usually bound by anything which his agent does after termination of the agency. However, where the agency is created by deed, both an agent and a third party are given statutory protection in respect of transactions effected after termination, provided that they were unaware of this.[4]

1   *Chappell v Bray* (1860) 6 H & N 145.
2   *Farrow v Wilson* (1869) LR 4 CP 744; *Pool v Pool* (1889) 58 LJP 67.
3   *Yonge v Toynbee* [1910] 1 KB 215, CA.
4   Powers of Attorney Act 1971, s5.

Principal and third parties

17.30   If an agent makes an *authorised* contract on behalf of his principal then the principal is deemed to have made the contract. Indeed, if a principal is a disclosed principal, he alone is deemed to have entered into the contract—except in certain limited circumstances. A principal may sue and be sued on authorised contracts made by his agent. If a principal is undisclosed then both principal and agent can sue or be sued on the authorised contract. If a contract or other transaction, such as a disposition of property, is not authorised then it does not bind the principal but the agent may incur personal liability in respect thereof. An agent's authority may take various forms.

The authority of agents

Actual authority

17.31 An agent who has been expressly appointed may have both express and implied actual authority. An agent appointed by implied agreement has implied actual authority.

Express authority is the authority conferred by the agreement (which is usually a contract) creating agency. Implied authority consists of those terms which will be implied into the contract of agency by applying the usual rules for the implication of terms into contracts.[1] Certain types of implied actual authority are well recognised, for instance, incidental and customary authority.

Incidental authority has been described as conferring authority to do 'all subordinate acts incident to and necessary for the execution of [express] authority'.[2] Thus, incidental authority supplements the express authority of the agent and gives the agent authority to undertake tasks which are incidental to his authorised task. It is a question of fact in every case whether a particular action is incidental to the authorised purpose of the agent. For example, an agent authorised to sell land has incidental authority to sign a memorandum so as to satisfy the Law of Property Act 1925, s40.[3]

Customary authority means that an agent operating in a particular market or business has the authority which an agent operating in that market or business usually has.[4] If an agent has a particular position in his principal's business, such as company secretary or foreman, or in his own right, such as stockbroker or auctioneer, then he has a type of customary authority commonly called usual authority, which confers on him the authority to undertake any tasks which an agent in that position usually has authority to undertake.[5] In *Panorama Developments Ltd v Fidelis Furnishing Fabrics Ltd*,[6] a company appointed X their company secretary. As such he was an agent of the company, and the company was liable to pay for cars hired by X, even though he used them for his own and not the company's purposes, because hiring cars was within the customary usual authority of an agent holding the position of company secretary.

It should be noted that, as between principal and agent, express authority is paramount. An agent who disobeys an express instruction cannot avoid liability on the ground that his actions lay within, for example, his usual authority. However, as far as third parties are concerned, they are entitled to assume, until they have notice to the contrary, that the agent has whatever authority would usually be implied in the circumstances.

1 Paras 7.16 to 7.25 above.
2 *Collen v Gardner* (1856) 21 Beav 540.
3 *Rosenbaum v Belson* [1900] 2 Ch 267.
4 *Bayliffe v Butterworth* (1847) 1 Exch 425.

5 *Hely-Hutchinson v Brayhead Ltd* [1968] 1 QB 549, [1967] 3 All ER 98; affd on other grounds by the Court of Appeal.
6 [1971] 2 QB 711, [1971] 3 All ER 16, CA.

Ostensible authority

17.32 Ostensible authority may result in:

a. a person who is not an agent being regarded as an agent of a person for whom he acts or appears to act in a particular transaction; or

b. the extension of the authority of an agent.[1]

It does not extend the actual authority of the agent in relation to his principal.

1 The important case of *Freeman and Lockyer v Buckhurst Park Properties (Mangal) Ltd* [1964] 2 QB 480, [1964] 1 All ER 630, CA, reaffirmed that ostensible authority operates in these two ways.

17.33 Ostensible authority can arise when the alleged principal makes to a third party a representation of fact, usually by conduct, which the third party relies on, that a person is authorised to act as his agent.[1] If the third party can show that such was the case, the alleged principal cannot deny the authority of the person whom he has held out as being his agent. Thus, a person who permits someone to act on his behalf may find himself unable to deny that he is his agent. Ostensible authority can operate in a single transaction. For instance, if a person stands by and watches someone acting for him, he conveys the impression to a third party that the person is authorised to act for him. But ostensible authority can also operate in a series of transactions; if a person has frequently allowed an unauthorised person to act for him, he may be unable to deny that the person had ostensible authority to act for him in future transactions of a similar type. For example, if a company allows X to act as managing director, even though he has not been appointed as such, third parties are entitled to assume that he is managing director.

If there is a single transaction, the ostensible authority of the agent is to effect that transaction and no more. That is all the 'principal' has represented to the world that the agent has authority to undertake. If the 'principal' has allowed a person to act on his behalf more than once, that person has ostensible authority to effect such transactions and similar transactions in the future, and may also have ostensible usual authority. Ostensible usual authority means that where a person is held out as occupying a particular position, for example, managing director, then he will have all the usual authority that a person would have if properly appointed to that position.[1] If a person has invested an agent with ostensible authority, it is not necessarily limited to exactly the same transactions as those from which the ostensible authority arose. In *Swiss Air Transport Co Ltd v Palmer*,[2] an agent who was held out as having authority to ship wigs was held to have ostensible authority to arrange the shipment of wigs and other items over the same route, but not to buy himself an air-ticket.

1 *Freeman and Lockyer v Buckhurst Park Properties (Mangal) Ltd* [1964] 2 QB 480, [1964] 1 All ER 630, CA.
2 [1976] 2 Lloyd's Rep 604.

17.34 Ostensible authority is of great importance where a principal has restricted or terminated the actual authority of his validly appointed agent. As between principal and agent, the restriction or termination is binding, and the agent will be liable to his principal if he acts without actual authority. However, third parties are not bound by any restriction, provided that they are unaware of the restriction or termination.[1]

Acts within the ostensible authority of an agent bind the principal even if they are entered into for the agent's own purposes or are fraudulent, provided the fraud occurs while the agent is purporting to carry out what he is ostensibly authorised to do.[2]

1   *Trickett v Tomlinson* (1863) 13 CB NS 663.
2   *Lloyd v Grace Smith & Co* [1912] AC 716, HL.

17.35 Ostensible authority is based on the belief raised in the mind of the third party by the representation of the alleged principal that a particular person is his agent or that a properly appointed agent has authority in excess of his actual authority. It follows that a third party, who knows, or ought to know, that the alleged principal has not invested with authority the person whom he appears to hold out as his agent, cannot rely on the doctrine of ostensible authority—because he cannot say that he was led to believe that that person was the alleged principal's authorised agent.[1] This may cause particular difficulties with companies. The public documents of the company[2] may reveal that a person whom the company appears to be holding out as an agent is not an agent and lacks authority in respect of the matter in hand. Because these documents are open to public inspection, they are deemed to give notice to the whole world of this lack of authority even if, as is usual, a particular third party has not read them. This has been amended in relation to directors, but not other agents of the company, by the Companies Act 1985, s35. A company cannot now deny the ostensible authority of a director or person whom it has held out as director, by claiming that the public documents gave notice of any lack of authority. On the other hand, if the public documents *extend* the authority of an agent or a person held out as an agent of the company, the third party cannot rely on such extension unless he has read the public documents.

1   See, for example, *Overbrooke Estates Ltd v Glencombe Properties Ltd* [1974] 3 All ER 511, [1974] 1 WLR 1355; para 13.32 above.
2   Para 15.24 above.

17.36 It must be emphasised that ostensible authority only operates to make someone an agent with authority for the purposes of his dealings with third parties. It does not create an agency relationship, though it may prevent the 'principal' denying that a person was acting on his behalf.

The disclosed principal
17.37 A disclosed principal is one whose existence, though not necessarily his identity, is known to the third party at the time of contracting. To put it another way, a principal is disclosed wherever the third party is aware that he is dealing with an agent.

If the agent of a disclosed principal makes an authorised contract, the principal can almost invariably sue and be sued upon it.[1] Whether the agent also can sue or be sued on the contract is a question which we discuss in paras 17.41 to 17.46 below.

Contracts under seal form an exception to the general rule. At common law, the principal could not sue or be sued unless he was named as a party to the deed and it was executed in his name.[2] In equity, the principal could sue on a deed if the agent contracted as trustee for the principal and the agent was made co-plaintiff.[3]

Statute now provides that, if an agent executes a contract under seal on behalf of the principal, the principal can sue on it,[4] although there is authority to suggest that he must still be named in the deed.[5]

1   *Montgomerie v United Kingdom Mutual SS Association* [1891] 1 QB 370.
2   *Schack v Anthony* (1813) 1 M & S 573.
3   *Harmer v Armstrong* [1934] Ch 65, CA.
4   Powers of Attorney Act 1971, s7.
5   *Harmer v Armstrong* [1934] Ch 65, CA.

The undisclosed principal

17.38 If the third party is unaware that he is dealing with an agent, the principal is called an undisclosed principal. An undisclosed principal can sue and be sued on authorised contracts entered into on his behalf.[1] The agent can also sue and be sued on such contracts.[2] It may seem odd that the third party can be sued by someone with whom he did not know he was contracting and with whom he may not have wished to contract. To protect the third party certain limitations have been placed on the right of the undisclosed principal to sue.

1   *Scrimshir v Alderton* (1743) 2 Stra 1182; *Thomson v Davenport* (1829) 9 B & C 78.
2   *Saxon v Blake* (1861) 29 Beav 438.

Limitations on the right of the undisclosed principal to sue
17.39 An undisclosed principal cannot sue:

a. If he did not exist or lacked capacity at the time the agent contracted.[1]

b. If the contract expressly prohibits the intervention of an undisclosed principal.[2]

c. If the contract impliedly excludes the intervention of an undisclosed principal. For example, if the contract 'shows' the agent to be contracting as principal. In *Humble v Hunter*,[3] the agent of an undisclosed principal signed a charterparty as 'owner' of the ship. This contract was found impliedly to regard the agent as owner, and the true owner (the principal) could not sue on the contract. The logic of this decision may be questioned, for it might be said that the agent is 'shown' to be the principal in every case where the principal is undisclosed.

d. If the third party can establish that he had some reason for wishing to deal with the agent personally. For example, if the agent was a man of fine reputation and acknowledged skill, and the contract involved reliance on such integrity and skill.[4]

e. If the third party would have a defence to an action by the agent. This most commonly arises where the third party has paid the agent what is due under the contract (for example, by setting-off money which the agent owes the third party). However, this only prevents the undisclosed principal from suing where it is his conduct which has enabled the agent to appear to be dealing on his own account.[5]

f. If the third party's legal position would be materially worse as a result of the principal's intervention.[6] For example, where a person became a protected tenant of a flat, it was held that evidence could not be brought to show that she had made the lease as agent for an undisclosed principal, since this would increase the number of people who would be entitled to security of tenure under the Rent Act.[7]

Apart from these cases, an undisclosed principal can intervene on the contract, even where it is clear that the third party would have refused for personal reasons to deal with him, provided that there has been no positive misrepresentation.[8]

1   Para 17.4 above.
2   *United Kingdom Mutual SS Assurance Association Ltd v Nevill* (1887) 19 QBD 110, CA.
3   (1848) 12 QB 310.
4   *Greer v Downs Supply Co* [1927] 2 KB 28, CA.
5   *Cooke v Eshelby* (1887) 12 App Cas 271, HL.
6   *Collins v Associated Greyhound Racecourses Ltd* [1930] 1 Ch 1.
7   *Hanstown Properties Ltd v Green* (1977) 246 Estates Gazette 917, CA.
8   *Dyster v Randall & Sons* [1926] Ch 932.

Election

17.40   Where the third party is in a position to sue either the agent or the principal (eg where the agent has acted on behalf of an undisclosed principal), the third party may, if he takes action against one party, be deemed to have elected to pursue that party exclusively. In such a case, even if the third party fails to obtain satisfaction, he cannot turn to the other party.[1] 'Election' in this sense may be express or implied. An implied election will only occur if a third party with full knowledge of all the relevant facts indicates clearly which party he intends to hold liable on the contract.[2] What constitutes implied election is a question of fact—beginning legal proceedings,[3] demanding payment, and debiting an account[4] are all relevant but not conclusive factors. Where principal and agent are jointly liable, the third party may even obtain judgment against one of them without forfeiting his right to sue the other.[5]

1   *Paterson v Gandasequi* (1812) 15 East 62.
2   *Thomson v Davenport* (1829) 9 B & C 78.
3   *Clarkson, Booker Ltd v Andjel* [1964] 2 QB 775, [1964] 3 All ER 260, CA.
4   *Young & Co Ltd v White* (1911) 28 TLR 87.
5   Civil Liability (Contribution) Act 1978, s3.

Agents and third parties

17.41   As we have seen, where an agent makes an authorised contract on behalf of an undisclosed principal, the agent can sue and be sued upon the contract.[1] Where an agent makes an authorised contract on behalf of a disclosed principal, the general rule is that the agent cannot sue or be sued on the contract. However, in certain cases the agent is liable and entitled on the contract, either alone or jointly with the principal.

1   *Saxon v Blake* (1861) 29 Beav 438.

Contracts under seal

17.42   An agent who enters into a contract under seal is liable on it, even if he is known to be contracting as an agent.[1]

1   *Schack v Anthony* (1813) 1 M & S 573.

Trade usage

17.43   If a trade custom, not inconsistent with the contract, makes an agent liable on a contract the courts will give effect to that custom.[1]

1   *Barrow & Bros v Dyster, Nalder & Co* (1884) 13 QBD 635, DC.

Where the agent is in fact principal

17.44   If an agent contracts on behalf of a non-existent principal then the agent must be contracting on his own behalf.[1] If the agent purports to contract as agent but is in fact the principal, he can sue and be sued on the contract.[2] But, if X, a purported agent who is in fact a principal, appears to contract on behalf of a named principal, he cannot sue or be sued on the contract[3] (though he can be sued for breach of warranty of authority[4]). The agent can sue if he contracts on his own behalf and the contract indicates, but does not name, a principal and shows that the identity of the principal is not relevant.[5] The cases in this area are generally considered to be unsatisfactory.

1   See in relation to unformed companies, the Companies Act 1985, s36(4).
2   *Gardiner v Heading* [1928] 2 KB 284, CA.
3   *Fairlie v Fenton* (1870) LR 5 Exch 169.
4   Para 17.47, below.
5   *Schmaltz v Avery* (1851) 16 QB 655.

Other cases

17.45   Apart from these special cases, an agent may be jointly or solely liable on the contract entered into on behalf of his disclosed principal, if the contract expressly or impliedly reveals this to be the intention of the parties. Under the Partnership Act 1890, s5, a partner who contracts on behalf of the partnership is jointly liable with the rest of the partners on that contract. In other cases, whether there is an implied intention that an agent shall be jointly or solely liable on the contract is a question of construction.

Particular note is taken of the description of the agent in a written contract and of how the agent signed a written contract. If either the description of the agent in the document or the form of his signature makes it clear that he is acting merely as an agent, he is not liable on the contract.[1] If neither the document nor the signature describes him as an agent, he is liable on the contract,[2] even if he is known to be acting as an agent. If the contract is oral and the agent is known to be an agent, the above rules for written contracts do not apply and every case is determined by reference to its particular facts.[3] If an agent is liable on a contract he will probably also have the benefit of that contract, unless, as a matter of construction, the contract reveals that the agent is to be liable without having the benefit of the contract.

1   *Lucas v Beale* (1851) 10 CB 739.
2   *Basma v Weekes* [1950] AC 441, [1950] 2 All ER 146, PC.
3   *N and J Vlassopulos Ltd v Ney Shipping Ltd* [1977] 1 Lloyd's Rep 478, CA.

Rights of third parties against agents

On the contract

17.46 If the agent is jointly or solely liable on the contract, the third party can, subject to the doctrine of election,[1] sue the agent.

1 Para 17.40 above.

For breach of warranty of authority

17.47 If a person acts as agent, knowing that he has no authority, he is liable to the third party for breach of warranty of authority if he has represented to the third party that he had authority.[1] Purporting to act as agent constitutes a representation of authority, unless the third party knew or ought to have known of the lack of authority.[2]

Even if the agent genuinely and reasonably believes he has authority, when he has not, he may be liable to the third party.[3] In *Yonge v Toynbee*,[4] an agent acting on behalf of his principal was held liable for breach of warranty of authority when, entirely unknown to him, his authority had been terminated by the insanity of his principal. The third party can sue even if he has not entered into a contract, provided he has altered his position in reliance on the representation.

If the representation made by the agent is one of law, not fact, he is not liable if it is untrue.[5] An action for breach of warranty cannot lie if the principal ratifies the unauthorised act.

The amount of damages which may be awarded under this head is the amount which would put the third party in the same position as if the representation (of authority) had been true.[6] Therefore, if the third party could have recovered nothing from the principal, even if the agent had had authority (for example because the principal is insolvent), he can recover only nominal damages for breach of warranty of authority.

1 *Collen v Wright* (1857) 8 E & B 647.
2 *Halbot v Lens* [1901] 1 Ch 344.
3 *Yonge v Toynbee* [1910] 1 KB 215, CA.
4 [1910] 1 KB 215, CA.
5 *Beattie v Ebury* (1872) 7 Ch App 777, HL.
6 *Richardson v Williamson and Lawson* (1871) LR 6 QB 276.

In tort

17.48 An agent may be liable even if his principal is also vicariously liable. Therefore, an agent may be liable in deceit, or under the rules in *Hedley Byrne & Co Ltd v Heller & Partners Ltd*,[1] or, of course, for such actions as knocking down a third party by negligent driving. However, an agent may not be personally liable under the Misrepresentation Act 1967 unless he is a party to the contract which he makes on behalf of his principal.[2]

1 [1964] AC 465, [1963] 2 All ER 575, HL; para 19.13 below.
2 *Resolute Maritime Inc v Nippon Kaiji Kyokai, The Skopas* [1983] 2 All ER 1, [1983] 1 WLR 857; para 13.21 above.

Types of agent

Estate agent

17.49 The primary function of an estate agent is to effect an introduction between persons who wish to buy and sell land. His implied or ostensible authority, and thus the extent to which he can bind his principal, is very restricted. Unless expressly authorised, an estate agent cannot make a binding contract for the sale of his principal's property,[1] accept a pre-contract deposit[2] or appoint a sub-agent.[3] In fact, his implied authority is limited to the making of statements about the property. If a third party relies on a misrepresentation made to him by an estate agent, the principal cannot enforce the contract[4] and may be liable in damages.[5]

The relationship between an estate agent and his client is a unilateral contract.[6] The agent is under no positive duty to act (except, perhaps, where he is a 'sole agent'[7]) but, if he does act, he must display reasonable care and skill.[8] In order to be entitled to his commission, the estate agent must fulfil precisely the terms of his instructions, which may vary from the mere introduction of a person who is willing to purchase the principal's property to the completion of a sale. The law on this matter is complex, but it may be said that the courts seldom award an estate agent his commission unless there is an actual sale.[9]

1   *Chadburn v Moore* (1892) 61 LJ Ch 674.
2   *Sorrell v Finch* [1977] AC 728, [1976] 2 All ER 371, HL.
3   *John McCann & Co v Pow* [1975] 1 All ER 129, [1974] 1 WLR 1643, CA.
4   *Mullens v Miller* (1882) 22 Ch D 194.
5   *Gosling v Anderson* (1972) 223 Estates Gazette 1743, CA.
6   *Luxor (Eastbourne) Ltd v Cooper* [1941] AC 108, [1941] 1 All ER 33, HL; para 5.2 above.
7   *E Christopher & Co v Essig* [1948] WN 461.
8   *Prebble & Co v West* (1969) 211 Estate Gazette 831, CA.
9   For further discussion, see Murdoch *The Law of Estate Agency and Auctions* (2nd edn) pp 235–286.

Auctioneer

17.50   Unlike an estate agent, an auctioneer has implied authority to effect an actual sale of his principal's land or goods,[1] as well as to make statements about the property.[2] Further, an auctioneer can sign a memorandum of the contract of sale for the purpose of the Law of Property Act 1925, s40,[3] not only on his principal's behalf,[4] but also on behalf of the highest bidder.[5]

1   *Pickering v Busk* (1812) 15 East 38 at 43.
2   *Smith v Land and House Property Corpn* (1884) 28 Ch D 7, CA.
3   Paras 43.11–43.17 below
4   *Beer v London and Paris Hotel Co* (1875) LR 20 Eq 412 at 426.
5   *Sims v Landray* [1894] 2 Ch 318 at 320.

Mercantile agents or factors

17.51   A mercantile agent or factor is an agent 'having in the customary course of his business as such agent authority either to sell goods, or to consign goods for the purpose of sale, or to buy goods, or to raise money on the security of goods'.[1] The ostensible authority of an agent who fulfils this definition is discussed in para 29.6b below.

1   Factors Act 1889, s1.

Part III
The law of tort

Chapter 18

Introduction

Aims and functions of the law of tort

18.1 In this chapter we attempt to describe the subject matter of the law of tort and to distinguish it from other fields of legal liability. As we shall see, however, a formal definition of a tort gives little or no indication as to *why* certain conduct is treated as wrongful and, furthermore, it is extremely difficult to deduce any general principle underlying this whole area of law. Because of this, we shall begin with a brief description of the law of tort in terms of its function within the legal system and within society as a whole.

Wherever men live together, the acts, activities or omissions of one may cause losses of different kinds to another. Compensation for such losses may take a variety of forms; unemployment benefit from the state, sick pay from one's employer, the proceeds of a private insurance policy and so on. Apart from these sources, it is the law of tort which decides whether the primary loss should remain where it has fallen (on the plaintiff) or be transferred to the person who caused it (the defendant). It is important to appreciate that this is all that the law of tort can do; the loss which has occurred cannot be repaired but only allocated. In reaching a decision on this question, the law takes into account both the kind and the severity of the plaintiff's loss, and the defendant's reason for causing it: in short, it is for the law of tort to implement social policy by laying down the circumstances in which the loss *ought* to be transferred from one party to the other.

If a single main function can be ascribed to the law of tort, therefore, it is the provision of *compensation* for loss suffered, within the general confines of attempting to strike a fair balance between plaintiff and defendant. This is not to say, however, that there are no other aims to be fulfilled. The very fact that a defendant is not usually liable unless he is 'at fault' (in the sense of having deliberately or carelessly caused harm to the plaintiff) indicates an element of *punishment* for misconduct. The same principle, by enabling a careful defendant to avoid liability, also has a *deterrent* effect which plays a part in helping to prevent accidents. On a rather different note, there is no doubt that some parts of the law of tort reflect the preoccupation of former centuries with *preserving the peace*, and encouraging people to settle their disputes in court instead of by acts of private vengeance; it is, perhaps, for this reason that any form of trespass automatically gives rise to a right of action, whether or not any real damage has been done.

Balance of interests

18.2 Compensation, then, is the keynote. But compensation is not an end in itself (although a surprising number of laymen assume that an injured person is automatically entitled to claim damages from whoever injured him). What the law of tort seeks to achieve is, in truth, a just balance between the many conflicting interests which are inevitably found in any society. These conflicts are sometimes obvious. For example, where the tort of private nuisance is concerned, the courts are asked to reconcile A's right to use his land as he pleases with B's right not to be interfered with in the enjoyment of his own land. Similarly, the tort of defamation seeks to balance C's interest in his reputation with D's freedom of speech.

Other situations commonly dealt with by the law of tort do not raise the 'conflict of interests' question in quite such a naked fashion. It might, for example, be thought that the *careless* causing of harm would always be actionable, on the basis that nobody has a legitimate interest in acting unreasonably. However, even here, the familiar balance is in operation; the court may regard the particular interest of the plaintiff which has been infringed as too trivial to merit protection against merely careless invasions. Indeed, to take this to its logical conclusion, certain types of harm are not actionable even when *deliberately* inflicted, for society is just not prepared to give protection to the interests involved. For example, there is nothing tortious in our opening a supermarket next door to your established but uncompetitive grocer's shop, even if it is our earnest hope that this will quickly put you out of business.

If the balancing approach leads, on occasion, to exemption from liability for those who cause loss carelessly or deliberately, it may equally bring about the imposition of liability upon a defendant who, far from wishing to harm the plaintiff, has in fact taken all reasonable steps to avoid doing so. Suppose, for example, that a highly dangerous (and highly profitable) enterprise such as a chemical plant explodes, causing widespread damage in the neighbourhood. The law might well say that, provided all due care has been used in running the plant, the victims will have no grounds on which to claim damages. But might it not say instead, and with equal justification, that the risk of such losses should lie upon those who run chemical plants for profit, rather than upon those who merely happen to live in their vicinity?

Definition of a tort

18.3 A tort may be defined as the breach of a legal duty owed, independent of contract, by one person to another, for which a common law action for unliquidated damages may be brought. Such a definition is, however, of fairly limited value, since it does not help us to recognise the circumstances in which a legal duty will be imposed. Its major purpose, as we shall see in the next few paragraphs, is the formal one of excluding other types of liability.

If this definition contains one *positive* identifying feature, it is that of the 'common law action for unliquidated damages'; without the availability of this particular remedy, the defendant's liability does not lie within the law of tort. This is not to say, however, that an action for damages is the only remedy available to a plaintiff in tort, nor even that it is necessarily always the most important. Some torts, such as nuisance, lend themselves readily to control by the grant of an injunction. A person who has been wrongfully dispossessed of land or goods may obtain an order for their return, and a limited amount of 'self-help' (eg ejecting a trespasser) is tolerated by the courts in the interest of avoiding unnecessary litigation. Nonetheless, the possibility of damages on a common law basis must always be there and, further, these must be 'unliquidated', in the sense of being subject to assessment by the court rather than by prior agreement between the parties.[1]

1 As to *liquidated* damages, see paras 11.16 and 11.17 above.

Tort and crime

18.4 A tort is the breach of a legal duty which is owed by one person to another; a crime, on the other hand, is the breach of a legal duty which is owed to, and enforceable by, society as a whole. Thus, the true distinction between these two fields of law lies, not in their subject matter (for such things as assault, theft and careless driving may be both crimes and torts), but in the purpose of the legal proceedings to which each gives rise. The object of a criminal prosecution (which is usually instigated by the state) is to vindicate the rights of society against the offender by punishing him. Such compensation as he may be ordered to pay to his vicitim[1] is an afterthought; the court's attention is focussed primarily upon the question of what should be done with the defendant. The usual aim of a tort action, on the other hand, is to secure compensation for harm suffered by an individual plaintiff. It is true that, in very limited circumstances, a court is empowered to punish a defendant by ordering him to pay an extra sum in damages, over and above what is needed to compensate the plaintiff, but this is subsidiary to the main object of the proceedings.

1 Under the Powers of Criminal Courts Act 1973.

Tort and contract

18.5 It has been said that duties in tort are imposed automatically upon a person by law, while contractual duties arise only out of his voluntary acceptance. Both sides of this distinction, however, require some degree of qualification. In the first place, there are many tortious duties which come into effect only as a result of some voluntary act by the defendant (eg in permitting someone to enter his land, or offering him some advice). Second, while the *existence* of a contract depends upon the parties' agreement (although even this may be a question of interpreting their conduct rather than their secret thoughts), much of its *content* may be decided on by the general law, as in hire-purchase or sales of goods. Thus, any attempt to differentiate between the law of contract and the law of tort in terms of their sources is of little value.

A better distinction, perhaps, lies in the *purpose* of each field of law. Tort, as we have seen, aims to compensate the plaintiff for harm done to him; it does this by awarding as damages a sum which will, as far as possible, restore him to his original position. In actions for breach of contract, by contrast, the plaintiff's basic complaint is that he has not received some benefit which he was promised, and damages are generally designed to fulfil the plaintiff's expectation, by putting him into the position in which he would have been had the contract been performed.[1]

Theory apart, there are some significant practical distinctions between a breach of contract and a tort, with regard to such matters as the liability of minors, the awarding of punitive damages (available in tort alone) and claims against bankrupt defendants. Most important, the rules as to limitation of actions are different. The time within which a plaintiff must serve his writ (or automatically lose his case) generally runs, in contract, from the date of the breach, while in tort the relevant date is that on which damage is suffered.[2]

It sometimes happens that a defendant's conduct is capable of constituting both a tort and a breach of contract. For instance, a taxi driver who drives negligently and thereby injures his passenger is guilty of both a breach of contract (an implied term that he will convey the passenger with due skill and care) and the tort of negligence, as well as of a criminal offence. In such circumstances, at least where physical damage results, the law has always allowed a plaintiff to frame his case in whatever way he chooses (usually in tort, so as to gain the advantage of more generous limitation rules). Where the plaintiff's loss is purely financial, on the other hand, authority for giving him this freedom of choice is more equivocal, although in several cases the client of a professional adviser has been permitted to sue him in the tort of negligence.[3] However, the whole question of alternative causes of action has become rather confused, as a result of certain dicta of the Privy Council in *Tai Hing Cotton Mill v Liu Chong Hing Bank Ltd*.[4] It was there said that, where the parties are in a contractual relationship, there is nothing to the advantage of the law's development in searching for a liability in tort; indeed, that it is correct in principle and necessary for the avoidance of confusion in the law to adhere to the contractual analysis.

If taken literally, this dictum would rule out any action for negligence between the parties to a contract. However, such an interpretation would be inconsistent with a great number of previous cases and, consequently, we believe that a narrower interpretation is correct. This is simply that, where a contract imposes a duty of care upon one party towards the other, the *scope* of that duty is governed exclusively by the contract, and will be no wider if the action is framed in tort.

1 Para 11.3 above.
2 Paras 11.33 to 11.39 above, and 31.21 to 31.22 below.
3 Para 19.16 below.
4 [1985] 2 All ER 947 at 957, PC.

Tort and quasi-contract[1]

18.6 In some circumstances, a person who has been unjustly enriched at the expense of another may be compelled by law to make restitution. If A, for instance, pays money to B under certain mistakes of fact, B may be ordered to return it. This area of law falls outside the definition of a tort because A is not claiming unliquidated damages; nor, indeed, can it meaningfully be said that B has broken any legal duty in merely receiving the money.

1 Ch 16 above.

Tort and breach of trust

18.7 The obligations which a trustee owes to a beneficiary arise out of the trust relationship and may, if broken, lead to an award of damages. The whole matter, however, (including the principles on which these damages are assessed) is governed by equity, rather than by common law, and the administration of trusts is today a function of the Chancery Division of the High Court; tort, by contrast, is normally regarded as within the province of the Queen's Bench Division.

Scope of the law of tort

Interests protected

18.8 The kinds of harm which come within the law of tort are extremely diverse and, since the interests of the plaintiff which may be infringed vary greatly in importance, so does the degree of protection which the law affords them. Thus, for example, an interest which is regarded as relatively trivial may be protected only against intentional invasions, whereas more important interests may give rise to actions against a defendant whose conduct is merely negligent or even accidental.

The most important interest to be recognised by any legal system is that of personal security which, broadly speaking, involves freedom from both physical injury[1] and wrongful deprivation of liberty. This particular interest also finds expression in other less obvious ways, such as the protection of a person's reputation and of certain status-based rights, eg the right to vote. Of rather less importance, though still well protected, are interests in the ownership and possession of land and goods; even a relatively primitive legal system can easily comprehend and act upon the destruction, damage or deprivation of tangible objects.

As a general rule, since no man has a proprietary interest in another, A is not allowed to sue in respect of an injury to B. However, an important statutory exception to this principle permits the dependants of a deceased person to sue the person responsible for his death for the loss of their breadwinner.[2]

It takes a fairly sophisticated legal system to recognise the possibility of compensating a plaintiff for those effects of the defendant's conduct which are purely financial. Even where protection is given to such economic interests (eg by the torts of conspiracy, intimidation and interference with contract) it is usually limited to cases where the defendant's conduct is deliberate. By and large, as we shall see, the causing of financial loss through mere carelessness is not actionable.[3]

1 Including nervous shock: paras 19.34 to 19.36 below.
2 Fatal Accidents Act 1976; see para 31.11 below.
3 Paras 19.22 to 19.26 below.

Damnum absque iniuria

18.9 This Latin phrase, which means 'loss without legal injury', indicates that, unless the plaintiff suffers an invasion of a recognised interest, he cannot claim compensation for his losses under the law of tort. There is, for example, no right of privacy as such; consequently, a person who wishes to protect himself against unwanted intrusions must, in order to succeed, show that the defendant has committed some recognised tort such as trespass or nuisance. Similarly, while injury to the plaintiff's feelings may aggravate the damages to which he is entitled in respect of a known tort, as where the defendant trespasses on the plaintiff's land in order to hurl abuse at him, it is not of itself an interest which the law will protect.

Examples of loss falling outside the scope of the law of tort are not difficult to find. In *Day v Brownrigg*,[1] the defendant, wishing to spite the plaintiff, his next-door neighbour, changed the name of his house to match that of the plaintiff's. It was held that, since there was no interference with any trading interest of the plaintiff, this conduct was not actionable. In *Bradford Corpn v Pickles*,[2] the defendant, irritated by the plaintiffs' refusal to buy his land, excavated in such a way that water which would otherwise have percolated into the plaintiffs' reservoir instead collected on the defendant's property. The House of Lords held that, since the defendant was absolutely entitled to this water (unlike water flowing in a defined channel), the plaintiffs could not complain when he intercepted it. Finally, in *Perera v Vandiyar*,[3] a landlord harassed his tenant by cutting off the supply of gas and electricity to the flat. This was undoubtedly a breach of contract, but it was held by the Court of Appeal that, since the landlord did not actually enter the premises, he was not guilty of any tort.

1 (1878) 10 Ch D 294.
2 [1895] AC 587, HL.
3 [1953] 1 All ER 1109, [1953] 1 WLR 672, CA.

Iniuria sine damno

18.10   The other side of the coin consists of circumstances in which the defendant's conduct may be actionable as a tort, notwithstanding that it has caused no actual damage to the plaintiff. The torts which come within this principle are said to be actionable per se; they are trespass in all its forms and libel (but not usually slander). The reasons for treating these torts differently and imposing liability are purely historical.

General principle of liability

Tort or torts?

18.11   An argument on which much has been written over the years is whether the whole field of tortious liability rests upon any general principle, or whether it consists simply of a random collection of civil wrongs, each with its own elements of liability. The dispute may be summed up by asking whether there is a 'law of tort' or merely a 'law of torts', and the fact that among the leading textbooks both titles are to be found indicates that there is something at least to be said for both approaches.

The 'law of tort' theory suggests that the law will presume any causing of injury or damage to be actionable, unless there is some legal justification for it. This, of course, provokes the obvious criticism that it gives no indication as to what is a sufficient 'justification'. However, there are signs that modern courts do adopt this approach, albeit in a somewhat modified form; it is probably true to say that, where a defendant intentionally or negligently inflicts physical damage on the plaintiff or his possessions, he can expect to be liable unless there is some good reason (e g self-defence) for his action.

The 'law of torts' theory, which compels every plaintiff to find an appropriate pigeonhole for his complaint, is perhaps attractive if the law is considered at any given moment, without any reference to its past or future development. In its extreme form, however, it fails to allow for what undoubtedly occurs, namely, the creation by judges from time to time of new torts. Outstanding among these are *Lumley v Gye*,[1] in which the courts for the first time recognised that, if A induces B to break his contract with C, an action *in tort* will lie against A, and *Fletcher v Rylands*,[2] where liability even in the absence of negligence was imposed upon a landowner for the escape of dangerous objects from his property. In more recent times, the rapid development of the tort of negligence is far better explained as the coherent exposition of a general principle than as the arbitrary creation of new pigeonholes.

If the 'law of tort' theory has its merits, these should not be over-stressed; the very existence of different torts, each with its own elements of liability, serves to indicate that no simple principle can be found to underlie the whole field of law. Nor is this surprising; as we have already seen, the function of the law of tort is to resolve the conflicts of interest which necessarily arise between members of society and, since these interests may vary greatly in importance, so the appropriate balance to be struck between them will alter. Any attempt to reduce to a single sentence all the policy factors which may play a part in judicial decisions would result in a proposition so generalised as to be practically meaningless.

1   (1853) 2 E & B 216.
2   (1866) LR 1 Ex 265.

Mental element

18.12   A major obstacle in the way of any attempt to deduce a general principle of liability from the law of tort is the fact that different torts depend upon different mental elements on the part of the defendant. Three levels are involved. In the first place, some torts (such as assault, false imprisonment and deceit) depend upon proof of intention, that is to say, that the defendant was aware of the likely consequences of his act and in fact desired those consequences. It is of course impossible to be absolutely certain of what a person wants but this, like so much else, can be proved to the satisfaction of a court by evidence as to what he says and does. Further, for the purposes of the law of tort 'recklessness' is equivalent to intention. This covers cases where the defendant is well aware of the risks inherent in what he is doing and those where, while not actually wanting to injure the plaintiff, he is totally indifferent to the possibility.

The second mental element which may be relevant to the law of tort is negligence, which normally signifies a blameworthy failure to appreciate and guard against the likely consequences of one's acts or omissions.[1] This concept, which today governs liability in the great majority of cases, involves testing the defendant's conduct against the objective yardstick of the hypothetical 'reasonable man'; if it falls short of that standard, the defendant is liable, whatever his subjective state of mind.

Third, certain torts are based upon what is termed 'strict liability'. This means that a defendant is liable for the consequences of his actions, even though he neither desired nor ought reasonably to have foreseen and avoided them. Naturally, the law requires fairly strong reasons for imposing this type of liability; these may lie in the importance of the plaintiff's interest which is to be protected, the inherently risky nature of the defendant's activity or (in modern times) perhaps the ease with which the defendant may absorb the loss (e g by insuring against it and passing on the cost to his customers). This kind of liability includes the rule in *Rylands v Fletcher*,[2] liability for animals[3] and breach of statutory duty;[4] the vicarious liability of an employer for torts committed by his employees is also strict.[5]

1   Ch 20 below.
2   Paras 27.2–27.13 below.
3   Ch 28 below.
4   Ch 24 below.
5   Paras 30.3–30.18 below.

Motive

18.13   'Intention' signifies a person's desire for certain consequences; his 'motive', on the other hand, tells us *why* he wants them to occur. Broadly speaking, the law of torts is not concerned with motive; it asks only what the defendant has done, not why. Occasionally, however, a good motive will excuse acts which would otherwise be unlawful. This is of particular relevance in relation to torts such as conspiracy and inducement to break a contract, which protect the plaintiff's economic interests.

As a general rule, a bad motive is no more relevant than a good one; if A is exercising a legal right, the law does not enquire why he chooses to do so. This principle, which helps to explain the case of *Bradford Corpn v Pickles*,[1] was also applied by a majority of the Court of Appeal in *Chapman v Honig*.[2] The defendant in that case was a landlord who, incensed that the plaintiff, his tenant, had given evidence against him on behalf of another tenant, served the plaintiff with a valid notice to quit. This, it was held, could not be regarded as wrongful, even though the defendant had clearly acted out of spite.

It is important to appreciate that evil motives are ignored only where the defendant is exercising an absolute legal right. In other cases, where his rights are qualified or limited, a bad motive may be the factor which tips his conduct over the line into what is unlawful. The tort of nuisance, for instance, permits a landowner to make some noise on his own land, provided that the interference which is thereby caused to his neighbours is not unreasonable; in deciding what noise level is acceptable, it is legitimate to ask why the noise is being made. In *Hollywood Silver Fox Farm Ltd v Emmett*,[3] the defendant fired guns near where his land adjoined that of the plaintiffs, frightening the plaintiffs' silver foxes and ruining their breeding season. A landowner is of course usually entitled to shoot over his own land; here, however, the defendant's actions were motivated by malice, and he was therefore held liable in nuisance.

1   [1895] AC 587, HL; para 18.9 above.
2   [1963] 2 QB 502, [1963] 2 All ER 513, CA.
3   [1936] 2 KB 468, [1936] 1 All ER 825.

Fault liability

18.14   Although, as we have said, it is impossible to reduce the law of tort to a single principle, there is no doubt that one particular idea has, over the last century, come to occupy a position of great dominance. This is the notion that a person's liability should be related to his 'fault', in the sense of intentional or negligent causing of harm. This principle, and its important corollary, that a person should not be liable *unless* he is 'at fault', became prominent at the time of the Industrial Revolution, when its moral appeal coincided with important vested interests. After all, the vast increases which took place at this time in both traffic and industrial activity were bound to lead to more accidents and, if liability for these were strict, development would thereby be retarded. Accordingly, 'no liability without fault' became the popular cry, and inevitable casualties were regarded merely as the unfortunate price of progress.

Today, 'fault' is established as the major criterion of liability in the law of tort. There remain areas where a person 'at fault' is not legally liable, and others in which liability may be imposed upon one whose conduct is 'faultless'. However, such areas are increasingly seen as anomalous and, whether by legislation or judicial decision, are gradually being whittled away.

Arguments for fault liability

18.15 Apart from the rather cynical view described above, that strict liability is undesirable because it impedes industrial progress, attempts to justify fault liability are usually based upon what is felt to be morally right, namely that a 'wrongdoer' should pay for the consequences of his misconduct. As we shall see, damages in practice are not paid from the funds of the individual defendant in all, or even most, tort cases; nevertheless, there is no doubt that ideas of 'personal responsibility' and 'justice' strike a strong chord with the public in general.

Allied to this is the notion that making a person responsible for his fault has a valuable deterrent effect; if the defendant knows that by taking care he can avoid liability, he is more likely to do so than if he would be strictly liable in any case. Thus, the argument goes, the punitive effect of an award of damages operates as a useful means of moulding people's conduct in areas where accidents are likely to occur.

18.16 The twin goals of fairness and deterrence might seem of overwhelming importance in assessing the value of fault liability. In practice, however, it is extremely doubtful whether the operation of the law in its present form comes near to achieving either aim, for a variety of reasons. Since, for example, the vast majority of tort cases arise out of accidents on the roads or at work, it is only rarely that the person actually at fault will have to meet the damages awarded out of his own pocket. If he drives a car negligently, his liability in tort (at least as regards the causing of death or personal injury) is bound to be covered by insurance; if he causes damage in the course of his employment, the doctrine of vicarious liability enables the plaintiff to claim directly against the tortfeasor's employer (who is probably insured against just this contingency). If, then, the actual tortfeasor does not have to pay, how is he deterred? And why should the ability of the plaintiff to obtain compensation from an insurance company depend upon whether or not the defendant (a third party) is 'at fault'?

The effectiveness of this so-called 'deterrent' may be questioned upon other grounds. First, since damages are assessed on the basis of the plaintiff's loss, rather than the seriousness of the defendant's conduct, it may be objected that the 'punishment' does not fit the 'crime'. Second, the idea of 'fault' itself bears an unreal air, for the courts, well aware of any insurance fund standing behind the defendant, are more likely to convict him of negligence in order to secure compensation for the plaintiff. This is done by demanding from the 'reasonable man' a standard of conduct so high that the defendant may well fail to achieve it even where no moral blame attaches to him. Indeed, this distortion of the meaning of 'fault' is accentuated by the courts' refusal to take into account such medically established factors as a person's 'accident-proneness'. And yet, if a defendant is genuinely prone to accidents, will civil liability deter him? For that matter, is he even 'at fault' in any meaningful sense?

Criticisms of fault liability

18.17 If the main argument in favour of fault liability, that it does justice as between plaintiff and defendant, can thus be exposed as fallacious, then the whole concept falls to be judged simply as a method of compensating the victims of accidents and, as such, it is susceptible to a number of severe criticisms. In the first place, it is estimated that the cost of administering the system (legal fees, the whole apparatus of insurance, etc) is roughly the equivalent of the compensation actually paid; that is to say that, out of every pound paid by motorists for liability insurance, for example, no more than 50p reaches accident victims as compensation. By comparison, a system of direct benefits, such as social security, has an administrative cost of approximately 10% of its turnover.

If fault liability is expensive, it is also highly inefficient, in that it depends upon a detailed investigation of facts (either by lawyers or by insurers), which usually takes place long after the event. Human memory being what it is, researchers have suggested that one out of every two tort cases is decided on 'facts' which never actually occurred; if this is true, it deprives 'fault' of much of its meaning.

In social terms, perhaps the most telling criticism of fault liability is that it leaves totally uncompensated those accident victims who are unable to make out a case in tort. Where it is genuinely a question of whether or not an individual defendant shall pay an individual plaintiff, this is of course perfectly reasonable. As we have said, however, this is seldom the case today, and it can be strongly argued therefore that fault liability merely serves to create an artificial and arbitrary distinction between two classes of victim. After all, the pedestrian who is run over suffers exactly the same injuries, whether or not the driver took reasonable care to avoid him. Does it not seem capricious, at least when one considers accidents as a whole, that his ability to obtain compensation from the driver's insurance company should depend upon such an elusive and unreliable concept as 'fault'?

Tort in context

Other compensation systems

18.18 This part of the book is concerned with the law of tort, rather than with compensation as a whole. Nevertheless, the role of tort cannot be fully understood unless some attention is paid to the other methods which exist, or which might be introduced, to bring about the payment of compensation to those who suffer losses of various kinds. It should be noted that 'liability insurance', such as is carried by all drivers of motor vehicles, is not an alternative compensation system, but simply a method of ensuring that tort damages, once awarded, are actually paid; a plaintiff's recovery of compensation by this route depends upon his ability to make out a case in tort against the defendant.

Apart from the law of tort, there are two obvious sources of monetary compensation. In the first place, almost any kind of potential damage, from death to loss of business through bad weather, may be the subject of private (loss) insurance. This is not a matter of liability (nor, indeed, of a defendant); if the stated event occurs, the insurer pays out. Under this heading are included, not only actual insurance policies taken out by individuals, but also schemes giving such 'fringe benefits' as sick pay or disablement pensions to employees.

The second major source of compensation is the social security system; this contains a large number of different benefits, most of which are designed to cover the financial consequences of accident or disease. The system is extremely complex and is constantly under review. However, an important general point is that injuries (including certain diseases) contracted *at work* are more generously compensated than the rest, which are simply dealt with in the same way as sickness.

A mixed system in operation

18.19 Of the compensation which is paid in the United Kingdom in respect of accidents causing personal injury or death, approximately one-half comes from the social security system, one-quarter from private insurance and one-quarter from the law of tort. Interestingly, however, the tort damages are shared among a mere $6\frac{1}{2}\%$ of accident victims, which makes these a privileged minority; the discrepancy arises because tort, unlike social security, places no fixed 'ceiling' on awards, and also because tort damages on a generous scale may be awarded for such non-financial losses as pain and suffering.

The favoured position of tort victims is accentuated by the fact that, broadly speaking, their damages are not reduced to take account of any private insurance benefits (except occupational sick pay) which accrue to them as a result of their injuries; some reduction in damages is made on account of social security benefits, but the overall position is nonetheless that, in financial terms at least, the victim of a tort may receive far more than he has lost.

In most people's scale of values, property damage ranks well below personal injury, and the case of the uncompensated victim is not regarded as such a pressing social problem. This has two practical consequences: little or no state aid is available to those whose goods or land are damaged, and liability insurance in respect of causing such loss is not compulsory. It might be thought that these factors would render the law of tort vitally important in this area; in fact, however, its significance is greatly reduced by the widespread use of private loss insurance, such as 'comprehensive' motor cover and 'house and contents' policies, and by the fact that many liability insurance policies do cover property damage.

The future

18.20　In recent years, many countries have expressed varying degrees of dissatisfaction with fault liability as a means of transferring compensation to the victims of accidents, at least in cases of death or personal injury. Most of the proposals for reform which have been voiced fall into one of two categories. First, it has been suggested that more use should be made of strict liability, based upon ideas of risk and backed by compulsory insurance. This would mean, for example, that a road accident victim would have an automatic right of action against a driver's insurance company, irrespective of whether the driver was at fault; it would, however, still deny compensation to those injured by risks not attributable to any particular class of defendants.

Second, and more radical, are suggestions that the future of compensation lies in direct benefit schemes, based either on private insurance or on social security. In the USA, for example, about one-half of the states operate an automatic compensation scheme, run by private insurance companies, in respect of road accidents. In the UK, too, automatic compensation flows from the state in respect of industrial injuries.

The direct benefit schemes mentioned above operate in addition to the possibility of the victim making a claim in tort, but an even greater step has been taken in New Zealand where, in 1972, an automatic compensation scheme for the victims of all accidents *replaced* the law of tort as regards death and personal injury. The benefits under this scheme cover approximately 80% of lost earnings; the balance can of course be covered by private insurance if the individual so wishes. As far as non-financial losses, such as pain and suffering, are concerned, benefits under the scheme are considerably lower than an award of tort damages would have been, but this is generally regarded as a reasonable price to pay for ensuring that everyone's financial losses are more or less covered.

The Pearson Commission Report

18.21　After an exhaustive inquiry lasting five years, the Royal Commission on Civil Liability and Compensation for Personal Injury, under the chairmanship of Lord Pearson, finally produced its Report[1] in April 1978. Many people expected it to recommend changes in the UK along the lines of those in New Zealand, but this did not happen; in so far as the Report has a single theme, it is the continuance of a mixed system of compensation, though with increased reliance upon social security.

Of prime importance among the Commission's 188 recommendations are that automatic direct compensation should be introduced for the victims of road accidents, at the rates current in the 'industrial injuries' scheme, and that the latter should be extended to cover accidents to persons on their way to and from work. However, impressed by arguments that the law of tort fosters a sense of responsibility, a majority of the Commission felt that these two classes of victims should retain their right to sue in tort for losses over and above the new scheme's limits. As for ante-natal injury,[2] the Commission found difficulty with questions of proof, and concluded that the best solution would be a special disability income for *all* severely handicapped children.

Apart from these areas, it was suggested that the *basis* for compensation should remain largely unaltered, although the Commission proposed the introduction of strict liability in a number of special cases; these are defective products, railway accidents, volunteers for medical research, state-recommended vaccination[3] and 'exceptional risks' (to be listed by statutory instrument).[4]

Of the Pearson Commission's other recommendations, most were aimed at improving both the existing methods of compensation and the relationships between them, rather than at making any major alterations to the system as a whole. The assessment and payment of tort damages received special scrutiny, and we shall in due course consider the major recommendations which were made in this respect.[5]

1 Cmnd 7054, 1978.
2 The original appointment of the Royal Commission was largely in response to public concern generated by the thalidomide tragedy.
3 Implemented by the Vaccine Damage Payments Act 1979.
4 See para 27.1 below.
5 See paras 31.6 to 31.9 below.

Chapter 19
Negligence—duty of care

19.1 Of all the torts which are recognised by the common law, the most important by far is negligence. Indeed, the idea that careless conduct *as such* should form a basis for legal liability seems today almost self-evident. Surprisingly, however, the emergence of negligence as a tort in its own right is a comparatively recent development; it is only in the last 150 years or so that the attention of the law has been focussed upon the *standard* of a defendant's conduct rather than its *type*, and attempts to deduce general principles in this area are largely confined to an even shorter period, namely the last half-century.

Dictionary definitions of negligence tend to speak in terms of 'want of proper care and attention' or 'carelessness', thus stressing the mental element involved. As we shall see, however, the law of tort is concerned rather with negligence *as conduct*. A man is considered to be negligent whenever his conduct falls below the standard which is set by the law, usually that of the 'reasonable man'. Thus (and it is vital that this be appreciated from the outset) a person may be held guilty of negligence in circumstances where he personally could not possibly have avoided causing the damage in question (for example, because he was not sufficiently intelligent to appreciate the risks inherent in his conduct, or because he could not afford to take the necessary steps to avert the danger). In this sense of conduct which is not up to par, negligence may be either a tort in itself or a mode of committing various other torts, such as trespass or nuisance, which do not require a plaintiff to establish that the defendant positively intended to cause him harm.

19.2 As an independent tort, negligence may be defined as the breach of a legal duty to take care, owed by the defendant to the plaintiff, which results in damage to the plaintiff. There are thus three elements of liability, each of which must be proved by the plaintiff if his action is to succeed:

a. a duty of care owed by the defendant to the plaintiff;

b. breach by the defendant of his duty;

c. damage to the plaintiff which is caused by the defendant's breach.

At first sight, this definition appears almost limitless in scope, at least in comparison with other torts, which tend to be restricted to a particular factual situation, such as *Rylands v Fletcher*,[1] or to protect only one interest of the plaintiff, such as libel and slander.[2] However, the law does not suggest that a person should always and in all circumstances be liable for all the consequences of his carelessness; such a burden would, it is thought, be an intolerably heavy one. The problem, therefore, is one of exclusion, and two of the elements of liability mentioned above are used by the courts to keep the tort of negligence within reasonable bounds. In the first place, however careless a defendant may have been, he is not legally liable to the plaintiff unless he owed him a legal *duty* to be careful. Second, even where the defendant is in breach of a duty of care, certain of the consequences of his breach are regarded by the courts as *too remote* to be actionable in law.[3]

1 Paras 27.2 to 27.13 below
2 Paras 29.16 to 29.24 below.
3 Remoteness of damage is dealt with in ch 21 below.

Duty of care

19.3 We have already noted that not all careless conduct of the defendant is of legal relevance, but only that which occurs when the defendant is under a duty to take care. This emphasis on duty is perhaps best understood from a historical perspective. Most legal systems find it easier to prohibit persons from positively causing harm than to make them take steps to prevent it from occurring. In its early days, the common law had quite enough to contend with in the field of intentional wrongdoing; its excursions into areas of unintended harm concerned mainly the subject matter of existing torts, such as trespass or nuisance. Later, when the law began to create positive obligations to take care, it did so in the context of various relationships whose common feature was that one party reasonably relied on the other to exercise the care and skill appropriate to his trade or profession; in this way liability for negligence was imposed upon the 'common callings' such as innkeepers, surgeons and attorneys, all of whom were said to owe a duty of care.

19.4 At about the time of the Industrial Revolution, the scope of negligence as a basis of legal liability increased dramatically, and it spread into areas where the 'relationship' between the parties was far more tenuous than in the case of the 'common callings', for example between one highway user and another. No doubt there was a general underlying feeling that a person *ought* to be liable simply because he unreasonably caused harm to another; the language of the law, however, continued to be that of 'duty'. A plaintiff who wished to sue in negligence was required either to show that his case fell within an existing category of duty, or to persuade the court that a new duty should be recognised to cover it. As a result, it has been said, this area of law was built up in 'disconnected slabs', as new duties were created to cover more situations.

Donoghue v Stevenson

19.5 The idea of 'duty of care' served a very useful practical purpose in the formative period of negligence as a tort, for it enabled the courts to exclude certain classes of plaintiff who were regarded as unmeritorious, such as trespassers, and certain types of injury which were not thought important enough to deserve protection, such as where the plaintiff's loss was purely financial. Conceptually, however, it was unsatisfactory, since there appeared to be no general principle underlying a judge's decision of 'duty' or 'no duty'. An attempt to deduce such a general principle was eventually made in 1932 in the leading case of *Donoghue v Stevenson*.[1] The facts of that case were that the appellant was treated by a friend, in a café, to a bottle of ginger beer manufactured by the respondents. Having poured out and drunk part of the contents, the appellant discovered that the bottle contained a partially decomposed snail; this discovery, she claimed, caused her severe nervous shock and (later) an attack of gastroenteritis. Since the appellant had no contract with the proprietor of the café, she sued the manufacturers of the ginger beer, who argued that their duty in respect of products was owed only to those to whom they sold them. In rejecting this argument, a majority of the House of Lords laid down that, in normal circumstances, a manufacturer owes a duty of care to the ultimate consumer of his products, notwithstanding the absence of any contractual relationship between them. In short, whatever else it may have done, *Donoghue v Stevenson* undoubtedly added a new duty to the existing list.

1 [1932] AC 562, HL.

19.6 The main importance of *Donoghue v Stevenson* for present purposes, however, lies in the speech of Lord Atkin, in which an attempt was made to formulate a *general* test for ascertaining whether or not a relationship is sufficient to found a duty of care. Having pointed out that 'the rule that you are to love your neighbour becomes, in law, you must not injure your neighbour', Lord Atkin went on to consider the 'duty' question in these terms: 'Who, then, in law is my neighbour? The answer seems to be— persons who are so closely and directly affected by my act that I ought reasonably to have them in contemplation as being so affected when I am directing my mind to the acts or omissions which are called in question.'

If taken at face value, this approach would impose a duty of care upon a defendant whenever he ought reasonably to have foreseen injury, loss or damage to the plaintiff. This is manifestly not the real position for, as was recognised by Lord Reid in *Home Office v Dorset Yacht Co Ltd*,[1] there are a number of areas in which the question 'duty or not?' depends, not upon some purely mechanical test, but upon wider considerations of public policy. Nonetheless, Lord Atkin's 'foreseeability' test still has an important part to play in determining whether or not a duty of care exists, as we now explain.

1 [1970] AC 1004 at 1027, [1970] 2 All ER 294 at 297, HL.

Anns v Merton London Borough Council
19.7 The most important and influential judicial analysis of the 'duty of care' question in recent years is that which was carried out by Lord Wilberforce in *Anns v Merton London Borough Council*.[1] In his speech in this case, the learned judge made it clear that there is no 'closed list' of duty-situations, so that the success of a plaintiff's action does not necessarily depend upon proof that it falls within the facts of a previous case. The task of the judge faced with a novel type of claim has rather to be tackled in two stages. 'First one has to ask whether, as between the alleged wrongdoer and the person who has suffered damage there is a sufficient relationship of proximity or neighbourhood such that, in the reasonable contemplation of the former, carelessness on his part may be likely to cause damage to the

latter, in which case a prima facie duty of care arises. Second, if the first question is answered affirmatively, it is necessary to consider whether there are any considerations which ought to negative, or to reduce or limit the scope of the duty or the class of persons to whom it is owed or the damages to which a breach of it may give rise.'

1   [1978] AC 728 at 751, [1977] 2 All ER 492 at 498, HL.

19.8   Today, a trial judge who is asked to extend the tort of negligence into a new area will almost invariably adopt the two-stage approach to the case suggested by Lord Wilberforce. 'Proximity' is a word which figures prominently in modern cases and, as a result, the part played by 'foreseeability' in deciding whether or not a duty of care exists is not as critical as was once thought. However, it should not be overlooked that, in one sense at least, foreseeability is crucial—if it is *not* foreseeable to the defendant that the plaintiff may suffer damage, then no considerations of policy can justify the imposition of a duty of care upon him. In short, foreseeability undeniably operates as an *exclusionary* test for the existence of a duty of care.

This point may be illustrated by the famous case of *Bourhill v Young*[1] in which a motor cyclist carelessly collided with a car and was killed. An action was brought against his estate by a woman who suffered nervous shock as a result of hearing the crash while alighting from a tram and, later, seeing a pool of blood on the road. It was held by the House of Lords that, since it was not foreseeable that she would suffer injury of any kind (either by impact or through shock alone), no duty of care was owed to her and she could not recover damages.

1   [1943] AC 92, [1942] 2 All ER 396, HL.

19.9   It must be admitted that, in practice, the courts in recent years have tended to emphasise the first stage of Lord Wilberforce's test rather than the second. Thus, where the defendant ought to have foreseen some injury to the plaintiff, he is unlikely to convince a court that policy considerations justify not imposing a duty of care upon him. The questions of whether the defendant ought to have foreseen the *type* of injury caused, or the *manner* in which it was inflicted, are dealt with under the heading of 'remoteness of damage' in paras 21.18 and 21.19 below.

19.10   For the remainder of this chapter we shall consider a number of important areas in which, for one reason or another, the existence or non-existence of a duty of care cannot be dealt with simply on the basis of what the defendant ought to have foreseen. In some of these cases, as we shall show later, there is no duty at all; in others, there is a duty but it is artificially restricted in some way.

Negligent statements

Physical injury

19.11   There is no reason in principle for drawing a distinction between physical damage which is caused by negligent acts and that which is caused by negligent words, although judges have from time to time expressed concern at the enormous scope of liability to which the latter might give rise. A favourite example (which fortunately remains hypothetical) is that of a marine hydrographer who, by negligently stating incorrectly the position of a particular rock, might be held liable for the loss of an ocean liner and all that it contains. However, notwithstanding these misgivings, it seems safe to say that, in relation to injury to the person or to property, the law does not distinguish between acts and words. In *Sharp v Avery*,[1] the defendant, a motor cyclist, offered to lead a second motor cycle, on which the plaintiff was a passenger, along a road which the defendant claimed to know. When the defendant went off the road at a bend and drove on to a piece of waste ground, the second motor cycle followed, and the plaintiff fell off and was injured. The Court of Appeal held that the defendant had assumed a duty of care towards the plaintiff, by his assurance that he knew the way and might safely be followed.

1 [1938] 4 All ER 85, CA.

Financial loss

19.12 Where the effect of a defendant's negligent words is simply to cause *financial* loss to the plaintiff, the legal position is more complicated; two factors in particular have restricted the development of the tort of negligence in this area, so as to prevent the imposition of a test based purely on foreseeability. In the first place, the realisation that words may be used over and over again, reaching unsuspected audiences without losing their power, has led to fears that a single slip might expose a defendant to unlimited liability. Second, there has undoubtedly been a feeling underlying many of the decisions that the right to complain of financial loss suffered through following a person's advice should be restricted to those who have paid for the advice and that a professional man should be liable to his client but to no-one else. By contrast, it is generally accepted that a person may expect not to be physically injured by others, whether or not he has paid them.

For some three-quarters of a century the possibility of development in this field was overshadowed by the decision of the House of Lords in *Derry v Peek*,[1] in which it was held that, in the absence of fraud, company directors were not liable for false statements made in a prospectus.[2] In *Candler v Crane, Christmas & Co*,[3] a majority of the Court of Appeal held that the 'neighbour' principle laid down by *Donoghue v Stevenson*[4] made no difference to this situation, so that a duty of care in respect of words was restricted to cases of physical damage, contractual relationships and certain other 'fiduciary' relationships (eg that between trustee and beneficiary) which were recognised by equity.[5]

1 (1889) 14 App Cas 337, HL.
2 The actual decision was immediately reversed by statute; see now Companies Act 1985, ss 67 and 68.
3 [1951] 2 KB 164, [1951] 1 All ER 426, CA.
4 Para 19.6 above.
5 *Nocton v Lord Ashburton* [1914] AC 932, HL.

19.13 *Hedley Byrne v Heller* The breakthrough, in the sense of recognition by the courts that the law of tort might give a remedy in the case of negligent statements causing financial loss, finally came with the decision of the House of Lords in the leading case of *Hedley Byrne & Co Ltd v Heller & Partners Ltd*.[1] The plaintiffs, a firm of advertising agents, were asked to arrange advertising space on behalf of Easipower, a client. Since, in accordance with trade practice, the plaintiffs would incur personal responsibility for paying for this space, they asked their bankers to check on Easipower's credit-worthiness. An enquiry was made of the defendants, who were Easipower's bankers and financial backers, and they replied 'without responsibility' that Easipower was 'a respectably constituted company, considered good for its ordinary business engagements'. Relying on this reference, the plaintiffs went ahead with the contracts; when, shortly afterwards Easipower became insolvent, the plaintiffs lost some £17,000. It was held, at first instance and in the Court of Appeal, that the defendants were not liable because, although they had been careless, they did not owe the plaintiffs any duty of care.

On appeal, the House of Lords held that the disclaimer ('without responsibility') prevented a duty from arising in the present case.[2] However, after an exhaustive review of the authorities, it was laid down that in an appropriate case a duty could arise. As to what would be an 'appropriate case', the test could not, it was said, be simply that of foreseeability, for this would impose an unacceptably heavy burden upon professional advisers. What was required was evidence of a 'special relationship' between the parties, arising out of an *assumption of responsibility* by the defendant.

The circumstances in which a court might expect to find a 'special relationship' and, with it, a duty of care were the subject of a wide range of opinions in the House of Lords; Lord Devlin, for example, took the narrow view that only a relationship which was 'equivalent to contract' would suffice. This apparently means that all the elements of a contract are present in the relationship, with the exception of consideration. It seems, however, that the decision may support a wider principle, namely, that a duty of care will arise whenever the defendant realises or ought to realise that his skill and care are being relied upon, provided both that there is such reliance and that the reliance is reasonable in the circumstances. Thus, for example, it is highly unlikely that a person would be held liable in respect of words casually uttered on a social occasion, and it may be that the defendant must be shown to have given the advice with a particular transaction in mind.[3] Further, it has recently been held that, where the information or advice is not specifically requested, as where it is contained in advertisements published by a manufacturer, the mere fact that a person may be expected to rely on it is not sufficient to establish a 'special relationship'.[4]

1 [1964] AC 465, [1963] 2 All ER 575, HL.
2 Such a disclaimer would now, at least in business circumstances, probably be subject to the provisions of the Unfair Contract Terms Act 1977; paras 9.41–9.53 above.
3 *Candler v Crane, Christmas & Co* [1951] 2 KB 164 at 183–184, [1951] 1 All ER 426 at 435, CA.
4 *Lambert v Lewis* [1982] AC 225, [1980] 1 All ER 978, CA. This point was not raised on appeal to the House of Lords.

19.14 *Hedley Byrne v Heller* was undoubtedly a decision of major importance in expanding the frontiers of negligence, and subsequent courts have by and large adopted a liberal approach in basing new duties upon this broad principle. A striking exception, however, is the decision of the Privy Council in *Mutual Life and Citizens Assurance Co v Evatt*,[1] in which a policyholder in the defendant company asked for advice as to the financial stability of an associated company, in which he had invested money. The

Australian courts regarded this as a 'special relationship', but a bare majority of the Privy Council held that, in the absence of an express undertaking to use care, a duty of care would only arise if *either* the defendant had a direct financial interest in the transaction on which he was advising[2] *or* the advice given was of a type which the defendant was in business to give. It should be noted, however, that, in a strong dissent, Lords Reid and Morris (both of whom had sat in *Hedley Byrne v Heller*) thought that a person giving advice outside the scope of his business or profession should still owe a duty of care, although the standard demanded of him might well be lower.

The logic involved in exempting an 'amateur' from any duty of care at all seems highly suspect, and it is perhaps not surprising that the Court of Appeal has twice expressed a preference for the reasoning of the minority in *Evatt's* case.[3]

The limits of the *Hedley Byrne* doctrine were further explored in the case of *Argy Trading Development Co Ltd v Lapid Developments Ltd.*[4] A lease of part of a warehouse placed the obligation to insure against fire upon the tenants; in fact, however, the landlords had a block policy which covered the whole building, so the tenants simply paid the landlords a proportionate part of the premiums. Some time later the landlords allowed the policy to lapse without telling the tenants, who consequently found themselves uninsured when fire gutted the building. In an action for negligence it was held that, although the relationship between the parties was such that the landlords owed the tenants a duty of care, this merely meant that they must not give inaccurate information as to the insurance position *at the time*; they were under no positive duty to notify the tenants of a change of circumstances.

Recent cases tend to indicate that the idea of *Hedley Byrne* as resting upon a duty restricted to 'special relationships' may be a thing of the past. Both the High Court[5] and the Court of Appeal[6] have held advisers liable in negligence to non-clients where, in truth, little more could be said than that reliance by the plaintiff on their advice, and his consequent loss, were foreseeable. In each case the court found a relationship of sufficient 'proximity' to justify the imposition of a duty of care.

As a pointer to the future development of this area of law, it is worth mentioning a recent decision of the New Zealand Court of Appeal in which two government ministers were held liable for negligently giving *assurances* that a company would receive financial support from the state in setting up industries in an underdeveloped area.[7] If this principle were to become established, it could lead to liability in tort wherever a promise was negligently given (and then left unfulfilled). This would be tantamount to enforcing a promise for which the plaintiff had given no consideration, something which would undermine an important principle of the law of contract.[8]

1 [1971] AC 793, [1971] 1 All ER 150, PC.
2 As in *Anderson (WB) & Sons Ltd v Rhodes (Liverpool) Ltd* [1967] 2 All ER 850.
3 *Esso Petroleum Co Ltd v Mardon* [1976] QB 801, [1976] 2 All ER 5, CA; *Howard Marine and Dredging Co Ltd v A Ogden & Sons (Excavations) Ltd* [1978] QB 574, [1978] 2 All ER 1134, CA.
4 [1977] 3 All ER 785, [1977] 1 WLR 444.
5 *Yianni v Edwin Evans & Sons* [1982] QB 438, [1981] 3 All ER 592.
6 *JEB Fastners Ltd v Marks Bloom & Co* [1983] 1 All ER 583, CA.
7 *Meates v A-G* [1983] NZLR 308.

8   See paras 6.3 to 6.22 above.

19.15   We suggested above that the Privy Council's attempt in *Mutual Life* to restrict liability to professional advisers is incorrect. Nonetheless, there is no doubt that the greatest impact of *Hedley Byrne v Heller* has been felt in the professional sphere, mainly because in this context reliance by a person upon advice given to him by another is most likely to be judged 'reasonable'.

Of the various advisers who have been held to owe a duty of care to persons other than their clients, we may take five examples. In *Computastaff Ltd v Ingledew Brown Bennison and Garrett,*[1] an estate agent employed by a landlord of office property was held to owe a duty of care to a prospective tenant in respect of information about the property which the agent passed on. In *Singer and Friedlander Ltd v John D Wood & Co,*[2] valuers making a valuation of development land were held to owe a duty of care, not only to the developers (who paid their fee), but also to the merchant bank which advanced money to the developers in reliance on the valuation. In *Yianni v Edwin Evans & Sons,*[3] a valuer instructed by a building society to value a house for mortgage purposes was held to owe a duty of care to the house-buyer. In *JEB Fastners Ltd v Marks Bloom & Co,*[4] accountants preparing a set of company accounts were held to owe a duty of care to a potential investor, to whom the accountants realised the accounts were likely to be shown. And in *Ross v Caunters,*[5] a solicitor who drafted his client's will was held to owe a duty of care to those who were intended to benefit under the will. This last case is especially interesting in that liability was imposed upon the solicitor, even though it could not be said that the beneficiaries had 'relied' upon any 'advice' which he had given.

1   (1983) 268 Estates Gazette 906.
2   (1977) 243 Estates Gazette 212.
3   [1982] QB 438, [1981] 3 All ER 592.
4   [1983] 1 All ER 583, CA.
5   [1980] Ch 297, [1979] 3 All ER 580.

Smith v Bush

19.16   *Contract and tort* Hedley Byrne v Heller has naturally been of the greatest importance to persons who, because they were in no contractual relationship with an adviser, would previously have been unable to sue him. A less obvious result of the decision, however, has been to improve the lot of *clients* adversely affected by a professional adviser's negligence. Such persons were, of course, already owed a *contractual* duty of care and skill but, in certain circumstances, this might be of less value to them than if the duty arose in tort. In particular, the rules governing limitation of actions (that is the period within which the plaintiff must issue his writ) are often more favourable in tort.[1] The question which fell to be decided after 1964 was whether, in such a case, the client might choose to frame his cause of action in tort.

Suggestions were made in a number of cases to the effect that a professional man causing financial loss to his client could only be sued in contract, but this reasoning seemed inconsistent with the decision of the Court of Appeal, in *Esso Petroleum Co Ltd v Mardon,*[2] that a statement made during pre-contractual negotiations could be sued upon both as a misrepresentation (contractual) and in negligence (tortious). Accordingly, in *Batty v Metropolitan Property Realisations Ltd,*[3] it was held by the Court of Appeal that a property developer who negligently arranged for a house to be built on unstable land was liable to the purchaser in both contract and tort.

The relationship between an adviser and his client was exhaustively analysed by Oliver J, in *Midland Bank Trust Co Ltd v Hett, Stubbs and Kemp*,[4] where a solicitor's negligent failure to register an option on behalf of a client rendered it unenforceable. It was argued for the solicitor that his liability was purely contractual and that, since his failure to register the option had taken place more than six years before the issue of a writ against him, the client's action was statute-barred. It was held, however, that the client was entitled to claim in tort, thereby obtaining the benefit of more generous limitation rules (in this case, the period began to run only when damage was done, ie when the option became unenforceable because the land was sold).

The present legal position has been rendered rather unclear by certain dicta of the Privy Council in *Tai Hing Cotton Mill Ltd v Liu Chong Hing Bank Ltd*.[5] Taken literally these dicta would mean that a client's rights are now governed exclusively by his contract with his professional adviser and that an action in tort for negligence is not possible. However, as stated above,[6] we believe that a narrower interpretation is the correct one.

1 See chs 11 above and 31 below.
2 [1976] QB 801, [1976] 2 All ER 5, CA.
3 [1978] QB 554, [1978] 2 All ER 445, CA.
4 [1979] Ch 384, [1978] 3 All ER 571.
5 [1985] 2 All ER 947 at 957, PC.
6 Para 18.5 above.

19.17 *Statutory powers* Apart from its main effect of imposing liability upon those who make statements as such, *Hedley Byrne v Heller* has also been relied upon by the courts in holding that public bodies such as local authorities, in the exercise of certain statutory powers, may owe a duty of care to persons adversely affected. Indeed, this area of liability has been developed in a way which goes beyond the original *Hedley Byrne* formula. In *Ministry of Housing and Local Government v Sharp*,[1] for example, a clerk employed at a local land registry negligently issued a 'clear' certificate of search to the prospective purchaser of a plot of land; as a result, the plaintiffs' charge over that land became unenforceable. It was held that the clerk owed a duty of care to the plaintiffs notwithstanding that (a) they had not *requested* the information concerned, and (b) the clerk had not *voluntarily* assumed responsibility but had acted under a statutory duty. Similarly, in *Anns v Merton London Borough Council*,[2] it was held that a local authority building inspector owed a duty of care to the future occupiers of a building which he inspected and that, if expensive repairs were to become necessary because of defective foundations which he failed to notice, he and his employers would be liable to compensate the occupiers for the cost of carrying these out.

Recent years have seen a marked increase in negligence actions against local authorities and other public bodies, arising out of the performance of their statutory functions. In *Fellowes v Rother District Council*,[3] it was suggested that such an action can only succeed where the plaintiff can satisfy the court:

a. that the act complained of was not within the limits of a discretion bona fide exercised under the relevant power. For instance, a decision to promote widespread vaccination against whooping cough would lie within this area of discretion and could not therefore be challenged in negligence;[4]

b. that having regard to all the circumstances, including the legislation creating the relevant power, there was sufficient proximity to create a duty of care on the defendant and no policy ground for negating or reducing such duty of care. For example, policy would negative a claim by a property developer, who builds in breach of the building regulations, that the building inspector owed him a duty of care to prevent him from so doing;[5] and

c. that it was reasonably foreseeable by the defendant, or by those for whom he was vicariously responsible, that the act complained of was likely to cause damage of the type actually suffered by the plaintiff.

1 [1970] 2 QB 223, [1970] 1 All ER 1009, CA.
2 [1978] AC 728, [1977] 2 All ER 492, HL.
3 [1983] 1 All ER 513 at 522.
4 *Department of Health and Social Security v Kinnear* (1984) Times, 7 July.
5 *Governors of the Peabody Donation Fund v Sir Lindsay Parkinson & Co Ltd* [1985] AC 210, [1984] 3 All ER 529, HL.

Judicial process

19.18 Despite the tremendous expansion in liability for negligent state-ments which has taken place since 1964, certain areas remain unaffected. For example, it is well settled that judges, barristers, solicitors, jurors and witnesses enjoy an absolute immunity from any form of civil action being brought against them in respect of anything they say or do in court during the course of a trial. However, immunity is not conferred upon everyone connected with legal proceedings. A sequestrator, for example, owes a duty of care to the owner of property which he administers, notwithstanding that he is acting as an officer of the court.[1]

We now consider some of the effects of this rule.

1 *I R C v Hoogstraten* [1984] 3 All ER 25, [1984] 3 WLR 933, CA.

Barristers

19.19 When professional men were liable for negligence in contract alone, it was not possible for an action to be brought against a barrister, for it had long been established that there was no contractual relationship between a barrister and his client. When *Hedley Byrne v Heller* opened up the possibility of an action in tort, therefore, the question of the barrister's immunity arose for re-examination, and this was carried out by the House of Lords in *Rondel v Worsley*,[1] where the plaintiff, who had been sentenced to 18 months' imprisonment for causing grievous bodily harm, sought to claim damages for negligence from the barrister who had unsuccessfully defended him on that occasion. The House of Lords unanimously held that, on grounds of public policy, no action would lie against a barrister for negligence in the conduct of a case in court. The reasons given for this continued immunity (which, it was said, is quite unconnected with the absence of a contractual relationship) were that a barrister's *primary* duty lies, not to his client, but to the court to secure the true administration of justice (which may compel him, on occasion, to disclose matters unfavourable to his case); that a barrister, unlike a solicitor, cannot pick and choose his clients, but must act for anyone, however offensive, who pays his fee; and that there must at some point be an end to litigation (and an action against a barrister would always necessitate to some extent a retrial of the original case).

It is important to note that the immunity conferred by *Rondel v Worsley* does not extend to those aspects of a barrister's work which are unconnected with the conduct of a case in court; in drafting documents, for example, or in giving an opinion on a point of law, a duty of care in tort is owed to the client. On the other hand, the immunity which covers his work in connection with litigation does not stop short at the door of the courtroom; it applies also to certain pre-trial work. The test, according to a majority of the House of Lords in *Saif Ali v Sydney Mitchell & Co*,[2] is whether the particular work is so intimately connected with the conduct of the cause in court that it can fairly be said to be a preliminary decision affecting the way that cause is to be conducted when it comes to a hearing.

1 [1969] 1 AC 191, [1967] 3 All ER 993, HL.
2 [1980] AC 198, [1978] 3 All ER 1033, HL.

Solicitors
19.20 In both *Rondel v Worsley* and *Saif Ali v Sydney Mitchell & Co*, the view was expressed by a majority of the House of Lords that, where a solicitor is acting in court as an advocate, he is entitled to the same immunity as a barrister from an action in negligence. Beyond this, however, a solicitor undoubtedly owes a duty of care and, as we have seen, it appears that he may be liable to his client in both contract and tort[1] and to third parties in tort.[2]

1 *Midland Bank Trust Co Ltd v Hett, Stubbs and Kemp* [1979] Ch 384, [1978] 3 All ER 571; para 19.16 above.
2 *Ross v Caunters* [1980] Ch 297, [1979] 3 All ER 580; para 19.15 above.

Arbitrators and valuers
19.21 The undoubted immunity of judges[1] has been extended to certain other persons who exercise a judicial or quasi-judicial function. It was for a long time thought that, as well as arbitrators, this protection covered persons who were merely in the position of arbitrators (ie those who were not formally appointed). Indeed, it was even said that any person determining a question which compelled him to hold the scales fairly between two other persons would be immune from an action in negligence. If correct, this would include any case in which the parties agree to be bound by the decision of a valuer appointed jointly by them both.

Two recent decisions of the House of Lords indicate that the immunity of arbitrators and 'quasi-arbitrators' is not as wide-ranging as had previously been thought, although the present limits are not altogether clear. In *Sutcliffe v Thackrah*,[2] the defendant, an architect, was employed to supervise the construction of a house which was being built for the plaintiff. The defendant negligently certified certain work as having been properly executed, whereupon the plaintiff paid the builders. The work had not in fact been done but the plaintiff was unable to recover his money as the builders had become insolvent, whereupon the plaintiff sued the defendant in negligence. The defendant claimed to be entitled to immunity as a 'quasi-arbitrator' (on the basis that he was deciding a question which affected the parties' rights), but the House of Lords held that this exists only where a person is engaged in settling a specific dispute, present or future. Nor did it matter that, in issuing certificates, the architect owed a duty to the builders to act honestly; this duty, said the House of Lords, in no way conflicted with the duty of care which he owed to his client.

In *Arenson v Casson, Beckman, Rutley & Co*,[3] the plaintiff, on entering his uncle's business, was given a number of shares in the private company which operated it. It was agreed that, if the plaintiff left the business, he would sell the shares to his uncle at whatever the defendants, who were the company's auditors, decided was a fair value. This eventually came to be done, but the plaintiff subsequently complained that the true value of his shares was six times the 'fair value' placed on them by the defendants. The Court of Appeal by a majority held that the defendants owed no duty of care in making this valuation, but their decision was unanimously reversed by the House of Lords, who took the opportunity to consider the general question of 'quasi-arbitrators'. Their Lordships agreed that immunity in this area did not depend simply on whether or not the defendant was formally appointed an arbitrator; indeed, two members of the House of Lords could see no reason in principle why an arbitrator should be immune. What mattered, according to the majority, was whether the defendant was appointed to settle an existing dispute by judicial means, so as to bind the parties by his decision.[4]

Although there is much to be said in theory for linking immunity to function rather than to the formal question of whether the defendant is an arbitrator or not, it should not be overlooked that a party who is dissatisfied with the result of an arbitration has a limited right of appeal to the courts,[5] and it might therefore be argued that he does not need to be able to sue the arbitrator in negligence. A valuation, on the other hand, does not appear to be open to challenge[6] (at least where the valuer gives no reason for his decision[7]), and to hold the valuer immune would thus be to deprive a dissatisfied party of all remedies.

1 See *Sirros v Moore* [1975] QB 118, [1974] 3 All 776, CA.
2 [1974] AC 727, [1974] 1 All ER 859, HL.
3 [1977] AC 405, [1975] 3 All ER 901, HL.
4 See *Palacath Ltd v Flanagan* [1985] 2 All ER 161 for the position of a surveyor determining a rent under a rent review.
5 Para 2.45 above.
6 *Campbell v Edwards* [1976] 1 All ER 785, [1976] 1 WLR 403, CA (valuer appointed jointly by landlord and tenant to fix the surrender value of the lease).
7 A 'speaking' valuation containing an error of law on its face may be challenged: *Burgess v Purchase & Sons (Farms) Ltd* [1983] Ch 216, [1983] 2 All ER 4.

Economic loss

19.22 Where a person suffers physical injury, or where property in which he has an interest is damaged, any action in negligence which he brings will, if successful, entitle him to damages for the financial consequences (e g loss of earnings in the case of personal injury, the cost of repairing goods, etc). As a general rule, however, no damages may be recovered for *pure* economic or financial loss, even where this is foreseeable, which results from the defendant's negligence. In *Cattle v Stockton Waterworks Co*,[1] the plaintiff was employed under a fixed-price contract to build a tunnel through an embankment. His costs were greatly increased by water which escaped from the defendants' negligently laid main, and he sued in negligence to recover this loss. It was held that the claim must fail, since no damage had been done to any property of the plaintiff; to allow his action would, the court pointed out, mean opening the door to every employee who had lost wages as a result of the flooding.

The principle that no damages will be awarded for the negligent causing of pure economic loss, which was approved by the House of Lords in *Simpson v Thomson*,[2] has come under attack in recent years as tending to produce results which are both harsh and illogical. Particular criticism has been levelled at the distinction drawn between *pure* economic loss and that which is *consequential* upon property damage; this distinction is often a fine one, as is illustrated by the case of *Spartan Steel and Alloys Ltd v Martin & Co (Contractors) Ltd*.[3] The defendants there negligently severed an electricity cable laid under the highway, thus cutting off power to the plaintiffs' foundry. Molten metal which was passing through a furnace threatened to solidify, which would have damaged both the metal and the furnace, and so the plaintiffs had to incur expense (and damage the metal) in removing it. Furthermore, the loss of power meant that four more 'melts' which were planned could not be carried out, so that the plaintiffs lost their expected profits. The Court of Appeal by a majority held that, while the defendants were liable for the physical damage and consequential loss of profit on the melt which had already been in progress, the inability to go ahead with the other four melts was pure economic loss and was therefore irrecoverable. It should also be noted that, if the metal had solidified in the furnace and production had been held up while it was cleaned out, the loss of profits would have been classed as *consequential* economic loss and thus recoverable.[4]

Despite the criticism of the 'economic loss' rule, the only general inroad which has been made into it is the recognition by the House of Lords in *Hedley Byrne & Co v Heller & Partners Ltd*[5] that an action may lie for economic loss caused by negligent words. However, the courts are showing an increasing awareness of the fact that the cases on pure economic loss fall into different categories and raise different problems, and that it may be inappropriate therefore to treat them all as subject to the same rule. Some of these categories we now consider.

1   (1875) LR 10 QB 453.
2   (1877) 3 App Cas 279, HL.
3   [1973] QB 27, [1972] 3 All ER 557, CA.
4   *SCM (UK) Ltd v WJ Whittall & Son Ltd* [1971] 1 QB 337, [1970] 3 All ER 245, CA.
5   [1964] AC 465, [1963] 2 All ER 575, HL.

Dependent interests
19.23   The *Cattle* and *Spartan Steel* cases mentioned above represent the classic type of pure economic loss case; that in which physical damage to the property of A causes financial loss to B, who was in some way dependent upon it. The main reason why damages are not available in such cases is the judicial fear of opening the floodgates; the financial consequences of a single incident may be felt by a great number of people, and begin to measure the losses which might be caused by a single excavator *& Co v Foot and Mouth Disease Research Institute*,[1] it was held that, while a person whose negligence caused an outbreak of cattle disease would be

liable to farmers who owned the affected cattle, he would not be liable to auctioneers who lost business when the local cattle markets were closed.

The lack of protection which the law gives to such 'dependent interests' is also shown by the case of *Kirkham v Boughey*,[2] where the plaintiff and his wife were both injured in an accident caused by the negligence of the defendant. When the plaintiff recovered from his injuries, he gave up a highly-paid job in order to be near his wife, who was still in hospital. It was held that the plaintiff's loss of earnings resulted, not from his own injuries, but from those of his wife: *his* loss, therefore, was in this respect a purely financial one and thus irrecoverable.

The 'floodgates' argument is nowadays largely discredited, but the position taken by the law in cases such as *Spartan Steel* is also supported by another approach which, if it does not do 'justice' between the parties, at least makes sense in general economic terms. This argument points out that, if an industrialist is unable to sue for lost production when the defendant negligently cuts off the power to his factory, he will insure against the possibility of that loss and pass on the cost of the premium to his customers. Conversely, if the plaintiff *were* allowed to sue, the defendant would have to take out liability insurance against the possibility of *causing* the harm. In terms of efficiency, it is better for the risk to be borne by the factory owner's insurance, since it is easier to quantify. After all, the loss of a day's production may be fairly accurately assessed, but how does one begin to measure the losses which might be caused by a single excavator cutting off power to an industrial estate or even to a whole town?

Rightly or wrongly, courts throughout the Commonwealth have consistently refused protection to dependent interests of the type now under discussion. This makes all the more remarkable the decision of the High Court of Australia in *Caltex Oil (Australia) Pty Ltd v The Dredge 'Willemstad'*.[3] The defendants there negligently fractured a submarine pipeline, owned by an oil refinery company, which was used to transport oil belonging to the plaintiffs from the refinery to their depot. The plaintiffs had no proprietary interest in the pipeline but, while it was out of use, they incurred very heavy costs in transporting their oil by alternative means. The High Court of Australia unanimously held that the defendants were liable in negligence for these costs.

In reaching their decision, the judges ruled that economic loss of this kind can only be recovered where there are 'special factors' present. Here it was held that the physical proximity of the plaintiffs' depot to the pipeline, and the fact that they were in effect engaged in a common business venture with the refinery company, justified the imposition of a duty of care upon the defendants for the plaintiffs' benefit. However, the Privy Council has recently declined to follow the lead of this case in holding that, where a ship is negligently damaged, it is only the owner who can claim damages, and not a 'time charterer', who has a mere contractual right to use the vessel.[4]

1 [1966] 1 QB 569, [1965] 3 All ER 560.
2 [1958] 2 QB 338, [1957] 3 All ER 153.
3 (1976) 136 CLR 529.
4 *Candlewood Navigation Corpn Ltd v Mitsui OSK Lines Ltd* [1985] 2 All ER 935, [1985] 3 WLR 381, PC.

Other cases

19.24 The negligence of A in respect of B or B's property may operate in other ways to inflict economic loss upon C. For example, C may be an insurer who has to compensate B for his damaged property, or an employer who has to continue paying B's wages while he is injured and unable to work. The law has again generally denied recovery in such cases,[1] but change may be in the air. In *Lambert v Lewis*,[2] a driver, who was held liable in negligence for a road accident caused when a trailer became detached from his vehicle, recovered in turn (under what is now the Sale of Goods Act, s14[3]) from the dealer who had sold him the defective towing hitch which was responsible. The dealer could not identify the wholesaler from whom he had bought the hitch, and so sued the manufacturer in tort for negligence. The Court of Appeal held that the retailer's loss was a purely financial one and, on what were described as grounds of common sense, not recoverable. On appeal to the House of Lords, it was held that the retailer was not liable to the driver and thus that he had no reason to sue the manufacturer. However, it was strongly hinted that, if a retailer were held directly liable to a consumer for personal injury (in contrast to the indirect form of liability involved in this case) then he *would* be able to recoup his loss by suing the manufacturer in negligence.

Yet another category of economic loss case is where A negligently damages property which belongs to B at the time that the damage occurs but which is thereafter transferred to C. Assuming that C has paid a price for the property which is based upon its undamaged value, he is the obvious loser in this situation; however, problems arise due to the fact that his loss is classified as economic. It is clear that B can recover damages in such circumstances (although it appears that he must then hand over those damages to C[4]); however, the present weight of authority is against permitting C to recover damages from A in his own right.

This problem arises in slightly different ways depending on whether the property in question is land or goods. In relation to land (or, more specifically, to a building which is defective due to the negligence of A), the damage may occur in an undiscoverable form during the ownership of B, only to be revealed after he has sold the building to C. In such a case, the House of Lords has held that, since a person's right to sue in negligence arises as soon as the damage occurs,[5] it is B and not C who can recover damages in respect of the defect.[6]

In relation to goods, cases have arisen in which cargo in the process of being sold is damaged by negligence for which the carrier is responsible, at a time when that cargo is still owned by the seller but is at the risk of the buyer (in the sense that he must nevertheless pay the full price for it). In *Leigh & Sillavan Ltd v Aliakmon Shipping Co Ltd*,[7] the Court of Appeal by a majority held that the buyer in these circumstances cannot recover damages from the carrier. The majority view in the Court of Appeal was based, not on any fear of opening the floodgates, but rather on the feeling that the carrier should not be made liable beyond what he has positively undertaken. Contracts of carriage usually incorporate exemption and limitation clauses, and it was felt that it would be unjust to allow the buyer to circumvent these by bringing an action in tort. Interestingly, the dissenting judge maintained that the buyer's tort action would itself be subject to any such clauses, on the principle that the buyer should have no greater rights against the carrier than the seller would have done.

---

1   *Simpson v Thomson* (1877) 3 App Cas 279.

2 [1982] AC 225, [1981] 1 All ER 1185, HL.
3 Para 7.18 above.
4 *The Albazero* [1977] AC 774, [1976] 3 All ER 129, HL.
5 *Pirelli General Cable Works Ltd v Oscar Faber & Partners* [1983] 2 AC 1, [1983] 1 All ER 65, HL; para 31.21 below.
6 *GUS Property Management v Littlewoods Mail Order Stores* 1982 SLT 533, HL.
7 [1985] QB 350, [1985] 2 All ER 44, CA.

Defects of quality
19.25   In *Donoghue v Stevenson*[1] it was clearly laid down that a manufacturer of defective goods, who was guilty of a breach of contract vis-à-vis the person to whom he supplied those goods, could at the same time be liable in the tort of negligence to a third party (the consumer) who suffered injury or whose property was damaged. What the House of Lords did *not* decide (and was not asked to consider) was whether a consumer could recover damages from the manufacturer where the goods in question did no actual harm but were simply defective, in the sense of not being of the quality one would normally expect. (This would be classified as pure economic loss, since the consumer would not have received value for money.) It has generally been assumed that such a claim will not succeed, since the question of quality is one to be determined on the basis of *contract* alone and, indeed, judges in those cases where negligent builders have been held liable for the cost of repair have been careful to confine their statements of principle to *dangerous* defects, ie those which threaten the safety of person or property.[2]

Two recent cases suggest that in this area, too, opinions may soon have to be revised. In *Ross v Caunters*,[3] a solicitor who had drawn up his client's will in favour of the plaintiff negligently failed to notice that the plaintiff's husband was one of the witnesses, and that the plaintiff was thereby disqualified from inheriting. In holding the solicitor liable to the plaintiff for her lost legacy, Megarry V-C pointed out that neither the testator nor his estate could sue the solicitor for more than nominal damages, since neither had suffered any loss. Consequently, unless the disappointed beneficiary were allowed to sue, the solicitor's negligence would expose him to no liability at all.

The complaint in *Ross v Caunters* concerned the quality of services; that in *Junior Books Ltd v Veitchi Co Ltd*[4] related to the standard of a product. The plaintiffs there commissioned the construction of a factory and nominated the defendants as sub-contractors to lay a special floor in the main production area. The defendants thereupon made a contract with the main contractors, but had no direct contractual links with the plaintiffs. The floor proved to be defective (though not dangerous) and the plaintiffs brought an action in negligence against the defendants for its replacement cost and certain consequential losses. The House of Lords by a majority held that, on the particular facts of the case (notably the plaintiffs' selection of the defendants, and their reliance upon the latters' skill and judgment), there was sufficient proximity between the parties to raise a duty of care. However, the majority denied that there would be sufficient proximity in a normal case of a manufacturer and a consumer. In accordance with this dictum, the Court of Appeal has since held that a consumer cannot recover damages from a manufacturer in respect of pure economic loss caused by a defective product.[5]

1 [1932] AC 562, HL; para 19.5 above.
2 *Dutton v Bognor Regis U D C* [1972] 1 QB 373, [1972] 1 All ER 462, CA; *Anns v Merton*

London Borough Council [1978] AC 728, [1977] 2 All ER 492, HL; para 23.26 below.
3 [1980] Ch 297, [1979] 3 All ER 580.
4 [1983] 1 AC 520, [1982] 3 All ER 201, HL.
5 *Muirhead v Industrial Tank Specialities Ltd* [1985] 3 All ER 705, [1985] 3 WLR 993, CA.

19.26 The two cases discussed above raise formidable problems, both theoretical and practical, for the law. As to theory, the fact that the defendant's negligence toward A is measured by the terms of his contract with B means that, in effect, A is suing for the breach of a contract to which he is not a party. This of course is contrary to the doctrine of privity of contract,[1] a point expressly acknowledged by Walton J in *Balsamo v Medici*.[2] A principal there sought to sue his sub-agent in negligence for having lost a sum of money with which he had been entrusted. The sub-agent was clearly guilty of negligence and would have been liable to the main agent; however, the learned judge held that to permit the *principal* to sue would abrogate the doctrine of privity altogether, something which he was not prepared to allow.

In practical terms, difficulties arise in the *Junior Books* type of case where either the main contract or the sub-contract contains an exemption clause. Can a client who brings a direct action against the sub-contractor in tort for negligence be permitted to outflank such restrictions upon liability? In *Southern Water Authority v Carey*,[3] it was held that an exemption clause in the *main* contract sufficed to show that there was no 'proximity', and therefore no duty of care, between client and sub-contractor. In *Leigh & Sillavan Ltd v Aliakmon Shipping Co Ltd*,[4] the dissenting judge, Goff LJ, thought that the client's claim would also be subject to any relevant clauses in the *sub-contract* (the overriding principle being that the sub-contractor should be no worse off against the client than he would have been against the main contractor). However, the majority of the Court of Appeal held that a tort action could not be restricted in this way and, indeed, this was one of their main reasons for holding that no action in negligence could be brought.

1 See paras 6.23 to 6.31 above.
2 [1984] 2 All ER 304, [1984] 1 WLR 951.
3 [1985] 2 All ER 1077.
4 [1985] QB 350, [1985] 2 All ER 44, CA; para 19.24 above.

Omissions
19.27 Most simple definitions of negligence draw no distinction between a defendant's acts and his omissions; in either case, it is said, he is responsible for the foreseeable consequences. It is undoubtedly true that an admitted duty of care is as frequently broken by omission as by positive conduct (where a motorist fails to give a signal, for example, or a valuer does not check his figures). However, cases in which the duty of care itself consists of an obligation to take positive action are highly infrequent. It has, for example, often been said that, in the absence of a prior legal relationship, there will be no liability involved in watching a blind man walk over a cliff edge, or a child drown in shallow water. So reluctant, indeed, is the common law to impose affirmative duties where there is not already a legal relationship between the parties that it has adopted the logical consequence that a person who would not be liable for failing to act at all is equally not

liable for acting negligently, provided that he does not thereby make the plaintiff's position worse. In *East Suffolk Rivers Catchment Board v Kent*,[1] the plaintiff's farm was flooded by the bursting of a sea wall. The defendants, who had a statutory power (but no statutory duty) to repair the wall, adopted such inefficient methods of doing so that the land remained under water for an unnecessarily long time. Despite a strong dissent from Lord Atkin, the House of Lords held that the defendants were not liable in negligence, for they had not created any new source of loss to the plaintiff, but had simply failed to reduce a loss which had already occurred and for which they were not responsible.

1 [1941] AC 74, [1940] 1 All ER 527, HL.

19.28 Lying at the root of the law's refusal to impose liability for pure omissions is the traditional view that, while every man should be protected against being positively harmed by his neighbour, he should not be entitled to demand benefits from that neighbour unless he has paid for them. As a result, positive duties are normally excluded from the sphere of tort and assigned to that of contract, with the latter's requirement of consideration.[1] It may be that it takes a more sophisticated (and more affluent) society to translate humanitarian ideals into legal obligations; whatever the reason, there is no doubt that the old rule of no liability for nonfeasance is today under attack from several directions. It has, for example, been suggested that a person who, by starting to rescue the plaintiff from danger, induces other would-be rescuers to give up their attempts, places himself under a legal duty to carry through what he has begun.

The courts today are fairly willing to find that there is already a sufficient relationship between the plaintiff and the defendant to found a duty of care, so that the defendant's failure to act may be treated as a mere breach of that duty. In *Goldman v Hargrave*,[2] for example, a tall redgum tree on the defendant's land caught fire after being struck by lightning. The defendant could not of course be blamed for this, but he was held liable in negligence for leaving the fire to burn itself out, with the result that it spread to the plaintiff's land. In *Barnett v Chelsea and Kensington Hospital Management Committee*,[3] the plaintiff's husband went to the casualty department of a hospital, complaining of vomiting and violent stomach pains; the doctor on duty, who was himself feeling unwell, refused to examine him. In an action against the hospital authority for negligence[4] it was held that a duty of care was owed; the question was left open whether the hospital might lawfully have closed its doors altogether.

A striking example of the more liberal approach adopted by modern courts is to be found in the Canadian case of *Horsley v Maclaren, The Ogopogo*,[5] where a guest on board a private boat fell into an icy lake and drowned. Following an abortive rescue attempt by the boat owner, a second passenger dived in to attempt a rescue but he, too, was drowned. The Supreme Court held, first, that the owner of the boat owed a positive duty to his guests to rescue them from the perils of the voyage (even where he was not at fault) and, second, that he owed a duty of care to other potential rescuers not to make such an incompetent rescue attempt that they would be led to put themselves in danger.

1 Paras 6.3 to 6.22 above.
2 [1967] 1 AC 645, [1966] 2 All ER 989, PC.
3 [1969] 1 QB 428, [1968] 1 All ER 1068.

4   Which failed on the ground of causation; see para 21.3 below.
5   [1971] 2 Lloyd's Rep 410.

19.29   The idea propounded in *East Suffolk Rivers Catchment Board v Kent*[1] that, if there is no duty to act at all, there can be no duty to act carefully, received close attention from the House of Lords in the case of *Anns v Merton London Borough Council*,[2] in which the purchasers of flats sued the local authority, alleging that their building inspector had negligently failed to notice that the foundations were defective. The defendants argued that, while they had a statutory *power* to carry out building inspections, they were not under any *duty* to do so, and could not therefore be held liable if inspections were carried out carelessly. The House of Lords, pointing out that the *East Suffolk* case was decided before the idea of a general duty of care had gained widespread approval, said that, although a local authority was not bound to conduct building inspections, it *was* bound to decide, responsibly and after due consideration, whether or not to have them. As a result, the *East Suffolk* 'rule' in no way prevented a duty of care in carrying out inspections from arising out of the present facts.

The present state of the law regarding omissions is not easy to summarise. However, it may well be that, while a pure omission can still not be made the basis of liability in negligence, the courts will prove increasingly ready to find that a defendant has, by his conduct, voluntarily undertaken a duty of care (which can then be breached by an omission).

1   [1941] AC 74, [1940] 3 All ER 527, HL; para 19.27 above.
2   [1978] AC 728, [1977] 2 All ER 492, HL.

Damage caused by third parties
19.30   The general principle of non-liability for an omission to act finds specific expression in the rule that, in the absence of special circumstances, the defendant is not to be held responsible for harm deliberately done to the plaintiff by an independent third party, even where such harm is foreseeable. Thus, in *Deyong v Shenburn*,[1] where an actor's clothes were stolen from his dressing-room, it was held that he could not sue the management of the theatre in respect of the admittedly inadequate security precautions. Similarly, in *Moorgate Mercantile Co Ltd v Twitchings*,[2] where a finance company carelessly failed to register a hire purchase agreement concerning a car, it was held by a majority of the House of Lords that the company owed no duty of care to future purchasers; they were accordingly not liable when the hire purchaser, fraudulently concealing the existence of the agreement, 'sold' the vehicle to a dealer. Again in *Perl (P) (Exporters) Ltd v Camden London Borough Council*,[3] where a dilapidated and insecure building owned by the defendants was used by thieves to gain access to the plaintiffs' adjoining shop, the defendants were held not liable for the theft, even though it was a foreseeable consequence of the state of their property.

1   [1946] KB 227, [1946] 1 All ER 226.
2   [1977] AC 890, [1976] 2 All ER 641, HL.
3   [1984] QB 342, [1983] 3 All ER 161, CA. See also *Lamb v Camden London Borough Council* [1981] QB 625, [1981] 2 All ER 408, CA. Cf. *Ward v Cannock Chase District Council* [1985] 3 All ER 537.

19.31   The cases in which the courts have found reason to depart from the above rule, and to hold a defendant liable in negligence to the plaintiff for harm deliberately caused by a third party, fall into two main groups. First, there are those in which some relationship exists between the defendant and the *plaintiff*, such that the plaintiff may reasonably expect to be given some protection. For example, an employer may be liable for exposing his employee to injury in a foreseeable wages snatch,[1] and a decorator working alone in a client's house may be liable for a theft which occurs when he leaves it empty and unlocked.[2] Second, there are those in which some relationship exists between the defendant and the *third party*, such that it is reasonable to expect the defendant to control him. For example, an institution which assumes control of a potentially dangerous person such as a violent lunatic[3] or a borstal inmate[4] may be liable for negligently permitting its charge to escape and cause damage.

Whether a duty of care can arise in cases which do not fall into either of these categories is not yet settled, although there have been suggestions that this may occur where there is an exceptionally high degree of foreseeability that, unless preventive measures are taken, the threatened harm will be done.[5]

1 *Charlton v Forrest Printing Ink Co Ltd* [1980] IRLR 331, CA (on the facts, employers not negligent).
2 *Stansbie v Troman* [1948] 2 KB 48, [1948] 1 All ER 599, CA.
3 *Holgate v Lancashire Mental Hospitals Board* [1937] 4 All ER 19.
4 *Home Office v Dorset Yacht Co* [1970] AC 1004, [1970] 2 All ER 294, HL.
5 See, for example, *Perl (P) (Exporters) Ltd v Camden London Borough Council* [1984] QB 342, [1983] 3 All ER 161, CA.

Land law
19.32 Among the exceptional cases, in which the foreseeability test propounded by Lord Atkin in *Donoghue v Stevenson*[1] cannot be relied upon without more to impose a duty of care, is 'a long chapter of the law determining in what circumstances owners of land can, and in what circumstances they may not, use their proprietary rights so as to injure their neighbours.'[2] The English courts, while recognising that the tort of negligence might have made a considerable impact upon this area of the law if it had been virgin territory, have proved on the whole surprisingly reluctant to reshape existing principles of liability and non-liability by reference to duties of care. In *Langbrook Properties Ltd v Surrey County Council*,[3] for example, the defendants, who were engaged in repositioning water mains, pumped out water which was percolating through the soil, thus causing subsidence on the plaintiffs' land. It was held that, since the defendants would not have been liable had they abstracted the water maliciously,[4] it would be highly illogical if they were made liable for doing it negligently. More remarkable is the case of *Smith v Scott*[5] in which the plaintiffs, the peaceful tenants of a council house, complained of various acts of trespass and nuisance carried out by a family of known troublemakers whom the local authority had housed in the adjoining property. It was held that, since a landlord's liability for nuisances caused by his tenants is based on the concept of 'authorisation', the local authority, having taken an express covenant not to commit nuisance from these troublemakers, could not be liable; it was irrelevant that the effects upon the plaintiffs were foreseeable to the point of being almost inevitable.

1 [1932] AC 562, HL; para 19.6 above.
2 *Home Office v Dorset Yacht Co* [1970] AC 1004 at 1026, [1970] 2 All ER 294 at 297, HL.
3 [1969] 3 All ER 1424, [1970] 1 WLR 161.
4 *Bradford Corpn v Pickles* [1895] AC 587, HL; paras 18.9 and 18.13 above.
5 [1973] Ch 314, [1972] 3 All ER 645.

19.33 We have already noted that traditional immunities are increasingly under attack from both the legislature and the judiciary. In some instances a full duty of care is imposed; in others, the duty is of a more restricted kind. In the present context, the following developments are particularly worthy of note:

a. The particular application of 'caveat emptor' which protected an owner-builder against all liability for defective premises has now, it appears, been abolished twice over.[1]

b. Although an occupier of premises has never been free to injure trespassers deliberately or recklessly, his duty towards them, until recently, went no further than this. However, the House of Lords improved their lot considerably,[2] and a recent statute has conferred still greater protection upon them.[3]

c. The common law imposed no duty on a farmer to prevent his domestic animals from straying on to the highway, so that, if an accident was caused in this way, the road-user was left without a remedy. Legislation has now brought this area within the tort of negligence.[4]

d. It used to be the law that a person was liable only for *positively* interfering with his neighbour's right of support.[5] However, liability has recently been extended to someone who merely allowed his property to fall into disrepair with the result that the neighbouring property was no longer supported.[6]

e. The duty of a mortgagee to obtain the best possible price for the property when he realises his security[7] is now owed, not only to the mortgagor, but also to any guarantor of the mortgage debt.[8]

1 By the Defective Premises Act 1972 and *Anns v Merton London Borough Council* [1978] AC 728, [1977] 2 All ER 492, HL; paras 23.25 to 23.29 below.
2 *British Railways Board v Herrington* [1972] AC 877, [1972] 1 All ER 749, HL; para 23.20 below.
3 Occupiers' Liability Act 1984; paras 23.21 to 23.24 below.
4 Animals Act 1971, s8; para 28.4 below.
5 See para 40.42 below.
6 *Bradburn v Lindsay* [1983] 2 All ER 408.
7 See para 41.25 below.
8 *Standard Chartered Bank v Walker* [1982] 3 All ER 938, [1982] 1 WLR 1410, CA.

Nervous shock

19.34 Where a person is in a position to claim damages for bodily injury, some compensation in respect of any accompanying shock to his nervous system is normally recoverable under the heading of 'pain and suffering'.[1] Where, however, there is no 'impact injury', an action in respect of *pure* nervous shock which is alleged to have been caused by the defendant's conduct gives rise to legal difficulties. The courts have adopted a highly restrictive approach to such claims, for two main reasons: first, the fear of counterfeit actions (made possible by the comparative imprecision of psychiatry as a branch of medical science); and second, the familiar 'floodgates' argument, that a defendant cannot be expected to bear the brunt of liability not only to an accident victim but also to a wide circle of distressed relatives and friends.

In an effort to solve the first of these problems (the possibility of fraudulent claims based on no real evidence) the courts at one time insisted that shock, to be compensatable, must result in some physical manifestation, for example, a miscarriage or coronary thrombosis. More recently there has been a greater willingness to accept medical evidence of recognisable psychiatric illnesses, such as prolonged depression or neurosis.[2] Indeed, a woman in a recent case, who had seen her husband seriously injured in a coach crash, was awarded damages for what the judge described as 'ordinary shock', without any medical or psychiatric evidence.[3]

Generally speaking, however, 'nervous shock' in law is a fairly limited concept, as is illustrated by *Hinz v Berry*.[4] The plaintiff in that case was picnicking in a lay-by with her husband, four children and four foster-children. While the plaintiff picked flowers in an adjoining field, the defendant's negligently driven car crashed into the family party, killing the husband and injuring most of the children. As a result of this incident, the plaintiff suffered a prolonged morbid depression, for which she was awarded £4,000 damages against the defendant. This may seem a somewhat low figure for what were undoubtedly fairly serious consequences to the plaintiff, but the Court of Appeal regarded it as rather on the high side; as the court pointed out, the plaintiff was being compensated only for *shock*, and not for grief and sorrow, worry about the children, financial stress or the difficulties of adjusting to a new life. Of course, it is not suggested that these various strands, which together produce the plaintiff's distress, can be accurately disentangled, but rather that damages will normally be kept at a fairly low level (though an extremely serious case recently resulted in an award of £22,500[5]).

Particular problems are caused in shock cases by hypersensitive plaintiffs, ie those whose mental or emotional state renders them especially susceptible to nervous disorder. It seems that, if the shock results solely from this special sensitivity (that is to say, the incident would not have affected a normal robust person) then the plaintiff cannot recover. If, however, a normal person would have been affected, then the plaintiff is entitled to damages for the full effect upon him.[6]

1   Para 31.6 below.
2   *Chadwick v British Transport Commission* [1967] 2 All ER 945, [1967] 1 WLR 912.
3   *Whitmore v Euroways Express Coaches Ltd* (1984) Times, 4 May.
4   [1970] 2 QB 40, [1970] 1 All ER 1074, CA.
5   *Brice v Brown* [1984] 1 All ER 997.
6   *Chadwick v British Transport Commission* [1967] 2 All ER 945, [1967] 1 WLR 912.

19.35   The second of the judicial fears mentioned above is the simple one of opening up too wide an area of liability. In the past the courts attempted to solve this problem by insisting that 'foreseeability' alone did not sufficiently limit the duty of care, and that further artificial controls were necessary. The particular 'controls' which were used for this purpose no longer form an absolute bar to the recovery of damages, but they remain of some relevance, as we explain in the next paragraph.

In two situations damages for nervous shock have always been available. These are, first, where the shock is caused intentionally or recklessly (as by a perverted practical joke[1]) and, second, where the plaintiff's shock results from fear for his own safety.[2]

1   *Wilkinson v Downton* [1897] 2 QB 57.
2   *Dulieu v White & Sons* [1901] 2 KB 669.

19.36   Most of the difficulties which beset actions for nervous shock are found in those cases where the plaintiff has witnessed or been told about some accident to another person. In *McLoughlin v O'Brian*,[1] for instance, the plaintiff's young daughter was killed, and her husband and two other children seriously injured, in a road accident some two miles from their home. A neighbour broke the news to the plaintiff and took her to the local hospital where, on seeing the state of her family, she suffered severe and persisting shock. The House of Lords held that the plaintiff was entitled to recover damages from the driver whose negligence had caused the accident and, in so holding, took the opportunity to clarify the law on this point.

The House of Lords ruled that the sole test in 'nervous shock' cases is whether or not shock to the plaintiff was foreseeable. In deciding this point, special attention will be given to three aspects of the case, although these are not, as had previously been thought, conclusive as to the recoverability of damages. The three factors in question are:

a. the closeness of the emotional tie between the plaintiff and the person physically injured. Relationship by blood or marriage is not essential, although the few cases in which someone beyond the family barrier has recovered damages for shock have contained additional factors which rendered the shock especially likely to occur;[2]

b. the plaintiff's physical proximity to the scene of the accident;[3] and

c. whether the plaintiff saw or heard the accident personally or merely learned about it later from a third party.[4]

1   [1983] AC 410, [1982] 2 All ER 298, HL.
2   See *Dooley v Cammell Laird & Co Ltd* [1951] 1 Lloyd's Rep 271; *Galt v British Railways Board* (1983) 133 NLJ 870; *Chadwick v British Transport Commission* [1967] 2 All ER 945, [1967] 1 WLR 912.
3   See *Bourhill v Young* [1943] AC 92, [1942] 2 All ER 396, HL.
4   See *Hambrook v Stokes Bros* [1925] 1 KB 141, CA; *Boardman v Sanderson* [1964] 1 WLR 1317, CA.

Chapter 20
Negligence—breach of duty

20.1 Once a court decides that a particular defendant owed a duty of care to a particular plaintiff, the next question is whether or not that duty was broken. The test to be applied is this: did the defendant act reasonably in all the circumstances of the case? It should be noted from the outset that, while 'reasonableness' is of course capable of great flexibility (and subtle differences of fact between one case and another may lead the court to apparently conflicting conclusions), the legal standard itself is always the same. Further, this standard of 'reasonableness' is the only one known to the law of tort; such concepts as 'gross negligence' have no part to play.

We have already remarked that the tort of negligence imposes an objective standard of conduct. What is required of a person, if he is to avoid liability, is not that he does his best, but that he does what is reasonable. At first glance, this may appear rather harsh, in that a defendant is sometimes found 'guilty' in circumstances where no moral blame attaches to him. It should not be overlooked, however, that a court which permitted itself the luxury of sympathising with such a defendant to the extent of acquitting him of negligence would, in effect, be condemning an equally innocent plaintiff to shoulder his own loss. Add to this the fact that the majority of modern defendants are either insured against liability or backed by employers who are so insured, and the courts' insistence upon the objective standard is easy to understand.

The prevalence of liability insurance is also one of the factors which have led the courts to impose, under the guise of 'reasonableness', standards of conduct which are rather higher than most people can consistently achieve. Another is undoubtedly the feeling that, while to set an impossibly high standard would be self-defeating, the aim of the law should always be an overall improvement in performance, for the reduction of accidents is to everyone's benefit. Interestingly, however, the courts are more lenient when considering the conduct of a plaintiff for the purpose of deciding whether his damages should be reduced on the ground of contributory negligence.[1] In theory, the test to be applied is again that of 'reasonableness', but here the imposition of a high standard would tend to restrict compensation rather than to increase it, and this would run counter to modern trends.

1 See para 22.11–22.16 below, especially para 22.13.

20.2 An important point (and one which is all too frequently over looked) is that decisions on 'breach of duty' are matters of fact and, consequently, not of binding authority for the future. Thus, the fact that a driver in one case is held to have been negligent in turning right without giving a signal does not mean that such conduct will automatically amount to negligence in another case. Indeed, it has even been held that, in extreme circumstances, a person may be driving a vehicle 'reasonably' despite the fact that he is exceeding the speed limit.[1]

When civil actions were tried by a judge and jury, the reasonableness or otherwise of the defendant's conduct was one of the matters which fell to the jury to decide. In order to assist these laymen in reaching their verdict (which involved them in the application of a legal standard), judges referred to such hypothetical creatures as 'the man in the street', 'the man of ordinary prudence' and, most famously, 'the man on the Clapham omnibus'. The jury would then be asked to measure the conduct of the actual defendant against what might have been expected of his mythical counterpart. As Alderson B put it in *Blyth v Birmingham Waterworks Co*:[2] 'Negligence is the omission to do something which a reasonable man, guided upon those considerations which ordinarily regulate the conduct of human affairs, would do, or doing something which a prudent and reasonable man would not do.'

Negligence actions are no longer tried by jury but the judge has to carry out exactly the same process of evaluation, and the 'reasonable man' therefore remains relevant. In considering whether the defendant's conduct has reached the requisite standard, various personal attributes of the defendant will be taken into account, and these we consider under the heading of 'The reasonable man'. Further, modern courts frequently evaluate a person's conduct by reference to the risk which it creates, and this we discuss under the heading of 'The principle of risk'.

1   *Barna v Hudes Merchandising Corpn* (1962) 106 Sol Jo 194, CA.
2   (1856) 11 Exch 781 at 784.

The reasonable man

Intellectual and emotional characteristics
20.3   As a general rule, no allowance is made in law for any lack of intelligence or emotional restraint on the part of a particular defendant. Indeed, the majority opinion of both judges and writers is that, where appropriate, liability in negligence should be imposed upon a lunatic, notwithstanding his obvious inability to act 'reasonably', on the ground that to excuse him would be unfair to the victims of his actions. Similar reasoning (supported in this instance by the comforting presence of compulsory insurance) has been used where the defendant is inexperienced rather than unintelligent; it was held by the Court of Appeal in *Nettleship v Weston*[1] that a learner-driver is negligent if he or she does not achieve the standard of an ordinarily competent and experienced driver.

1   [1971] 2 QB 691, [1971] 3 All ER 581, CA.

Physical defects
20.4   Although a person's psychological make-up is thus irrelevant to his liability in negligence, the courts are rather more prepared to make some allowances in the case of a defendant who suffers from some recognisable physical impediment. This may be simply because of the comparative ease

with which such a disability may be proved to exist.[1] However, whatever the reason there is no doubt that a person who is blind or who has only one leg will be judged by what may reasonably be expected from someone in that condition. This, it should be noted, is two-edged. While a disabled person may not be held negligent for failing to achieve the same standard of agility or awareness as a normal person, he must recognise his own limitations and refrain from activities which, because of his condition, are fraught with special risk.

The law here attempts to strike some sort of compromise between the interest of the handicapped in leading a full and active life, and the safety of the general public. Once again, where insurance is present it tends to tilt the scales against the defendant. In *Roberts v Ramsbottom*,[2] where a driver suffered a stroke which left him unable to drive safely but also unable to appreciate his incapacity, he was nevertheless held liable in negligence for the resulting accident. Further, while a driver is not liable if he suffers an unforeseeable total collapse at the wheel, a court might well be quick to find that he was negligent in driving at all, in the light of prior symptoms.

1 Cf the reluctance of the courts to award damages for nervous shock, as compared with physical injury; paras 19.34 to 19.36 above.
2 [1980] 1 All ER 7, [1980] 1 WLR 823.

Age

20.5 It is comparatively unusual to find an action in negligence being brought against a child, in view of the difficulties involved in obtaining satisfaction. Even assuming that liability is established, it is highly unlikely that the child will have either adequate personal funds or insurance cover, and the law does not make parents vicariously responsible for the torts of their children. Nevertheless, the 'reasonableness' or otherwise of a child's conduct not infrequently falls to be considered by the courts in the context of alleged contributory negligence, and it is well settled that full account is to be taken of age. In *Gough v Thorne*,[1] for example, a 13-year-old girl was beckoned across the road by the driver of a stationary lorry. Relying entirely upon this signal, she stepped out past the lorry and was knocked down by a negligently driven car. The trial judge held that her failure to look out for vehicles overtaking the lorry amounted to contributory negligence but the Court of Appeal, while accepting that this would be true in the case of a more experienced adult, held that a child of this age could not be faulted for trusting her elders. A similar decision was reached by the Court of Appeal in *Foskett v Mistry*,[2] where a sixteen-year-old youth ran across a road without looking and was struck by a car. He was held to bear three-quarters of the blame for this accident; an adult would have been totally responsible.

In contributory negligence cases, the lenient approach to children has the desirable effect of enlarging the overall scope of compensation. To give similar latitude in the rare cases where a child is sued would, of course, have the opposite effect. Nevertheless, it is clear that this is the correct approach to adopt, although even a child must achieve certain standards. In *Watkins v Birmingham City Council*,[3] a ten-year-old boy, while distributing school milk to various classrooms, left his tricycle in a position where a teacher fell over it. This was held to constitute negligence, a finding which was not challenged in the Court of Appeal, where the decision was reversed on another ground.[4]

Although there is less authority than in respect of children, it seems that an elderly litigant is also to be judged in the light of his age. In *Daly v Liverpool Corpn*,[5] where a collision occurred between the plaintiff, a 69-year-old pedestrian, and the defendants' bus, it was held that a charge of contributory negligence against the plaintiff must take her age into account. As Stable J remarked: 'I cannot believe that the law is quite so absurd as to say that, if a pedestrian happens to be old and slow and a little stupid, he or she can only walk about his or her native country at his or her own risk.'

1   [1966] 3 All ER 398, [1966] 1 WLR 1387, CA.
2   [1984] RTR 1, CA.
3   (1975) Times, 1 August, CA.
4   See para 30.7 below.
5   [1939] 2 All ER 142.

Knowledge of other people

20.6   In order to attain the standard which the law demands of the reasonable man, the defendant must take into account and make due allowance for those shortcomings of others which are reasonably to be foreseen. As an obvious example, if it is foreseeable that blind persons will use a city pavement, the reasonable man who excavates there will erect a barrier sufficient to protect them, and not merely one which is sufficient to safeguard those who can see it.[1]

The whole idea of contributory negligence recognises that the negligence of one person does not automatically absolve another from his duty to take care. In *London Passenger Transport Board v Upson*,[2] for example, it was held that the reasonable pedestrian must have regard to the possibility that a driver will not take as much care for his safety as he should.

There may indeed be extreme cases in which a defendant ought to foresee and guard against even the *criminal* misconduct of others although, as we have seen,[3] the law is reluctant to impose a duty of care in such circumstances.

1   *Haley v London Electricity Board* [1965] AC 778, [1964] 3 All ER 185, HL.
2   [1949] AC 155, [1949] 1 All ER 60, HL.
3   Paras 19.30–19.31 above.

Professional standing

20.7   Unlike most of the factors so far considered, which may lead a court to expect rather less of a defendant than of other people, a person's status within a trade or profession may mean that he has to achieve a *higher* standard than others, in the sense of displaying skill as well as care. As to the *degree* of skill which must be shown, this is whatever may be expected of a reasonably competent practitioner, rather than a leading specialist (although a defendant who sets himself up as a specialist will be judged accordingly[1]). In *Roe v Minister of Health*,[2] the plaintiff underwent minor surgery in 1947, during which he became partially paralysed as a result of being injected with a contaminated anaesthetic. The danger of such contamination was appreciated by very few doctors until about 1951, after which the profession in general took action to prevent it from happening again. In acquitting the hospital staff of negligence, Denning LJ pointed out that: 'We must not look at the 1947 accident with 1954 spectacles'.

Where a person acts in accordance with what is the generally accepted practice of his profession, he is unlikely to be found negligent,[3] although there have been occasions on which a court has declared such common practice to be unreasonable.[4] The converse is also true, namely that a person who ignores the usual procedures runs an increased risk of being judged negligent.[5] What, then, of the case in which professional opinion is split? In *Bolam v Friern Hospital Management Committee*[6] McNair J made it clear that it was not for the court to select one body of opinion as correct and to discount all others; the question was simply whether it could be said that no reasonably competent practitioner could possibly hold the view which the defendant preferred. This statement of principle was approved by the House of Lords in *Maynard v West Midlands AHA*.[7]

It should always be remembered that a professional man's duty is to be skilful and careful, not necessarily to be correct. Nevertheless, it is not true to say that an error of judgment cannot amount to negligence; the vital question is whether the error is one which a reasonably competent practitioner would not have made.[8]

1 *Duchess of Argyll v Beuselinck* [1972] 2 Lloyd's Rep 172; cf *Wimpey Construction UK Ltd v Poole* (1984) Times, 3 May.
2 [1954] 2 QB 66, [1954] 2 All ER 131, CA.
3 *Morton v William Dixon Ltd* 1909 SC 807 at 809.
4 See, for example, *Edward Wong Finance Co v Johnson, Stokes and Master* [1984] AC 296, PC.
5 See, for example, *Clark v MacLennan* [1983] 1 All ER 416.
6 [1957] 2 All ER 118, [1957] 1 WLR 582.
7 [1985] 1 All ER 635, [1984] 1 WLR 635, HL.
8 *Whitehouse v Jordan* [1981] 1 All ER 267, [1981] 1 WLR 246, HL. See also para 20.8 below.

20.8 *Valuers* Although it was not until the decision of the House of Lords in *Hedley, Byrne & Co Ltd v Heller & Partners Ltd*[1] that it became possible for a negligent valuer to be sued in tort, it had long been settled that a claim in contract would lie at the suit of a dissatisfied client. Consequently, in seeking guidance as to how a valuer's *legal* duty (to use such care and skill as is reasonable) should be translated into *practical* terms, decisions of the courts both before and after 1964 are of equal relevance.

In the first place, it must be stressed that valuation is not an exact science, and that to be wrong is not necessarily to be negligent.

'The law does not require any man, valuer of public-houses or any other expert agent, to be perfect. The law does not say that in any branch of intelligent operation, intelligent skill, there is necessarily one defined path which must be strictly followed, and that if one departs by an inch from that defined path one were necessarily at fault'.[2]

Even more in point are the words of Goddard LJ, in *Baxter v F W Gapp & Co Ltd*:[3]

'Valuation is very much a matter of opinion. We are all liable to make mistakes, and a valuer is certainly not to be found guilty of negligence merely because his valuation turns out to be wrong. He may have taken too optimistic or too pessimistic a view of a particular property. One has to bear in mind that, in matters of valuation, matters of opinion must come very largely into account'.

Nevertheless, a sizeable error will require some explanation, and it has been said that a valuation which departs from the 'correct' figure (as found by the judge with the help of expert witnesses) by more than 10 or 15% 'brings into question the competence of the valuer and the sort of care he gave to the task of valuation'.[4]

Assuming that a valuer has reached a wrong conclusion, damages for negligence can only be recovered if it is established that the error was due to a lack of reasonable care and skill. This has on occasion been found in such matters as the failure to know (and to keep up to date with) the principles of law which affect the type of valuation in question;[5] a survey too superficial to reveal obvious defects in the property;[6] and (where the complaint was of an under-valuation) the overlooking of a potential market.[7]

As far as the actual valuation process is concerned, the courts are careful not to lay down restrictive rules, since it is appreciated that an experienced valuer may often operate intuitively. Hence, the absence of comparables or detailed calculations does not of itself indicate negligence.[8] On the other hand, a valuer who does not trouble to visit the site which he is to value,[9] or who (after only three months' experience, all of it limited to property worth less than £33,000) nonchalantly values a house at £100,000 without seeking confirmation from a more experienced colleague,[10] is unlikely to attract the sympathy of a judge when it is alleged that he was lacking in reasonable care and skill.

1　[1964] AC 465, [1963] 2 All ER 575, HL; para 19.13 above.
2　*Love v Mack* (1905) 92 LT 345 at 349.
3　[1938] 4 All ER 457 at 459.
4　*Singer and Friedlander Ltd v John D Wood & Co* (1977) 243 Estates Gazette 212 at 213.
5　*Weedon v Hindwood, Clarke and Esplin* (1974) 234 Estates Gazette 121.
6　*Philips v Ward* [1956] 1 All ER 874, [1956] 1 WLR 471, CA.
7　*Bell Hotels (1935) Ltd v Motion* (1952) 159 Estates Gazette 496.
8　*Corisand Investments Ltd v Druce & Co* (1978) 248 Estates Gazette 315 at 319.
9　*Singer and Friedlander Ltd v John D Wood & Co* (1977) 243 Estates Gazette 212.
10　*Kenney v Hall, Pain and Foster* (1976) 239 Estates Gazette 355.

20.9　The obligation to display professional skill as well as reasonable care is imposed, not only upon those who are actually members of that profession, but also on those who attempt to take on work which requires professional skill.[1] In *Freeman v Marshall & Co*,[2] the plaintiff complained of a survey carried out for him by the defendant, in which he failed to diagnose rising damp. The defendant argued that, since he was unqualified and had little knowledge of structures, he had done all that could be reasonably expected of him. It was held, however, that, by advertising himself as an estate agent, valuer and surveyor, and by undertaking a structural survey, he had laid claim to the necessary expertise and must be judged accordingly.

Many jobs may as reasonably be undertaken by semi-skilled or unskilled persons as by professionals. Where this is so, the courts will not necessarily judge the defendant by the standard of the most skilled person who might be expected to do the work. In *Philips v William Whiteley Ltd*,[3] for example, a jeweller pierced a woman's ears. The instruments used were disinfected, although not to the standard which a surgeon would be expected to achieve, and she developed an abscess. It was held that, since this operation was frequently performed by jewellers, the defendants fell to be judged by the standards of a reasonable jeweller, and not those of a reasonable surgeon. A similar decision was reached in the case of *Wells v Cooper*,[4] where a door handle fitted by the defendant householder, who was an amateur carpenter of some experience, came off, with the result that the plaintiff was injured. The Court of Appeal held that, since this was the sort of job which the reasonable householder might be expected to do for himself, the defendant was to be judged by amateur, and not professional, standards.

Whether the generosity which these two cases showed to defendants will be repeated in future must be regarded as open to doubt in the light of *Nettleship v Weston*,[5] where the Court of Appeal, no doubt influenced by their awareness of available insurance, held that the standard which a learner-driver must achieve, if he is not to be held negligent, is not that of a 'reasonable learner', but that of a reasonable experienced driver.

1 Some jobs (e g lift maintenance: *Haseldine v C A Daw & Son Ltd* [1941] 2 KB 343, [1941] 3 All ER 156, CA) so obviously require an expert that a defendant who attempts to carry them out himself is almost bound to be regarded as negligent.
2 (1966) 200 Estates Gazette 777.
3 [1938] 1 All ER 566.
4 [1958] 2 QB 265, [1958] 2 All ER 527, CA.
5 [1971] 2 QB 691, [1971] 3 All ER 581, CA.

The principle of risk

20.10 The traditional view of negligence is concerned primarily with the hypothetical 'reasonable man' and what he ought to have foreseen. More recently, courts have tended to look at a situation as a whole and to consider where the risks inherent in the defendant's activity are such as to outweigh its value (if any) or the difficulty of rendering it safe. In conducting this balancing operation a court will take into account some or all of the following matters:

a. the likelihood that the activity in question will cause injury or damage;

b. the seriousness of the injury that may result if the risk materialises.

Against these factors may be set:

c. the value, social utility or other desirability of the activity; and

d. the cost and practicability of taking steps to reduce or eliminate the danger.

Likelihood of injury

20.11 As Lord Dunedin remarked in *Fardon v Harcourt-Rivington*:[1] 'People must guard against reasonable probabilities, but they are not bound to guard against fantastic possibilities'. This means that a risk may be so remote that the reasonable man is quite justified in ignoring it altogether, and perhaps the most famous example of this is the case of *Bolton v Stone*,[2] where the plaintiff was injured by a cricket ball which a visiting batsman had struck more than 100 yards, clearing a high fence on the way. The evidence indicated that shots of this kind had occurred on the ground no more than six times in 28 years and the House of Lords held that, while the risk was clearly foreseeable, from the very fact that there had been such shots in the past, it was sufficiently remote that the defendants might reasonably ignore it. While this principle has subsequently been accepted, it should not be overlooked that the conduct of the defendants in that case (playing cricket) was considered by the House of Lords to be socially valuable; hence, there was a second reason for holding the defendants not liable.

1 (1932) 146 LT 391 at 392.
2 [1951] AC 850, [1951] 1 All ER 1078, HL.

Seriousness of consequences

20.12   Quite apart from the probability or improbability that a particular type of accident will occur, a court assessing a defendant's conduct may justifiably consider the gravity of the potential consequences. This principle was laid down by the House of Lords in *Paris v Stepney Borough Council*,[1] where a one-eyed garage hand was struck in his remaining eye by a metal chip and became completely blind. It was not the practice of the employers to supply their workmen with safety goggles, since they regarded the risk of eye injury as extremely remote. The House of Lords held that, although this approach was justifiable in relation to normal, two-eyed employees, special precautions should have been taken in the plaintiff's case, since he had so much more to lose.

1   [1951] AC 367, [1951] 1 All ER 42, HL.

Value of conduct

20.13   The number of accidents which occur every day could be drastically reduced if certain steps were taken. As a simple example, it is obvious that road accidents would be far less likely to happen if everyone drove at no more than ten mph. Can it then be said that anyone who exceeds that speed is automatically guilty of negligence, since he has thereby increased the risk of injury to other road users? The answer to this question is of course that the reasonable man would regard the increased risk as justified, in view of the enormous inconvenience which would be caused to the general public if all traffic were to move at a snail's pace.

The principle that important ends may be held to justify risky means was invoked in *Daborn v Bath Tramways Motor Co Ltd*,[1] where it was held that the use of a left-hand drive vehicle as an ambulance in wartime was reasonable (in view of the shortage of suitable transport), notwithstanding the dangers which it created to other road users when turning right without giving any signal. In *Watt v Hertfordshire County Council*,[2] a heavy jack, which was needed to rescue a woman trapped under a bus, was carried on a lorry not suited to the purpose. During the journey the jack shifted, injuring the plaintiff, a fireman. The Court of Appeal held that the fire brigade's decision to use this unsuitable vehicle was a reasonable one, having regard to the emergency.

1   [1946] 2 All ER 333, CA.
2   [1954] 2 All ER 368, [1954] 1 WLR 835, CA.

Cost of precautions

20.14   In deciding whether a defendant has dealt adequately with a particular risk, the courts will have regard to the ease with which that risk could have been reduced or eliminated. This is not simply a matter of money, although financial considerations are undoubtedly of importance; it also covers questions of convenience and practicability. In extreme cases, where the risk is a very serious one, it may be that the only course of action open to the reasonable man is to cease altogether the dangerous activity, although the courts are reluctant to impose such a heavy burden.[1] In *Withers v Perry Chain Co Ltd*,[2] for example, a woman who was susceptible to dermatitis (caused by contact with grease) was given the driest work which her employers had available; nevertheless, she again contracted the disease. Her argument that the defendants should have dismissed her for her own protection was rejected by the Court of Appeal, who held that such a drastic step could not possibly be justified by the relatively minor risk to which she was exposed.

At the other end of the scale, a person may be held liable for failing to eliminate even a small risk, if he could have done so with ease. As Lord Reid put it:[3] 'It does not follow that, no matter what the circumstances may be, it is justifiable to neglect a risk of such a small magnitude. A reasonable man. . . would not neglect such a risk if action to eliminate it presented no difficulty, involved no disadvantage, and required no expense'.

By and large, the objective standard of reasonable care applies to questions of cost and inconvenience as it does to other factors in the assessment of negligence. Thus, once a court decides that a reasonable man would have taken certain precautions (ie that they were not too costly in relation to the risk) a defendant who did not do so is liable, even if he personally could not afford them. In recent times, however, a degree of subjectivity has been introduced for the benefit of an occupier upon whose land a danger arises through natural causes (and for which, therefore, he is not to blame). Where this happens, it has been held that the occupier may avoid liability to a neighbour by establishing that the actions necessary to eliminate the danger would have been beyond his personal means.[4]

1 See *Bolton v Stone* [1951] AC 850, [1951] 1 All ER 1078, HL; para 20.11 above.
2 [1961] 3 All ER 676, [1961] 1 WLR 1314.
3 *The Wagon Mound (No 2)* [1967] 1 AC 617 at 642, [1966] 2 All ER 709 at 718.
4 *Goldman v Hargrave* [1967] 1 AC 645, [1966] 2 All ER 989, PC.

The proof of negligence
20.15 In matters of negligence the burden of proof, as is usual in civil cases, lies on the plaintiff. This means that it is for the plaintiff to bring evidence which establishes on the balance of probabilities that the defendant has been careless.

One specific rule of evidence is worthy of note. By virtue of the Civil Evidence Act 1968, s11, a criminal conviction for an offence which involves negligence (eg driving without due care and attention) is to be regarded in subsequent civil proceedings as sufficient evidence of negligence. This means that, in subsequent civil proceedings, the defendant's negligence will be presumed, although it is still open to him to rebut this presumption.

Res ipsa loquitur
20.16 In attempting to prove negligence against the defendant, a plaintiff is entitled to rely on circumstantial evidence as much as on that which is direct. Indeed, in many of the situations in which allegations of negligence are most common, the plaintiff will be forced into this position, since the details of the accident will be known only to the defendant. Where this occurs, the plaintiff may gain assistance from the maxim '*res ipsa loquitur*' ('the thing speaks for itself'). The operation of this maxim is illustrated by the leading case of *Scott v London and St Katherine Docks Co*,[1] in which the plaintiff, who was walking past the defendant's warehouse, was injured when six bags of sugar fell on him. Neither party could offer any explanation of this occurrence, and the trial judge held that there was not enough evidence to allow the case to go to the jury. However, on appeal, this decision was held to be incorrect, and the following principle was laid down by Erle CJ: 'There must be reasonable evidence of negligence. But

where the thing is shown to be under the management of the defendant or his servants, and the accident is such as in the ordinary course of things does not happen if those who have the management use proper care, it affords reasonable evidence, in the absence of explanation by the defendants, that the accident arose from want of care'.

It is clear, then, that for *res ipsa loquitur* to apply, it must be shown that:

a.   the thing which did the damage was under the management and control of the defendant or someone for whom the defendant was responsible; and

b.   the occurrence was such as would ordinarily indicate negligence.

1   (1865) 3 H & C 596.

20.17   *Control by the defendant*   The mere fact that an unauthorised person could have tampered with the thing which causes injury to the plaintiff will not preclude reliance on *res ipsa loquitur*, provided that such intervention is improbable. Thus, where a railway passenger fell from a moving train immediately after leaving the station, it was held that the carriage doors could be regarded as under the control of the railway company.[1] However, the opposite conclusion was reached in the case of a child falling from the corridor of a train which had travelled a considerable distance since its last stop.[2]

1   *Gee v Metropolitcan Rly Co* (1873) LR 8 QB 161.
2   *Easson v London North Eastern Rly Co* [1944] KB 421, [1944] 2 All ER 425, CA.

20.18   *Inference of negligence*   The facts which may give rise to the application of *res ipsa loquitur* are infinitely varied. Apart from the obvious example of objects falling from the upper floors of buildings,[1] the doctrine has been invoked in cases of railway collisions,[2] an aircraft which crashed on taking off[3] and the sudden and violent skid of a motor vehicle.[4] In *Ward v Tesco Stores Ltd*,[5] where a supermarket customer slipped on some yoghourt which had been spilled on the floor, a majority of the Court of Appeal reached the somewhat doubtful conclusion that, in the absence of further evidence as to how the yoghourt came to be on the floor, its presence there could be attributed to negligence on the part of the defendants.

In practical terms, *res ipsa loquitur* is of most benefit to the plaintiff who is injured by a process, the details of which he does not understand, or who cannot show which of the defendant's employees it was who was guilty of negligence. Such plaintiffs include consumers injured by defective products (eg *Grant v Australian Knitting Mills Ltd*,[6] where the plaintiff contracted dermatitis from a new pair of underpants) and patients whose condition is rendered worse rather than better by the medical treatment which they receive (eg *Cassidy v Ministry of Health*,[7] where hospital treatment of the plaintiff's two stiff fingers left him with four stiff fingers).

1   *Scott v London and St Katherine Docks Co* (1865) 3 H & C 596; para 20.16 above.
2   *Skinner v London, Brighton and South Coast Rly Co* (1850) 5 Exch 787.
3   *Fosbroke-Hobbes v Airwork Ltd and British American Air Services Ltd* [1937] 1 All ER 108.
4   *Richley v Faull* [1965] 3 All ER 109, [1965] 1 WLR 1454.
5   [1976] 1 All ER 219. [1976] 1 WLR 810, CA.
6   [1936] AC 85, PC.
7   [1951] 2 KB 343, [1951] 1 All ER 574, CA.

20.19   *Effect of the maxim*   The precise effect of *res ipsa loquitur* upon a negligence action is a matter of some controversy. As originally conceived it *entitled* a plaintiff to have the case considered by the jury; it did not, however, *compel* the jury to find in the plaintiff's favour. Now that the civil jury has virtually disappeared, and questions of law and fact alike are tried by the judge alone, the courts have tended to elevate the maxim to the status of a legal presumption,[1] with the result that a plaintiff who makes out his case in this way is *bound* to succeed unless the defendant can rebut this presumption (by genuine evidence, not mere conjecture).

Once a particular thing is held to 'speak for itself', the defendant has two alternative ways of avoiding liability, although neither of these is easy to achieve. In the first place, it may be possible for the defendant to establish the true cause of the accident and to show that this is independent of any negligence on his part. In *Henderson v Henry E Jenkins & Sons*,[2] where a man was killed by a runaway lorry, the defendants, who were owners of the lorry, proved that concealed corrosion in a pipe had caused the brakes to fail. The defendants also showed that they had complied with the recommended maintenance schedules in respect of this vehicle, but the House of Lords held that even this was not sufficient to rebut the presumption of negligence which had been raised against them. In order to do this, they would have had to establish that nothing had happened to the lorry throughout its history which would call for extra precautions to be taken.[3]

The second way in which a defendant may avoid liability is by proving to the satisfaction of the court that, although the cause of the accident remains unknown, the defendant has not been in any way guilty of negligence. The burden of proof on the defendant in such a case is an extremely heavy one, especially where the evidence consists of little more than his word.[4]

1   See *Moore v R Fox & Sons* [1956] 1 QB 596, [1956] 1 All ER 182, CA; *Henderson v Henry E Jenkins & Sons* [1970] AC 282, [1969] 3 All ER 756, HL and *Colvilles Ltd v Devine* [1969] 2 All ER 53, [1969] 1 WLR 475, HL.
2   [1970] AC 282, [1969] 3 All ER 756, HL.
3   Rather less is expected of a private motorist: *Rees v Saville* [1983] RTR 332, CA.
4   See, for example, *Ludgate v Lovett* [1969] 2 All ER 1275, [1969] 1 WLR 1016, CA.

Chapter 21
Negligence—the causing of damage

21.1 The mere fact that a defendant acts carelessly towards a plaintiff is not enough to render him liable in tort. In order to succeed in an action, the plaintiff must prove that he has suffered damage and, further, that this was *caused* by the defendant's breach of duty.

It is essential to appreciate from the very first that 'causation' in legal terms has a rather more restricted meaning than that which is given to it in a scientific or metaphysical context. To take a simple example: A is walking past some scaffolding when a brick falls on his head. From the purely *factual* point of view, we may say that A's injuries are caused by his presence there; by the act of a workman who leaned against the stack of bricks; by the action of a labourer who placed the stack in that position; by the decision of the owners to have their building repaired at that time; and so on. Add to these such passive causes (no less essential to the accident) as the law of gravity (without which the brick would have floated safely away) and the regrettable truth that bricks are harder than skulls, and the complexity of factual causation is apparent.

Fortunately, perhaps, the lawyer is concerned not to identify all the causes of an accident, but merely to consider whether any or all of a small number of identified conditions (normally the acts or omissions of the parties to a lawsuit) may be regarded as sufficiently important to rank as *legal* causes and thus to attract responsibility. This task, clearly, is one of selection in which the judge, aided by common sense and human experience, arrives at what in the end is a value judgment.

21.2 Causation in law is really two problems in one. In the first place, there must be a factual enquiry in order to ascertain whether the conduct of a particular individual (usually the defendant) can be regarded as a cause of loss; if it cannot be so regarded, society could hardly justify making the defendant liable for the plaintiff's misfortune. Second, assuming that the first question receives an affirmative answer, the law must decide whether the defendant's conduct and the plaintiff's damage are sufficiently closely connected that liability *ought* to be imposed. The reason for this second enquiry is that: 'The law cannot take account of everything that follows a wrongful act; it regards some subsequent matters as outside the scope of its selection, because "it were infinite to trace the cause of causes", or consequence of consequences'.[1] If human activity is not to grind to a complete halt, a line has to be drawn beyond which a wrongdoer is not to be held liable; where that line is drawn depends upon public policy and the good sense of the judge.

An example may make this clear. Suppose that A negligently breaks B's arm. Obviously A is liable for such consequences as B's loss of earnings and medical expenses, and also for the pain which B suffers. What is the position, however, if B is run over by a car on his way to hospital to have the arm set? Or if a post-operative infection causes the arm to be amputated? Or if a boat in which B is travelling a month later sinks, and B is drowned because he cannot swim to safety? Or if, in a fit of depression at being unable to play cricket for his country, B commits suicide? All these catastrophes can in factual terms be traced back to A's original negligence. But should he be made responsible for them?

Where it is concluded that a particular consequence of the defendant's breach of duty is not sufficiently connected to it to found liability, this may be expressed by saying that the conduct is not a 'legal cause' or, as is more common today, that the item of damage is 'too remote'. Indeed, the question of 'remoteness of damage' is nowadays so frequently the focus of the courts' attention that there is perhaps a tendency to overlook the continuing need to prove factual causation first.

We shall consider the topics of causation and remoteness of damage under three headings. First, there is the question of factual causation. Second, although this is in truth merely a part of the general issue, we shall adopt the common practice of dealing separately with those cases where it is alleged that the effect of the defendant's breach has been wiped out by some 'intervening cause'. Finally, we shall consider attempts which have been made by the courts to reduce the question of 'remoteness' to a statement of legal principle.

1   *Liesbosch Dredger v SS Edison* [1933] AC 449 at 460, HL.

Causation in fact

The 'but for' test

21.3   In establishing whether or not the defendant's act was a *factual* cause of the plaintiff's injury, the 'but for' test is that which is most widely accepted by the courts. According to this test (which, as we show later, is subject to some important exceptions) the question to be asked is whether the damage would have happened *but for* the defendant's breach of duty. If the answer is that it would not, then that breach may be said (factually at least) to have been a cause of it.[1] If, however, it would have happened anyway, then the defendant's breach is not a cause.

The operation of the 'but for' test is strikingly shown by the case of *McWilliams v Sir William Arrol & Co Ltd*,[2] in which a steel erector fell to his death from a tower on which he was working. His employers had failed in their statutory obligation to provide him with a safety belt. Nevertheless, his widow's action was successfully answered by showing 'to a high degree of probability' that, even if a belt had been provided, the deceased would not have worn it and would therefore in any event have fallen.[3] Similarly, in *Barnett v Chelsea and Kensington Hospital Management Committee*,[4] a casualty doctor's negligent refusal to examine a poisoned night-watchman was held not to be a cause of his death, since the evidence established that accurate diagnosis would have been too late to save him.

In deciding what *would* have happened but for the defendant's intervention, the court is of course entering the realm of conjecture. It appears, nonetheless, that a finding on the balance of probabilities is decisive. In *Cutler v Vauxhall Motors Ltd*,[5] the plaintiff, who suffered from an unsuspected varicose condition, grazed an ankle in circumstances which rendered the defendants liable. The graze led to an ulcer, and the plaintiff was forced to undergo an operation to strip the veins. A majority of the Court of Appeal held that, since the plaintiff would probably have required this operation anyway at a later date, the defendants were not liable for it; they had merely accelerated it, rather than caused it to happen. Russell LJ however, dissented on the ground that the defendants has turned into a certainty what was previously a mere possibility.

It should be remembered that the 'but for' test is essentially *exclusive* in nature. A cause which does not satisfy this requirement *cannot* be a legal cause; one which does satisfy it may be treated as legally operative if a court regards it as sufficiently important. In *Rouse v Squires*,[6] for example, a negligently driven lorry 'jack-knifed' and blocked two lanes of a motorway. In trying to avoid it, a second lorry, also negligently driven, skidded and killed a bystander. The accident would obviously not have happened but for the presence of both lorries, and the Court of Appeal held that both drivers were liable.[7] In *Dymond v Pearce*,[8] by contrast, where a motor cyclist injured his pillion passenger by negligently driving into a parked lorry, it was held that the lorry's presence, although again a necessary condition for the accident, was not a *legal* cause of it; responsibility here was attributed solely to the motor cyclist.

1   Note that the defendant is in no way excused merely because other factors were *also* necessary.
2   [1962] 1 All ER 623, [1962] 1 WLR 295, HL.
3   In view of the courts' natural bias against a defendant who is admittedly in breach of a safety regulation, such an argument is unlikely to succeed unless the evidence is overwhelming.
4   [1969] 1 QB 428, [1968] 1 All ER 1068.
5   [1971] 1 QB 418, [1970] 2 All ER 56, CA.
6   [1973] QB 889, [1973] 2 All ER 903, CA.
7   Liability was apportioned at 25% to the first driver and 75% to the second.
8   [1972] 1 QB 496, [1972] 1 All ER 1142, CA.

Proof

21.4   There is sometimes a tendency to assume that causation in the factual sense is an absolute, either definitely there or definitely absent. This assumption, however, is erroneous; in matters of causation, as in all other elements of liability, it is for the plaintiff to prove his case on the balance of probabilities. In *Metropolitan Rly Co v Jackson*,[1] for example, a railway passenger's hand was crushed when a porter, without negligence, slammed the door of the compartment. The plaintiff's hand was in that position because he was standing up to prevent more people from entering the compartment, which the defendants had negligently permitted to become overcrowded. The plaintiff claimed that his injury could be attributed to this original negligence, but the House of Lords held that the evidence did not justify this conclusion.

Modern courts frequently resolve causal doubts in favour of the plaintiff, probably out of natural sympathy for one who is, after all, the innocent victim of an admitted wrongdoer. A decision of great importance was reached by the House of Lords in *McGhee v National Coal Board*,[2] where the plaintiff's job exposed him to abrasive brick dust. The plaintiff contracted dermatitis and claimed that this was due to the defendants' failure to provide washing facilities on site, as a result of which he had to cycle home each day still caked with dust and sweat. It was held that, although a positive connection could not be established between the defendants' failure and the plaintiff's injury (since the precise causes of dermatitis remain a medical mystery), it was sufficient to impose liability that they had materially increased the risk.

1 (1877) 3 App Cas 193, HL.
2 [1972] 3 All ER 1008, [1973] 1 WLR 1, HL.

Multiple causes

21.5 The 'but for' test is, unfortunately, apt to lose its potency in the very situations in which causation becomes most difficult. Suppose, for example, that two independent fires, negligently lit by A and B, together destroy C's house. Are A and B each to evade liability by claiming that the house would in any event have been destroyed by the other fire? No legal system could tolerate such an absurdity and so both are liable in full. Of course, this does not mean that the plaintiff can recover double damages. He may take his compensation as he chooses (all from one defendant, or some from each) and, once he has done so, the defendants may seek contribution from each other in proportions assessed by the court.[1]

Where there is only one defendant, because the other cause is innocent,[2] the arguments in favour of the plaintiff are far less strong. Indeed, to allow a plaintiff to claim for losses which would in any case have come about may smack of giving him an undeserved windfall.

In the example of the two fires, *either* cause would have sufficed to bring about the damage in question. The same applies, however, where *both* are necessary (for instance, where a passenger is injured in a collision caused by two negligent drivers). Thus, the defendants in *Bonnington Castings Ltd v Wardlaw*[3] were held liable in full when their employee contracted silicosis after inhaling noxious dust over a long period, notwithstanding that part of the noxious dust came from a source for which the defendants were not responsible.

1 Paras 31.14 and 31.15 below.
2 As in *Cutler v Vauxhall Motors Ltd* [1971] 1 QB 418, [1970] 2 All ER 56, CA (para 21.3 above); or *Jobling v Associated Dairies Ltd* [1982] AC 794, [1981] 2 All ER 752, HL (para 21.6 below).
3 [1956] AC 613, [1956] 1 All ER 615, HL.

Overlapping injuries

21.6 In the last paragraph we were concerned with the plaintiff who suffers one item of loss as a result of two or more independent causes. Slightly different is the case where the same injuries, or ones which overlap each other, are caused on separate occasions. The rule here is that the first cause in time is treated as legally operative to the exclusion of all others. In *Performance Cars Ltd v Abraham*[1] the defendant damaged the plaintiffs' car in such a way that it required a respray. In fact, however, as the result of a previous accident, it already required a respray, and it was accordingly held that the defendant could not be said to have caused this item of damage.

The principle of this case is that the second tortfeasor takes his victim as he finds him (ie in a damaged state). The effect which this has upon the liability of the *first* tortfeasor was considered in the important case of *Baker v Willoughby*[2] in which the defendant was responsible for negligently injuring the plaintiff's leg and, thereby reducing his earning capacity. Some time later, but before the case came to trial, the plaintiff was shot by robbers and his injured leg had to be amputated. The question was whether the defendant's liability for loss of earnings ceased at the time of the amputation. The Court of Appeal held that it did, on the ground that the second injury effectively 'swallowed up' the first. The House of Lords, however, pointed out that, since the robbers, if sued, would be liable only for depriving the plaintiff of an already damaged leg, this solution would leave him out of pocket. It was accordingly held that, in assessing the defendant's liability, the second injury was to be ignored.

It should be noted that the approach adopted in *Baker v Willoughby* does not apply where the other cause of injury is natural, rather than tortious. In *Jobling v Associated Dairies Ltd*,[3] it was held that a plaintiff's damages for loss of earnings should only compensate him up to the date on which an earlier injury would in any case have rendered him totally disabled. The House of Lords there pointed out that any other result would over-compensate the plaintiff, and suggested that the *Baker v Willoughby* approach is only justifiable in order to prevent the plaintiff from falling between two tortfeasors.

1 [1962] 1 QB 33, [1961] 3 All ER 413, CA.
2 [1970] AC 467, [1969] 3 All ER 1528, HL.
3 [1982] AC 794, [1981] 2 All ER 752, HL.

Intervening causes

21.7 Particular problems arise in those cases where the defendant's wrongful act and the plaintiff's injury are separated by what has been called 'the conscious act of another volition'. The question for the court to decide is whether such an act, which may be that of a third party or of the plaintiff himself, is of so overwhelming a nature as to 'break the chain of causation' and thus to free the defendant from liability. If it is of such magnitude it is called a *novus actus interveniens* or 'intervening act'. A decision on this question cannot be made upon factual or scientific grounds, since the defendant's conduct is undoubtedly a cause in that sense. The judge, therefore, is exercising a function of *evaluating* the conduct in the light of supervening events, in order to decide whether partial or total responsibility *ought* still to attach to the defendant.

Before we consider whether the test of *novus actus interveniens* can be reduced to a legal principle, we shall look at a number of examples drawn from decided cases. For the sake of convenience we divide these into two categories, namely acts of third parties and acts of the plaintiff.

Conduct of a third party
Blameless actor
21.8 The chain of causation will seldom, if ever, be held to have been

broken by the act of a third party who, for one reason or another, cannot be regarded as fully responsible for his actions. Where, for example, the defendant's negligence consists of leaving his horse untethered in the street, he cannot avoid liability by pointing out that it was stampeded by mischievous children.[1] Similarly, the unthinking action of a person in an emergency will not be regarded as 'the conscious act of another volition'. In *Scott v Shepherd*,[2] the defendant threw a lighted squib in a crowded market. Two people in turn, seeking to protect themselves and their goods, picked up the squib and threw it away; it finally exploded in the plaintiff's eye. The defendant was held liable.

The 'emergency principle' can on occasion be extended beyond the instinctive reactions of an endangered person to cover also his reasonable, albeit mistaken, decisions. In *The Oropesa*,[3] one of the many maritime collision cases to have raised this point, the master of a badly damaged ship launched a boat in heavy seas towards the *Oropesa*, which had been responsible for the collision, in order to discuss salvage. The boat overturned and a seaman was drowned. It was held that the death could be attributed to the negligence of the *Oropesa*; the decision of the other ship's master, at a time when 'the hand of the casualty lay heavily' upon him, could not be said to break the chain of causation.

It should not be thought that a decision taken in an emergency is necessarily immune from challenge on the ground of negligence. In *Knightley v Johns*,[4] where a police motor cyclist was injured when ordered by his inspector to ride through a tunnel against the traffic following an accident, it was held that the inspector's negligence in giving this order broke the chain of causation between the motorist whose negligence caused the original accident and the motor cyclist.

1   *Haynes v Harwood* [1935] 1 KB 146, CA.
2   (1773) 2 Wm Bl 892.
3   [1943] P 32, [1943] 1 All ER 211, CA.
4   [1982] 1 All ER 851, [1982] 1 WLR 349, CA.

Blameworthy actor

21.9 It was at one time thought that any deliberate, conscious act by a person of full capacity, in circumstances where there is no emergency, would operate as a *novus actus interveniens*, but there is no doubt that the law today is far more ready to trace liability back to the defendant, notwithstanding a highly unreasonable intervening act. In *Philco Radio Ltd v J Spurling Ltd*,[1] the defendants negligently misdelivered cases of highly inflammable material to the plaintiffs' premises. A typist employed by the plaintiffs touched a case with a lighted cigarette (intending to do minor damage, although unaware of the true contents) and a serious explosion and fire resulted. The defendants were held liable, notwithstanding the typist's act. Indeed, in extreme cases it has been held that even a deliberate criminal act may not break the chain of causation. This is shown by *Stansbie v Troman*,[2] where a decorator, who was working alone in the plaintiff's house, left it unlocked and unoccupied for two hours. He was held liable for a theft of jewellery which occurred during his absence.

1   [1949] 2 All ER 882, CA.
2   [1948] 2 KB 48, [1948] 1 All ER 599, CA.

Conduct of the plaintiff

21.10 Principles similar to those which govern the conduct of a third party may also apply to an intervening act of the plaintiff himself, which may be held by the court to be so unreasonable that the effect of the defendant's original wrongdoing is entirely wiped out. In *McKew v Holland and Hannen and Cubitts (Scotland) Ltd*,[1] for example, an accident for which the defendants were responsible left the plaintiff's leg with a tendency to collapse suddenly and without warning. When, a few days later, knowing of this tendency, the plaintiff attempted to descend a steep staircase without assistance, it was held that he was entirely to blame for his resulting fall. On the other hand, in *Pigney v Pointers Transport Services Ltd*,[2] the defendants were held liable when serious head injuries, for which they were responsible, led several months later to the plaintiff's suicide.

Decisions upon the effect of the plaintiff's conduct are frequently dealt with in terms of *volenti non fit injuria* (ie whether the plaintiff has consented to bear the legal risk of injury)[3] rather than as matters of causation. In modern times, however, an even more common tendency is to treat the case as one of contributory negligence[4] in order to enable a more flexible decision to be reached. Under this regime a court can hold that the plaintiff's conduct, while not so outrageous as to exonerate the defendant entirely, is nevertheless a sufficiently significant cause of his injury that he should, by suffering a reduction in the damages awarded, be made to bear a proportion of his own loss.

In a number of cases, it can safely be said that the plaintiff's conduct will not affect causation (nor, indeed, amount to contributory negligence); these are considered below.

1 [1969] 3 All ER 1621, HL.
2 [1957] 2 All ER 807, [1957] 1 WLR 1121. Cf *Hyde v Tameside Area Health Authority* (1981) Times, 16 April, CA.
3 Paras 22.2–22.10 below.
4 Paras 22.11–22.16 below.

Rescue cases

21.11 The act of a person who knowingly courts danger in attempting to rescue persons or even property[1] will not normally constitute a *novus actus interveniens*. In *Haynes v Harwood*,[2] for example, the owner of a runaway horse was held liable to a policeman who was injured in attempting to stop it in a crowded street. Where, however, the rescue attempt is unreasonable, for example because the danger outweighs the value of what is threatened, the chain of causation may be broken. In *Cutler v United Dairies (London) Ltd*,[3] the plaintiff was injured in helping the driver of a milk float whose runaway horse had come to rest safely in a field. The Court of Appeal held that, since the danger was over at the time of the plaintiff's intervention, he must be regarded as having caused his own injury. A rescuer has also been held to be a *partial* cause of his own injury and thus to be guilty of contributory negligence,[4] although this related to the manner in which he went about the rescue rather than his initial decision to attempt it.[5]

1 *Hyett v Great Western Rly Co* [1948] 1 KB 345, [1947] 2 All ER 264, CA.
2 [1935] 1 KB 146, CA.
3 [1933] 2 KB 297, CA.
4 Paras 22.11–22.16 below.
5 *Harrison v British Railways Board* [1981] 3 All ER 679.

Emergencies

21.12 Like third parties, whom we discussed in para 21.8 above, plaintiffs who are faced with an emergency are given considerable latitude by the courts in the sense that an instinctive decision, albeit one which turns out to be wrong, will not break the chain of causation unless it is totally unreasonable. In *Jones v Boyce*,[1] the defendant's negligence led the plaintiff to believe that his stagecoach, in which the plaintiff was a passenger, was about to overturn. The coach did not in fact overturn but the plaintiff, in jumping to safety, broke his leg. The defendant was held liable.

1 (1816) 1 Stark 493. See also *Colvilles Ltd v Devine* [1969] 2 All ER 53, [1969] 1 WLR 475, HL.

Legal rights

21.13 The generous treatment which is given by the courts to endangered plaintiffs is also reflected in their attitude towards those who act in defence of their legal rights, where these are infringed by the defendant. In *Clayards v Dethick and Davis*,[1] for example, the defendant unlawfully dug a trench in such a way that the sole access to the plaintiff's stables became dangerous. When a horse which the plaintiff attempted to lead out was injured, the defendant was held liable; it could not be said that the plaintiff had caused his own loss, since this was a risk which he was perfectly entitled to take in exercising his right of way.

A reminder of the discretion which the judge exercises in this field is provided by the celebrated case of *Sayers v Harlow UDC*,[2] where the plaintiff was injured in trying to climb out of a public convenience in which the defendants' negligence, in having no handle on the inside of the door, had immured her. It was held that, since the plaintiff's predicament was one of inconvenience rather than danger, her action was unreasonable; she should, it was held, have endured her loss of liberty rather than run this risk. Nonetheless, her negligence could not be said to have wiped out altogether the effects of the defendants' negligence, and so the plaintiff was held to be 25% responsible for her injuries.

1 (1848) 12 QB 439.
2 [1958] 2 All ER 342, [1958] 1 WLR 623, CA.

Test of novus actus interveniens

21.14 It is clear, from the cases mentioned above, that the question whether an intervening act breaks the chain of causation and so exculpates the defendant cannot be made to turn simply on whether or not it was 'the conscious act of another volition'. It must indeed be regarded as highly doubtful whether a single satisfactory test can be devised; most of the judicial attempts to do so have concentrated either upon the *foreseeability* of the intervening act or upon its *reasonableness*. In so far as these tests are designed to show what *is* a *novus actus interveniens*, rather than what is not, they are patently inadequate. The conduct of the typist, for example, in *Philco Radio Ltd v J Spurling Ltd*[1] must, by any rational standards, be regarded as both unreasonable and unforeseeable; yet the chain of causation remained unbroken.

The converse proposition, that a foreseeable/reasonable act does *not* exonerate the defendant, is much closer to the truth. Even here, however, there are exceptions. In *Quinn v Burch Bros (Builders) Ltd*[2] the plaintiff fell from an unstable trestle, which he was using because the defendants had failed in their contractual duty to provide him with a stepladder. The Court of Appeal held that the plaintiff's unreasonable decision to adopt this dangerous practice was the sole cause of his injury, even though it was foreseeable. It should be noted that it was not open to the court to reduce the damages on the ground of contributory negligence by the plaintiff. The action was one for pure breach of contract, and the Law Reform (Contributory Negligence) Act 1945 therefore had no application.[3]

At the end of the day, it seems that no single legal test can be devised which will accurately predict the outcome of what is essentially a practical, common sense enquiry. The question is whether, in the opinion of the judge, the intervening cause can be regarded as arising in the ordinary course of things out of the risks created by the defendant's breach of duty, or whether it is so powerful and overwhelming that it relegates the defendant's conduct from the status of 'cause' to being merely part of the surrounding circumstances.

1   [1949] 2 KB 33, [1949] 2 All ER 882, CA; para 21.9 above.
2   [1966] 2 QB 370, [1966] 2 All ER 283, CA.
3   See paras 11.15 above and 22.12 below.

Remoteness of damage

21.15   Even where it can be shown that the defendant's breach of duty is a factual cause of the plaintiff's injury, and that no intervening cause has deprived it of relevance, it is still not certain that the defendant will be held responsible for a particular consequence. In attempting to keep liability for a single act of negligence within bounds, the law treats certain results as 'too remote' from the original tort to found an action.[1] The way in which consequences are divided into the categories of 'proximate' and 'remote' is, in truth, a matter of evaluation in which the judge's personal experience, common sense and notions of public policy all play their part. For instance, the courts have recently had to consider whether a defendant should be liable when the plaintiff's head injuries cause a personality change which leads to divorce or to his becoming a sex offender.[2] Such decisions are obviously highly subjective, and yet it is in the nature of lawyers to attempt to relate them to some general principle. In pursuit of a general principle to govern the question whether or not a given consequence of the defendant's negligence is 'too remote' from it to be actionable, English law has wavered between two different 'tests'.

1   The same principle applies to actions for breach of contract, although the detailed rules are different; paras 11.5–11.10 above.
2   *Jones v Jones* [1984] 3 All ER 1003, [1984] 3 WLR 862, CA; *Meah v McCreamer* [1985] 1 All ER 367. Both plaintiffs were successful.

The 'directness' test

21.16   In 1921 the Court of Appeal laid down the rule that, once a defendant was shown to have committed an act of negligence against a plaintiff, he was liable for all the *direct* consequences of that act, whether or not they were *foreseeable*. It is important to realise that this test did not render the question of foreseeability totally irrelevant for, unless the circumstances were such that the defendant ought to have foreseen some kind of injury or damage to the plaintiff, he could not be said to have been negligent at all. What the test meant was that, once it could be shown that *some* damage to the plaintiff was foreseeable, whether or not this actually materialised,[1] the defendant was liable for *all* the damage caused by him, however unforeseeable this might be in kind or extent, or in the manner of its infliction. Foreseeability of the 'kind' of damage actually suffered was required only in the sense that a distinction was drawn between personal injury and damage to property.

The operation of the 'directness' test is exemplified by the case of *Re Polemis and Furness, Withy & Co,*[2] in which it was established. The defendants in that case, having chartered the plaintiffs' ship, used it to carry tins of petrol. Unknown to anyone, petrol vapour leaked from these tins, so that, when the defendants' employees carelessly caused a plank to fall into the hold, and this struck a spark, the ship was completely destroyed by fire. It was found as a fact that the reasonable man would not have foreseen the possibility of fire, although he would have foreseen the possibility of other forms of damage from the plank's impact. The Court of Appeal held that the possibility of this relatively minor damage was enough to render the employees, and through them the defendants, guilty of negligence in dropping the plank. Given this, the defendants were liable in full for the ship's loss, notwithstanding the unforeseeable way in which this occurred.

An important limitation was placed upon the *Re Polemis* principle in *Liebosch Dredger v SS Edison,*[3] where the plaintiff's dredger was sunk by the negligence of the defendants. The plaintiffs were at that time engaged in performing contract work which, on pain of heavy penalty clauses, they had to complete within a given time. Consequently, they required a substitute dredger immediately and, being too poor to buy one, had to hire one at exorbitant rates. The House of Lords held that, while the plaintiffs were entitled to claim from the defendants the cost of buying a suitable replacement dredger, the hire charges were too remote, since these resulted from the plaintiffs' own lack of funds. The plaintiffs' argument based on *Re Polemis* was rejected; this principle, it was said, applied only to the direct *physical* consequences of a negligent act.

1   *Thurogood v Van Den Berghs and Jurgens Ltd* [1951] 2 KB 537, [1951] 1 All ER 682, CA.
2   [1921] 3 KB 560, CA.
3   [1933] AC 449, HL.

The 'foreseeability' test

21.17 Despite criticisms of it as being both unjust and illogical, the 'directness' test was applied by the courts for 40 years until, in the case of *Overseas Tankship (UK) v Morts Dock and Engineering Co*[1] (commonly known as *The Wagon Mound*), the Privy Council declared it to be wrong. The facts of that case were that the defendants negligently spilled large quantities of fuel oil into Sydney Harbour while their ship was being bunkered. Wind and tide carried this oil to the plaintiffs' wharf where two ships were being repaired by means of oxy-acetylene welding. The plaintiffs ceased welding because of the fire risk but, on being assured by experts that fuel oil spread thus thinly on cool water would not ignite, recommenced; as a result a catastrophic fire badly damaged both the wharf and the ships. The Australian courts held that, since *some* damage to the plaintiffs' wharf was foreseeable, viz the fouling of the slipways, the defendants were also responsible (on the basis of *Re Polemis*) for the damage done by fire, notwithstanding that this was unforeseeable. However, on appeal, the Privy Council held that 'foreseeability' must embrace, not only the *fact* of injury, but also its kind; therefore, in this case, the defendants were not liable for the damage done by fire, since it was unforeseeable.

In *Overseas Tankship (UK) v Miller SS Co Pty*[2] (commonly known as *The Wagon Mound* (*No 2*)), a second action arose out of the same incident, this time brought by the owners of the damaged ships. The evidence which was put before the trial judge on this occasion[3] indicated that a reasonable ship's officer would have regarded fire as a possibility, albeit a slight one. The Privy Council held that, so long as the risk was not so remote that a reasonable man would brush it aside as far-fetched, it was foreseeable enough; accordingly, the defendants were held liable.

Two claims have been made for the *Wagon Mound* doctrine. In the first place, it has been said to be logically superior to *Re Polemis* in that it applies the same test to remoteness of damage as that which governs the initial question of breach of duty. On close examination, however, it may be doubted whether the 'foreseeability' test is applied in quite the same way in these two areas. Where breach of duty is concerned, a court is concerned to assess *how foreseeable* the damage was, and to balance this against other factors.[4] Where remoteness of damage is concerned, the principle appears to be that the defendant is liable if the damage in question was at all foreseeable; the degree of foreseeability is not relevant.

Apart from being arguably more logical than *Re Polemis*, the *Wagon Mound* principle is also said to be more just, since it is unfair to expose a defendant who is guilty of a trivial act of negligence to liability for the serious unforeseeable consequences of that act. This, however, prompts the question: given that the unforeseeable loss must fall on someone, is it more just to place it on the defendant, who is at least guilty of some negligence, or on the plaintiff, who is guilty of none at all? In truth, the answer is a matter of policy, and depends upon whether plaintiffs or defendants are to be favoured.

Whatever the respective merits of the two tests, and despite the fact that decisions of the Privy Council are theoretically of persuasive authority only, there can be no doubt that, in the eyes of English judges, 'directness' has now been superseded by 'foreseeability'. The practical effects of this change can best be measured by considering separately the three identifying characteristics of any particular consequence in respect of which damages may be claimed. These are the *kind* of damage, the *manner* of its infliction and its *extent*. As we shall see, the interpretation which since 1961 has been given to 'foreseeability' in this area means that the change brought about by the *Wagon Mound* principle is less fundamental than might have been expected.

1 [1961] AC 388, [1961] 1 All ER 404, PC.
2 [1967] 1 AC 617, [1966] 2 All ER 709, PC.
3 Why the evidence in the two cases was different is not easy to see. It may be, however, that the plaintiffs in *Wagon Mound* (*No 1*) did not really *want* to establish that the fire was foreseeable, lest they be held contributorily negligent for continuing with their welding.
4 Paras 20.10–20.14 above.

Kind of damage
21.18 Under *Re Polemis*, the requirement of foreseeability extended to the

kind of damage in issue only in the very broad sense that the law distinguished between injury to the person and to property. Since *Wagon Mound*, however, it is clear that the categories are narrower (foreseeability of damage by fouling, for example, will not render a defendant liable for damage by fire). The extent to which this represents a change in the law depends upon how precisely these classes are defined, and the general trend of decisions since 1961 has undoubtedly been against the drawing of over-nice distinctions. In *Bradford v Robinson Rentals Ltd*,[1] for example, a van driver, sent by his employers on a long journey in exceptionally cold weather in an unheated vehicle, suffered frostbite. It was held that, even if frostbite itself was unforeseeable, it was insufficiently akin to other foreseeable injuries from cold and fatigue to permit recovery.

1 [1967] 1 All ER 267, [1967] 1 WLR 337.

Manner of infliction of damage
21.19 The approach of judges to the question of how damage is caused has, by and large, shown the same generosity as that which characterises their treatment of 'kind of damage'. Once again, foreseeability of the general outline, rather than of precise details, is all that is required. There has, for example, been a readiness to impose liability upon the defendant where an injury which he has caused to the plaintiff leads to a second accident,[1] to medical treatment with adverse effects[2] or to even more unlikely consequences.[3]

The general attitude of the courts is well illustrated by the case of *Hughes v Lord Advocate*[4], where employees of the Post Office left an open manhole covered by a canvas shelter and surrounded by paraffin warning lamps. An eight-year-old boy took one of these lamps into the shelter, where he accidentally knocked it down the hole; there was a violent explosion and the boy was severely burned. The Scottish courts held that the defendants were not liable, on the ground that, while injury by burning was foreseeable, the explosion was not. The House of Lords, however, held that such a distinction was too fine to be accepted, and that the accident fell within the area of risk which the defendants had created.

The occasional decision stands out as taking a much narrower line, although it may for that very reason be regarded with some doubt. One such is *Doughty v Turner Manufacturing Co Ltd*,[5] where the defendants' employee negligently dropped an asbestos cement cover into a cauldron of molten liquid. There was no splash, but two minutes later, due to an unforeseeable chemical reaction, the liquid erupted and the plaintiff was burned. The Court of Appeal held that, even if injury by splashing were foreseeable, this eruption was not; not could it be treated as a mere variant of the foreseeable risk. The defendants were accordingly not liable.

1 *Wieland v Cyril Lord Carpets Ltd* [1969] 3 All ER 1006.
2 *Robinson v Post Office* [1974] 2 All ER 737, [1974] 1 WLR 1176, CA.
3 See *Jones v Jones* [1984] 3 All ER 1003, [1984] 3 WLR 862, CA; *Meah v McCreamer* [1985] 1 All ER 367, para 21.15 above.
4 [1963] AC 837, [1963] 1 All ER 705, HL.
5 [1964] 1 QB 518, [1964] 1 All ER 98, CA.

Extent of damage
21.20 The *kind* of damage, then, and the *manner* in which it is caused, must both be reasonably foreseeable, albeit in only a general sense. By

contrast, the *extent* of the damage so caused need not be foreseeable at all. In *Vacwell Engineering Co Ltd v BDH Chemicals Ltd*,[1] for example, the defendants negligently failed to warn the plaintiffs that a chemical which they had supplied was liable to explode on contact with water. An employee of the plaintiffs placed a large quantity of this substance in a sink. This resulted in a violent explosion, which extensively damaged the plaintiffs' premises. It was found that, while a minor explosion was foreseeable, one of this magnitude was not; nevertheless, the defendants were held liable for all the damage.

The best-known illustrations of the principle that the extent of damage is not subject to the requirement of foreseeability are the so-called 'egg-shell skull' cases, in which the defendant is held fully liable when the plaintiff's injuries are aggravated by some inherent defect such as haemophilia, notwithstanding that the defendant could not possibly have foreseen this. The basis for these decisions is the rule that 'a tortfeasor takes his victim as he finds him', a rule which was held, in *Smith v Leech Brain & Co Ltd*,[2] to have survived *The Wagon Mound*. The defendants in that case negligently caused an employee's lip to be burned by molten metal. This burn activated an unsuspected pre-malignant cancerous condition which, three years later, led to the man's death. The defendants were held liable, not only for the initial burn, but also for the death.

Although the 'egg-shell skull' principle has been applied to plaintiffs with a weak heart,[3] an allergy to certain vaccine[4] and even an 'egg-shell personality',[5] the House of Lords ruled in 1933 that it could not be extended to a plaintiff's financial state.[6] Consequently, if the loss caused to a plaintiff was aggravated due to his lack of means, the additional loss could not be treated as having been caused by the defendant. In recent years, the courts appear to have retreated somewhat from this position; on several occasions, the Court of Appeal has distinguished *Liesbosch Dredger v S S Edison* on grounds which are unconvincing. For example, in *Dodd Properties (Kent) Ltd v Canterbury City Council*,[7] the plaintiffs sued the defendants for the cost of repairing their garage, which the defendants had negligently damaged. By the time the case came to court, the cost of repairs had escalated and the defendants claimed that they were liable only for what the repairs would have cost if put in hand at an earlier date. The Court of Appeal held that, while pure lack of funds would have given the plaintiffs no excuse to delay (and would thus have restricted their claim to the lower figure), their *decision* to delay until they had recovered damages (based upon principles of 'cash flow') was a reasonable one. The defendants were therefore liable in full.

1   [1971] 1 QB 111n, [1970] 3 All ER 553n, CA.
2   [1962] 2 QB 405, [1961] 2 All ER 1159.
3   *Love v Port of London Authority* [1959] 2 Lloyd's Rep 541.
4   *Robinson v Post Office* [1974] 2 All ER 737, [1974] 1 WLR 1176, CA.
5   *Malcolm v Broadhurst* [1970] 3 All ER 508.
6   *Liesbosch Dredger v SS Edison* [1933] AC 449, HL; para 21.16 above.
7   [1980] 1 All ER 928, [1980] 1 WLR 433, CA; para 31.13 below.

Chapter 22

Defences to negligence

22.1 The defendant in a negligence action may, of course, seek to defeat the plaintiff's claim by arguing that one of the essential elements of liability is missing. He may, for example, be able to show the court that no duty of care was owed, or that his carelessness did not cause the plaintiff's loss. In so doing, the defendant is not really establishing a defence; rather the plaintiff is failing to make out his case.

Apart from producing arguments of the kind outlined above, the defendant may seek to rely on either or both of two specific defences. These are, first, *'volenti non fit injuria'*, the rule that a person cannot complain of harm to which he has expressly or impliedly consented, or of which he has assumed the legal risk; and, second, contributory negligence, which applies where the plaintiff is partly responsible for his own injury. A significant difference between these defences is that a plea of *volenti*, if successful, defeats the plaintiff's action altogether; contributory negligence, on the other hand, is no longer a complete answer but, since 1945, leads only to a reduction in the damages awarded. Not surprisingly, in view of the added flexibility which apportionment brings, the courts prefer to base their decisions on contributory negligence; as a result, it is nowadays comparatively rare to find *volenti* successfully pleaded.

We shall now consider these two defences. It should be noted that, notwithstanding the title of this chapter, they apply across a wide area of the law of tort, although it is in relation to negligence that most problems arise.

Volenti non fit injuria

Consent
22.2 Although some writers regard the essence of this defence as being the plaintiff's *submission to injury* (a question of fact to be deduced from his conduct), the majority hold to the traditional view that it depends upon his (possibly fictitious) *consent*. This approach is at its most straightforward in relation to intentional torts such as trespass to the person; a boxer cannot complain of a fair punch, for example, nor a patient of the invasion of his body which is inherent in a surgical operation.[1] Consent, however, has its limits; even a participant in a fist fight may not be precluded from claiming damages if his antagonist inflicts serious injury with a savage blow which is quite out of proportion to the occasion.[2]

In torts of strict liability, too, few theoretical complexities are raised by *volenti*, although the terminology here is different. A plaintiff will lose his case wherever it can fairly be said that he has *assumed the legal risk* of being injured. Thus, a person who keeps a dog which he knows to be vicious takes the legal risk that it will bite someone; but that legal risk will be transferred to the shoulders of anyone who ignores a clear 'Beware of the Dog' notice.[3]

1 See para 22.3 below.
2 *Lane v Holloway* [1968] 1 QB 379, [1967] 3 All ER 129, CA.
3 *Cummings v Granger* [1977] QB 397, [1977] 1 All ER 104, CA.

Knowledge

22.3 Full knowledge of the nature and extent of a risk is a legal prerequisite of a person's consent to run it. In this context *actual* knowledge is what counts; thus in *Sarch v Blackburn*,[1] where the plaintiff was bitten by the defendant's dog, his right to recover damages was held to be unaffected by a large 'Beware of the Dog' notice, since he could not read.

The House of Lords has recently considered the effect of a surgeon's failure to warn a patient of the risks inherent in a proposed operation. Many American states have a doctrine of 'informed consent' whereby, if the patient is not given full information, his or her consent is vitiated and the operation becomes a trespass, even if carried out with all due care and skill. In *Sidaway v Board of Governors of the Bethlem Royal Hospital and Maudsley Hospital*,[2] the House of Lords held that this doctrine has no place in English law; a surgeon's duty to warn is merely part of the duty of care which he owes to his patient and is judged in the same way as any other aspect of his job.

Where a person's consent is obtained by fraud, it is usually said to be no defence, since he will lack the necessary knowledge. However, in the Irish case of *Hegarty v Shine*,[3] where the plaintiff sued her lover for trespass to the person (he had infected her with venereal disease), it was held that the defendant's concealment of his condition was not enough to vitiate her consent to intercourse; the fraud did not go to the nature of the act, but concerned a collateral detail.[4]

Knowledge is a necessary condition of this defence, but knowledge alone is not sufficient to show consent. A plaintiff may be fully entitled to undertake a risk of which he is aware, for example to keep his job,[5] effect a rescue[6] or exercise his legal right which the defendant has infringed.[7]

1 (1830) 4 C & P 297. See also *Harrison v Vincent* [1982] RTR 8; *Latchford v Spedeworth International Ltd* (1983) Times, 11 October; para 22.7 below.
2 [1985] 1 All ER 643, [1985] 2 WLR 480, HL.
3 (1878) 4 LR Ir 288, 14 Cox CC 124.
4 This refinement, introduced from the criminal law, seems wholly out of place as between the parties to a civil action; we think that any fraud should suffice to defeat consent.
5 Para 22.8 below.
6 Paras 22.9 to 22.10 below.
7 See *Clayards v Dethick and Davis* (1848) 12 QB 439; para 21.13 above.

Voluntariness

22.4 To be of any legal effect, a person's consent to assume a risk must be fully and freely given. There must be no pressure upon him sufficient for it to be said that his free will was impaired. For example, in cases of employer and employee,[1] it is usually said that economic pressure on the employee not to lose his job prevents the implication that he assumes the risks inherent in it. Similarly, in rescue cases,[2] *volenti* is ruled out by the moral obligation on the plaintiff to go to the aid of someone in danger.

1 Para 22.8 below.
2 Paras 22.9 and 22.10 below.

Consent in negligence cases

22.5 *Express consent* It is in relation to negligence, and those other torts where liability is based upon lack of care, that most difficulties are found. Nor is this surprising. A finding of *volenti* means, in effect, that the plaintiff has licensed the defendant to commit a tort against him, and the very idea of the plaintiff agreeing to allow the defendant to be negligent seems highly unrealistic.

Where the plaintiff is alleged to have consented expressly to negligence on the part of the defendant, the case is usually concerned with an exemption clause, although a non-contractual waiver is in principle also effective.[1] However, statute has now deprived the latter of one of its most important practical applications, namely, 'Ride at your own risk' as regards passengers in motor vehicles, at least where passenger insurance is compulsory.[2] Further, the extent to which liability for negligence may be excluded by a contract term or notice is heavily restricted,[3] and the Unfair Contract Terms Act 1977, s2(3) makes it clear that a person's agreement to or awareness of a purported exemption clause does not in itself lead to the conclusion that he assumes any risk.

1 *Buckpitt v Oates* [1968] 1 All ER 1145.
2 Road Traffic Act 1972, s148(3).
3 Paras 9.41–9.53 above.

22.6 *Implied consent* Attempts to show that the plaintiff by his conduct has clearly undertaken to bear the consequences of the defendant's negligence are seldom successful. The circumstances in which such a plea is most likely to be accepted are where the defendant's negligence take place first, so that its full effects are visible to the plaintiff before he puts himself in danger. In *Cutler v United Dairies (London) Ltd*,[1] due to negligence for which the defendants were responsible, a horse ran away into a field. There was no danger, but the driver called for assistance in pacifying the animal, and the plaintiff was injured in helping him. The Court of Appeal held that the plaintiff had obviously assumed the risk and could not, therefore, recover damages.

The very idea of the plaintiff taking on the risk that the defendant will in future act negligently towards him is one which judges dislike; indeed it has been suggested on more than one occasion that *volenti* can never apply to neglience in the simple sense of a duty of care based upon foreseeability.[2] This may overstate the case, but it is worth remembering that the vital question is not whether the plaintiff foolishly risked injury, but whether he agreed in effect that the *legal* risk of loss should be upon him and not upon the defendant.

1 [1933] 2 KB 297, CA; para 21.11 above.
2 *Dann v Hamilton* [1939] 1 KB 509 at 512, [1939] 1 All ER 59 at 60; *Wooldridge v Sumner* [1963] 2 QB 43 at 69, [1962] 2 All ER 978 at 990, CA. See, however, *Ashton v Turner* [1981] QB 137, [1980] 3 All ER 870.

22.7 *Variable duties* Although the courts by and large have hesitated to put the plaintiff out of court altogether on the ground of *volenti* in cases where the defendant is clearly at fault, there is undoubtedly some sympathy for the view that the plaintiff's carelessness for his own safety should not go entirely unmarked. Nowadays, of course, this can be achieved through the medium of apportionment for contributory negligence. Quite apart from this, however, the courts have flirted with the idea that the relationship between the parties, and their appreciation of the risks involved in a particular enterprise, may make it fair to impose something less than a full duty of care upon the defendant. In *Wooldridge v Sumner*,[1] for example, a competitor at the National Horse Show took a corner too fast, injuring a photographer who was standing in the arena. In holding the defendant not liable, a majority of the Court of Appeal laid down that no duty of reasonable care was owed, and that, since the photographer (and indeed any other spectator) would not expect a competitor to consider his interests, liability could only be imposed if the defendant had shown 'reckless disregard of the spectator's safety'.

The 'reckless disregard' test has been applied subsequently, but its limits should be noted. In *Harrison v Vincent*,[2] a sidecar passenger was injured when a mechanical defect caused the defendant to lose control of the motor cycle combination during a race. The Court of Appeal held that anything done in the flurry and excitement of the sport (ie the actual riding of the machine) should be judged on the *Wooldridge v Sumner* principle; the mechanical preparations, however, done in the calm of the workshop fell within the normal rules of negligence. Defects in course design or safety are also subject to the normal rules.[3]

Although the introduction of various levels of duty within the general scope of negligence raises theoretical complexities, it proponents claim that it achieves a relatively just result. Nonetheless, it has not been universally accepted by judges as the correct approach. In *Wilks v Cheltenham Home Guard Motor Cycle and Light Car Club*,[4] where a spectator at a motor cycle scramble was injured when a machine inexplicably jumped over a safety rope, it was said that even a competitor must exercise reasonable care, although what is reasonable depends upon all the circumstances, including the fact that he is expected to go all out to win. Similarly, in *Nettleship v Weston*,[5] where a learner driver crashed into a lamp-post and injured her instructor, the Court of Appeal rejected the argument that the instructor must necessarily be taken to accept a lower standard of skill from his pupil than from an experienced driver. Here, the instructor, by requiring an assurance that his pupil had passenger insurance, had shown that he did not accept any legal risk of injury. Indeed, the court held that, in assessing the defendant's conduct, no allowance at all was to be made for the fact that she was only learning to drive.

1 [1963] 2 QB 43, [1962] 2 All ER 978, CA.
2 [1982] RTR 8.
3 *Harrison v Vincent* [1982] RTR 8; *Latchford v Spedeworth International Ltd* (1983) Times, 11 October
4 [1971] 2 All ER 369, [1971] 1 WLR 668, CA. See also *Condon v Basi* [1985] 2 All ER 453 (footballer's duty of care to opponent).
5 [1971] 2 QB 691, [1971] 3 All ER 581, CA; paras 20.3 and 20.9 above.

Employment cases
22.8 If the mere awareness of a risk signified consent to run it, *volenti*

would seem particularly applicable to cases of injuries sustained in the course of employment. Indeed in the early nineteenth century, when society regarded the growth of industry as more important than the safety of the workforce, the view was often taken that a workman who continued to do his job in the face of clear danger could not recover damages for either negligence or breach of statutory duty if he was subsequently injured. A more humane era, however, was ushered in by the leading case of *Smith v Baker & Sons*[1] where the plaintiff, who was working in a cutting, was injured when a crane dropped a stone on him. For several months this crane had swung its loads over the plaintiff's head, and at no time had any warning been given that it was about to do so. The House of Lords held that the plaintiff could not be said to have accepted the risk merely by virtue of continuing to work for the defendant with knowledge of it.

The principle of *Smith v Baker* was extended beyond the strict field of employer and employee in *Burnett v British Waterways Board*,[2] where the plaintiff had to use the defendants' facilities in the course of his employment. A notice of which the plaintiff was aware disclaimed responsibility for any injury sustained, but the Court of Appeal held that this was not binding on the plaintiff, who had no free choice in the matter.

The desire of the courts to protect employees from being forced by economic pressures to submit to risks means that an employer who is guilty of negligence will today find it almost impossible to plead *volenti*. Further, one who is personally in breach of a statutory duty will certainly not be allowed to do so, since it would be totally opposed to public policy to permit someone to contract out of the statute.[3] Even in this enlightened age, however, there may be extreme cases in which the use of the defence against an employee would not offend public policy, and one such was *ICI Ltd v Shatwell*.[4] That case concerned two shot-firers who, in flagrant breach of statutory duties which were imposed upon them personally, tested a firing circuit without taking cover. When an explosion injured one of the men, he claimed that his employers were vicariously liable for his colleague's breach of statutory duty. The House of Lords held that, since the employers were morally innocent in this matter (having done everything in their power to see that these regulations were obeyed) and since they were personally not guilty of any tort, the defence of *volenti* was open to them and they were, therefore, not liable.

1   [1891] AC 325, HL.
2   [1973] 2 All ER 631, [1973] 1 WLR 700, CA.
3   *Baddeley v Earl Granville* (1887) 19 QBD 423, DC.
4   [1965] AC 656, [1964] 2 All ER 999, HL.

Rescue cases

22.9   At first sight, *volenti* would seem highly apposite to the case of someone who risks (and receives) injury in attempting to rescue another person[1] from danger. Such a rule, however, would hardly encourage humanitarian conduct and, not surprisingly, the law does not apply it. In *Haynes v Harwood*,[2] for example, where a policeman was injured in stopping a runaway horse in a crowded street, it was held that the defendant, whose negligence had permitted the horse to run away, could not avoid liability by claiming that the policeman had voluntarily incurred the risk.

The theoretical basis on which a rescuer is allowed to recover damages is that, because he acts under some form of moral compulsion, he lacks the necessary free will to assume the risk. It has been suggested that the plaintiff in *Haynes v Harwood* was under a legal obligation to act as he did, by virtue of his status as a policeman. This, however, does not seem crucial; in *Chadwick v British Transport Commission*,[3] a person who volunteered to help in the wreckage of a disastrous train crash was awarded damages for nervous shock, although it could not be said that he owed anyone a legal duty to act in this way.

1 Or property; *Hyett v Great Western Rly Co* [1948] 1 KB 345, [1947] 2 All ER 264, CA.
2 [1935] 1 KB 146, CA; para 21.11 above.
3 [1967] 2 All ER 945, [1967] 1 WLR 912.

22.10 It is now settled that an action brought by an injured rescuer is quite independent of any claim by the person rescued. It rests on a separate duty of care which is owed to the rescuer personally by whoever causes the danger and hence the rescue. As a result, a rescuer is not adversely affected by any defect in the claim of the person rescued, such as contributory negligence, or the fact that the person is a trespasser.[1]

The legal independence of the rescuer's claim has further consequences. For instance, a person who negligently endangers himself may be liable to a rescuer, if the circumstances are such as to render a rescue attempt foreseeable.[2] And the Supreme Court of Canada has also held that a rescuer who so bungles the job that someone is induced to make a second attempt may be liable to the second rescuer if he is injured.[3]

1 *Videan v British Transport Commission* [1963] 2 QB 650, [1963] 2 All ER 860, CA.
2 *Harrison v British Railways Board* [1981] 3 All ER 679.
3 *Horsley v Maclaren, The Ogopogo* [1971] 2 Lloyd's Rep 410.

Contributory negligence

22.11 At common law a plaintiff who, by failing to take reasonable care of himself, contributed to his own injury could recover nothing at all from the defendant whose tort would otherwise have been regarded as the legal cause. The obvious harshness of this rule led to a number of decisions denying that plaintiffs were contributorily negligent, despite evidence to the contrary. These decisions must be regarded as doubtful now that the rule itself has been removed by statute.

The 1945 Act

22.12 The present law on contributory negligence is governed by the Law Reform (Contributory Negligence) Act 1945, s1(1) of which provides that where a person suffers damage as the result partly of his own fault and partly of the fault of another person, the damages recoverable by him shall be reduced to such extent as the court thinks just and equitable having regard to the claimant's share in the responsibility for the damage.

Interestingly, the Act speaks, not of negligence but of *fault*. According to s4, this means 'negligence, breach of statutory duty or other act or omission which gives rise to a liability in tort or would, apart from this Act, give rise to the defence of contributory negligence'. Clearly, then, this defence is available not only in cases of negligence, but also in a number of other torts.

It does not operate, however, in cases where the defendant intends to cause injury.[1]

The 1945 Act is clearly inapplicable to actions based purely on a breach of contract.[2] What has not yet been authoritatively decided, however, is the precise legal position where a plaintiff's claim might equally well be framed in tort (for negligence) or for breach of contract. Assuming that the plaintiff has a choice as to how he will frame his action,[3] it seems absurd that he should be able to evade the defence of contributory negligence by suing in contract rather than in tort. Nonetheless, it has been held in one case[4] that this may indeed be done, although the statements of law found in other cases are rather more equivocal.[5]

1 *Lane v Holloway* [1968] 1 QB 379, [1967] 3 All ER 129, CA.
2 Para 11.15 above.
3 See *Tai Hing Cotton Mill Ltd v Liu Chong Hing Bank Ltd* [1985] 2 All ER 947, [1985] 3 WLR 317, PC; para 18.5 above.
4 *Marintrans AB v Comet Shipping Co Ltd, The Shinjitsu Maru No 5* [1985] 3 All ER 442, [1985] 1 WLR 1270.
5 See *Basildon District Council v J E Lesser (Properties) Ltd* [1985] QB 839, [1985] 1 All ER 20.

Standard of care

22.13 When a defendant alleges that the plaintiff was contributorily negligent, he is not called upon to show that the plaintiff owed him a legal duty; contributory negligence consists simply of failing to take such care of oneself as is reasonable in all the circumstances of the case. As a result, the plaintiff's conduct is to be evaluated in much the same way as is a defendant's for the purpose of establishing a breach of a duty of care.[1] Indeed, many of the factors which we considered in that context (such as the standard of care demanded of children, and the extent to which the reasonable man must foresee negligence in others) are of special relevance here. So too, those cases where the plaintiff's conduct tends not be be regarded as a *novus actus interveniens*[2] (such as rescue attempts, or the plaintiff's instinctive reactions to an emergency) may well today give rise to a finding of contributory negligence.[3] There, the plaintiff's lack of care does not overwhelm the defendant's breach in causative terms, but operates alongside it.

In considering the defence of *volenti* we noted that knowledge of a risk is not the same, in legal terms, as acceptance of it.[4] Such knowledge may, however, lead a court to the conclusion that the plaintiff was contributorily negligent in failing to take avoiding action. In *Owens v Brimmell*,[5] for example, a passenger in a car who knew that his driver had been drinking heavily lost 20% of his damages when the driver negligently crashed the car and the passenger was injured. So too, in *Gregory v Kelly*,[6] the plaintiff was held to be contributorily negligent in travelling in a car when he knew that the footbrake did not work.

Theoretically, at least, the standard to which the plaintiff must conform is identical to that which is demanded of the defendant. In practice, however, this is not strictly true, for plaintiffs are treated rather more leniently. As to why this should be so, various reasons have been suggested. In the first place, it seems legitimate to argue that conduct which endangers others is more serious than conduct which only endangers oneself, and that consequently a defendant must take greater steps to keep the risk within bounds. Second, there is no doubt that modern trends are towards increasing the availability of compensation and that both the raising of standards for defendants and the lowering of those for plaintiffs are means to this end. Third, in the specific case of industrial safety regulations, the courts feel that it would be wrong to use apportionment so as to deprive a workman of their intended benefit, especially where his 'fault' consists of inattention to a job which is boring, tiring and repetitious.[7]

1 Ch 20 above.
2 Paras 21.10 to 21.13 above.
3 See *Harrison v British Railways Board* [1981] 3 All ER 679; para 21.11 above.
4 Para 22.3 above.
5 [1977] QB 859, [1976] 3 All ER 765.
6 [1978] RTR 426.
7 See, for example, *Mullard v Ben Line Steamers Ltd* [1971] 2 All ER 424 at 428, CA.

Causation

22.14 It is not enough for a defendant to show that the plaintiff failed to take reasonable care of himself; the lack of care must also be shown to have contributed, at least in part, to the plaintiff's damage. This is simply a matter of causation, although it is worth mentioning that modern courts, secure in the knowledge that they can dispense justice through the medium of apportionment, are more ready to regard the plaintiff's conduct as a legal cause than were their predecessors when such a finding would have defeated the action altogether.

It should be noted that the plaintiff's fault need not contribute to the accident, but only to the damage. Thus, a moped rider who was in no way responsible for a collision nevertheless lost 15% of his damages, since the evidence established that his injuries would have been substantially less severe had he worn a helmet.[1] After a good deal of hesitation on the part of trial judges, the Court of Appeal held that the same principle applied to seat belts in motor vehicles;[2] failure by a driver or front-seat passenger to wear a seat belt would normally lead to a reduction in damages of between 15 and 25%, depending on whether the injuries would have been substantially or even totally avoided (and irrespective of what other injuries the seat belt itself might have caused[3]). The Court of Appeal recognised that there might be circumstances such as pregnancy, extreme corpulence, or a phobia about being trapped,[4] in which it might not be unreasonable to travel without a belt. However, now that Parliament has made their use compulsory,[5] it is doubtful whether such loopholes still apply.

Since the attribution of legal cause is really, as we have seen,[6] a matter in which the judge exercises a choice, no hard and fast rules can be laid down. An important factor, however, is that of *risk*; if the plaintiff's damage does not fall within the scope of the risk to which he unreasonably exposed himself, then his negligence is not contributory. In *Jones v Livox Quarries Ltd*,[7] an employee who stood, contrary to instructions, on the back of a moving traxcavator was injured when another vehicle collided with it. The plaintiff argued that his negligence did not contribute to his injuries, since the only risk he had undertaken was that of falling off. The Court of Appeal, while accepting that he would not have been in any way to blame if, during his unauthorised ride, he had been shot by a negligent sportsman, nevertheless felt that the actual accident was within the risk. Accordingly damages were reduced by 20%. A similar problem faced the House of

Lords in *Westwood v Post Office*,[8] where an employee was killed when he ignored a notice which read: 'Authorised personnel only', entered a lift motor room and fell through a defective trapdoor. A bare (3–2) majority held that, since the notice gave no indication of danger, let alone of the specific danger, the trespasser's only fault was disobedience, and not contributory negligence.

1 *O'Connell v Jackson* [1972] 1 QB 270, [1971] 3 All ER 129, CA.
2 *Froom v Butcher* [1976] QB 286, [1975] 3 All ER 520, CA.
3 *Patience v Andrews* [1983] RTR 447.
4 *Condon v Condon* [1978] RTR 483.
5 Road Traffic Act 1972, s33A.
6 Paras 21.7–21.14 above.
7 [1952] 2 QB 608, CA.
8 [1974] AC 1, [1973] 3 All ER 184, HL.

Identification
22.15 In some circumstances, A may be 'identified' with B for the purposes of contributory negligence. Where this is so, it means that any damages which are awarded to A in an action against a third party may be reduced because of the contributory negligence of B. For example, if a lorry is involved in a collision with another vehicle due to the negligence of both drivers, any damages which the lorry driver's employers (as owners of the lorry) claim from the other driver may be reduced on the ground of their employee's contributory negligence.

This doctrine of 'identification' applies wherever there is a relationship sufficient to impose vicarious liability[1] and to a claim by dependants under the Fatal Accidents Act 1976, where the deceased was partly to blame for his own death.[2]

1 Ch 30 below.
2 Para 31.11 below.

Apportionment
22.16 Section 1(1) of the 1945 Act instructs the court to reduce the plaintiff's damages to such an extent as is just and equitable in view of the plaintiff's 'share in the responsibility for the damage'. No statutory guidance is given for this process, but two factors are clearly regarded by the courts as relevant. The first of these, naturally, is the degree of fault which may be attributed to each party. This, however, cannot be the sole criterion for, in a case where the defendant is strictly liable (eg for a breach of statutory duty), it would lead to the absurd conclusion that a slightly negligent plaintiff receives nothing at all. Thus a second factor, that of 'causative importance', must also be considered.[1]

It should not be thought that equal carelessness compels equal division. For example, it is not unreasonable to place a greater burden upon a negligent motorist than upon an equally negligent pedestrian, since the conduct of the former entails grave risks to others as well as to himself. All that can be said is that the courts use their flexible power to the full; reductions have ranged from a mere 5% in the case of a passenger whose failure to wear a seat-belt was itself partly the driver's fault[2] to 80% where safety regulations were deliberately flouted by a workman and his collea-gue.[3] Indeed, the Court of Appeal has even upheld a finding that an injured workman was 100% 'contributorily negligent'[4] although, in such a case, it might be preferable to say that he was the sole cause of his injuries.

1   *Stapley v Gypsum Mines Ltd* [1953] AC 663 at 682, [1953] 2 All ER 478 at 486, HL.
2   *Pasternack v Poulton* [1973] 2 All ER 74, [1973] 1 WLR 476.
3   *Stapley v Gypsum Mines Ltd* [1953] AC 663, [1953] 2 All ER 478, HL.
4   *Jayes v I M I (Kynoch) Ltd* [1985] ICR 155, CA.

Chapter 23
Liability for dangerous premises

23.1 In this chapter we consider a number of way in which tortious liability may arise out of the condition of premises (land, buildings and other structures). Central to this area of law is the statutory duty which is owed by every occupier of land to his lawful visitors. In addition, a somewhat lower duty (also now governed by statute) is owed to trespassers. In two further cases, defective premises may serve as a ground of liability for those who are no longer occupiers: landlords who are in breach of their repairing obligations, and persons who sell or let property in a dangerous condition.

It is important to appreciate that this chapter is concerned only with injury or damage which is caused on the land itself. Dangerous premises may, of course, cause damage to persons or goods on adjoining property or on the highway. However, where this is so a claim in respect of the damage falls under the heading of nuisance and will be considered when that tort is discussed.[1]

1 Ch 26 below.

Lawful visitors

Scope of the duty
23.2 Before 1957, the common law which governed the liability of an occupier to his lawful visitors was complex to an unsatisfactory degree. Different classes of visitor (eg those in whose visit the occupier had a material interest, and those whose presence was merely permitted) were owed different standards of duty, a state of affairs which led to fine and often technical distinctions being drawn in borderline cases. Fortunately, most of these differences may now be forgotten, for the law has been restated on a simpler and more rational basis by the Occupiers' Liability Act 1957.

Section 2(1) of that Act provides: 'An occupier of premises owes the same duty, the "common duty of care", to all his visitors, except in so far as he is free to and does extend, restrict, modify or exclude his duty to any visitor or visitors by agreement or otherwise'.

Most of the litigation in this area concerns personal injury or death, but the Act of 1957 makes it clear that the occupier's duty is not restricted in law; s1(3) provides that the statutory rules also apply to the obligations of a person occupying or having control over any premises or structure in respect of damage to property, including the property of persons who are not themselves his visitors. Further, where damage to property is proved, the occupier's liability extends also to consequential financial loss, such as the expense of salvaging damaged goods.[1]

1 *A M F International Ltd v Magnet Bowling Ltd* [1968] 2 All ER 789, [1968] 1 WLR 1028.

Exclusion of liability by contract

23.3 Section 2(1) clearly envisages that an occupier may exclude or restrict the duty which he would otherwise owe to a visitor. However, the qualification 'in so far as he is free to' indicates that there are circumstances in which the occupier is denied this freedom. It seems, for instance, that an innkeeper is not permitted to exclude his liability for damage to the property of guests.[1] Further, while s5 of the Act of 1957 makes a contract between the occupier and a visitor decisive as to the rights of the latter, s3 provides that a person entering premises under a contract to which he is not a party may not be adversely affected by the terms of that contract.[2]

Any attempt by an occupier to exclude or restrict his duty by means of a contractual term is subject to the rules which govern exemption clauses.[3] Of fundamental importance is the Unfair Contract Terms Act 1977. This, when it applies, prohibits the exclusion or restriction of liability for personal injury or death altogether, and makes the exclusion or restriction of liability for other kinds of damage subject to a test of 'reasonableness'. The provisions of this Act are considered in detail elsewhere;[4] for present purposes it is sufficient to state that its operation is limited to duties which arise 'from the occupation of premises used for business purposes of the occupier'. However, a relaxation of the rules, which was introduced by the Occupiers' Liability Act 1984, s2, permits a 'business occupier' to exclude or restrict liability to those whom he permits to enter his land for recreational or educational purposes which do not themselves form part of his business. A private occupier is not affected by the Unfair Contract Terms Act, but any attempt which he makes to exclude or restrict his liability by means of a contract term must still satisfy the stringent requirements of common law.

1 *Williams v Linnit* [1951] 1KB 565, [1951] 1 All ER 278, CA; see now the Hotel Proprietors Act 1956, s2(3).
2 Para 23.12 below.
3 Paras 9.24–9.53 above.
4 Paras 9.41–9.53 above.

Exclusion of liability by notice

23.4 Occupiers not infrequently seek to exclude or restrict their liability by displaying prominently on their premises notices which state, for example: 'Entry at Own Risk' or 'No Liability is Accepted for any Injury or Damage'. In principle, it appears that this practice is effective. The leading case is *Ashdown v Samuel Williams & Sons Ltd,*[1] in which the defendants, who owned and occupied a dockyard estate containing railway sidings, erected notices around their land, stating that persons entering did so at their own risk. The plaintiff (who was held to be a lawful visitor) took a short cut to work across the land and was injured by the shunting of trucks, which was negligently carried on by the defendants' employees. It was held by the Court of Appeal that the notices were effective to exclude the defendants' liability.

Ashdown v Williams was decided before the Occupier's Liability Act 1957 became law and, in view of the criticism which the decision received, doubts were expressed as to whether it had survived the Act. In *White v Blackmore*,[2] however, it was followed by a majority of the Court of Appeal, who held that the Act's reference to exclusion of liability 'by agreement or otherwise' clearly covered this situation.

The principle which underlies both *Ashdown v Williams* and *White v Blackmore* is that, since an occupier is entitled to say: 'Keep Out', he is equally entitled to impose conditions upon which persons may enter.[3] This principle is quite distinct, therefore, from two other defences which may be available to an occupier, namely, that he gave a visitor a sufficient warning of a danger to make him reasonably safe,[4] and that the visitor voluntarily accepted the risk of injury.[5] Nevertheless, a desire to limit the effectiveness of 'Own Risk' notices led Lord Denning to blur these concepts. In *White v Blackmore*, for instance, Lord Denning held that a notice was insufficient to *exclude* liability because it did not adequately *warn* of the danger in question. And in *Burnett v British Waterways Board*,[6] where a lighterman had to enter the defendants' dock in the course of his employment, Lord Denning said (by analogy with the rules of *volenti non fit injuria*[7]) that he was not bound by a notice excluding the defendants' liability. We do not think that these dicta represent the law in its present state. It should be noted, in relation to business premises, that the rules stated above have now been altered by the Unfair Contract Terms Act.[8] As a result, *Ashdown v Williams* and (possibly) *White v Blackmore* would be decided differently today.[9]

1 [1957] 1 QB 409, [1957] 1 All ER 35, CA.
2 [1972] 2 QB 651, [1972] 3 All ER 158, CA.
3 For this reason it seems that a notice excluding liability will be of no effect against a person who enters the premises by some legal right.
4 S2(4)(a): para 23.16 below.
5 S2(5): para 23.18 below.
6 [1973] 2 All ER 631, [1973] 1 WLR 700, CA.
7 Paras 22.2 to 22.10 above, especially para 22.8.
8 Paras 9.42 and 23.3 above.
9 It may also be that a visitor's rights would today be restricted, rather than totally excluded; see para 23.24 below.

Occupier

23.5 The Occupiers' Liability Act 1957 contains no definition of 'occupier'; indeed, the common law position is expressly preserved by s1(3). Traditionally, this question has been approached on a common sense basis, so that the realities of the situation, rather than the technicalities of land law, are decisive. Thus, for example, on a large-scale building project, the contractors may well be held to be 'occupiers' of the site (either alone or jointly with the owner).[1] Similarly, in a Canadian case where an auction was conducted on a farm, both the farmer and the auctioneer were held to be occupiers of the barn in which it took place.[2]

The most important single factor used in deciding who is an occupier is that of *control*. This need be neither entire nor exclusive but, unless a person is sufficiently in control of premises to realise that carelessness on his part may lead to a visitor being injured, he cannot be regarded as an occupier. It is on the basis of the 'control test'[3] that liability has been imposed upon a fairground concessionaire (who had no interest in the property)[4] and upon a local authority which, having acquired a house by compulsory purchase, ordered the resident to leave by serving a notice of intention to enter.[5] In the latter case, the local authority did not actually take possession, but the Court of Appeal held that their statement of intention to do so showed sufficient control, so that their responsibility began as soon as the previous resident left. Similarly, where the owner of premises licenses another to use them, it may well be that he retains sufficient control to be treated as an occupier,[6] and it is then a question of fact whether the licensee is an occupier as well. On the other hand, where property is leased,[7] it is the tenant, and not the landlord, who is the occupier, although a landlord who is in breach of his repairing obligations may incur liability under a separate provision.[8] The landlord will also be regarded as the occupier of 'common parts', such as lifts and staircases in a block of flats, notwithstanding that he cannot deny access to these areas to his tenants' families or guests.[9]

1 *AMF International Ltd v Magnet Bowling Ltd* [1968] 2 All ER 789, [1968] 1 WLR 1028.
2 *Couch v McCann* (1977) 77 DLR (3d) 387.
3 Laid down in *Cavalier v Pope* [1906] AC 428 at 433, HL.
4 *Humphreys v Dreamland (Margate) Ltd* (1930) 144 LT 529, HL.
5 *Harris v Birkenhead Corpn* [1976] 1 All ER 341, [1976] 1 WLR 279, CA.
6 *Wheat v E Lacon & Co Ltd* [1966] AC 552, [1966] 1 All ER 582, HL.
7 For the distinction between a lease and a licence, see para 38.3 below.
8 Para 23.30 below.
9 *Moloney v Lambeth London Borough Council* (1966) 64 LGR 440.

Multiple occupation
23.6 The courts have repeatedly held that neither 'occupation', nor the 'control' on which it is based, need be exclusive and that consequently there may be more than one occupier of the same premises. In *Fisher v CHT Ltd*,[1] for example, X owned a gaming club; a restaurant on the premises was held under licence by Y, who ran it as a separate business. Although detailed control over the restaurant was in the hands of Y, its sole entrance was through X's premises, and X had a right of entry. When a workman was injured in the restaurant, both X and Y were held liable as occupiers.

The leading case on the subject of multiple occupation is *Wheat v E Lacon & Co Ltd*[2] which concerned a fairly common situation, namely, that of a resident manager of a public house. The brewers allowed their manager and his wife (who occupied part of the premises as licensees) to take in paying guests, and one of these guests was killed when he fell down the unlighted back stairs. Although an action by the guest's widow failed on the ground that there had been no negligence, the House of Lords reached some important conclusions on the question of occupation. The brewers, it was held, were to be regarded as occupying the residential part of the premises, either *vicariously* (through their employee, the manager) or because they retained *control*. The manager, too, was an occupier of the relevant part. Both occupiers owed visitors a duty of care; the *content* of their duties, however, might well differ. For example, the structure of the property would probably be the responsibility of the brewers, while liability for defective carpeting in the manager's flat would more appropriately be imposed upon the manager himself.

1 [1966] 2 QB 475, [1966] 1 All ER 88, CA.
2 [1966] AC 552, [1966] 1 All ER 582, HL. See also *Stone v Taffe* [1974] 3 All ER 1016, [1974] 1 WLR 1575, CA.

Premises

23.7 The Occupiers' Liability Act 1957 does not define what is meant by 'premises', although these clearly include land and buildings. In addition, it is provided by s1(3)(a) that the statutory rules shall regulate 'the obligations of a person occupying or having control over any fixed or moveable structure, including any vessel, vehicle or aircraft', a list which seems apt to include both such permanent structures as grandstands[1] or pylons,[2] and more temporary erections such as scaffolding[3] or ladders.[4] However, in *Wheeler v Copas*,[5] it was held that the Act did not apply to a farmer who lent an unsuitable ladder to a bricklayer; the farmer could not be said to remain in 'occupation' of the ladder once it was lent. As far as 'vessels, vehicles or aircraft' are concerned, it appears that the Act covers only damage caused by defective *structure* and not that which results from, say, negligent *driving*.

1 *Francis v Cockrell* (1870) LR 5 QB 501.
2 *Kenny v Electricity Supply Board* [1932] IR 73.
3 *Pratt v Richards* [1951] 2 KB 208, [1951] 1 All ER 90n.
4 *Woodman v Richardson* [1937] 3 All ER 866, CA.
5 [1981] 3 All Er 405.

Visitor

23.8 The simplification of occupiers' liability by the Act of 1957 leaves untouched one vital distinction, namely, that between a lawful visitor and a trespasser; the statutory 'common duty of care' is owed only to the former. The most frequently cited definition of a trespasser is 'he who goes on the land without invitation of any sort and whose presence is either unknown to the proprietor or, if known, is practically objected to'.[1] This category embraces a wide variety of entrants, from the burglar or poacher to the lost rambler or wandering child.

Whether or not a person is *expressly* permitted to enter premises is, of course, simply a question of fact. Difficulties arise, however, where it is alleged that the occupier has *impliedly* given permission. As a general rule, the courts are reluctant to reach such a conclusion, as is illustrated by the case of *Great Central Rly Co v Bates*,[2] in which a policeman, seeing a warehouse door open at night and going in to investigate, was held to be a trespasser. On the other hand, the mere existence of a path to one's front door is a tacit invitation to members of the public wishing to conduct lawful business with the occupier, although this licence extends no further than the front door.[3] Further, even this implication can be excluded by a clearly displayed notice which states, for example: 'No salesmen'. In the entertaining case of *Snook v Mannion*,[4] however, a householder's remark to two police officers, couched in gynaecological terms, was held to constitute mere vulgar abuse rather than a valid revocation of their implied permission to be on the premises.

Particular problems are caused by cases of repeated trespass, for instance where the occupier's land is frequently used by members of the public as a short cut, or for picnicking. No permission can be inferred if the occupier takes reasonable steps to keep such people out.[5] Even if he takes no steps, however, it seems that *acquiescence*, rather than mere *knowledge*, is what must be proved; as Lord Goddard put it: 'How is it to be said that he had licensed what he cannot prevent?'[6] Nonetheless, in extreme cases, failure to take action may amount to permission, as it did in *Lowery v Walker*,[7] where a farmer's field had been used as a short cut to the local railway station for some 35 years. The farmer occasionally turned people back but otherwise took no action until, without warning, he put a savage horse in the field. The plaintiff, who was attacked and injured by this horse, was held by the House of Lords to be a lawful visitor and therefore entitled to sue the farmer for damages.

Now that trespassers themselves receive a much greater measure of protection in law,[8] it may well be that the courts will no longer strain to infer a licence as they did in *Lowery v Walker*. The same may also be true of the doctrine of 'allurement', whereby a child who was 'enticed' on to the defendant's land by something dangerous and attractive might be treated as a licensee rather than as a trespasser. In *Cooke v Midland Great Western Rly of Ireland*,[9] for example, children frequently played on the defendants' turntable; indeed, a well worn track led to it through a gap in the hedge which bordered a nearby road. When the turntable, which was kept unlocked, moved and crushed a four-year-old boy, the House of Lords held that he was not to be regarded as a trespasser.

1   *R Addie & Sons (Collieries) Ltd v Dumbreck* [1929] AC 358 at 371, HL.
2   [1921] 3 KB 578.
3   *Robson v Hallet* [1967] 2 QB 939, [1967] 2 All ER 407, DC.
4   [1982] RTR 321, DC.
5   *Hardy v Central London Rly Co* [1920] 3 KB 459, CA.
6   *Edwards v Railway Executive* [1952] AC 737 at 746, [1952] 2 All ER 430, HL.
7   [1911] AC 10, HL.
8   Paras 23.21 to 23.24 below.
9   [1909] AC 229, HL.

Limited permission

23.9 The permission, whether express or implied, by which a person enters premises may be limited in scope. If this is so, and the permission is exceeded, that person ceases to be a lawful visitor and becomes a trespasser.

The limitations which may be placed upon a licence to enter take various forms, of which the most common relates to area. A hotel guest, for example, becomes a trespasser if he chooses to go through a door marked 'Private'. In *Westwood v Post Office*,[1] an employee who disregarded a notice on a door which stated: 'Authorised personnel only' was held to be a trespasser when he fell through a defective trapdoor in the room and was killed. On the other hand, where a limitation is not clearly shown, a visitor is given a certain amount of leeway. Thus, in *Pearson v Coleman Bros*,[2] a little girl was held to be a licensee when, in searching for a lavatory at a circus, she strayed into the zoo area and was mauled by a lion.

Permission may also be limited as to time, in which case it seems that, to be effective, the limitation must be brought to the entrant's notice. In *Stone v Taffe*,[3] where the manager of a public house gave an unauthorised after-hours party, it was held that the brewers were not entitled to treat a guest as a trespasser, as he did not know that they objected to this practice, This seems surprising since, as a general rule, a person may be a trespasser without being aware of it.[4]

The third limitation which may be placed upon permission to enter premises relates to the purpose of entry; a person may become a trespasser by abusing his licence. This rule, which Scrutton LJ summarised by saying: 'When you invite a person into your house to use the staircase, you do not invite him to slide down the banisters',[5] was applied by the Court of Appeal in *R v Jones and R v Smith*.[6] The two defendants in that case were accused of
380

stealing two television sets from the house of Smith's father; they could only be convicted of burglary under the Theft Act 1968 if they had entered the house 'as trespassers'. Smith's father gave evidence that his son had unrestricted permission to enter it; it was held, however, that the general permission had been exceeded in this case, so that both defendants were trespassers.

1 [1973] QB 591, [1973] 1 All ER 283, CA; revsd on other grounds [1974] AC 1, [1973] 3 All ER 184, HL.
2 [1948] 2 KB 359, [1948] 2 All ER 274, CA.
3 [1974] 3 All ER 1016, [1974] 1 WLR 1575, CA.
4 Para 25.1 below.
5 *The Carlgarth* [1927] P 93 at 110, CA.
6 [1976] 3 All ER 54, [1976] 1 WLR 672, CA.

Entry as of right
23.10 It is provided by the Occupiers' Liability Act 1957, s2(6) that 'persons who enter premises for any purpose in the exercise of a right conferred by law are to be treated as permitted by the occupier to be there for that purpose, whether they in fact have his permission or not'. As a result, whatever may be the personal feelings of the occupier, he owes the common duty of care to any of a host of officials who have statutory powers of entry (eg police, firemen, inspectors of the Health and Safety Executive, electricity board officials, etc). Similarly, where a local authority provides such facilities as parks, playgrounds, lavatories or libraries, it seems that persons using these are lawful visitors.

An exception to the above rule is contained in s1(4) of the Act of 1957. Persons who enter property by virtue of an access agreement or order made under the National Parks and Access to the Countryside Act 1949 may not be sued for trespass but, if injured, they may not claim the rights of a visitor.[1] This is presumably because, if access agreements subjected land-owners to undue burdens, few would be made.

1 They will now fall within the Occupiers' Liability Act 1984: see para 23.21 below.

Rights of way
23.11 Where a person uses a *public* right of way across land he is, of course, not guilty of the tort of trespass. Nonetheless, he was not treated by the common law as a visitor to the land, and the occupier therefore owed him no positive duty to make the way safe. In *Greenhalgh v British Railways Board*,[1] it was held by the Court of Appeal that this rule had not been altered by the Occupiers' Liability Act 1957, so that a woman who was injured when she tripped in a pothole on a railway bridge could not recover damages from the owners of the bridge, notwithstanding that it was crossed by a public footpath. Furthermore, the user of a public right of way cannot even take advantage of the statutory duty which an occupier of land owes to trespassers and other uninvited entrants,[2] for the Occupiers' Liability Act 1984, s1(7) specifically provides that that duty is not owed to persons using the highway.

The occupier's immunity in such cases is subject to two qualifications. In the first place there may be liability where the danger arises not from the condition of the way itself, but from activities which are carried on by the occupier on the same or adjoining land. In *Thomas v British Railways Board*,[3] for example, the defendants were held liable when their failure to repair a stile allowed a two-year-old girl to stray on to a railway line, where she was struck by a train. Second, where a right of way is maintainable at the public expense, the relevant highway authority is now under a positive statutory duty to repair and maintain the way.[4]

A person using a *private* right of way across land is likewise not treated, either by the common law or under the Occupiers' Liability Act 1957, as a visitor to the land.[5] However, he is now entitled to the more limited protection which is afforded to trespassers and other uninvited entrants by the Occupiers' Liabilitity Act 1984.[2]

1 [1969] 2 QB 286, [1969] 2 All ER 114, CA.
2 See para 23.21 below.
3 [1976] QB 912, [1976] 3 All ER 15, CA.
4 Highways Act 1980.
5 *Holden v White* [1982] QB 679, [1982] 2 All ER 328, CA.

Visitors under contract
23.12 Persons who enter premises under some contract are subject to two specific provisions of the Act of 1957. First, where the contract is made between the occupier and the visitor (eg where entry is by ticket), s5 provides in effect that the visitor's rights depend upon the terms of that contract although, if the contract is silent on this point, the common duty of care will apply. However, this provision must now be read subject to the Unfair Contract Terms Act 1977, which contains severe restrictions on the use of exemption clauses where premises are 'business premises'.[1] The Law Reform (Contributory Negligence) Act 1945 (which empowers a court to reduce the damages of a plaintiff who is partly to blame for his injuries, rather than to reject his claim altogether) does not apply to actions for breach of contract.[2] This would appear to mean that a contractual visitor who is guilty of contributory negligence will fail altogether, but it has been held that a person whose claim is jeopardised on this ground may, if he prefers, base his action on the Occupiers' Liability Act 1957, s2.[3]

Section 3 of the Act of 1957 deals with persons who enter premises under some contract to which they are not party. For instance, where an occupier employs a firm of builders to work on his house, the actual workmen are not normally parties to the contract under which the work is done. So too, a lease may grant access to 'common parts' of the landlord's building, such as staircases and lifts, not only to tenants, but also their families and guests. In all such cases, it is provided that, while the visitor may take the benefit of any additional obligations which the contract imposes upon the occupier, his rights may not be reduced below the level which is imposed by the common duty of care.

1 Paras 9.42 and 23.3 above.
2 Para 22.12 above.
3 *Sole v W J Hallt Ltd* [1973] QB 574, [1973] 1 All ER 1032.

The common duty of care
23.13 The duty which an occupier owes to his lawful visitors is defined by the Occupiers' Liability Act 1957, s2(2) as 'a duty to take such care as in all the circumstances of the case is reasonable to see that the visitor will be reasonably safe in using the premises for the purpose for which he is invited or permitted by the occupier to be there'. Apart from noting that the duty is to make the *visitor*, rather than the *premises*, safe, little need be said about this definition; it is a straightforward application of negligence principles.

Indeed, the Act might well have stopped there, leaving the courts to work out the details; in fact, however, certain areas which had caused problems before 1957 are specifically dealt with, and these we consider in the next five paragraphs.

Children

23.14 In pointing out that the carefulness or otherwise which may be expected of a visitor is relevant to the occupier's duty towards him, s2(3)(a) provides that 'an occupier must be prepared for children to be less careful than adults'. That children are especially at risk is obvious. For example, in *Moloney v Lambeth London Borough Council*,[1] the defendants were held liable to a four-year-old who fell through a gap in a staircase balustrade too small to have endangered an adult.

A particular problem with children is that, even when on premises lawfully, they may be tempted by some dangerous and attractive object to exceed the scope of their permission. If this leads to injury, it is well established that the occupier may not use the child's technical trespass as a ground for avoiding liability. Thus in *Glasgow Corpn v Taylor*,[2] where a seven-year-old boy stole some attractive berries from an unfenced bush in a public park, it was held that his death by poisoning disclosed a good cause of action.

In relation to very young children, to whom almost anything is dangerous but who cannot understand warnings, the law seeks to balance the duty of the occupier with that of the parent. At one time the courts used the fiction of the 'conditional licence', by which the child could be treated as a trespasser unless accompanied by a responsible person, but the better view is that an occupier, in taking precautions for the safety of small children, is entitled to assume that their parents, too, will take care. This approach was adopted by Devlin J in *Phipps v Rochester Corpn*,[3] where a five-year-old boy went blackberrying with his sister, aged seven, on a large grassy space forming part of the defendants' building site. The defendants were well aware that children frequently played in this place, so that they were to be regarded as lawful visitors.[4] When the boy fell into a trench and broke his leg, it was held that the defendants were not liable, since this was the kind of danger from which the occupier might expect a reasonable parent to protect his child.

1 (1966) 64 LGR 440.
2 [1922] 1 AC 44, HL.
3 [1955] 1 QB 450, [1955] 1 All ER 129. See also *Simkiss v Rhondda Borough Council* (198) 81 LGR 460, CA.
4 See para 23.8 above.

Specialists

23.15 It is provided by s2(3)(b) that 'an occupier may expect that a person, in the exercise of his calling, will appreciate and guard against any special risks ordinarily incident to it, so far as the occupier leaves him free to do so'. One important effect of this is that an occupier whose property becomes dangerous will not normally be liable to persons who come for the very purpose of repairing it. However, where a fire is caused by the occupier's negligence and a fireman is injured, he may recover damages from the occupier provided that his presence at the fire was foreseeable and that he would be at risk despite exercising all the skill of his calling.[1]

Whether or not a risk is 'incident to a person's calling' is a question of fact, but some guidance may be obtained from a comparison of two decisions. In *Howitt v Alfred Bagnall & Sons Ltd*,[2] a clerk of works fell from scaffolding on which he was standing to inspect roof repairs. The occupiers were held not liable, for the scaffolding was not defective; the only risk lay in using it at all, and this was inherent in the man's job. In *Woollins v British Celanese Ltd*,[3] on the other hand, a post office engineer fell through some hardboard roofing at the defendants' factory. It was held by the Court of Appeal that, while he could be expected to guard against live wires, the structure of the building was not connected with his job; he was therefore able to recover damages.

1 *Salmon v Seafarer Restaurants Ltd* [1983] 3 All ER 729, [1983] 1 WLR 1264.
2 [1967] 2 Lloyd's Rep 370.
3 (1966) 1 KIR 438, CA.

Warnings
23.16 A reminder that an occupier's duty is to render his *visitor* safe, rather than his *premises*, is given by s2(4)(a), which provides: 'Where damage is caused to a visitor by a danger of which he had been warned by the occupier, the warning is not to be treated without more as absolving the occupier from liability, unless in all the circumstances it was enough to enable the visitor to be reasonably safe'. The legal effect of compliance with this provision is that the common duty of care is fulfilled, which has two important consequences in deciding whether or not a warning is valid. First, the warning must come from the occupier himself,[1] although a warning from another source may lead to the conclusion that a visitor either assumes the risk of injury or is contributorily negligent. Second, it must be adequate, in the sense of both specifying the particular danger sufficiently clearly that the visitor can avoid it and being visible. In *Woollins v British Celanese Ltd*,[2] a warning hidden behind a door was held to be inadequate.

1 *Bunker v Charles Brand & Son Ltd* [1969] 2 QB 480, [1969] 2 All ER 59.
2 (1966) 1 KIR 438, CA.

Independent contractors
23.17 Prior to 1957 there was some doubt as to whether an occupier was liable in respect of dangers on his land which were attributable to the fault of an independent contractor. In order to clarify this point, s2(4)(b) provides:

> 'Where damage is caused to a visitor by a danger due to the faulty execution of any work of construction, maintenance or repair by an independent contractor employed by the occupier, the occupier is not to be treated without more as answerable for the danger if in all the circumstances he had acted reasonably in entrusting the work to an independent contractor and had taken such steps (if any) as he reasonably ought in order to satisfy himself that the contractor was competent and that the work had been properly done'.

This, in effect, gives statutory approval to two earlier decisions of the Court of Appeal. In *Haseldine v CA Daw & Son Ltd*[1] the plaintiff was injured when a lift in the defendants' block of flats fell to the bottom of the shaft. The accident resulted from negligent work by the firm of specialist engineers employed by the defendants to service the lift and it was held that, since the defendants had no reason to doubt the competence of their contractors, they had in no way failed in their duty towards the plaintiff.

The wording of s2(4)(b) also endorses the principle laid down in *Woodward v Hastings Corpn*[2] that, if an occupier chooses to leave to an independent contractor jobs which he could and should do for himself, he remains personally responsible for their proper execution. In that case a school cleaner (who was assumed to be an independent contractor) swept the snow from a step and carelessly left it in a dangerously icy condition. It was held that the local authority were liable in negligence to a person who slipped on the step, since this was not a specialist task.

Even where it is reasonable to entrust the work to an independent contractor, the occupier must take reasonable steps to see that the work is properly done. The courts do not demand much from an occupier in this connection where he cannot be expected to understand the intricacies of the job, but it has been held that on a large-scale construction job, for instance, the occupier may be obliged to appoint a qualified architect or surveyor to supervise the work.[3] In such a case the architect or surveyor would himself be an independent contractor to the occupier.

1 [1941] 2 KB 343, [1941] 3 All ER 156, CA.
2 [1945] KB 174, [1944] 2 All ER 565, CA.
3 *AMF International Ltd v Magnet Bowling Ltd* [1968] 2 All ER 789, [1968] 1 WLR 1028.

Volenti non fit injuria

23.18 Section 2(5) makes it clear that an occupier is not liable to a visitor in respect of risks which the latter willingly assumes. Thus, in *Simms v Leigh Rugby Football Club Ltd*,[1] where a professional Rugby League player was thrown against a concrete wall which surrounded the defendants' pitch, it was held that he could not recover damages for the injuries received: since the ground satisfied the League rules, it had to be assumed that players had accepted the risks inherent in playing on it.

Since s2(5), in effect, applies the common law defence of *volenti non fit injuria*, the rules which govern that defence are applicable.[2] In particular, it will not protect an occupier if the visitor has no real choice in the matter; for example, where his employer orders him to enter the premises[3] or to incur the risk.[4]

It should also be noted that, although the Act is silent on the point, it has frequently been held that the defence of contributory negligence is available to an occupier.

1 [1969] 2 All ER 923. Cf *Harrison v Vincent* [1982] RTR 8, CA; para 22.7 above.
2 Paras 22.2 to 22.10 above.
3 *Burnett v British Waterways Board* [1973] 2 All ER 631, [1973] 1 WLR 700, CA.
4 *Bunker v Charles Brand & Son Ltd* [1969] 2 QB 480, [1969] 2 All ER 59.

Trespassers

23.19 The Occupiers' Liability Act 1957 applies only to lawful visitors; hence, injuries to trespassers were governed by the common law, which had to deal with two separate problems. First, there is the trespasser who is injured by the very steps which the occupier has taken to keep him out. The position here seems to be that static deterrents, such as broken glass or spikes on top of a wall, are permissible;[1] concealed instruments of retribution (such as man-traps or spring-guns), on the other hand, are not allowed,[2] although a trespasser who enters with full knowledge of their presence may be held to have assumed the risk of injury.[3]

The second issue concerns the trespasser who is injured by the condition of the premises or by an activity which is carried on there. In such a case the law must attempt to strike a balance between the right of anybody, even a trespasser, to expect civilised behaviour from others, and the freedom of a landowner to use and enjoy his property as he wishes. Until recently, the scales were heavily weighted in favour of landowners, as is shown by the case of *R Addie & Sons (Collieries) Ltd v Dumbreck*,[4] in which a four-year-old trespasser was killed when a haulage wheel on which he was playing was started up. The colliery employees who started the machinery knew that children often played on it, but did not bother to check that all was clear; nonetheless, the House of Lords held that the colliery was not liable. It was said that a trespasser takes the land as he finds it, and an occupier's duty is limited to not injuring him intentionally or recklessly. That this was a borderline decision was made clear within a year, when the House of Lords came to the opposite conclusion on similar facts. This time the employees who started up machinery could, by merely turning round, have seen children on it, and they were held reckless for failing to take this simple step.[5]

The *Addie* rule, which drew no distinction between a vicious intruder and a playful four-year-old, was regarded by many judges as too harsh, and frequent attempts were made to evade it, for example by a strained finding of 'implied permission'.[6]

1 *Deane v Clayton* (1817) 7 Taunt 489.
2 *Bird v Holbrook* (1828) 4 Bing 628.
3 *Ilott v Wilkes* (1820) 3 B & Ald 304.
4 [1929] AC 358, HL.
5 *Excelsior Wire Rope Co Ltd v Callan* [1930] AC 404, HL.
6 Para 23.8 above.

Common humanity

23.20 The law on trespassers underwent a radical change in *British Railways Board v Herrington*,[1] in which a six-year-old boy went on to an electrified railway line and was severely burnt by the live rail. The line ran between two areas of National Trust land and it was clear, from gaps in the fences and a well-trodden path, that people were habitually taking a short cut across the line at this point. Children had indeed been seen on the track by employees of the defendants but, apart from informing the police, the defendants had taken no action to prevent further trespass. On these facts the Court of Appeal held that the defendants were reckless and, while the House of Lords disagreed with this assessment of the defendants' conduct, they nevertheless decided that it fell short of the standard which the law would now demand of an occupier where trespassers are concerned. This standard, said the House of Lords, was considerably higher than the 'intention or recklessness' level of *Addie*, while not as stringent as a duty of reasonable care; the occupier was bound to act towards a trespasser with 'common humanity'. In deciding whether or not the occupier had fulfilled this obligation, a fairly subjective test would be applied; no more would be demanded of the occupier than might reasonably be expected of a person with his knowledge, skill and resources.

1 [1972] AC 877, [1972] 1 All ER 749, HL.

Occupiers' Liability Act 1984

23.21 Exactly what was meant by 'common humanity', and how it differed from 'reasonable care', are questions with which we need no longer concern ourselves. Fears that the new standard would prove vague and uncertain, and hence provoke much litigation, led to a recommendation from the Law Commission that the matter be governed by statute, and this was duly done with the enactment of the Occupiers' Liability Act 1984. *It is important to note that this Act applies, not only to trespassers, but to all 'persons other than [the occupier's] visitors*; it thus embraces persons entering under the National Parks and Access to the Countryside Act 1949[1] and also those using a *private* right of way. However, the Act specifically excludes persons using a *public* right of way. The net result appears to be that, while *Greenhalgh v British Railways Board*[2] remains good law, the effect of *Holden v White*[3] is reversed.

1   See para 23.10 above.
2   [1969] 2 QB 286, [1969] 2 All ER 114, CA: para 23.11 above.
3   [1982] QB 679, [1982] 2 All ER 328, CA: para 23.11 above.

Scope of the duty

23.22 In attempting to strike the right balance between the interests of an occupier[1] of premises[2] and those of his 'non-visitor', s1(3) of the Act provides that the occupier shall only owe a duty to such a person if

a.   he is aware of a danger or has reasonable grounds to believe that it exists;

b.   he knows or has reasonable grounds to believe that the other person is in the vicinity of the danger or that he may come into that vicinity; and

c.   the risk is one against which he may reasonably be expected to offer the other person some protection.

The overall effect of this formulation appears to be that, while the occupier is not bound to inspect his property to see whether or not it is safe for trespasser and other uninvited entrants, he is assumed to be able to recognise a danger whenever what he *actually* knows should lead him to the conclusion that one exists.

It is important to note that the new statutory duty applies only to 'injury', which is defined to include death, disease and any impairment of physical or mental condition. The Act specifically provides that there is no liability for any loss of or damage to property (s1(8)).

1   'Occupier' bears the same meaning as it does for the purpose of the Occupiers' Liability Act 1957; see paras 23.5 to 23.6 above.
2   'Premise' bears the same meaning as it does for the purposes of the Occupiers' Liability Act 1957; see para 23.7 above.

Defences

23.23 The 1984 Act provides an occupier with two defences against liability similar to those available under the 1957 Act. First, s1(5) provides that the occupier's duty may be discharged by taking such steps as are reasonable 'to give warning of the danger concerned or to discourage persons from incurring the risk'.[1] Second, s1(6) makes it clear that the defence of *volenti non fit injuria* (assumption of risk) is applicable.[2] Although it is not specifically mentioned, it seems likely that the defence of contributory negligence would also apply.[3]

1 See para 23.16 above.
2 See paras 22.2 to 22.10 and para 23.18 above.
3 See paras 22.11 to 22.16 above.

Exclusion of liability

23.24 We have already considered the extent to which an occupier may, by putting up a notice, exclude or restrict his liability to lawful visitors.[1] The 1984 Act gives no guidance whatever as to whether the rights of 'non-visitors' may be similarly affected, and the arguments for and against seem fairly well balanced. On the one hand, since a trespasser has no permission to enter, it would be nonsensical to suggest that he enters subject to a condition that the occupier shall not be liable to him. Furthermore, there is the practical argument that a visitor is more likely than a trespasser actually to see a notice; after all, this will normally be at the gate, while the trespasser may well climb over the fence. On the other hand, it would be bizarre if a lawful visitor were to be placed in a worse position, legally speaking, than a trespasser. A possible solution would be for the courts to hold that, while the rights of a lawful visitor may be excluded by an appropriate notice, he is then left with rights equivalent to those enjoyed by a trespasser under the 1984 Act, and that neither lawful visitor nor trespasser may suffer any further reduction of their rights.

1 Para 23.4 above.

Vendors and lessors

Caveat emptor

23.25 Where legal liability is concerned, there is no logical reason for distinguishing between dangerous houses and dangerous goods. Nevertheless, such a distinction is recognised by the law, as a result of a doctrine known as '*caveat emptor*' or 'let the buyer beware'. This doctrine, which was long ago virtually abolished in relation to sales of goods, has until recently maintained a stranglehold on sales and leases of lands sufficient to resist any attempt to introduce ideas of consumer protection into this area.

The effects of *caveat emptor* are manifold; it means, for example, that, while an implied contractual term requires *goods* to be of reasonable quality, no such protection exists for the buyer of a completed house, although terms as to quality are implied in contracts for the sale of a house to be built or completed[1] and for the letting of furnished property.[2] For present purposes, the importance of *caveat emptor* lies in the fact that for centuries a vendor or lessor of real property owed no duty of care in respect of defects in the property, either to his purchaser or tenant or to anyone else. In relation to dangers which the vendor/lessor has not positively created, this (for the moment at least) remains the law. In *Rimmer v Liverpool County Council*[3] the Court of Appeal held, albeit reluctantly, that this principle was based on authority of the House of Lords[4] and could thus only be changed by that court.

The undeserved and anomalous immunity of the owner used even to protect a person in respect of dangers which he had positively created; no action in negligence could be brought against an owner-builder[5] or a landlord whose tampering made the premises dangerous before they were let.[6] The extent of the anomaly is emphasised by the fact that the *mere* builder of a house (ie one who did not own it, but who simply worked as a contractor) owed the same duty of care to future users as a manufacturer of goods owes to consumers.[7]

Reform was long overdue and, in the early 1970's, it duly arrived. Unfortunately, however, it came almost simultaneously from two independent sources (parliament and the courts) and, since their efforts were in no way harmonised, the resulting law is somewhat uncertain.

1 *Hancock v B W Brazier (Anerley) Ltd* [1966] 2 All ER 901, [1966] 1 WLR 1317, CA; para 7.23 above.
2 *Smith v Marrable* (1843) 11 M & W 5; para 37.4 below.
3 [1985] QB 1, [1984] 1 All ER 930, CA.
4 *Cavalier v Pope* [1906] AC 428, HL.
5 *Otto v Bolton and Norris* [1936] 2 KB 46, [1936] 1 All ER 960.
6 *Davis v Foots* [1940] 1 KB 116, [1939] 4 All ER 4, CA.
7 *Sharpe v E T Sweeting & Son Ltd* [1963] 2 All ER 455, [1963] 1 WLR 665.

Judicial reform

23.26 In *Dutton v Bognor Regis U D C*,[1] the plaintiff was the second owner of a house which, a mere two years after being completed, developed alarming cracks in walls and ceilings. It was discovered that the house had been built on the site of an old rubbish tip and that, because of this, its foundations were inadequate. In view of the difficulties mentioned in the last paragraph, the plaintiff settled her claim against the owner-builder for a small sum, and sued the local authority for the negligence of their building inspector in passing the foundations. In upholding this claim, a majority of the Court of Appeal took the opportunity to state their opinion that the builder would, if sued, have been liable. This suggested reversal of the previous legal position received a good deal of criticism on various grounds. However, in the similar case of *Anns v Merton London Borough Council*,[2] it was unanimously approved by the House of Lords and must now be regarded as the law.

Although the last few years have seen numerous cases in which builders have been sued on this basis, the exact scope of their liability remains unclear. The duty of the *local authority* in 'defective building' cases is certainly limited to ensuring that the builder complies with the building regluations and, since these are designed to prevent danger to the health or safety of occupiers, it has been held that only an endangered occupier can claim, and then only for the cost of restoring the building to a condition in which it is no longer a danger.[3] This requirement of 'danger' has also been applied to the liability of the *builder*; it is noteworthy that in *Junior Books Ltd v Veitchi Co Ltd*,[4] where a sub-contractor was held liable to the main contractor's client for *non-dangerous* defects, the House of Lords were at pains to stress the closeness of the relationship between the parties, and to distinguish this from the normal case of a negligent builder. However, it is fair to say that the courts take a liberal view of what amounts to a sufficient 'danger' for this purpose;[5] further, it is not difficult to find cases in which the damages awarded are clearly based on the entire diminution in value of the property.[6]

There is no doubt that the courts appear willing to expand this area of liability. In *Hone v Benson*,[7] it was held that the vendors of a restaurant owed a duty of care to the purchasers in respect of a central heating system, notwithstanding that they had, without any qualifications or experience, done the job themselves. And, in *Batty v Metropolitan Property Realisa-*

tions Ltd,[8] the Court of Appeal imposed liability on both the builders and the developers of a housing estate on land which was liable to slip, even though the danger was not discoverable from an inspection of the development land itself.

1   [1972] 1 QB 373, [1972] 1 All ER 462, CA.
2   [1978] AC 728, [1977] 2 All ER 492, HL.
3   *Peabody Donation Fund (Governors) v Sir Lindsay Parkinson & Co Ltd,* [1984] All 3 ER 529, [1984] 3 WLR 953, HL.
4   [1983] 1 AC 520, [1982] 3 All ER 201, HL; para 19.25 above.
5   *Ketteman v Hansel Properties Ltd* [1985] 1 All ER 352, [1984] 1 WLR 1274, CA.
6   *Batty v Metropolitan Property Realisations Ltd* [1978] QB 554, [1978] 2 All ER 445, CA.
7   (1978) 248 Estates Gazette 1013.
8   [1978] QB 554, [1978] 2 All ER 445, CA.

Defective Premises Act 1972
23.27   The Act, which came into operation on 1 January 1974, contains two provisions of relevance in the present context. Section 1(1) provides that a person taking on work for or in connection with the provision of a dwelling (whether the dwelling is provided by the erection or by the conversion or enlargement of a building) owes a duty—

a.   if the dwelling is provided to the order of any person, to that person; and

b.   without prejudice to paragraph (a) above, to every person who acquires an interest (whether legal or equitable) in the dwelling,

to see that the work which he takes on is done in a workmanlike or, as the case may be, professional manner, with proper materials and so that as regards that work the dwelling will be fit for habitation when completed. This provision, which does not apply to work 'taken on' before 1 January 1974,[1] affects, not only builders, but also architects, surveyors, subcontractors, and the developer who arranges for someone else to do the work.[2] It does not, however, apply to a manufacturer or supplier of standard components, nor to a builder who works entirely to a specification which he is given.[3]

The duty imposed by s1(1) is not a duty of care, but rather a statutory version of the strict (ie independent of negligence) warranty which the common law implies into contracts to build and sell a dwelling.[4] The benefit of this duty, which cannot be contracted out of,[5] is now extended beyond the contracting party to anyone who subsequently acquires an interest in the property. On the face of it, this provision seems to be of great potential importance, but its operation is severely curtailed by s2, which excludes all dwellings covered by an 'approved scheme'. The scheme in question is that administered by the National House-Building Council,[6] under which, as amended in 1979, the vendor-builder undertakes to remedy defects in the first two years and the Council provides insurance against major structural defects in the next eight years. The vast majority of new houses are covered by the N H B C Scheme and, as a result, s1 of the Act will be of importance mainly in respect of conversions and alterations, where the Scheme does not apply.

1   *Alexander v Mercouris* [1979] 3 All ER 305, [1979] 1 WLR 1270, CA.
2   S1(4).
3   S1(2) and (3).
4   Para 7.23 above.

5 S6(3).
6 The House-Building Standards (Approved Scheme etc) Order 1973, SI 1973/1843.

23.28 The Defective Premises Act 1972, s3(1) provides: 'Where work of construction, repair, maintenance or demolition or any other work is done on or in relation to premises, any duty of care owed, because of the doing of the work, to persons who might reasonably be expected to be affected by defects in the state of the premises created by the doing of the work shall not be abated by the subsequent disposal of the premises by the person who owed the duty'. This provision was intended to abolish the owner-builder's immunity but, since its wording is more restricted than the rule laid down by the House of Lords in *Anns v Merton London Borough Council*,[1] it seems unlikely that it will in practice be used.

1 [1978] AC 728, [1977] 2 All ER 492, HL; para 23.26 above.

Present law
23.29 The interaction of the tort of negligence with the Defective Premises Act, s1 is not altogether clear. In the limited area of its application, the statute has the undoubted advantage of imposing strict liability. Further, it would probably cover a case where a house is defective without being dangerous, which appears to fall outside the scope of the common law. The major disadvantage of the Act, however, lies in the period which it lays down for the purpose of limitation of actions; this is six years from completion of the dwelling. In the tort of negligence, by contrast, time normally does not start to run against the plaintiff until damage actually occurs.[1] This is obviously a matter of great importance since defects in, say, foundations may not cause any real damage to the structure of the building for many years.

At present, therefore, actions against a builder are more likely to be founded upon the tort of negligence than on the Act. In future, however, it may be that both are superseded by a claim for breach of statutory duty based upon the building regulations, which would have the advantage for the plaintiff that he would not be required to show negligence, merely the breach of one of a large number of detailed rules. It was suggested by Lord Wilberforce in *Anns* that such an action could already be brought, and, even if this is not correct,[2] specific provision for it (in relation to the next generation of building regulations) is made by the Building Act 1984, s38.

1 *Pirelli General Cable Works Ltd v Oscar Faber and Partners* [1983] 2 AC 1, [1983] 1 All ER 65, HL; para 31.21 below.
2 See para 24.3 below.

Repairing obligations
23.30 The preceding paragraphs, which dealt with premises which are defective when disposed of, apply equally to vendors and lessors. In respect of defects which arise later, however, the position of the lessor requires separate treatment, since he may be under an obligation to repair. At common law, the breach of a repairing obligation was actionable by the tenant alone;[1] a visitor who was injured could neither recover damages for breach of the landlord's contractual obligation to repair the demised premises, nor treat the landlord as 'occupier' of these premises.[2] This

unsatisfactory state of affairs was remedied by the Defective Premises Act 1972, s4[3], which provides:

'Where premises are let under a tenancy which puts on the landlord an obligation to the tenant for the maintenance or repair of the premises, the landlord owes to all persons who might reasonably be expected to be affected by defects in the state of the premises a duty to take such care as is reasonable in all the circumstances to see that they are reasonably safe from personal injury or from damage to their property caused by a [defect within the repairing obligation]'.

The effect of s4 is that an injured person (who may be a visitor, trespasser or even someone off the premises) may sue the landlord for injury or damage caused by a defect which the landlord is under an obligation to repair. Further, while the landlord might be able to answer a claim by the *tenant* on the ground that the latter had failed to notify him of the defect,[4] this will be no defence against a third party, provided that the landlord knew or ought to have known of the defect. It is important to note that s4 also applies to the many cases where a landlord, although under no duty to repair the premises, nonetheless has an express or implied right to do so.[5]

1   *Cavalier v Pope* [1906] AC 428, HL.
2   Para 23.5 above.
3   Replacing the more limited provisions of the Occupiers' Liability Act 1957, s4.
4   Para 37.13 below.
5   See, for example, *Mint v Good* [1951] 1 KB 517, [1950] 2 All ER 1159, CA.

Chapter 24
Breach of statutory duty

24.1 Vast and increasing areas of modern life are controlled by legislative rules, in the form of either Acts of Parliament or (more commonly) regulations made under them. It frequently comes about, therefore, that an act which causes injury or damage to another also constitutes a breach of some statutory obligation. This naturally renders the person concerned liable to whatever penalty is prescribed by the statute, but our present concern is with the effect (if any) which the statutory breach has upon his liability to pay damages to the plaintiff.

In contrast with many other legal systems, which regard the fact that a defendant has contravened a statutory rule as relevant only to the question whether or not he has acted negligently, English law takes the view that 'breach of statutory duty' may itself be a tort, quite independent of negligence on the part of the defendant, and with its own elements of liability and defences. However, it is not suggested that every statutory obligation gives rise to a civil action, for such is the bulk of modern legislation that the universal imposition of liability would, it is thought, be an unacceptably heavy burden. Thus, a preliminary task for a plaintiff who wishes to frame his action in this way (in order to recover damages without the need to prove negligence) is to satisfy the court that the rule or regulation in question is indeed one for whose breach damages may be awarded.

Existence of civil liability
24.2 In some (albeit regrettably few) cases, parliament makes it clear that the breach of a particular statute or regulation either does[1] or does not[2] give rise to civil liability. Usually, however, no specific mention is made of the point, and the question is therefore left for determination by the courts upon an interpretation of the relevant provision. Although, in reaching their decisions, the courts claim to be giving effect to the intention of parliament, it is probably more sensible to recognise from the outset that parliament's silence indicates a lack of any positive intention, and that the judges are in reality playing a creative role on the basis of policy. Thus, while the following criteria are sometimes stated to be useful guides in such cases, they are in truth more helpful in justifying a decision than in reaching it.

In seeking the 'intention of parliament', the courts sometimes claim to gain assistance from a consideration of what, if any, sanction has been laid down for a breach of the provision in question. In particular, it is probably true to say that, if no sanction at all is mentioned, this points strongly to the existence of a civil action for, without it, the duty would be wholly unenforceable at law.[3] Of less importance is the alleged presumption[4] that statutes passed for the benefit of a particular class of persons give rise to a civil action, whereas those which benefit the public in general do not. If this were indeed so, then the crime of harassment[5] would surely permit a distressed tenant to claim damages. However, in *McCall v Abelesz*,[6] the Court of Appeal held that no such claim would lie. It appears that only performers, and not record companies, may recover damages from a person who commits a criminal offence by making unauthorised recordings of live performances.[7]

It seems in practice that the courts are most likely to allow an action for breach of statutory duty in areas where duties already exist at common law, since the judges tend to shy away from what would amount to the creation of new kinds of legal right. In *Atkinson v Newcastle Waterworks Co*,[8] for instance, the defendants, in breach of a statutory rule for which they could be fined £10, failed to maintain the prescribed pressure of water in their mains. As a result, a fire in the plaintiff's property could not be extinguished. It was held by the Court of Appeal that parliament could not have intended to make the defendants virtual insurers of every property in the city and that consequently no civil action lay for breach of this duty. A similar decision was reached by the House of Lords in *Cutler v Wandsworth Stadium Ltd*,[9] where an individual bookmaker unsuccessfully claimed damages from the defendants for breach of their statutory duty to make space available for bookmakers at their greyhound racing track.

An interesting recent development has been the acceptance by the House of Lords[10] that, where legislation of the European Communities is 'directly applicable',[11] it may confer upon individuals a right of action similar to that for breach of statutory duty. In deciding whether or not this is the case, the courts do not, of course, refer to the 'intention of parliament', but nonetheless give attention to the criteria mentioned above. It has further been held that, even where a right of this kind is held to exist, it does not necessarily entitle a person aggrieved to recover damages; some other remedy may be appropriate.[12]

1 Eg the Nuclear Installations Act 1965 and the Consumer Safety Act 1978.
2 Eg the Guard Dogs Act 1975.
3 *Thornton v Kirklees Metropolitan Borough Council* [1979] QB 626, [1979] 2 All ER 349, CA.
4 *Lonrho Ltd v Shell Petroleum Co Ltd* [1982] AC 173, [1981] 2 All ER 456, HL.
5 Protection from Eviction Act 1977, s1.
6 [1976] QB 585, [1976] 1 All ER 727.
7 *Ex p Island Records Ltd* [1978] Ch 122, [1978] 3 All ER 824, CA; *RCA Corpn v Pollard* [1982] 3 All ER 771, CA; *Rickless v United Artistes Corpn* (1985) Times, 17 June.
8 (1877) 2 Ex D 441, CA.
9 [1949] AC 398, [1949] 1 All ER 544, HL.
10 *Garden Cottage Foods Ltd v Milk Marketing Board* [1984] AC 130, [1983] 2 All ER 770, HL.
11 See paras 3.29–3.32 above.
12 *Bourgoin SA v Ministry of Agriculture, Fisheries and Food* [1985] 3 All ER 585, CA.

24.3 Although attempts to relate the 'intention of parliament' to any coherent principle are unsatisfactory, the actual decisions reached by the courts have been remarkably consistent in allowing a civil right of action for the breach of any industrial safety regulation. Indeed, when the new generation of such regulations is passed under the Health and Safety at Work etc Act 1974, the position will become even clearer because s47(2) of that Act provides that damages may be awarded for any breach except in so far as the regulations themselves provide otherwise.

Outside the field of industrial safety, the prevailing judicial attitude towards claims for breach of statutory duty has been one of considerable reluctance. In matters of road safety, for example, where regulations abound, it might have been thought desirable to introduce this form of liability, so that accident victims might recover compensation without the uncertainties of an action in negligence. However, in *Phillips v Britannia Hygienic Laundry Co Ltd*,[1], where an accident was caused by the defective condition of the defendants' van (which was not due to any negligence on their part), the Court of Appeal rejected a claim based on the Motor Vehicles (Construction and Use) Regulations, which made the use of the vehicle in this condition an offence of strict liability. Likewise, in *Coote v Stone*,[2] it was held that no damages could be awarded for a breach of 'Clearway' parking regulations. These decisions undoubtedly represent the general trend, but there are two notable exceptions; in *Monk v Warbey*,[3] a car owner was held liable for allowing an uninsured person to drive, since the latter was unable to pay damages to a victim of his negligent driving; and, in *London Passenger Transport Board v Upson*,[4] a driver was held civilly liable for failing to give precedence to a pedestrian on a crossing.

Another field in which the courts might profitably have adopted a more robust approach is that of consumer protection. However, once again the opportunity has not been taken, so much so that, in *Biddle v Truvox Engineering Co Ltd*,[5] it was held that no damages could be awarded against the seller of a dangerously unfenced machine in respect of his breach of the Factories Acts. It has been suggested that a house owner might recover damages from a builder for a breach of building regulations,[6] but the position is unclear.[7]

Once the plaintiff satisfies the court that the statutory duty in question *is* one in respect of which a civil action may be brought, he must establish certain elements of liability in order to win his case; these we now consider.

1   [1923] 2 KB 832, CA.
2   [1971] 1 All ER 657, [1971] 1 WLR 279, CA.
3   [1935] 1 KB 75, CA.
4   [1949] AC 155, [1949] 1 All ER 60, HL.
5   [1952] 1 KB 101, [1951] 2 All ER 835.
6   *Anns v Merton London Borough Council* [1978] AC 728, [1977] 2 All ER 492, HL; see para 23.29 above.
7   *Eames London Estates Ltd v North Hertfordshire District Council* (1981) 259 Estates Gazette 491; cf *Worlock v SAWS* (1981) 260 Estates Gazette 920.

Elements of liability
Class protected

24.4 As we have seen, a person cannot sue for breach of statutory duty *merely* because he is a member of the class for whose protection the duty was imposed. Assuming, however, that a class-protecting statute does give rise to a civil right of action, it is clear that this is available only to the class in question. A good illustration of this point is the case of *Hartley v Mayoh & Co Ltd*,[1] in which a fireman was killed by electrocution while fighting a fire at the defendants' factory. In an action by the fireman's widow it was held that the breach by the defendants of wiring regulations was irrelevant, since these were expressed to be for the benefit of 'persons employed' at the factory, and this did not include the fireman.

In *Hartley v Mayoh* the protected class was expressly defined; where this is not so, the courts are usually reluctant to impose their own limitations. In *Westwood v Post Office*,[2] for example, a defective trapdoor, the condition of which constituted a breach of the Offices, Shops and Railway Premises Act 1963, led to the death of an employee at a telephone exchange. The trapdoor was in fact in a part of the premises which the deceased was not permitted to enter and it was argued by the defendants that, while the statute protected most employees, it did not cover trespassers. It was held by the House of Lords, however, that the employee's trespass did not deprive him of statutory protection.

1   [1954] 1 QB 383, [1954] 1 All ER 375, CA.
2   [1974] AC 1, [1973] 3 All ER 184, HL; para 23.9 above.

Type of injury
24.5   Just as the tort of negligence is concerned only with those consequences of a person's carelessness which fall within the risk which he has created, so the plaintiff in an action for breach of statutory duty must show that the injury or damage which he has suffered is of a type which the statute is designed to prevent. The classic example is *Gorris v Scott*,[1] in which the absence of pens on the deck of the defendant's ship allowed the plaintiff's sheep to be swept overboard in a storm. Although pens were required by statute, this was held to be of no assistance to the plaintiff, for their purpose was merely to reduce the spread of disease among the animals. This principle also led to a rather harsh decision in *Close v Steel Co of Wales Ltd*,[2] where it was held that, since the duty to fence dangerous machinery is designed to 'keep the worker out', it is of no relevance where the absence of a guard allows part of the machine to fly out and cause injury.

It is obvious that, the more precisely the purpose of a statute is interpreted by judges, the fewer cases will fall within it. The modern tendency, however, is to define the protected risk in fairly broad terms, an approach rather similar to that adopted towards the questions of how damage is caused in the tort of negligence.[3] Thus, in *Grant v National Coal Board*,[4] where a statutory breach allowed rock to fall from a mine roof, it was held that a miner could sue for injuries received when the bogie in which he was travelling was derailed by the fallen rock. So too, in *Donaghey v Boulton and Paul Ltd*,[5] the defendants failed in their statutory duty to supply an employee with 'crawling boards' when he was working on a fragile asbestos roof. The employee fell, not through the asbestos, but through a hole in the roof adjacent to it. It was argued that this was outside the object of the statute, which was limited to fragile roofs, but the House of Lords rejected so narrow an interpretation and held that damages should be awarded.

1   (1874) LR 9 Exch 125.
2   [1962] AC 367, [1961] 2 All ER 953, HL.
3   See *Hughes v Lord Advocate* [1963] AC 837, [1963] 1 All ER 705, HL; para 21.19 above.
4   [1956] AC 649, [1956] 1 All ER 682, HL.
5   [1968] AC 1, [1967] 2 All ER 1014, HL.

Breach by defendant

24.6 If the law regarded a breach of statutory duty merely as evidence of a person's negligence, then it might treat the near infringement of a regulation in the same way. As we have seen, however, English law takes the view that breach of statutory duty is a separate tort; consequently, only an actual breach is relevant. In *Chipchase v British Titan Products Co Ltd*,[1] the plaintiff fell from a working platform only 9 in wide; had it been a few inches higher, statute would have required a width of 34 in. On these facts the defendants were held not liable for either negligence or breach of statutory duty.

In deciding whether or not a particular obligation has been broken, it is important to realise that the standard of conduct required may vary, because of either the words used or their interpretation by the courts. For example, in *Ministry of Housing and Local Government v Sharp*,[2] the Court of Appeal differed as to whether the duty of a local land registrar in issuing certificates of search was absolute or, as the majority held, one of reasonable care. A duty qualified by such words as 'so far as is reasonably practicable' is, it appears, equivalent to one of reasonable care; at the other extreme, an unqualified duty may be held to impose an absolute obligation. In *John Summers & Sons Ltd v Frost*,[3] for instance, it was held by the House of Lords that a grinding wheel could not be described as 'securely fenced', as required by statute, if any part of the wheel remained exposed, even though to cover it completely would render it unusable.

Between these two levels lies an obligation 'to take such steps as may be necessary'. In deciding what steps are necessary, the courts consider only such dangers as the defendant ought reasonably to have foreseen. If this test establishes that steps *are* necessary, however, the defendant's obligation to take those steps is an absolute one.[4]

1   [1956] 1 QB 545, [1956] 1 All ER 613, CA.
2   [1970] 2 QB 223, [1970] 1 All ER 1009, CA.
3   [1955] AC 740, [1955] 1 All ER 870, HL.
4   *Brown v National Coal Board* [1962] AC 574, [1962] 1 All ER 81, HL.

Causation

24.7 As with any action in tort, the plaintiff must establish that the defendant's breach of duty was a legal cause of his injuries. With one exception the law on this matter, although complex, is no different from that which governs cases of negligence and which we have already considered.[1] The exception is where a statute is so drafted as to place identical duties on two parties (usually employer and employee) in such terms that an act or omission by one party constitutes a breach by both of them. In such a case, where a statute states baldly that something 'shall be done', failure to do it puts both parties in breach, even though the 'fault' is of one party alone. In *Ginty v Belmont Building Supplies Ltd*,[2] for example, it was provided by statute that, when work was being done on fragile roofs, crawling boards 'shall be used'. The defendants supplied such boards, together with full instructions as to their use, to the plaintiff, an experienced workman whom they employed, but he decided not to use the boards and consequently fell through the roof. This breach of statutory duty was undoubtedly one for which both plaintiff and defendants could have been criminally liable. However, it was held that the plaintiff was not entitled to claim damages from defendants, for their breach of statutory duty consisted entirely of his own breach.

It is important to note that the decision in *Ginty* can only exonerate a defendant where the plaintiff is the sole cause of his own misfortune; if any kind of independent or 'extra' fault can be attributed to the defendant, he will be liable, although the plaintiff is likely in such a case to lose a substantial proportion of his damages on the ground of contributory negligence. In *Boyle v Kodak Ltd*,[3] for instance, the House of Lords held the defendant employers two-thirds to blame for an accident at work, since they had failed to provide the plaintiff with adequate supervision or instruction in the relevant regulations. And, in *McMath v Rimmer Bros (Liverpool) Ltd*,[4] where the plaintiff fell from a ladder which no-one was 'footing', his employers were held liable for 50% of his damages, since the absence of anyone to foot the ladder was attributable to their fault.

1 Ch 21 above.
2 [1959] 1 All ER 414.
3 [1969] 2 All ER 439, [1969] 1 WLR 661, HL.
4 [1961] 3 All ER 1154, [1962] 1 WLR 1, CA.

Defences
24.8 In principle, the defence of *volenti non fit injuria*[1] is available in actions for breach of statutory duty. However, for reasons of public policy it has long been settled that an employer may not use it against his employee when the employer is personally in breach of his own statutory obligation.[2] In cases where the employer is not personally in breach, but is made vicariously liable for breach by his employees of statutory duties which are laid upon them, he may use the defence.[3]

There is no doubt that the defence of contributory negligence[4] is available (and it should be noted that the plaintiff's 'fault' for this purpose may itself consist of some breach of statutory duty). However, if too liberally used, this defence would deprive many employees of the benefit of regulations specifically designed for their protection. Consequently, in dealing with industrial accident cases, the courts are careful to make full allowance for problems of fatigue, repetition, boredom and the like.[5]

Where the defendant is personally under a statutory duty, it is no defence for him to show that he delegated its performance to the plaintiff. However, if the plaintiff's conduct is the sole cause of his injury, the defendant may avoid liability on the basis of the rule in *Ginty v Belmont Building Supplies Ltd*.[6] Alternatively, there is nothing to prevent a court from saying that, notwithstanding the defendant's breach, the plaintiff's contributory negligence is so serious as to amount to 100%.[7]

1 Paras 22.2 to 22.10 above.
2 *Baddeley v Earl Granville* (1887) 19 QBD 423, DC.
3 *Imperial Chemical Industries Ltd v Shatwell* [1965] AC 656, [1964] 2 All ER 999, HL; para 22.8 above.
4 Paras 22.11–22.16 above.
5 See *Caswell v Powell Duffryn Associated Collieries Ltd* [1940] AC 152, [1939] 3 All ER 722, HL; *Mullard v Ben Line Steamers Ltd* [1971] 2 All ER 424, [1970] 1 WLR 1414, CA.
6 [1959] 1 All ER 414; para 24.7 above.
7 *Jayes v IMI (Kynoch) Ltd* [1985] ICR 155, CA; para 22.16 above.

Chapter 25

Trespass to land

25.1 This tort may be said to consist of a direct intrusion upon land in the possession of the plaintiff. Certain elements of the definition require amplification but, before this is done, a number of general points may be made. First, despite the multitude of notices proclaiming that 'Trespassers will be prosecuted', trespass in itself is not a crime.[1] It is, however, civilly actionable per se, that is, without any need to prove that damage has been done,[2] a rule dating from the time when the law's primary concern was to preserve the peace. In this respect it differs from the tort of nuisance (in which the plaintiff must prove damage) and, since both torts may consist of causing objects to enter the plaintiff's land, it is important to appreciate the distinction between them. This lies in the fact that trespass applies only to *direct* invasions. Thus, the man who chops down his tree so that it falls into his neighbour's garden commits trespass; if he merely allows its roots or branches to grow across the boundary, this is nuisance.[3]

If the intrusion of the defendant, or of some object propelled by him, is accidental, in the sense that he did not intend it and took reasonable steps to prevent it, it seems that he has the defence of inevitable accident.[4] Thus, in *League Against Cruel Sports Ltd v Scott*,[5] it was held that the master of a hunt would only be liable for trespass by the hounds if he either intended them to enter the plaintiff's land or negligently failed to prevent them from so doing. On the other hand, if the defendant acts deliberately, it is no defence to show that he did not mean to trespass (eg because he was mistaken). Thus, in *Basely v Clarkson*,[6] a man was held liable in trespass when, in mowing his grass, he crossed an ill-defined boundary and mowed some of the plaintiff's.

1 Except where statute so provides, eg on railway property (Railway Regulation Act 1840) or where the trespasser has an offensive weapon (Criminal Law Act 1977).
2 *Entick v Carrington* (1765) 19 State Tr 1029.
3 *Lemmon v Webb* [1894] 3 Ch 1, CA.
4 So held in relation to trespass to goods in *National Coal Board v J E Evans & Co Ltd* [1951] 2 KB 861, [1951] 2 All ER 310, CA; para 29.2 below.
5 [1985] 2 All ER 489, [1985] 3 WLR 400.
6 (1681) 3 Lev 37.

Land
25.2 In normal circumstances, the possession of land carries with it possession of all underlying strata and of the airspace above, so that the possessor may sue in trespass for intrusion at any level. Sometimes,

399

however, horizontal divisions are made (eg in a block of flats, or where minerals are sold) and, where this is so, the possessor of the affected area is alone able to sue. Thus, for example, where X possesses land over which Y has rights of pasture, X may sue anyone who drives tent-pegs into the soil;[1] but only Y may take action against a person who rides across the grass.[2]

As far as the airspace above the land is concerned, it is clear that an unauthorised invasion of this is trespass, at least where it is not above the maximum height necessary for the occupier's ordinary use and enjoyment of his land and buildings. This may include, for example, a projecting advertisement[3] or the swinging jib of a crane.[4] In *Bernstein v Skyviews and General Ltd*,[5] however, the defendants were held not liable when they flew several hundred feet above the plaintiff's house to take unauthorised photographs of it with a view to selling them to the plaintiff.

Overflight is also subject to the Civil Aviation Act 1982 which, broadly speaking, prevents the landowner from claiming in either trespass or nuisance for the mere fact of the flight, provided that this is at a height which is reasonable, having regard to wind and weather. In *Bernstein's* case, notwithstanding the purpose of their flight, the defendants were allowed to rely on this defence. However, if any material damage is caused, liability for this is strict.

1 *Cox v Glue* (1848) 5 CB 533.
2 *Cox v Mousley* (1848) 5 CB 533.
3 *Kelsen v Imperial Tobacco Co (of Great Britain and Ireland) Ltd* [1957] 2 QB 334, [1957] 2 All ER 343.
4 *Woollerton and Wilson Ltd v Richard Costain Ltd* [1970] 1 All ER 483, [1970] 1 WLR 411.
5 [1978] QB 479, [1977] 2 All ER 902.

Intrusion

25.3 Perhaps the most obvious form of trespass to land is entry by the defendant himself. The slightest crossing of the boundary (such as a hand across the threshold[1]) is sufficient but, in the absence of such a crossing (or at least some contact with the fabric of the property), there is no trespass. Thus, where a landlord cuts off mains services to a tenant's flat from a point outside the flat, he may be guilty of a breach of contract and of the criminal offence of harassment,[2] but his conduct does not constitute the tort of trespass.[3] It was at one time thought that, since no action for breach of statutory duty may be based upon the Protection from Eviction Act 1977 or its predecessors,[4] a tenant who was harassed in this way would be unable to claim exemplary damages.[5] However, such action by a landlord is likely to constitute the tort of nuisance, and the Court of Appeal has held that exemplary damages may be awarded where this is the case.[6]

A person who is permitted or legally entitled to enter land may, by exceeding or abusing his right, become a trespasser.[7] This rule is especially important in relation to public or private rights of way, which extend only to reasonable passage; thus, in *Hickman v Maisey*,[8] the defendant, who had patrolled a 15-yard stretch of highway across the plaintiff's land in order to spy on racehorse trials there, was held to be a trespasser. In such cases, action may be taken by the owner of the subsoil (which today often means a highway authority).

A common form of trespass consists of directly causing objects to enter the plaintiff's land. Once again, the most trivial invasion will suffice, such as leaning a ladder against the plaintiff's wall.[9]

1 *Franklin v Jeffries* (1985) Times, 11 March.
2 Protection from Eviction Act 1977, s1.
3 *Perera v Vandivar* [1953] 1 All ER 1109, [1953] 1 WLR 672, CA.
4 *McCall v Abelesz* [1976] QB 585, [1976] 1 All ER 727, CA.
5 Para 31.2 below.
6 *Guppys (Bridport) Ltd v Brookling* (1983) 269 Estates Gazette 846, 942, CA.
7 Para 23.9 above.
8 [1900] 1 QB 752, CA.
9 *Westripp v Baldock* [1939] 1 All ER 279.

Trespass ab initio

25.4 A person who, having entered land under some legal authority (not merely by permission of the owner), then abuses that authority may be treated as a trespasser from the moment of entry. This fiction, which has the effect of inflating the damages awarded, does not apply where the subsequent abuse consists of an omission,[1] nor where some justification remains for the entry (e g where police seize some documents unlawfully and others lawfully[2]). Whether the doctrine, which was originally devised to protect citizens against the abuse of power by officials, retains any usefulness has been doubted by the Court of Appeal.[3]

1 Such as failure to pay for food ordered and consumed: *Six Carpenters' Case* (1610) 8 Co Rep 146a.
2 *Elias v Pasmore* [1934] 2 KB 164.
3 *Chic Fashions (West Wales) Ltd v Jones* [1968] 2 QB 299, [1968] 1 All ER 229, CA.

Possession

25.5 Trespass to land is a wrong to the plaintiff's *possession* rather than to his *ownership*. As a result, where land is let, only the tenant may take action against a trespasser, except that where permanent damage is done to the property the landlord may sue.[1] For the same reason, a tenant who fails to quit the premises when his lease expires is not thereby guilty of trespass.[2] Conversely, where land is occupied under licence, the licensee normally[3] lacks the exclusive possession of the property which is necessary to found an action in trespass;[4] this remains in the hands of the licensor.

The common law's emphasis upon the protection of possession (based on its concern with preserving the peace) is such that even one whose possession is wrongful may sue in trespass any other wrongdoer who disturbs him,[5] and it is no defence for the latter to show that the true right to possession lies with a third party. The only person who may override such wrongful possession is the true owner, or someone acting on his behalf.[6]

The question of what constitutes possession in law receives different answers in respect of different types of property. It is the occupation of a house which counts, but the possession of open land may depend upon evidence of actual use. If, as frequently happens in trespass actions, possession is disputed,[7] the law presumes in favour of the person with title[8] even if, on investigation, that title proves to be defective.[9]

A person who is not actually in possession of land cannot sue for trespass, even though he has an immediate right to possession. When he eventually enters upon the land, however, he is deemed by the doctrine of 'trespass by relation' to have been in possession from the moment his right accrued, and he can therefore claim in respect of trespass committed in the interim.

1 *Jones v Llanrwst UDC* [1911] 1 Ch 393.
2 *Hey v Moorhouse* (1839) 6 Bing NC 52.
3 But see Ch 38 below.
4 *Hill v Tupper* (1863) 2 H & C 121.
5 *Nicholls v Ely Beet Sugar Factory* [1931] 2 Ch 84, CA.
6 *Delaney v T P Smith Ltd* [1946] KB 393, [1946] 2 All ER 23, CA.
7 Especially where one party claims to have acquired title against the other by adverse possession; ch 42 below.
8 *Jones v Chapman* (1849) 2 Exch 803.
9 *Fowley Marine (Emsworth) Ltd v Gafford* [1968] 2 QB 618, [1968] 1 All ER 979, CA.

Defences
25.6   An act cannot be a trespass if it is legally justified, and justification in this context may arise in various ways. Statutory powers of entry are conferred, not only on the police, but also on a myriad of officials, such as inspectors of the Health and Safety Executive, trading standards officers and VAT inspectors. Indeed, an access agreement or order made under the National Park and Access to the Countryside Act 1949 entitles anyone to enter the land concerned, provided that he complies with the specified conditions. Further, it is hardly necessary to point out that a person exercising a public or private right of way is not a trespasser unless he abuses or exceeds that right.[1]

Common law recognises the right of an owner of goods to retake them from the land of another, at least where that other is wrongfully responsible for their presence there.[2] Further, apparent acts of trespass may be justified by necessity (defence of the realm or the preservation of life or property) provided that they are in reasonable proportion to the threatened harm and that the need to trespass is not brought about by the defendant's own negligence.[3] This defence is kept within strict limits; homelessness, for example, is no excuse for 'squatting' in vacant premises.[4]

Apart from rights of way, certain other rights over land (such as easements, profits à prendre and local customary rights[5]) may entitle someone to do what would otherwise be a trespass. Indeed, a bare permission or licence will also have this effect. Once such a licence is validly revoked[6] any further intrusion is a trespass, although the licensee cannot be compelled to undo what he has done. Thus, in *Armstrong v Sheppard and Short Ltd*,[7] where the plaintiff withdrew the permission which he had given the defendants to lay and use a sewer under his land, it was held that further use of the sewer was a trespass, although the defendants could not be compelled to remove the sewer itself.

1 Paras 23.9 and 25.3 above.
2 *Patrick v Colerick* (1838) 3 M & W 483.
3 *Rigby v Chief Constable of Northamptonshire* [1985] 2 All ER 985, [1985] 1 WLR 1242.
4 *Southwark London Borough Council v Williams* [1971] Ch 734, [1971] 2 All ER 175, CA. See also *John Trenberth Ltd v National Westminster Bank Ltd* (1979) 253 Estates Gazette 151, para 25.8 below.
5 Ch 40 below.
6 This complex and difficult topic is dealt with in para 38.7 below.
7 [1959] 2 QB 384, [1959] 2 All ER 651, CA.

Remedies

Damages

25.7   Where the plaintiff's land is harmed, he is entitled to claim damages, and these will be based either on the amount by which the value of the property is diminished or, more commonly, the cost of reinstating it to its former condition.[1] Even where the land itself is not damaged, the plantiff is entitled to claim for the loss of use of his property, and here the appropriate measure is its ordinary letting value,[2] whether or not it appears likely that the plaintiff could have let it.[3]

It should be noted that where the defendant is guilty of a *continuing* trespass (e g by remaining in occupation of or leaving his goods on the plaintiff's land) he is liable to successive actions until he ceases the offence.[4] Where, however, the trespass is a single act (such as the digging of a hole in the plaintiff's land), the fact that its *effects* continue does not lead to the same result; here damages are awarded once and for all.[5]

1   Para 31.12 below.
2   *Whitwham v Westminster Brymbo Coal Co* [1896] 2 Ch 538, CA.
3   *Swordheath Properties Ltd v Tabet* [1979] 1 All ER 240, [1979] 1 WLR 285, CA.
4   *Holmes v Wilson* (1839) 10 Ad & El 503.
5   *Clegg v Dearden* (1848) 12 QB 576.

Injunction

25.8   Where trespass is continuous or repetitive, the plaintiff will usually be entitled to an injunction ordering the defendant to cease the offending activity. However, it should be remembered that the injunction is a discretionary remedy and, in special circumstances (for example where the court disapproves of the plaintiff's conduct), no injunction will be granted.[1] Furthermore, it is possible in an appropriate case for the court to grant an injunction but to limit its operation in some way. In *Woollerton and Wilson Ltd v Richard Costain Ltd,*[2] for instance, the plaintiffs refused to give permission for the defendants, who were engaged in a building project, to swing their crane over the plaintiffs' property except on payment of a very large sum of money. When the defendants declined to pay but continued to swing the crane, the plaintiffs sued them in trespass. They were duly awarded an injunction but the judge suspended its operation for a time sufficient to enable the defendants to complete the project.

Not every judge is as sympathetic to the difficulties which an injunction would cause to a defendant. In *John Trenberth Ltd v National Westminster Bank Ltd,*[3] the defendants could not repair their dangerously dilapidated building without entering the plaintiffs' premises, but the plaintiffs refused to permit them to do so. It was held that the plaintiffs were entitled to prevent any trespass by the defendants by obtaining an immediate injunction.

1   *Tollemache & Cobbold Breweries Ltd v Reynolds* (1983) 268 Estates Gazette 52, CA.
2   [1970] 1 All ER 483, [1970] 1 WLR 411.
3   (1979) 253 Estates Gazette 151.

Action of ejectment

25.9   This ancient action, now more commonly called the action for the recovery of land, enables the plaintiff to regain actual possession of his land.[1] It has often been said that, whereas a plaintiff seeking damages need only show that he had possession, one who seeks to recover his land must prove his title. However, in practice it seems that proof of prior possession by the plaintiff raises a presumption of title which the defendant (unless he himself is entitled to the land) will find almost impossible to rebut.[2] Whether proof that true title rests with a third party will suffice to defeat the plaintiff's claim is a matter of great controversy; even if it does, however, it is of no avail to a defendant whose possession is wrongful as against the plaintiff or is derived from him.

A person who seeks to recover his land in this way frequently joins to his action a claim for mesne profits (any profit gained by the defendant from his wrongful occupation, together with damages for any harm done). Such a claim normally depends upon possession of the property by the plaintiff, but where he succeeds in recovering possession he may then rely on the doctrine of trespass by relation.[3]

1   A special summary procedure is available against persons who are unidentified, such as 'squatters' or 'sitters-in': RSC Ord 113.
2   *Asher v Whitlock* (1865) LR 1 QB 1.
3   Para 25.5 above.

Self-help
25.10   As an alternative to taking legal action, the person in possession of land is entitled to use a reasonable degree of force to eject a trespasser or to deny him entry.[1] As far as the law of tort is concerned, it seems that a person wrongfully dispossessed may similarly attempt to recover his property. In this case, however, great care must be taken to avoid a breach of the criminal law. A residential tenant who refuses to quit, for example, cannot be evicted without a court order. Further, the Criminal Law Act 1977 makes it an offence for anyone except a 'displaced residential occupier' to use or threaten violence in order to secure entry to property.

1   *Hemmings v Stoke Poges Golf Club* [1920] 1 KB 720, CA.

Chapter 26
Nuisance

26.1 The meaning in law of the word 'nuisance' is surrounded by confusion. In so far as it is capable of a short definition, this is simply 'annoyance' or 'harm', which is of very little help. It does, however, convey the idea that this area of the law of tort is concerned more with the effect of something upon the plaintiff than with the conduct of the defendant. The truth is that the subject matter of nuisance is of enormous breadth, linking together such diverse activities as running a fish-and-chip shop or a brothel, digging a trench in the street and letting one's trees overhang a neighbour's garden. When it is further appreciated that liability is not based on any single standard of conduct, such as negligence, the complexity of nuisance is easy to envisage.

A large part of the confusion over 'nuisance' is caused by the fact that the term is used to describe several different areas of liability which have relatively little in common. First, and perhaps most important as far as the law of tort is concerned, a *private nuisance* consists of any unlawful interference with a person's land, or with his use and enjoyment of that land. Within this category there also falls any interference with a person's rights over land, such as easements or profits.[1] Second, and quite separate, a *public nuisance* is a criminal offence, consisting of an activity which endangers or inconveniences the public in general, or which obstructs the exercise of public rights. The relevance of this class of nuisance to the law of tort is that damages may be awarded to any individual who suffers loss or damage over and above that which is incurred by the general public. Third, and not within the law of tort at all, is a *statutory nuisance* under various Acts of Parliament, such as the Control of Pollution Act 1974, the aim of which is to protect the environment. Enforcement in respect of this type of nuisance is in the hands of public bodies such as local authorities.

1 Discussion of these rights belongs to land law; see Ch 40 below.

Private nuisance
26.2 It has been said, and often repeated, that 'private nuisances, at least in the vast majority of cases, are interferences for a substantial length of time by owners or occupiers of property with the use or enjoyment of neighbouring land'.[1] The main function of the law here is to balance the conflicting interests of neighbours, and to decide at what point an interference becomes intolerable and therefore actionable. For ease of exposition we shall consider first the types of interference which are capable of

constituting a nuisance, before discussing the factors which may render such interference 'unlawful'. It will also be necessary to deal with the questions of who is protected by this tort, and who may be liable for it. Finally, mention will be made of certain defences to liability, and the remedies which are available to a successful plaintiff.

1   *Cunard v Antifyre Ltd* [1933] 1 KB 551 at 557.

Interference
Damage to land
26.3   A person who *directly* causes something to enter the plaintiff's land is, of course, guilty of the tort of trespass.[1] Where the element of directness is lacking, however, the appropriate tort is private nuisance. Thus, for example, while it would be trespass to plant a tree in the plaintiff's garden, it is nuisance when the roots or branches of trees which the defendant has planted on his own land grow across the boundary.[2] Similarly, to build a wall on the plaintiff's land is a trespass, but to allow one's own wall to become so dilapidated that it falls on to the plaintiff's land is a nuisance.[3] Indeed, an occupier of land may become liable for nuisances which exist on it in circumstances where he cannot be said to have caused anything, even indirectly.[4]

The simplest case within this category of 'damage to land' is one in which something tangible is allowed to enter the plantiff's property. A defendant has been held liable, for example, for allowing his drain to become blocked, with the result that water overflows on to neighbouring land.[5] It is clear, however, that damage may also be caused intangibly, as when vibrations shake the foundations of the plaintiff's building,[6] or fumes from a factory kills his shrubs.[7] These cases also show that nuisance protects crops and buildings as well as the land itself; in *Farrer v Nelson*,[8] for instance, a person who overstocked his land with pheasants was held liable for the effect upon his neighbour's crops.

As we shall see, the tort of private nuisance protects only the occupier of land. Consequently, no action may be brought by a visitor who is injured or whose goods are damaged. The occupier, however, may claim damages in respect of his goods, as in *Halsey v Esso Petroleum Co Ltd*,[9] where smuts from an oil depot damaged the plaintiff's lines of washing. Further, although there is no decision directly in point, it is generally accepted that the occupier can recover damages for personal injury, e g if he is made ill by fumes which render his house an unhealthy place in which to live.

1   Ch 25 above.
2   *Lemmon v Webb* [1894] 3 Ch 1, CA.
3   *Brew Bros Ltd v Snax (Ross) Ltd* [1970] 1 QB 612, [1970] 1 All ER 587, CA.
4   Para 26.14 below.
5   *Sedleigh-Denfield v O'Callaghan* [1940] AC 880, [1940] 3 All ER 349, HL.
6   *Hoare & Co v McAlpine* [1923] 1 Ch 167.
7   *St Helen's Smelting Co v Tipping* (1865) 11 HL Cas 642, HL.
8   (1885) 15 QBD 258.
9   [1961] 2 All ER 145, [1961] 1 WLR 683.

Use and enjoyment
26.4   Arguably the most important feature of private nuisance is that it protects a person's use and enjoyment of his land. In this respect it is unique, whereas actual damage to land may well also come within other

torts. Even where no physical damage is done, an occupier is entitled to complain if the use to which he wishes to put his property is unreasonably curtailed by the activities of the defendant. It is on this basis that action in nuisance may be taken in respect of smoke from a factory chimney,[1] the offensive smell from neighbouring stables[2] or the noise from a children's playground.[3] Indeed, the law takes account of even more subtle attacks upon the plaintiff's enjoyment of his land, or upon its amenity. Thus, the picketing of a person's premises from the highway, it is does not fall within the statutory protection given to certain industrial activities, may constitute a nuisance,[4] and the use of high-class residential premises for prostitution may be a nuisance to neighbours.[5]

The 'use' of land to which private nuisance applies is not merely that of a domestic residence; the agricultural, commerical or industrial occupier is also protected. There seems no reason to exclude any lawful use, so that the dictum of Buckley J in *Bridlington Relay Ltd v Yorkshire Electricity Board*,[6] that a purely recreational use (in that case television reception) is outside the scope of this tort, appears incorrect.

1 *Crump v Lambert* (1867) LR 3 Eq 409.
2 *Rapier v London Tramways Co* [1893] 2 Ch 588, CA.
3 *Dunton v Dover District Council* (1977) 76 LGR 87.
4 *Hubbard v Pitt* [1976] QB 142, [1975] 3 All ER 1, CA.
5 *Thompson-Schwab v Costaki* [1956] 1 All ER 652, [1956] 1 WLR 335, CA. See also *Laws v Flonnplace Ltd* [1981] 1 All ER 659 (sex shop in predominantly residential area).
6 [1965] Ch 436, [1965] 1 All ER 264.

Unlawfulness

Degree of interference

26.5 Private nuisance, then, consists of an interference. However, not every interference is a nuisance, for it would be futile to demand *absolute* silence or absence of smell from neighbours; they must be allowed the occasional party or garden bonfire. The law seeks to apply the broad principle of 'give and take', or 'live and let live'; as Lord Wright put it in *Sedleigh-Denfield v O'Callaghan*:[1] 'A balance has to be maintained between the right of the occupier to do what he likes with his own, and the right of his neighbour not to be interfered with'.

In striking this balance, a wide variety of factors have to be considered. One of the most important, and also the most obvious, is the seriousness of the inteference in question. Where actual physical damage is caused, a fairly minor interference is sufficient to constitute nuisance but, where the plaintiff complains of interference with his use and enjoyment, rather more is required. It has been said that there must be 'an inconvenience materially interfering with the ordinary comfort physically of human existence, not merely according to elegant or dainty modes and habits of living, but according to plain and sober and simple notions among the English people'.[2] The matter here is purely one of degree, as appears from the following two cases. In *Heath v Brighton Corpn*,[3] a buzzing noise from a power station, which disturbed a church congregation in a poor area, was held insufficient to be a nuisance. In *Haddon v Lynch*,[4] on the other hand, the persistent and early ringing of church bells on Sunday mornings was held to be actionable.

It is obvious that the judge in a nuisance action has a wide discretion, and he not infrequently decides to view the property for himself. In *Penn v Wilkins*,[5] for example, an excursion to Hertfordshire by Megarry J was enough to convince the learned judge that the periodic emptying of the defendant's cesspit was not so offensive as to be a nuisance.

1 [1940] AC 880 at 903, [1940] 3 All ER 349 at 364, HL.
2 *Walter v Selfe* (1851) 4 De G & Sm 315 at 322.
3 (1908) 98 LT 718.
4 [1911] VLR 230.
5 (1974) 236 Estates Gazette 203.

Sensitivity

26.6 The fact that a person is abnormally sensitive, or that he puts his property to an abnormally sensitive use, does not entitle him to a greater freedom from interference than anyone else. This rule, which is really no more than an application of the general principle outlined in the previous paragraph, is illustrated by *Robinson v Kilvert*,[1] in which heat from the defendant's premises damaged the plaintiff's stocks of brown paper. The amount of heat was not unreasonable; the damage was caused because the paper was unduly sensitive. The defendant was accordingly not liable. So too, in *Bridlington Relay Ltd v Yorkshire Electricity Board*,[2] where the plaintiffs 'piped' television signals from their aerial mast to members of the public, they claimed to be entitled to a greater freedom from interference than the average domestic user on the basis that, unless they could offer a superior signal, they would have no customers. Not surprisingly, this claim was rejected.

Although the law gives no *extra* protection to the sensitive, it does not abandon them altogether. If an interference is sufficiently substantial to constitute nuisance by ordinary standards, the plaintiff may claim damages for the effect it has upon his sensitive use of property, such as the growing of delicate orchids.[3]

1 (1889) 41 Ch D 88, CA.
2 [1965] Ch 436, [1965] 1 All ER 264.
3 *McKinnon Industries Ltd v Walker* [1951] 3 DLR 577 at 581.

Locality

26.7 In assessing the standard of comfort to which the plaintiff is legally entitled, the character of the neighbourhood is an important factor. In *Halsey v Esso Petroleum Co Ltd*,[1] for instance, where the plaintiff complained of the nightly noise of tankers driving in and out of the defendants' oil depot, the judge regarded it as crucial that the depot was situated in a quiet residential part of Fulham. Even a noisy area, however, has some standards. For example, in *Polsue and Alfieri Ltd v Rushmer*,[2] the plaintiff, who lived in Fleet Street, was held entitled to complain of the nightly noise from a new printing press which the defendants had installed.

An interesting point was raised in the case of *Allen v Gulf Oil Refining Ltd*,[3] in which a massive oil refinery, constructed under the authority of an Act of Parliament, caused severe dislocation of the environment. It was pointed out by Lord Wilberforce that, even if claims in nuisance were not completely defeated by the defence of statutory authority,[4] the appropriate standard of comfort for this locality was to be based on what parliament had clearly authorised it to become, rather than on what it had been before the refinery was built.

It should be noted that, where physical damage is caused to the plaintiff's property, the locality is irrelevant. Thus, in *St Helens Smelting Co v Tipping*,[5] where the plaintiff's shrubs were killed by fumes from the defendants' smelting works, the House of Lords regarded it as no defence that the area was devoted to such industrial activity.

1 [1961] 2 All ER 145, [1961] 1 WLR 683.
2 [1907] AC 121, HL.
3 [1981] AC 101, [1981] 1 All ER 353, HL.
4 Para 26.16 below.
5 (1865) 11 HL Cas 642, HL.

Continuity
26.8 In most cases of private nuisance, especially those in which the plaintiff's 'use and enjoyment' are affected, the interference of which he complains has an element of continuity or repetition. This is perfectly reasonable; the dust from building operations lasting years, or the noise from nightly revelries, may well be intolerable, whereas interference of a shorter or more sporadic nature might not be. Even if the temporary nature of an interference does not prevent it from being a tort at all, it may well mean that no injunction will be granted.[1] It should not be thought, however, that an isolated incident can never be a basis for liability; where actual damage results, as where a dilapidated building falls on to the plaintiff's land, there is no need for a repetition before action can be taken. In such a case it could of course be said that, although the damage itself is momentary, it results from a continuing state of affairs for which the defendant is responsible. Thus in *Spicer v Smee*,[2] where defective wiring in the defendant's bungalow caused a fire which spread to the plaintiff's property, the defendant was held liable in nuisance. In *British Celanese Ltd v A H Hunt (Capacitors) Ltd*,[3] where light strips of metal foil, which were stored over a period of time on the defendants' land, blew on to adjoining property and caused damage, liability in nuisance was again imposed. In *SCM (UK) Ltd v W J Whittall & Son Ltd*,[4] on the other hand, where a workman negligently severed a cable and thus cut off the electricity supply to the plaintiff's factory, it was held that the defendants could not be liable in nuisance. Here there was no 'state of affairs', but simply an isolated act of negligence.

1 *Swaine v G N Rly* (1864) 4 De GJ & S 211.
2 [1946] 1 All ER 489.
3 [1969] 2 All ER 1252, [1969] 1 WLR 959.
4 [1970] 2 All ER 417, [1970] 1 WLR 1017, CA.

Utility of the defendant's conduct
26.9 A frequent plea of defendants in nuisance actions is that the offending activity is being carried on for the benefit of the public. This can undoubtedly have some bearing on the degree of interference which the plaintiff can be expected to put up with (the noise and dust which usually accompanies demolition and rebuilding, for example, would certainly be actionable if caused for no good reason). However, it cannot be a complete defence, for the courts will not allow the public interest to ride roughshod over private rights. In *Adams v Ursell*,[1] for instance, the smell from a fried-fish shop was held to be a nuisance, notwithstanding its value in supplying good food in a poor neighbourhood. Even more striking is the case of *Shelfer v City of London Electric Lighting Co*,[2] in which vibrations from the

building of a power station damaged the plaintiff's house. The Court of Appeal held that the plaintiff was entitled to an injunction to stop the work, even though the laudable purpose of the building was to bring electric light to the City of London.

It may be that courts today are more willing than their predecessors to give weight to the public interest, at least to the extent of refusing to order the complete termination of a beneficial activity. In *Miller v Jackson*,[3] for example, the plaintiff bought a new house next to the ground on which the village team had played cricket for some 70 years. The Court of Appeal held, by a majority, that the danger from cricket balls constituted a nuisance; nevertheless, in view of the social value of the ground to the community, the plaintiff was denied an injunction, and left to his remedy in damages. Likewise, in *Dunton v Dover District Council*,[4] where the plaintiff complained of the noise from a children's playground next to his hotel, the judge refused to order its closure, but restricted its opening times and the age-group of children permitted to use it. However, not every plea of 'public interest' is successful. In *Kennaway v Thompson*,[5] the Court of Appeal granted an injunction which drastically curtailed the activities of a motor boat racing club, preferring to protect the interest of a neighbouring resident who complained about the noise.

1 [1913] 1 Ch 269.
2 [1895] 1 Ch 287, CA.
3 [1977] QB 966, [1977] 3 All ER 338, CA.
4 (1977) 76 LGR 87.
5 [1981] QB 88, [1980] 3 All 329, CA.

Order of events
26.10 Notwithstanding a recent attack,[1] the rule seems settled that a plaintiff is not precluded from complaining of a nuisance merely because he came to it with his eyes wide open. In *Sturges v Bridgman*,[2] a doctor was held entitled to complain of the noise from machinery used by the defendant on adjoining premises, even though this caused him no inconvenience until he chose to build a consulting room at the end of his garden.

1 By Lord Denning MR in *Miller v Jackson* [1977] QB 966, [1977] 3 All ER 338; the majority of the Court of Appeal upheld the established rule.
2 (1879) 11 ChD 852, CA.

The defendant's state of mind
26.11 The question whether liability in nuisance depends upon proof of any particular mental element on the part of the defendant is one of the most difficult and complex aspects of this tort. What may safely be said is that the more blame (in the moral sense) which can be attached to the defendant, the less likely it is that the plaintiff will be expected to tolerate the interference in question. Thus, in *Christie v Davey*,[1] where the defendant banged a tray on the party wall in order to disrupt the plaintiff's music lessons, his malice was held to render this noise actionable as a nuisance, even though the volume itself might not have done so. Even clearer is *Hollywood Silver Fox Farm Ltd v Emmett*,[2] where the defendant fired guns near the boundary of his land for the specific purpose of disturbing the breeding season of the plaintiffs' silver foxes. This was held to be actionable, although it could hardly be said that the sound of gunfire would normally amount to a nuisance, unless unduly prolonged. However, it

should be noted that malice cannot make unlawful something which the defendant has an *absolute* right to do, such as the abstraction of percolating water from beneath his own land.[3]

Of less weight than malice, although still relevant to this question, is the possibility that the defendant has been negligent in failing to keep the interference to a minimum. If building operations cause more dust and noise than necessary,[4] or children in a day nursery are permitted to make excessive noise,[5] the defendant's lack of care may lead a court to the conclusion that the plaintiff cannot be expected to put up with the consequences.

Although malice and negligence may thus both be highly relevant to liability in nuisance, it does not seem that either is essential. The courts have repeatedly stressed that, if the interference caused by an activity is substantial enough to be a nuisance, the defendant cannot evade liability merely by showing that he took all reasonable steps to reduce it. The smell from stables[6] or from a fried-fish shop[7] and the noise from a hotel kitchen[8] have all founded a successful action in nuisance against defendants who had taken all due care. The same is true where actual damage is caused; for example, where building works infringe a neighbour's right of support, it is no defence to show that the works were carried out without negligence.[9] In all these cases, however, the defendant was held liable *as creator* of the nuisance. As we shall see, where the defendant is sued *as occupier* of the land from which the nuisance emanates, proof that he has not taken reasonable care is normally essential to liability.[10]

The confusion which surrounds this point cannot be said to have been dispelled by the decision of the Privy Council in *The Wagon Mound (No 2)*[11] that, while 'negligence in the narrow sense' might not always be needed for an action in nuisance, 'fault of some kind' is almost invariably necessary. What is meant by 'fault' is this context is far from clear. However, an important consequence of the decision is that, since 'fault' involves 'foreseeability', the rules as to remoteness of damage in nuisance are identical to those in negligence.[12]

1 [1893] 1 Ch 316.
2 [1936] 2 KB 468, [1936] 1 All ER 825.
3 *Bradford Corpn v Pickles* [1895] AC 587, HL.
4 *Andreae v Selfridge & Co Ltd* [1938] Ch 1, [1937] 3 All ER 255, CA.
5 *Moy v Stoop* (1909) 25 TLR 262.
6 *Rapier v London Tramway Co* [1893] 2 Ch 588, CA.
7 *Adams v Ursell* [1913] 1 Ch 269.
8 *Vanderpant v Mayfair Hotel Co Ltd* [1930] 1 Ch 138.
9 *Brace v South-East Regional Housing Association Ltd* (1984) 270 Estates Gazette 1286, CA.
10 Para 26.14 below.
11 [1967] 1 AC 617, [1966] 2 All ER 709, PC.
12 For these rules, see paras 21.17–21.20 above.

Who is protected?

26.12 The tort of private nuisance exists for the protection of those who are in possession or occupation of land. Even a limited interest, such as a weekly tenancy,[1] will suffice (although someone with such an interest will only be granted an injunction in serious cases); indeed, the courts have suggested that, as is the case in trespass,[2] the plaintiff need only be in actual possession of the land.[3] However, without such possession or occupation it is clear that no action will lie, which can lead to certain anomalies. Thus, in *Malone v Laskey*,[4] where vibrations from the defendant's premises caused a cistern in the house next door to fall and injure the tenant's wife, it was held that she could not claim damages for her injuries in nuisance.

The requirement of possession serves to exclude actions by the landlord of property, at least in respect of temporary interferences with its use and enjoyment, even if the effect of these is to reduce its letting value.[5] The landlord can, however, sue to protect his reversionary interest against either physical damage or such nuisances as may, by the doctrine of prescription,[6] operate to deprive him of rights or burden his land with obligations.[7]

Where, as frequently happens, a nuisance continues over a period, it is quite possible for its effects to be felt by successive owners or occupiers of the same property. The implications of this were considered in *Masters v Brent London Borough Council*,[8] where the roots of the defendants' lime tree encroached and damaged the foundations of a house. The plaintiff, having bought the house, paid for the necessary repairs and then sued the defendants for the cost. However, the defendants raised the defence that the damage had occurred during the ownership of the plaintiff's predecessor. Talbot J, having decided that some damage continued to occur during the plaintiff's ownership, held that this entitled him to claim for whatever losses he had actually suffered (ie the full cost of repair).

1 *Jones v Chappell* (1875) LR 20 Eq 539.
2 Para 25.5 above.
3 *Newcastle-under-Lyme Corpn v Wolstanton Ltd* [1947] Ch 427, [1947] 1 All ER 218, CA.
4 [1907] 2 KB 141, CA.
5 *Simpson v Savage* (1856) 1 CBNS 347.
6 *Paras 40.28–40.36 below.*
7 *Jones v Llanrwst UDC* [1911] 1 Ch 393.
8 [1978] 1 QB 841, [1978] 2 All ER 664.

Who is liable?

Creator

26.13 Although most nuisance actions are brought against the occupier of the offending land, there seems no reason to restrict liability to such a person. In principle, if someone actually *creates* a nuisance, whether on his own land, the land of another, or the public highway, he should be answerable for it. This was certainly assumed to be the case in *Hall v Beckenham Corpn*,[1] where the plaintiff complained of noise from model aeroplanes in a public park, although the individual enthusiasts were not in fact sued in that case. Further, where a person creates a nuisance on his own land, he remains liable for it, even where he subsequently parts with possession of the property and so becomes unable to prevent its continuance.[2]

1 [1949] 1 KB 716, [1949] 1 All ER 423.
2 *Thompson v Gibson* (1841) 7 M & W 456.

Occupier

26.14 Quite apart from the possibility that he may actually create a nuisance, an occupier may be held responsible simply because a nuisance exists upon his land, whether this arises from natural causes or from the actions of other persons. An extreme example of this is *Russell v Barnet*

London Borough Council,[1] in which a highway authority was held liable to a householder for damage caused by the roots of trees growing in the street, notwithstanding that the trees actually belonged to the householder! The general rule where the occupier is not personally responsible for the creation of the nuisance is that he is only liable where, with knowledge or the means of knowledge of its existence, he fails to take reasonable steps to abate it. In *Sedleigh-Denfield v O'Callaghan,*[2] for example, a drainage pipe, which had been negligently laid in the defendants' ditch by trespassers, became blocked, with the result that water overflowed on to the plaintiff's land. The defendants were held liable, for they had known of the pipe for three years and should have appreciated the danger. In *St Anne's Well Brewery Co v Roberts,*[3] on the other hand, part of the city wall of Exeter which was owned by the defendant collapsed and demolished the plaintiff's inn. The cause of this collapse was excavations which had been carried out by the defendant's predecessor. Since the defendant did not and could not know of these, he was held not liable.

The principle of these cases, in which nuisance is caused by the acts of others, has also been applied to nuisances which arise naturally, such as fire caused by lightning striking a tall tree[4] or earth falling from a geological mound.[5] Indeed, the courts here, aware that an 'innocent' occupier should not be subjected to too heavy a burden, have held that, in deciding whether he has acted reasonably, regard should be had to his individual circumstances, such as his financial resources.

There is one anomalous exception to the general rule that an occupier's liability is based on negligence. It was laid down by the Court of Appeal, in the much-criticised case of *Wringe v Cohen,*[6] that, where premises abut upon a highway, the occupier (and landlord, if he is under a duty to repair) is strictly liable for damage resulting from disrepair, whether this is caused to neighbouring property or to the highway.[7] The extent of this liability is uncertain, since the court excluded cases in which the damage resulted from either the act of a trespasser or the secret and unobservable processes of nature.

The common thread which joins all these cases is that the nuisance is created neither by the occupier nor by anyone for whom he is answerable. Where the nuisance arises out of the activities of a visitor, for example, it seems that the occupier will be liable, provided that this is a foreseeable consequence of what he has permitted the visitor to do. Thus in *A-G v Stone,*[8] the defendant, who had allowed gypsies to camp on his land, was held liable when the noise and insanitary conditions of their camp constituted a nuisance. The same principle applies where work carried out on the occupier's behalf by an independent contractor causes a nuisance; if this consequence is foreseeable from the nature of the work, as where support is withdrawn from neighbouring property,[9] the defendant will be liable. In *Matania v National Provincial Bank Ltd,*[10] for instance, building operations carried on by a contractor on behalf of the occupier of a building's first floor involved a clear risk of nuisance by noise and dust to the occupiers of higher floors. When this happened, the occupier was held liable for it.

1 (1984) 271 Estates Gazette 699.
2 [1940] AC 880, [1940] 3 All ER 349, HL.
3 (1928) 140 LT 1, CA.
4 *Goldman v Hargrave* [1967] 1 AC 645, [1966] 2 All ER 989, PC.

5   *Leakey v National Trust for Places of Historic Interest or Natural Beauty* [1980] QB 485, [1980] 1 All ER 17, CA.
6   [1940] 1 KB 229, [1939] 4 All ER 241, CA.
7   In the latter case the occupier would be liable for public nuisance; para 26.23 below.
8   (1895) 12 TLR 76. See also *Page Motors Ltd v Epsom and Ewell Borough Council* (1982) 80 LGR 337.
9   *Bower v Peate* (1876) 1 QBD 321.
10 [1936] 2 All ER 633, CA.

Landlord

26.15   Where a nuisance exists on premises which are let, the usual person to be sued is the tenant; whether or not he is liable depends upon the rules as to an occupier's responsibility which we have just discussed. In certain circumstances, however, the landlord may also be liable, although it is important to realise that this in no way exonerates the tenant. In the first place, the landlord is legally responsible whenever he can be said to have 'authorised' his tenant to commit nuisance. This will be so where the nuisance arises from the normal use of the land by the tenant for the very purpose for which it is let, as in *Harris v James*,[1] where the plaintiff complained of blasting and smoke from a lime quarry, or *Sampson v Hodson-Pressinger*,[2] where perfectly normal use of a top-floor flat caused an intolerable amount of noise to the tenant of the flat below. It should be emphasised, however, that it is *authority*, and not merely *foreseeability*, which must be established. Thus, in *Smith v Scott*,[3] where a local authority housed a 'problem' family next to the plaintiffs, it was held that the local authority were not liable for the foreseeable nuisances which ensued, since, having made their tenants covenant not to commit nuisance, they could hardly be said to have authorised them to do so.

Where nuisance arises, not from the use to which the property is put, but from the state of repair in which it is let, the landlord is liable if he knows or ought to know of its state at the commencement of the tenancy.[4] Further, this liability is in no way diminished by the fact that the tenant covenants to put the premises into repair, because such a covenant cannot be allowed to restrict the rights of third parties.[5]

In cases where the property falls into disrepair, and thus becomes a nuisance, during the currency of the lease, the landlord is only responsible if he has a duty to repair[6] or a right to enter and do repairs.[7] The common law on these points is somewhat uncertain, and it may in practice be safer for plaintiffs to rely on the similar provisions which are now contained in the Defective Premises Act 1972, s4.[8]

The general rule is that a landlord, like an occupier, is only liable for nuisance by disrepair where he knows or ought to know of it. Once again, however, the case of *Wringe v Cohen*[9] lays down that, if the premises adjoin a highway, liability is strict.

1   (1876) 45 LJQB 545.
2   [1981] 3 All ER 710, CA.
3   [1973] Ch 314, [1972] 3 All ER 645; para 19.32 above.
4   *St Anne's Well Brewery Co v Roberts* (1928) 140 LT 1, CA.
5   *Brew Bros Ltd v Snax (Ross) Ltd* [1970] 1 QB 612, [1970] 1 All ER 587, CA.
6   This may be express or implied, eg under the Landlord and Tenant Act 1985, ss11–14; para 37.4 below.
7   *Heap v Ind, Coope and Allsopp Ltd* [1940] 2 KB 476, [1940] 3 All ER 634, CA. This may be implied, eg in a weekly tenancy: *Mint v Good* [1951] 1 KB 517, [1950] 2 All ER 1159, CA.
8   Para 23.30 above.
9   [1940] 1 KB 229, [1939] 4 All ER 241, CA.

Defences
Statutory authority

26.16 A high proportion of actions in nuisance arise out of activities of local authorities and other public or quasi-public bodies, which are carried on under the auspices of a statute. Such bodies may have a defence against liability where they can prove that the nuisance they have created is an inevitable consequence of what the statute ordered or empowered them to do, in the sense that it would occur despite the use of all reasonable care and skill, according to the state of scientific knowledge at the time.[1] However, the position may be further affected if, as is common, the statute in question contains a specific statement to the effect that liability for nuisance is, or is not, excluded.

The case law on statutory authority as a defence is complex, but an attempt was made to rationalise it in the case of *Department of Transport v North West Water Authority*[2] where the following propositions, formulated by the trial judge, were endorsed by the House of Lords:

a.   In the absence of negligence, a body is not liable for a nuisance caused by its performance of a statutory *duty*.[3]

b.   This is so, even if the statute in question expressly imposes liability for nuisance.[4]

c.   In the absence of negligence, a body is not liable for a nuisance caused by its exercise of a statutory *power*, where the statute does not expressly impose liability upon it.[5]

d.   Even without negligence, a body is liable for a nuisance caused by its exercise of a statutory power, if the statute expressly imposes liability upon it.[6]

e.   In all cases, immunity depends upon proof that the work has been carried out, or the operation conducted, with all reasonable regard and care for the interests of other persons.[7]

In deciding whether or not a particular nuisance has been 'authorised' by a statute, the terms of that statute must be interpreted, and it is important to appreciate that 'authority' may be conferred either expressly or by implication. In the leading case of *Hammersmith and City Rly Co v Brand*,[8] for instance, where a railway company was expressly authorised to use railway engines, it was held by the House of Lords that no action in nuisance would lie against it in respect of damage caused by vibrations from passing trains. In the recent case of *Allen v Gulf Oil Refining Ltd*,[9] the express authority of the defendants was limited to acquiring land and there *constructing* an oil refinery. A majority of the House of Lords, reversing the decision of the Court of Appeal, held that there was also, by implication, authority to *operate* a refinery, so that no action in nuisance would lie in respect of the inevitable consequences (smell, noise, vibrations, etc) of its operation.

In the last two cases, the defendants were empowered to carry on the activity in question in a specific place. Frequently, however, this is not so, the defendants in question having a wide discretion under the statute as to the place and method of exercising their power. In such a case, a court is less likely to take the view that any nuisance arising from the exercise of the discretion is 'inevitable'. Thus, in *Metropolitan Asylum District Managers v*

Hill,[10] it was held that a general authority to build hospitals did not protect the defendants from liability when they chose to site a smallpox hospital in a residential area.

Where the 'statutory authority' is to carry out, not a specific undertaking, but such works of a particular kind as may from time to time be necessary, the courts are not over-zealous in their protection of private rights under the tort of nuisance. This is because, when parliament has seen fit to confer an administrative discretion upon a public body, the bona fide exercise of that discretion should be challenged only through administrative channels, and not through the ordinary courts of law.[11]

1   *Manchester Corpn v Farnworth* [1930] AC 171, HL.
2   [1984] AC 336, [1983] 3 All ER 273, HL.
3   *Hammond v St Pancras Vestry* (1874) LR 9 CP 316.
4   *Smeaton v Ilford Corp* [1954] Ch 450, [1954] 1 All ER 923.
5   *Dunne v North Western Gas Board* [1964] 2 QB 806, [1963] 3 All ER 916, CA.
6   *Charing Cross West End and City Electric Supply Co v Hydraulic Power Co* [1914] 3 KB 772, CA.
7   *Allen v Gulf Oil Refining Ltd* [1981] AC 1001, [1981] 1 All ER 353, HL.
8   (1869) LR 4 HL 171, HL.
9   [1981] AC 1001, [1981] 1 All ER 353, HL.
10 (1881) 6 App Cas 193, HL.
11 *Marriage v East Norfolk Rivers Catchment Board* [1950] 1 KB 284, [1949] 2 All ER 1021, CA.

Prescription

26.17 It seems in principle that the right to commit certain private nuisances may be acquired by 20 years' use, under the doctrine of prescription. For this to be so, however, the right in question must be capable of forming the subject matter of an easement,[1] such as the right to send smoke through flues in a party wall.[2] It is generally thought that this requirement excludes the possibility of prescription in respect of such variable nuisances as noise and smells, although the cases on these matters have all been decided on other grounds. In *Sturges v Bridgman*,[3] for example, where a doctor complained of noise from a next-door business, the defendant claimed to have carried on trade there for over 20 years. This, however, was held to be irrelevant, for the defendant's activity had not existed *as a nuisance* for 20 years; it had only become one when the plaintiff built a consulting room at the end of his garden.

1   Paras 40.6–40.9 below.
2   *Jones v Pritchard* [1908] 1 Ch 630.
3   (1879) 11 ChD 852, CA.

Other defences

26.18 The defences of *volenti non fit injuria* and contributory negligence, which we have already considered in relation to negligence,[1] are clearly capable of applying to nuisance, at least where the plaintiff sues in respect of a single incident causing personal injury or damage to property. Where, however, the gist of the plaintiff's complaint is the general effect upon him of the defendant's unreasonable use of land, these defences seem of little relevance. In particular, it is certainly no defence to prove that the plaintiff came to an existing nuisance,[2] nor that he could have reduced its effects, e g by shutting his windows against noise.

One line of argument which does not provide a defence to an action in private nuisance is that the defendant is merely one contributor to the plaintiff's discomfort. Even if the interference is only sufficient to constitute a nuisance when combined with others, the defendant is fully liable as, indeed, are all guilty parties. In *Lambton v Mellish*,[3] for instance, where the plaintiff suffered from the combined effects of two rival fairground organs, it was held that he was entitled to an injunction, although neither organ was making sufficient noise to constitute a nuisance in itself.

1 Ch 22 above.
2 Para 26.10 above.
3 [1894] 3 Ch 163; *Pride of Derby and Derbyshire Angling Association Ltd v British Celanese Ltd* [1953] 1 Ch 149, [1953] 1 All ER 179.

Remedies

Damages

26.19 Although private nuisance is in theory actionable only on proof that the plaintiff has suffered damage, the necessary damage will sometimes be presumed to exist. For example, the mere fact that the cornice of the defendant's house projects over the plaintiff's land is sufficient to found an action, without the need to prove that water falls from it.[1] So too, any interference with a proprietary right of the plaintiff is automatically actionable; if this were not so, continued inteference might eventually lead to the loss of the right altogether.[2]

Once it is established that the defendant is guilty of nuisance, the plaintiff is entitled to claim damages for any resulting loss, provided that this is of a foreseeable kind.[3] As we have seen,[4] the relevant 'kinds' of damage are those which protect the usual interests in the safety of person, goods and land, together with the intangible 'use and enjoyment' of the plaintiff's property. The last category is obviously difficult to express in monetary terms; the courts sometimes use the analogy of personal injury cases, so that damages for noise reflect those for deafness[5] and damages for smell reflect those awarded for loss of that sense.[6]

1 *Fay v Prentice* (1845) 1 CB 828.
2 *Nicholls v Ely Beet Sugar Factory Ltd* [1936] Ch 343, CA.
3 *The Wagon Mound (No 2)* [1967] 1 AC 617, [1966] 2 All ER 709, PC.
4 Paras 26.3–26.4 above.
5 *Chadwick v Keith Marshall* [1984] CLY 1037.
6 *Bone v Seale* [1975] 1 All ER 787, [1975] 1 WLR 797, CA.

Injunction[1]

26.20 A commonly sought remedy in nuisance actions is that of injunction, whereby the plaintiff asks the court to order the termination of the offending activity. The award of this remedy lies in the discretion of the court, and it will seldom be granted in respect of injury which is trivial or temporary.[2] In more serious cases, however, the courts have displayed a notable tendency to grant an injunction even when the defendant's activity has public value,[3] which seems rather surprising in view of their statutory power to award damages in lieu of the injunction sought.[4]

1 Paras 31.16 to 31.18 below.
2 *A-G v Sheffield Gas Consumers Co* (1853) 3 De GM & G 304.
3 Para 26.9 above.
4 Para 31.18 below.

Abatement

26.21   The law has for centuries recognised the right of a person affected by a nuisance to take matters into his own hands and abate (ie remove) it. In a more sophisticated age, however, such self-help remedies are treated by the courts with suspicion and dislike (if for no other reason than that they may lead to a breach of the peace), and anyone exercising this right must therefore take great care not to exceed what the law permits. Where, for example, the defendant's tree overhangs the plaintiff's land, the plaintiff may lop off its branches;[1] he must not, however, keep the fruit.[2] Further, where abatement involves entry on to the defendant's land, notice must first be given, except in an emergency.[3] And the overall requirement that damage be kept to a minimum means that, where there are alternative methods of abating a nuisance, the less mischievous must be chosen.[4]

1   *Lemmon v Webb* [1895] AC 1, HL.
2   *Mills v Brooker* [1919] 1 KB 555.
3   *Jones v Williams* (1843) 11 M & W 176.
4   *Lagan Navigation Co v Lambeg Bleaching Co* [1927] AC 226, HL.

Public nuisance

26.22   If the forms of private nuisance are manifold, the subject matter of public nuisance is quite astonishing in its variety, partly because it is not limited to interference with land. Public nuisances fall into two broad categories. First, the kind of interference, such as noise, smoke, etc. which is commonly a private nuisance will also become a public nuisance if it affects a sufficiently substantial neighbourhood or section of the public. Whether or not this is so is a question of fact;[1] thus, in *R v Lloyd*,[2] where only three people complained of noise, the defendant was held not guilty of public nuisance. Second (which is its original form), public nuisance may consist of interference with the exercise of public rights, for instance by obstructing a highway or navigable river. Within these two classes, liability has been imposed on such diverse activities as blasting operations causing widespread vibrations, dust, splinters and noise,[3] organising a pop festival which causes noise, traffic congestion and general inconvenience,[4] and selling impure food.[5]

It must be remembered that public nuisance is essentially a matter of criminal law.[6] However, as we shall see, a private individual may in some circumstances seek damages for the effect which a public nuisance has on him. Further, where the relevant criminal penalties are felt to be inadequate, the Attorney General is empowered to bring what is called a relator action for an injunction to have the offending activity terminated.

Public nuisance, like private nuisance, involves the courts in the task of balancing conflicting interests in accordance with the general idea of 'reasonableness'. Therefore, a person is not *automatically* liable when queues form outside his shop and obstruct the highway, since these may be due to circumstances beyond his control, such as wartime shortages.[7] Liability will be imposed, however, on a theatre proprietor who takes no steps at all to reduce large nightly queues,[8] or on a shopkeeper who, by selling ice cream from a window, instead of inside the shop, positively increases the likelihood of obstruction.[9] Again, as with private nuisance, the court must apply the principle of 'give and take'. A builder may erect hoardings or scaffolding in the street,[10] vans may load and unload outside business premises[11] and vehicles may break down,[12] without liability arising in public nuisance. Indeed, where personal injury results from such an obstruction, as where the plaintiff collides at night with a parked vehicle, the modern tendency is to impose liability upon the defendant only where he has been negligent in causing the danger,[13] although it is not clear whether it is for the plaintiff to establish negligence or for the defendant to disprove it. Where, however, the obstruction is unreasonable in size or extent, as where a vehicle which has broken down is left for a long period in an unlighted or otherwise dangerous condition, the defendant will be liable in public nuisance.[14]

1 *A-G v P Y A Quarries Ltd* [1957] 2 QB 169, [1957] 1 All ER 894, CA.
2 (1802) 4 Esp 200.
3 *A-G v P Y A Quarries Ltd* [1957] 2 QB 169, [1957] 1 All ER 894, CA.
4 *A-G for Ontario v Orange Productions Ltd* (1971) 21 DLR (3d) 257.
5 *Shillito v Thompson* (1875) 1 QBD 12.
6 A very important consequence of this is that a public nuisance can never be legalised by prescription.
7 *Dwyer v Mansfield* [1946] KB 437, [1946] 2 All ER 247.
8 *Lyons, Sons & Co v Gulliver* [1914] 1 Ch 631, CA.
9 *Fabbri v Morris* [1947] 1 All ER 315, DC.
10 *Harper v G N Haden & Sons Ltd* [1933] Ch 298, CA.
11 *Trevett v Lee* [1955] 1 All ER 406, CA.
12 *Maitland v Raisbeck and R T and J Hewitt Ltd* [1944] KB 689, [1944] 2 All ER 272, CA.
13 *Dymond v Pearce* [1972] 1 QB 496, [1972] 1 All ER 1142, CA.
14 *Ware v Garston Haulage Co Ltd* [1944] 1 KB 30, [1943] 2 All ER 558, CA.

Highways

26.23 It is obvious from the previous paragraph that public nuisance frequently concerns the highway. In the first place, any obstruction, whether total or partial, of the highway is actionable, except where it can be justified on the broad ground of 'reasonableness'. Second, it is a public nuisance to carry on any activity, or to allow property to fall into a state, whereby users of the highway are endangered. This includes the creation of such obvious hazards as a pool of acid[1] or a pile of rubbish,[2] and the emission of large clouds of smoke from neighbouring premises[3] or defective vehicles[4] which obscure the vision of drivers. In *Castle v St Augustine's Links*,[5] liability was imposed upon a golf club which so sited one of its tees that golfers often sliced balls on to an adjoining public road. A person may be liable for public nuisance even where the danger which he has created is not technically on the highway at all, provided that a passer-by may be endangered without making a substantial detour. Thus, for example, an unfenced excavation at the very edge of the road, or sharp outward-pointing spikes on a boundary fence,[6] can constitute a public nuisance.

Where danger arises from work which is being done on or in the highway itself, such as excavations, it is important to note that the defendant is liable even where he is not negligent and, further, that he is responsible for any default of his independent contractor.[7]

The mere fact that a person's building or tree projects over the highway does not render him guilty of a public nuisance, unless it is such as to interfere with reasonable passage. Where, however, it falls and does damage, there may undoubtedly be liability, although the basis of this is disputed. It seems that, where *trees* are concerned, the occupier is not liable unless he had reason to suspect the danger;[8] nor is he responsible for the negligence of his independent contractor, e g in felling operations.[9] Where *buildings* collapse, liability appears to be strict, whether these project over[10] or merely adjoin[11] the highway.

As regards dangers arising from the condition of the highway itself, such as potholes or uneven flagstones, common law imposed no liability upon anyone for a mere failure to repair. In relation to highway authorities, this immunity was anomalous, and it was removed by statute in 1961. Under this provision (which is now contained in the Highways Act 1980), a highway authority may be liable in negligence, nuisance or breach of statutory duty for damage caused by its failure to maintain or repair a highway, subject to a statutory defence of proving that all reasonable care had been taken, by independent contractors or employees of the highway authority, to make the particular highway safe for the type and volume of traffic which might reasonably be expected to use it.

1 *Pope v Fraser and Southern Rolling and Wire Mills Ltd* (1938) 55 TLR 324.
2 *Almeroth v Chivers & Sons Ltd* [1948] 1 All ER 53, CA.
3 *Holling v Yorkshire Traction Co* [1948] 2 All ER 662.
4 *Tysoe v Davis* [1984] RTR 88.
5 (1922) 38 TLR 615.
6 *Fenna v Clare & Co* [1895] 1 QB 199, DC.
7 *Holliday v National Telephone Co* [1899] 2 QB 392, CA; see para 30.22 below.
8 *Caminer v Northern and London Investment Trust Ltd* [1951] AC 88; [1950] 2 All ER 486, HL. What this means in practical terms is well illustrated by *Quinn v Scott* [1965] 2 All ER 588, [1965] 1 WLR 1004.
9 *Salsbury v Woodland* [1970] 1 QB 324, [1969] 3 All ER 863, CA.
10 *Tarry v Ashton* (1876) 1 QBD 314.
11 *Wringe v Cohen* [1940] 1 KB 229, [1939] 4 All ER 241, CA.

Action for damages
26.24 The fact that a person is inconvenienced by a public nuisance does not of itself entitle him to recover damages in respect of it.[1] In order to claim damages, he must show that he has suffered some 'particular' damage, over and above that which is sustained by the public in general. This requirement is obviously satisfied by personal injuries, and, in *Halsey v Esso Petroleum Co Ltd*,[2] it was held that the plaintiff was entitled to complain of smuts from the defendants' oil depot, since these had caused actual damage to the paintwork of his car, which was parked in the street outside his house. In such cases, the damage to the plaintiff is of a different *kind* from that suffered by other persons, but it seems that a substantial difference in *extent* is also sufficient to found an action. In the Irish case of *Boyd v Great Northern Rly Co*,[3] for instance, a doctor with a busy practice recovered damages when he was delayed for 20 minutes at a level crossing, while in *Rose v Miles*,[4] where the defendant obstructed a creek and thus trapped the plaintiff's barges, the plaintiff was able to recover the considerable cost of unloading the cargo and transporting it by land. Again, in *Tate & Lyle Industries Ltd v Greater London Council*,[5] where the defendants caused serious siltation in navigable reaches of the River Thames, the plaintiffs recovered for losses caused by the inability of large vessels to load and unload at their sugar refinery.

The obstruction of streets not infrequently leads to complaints by neighbouring tradesmen of loss of custom. Where access to the plaintiff's premises is blocked, this certainly gives rise to an action for damages.[6] Where the obstruction is further away, the legal position is less clear, although the better view is that an affected tradesman can sue,[7] provided that the effect of the obstruction upon his business is foreseeable and therefore not too remote.[8]

1   *Winterbottom v Lord Derby* (1867) LR 2 Exch 316.
2   [1961] 2 All ER 145, [1961] 1 WLR 683.
3   [1895] 2 IR 555.
4   (1815) 4 M & S 101.
5   [1983] 2 AC 508, [1983] 1 All ER 1159, HL.
6   *Fritz v Hobson* (1880) 14 ChD 542.
7   *Wilkes v Hungerford Market Co* (1835) 2 Bing NC 281.
8   *The Wagon Mound (No 2)* [1967] 1 AC 617, [1966] 2 All ER 709, PC; paras 21.17 to 21.20 above.

Statutory nuisance

26.25   Although we are now moving outside the scope of the law of tort, an account of nuisance would be misleading without some reference to an impressive range of statutory provisions, the overall purpose of which is to minimise environmental damage. Unhealthy premises, provided that they affect persons outside,[1] noise, and the pollution of land, sea and air, are all covered by an elaborate system of administrative control, the enforcement of which is usually in the hands of local authorities and which is carried out by means of criminal prosecution. While some of these provisions give rise to an action for damages by any individual who is affected, the vast majority do not; nevertheless, a person aggrieved may, by complaining to the appropriate enforcement authority, achieve what he most wants, namely, the termination of the offending activity.

1   *National Coal Board v Neath Borough Council* [1976] 2 All ER 478, DC.

Chapter 27
Strict liability

27.1 We said earlier that the basic function of the law of tort is to allocate responsibility for various kind of loss or damage which result from human activity. We also noted that the common law usually takes the view that, unless the defendant has been at fault in causing loss to the plaintiff, the loss should lie where it has fallen. What we shall consider in this and the next chapter are several situations in which liability may be imposed upon a defendant who is not guilty of any 'fault', in the legal sense of causing harm intentionally or negligently.

It should be appreciated from the outset that there is nothing either harsh or illogical in these departures from the normal requirement of fault. The law in effect says of certain high-risk activities that, while it is in the public interest that they be carried on, this can only be on the basis that the losses which they are statistically bound to cause are borne by those who carry on the activities themselves, and not by those innocent members of society on whom they happen to fall. Indeed, were this not so, it would be tantamount to saying that either the unfortunate victims, or society in general (through state benefits paid to those victims) must subsidise the activity in question.

If strict liability (ie liability without fault) has a legitimate place even in a system which is largely fault-based, the vital question becomes: to which activities should it be applied? From a purely logical point of view, there is much to be said for the view of the Law Commission[1] that all 'ultra-hazardous activities' should attract this form of liability.[2] However, as the law now stands, strict liability is applied in a piecemeal fashion. The major areas of application are under the limited doctrine of *Rylands v Fletcher*, and the special rules relating to the escape of fire. We shall also note briefly some cases in which statute has intervened and (in the next chapter) the principles which govern liability for damage done by animals.

1 Report on Civil Liability for Dangerous Things and Activities, Law Com No 32 (1970).
2 Compare the proposals of the Royal Commission on Civil Liability and Compensation for Personal Injury; para 18.21 above.

Rylands v Fletcher
27.2 The facts of this celebrated case were that the defendants employed reputable independent contractors to construct a reservoir on their land, for the purpose of supplying water to their mill. In the course of construction, the contractors discovered some disused mine shafts on the reservoir site but negligently failed to seal these properly, with the result that water

422

flowed down the shafts and flooded the plaintiff's mine, which connected with the disused workings. No negligence was found against the defendants themselves and, at first instance, they were held not liable for the damage caused. On appeal, however, the plaintiff was successful, upon grounds stated by Blackburn J:[1]

> 'We think that the true rule of law is, that the person who for his own purposes brings on his lands and collects and keeps there anything likely to do mischief if it escapes, must keep it in at his peril, and, if he does not do so, is prima facie answerable for all the damage which is the natural consequence of its escape. He can excuse himself by showing that the escape was owing to the plaintiff's default; or perhaps that the escape was the consequence of *vis major*, or the act of God; but as nothing of this sort exists here, it is unnecessary to inquire what excuse would be sufficient'.

This decision, together with the reasoning on which it was based, was expressly approved and upheld by the House of Lords,[2] although Lord Cairns LC rather complicated matters by stressing the importance of the fact that the defendants were at the relevant time putting their land to a 'non-natural use'. This qualification has subsequently been treated as one of the main elements of liability under the rule in *Rylands v Fletcher*, and we shall deal with it as such. In addition, since Blackburn J clearly recognised that *some* defences were available against this form of strict liability, we shall consider a number which have proved successful in later cases.

1   (1866) LR 1 Exch 265 at 279.
2   (1868) LR 3 HL 330, HL.

Elements of liability
Land
27.3   An important part of the rule as laid down, and one which has helped to prevent it from developing to cover dangerous activities in general, is the requirement that the escaping object be something which the defendant has brought on to his land. This does not mean, however, that liability is imposed only upon the freehold owner, or even the occupier, of the land in question. If a licensee, for example, introduces a dangerous substance on to land which he is permitted to use, he may be liable under *Rylands v Fletcher* for its subsequent escape, provided that it is then still under his (ineffective) control.[1] In such a case, it seems that the owner who is not in occupation is only liable if he has expressly or impliedly authorised the accumulation.[2]

The requirement that the defendant be in occupation of land has been slightly relaxed, so as to bring within the rule those who have a right to lay pipes, cables, etc under the land of others or under the public highway. Indeed, an 'escape' in such circumstances may render the defendant liable, not only to neighbouring landowners,[3] but also to other public bodies with similar rights.[4]

Whether the rule is capable of any further expansion must be regarded as doubtful, although it may possibly apply where a dangerous thing escapes from the highway on to which the defendant has brought it.[5]

1   *Rainham Chemical Works v Belvedere Fish Guano Co* [1921] 2 AC 465, HL.
2   *St Anne's Well Brewery Co v Roberts* (1928) 140 LT 1, CA.
3   *Northwestern Utilities Ltd v London Guarantee and Accident Co Ltd* [1936] AC 108, PC.

4   *Charing Cross Westend and City Electric Supply Co v Hydraulic Power Co* [1914] 3 KB 772, CA.
5   *Rigby v Chief Constable of Northamptonshire* [1985] 2 All ER 985, [1985] 1 WLR 1242.

Accumulation

27.4   Blackburn J spoke of the person who 'for his own purposes brings on his lands and collects and keeps there' something which, if it escapes, will be dangerous. Subsequent cases support this idea that the defendant is strictly liable only for artificial accumulations, and not for either natural material, such as earth, or material which accumulates naturally, such as rainwater. For instance, in *Giles v Walker*,[1] an occupier who ploughed up forest land was held not liable for the subsequent spontaneous crop of thistles which spread to the plaintiff's land.[2] So too, in *Pontardawe RDC v Moore-Gwyn*,[3] it was held that *Rylands v Fletcher* had no application to a fall of rock from an outcrop due to the natural process of erosion. Again, where water is naturally on the defendant's land, the plaintiff cannot complain that the defendant's normal working of mines causes it to flow on to his land.[4]

Not surprisingly, an occupier who actively causes natural material to 'escape' will be liable under *Rylands v Fletcher*.[5] For example, in *Miles v Forest Rock Granite Co (Leicestershire) Ltd*,[6] liability was imposed upon the defendants for damage done by the escape of rock caused by their blasting operations. A similar decision was reached in *Baird v Williamson*,[7] where the defendant pumped water which was naturally in his mine to a level from which it flowed into the plaintiff's mine.

Although strict liability can thus only apply to the artificial collection of material, or to artificially causing the escape of natural material, recent decisions make it clear that a duty of care is placed upon an occupier whose land becomes a danger to his neighbour through natural causes.[8] Thus the occupier will be liable if, when he knows or ought to know of the damage, he fails to take reasonable steps to abate it.

The requirement that the accumulation be for the defendant's own purposes should not be taken too literally, as restricting *Rylands v Fletcher* to cases where the defendant acquires some personal benefit. It has been held to apply, for example, to a local authority compelled by statute to receive sewage into its sewers,[9] although the liability of statutory undertakers was doubted by the Court of Appeal on precisely this ground in *Dunne v North Western Gas Board*.[10]

1   (1890) 24 QBD 656.
2   Contrast *Crowhurst v Amersham Burial Board* (1878) 4 ExD 5, where the defendants actually planted a poisonous tree.
3   [1929] 1 Ch 656.
4   *Smith v Kenrick* (1849) 7 CB 515, approved in *Rylands v Fletcher*.
5   If his act is *deliberate*, the appropriate tort is trespass: *Rigby v Chief Constable of Northamptonshire* [1985] 2 All ER 985, [1985] 1 WLR 1242.
6   (1918) 34 TLR 500, CA.
7   (1863) 15 CBNS 376, again approved in *Rylands v Fletcher*.
8   *Goldman v Hargrave* [1967] 1 AC 645, [1966] 2 All ER 989, PC; *Leakey v National Trust for Places of Historic Interest or Natural Beauty* [1980] QB 485, [1980] 1 All ER 17, CA; para 26.14 above.
9   *Smeaton v Ilford Corpn* [1954] Ch 450, [1954] 1 All ER 923.
10   [1964] 2 QB 806, [1963] 3 All ER 916, CA.

Dangerous things

27.5   As originally stated, the rule in *Rylands v Fletcher* applies only to such things as are likely to do mischief if they escape. The difficulty with this restriction is that almost anything is capable of causing damge in some circumstances; further, by definition, the very fact that the plaintiff sues indicates that the object in question *has* caused damage. In practice, therefore, the courts appear largely to have ignored this point and to have instead used the question of 'non-natural user' as a means of keeping the defendant's liability within reasonable bounds.

Among the many things which have given rise to strict liability are water in bulk,[1] gas,[2] electricity,[3] sparks,[4] acid smuts[5] and poisonous vegetation.[6] *Rylands v Fletcher* has also been held to apply to fire[7] and explosions,[8] notwithstanding that the thing which escapes in such cases is not necessarily the same as that which the defendant has accumulated. All these seem to fall fairly within the rule as originally laid down, but some other candidates for inclusion have stretched it more than a little. In *Firth v Bowling Iron Co*,[9] for example, the defendants were held liable for a rusty wire fence which flaked on to the plaintiff's land and poisoned his cattle, while, in *Hale v Jennings Bros*,[10] the principle was invoked where a chair from a fairground 'chair-o-plane' became detached from the roundabout and, complete with its occupant, flew off and injured the occupier of a nearby booth. Even a falling flagpole[11] has been held to come within *Rylands v Fletcher*, although its application to vibrations,[12] where the invasion is intangible, has been criticised. Most extreme of all is perhaps the case of *A-G v Corke*,[13] where the doctrine was applied to human beings so as to justify the grant of an injunction against a man who allowed caravan dwellers to use his field, when these committed various acts of nuisance in the neighbourhood. The dubious nature of this decision is emphasised by the fact that liability could in any case have been imposed on the simple ground of nuisance.[14]

1   *Ryland v Fletcher* itself.
2   *Northwestern Utilities Ltd v London Guarantee and Accident Co Ltd* [1936] AC 108, PC.
3   *National Telephone Co v Baker* [1893] 2 Ch 186.
4   *Jones v Festiniog Rly Co* (1868) LR 3 QB 733.
5   *Halsey v Esso Petroleum Co Ltd* [1961] 2 All ER 145, [1961] 1 WLR 683.
6   *Crowhurst v Amersham Burial Board* (1878) 4 ExD 5.
7   *Mason v Levy Auto Parts of England Ltd* [1967] 2 QB 530, [1967] 2 All ER 62.
8   *Rainham Chemical Works v Belvedere Fish Guano Co* [1921] 2 AC 465, HL.
9   (1878) 3 CPD 254.
10 [1938] 1 All ER 579, CA.
11 *Shiffman v Hospital of the Order of St John of Jerusalem* [1936] 1 All ER 557.
12 *Hoare & Co v McAlpine* [1923] 1 Ch 167.
13 [1933] Ch 89.
14 *A-G v Stone* (1895) 12 TLR 76; para 26.14 above.

Escape

27.6 Any possibility of building, upon the foundation of *Rylands v Fletcher*, a general principle of liability for ultra-hazardous activities is ruled out by the courts' insistence that the damage complained of be suffered *outside* the land on which the defendant accumulates his dangerous things. In *Ponting v Noakes*,[1] for instance, the plaintiff was unable to recover damages when his horse reached over the boundary of the defendant's land, ate some poisonous vegetation which grew there and died. This principle was unanimously endorsed by the House of Lords in *Read v J Lyons & Co Ltd*,[2] where the plaintiff, a munitions inspector, was injured by the explosion of a shell at the defendants' armaments factory. It was admitted that such shells were 'dangerous things'; nevertheless it was held that, in the absence of either negligence or an 'escape', the defendants were not liable.

In deciding whether there has been a sufficient 'escape', the courts are concerned, not with the niceties of land law, but with the simple question of fact whether something has escaped from a place where the defendant has control to a place where he has not. As a result, a landlord may be liable to his own tenant (or, possibly, his licensee) when something escapes from that part of the property which he has retained to that part which is in the occupation of the plaintiff.[3]

1 [1894] 2 QB 281.
2 [1947] AC 156, [1946] 2 All ER 471, HL.
3 *Hale v Jennings Bros* [1938] 1 All ER 579, CA.

Non-natural use

27.7 In laying down the rule in *Rylands v Fletcher*, Blackburn J stressed the importance of the fact that the defendants had brought on to their land something which was not naturally there. This element of liability, like all the others, was expressly approved by Lord Cairns LC, in the House of Lords, but the additional point was made that the defendant must be engaged in a 'non-natural' use of his land. This may have been meant simply as another way of expressing Blackburn J's point. However, subsequent courts have treated it as a separate issue. Thus, the simple question of fact whether the accumulation is natural or artificial is no longer sufficient; the judge must now also decide whether the use to which the defendant puts his land is 'natural' or 'non-natural'.

The effect of this requirement is to introduce a great deal of flexibility into this area of law, because the courts are free not to impose strict liability upon a person whose use of land, although artifical, is an ordinary and usual one. The result of this discretion has been to tie *Rylands v Fletcher* more closely to the idea of exceptional risk, and it has been suggested that a 'non-natural' use is one which brings with it increased danger to others and is not merely the ordinary use of the land or such a use as is proper for the general benefit of the community.[1]

It is impossible to predict accurately how courts will make what is in effect a value judgment. Nevertheless, some insight into judicial attitudes may be gained from previous decisions. Thus, while domestic water supply[1] or electric wiring,[2] or a fire in a grate,[3] are all 'natural', similar utilities carried in bulk are not.[4] So too, trees (whether planted or self-sown) are regarded as 'natural'[5] unless they are poisonous.[6] It should not be thought, however, that the dividing line lies between what is domestic or agricultural, on the one hand, and what is industrial, on the other. Modern courts have proved increasingly ready to hold that a defendant's use of land is 'natural', with the result that he is not liable, in the absence of negligence, to compensate an injured plaintiff. It is on this basis that *Rylands v Fletcher* has been held not to apply to the ordinary working of mines and minerals,[7] nor to a light engineering factory on an industrial estate.[8] It has even been suggested, on rather questionable policy grounds, that a munitions factory in time of war is a 'natural' use of land.[9]

1 *Rickards v Lothian* [1913] AC 263 at 279, PC.
2 *Collingwood v Home and Colonial Stores Ltd* [1936] 3 All ER 200, CA.
3 *Sochacki v Sas* [1947] 1 All ER 344.
4 *Smeaton v Ilford Corpn* [1954] Ch 450, [1954] 1 All ER 923 (sewage).

5 *Noble v Harrison* [1926] 2 KB 332.
6 *Crowhurst v Amersham Burial Board* (1878) 4 ExD 5.
7 *Rouse v Gravelworks Ltd* [1940] 1 KB 489, [1940] 1 All ER 26, CA.
8 *British Celanese Ltd v A H Hunt (Capacitors) Ltd* [1969] 2 All ER 1252, [1969] 1 WLR 959.
9 *Read v J Lyons & Co Ltd* [1947] AC 156 at 170, 174, 187, [1946] 2 All ER 471 at 475, 478, 484, HL.

Damage

27.8 A defendant in *Rylands v Fletcher* is liable for 'all the damage which is the natural consequence' of the escape. This formulation does not indicate the appropriate test for remoteness, but it is suggested that this should be 'foreseeability', even though forseeability is irrelevant to liability itself.

As to the *kinds* of damage which are actionable, the major question is whether the kinship of *Rylands v Fletcher* with private nuisance means that this tort too should protect only an occupier of land.[1] The weight of authority suggests that it is not so limited; thus in *Halsey v Esso Petroleum Co Ltd*,[2] the plaintiff was able to claim for damage caused to the paintwork of his car, which was parked in the street, by acid smuts from the defendants' oil depot. So too, in *British Celanese Ltd v A H Hunt (Capacitors) Ltd*,[3] where strips of metal foil blew from the defendants' land on to an electricity substation, and the resulting power cut caused damage in the plaintiffs' factory, it was held to be no defence that nothing had 'escaped' on to the plaintiffs' land.

It is uncertain whether damages may be recovered in respect of personal injuries, at least those suffered by a non-occupier. Dicta in *Read v J Lyons & Co Ltd*[4] suggest that such an action depends on proof of negligence. Once again, however, there is authority in favour of liability, whether to an occupier[5] or a non-occupier.[6]

Whether or not it may be described as a 'natural consequence', it is settled that no damages may be claimed under *Rylands v Fletcher* for pure economic loss.[7]

1 Para 26.12 above.
2 [1961] 2 All ER 145, [1961] 1 WLR 683.
3 [1969] 2 All ER 1252, [1969] 1 WLR 959.
4 [1947] AC 156 at 174, 178, 180, [1946] 2 All ER 471 at 478, 480, 481, HL.
5 *Hale v Jennings Bros* [1938] 1 All ER 579, CA.
6 *Miles v Forest Rock Granite Co (Leicestershire) Ltd* (1918) 34 TLR 500, CA; *Shiffman v Hospital of the Order of St John of Jerusalem* [1936] 1 All ER 557; *Perry v Kendricks Transport Ltd* [1956] 1 All ER 154, [1956] 1 WLR 85, CA.
7 *Cattle v Stockton Waterworks Co* (1875) LR 10 QB 453; *Weller & Co v Foot and Mouth Disease Research Institute* [1966] 1 QB 569; [1965] 3 All ER 560. See paras 19.22 to 19.26 above.

Defences

Consent of the plaintiff [1]

27.9 Where the plaintiff consents to the presence of the source of danger, the defendant is not liable unless he is negligent. Such consent is rarely express;[2] circumstances may however lead to the inference that it has been given. As to what circumstances will suffice, the position is confused, partly because nearly all the cases have concerned an escape of water from an upper floor to a lower, and could therefore have been decided on the basis that the installation in question was a natural use of land.[3] Apart from this, two main threads emerge from the cases as reasons for holding that the plaintiff has consented. First, and despite its apparent conflict with the principle that 'coming to a nuisance' is no defence,[4] the plaintiff (at least where he is the defendant's tenant) cannot complain of the condition of his or the landlord's property at the commencement of the lease.[5] Second, consent to a dangerous installation will more easily be implied where it is maintained for the benefit of the plaintiff as well as the defendant.[6] This latter factor, however, is not conclusive, so that a consumer of gas is not precluded from suing the statutory undertakers by the fact that he benefits from the supply.[7]

It should be emphasised that the consent which is implied in these cases merely precludes the plaintiff from bringing an action under the rule in *Rylands v Fletcher*. Where the defendant is guilty of negligence, he remains liable,[8] unless the circumstances are so extreme that the plaintiff can be said to have assumed the risk of this.

1 Paras 22.2 to 22.4 above.
2 It was in *A-G v Cory Bros & Co Ltd* [1921] AC 521, HL.
3 *Rickards v Lothian* [1913] AC 263, PC; para 27.7 above.
4 Para 26.10 above.
5 *Kiddle v City Business Properties Ltd* [1942] 1 KB 269, [1942] 2 All ER 216.
6 *Gill v Edouin* (1895) 72 LT 579, CA.
7 *Northwestern Utilities Ltd v London Guarantee and Accident Co Ltd* [1936] AC 108, PC.
8 *A Posser & Son Ltd v Levy* [1955] 3 All ER 577, [1955] 1 WLR 1224, CA.

Default of the plaintiff and hypersensitivity
27.10 The doctrine of causation applies as much to *Rylands v Fletcher* as to any other tort. Thus, if the true legal cause of damage is some act or default of the plaintiff himself, no action will lie. In *Dunn v Birmingham Canal Navigation Co*,[1] for example, where a mine-owner, fully aware of the danger, worked his mine directly under the defendants' canal, he was held unable to sue in respect of the resulting flood. It also appears that, if the plaintiff is *partly* responsible for the damage, his damages may be reduced on the ground of contributory negligence.[2]

Where damage is caused by the hypersensitivity of the plaintiff or his property, it seems (by analogy with nuisance[3]) that the defendant should not be liable. This, in *Eastern and South African Telegraph Co Ltd v Cape Town Tramways Companies Ltd*,[4] where the escape of minute electric currents from the defendants' tramway system interfered with the plaintiffs' submarine telegraph cable, the plaintiffs failed to recover damages. Where, however, the plaintiff is not actively responsible for the 'sensitivity', the position is less clear. For example, in *Hoare & Co v McAlpine*,[5] it was said to be no defence to an action for causing damage by vibrations that the plaintiffs' building was old and unstable.

1 (1872) LR 7 QB 244.
2 Paras 22.11–22.16 above.
3 Para 26.6 above.
4 [1902] AC 381, PC.
5 [1923] 1 Ch 167.

Act of God
27.11 The defendant is not exempted from liability merely because an escape was unforeseeable (if this were not so there would be no difference between *Rylands v Fletcher* and negligence). Nevertheless, the law recog-

nises that there may be a natural catastrophe so overwhelming that even a system of strict liability should not hold the defendant responsible. Thus, where the escape is due to an operation of natural forces 'which no human foresight can provide against, and of which human prudence is not bound to recognise the possibility',[1] there is no liability. In *Nichols v Marsland*,[2] the defendant created artificial lakes on his land by damming a natural stream. A rainstorm of unprecedented violence broke down the banks which he had built, and the resulting flood swept away the plaintiff's bridges. The defendant was held not liable, on the basis that the storm constituted an act of God.

Nichols v Marsland appears to be the only reported English case in which the defence has succeeded, and even that decision has subsequently been heavily criticised. In *Greenock Corpn v Caledonian Rly Co*,[3] it was held by the House of Lords that, whatever the English position might be, an extraordinary rainfall in Scotland was no act of God!

1   *Tennent v Earl of Glasgow* 1864 2 Macph 22 at 26, HL.
2   (1876) 2 ExD 1, CA.
3   [1917] AC 556, HL.

Act of a stranger

27.12   Although difficult to reconcile with the theory of strict liability, it is well established that a defendant is not liable under *Rylands v Fletcher* where the escape is due to the deliberate and unforeseeable intervention of a 'stranger', that is, someone over whom he has no control. This may be a person unknown who blocks up the waste-pipe of a washbasin and leaves the taps running;[1] a trespassing child who drops a lighted match into the petrol tank of a motor vehicle;[2] or even a neighbour who, by emptying his reservoir into the stream which feeds the defendant's reservoir, causes the latter to flood the plaintiff's land.[3] The defendant is responsible, however, for the acts of his employees, unless they go where they are expressly forbidden,[4] and, of course, for his independent contractors.[5] Further, it appears that he may be liable for the actions of anyone lawfully on his land. For example, in *Hale v Jennings Bros*,[6] where a chair flew off a fairground 'chair-o-plane', it was held to be no defence that this was due to tampering by the person who was riding in it.

A defendant is responsible, even for the intervention of a 'stranger', if he ought reasonably to have anticipated the danger and taken steps to prevent the accident. In *Northwestern Utilities Ltd v London Guarantee and Accident Co Ltd*,[7] for example, the plaintiffs' hotel was destroyed by fire after gas escaped from the defendants' main and exploded. The main had fractured when support was withdrawn from it during the construction of a sewer. The Privy Council held the defendants liable, for they were aware of the construction work and should have appreciated the very grave danger which this involved.

1   *Rickards v Lothian* [1913] AC 263, PC.
2   *Perry v Kendricks Transport Ltd* [1956] 1 All ER 154, [1956] 1 WLR 85, CA.
3   *Box v Jubb* (1879) 4 ExD 76.
4   *Stevens v Woodward* (1881) 6 QBD 318, DC (employee caused a flood by leaving the taps running in a lavatory which he was not permitted to use).
5   *Rylands v Fletcher* itself.
6   [1938] 1 All ER 579, CA.
7   [1936] AC 108, PC.

Statutory authority

27.13 Where a person's activity is specifically authorised by statute, he cannot be liable under *Rylands v Fletcher* for any damage which it causes, although he will be liable if he is negligent.[1] Whether or not the activity is authorised depends upon the statute in question, and the principles of interpretation which are used by the courts are similar to those which apply in cases of nuisance.[2] In *Green v Chelsea Waterworks Co*,[3] for example, the defendants were under a statutory *duty* to maintain a certain pressure of water in their mains, and the statute, unlike many of its kind, did not expressly state that they would be liable for any nuisance caused.[4] When a main burst, it was held that they were not liable in the absence of negligence. By contrast, in *Charing Cross Westend and Electric Supply Co v Hydraulic Power Co*,[5] the defendants merely had a statutory *power* to carry water in mains, and they were specifically made liable for nuisance. It was held that the statute did not exempt them from strict liability under *Rylands v Fletcher* in respect of a burst main.

The argument that liability in respect of an activity which parliament has authorised should only be for negligence is, at first glance, an attractive one.[6] On a closer examination, however, some of its consequences seem rather more questionable. In *Pearson v North Western Gas Board*,[7] for instance, the plaintiff was seriously injured, her husband killed and her home destroyed, by an explosion of gas which had escaped from the defendants' main. Since the defendants were not guilty of any negligence, they were held not to be liable. It may well be that the provision of gas to consumers is a valuable benefit to society but, if so, there seems no good reason why the cost of this benefit should fall on Mrs Pearson rather than on society in general (or better still, on consumers of gas, in the form of higher prices which would reflect the cost of insuring against strict liability).

1 *Manchester Corpn v Farnworth* [1930] AC 171, HL.
2 Para 26.16 above.
3 (1894) 70 LT 547, CA.
4 Even if there had been such a provision, the defendants would probably not have been liable: *Department of Transport v North West Water Authority* [1984] AC 336, [1983] 3 All ER 273, HL.
5 [1914] 3 KB 772, CA.
6 See *Dunne v North Western Gas Board* [1964] 2 QB 806, [1963] 3 All ER 916. CA.
7 [1968] 2 All ER 669.

Fire

27.14 Common law has for centuries imposed a form of strict liability upon anyone from whose property fire is allowed to spread and cause damage,[1] unless this is due to an act of God[2] or the intervention of a 'stranger'. The latter defence covers only those over whom the occupier has no control, so that liability has been imposed upon an occupier for the negligence of an employee who allowed a fire to spread,[3] an independent contractor who used a blowlanp to thaw frozen pipes and set fire to their lagging,[4] and even a golf club guest who dropped a lighted match.[5] In *H and N Emanuel Ltd v G L C*,[6] a demolition contractor, on the defendants' land with their permission, lit a bonfire to burn rubbish; this was known to be his normal practice, although the contract specifically prohibited the lighting of fires on site. When sparks carried to the plaintiffs' property and caused damage, the defendants were held liable.

As we shall see, actions for the spread of fire are today usually governed by statute. Where this is not so, however, the common law rule still applies. Thus, for example, in *Mansel v Webb*,[7] the defendant was held strictly liable for the escape of sparks from his steam engine on the highway.

1   *Beaulieu v Finglam* (1401) YB 2 Hen 4, fo 18, pl 6.
2   *Turberville v Stamp* (1697) 1 Ld Raym 264.
3   *Musgrove v Pandelis* [1919] 2 KB 43, CA.
4   *Balfour v Barty-King* [1957] 1 QB 496, [1957] 1 All ER 156, CA.
5   *Boulcott Golf Club Inc v Engelbrecht* [1945] NZLR 556.
6   [1971] 2 All ER 835, CA.
7   (1918) 88 LJKB 323, CA.

27.15   The Fires Prevention (Metropolis) Act 1774, s86 provides that no action shall be brought against any person in whose premises, or on whose estate, any fire shall accidentally begin. In view of the way in which this provision (which, in spite of its title, applies throughout the country) has subsequently been interpreted, the extent to which it modifies the common law rule is somewhat uncertain. In *Filliter v Phippard*,[1] 'accidentally' was said to refer only to a fire produced by mere chance or incapable of being traced to any cause. This rules out protection where the defendant negligently allows a fire to spread;[2] but it seems that a person may avoid liability, even for a fire which he has deliberately lit, provided that he is not guilty of any negligence. Thus in *Sochacki v Sas*,[3] a lodger who left his room for two or three hours with a fire burning was held not liable when a coal jumped out and set the house alight, since there was no evidence that the fire was too large for the grate. The operation of the statute is also shown by *Collingwood v Home and Colonial Stores Ltd*,[4] in which fire broke out at the defendants' shop as a result of defective electric wiring. In the absence of any negligence on the part of the defendants, they were held not liable.

It should be noted that, even where a fire is caused by an act of God or of a 'stranger', the defendant may still incur liability if, with knowledge of the danger on his land, he fails to take reasonable steps to abate it.[5]

1   (1847) 11 QB 347.
2   *Musgrove v Pandelis* [1919] 2 KB 43, CA.
3   [1947] 1 All ER 344.
4   [1936] 3 All ER 200, CA.
5   *Goldman v Hargrave* [1967] 1 AC 645, [1966] 2 All ER 989, PC.

27.16   Apart from the special rules outlined above, it is established that either fire itself,[1] or the combustible material on which it feeds,[2] may be treated as a 'dangerous thing' for the purposes of the rule in *Rylands v Fletcher*. This might appear to be of great significance in view of the much-criticised decision of the Court of Appeal, in *Musgrove v Pandelis*,[3] that the Fires Prevention (Metropolis) Act 1774 provides no defence to such an action. In practice, however, the benefits to the plaintiff may be more apparent than real. In the first place, either fire[4] or its cause[5] may be held to be a 'natural use' of land, in which case *Rylands v Fletcher* does not apply. Second, where the defendant accumulates materials, it has been held that liability under *Rylands v Fletcher* depends on proof both that they were likely to ignite and that the resulting fire was likely to spread.[6] If this is correct, liability in such cases is no different from ordinary negligence.

1   *Jones v Festiniog Rly Co* (1868) LR 3 QB 733.
2   *Mason v Levy Auto Parts of England Ltd* [1967] 2 QB 530, [1967] 2 All ER 62.
3   [1919] 2 KB 43, CA.
4   *Sochacki v Sas* [1947] 1 All ER 344.
5   *Collingwood v Home and Colonial Stores Ltd* [1936] 3 All ER 200, CA (electric wiring).
6   *Mason v Levy Auto Parts of England Ltd* [1967] 2 QB 530, [1967] 2 All ER 62.

Statutory liability

27.17   One of the features of an industrialised urban society is that a single accident may disastrously affect an enormous number of people. A collapsing slag-heap, an explosion at a chemical plant or a crippled oil tanker, all may cause severe injury and damage over a wide area. In recent years, governments have sought by various statutes to provide for the possibility of certain of these incidents, and the provisions have often included the imposition of some form of strict liability for the consequences. Of special importance in this connection are the Nuclear Installations Act 1965 (liability of the licensee of a nuclear site for injury or damage resulting from the radioactive, toxic, explosive or otherwise hazardous properties of nuclear matter, or from radiations emitted from waste); the Merchant Shipping (Oil Pollution) Act 1971 (liability of shipowners for damage caused by the escape or discharge of persistent oil from a ship); and the Control of Pollution Act 1974 (liability for injury or damage caused by the deposit of poisonous, noxious or polluting waste on land). The forms of liability, and the defences available, vary from one statute to another, but they may all be regarded as strict, in the sense that the absence of negligence provides no defence.

Chapter 28
Animals

28.1 Considered merely as a kind of property, animals occupy no special place in the law of tort. A noisy farmyard is as much a nuisance as a noisy factory, and negligence applies to riding a horse as it does to driving a car. This, however, is only part of the story; unlike other goods, animals have minds and instincts of their own, which may lead them to cause damage in various ways, from ravaging a turnip field to biting a postman's leg. Not surprisingly, therefore, the common law has for centuries adopted special rules of strict liability for harm done by animals, in addition to actions which may arise from the application of ordinary tort principles.

In modern times, there is perhaps less justification for subjecting animals to a special code. Society is more industrial and less agricultural; fences are more efficient; and transport systems are no longer reliant on the horse and the ox. As a result of such developments, the Law Commission was asked to examine the working of the common law rules, which had been much criticised on the grounds of complexity and obscurity. The resulting Report[1] concluded that the basic forms of strict liability should be retained, but recommended numerous changes of detail, most of which were put into effect by the Animals Act 1971. Unless otherwise specified, all statutory references in this Chapter are to that Act.

In this Chapter we consider first the application of the general law of tort to damage caused by animals, before discussing the three kinds of strict liability which are now governed by the Act: liability for dangerous animals, straying livestock and the worrying of livestock by dogs.

1 Civil Liability for Animals, Law Com No 13 (1967).

Liability at common law
28.2 Most torts are capable of arising out of the acts of an animal, although some lend themselves more readily than others to this form of commission. It is, for example, an undoubted assault and battery to set one's dog on somebody, and there seems no reason why teaching a parrot to repeat slanderous material should not lead to liability in defamation. Of more practical importance, the action of fox hunters in riding across a farmer's land in spite of his protests has been held to constitute trespass[1] and, while direct authority is lacking, the application of *Rylands v Fletcher*[2] to both vegetation and human beings leaves little doubt that it could also be used in cases of escaping animals, subject to the question of 'non-natural user'.[3]

1   *Paul v Summerhayes* (1878) 4 QBD 9, DC. See also *League Against Cruel Sports Ltd v Scott* [1985] 2 All ER 489, [1985] 3 WLR 400; para 25.1 above.
2   Paras 27.2 to 27.13 above.
3   Para 27.7 above.

Nuisance

28.3   The tort of nuisance is one in which animals frequently play a part. The smell of pigs[1] or the crowing of cockerels[2] may be actionable, while the obstruction of a highway by 24 cows has been held to be a public nuisance.[3] Where the gist of the complaint is the invasion of the plaintiff's land by numbers of wild animals (rats, rabbits, etc) escaping from the defendant's property, liability has traditionally been dependent upon whether the defendant is in any way responsible for their accumulation. Thus, in *Farrer v Nelson*,[4] a defendant who overstocked his land with pheasants was held liable for damage to his neighbour's crops. On the other hand, there was no liability in *Seligman v Docker*,[5] where the increase in the pheasant population of the defendant's property was due simply to good weather. It should be noted, however, that even inaction may nowadays give rise to liability if the defendant, with knowledge of the danger, fails to take reasonable steps to avert it.[6]

1   *Aldred's Case* (1610) 9 Co Rep 57b.
2   *Leeman v Montagu* [1936] 2 All ER 1677.
3   *Cunningham v Whelan* (1917) 52 ILT 67.
4   (1885) 15 QBD 258.
5   [1949] 1 Ch 53, [1948] 2 All ER 887.
6   *Goldman v Hargrave* [1967] 1 AC 645, [1966] 2 All ER 989, PC.

Negligence

28.4   Damage done by animals, like other kinds of damage, most commonly gives rise to claims in negligence. There is no doubt that a person in charge of an animal is under a general duty of care to keep it from causing harm, and this can be of great assistance to a plaintiff who is unable to establish the necessary elements of strict liability under the Animals Act.[1] In *Gomberg v Smith*,[2] for example, a defendant who took his St Bernard for a walk in the street without a lead was held liable when it collided with and damaged the plaintiff's van. The dog in that case was merely clumsy, but the same principle may apply to a deliberate attack. For example, in *Aldham v United Dairies (London) Ltd*,[3] the defendants were held liable in negligence for leaving their pony unattended in the street for so long that it became restive and bit a passer-by.

There is no strict liability for livestock which stray from the highway,[4] but anyone who brings an animal on to the highway owes a duty of care to adjoining landowners. Thus in *Gayler and Pope Ltd v B Davies & Son Ltd*,[5] where the defendants left their pony and milk van unattended in the street, they were held liable when it bolted and crashed through a draper's shop window. In *Tillett v Ward*,[6] by contrast, where an ox which was being driven along a street strayed into an ironmonger's, the defendant was found to have taken all reasonable care and was therefore not liable.

Common law recognised one exception to the general principle of liability for negligence in relation to animals, namely, that an occupier of land owed no duty of care to highway users to fence his land or otherwise to prevent his domestic animals from straying and causing damage. Always regarded as anomalous, this rule attracted immense criticism when the invention of the internal combustion engine greatly increased the speed and volume of traffic on the roads. The immunity has now been abolished by the Animals Act 1971, s8(1) so that here, as elsewhere, the tort of negligence prevails. It should be emphasised, however, that s8(1) does not impose a universal obligation to fence; in areas such as the Welsh mountains, for example, motorists may be expected to look out for straying sheep, and the cost to farmers of fencing every roadside would be prohibitive. Section 8(2) attempts a compromise, by providing that a person is not to be regarded as negligent by reason only of placing animals on unfenced land if:

a. the land is common land, or

b. it is situated in an area where fencing is not customary, or

c. it is a town or village green;

and he has a right (which includes permission from someone else who has a right[7]) to place the animals on that land.

This is not a return to the old immunity since, even in these areas, road and traffic conditions may be such that it *is* negligent to allow one's animals to stray.

1   See, e g *Draper v Hodder* [1972] 2 QB 556, [1972] 2 All ER 210, CA; para 28.7 below.
2   [1963] 1 QB 25, [1962] 1 All ER 725, CA.
3   [1940] 1 KB 507, [1939] 4 All ER 522, CA.
4   Para 28.9 below.
5   [1924] 2 KB 75.
6   (1882) 10 QBD 17.
7   *Davies v Davies* [1975] QB 172, [1974] 3 All ER 817, CA.

Dangerous animals
Classification of species
28.5   The Animals Act 1971, like the common law, makes the keeper of a 'dangerous animal' strictly liable for all the damage it causes. The Act also follows the common law in treating two different kinds of animal as 'dangerous' for this purpose. First, certain species (lions, tigers, etc) are regarded as so obviously dangerous that all their members automatically attract strict liability. Second, members of other less dangerous species may attract strict liability as individuals by exhibiting dangerous tendencies, but only when their keepers are aware of these tendencies.

The classification of species is thus clearly of prime importance, and this is dealt with by s6(2), which provides that a dangerous species is a species:[1]

a. which is not commonly domesticated in the British Islands; and

b. whose fully grown animals normally have such characteristics that they are likely, unless restrained, to cause severe damage or that any damage they may cause is likely to be severe.

The wording of this definition seems apt to include both animals which are normally fierce (such as bears, tigers and gorillas) and animals which, though normally docile, are likely to cause severe damage if they cause damage at all. An elephant, for instance, is unlikely to cause damage, but its sheer bulk makes it dangerous on the occasions when it does get out of control. It also appears that a species may be 'dangerous' on account of the threat which it poses to property; this could even include, for example,

435

rabbits, squirrels and Colorado beetles, provided that the damage which they are likely to cause can be described as 'severe'.

It is important to appreciate that, once a species is classified as 'dangerous', no allowance is made for the amiable nature of a particular individual. A circus elephant may be as tame as a cow and, because of its training, much easier to control; nevertheless, since the species satisfies s6(2), the individual is 'dangerous' in law.[2]

A species which does not satisfy the statutory definition contained in s6(2) is automatically a 'non-dangerous species'.

1   This includes sub-species and variety: s11.
2   *Behrens v Bertram Mills Circus Ltd* [1957] 2 QB 1, [1957] 1 All ER 583.

Dangerous species

28.6   Section 2(1) provides that where any damage is caused by an animal which belongs to a dangerous species, any person who is a 'keeper' of the animal is liable for the damage, except as otherwise provided by the Act. This wide form of strict liability is not limited to such damage as results from the animal's dangerous characteristics, since it also includes, for example, injuries caused by the blunderings of a frightened elephant, or a disease transmitted by an infected rat. So too, a person who suffers nervous shock on being faced by an escaped tiger, or who falls and breaks his leg in running away from it, can recover damages under this provision. It has even been held applicable to someone falling from a swaying camel, although the plaintiff's claim under s2(1) failed on the ground that she had voluntarily assumed the risk.[1].

Liability under s2 is imposed upon the animal's 'keeper', defined in s6(3) as someone who 'owns the animal or has it in his possession; or is the head of a household of which a member under the age of 16 owns the animal or has it in his possession'. That sub-section further provides that a person who loses the ownership or possession of an animal continues to be its 'keeper' unless and until someone else fulfils the definition. Thus, if a person's pet fox escapes and reverts to the wild, he remains responsible for its activities. Where, however, a person takes possession of an animal *merely* to prevent it from causing damage or to return it to its owner, he does not thereby become its 'keeper'.[2]

1   *Tutin v Mary Chipperfield Promotions Ltd* (1980) 130 NLJ 807. The plaintiff recovered damages on the ground of negligence.
2   S6(4).

Non-dangerous species

28.7   The strict liability which attaches to dangerous species also encompasses other individual animals with known dangerous characteristics, although in such a case the keeper is liable, not for all the damage done, but only for that which results from those dangerous characteristics. This is laid down by s2(2), which provides that where damage is caused by an animal which does not belong to a dangerous species, a keeper of the animal is liable for the damage, except as otherwise provided by the Act, if:

a.   the damage is of a kind which the animal, unless restrained, was likely to cause or which, if caused by the animal, was likely to be severe; and

b.   the likelihood of the damage or of its being severe was due to characteristics of the animal which are not normally found in animals of the same species or are not normally so found except at particular times or in particular circumstances; and

c. those characteristics were known to that keeper or were at any time known to a person who at that time had charge of the animal as that keeper's servant or, where that keeper was the head of a household, were known to another keeper of the animal who was a member of that household and under the age of 16.

The essence of this provision is that strict liability is imposed on a 'keeper' (as defined above) where he, or someone for whom he is responsible, knows of some abnormal characteristic which renders his animal dangerous. This abnormality (which applies to nervous unpredictable animals as well as vicious ones[1]) may be permanent or periodic, such as the tendency of a bitch with pups to be aggressive towards humans.[2]

A 'keeper' is only liable under s2(2) where he, or certain of his family or his employees, knows that the animal in question is dangerous. Such knowledge is usually gained as the result of a previous attack, but this is not the only possibility. For example, in *Worth v Gilling*[3] it was sufficient that the defendant's dog habitually ran at passers-by to the limit of its chain, barking and trying to bite them. A horse's tendency to bite other horses, however, is not necessarily evidence that it is dangerous to people.[4]

Where the conditions of s2(2) are satisfied, reasonable care is no defence; the defendant keeps the animal at his peril. The question of negligence may, however, be highly relevant in cases where, for some reason, s2(2) does not apply, a point well illustrated by *Draper v Hodder*[5]. The three-year-old plaintiff in that case was attacked and seriously injured by a pack of Jack Russell terrier puppies which the defendant, a neighbouring breeder, allowed to wander on his own and the plaintiff's property. It is well known that Jack Russells in a pack are liable to attack, but the defendant was not strictly liable for this, because he had no actual knowledge that any particular dog was dangerous. Nevertheless, it was held by the Court of Appeal that he was clearly guilty of negligence in failing to take any steps to control what the reasonable man would regard as a serious danger.

1   *Wallace v Newton* [1982] 2 All ER 106, [1982] 1 WLR 375.
2   See *Barnes v Lucille Ltd* (1907) 96 LT 680.
3   (1866) LR 2 CP 1.
4   *Glanville v Sutton & Co Ltd* [1928] 1 KB 571.
5   [1972] 2 QB 556, [1972] 2 All ER 210, CA.

Defences
28.8   Although strict (ie independent of negligence), liability under s2 in respect of both dangerous and non-dangerous species is not absolute, since the Act expressly recognises four possible defences. Section 5(1) provides that a plaintiff cannot claim in respect of any damage which is due wholly to his own fault, as where he provokes a fierce dog, or reaches into a leopard's cage; if the plaintiff is partly responsible for his own injuries, his damages may be reduced on the ground of contributory negligence.[1]

The defence of *volenti non fit injuria*[2] is made applicable to actions under s2 by s5(2), a provision which may be of great importance in practice since the exclusion of this type of liability is not subject to the Unfair Contract Terms Act 1977.[3] The scope of this defence is, however, subject to the restriction in s6(5) that a keeper's employee is not to be treated as voluntarily accepting any risk which is incidental to his employment.

Section 5(3) lays down special rules for injured trespassers by providing that, where damage is caused by 'an animal kept on any premises or structure to a person trespassing there', the keeper is not liable under s2 provided either that the animal was not kept there for the protection of persons or property or that, if it was so kept, it was reasonable to keep it there. Thus, a trespasser injured by an animal in a zoo or a safari park would probably not succeed in a claim under s2,[4] for the animal would not be kept for protection. As to animals which it is reasonable to keep for protection, this is in practice most likely to apply to dogs. The Guard Dogs Act 1975, which makes it a criminal offence to have a guard dog on premises unless it is either secured or under the control of a handler, does not give rise to civil liability. However, it is thought that a court would regard someone as 'unreasonable' for the purpose of the Animals Act 1971, s5(3) if he kept a dog in contravention of the Guard Dogs Act.

All the defences mentioned above were considered in the case of *Cummings v Granger*[5] where an untrained alsatian, kept by the defendant to guard his scrapyard, attacked the plaintiff who, despite seeing a large 'Beware of the Dog' notice and knowing that the dog was there, entered the yard as a trespasser. The trial judge held that keeping the dog in these circumstances was unreasonable and that the defendant was accordingly liable, although he reduced the plaintiff's damages on the ground of contributory negligence. The Court of Appeal, however, took a rather more robust view of the rights of Englishmen to defend their castles. While agreeing that the damage could not be treated as wholly due to the plaintiff's fault, the Court of Appeal held both that keeping the dog was reasonable[6] and that the plaintiff had in any case voluntarily accepted the risk of injury.

1   S10; paras 22.11 to 22.16 above.
2   Paras 22.2 to 22.10 above.
3   Paras 9.41–9.53 above.
4   An action might nevertheless lie under the Occupiers' Liability Act 1984; paras 23.21 to 23.24 above.
5   [1977] QB 397, [1977] 1 All ER 104, CA.
6   These events preceded the coming into force of the Guard Dogs Act 1975.

Straying livestock
28.9   Section 4(1) of the Act provides that where livestock belonging to any person strays on to land in the ownership or occupation of another and:

a.   damage is done by the livestock to the land or to any property on it which is in the ownership or possession of the other person; or

b.   any expenses are reasonably incurred by that other person in keeping the livestock while it cannot be restored to the person to whom it belongs or while it is detained in pursuance of s7 of the Act, or in ascertaining to whom it belongs;

the person to whom the livestock belongs is liable for the damage or expenses, except as otherwise provided by the Act.

For the purpose of this provision, s11 defines 'livestock' as 'cattle, horses, asses, mules, hinnies, sheep, pigs, goats and poultry [which means the domestic varieties of fowls, turkeys, geese, ducks, guinea-fowls, pigeons, peacocks and quails], and also deer not in the wild state'.

This action, which protects both the owner and occupier of land, but which imposes liability only upon the possessor of livestock, covers damage, not only to the plaintiff's land and crops, but also to his goods, which includes animals. As a result, the plaintiff is entitled to damages, not only where his own animals are attacked, but also for other consequences such as infection[1] or the serving of a thoroughbred heifer by a bull of low birth.[2]

Where livestock stray on to the highway, it seems that the owner or occupier of the land across which the highway passes may claim under s4(3).[3] A mere *user* of the highway, however, has no such right and must, in order to recover damages (eg where straying livestock cause a road accident), establish negligence.[4] Further, where livestock lawfully on the highway stray from it, liability again depends on negligence; s4 is expressly excluded.[5]

1 *Theyer v Purnell* [1918] 2 KB 333.
2 *McLean v Brett* (1919) 49 DLR 162.
3 *Durrant v Child* (1611) 1 Bulst 157.
4 See Animals Act 1971, s8; para 28.4 above.
5 S5(5).

Defences

28.10 Liability under s4 is strict, but certain defences are recognised by the Act. A plaintiff will fail altogether in his claim if the damage he suffers is wholly due to his own fault;[1] if it is partly due to his fault, his damages may be reduced on the ground of contributory negligence.[2]

The vexed question of duties to fence is dealt with by s5(6), which provides that, while a mere failure on the plaintiff's part to fence out the defendant's livestock does not amount to 'fault' on his part, the defendant is nonetheless not liable where it is proved that the straying of the livestock on to the land would not have occurred but for a breach by any other person, being a person having an interest in the land, of a duty to fence. This it should be noted, is not limited to the obvious case of the plaintiff who owes a fencing obligation to the defendant, since it also provides a defence where the plaintiff owes a legal duty to a third party, or where the duty is owed *by* a third party with an interest in the plaintiff's land (eg his landlord).

The defences of act of God, intervention by a 'stranger' and *volenti non fit injuria*, all of which previously applied at common law, are not available in an action under s4.

1 S5(1).
2 S10; paras 22.11 to 22.16 above.

Detention and sale

28.11 In an attempt to provide a simple means of settling trivial disputes over straying animals without the need for legal action, s7 creates a statutory power of detention and sale. Under this provision, an occupier may detain any livestock which strays on to his land and which is not under anyone's control, provided he gives notice within 48 hours to the police and to the possessor of the livestock, if known. He must also treat the livestock with reasonable care, which includes feeding and watering it. The person entitled to possession of the livestock may demand its return but, if the detainor has a claim under s4 for damage done by straying cattle, or for expenses incurred, this must first be met. It has been held that a local authority on to whose land animals frequently strayed was justified in making standard charges to cover their costs, rather than working out the exact expense caused by each stray.[1]

Once livestock has been lawfully detained for 14 days, then, provided neither party has commenced legal proceedings, the detainor may sell it at a market or by public auction and keep the amount of his claim under s4 out of the net proceeds of sale.

1 *Morris v Blaenau Gwent District Council* (1982) 80 LGR 793, CA.

Dogs worrying livestock
Liability for dogs
28.12 The worrying of livestock by dogs has long been a special problem and the Animals Act, 1971, s3, which deals with this, merely repeats with some modifications the rules laid down by earlier statutes. Section 3 provides that where a dog causes damage by killing or injuring livestock, any person who is a keeper of the dog is liable for the damage, except as otherwise provided by the Act. For this purpose, 'livestock' includes the same animals as for the purpose of s4,[1] but also includes pheasants, partridges and grouse in captivity; the meaning of 'keeper' is the same as under s2.[2]

The effect of this provision, which makes a keeper liable without negligence and without any knowledge of his dog's dangerous characteristics, is to confer a greater degree of protection upon livestock than upon human beings, an interesting reflection of the Englishman's scale of values! However, as with the other forms of strict liability under the Act, a plantiff's claim may fail wholly under s5(1),[3] or partly under the doctrine of contributory negligence. Section 5(4) also provides a defence where the attack takes place on land to which the livestock have strayed, so long as the presence of the dog there is authorised.

1 Para 28.9 above.
2 Para 28.6 above.
3 Para 28.8 above.

Protection of livestock
28.13 At common law, a person whose animals were under attack was not restricted to taking legal action against the owner of the attacking animal; he could in certain circumstances act immediately in the defence of his property, even if this involved killing or injuring the attacker. The common law rules on this matter, which were laid down in the case of *Cresswell v Sirl*,[1] applied to all kinds of animal, both attacking and attacked, provided only that the latter belonged to the person acting in their defence; there was therefore no right to shoot a dog which was attacking *wild* animals on the defendant's land.[2]

The common law rules remain in force but, in relation to a somewhat narrower area, namely, the worrying[3] of *livestock* by *dogs*, the Animals Act 1971, s9 confers even greater protection upon a person who takes matters into his own hands. According to this provision, it is a defence to an action for killing or injuring a dog that the defendant was entitled to act for the protection of livestock, that he did so act and that, within 48 hours of the incident, he notified the police.

A person is entitled to act for the protection of livestock if, and only if, either the livestock or the land on which it is belongs to him, or if he is acting with the authority of such a person. However, if the circumstances in which a dog attacks livestock are such that the dog's keeper would have a defence under s5(4),[4] then s9 does not permit anyone to act for the protection of the livestock by killing or injuring the dog. The conditions under which the defendant may otherwise act are clearly stated by s9, with the proviso that the defendant is protected if he reasonably believes them to be satisfied. These conditions are that either

a.   the dog is worrying or is about to worry the livestock and there are no other reasonable means of ending or preventing the worrying; or

b.   the dog has been worrying livestock, has not left the vicinity and is not under the control of any person and there are no practicable means of ascertaining to whom it belongs. The effect of this is that, in some cases, a stray dog may be shot even when it has ceased to be a danger to livestock. This represents the major difference between the statutory rules and those of common law.

1   [1948] 1KB 241, [1947] 2 All ER 730, CA.
2   *Gott v Measures* [1948] 1 KB 234, [1947] 2 All ER 609, DC.
3   This probably includes not only an actual attack, but also chasing in such a way as is likely to cause injury.
4   Para 28.12 above.

Chapter 29
Other torts

Interference with goods

29.1 In its application to the protection of interests in goods, the law of tort is extremely complex and technical, largely because there is substantial overlap between a number of different torts, each of which has its own elements of liability. In 1971 the Law Reform Committee recommended radical revision of this part of the law, based on a single tort of 'wrongful interference'.[1] Unfortunately, the resulting Torts (Interference with Goods) Act 1977, although implementing some of the Committee's proposals and thereby removing the worst anomalies, is nothing like a complete codification. It is necessary, therefore, for us to deal separately with the torts of trespass to goods and conversion, before considering the question of remedies, the sphere in which the new Act is of most importance. Unless otherwise stated, all statutory references in this part of the chapter are to the Torts (Interference with Goods) Act 1977.

1 18th Report, Cmnd 4774.

Trespass to goods

29.2 Trespass to goods consists of any direct physical interference with goods in the possession of another person. This obviously covers acts of damage, such as beating an animal;[1] less obviously, perhaps, it includes merely moving chattels from one place to another. Thus, in *Kirk v Gregory*,[2] where the defendant removed jewellery of a recently deceased person to what he thought was a place of safety, he was held guilty of trespass. Indeed, on the basis that all forms of trespass are actionable per se (ie without proving damage), it seems that merely touching something may constitute trespass to goods, although it has been argued that this does not apply to unintentional contacts which cause no damage.

At one time, the defendant's mental element was quite irrelevant to his liability in trespass. Today, however, it is clear that he will not be liable in the absence of intention or negligence. What is not clear is whether, in the case of unintentional trespass, the onus is on the plaintiff to prove negligence[3] or on the defendant to disprove it.[4] Either way, it should be stressed that, provided the defendant intended to do the act in question, mistake is no defence. Thus, in *Wilson v Lombank Ltd*[5] the plaintiff was in possession of a car which, unknown to him, belonged to X. The defendants, honestly believing that the car was theirs, repossessed it, but returned it to X on discovering the truth. The defendants were held liable in trespass.

It is important to note that trespass in all its forms protects possession rather than either the right to possession or even ownership. For example, where A hires goods from B, only A may sue a third party in trespass.[6] However, an employer may have legal possession through the custody of his employee; similarly, where A's goods are in the hands of B for some purpose, but A has an immediate right to their return, both A and B may bring actions of trespass against a third party.[7]

1 *Slater v Swann* (1730) 2 Stra 872.
2 (1876) 1 ExD 55.
3 As it is in trespass to the person: *Fowler v Lanning* [1959] 1 QB 426, [1959] 1 All ER 290; *Letang v Cooper* [1965] 1 QB 232, [1964] 2 All ER 929, CA.
4 As was held in relation to goods in *National Coal Board v J E Evans & Co (Cardiff) Ltd* [1951] 2 KB 861, [1951] 2 All ER 310, CA.
5 [1963] 1 All ER 740, [1963] 1 WLR 1294.
6 *Lotan v Cross* (1810) 2 Camp 464.
7 *Nicolls v Bastard* (1835) 2 Cr M & R 659.

Conversion

29.3 The tort of conversion is difficult if not impossible to define accurately, largely because it can be committed in so many different ways. Nevertheless, one feature seems common to all instances, namely, some act in relation to the plaintiff's goods which constitutes a denial of his rights to those goods. As we shall see, this 'denial' need not be deliberate, for conversion can be committed unwittingly. However, some element of denial is necessary. Consequently, in *Fouldes v Willoughby*,[1] where the defendant wrongfully unloaded the plaintiff's horses from his ferry in the course of an argument, it was held that, while this might be a trespass, it could not amount to conversion. On the other hand, to deprive a person of most of the rights of ownership, including the right to possession, for an indefinite period, is clearly conversion, even where the defendant is prepared to acknowledge the ownership itself.[2]

Perhaps ironically, 'denial of title', although an essential element of conversion, is not *in itself* conversion;[3] there must be some act in relation to the goods, albeit by a paper transaction.[4] In most cases, this 'act' will be a positive one, but s2 of the 1977 Act contains an important exception. According to that provision, a person is liable in conversion if, having been entrusted with the possession of goods belonging to another, he negligently allows them to be lost or destroyed.

We may now turn to consider the various ways in which conversion may be committed.

1 (1841) 8 M & W 540.
2 *Howard E Perry & Co Ltd v British Railways Board* [1980] 2 All ER 579, [1980] 1 WLR 1375.
3 Common law doubts have been settled by s11(3) of the 1977 Act.
4 As in *Hiort v Bott* (1874) LR 9 Exch 86.

Forms of conversion

29.4 *Dealing with goods* A person lawfully in possession of goods belonging to another is guilty of conversion if he deals with those goods in a manner which is inconsistent with the owner's rights. This includes, for example, the common case where a person to whom goods have been let on hire purchase sells them before all the instalments have been paid.[1]

It is important to appreciate that dishonesty is by no means essential to liability; in the leading case of *Hollins v Fowler*,[2] a cotton broker, who had bought and resold cotton in good faith and had taken only a commission on the deal, was held liable in conversion when it transpired that the seller had obtained the cotton from the plaintiff by fraud and therefore had no right to sell it. However, where the defendant does not transfer possession of the goods, as where he merely carries out a transaction on paper, he is *not* liable in conversion unless the effect of that transaction is to confer title upon the buyer,[3] as on a sale in market overt.[4]

The innocent employee of a rogue who assists in a conversion is himself liable;[5] but not the innocent packer, carrier or warehouseman who deals only with the *custody* of goods and has no effect upon their *possession*.[6] This distinction has caused some difficulty in the case of an auctioneer. Clearly, if he knocks down and delivers goods which his client has no right to sell, he is liable to the true owner,[7] but what is the position if he merely negotiates a private sale between two parties, both of whom are present? It used to be thought[8] that the auctioneer in such a case would be a mere 'conduit', but this has now been disapproved by the Court of Appeal in a case where a car auctioneer arranged a private sale of a vehicle on the same terms as if it had been auctioned, and took a commission on it.[9] In such cases, therefore, the auctioneer is liable in conversion.

There are a number of common law and statutory powers under which a person may sell goods which do not belong to him, without becoming liable in conversion. We discuss some of the more important of these powers in para 29.6 below.

1   *Union Transport Finance Ltd v British Car Auctions Ltd* [1978] 2 All ER 385, CA.
2   (1875) LR 7 HL 757, HL.
3   *Lancashire Waggon Co Ltd v Fitzhugh* (1861) 6 H & N 502.
4   Para 29.6f below.
5   *Stephens v Elwall* (1815) 4 M & S 259.
6   *Hollins v Fowler* (1875) LR 7 HL 757, HL.
7   *Consolidated Co v Curtis & Son* [1892] 1 QB 495.
8   On the authority of *National Mercantile Bank Ltd v Rymill* (1881) 44 LT 767, CA.
9   *R H Willis & Son v British Car Auctions Ltd* [1978] 2 All ER 392, [1978] 1 WLR 438, CA.

29.5 *Receipt of goods* Obviously a person who knowingly receives stolen goods is guilty of conversion, for it is difficult to envisage a clearer denial of an owner's title. However, any intentional receipt of the plaintiff's goods without lawful justification is also conversion, even though the defendant may be unaware of any problem. Thus, where the defendant, however innocently, buys goods from someone who has no right to sell them, he is liable in conversion to the true owner[1] unless the circumstances of the sale are such that he acquires title to the goods under some common law or statutory rule.[2] The same is true where goods are pledged with the defendant.[3]

As for the receipt of unsolicited goods, this of itself does not amount to conversion or any other tort. Indeed, in certain circumstances a person to whom unsolicited goods are sent with a view to his acquiring them may, after six months, treat them as an unconditional gift.[4] Apart from this, however, an unintentional recipient is under no positive duty to take care of the goods,[5] though he will be liable if he wilfully damages or destroys them.

If he attempts to return the goods and, as a result, they are lost or damaged, he is not guilty of conversion unless he acts unreasonably.[6] Thus, in *Elvin and Powell Ltd v Plummer Roddis Ltd*,[7] where a rogue first induced the plaintiffs to deliver goods to the defendants and then, posing as the plaintiffs, collected them from the defendants, it was held that the defendants were not guilty of negligence and were therefore not liable.

1 *Cundy v Lindsay* (1878) 3 App Cas 459, HL; para 12.11 above.
2 Para 29.6 below.
3 1977 Act, s11(2).
4 Unsolicited Goods and Services Act 1971.
5 *Howard v Harris* (1884) Cab & El 253.
6 *Hiort v Bott* (1874) LR 9 Exch 86.
7 (1933) 50 TLR 158.

29.6 *Transfer of title by non-owner* Contrary to popular belief, a person who buys goods from someone who has no right to sell them does not acquire title merely because he acts in good faith. The general rule, which is now contained in the Sale of Goods Act 1979 (SGA), s21, is that the buyer acquires no better title than his seller had. As a result, by virtue of the rules discussed above, both buyer and seller are liable in conversion to the true owner.

The general rule is subject to a number of exceptions, with which we now deal. Two points should be noted. First, it is impossible here to give more than a bare outline of the law, and readers seeking further details should refer to one of the specialist works on sale of goods or personal property. Second, apart from the examples given at h, below, these rules protect only the innocent *buyer*; the person who *sells* the goods without any right to do so remains liable in conversion to their owner. The exceptions are:

a. *Agency* Obviously an authorised agent may sell his principal's goods, but the SGA, s21(1) recognises a wider principle, namely, that an owner of goods may be estopped or precluded by his own conduct from denying that the seller was authorised to sell them. This occurs when the owner in some way enables another person to appear as if he owns the goods. There have been many cases on the question of what conduct will have this effect; perhaps the most important point to emerge is that the true owner is not estopped merely because he allows someone else to have possession of his goods.

b. *Factors Act* Where a mercantile agent[1] is in possession of goods with the consent of their owner, the Factors Act 1889, s2(1) enables him to pass a good title to an innocent third party by any sale, pledge or other disposition which he makes in the ordinary course of his business.

c. *Seller in possession* Where a person, having sold goods to A, continues to hold possession of them, the SGA, s24 enables him, in certain circumstances, to pass good title by a second disposition of the goods to B. It is important to note that, in this case, there must be, not merely a paper transaction, but an actual delivery to B of either the goods or documents of title to them.

d. *Buyer in possession* Where a person, having bought or agreed to buy

445

goods, is allowed by the seller to take possession of them (for example, before he has paid the price), he is empowered by the SGA, s25 to pass good title to a third party in any circumstances in which a mercantile agent could pass it.[2] Once again, an actual delivery of the goods or documents of title is necessary. It is important to appreciate that a person who is in possession of goods under a hire purchase or conditional sale agreement does *not* come within this provision.

e. *Voidable title* A person whose title to goods is voidable, for example, because he obtained them by fraud, may, provided his title has not already been avoided, pass a good title to an innocent buyer by virtue of the SGA, s23.

f. *Market overt* An archaic rule, preserved in the SGA, s22, confers good title upon the innocent buyer of goods in 'market overt'. This means any open, public market which is properly constituted by charter, custom or statute and, in addition, any shop within the City of London. In order to attract the operation of this rule, the sale must comply with certain conditions, such as taking place between sunrise and sunset, which are designed to ensure that it is open and public. Further, it must be in accordance with any usages of the particular market. The great importance of this provision, unlike those already considered, is that a buyer may acquire title even to stolen goods.

g. *Motor vehicles* As we said under d. above, an unauthorised disposition of goods which are subject to a hire-purchase or conditional sale agreement is not normally effective to pass title. However, if the item in question is a motor vehicle, its transfer to a private individual by way of sale or hire-purchase is protected by the Hire-Purchase Act 1964, Part III.[3] Further, if the unauthorised transfer is to a trade purchaser, its subsequent transfer to an innocent private buyer attracts the statutory protection.

h. *Special powers* There are numerous rules, both common law and statutory, which enable A to sell goods belonging to B. Their importance lies in the fact that, not only does the buyer obtain good title, but the seller too is free from any liability to the true owner. Among the more important powers are those of a pledgee to sell unredeemed pledges;[4] of an innkeeper to sell a guest's goods in payment of his bill;[5] and of any person with whom goods are deposited (eg for repair) to sell them in certain circumstances if the depositor fails to collect them.[6] In most of these cases, certain statutory formalities must be complied with, or a court order sought. The effect of a sale under any of these powers is that the buyer obtains a title which is good against the pledgor, hotel guest or depositor, as the case may be. However, where the High Court exercises its jurisdiction to order a sale of goods for good reason (eg because they are perishable),[7] the buyer obtains a title which is good against the whole world.

1 Para 17.51 above.
2 See b. above.
3 Reproduced with minor changes in the Consumer Credit Act 1974, Sch 4.
4 *Re Richardson, Shillito v Hobson* (1885) 30 Ch D 396 at 403, CA; Consumer Credit Act 1974, ss 114–122.
5 Innkeepers Act 1878, s1.

6 Torts (Interference with Goods) Act 1977, ss 12 and 13.
7 RSC Ord 29, r4.

29.7 *Other cases* Merely to damage goods is not conversion, though it is usually trespass. However, wilful *destruction* is conversion, as in *Richardson v Atkinson*,[1] where the defendant drew some liquor from the plaintiff's cask and topped it up with water, thereby destroying the identity of the whole. Further, the defendant is liable if he uses goods in a way which is likely to lead to their loss by the plaintiff. Thus, the use of a borrowed car for smuggling watches is conversion, since the vehicle may be liable to confiscation by the Customs authorities.[2]

Perhaps the most obvious of all cases of conversion is a refusal to hand over goods to the person entitled to them.[3] In some circumstances, however, a delay in handing them over may be reasonable; where, for example, A finds property which B claims to have lost, A may lawfully detain the goods while B establishes his ownership.[4]

1 (1723) 1 Stra 576.
2 *Moorgate Mercantile Co Ltd v Finch and Read* [1962] 1 QB 701, [1962] 2 All ER 467, CA.
3 *Finlayson v Taylor* (1983) 133 NLJ 720.
4 *Alexander v Southey* (1821) 5 B & Ald 247.

Plaintiff's right to sue
29.8 Unlike trespass to goods, which requires actual possession on the part of the plaintiff, conversion is actionable by someone with a mere right to possession. For example, in *Manders v Williams*,[1] where a publican was bound to return beer barrels to the brewers, it was held that this gave them an immediate right to possession as soon as the barrels were empty, and they could therefore sue a third party in conversion. In other cases, a wrongful act by a person in possession of goods (such as the sale of a vehicle which is let on hire purchase) may revive the owner's right to possession and enable him to sue either that person or anyone deriving title from him.[2]

Where goods are the subject of co-ownership, each owner is entitled to possession of the whole, and his exercise of that right cannot be conversion. However, a co-owner will be liable if he destroys the goods, disposes or purports to dispose of them, or does anything else which is equivalent to destroying the interests of the other co-owners.[3]

1 (1849) 4 Exch 339.
2 *Union Transport Finance Ltd v British Car Auctions Ltd* [1978] 2 All ER 385, CA.
3 Torts (Interference with Goods) Act 1977, s10.

29.9 *Finders* Where goods are found, it seems that the finder acquires a right to possession sufficient to enable him to bring an action for conversion against any third party who wrongfully dispossesses him, but not, of course, against the true owner. Thus, a chimney-sweep's boy who found a jewel was entitled to sue a goldsmith, to whom he had taken it for valuation, for its return,[1] whereas the purchaser of a house who found a biscuit tin full of money in the loft had to return it to the vendor's executors.[2] An exception to this general principle is that, where goods are found by someone in the course of his employment, his employer has a better claim to them than the finder himself.[3]

The law has met with considerable difficulty in deciding between the claims of a finder of goods and those of the person in possession of the land on which they are found. As a general rule, the latter has prevailed, at least in respect of anything fixed or buried, such as a wall safe in a demolished building[3] or gold rings embedded in mud at the bottom of a pool.[4] The principle appears to be that the occupier is presumed to intend to assume control over the contents of his land, even those of whose presence he is not specifically aware. However, this presumption may be rebutted, as where the 'occupier' has never in fact been in occupation of the property.[5] It was also rebutted in *Bridges v Hawkesworth*,[6] where banknotes were found lying on the floor of a shop. It was held that, since the public had unrestricted access to the shop, the shopkeeper had never acquired any sort of right to the notes, and the finder was therefore entitled to them. This decision has been greatly criticised, but it was followed by the Court of Appeal in *Parker v British Airways Board*,[7] where a passenger who found a gold bracelet in an executive lounge at Heathrow Airport was held to have a better title to it than the airline. It was said that, when the object in question is not fixed or buried, the occupier takes priority only where he has previously manifested the intention to exercise control over everything on the land.

As between the occupier and the freehold owner of the land on which goods are found, the occupier is normally in a stronger position, since what is in issue is the right to possession. Again, however, it depends on the facts, so that a prehistoric boat was held to belong to a landlord rather than to his tenant, since it had clearly been buried in his land long before the commencement of the lease.[8]

1   *Armory v Delamirie* (1722) 1 Stra 505.
2   *Moffatt v Kazana* [1969] 2 QB 152, [1968] 3 All ER 271.
3   *London Corpn v Appleyard* [1963] 2 All ER 834, [1963] 1 WLR 982.
4   *South Staffordshire Water Co v Sharman* [1896] 2 QB 44.
5   *Hannah v Peel* [1945] KB 509, [1945] 2 All ER 288.
6   (1851) 21 LJQB 75.
7   [1982] QB 1004, [1982] 1 All ER 834, CA.
8   *Elwes v Brigg Gas Co* (1886) 33 Ch D 562.

Defences

29.10   Two provisions of the 1977 Act are worthy of mention. In the first place, s11(1), in order to resolve a doubt at common law, provides that contributory negligence is no defence in proceedings founded on conversion or on intentional trespass to goods. However, it continues to be a defence in cases of unintentional (ie negligent) trespass. Second, and more important, s8 abolishes the rule that a defendant may not set up the title of a third party in answer to the plaintiff's action. Henceforth this may be done, the intention of the Act being that the third party should join the action so that the relative claims of all interested parties can be dealt with at the same time.

Remedies

Damages

29.11   *Measure of damages*   Where goods are destroyed or damaged, the damages which may be awarded for trespass or conversion are no different from those for any other tort,[1] so that the plaintiff may recover the value (or the reduction in value) of the goods at the time of the tort, together with any consequential damage such as the loss of use or the hire of a replacement.

Where goods are misappropriated by an act of conversion, as where the defendant either keeps the goods or wrongfully sells them to a third party, the plaintiff is entitled to claim their full value at the date of conversion, even if he has only a limited interest.[2] If the market value falls before the date of judgment, the plaintiff is unaffected; if it rises, he is entitled to additional damages to reflect this, provided that he has not failed to mitigate his loss by obtaining a replacement.[3]

Where the plaintiff is deprived of his goods for a period, he is entitled to claim for whatever loss he suffers. Thus, if he would have hired out the chattel at a proft, damage will reflect the hire charges.[4] However, a plaintiff who can show no actual loss is entitled only to nominal damages. There is no rule which makes the defendant liable merely because the market value of the goods has fallen while they were in his possession.[5]

It should be noted that, where the plaintiff is compensated, by an award of damages or by the settlement of his action, for the whole of his interest in goods (even if subject to a reduction for contributory negligence), payment in full of the damages or the settlement operates to extinguish that interest.[6]

1   Para 31.12 below.
2   *The Winkfield* [1902] P 42, CA.
3   *Sachs v Miklos* [1948] 2 KB 23, [1948] 1 All ER 67, CA.
4   *Hillesden Securities Ltd v Ryjack Ltd* [1983] 2 All ER 184, [1983] 1 WLR 959.
5   *Brandeis Goldschmidt & Co Ltd v Western Transport Ltd* [1981] QB 864, [1982] 1 All ER 28, CA.
6   1977 Act, s5.

29.12   *Improvements*   Where a person improves goods, in the honest belief that he has title to them, s6 of the 1977 Act provides that any damages which he subsequently has to pay for conversion shall be reduced to take account of the improvement. A similar allowance is made in respect of any innocent purchaser who derives title from an 'improver', on the basis that such a person may be presumed to have paid an enhanced price. On the other hand, when that innocent purchaser sues his seller for failing to pass good title, the damages which he obtains must again be reduced on account of the improvement.

29.13   *Double liability*   As we have seen, a person with mere possession, or even a right to possession, of goods may recover their full value as damages for conversion,[1] and it is therefore quite possible for a defendant to be liable twice over in respect of the same act. Section 7 of the 1977 Act provides that, where both claimants are parties to the same action, the relief given by the court shall avoid such 'double liability'. Further provisions seek to ensure that, even where a claim is made by a single plaintiff, he is not unjustly enriched at the expense either of other claimants or of the defendant.

1   *The Winkfield* [1902] P 42, CA.

Recovery of goods
29.14   Section 3 of the 1977 Act empowers a court, in any case where the defendant is in possession of goods, to make a specific order for their return to the plaintiff. This remedy is at the court's discretion and cannot therefore

be demanded by the plaintiff. However, the plaintiff can choose *either* a form of order which gives the defendant the option of returning the goods or paying their value *or* damages, in which case the defendant has no option to return the goods instead.

It should be noted that s4 empowers the court to order that goods be handed over to the plaintiff or to any other person, pending proceedings for wrongful interference with those goods. This power is not restricted to cases in which there is a danger that the goods will otherwise be disposed of or destroyed.[1]

1   *Howard E Perry & Co Ltd v British Railways Board* [1980] 2 All ER 579, [1980] 1 WLR 1375.

Self-help

29.15   Where a person has been wrongfully deprived of his goods, the common law permits him to retake them[1] either from the original tortfeasor or from a third party into whose possession they have come (provided of course that the third party has not acquired title). As against the original tortfeasor at least, the owner may use such force as is reasonable.[2]

In retaking his goods, the owner is allowed to enter the land of the original tortfeasor.[3] However, whether he may enter other land is very unclear, and it must be regarded as inadvisable.[4]

1   But statute (eg the Consumer Credit Act 1974) may not.
2   *Blades v Higgs* (1861) 10 CBNS 713, (1865) 11 HL Cas 621.
3   *Patrick v Colerick* (1838) 3 M & W 483.
4   See *Anthony v Haney* (1832) 8 Bing 186.

Defamation

29.16   The personal protection which is afforded by the law of tort extends, through defamation, to the reputation of all *living* persons;[1] a man may be entitled to very substantial damages if his good name is wrongfully attacked. In giving this protection, the law attempts to strike a balance between the individual's interest in his reputation and the general public interest in freedom of speech. Not surprisingly, where two such important interests are in conflict, the resulting law is excessively technical and complex.

For reasons which are largely historical, defamation is two torts rather than one. If a defamatory 'statement' is in permanent form, it is a libel; if transient, it is a slander. Libel therefore includes writing, pictures, statues, waxworks and (by statute) broadcasting and theatre performances; further, it has been held that a film sound track is libel.[2] The practical importance of the distinction is that, while libel is always actionable per se, a plaintiff in slander must prove damage (eg the loss of a job or of hospitality), except in the case of imputations:

a.   of a criminal offence punishable with imprisonment;

b.   of an infectious disease;

c.   of unchastity in women; or

d.   of unfitness for any office actually held by the plaintiff.

1 Including corporations and partnerships, but not usually unincorporated associations: *Electrical, Electronic, Telecommunication and Plumbing Union v Times Newspapers Ltd* [1980] QB 585 at 595, [1980] 1 All ER 1097 at 1100.
2 *Youssoupoff v Metro-Goldwyn-Mayer Pictures Ltd* (1934) 50 TLR 581, CA.

Elements of liablity
Defamatory meaning
29.17 The traditional view of a defamatory statement is that it is one which brings 'hatred, contempt or ridicule' upon the plaintiff, or which tends to lower him in the eyes of people in general (who for this purpose are conclusively presumed to be honest and right-thinking[1]). However, a false allegation that the plaintiff is insane, or has been raped,[2] is defamatory, notwithstanding that these are matters for sympathy rather than censure; the test here is whether it would cause people to shun or avoid the plaintiff.

Words can, of course, have more than one meaning, and where, as is usual in defamation cases, trial is by judge and jury, it is for the jury to decide whether one or all of the ordinary meanings of the words used are defamatory.[3] Sometimes however, the plaintiff alleges that words which appear harmless are defamatory of him because of additional facts known to persons to whom the words were addressed;[4] in such a case it is for the plaintiff to prove these facts and to specify the persons concerned. Thus, to use a caricature of a famous amateur golfer in an advertisement for chocolate may support the innuendo that he is making money out of his sporting reputation;[5] and the inference to be drawn from the placing of a waxwork effigy of the plaintiff in close proximity to a number of effigies of famous criminals is obvious.[6]

1 *Byrne v Deane* [1937] 1 KB 818, [1937] 2 All ER 204, CA.
2 *Youssoupoff v Metro-Goldwyn-Mayer Pictures Ltd* (1934) 50 TLR 581, CA.
3 *Lewis v Daily Telegraph Ltd (No 2)* [1964] 2 QB 601, [1964] 1 All ER 705, CA.
4 At the time they were addressed: *Grappelli v Derek Block (Holdings) Ltd* [1981] 2 All ER 272, [1981] 1 WLR 822, CA.
5 *Tolley v J S Fry & Sons Ltd* [1931] AC 333, HL.
6 *Monson v Tussauds Ltd* [1894] 1 QB 671, CA.

Reference to plaintiff
29.18 The plaintiff must prove that the defendant's statement refers to him. This seldom presents a problem, but two points are worthy of note. First, a general statement about a class (eg 'all students are immoral') gives no right of action to any individual, unless the class is so small that the statement may be regarded as applying to each member.[1] Second, reference to the plaintiff may be completely accidental, as where the defendant uses what he believes to be a fictitious name or, worse still, where a true statement about X (eg that he has been convicted of a crime) is reasonably believed by others to refer to his namesake.[2] However, in such a case the defendant may, provided he has not been negligent, make a prompt offer to publish a correction and apology; if he does this then, within certain limitations, he may have a defence against subsequent proceedings by virtue of the Defamation Act 1952, s4.

1 *Knuppfer v London Express Newspaper Ltd* [1944] AC 116, [1944] 1 All ER 495, HL.
2 *Newstead v London Express Newspaper Ltd* [1940] 1 KB 377, [1939] 4 All ER 319, CA.

Publication
29.19 Since defamation is an injury to reputation, it must be proved that

the statement was published to someone other than the plaintiff himself (or, for reasons of public policy, the defendant's spouse[1]). However, the idea of 'publication' does not connote any intention to pass on information for the purpose of discrediting the plaintiff. Hence a businessman 'publishes' a slander to his secretary when he dictates a letter to her, and an author publishes a libel to his editor and even to his printer. In such a case, the defendant is also liable in respect of every further publication which he intends or has reason to expect.[2]

Every repetition of a defamatory statement is a fresh publication,[3] a rule which serves to impose liability, not only on authors, but also on editors, newspaper owners, printers, publishers and even mere distributors of printed matter such as libraries and newsagents. However, those who are concerned only with distribution may have a defence if they can prove that they knew of no libel and were not negligent.[4]

It should be noted that a plaintiff who actually consents to the publication of certain material cannot thereafter allege that it is defamatory of him.[5]

1 *Wennhak v Morgan* (1888) 20 QBD 635.
2 *Cutler v McPhail* [1962] 2 QB 292, [1962] 2 All ER 474.
3 *Duke of Brunswick v Harmer* (1849) 14 QB 185.
4 *Vizetelly v Mudie's Select Library Ltd* [1900] 2 QB 170, CA.
5 *Chapman v Lord Ellesmere* [1932] 2 KB 431, CA.

Defences
Justification
29.20 Defamation gives no protection to a reputation which the plaintiff does not merit; hence it is an absolute defence to prove that the offending statement is true. By the Defamation Act 1952, s5, the precise accuracy of every ingredient need not be established, provided that what cannot be proved does no harm in the light of what can. It should be noted that justification must be 'as broad as the charge'; hence, the defendant who says of the plaintiff: 'X told me that ...' must prove the truth of X's remark, not merely that it was made.[1]

1 *'Truth' (NZ) Ltd v Holloway* [1960] 1 WLR 997, PC.

Fair comment
29.21 The public interest in free speech demands that people should be allowed to comment, whether favourably or unfavourably, on matters of general interest; criticism must not be stifled. In order to raise the defence of fair comment, a defendant must prove:

a. that the matter commented upon was of public interest. This is a wide area ranging from politics to art;

b. that any facts on which the comment was based were true; and

c. that the comment was fair. This means that it must have been honestly believed, even if wrong, exaggerated or prejudiced.[1]

Even then the defence may fail, if the plaintiff can show that the defendant was actuated by malice in making the statement. In this context, 'malice' means an evil motive, such as personal spite against the plaintiff.[2]

1 *Slim v Daily Telegraph Ltd* [1968] 2 QB 157 at 170, [1968] 1 All ER 497, CA.
2 *Thomas v Bradbury, Agnew & Co Ltd* [1906] 2 KB 627.

Privilege

29.22 *Absolute privilege* In some (obviously limited) circumstances, the principle of free speech is regarded as so vital that actions for defamation are completely ruled out. The most important of these cases are:

a. statements made in parliament;

b. anything said in judicial proceedings, provided it is relevant;

c. professional communications between solicitor and client; and

d. official communications between officers of state.

29.23 *Qualified privilege* In some circumstances, where free speech is not quite so highly prized, the defendant may be entitled to the benefit of a more restricted defence. The extent of this defence is perhaps the most difficult and uncertain area of the law of defamation, but it seems that it will apply in the following cases:

a. where some 'common interest' binds the defendant and the person to whom the statement is made, for example where a character reference is given;

b. where the defendant is under a legal or moral duty to pass on the information; and

c. where the defendant seeks to protect his own interests by passing on information to the proper authorities.

Although qualified privilege is lost if the statement is published to an unnecessarily wide audience,[1] publication in the ordinary course of business (eg by a businessman to his secretary) attracts an 'ancillary privilege'.[2]

Unlike absolute privilege, qualified privilege is defeated by evidence of malice which, in this context, means either lack of honest belief in the statement or the use of a privileged occasion for an irrelevant and improper purpose.[3]

1 *Watt v Longsdon* [1930] 1 KB 130, CA; *Chapman v Ellesmere* [1932] 2 KB 431, CA.
2 *Bryanston Finance Ltd v de Vries* [1975] QB 703, [1975] 2 All ER 609, CA.
3 *Horrocks v Lowe* [1975] AC 135, [1974] 1 All ER 662, HL.

29.24 *Privileged reports* Certain reports of parliamentary[1] or judicial[2] proceedings are absolutely privileged by statute. However, even where the statutory conditions are not met (for example, because the report is a mere extract) there is qualified privilege at common law.

Reports and publications of the Parliamentary Commissioner for Administration[3] are absolutely privileged under the Parliamentary Commissioner Act 1967.

Finally, the Defamation Act 1952[4] lists certain topics of public interest, newspaper or broadcast reports of which attract qualified privilege. In some cases, which are specified by the Act, this is subject to the defendant's willingness to publish a statement by way of explanation or contradiction of what is in the report.

1 Parliamentary Papers Act 1840.
2 Law of Libel Amendment Act 1888.
3 Para 4.26 above.
4 S7 and Sch.

Chapter 30
Vicarious liability

30.1 In certain circumstances the law of tort makes A responsible for damage which is done by B. Several of these circumstances have nothing at all to do with what can be called 'true' vicarious liability. In the first place, A may have specifically authorised or incited B to commit the tort in question; if so, A is regarded in law as having committed it himself. Second, B may have purported to act on A's behalf, though without any authority to do so; if A, with full knowledge of all material facts, thereafter ratifies or accepts what B has done, he again incurs personal responsibility for it. Third, there are many situations in which some personal failure on A's part may lead through B's conduct to the causing of harm. For instance, where an independent contractor causes damage to the plaintiff, this may turn out to be because his client has carelessly entrusted to him a job beyond his capabilities, or has given him inadequate instructions; if so, the client is liable, not for the contractor's negligence, but for his own.

The three types of liability mentioned above are fairly straightforward, but there is a fourth which causes rather more problems. Although, as we shall show later, A is not usually responsible for torts committed by his independent contractor, the law will sometimes regard A's personal duty towards the plaintiff as a 'non-delegable' one; this means that, if A chooses to delegate performance of the duty to another, he does so at his own risk and is responsible for his delegate's negligence. The circumstances in which duties are 'non-delegable' in this respect are dealt with in paras 30.19 to 30.26, below under the heading of 'Independent contractors'.

If none of these things is truly 'vicarious liability', then what is the meaning of that term? The answer to this question is that vicarious liability applies where A is made to answer for the tort of B because:

a. there is a particular relationship between A and B; and

b. the tort is in some way connected to that relationship.

In practice, the only relationship which gives rise to a general principle of vicarious liability is that of employer and employee; here, the necessary connection between the tort and the relationship is that the employee must have committed the tort 'in the course of his employment'. A much more limited form of vicarious liability applies as between principal and agent[1] and between partners.[2] However, these instances apart, the law is slow to make A answer for the actions of B, as may be seen from the fact that a superior employee is not vicariously liable for the torts of his subordinate,[3] nor a parent for those of his child, although in either of these cases liability may be imposed for one or the other reasons outlined above.

1 Paras 30.16–30.18 below.
2 For torts committed 'in the ordinary course of the business of the firm': Partnership Act 1890, s10.
3 *Stone v Cartwright* (1795) 6 Term Rep 411.

Basis of vicarious liability

30.2 The generally accepted view of vicarious liability is that all the elements of a tort must be proved against B, and that A is then answerable for it. The alternative theory, that it is A's own duty which is breached by B's conduct, is today largely discredited. Nevertheless, attention should be drawn to two odd cases in which the 'employee's tort' theory is hard pressed to explain what is undoubtedly the legal result. First, it is established that an employer may be vicariously liable even in circumstances where the employee himself would, if sued, have had a personal immunity.[1] Second, where an employee gives an unauthorised invitation to the plaintiff to enter the employer's premises, and he is injured there, the plaintiff's rights against the employer are those of a trespasser,[2] notwithstanding that vis-à-vis the employee his presence is lawful.[3]

1 *Broom v Morgan* [1953] 1 QB 597, [1953] 1 All ER 849, CA (employer liable for injury by employee to employee's wife, at a time when tort actions between spouses were not allowed).
2 Paras 23.19–23.24 above.
3 *Conway v George Wimpey & Co Ltd (No 2)* [1951] 2 KB 266, [1951] 1 All ER 363, CA.

Employer and employee

30.3 As we have already seen, the relationship of employer and employee is the only one to which the law attaches a *general* principle of vicarious liability. It may be said that an employer is responsible for any tort which is committed by his employee in the course of his employment. This obviously raises two questions: who is an employee and what is the course of employment?

Who is an employee?

30.4 Since an employer is not usually responsible for the torts of an independent contractor to whom he entrusts work, it is obvious that the distinction between an employee and an independent contractor is of paramount importance. Indeed, it is not only in relation to vicarious liability that this distinction is relevant; among other things, it may also serve to indicate whether the 'worker' is protected under industrial safety legislation, and whether the duty to pay national insurance contributions falls upon him or upon his 'employer'.

It is said that an employee works under a contract *of service*, an independent contractor under a contract *for services*. This, however, merely restates the problem in different words, for it gives no clue as to how these two kinds of contract are to be distinguished. Nor is the terminology of the contract itself decisive (though it is relevant) since, if the court decides that the relationship as a whole falls into one category, it will be treated as such, notwithstanding that the parties have called it by another name. Thus, for example, in *Ferguson v John Dawson & Partners (Contractors) Ltd*,[1] where a building worker was expressly described as a 'labour only sub-contractor', a majority of the Court of Appeal held that the relationship between the parties was nevertheless that of employer and employee.

It is perhaps worth stating at this point that, while the formulation of a precise yet simple test for distinguishing employees from independent contractors has caused serious problems, it is not usually difficult to see on which side of the line a particular case falls. As Lord Denning has said,[2] it is often easy to recognise a contract of service when you see it, but difficult to say wherein the distinction lies. A ship's master, a chauffeur and a reporter on the staff of a newspaper are all employed under a contract of service; but a ship's pilot, a taxi driver, and a newspaper contributor are employed under a contract for services.

Of the many attempts which judges and writers have made to lay down some criteria by which a contract of service may be recognised, one of the best known is that of Lord Thankerton in *Short v J and W Henderson Ltd*:[3]

a. the employer's power of selection of his employee;

b. the payment of wages or other remuneration;

c. the employer's right to control the method of doing the work; and

d. the employer's right of suspension and dismissal.

It should always be borne in mind, however, not only that this list is far from exhaustive (one writer has identified no fewer than 15 relevant factors), but also that the feature which is in one case decisive may in the next be overwhelmed by other features which point to the opposite conclusion.

1 [1976] 3 All ER 817, [1976] 1 WLR 346, CA.
2 *Stevenson, Jordan and Harrison Ltd v Macdonald and Evans* [1952] 1 TLR 101 at 111, CA.
3 (1946) 62 TLR 427 at 429.

Control test
30.5 The foregoing discussion serves to show that there is no single, simple test by which employees and independent contractors may be distinguished. It used at one time to be thought that such a test did exist, in the degree of control which the employer was entitled to exercise over each category. An independent contractor, it was said, could be told only *what* he was to do, whereas an employee was subject to the command of his employer as to the *manner* in which he should do his work.[1] However, modern conditions, especially the widespread employment by corporations of highly skilled and qualified personnel, have shown up the inadequacy of this test. For example, it cannot be doubted that a ship's captain works under a contract of service, but it would be ludicrous to suggest that his employers are in a position to tell him exactly how to do his job. Indeed, many people today are employed for the precise reason that they possess some skill which their employer does not; in such circumstances the 'control' test is clearly of little use.

1 *Yewens v Noakes* (1880) 6 QBD 530 at 532.

Other criteria

30.6 If 'control' alone is not decisive, the same is even more true of the other criteria mentioned above. The employer's rights of appointment and dismissal, which were regarded as characteristic of a contract of service in *Short v Henderson*, seem equally applicable to independent contractors, while the type of remuneration paid, although helpful, is far from conclusive. After all, an employee is usually paid a wage based on time, but may be on 'piece work'. An independent contractor is more commonly paid for results, but may be on an hourly rate.

Function of employee

30.7 It has been suggested that, instead of looking at the individual rights and duties which make up a contract of service or one for services, the courts should consider the *function* of the particular 'worker', since one feature which seems to run through the instances is that, under a contract of service, a man is employed as part of the business, and his work is done as an integral part of the business; whereas under a contract for services, his work, although done for the business, is not integrated into it but is only accessory to it.[1] This 'organisation' test certainly serves to explain a number of cases in which a contract of service has been held to exist despite the lack of any real 'control' by the employer, especially those in which, contrary to earlier authority, hospitals were held liable for the negligence of highly qualified staff.[2] However, in marginal cases, it seems merely to replace one difficult question: 'Is the man an employee?' with another: 'Is he part of the employer's organisation?'

Concentration upon the actual work which is done by a particular individual should not be allowed to obscure the fact that vicarious liability depends upon the existence of a contract of service. In *Watkins v Birmingham City Council*,[3] where a schoolteacher was injured due to the negligence of a ten-year-old milk monitor, the trial judge held the local authority vicariously liable on the ground that the boy was doing a job which would otherwise have been done by a paid employee. However, the Court of Appeal reversed this decision, holding that the boy was delivering the milk as a pupil and not as an employee.

1   *Stevenson, Jordan and Harrison Ltd v Macdonald and Evans* [1952] 1 TLR 101 at 111, CA.
2   *Cassidy v Ministry of Health* [1951] 2 KB 343, [1951] 1 All ER 574, CA.
3   (1975) Times, 1 August, CA.

'Business' test

30.8 In a number of recent cases, the courts have adopted a slightly different approach to this problem, by considering whether it may fairly be said that the 'worker' is in business on his own account.[1] Although this has links with the 'function' test described above, it seems that the courts are concerned, not so much with the nature of the work done, but more with such questions as whether the person works on his own premises or with his own equipment, whether he hires his own helpers and can delegate the task to them, whether he works for a number of 'employers', what degree of financial risk he takes, what degree of responsibility he has for investment and management, and to what extent, if at all, he has an opportunity to profit from his own sound management.

Many of these factors were considered in *Ready-Mixed Concrete (South-East) Ltd v Minister of Pension and National Insurance*,[2] a case concerning the drivers of lorries designed for the delivery of concrete. The drivers bought their own vehicles, although they could not alter or sell them without the company's consent, and they were obliged to maintain them and to use them exclusively for the company. The company was responsible for obtaining orders and supplying concrete, and it paid the drivers a rate based on mileage. After a thorough review of the authorities, MacKenna J held that the drivers were not employees of the company, but independent contractors, so that the company was not responsible for the payment of their national insurance contributions.

In conclusion, it is worth remembering that most of the modern decisions on the question of who is an employee have been concerned, not with vicarious liability, but with other aspects of employment law. It may well be that, should a borderline case arise in which possible vicarious liability is in issue, a desire to see that the plaintiff receives compensation will sway the court towards the conclusion that the relevant relationship is a contract of service.

1   *Market Investigations Ltd v Ministry of Social Security* [1969] 2 QB 173, [1968] 3 All ER 732.
2   [1968] 2 QB 497, [1968] 1 All ER 433.

Borrowed employees

30.9   A particular problem may arise in cases where an individual employee is lent (or, more commonly, hired) by his general employer to a third party. If the employee commits a tort while working for the third party (albeit not under a contract of employment), the question is where the burden of vicarious liability is to fall. It might have been thought that both 'employers' should be liable, but the common law insists that the responsibility falls upon one alone.

In *Mersey Docks and Harbour Board v Coggins and Griffith (Liverpool) Ltd*,[1] a mobile crane, complete with its driver, was hired by the harbour board to a firm of stevedores. The driver was paid by the board but, for the period of hire, was subject to the detailed control of the stevedores. When the driver negligently injured a third party, the House of Lords held that vicarious responsibility must rest with the harbour board; this primary liability could, it was said, be transferred in an appropriate case, but the burden of proof upon a general employer would be a heavy one. This heavy burden is perhaps most likely to be satisfied in cases where the employee in question is an unskilled labourer, since it is then more realistic to treat 'control' as having been passed on.

A statement in the contract of hire itself to the effect that any vicarious liability shall attach to the special employer has no effect upon the rights of an injured plaintiff. Prima facie it is conclusive as to the position of the two employers,[2] although it may be regarded as an indemnity or exemption clause and thus subject to the text of 'reasonableness' under the Unfair Contract Terms Act 1977.[3]

1   [1947] AC 1, [1946] 2 All ER 345, HL.
2   *White (Contractors) Ltd v Tarmac Civil Engineering Ltd* [1967] 3 All ER 586, [1967] 1 WLR 1508, HL.
3   See *Phillips Products Ltd v Hyland* (1984) 129 Sol Jo 47, CA.

Course of employment

30.10   The mere existence of an employer and employee relationship is not sufficient to create vicarious liability; it would, of course, be wholly unjust if the employer were to be made responsible for every wrongful act of his employees. On the other hand, to limit the employer's liability to those cases in which the employee is actually carrying out his instructions would be to deprive the law of an extremely useful doctrine since the number of employers who specifically authorise the commission of torts is very small. What is needed is some intermediate limitation, and this is found in the rule that, for an employer to be liable, the employee must be shown to have committed the tort 'in the course of his employment'. As to what is meant by this expression, *Salmond on Torts*,[1] in a passage which has often been judicially approved, explains that an employer, as opposed to the client of an independent contractor, is liable even for acts which he has not authorised, provided they are so connected with acts which he has authorised that they may rightly be regarded as modes—although improper modes—of doing them. In other words, an employer is responsible not merely for what he authorises his employee to do, but also for the way in which he does it. On the other hand, if the unauthorised and wrongful act of the employee is not so connected with the authorised act as to be a mode of doing it, but is an independent act, the employer is not responsible: for in such a case the employee is not acting in the course of his employment, but has gone outside it.

The idea that an unauthorised act may found vicarious liability if it can be treated as a mode of performing an authorised act means that a court, in seeking to determine the scope of an employee's employment, must first discover what acts are authorised and then consider what, if any, connection exists between an authorised act and the tort in question. Looked at in this light, the decision of the House of Lords in *Century Insurance Co Ltd v Northern Ireland Road Transport Board*[2] appears inevitable. The employee in that case was the driver of a petrol tanker who, while delivering petrol to a garage, lit a cigarette and dropped the match. The driver's employers sought to avoid liability for the resulting fire by claiming that they did not employ men to smoke. Not surprisingly, this argument was rejected for, given that the driver was specifically authorised to deliver petrol, it would be difficult to think of a more negligent mode of doing so.

The need to find an authorised act, with which the unauthorised tort can be linked, may be illustrated by cases in which a vehicle owned by the employer is driven by an employee who has no specific authority to do so. In *Beard v London General Omnibus Co*,[3] where a conductor took it upon himself to turn a bus round for its return journey, it was held that his negligent driving which caused an accident was outside the scope of his employment, since he was not permitted to drive. His employers were therefore not vicariously liable. In *Ilkiw v Samuels*,[4] on the other hand, where a lorry driver allowed an incompetent person to drive it, it was held that the *lorry driver's* negligence fell within the course of his employment, for his job involved taking care of the vehicle. As a result, the lorry driver's employers were liable to a person injured in the ensuing accident. There is no doubt that modern courts take a fairly liberal view of what is 'authorised'. Nevertheless, the decision in *Kay v ITW Ltd*[5] must be considered very close to the borderline. The employee there was a storekeeper whose duties included returning a fork-lift truck to a warehouse. Finding the warehouse door blocked by a five-ton lorry which belonged to another firm, the storekeeper attempted to move it and, in so doing, negligently injured the plaintiff. After some hesitation, the Court of Appeal came to the conclusion that the employers were vicariously liable, for this misguided act fell just within the course of the storekeeper's employment.

1   (18th edn) p 437.
2   [1942] AC 509, [1942] 1 All ER 491, HL.
3   [1900] 2 QB 530, CA.
4   [1963] 2 All ER 879, [1963] 1 WLR 991 CA.
5   [1968] 1 QB 140, [1967] 3 All ER 22, CA.

Implied authority
30.11   In considering exactly what acts of an employee may be regarded as 'authorised', it is important to realise that an employer's permission may be implied rather than express and, further, that this may well be so even in relation to acts which benefit the employee rather than the employer. To take a simple example, an employee has implied authority to use lavatories, washbasins and so on, while at work. If he negligently leaves a tap running and thereby floods adjoining premises, his employer will be vicariously liable; he cannot argue that the employee was not in the course of his employment because he was not actually working at the time.[1] A similar principle applies to meals, tea breaks and the like, provided either that they are taken on the premises, or that the employee is travelling on the employer's business. For example, in *Harvey v R G O'Dell Ltd*,[2] an employee sent out on an all-day job was held to be within the course of his employment when riding his motor-cycle into a neighbouring town to have lunch.

As far as travel to and from one's place of work is concerned, the law normally draws a distinction between those parts of the journey which take place on and off the employer's premises. In *Staton v National Coal Board*,[3] for example, a first-aid man was held to be within the course of his employment when cycling across a factory yard to collect his pay. In *Nottingham v Aldridge*,[4] on the other hand, an apprentice was held to be outside the scope of his employment while driving to a GPO training establishment after a week-end at home, even though, by giving a lift to a fellow-apprentice, he qualified for a mileage allowance from his employers. Occasionally the distinction is not maintained. In *Harrison v British Railway Board*,[5] for example, a station foreman who attempted to board a moving train in order to leave work before his shift officially ended was held not be acting within the course of his employment.

1   *Ruddiman & Co v Smith* (1889) 60 LT 708, DC.
2   [1958] 2 QB 78, [1958] 1 All ER 657.
3   [1957] 2 All ER 667, [1957] 1 WLR 893.
4   [1971] 2 QB 739, [1971] 2 All ER 751.
5   [1981] 3 All ER 679.

Ostensible authority
30.12   In certain circumstances an employer may incur vicarious liability, not because he has actually (even impliedly) authorised his employee to commit a particular act, but because he has given third parties the impression that this is so. Where this happens, and a third party relies upon

the appearance, the employer will in effect be estopped from denying that authority exists. As a result, liability for a tort of the employee may be attributed to the employer, notwithstanding that it was committed purely for the employee's own benefit, or that it had been specifically prohibited by the employer.

The leading case on the subject of ostensible authority is *Lloyd v Grace, Smith & Co,*[1] in which the plaintiff, a widow, sought advice from a firm of solicitors about certain property which she had inherited. She dealt entirely with the solicitors' managing clerk, who fraudulently induced her to sign documents which transferred the property to him. The clerk then misappropriated it. It was held by the House of Lords that the solicitors were responsible for this fraud; having permitted their employee to deal unsupervised with clients, they were liable for any tort which he might commit in what appeared to be the course of his employment.

1 [1912] AC 716, HL.

Prohibitions

30.13 What, if any, is the effect upon an employer's vicarious liability of proof that he had forbidden his employee to do the thing which caused the damage? An instinctive reaction to this question might well be that such a prohibition must exclude the employer's liability, since the employee can hardly be said to be acting within the course of his employment when disobeying a specific instruction. A moment's reflection, however, will serve to show that such a conclusion would soon lead to the end of vicarious liability for all practical purposes, since every employer would simply insert a term into all contracts of employment to the effect that 'the employee is forbidden to commit any tort'.

A prohibition, then, cannot be allowed automatically to exonerate the employer. In order to understand how this can be so, it is necessary to remember that vicarious liability applies, not only to authorised acts, but also to unauthorised modes of performing authorised acts.[1] Therefore, the question which has to be asked is whether the employer has prohibited the act itself (in which case the employee cannot be within the course of his employment when performing it) or merely a mode of carrying it out. As was stated by Lord Dunedin, in *Plumb v Cobden Flour Mills Co Ltd,*[2] 'There are prohibitions which limit the sphere of employment, and prohibitions which only deal with conduct within the sphere of employment.'

Recognition that an employer may be legally responsible, even for conduct of his employee which he has banned, came as long ago as 1862, in the leading case of *Limpus v London General Omnibus Co.*[3] There, a bus driver, in attempting to obstruct a bus belonging to a rival company (a practice which his employers had expressly forbidden), caused an accident. Notwithstanding the prohibition, the employers were held vicariously liable, since the driver's negligence was undeniably committed in the course of performing an authorised act, namely, driving the bus. By contrast, where the prohibition is such as to remove all authority from the employee, he cannot then be said to act within the course of his employment. In *Kooragang Investments Pty Ltd v Richardson & Wrench Ltd,*[4] for example, a staff valuer was held to have gone outside the course of his employment in carrying out valuations for a client whom his employers had 'black-listed'. Likewise, in *Stevens v Woodward,*[5] an employee entered a washroom on the employer's premises, which he was not permitted to use, and, by leaving a tap running, caused a flood. The employer was held not liable because, if the employee's very presence in the washroom was forbidden, there was no 'authorised act' in the course of which his tort could be committed. The effect of the prohibition in this case was to prevent any implication of authority.[6] However, it should be noted that *ostensible* authority cannot be removed by a prohibition unless the third party is aware of it.

The difference between prohibiting a class of acts, and prohibiting a mode of carrying out permitted acts, is simply one of degree. Much depends upon how precisely a court defines the scope of the employee's employment in the first place, and the modern tendency is to adopt a fairly liberal approach. In *LCC v Cattermoles (Garages) Ltd,*[7] for example, a garage hand was expressly forbidden to drive customers' vehicles, although he was allowed (and, indeed, expected) to move them around the premises by hand. When he drove a customer's car and caused an accident, his employers argued that he was acting outside the course of his employment. The Court of Appeal, however, held the employers vicariously liable, on the ground that their employee was authorised to move cars; the prohibition applied only to the method which he used.

Particular problems have been raised by cases in which a driver has negligently injured someone to whom he has given a lift contrary to his employer's instructions. Clearly the invitation is unauthorised, but the injury is actually caused by negligent driving, which is precisely what the man is employed to do. In *Twine v Bean's Express Ltd,*[8] the Court of Appeal held the employer not liable since, while the employee could be regarded as within the course of his employment vis-à-vis other road users, he must be treated as outside it vis-à-vis his unauthorised passenger. Once again, however, the modern approach seems to be a rather more broad one. In *Rose v Plenty,*[9] a milk roundsman took a young boy on the float to help with deliveries, strictly against the instructions of his employers. When, due to the milkman's negligent driving, the boy was injured, a majority of the Court of Appeal held the employers liable on the ground that, in taking him on, the employee was doing in an unauthorised way what he was authorised to do, namely, deliver the milk.

1   Para 30.10 above.
2   [1914] AC 62 at 67.
3   (1862) 1 H & C 526.
4   [1982] AC 462, [1981] 3 All ER 65, PC.
5   (1881) 6 QBD 318, DC.
6   Cf *Ruddiman & Co v Smith* (1889) 60 LT 708, DC, para 30.11 above.
7   [1953] 2 All ER 582, [1953] 1 WLR 977, CA.
8   (1946) 175 LT 131, CA.
9   [1976] 1 All ER 97, [1976] 1 WLR 141, CA.

Intentional wrongdoing
30.14   Given that prohibited conduct may still be held to fall within the course of an employee's employment, it should come as no surprise that the same is true of wrongs intentionally committed. Once again, the important question is whether the employee can be said to be doing wrongfully what he is employed to do lawfully. Thus, in *Moore v Metropolitan Rly Co,*[1] where a railway official arrested the plaintiff in the mistaken belief that he had not paid his fare, the railway company were held liable. In *Abrahams v*

Deakin,[2] on the other hand, it was held that a barman had no implied authority to give someone into custody on a mistaken charge of attempting to pass bad money; in taking this step, the barman was furthering the course of justice rather than protecting the interests of his employer, for the attempt had failed.

A similar distinction can be found in cases of assaults committed by employees. There may well be vicarious liability in respect of excessive corporal punishment administered by a schoolteacher;[3] a blow given by a driver to a boy whom he suspects of stealing sugar from a cart;[4] or an over-zealous ejection of a troublemaker by a dance-hall 'bouncer'.[5] On the other hand, the short-tempered petrol pump attendant[6] or bus conductor[7] who strikes a customer in the course of an argument will not normally render his employer responsible, even where the original cause of the dispute is connected with the employer's business.

The most difficult cases are those in which the employee has quite clearly acted for his own benefit. As we have seen from the case of *Lloyd v Grace, Smith & Co*,[8] this fact alone does not exonerate the employer, and the same principle has been applied to torts other than deceit. In *Morris v C W Martin & Sons Ltd*,[9] the defendants, a firm of specialist cleaners, entrusted the plaintiff's mink coat to one of their employees. Instead of cleaning the garment, the employee stole it, and the defendants were held liable for this act of conversion. However, it should be noted that, had a third party or even another employee been guilty of the theft, the defendants would not have been liable; only in relation to the employee to whom the coat had actually been entrusted could it be said that he had done wrongfully what he was employed to do. Similar reasoning underlies the case of *Photo Production Ltd v Securicor Transport Ltd*,[10] where a patrolman employed by the defendants deliberately started a fire in one of the factories which it was his duty to visit. The House of Lords had no hesitation in holding that this tort was committed in the course of the patrolman's employment, so that his employers must in principle answer for it.[11]

1 (1872) LR 8 QB 36.
2 [1891] 1 QB 516, CA.
3 *Ryan v Fildes* [1938] 3 All ER 517.
4 *Poland v John Parr & Sons* [1927] 1 KB 236, CA.
5 *Daniels v Whetstone Entertainments Ltd* [1962] 2 Lloyd's Rep 1, CA.
6 *Warren v Henlys Ltd* [1948] 2 All ER 935.
7 *Keppel Bus Co Ltd v Sa'ad bin Ahmad* [1974] 2 All ER 700, [1974] 1 WLR 1082, PC.
8 [1912] AC 716, HL; para 30.12 above.
9 [1966] 1 QB 716, [1965] 2 All ER 725, CA. *See also Nahhas v Pier House (Cheyne Walk) Management Ltd* (1984) 270 Estates Gazette 328.
10 [1980] AC 827, [1980] 1 All ER 556, HL.
11 On the facts, an exemption clause protected them; see para 9.31 above.

Liability of employee

30.15 It should be emphasised that the vicarious liability of an employer in no way displaces the employee's own legal responsibility for the tort which he has committed. In practice, of course, a victim will almost invariably choose to sue the employer, since this increases the chance that any judgment in his favour will actually be satisfied. Nonetheless, and despite criticism that it leads to inefficient distribution of losses and the need for double insurance against the same risk, there is no doubt that the employee is personally liable, if sued.

Indeed, this does not represent the only danger to an employee who commits a tort in the course of his employment since, legally at least, he may be liable to reimburse his employer for the damages which the latter has been forced to pay because of his vicarious liability. This may arise under the Civil Liability (Contribution) Act 1978, since employer and employee are joint tortfeasors.[1] Apart from this, however, it was laid down by the House of Lords in *Lister v Romford Ice and Cold Storage Co Ltd*,[2] that the employer (or his insurers) can sue the employee on the basis of an implied term in his contract of employment that he will indemnify his employer against any liability incurred by the employer as a result of his wrongful acts.[3]

If the *Lister* principle were to become a regular practice, vicarious liability as it operates today would be seriously undermined. In the opinion of an inter-departmental committee which considered the possibility, this would be a bad thing and, as a result of governmental threats to introduce legislation to reverse *Lister*, employers' and insurers' organisations promised that they would not exercise their rights of indemnity against individual employees except in cases of collusion or wilful misconduct.

1   Paras 31.14 and 31.15 below.
2   [1957] AC 555, [1957] 1 All ER 125, HL.
3   See para 7.23 above.

Principal and agent

30.16   As stated at the beginning of this chapter, there is no general rule of law by which a principal is responsible for the torts of his agent, unless the relationship of employer and employee exists between them. Nevertheless, in two specific instances, and for widely differing reasons, the courts have imposed such liability.

Statements

30.17   From the legal point of view, the most important characteristic of an agent is that he is authorised to make contracts or dispose of property on behalf of his principal, and thereby to create obligations which the principal is bound to honour. Central to this function is the agent's role in making statements for his principal and, as a result, it has long been established that the principal is liable when these statements turn out to be false, even though the cause of action to which they give rise is tortious in nature rather than contractual.

The principle of liability is settled, but its extent is rather less clear. In *Mullens v Miller*,[1] the client of an estate agent was held liable for a *fraudulent* statement about the property, made by the agent to a prospective purchaser. In *Gosling v Anderson*,[2] another estate agent's client had to pay damages in respect of a *negligent* statement. It may even be that a principal would be held liable for *defamatory* statements made by his agent.[3]

1   (1882) 22 Ch D 194.
2   (1972) 223 Estates Gazette 1743, CA.
3   *Colonial Mutual Life Assurance Society Ltd v Producers and Citizens Assurance Co of Australia Ltd* (1931) 46 CLR 41.

Vehicles

30.18 In an attempt to ensure that the victims of road accidents do not go uncompensated for the lack of a defendant who is solvent or insured, English law treats the owner of a motor vehicle as vicariously liable for the negligence of anyone who is driving it with his consent and on his behalf.[1] Although the owner's presence in the vehicle is not required, he will not be liable unless the 'agent's' journey is undertaken both with his consent and for his benefit. Thus, in *Morgans v Launchbury*,[2] where a husband, too drunk to drive home in his wife's car, asked a friend to drive him, it was held by the House of Lords that the wife was not liable for the friend's negligent driving to passengers who were injured.

The importance of this form of vicarious liability has been greatly reduced by the introduction of legislation making it compulsory for every driver to be insured against liability for causing personal injury or death to other road users (including passengers). Nevertheless, it may still be relevant where damage is caused to property, such as other vehicles, or where the accident takes place off public roads and there is no insurance.

1 *Ormrod v Crosville Motor Services Ltd* [1953] 2 All ER 753, [1953] 1 WLR 1120, CA.
2 [1973] AC 127, [1972] 2 All ER 606, HL.

Independent contractors
General principle
30.19 As a general rule, a person who entrusts work to an independent contractor (hereafter referred to as the 'client') is not legally responsible for any torts committed by the contractor or the contractor's employees in the course of carrying out that work. Where, for example, the police arrange for an abandoned car to be towed away, and the car is damaged due to the negligence of the garage to whom the job is entrusted, it is the garage alone which is liable.[1] The client will, of course, be liable for any tort which he authorises or ratifies, and he may also be liable if he has been personally negligent in selecting an incompetent contractor, giving him inadequate instructions[2] or failing to exercise reasonable supervision.[3] However, apart from these possibilities there are a number of cases, which may be increasing, in which the law is prepared to say that the client owes a personal, 'non-delegable' duty to third parties, so that, while entitled to delegate performance of such a duty to another, he remains responsible for its due fulfilment.

The standard of liability which is imposed by these non-delegable duties is not entirely uniform. In some instances, such as under *Rylands v Fletcher* and many statutes, the client's duty is a strict one, in the sense that it can be broken even when there is no negligence on anyone's part. Other cases, such as the duty of a bailee of goods, depend upon proof that someone is negligent; the client here may be said to owe a duty that reasonable care be taken. As to the category in which a particular duty should be placed, there seems to be no coherent principle. Indeed, the same can be said of non-delegable duties as a whole, which seem to have evolved to meet particular situations, rather than being deduced from any general idea of the circumstances in which the client of an independent contractor ought to be liable. With this in mind we may now consider the major duties which the law treats as non-delegable.

1   *Rivers v Cutting* [1982] 3 All ER 69, [1982] 1 WLR 1146, CA.
2   *Robinson v Beaconsfield RDC* [1911] 2 Ch 188, CA.
3   *AMF International Ltd v Magnet Bowling Ltd* [1968] 2 All ER 789, [1968] 1 WLR 1028; see para 23.17 above.

Non-delegable duties

Statutory duties

30.20   Many, if not most, of the statutory duties which give rise to civil liability[1] are non-delegable. In *Gray v Pullen*,[2] for example, where the defendants were obliged by statute to reinstate the highway after laying a drain in it, they were held liable when their independent contractor failed to do so.

Furthermore, it seems that a person with a statutory power (to do something which would otherwise be unlawful) delegates the exercise of this at his peril. Thus, in *Darling v A-G*,[3] where the Ministry of Works employed a contractor to drill trial bore holes on the plaintiff's land, the Ministry was held liable for the contractor's negligence in leaving a pile of timber there which injured the plaintiff's horse.

1   Ch 24 above.
2   (1864) 5 B & S 970.
3   [1950] 2 All ER 793.

Withdrawal of support

30.21   Where a landowner has a right to have his land or buildings supported by those of his neighbour,[1] he may sue if that support is withdrawn by the neighbour himself or by his independent contractor. This principle, which was established in *Bower v Peate*,[2] was perhaps the first non-delegable duty to be recognised by common law.

1   Para 40.42 below.
2   (1876) 1 QBD 321.

Operations on the highway

30.22   Where work is done by an independent contractor on or under the highway, the client is liable if the contractor negligently causes damage to a highway user, for example by leaving an unlighted heap of soil in the road,[1] or to the occupier of adjoining premises, for example by fracturing a gas main and thus causing an explosion.[2] This principle extends to the negligent repair by a contractor of an overhanging lamp which consequently falls on a passer-by;[3] it does not, however, cover the negligent felling of trees *near* a highway[4] nor, for reasons which are unexplained, the negligent repair by a contractor of a motor vehicle which the employer then drives along the road.[5]

1   *Penny v Wimbledon UDC* [1899] 2 QB 72, CA.
2   *Hardaker v Idle District Council* [1896] 1 QB 335, CA.
3   *Tarry v Ashton* (1876) 1 QBD 314.
4   *Salsbury v Woodland* [1970] 1 QB 324, [1969] 3 All ER 863, CA.
5   *Phillips v Britannia Hygienic Laundry Co Ltd* [1923] 1 KB 539, DC.

Strict liability

30.23   In chs 27 and 28 we considered a number of areas in which the common law imposes strict liability, notably the rule in *Rylands v Fletcher*, the escape of fire and damage of various kinds caused by animals. In all these cases a client may be held responsible for the default of his independent contractor.

Extra-hazardous acts

30.24 In *Honeywill and Stein Ltd v Larkin Bros Ltd*,[1] the defendants, a firm of photographers, were employed by the plaintiffs to take pictures inside a cinema owned by third parties. Due to the negligence of the defendants in the use of magnesium flares (which were then necessary for indoor photography), the premises were damaged by fire. It was held by the Court of Appeal that, since this was a 'dangerous operation', the plaintiffs' duty in respect of it was a non-delegable one, and they were accordingly liable. A similar line of thinking can be found in *Matania v National Provincial Bank Ltd*,[2] where noise and dust from building works caused a nuisance; the builders' clients were held liable, since this was no mere ordinary building operation, but an extensive job involving a high risk of nuisance.

The problem with cases like these is that, by attaching important legal consequences to what is only a difference of degree, they lead to confusion and uncertainty in the law. After all, when exactly does an operation become 'dangerous' or an act 'extra-hazardous'? It may well be that the courts will in future decline to follow this particular lead.

1 [1934] 1 KB 191, CA.
2 [1936] 2 All ER 633, CA.

Other cases

30.25 Of the other situations in which courts have declared a person's duty to be non-delegable, so as to fix him with responsibility for the default of his independent contractor, three worthy of note are the duty of a contractual bailee to safeguard his bailor's goods;[1] the duty of every employer to take care for the safety of his employees;[2] and (probably) the duty of a hospital to look after its patients.[3] The emphasis in all these cases is on the relationship between the *client* and the victim, and it may well be that courts will be increasingly ready to find that a client has 'undertaken' a non-delegable duty, at least where he and the victim are parties to a contract.[4]

1 *British Road Services Ltd v Arthur V Crutchley & Co Ltd* [1968] 1 All ER 811, CA.
2 *Sumner v William Henderson & Sons Ltd* [1964] 1 QB 450, [1963] 1 All ER 408.
3 *Cassidy v Ministry of Health* [1951] 2 KB 343, [1951] 1 All ER 574, CA.
4 See *Rogers v Night Riders* [1983] RTR 324, CA.

Collateral negligence

30.26 Even in circumstances where the law recognises a non-delegable duty, it is usually said that the client is not responsible for *casual* or *collateral* negligence of the independent contractor, but only for negligence in the very act which he is employed to carry out. Thus in *Padbury v Holliday and Greenwood Ltd*,[1] where a workman employed by sub-contractors negligently left an iron tool on a window-sill and it fell on to a passer-by, the clients of the sub-contractors were held not liable.

The difficulty of deciding when negligence is truly 'collateral' is well illustrated by *Holliday v National Telephone Co*,[2] where the defendants, who were laying telephone wires under a street, employed a plumber to make certain connections. The plumber negligently dipped his blowlamp into molten solder, and a passer-by was injured by the resulting explosion. The Divisional Court thought that this was about as typical a case of casual negligence as it was possible to imagine, but the Court of Appeal held that this was negligence in the very act which the contractor was engaged to perform!

1   (1912) 28 TLR 494, CA.
2   [1899] 2 QB 392, CA.

Chapter 31
Remedies

Damages

31.1 The availability of an action for damages is the hallmark of a tort; the absence of such a remedy is what serves to distinguish other civil wrongs, such as breach of trust. Nevertheless, and despite the fact that an award of damages is the plaintiff's objective in the vast majority of cases, this is not the only remedy which may be obtained; an injunction to restrain the continuance of a nuisance, or an order for the specific recovery of land or goods, may be of more practical importance in a particular case.

It should be emphasised that damages are available even in respect of those torts which are actionable per se, that is without the need to prove that the plaintiff has suffered any actual loss. In such a case, the sum awarded may, but need not, be nominal. This is not so, however, where other torts are concerned; here the plaintiff is called upon to establish his loss and, having done so, he is entitled to be compensated for it.

Kinds of damages

31.2 As a general rule, the sole object of awarding damages to a plaintiff is to compensate him for the loss which he has suffered as a result of the defendant's tort. With a few minor exceptions, matters such as the punishment of the defendant, or the restoration of benefits which he has wrongfully obtained, have no place in the law of tort. It should also be noted that, whereas damages for breach of contract generally endeavour to put the plaintiff, in monetary terms, into the position in which he would have been had the contract been performed,[1] and thus take into account any profit which he would have made from the bargain, damages for tort attempt to restore the plaintiff to his original position (as if the tort had not been committed at all).

In a number of instances, the courts may depart, or appear to depart, from the principle of compensation in assessing the amount of damages to be awarded to a successful plaintiff. For example, where the plaintiff has a bare legal claim, but the court feels that he is morally wrong to pursue it, he may be awarded *contemptuous* damages, usually the smallest coin of the realm. In such a case the plaintiff will probably be ordered to pay his own costs, which means that he will end up out of pocket to a considerable extent.

Not to be confused with contemptuous damages are nominal damages, which are awarded in respect of torts actionable per se to mark the infringement of the plaintiff's legal rights, in cases where no actual loss has been incurred. An award of, say, £2 for trespass in no way signifies that the court is critical of the plaintiff for bringing the case; on the contrary, such an award is frequently accompanied by an injunction restraining the defendant from committing further acts of trespass.

In any case where damages are incapable of precise assessment in money terms (eg trespass or assault), the manner in which the defendant commits the tort may be taken into account by the court and, if this is such as to injure the plaintiff's dignity or pride, *aggravated* damages may be awarded. Indeed, even where the plaintiff *has* suffered a quantifiable financial loss (eg where he has been defrauded by the defendant) he may receive an additional sum for injury to his feelings.[2] It should be noted that, while aggravated damages are in theory compensatory, they seek to give redress for something which would not be actionable if it stood alone. Thus, an insult itself cannot bring damages; but, if the defendant trespasses on the plaintiff's land in order to insult him, this may aggravate the damages which are awarded in respect of the trespass.

Quite apart from any question of aggravation, there remains the possibility that, where the defendant's conduct is particularly outrageous, the court may order him to pay *exemplary* (or *punitive*) damages, over and above what is necessary to compensate the plaintiff, for the specific purpose of punishing the defendant and of teaching him that 'tort does not pay'. Such damages may be criticised on the grounds that the defendant is being punished for what is not a crime without the benefit of a criminal trial and, further, that such a 'fine' should be paid to the state rather than to the plaintiff who, after all, has already received sufficient to compensate him for his loss. Nevertheless, the power to award exemplary damages is well established, although the House of Lords has laid down[3] that it should only be exercised in three classes of case:

a. where statute authorises such an award;

b. in cases of oppressive, arbitrary or unconstitutional acts by the servants of the government (such as assault or wrongful arrest by police officers, who are regarded for this purpose as the servants of the government[4]); or

c. where the defendant has quite cold-bloodedly decided to infringe the plaintiff's rights after calculating that his profit in doing so will outweigh any compensation he may be ordered to pay. This has been held to include such cases as the publication of a book containing sensational libels in order to boost sales,[5] and the eviction of a protected tenant by a landlord anxious to turn his flat to more profitable use.[6]

1 Para 11.3 above
2 *Archer v Brown* [1984] 2 All ER 267, [1984] 3 WLR 350.
3 *Rookes v Barnard* [1964] AC 1129, [1964] 1 All ER 367, HL.
4 *White v Metropolitan Police Commissioner* (1982) Times, 24 April.
5 *Cassell & Co Ltd v Broome* [1972] AC 1027, [1972] 1 All ER 801, HL, in which it was held to be irrelevant that no profit was in fact made.
6 *Drane v Evangelou* [1978] 2 All ER 437, [1978] 1 WLR 455, CA (trespass); *Guppys (Bridport) Ltd v Brookling* (1983) 269 Estates Gazette 846, CA (nuisance).

Personal injury

31.3 The rules which govern the assessment of damages for personal injury are complex and, in many respects, controversial; no more than an outline can be given here, although we have tried to draw attention to some at least of the reforms suggested by the Pearson Commission[1]. One of the major problems is that the 'loss' which flows from an injury falls into two very different categories. In the first place, the plaintiff may suffer *pecuniary* loss, such as medical expenses or loss of earnings; the guiding principle here is that he is entitled, so far as is possible, to full restitution of what he has lost. Second, however, there is *non-pecuniary* loss, which takes in such matters as pain and suffering and loss of amenity. It is obviously impossible to place a precise monetary value upon such things and, as a result, the law adopts the principle that compensation should merely be 'fair and reasonable', which involves attempting to devise a scale of injuries (a lost leg is worth more than a lost eye, etc) and also maintaining some degree of consistency between the amounts awarded in similar cases. With these points, and especially these two categories, in mind we may now consider the various heads of damage under which personal injury awards are usually itemised.

1 See para. 18.21 above.

Loss of amenity

31.4 The plaintiff is entitled to an award of damages in respect of the extent to which his injuries render him unable or less able to do what he previously enjoyed. Under this heading compensation may be awarded, for example, in respect of a lost limb or the impairment of senses or of sexual function. The more serious the deprivation, the greater the plaintiff's awareness of it, and the longer he is likely to have to endure it, are all factors which tend to increase the size of the award. In *Daly v General Steam Navigation Co Ltd*,[1] a woman whose injuries made it difficult and painful to keep house for her family recovered under this head for the period preceding the trial; as to the future, she was held entitled to the estimated costs of employing a housekeeper, whether or not she in fact intended to employ one.

Although this category is in truth concerned with a person's lost enjoyment of life, it was laid down by the House of Lords, in *H West & Son Ltd v Shephard*,[2] that it represents an objective loss. Consequently, even someone rendered immediately and permanently unaware of his loss may be entitled to a considerable sum.[3] This has been criticised as being of benefit only to the plaintiff's dependants, and the Pearson Commission recommended that unconscious plaintiffs should not be compensated in this way.

1 [1980] 3 All ER 696, [1981] 1 WLR 120, CA.
2 [1964] AC 326, [1963] 2 All ER 625, HL.
3 £35,000 in *Croke v Wiseman* [1981] 3 All ER 852, [1982] 1 WLR 71, CA.

Loss of expectation of life

31.5 A plaintiff's entitlement to damages (usually a small 'conventional' sum) for the fact that his life expectancy has been reduced has now been abolished by the Administration of Justice Act 1982, s1(1). However, this does not prevent him from claiming in respect of either the suffering caused by his awareness of his reduced life span (s1(1)(b)) or what he could have earned during the 'lost years' (s1(2)).

Pain and suffering

31.6 This category, which by definition cannot apply to plaintiffs rendered permanently unconscious, includes not only the physical pain of the injury and subsequent surgical operations, but also mental anguish arising out of disability or disfigurement. Further, distress caused by the plaintiff's awareness of his loss of amenity may lead to additional damages being awarded even though, as we have seen, the loss itself is treated as objective.

As a general rule, the courts do not separate 'pain and suffering' from 'loss of amenity', but award a global sum to cover both categories. Where very severe injuries are involved, this can be a considerable amount; the Court of Appeal's 'guideline' for the average case of total paralysis is £75,000.[1]

Since pain cannot be accurately quantified, it could be argued that to give the plaintiff a sum of money because he has suffered is futile. It seems, however, that public opinion regards such damages as necessary to secure 'justice'. The Pearson Commission did not disagree with this view, but recommended, as a means of excluding minor claims, that no damages should be awarded in respect of any non-pecuniary loss suffered in the first three months following the injury.

1 *Housecroft v Burnett* (1985) Times, 7 June, CA.

Medical and other expenses

31.7 The plaintiff is entitled to claim the cost, both past and future, of medical and nursing care including, where appropriate, the expense of living in a suitable institution or of adapting his own home to his needs. Reasonable steps must be taken to keep the expense to a minimum, although it is not unreasonable to care for a severely injured person at home because he could be catered for more cheaply than in an institution.[1] Nor can the defendant argue that the plaintiff should have made use of National Health Service facilities,[2] although the Pearson Commission recommended that a plaintiff seeking to recover for private medical fees should be called upon to show that it was reasonable to incur them. Where the plaintiff has to live in an institution, a sum representing his normal living expenses must be deducted from the damages awarded under this head, since these will no longer be incurred.[3]

Problems have arisen in the past where necessary nursing services have been rendered to a seriously disabled plaintiff by a close relative, as where a mother has given up a job in order to look after her crippled child. Notwithstanding that the plaintiff in such a case is under no legal obligation to pay for these services, it has now been held by the Court of Appeal[4] that he can recover a reasonable sum in respect of them from the defendant.

1 *Rialas v Mitchell* (1984) Times, 17 July, CA.
2 Law Reform (Personal Injuries) Act 1948, s2(4).
3 *Lim Poh Choo v Camden and Islington Area Health Authority* [1980] AC 174, [1979] 2 All ER 910, HL.
4 *Donnelly v Joyce* [1974] QB 454, [1973] 3 All ER 475, CA.

Loss of earnings
31.8 Earnings which the plaintiff has lost up to the date of the trial are relatively easy to measure, but loss of future earnings must also be compensated, and here assessment is far less certain, especially where it appears that the plaintiff will never be able to work again. In such cases, the courts, having firmly refused to enter into detailed actuarial calculations,[1] simply multiply their prediction of the plaintiff's average annual income (net of income tax and national insurance contributions) by an appropriate multiplier. This is not simply the number of years' earnings which have been lost, but is discounted to reflect the chance of an earlier death and the benefit of having an immediate lump sum; it is not increased, however, to offset inflation.[2]

Where a person's life expectancy is substantially reduced as a result of a tort, it is course likely that he will thereby be deprived of the opportunity to earn money during the 'lost years'. At one time no damages could be awarded for loss of earnings during this period, but the law was changed by the House of Lords in *Pickett v British Rail Engineering Ltd*,[3] and this has now been given statutory force by the Administration of Justice Act 1982, s1(2). As a result of this provision, a *living* plaintiff[4] can recover for prospective earnings during the 'lost years', although a deduction must be made in respect of what he would have spent on his own support during that time. However, the courts will not make an award of this kind to a very young plaintiff, on the grounds that his loss is too speculative.[5]

Much of the uncertainty which surrounds this particular head of damage arises from the fact that, since damages are paid as a lump sum, they must be assessed in advance. One of the Pearson Commission's more far-reaching proposals was that the normal practice should be periodic payments, reviewable if circumstances change. While this has not been implemented, the Administration of Justice Act 1982, s6 brings about a more limited reform. In cases where there is a chance that the plaintiff's condition will deteriorate at some time in the future, the court is empowered to make an initial award on the basis that this will not happen, the plaintiff being at liberty to seek additional damages if it does.

1 *Mitchell v Mulholland (No 2)* [1972] 1 QB 65, [1971] 2 All ER 1205, CA.
2 *Cookson v Knowles* [1979] AC 556, [1978] 2 All ER 604, HL.
3 [1980] AC 136, [1979] 1 All ER 774, HL.
4 The claim does not pass to the deceased's estate: see para 31.10 below.
5 *Croke v Wiseman* [1981] 3 All ER 852, [1982] 1 WLR 71, CA.

Collateral benefits
31.9 A person who is injured in an accident may, as a result of this, receive sums of money from a wide variety of sources. It may be, for example, that he has insured himself against this contingency, he may receive sick pay or a pension from his employer, or he may be entitled to various social security benefits. To what extent, if at all, should this be regarded as relevant when the plaintiff comes to claim damages from the defendant in respect of his loss of earnings? Should the plaintiff be allowed to recover full damages and to keep his other benefit, and thereby be doubly compensated? Should damages be reduced, so that the defendant reaps the benefit of a payment designed to help the plaintiff? Or should the law seek to ensure that the money is in some way returned to the collateral fund?

To these questions, English law has no simple answers, largely because it has dealt with each type of 'collateral benefit' as it has arisen, without attempting to lay down any general principles. Broadly speaking, the present position is that one-half of all state benefits received in the five years following the accident have to be deducted from the damages awarded,[1] as do wages, sick pay and the like to which the plaintiff is actually entitled, together with any saving on living costs where the plaintiff is maintained at public expense in an institution.[2] The product of private insurance, or a charitable payment, on the other hand, is non-deductible.[3] On the very borderline is a pension; in *Parry v Cleaver*,[4] this was held by a bare majority of the House of Lords to be non-deductible, on the ground that it is not intended to be an equivalent of wages lost and cannot therefore be said to reduce the loss which the plaintiff has suffered.

1 Law Reform (Personal Injuries) Act 1948, s2. The Pearson Commission recommended that virtually all state benefits should be deducted from damages awarded in respect of lost earnings.
2 Administration of Justice Act 1982, s5.
3 *Bradburn v Great Western Rly Co* (1874) LR 10 Exch 1.
4 *Parry v Cleaver* [1970] AC 1, [1969] 1 All ER 555, HL.

Death
31.10 The Law Reform (Miscellaneous Provisions) Act 1934 provides that most tort actions (except defamation) survive for and against the estates of the parties. However, the Administration of Justice Act 1982, s4 provides that a deceased person's estate may not be awarded damages for bereavement,[1] exemplary damages[2] or damages for loss of earnings during the 'lost years'.[3] Apart from this, where an action is brought on behalf of a deceased person, the damages awarded are such as he could have recovered if he had not died, which means that the headings considered above under 'personal injury' are again relevant, at least as regards the period between the tort and death.

1 Para 31.11 below.
2 Para 31.2 above.
3 Para 31.8 above.

Fatal accidents
31.11 At common law, no tort action could be brought by A on the ground that the death of B had caused him loss. However, a statutory right of action for the dependants of a person who is killed by a tort has long been in existence and is currently governed by the Fatal Accidents Act 1976, as amended by the Administration of Justice Act 1982, s3. 'Dependants' for this purpose bears a wide meaning, including spouses, all ascendants and descendants, brothers and sisters, uncles and aunts and their issue (provided, of course, that they truly were dependent upon the deceased). Moreover, since 1982, the Act has extended to a former or 'common law' spouse of the deceased, although the amount of damages payable to the latter must reflect the fact that he or she had no legal right to financial support by the deceased.

The cause of action given by the Fatal Accidents Act is quite separate from that which may have survived for the benefit of the estate itself. Normal practice is for the action to be brought by the personal representative of the deceased, on behalf of all the dependants; the court will then assess the total liability of the defendant before apportioning the damages between the various dependants. Since the action is an independent one, it has its own limitation period[1] of three years from the date of death. Further, it seems that where a dependant has through his own fault contributed to the causing of death, for example by negligent driving, *his* damages, though not those of other dependants, may be reduced on the ground of contributory negligence.

Although the action is thus separate, it is still subject to the principle that it can only be brought where the deceased himself could have sued if he had been injured rather than killed. As a result, if the deceased had already sued to judgment or settled his claim against the defendant, or if his action was barred by time or by an exemption clause, the dependants' rights are also defeated. So too, if the deceased was guilty of contributory negligence, damages awarded under the Fatal Accidents Act will suffer an appropriate reduction.

It is important to appreciate that the main purpose of this statutory cause of action is to compensate the dependants, not for their grief at losing a loved one, but for the loss of some benefit which has a monetary value (including, for example, services performed by a wife and mother[2] or unpaid help given by a son to his father's work[3]) and which would have come to the dependants because of their relationship with the deceased.[4] However, since 1982 there has been a limited exception to this principle, in that damages for 'bereavement' (a fixed sum of £3,500, subject to alteration by statutory instrument) may be awarded to the widow(er) or, where the deceased is an unmarried minor, to his parents.

In deciding how much to award for loss of dependency, the court must try to assess what the position would have been had the deceased lived and, in carrying out this task, the prospects of both the deceased and the dependants are of course relevant. However, in one area good taste has intervened, since the court is no longer required to consider a widow's prospects, if any, of remarriage.

Section 4 of the 1976 Act provides that, in assessing damages, no account is to be taken of any benefits which accrue to the dependant in question as a result of the death (by way of inheritance, insurance policies, etc).

1 Paras 31.20–31.22 below.
2 *Mehmet v Perry* [1977] 2 All ER 529, DC.
3 *Franklin v South Eastern Rly Co* (1858) 3 H & N 211.
4 Funeral expenses incurred by the dependants are also recoverable: Fatal Accidents Act 1976, s3(3).

Damage to property
Measure of damages
31.12 A person may sue in tort on the ground that his property has been destroyed, damaged or misappropriated. In assessing damages in each case the courts will apply similar principles, whether the property in question consists of goods or land (although, in practice, total destruction is found only in relation to goods). The basic rule, once again, is that the plaintiff is entitled to full restitution in money terms of what he has lost.

Where property is totally destroyed, the usual measure of damages is at least the full value to the plaintiff of that property at the time and place of its destruction. This 'value', in the case of a profit-earning chattel such as a ship, should take into account its profitability at the time, in the light of its current engagements.[1] However, if the plaintiff receives this sum he may yet be out of pocket, in that the acquisition of a suitable replacement may take time; in such a case, damages for loss of profit, or simply loss of use, may also be recovered.

Where property is damaged, the court has an obvious choice of two possible measures to award: either the amount by which the value of the property has been reduced, or the cost of repairing it (which may, but need not, be the same). In the case of goods, the courts have usually been prepared to award the cost of repair, provided that this is reasonable. For example, the owner of a badly damaged car will not normally be allowed the cost of repair where this exceeds the 'write-off' value of the vehicle.[2] A similar principle applies in respect of damage to land and buildings, so that the cost of reinstatement is usually appropriate, provided that the plaintiff's decision to repair is a reasonable one. Thus, in *Hollebone v Midhurst and Fernhurst Builders*,[3] where the plaintiff's house was damaged by fire, the judge held that the plaintiff was fully entitled to decide to rebuild what was in effect a unique property. That case also laid down that a plaintiff need not suffer any deduction from his damages in respect of 'betterment', ie the amount by which the value of the restored property exceeds its pre-accident value. Where the plaintiff has no intention of repairing the building (as in *C R Taylor (Wholesale) Ltd v Hepworths Ltd*,[4] where fire damaged a disused billiards hall on a site which the plaintiffs had always intended to redevelop) damages should only reflect the diminution in value of the property. This is also true of cases where the cost of reinstatement would be out of all proportion to the loss suffered. In *Jones v Gooday*,[5] for example, where the defendant wrongfully removed soil from the plaintiff's field, the plaintiff was awarded only the amount by which the value of the field was reduced, and not the much greater cost of restoring it to its original condition. In *Heath v Keys*,[6] where the defendant wrongfully dumped spoil on a small area of woodland owned by the plaintiff, the award was something of a compromise; not the full cost of restoring the site to its original condition, but enough to pay the costs involved in removing most of the spoil and tidying the site (in addition to the diminution in value which would remain).

Quite apart from the damages discussed above, a plaintiff is entitled to compensation for loss of profits or loss of use during the time taken to effect repairs, which may be assessed on the basis of the cost of hiring a reasonable substitute. What is 'reasonable' is a question of fact, and may even include a 'prestige' car.[7] It is important to note that the plaintiff is not required to show that he has actually suffered from the non-availability of his property. Consequently, in *The Mediana*,[8] where a damaged lightship was replaced for a time by a substitute which the plaintiffs kept for just such an emergency, they were nevertheless awarded substantial damages for loss of use.

Where goods are misappropriated, or land is wrongfully occupied, special rules regarding the assessment of damages come into play; these are discussed in the context of the particular torts concerned.[9]

1 *Liesbosch Dredger v SS Edison* [1933] AC 449, HL.
2 *Darbishire v Warran* [1963] 3 All ER 310, [1963] 1 WLR 1067, CA.

3 [1968] 1 Lloyd's Rep 38.
4 [1977] 2 All ER 784, [1977] 1 WLR 659.
5 (1841) 8 M & W 146.
6 (1984) Times, 28 May.
7 *Daily Office Cleaning Contractors v Shefford* [1977] RTR 361, DC.
8 [1900] AC 113, HL.
9 Paras 25.7 and 29.11 above.

Date of assessment
31.13 Times of rampant inflation have given rise to a particular problem
in cases where damages are to be assessed on the basis of cost of repair. In
Dodd Properties (Kent) Ltd v Canterbury City Council,[1] for example, the
plaintiffs' garage was seriously damaged in 1968 by building works carried
on by the defendants on adjoining property, in such circumstances that the
defendants were clearly liable. The cost of repairing the garage in 1968
would have been £10,800. In 1970, which was the earliest possible date by
which repairs could have been started, the cost would have been £11,300.
By 1978, however, when the plaintiffs' action was tried, the cost had
rocketed to £30,000! It was obviously of crucial importance to decide which
date should be taken for the purpose of assessing damages. The Court of
Appeal held that, while the basic rule in tort is that damages are to be
assessed when they occur, this must not be allowed to penalise a plaintiff. In
the 'cost of repair' cases, therefore, the appropriate date is that on which
the plaintiff ought reasonably to have repaired the property. Here, the
plaintiffs had chosen for financial reasons not to start repairs until they had
recovered damages from the defendants and, despite the defendants' plea
that lack of funds could not excuse the plaintiffs' failure to put the repairs in
hand,[2] they were held to be entitled to the much higher sum which
represented this cost at the time of the trial.

1 [1980] 1 All ER 928, [1980] 1 WLR 433, CA.
2 Based on *Liesbosch Dredger v SS Edison* [1933] AC 449, HL; paras 21.16, 21.20 above.

Joint and several tortfeasors
31.14 Where the plaintiff is injured by the tortious conduct of more than
one person, the first question to be asked is whether the damage which he
has suffered is capable of being clearly divided among those who are to
blame. If a relationship of cause and effect can be shown between each
tortfeasor and some identifiable part of the plaintiff's loss, then each is
liable only for what he himself has caused. More commonly, however, the
plaintiff's loss will be found to be indivisible and, where this is so, the rule is
that the plaintiff is entitled to recover damages *in full* from any or all of the
tortfeasors (subject, of course, to the proviso that he cannot recover more
in total than he has lost). Thus, for example, if the plaintiff is injured by the
combined negligence of A and B in such circumstances that the court
regards A as three-quarters and B as one-quarter to blame, the plaintiff may
nevertheless choose to sue B alone and may recover full damages. The
importance of this principle is seen in cases where A is insolvent and
uninsured; the loss then falls upon B, who is after all guilty of *some* fault,
rather than upon the plaintiff, who is completely innocent.
   In practice, it is desirable that the plaintiff should bring all the defendants
into court in one action and, to encourage him to do so, the common law
laid down the rule that judgment (even if unsatisfied) against one 'joint

tortfeasor' barred subsequent proceeding against the others. This rule has been abolished, but the plaintiff is still unable to recover his costs in subsequent proceedings unless the court finds that there were reasonable grounds for bringing them.[1]

1 Civil Liability (Contribution) Act 1978, s4.

Contribution

31.15 At common law, if a plaintiff chose to sue one tortfeasor and not others, the loss lay where it fell; the others could not be ordered to make any contribution to the damages paid. This rule was, however, abolished in relation to tort in 1935 and in relation to other types of liability, such as breach of contract and breach of trust, in 1978. The rules governing contribution are contained in the Civil Liability (Contribution) Act 1978. Of course, no order for contribution can be made against a tortfeasor unless he is party to an action. As we have seen, the 'costs sanction' encourages the plaintiff to join all defendants in the first place and, even where this is not done, one defendant can bring in others as third parties, in order that the liability of each may be determined in a single action.

The right of one defendant (D1) to claim contribution from another (D2) is independent of the plaintiff's right of action. Thus, the fact that the *plaintiff's* claim against D2 would have barred by lapse of time[1] is irrelevant, provided that D1 himself brings his action for contribution within two years of the date on which his right arises (normally the date on which D1 pays compensation to the plaintiff).

In assessing the amount of contribution, the court is instructed to do what is 'just and equitable', and it seems that, in arriving at a fraction or percentage, it will rely on the same factors as in cases of contributory negligence.[2] However, it should be noted that D2 cannot be ordered to pay more to D1 than he would have had to pay the plaintiff (eg where his contract with the plaintiff contained a clause which limited his liability): nor does the Civil Liability (Contribution) Act prevail against a right of indemnity which is contained in a contract between the tortfeasors.

1 Paras 31.20–31.22 below.
2 Para 22.16 above.

Injunction

31.16 An injunction is a specific decree of the court which orders the defendant to do or, more commonly, not to do something. Like all equitable remedies it is not available as of right, but lies in the discretion of the court. As a result, it is unlikely to be granted where damages would be an adequate remedy, where the harm suffered by the plaintiff is of a very trivial or temporary nature,[1] or where the plaintiff has actually or apparently acquiesced in the defendant's tort. For example, in *Armstrong v Sheppard and Short Ltd*,[2] the plaintiff assented in principle to the laying of a sewer by the defendants under certain land near his house, unaware that he in fact owned it; upon discovering the truth, he sued the defendants in trespass. The Court of Appeal held that, since the defendants had been misled and the harm was trivial, the plaintiff was not entitled to an injunction but only to damages.

1   *A-G Sheffield Gas Consumers Co* (1852) 3 De GM & G 304.
2   [1959] 2 QB 384, 2 All ER 651, CA.

Kinds of injunction

31.17   A *prohibitory* injunction, the most common kind, is an order to the defendant to stop certain conduct which represents a continuing or repetitive infringement of the plaintiff's legal rights (eg by the commission of trespass or nuisance). In the absence of special circumstances, the grant of such an injunction is almost automatic, though its operation may on occasion be suspended for a period to enable the defendant to make alternative arrangements.

By contrast, a *mandatory* injunction (which orders the defendant to take positive steps to repair the wrong he has done) is reserved for those few cases in which the plaintiff will suffer very serious harm unless the injunction is granted. Further, unless the defendant has acted in flagrant disregard of the plaintiff's rights, the court must weigh up what it will cost the defendant to comply with the order. Thus, in *Redland Bricks Ltd v Morris*,[1] where the defendants' excavations on their own land had caused subsidence of part of the plaintiff's land and danger to the rest, the House of Lords refused to order the defendants to restore support, since the cost of doing this would be greater than the total value of the plaintiff's land.

In matters of urgency, where the preservation of the status quo is important to save the plaintiff from further loss, the court may grant him an *interlocutory* injunction, a provisional order until a full trial takes place. Since the defendant may lose money because of this order, and then turn out to have been in the right all along, the plaintiff may be compelled to give an undertaking that in such circumstances he will pay compensation. The principles on which a court should exercise its discretion in relation to interlocutory injunctions were laid down by the House of Lords in the case of *American Cyanamid Co v Ethicon Ltd*.[2] Briefly, these are that, if there is a serious question to be tried, the court must consider all the circumstances, particularly whether the preservation of the status quo is important, and whether the defendant will be adequately protected by the plaintiff's undertaking to pay damages.

In rare cases, where the plaintiff's cause of action depends on proof of damage, the court may issue an injunction *quia timet* before such damage had actually occurred. In effect, this means that the defendant is liable before a complete tort has been committed; not surprisingly, therefore, such an order is only granted where damage is almost certain to occur and where it is imminent.

1   [1970] AC 652, [1969] 2 All ER 576, HL.
2   [1975] AC 396, [1975] 1 All ER 504, HL.

Damages in lieu of injunction

31.18   In any case where an injunction is claimed, the court has a statutory discretion to refuse the injunction and award damages in substitution for it. In effect, such an order allows the defendant to purchase the right to commit a tort against the plaintiff. Consequently, the discretion is to be used sparingly. It has been suggested that the court should only act in this way where it is shown that the injury to the plaintiff is small, capable of estimation in money terms and adequately compensated by damages and that an injunction would cause great hardship to the defendant.[1]

1   *Shelfer v City of London Electric Lighting Co* [1895] 1 Ch 287 at 322, CA.

Other remedies

31.19   In the vast majority of tort cases which come to court, the plaintiff is seeking either damages or an injunction. However, in some circumstances other remedies may be of greater value, particularly an order for the specific restitution of land[1] or goods.[2]

Although not popular with the courts (and therefore strictly controlled) a certain amount of self-help is tolerated, in the interest of avoiding unnecessary litigation. Examples of this principle, all of which we have considered at the appropriate place, are the ejection of a trespasser and re-entry on to land,[3] the abatement of a nuisance,[4] the detention of straying livestock,[5] the killing of a marauding dog[6] and the retaking of goods belonging to the plaintiff.[7]

1   Para 25.9 above.
2   Para 29.14 above.
3   Para 25.10 above.
4   Para 26.21 above.
5   Para 28.11 above.
6   Para 28.13 above.
7   Para 29.15 above.

Limitation of actions

31.20   Any civil action will be barred by lapse of time unless the writ by which it commences is issued within the prescribed limitation period. The rules which govern this matter are entirely statutory, the relevant Act being the Limitation Act 1980. For present purposes, the main limitation periods are twelve years (recovery of land and contracts under seal); six years (breach of simple contracts and tort); and three years (actions of any kind in respect of personal injuries).

Commencement of limitation period

31.21   Whatever the period may be, the basic rule is that it starts on the day when the plaintiff's cause of action accrues. In contract cases, this is almost invariably the date of the defendant's breach, and the same is true of those torts which are actionable per se. On the other hand, where proof of damage forms part of the tort itself, as in cases of negligence or nuisance, the cause of action does not arise until the damage occurs and, accordingly, time does not start to run until that date. It is apparent, therefore, that it may sometimes be to a plaintiff's advantage to be able to sue in tort rather than in contract, and this is what gives such importance to those recent decisions which have held professional men liable to their clients in the tort of negligence as well as for breach of contract.[1] However, the advantage of a tort action is not always as marked as might be supposed. For example, where a solicitor gives negligent advice to a client, as a result of which the client executes an imprudent mortgage of her property, it has been held that the damage is suffered as soon as the mortgage is executed and not just when the property is later seized by the mortgagee.[2]

A particular problem may arise in cases where injury or damage is not discovered (or, indeed, discoverable) by the plaintiff until some considerable time after it first occurs. It was recognised by the House of Lords in *Cartledge v E Jopling & Sons Ltd*,[3] a case concerning a lung disease contracted over a long period of time by workers in a particular industry, that a man's right of action might well be barred by time before he could possibly know that it existed, but this potentially harsh rule has been alleviated by statute, at least where personal injuries are concerned. The Limitation Act 1980 provides that the three-year period in such cases shall not begin until the plaintiff has knowledge of a number of material facts, of which the most important are the significance of his injury (that is, that it is serious enough to justify taking legal action) and its attributability to the defendant.

The problem of hidden damage is not confined to personal injury cases; negligence in building houses (eg where the foundations are inadequate) is another obvious example. Prior to 1983, there was some authority for the view that time did not begin to run against a plaintiff in such a case until damage became reasonably discoverable.[4] However, in *Pirelli General Cable Works Ltd v Oscar Faber & Partners*,[5] the House of Lords laid down that the correct starting-point is when the damage actually *occurs*, whether or not it is then visible. Indeed, it was said obiter that, if the building can be shown to have been 'doomed from the start',[6] then time for the purpose of the Limitation Act would run from an even earlier moment, namely, that at which the building is completed. The law which governs limitation of actions in 'negligent building' cases is generally regarded as unsatisfactory, and a Bill to amend it is currently before Parliament.

'Continuing' torts, such as certain kinds of trespass[7] or nuisance, give rise to a fresh right of action every day until they are abated. One consequence of this is that a plaintiff is entitled to sue for everything which has occurred during the past six years, even if the tort was first committed outside that period or, indeed, before he acquired the property in question.[8]

1 Para 19.16 above. Note however, the doubts expressed by the Privy Council in *Tai Hing Cotton Mill Ltd v Liu Chong Hing Bank Ltd* [1985] 2 All ER 947 at 957, PC, para 18.5 above.
2 *Forster v Outred & Co* (1982) 2 All ER 753, [1982] 1 WLR 86, CA. See also *Baker v Ollard & Bentley* (1982) 126 SJ 593, CA. Cf *Mathew v Maughold Life Assurance Co Ltd* (1985) Times, 23 January.
3 [1963] AC 758, [1963] 1 All ER 341, HL.
4 *Sparham-Souter v Town and Country Developments (Essex) Ltd* [1976] QB 858, [1976] 2 All ER 65, CA.
5 [1983] 2 AC 1, [1983] 1 All ER 65, HL.
6 Which will seldom if ever be the case: see *Dove v Banhams Patent Locks Ltd* [1983] 2 All ER 833, [1983] 1 WLR 1436.
7 Para 25.7 above.
8 See *Masters v Brent London Borough Council* [1978] QB 841, [1978] 2 All ER 664.

Extension of time

31.22 It is provided by the Limitation Act 1980 that in certain circumstances the limitation period may either begin to run from a later date than normal or may simply be extended.

a. Where there is fraud, concealment or mistake,[1] the limitation period does not begin to run until this has been or ought to have been discovered by the plaintiff. The question of 'concealment' has arisen in a number of cases where defects in a building which are due to negligence by the builder have been covered up in the course of the construction work and have not come to light until many years later. It has been held that the mere fact that a builder continues with his work after something shoddy or inadequate has been done does not necessarily amount to 'concealment' for this purpose.[2] The question is whether in all the circumstances it was unconscionable for the builder to proceed with the work so as to cover up the defect.[3]

b. Where the plaintiff is a minor or is mentally ill, the limitation period does not begin to run until the removal of his disability or his death, whichever event occurs first.[4] This provision has been held to apply where the plaintiff's unsoundness of mind is caused by the accident in respect of which he sues.[5]

c. A sweeping change in the law governing limitation of actions was introduced by the Limitation Act 1980, s33. This provision, which applies to all actions brought in respect of personal injuries, empowers the court simply to override the normal three-year period if it appears equitable to do so. In deciding how to exercise its discretion in this way, the court is instructed to have regard to all the circumstances of the case, and in particular to the extent to which each party would be prejudiced by an adverse decision, to the conduct of each party since the accident, and to the length and reasons for the delay.[6]

1 Para 11.36 above.
2 *William Hill Organisation Ltd v Bernard Sunley & Sons Ltd* (1983) 22 BLR 8, CA.
3 *Applegate v Moss* [1971] 1 QB 406, [1971] 1 All ER 747, CA.
4 Para 11.35 above.
5 *Kirby v Leather* [1965] 2 QB 367, [1965] 2 All ER 441, CA.
6 See *Thompson v Brown Construction (Ebbw Vale) Ltd* [1981] 2 All ER 296, [1981] 1 WLR 744, HL.

Theft
31.23 Special provisions apply to the tort of conversion, where this takes the form of theft. As far as the thief and anyone who derives title from him are concerned (except a purchaser in good faith), time does not run at all.[1] Hence, on discovering his goods at any time, the true owner may take action to recover them or their value. In favour of a purchaser of the stolen goods in good faith, the six-year period begins to run on the date of purchase, since this is when he commits conversion.

1 Limitation Act 1980, s4.

Injunctions
31.24 Injunctions are equitable remedies and their award, therefore, is not subject to the provisions of the Limitation Act. However, equity has its own rules concerning delay, and these we discussed in para 11.40 above.

Part IV
Land law

Chapter 32
Land and its ownership

32.1 The study of land law is the study of the law relating to the rights and interests (ie 'bundles of rights') which people may have in respect of land. It deals with the nature of these rights and interests and with how they are created, transferred to other people and enforced against them. Those who are students of valuation may be conversant with the idea that when we speak of land being bought, sold or valued, we are not strictly referring to the physical entity itself, but rather to abstract interests which people may have in the property. We would stress, however, that although land law can be viewed as essentially concerned with abstract rights and interests, its practical context of houses and flats, offices and shops, factories and farms should be borne in mind when studying its rules.

32.2 For the purposes of exposition, we may broadly divide interests in land into those in respect of one's own land and those in respect of another's. The former category we shall call 'ownership interests'; it may be divided into that which in effect gives absolute ownership of the land,[1] popularly referred to as the freehold interest, and those which give rise to a more limited ownership, of which the main example is the leasehold interest. The two main ownership interests, then, are the freehold and the leasehold, though other forms exist, such as the life interest. These ownership interests may be enjoyed exclusively or concurrently with other owners.[2]

As well as these ownership interests, a person may have interests in respect of another's land, such as a private right of way over neighbouring land (a species of easement[3]), a right to prevent the neighbour building on his land (an example of a restrictive covenant[4]), or a mortgage on land granted as security for a loan to its owner.[5]

---

1 For the notion that, as between rival claimants, ownership is not absolute but relative, see para 42.1 below.
2 Ch 36 below.
3 Ch 40 below.
4 Ch 39 below.
5 Ch 41 below.

32.3 What makes land law a subject of some complexity, and what makes buying and selling interests in land potentially more complicated than buying and selling a car, is that it is possible for a number of these interests to exist simultaneously in respect of one piece of land. For example, A may have a life interest in the property, B may have the right to enjoy the freehold on A's death (a right of future enjoyment having a present market value,[1] and C may have a 21-year lease of the property. Meanwhile X, a neighbour, may have the benefit of a covenant restricting development on the property; Y may have a private right of way across it, and Z may have a mortgage on C's leasehold interest. Before further considering these rights and interests, we briefly consider what exactly the law regards as being land.

1   Paras 35.6 to 35.8 below.

What is land?
32.4   Land, the thing in respect of which all these rights and interests can be enjoyed, includes more than just the surface of the earth.[1] According to the case of *Mitchell v Moseley*,[2] 'the grant of land includes the surface and all that is [above]—houses, trees and the like— ... and all that is [below], ie mines, earth, clay, etc'. On this basis, in *Grigsby v Melville*,[3] where the conveyance to the plaintiff of his semi-detached house was of 'all that dwelling-house and premises situate on the west side of Church Hill', it was held that the plaintiff acquired ownership of the cellar beneath his house, even though it could not be reached from the house but only from the adjoining property. He became owner of all the land above and below the surface.[4] In law, land includes physical things such as fixtures and things growing naturally on the land (which we consider in the following paragraphs): it also includes certain 'incorporeal' rights, such as easements.[5]

1   See Law of Property Act 1925, s205.
2   [1914] 1 Ch 438, CA.
3   [1973] 3 All ER 455, [1974] 1 WLR 80, CA.
4   See paras 32.9–32.10 and paras 43.36–43.43 below.
5   Law of Property Act 1925, s205.

Fixtures
32.5   It is sometimes said that whatever is attached to the land becomes part of the land, but the law is not as straightforward as this. Whether or not something which is attached to the land becomes part of the land depends on all the circumstances, two of which are particularly important: the degree of annexation and the purpose of annexation[1] (or, in other words, how securely the thing is attached to the land and the reasons behind its being attached). The law appears to be that if something is fixed to the land it is presumed to be land, and the more firmly it is fixed the stronger this presumption becomes. However, this presumption may be rebutted by evidence that it was not the intention behind fixing the thing to the land that it should become a permanent part of the land. For example, a poster pinned to the wall of a student's room would not be intended to become a permanent part of the land, and would not be a 'fixture'. If a chattel is resting on land by its own weight it is presumed to retain its character as a chattel and not to become part of the land, although this may be rebutted by evidence of intention. Thus, to take an example given in *Holland v Hodgson*,[2] a pile of stones stacked up in a builder's yard would not be part of the land, but the same stones forming a dry stone wall would.

1   *Holland v Hodgson* (1872) LR 7 CP 328.
2   (1872) LR 7 CP 328.

32.6 Further illustrations of whether a chattel fixed to the land has nonetheless retained its chattel nature or has become a fixture, ie a part of the land, are provided by the following cases. *Leigh v Taylor*[1] concerned tapestries which were put on the walls of a house by being fixed to a framework of wood and canvas which was nailed to the walls, each tapestry then being surrounded by a moulding, itself attached to the wall. The House of Lords held that the tapestries did not become part of the land and thus pass with it as fixtures, but remained chattels, since the reason they were fixed to the wall was so that they might be better enjoyed as chattels. In contrast, in *Reynolds v Ashby & Son*,[2] the House of Lords held that machines which were let into concrete beds in the floor of a factory and fixed by nuts and bolts, but which could be removed without difficulty, became fixtures, since the purpose of annexation was to complete and use the building as a factory.

1 [1902] AC 157, HL.
2 [1904] AC 466, HL.

Things growing on the land

32.7 Things which grow naturally on the land (such as grass) and plants and trees which, though they may need attention when first planted, do not need attention each year to produce a crop, such as apple trees, are known as *fructus naturales* and are regarded as part of the land. On the other hand, cultivated crops, such as wheat and potatoes, which are known as *fructus industriales*, are not regarded as part of the land.

Importance of definition of land

32.8 It is important to know whether something attached to, or growing on, land is regarded as being part of the land for the following reasons:

a. A conveyance of land operates to pass to the purchaser all the vendor's land, including fixtures and *fructus naturales*, unless excluded by the contract for sale.[1]

b. The terms of a contract for the sale of land, but not of one for the sale of goods, must be evidenced in writing.[2]

c. Where land is mortgaged, the security includes all fixtures (unless specifically excluded) and *fructus naturales*.

d. Fixtures added by a tenant under a lease become part of the land and are therefore regarded as belonging to the freeholder, who has absolute ownership of the land. The effect of this last rule is modified, however, in that a tenant is permitted to remove any domestic fixtures that he has attached and which can be removed without substantial damage to the fabric of the building, any fixtures which he has attached for the purposes of his business, and, under the Agricultural Holdings Act 1948, agricultural fixtures. In this last case, the Act provides that fixtures which the tenant has a right to remove remain his property and do not belong to the landlord.

1 Law of Property Act 1925 (LPA), s62.
2 LPA, s40(1); paras 43.11 to 43.17 below.

The physical extent of a landowner's rights

32.9 We saw in para 32.4 above, that, according to *Mitchell v Moseley*,[1] land includes not only the surface but also what is above and what is below the surface. Prima facie, the rights of a landowner extend over all the land as so defined. This is expressed in the Latin maxim, *cuius est solum, eius est usque ad coelum et ad inferos*, which may be translated as 'he who owns the surface also owns indefinitely upwards and downwards from the surface'. This maxim must not be regarded as containing the legal definition of land but rather as being a somewhat imprecise expression of the rights of a freeholder[2] or, subject to certain exceptions, any other landowner. Nor should it be taken to preclude an owner from expressly splitting up his land by means of horizontal boundaries, as may occur on the sale of flats or mineral rights. However, the maxim at least makes it clear that the rights of a landowner normally extend above and below the surface; but it is clearly fanciful to treat it as meaning that the landowner's rights extend upwards to the heavens and downwards to the centre of the earth, a notion which would lead to the absurdity of a trespass at common law being committed every time a satellite passes over a suburban garden.[3] On the other hand, the limits which may realistically be put on the height and depth to which the landowner's rights extend are not easy to determine.

1 [1914] 1 Ch 438, CA.
2 Paras 32.14 and 32.15 below; *Railways Commissioner v Valuer-General* [1974] AC 328, [1973] 3 All ER 268, PC.
3 *Bernstein v Skyviews and General Ltd* [1977] 2 All ER 902 at 907.

Limitations on the extent of the owner's rights

32.10 Certain limitations on the extent to which the *cuius est solum* maxim can be taken literally as a statement of the physical extent of the rights of a landowner will be dealt with briefly here.

a. *Airspace* We have suggested in para 25.2 above, that, following *Bernstein v Skyviews and General Ltd*,[1] the rights of a landowner as regards the airspace above the surface of his land are restricted to such a height as is necessary for the ordinary use and enjoyment of the land and the structures on it. However, this begs the question of how high that is in any particular case. This means that whether or not a trespass to airspace has been committed in any particular instance depends on the facts of each case.

b. *Minerals* The conventional view is that the landowner's rights do indeed extend to the earth's core, and as mining techniques improve this may not be so fanciful. It certainly constitutes a trespass to tunnel into adjoining land to exploit minerals.[2] Although the general rule is that the landowner is entitled to the minerals under his land, there are exceptions, of which the following are examples. All gold and silver in gold and silver mines belong to the Crown; therefore such a mine cannot be worked by an individual even on his own land without a licence from the Crown.[3] Oil and natural gas in underground strata belong to the Crown.[4] Coal is vested in the National Coal Board.[5]

c. *Things found on or under the land* In the absence of evidence as to the true owner, the law presumes that the landowner, if he is in possession of the land, is entitled as against the finder to

i things fixed or buried in the land; and

ii things on the land *where he manifests an intention to exercise control over the property and the things in it.*[6]

However, treasure trove, that is gold or silver, in the form of coins, or plate or bullion, which has been deliberately hidden rather than casually lost or abandoned, and of which the true owner is unknown, belongs to the Crown.[7]

d. *Wild animals* Animals which live wild on one's land cannot be owned but, once killed on the land, they become the property of the landowner,[8] whether killed by the landowner in the exercise of his common law,[9] if not moral, right to kill and take wild animals found on his land, or by a trespasser such as a poacher.[10]

e. *Water* Water standing on the land in a pond or lake is part of the land and belongs to the landowner. Water percolating in undefined channels or flowing in defined channels through or past his land cannot be the subject of ownership but, although the landowner does not own the water, he has certain rights in relation to it. The most important of these is the right of abstraction. The Water Resources Act 1963 lays down the general rule that the landowner may only abstract water from a 'source of supply' in pursuance of a licence obtained from the local water authority. Rivers, streams and water in underground strata all constitute 'sources of supply', as do those lakes, ponds or reservoirs which discharge into rivers or streams. However, a licence is not required:

i for the abstraction of a quantity of water not exceeding 1,000 gallons if it does not form part of a continuous operation, or of a series of operations, whereby in the aggregate more than 1,000 gallons of water are abstracted;[11]

ii where water is abstracted in the course of land drainage, or where it is necessary to prevent interference with mining, engineering or building operations;

iii in the case of underground strata, for the abstraction of water for the domestic supply of the landowner's household;

iv in the case of rivers and streams and other inland water, for the abstraction by the owner of contiguous land of water for the domestic and agricultural purposes of that land. However, spray irrigation requires a licence.

Where no water authority licence is required, a landowner is quite at liberty to abstract water percolating in undefined channels through underground strata, to the full extent of his needs, even if this prevents any reaching his neighbour's land. Should the neighbour suffer damage as a result, he has no remedy.[12]

Where the owner of land contiguous with a river or stream (the riparian owner) needs no water authority licence for his proposed abstraction, he is nonetheless limited in what he may take by the common law. He is free to abstract what he needs for his domestic purposes and for his cattle without regard to the effect which his use will have on landowners downstream,[13] but abstraction for other purposes (which must be connected with the land) is subject to the requirement that the water is put back in substantially the same volume and quality. The reason for this limitation is that at common law each riparian owner has the right to the flow of the river or stream unaltered in quantity and quality, and may enforce this right against owners upstream by an action in nuisance.[14] If water is abstracted in pursuance of a water authority licence, the riparian owner has a defence to such an action.[15]

The riparian owner also has the right to fish in non-tidal waters, even where they are navigable rivers.[16]

1   [1977] 2 All ER 902.
2   See *Bulli Mining Co v Osborne* [1899] AC 351, PC.
3   *A-G v Morgan* [1891] 1 Ch 432, CA.
4   Petroleum (Production) Act 1934.
5   Coal Act 1938; Coal Industry (Nationalisation) Act 1946.
6   Para 29.9 above.
7   *A-G of Duchy of Lancaster v G E Overton (Farms) Ltd* [1982] Ch 277, CA.
8   *R v Townley* (1871) LR 1 CCR 315.
9   Statute makes it an offence to kill certain wild animals: see, for example, Wildlife and Countryside Act 1981, s9.
10 *Blades v Higgs* (1865) 11 HL Cas 621, HL.
11 See *Cargill v Gotts* [1981] 1 All ER 682 at 686.
12 *Bradford Corpn v Pickles* [1895] AC 587, HL; para 18.9 above; *Langbrook Properties Ltd v Surrey County Council* [1969] 3 All ER 1424, [1970] 1 WLR 161; para 19.32 above.
13 *Miner v Gilmour* (1858) 12 Moo PCC 131.
14 *John Young & Co v Bankier Distillery Co* [1893] AC 691, HL; *Tate & Lyle Industries Ltd v Greater London Council* [1983] 2 AC 509, [1983] 1 All ER 1159, HL.
15 Water Resources Act, s31.
16 *Cooper v Phibbs* (1867) LR 2 HL 149, HL; *Pearce v Scotcher* (1882) 9 QBD 162, DC.

Estates and tenure

32.11   Having considered the legal nature of land and the physical extent of a landowner's rights, we now return to the nature of what we have called ownership interests in land. Ownership of land can be split up into interests of different durations, a notion expressed in English law by the doctrine of *estates*. Thus, rather than speak of owning land in perpetuity or for life, we speak of owning a particular *estate*[1] in the land. Furthermore, to be more accurate, we should speak not of *owning* land for a particular estate but of *holding* land for a particular estate. The reason for this is that, as a matter of legal theory—and it has almost no practical significance—all land is regarded as being 'owned' by the Crown, individual subjects of the Crown merely 'holding' particular estates from the Crown. This is the doctrine of *tenure*. We shall now briefly consider these two historical building blocks of English land law, the doctrine of tenure and the doctrine of estates.

1   The term is *not* here used in the same sense as in 'estate management'.

Tenure

32.12   Feudalism, in which tenure (from the Latin, *tenere*, to hold) was the basic element, formed the basis of society after the Norman Conquest. The social structure was based on grants of land by the king (to whom all land was regarded as belonging as the spoils of victory) to his followers, not as theirs to own, but to 'hold of' him (or 'have possession of' from him) as their superior lord in return for their performing certain services, such as furnishing the king with armed horsemen or with provisions. These 'tenants-in-chief' in their turn granted land to other 'tenants' to hold of them as superior lords in return for services, and so on. Each tenant, then, held land in return for providing services to his lord. The theoretical possibility of creating an ever-increasing tenurial chain, with every grant of land involving the grantor and grantee in a tenurial relationship, was eventually cut short by the Statute *Quia Emptores* 1290. This statute, which is still law, had the effect that on every grant of freehold land, the grantee would step into the grantor's position on the feudal ladder and would not hold the land as tenant of the grantor as superior lord. *Quia Emptores* marked the beginning of the contraction of the tenurial system. Succeeding centuries saw a gradual decline in the practical significance of the system of tenure, with the benefits and obligations of tenure gradually disappearing, so that all that remains today is the legal theory that land is not owned outright but held of the Crown.

Estates

32.13 Although we referred in the last paragraph to the tenant holding land, it is more accurate to speak of the tenant holding an *estate* in land, ie holding an interest of a particular duration in the land. The two most important estates are what are popularly referred to as the freehold and the leasehold. Historically, the law recognised other estates, in particular the fee tail and the life estate. The social importance of these has declined considerably over the years, and a change in the legal machinery for giving effect to them means that we shall postpone our discussion of them until ch 35, concentrating in succeeding paragraphs on the freehold and the leasehold.

Freehold: the fee simple absolute in possession

32.14 The technical legal term for the freehold is the estate in fee simple absolute in possession.[1] The significance of this term is as follows. 'Fee' denoted, *historically*, an estate of inheritance, that is, an estate which, prior to the reforming property legislation of 1925, passed on the death of the current owner to his heir. This type of fee was described as a fee 'simple' to distinguish it from the other variety of inheritable fee, the fee tail,[2] under which the class of persons who *might* inherit was cut down to include only the direct lineal descendants of the person originally granted the land (or that person and a particular spouse). The aim of the fee tail was to ensure that land was kept in the family. The term 'absolute' distinguishes this type of fee simple from the, rarely encountered, conditional and determinable fees simple, which we discuss in ch 35. The words 'in possession' mean that the landowner must either be physically in possession of the land or in receipt of the rents and profits of the land,[2] and they distinguish a *present* ownership interest from future enjoyment of the land, a topic which we reserve until ch 35.

1 LPA, s1.
2 Para 35.4 below.
3 Or have the right to physical possession or the income of the land, LPA, s205(1).

The characteristics of the fee simple absolute in possession

32.15 A tenant in fee simple absolute in possession is, in law, equivalent to an absolute owner. He has complete freedom of 'alienation' during his lifetime or under his will; in other words, he can transfer ownership of his property as he wishes. He can carve lesser interests, which we earlier referred to as limited ownership interests, out of his freehold, and can grant rights over it to others.

Leasehold: the term of years absolute

32.16 The leasehold interest is the second of the two estates recognised at law. The nomenclature used in the LPA, s1 for the leasehold interest is 'the term of years absolute'. This phrase need not detain us; it can be regarded as having no meaning other than to denote a leasehold interest. A person has a leasehold interest in land where another, the landlord or lessor, grants him exclusive possession of property, as tenant or lessee, for a definite or certain period[1] or for a period which, subject to statute,[2] can be rendered certain. The leasehold interest acquired by the tenant or lessee is known variously as a 'tenancy'—generally where it is of short duration, as in weekly, monthly or yearly tenancies—or as a 'lease', 'term of years' or 'term certain'—generally where it is of longer, fixed, duration, perhaps of 21 or 99 years. Having granted, or 'let' or 'leased' or 'demised' the property, the lessor is said, somewhat inaccurately, to retain the 'reversion' on the lease,[3] on the basis that physical possession of the land will revert to him on the ending of the lease. In the eyes of the law, of course, he is still regarded as being in possession in that he is in receipt of the rents and profits of the land.[4]

1 The term may be discontinuous, as where a holiday home is let on a 'time-share' basis for one week per year for 80 years: *Cottage Holiday Associates Ltd v Customs and Excise Comrs* [1983] QB 735.
2 Paras 37.24 to 37.28 below.
3 See also para 35.8 below.
4 LPA, s205(1) (xix); paras 32.14 above and 35.6 below.

Characteristics of Leasehold Interests

Exclusive possession

32.17 For a person to be regarded as having a leasehold interest in property, it is essential that he should have exclusive possession of it. That is, he must have the right to exclude all others from the property, even the landlord himself. It is a fundamental principle that the landlord may only enter the property in pursuance either of an agreement with the tenant or of a right of entry[1] accorded to him by the lease. Without exclusive possession there can be no lease, only a licence. The latter confers only a personal permission to occupy property but does not give the occupier a stake in the property.[2] We consider the lease/licence distinction further at para 38.3 below.

1 Paras 37.15 and 37.22 below.
2 *Marchant v Charters* [1977] 3 All ER 918, [1977] WLR 1181, CA.

Duration certain, or capable of being made so

32.18 The requirement that the maximum duration of a lease must be ascertained at the outset is reflected in the phrase sometimes applied to long leases, namely, 'term certain'. A term cannot be certain if, for example, it is expressed to last for the duration of the war. A purported lease to that effect was thus declared to be void by the Court of Appeal in *Lace v*

Chantler.[1] The desired object could have been achieved, it may be noted, had the parties expressed the lease to be for, say, 99 years determinable on the ending of the war.

Periodic tenancies—for example, weekly, monthly or yearly tenancies—do not determine (end) automatically at the end of the period, be it week or month or year, but continue from week to week, month to month, year to year, until ended by appropriate notice.[2] Thus, in one sense, at the outset of the tenancy its maximum duration is unknown. It follows that the simple statement that the maximum duration of a term must be certainly known in advance of its taking effect does not directly apply to periodic tenancies.[3] Furthermore, it is open to the parties to such a tenancy to prevent one side determining the tenancy for an uncertain period.[3] However, a provision purporting to prohibit absolutely the giving of notice by one party is repugnant to the nature of the tenancy and therefore invalid.[4]

1 [1944] KB 368, [1944] 1 All ER 305, CA.
2 Paras 32.27 and 32.28 below, and note, in particular, para 37.25, as to statutory regulation of the termination of residential tenancies.
3 *Re Midland Rly Co's Agreement* [1971] Ch 725 at 732, [1971] 1 All ER 1007.
4 *Centaploy Ltd v Matlodge Ltd* [1974] Ch 1, [1973] 2 All ER 720.

32.19 *Leases for life* Prior to 1926, it was possible to create a lease for life, despite the fact that such a term is far from certain. As a result of the LPA, s149(6), an attempt to create such a lease now results in the grant of a 90-year term which may be ended after the death of the lessee by one month's notice in writing given on one of the usual quarter days (25 March, 24 June, 29 September, and 25 December) either by the lessor or by the person in whom the leasehold interest has vested. This same rule is made to apply to leases determinable on the marriage of the lessee.

32.20 *Perpetually renewable leases* Again, prior to 1926, it was permissible to grant a lease conferring on the lessee the right to have the lease renewed on the expiry of the existing term over and over again. Such leases were, by the Law of Property Act 1922, s145 and Sch 15 converted into terms of 2,000 years commencing with the beginning of the then existing term. Any perpetually renewable lease granted since 1926 is likewise to take effect as a 2,000 year term. The term created by the statute is subject, in addition to the terms of the original lease, to the provision that the lessee may terminate the lease on ten days' notice ending on a date on which it would have expired had it not been converted; to the requirement that every transfer of the lease must be registered with the landlord, and to the provision that, if the lease is assigned, the lessee will not be liable for breaches of covenant committed thereafter.[1] It is, of course, highly unlikely that a lessor would today expressly create a perpetually renewable lease. However, such a lease may be created inadvertently, as is demonstrated by *Caerphilly Concrete Products Ltd v Owen*,[2] where a lessor granted a lease, for a term of five years at a rent of £10 per annum, containing a covenant to renew the lease at the same rent and subject to the same covenants, including the covenant to renew, with the result that the lease was perpetually renewable; the lessor had accidentally created a 2,000-year term at a rent of £10 per annum.

As to provisions for the renewal of leases generally, it is provided that the parties may not agree to renew a lease for a period longer than 60 years after the expiry of the original term.[3]

1　See para 39.4 below.
2　[1972] 1 All ER 248, [1972] 1 WLR 372, CA.
3　LPA 1922, Sch 15.

32.21 *Reversionary leases* A person may not create, or make a contract to create, a lease which is to take effect in possession more than 21 years after the date of the lease.[1] A lease which is intended to take effect at some time after the date of the lease is called a reversionary lease.

1　LPA, s149(3).

Created in proper form
32.22 We reserve discussion of how leases are created until paras 33.3 to 33.9 below.

Particular types of tenancy
32.23 We first consider two anomalous tenancies, the tenancy at will and the tenancy at sufferance.

Tenancy at will
32.24 A tenancy at will occurs where a person is let into possession of property as a tenant by the landlord on the basis that either side may terminate the arrangement whenever he wishes. It may arise where a purchaser of property is permitted to occupy the property prior to completion of the transaction or, subject to statute,[1] where a lessee under a fixed term lease is allowed to remain on the expiry of the term while the parties discuss the granting of a new term. Consequently, it has been suggested by Scarman LJ in *Heslop v Burns*,[2] that it may be that the tenancy at will can now serve only one legal purpose, and that is to provide for occupation of property during a period of transition. It will be noted that a tenancy at will does not satisfy the requirement of certainty of duration. It has thus been suggested that a tenancy at will does not constitute an estate in land at all but is merely a relationship of tenure,[3] which can be terminated forthwith by notifying the other party. Although a tenancy at will normally arises by implication, such a tenancy may be expressly granted, as in *Manfield & Sons Ltd v Botchin*[4] where such a tenancy was granted pending the landlord's application for planning permission to develop the site. A tenancy at will may also provide for the payment of rent by the tenant, even though, as we point out in para 32.27 below, the payment of rent might otherwise give rise to the implication of a periodic tenancy. If no provision is made for rent to be paid, the landlord is entitled to compensation for the use and occupation of the property.

1　Paras 37.25 to 37.28 below.
2　[1974] 3 All ER 406 at 416.
3　Paras 32.11 to 32.12 above.
4　[1970] 2 QB 612, [1970] 3 All ER 143.

Tenancy at sufferance
32.25 A tenant at sufferance is, at common law, someone who wrongfully remains in possession ('holds over') without the landlord's consent after his tenancy has come to an end. Such a person is in effect a trespasser. The landlord may at any time claim possession of the property. The tenant at sufferance is essentially in the position of a 'squatter',[1] though liable under

statute[2] to pay either a payment calculated at double the rental value of the property or, in certain circumstances, double the rent which he paid under the lease, for holding over in the face of a notice to quit.

1 Ch 42 below.
2 Landlord and Tenant Act 1730; Distress for Rent Act 1737.

Periodic tenancies

32.26 *By implication* A person in occupation of property, perhaps by virtue of holding over after the expiry of a previous tenancy, may, if he pays rent which is accepted by the landlord, be held to acquire by implication a periodic tenancy. The period of the tenancy is the period according to which the rent is calculated. Thus if the rent is fixed at £1,000 per annum, a yearly tenancy arises even if the rent is paid at more frequent intervals; if rent is fixed at £20 per week, a weekly tenancy arises.[1] As the case of *Manfield & Sons Ltd v Botchin*[2] shows, there is no room for the implication of a periodic tenancy where the parties expressly provide that the tenancy should remain at will. Furthermore, recent cases have shown that, in a case where a tenant holds over on the determination of a previous tenancy, although a common and reasonable inference from the acceptance of rent would normally be that a periodic tenancy has been created, in these days of statutory controls over the landlord's right to possession (for example under the Rent Act 1977[3]) such an inference will not so readily be drawn as in the past it would have been. All the circumstances, particularly the background of statutory control, must be taken into account.[4]

1 See *Ladies' Hosiery and Underwear Ltd v Parker* [1930] 1 Ch 304.
2 Para 32.24 above.
3 Para 37.25 below.
4 *Harvey v Stagg* (1977) 247 Estates Gazette 463, CA; *Longrigg, Burrough and Trounson v Smith* (1979) 251 Estates Gazette 847,CA.

32.27 *Yearly tenancy* A yearly tenancy may be created either expressly or by implication arising from the payment and acceptance of rent, as described in para 32.26 above. Where a yearly tenancy is held to arise by implication in a case where the tenant has held over on the ending of a previous lease, the terms of that lease will apply to the yearly tenancy, so far as consistent therewith.[1] At a common law, in the absence of contrary agreement, a yearly tenancy is terminable by either side giving half a year's notice expiring at the end of a year of the tenancy. Notice once given cannot be withdrawn, though the parties may enter into some new agreement. If not terminated by notice, the tenancy continues from year to year.[2]

1 See *Godfrey Thornfield Ltd v Bingham* [1946] 2 All ER 485.
2 See also paras 37.24 to 37.28 below, for statutory modifications.

32.28 *Other periodic tenancies* Again such tenancies, weekly, monthly, quarterly, etc., may be created expressly or arise by implication from the payment and acceptance of rent. Unless terminated by notice they run from week to week, month to month, etc. A full week's, or month's, or quarter's, notice is required to end the tenancy at common law.[1]

1 But see, in particular, para 37.25 below, for the Protection from Eviction Act 1977 and the Rent Act 1977.

496

Tenancy by estoppel

32.29 Where a person who has no power to do so purports to grant a lease or tenancy, he and his 'tenant' are estopped[1] from denying the validity of the 'lease'; neither can deny its validity. Thus as between the parties, a tenancy by estoppel has all the features of a valid tenancy; it will similarly bind assigns of the parties but will not bind third parties. A tenancy by estoppel could arise where a purchaser of land is allowed into possession prior to completion of the transaction and then purports to grant a lease, or where a mortgagor (borrower) purports to grant a lease in excess of the powers conferred on him by statute and the mortgage deed.[2] In the former case, the subsequent acquisition of the freehold estate by the purchaser is said to 'feed the estoppel' and confers on the tenant a valid tenancy.

1   Para 6.15, n2 above.
2   Para 41.37 below.

Bringing leases to an end

32.30   A leasehold interest may terminate in the following ways:

a. *by forfeiture,* which we consider in paras 37.15 to 37.18 and 37.22 below;

b. *by surrender,* which occurs where the tenant's interest is 'swallowed up' by his immediate landlord's reversion and is thus extinguished. Surrender of a leasehold interest may be effected expressly by deed, or by implication—as where the tenant gives up possession and the landlord accepts this as surrender, or where the tenant accepts a new lease from the landlord during the currency of the existing tenancy;

c. *by merger,* which occurs where either the landlord's and the tenant's interests are acquired by a third party in the same capacity, or where the tenant acquires the landlord's reversion;

d. *by expiry.* At common law a lease for a fixed term of years comes to an end when that term expires. The common law position is, however, much affected by statute;

e. *by notice.* We discussed the termination of periodic tenancies by notice in paras 32.27 and 32.28 above. A lease for a fixed term may not be determined by notice unless there is an express provision to that effect. The termination of leases by notice is also considerably affected by statute.

f. *by enlargement.* The LPA, s153 provides that where a lease has been granted for a term of not less than 300 years, of which not less than 200 years are left unexpired, and either no rent or no rent having any money value is payable, the term of years may be enlarged into a fee simple (freehold) by the tenant executing a deed to that effect. Such a combination of circumstances is no doubt unlikely.

In addition, a lease can be terminated by frustration, a matter discussed in para 10.9 above.

We consider how the common law concerning termination of leases has been altered by statute in paras 37.24 to 37.28 below.

Chapter 33

Law and equity

33.1 The Law of Property Act 1925, s1 distinguishes between legal estates and interests on the one hand, and equitable interests on the other. The freehold, or fee simple absolute in possession, and the leasehold, or term of years absolute, are now, by virtue of that section, the only estates that can exist at law. They are the two *legal estates*. Those estates, such as the life estate, which were formerly recognised by the law, today take effect as *equitable interests*.[1] The section also provides that certain rights in respect of another's land can exist at law. The more important of these are easements[2] (rights of way, rights of support and the like) which have been granted for a period equivalent to a fee simple absolute in possession or term of years absolute, and charges by way of legal mortgage,[3] the most common device for mortgaging land. These are referred to as *legal interests*. Those rights over another's land which do not take effect as legal interests are *equitable interests*.

1 Para 35.3 below.
2 Ch 40 below.
3 Para 41.7 below.

What is an equitable interest?
33.2 An equitable interest is an interest derived from the rules of equity (ie those principles of law which originated in the decisions of the former Court of Chancery[1]). In a nutshell, the differences between that which is an equitable interest in land and that which is legal lie in the rules for the creation and for the enforceability of the two types of right. We consider first the rules relating to the *creation* of legal and equitable rights in land.

1 Paras 1.9 and 1.10 above.

Creation of legal and equitable interests
33.3 One way in which we can express the difference between legal estates and interests, on the one hand, and equitable interests, on the other, is by saying that legal estates and interests require formality for their creation, while equitable interests may be created informally. The general rule for legal estates and interests, which is laid down by the LPA, s52(1), is that they must be created and conveyed by means of a deed. A deed is a document which is 'signed, sealed and delivered'. The use of wax seals on

deeds is rare today, a disc of red adhesive paper usually being employed instead, and, apparently, a document purporting to be a deed is capable in law of being such although it has no more than an indication of where the seal should be.[1] Again, the requirement of delivery is misleading, for no actual delivery is necessary, merely some act or words by the maker of the document showing an intent to be bound.[2] Nonetheless, it remains the basic rule that the creation of legal estates and interests requires the formality of a deed.

1 *First National Securities Ltd v Jones* [1978] Ch 109, [1978] 2 All ER 221.
2 *Vincent v Premo Enterprises (Voucher Sales) Ltd* [1969] 2 QB 609, [1969] 2 All ER 941, CA.

33.4 One important exception to this general rule is that leases taking effect in possession[1] for a term not exceeding three years (for example, periodic leases such as yearly or weekly tenancies) may be created orally or in writing so long as they are at the best rent reasonably obtainable and not for a lump sum payment. This is provided for by the LPA, s54(2). Within this exception also falls the creation of a periodic tenancy by implication, arising from going to possession and paying rent which is accepted.[2] Another exception to the general rule relates to the acquisition of a legal estate in the land by virtue of adverse possession of the land for the statutory limitation period, a topic which we consider in ch 42 below.

1 Para 32.14 above.
2 Para 32.27 above.

33.5 The LPA, s53 states the general rule that equitable interests, although not requiring the formality of a deed, must be created or transferred by signed writing. An exception to this is that certain equitable interests may come into existence as a result of the operation of some rule of law.[1] Furthermore, s53 does not affect the doctrine of part performance[2] or the creation of resulting,[3] implied or constructive trusts.[4] An important point to note is that an attempt to create an estate or interest which fails in the eyes of the law because the formality of a deed is not gone through, nonetheless may give rise to an interest in the eyes of equity. We can illustrate this by reference to informal leases, ie leases not created in accordance with the formality required by law.

1 See, for example, para 38.10 below.
2 Para 43.18 below.
3 Para 36.12 below.
4 Para 38.15 below.

Informal leases
33.6 Even if the parties to a lease of more than three years' duration do not comply with the requirement of the LPA, s52(1) that the transaction should be effected by deed, the lack of a seal need not be fatal. For equity regards the transaction as being an agreement to create a lease. If the terms of such an agreement are evidenced in writing, as required by the LPA, s40(1),[1] or if there have been sufficient acts of part performance[2] (as there will be if the tenant went into possession following the agreement), equity will in the normal case grant specific performance of the agreement, requiring that a formal lease be created. In this way, equity can remedy the

failure to create a formal lease. What is the position, however, if neither party goes to court to seek this remedy for their failure to comply with the LPA, s52? (This, of course, would be quite likely since the parties' failure to use a deed may well have arisen from the fact that they did not appreciate that one was necessary.) In this case, 'equity looks on that as done which ought to be done', ie equity regards that which ought to be done as having already been done. What ought to be done in the case of an agreement for a lease is that is should be implemented (as it would be were specific performance granted). Equity therefore regards the situation as if the agreement had been implemented and a lease granted. Therefore, in the eyes of equity, an informal lease (and indeed a 'genuine' agreement to grant a lease) is regarded as a lease. But this lease is a *creature of equity*; it is an equitable lease, which, as we shall see, falls short of a legal lease in some respects.

1 Para 43.11 below.
2 Paras 43.18 and 43.19 below.

33.7 To illustrate the operation of this principle, suppose L grants to T a seven year lease in writing. Such a lease, not falling within the exception to the general rule for legal estates under the LPA, s54(2),[1] should have been made by deed.[2] Suppose further that, the parties not being aware that they have failed to comply with the proper formalities, T goes into possession and pays rent which L accepts. At law, a periodic tenancy arises by implication.[3] Equity, however, regards the matter differently. It treats the informal seven year lease as an agreement to grant a seven year legal lease which can be specifically enforced. However, if specific performance is not sought, equity regards T as having a seven year equitable lease provided that the agreement is specifically enforceable.[4]

1 Para 33.4 above.
2 Para 33.3 above.
3 Para 32.26 above.
4 Para 11.27 above.

33.8 In the case of *Walsh v Lonsdale*,[1] the parties entered into an agreement that Lonsdale would grant Walsh a seven-year lease of a mill. The agreement provided that Walsh was to pay rent annually in advance. The required deed was never drawn up, but Walsh went into possession, paying rent quarterly in arrears. The essential question in this case was whether Lonsdale was entitled to demand the payment of rent annually in advance in accordance with the terms of their agreement or whether Walsh held under a legal periodic tenancy, paying rent in arrears. It was held that Lonsdale could demand the rent in advance, since where the rules of equity and law conflict, equity prevails;[2] therefore the court had to adopt the view of equity that Walsh and Lonsdale were parties to a seven-year equitable lease on the terms of their agreement. Such a decision, although adverse to Walsh on the facts, could be of benefit to a tenant in his position where the landlord seeks to turn him out by notice appropriate to ending a periodic tenancy.[3]

1 (1882) 21 Ch D 9.
2 Supreme Court Act 1981, s49.

3   Paras 32.27 and 32.28 above; but see paras 37.25–37.28 below.

33.9   It has been said that, as a result of the decision in *Walsh v Lonsdale*,[1] an agreement for a lease is as good as a lease. There are however some important differences between a legal lease and an equitable lease. First, equity will only look on the parties to an informal lease or an agreement for a lease as having a lease where it considers that specific performance ought to be granted. Specific performance is a discretionary remedy.[2] So, for example, should the tenant go into possession under the agreement and immediately break one of its terms, equity would refuse him specific performance of the agreement.[3] He would not then have a lease in the eyes of equity, although a legal periodic tenancy might have arisen through the payment and acceptance of rent.

Second, an informal lease, being regarded as a contract to grant a lease, constitutes 'a contract to convey or create a legal estate' which in turn, as we shall see, constitutes a species of equitable interest known as an estate contract. Unlike a legal lease, this must be registered if it is to be enforceable against subsequent purchasers of the legal estate.[4] Since the parties to an informal lease may well have been unaware of the legal requirement for creating a legal lease, they may also be unaware that an equitable lease should be registered as an estate contract. Thus, where the tenant fails to register his estate contract and the landlord subsequently sells the freehold to a third party, the third party will not be bound by the tenant's equitable lease, although he will be bound by any legal periodic tenancy which has arisen by implication, as this does not require registration. However, subject where appropriate to the Rent Act 1977, he can terminate such a tenancy by notice.[5]

Further, informal and formal leases differ in that certain easements which may, by virtue of the LPA, s62 by implied on the grant of a lease may not be implied where there is only an informal lease.[6]

Finally, it is not possible to enforce covenants contained in an informal lease against an assignee of the tenant.[7]

1   (1882) 21 Ch D 9, CA.
2   Para 11.27 above.
3   *Coatsworth v Johnson* (1886) 55 LJQB 220.
4   Where appropriate under the Land Charges Act 1972, para 33.23 below, or as a minor interest under the Land Registration Act 1925, para 34.21 below.
5   This discussion is subject to the caveat that where the title to the freehold is registered under the Land Registration Act 1925, which we discuss in ch 34 below, then, if the tenant is in occupation under the lease, his rights under the equitable lease will bind the purchaser as an overriding interest.
6   Para 40.26 below.
7   Para 39.7 below.

Protection and enforcement of equitable interests

33.10   The second difference between legal and equitable interests is that equitable interests are essentially weaker, needing protection before they can be enforced against third parties. We can begin to understand this difference as regards protection and enforcement by reference to the concept of a 'trust'. The idea which lies behind the trust is that of separating the management of property from the enjoyment of its benefits, such as possession of it and income from it. The device is said to have originated in the practice of those going on Crusades of granting their land to trusted friends to hold for the benefit of their wives and children while they were away, and in the practice of granting land to be held for the benefit of Franciscan friars, who by the rules of their Order, could not themselves hold land. In the eyes of the common law, only those to whom the land was conveyed had rights in respect of it, rights which the common law would enforce against all comers. The Court of Chancery, however, recognised that the persons to whom the land was conveyed (who are now known as trustees) were in conscience bound to observe the trust placed in them. The Chancellor obliged the trustees to deal with the land in accordance with the wishes of the person whom it was intended to benefit (whom we now call the beneficiary), and to permit him to take the income of the land. That the beneficiary had these rights against the trustees effectively meant that the trustees had only the bare legal ownership of the land, whilst the beneficial ownership lay with the beneficiary. However, the beneficiary's rights against the trustees would be of little avail if he could be deprived of the benefits of the land by, for example, the trustees giving the land to someone else. Gradually, the Chancellor came to hold that there were others besides the original trustees who were in conscience bound to give effect to the rights of the beneficiary. The beneficiary's rights came to be enforceable against a trustee's heir, against someone to whom a trustee left the land by will, against someone to whom the trustees gave the land, and against someone who bought the land knowing that the beneficiary was entitled to the benefit of it. As the class of persons against whom the beneficiary could enforce his rights was extended the effect was that his beneficial interest recognised by equity became almost as good as the interest which the trustees held in the land (the legal estate), their rights to which were enforceable against all comers. However, the Court of Chancery stopped short of enforcing the beneficiary's rights against the whole world for, while legal rights were so enforceable, equitable rights were enforceable against the whole world except *a bona fide purchaser of a legal estate for value without notice of the equitable interest*.

In addition to beneficial interests under a trust, equity had, over the years, come to recognise a number of rights in respect of land which were not recognised by the common law; for example the restrictive covenant.[1] The decision in *Pilcher v Rawlins*[2], in 1872, made it clear that the rule that equitable rights were not enforceable against a bona fide purchaser of a legal estate without notice of their existence applied to all equitable interests. Furthermore, it is established by the decision in *Wilkes v Spooner*[3] that, if the legal estate is acquired by a purchaser for value without notice, the equitable interest of which he has no notice is effectively destroyed. It cannot be enforced against a subsequent purchaser who, unlike the bona fide purchaser, knows of the existence of the equitable interest.

1   Ch 39 below.
2   (1872) 7 Ch App 259.
3   [1911] 2 KB 473, CA.

33.11   At the time of *Pilcher v Rawlins*[1] it was entirely correct to state that the difference between a legal interest and an equitable interest in land lay in the fact that the latter cannot be enforced against a purchaser for value of the legal estate without notice. However, such a statement does not entirely accurately reflect the distinction today.

The fact that an equitable interest in land could be lost if the legal estate was acquired for valuable consideration by someone without notice of its existence made it somewhat vulnerable. Furthermore, and conversely, as a purchaser might be deemed to have notice of an equitable interest unless prior to his purchase he made reasonable inquiries and inspections relating to the land,[2] he was at risk of being bound by an undiscovered equitable interest unless he had made proper pre-purchase inquiries. Two solutions were adopted to ease the lot of both parties. In the case of some equitable interests which might loosely be regarded as 'commercial', the concept of registration was introduced. The essence of this is that if the interests are protected by being registered they bind the purchaser, since he is deemed to be fixed with notice of them; if they are not, they do not bind. A purchaser knows that prior to his purchase he must search the register to discover whether any of these interests bind him. This policy was implemented by the Land Charges Act 1925.[3]

The second solution relates to those equitable interests of a 'family' nature, such as successive limited ownership interests under a trust designed to keep land in the family. In the case of this type of equitable interest it was felt unnecessary that they should bind a purchaser at all, and undesirable that the legal estate should in perpetuity be encumbered with a string of successive beneficial interests. Consequently, the solution of 'overreaching' was adopted.[4] 'Overreaching' is the process whereby, on the sale of the land, the successive beneficial interests under the trust cease to bind the land, and are satisfied thenceforth out of the proceeds of sale instead. The proceeds of sale are invested by the trustees, the beneficiaries then being entitled to the income from that investment for the duration of their interests.

It is important to note that these two devices for protecting and enforcing certain equitable interests do not between them cover the whole field of equitable interests, since while some equitable rights depend for their enforcement upon protection by registration under the Land Charges Act and others are protected by the concept of overreaching, a further group still depend for their protection upon the original doctrine of notice, i e they are only enforceable against a purchaser of the legal estate for value if he has notice. Examples of this last group are pre-1926 equitable easements and pre-1926 restrictive covenants, which are specifically excluded from the Land Charges Act.

1 (1872) 7 Ch App 259.
2 Para 33.16 below.
3 Paras 33.20 to 33.30 below.
4 Para 35.25 below.

33.12 Unfortunately, the picture we have painted in the preceding paragraph still represents only part of the story. In 1926, a radically different system of protection and enforcement of all interests in land, legal and equitable, was introduced under the Land Registration Act 1925. The implementation of the scheme of registration of *title* to land under this Act is a very gradual process, though more than half the land in England and Wales is now in a compulsory registration area under the Act. Where that Act applies, quite different rules apply to the creation, transfer and protection of interests in land. We consider the scheme of the Land Registration Act 1925 in the next chapter.

33.13 We now return to the rules relating to the protection of equitable interests where the Land Registration Act does not apply, where, as we have said, equitable interests may be divided into three groups: those protected by notice, those protected by registration under the Land Charges Act, and those protected by overreaching. We deal first with the doctrine of notice and then the Land Charges Act 1972. We postpone further consideration of the concept of overreaching until ch 35, below.

The doctrine of notice

33.14 Legal rights are good against the whole world; equitable rights are good against the whole world except a bona fide purchaser of a legal estate for value without notice. To fall within the exception, a purchaser must have acted bona fide, 'in good faith'; he must have acted honestly, and genuinely be without notice. The word 'purchaser' bears an extended meaning in law encompassing all those who acquire an interest in land other than on intestacy[1] and includes a lessee and a mortgagee. However, the purchaser must acquire the legal estate 'for value', ie for valuable consideration[2] or in consideration of marriage. Thus, where a person acquires the legal estate as a gift he will be bound by any equitable interests, even if he has no notice of them.

The purchaser must acquire a 'legal estate', a concept which for this purpose includes both legal estates and legal interests. Where a purchaser acquires for value an equitable interest, for example where a beneficiary under a trust assigns his equitable interest to another, the latter will be bound by prior equitable interests affecting the equitable interest, such as an equitable mortgage,[3] whether or not he has notice of them. The rule here is that 'where the equities are equal the first in time prevails'.

A purchaser of a legal *or* equitable interest will take free of 'mere equities' of which he has no notice. These are equitable rights falling short of equitable interests but ancillary to or dependent on some interest in land; eg a right to rectification of a conveyance for mistake or to set aside a conveyance on grounds of fraud.[4]

We now turn to the concept of notice itself, of which there are three varieties: actual notice, constructive notice and imputed notice.

1 Ie where a person dies leaving no effective will.
2 See ch 6 above.
3 Para 41.9 below.
4 *National Provincial Bank Ltd v Ainsworth* [1965] AC 1175, [1965] 2 All ER 472, HL; compare *Blacklocks v J B Developments (Godalming) Ltd* [1982] Ch 183, [1981] 3 All ER 392 and *Smith v Jones* [1954] 2 All ER 823, [1954] 1 WLR 1089.

Actual notice

33.15 A purchaser has actual notice of an equitable interest if he knows about it. In addition, registration of those equitable interests required to be registered under the Land Charges Act is deemed to give actual notice to a purchaser.[1]

1 LPA, s199(1)(i).

Constructive notice

33.16 If actual notice were the only type of notice, a purchaser could avoid knowledge of an equitable interest, and thus avoid its binding him, by failing to inspect the land he was buying or by failing to investigate the title to it. However, by LPA, s199(1), a purchaser has constructive notice of an equitable interest if its existence 'would have come to his knowledge if such inquiries and inspections had been made as ought reasonably to have been made'.[1] The onus is thus on the purchaser to make reasonable inquiries and inspections. We shall consider in detail what is required of him in ch 43, below, but some comments will be made at this stage. In unregistered land,[2] conveyancing proceeds by investigating the documentary evidence relating to the vendor's ownership of the land he is selling. The investigation begins with what is termed 'a good root of title',[3] generally a previous conveyance of the land, at least 15 years old,[4] and proceeds by scrutiny of all the documentary links in the chain from that document to the time of sale. In essence, a purchaser who fulfils this requirement, *and* inspects the land, will make 'such inquiries and inspections . . . as ought reasonably to have been made'.

1 LPA, s199(1)(ii)(a).
2 As opposed to land to which the Land Registration Act applies, ch 34 below.
3 Para 43.29 below.
4 LPA, s44(1), as amended by LPA 1969, s23.

33.17 In the case of a purchaser of leasehold property, there are certain restrictions on the extent to which he can investigate the evidence relating to his vendor's ownership of the land. First, he has no right to investigate the title to the freehold. Second, he is otherwise limited in his investigation to seeing only the lease or sub-lease and, where appropriate, the assignment thereof under which his vendor holds.[1] It is possible however for the contract between vendor and purchaser to exclude these restrictions and provide for a fuller investigation of title. If the restrictions are not contracted out of, the purchaser will nonetheless not be affected with notice of any equitable interest which he might have discovered had he contracted for a more thorough investigation of his vendor's title.[2] However, this causes the problem that an equitable property right affecting the freehold and requiring protection by notice, for example a pre-1926 restrictive covenant, might effectively be lost on the grant of a lease out of the freehold since the lessee may not have notice of it.

1 LPA, s44.
2 LPA, s44(5).

33.18 A further aspect of constructive notice is the doctrine of *Hunt v Luck*,[1] whereby a person's occupation of property constitutes constructive notice of his rights in respect of the property. Thus, a purchaser, on inspecting the property, should make inquiries of any person in occupation, other than his vendor, to establish whether that person has any rights in the property. Failure to do so will give him constructive notice of any rights needing protection by notice which the person in occupation may have.[2]

1 [1901] 1 Ch 45; affd [1902] 1 Ch 428, CA.
2 Para 36.17 below.

Imputed notice

33.19 Any notice, actual or constructive, which is acquired or deemed to be acquired by a solicitor or other agent acting for the purchaser in the transaction is imputed to the purchaser.[1]

1 LPA, s199(1)(ii)(b).

The Land Charges Act 1972

33.20 Pending the complete introduction of registration of title under the Land Registration Act 1925, a process requiring many years, some improvements were needed in the unregistered system of conveyancing. Of particular importance was the reduction of the impact of the doctrine of notice, both to enable a purchaser better to discover interests affecting the land and to enable those entitled to those interests to fix the purchaser with notice of their existence. This policy was given effect by the Land Charges Act 1925, now repealed and consolidated by the Land Charges Act 1972.

33.21 The Land Registry, headed by the Chief Land Registrar, as well as operating the system of registration of title under the Land Registration Act 1925, also maintains a Land Charges department operating the Land Charges Act 1972. This department keeps on computer at Plymouth the five registers required to be maintained under the 1972 Act. Of these the most important is the Land Charges Register. However, mention may also be made of the Register of Pending Actions and the Register of Writs and Orders affecting Land. The Register of Pending Actions contains particulars of any court action or proceedings whereby some proprietary right in the land is claimed and also particulars of any bankruptcy petition. The Register of Writs and Orders contains details not only of any court order enforcing a judgment in respect of the land, but also of receiving orders in bankruptcy. The purpose of the registers is clear: an intending purchaser will, on searching them, be warned, for example, that someone has started proceedings to enforce some right in respect of the land, or that a court has made an order relating to it. Furthermore, if he is dealing with someone who is insolvent, he is alerted to the fact.

Land Charges Register

33.22 This register is a register of six classes of charge or obligation affecting land, Classes A to F. Classes A, B and E need not concern us.

33.23 *Class C land charges* The Land Charges Act 1972, s2(4) lists four rights in respect of another's land falling within Class C.

a. *A puisne mortgage (Class C (i))* A puisne (pronounced 'puny') mortgage is a *legal* mortgage not protected by deposit of title deeds, ie the documentary evidence relating to the ownership of the land. This is an exception to the rule that legal rights in unregistered land are good against the whole world, for it is a legal right, yet it requires to be protected by registration. We shall return to this right in our discussion of mortgages.[1] Suffice it to say now that a *first* mortgagee (lender) is entitled to possession of the landowner's title deeds.[2] Subsequent intending purchasers or mortgagees of the land are thus put on their guard by the absence of title deeds that the property is subject to a mortgage. In order to warn intending purchasers and mortgagees as to mortgages not protected by deposit of title deeds (e g second or subsequent mortagages) registration as a land charge was felt necessary for otherwise such mortgages, being legal, would have bound purchasers who had no means of knowing of their existence.

b. *Limited owner's charge (Class C (ii))* This equitable charge arises where a limited owner, a person having a limited ownership interest taking effect under a trust, pays out of his own pocket capital transfer tax, payable in respect of the transfer of the land following the death of the previous limited owner, without resorting to the land or any capital subject to the trust. The charge puts the limited owner in much the same position as if he had lent money to the estate on a mortgage.

c. *General equitable charge (Class C (iii))* The only important right falling within this class is an equitable mortgage of a legal estate (ie a mortgage not made according to the formalities required for creating a legal mortgage[3]) so long as it is not protected by deposit of title deeds.

d. *Estate contract (Class C (iv))* 'An estate contract is a contract by an estate owner, or by a person entitled at the date of the contract to have a legal estate conveyed to him, to convey or create a legal estate'.[4] Falling within this class are contracts for the sale of the freehold and agreements for a lease,[5] so long as the contract is enforceable within the terms of the LPA, s40.[6] If the intending purchaser or lessee wishes to prevent his right under the agreement being lost, should the land be sold to a third party, he must register it as an estate contract.

The definition of 'estate contract' also includes an option to purchase, an option to renew a lease,[7] and a right of pre-emption. An option to purchase is a continuing offer to sell the land, which the person granted the option has the right at any moment to convert into a contract for sale by notifying his acceptance of that offer. A right of pre-emption, or right of first refusal, gives the prospective purchaser no immediate rights. The possible vendor is required not to sell the land to anyone else without first giving the holder of the right of pre-emption the opportunity of purchasing. An option to purchase constitutes an equitable interest in land binding on subsequent purchasers if registered as an estate contract. A right of pre-emption does not in itself constitute an equitable interest in the land capable of binding successors of the grantor; but, if registered, it will bind someone who buys the land, for once the vendor takes steps to sell the land to someone else in breach of the right of pre-emption, it is converted into an option to purchase.[8]

A rough idea of the relative importance of these various Class C land charges is given by the statistics published by the Chief Land Registrar for 1984–85 showing that there were in that year 162, 714 Class C (i) registrations, 144 Class C (ii), 6,186 Class C (iii) and 29,403 Class C (iv).

1 Para 41.40 below.
2 LPA, ss85 and 86; para 41.40 below.
3 Para 41.11 below.
4 Land Charges Act 1972, s2(4).
5 Paras 33.6 to 33.9 above.
6 *Mens v Wilson* (1973) 231 Estates Gazette 843; paras 43.11 to 43.19 below.

33.23–33.25 *Law and equity*

7   *Taylor Fashions Ltd v Liverpool Victoria Trustees Co Ltd* [1982] QB 133n, [1981] 1 All ER 897.
8   *Pritchard v Briggs* [1980] Ch 338, [1980] 1 All ER 294, CA.

33.24   *Class D land charges*   The Land Charges Act 1972, s2(5) lists three Class D land charges:

a. *An Inland Revenue charge for capital transfer tax (Class D (i)).*

b. *A restrictive covenant (Class D (ii))*   This important class refers to covenants or agreements restricting the use of land, other than those made before 1 January 1926 and those made between a landlord and his tenant, neither of which are registrable as land charges, and depend for their protection in unregistered land on the doctrine of notice: they cannot affect a purchaser of the legal estate for value without notice. We consider restrictive covenants in detail in ch 39 below.

c. *An equitable easement (Class D (iii))*   The statute defines this class of right as 'an easement, right or privilege over or affecting land created or arising on or after 1 January 1926 and being merely an equitable interest'.[1] This class of right appears, despite its potentially wide definition, to be limited to equitable easements and profits.[2] In *E R Ives Investment Ltd v High*,[3] the Court of Appeal held that a right in land arising from the doctrine of proprietary estoppel[4] did not fall within the definition, nor, according to the House of Lords, in *Shiloh Spinners Ltd v Harding*,[5] does an equitable right of entry (used to enforce compliance with positive covenants not in themselves enforceable).[6]

1   Land Charges Act 1972, s2(5).
2   Ch 40 below.
3   [1967] 2 QB 379, [1967] 1 All ER 504, CA.
4   Paras 38.10–38.13 below.
5   [1973] AC 691, [1973] 1 All ER 90, HL.
6   Para 39.13 below.

33.25   *Class F land charges*   Under Class F is registered a charge affecting any land by virtue of the Matrimonial Homes Act 1983.[1] This Act, which consolidates earlier legislation, gives a spouse who does not own the freehold or leasehold in the matrimonial home certain statutory rights of occupation in respect of it. These are:

a. if she, or he, is in occupation, the right not to be evicted or excluded from the home by the owning spouse, except with a court order;

b. if not in occupation, the right, with leave of the court, to enter and occupy the house.[2]

These rights end on the death of the owning spouse or on the ending of the marriage (unless in the event of a matrimonial dispute the court has earlier directed otherwise).[3] A spouse who wishes to protect his or, more likely, her statutory rights of occupation (usually only where there is an actual or impending dispute) should register a Class F land charge. Such registration can be effected without the knowledge of the owning spouse and could be used to frustrate a sale of the matrimonial home by a non-owning spouse who wishes to remain in occupation,[4] but not by a spouse who has no wish to occupy.[5] Registration may be cancelled on death, or on the ending of the marriage, or on a court order, for which a successor to the owning spouse may apply.[6] Where a spouse who does not own the freehold or leasehold nonetheless holds an equitable co-ownership interest in the property[7] there appears to be little to be gained from the registration of a Class F charge.[8]

1 Land Charges Act 1972, s2(7).
2 Matrimonial Homes Act 1983 s1(1).
3 Ibid, s2(4).
4 *Wroth v Tyler* [1974] Ch 30, [1973] 1 All ER 897.
5 *Barnett v Hassett* [1982] 1 All ER 80, [1981] 1 WLR 1385.
6 Matrimonial Homes Act 1983, ss2(5) and 5(1).
7 Para 36.12 below.
8 Paras 36.17 and 36.18 below.

Registration and failure to register

33.26 Registration of a land charge is deemed to constitute actual notice;[1] it does not confer validity on an otherwise invalid right in respect of another's land. Failure to register only affects the enforceability of the charge against a subsequent purchaser of the land affected, it does not affect its enforceability between the original parties. The extent of unenforceability caused by a failure to register depends on which of two groups the charge falls into. Non-registration of a charge within Classes C (i)–(iii) and F renders the right void against a purchaser for valuable consideration of *any* interest in the land.[2] Non-registration of a charge within Classes C (iv) and D renders the interest void against a purchaser *of the legal estate for money or money's worth*.[3]

If follows that an unregistered estate contract, restrictive covenant or equitable easement will bind a purchaser of the legal estate without notice whose only consideration is marriage, or a purchaser of an equitable interest, even if he has no notice of it (being first in time),[4] and that in no case does non-registration of a charge affect its enforceability against a donee, devisee (ie a donee under a will) or squatter. It should be remembered that the term 'purchaser' includes a lessee and a mortgagee.[5]

If a charge is declared to be void as against a purchaser as a result of non-registration then the purchaser will not be affected by it even though he has notice of it, even if he expressly takes subject to it.[6] Furthermore, in *Hollington Bros Ltd v Rhodes*,[7] it was held that where land was acquired expressly subject to such tenancies as may affect the premises the purchaser was not affected by an agreement for a lease since it had not been registered as a Class C (iv) land charge.[8] Harman J said that, although on the face of it, it might seem wrong that a purchaser who knows perfectly well of rights subject to which he is expressed to take should be able to ignore them, he did not see how something declared by statute to be void could be made valid again. In *Midland Bank Trust Co v Green*,[9] a husband conveyed the legal estate in his farm, worth £40,000, to his wife, for £500, with the intention of defeating an option to purchase which he had earlier granted to his son but which his son had not registered.[10] The House of Lords held that the option was void against the wife for non-registration. She was a genuine 'purchaser for money or money's worth of a legal estate in the land'.[11] She took an interest (in fee simple) in the land 'for valuable consideration' (a term of art which precludes any inquiry as to adequacy)—so she was a purchaser within s17 of the Act; and she was a purchaser for money, £500.

The statute imposed no requirement that she should have acted in good faith. In any event, the House held, it was not fraud or a lack of good faith to take advantage of legal rights conferred by Act of Parliament.

Despite these two cases, it was held in the controversial case of *Lyus v Prowsa Developments Ltd*,[12] where a purchaser acquired land expressly subject to a specified unregistered estate contract (as opposed to 'subject to such rights as may affect the land', as in *Hollington v Rhodes*), that the purchaser became a constructive trustee[13] in favour of the person entitled under the estate contract, for to hold otherwise would be to permit the purchaser fraudulently to renege on the positive stipulation to give effect to the contract subject to which he acquired the land. Furthermore, in *Taylor Fashions Ltd v Liverpool Victoria Trustees Co Ltd*[14] it was made clear that the principle of proprietary estoppel[15] may in appropriate circumstances operate to prevent a purchaser denying the validity of a land charge declared by the Land Charges Act to be void.

1   LPA, s198(1).
2   Land Charges Act 1972, s4(5).
3   Ibid, s4(6).
4   See *McCarthy and Stone Ltd v Julian S. Hodge & Co Ltd* [1971] 2 All ER 973.
5   Land Charges Act 1972, s17.
6   LPA, s199.
7   [1951] 2 All ER 578n.
8   Para 33.23 above.
9   [1981] 1 All ER 153, HL.
10 As an estate contract.
11 Land Charges Act 1972, s4(6).
12 [1982] 2 All ER 953, [1982] 1 WLR 1044.
13 Para 38.15, below.
14 [1982] QB 133n, [1981] 1 All ER 897.
15 Para 38.10 below.

The registration machinery
33.27 It is a fundamental defect of the system of registering interests in unregistered land that the registration is made, not against the land affected, but against the name of the owner of the legal estate.[1] Thus, a purchaser intending to buy 42 Acacia Avenue cannot look up 42 Acacia Avenue (or its reference number) in the Land Charges Register to discover, for example, whether it is affected by an option to purchase; instead, he must make a search against the names of all the owners of the legal estate of 42 Acacia Avenue since 1 January 1926.[2]

The major problem to which this system could conceivably give rise is that a purchaser may not be able to ascertain the names of all the estate owners since 1925 against which to search. This theoretical problem is made worse by the LPA 1969, s23 which reduced the minimum period in respect of which the purchaser is required to investigate the vendor's title to 15 years (from 30 years).[3] So, although a purchaser may only be able to investigate the title going back to a good root of title 15 or so years old, he will be deemed to have actual notice of registered land charges going back to 1926.[4]

This problem is relieved as a matter of conveyancing practice by keeping copies of all official certificates of search of the register[5] received by purchasers in the past together with the title deeds, thus revealing the relevant names. However, should this practice break down in a particular case, the LPA 1969, s25 provides that if a purchaser suffers loss by reason of the land being affected by a land charge of which he had no actual knowledge, which was registered against a name not discoverable from the relevant title, he is entitled to compensation payable by the Chief Land Registrar out of public funds.

1 Land Charges Act 1972, s3(1).
2 When the Land Charges Act 1925 came into force.
3 Para 43.29 below.
4 LPA; s198; para 33.26 above.
5 Para 43.30 below.

33.28 As we stated in para 33.17 above, the purchaser of a leasehold interest and a sub-lessee are prevented by the LPA, s44, unless they contract otherwise, from investigating the title to the freehold, being limited to investigation of the lease or sub-lease and any assignment of it under which the other contracting party holds. Although s44(5) provides that nonetheless they are not to be affected with notice of any equitable interest which they might have discovered had they contracted for a more thorough investigation of the title, this does not affect the LPA, s198, under which the purchaser is deemed to have actual notice of a registered land charge.[1] It follows that although a lessee may not be in a position to investigate fully the lessor's title and discover the names of previous estate owners, he may be bound by an undiscovered and undiscoverable registered land charge, such as a restrictive covenant. To add insult to injury, the compensation scheme under the LPA 1969, s25 does not in general apply to lessees and sub-lessees affected by land charges which they could not discover because of the LPA, s44.[2]

1 *White v Bijou Mansions Ltd* [1937] Ch 610, [1937] 3 All ER 269.
2 LPA 1969, s25(9) and (10).

33.29 *Searches* A purchaser may make a search of the register in person[1] but it is usual to request an official search. The latter is the preferable course since it results in an official certificate of search which is conclusive in favour of the purchaser,[2] so that he takes free of any registered land charges which the certificate fails to disclose. Furthermore, an official search confers a priority period of 15 working days:[3] no charge registered within 15 working days of the issue of an official search certificate will bind the purchaser if he completes the purchase within that period.

1 Land Charges Act 1972, s9.
2 Ibid, s10.
3 Ibid, s11.

33.30 An official search certificate is only conclusive in favour of a purchaser where his application gives no reasonable scope for misunderstanding in the Registry.[1] Where a building society requested a search of the register giving, apparently because of a clerical error, the wrong name (Francis Davis Blackburn) for the estate owner (Francis David Blackburn), the 'nil certificate' which resulted was not conclusive in their favour, even though in the particular case the registered estate contract by which the building society was held to be bound, had itself been registered against a name (Frank David Blackburn) which not the full and correct name of the estate owner.[2] Such an inaccurate registration is thus not a total nullity, being effective where there is a failure to search or where a search is made against some other incorrect name.

1 *Du Sautoy v Symes* [1967] Ch 1146, [1967] 1 All ER 25.
2 *Oak Co-operative Building Society v Blackburn* [1968] Ch 730, [1968] 2 All ER 117, CA.

Interests outside the Land Charges Act

33.31 We think it worth reiterating that, although the Land Charges Act has considerably reduced the importance of the doctrine of notice as the vehicle for the protection of equitable interests, it has not totally superseded it. The Act itself shows that there are rights, namely pre-1926 equitable easements and restrictive covenants, and covenants in a lease, to which the doctrine of notice still applies. Further, decisions of the courts, such as *E R Ives Investment Ltd v High*[1] and *Shiloh Spinners Ltd v Harding*,[2] demonstrate that there are other equitable rights which are not within the Land Charges Act and which are not overreached on sale and are thus dependent on the doctrine of notice. Of course, there is one major area where the Land Charges Act *and* the doctrine of notice have no application, and that is where the Land Registration Act 1925 applies.

1 [1967] 2 QB 379, [1967] 1 All ER 504, CA; para 33.24 above.
2 [1973] AC 691, [1973] 1 All ER 90, HL; para 33.24 above.

Chapter 34
Land Registration Act

34.1 At the commencement of this Part of the book we stated that land law is concerned with the nature of the rights a person may have in respect of land, with the enforcement of those rights, and with their creation and transfer. So far we have outlined the nature of the two main ownership interests in land, the freehold and the leasehold; the nature of other rights will be considered in due course. We have also noted that the categorisation of interests in land as legal or equitable relates primarily to their mode of creation and their enforceability. Although conveyancing, the process of transferring interests in land, will be considered in a later chapter, we must point out here that there exist two quite separate forms of machinery for transferring land: one of them, the unregistered system, aspects of which we have already touched on, is gradually being replaced by the other, the registered title system.

The registered title system, governed by the Land Registration Act 1925, hereafter the LRA, applies to considerably more than half of all conveyancing transactions, and the Act now applies to all urban land and will eventually cover the whole of England and Wales. We deal with the registered system of conveyancing at this stage because, although its purpose is to improve on the machinery of conveyancing under the unregistered system, it has a major impact on the creation and enforceability of interests in land to which it applies. It should be noted, however, that although the LRA affects the enforceability, creation and transfer of interests in land, it does not affect the *nature* of the rights which may exist in relation to the land to which it applies.

34.2 It will be recalled that the unregistered system of conveyancing requires that a vendor prove to a purchaser his right to the property he is purporting to sell, ie prove his title to the land, by reference to the deeds and documents relating to the land. The purchaser of land under that system is bound by those interests relating to the land which are legal, by those interests registered in the Land Charges Register under the Land Charges Act, and by those equitable interests not required to be so registered (other than those which may be overreached) of which he has notice, actual, constructive or imputed. The distinction between legal and equitable interests is thus centrally important in the unregistered system, albeit that its importance is reduced by the existence of the Land Charges Register.

The registered system replaces proof of title by reference to deeds, with proof of title by reference to a state register of title whereby the state effectively guarantees a vendor's title to land. However, in replacing title deeds with a state register, this system goes further. It substitutes a new scheme of protection of interests in land for that applicable under the unregistered system. Under this scheme the distinction between legal and equitable interests is of considerably reduced significance, the doctrine of notice plays no part, and the Land Charges Register is totally inapplicable.

For the purposes of the registered system of conveyancing, the LRA divides interests in land into three basic categories: registered interests, overriding interests and minor interests. This classification is superimposed on the existing threefold classification of interests into legal estates, legal interests and equitable interests, but, it should be noted, there is not an exact correspondence.

Registered interests

34.3 The scheme which we have referred to as the registered system of conveyancing is usually known as the 'registered land' scheme, from the name of the governing Act. This is, however, something of a misnomer, for what is registered is not the land itself, but the title to the land, ie the evidence of the owner's right to the land. The only interests in land in respect of which a proprietor (to use the terminology of the Act) can be substantively registered, ie which can have their own separate and distinct title registers, are freeholds and leaseholds having more than 21 years to run.[1] The Land Registry, which operates the machinery of the Act, contains separate registers of the titles to freehold and leasehold land (where the term has more than 21 years to run) to which the LRA applies.

1   LRA, ss 2, 4 and 8. (Leases containing an absolute prohibition against dealings cannot be registered.)

Compulsory registration

34.4 We have said that the LRA now applies to all urban areas and will eventually apply to the whole country. This does not mean that, as and when the Act is made to apply to a particular area, the titles to all substantively registrable interests within that area thereby automatically and immediately become registered in the Land Registry. Rather, what happens is that, by Order in Council,[1] areas of the country are, from time to time, made compulsory registration areas within the terms of the Act.[2] Thereafter, on the occurrence of certain specified transactions, the title to freeholds, and certain leaseholds, must be registered.[3]

1   Para 3.11 above.
2   LRA, s120.
3   Ibid, s123.

34.5 The specified transactions which give rise to a requirement for first registration of title are:

a. a conveyance on sale of freehold land;[1]

b. a grant of a lease or sub-lease of more than 21 years where the title to the reversion is already registered;[2]

c. a grant of a lease or sub-lease of 40 years or more where the title to the reversion is not yet registered;[3]

d. an assignment on sale of a lease having 40 years or more to run.[3]

It should be noted that in a. and d. the transaction must be 'on sale'. Consequently, if, for example, a freehold is given away or bequeathed, the occasion for first registration does not arise. The details of the conveyancing process will be considered in ch 43 below. Suffice it to say for the moment that on the occasion of first registration of a freehold interest, or of a leasehold interest where the title to the landlord's reversion is not already registered, the procedure followed is that of unregistered conveyancing. Thereafter the purchaser or his solicitor applies to the Chief Land Registrar (hereafter, 'the Registrar'), at the appropriate District Land Registry, for first registration, enclosing all relevant title deeds and documents. On being satisfied as to these, the Registrar will then register the title.

Should the purchaser in this case fail to apply for first registration, the transaction becomes void as to the passing of the legal estate after two months[4] (unless the Registrar exercises his power to extend this period if sufficient cause for the delay is shown) and the legal estate reverts to the vendor who will hold it on trust for the purchaser. The latter will then have the right to have the legal estate conveyed to him again and this time he should have his title to it registered; in the meantime, however, the marketability of the title is seriously impaired.

1   LRA, s123.
2   Ibid, ss 19(3) and 22(2).
3   Ibid, s123. Note that first registration is also compulsory, even outside compulsory registration areas, where a public sector tenant buys his house under the right to buy provisions of the Housing Act 1985; ibid s, 154.
4   Ibid. (Under the Land Registration Rules 1925, r 73(2) a mortgagee may apply for first registration on behalf of the proprietor).

Registered dealings

34.6 It is most important to realise that once first registration of an interest has taken place all dealings in respect of it are governed by the LRA. Any subsequent transfer of the registered interest must be completed by registration, ie by the Registrar entering the transferee of the land on the register as proprietor.[1] Similarly, where a leasehold interest of more than 21 years is created out of a registered estate, the lessee should be registered as proprietor of the leasehold interest. The grant of the lease should also be noted on the landlord's title register,[2] and this will be done automatically by the Registrar on the lessee's application for first registration. It is important to realise that unless and until these dispositions are completed by registration, no legal estate passes. The purchaser will only have a minor interest capable of being overridden if not protected (paras 34.21 to 34.25 below) or, if in occupation, an overriding interest (para 34.20 below). It should again be stressed that once registration has taken place the enforceability and protection of interests benefiting or affecting the registered estate are governed by the provisions of the LRA which we discuss in this chapter, and not by the rules discussed in ch 33 above.

1   LRA, ss 19(1) and 22(1).
2   Ibid, ss 19(2) and 22(2).

Voluntary registration

34.7 Voluntary registration of title to freehold land, or leasehold land where the term has more than 21 years to run, is possible in areas of compulsory registration.[1] It is thus not absolutely necessary to wait until one of the transactions specified in s123 occurs before first registration. Voluntary registration of title is also possible outside compulsory registration areas but only: a. in a case where the title deeds to the land have been lost or destroyed, or b. in the case of residential, industrial or commercial developments of at least 20 units.[2]

1   LRA, ss 4 and 8.
2   Land Registration Act 1966.

Classes of title

34.8 An application to the Registrar for registration of title to land is made for one of three classes of title: absolute, good leasehold, and possessory. A fourth class, qualified title, may be given where the Registrar is unable to grant the class of title originally applied for.

Absolute

34.9 *Freehold* Absolute title is applied for and granted in the vast majority of cases involving freehold land. Registration as proprietor of freehold land with absolute title vests in the proprietor the freehold estate together with all rights belonging to it (for example, easements such as rights of way) subject to:

a. entries on the register; and

b. overriding interests.[1]

Absolute title will be given where the applicant proves his title to the satisfaction of the Registrar. It is not quite accurate to say that registration with absolute title affords an absolute state guarantee of the registered proprietor's title, for there exists the possibility that the register may be rectified, ie amended if it does not show what should be the true state of affairs.[2] However, subject to this possibility, registration with absolute title effectively guarantees that the registered proprietor is entitled to the legal estate together with appurtenant rights and subject only to overriding interests and interests entered on the register.[3] Thus, such registration can, again subject to the possibility of rectification, have the effect of removing any defect in the title which existed prior to registration, even vesting in the proprietor a title which the vendor could not convey. Consequently, as the case of *Epps v Esso Petroleum Co Ltd*[4] shows, if by a conveyancing error caused by unclear boundaries, X conveys to Y land, a strip of which he has already conveyed to Z under the unregistered system, the registration of Y as first registered proprietor of the land including the strip, vests in him the freehold in the strip, thereby depriving Z of the legal estate in land which had already been conveyed to him. Rectification of the register may be ordered to correct this error, but there are many cases where rectification will not be ordered,[5] although an indemnity may be payable by the Registrar in such a case.[6]

1   LRA, s5.
2   Para 34.28 below.

3 Cf effect of registration with other classes of title.
4 [1973] 2 All ER 465, [1973] 1 WLR 1071.
5 Para 34.28 below.
6 Para 34.29 below.

34.10 *Leasehold* It is possible for absolute title to be accorded in respect of leasehold interests, but this can only be done where the Registrar is satisfied not only as to title to the lease but also as to title to the freehold and any intermediate leasehold interests.[1] Only in such a case could the Registrar guarantee that the lease was validly granted. However, since a lessee has no right to call for proof of his landlord's title,[2] he will not be in a position to satisfy the Registrar as to the landlord's title, unless he has, exceptionally, contracted with his landlord for the production of the latter's title deeds. On the other hand, if the freehold and any leasehold reversions are already registered, an application for registration with absolute title to a leasehold interest may be made, for the Registrar will then be in a position to satisfy himself as to these superior titles. Registration with absolute title vests in the proprietor the leasehold interest together with all rights belonging to it, subject to

a. covenants in the lease (express or implied);

b. entries on the register; and

c. overriding interests.[3]

Apart from the obvious advantage of guaranteeing that the lease was validly granted, registration with absolute title carries the further advantage that restrictive covenants which appear on the registers of superior titles are entered on the leasehold title register. All lessees are bound by valid restrictive covenants entered on the register of superior titles even if they are, because of the restrictions on the investigation of leasehold title under the LPA, s44, unable to discover their existence. When the lessee is registered with absolute title under the LRA he will at least be able to discover the details of the covenants which bind him, as will subsequent purchasers of the lease.

1 LRA, s8.
2 LPA, s44; para 33.17 above.
3 LRA, s9.

Good leasehold
34.11 Where it is not possible for a proprietor of a leasehold interest to be registered with absolute title, because the Registrar cannot satisfy himself as to the landlord's title, application may be made for registration with good leasehold title. Registration with good leasehold title vests the leasehold interest in the proprietor subject to:

a. entries on the register and

b. overriding interests, but it does not guarantee that the lease was validly granted, for the interest is also subject to

c. rights or interests affecting the landlord's title to grant the lease.[1]

1 LRA, s10.

Possessory
34.12 Where an applicant cannot prove his title by reference to title deeds,

being unable to produce them, or where title is based on adverse possession (squatting),[1] application may be made for registration with possessory title. Such applications are infrequent. Registration with possessory title has the same effect as registration with absolute title except that in addition to entries on the register and overriding interests, the registered interest is also subject to any adverse rights or interests existing at the time of registration.[2] In other words, the title to the land is only guaranteed in respect of dealings *after* first registration. So, for example, a restrictive covenant binding the land prior to registration remains binding, albeit neither overriding nor entered on the register.

1   Ch 42 below.
2   LRA, ss 6 and 11.

Qualified
34.13   In a few rare cases, the Registrar may decide that he is unable to grant the title applied for because of some specific defect in the title. In such a case, the applicant for registration may, on application, be registered with a qualified title. The effect of registration with a qualified title is the same as the effect of registration with absolute title except that in addition to entries on the register and overriding interests, the registered interest is also subject to a specific qualification stated in the register, for example any rights arising before a specified date or under a specified document.[1]

1   LRA, ss 7 and 12.

Cautions against first registration
34.14   A person who has an interest in land which may be lost if another person is registered as proprietor may lodge a caution with the Registrar under the LRA, s53. This entitles him to notice of any application that may be made for registration of an interest affecting his rights. He then has 14 days in which to oppose the registration if he wishes, otherwise registration will be effected.[1]

1   See also para 34.24 below.

Upgrading of title
34.15   a. Where freehold land has been registered for 15 years with possessory title, the Registrar must, on application, upgrade the title to absolute title, if he is satisfied that the proprietor is in possession.[1]

b. Where leasehold land has been registered for ten years with possessory title, the Registrar must, on application, upgrade the title to good leasehold title, if he is satisfied that the proprietor is in possession.[1]

c. Where leasehold land has been registered for at least ten years with good leasehold title, the Registrar may, on application, upgrade the class of title to absolute title, if he is satisfied that the proprietor, or successive proprietors, have been in possession during that period.[2]

d. On a transfer for valuable consideration of land registered with a qualified, good leasehold or possessory title, the Registrar may, if he is satisfied with the title, upgrade it to absolute or good leasehold as appropriate.[3]

A caution may be lodged against coversion of a title, to prevent rights being lost as a result.[4]

1   LRA, s77(3)(b).
2   Ibid, s77(4).
3   Ibid, s77(2).
4   Ibid, s54. Land Registration Rules, r215(2). See para 34.24 below.

The register

34.16   The register of each title is kept on a card index at the appropriate District Land Registry. Each register of title is divided into three parts: the Property Register, the Proprietorship Register and the Charges Register.[1]

a. *Property Register*
This part of the register contains a description of the land, states whether it is freehold or leasehold, and refers to a filed plan of the land.[2] Where the land is leasehold, brief particulars of the lease are set out. The Property Register also contains notes of any rights which benefit the land, such as easements.
   The filed plan is prepared from the plans and description of the land in the title deeds and is based on the Ordnance Map. It denotes the land comprised in the title by red edging. Boundaries shown in the filed plan are general, not fixed, boundaries; that is they do not purport to show the exact line of the legal boundary.[3]

b. *Proprietorship Register*
This part states the class of title with which the land is registered, the name and address of the registered proprietor, together with any cautions, inhibitions and restrictions[4] affecting the proprietor's right to deal with the land.[5]

c. *Charges Register*
This part contains entries and notices of rights and interests which adversely affect the title, such as restrictive covenants, easements, mortgages and registered leases.[6]

1   Land Registration Rules, r2.
2   Ibid, r3.
3   Ibid, r278; para 43.37 below
4   Paras 34.22 to 34.25 below.
5   Land Registration Rules, r6.
6   Ibid, r7.

Land certificates

34.17   A copy of the register and filed plan, called the Land Certificate, is given to the registered proprietor.[1] Although this document affords some evidence of title,[2] at any one time it may not correspond exactly with the register itself because some entries may be made on the register without the certificate being lodged at the registry for amendment,[3] and therefore it is the register which is the proof of title. Where the registered property is mortgaged by means of a registered charge,[4] the Land Certificate is retained by the Registry and the mortgagee (lender) is issued with a Charge

Certificate[5] which is likewise a copy of the register together with the deed of charge.

1   LRA, s63.
2   Ibid, s68.
3   See para 34.24 below.
4   Para 41.8 below.
5   LRA, s65.

Inspection of the register
34.18   The proprietor's register of title is not open to public inspection (just as, in unregistered land, his title deeds would not be) and his authority to inspect must be obtained.[1] The Land Registry maintains a Public Index Map showing the position and extent of every registered estate, and a list of pending applications for first registration. An official search of these will reveal whether a particular piece of land is registered or not, and, if registered, whether as freehold or leasehold, the date of and parties to the lease. If the land is not registered, cautions against first registration and pending applications for registration will be revealed.[2]

1   LRA, s112.
2   Land Registration Rules, rr8, 10, 12 and 286.

Overriding interests
34.19   Overriding interests are rights and interests which do not appear on the register of title but are nevertheless binding on a purchaser of registered land. In this respect, overriding interests are like legal interests in unregistered conveyancing, though in fact the category of overriding interests includes legal and equitable rights. Consequently, a proprietor's register of title does not provide a complete picture of the rights affecting the title and so further inspection of the land and inquiries of the vendor will be necessary to discover the full picture, including overriding interests. These rights are listed in the LRA, s70(1); among the more important are:

a. legal easements, and legal or equitable profits à prendre;[1]

b. rights acquired or in the course of being acquired under the Limitation Act[2] (ie 'squatters' rights');

c. the rights of every person in actual occupation of the land (or in receipt of the rents and profits thereof) except where inquiry is made of such person and the rights are not disclosed;[3]

d. leases for a term not exceeding 21 years at a rent, no lump sum or premium ('fine') being paid.[4]

The existence of the category of overriding interests, which bind the purchaser despite not being entered on the register, clearly invalidates any idea that the registered land scheme ensures that all interests affecting the land should be discoverable from the state register. However, albeit that the extent of the rights which may be protected as being overriding appears considerable, in practice a purchaser may well find that many potential overriding interests are in fact entered on the register. Thus adverse easements (such as rights of way across the registered land) which appear on the title at the time of first registration must be noted on the register of title.[5] Again, easements created by a registered proprietor must be completed by registration.[6] Finally, the Registrar has a discretion to note any overriding interests on the register.[7] Once noted on the register the interest ceases to be overriding.[8]

1 LRA, s70(1)(a). In *Celsteel Ltd v Alton House Holdings Ltd* [1985] 2 All ER 562, [1985] 1 WLR 204 it was held that the Land Registration Rules, r258 extends the category of overriding interests to include equitable easements. This may not be correct, however, because the wording of this rule suggests that it was intended merely to include as overriding interests easements within the LPA, s62; para 40.22 below.
2 Ibid, s70(1)(f); para 42.5 below.
3 Ibid, s70(1)(g); para 34.20 below.
4 Ibid, s70(1)(k).
5 Ibid, s70(2); *Re Dances Way, West Town, Hayling Island* [1962] Ch 490, [1962] 2 All ER 42.
6 LRA, ss 19(2) and 22(2).
7 Ibid, s70(3).
8 Ibid, s3(xvi).

Rights of every person in actual occupation
34.20   This is potentially the most extensive category of overriding interest. The relevant provision (the LRA, s70(1)(g)) may be regarded as the registered land equivalent of the doctrine in *Hunt v Luck*,[1] whereby a purchaser has constructive notice of the rights of any person in occupation of land. However, s70(1)(g) extends this doctrine by including, amongst those whose rights are protected, persons in receipt of the rents and profits of land. Furthermore, while the doctrine of *Hunt v Luck* cannot save an unregistered land charge from invalidity,[2] s70(1)(g) can,[3] for it makes no difference that the right protected by occupation might also have been protected as a minor interest on the register.[4] The only rights which can be protected by actual occupation under s70(1)(g) are 'rights with reference to land which have the quality of being capable of enduring through different ownerships of the land according to normal conceptions of title to real property'.[5] Examples include unregistered estate contracts (thus putting a tenant in occupation under an unregistered agreement for a lease in a better position in registered than in unregistered land[6]), a right to rectification[7] and interests under a resulting trust and a trust for sale. Beneficial interests under a strict settlement cannot constitute overriding interests,[8] nor can a spouse's rights of occupation under the Matrimonial Homes Act: these must be protected as minor interests.

The extent of the protection afforded by s70(1)(g) is illustrated by *Hodgson v Marks*.[9] Mrs Hodgson, the freehold owner of a house, transferred it, *gratis*, to her lodger, Evans. This was not intended to be an outright gift, for the parties agreed that although Evans was to become the registered proprietor, the beneficial (equitable) ownership was to remain in Mrs Hodgson; in other words, Evans was to hold the land on (resulting) trust for Mrs Hodgson. The parties continued to live in the house as if nothing had changed: Mrs Hodgson as if owner and Evans as if lodger. Evans then sold the house to Marks who became registered proprietor. Marks was aware of Mrs Hodgson's presence in the house but not of any rights she might have in respect of it. Mrs Hodgson's interest under the trust could only bind Marks if it was protected by an entry on the register, which it was not, or if it was an overriding interest by virtue of her occupation of the property. The Court of Appeal held that she was in actual occupation of the property and her rights under the trust constituted an overriding interest. The court held that simply because the vendor is, or appears to be, in occupation of the property does not mean that no one else can be in actual occupation. Who is in 'actual occupation' is a question of fact,[10] depending on the circumstances, 'and a wise purchaser or lender will take no risks'.[11] In other words, a purchaser of registered land should enquire of all those who are or appear to be in actual occupation of the property, including, for example, resident grannies and adult offspring, as to whether they have any rights in the land; the vendor's word should not be accepted.[11] Furthermore, since the sub-section protects the rights of those in receipt of rents and profits, the purchaser must also ask the occupier 'To whom do you pay your rent?'.[12] If the answer to that question is someone other than the vendor, the purchaser must then enquire as to the rights of that person.

It is now clear, from *Williams and Glyn's Bank Ltd v Boland*,[13] that a wife may be in actual occupation of property for the purposes of this provision albeit her registered proprietor husband is also in occupation. Her occupation is not to be regarded simply as a shadow of his. Once it is found that a wife is in actual occupation, it is clear that a prospective purchaser or lender should make inquiry of the wife. If she has rights in the land (eg as an equitable co-owner[14]) and discloses them he takes subject to them. If she does not disclose them, he takes free of them. Anyone who lends money on the security of a matrimonial home should make sure that the wife agrees to it, or go to the house and make enquiries of her.[15]

Boland's case and *Hodgson v Marks*, whilst doing much to protect the security of wives and other occupiers, do little to facilitate conveyancing and to protect purchasers and mortgagees. The reasons for this lie in two particular problems: that of determining who, besides the vendor/mortgagor, is in actual occupation, given that the vendor's word should not be accepted as conclusive; and that a purchaser is bound by overriding interests existing at the date of registration of his interest, giving rise to the possibility that a person with rights in the land may go into occupation after completion of the purchase but prior to registration.[16] Reform of this area of the law has been proposed[17] and can be expected sooner or later, but attempts have thus far foundered.

1 [1902] 1 Ch 428, CA; para 33.18 above.
2 Land Charges Act 1972, s4(5) and (6).
3 *Webb v Pollmount* [1966] Ch 584, [1966] 1 All ER 481.
4 *Williams and Glyn's Bank Ltd v Boland* [1980] 2 All ER 408, [1980] 3 WLR 138, HL.
5 *National Provincial Bank Ltd v Ainsworth* [1965] AC 1175 at 1226.
6 Para 33.26 above. *Kling v Keston* (1985) 49 P&CR 212.
7 *Blacklocks v JB Developments (Godalming) Ltd* [1982] Ch 183, [1981] 3 All ER 392.
8 LRA s86(2).
9 [1971] Ch 892,[1971] 2 All ER 684, CA.
10 See *Williams & Glyn's Bank Ltd v Boland* [1980] 2 All ER 408 at 413.
11 *Hodgson v Marks* [1971] Ch 892 at 932.
12 *Strand Securities Ltd v Caswell* [1965] Ch 958, [1965] 1 All ER 820, CA.
13 *Williams and Glyn's Bank Ltd v Boland* [1980] 2 All ER 408, [1980] 3 WLR 138, HL.
14 Para 36.12 above.
15 *Williams and Glyn's Bank Ltd v Boland* [1979] 2 All ER 697 at 706.
16 LRA, ss 5, 9, 20, 23.
17 Law Com No 115 (1982).

Minor interests
34.21 Essentially, the category of minor interests includes all those interests which are not registered or overriding. In particular, it includes:

a. beneficial interests under a settlement or trust for sale;

b. rights which in unregistered land would be protected under the Land Charges Act 1972 or under the doctrine of notice;[1] and

c. interests created by dispositions by a registered proprietor which have not been completed by registration as required by the Act.[2]

These minor interests must be protected by entry on the register, otherwise, unless they are overriding within s70(1)(g), a purchaser will take free of them. There are four methods of protecting a minor interest by entry on the register.

1 Paras 33.22 to 33.25 and 33.31 above.
2 LRA, s101.

Restriction
34.22 A restriction is entered in the Proprietorship Register of the register of title by, or with the consent of, the registered proprietor himself. Its object is to prevent dealings with the land unless a specified requirement has been complied with, for example, obtaining the consent of a particular person. Its use is particularly to protect beneficial (equitable) interests under a settlement or trust for sale.[1]

1 LRA, s58. See, for example, paras 35.15 and 35.29 below.

Notice
34.23 A notice[1] is used especially to protect rights which in unregistered land would be protected under the Land Charges Act, eg a restrictive covenant. Also noted on the Register are adverse easements and leases subsisting at the time of first registration or created by registered disposition. For a notice to be entered the proprietor of the land affected must lodge his Land Certificate at the Registry.[2] If the land is mortaged by registered charge the Land Certificate will, however, already be lodged at the Registry,[3] so that the proprietor's co-operation is not always needed. However, where the Land Certificate is lodged at the Registry, the proprietor will be given an opportunity to object to a notice being entered on the register, except in the case of notice of a non-owning spouse's rights under the Matrimonial Homes Act.[4]

A disposition by a registered proprietor takes effect subject to all rights protected by a notice, but as with registration of a land charge under the Land Charges Act in unregistered land, the entry of a notice does not confer validity on an otherwise invalid interest.

1 LRA, ss 48–52.
2 Ibid, s64.
3 Ibid, s65; para 41.8 below.
4 Para 33.25 above.

Caution
34.24 There are two forms of caution. Cautions against first registration have already been considered;[1] the other form is known as a caution against dealings.[2] Such a caution is entered in the Proprietorship Register; there is

no requirement that the Land Certificate be produced. The caution, as opposed to the notice, may thus be described as a hostile entry on the register, since the co-operation of the proprietor is not required. A cautioner must have a claim to an enforceable right or interest in the land.[2] Entry of a caution entitles the cautioner to be notified of proposed dealings with the land and to enter an appearance within fourteen days to object.[3] The Register has a wide discretion as to giving effect to the cautioner's claim.[4]

1 Para 34.14 above.
2 LRA, s54.
3 LRA, s55.
4 Land Registration Rules r220.

Inhibition

34.25 The use of inhibitions is very rare. An inhibition prevents all dealings with the land for a specified period.[1] The main use of inhibitions is in connection with bankruptcy. When a receiving order has been made in bankruptcy proceedings, a bankruptcy inhibition is automatically entered in the register prohibiting dealings until a trustee in bankruptcy is registered as proprietor.[2]

1 LRA, s57.
2 LRA, s61(3); Land Registration Rules r180.

Irrelevance of doctrine of notice

34.26 It is hoped it will have become apparent that the scheme of the LRA is that the law as to notice has no application to registered land. All a purchaser has to do is consult the register; from any burden not entered on the register, with the one exception of overriding interests, he takes free.[1] This is confirmed, for example, by s20 which provides that the purchaser of registered land is bound by entries on the register and overriding interests but takes free from all other estates and interests whatsoever; by s59(6) which provides that a purchaser is not bound by an unprotected minor interest even if he has notice of it, and by s74 which provides that a person dealing with a registered estate is not to be affected by notice of any trust. Nonetheless, it has been held that a purchaser may be bound by an interest not overriding nor entered on the register by virtue of the device of the constructive trust, as in *Lyus v Prowsa Developments Ltd*[2] which we discuss in para 33.26 above. It also appears that in appropriate circumstances a registered proprietor may be estopped from denying that he is bound by an unprotected minor interest.[3]

Finally, it should be noted that, since minor interests take effect in equity,[4] priority between competing minor interests follows the rule 'where the equities are equal the first in time prevails' and is thus determined by the order of creation, not of registration.[5]

1 *Williams and Glyn's Bank Ltd v Boland* [1981] AC 487, [1980] 2 All ER 408, HL.
2 [1982] 2 All ER 953, [1982] 1 WLR 1044; see also *Peffer v Rigg* [1978] 3 All ER 745, [1977] 1 WLR 285.
3 *Taylor Fashions Ltd v Liverpool Victoria Trustees Co* [1983] QB 133n, [1981] 1 All ER 897, paras 38.10–38.11 below.
4 LRA, s2(1).
5 *Barclays Bank Ltd v Taylor* [1973] Ch 137, [1973] 1 All ER 752, CA.

Leases

34.27 It is appropriate at this point to take stock of how leases may be protected in registered land. It is a complex picture. Leases for more than 21 years should be substantively registered where the superior title is registered and should also be noted on that title.[1] Where the superior title is not registered, first registration of leases of 40 years or more is required.[2] Leases of 21 years or less are overriding interests if at a rent.[3] However if a fine is taken, ie if a premium is paid for the lease, a lease of 21 years or less requires protection as a minor interest. Any lease which contains an absolute prohibition against dealings by the lessee during his lifetime may be overriding if within the LRA, s70(1)(k) but it may not be substantively registered.[4] An agreement for a lease constitutes an estate contract and must be protected as a minor interest. Where a lease is not substantively registered in a case where it should be, it takes effect as a minor interest.[5] Finally, it must also be remembered that even where a leasehold interest is not substantively registered (or protected as a minor interest) as it should be, it will be protected as an overriding interest where the tenant is in actual occupation of the property.[6]

1 LRA, ss 19(2) and 22(2).
2 Ibid, s123.
3 Ibid, s70(1)(k).
4 Ibid, s8(2).
5 Ibid, s101.
6 Ibid, s70(1)(g).

Rectification and indemnity

Rectification

34.28 It was pointed out earlier that registration with absolute title does not, despite the name, absolutely guarantee the title, for there remains the possibility that the register of title may be rectified (either by court order or by the Registrar). The LRA, s82(1) lists eight cases in which the register may be rectified including:

a. where an entry on the register was obtained by fraud;

b. where two or more persons are, by mistake, registered as proprietors of the same registered estate;

c. where a legal estate has been registered in the name of a person who, if the land had not been registered, would not have been the estate owner; and

d. in any other case where, by reason of any error or omission in the register, or by reason of any entry made under a mistake, it may be deemed just to rectify the register.

It follows that, prima facie, there is a wide discretion to rectify the register. However, the LRA, s82(3)[1] provides that this discretion cannot be exercised so as to affect a proprietor who is in possession,[2] except in four cases:

a. to give effect to a court order (eg that another person is in fact entitled to the land);

b. to give effect to an overriding interest;[3]

c. where the proprietor has caused or substantially contributed to the error or omission by fraud or lack of proper care;

d. where it would be unjust not to rectify.

Rectification was unsuccessfully sought against a proprietor in possession in *Epps v Esso Petroleum Co Ltd*[4] which we referred to, in relation to registration with absolute title, in para 34.9 above. Esso had been registered as proprietors of a plot of land, a strip of which had previously been conveyed to Epps under the unregistered system. Epps sought to have the register rectified so as to exclude the strip of land from Esso's title. As Esso were in possession, the discretion to rectify could only be exercised if the case fell within the four exceptions under s82(3). Epps contended that the case fell within exceptions b. and d. above. He claimed that his right to the land constituted an overriding interest within the LRA, s70(1)(g) as he was in actual occupation of the strip of land, since for many years he and his predecessors had parked their cars on the strip. This claim was rejected, the court holding that parking a car on the strip did not amount to 'actual occupation' of it, since the car did not actually occupy the whole, or a substantial, or any defined part of the land for the whole or any defined time. Since Epps was therefore not in actual occupation of the strip, his rights in respect of it could not constitute an overriding interest within s70(1)(g).[5] Furthermore, the court held that on the facts a refusal to rectify would not be unjust, since justice lay entirely with Esso. There had been nothing in the conveyance or on the site which would lead them to realise that there had been a double conveyance of the disputed strip; indeed, the evidence pointed to the strip belonging to them. Epps on the other hand had failed to make proper enquiries prior to his purchase even though it was apparent there might be boundary problems.

In *Freer v Unwins Ltd*,[6] where, on the grant of a 21-year lease of a shop,[7] the register of the landlord's freehold title did not show a restrictive covenant binding on the land, subsequent rectification of the register of the freehold title to show the covenant was held not to affect the lessee, whose lease took effect subject only to overriding interests and entries on the register *at the time the lease was granted.*[8]

1 As amended by the Administration of Justice Act 1977, s24.
2 This expression includes being in actual receipt of rents and profits.
3 See *Epps v Esso Petroleum Co Ltd* [1973] 2 All ER 465, [1973] 1 WLR 1071.
4 [1973] 2 All ER 465, [1973] 1 WLR 1071.
5 Para 34.20 above.
6 [1976] Ch 288, [1976] 1 All ER 634.
7 Which, though not requiring substantive registration, is treated as a registered disposition; LRA, ss 19(2) and 22(2).
8 LRA, s20(1); para 34.26 above. The registered proprietor's title would be affected from the date of the entry of the notice, LRA, s50(2).

Indemnity

34.29 In a sense it is the indemnity provisions of the LRA which give rise to registration being regarded as a state guarantee of title. Although registration does not absolutely guarantee the title, since there is always the possibility that the register will be rectified, anyone who suffers loss as a result of rectification of the register is entitled to an indemnity paid by the Registrar from moneys provided by parliament.[1] Likewise, anyone who suffers loss because the register is *not* rectified to remove some error or omission[2] is entitled to be indemnified, as is anyone suffering loss by reason of the loss or destruction of any document lodged at the Registry or by reason of an error in any official search of the register.[3]

No indemnity is payable where the applicant caused or substantially contributed to the loss by fraud or lack of proper care.[4] Nor, importantly, is an indemnity payable where the register is rectified to give effect to an overriding interest. This is because the registered proprietor's title has from the start been subject to the overriding interest; after rectification he is, strictly, in no worse position than he was in all along. In *Re Chowood's Registered Land*,[5] a vendor conveyed a plot of land including a strip which had in fact been acquired by someone else by adverse possession. The purchaser's register of title was rectified to give effect to that person's overriding interest[6] by removing the strip from the title, but the purchaser was not entitled to an indemnity.

Another gap in the indemnity provisions is shown by *Freer v Unwins Ltd*.[7] Freer, although in no way at fault, not only was unable to enforce the restrictive covenant against the lessee, Unwins, but was not entitled to an indemnity because of the Registry's mistake, since his loss resulted not from rectification of the register but from the fact that the covenant was not entered on the register of the freehold title when the lease was granted. Finally, as a general rule, where a claim to indemnity arises because of the registration of an estate in land with an absolute or good leasehold title, the claim is enforceable only for six years after the registration,[8] a provision which operated to deprive the plaintiff of an indemnity in the case of *Epps v Esso Petroleum Co Ltd*. The limitation period for a claim to an indemnity is otherwise six years from when the claimant becomes aware, or ought to have become aware, of his right to make a claim.[8]

1   LRA, s83(1).
2   Ibid, s83(2).
3   Ibid, s83(3).
4   LRA, s83(5)(a).
5   [1933] Ch 574.
6   Para 34.19b above.
7   [1976] Ch 288, [1976] 1 All ER 634.
8   LRA, s83(11).

Chapter 35

Settlements

35.1 In this and the next chapter we shall consider the following related topics:

a. the nature of what we have referred to as limited ownership interests in land (other than leaseholds), and of future enjoyment of land;

b. the machinery whereby the law provides for successive ownership interests in land to take effect, and

c. the machinery of the law for dealing with concurrent ownership interests in land (in other words, co-ownership of land).

Limited ownership and future enjoyment

Limited ownership interests
35.2 The two main forms of ownership interest in land are the freehold and the leasehold. The freehold interest is equivalent to absolute ownership of land, whereas the leasehold interest is a form of limited ownership. The leasehold interest has a certain duration (or a duration capable of being rendered certain). However, there are other forms of limited ownership interest, which differ from a leasehold interest in that they are of uncertain duration. These other limited ownership interests are not frequently encountered; they are, primarily, the life interest and the entailed interest, and, equally rare, the conditional fee simple and the determinable fee simple. The nature of these interests will now briefly be considered, but their operation cannot fully be understood apart from the law relating to settlements.

The life interest
35.3 As its name makes clear, a life interest occurs where land is granted to someone for his life.[1] Such a person's rights of enjoyment of the land are more limited than those of a freeholder. Like a leaseholder he is subject to the doctrine of waste which provides for liability for substantially altering the premises where this is to the detriment of those who will succeed the 'life tenant', as he is known.[2] He will be liable at common law for voluntary waste (which we discuss at para 37.6 below), unless, as is possible, the grant of the life interest stipulates that the life tenant shall be 'unimpeachable of waste', ie that he shall not be liable for waste at common law. Where this is done, equity will intervene by injunction to prevent acts of equitable waste,

i e acts of gross damage to the property, as in *Vane v Barnard*,[3] where the life tenant of a castle had stripped the property of all its wood, glass, lead and so on, leaving it simply a shell. Should a life tenant sell his interest, he clearly cannot create a greater interest than his own; consequently, the purchaser will receive only an interest for the life of the grantor (an interest *pur autre vie*).

1 For leases for life, see para 32.19 above.
2 Para 37.6 below.
3 (1716) 2 Vern 738.

The entailed interest

35.4 The entailed interest (known historically as the 'fee tail') derived particularly from the statute *De Donis Conditionalibus* 1285. Like the fee simple absolute in possession (freehold), it is a fee, i e an interest which can be inherited (unlike the life interest). However, the fee is *taillé* or cut down, so that on the death of the person entitled to it (the 'tenant in tail'), it can pass *only* to his lineal descendant: originally, no action by the tenant in tail could prevent this automatic inheritance. The idea behind the entailed interest, then, is that it should forever pass from father to eldest son, thus keeping the land in the family. An entailed interest is created by granting land 'to X in tail' or 'to X and the heirs of his body'. It may be general or special: in the latter case it passes on death only to the lineal descendant of the tenant in tail and a particular wife. A tenant in tail is now given power by the Fines and Recoveries Act 1833 to 'bar the entail', that is, to convert the entailed interest into a fee simple absolute by executing a deed known as a 'disentailing assurance'. A tenant in tail is not subject to the doctrine of waste.

Conditional and determinable fees

35.5 Both these interests are forms of fee simple, giving the owner the same rights as the owner of a fee simple absolute. However, the determinable fee *automatically* comes to an end should some specified event occur (reverting to the grantor as a fee simple absolute), while a conditional fee *may be cut short by the grantor or his heirs exercising a right of entry*[1] should some condition specified for its exercise occur. For example, a conveyance of a building in fee simple *until* it ceases to be used as a hospice creates a determinable fee; a conveyance of a building in fee simple *on condition that* it is always used as a hospice creates a conditional fee. Determinable fees may be recognised by words, such as 'until' or 'as long as', which mark out time; conditional fees may be recognised by words, such as 'on condition that' or 'provided that', which lay down conditions.

1 Para 39.13 below.

Future enjoyment

35.6 The difference between the leasehold interest and the forms of limited ownership interest considered in the foregoing paragraphs is not only that the former is of a certain duration whilst the duration of the latter is always uncertain. If a landowner grants a lease, he is regarded as remaining in possession of the land throughout the duration of the lease by virtue of the fact that he receives the rents and profits of the land.[1] However, if a landowner grants, for example, a life interest, then once that interest takes effect, the grantor's interest is no longer in possession; it is the life tenant who is entitled to the possession, income and profits of the land: only in the future, when the life interest ends, will the grantor enjoy possession of the land.

1   LPA, s205(1); para 32.14 above.

Vested and contingent interests

35.7   Where, as in the last example, the grantor of a limited interest has a right to future enjoyment of the land, on the ending of the limited interest, he is said to have a *vested* right to future enjoyment of the land. Wherever a person unconditionally owns the right to enjoy land in the future, he has a vested interest in the land. Future enjoyment may, however, be *contingent*, ie the right to enjoyment of the land in the future may depend on the occurrence of some contingency or uncertain event. A landowner who in his will leaves the freehold interest in a plot of land 'to the first of my grandchildren to marry' or 'to my young nephew when he reaches 21' creates a contingent interest. In each case, uncertainty surrounds whether the interest will fall into possession: no grandchild, if there are any, may marry; the nephew may not reach 21. If a landowner, by the terms of his conveyance or his will, creates vested interests, the 'destiny' of the land, so to speak, is known and established, for it will be certain who, if anyone, will be entitled to the land and that each interest in the land will take effect as soon as the previous one ends. Where the landowner creates contingent interests (and if he attempts to control what is to happen to the land far into the future he is bound to create contingent interests), the destiny of the land is uncertain. On the face of it, where it is not known who will become entitled to the land on the ending of a particular limited interest or whether a future interest will take effect as soon as the previous interest ends, the land becomes effectively 'sterilised'—withdrawn from the market—and there can be no dealings with it, until the contingency occurs which will make the destiny of the land certain. It is the policy of the law that land should be freely alienable and that a man should not be able to sterilise dealings with his land for a period of time well into the future. This policy is given effect in particular by the doctrine of overreaching,[1] to a limited extent by the right to bar an entail, and also by the rule against remote vesting (or *rule against perpetuities*). This rule provides that the contingency on which the vesting of an interest depends must occur within the period laid down by the law, otherwise the grant of the interest is void.[2] In this way property is not removed from the market for an unacceptably long time because the contingency, upon which its destiny depends, must occur within a specified period.

1   Para 35.25 below.
2   For dispositions taking effect after 15 July 1964 the period is either that specified by the settlor up to 80 years or is determined by reference to the duration of the lives of certain specified individuals plus 21 years: Perpetuities and Accumulations Act 1964.

Reversions and remainders

35.8   The right to future enjoyment of property may exist as a reversion or a remainder. Suppose X, the owner of Oaklands, grants a life interest in Oaklands to Y. When that interest takes effect, X ceases to have a present interest in the land, having only a right to enjoyment of the land in the future. This interest in the land is known as a 'reversion'.[1] When Y dies,

Oaklands will *revert* to X. If X grants a life interest in Oaklands to Y and the freehold to Z on Y's death, X will cease to have any interest in the land, Y will have a present life interest and Z a freehold 'remainder'. When Y dies, the land will *remain away* from the original grantor, X. A series of interests in the land may be granted in remainder (eg in the case of a grant by X 'to A for life, to B for life, to C in fee simple', B and C's interests are in remainder since on the ending of the previous interest the land remains away from the grantor); there can only be one reversion. A reversion is always in fee simple and always in favour of the original grantor of the limited interests. A reversion is vested; a remainder may be vested or contingent. If a limited interest or a succession of limited interests is created out of land and the freehold is not expressly disposed of, then it automatically reverts to the grantor or his heirs on the ending of the limited interests.

1 Cf landlord's 'reversion', and reversionary leases; paras 32.16 and 32.21 above.

Existence behind a trust

35.9 The fee simple absolute in possession and the leasehold (term of years absolute) are the only legal estates. All other ownership interests are therefore equitable interests. Where a freeholder grants a limited interest in land, other than a leasehold interest, the freehold can then only exist in reversion or in remainder after the limited interest. In each case it is no longer a fee simple absolute *in possession* as it will not be enjoyed until the future; it is therefore no longer a legal estate. Thus limited ownership and rights to future enjoyment take effect *in equity*, and they do so by virtue of a trust. Under the trust, the legal and equitable ownership of the land is split up. The legal estate in the land (almost invariably the fee simple absolute in possession) is held on trust to give effect to the limited ownership interest(s) in equity. Whenever a landowner creates limited ownership interests (other than leaseholds) out of his interest in the land, the succession of interests thus created takes effect under a trust, and is known as a settlement.

Settlements

35.10 A settlement exists whenever successive interests in land are created. For example, if a landowner wishes to give his widow a life interest in his property after he dies, with remainder to his children, he creates a settlement.

Two forms of settlement exist, the strict settlement and the trust for sale. Both are forms of trust: the successive interests exist in equity, the legal estate in the land being held on trust. Today, both these forms of settlement may be regarded as different forms of machinery for achieving the same object, namely, dealing with successive interests in land. Historically, they were established with rather different aims. The purpose of the strict settlement was to ensure that the family estates passed on to successive generations of the same family, as witness the common form of settlement in which the landowner 'settled' on himself a life interest followed by an entailed interest for his eldest son. (However, since the eldest son could convert the entailed interest into a fee simple by 'barring the entail', it was necessary to induce him to re-settle the land on himself for life and his eldest son in tail: by this process of settlement and re-settlement the land was kept in the family. Any attempt to avoid this problem by creating a long string of life interests for the eldest son and the eldest son's eldest son, etc would ultimately fall foul of the rule against remote vesting of contingent interests.)[1] Historically, the purpose of the trust for sale was not keeping land in the family, but, as its name suggests, selling it and providing for future generations out of the investment income of the proceeds of sale.

The present day picture differs rather radically from the past for three reasons: first, changes in society marked by the decline in land-holding as a form of wealth (and as a means to power), paralleled by the rise in industrial wealth; second, an increasing desire that the marketability of land should not be inhibited and thus that it should be possible to sell land free from successive limited interests; third, taxation. Our tax structure does not favour the creation of successive interests in land. Those who create a settlement today must bear in mind the need to preserve the family wealth in a form which attracts as little taxation as possible. The considerable impact in particular of capital transfer tax in this area is beyond the scope of this book; our concern is with the machinery which the law employs to regulate successive interests in land, given that a settlement has been created.

Though comparatively few strict settlements may be created today, one may well be created accidentally. For example, a man who in a 'home-made' will leaves his house to his widow for the rest of her life then to his son after her death, creates a strict settlement, with all the machinery of the Settled Land Act (which we consider in the ensuing paragraphs) that that entails. The machinery of the trust for sale is of central importance in land law, again not so much because landowners deliberately settle land employing that machinery, but because the law adopts the same machinery to deal with concurrent interests in land, ie co-ownership—and the majority of homes are today co-owned.

1 Para 35.7 above.

The strict settlement
35.11 We consider here the machinery provided under the Settled Land Act 1925 (SLA) for the regulation of successive interests. The relevance of this topic lies not only in the fact that such strict settlements still exist and are occasionally expressly created, but also in the fact that whenever a landowner creates a limited interest (other than a lease) the SLA machinery automatically applies unless he expressly states that the trust for sale machinery of the Law of Property Act is to apply.

What is a strict settlement?
35.12 The SLA, s1 provides that a strict settlement exists where, and is a deed, agreement or instrument whereby:

a. successive interests in land are created; or

b. a person is granted, in possession,
i   an entailed interest;
ii   a conditional fee;
iii a determinable fee;
iv a fee simple or a term of years, where that person is a minor; or

c. a person is granted a contingent freehold or leasehold interest (eg 'to A when he reaches 21' or 'to B when he marries'); or

d. land is made subject to family charges, ie where the payment of money is charged on land to make provision for members of the family other than the one who is actually entitled to the land. These sums are paid by the person entitled to the land out of the regular income of the property.

The definition of a strict settlement specifically excludes trusts for sale. Thus, except where a trust for sale is expressly created, the creation of limited ownership interests (other than leases) brings the SLA into play, as does any grant of land to a minor or subject to family charges.

Tenant for life
35.13 The peculiarity of the strict settlement is that the legal estate in the land is held not, as one would expect, by the trustees, but by the tenant for life. The tenant for life is the person who is at present beneficially entitled under the settlement to possession of the settled land.[1] Thus, if land is granted to A for life and then to B in tail, A is the first tenant for life, B the next, B's lineal descendant the next. The tenant for life has extensive powers of dealing with the settled property, but, of course, his beneficial ownership interest in the land is limited, not absolute; consequently he does not hold the legal estate simply for his own benefit but must take into account the interests of everyone entitled under the settlement.[2] The tenant for life holds the legal estate on trust; he is at one and the same time a trustee and a beneficiary.

Although the legal estate is held by the tenant for life, there are in fact trustees of the settlement, whose function is to oversee the trust and to ensure that the terms of the settlement itself and of the SLA are carried out. There are two cases where the legal estate is not held by the tenant for life: where the tenant for life is a minor[3] and where there is in fact no tenant for life at present (as, for example, where land is granted 'to A when he marries' and A is not yet married).[4] In both cases the legal estate is held by a 'statutory owner'.[5] Normally, the trustees would act as statutory owner.

1   SLA, s19.
2   Ibid, s107.
3   Ibid, s26.
4   Ibid, s23.
5   Ibid, s117(1)(xxvi).

Creating a settlement
35.14 *Unregistered land* A strict settlement must be created by the use of two documents: the trust instrument, which contains the terms of the trust, and the principal vesting deed, which vests the legal estate in the tenant for life.[1] The object of requiring two documents is to 'keep the trust off the title'; in other words, the detailed terms of the settlement, which are contained in the trust instrument, do not form part of the title deeds of the land.

Unless the strict settlement is created by two documents, no legal estate passes to the tenant for life and he therefore has no power to deal with it.[1] Any purported dealing with the land by a tenant for life before a vesting deed has been executed takes effect only as a contract to carry out the transfer once a vesting deed has been executed.[2] (This contract should be protected by registration as an estate contract in the Land Charges Register.) It must be remembered that a strict settlement may be created accidentally, as by burdening land with family charges or by creating a succession of interests in a 'home-made' will. In such a case the legal estate in the land cannot be dealt with unless and until a vesting deed has been executed and the other requirements of the SLA complied with.

1 SLA, s4.
2 SLA, s13.

35.15 *Registered land* Where the land is registered, the tenant for life is registered as proprietor and the other beneficial interests under the settlement take effect as minor interests protected by a restriction entered in the Proprietorship Register.[1] Where a settlement is created out of registered land it is created by two documents: a trust instrument, as before, and a vesting 'transfer' in statutory form. The settlor or his personal representatives should apply for restrictions to be entered in the Proprietorship Register of the tenant for life, to the effect that no disposition of the land by the proprietor under which capital money arises is to be registered unless the money is paid to at least two trustees or a trust corporation,[2] and, further, that no disposition is to be registered unless it is authorised by the SLA or the settlement itself. It must be remembered that it is registration and not the vesting transfer which vests the legal estate in the tenant for life.

1 LRA, s86.
2 Para 35.24 below.

The powers of the tenant for life

35.16 Although the legal estate is vested in the tenant for life, being a limited owner he does not have complete freedom of action in his dealings with the land. The range of his powers is laid down by the SLA, although it may be extended, but not cut down,[1] by the terms of the settlement itself. In exercising his powers, the tenant for life must have regard to the interests of all the beneficiaries under the settlement, although in applying this requirement the courts are reluctant to impede the exercise of the statutory powers.[2] Any provision in the settlement having the effect of discouraging the tenant for life from exercising his powers is void.[1] It should be remembered that a tenant for life who has a life interest (as opposed to any other form of limited interest) may be subject, in addition to the restrictions of the SLA, to the doctrine of waste.

1 SLA, s106.
2 SLA, s107; *Wheelwright v Walker* (1883) 23 Ch D 752.

35.17 *Sale* The tenant for life may sell the legal estate in the land and may sell easements, profits or other rights over the land.[1] The purchase money must be paid to at least two trustees or to a trust corporation.[2] The tenant for life must get the best price reasonably obtainable.[3] He can be prevented by injunction from selling at a lower price, but if he does so he can be made liable for the difference. A purchaser dealing in good faith with a tenant for life (whether or not he knows he is dealing with a tenant for life[4]) is, however, conclusively presumed to have given the best price and to have otherwise complied with the Act.[5] Therefore no action can be taken against him, only against the tenant for life, if, for example, the sale is at a price less than the best reasonably obtainable.

1 SLA, s38.
2 Ibid, s94.
3 Ibid, s39.
4 *Re Morgan's Lease, Jones v Norsesowicz* [1972] Ch 1, [1971] 2 All ER 235.
5 SLA, s110(1).

35.18 *Leasing* A tenant for life may grant leases of the settled land, for up to 999 years in the case of building leases and forestry leases, for up to 100 years in the case of mining leases and, in any other case, for up to 50 years.[1] His power to grant residential leases is thus somewhat restricted. These leases must be at the best rent reasonably obtainable taking into account any fine (ie premium or lump sum payment).[2] A premium or lump sum payment represents capital and, like any capital money arising under a settlement, is therefore payable to the trustees.[3] In the normal case,[4] rent represents income, which is payable to the tenant for life.

1 SLA, s41.
2 Ibid, s42.
3 Ibid, ss18 and 42.
4 Except mining leases where a proportion of the rent is treated as capital.

35.19 *Mortgaging* The tenant for life can mortgage the legal estate only for certain specified purposes, including paying for authorised improvements to the settled land.[1] The tenant for life may not mortgage the land for his own benefit.

1 SLA, s71.

35.20 With one exception,[1] the tenant for life does not usually require the consent of the trustees before he can exercise his powers of sale, leasing and mortgaging, but he is required to give them written *notice* at least one month before the transaction. There must be at least two trustees or a trust corporation to receive the notice.[2]

1 Sale of a principal *mansion* house, SLA, s65.
2 SLA, s101.

35.21 *Improvements to the land* Whilst the cost of day-to-day maintenance of settled property must be paid for out of the income of the land, or the pocket of the tenant for life, the cost of improvements which will affect the capital value of the land may be paid for out of capital or from money raised by mortgaging the settled land.[1]

1 SLA, ss83 and 84, Sch 3.

35.22 *Capital investment* Any money regarded as capital is payable to the trustees of the settlement[1] who must apply it in one of the ways listed in the SLA, s73. Income produced by investment of the capital is payable to the tenant for life. It is for the tenant for life to choose how, within the limits of s73, the capital is to be employed, though if he makes no decision, the choice is left to the trustees.[2]

1 SLA, s18.
2 Ibid, s75.

35.23 *Unauthorised dispositions* The tenant for life can only deal with the legal estate in accordance with the SLA and any wider powers conferred by the trust instrument. The SLA, s18 renders any unauthorised disposition by the tenant for life void, except for the purposes of conveying or creating such equitable interests as tenant for life could create from his own limited equitable interest. For example, should the tenant for life purport to grant a 99-year residential lease the transaction would be void.

The trustees of the settlement

35.24 Trustees for the purposes of the SLA will normally be appointed by the settlement itself which also deals with the replacement of trustees.[1] If the matter is not dealt with by the settlement, the Act provides who are to be trustees.[2] There cannot be more than four trustees and there should be at least two, or a trust corporation.[3] It is quite permissible for the tenant for life to be one of the SLA trustees. In such a case he has two quite distinct capacities and his role in the one should not be confused with his role in the other. It must be emphasised that the trustees do not hold the legal estate. Their function is to oversee the working of the settlement and, in particular, to receive and invest capital money.[4]

1 Para 35.14 above.
2 SLA, s30.
3 Trustee Act 1925, ss34 and 39; SLA, s94. The term 'trust corporation' includes the Public Trustee and companies, such as banks, incorporated to undertake trust business and having an issued capital of at least £250,000.
4 Para 35.22 above.

Overreaching

35.25 If a purchaser of settled land from the tenant for life complies with the requirements of the SLA, the beneficial interests under the settlement are 'overreached', that is they are transferred from the land to the purchase money.[1] The beneficial interests cease to bind the land, so that the purchaser is not concerned with them, and thenceforth bind the capital money. Any capital money arising under the settlement is treated as if it were land, and is subject to the same trusts as the land.[2]

For the beneficial interests to be overreached, the main requirement which a purchaser of settled land must comply with is to pay the purchase money to at least two trustees or a trust corporation.[3] The trustees will then invest the money[4] and the tenant for life will receive the investment income for his life, as will the next tenant for life and so on. When the settlement ends the capital money goes to the person who would otherwise have been absolutely entitled to the land. By the process of overreaching the beneficial interests are satisfied without impairing the marketability of the land.

A purchaser who complies with the Act takes the legal estate free not only from the beneficial interests under the settlement but also from any family charges under the settlement and any limited owner's charge[5] and general equitable charges[5] affecting the land, even though these are protected by registration.[6] All these interests and charges are transferred to the purchase money but, of course, other interests affecting the land, eg leases and easements, will continue to bind the land according to normal principles.

1 SLA s72.
2 Ibid, s75.
3 Ibid, ss18 and 94.
4 Para 35.22 above.
5 Para 33.23 above.
6 SLA, s72.

Trusts for sale

35.26 Although the trust for sale is another means of dealing with successive interests in land, i e another form of settlement, it is important in practice for other reasons. In particular, if land is concurrently owned by two or more people, as is the case with most matrimonial homes, which are jointly owned by husband and wife, the legal estate is held on trust for sale. In this chapter we consider the trust for sale as a device for settling land. In the next chapter, we consider the trust for sale in the context of co-ownership.

The express trust for sale is perhaps the more common form of settling land. The main points of difference between it and a strict settlement are:

a. in the trust for sale, the legal estate and the powers in relation to it are vested in the trustees and not in the present beneficiary;

b. the trust for sale is governed by the LPA and *not* by the SLA, being expressly excluded from the definition of a strict settlement.[1]

1 SLA, s1.

What is a trust for sale?

35.27 Under a trust for sale, land is conveyed to trustees on trust to sell it and invest the proceeds for the benefit of particular beneficiaries. In order for a settlement of land to qualify as a trust for sale within the LPA it must be an '*immediate binding trust for sale*'.[1] If it is not, the land is subject to a strict settlement within the SLA. Consequently the settlor must impose a 'trust' for sale, which means that he must impose on the trustees a *duty* to sell the property and not merely give them a *power* to sell. If the trustees are given only a power to sell, the settlement falls within the SLA, the trustees become SLA trustees,[2] and the power of sale is in fact vested in the tenant for life.

The trust for sale must be 'immediate', in that the obligation to sell arises immediately on the creation of the trust. An instruction not to sell for 20 years is inconsistent with an immediate trust for sale. It should be noted however, that although under a trust for sale a *duty* to sell arises immediately, it is not a duty to *sell* immediately. The trustees have power to postpone sale (unless a contrary intention appears from the terms of the trust)[3] until a suitable moment arises. In *Re Mayo*,[4] one of three trustees for sale applied to court for an order of sale[5] because the other trustees would not agree to sell. The court ordered sale on the basis that the trust for sale must prevail unless all the trustees agree to postpone. It follows that any one trustee can require that the duty to sell be carried out, but all the trustees must agree to exercise the power of postponement. This simple rule does not apply, however, where the circumstances in which the trust was created show an intention that the land should be retained.[6] The abstruse meaning given by certain cases[7] to the term 'binding' need not detain us, being confined to determining whether the LPA or the SLA applies where a trust for sale has apparently been imposed in relation to land which has been the subject of a strict settlement.

1   LPA, s205(1)(xxxix).
2   SLA, s30.
3   LPA, s25.
4   [1943] Ch 302, [1943] 2 All ER 440.
5   LPA, s30; para 36.16 below.
6   Para 36.16 below.
7   See *Re Norton* [1929] 1 Ch 84 and *Re Sharpe's Deed of Release* [1939] Ch 51.

Creating a trust for sale

35.28   *Unregistered land* Almost invariably an express trust for sale is created by two documents: a conveyance of the land to the trustees on trust for sale, and a trust instrument containing the details of the beneficial interests in the proceeds of sale. As with the strict settlement, the object is to keep the trusts off the title, for again the purchaser who complies with the statutory requirement of payment of the purchase price to two trustees is not affected by the beneficial interests.[1] However, there is no legal requirement that a landowner who creates a trust for sale during his lifetime should employ two documents; one document conveying the land to the trustees (between two and four, or a trust corporation) and containing the detailed terms of the trust will suffice.

1   Cf para 35.25 above, but see para 35.37 below.

35.29   *Registered land* Where registered land is the subject of a trust for sale, it is the trustees who are registered as proprietors.[1] All references to the trust must be kept off the register,[2] the trust instrument being kept separately, but a purchaser is warned of the existence of the trust, and the beneficial interests are protected,[3] by the entry of a restriction in the Proprietorship Register. This states that no disposition by one proprietor (trustee) of the land under which capital money arises is to be registered without an order of the Registrar or the court.[4] Capital money must be paid to two trustees[5] and the restriction ensures this is complied with.

1   LRA, ss94 and 95.
2   Ibid, s74.
3   See also para 36.20 below.
4   LRA, s58.
5   Or to a trust corporation, LPA, s27.

Restraints on sale or other dispositions

35.30   *Consents* The settlor may impose a requirement that before the property can be sold the trustees must first obtain the consent of one or more specified individuals, including, in all likelihood, the present beneficiary or future beneficiaries. In this way, the settlor may more effectively ensure that the land is kept in the family and not sold than if he had imposed a strict settlement, for there is little restraint on the power of a tenant for life under a strict settlement to sell the land. Sale or any other disposition without the requisite consents constitutes a breach of trust and may be restrained by injunction. However, if the trust requires that the consent of more than two persons be obtained, *a purchaser* need only ensure that two such persons have consented to the sale (or lease or other disposition).[1] If a requisite consent cannot be obtained, any person interested under the trust may apply to the court for an order giving effect to, or directing the trustees to give effect to, the proposed transaction.[2]

1   LPA, s26.
2   Ibid, s30.

35.31   *Consultation* The settlor may expressly require that the trustees consult the present beneficiary or beneficiaries as to sale or any other disposition of the property and give effect to their wishes, so far as that is consistent with the general interests of the trust.[1] Where the requirement of consultation applies, a purchaser need not ensure that it has been complied with.[1]

1   LPA, s26(3). See also para 36.15 below.

Powers of the trustees
35.32   The LPA, s28 provides that the trustees for sale are to have in respect of the land the powers given by the SLA to the tenant for life *and* to the strict settlement trustees, subject to any consents required by the trust. This means that while the trustees have full powers of management,[1] they are restricted as to sale, leasing and mortgaging the land in the same way as a tenant for life would be.[2] However, in the case of unregistered land it is common to provide expressly that the trustees should have the powers of an absolute owner, though possibly subject to consents. Again, in registered land, the trustees, as registered proprietors, automatically have those powers, unless a restriction limiting their powers (or requiring consents) is entered on the register by them.

1   LPA, s28; SLA, s102.
2   Paras 35.16 to 35.19 above.

35.33   Capital money arising by virtue of any disposition of the property is, unless applied in one of the ways specified in the SLA, s73,[1] invested in trustee securities, the income going to the present beneficiary.[2] Money treated as income, such as rent from leases,[3] is also payable to the present beneficiary. Any land acquired by the trustees for sale must be held by them on trust for sale. Once all the land subject to the trust for sale has been sold, the trustees cease to be trustees for sale and become ordinary trustees of the resulting capital. Their powers are then limited to investment of the capital in trustee securities.[4]

1   Para 35.22 above.
2   LPA s28.
3   Para 35.18 above.
4   *Re Wakeman* [1945] Ch 177, [1945] 1 All ER 421.

35.34   *Delegation* Instead of selling the property and providing the present beneficiary with the investment income, or leasing it and passing the rent (after deduction of the cost of repairs, insurance and outgoings)[1] to the present beneficiary as income, the trustees may simply allow the beneficiary to reside in the property if appropriate. Furthermore, the trustees may delegate their powers of leasing and management to the present beneficiary. Such a delegation must be in writing signed by the trustees so that, for example, evidence of the delegation can be given to a lessee. The delegation can be revoked at any time.[2] If delegation occurs, the beneficiary is in some respects in the same position as a tenant for life under a strict settlement though the delegation is revocable and, of course, the beneficiary has no power to sell the land.

1 LPA, s28
2 Ibid, s29.

35.35 *Order of the court* If the trustees refuse to sell or to exercise any of their powers of management or to delegate those powers, or any required consent is refused, any person interested under the trust may apply for a court order giving effect to the proposed transaction. The court has a complete discretion as to what order to make.[1]

1 LPA, s30; see para 36.16 below, where this topic is considered in detail.

Conversion

35.36 The doctrine of conversion is another illustration[1] of the maxim, 'equity looks on that as done which ought to be done'. In the case of the trust for sale what should be done is that the land should be sold, and the beneficial interests should be satisfied out of the purchase money. Equity is therefore said to regard the situation as if the land had been sold and to treat the beneficial interests as being in the purchase money and not in the land. The moment a trust for sale is created, the beneficial interests are, in the eyes of equity, converted from interests in land to interests in money. One clear effect of this doctrine is that beneficial interests under a trust for sale are classified as personal property rather than real property, 'monied' rather than 'landed' property. Thus, should an individual by will leave 'all my personal property to X' and 'all my real property to Y', this phrase will serve to pass an interest under a trust for sale to X.[2]

Were the courts to press the doctrine of conversion to its logical conclusion by always treating the beneficial interests under a trust for sale as interests in money rather than in land, it would be 'just a little unreal'[3] and it could have an adverse impact on the rights of the beneficiaries. The courts have therefore been willing to hold that a beneficiary under a trust for sale has a right subsisting in reference to the land and affecting the legal estate and hence has a right capable of being an overriding interest within the LRA, s70(1)(g).[4] Equally he is a person 'interested . . . in any land'[5] and is thus entitled to lodge a caution against dealings under that Act. Whether or not the expression 'interest in land' in an Act of Parliament is apt to cover interests under a trust for sale depends on the context of the Act, and no hard and fast rule can be laid down.[6]

1 Para 33.6 above.
2 See *Re Cook, Beck v Grant* [1948] Ch 212, [1948] 1 All 231.
3 *Williams and Glyn's Bank Ltd v Boland* [1980] 2 All ER 408 at 415.
4 *Williams and Glyn's Bank Ltd v Boland* [1980] 2 All ER 408, [1980] 3 WLR 138, HL; para 34.20 above. See also *City of London Building Society v Flegg* (1985) Times, 23 December.

5 *Elias v Mitchell* [1972] Ch 652, [1972] 2 All ER 153.
6 *Elias v Mitchell* [1972] Ch at 664. See also *Cooper v Critchley* [1955] Ch 431, [1955] 1 All ER 520, CA (interest under trust for sale an 'interest in land' within the LPA, s40).

Purchasing land held on trust for sale

35.37 The trustees must together join in any conveyance of the land and the purchaser must pay the purchase money to at least two trustees (or a trust corporation).[1] If the purchaser pays the money to the trustees he takes free of the beneficial interests under the trust,[1] which are overreached.[2] Where sale is subject to more than two specified consents, the purchaser's title is not affected provided two consents have been obtained.[3] Likewise, where the land is sold in breach of a requirement of consultation, the purchaser's title is not affected. A complete picture of the law as to the purchase of land subject to a trust for sale requires consideration of the situation where the legal estate is held by one trustee (not being a trust corporation) only. This we postpone until paras 36.17 to 36.20 below.

1 LPA, s27.
2 LPA, s2. Note, however, the highly controversial decision of the Court of Appeal in *City of London Building Society v Flegg* (1985) Times, 23 December, from which it could be argued that the overreaching provisions of the LPA do not apply where the beneficiaries under the trust for sale are in actual occupation of the land; see LPA, s14. At the time of writing the decision is under appeal.
3 Ibid, s26.

Chapter 36

Co-ownership

36.1 In this chapter we consider the law relating to concurrent interests in land, ie simultaneous ownership of a freehold or leasehold estate in land by two or more people, which is an extension of the law of trusts for sale.

There are two forms of co-ownership: joint tenancy and tenancy in common. ('Tenancy' in this context may be regarded as meaning 'ownership'.) Both forms may exist in relation to freehold or leasehold interests.

Joint tenancy

36.2 The essential characteristics of joint tenancy are:

a. the right of survivorship; and

b. the 'four unities'.

The right of survivorship

36.3 Where co-ownership takes the form of joint tenancy, a joint tenant's interest in the land passes automatically on his death to the surviving joint tenants (and so on, until there is one survivor who is the sole owner of the land). This is the right of survivorship; the ultimate survivor takes all. Should a joint tenant purport to leave his interest in the land by will, this disposition has no effect. Nor do the rules of intestacy, which apply where a person dies leaving no effective will, take precedence over the right of survivorship.

The four unities

36.4 The 'four unities' are the unities of possession, interest, title and time; if one of them is missing there cannot be a joint tenancy. Joint tenants share possession of the land, together having one interest in the land, deriving the one title to the property at the same time.

a. *Unity of possession* Joint tenants enjoy unity of possession; each has the right to possession of all of the co-owned land. No one joint tenant can exclude the others from any part of the land. A co-owner cannot, by the very nature of co-ownership, point to one part of the land and say 'that is mine and no one else's.'

b. *Unity of interest* Where there is joint tenancy, each co-owner is entitled jointly with the other joint tenants to the entire interest in the property. There is one interest, freehold or leasehold, to which they are all entitled.

c. *Unity of title* Joint tenants derive title to the property under the same document (or by simultaneously taking possession and acquiring it by adverse possession).[1]

d. *Unity of time* For a joint tenancy to exist the co-owners must not have interests commencing at different times.

1 Ch 42 below.

Tenancy in common

No right of survivorship

36.5 If co-ownership takes the form of tenancy in common, the interest of each co-owner does not automatically pass to the surviving co-owners. The reason is that each tenant in common has a fixed share in the land. On his death this may be passed on, by his will, to whomsoever he chooses (or, in the event of his leaving no will, passes to the person(s) specified by the rules of intestacy). Although each tenant in common has a fixed share, the land is not, of course, physically divided to give effect to those shares; land subject to tenancy in common is referred to in the LPA as being held 'in undivided shares'.

Four unities not essential

36.6 Unity of possession is an essential characteristic of co-ownership, whatever form it takes, for there is clearly no co-ownership where a person possesses land to the exclusion of all others. However, the other unities are not essential to tenancy in common, although they may be present.

How to recognise a tenancy in common

36.7 A tenancy in common exists—

a. *Where land is co-owned, but one of the unities of interest, title or time is absent.*

b. *Where, in the grant of the land to the co-owners, 'words of severance' are used.* 'Severance' is the term used to describe destruction of the essential unity which characterises joint tenancy. Any words which demonstrate that each co-owner is to take a particular share in the property are 'words of severance': eg 'to A and B in equal shares', 'to be divided amongst A and B' and, obviously, 'to A and B as tenants in common'. In *Re North, North v Cusden*[1] land was left in a will to two sons on condition that they paid to their mother the sum of ten shillings weekly 'in equal shares'. It was held that the sons should likewise hold the property 'in equal shares', ie as tenants in common. In addition, of course, words which confer unequal shares (eg 'two-thirds to A, one-third to B') create a tenancy in common.

c. *Where equity infers it.* In certain cases equity infers the existence of a tenancy in common despite the presence of the four unities and the absence of words of severance. The rationale is that the right of survivorship, which benefits the co-owner who lives longest, might operate particularly unfairly in these cases, for example—

i where the purchase price for the land was provided by the co-owners in *unequal* shares. The co-owners are then regarded as holding the land in undivided shares proportionate to their contributions.

ii where the land was acquired by business partners as part of the assets of the partnership.

iii where money is lent by co-mortgagees. As between themselves, co-mortgagees are regarded as being tenants in common in relation to their interest in the land. The loan is repaid however into a joint account and the survivor can thus give a complete discharge for all money due.[2]

iv where the co-owners hold the land for their several individual business purposes.[3]

In each of these cases, equity presumes that each co-owner will wish to have the fullest ability to realise his investment. However, there is only a *presumption* of tenancy in common, which can be rebutted.

1 [1952] Ch 397, [1952] 1 All ER 609.
2 LPA, s111.
3 *Malayan Credit Ltd v jack Chia–MPH Ltd* [1986] 1 All ER 711, PC.

The machinery for effecting co-ownership
Tenancy in common

36.8 A tenancy in common cannot exist in relation to a legal estate;[1] consequently, it takes effect only in equity. If land is conveyed to a number of people as tenants in common, the LPA provides that the conveyance takes effect as if it were a conveyance of the legal estate to the co-owners (or, if there are more than four, to the first four named in the conveyance) as *joint tenants* on *trust for sale* to give effect to the rights of the co-owners as *tenants in common in equity*.[2] Tenancy in common can only exist behind a trust for sale which either is imposed by the LPA or may be expressly created; it takes effect in relation to the beneficial, equitable interest in the land, but not the legal estate. It will be seen that the key to an understanding of the machinery of co-ownership is to consider separately the position of the co-owners in relation to the legal estate in the land (be it freehold or leasehold) and their position in relation to the equitable interests existing behind the curtain of the trust.

Thus, if land is granted to A, B and C in equal shares (words of severance) they will hold the legal estate as joint tenants and be trustees to give effect to their tenancy in common in equity:

The 'curtain' of the trust

A, B, C — legal JT (joint tenancy)

A, B, C — equitable TiC (tenancy in common)

Should C die, his individual share under the tenancy in common may pass under his will or on intestacy (say to X); but the right of survivorship operates in respect of the joint tenancy of the legal estate:

A, B — legal JT

A, B, X — equitable TiC.

1   LPA, s1(6).
2   Ibid, ss34 and 35.

Joint tenancy

36.9   For reasons which will become apparent,[1] a beneficial joint tenancy also takes effect behind a trust for sale, whether express or imposed by statute.[2] As in the case of tenancy in common there is a splitting of the legal and equitable ownership. The co-owners (or the first four of them) hold the legal estate as joint trustees for sale for themselves as *joint tenants* in equity:

A, B, C — legal JT
_____
A, B, C — equitable JT

Should C die, the right of survivorship operates in respect of the joint tenancy both at law and in equity:

A, B — legal JT
_____
A, B — equitable JT

1   Paras 37.10 and 37.12 below.
2   LPA, s36.

Conveyancing advantages

36.10   The use of the trust for sale to give effect to co-ownership avoids complexity in conveyancing. A purchaser of land which is co-owned need not concern himself with the equitable interests behind the curtain of the trust, no matter how many; they are off the title (or off the register).[1] Furthermore as the trustees hold the legal estate as joint tenants, there is unity of title, ie only one title (or register of title) for the purchaser to investigate. A purchaser need only ensure that he pays the purchase money to two trustees to be free of the equitable co-ownership interests which are overreached by the conveyance.[2] To illustrate, suppose land is conveyed to A, B, C, D and E as tenants in common. This takes effect as follows:

A, B, C, D — legal JT
_____
A, B, C, D, E — equitable TiC

Suppose A dies, leaving his interest in the land to X. The position now is:

B, C, D — legal JT
_____
X, B, C, D, E — equitable TiC

On a sale of the land, a purchaser would only be concerned to investigate the single title (or register of title) of B, C and D. He would not be concerned with the beneficial interests in general or with what has happened to A's interest in the land, in particular. If he pays the purchase price to three of the trustees, B, C and D, the complexity in relation to the beneficial ownership of the land need not concern him, for the conveyance overreaches the beneficial interests.

1 Paras 35.28 and 35.29 above.
2 Para 35.37 above.
Note, however, *City of London Building Society v Flegg* (1985) Times, 23 December, CA, in which it was held that the overreaching provisions of the LPA do not apply where beneficial co-owners are in actual occupation of the land; see LPA, s14. In any event, it was held, the interest of a co-owner in actual occupation of property constitutes an overriding interest in registered land, incapable of being overreached even where the purchase money is paid to two trustees. This highly controversial decision is under appeal at the time of writing.

Severance

36.11 Severance means converting an equitable joint tenancy into an equitable tenancy in common. Only an equitable joint tenancy can be severed, of course, for to sever a legal joint tenancy would be to create a legal tenancy in common, which cannot exist.[1] There are five methods of severing an equitable joint tenancy. In the first two methods, severance is effected by destroying one of the four unities.[2]

a. *Acquiring a greater interest in the land* All the joint tenants have one interest in the land; if one acquires another interest, the unity of interest is destroyed. This is only of significance where the parties are joint tenants for life under a strict settlement.[3] Thus if A and B are joint tenants for life and A subsequently acquires the freehold reversion, A's life interest and the reversion merge and A no longer has the same interest as B. During B's life, the two are tenants in common.

b. *By assignment of the equitable interest* A purported disposition by a joint tenant of his equitable interest on death has no effect because of the right of survivorship. But an assignment of that interest by the joint tenant during his lifetime effects a severance by destroying the unity of title, since the assignee derives title under a different document from the original co-owners. Thus, if A, a joint tenant with B and C, assigns his equitable interest in the land to X, X takes as tenant in common. As between themselves, B and C remain joint tenants, for between them the four unities remain:

i. A, B, C — legal JT
    ─────────────────
    A, B, C — equitable JT

ii. A, B, C — legal JT
    ─────────────────
    X, B, C — equitable
       ⌐ ⌐
       │ JT
       └─┘
    ───
    TiC

X becomes a tenant in common, having a one-third share, with B and C who are joint tenants of a two-thirds share. Note that the position with regard to the legal estate is not affected by A's assignment of his equitable interest. A will no doubt wish to drop out of the picture, having assigned his equitable interest in the land, thus A, B and C as trustees should convey the legal estate to X, B and C to give effect to the requisite trusts. Note that a specifically enforceable contract to sell his interest to X would equally effect a severance of A's interest.

c. *By mutual agreement to sever* Equitable joint tenants may by mutual agreement sever that joint tenancy. The agreement itself converts the joint tenancy into a tenancy in common.

d. *By notice in writing* An equitable joint tenant may sever the joint tenancy by giving a notice in writing to that effect to the other joint tenant(s).[4] This provision applies only where land is vested in joint tenants beneficially, ie where the joint tenants hold both the legal estate and the equitable interests. However, where land is granted to more than four people as joint tenants, the legal estate is vested only in the first four. It would seem then that in such a case this method of severance is not possible, since not all the joint tenants hold the legal estate.

The case of *Re Draper's Conveyance, Nihan v Porter*[5] provides an illustration of severance by notice in writing. A husband and wife had been joint tenants of their home. After they were divorced, the wife issued a summons seeking a court order[6] that the property be sold. The order was granted, but the husband remained in occupation and no sale was ever effected. The husband subsequently died intestate. By the operation of the right of survivorship the wife was thus the sole surviving trustee of the legal estate.[7] However, the question was what was the position in relation to the equitable interest? Who was beneficially entitled to the property? Was the wife, by survivorship, solely entitled in equity; or had her action in seeking a court order severed the joint tenancy, thus creating a tenancy in common and leaving the wife trustee for herself and her late husband's estate as tenants in common? The court held that the latter was the case; the wife was not solely entitled to the property. It was successfully argued for the husband's estate that severance was effected either because in seeking the order of sale the wife had exhibited an intention to realise her share of the property, which in itself was sufficient to effect severance, or because the issue of the summons constituted the giving of a written notice to sever. In *Burgess v Rawnsley*,[8] only this second ground for the decision was approved by the Court of Appeal. In *Harris v Goddard*[9] it was held that a written notice which only expresses a desire to bring about severance at some time in the future will not suffice. Furthermore, the notice must exhibit a desire to *sever*—ie to separate off the share of the joint tenant. Hence the wife's application in a divorce petition for the court to exercise its powers under the Matrimonial Causes Act (para 36.17 below) in respect of the house did not operate as a notice to sever.

e. *Course of dealings* It was held in *Burgess v Rawnsley* that an uncommunicated declaration of an intention to sever, and realise one's share, is insufficient to bring about severance, but, following *Williams v Hensman*,[10] a course of dealings between the parties sufficient to indicate a *shared* intention to sever will bring about severance.[10]

1 LPA, s1(6); para 36.8, above.
2 Para 36.4 above.
3 Para 36.23 below.
4 LPA, s36(2).
5 [1969] 1 Ch 486, [1967] 3 All ER 853.
6 Cf para 36.16 below.
7 Para 36.19 below.
8 [1975] Ch 429, [1975] 3 All ER 142, CA.
9 [1983] 3 All ER 242, [1983] 1 WLR 1203, CA.
10 *Williams v Hensman* (1861) 1 John & H 546.

Co-ownership by implication

36.12 In certain circumstances, where land is conveyed to one person alone, the courts may imply co-ownership. In general the principle according to which this is done is an elaboration of the doctrine of resulting trusts,[1] under which property results to or comes back to the person who advances the purchase money (otherwise than as a gift or loan[2]), if it is not actually conveyed into his or her name.[3] Much of the case law has arisen in the context of the matrimonial home or the quasi-matrimonial home (by which we mean where a couple live together as if man and wife): the property is conveyed in the name of one partner only (usually the man) but the other claims a share. There is no principle in English law of community of property or family assets whereby property belonging to either spouse is regarded as family property, thus the claim to a share must, in general, be based on a claim to an interest under a resulting trust.

The cases show that a resulting trust in favour of the party claiming a share will be found to exist only where the court is satisfied that it was the parties' common intention, as evidenced by actual agreement or more likely inferred from the parties' conduct and the surrounding circumstances, that the beneficial (equitable) interest was to be shared in some proportion or other.[4] Such an intention can only be inferred where the party claiming a share makes a real or substantial financial contribution towards the acquisition of the property. This might be, for example, by paying part of the purchase price or contributing regularly to the mortgage instalments or paying off part of the mortgage or making substantial financial contributions to the family expenses so as to enable the mortgage instalments to be paid.[5] In the case of *married* couples it is specifically provided, by the Matrimonial Proceedings and Property Act 1970, s37 that, subject to any contrary agreement between the spouses, a substantial contribution in money or money's worth to the improvement of the property entitles a spouse to a share (or, as the case may be, enlarged share) in the beneficial interest in the property. Where the parties have actually agreed that the beneficial interest should be shared, such agreement must be evidenced in writing signed by the legal owner or there must be evidence that the other party has acted to his or her detriment by reason of the common intention as to joint ownership.[6]

It has universally been accepted by the courts that, where co-ownership is implied on this resulting trust basis, the legal estate is held by the sole legal owner on *trust for sale* for himself and the other co-owner(s) in equity as joint tenants or tenants in common, as the case may be. This clearly accords with the scheme of the 1925 legislation[7] although the legislation does not specifically provide for the case of co-ownership by implication.

1 Occasionally the courts speak of imposing a constructive trust (para 38.15, below), *Eves v Eves* [1975] 3 All ER 768 [1975] 1 WLR 1338, CA; 'whether [such a] trust . . . is described as implied, constructive or resulting does not greatly matter', *Burns v Burns* [1984] 1 All ER 244 at 251.
2 *Re Sharpe, a bankrupt* [1980] 1 All ER 198, [1980] 1 WLR 219.
3 *Dyer v Dyer* (1788) 2 Cox Eq Cas 92.
4 *Gissing v Gissing* [1971] AC 886, [1970] 2 All ER 780, HL.
5 *Burns v Burns* [1984] Ch 317, [1984] 1 All ER 244, CA.
6 LPA, s53(1)(b); *Midland Bank Ltd v Dobson* [1985] NLJ Rep 751, CA.
7 LPA, ss34–36; SLA, s36; *Bull v Bull* [1955] 1 QB 234, [1955] 1 All ER 253, CA.

Quantifying the co-owners' beneficial shares

36.13 It is today commonly the case that property conveyed to co-owners is conveyed to them on *express* trust for sale as joint tenants or tenants in common as the case may be. In such cases there will therefore be an express declaration as to what the beneficial share of each co-owner is to be.[1] Where however there is no express declaration of trust we have seen that the LPA provides that a conveyance to co-owners takes effect as a conveyance on trust for sale; likewise, where co-ownership is implied, the sole legal owner holds on trust for sale. In these latter cases the question arises of quantifying the co-owners' shares in equity. Where the property is bought outright and not on a mortgage then the extent of their respective shares will depend on a more or less precise arithmetical calculation of the extent of their contributions to the purchase price. Where on the other hand and as is more usual nowadays the property is bought with the aid of a mortgage then the court has to assess each of the parties' respective contributions in a broad sense; nevertheless the court is only entitled to look at the financial contributions, or their real or substantial equivalent, to the acquisition of the property. Only when there is no evidence on which a court can reasonably draw an inference about the extent of the shares of the parties should it fall back on the maxim 'equality is equity' and hold that the beneficial interest belongs to the parties in equal shares.[2] In such a case, at least where the property has been conveyed to all the co-owners, equity follows the law and they will hold as joint tenants in equity.[3] In all other cases, the co-owners will be tenants in common in equity.[4]

1 Goodman v Gallant [1986] 1 All ER 311, CA[3]
2 *Burns v Burns* [1984] 1 All ER 244 at 264–265.
3 *Walker v Hall* (1984) 14 Fam Law 21, CA.
4 Para 36.7c above.

Occupation of co-owned land

36.14 It was accepted by the House of Lords in *Williams and Glyn's Bank v Boland*,[1] following the decision of the Court of Appeal in *Bull v Bull*,[2] that a co-owner in equity has a right to occupy the property. Yet a theoretical objection to this has been put forward, namely that since the co-owner's interest takes effect under a trust for sale, it is (by virtue of the doctrine of conversion[3]) an interest in the proceeds of sale and not a beneficial interest in the land which would entitle the co-owner to occupy the land. This is in fact another area where the courts ignore the full theoretical impact of the doctrine of conversion. Where the property was patently acquired to provide a home the courts will permit occupation; but where it is clear that the prime object of the trust was that the property should be sold, the courts will deny a beneficial co-owner the right to occupy the property and thereby hinder sale.[4]

In the context of the matrimonial home, an attempt to avoid some of the theoretical difficulties over the right to occupy the property is made by the provisions of the Matrimonial Homes Act 1983, which gives all non-owning spouses *including* those who are beneficial co-owners by implication (the legal estate being vested in the other spouse alone) the right to occupy the home.[5] This right is 'in essence a personal and non-assignable statutory right not to be evicted from the matrimonial home in question during marriage or until the court otherwise orders; and this right constitutes a charge on the estate or interest of the owning spouse which requires protection against third parties by registration'.[6] As we shall see, *Boland's* case renders reliance on this right unnecessary in the case of a spouse in occupation.[6]

1 [1980] 2 All ER 408, [1980] 1 WLR 138, HL; para 36.18 below.
2 [1955] 1 QB 234, [1955] 1 All ER 253, CA.
3 Para 35.36 above.
4 *Barclay v Barclay* [1970] 2 QB 677, [1970] 2 All ER 676, CA.
5 Para 33.25 above.
6 *Wroth v Tyler* [1974] Ch 30, [1973] 1 All ER 897.

Sale of co-owned land
Consultation
36.15 By the LPA, s26(3),[1] the trustees for sale must consult the existing adult equitable co-owners and, so far as is consistent with the general interests of the trust, give effect to their wishes, or, in the case of dispute, the wishes of the majority according to the value of their interests. However, this requirement does not apply where the land has been expressly conveyed to the co-owners on trust for sale unless it is expressly incorporated. In many cases of co-ownership, the trustees and the beneficiaries will be the same people, in which case the co-owners having the greatest share will normally carry the day. However, if there is deadlock as to, for example, whether the land should be sold, and one or more of the trustees refuses to sell, any person interested in the land may apply for a court order of sale under the LPA, s30.

1 Para 35.31 above.

Court order
36.16 Under the LPA, s30, 'If the trustees for sale refuse to sell ... any person interested may apply to the court for [an] order for giving effect to the proposed transaction or for an order directing the trustees for sale to give effect thereto, and the court may make such order as it thinks fit.' The court has a wide discretion as to whether or not to make an order on an application under s30. In *Re Buchanan-Wollaston's Conveyance*,[1] four

people purchased a plot of land adjacent to their homes in order to keep it free from development. All four agreed that the land should be dealt with only in accordance with the wishes of the majority. One co-owner subsequently left the neighbourhood and sought a court order that the land should be sold. The court refused to order sale. Having regard to the circumstances, particularly the agreement between the co-owners, it was not right and proper to order sale at that particular time. On the face of it, this decision appears to be inconsistent with *Re Mayo, Mayo v Mayo*,[2] where it was held that unless all the trustees concur in postponing sale the trust will prevail and the land must be sold. In *Jones v Challenger*,[3] however, the court explained that in *Re Mayo* the simple and fundamental principle was applied that in a trust for sale there is a duty to sell and a power to postpone, with the result that one trustee can call on the others to perform a duty but all must agree to exercise the power. However, this principle cannot prevail where the trust itself, or the circumstances in which it was made, show that there was a collateral object besides that of sale. In *Re Buchanan-Wollaston's Conveyance*, the land was bought for the express purpose of keeping it as an open space. That collateral object still subsisted at the time of the application for sale and therefore sale was refused.

Once again, the bulk of litigation in this area in recent years has concerned the matrimonial or, more particularly, quasi-matrimonial home.[4] In such cases, the issue generally arises on the breakdown of the relationship where one party wishes the co-owned home to be sold to realise his or her share, while the other wishes it to be retained to provide a roof over his or her head. Nowadays, where the parties were *married*, the court has power, under the Matrimonial Causes Act 1973, ss24 and 25 as amended,[5] on or after granting a decree of divorce, nullity or judicial separation, to make an order 'adjusting' the spouses' respective property rights (for example by transferring an interest from one to the other). In exercising its discretion under this provision the court should take into account all the circumstances, particularly the welfare of any children of the family, but also including the financial resources and needs of the parties. Where appropriate, applications should therefore be made under the Matrimonial Causes Act and not under the LPA, s30.[6]

In contrast, where the 1973 Act does not apply, for example in the case of unmarried couples, there is no jurisdiction under s30 to do what is fair and reasonable.[7] In the first place the court cannot assist a party who has no beneficial interest in the property, even though, for example, the parties have lived together as if married for many years.[8] Second, the court cannot under s30 adjust the parties' interests in the property. Although the discretion conferred by s30 is wide, it seems it does not enable the court to make orders where an order for sale is not made.[9]

As Kerr LJ said in *Bernard v Josephs*,[10] under s30 the principle according to which the courts act is that once the purpose of the trust has come to an end, a sale can be insisted on by any of the beneficiaries unless the court considers that it is inequitable for him to realise his investment. In *Re Evers's Trust, Papps v Evers*,[11] for example, the court found that the property was purchased by the parties, who had lived together as man and wife, as a family home and that that purpose still subsisted after the relationship ended, since the woman still needed a home for herself and the children, whilst on the other hand the man had no pressing need to realise his investment. The court therefore refused to order sale, on the woman undertaking to pay the mortgage and outgoings and to indemnify the man in respect of her occupation. In *Bernard v Josephs*,[12] where there were no children and the relationship had ended, an order for sale was made, but was postponed on the parties agreeing that the man, who remained in occupation, would buy the woman out. In *Dennis v McDonald*[13] sale was refused, but the man, who remained in occupation with some of the children, was ordered to pay the woman an 'occupation rent' as compensation for having excluded her from the property.

These cases show the courts achieving a certain flexibility, balancing the interests of the parties, in their application of s30. However, different considerations will in general apply where an application under the section is made by a trustee in bankruptcy in whom one co-owner's interest has vested on the making of a bankruptcy order. In all but exceptional cases[14] the court will order sale, preferring the interests of the creditors in receiving what is owed to them from the proceeds of sale to the interests of the co-owners in retaining a home.[15]

1 [1939] Ch 217; affd [1939] Ch 738, [1939] 2 All ER 302, CA.
2 [1943] Ch 302, [1943] 2 All ER 440. Para 35.27 above.
3 [1961] 1 QB 176, [1960] 1 All ER 785, CA.
4 Para 36.12 above.
5 Matrimonial and Family Proceedings Act 1984, s3.
6 *Williams v Williams* [1977] 1 All ER 28, [1976] Ch 278, CA.
7 *Re Evers's Trust, Papps v Evers* [1980] 3 All ER 399, CA.
8 *Burns v Burns* [1984] 1 All ER 244, CA; para 36.12 above.
9 *Dennis v McDonald* [1981] 2 All ER 632; affd [1982] 1 All ER 590, CA.
10 [1982] 3 All ER 162, CA.
11 [1980] 3 All ER 399, CA.
12 [1982] 3 All ER 162, CA. Compare *Stott v Ratcliffe* (1982) 126 Sol Jo 310.
13 [1981] 2 All ER 632; affd [1982] 1 All ER 590, CA.
14 *Re Holliday (a bankrupt)* [1980] 3 All ER 385, CA.
15 *Re Lowrie (a bankrupt)* [1981] 3 All ER 353.

Sale by a sole trustee

36.17   In a case of co-ownership by implication of *unregistered* land, where the legal estate is held by a single trustee, how are the beneficial co-ownership interests of those who do not hold the legal estate to be protected should the legal owner sell or otherwise dispose of the legal estate? The purchaser will not be in a position to comply with the LPA, s27(2), which requires that the purchase money be paid to at least two trustees,[1] since an examination of the title deeds will not show him that the land is co-owned in equity; the conveyance will therefore not overreach the beneficial interests. Is he then bound by the beneficial interests arising under the trust for sale for failing to comply with the requirement of paying the purchase price to at least two trustees?[2] The answer given in *Caunce v Caunce*[3] is that whether the purchaser is bound depends on *notice*. If the purchaser has notice, actual, constructive or imputed, of the equitable co-ownership interests he is bound by them, and takes the legal title subject to them. It follows that, under the doctrine of *Hunt v Luck*,[4] if the co-owner is in occupation of the property the purchaser will have constructive notice of his equitable rights under the trust for sale and will take subject to them. The view expressed in *Caunce v Caunce* that where the vendor is in occupation, the occupation of any other person which is not inconsistent with that of the vendor (eg his wife's) does not give constructive notice of that person's rights, was in effect rejected by the House of Lords in *Williams and Glyn's Bank v Boland*.[5]

1 Para 35.37 above.
2 LPA, s27(1).
3 [1969] 1 All ER 722, [1969] 1 WLR 286.
4 [1902] 1 Ch 428, CA; para 33.18 above.
5 2 All ER 408, [1980] 3 WLR 138, HL; para 34.20 above.

36.18 In the case of co-ownership by implication of *registered* land, the register of title of the sole legal owner will contain no sign of the existence of the equitable co-ownership interests, and a purchaser will not be affected by notice of the interests under the trust.[1] It might seem then, that unless the beneficial interests are protected by an entry on the register[2] (which in practice is unlikely) a purchaser will not be affected by them. However, it has been held, in *Williams and Glyn's Bank Ltd v Boland*,[3] that a co-owner in equity who is in actual occupation of the property will, in this situation, have an overriding interest within the LRA, s70(1)(g), subject to which the purchaser will take. Furthermore, the spouse of the legal owner is no exception to those protected.[4] Mrs Boland was, by virtue of her substantial contribution to its purchase price, an equitable tenant in common of the house which had been transferred into the sole name of her husband. He mortgaged the house to the bank which made no inquiries of Mrs Boland. On the husband defaulting, the bank started possession proceedings. It was held, however, that the wife's interest, being overriding, had priority over the bank's and it could not therefore obtain possession as against her.

It follows that it is important that those who purchase, or lend money on the security of, a house apparently owned solely by one spouse or cohabitee make enquiries of the other (if he or she is in actual occupation) as to his or her rights. Those who lend money on the security of a matrimonial or quasi-matrimonial home should seek the concurrence of both parties in the transaction no matter that one alone seems from the register or title deeds to be entitled to the property.[5] (It should be noted that the same problems arise where others, for example, parents, contribute to the purchase or extension of property but do not appear on the title.) The decision in *Williams and Glyn's Bank Ltd v Boland* also means that a wife who has an equitable interest in the matrimonial home, if she is in occupation, need not rely upon the much criticised protection afforded by the Matrimonial Homes Act 1983 to protect her right to occupy the property.[6]

1 LRA, s74.
2 Restriction, LRA, s58; caution, ibid, s54; notice, ibid, s49(2).
3 [1980] 2 All ER 408, [1980] 3 WLR 138, HL.
4 Cf *Caunce v Caunce* [1969] 1 All ER 722, [1969] 1 WLR 286; para 36.16 above.
5 Note, however, *Bristol & West Building Society v Henning* [1985] 2 All ER 606, CA and *Paddington Building Society v Mendelsohn* (1985) 50 P & CR 244, CA.
6 Para 33.25 above.

36.19 A further situation involving sale by a sole owner should also be noted: that is where a legal estate which was subject to a joint tenancy is now, by the right of survivorship, vested in a sole surviving trustee. If the sole trustee is solely entitled in law *and* in equity he may deal with the land as if it were not held on trust for sale.[1] However, in *unregistered* land, a purchaser of the land from him will know from the terms of the title deeds that the land has been the subject of co-ownership but, since dealings with the equitable interests are kept off the title, the purchaser will not know for certain whether the sole trustee is, by survivorship, also solely entitled in equity or whether the joint tenancy in equity has at some time been severed with the result that the sole trustee holds the land for himself and another or others as tenants in common. Prior to 1964, to ensure that he would not take the land subject to equitable interests arising under a tenancy in common, the purchaser would have required that a second trustee be appointed so that the LPA, s27(2)[2] might be complied with. Since that time, however, the Law of Property (Joint Tenants) Act 1964 has provided that, if the surviving trustee conveys the land, not as trustee, but as beneficial owner (ie as absolute owner) or if the conveyance contains a statement that the vendor is sole beneficial owner, the purchaser takes free of any equitable interests behind the trust for sale, unless a note recording that the joint tenancy in equity has been severed (ie turned into a tenancy in common) is attached to the conveyance. It follows that it is up to any equitable tenant in common whose interest arises by severance to protect the interest by having a memorandum of severance endorsed on the conveyance.

1   LPA, s36(2).
2   Para 35.37 above.

36.20   The Law of Property (Joint Tenants) Act 1964 does not apply to *registered* land. Where land is conveyed to joint tenants, the beneficial interests should be protected by the entry of a restriction in the proprietor-ship register.[1] So long as that restriction remains on the register, no disposition by a sole surviving trustee can be registered without an order of the Registrar or court, thus ensuring that the LPA, s27 is complied with. The restriction will remain in force until the sole surviving trustee procures its removal by satisfying the Registrar that he is the sole beneficial owner. Conceivably, he could procure its removal by fraud, in which case the beneficial interests would be capable of protection as overriding interests within s70(1)(g). The moral is that all purchasers should make enquiries of all persons in actual occupation.

1   Para 34.22 above.

Property investment

36.21   The machinery of co-ownership may be used as a means of enabling a number of persons or institutions to invest in a particular commercial property in the following way. The freehold or long leasehold of a property is conveyed to a trust corporation on express trust for sale to hold for the benefit of the investors as tenants in common in equity in proportion to the size of their investment. The trust for sale machinery enables each investor/co-owner to have an equitable interest in the proceeds of sale, the value of which should continually increase, together with income in the form of a share in the rents and profits arising from letting the property. Each tenant in common is free to assign his interest during his lifetime or on death. The trust for sale is made subject to the consents of the majority in value.[1] The court could dispense with these consents if an application for sale was made under the LPA, s30 by one of the tenants in common, but it is essential to the scheme that no one investor should be able to force sale at what the majority consider an inappropriate moment by means of an application to court. To this end, as in *Re Buchanan-Wollaston's Conveyance*² all the co-owners agree not to seek sale of the land save with the agreement of the majority. A purchaser of the property is not, of course, concerned with (and is not entitled to investigate) the interests of the investor/co-owners. He need only investigate the title or register of title of the trust corporation, paying the purchase money to it, whereupon the trust would no doubt be terminated and the proceeds divided amongst the tenants in common.

1   Para 35.30 above.
2   [1939] Ch 21.7; affd [1939] Ch 738, [1939] 2 All ER 302, CA.

Ending co-ownership

36.22   Co-ownership may be ended by partition of the land or by union of the concurrent interests in a single co-owner.

Partition of the land destroys the unity of possession without which there can be no co-ownership. The parties agree to divide the land between them, the trustees conveying a part to each.¹ Sale may be ordered under the LPA, s30² as a substitute for partition and this will be particularly appropriate if partition is impractical, as where the property consists of a single house.

Union of the interests in the land in a sole tenant may occur by survivorship or by one tenant acquiring the interests of the others.

1   LPA, s28.
2   Para 36.15 above.

Settled land

36.23   What happens if two or more people concurrently become entitled to settled land (e g to A for life, to B and C for their joint lives) depends on whether they become entitled as joint tenants or as tenants in common. If as the former, they are jointly treated as the tenant for life under the settlement which is governed by the SLA.¹ If as the latter, the strict settlement comes to an end, a trust for sale under the LPA then operates, the SLA trustees becoming trustees for sale and having the legal estate vested in them.²

1   SLA, s19.
2   SLA, s36; LPA, Sch 1, Part IV.

Chapter 37

Landlord and tenant

Rights and obligations of the parties to a lease

37.1 The primary source of the rights and obligations of the landlord and the tenant is, of course, the lease itself. The terms of the lease are referred to as 'covenants', whether or not the lease was made by deed,[1] albeit that strictly that word is reserved for contractual terms contained in a deed. It is possible, and quite likely in the case of a weekly or monthly tenancy, that nothing will be expressly agreed by the parties to the lease, other than its duration and the rent. In such a case, certain *minimal* terms will be implied by the law. It is therefore preferable that the parties should expressly agree at least that the lease should contain the 'usual' covenants, which we discuss in para 37.9 below.

We consider first the position of the parties in the absence of express terms governing their rights and obligations.

1 Paras 33.3 to 33.4 above.

Where no express terms
The landlord

37.2 *Implied covenant for quiet enjoyment* This obligation on the part of the landlord, implied in all leases as being a legal incident of the relationship,[1] is intended to secure for the tenant, not enjoyment of his tenancy free from the nuisance of noise, but enjoyment free from disturbance by adverse claimants to the property[2] and free from substantial physical interference by the landlord.[3] The landlord was held liable in damages for breach of this covenant in *Perera v Vandiyar*[4] where, with the object of driving the tenant out, he cut off the electricity and gas supplies to the premises. It should be noted that a landlord who indulges in such harassment will be guilty also of a criminal offence under the Protection from Eviction Act 1977, s1, as will a landlord who unlawfully evicts a tenant.

1 Paras 7.22–7.23 above.
2 *Hudson v Cripps* [1896] 1 Ch 265.
3 See *Browne v Flower* [1911] 1 Ch 219 (landlord not in breach of this covenant where another tenant, with landlord's consent, erected an iron staircase outside the plaintiff tenant's window seriously affecting the plaintiff's privacy); contrast *Owen v Gadd* [1956] 2

556

QB 99, [1956] 2 All ER 28 (landlord in breach of this covenant where he erected scaffolding outside the entrance to tenant's shop).
4 [1953] 1 All ER 1109, [1953] 1 WLR 672, CA. For the award of exemplary damages where the landlord's action constitutes a tort, see para 30.2 above.

37.3 *Non-derogation from grant*[1] A covenant is again implied in all leases that the landlord will not derogate from his grant. Indeed, it is a principle of general application that a grantor may not take away with one hand what he has given with the other.[2] Thus, if the landlord leases land to be used in a particular way, he must not so act in relation to land retained by him as to make the demised premises materially less fit for their intended use.[3] For example, a landlord, who leased to the tenant two floors of a block of flats for residential purposes and then leased the remainder to another tenant for business purposes, was held to have derogated from his grant to the first tenant in so doing.[4]

1 Para 40.13 below.
2 *Birmingham, Dudley and District Banking Co v Ross* (1888) 38 Ch D 295 at 313.
3 *Aldin v Latimer Clark, Muirhead & Co* [1894] 2 Ch 437; *Browne v Flower* [1911] 1 Ch 219.
4 *Newman v Real Estate Debenture Corpn Ltd and Flower Decorations Ltd* [1940] 1 All ER 131. See also *Aldin v Latimer Clark, Muirhead & Co*, para 40.13 below.

37.4 *Fitness for habitation, and repair of premises* The courts have not taken the step of implying, as a legal incident of the relationship of landlord and tenant, any covenant on the part of the landlord that the premises are and/or will remain fit for habitation. There is one exception: where premises are let *furnished*, a condition is implied that they are fit for human habitation at the commencement of the tenancy.[1] Further, in one other case, of little practical relevance, a covenant is implied *under statute*. Under the Landlord and Tenant Act 1985, s8, there is an implied condition in any letting of a dwelling-house at a rent not exceeding, in Greater London, £80 per annum, or elsewhere, £52, that the house is fit for human habitation at the commencement of the tenancy, and furthermore the landlord impliedly covenants that it will be kept so fit during the tenancy.[2] The landlord's obligation is limited to defects of which he has notice,[3] and which can be remedied at reasonable cost.[4] (It is worth noting that, under the Housing Act 1985, Part VI, local authorities have power to require landlords to render their property fit for human habitation if this can be done at reasonable cost. A tenant may thus call upon the local authority to exercise its powers rather than rely on any covenant in the lease.)

As to *repairs*, there is no generally implied covenant that the landlord shall carry out repairs. A statutory exception is contained in the Landlord and Tenant Act 1985, ss11 to 14, which provide that where a dwelling-house is let for less than seven years, the landlord impliedly covenants:

a. to keep the structure and exterior in repair; and

b. to keep in repair and proper working order the installations in the house for the supply of water, gas and electricity, for sanitation, and for space- and water-heating.

Again, the landlord is only liable for defects of which he has notice.[5] The landlord has the right, on giving 24 hours' written notice, to enter and view the premises at all reasonable times. Where parts of a building have been let to different tenants, 'dwelling house', for the purposes of the 1985 Act, means the part of the building demised, ie the particular flat and not the whole block. The landlord's obligation extends to anything which in the ordinary use of words would be regarded as part of the structure and exterior of the particular dwelling house.[6] Hence also, the reference to installations 'in the house' means within the physical confines of the flat and would not therefore include an external central heating boiler.[6]

In considering fitness for habitation, and repair, the following obligations of the landlord should also be noted. First, it was held in *Liverpool City Council v Irwin*[7] that where parts of a building (in this case, a high-rise block of flats) have been let to different tenants and the essential means of access, such as stairs and lifts, are retained by the landlord, a term may be implied that the landlord will take reasonable care to keep those parts reasonably safe and reasonably fit for use. Second, in *Rimmer v Liverpool City Council*[8] it was held that a landlord who designed and built the demised premises owed, in his capacity as designer and builder, a duty in the tort of negligence to the tenant (amongst others) to take reasonable care to ensure he would not suffer injury as a result of faults in the design and construction of the premises. Finally, the reader should note the obligations of a landlord under the Defective Premises Act 1972, s4 which we discuss at para 23.30 above.

1 *Smith v Marrable* (1843) 11 M & W 5.
2 In *Quick v Taff-Ely Borough Council* [1985] 2 All ER 321, the Court of Appeal, calling for a revision of the definition of low rent, remarked that this section must have remarkably little application. .
3 *McCarrick v Liverpool Corpn* [1947] AC 219, [1946] 2 All ER 646, HL.
4 *Buswell v Goodwin* [1971] 1 All ER 418, [1971] 1 WLR 92, CA.
5 *O'Brien v Robinson* [1973] AC 912, [1973] 1 All ER 583, HL.
6 *Campden Hill Towers Ltd v Gardner* [1977] QB 823, [1977] 1 All ER 739, CA; *Douglas-Scott v Scorgie* [1984] 1 All ER 1086, [1984] 1 WLR 716, CA.
7 [1977] AC 239, [1976] 2 All ER 39.
8 [1984] 1 All ER 930, [1984] 2 WLR 426, CA.

The tenant

37.5 We considered the freeholder's rights of alienation and of enjoyment of his property at paras 32.9, 32.10 and 32.15 above. The rights of a leaseholder will not be as extensive, being confined particularly by the covenants in the lease. In the absence of an express covenant, a tenant may assign his interest, ie grant his entire interest to another (the assignee) thus putting him in the position of tenant vis-à-vis the landlord,[1] or may sub-let (ie carve a lesser estate out of his own, putting himself in the position of landlord to the sub-lessee).[2] However, these rights are almost invariably subject to restriction, absolute or qualified, by the express terms of the lease.[3] As to the tenant's use of the premises, in the absence of express covenants, there are two restrictions imposed by the law: he must not commit voluntary waste, and, in the case of periodic tenancies, he is bound by an implied covenant to use the premises in a tenant-like manner.

1 Note that assignment must be by deed (LPA, s52(1)) even where the lease itself was not required to be created by deed (LPA, s54(2)); see para 33.3 above.
2 A purported sub-lease which passes the residue of the term takes effect as an assignment (even if, it appears, the sub-lease is not effected by deed).
3 Para 37.12 below.

37.6 *Waste* 'Waste' has been defined as 'any act which alters the nature of the land, whether for the better or for the worse'.[1] Where a tenant is liable for waste the landlord may sue for damages or an injunction.

Common law recognised two forms of waste, voluntary and permissive. Voluntary waste would be constituted by carrying out substantial alterations to the property, for example, by pulling down a building, or, as in *Marsden v Edward Heyes Ltd*,[2] by gutting the ground floor of a building to convert the entire area into a shop. Permissive waste is damage caused by omission or neglect, as by letting the premises go to ruin. All tenants are liable for voluntary waste. A tenant holding under a periodic tenancy is not liable for permissive waste but the point is probably covered by his obligation to use and deliver up the premises in a tenant-like manner.

1 Megarry and Wade, *The Law of Real Property* (5th edn) p 96. See also para 35.3 above.
2 [1927] 2 KB 1.

37.7 *Implied covenant to use the premises in a tenant-like manner* This covenant is implied in all periodic tenancies.[1] According to Denning LJ, as he then was, in *Warren v Keen*, 'The tenant must take proper care of the place ... he must do the little jobs about the place which a reasonable tenant would do. In addition, he must, of course, not damage the house, wilfully or negligently, and he must see that his family and guests do not damage it, and if they do, he must repair it'.[2]

1 *Marsden v Edward Heyes Ltd* [1927] 2 KB 1; *Warren v Keen* [1954] 1 QB 15, [1953] 2 All ER 1118, CA.
2 [1954] 1 QB 15 at 20, [1953] 2 All ER 1118. For example, the covenant does not necessarily oblige the tenant to lag water pipes. This depends on the circumstances, including the severity of the cold and the length of contemplated absences from home (*Wycombe Area Health Authority v Barnett* (1982) 264 Estates Gazette 619).

37.8 *Right to fixtures* For the tenant's right to fixtures, see para 32.8 above.

Express terms
The 'usual covenants'
37.9 Where, as is commonly the case in respect of longer leases, the grant of the lease itself is preceded by a contract to grant the lease and the contract does not specify the covenants to which the lease shall be subject, it is implied that the lease will contain 'the usual covenants'. Again, it is possible expressly to provide that the lease shall be subject to the usual covenants. The usual covenants always include those set out in *Hampshire v Wickens*,[1] namely: a covenant by the landlord for quiet enjoyment; a covenant by the tenant to pay rent subject to a proviso for re-entry by the landlord in the event of non-payment;[2] a covenant by the tenant to pay tenant's rates and taxes; a covenant by the tenant to keep and leave the premises in repair, and where the landlord has undertaken any obligation to repair, a covenant to permit him to enter and view the state of repair. What further covenants are usual is a question of fact[3] to be determined by reference to the nature of the premises, their situation, the purpose for which they are being let, the length of the term, the evidence of conveyancers and the books of precedents.[4]

1 (1878) 7 Ch D 555.

2   Para 37.36 below.
3   *Flexman v Corbett* [1930] 1 Ch 672.
4   *Chester v Buckingham Travel Ltd* [1981] 1 All ER 386.

Common express covenants
37.10   Covenants commonly found in leases include:

a. a covenant to pay rent;

b. a covenant against assignment, sub-letting or parting with possession;

c. repairing covenants;

d. covenants restricting the use of the premises;[1]

e. a covenant to insure. Either the landlord will covenant to insure the property on the basis that the tenant will pay the premiums, or the tenant will be required to insure the property, often with a named company, to its full value. Failure to keep the property insured constitutes a breach.[2]

1   Ch 39 below.
2   *Penniall v Harborne* (1848) 11 QB 368.

37.11   *Rent* The payment of rent, although a normal feature of leases, is not an essential legal requirement. The rent payable by a tenant, correctly known as 'rent*service*', deriving from the tenurial relationship between landlord and tenant, will generally take the form either of a rack rent or a ground rent. A rack rent is a rent equivalent or approximately equivalent to the annual value of the land at the commencement of the tenancy. A ground rent, a lesser sum commonly paid in the case of long leases, is paid where the land has been leased partly in consideration of a 'fine' (ie premium or lump sum payment) at the commencement of the lease, or in consideration of the tenant building on the land, this being reflected in the low rent. Unless otherwise expressly provided, rent is payable in arrears.

It is very common in the case of longer commercial leases to provide for rent review at intervals, for example, every five years. A well-drafted rent review clause should contain both a formula for determining the revised rent and machinery for agreeing the rent and resolving disputes between the parties (generally by way of reference to a chartered surveyor acting as expert and arbitrator[1]). Regrettably, many rent review clauses are not well-drafted and have given rise to much litigation concerning their construction. Particular problems have arisen in connection with provisions which set out a 'timetable' for carrying out the review procedure and with the interpretation of the formula provided for determining the rent.

Many review clauses provide a timetable for taking some or all of the steps in the review procedure which, if followed, will enable the revised rent to be settled not later than the review date. The first step in such a timetable is for the landlord to serve a 'trigger' notice on the tenant, proposing a revised rent. The question arose whether late service of this notice deprived the landlord of the right to a review. In *United Scientific Holdings Ltd v Burnley Borough Council*,[2] the House of Lords held that it did not; in other words, time is presumed not to be of the essence of the timetable provisions of a rent review clause,[3] unless the lease expressly or by implication provides otherwise. This decision led to further litigation as to when the circumstances would give rise to an implication that time was of the essence. Thus where a lease provided the same timetable for rent review and for the lessee's option to determine the lease (in respect of which time is of the essence[4]) it was held that by implication time was of the essence of the rent review.[5] It has further been held that where time is not of the essence, mere delay, however lengthy, and even delay plus hardship to the tenant, would not disentitle the landlord to exercise his contractual right to serve a 'trigger' notice.[6]

Ideally, the formula provided for determining the revised rent should specify the matters to be assumed (eg that the rent should be assessed on a 'willing lessor/willing lessee' basis) and the matters to be disregarded (eg the value of tenant's improvements) in assessing the rent. Again this is frequently not done, with the result that such issues have to be resolved by determining the proper construction of the particular clause. For example, where a rent review clause provided that the revised rent should be the sum 'assessed as a reasonable rent for the demised premises' this was held to require the fixing of a rent, assessed on an objective basis, for the demised premises as improved (albeit that the tenant had paid for these improvements).[7] On the other hand, where the clause referred to 'a rent to be agreed between the lessor and lessee', the court held that this meant a rent which would have been reasonable for this landlord and this tenant to have agreed; that is, a subjective rent. Consequently, it would be proper to ignore the valuation effect of improvements paid for by the tenant.[8]

1 See para 19.21 above.
2 [1978] AC 904, [1977] 2 All ER 62, HL.
3 See paras 8.11–8.14 above.
4 *United Scientific Holdings Ltd v Burnley Borough Council* [1978] AC 904, [1977] 2 All ER 62, HL.
5 *Al Saloom v Shirley James Travel Service Ltd* (1981) 259 Estates Gazette 420, CA.
6 *Amherst v James Walker Goldsmith and Silversmith Ltd* [1983] Ch 305, [1983] 3 All ER 1067, CA.
7 *Ponsford v HMS Aerosols Ltd* [1979] AC 63, [1978] 2 All ER 837, HL.
8 *Thomas Bates & Son Ltd v Wyndham's (Lingerie) Ltd* [1981] 1 All ER 1077, [1981] 1 WLR 505, CA.

37.12 *Assignment, sub-letting, or parting with possession* An *absolute* covenant against assignment or sub-letting, etc is more usually found in shorter residential tenancies. The commonly encountered *qualified* covenant prohibits assignment or sub-letting or parting with possession without the landord's licence or consent. It is, by statute, subject to the further qualification that that licence or consent must not be unreasonably withheld.[1] (The statute does not purport to forbid the use of absolute covenants against assignment, nor does it purport to invalidate a covenant which requires the tenant first to offer to surrender[2] his lease to the landlord should he wish to assign.[3]) In the event of the landlord unreasonably refusing consent the tenant may go ahead with the proposed assignment or sub-lease, or apply to court for a declaration that the refusal is unreasonable. The onus is on the tenant to show that consent was withheld unreasonably.

In considering whether the landlord unreasonably withheld consent, the court is to consider what was the purpose of the covenant and all the circumstances, including the statutory background, at the time when the consent is sought.[4] It has been held, for example, that the landlord's refusal of consent was reasonable where the proposed tenant would acquire rights under the Rent Act[4] or the Leasehold Reform Act,[5] which were not available to the existing tenant. If the refusal of consent is designed to achieve some collateral purpose, wholly unconnected with the terms of the lease, then it will be unreasonable, even if the purpose was in accordance with good estate management.[6] Thus it was unreasonable for a landlord to refuse consent where the reason was that the landlord was seeking to bring about the letting of the entire building, of which the demised premises formed part, to a single tenant.[6] Likewise, although it might be reasonable for the landlord to refuse his consent to an assignment on the ground of the purpose for which the proposed assignee intended to use the premises,[7] it would be unreasonable where the grounds had nothing to do with the relationship of landlord and tenant in regard to the subject matter of the lease;[8] for example, where the proposed use would have a depressing effect on rental levels of the landlord's adjacent property.[9]

Assignment or sub-letting in contravention of a covenant, whether absolute or qualified, does not affect the validity of the assignment or sub-lease, but may expose the assignee or sub-lessee to the risk of forfeiture.[10]

1 Landlord and Tenant Act 1927, s19(1); certain building and agricultural leases excepted. See *International Drilling Fluids Ltd v Louisville Investments Ltd.*
2 Para 32.31 above.
3 *Bocardo SA v S and M Hotels Ltd* [1979] 3 All ER 737, [1980] 1 WLR 17, CA. In *Allnatt London Properties Ltd v Newton* (1983) 265 Estates Gazette 601, the Court of Appeal held that in the case of business tenancies within the Landlord and Tenant Act 1954 (para 37.27 below) the agreement resulting from a landlord's acceptance of a tenant's offer to surrender under such a surrender-back clause is void. If that decision is correct there would seem to be no point in law in including such a surrender-back clause in a business lease.
4 *West Layton Ltd v Ford* [1979] QB 593, [1979] 2 All ER 657, CA; *Leeward Securities Ltd v Lilyheath Properties Ltd* (1984) 271 Estates Gazette 279, CA.
5 *Bickel v Duke of Westminster* [1977] QB 517, [1976] 3 All ER 801, CA; *Norfolk Capital Group Ltd v Kitway Ltd* [1977] QB 506, [1976] 3 All ER 787, CA.
6 *Bromley Park Garden Estates Ltd v Moss* [1982] 2 All ER 890, [1982] 1 WLR 1019, CA.
7 *Bates v Donaldson* [1896] 2 QB 241 at 244.
8 *Houlder Brothers & Co Ltd v Gibbs* [1925] Ch 575.
9 Cf *Anglia Building Society v Sheffield City Council* (1982) 266 Estates Gazette 311, CA.
10 *Old Grovebury Manor Farm Ltd v W Seymour Plant Sales & Hire Ltd (No 2)* [1979] 3 All ER 504, [1979] 1 WLR 1397, CA; and see para 37.16 below.

37.13 *Covenants to repair* A variety of covenants providing for the liability of landlord and tenant to repair the premises may be encountered. In the case of long leases, it is often provided that the full liability for repairing the premises is placed on the lessee. Also common, where premises are let to several tenants, are so-called 'clear leases', ie leases in which the tenants bear all the costs of repairing and maintaining the building (by way of service charges), so that the rent reaches the landlord clear of all expenses and overheads. In the case of shorter leases and tenancies, the tenant's liability tends to be restricted to an obligation to keep, and deliver up at the end of the term, the interior of the premises in a good and tenantable state of repair, perhaps 'fair wear and tear excepted'. In the case of shorter residential tenancies, the landlord is liable under the Landlord and Tenant Act 1985, as we have seen,[1] to keep in repair the exterior and service installations. It is again common to provide for the landlord to have the right to enter and view the state of repair.

Where an obligation is imposed on the tenant to 'keep in repair' he is obliged also first to put the premises in repair if necessary.[2] An obligation to keep property 'in good and tenantable repair' requires such repairs 'as taking into account the age, character and locality of the house, would make it reasonably fit for the occupation of a reasonably-minded tenant of the class that would be likely to want such a house'.[3] That is not to say that the standard of repair required is affected by a depreciation in the neighbourhood since the granting of the lease: the court must look to the character of the house and its ordinary use at the time of demise.[4] Repair connotes the idea of making good damage so as to leave the subject so far as possible as though it had not been damaged.[4] A covenant to repair may require renewal of subsidiary parts, but not of the whole,[5] and may extend to cover repairs necessitated by inherent defects in the premises. It should, however, be remembered that there must be disrepair before any question arises as to whether a covenant to repair requires the remedying of a design fault.[6] It is always a question of degree whether what the tenant is being asked to do can properly be described as repair, or whether on the contrary it would involve giving back to the landlord a wholly different thing from that which he demised.[7]

A covenant which contains a 'fair wear and tear' exception relieves the tenant from liability to repair damage caused by time and the elements or by normal and reasonable use. However, if such damage is likely to produce further damage if unremedied, as for example where a slate falls from the roof and water enters the premises as a result, the tenant is liable to remedy it.[8] In any case where the landlord is under an obligation to repair, his liability does not arise until he has notice of the defect.[9]

1 Para 37.4 above.
2 *Payne v Haine* (1847) 16 M & W 541.
3 *Proudfoot v Hart* (1890) 25 QBD 42, CA.
4 *Anstruther-Gough-Calthorpe v McOscar* [1924] 1 KB 716, CA.
5 *Lurcott v Wakely & Wheeler* [1911] 1 KB 905, CA.
6 *Quick v Taff-Ely Borough Council* [1985] 3 All ER 321, CA.
7 *Ravenseft Properties Ltd v Davstone (Holdings) Ltd* [1980] QB 12, [1979] 1 All ER 929.
8 *Regis Property Co Ltd v Dudley* [1959] AC 370, [1958] 3 All ER 491, HL.
9 *McCarrick v Liverpool Corpn* [1947] AC 219, [1946] 2 All ER 646, HL. Cf Defective Premises Act 1972, para 23.30 above.

Remedies for breach of covenant
For breach of covenants other than for payment of rent
37.14 For breach of covenants other than for payment of rent or for repair, the injured party may sue for damages or seek an injunction to restrain the breach, or, in the case of the landlord, claim forfeiture of the lease. Essentially, the same remedies apply in the case of a breach of a covenant to repair; we discuss certain important differences in para 37.19 below.

Forfeiture
37.15 The landlord's right to claim forfeiture of the lease arises either where the tenant is in breach of a covenant framed as a 'condition' (by using such phrases as 'provided always that' or 'on condition that') or where, as is invariably the case in a properly drafted lease, the lease contains a proviso for re-entry in the event of a breach of covenant. Such a right of re-entry is a proprietary right and as such is enforceable not only against the tenant but

also against assignees and sub-tenants (even where, as we explain in para 39.9 below, the covenant, breach of which occasions the re-entry, is not itself enforceable against the sub-tenant). In claiming forfeiture and exercising a right of re-entry the landlord is choosing to put an end to the tenant's interest in the property because of the breach. The landlord may, however, forfeit a lease as to part only of the demised premises where that part is physically separate and capable of being distinctly let.[1]

The landlord should normally go about forfeiture by bringing a court action for possession. An alternative is self-help, by peaceably re-entering on the land, *but*: a. a right of re-entry or forfeiture may not be enforced in respect of a lease of premises let as a dwelling otherwise than by proceedings in court while any person is lawfully residing in the premises;[2] and b. the landlord runs the possible risk of contravening the Criminal Law Act 1977, s6 which prohibits the use of violence to secure entry, or some other provision of the criminal law.

1 *GMS Syndicate Ltd v Gary Elliott Ltd* [1982] Ch 1, [1981] 1 All ER 619.
2 Protection from Eviction Act 1977, s2.

37.16 The LPA, s146 provides that a right of re-entry or forfeiture for breach of a covenant or condition *other than one for payment of rent* may not be enforced unless and until the lessor serves on the lessee a notice:

a. specifying the particular breach complained of; and

b. if the breach is capable of remedy, requiring the lessee to remedy it; and

c. in any case, requiring the lessee to make compensation in money for the breach,

and the lessee fails, within the reasonable time thereafter, to remedy the breach, if it is capable of remedy, and to make reasonable compensation in money, to the satisfaction of the lessor, for the breach.

The purpose of the notice is to give the tenant reasonable information about what, if anything, he has to do to avoid forfeiture. Despite the wording of the section, however, it has been held that the landlord's notice need not call for compensation if he does not require it.[1] Moreover, it has been held that certain breaches of covenant are incapable of remedy and that a notice in respect of such breaches therefore need not require a remedy. For example, breach of a covenant against immoral user, by using the demised premises as a brothel, is not capable of remedy, at least within a reasonable time, because merely stopping the immoral use would not remove the stigma cast on the premises; this 'stigma' might indirectly reflect on the landlord and be reflected in the value of the property.[2] Again, breach of a covenant against assignment or sub-letting is not capable of remedy.[3] It has been argued that breaches of any negative covenant such as one restricting use of the property are incapable of remedy[4] but this is doubtful. Whether a breach is capable of remedy depends on whether the harm that has been done to the landlord by the relevant breach is for practical purposes capable of being retrieved, by doing what is necessary to put the lessor back into the position he would have been in had no breach been committed. If this cannot be done within a reasonable time or at all, the breach is not capable of remedy.[5] Ordinarily, a breach of a positive covenant, such as a covenant to repair or to reconstruct premises by a certain date, is capable of remedy.[5] A landlord faced with the difficulty of knowing whether his s146 notice should or should not require that the breach specified be remedied is advised to require that the breach be remedied, 'if it is capable of being remedied'.[6] Even where the breach is not in fact capable of remedy, reasonable notice must still be given before proceeding to forfeiture[7] though this will naturally be shorter than where the breach is capable of remedy.

1   *Lock v Pearce* [1893] 2 Ch 271, CA.
2   *Rugby School (Governors) v Tannahill* [1935] 1 KB 87, CA; *Egerton v Esplanade Hotels, London Ltd* [1947] 2 All ER 88; *British Petroleum Pension Trust Ltd v Behrendt* (1985) 276 Estates Gazette 199, CA.
3   *Scala House and District Property Co Ltd v Forbes* [1974] QB 575, [1973] 3 All ER 308, CA. It should be noted that where the tenant has assigned the lease, albeit in breach of covenant, the s146 notice must be served on the assignee: *Old Grovebury Manor Farm Ltd v W Seymour Plant Sales and Hire Ltd (No 2)* [1979] 3 All ER 504, [1979] 1 WLR 1397, CA.
4   See *Rugby School (Governors) v Tannahill* [1934] 1 KB 695; *Scala House and District Property Co Ltd v Forbes* [1974] QB 575, [1973] 3 All ER 308, CA.
5   *Expert Clothing Service and Sales Ltd v Hillgate House Ltd* [1985] 2 All ER 998, [1985] 3 WLR 359, CA.
6   See *Glass v Kencakes Ltd* [1966] 1 QB 611, [1964] 3 All ER 807.
7   *Horsey Estate Ltd v Steiger* [1899] 2 QB 79, CA. Fourteen days' notice has been held sufficient in such cases, to enable the tenant to consider his position: *Civil Service Co-operative Society Ltd v McGrigor's Trustee* [1923] 2 Ch 347.

37.17   *Waiver* The landlord may not claim forfeiture of the lease for a breach of covenant where he has expressly or impliedly waived that breach. Implied waiver can only occur where the lessor, with knowledge of the facts upon which his right to re-enter arises, does some unequivocal act which, considered objectively, without regard to the landlord's motive or intention, could only be regarded as having been done consistently with the continued existence of the lease.[1] The onus is on the tenant to show that his breach of covenant has been waived. The act most commonly relied on as constituting waiver is the acceptance of rent. The very fact of acceptance of rent, even as a result of a clerical error, constitutes, as a matter of law, waiver of the breach so long as at the time the lessor had knowledge of the breach.[2] Equally a demand for future rent, with knowledge, constitutes waiver.[3] A waiver does not operate as a general waiver of the benefit of the particular covenant but only in respect of the particular breach.[4] If the breach is of a continuing nature, for example, failure to insure, continued breach after the waiver revives the right of re-entry.

1   *Matthews v Smallwood* [1910] 1 Ch 777 at 786; *Central Estates (Belgravia) Ltd v Woolgar (No 2)* [1972] 3 All ER 610, [1972] 1 WLR 1048, CA; *Expert Clothing Service and Sales Ltd v Hillgate House Ltd* [1985] 1 All ER 998, [1985] 3 WLR 359, CA.
2   *Central Estates (Belgravia) Ltd v Woolgar (No 2)* [1972] 3 All ER 610, [1972] 1 WLR 1048, CA.
3   *David Blackstone Ltd v Burnetts (West End) Ltd* [1973] 3 All ER 782, [1973] 1 WLR 1487. The demand must actually be communicated to the tenant. Furthermore, in the case of a statutory tenancy under the Rent Act (para 37.25 below) the landlord may demand rent so long as the tenancy continues (ie until it is determined by court order) hence such a demand does not constitute waiver: *Trustees of Henry Smith's Charity v Willson* [1983] QB 316, [1983] 1 All ER 73, CA.
4   LPA, s148.

37.18   *Relief* At any time from the service of the s146 notice until the landlord has recovered possession of the property,[1] the tenant may apply, under the LPA, s146(2) to the court for relief from forfeiture.[2] The court has a complete discretion as to whether or not to grant relief and on what terms, if any, it thinks fit.[3] In the normal case, then, the tenant has two opportunities to avoid forfeiture: first, compliance with the landlord's notice, and second, applying for relief. Even where a breach is incapable of remedy, the court may grant relief. Rarely, however, will relief be granted in the case of a breach of a covenant against immoral user.[4] A tenant may seek relief from forfeiture in respect of part only of the demised premises, so long as that part is physically separate and capable of being distinctly let.[5]

The destruction of the lessee's interest in land brought about by forfeiture entails also the destruction of any sub-leases granted by the lessee. This, of course, would involve considerable hardship to an innocent sub-lessee and so, under the LPA, s146(4) the sub-lessee is enabled to apply to court for relief in the form of an order vesting in him, on such terms as the court things fit, a lease held directly of the landlord in place of, and for a term not exceeding,[6] his sub-lease.[7]

There is some controversy as to whether the court has a general equitable jurisdiction to relieve from forfeiture in addition to that conferred by LPA, s146. Such a jurisdiction, exercisable even though the landlord has recovered possession, has been held to exist in respect of a breach by the lessee of a covenant to pay a sum of money due otherwise than as rent (eg by way of maintenance contribution).[8]

1 *Rogers v Rice* [1892] 2 Ch 170; *Pakwood Transport Ltd v 15 Beauchamp Place Ltd* (1978) 36 P & CR 112, CA.
2 This provision also applies where the landlord seeks possession in pursuance of a provision in the lease entitling him to give short notice to terminate the tenancy in the event of a breach of covenant; *Richard Clarke Ltd v Widnall* [1976] 3 All ER 301, [1976] 1 WLR 845, CA.
3 LPA, s146(2).
4 *Central Estates (Belgravia) Ltd v Woolgar (No 2)* [1972] 3 All ER 610, [1972] 1 WLR 1048, CA.
5 *GMS Syndicate Ltd v Gary Elliott Ltd* [1982] Ch 1, [1981] 1 All ER 619.
6 Subject to any statutory security of tenure, for example under Part II of the Landlord and Tenant Act 1954 (para 37.27 below); *Cadogan v Dimovic* [1984] 2 All ER 168, [1984] 1 WLR 609, CA.
7 The new lease cannot antedate the date of the court order: *Cadogan v Dimovic*, above; *Official Custodian for Charities v Mackey* [1985] Ch 168, [1984] 3 All ER 689.
8 *Abbey National Building Society v Maybeech Ltd* [1985] Ch 190, [1984] 3 All ER 262; but see *Smith v Metropolitan City Properties Ltd* (1985) 277 Estates Gazette 753.

Repairing covenants

37.19 Apart from forfeiture, the *landlord* is limited to a claim for damages in respect of a tenant's breach of a covenant to repair; he may not obtain an injunction or specific performance, as damages are regarded as an adequate remedy.[1] The measure of damages which he may obtain is limited to the amount by which the value of his reversion is reduced by virtue of the failure to repair.[2] Where the landlord has opted to forfeit the lease *and* sue for damages for breach by the tenant of a repairing covenant, the date of service of the writ for possession marks the landlord's decisive election to forfeit, puts an end to the covenants and fixes the date down to which damages may be claimed.[3]

Where the *tenant* sues for damages in respect of the landlord's breach, the object is to restore the tenant to the position he would have been in if there were no breach. Damages may thus include the cost of alternative accommodation, the cost of any repairs undertaken by the tenant and a sum to represent the unpleasantness of living in poor conditions. They will only be based on the diminution in the value of the tenant's interest where, to the landlord's knowledge, the tenant acquired the property to re-let or sell, or if the tenant is forced to sell by the state of the premises.[4] In the case of residential tenancies, there is no bar to the tenant being awarded specific performance,[5] and in any case the court has a general jurisdiction, which should be carefully exercised, to order a landlord to do some specific work pursuant to his covenant to repair.[6]

Whether a *landlord* seeks to pursue his remedy for breach of a repairing covenant by way of an action for damages or by way of forfeiture, he must, in certain cases, comply with the Leasehold Property (Repairs) Act 1938.[7] This Act applies to all leases, other than agricultural tenancies, granted for a term of seven years or more of which three years or more remain. Where the Act applies, not less than one month before bringing the action, the landlord must serve on the tenant a s146 notice containing, in addition to the requirements which we set out in para 37.16 above, a statement that the tenant may, within 28 days, serve on the landlord a counter-notice claiming the benefit of the 1938 Act. Should the tenant do this, the landlord cannot proceed further without leave of the court. The court has a discretion whether to grant leave but is debarred from doing so unless the landlord shows a prima facie case[8] that, for example:

a. the tenant's breach must be immediately remedied to prevent a substantial diminution in the value of his reversion, or that the breach has already brought about such a diminution; or

b. the breach requires immediate remedy to give effect to a bye-law or court order, etc; or

c. immediate repair would involve relatively smaller cost than would be involved were the work postponed; or

d. special circumstances render it just and equitable to grant leave.[9]

The landlord's s146 notice must, in specifying the breach complained of, state not simply that the covenant to keep in repair has been broken but how it has been broken, that is, it must fairly tell the tenant what he is required to repair.[10] This is commonly done by including a 'schedule of dilapidations' prepared by a surveyor. In the particular case of forfeiture for repairing covenants, the landlord must prove that the tenant had knowledge that the s146 notice had been served and that a reasonable time has elapsed since it came to the tenant's knowledge.[11]

Where a s146 notice is served on a tenant in respect of internal decorative repairs, he may apply to the court for relief from liability to carry out the repairs, which the court may grant if in all the circumstances it considers the notice unreasonable.[12] There are certain exceptions to this provision, including the case where there is an express covenant to put the property in decorative order and this has never been done.

1 Paras 11.26 and 11.32 above.
2 Landlord and Tenant Act 1927, s18(1).
3 *Associated Deliveries Ltd v Harrison* (1984) 272 Estates Gazette 321, CA.
4 *Calabar Properties Ltd v Stitcher* [1983] 3 All ER 759, [1984] 1 WLR 287, CA.

5   Landlord and Tenant Act 1985, s17.
6   *Jeune v Queens Cross Properties Ltd* [1974] Ch 97, [1973] 3 All ER 97.
7   Where a tenant fails to comply with a repairing covenant in a lease which confers on the landlord the right to enter and carry out the repairs and recover the cost from the tenant, an action by the landlord to recover the cost is a claim for a debt due under the lease, not a claim for damages. Hence the landlord does not require leave under the 1938 Act: *Hamilton v Martell Securities Ltd* [1984] Ch 266, [1984] 1 All ER 665; *Colchester Estates (Cardiff) v Carlton Industries plc* [1984] 2 All ER 601, [1984] 3 WLR 693.
8   *Land Securities plc v Metropolitan Police District Receiver* [1983] 2 All ER 254, [1983] 1 WLR 439.
9   Leasehold Property (Repairs) Act 1938, s1(5).
10 See *Fox v Jolly* [1916] 1 AC 1, HL.
11 Landlord and Tenant Act 1927, s18(2).
12 LPA, s147.

Non-payment of rent
37.20   In the event of non-payment of rent, the remedies available are distress, an action to recover the rent, and forfeiture.

Distress[1]
37.21   This is an ancient remedy, and is rarely resorted to. It is a 'self-help' remedy save in relation to tenancies falling within the Rent Act, where leave of the county court is required.[2] The right of distress is the right of the landlord, or rather his certificated bailiff, to enter the demised premises and impound chattels found there to provide security for the outstanding rent. Provided that notice is given to the tenant these goods may be sold after five days. The notice to the tenant should specify the rent due, the goods impounded, the place where they are impounded (if not on the demised premises, as they usually are), and when they will be sold unless the tenant pays what is owed. Certain goods, such as perishables, clothes and bedding up to the value of £100, and tools of the tenant's trade up to a total value of £150, if not in actual use, may not be impounded.

1   Distress for Rent Acts 1689 and 1737.
2   Rent Act 1977, s147; para 37.25 below.

Forfeiture
37.22   The landlord may claim forfeiture of the lease for non-payment of rent where either the requirement of payment is framed as a condition of the lease or, as is usual, the lease contains an express proviso for re-entry. At common law, the landlord cannot claim forfeiture without having first made a formal demand for the exact sum due, on the demised premises, between sunrise and sunset. This requirement is dispensed with, where the landlord brings proceedings for forfeiture, by the Common Law Procedure Act 1852, s210,[1] in cases where half a year's rent is in arrear and insufficient distrainable goods are to be found on the premises. The technicality of a formal demand is, in practice, normally avoided by expressly stating that the right of re-entry shall be exercisable once the rent is a specified number of days in arrear 'whether the same shall have been formally or legally demanded or not'. A s146 notice is not required in the case of forfeiture for non-payment of rent. The law as to enforcement of the right of re-entry and as to waiver expounded earlier is applicable.

Where the tenant owes at least half a year's rent, the landlord's action for forfeiture will be terminated if the tenant pays into court the arrears together with the landlord's costs.[2] Otherwise the court has an equitable, and, hence, discretionary, jurisdiction to grant relief where the tenant pays the rent due and the landlord's expenses.[3] Unlike the case of forfeiture for breach of some other covenant,[4] relief may in this case be granted even after the landlord has obtained judgment for possession, at least within six months thereafter.[5] A sub-lessee equally may apply for relief under this general equitable jurisdiction or, before the landlord recovers possession, under the terms of the LPA, s146(4).[6]

1 See also County Courts Act 1984, s139(1), for actions within the jurisdiction of the county court.
2 Common Law Procedure Act 1852, s212. See also County Courts Act 1984, s138, which applies even where half a year's rent is not owed.
3 See also Supreme Court Act 1981, s38.
4 Para 37. 18 above.
5 Common Law Procedure Act 1852, s210. Where peaceable re-entry is made—as opposed to under a court order—this limit may be extended. In the case of county court proceedings, different provisions for relief apply. The court's order for possession must be suspended for not less than four weeks (subject to extension) to allow the tenant time to pay the arrears and costs. Where the lessor recovers possession at any time after the making of the order, the lessee has six months from that date to apply to the court for relief: County Courts Act 1984, s138, as amended by the Administration of Justice Act 1985. Where the landlord makes a peaceable re-entry, the same six-month limit applies: County Courts Act 1984, s139.
6 Para 37.18 above. In the county court, sub-lessees may seek relief under the LPA, s146(4) or under the provisions of the County Courts Act.

Enforcement of covenants by and against assignees
37.23   We reserve until paras 39.2 to 39.8 below, our discussion of the rules relating to the enforcement of the covenants in a lease by and against assignees of the original parties.

Statutory control of leases and tenancies
37.24   The law of landlord and tenant as expounded so far in this chapter is, regrettably, only half the story, for today the law relating to leases is much modified and qualified by statute. This statutory regulation is divided broadly into three areas: residential tenancies, business tenancies and agricultural tenancies. The impact of the legislation is in two spheres in particular, rent control and security of tenure. The study of this area of law is an important part of the study of estate management. However, it is impossible in a book of this nature to give more than the following brief reference to the statutory regulation of landlord and tenant.

Residential tenancies
37.25   The Rent Act 1977 applies to certain lettings of dwelling-houses, excluding, for example, houses above a certain rateable value, houses let at a low rent,[1] tenancies where the rent includes an element for board or attendance, which in the case of attendance (such as cleaning the rooms) must be substantial, lettings to students by universities and colleges, and

lettings where the landlord resides in another part of the same building (so long as this is not a purpose-built block of flats). Contractual tenancies protected by the Act are referred to as 'protected tenancies'.[2] Such tenancies may terminate, inter alia, by expiry, by forfeiture, or by notice, although in this connection it is important to note (as a qualification to our earlier discussion of the termination of periodic tenancies by notice) that the Protection from Eviction Act 1977, s5 provides that no notice by a landlord or a tenant to quit any premises let as a dwelling-house shall be valid unless it is in writing containing the prescribed information and given not less than four weeks before the date on which it is to take effect. However, on the termination of a protected contractual tenancy, there immediately arises a statutory tenancy,[3] on the same terms so far as consistent with the Act. This confers on the tenant, not an estate in the land, but a 'status of irremovability'.[4] Protected tenancies and statutory tenancies are together known as regulated tenancies.[5] The landlord of a regulated tenancy may not recover possession save by order of the court which will only be granted in accordance with the provisions of the Rent Act 1977, s98 and Sch 15. For example, the court has a discretion to order possession in cases of non-payment of rent or breach of some other covenant, or because the tenant is a source of nuisance or annoyance to adjoining occupiers. Furthermore, the court must order possession where, for example, the property was let by an owner-occupier who now requires the property for his residence. As regards rent control, the landlord or tenant of a regulated tenancy may apply to the rent officer for the area for the determination and registration of a fair rent, which must not be exceeded.[6]

The Rent Act also provides for 'restricted contracts', ie contracts which give a person the right to occupy a dwelling as a residence for a rent which includes payment for the use of furniture or services. The term also includes tenancies within the 'resident landlord exemption' from the definition of protected tenancies. The definition of a restricted contract applies to tenancies where the rent includes an element for board or a substantial element for attendance; and to licences, so long as exclusive occupation (though not exclusive possession[7]) of at least one room is conferred. The rent in respect of a restricted contract may be referred to a rent tribunal to determine a reasonable rent which, once registered, cannot be exceeded. For contracts entered into after 27 November 1980 there is no security of tenure save that a court making a possession order may postpone possession for up to three months.[8]

The Housing Act 1980 introduced a new form of residential tenancy, the protected shorthold tenancy, which enables landlords to create residential tenancies, of between one and five years, during which time the tenant has security but at the end of which the landlord will have the right to regain possession.[9] The Act further gives the Secretary of State power to approve bodies seeking to build rented accommodation which they may then let out on 'assured' tenancies outside the protection of the Rent Act. However, such 'assured' tenants have essentially the same security of tenure as business tenants. Finally, the Housing Act 1985, Part IV, provides for security of tenure for public sector tenants, for example, tenants of local authorities. Their 'secure tenancies' may not be terminated save by a court order for possession on grounds similar to those under the Rent Act.

1 Long tenancies at a low rent fall within Part I of the Landlord and Tenant Act 1954. See also Leasehold Reform Act 1967, para 37.26 below.
2 Rent Act 1977, s1.
3 Ibid, s2.
4 *Keeves v Dean* [1924] 1 KB 685 at 686.
5 Rent Act 1977, s18.
6 Ibid, Parts III and IV.
7 Paras. 32.17 and 38.3.
8 Rent Act 1977, ss 19–21, 77–81, 102A, 106A.
9 In Greater London, the letting must be at a fair rent.

Enfranchisement

37.26 By virtue of the Leasehold Reform Act 1967, as amended, where a tenant has occupied as his residence for three years a house which was originally let for a fixed term of over 21 years at a low rent, he can, by serving notice on the landlord, require that the freehold of the property be transferred to him, or alternatively that he be granted a new lease in substitution for his existing lease, for a term expiring 50 years from the expiry of the existing lease. This alternative is rarely sought. The notice takes effect as a contract for the sale or lease of the property. The price or rent to be paid is to be determined in accordance with the Act. In general the price to be paid is that which the freehold would realise on the open market subject to the tenancy as if it had been extended under the Act. The rent payable in the case of an extended lease is a ground rent based on the letting value of the site for the uses to which the premises have been put during the tenancy, subject to a review after 25 years.

Business tenancies

37.27 Business tenancies[1] are regulated by Part II of the Landlord and Tenant Act 1954. The term 'business' is very widely defined, to include a trade, profession or employment or any activity carried on by a body of persons.[2] The policy of the Act is to provide security of tenure for tenants who have established themselves in business in leasehold premises so that they can continue to carry on their business there. The Act provides that business tenancies are not determined by expiry or by notice but must be terminated by the landlord giving between six and twelve months' notice, in prescribed form, ending no sooner than the tenancy could or would have ended at common law. Unless so ended, the tenancy simply continues, subject, for example, to forfeiture. Should the landlord give notice as prescribed, the tenant may apply to court for a new tenancy.[3] The landlord may oppose such an application on certain statutory grounds: for example, because he intends to redevelop the property or intends to occupy the premises for the purposes of his business or as a residence.[4] The terms of any new tenancy granted may be such as agreed by the parties or, in default, as determined by the court.[5] Subject to certain statutory 'disregards', the rent is to be an open market rent.[6]

1 Excluding, for example, tenancies for a term not exceeding six months unless they contain a provision for renewal, or the tenant has been in occupation for more than 12 months.
2 Landord and Tenant Act 1954, s23.
3 Ibid, ss24 and 25.
4 Ibid, s30.
5 Ibid, ss33 and 35.
6 Ibid, s34.

Agricultural holdings

37.28 An agricultural holding is land (whether agricultural land or not), comprised in a contract of tenancy which is a contract for an agricultural tenancy. A contract for an agricultural tenancy is a contract of tenancy under which the whole of the land is let for use as agricultural land for the purposes of a trade or business. 'A contract of tenancy' is defined as a lease or agreement for a lease for a term of years or from year to year, but it is provided that any letting of land for use as agricultural land for an interest less than a tenancy from year to year, or any licence to occupy such land, is to take effect as if it were an agreement for a tenancy from year to year. A tenancy for a term of two years or more continues, on expiry, as a tenancy from year to year unless and until either party serves a notice to quit; this provision is modified where the tenant dies before the term expires and may be contracted out of, with approval of the Minister.[1] As a general rule, an agricultural tenancy may only be terminated by a notice to quit of at least 12 months. On the service of such notice by the landlord, the tenant may serve a counter-notice whose effect is to prevent the notice to quit operating without the consent of the Agricultural Land Tribunal. The Tribunal is to withhold consent if satisfied that in all the circumstances a fair and reasonable landlord would not insist on possession, but subject to this it may consent to the notice operating if, for example, the landlord proposes to terminate the tenancy in the interest of good husbandry or the sound management of the estate. In a number of cases the tenant may not serve a counter-notice and thus has no security, for example, where the land is required for a non-agricultural use for which planning permission has been granted.[2]

1 Agricultural Holdings Act 1948, ss1 to 3, as amended by the Agricultural Holdings Act 1984, Sch 3.
2 Agricultural Holdings (Notices to Quit) Act 1977, ss1 to 3, as amended by the Agricultural Holdings Act 1984.

Chapter 38
Licences

38.1 The classic definition of a licence relating to land states that a licence passes no interest in the land but only makes lawful what would otherwise be unlawful.[1] It would appear, then, that a licence to enter on, or to occupy, property is a personal arrangement between the licensor and the licensee under which the licensee acquires no interest in the property. If a licence creates no property interest but is dependent on the permission of the licensor, why is the topic of licences an important part of the study of land law? First, because occupation of land by virtue of a licence has been common as a substitute for occupation by virtue of a tenancy, as a means of avoiding legislation protective of the rights of tenants.[2] Second, because the courts have begun to invest certain types of use and occupation of land which are prima facie enjoyed by licence of the landowner with proprietary characteristics, in particular with the characteristic of being enforceable against subsequent owners of the land.[3]

1 *Thomas v Sorrell* (1673) Vaugh 330 at 351.
2 Eg Rent Act 1977, Landlord and Tenant Act 1954.
3 Paras 38.11–38.16 below.

38.2 The variety of possible licences is considerable. Nonetheless, licences may be broadly classified into those which are similar to leases (those relating to occupation of land) and those which are similar to easements (those relating to the use of another's land). The difference between licences and easements is considered at para 40.12 below.

Licences and leases distinguished
38.3 The issue we are concerned with here is not simply an academic question of the difference between a personal right and a proprietory right, but also the practical question of whether in a given case a person is in occupation of property as a licensee or as a tenant. A tenant may be entitled to the full protection of such legislation as the Rent Act 1977[1] or Part II of the Landlord and Tenant Act 1954,[2] a licensee is not.[3] In considering whether a transaction constitutes a licence or a tenancy, the court is to have regard not to the label ('lease' or 'licence') which the parties give to the document but to the substance of the transaction.[4] Prior to the House of Lords' decision in *Street v Mountford*,[5] it was, however, possible to assert categorically that 'it is the parties' intentions which are paramount'[6] in determining whether an agreement is a lease or a licence. But, as Lord

Templeman pointed out in a now famous dictum in *Street v Mountford*, 'The manufacture of a five-pronged implement for manual digging results in a fork even if the manufacturer . . . insists that he intended to make and has made a spade.'[7] In other words, if the parties' agreement has the hallmarks of a tenancy, it is a tenancy, no matter what the parties intend. Those hallmarks are, according to the House of Lords, exclusive possession, for a term, at a rent.[8] Since Mrs Mountford's agreement with Mr Street gave her exclusive possession of rooms owned by Mr Street at a rent for a term, she was a tenant even though she had signed the agreement as accepting that it was only a licence which gave her no protection as a Rent Act tenant.

The presence or absence of exclusive possession, then, is the key distinction between a lease and a licence. There may, however, be occasions when an occupier has exclusive possession yet is merely a licensee. Two such situations were referred to by the House of Lords in *Street v Mountford*. First, there is the case of a service occupier, ie an employee who occupies his employer's premises in order better to perform his duties as an employee. In such cases, the employee's possession is regarded as that of his employer. The second case is where there has been something in the circumstances, such as a family arrangement, an act of friendship or generosity, or such like,[9] which, as the House of Lords explained it, negatives any intention to enter into legal relations and hence negatives the existence of a tenancy. For example, in *Heslop v Burns*,[10] X allowed a family on whom he had taken pity to live, rent free, in a house owned by him. Throughout X's life, he and the family remained close friends. On his death his executors brought an action for possession of the house, which, if the family occupied as licensees rather than as tenants at will, the family could not resist. The court held that they were licensees: it was not possible to infer from the arrangement an intention to create legal relations. This case shows that where no legal relationship is intended, no tenancy can exist. Where, however, a legal relationship is intended, the parties may still create a contractual licence, so long as exclusive possession is not conferred.

Since it has always been clear that the absence of exclusive possession precluded the grant of a tenancy, it had become common for landlords wishing to avoid the provisions of protective legislation such as the Rent Acts to make use of agreements which explicitly did not confer exclusive possession, as for example in *Somma v Hazelhurst*.[11] In this case, H and his girlfriend each signed a separate agreement for the occupation of a bed-sit, which provided that their use of the rooms was to be 'in common with the Licensor and such other licensees as the Licensor may permit to use the rooms'. Although the Court of Appeal had concluded that the parties were only licensees, the House of Lords in *Street v Mountford* disapproved of the decision and others in similar vein,[12] on the basis that the agreement was clearly a 'sham device' or 'artificial transaction' designed to disguise the grant of a tenancy. So far as the House of Lords was concerned, courts need only inquire 'whether as a result of an agreement relating to residential accommodation the occupier is a lodger or tenant', and he will be a lodger only where 'the landlord provides attendance or services[13] which require the landlord or his servants to exercise unrestricted access to and use of the premises'. It would seem, then, that only in this latter case will there be no exclusive possession and hence no tenancy. If so, this is a narrowing of the concept of non-exclusive possession and one whose wider applicability is unclear

1   Para 37.25 above.
2   Para 37.27 above.
3   However, a residential licence of furnished premises may constitute a restricted contract, para 37.25 above.
4   *Shell-Mex and BP Ltd v Manchester Garages Ltd* [1971] 1 All ER 841 at 845.
5   [1985] AC 809, [1985] 2 All ER 289, HL.
6   *Matchams Park (Holdings) Ltd v Dommett* (1984) 272 Estates Gazette 549, CA.
7   [1985] AC 809 at 819.
8   [1985] AC 809 at 826.
9   *Facchini v Bryson* [1952] 1 TLR 1386 at 1389.
10 [1974] 3 All ER 406, [1974] 1 WLR 1241, CA.
11 [1978] 2 All ER 1011, [1978] 1 WLR 1014, CA.
12 *Sturolson & Co v Weniz* (1984) 272 Estates Gazette 326, CA; *Aldrington Garages Ltd v Fielder* (1978) 37 P & CR 461, CA.
13 Such as cleaning the room and changing the linen: *Marchant v Charters* [1977] 3 All ER 918, [1977] 1 WLR 1181, CA.

Classification and characteristics of licences

38.4   Licences may be bare licences, contractual licences, or licences protected by estoppel or in equity.

Bare licences

38.5   The guest whom you invited to dinner has, when he comes to dinner, a bare licence to be on your property. Your young neighbour, who with your permission enters your garden to retrieve his ball, is a bare licensee. When a householder lives in a dwelling-house to which there is a garden in front and does not lock the gate of the garden, it gives an implied bare licence to any member of the public who has a lawful reason for doing so to proceed from the gate to the front door or back door, and to inquire whether he may be admitted and to conduct his lawful business.[1] In each of these examples the right of the licensee to be on the land is dependent entirely on the permission, express or implied, of the landowner/licensor. Without that permission, the licensee would be a trespasser. The licensee has no claim to prevent the revocation of his licence so that the landowner may revoke the permission to be on the land at any time. The licensee does not immediately become a trespasser however. The law allows him a reasonable time to leave the premises by the most appropriate route.[1] Although the most common examples of bare licences are of the trivial variety mentioned above, it should be remembered that the category of 'bare licence' is a residual one; consequently any licence not falling within one of the following categories falls within this category.[2]

Clearly such a licence, being entirely dependent on the permission of the landowner, is neither assignable by the licensee nor enforceable against successors of the licensor.

1   *Robson v Hallett* [1967] 2 QB 939 at 953, 954 [1967] 2 All ER 407 at 414.
2   See, for example, *Horrocks v Forray* [1976] 1 All ER 737, [1976] 1 WLR 230; para 38.6 below.

Contractual licences
Nature

38.6 A licence to enter land is a contractual licence if it is conferred by contract; it is immaterial whether the right to enter the land is the primary purpose of the contract or is merely secondary.[1] An example of the former would be a contractual licence to occupy a room in a university hall of residence.[2] We have explained in para 38.3 above, that a contract which confers exclusive possession does not confer a licence. In this example, however, the services provided by the landowner necessitate unrestricted access and hence there is no tenancy, merely a licence. An example of a licence conferred as a secondary object of a contract is provided by *Hounslow London Borough Council v Twickenham Garden Developments Ltd*,[3] in which the primary object of the contract was that the defendants should build a housing estate for the plaintiffs; it was held that this necessarily conferred on the defendants a licence to enter the site. The contractual licence being an aspect of a contract, it must be shown that the essential requirements of a valid contract are present. In certain cases where there has been no express agreement between the parties, the courts have been able to discern the presence of the requirements of a contract and thereby imply the existence of a contractual licence between the parties. In *Tanner v Tanner*,[4] T had bought a house for his mistress and their children to live in. In moving into this house the mistress gave up her own flat. On his subsequent marriage to another woman, T sought to evict his mistress from the house. The Court of Appeal was able to imply from the conduct of the parties the existence of a contractual licence[5] for the mistress to live in the house until the children left school, the mistress having given consideration by giving up her own flat and looking after the children. By way of contrast, in *Horrocks v Forray*,[6] the court was unable to infer the necessary ingredients of a contract, in particular an intention to create legal relations, from the arrangement between a man and his mistress, whereby the former had for many years provided accommodation for the latter. Hence, having only a bare licence, she could not resist his executors' claim for possession of the house in which she lived.

1 *Hounslow London Borough Council v Twickenham Garden Developments Ltd* [1971] Ch 233 at 254, [1970] 3 All ER 326 at 343.
2 Or other 'lodger-type' agreements.
3 [1971] Ch 233, [1970] 3 All ER 326.
4 [1975] 3 All ER 776, [1975] 1 WLR 1346, CA.
5 These would appear obviously to have been no exclusive possession.
6 [1976] 1 All ER 737, [1976] 1 WLR 230, CA.

Revocability

38.7 A contractual licence is not an entity distinct from the contract which brings it into being, but merely a provision of that contract.[1] Thus the extent to which the licensor is free to revoke the licence depends on the terms, express or implied, of the contract. It is a question of construction of the particular contract whether a purported revocation by the licensor is or is not in breach of contract.[2] In the absence of express terms there is no general rule as to the revocability of a contractual licence,[3] although (where there is no other evidence of the parties' intentions) it appears that the courts will readily imply a term that the licence is revocable on reasonable notice being given;[4] what is 'reasonable' depending on the circumstances of the case.

If the licensor purports to revoke the licence in breach of contract, what is the licensee to do? He has a contractual right to remain on the property despite the wrongful revocation by the licensor and cannot be treated as a trespasser[5] (and, if he is forcibly removed as a trespasser, he may sue for damages for assault).[6] If it is practicable for the licensee to seek the assistance of the court, he may obtain an injunction to prevent his being turned out or, in a case where the licensor refuses to let him enter, an order of specific performance.[7] However, these orders are available only at the discretion of the court, and, for example, the court will not specifically enforce an agreement for two people to live peaceably under the same roof.[8] A licensee who cannot obtain an order enforcing the contractual licence, either because in the circumstances it is not practicable for him to seek one[9] or because the licence is not regarded as specifically enforceable, must, unless he can otherwise secure peaceable entry to the property, accept the termination of the licence as a fait accompli and sue for damages for breach of contract.

1 *Hounslow London Borough Council v Twickenham Garden Developments Ltd* [1971] Ch 233 at 254, [1970] 3 All ER 326 at 343.
2 *Millenium Productions Ltd v Winter Garden Theatre (London) Ltd* [1946] 1 All ER 678, CA; *Winter Garden Theatre (London) Ltd v Millenium Productions Ltd* [1948] AC 173, [1947] 2 All ER 331, HL.
3 *Australian Blue Metal Ltd v Hughes* [1963] AC 74 at 99.
4 *Winter Garden Theatre (London) Ltd v Millenium Productions Ltd* [1948] AC 173, [1947] 2 All ER 331, HL; *Chandler v Kerley* [1978] 2 All ER 942, [1978] 1 WLR 693, CA.
5 *Winter Garden Theatre (London) Ltd v Millenium Productions Ltd* [1948] AC 173, [1947] 2 All ER 331, HL.
6 See *Hurst v Picture Theatres Ltd* [1915] 1 KB 1, CA.
7 *Verrall v Great Yarmouth Borough Council* [1980] 1 All ER 839, [1980] 3 WLR 258, CA.
8 *Thompson v Park* [1944] KB 408 at 409, [1944] 2 All ER 477 at 479.
9 As where a customer is threatened with eviction from a theatre performance, or from a restaurant.

Enforceability against third parties
38.8 On principle, the current view that a contractual licence has no existence independent of the contract which creates it[1] means that the licensee cannot enforce his contractual right to remain on land against a successor of the licensor, for the arrangement between licensor and licensee is a personal contractual arrangement giving the licensee no interest in the land capable of binding the third party.[2] Thus, for example, the occupier of a hall of residence room under a contractual licence could not insist on remaining in the hall were it sold by the university to a third party; his remedy would lie in damages against the licensor.[3] On this view (which we think is the correct one), although a person may enjoy under the terms of a contractual licence rights akin to a lease or easement, the contractual licence does not possess that most important characteristic of an interest in land, that of being capable of binding third parties. However, two cases in particular stand out against this view. In *Errington v Errington and Woods*,[4] the Court of Appeal held that an arrangement whereby a father allowed his son and daughter-in-law to live in a house owned by him on the basis that they paid the mortgage instalments, constituted a contractual licence binding on the father's successor in title on his death and indeed against all comers except a bona fide purchaser for value without notice. In *Midland*

Bank Ltd v Farmpride Hatcheries Ltd[5] the Court of Appeal appears to have assumed, without discussion, that a contractual licence is capable of binding all but the bona fide purchaser. Notwithstanding these decisions, we do not think that it is legitimate to invest a contractual licence, without more, with the qualities of an equitable interest, although it may be possible for such a licence to be enforced against a third party if it can also be classified as falling within the next category of licences.

1 Para 38.7 above.
2 *Clore v Theatrical Properties Ltd* [1936] 3 All ER 483, CA.
3 *King v David Allen & Sons, Billposting Ltd* [1916] 2 AC 54, HL.
4 [1952] 1 KB 290, [1952] 1 All ER 149, CA. Although the contract in this case conferred exclusive possession, the House of Lords appears to have accepted in *Street v Mountford* (para 38.3 above) that this was not a case of a tenancy. It appears, however, that their Lordships regarded the arrangement as a contract by the father to sell the house.
5 (1981) 1260 Estates Gazette 493, CA.

Licences protected by estoppel or otherwise in equity
38.9 In this section we are concerned with cases in which a person who occupies or uses property under a licence (which may, indeed, be bare or contractual in its inception) is protected from having his enjoyment of the property terminated by the legal owner by the doctrine of proprietary estoppel or by some other equitable device, namely the doctrines of benefit and burden and of the constructive trust.

Proprietary estoppel

38.10 *Nature* 'Proprietary estoppel' is an equitable doctrine. An early statement of the doctrine is to be found in the judgment of Lord Kingsdown in *Ramsden v Dyson:*[1] 'If a man ... under an expectation, created or encouraged by the land[owner], that he shall have a certain interest, takes possession of such land, with the consent of the land[owner], and upon the faith of such ... expectation, with the knowledge of the land[owner], and without objection by him, lays out money upon the land, a court of equity will compel the land[owner] to give effect to such ... expectation'. In *Crabb v Arun District Council,*[2] the doctrine was shown to extend to cover not only expenditure by the licensee but also other acts to his detriment in reliance on the expectation encouraged by the landowner. In *Habib Bank Ltd v Habib Bank AG Zurich,*[3] the Court of Appeal, referring to 'archaic and arcane' distinctions in this branch of the law, stated that 'the more recent cases indicate ... that the application of the *Ramsden v Dyson* principle ... requires a very much broader approach which is directed rather at ascertaining whether, in particular individual circumstances, it would be unconscionable for a party to be permitted to deny that which, knowingly or unknowingly, he has allowed or encouraged another to assume to his detriment rather than to enquiring whether the circumstances can be fitted within the confines of some preconceived formula'.[4]

In *Greasley v Cooke*[5] the Court of Appeal held that once it is proved that a representation has been made by the landowner, which would tend to induce the licensee to act to his detriment, the onus is then on the landowner to prove that the licensee did not so rely on it.

1 (1855) LR 1 HL 129 at 170.

2   [1976] Ch 179, [1975] 3 All Er 865, CA.
3   [1981] 2 All ER 650, [1981] 1 WLR 1265, CA.
4   Ibid at 666.
5   [1980] 3 All ER 710, [1980] 1 WLR 1306, CA.

38.11 *Effect* The doctrine of proprietary estoppel operates to prevent what the court regards as the true arrangement envisaged by the parties being frustrated by their being left to their rights and duties at law.[1] Its effect is to give rise to what is, misleadingly, referred to as an 'equity' in favour of the licensee, which the court satisfies by making an order appropriate to give effect to that arrangement. In the majority of the cases, the arrangement between the parties gives rise, at law, only to a licence revocable at will. By virtue of proprietary estoppel, however, an 'equity' arises in favour of the licensee which the court may satisfy, according to the circumstances of the case, either positively, by conferring on the licensee a recognised property interest in the land, (eg the freehold),[2] or negatively by holding the licence to be protected from revocation by the 'equity' arising from the estoppel.[3] An example of the former is *Pascoe v Turner*,[4] where the plaintiff, on leaving the defendant for another woman, represented to the defendant that the house in which they had been living as man and wife was hers. On the faith of this, the defendant spent money on repairs and decoration. The plaintiff subsequently sought to 'determine her licence to occupy'. The Court of Appeal held, however, that the doctrine of proprietary estoppel gave rise to an 'equity' in favour of the defendant which, in the circumstances, could be satisfied only be declaring that the freehold of the property was vested in the defendant.[5] The alternative approach is shown by *Inwards v Baker*,[6] where a father allowed his son to build a bungalow for himself on the father's land, which the son did, by his own labour, and sharing the expense with his father. The father had, by an old unrevoked will, left the land to someone else, and on his death his executors claimed possession of the land from the son. This the Court of Appeal refused, holding that the son, having spent money on the land in the expectation of being allowed to stay there, was entitled to a licence to remain on the property for life or for so long as he wished the bungalow to be his home. This licence was protected from revocation by the 'equity' arising from the expenditure. Thus, this 'equity' bound not only the father but also, it was held, anyone other than a bona fide purchaser of the land for value without notice of the 'equity'.[7] In seeking to satisfy the 'equity' which arises from the licensee's expenditure on the land, the court claims to give effect to the true arrangement envisaged by the parties. It may thus be appropriate in certain cases to protect the licensee's occupation only until his expenditure on the land has been reimbursed.[8]

1   *Chandler v Kerley* [1978] 2 All ER 942 at 946.
2   Eg *Dillwyn v Llewellyn* (1862) 4 De GF & J 517; *Pascoe v Turner* below.
3   Eg *Inwards v Baker* below.
4   [1979] 2 All ER 945, [1979] 1 WLR 431, CA.
5   See also *Dillwyn v Llewellyn* (1862) 4 De GF & J 517.
6   [1965] 2 QB, [1965] 1 All ER 446, CA.
7   Paras 33.14 to 33.19 above.
8   *Dodsworth v Dodsworth* (1973) 228 Estates Gazette 1115, CA.

38.12 The doctrine of proprietary estoppel is not limited to cases of expenditure on the land of another; it also encompasses, for example, expenditure on one's own land in expectation of being granted some right over another's land. This is shown by *ER Ives Investment Ltd v High*,[1] where the defendant so constructed a garage on his land that it could be reached only across the yard of the neighbouring property. The neighbouring owners at that time, predecessors of the plaintiff, stood by and, indeed, encouraged[2] the defendant so to build his garage, knowing that he believed, as a result of prior transactions,[3] that he had a right of way across the yard. An 'equity' thus arose in the defendant's favour, enforceable against the plaintiff purchaser with notice, which was satisfied by allowing the defendant and his successors to have access to the garage across the yard. As we have said, *Crabb v Arun District Council*[4] shows, further that the doctrine extends to the situation where the licensee merely acts to his detriment in reliance on the expectation encouraged by the licensor. The plaintiff, believing himself entitled, as a result of negotiations with the defendant, to a right of way across the defendant's adjoining land, sold part of his land, leaving the remainder accessible only via this disputed right of way. The Court of Appeal held that the actions of the defendant, in encouraging the plaintiff so to act to his detriment, raised an 'equity' in favour of the plaintiff which would be satisfied by declaring that he was entitled to an easement of way[5] or equivalent irrevocable licence.

1 [1967] 2 QB 379, [1967] 1 All ER 504, CA.
2 [1967] 2 QB 379 at 399.
3 Para 38.14 below.
4 [1976] Ch 179, [1975] 3 All ER 865, CA.
5 Para 40.38 below.

38.13 Although an 'equity' is said to arise where a licence is protected by proprietary estoppel, it may be argued that a licence of the kind which arose in *Inwards v Baker*[1] and *ER Ives Investment Ltd v High*,[2] is a new species of equitable interest in land.[3] However, although, as these cases demonstrate, such rights possess the characteristic of equitable interests, that a purchaser of unregistered land with notice is bound by them, they do not necessarily possess all the characteristics which it may be assumed are inherent in a property interest. Thus, while the interest created in *Ives v High* would be assignable to subsequent purchasers of the benefited land, the interest created in *Inwards v Baker* is clearly not assignable. Again, at least prior to any court action over the matter, the existence of such a right would be difficult to ascertain. Even after the court has determined that the licence is protected by proprietary estoppel, conveyancing problems remain. It is clear that in unregistered land, the protection of the 'equity' depends on notice; the Land Charges Act 1972 is inapplicable.[4] In registered land, it is submitted that such a right may derive protection against subsequent purchasers of the land affected by virtue of being an overriding interest, in cases where, as in *Inwards v Baker*, the licensee—if that term is still appropriate—is in occupation of the property.[5] Where the licensee is not in occupation, as in *Ives v High*, the right must exist as a minor interest which would appear to be capable of protection by the entry on the register of a notice or caution against dealings.[6] The problem then exists that such an interest ought to be protected as soon as it comes into being, for otherwise the risk is run of a purchaser taking the land affected free from the licensee's rights—and yet the licensee may not be aware he has an 'equity' arising from proprietary estoppel and requiring protection by registration unless he is informed of the fact by a decision of the court. It is certainly the case that the 'equity' arising in these cases falls rather short of the requisites of a property interest suggested by Lord Wilberforce in *National Provincial Bank Ltd v Ainsworth*,[7] which are that it must be 'definable, identifiable by third parties, capable in its nature of assumption by third parties, and have some degree of permanence or stability'. At the very least, it must be agreed that in this area equity is displayed at its most flexible.[8]

1 Para 38.11 above.
2 Para 38.12 above.
3 See also *Plimmer v Wellington Corpn* (1884) 9 App Cas 699, PC, and note LPA, s4(1).
4 *Ives v High*; para 33.24 above.
5 LRA, s70(1)(g); para 34.20 above.
6 Paras 34.23 and 34.24 above. Such a right *may* be overriding within LRR, r258.
7 [1965] AC 1175 at 1248, [1965] 2 All ER 472 at 494, HL.
8 *ER Ives Investment Ltd v High* [1967] 2 QB 379 at 399, [1967] 1 All ER 504.

The doctrine of benefit and burden
38.14 Further illustrating equity's flexibility in this area, other aspects of the case of *ER Ives Investment Ltd v High*[1] demonstrate how the doctrine of benefit and burden, originally limited to those taking the benefit of a deed,[2] may be pressed into service to protect a licence from revocation both by the original licensor and his assignees. High's original neighbour W built a block of flats on his land, the foundations of which encroached on High's land by about one foot. High and W agreed that the foundations could remain where they were and that in return High could have a right of way across the yard of W's flats to gain access to a side road. W subsequently sold his property to X. While X owned the flats, High, to X's knowledge, built a garage in such a way that it could only be reached across the yard, and also contributed to the cost of resurfacing the yard. Later X sold the flats to Ives Ltd, expressly subject to High's right to cross the yard. Ives Ltd brought this action to restrain High from crossing the yard. The Court of Appeal, in addition to upholding High's right on the basis of proprietary estoppel,[3] held that, on the principal that 'he who takes the benefit must accept the burden', so long as the owners of the blocks of flats had the benefit of having their foundations in High's land, they had to allow High and his successors to have access over their yard. The converse equally applies: so long as High took the benefit of access across the yard, he had to permit the foundations to remain. This would suggest then that should High, for example, decide to abandon using the access across the yard, he could demand that the foundations be removed from his land, no doubt necessitating the demolition of the flats.

1 [1967] 2 QB 379, [1967] 1 All ER 504, CA.
2 Cf para 39.14 below; and see *Tito v Waddell (No. 2)* [1977] Ch 106 at 289ff.
3 Para 38.12 above.

Constructive trust
38.15 In *Binions v Evans*,[1] Lord Denning MR held a (contractual) licence to be protected from revocation by a purchaser with notice from the licensor by virtue of a constructive trust. The nature of a constructive trust

has never been clearly defined. A leading textbook[2] suggests that a constructive trust is a trust which is imposed by equity in order to satisfy the demands of justice and good conscience, without reference to any express or presumed intention of the parties. Even given the width of this definition it is clear that Lord Denning's judgment in *Binions v Evans* marks an extension of the concept. Her husband's former employers allowed old Mrs Evans to live in a cottage rent free for the rest of her life. The agreement spoke of her having a 'tenancy at will'[3] but went on to provide that the agreement could be terminated by the defendant giving four weeks' notice in writing. The employer subsequently sold the cottage to Binions expressly subject to Mrs Evans' 'tenancy'. In this action, Binions sought to evict Mrs Evans. The Court of Appeal unanimously held that the agreement between the employers and Mrs Evans was inconsistent with a tenancy at will. Lord Denning MR held that Mrs Evans had a contractual licence to remain in the property for life although he did not spell out the nature of the consideration furnished by her. When the plaintiffs purchased the house 'subject to' Mrs Evans' rights they became constructive trustees 'for the simple reason that it would be utterly inequitable for the plaintiff to turn the defendant out contrary to the stipulation subject to which they took the premises'.[4] Consequently, Binions held the cottage on trust to permit Mrs Evans to reside there during her life. The other two members of the Court of Appeal held, following a similar case, *Bannister v Bannister*,[5] that Mrs Evans was entitled to a tenancy for life under a strict settlement by virtue of the Settled Land Act 1925.[6] In view of the definition of a strict settlement in that Act,[7] and in view of the fact that such a decision would give Mrs Evans the power to sell the cottage, which can scarcely have been intended, this conclusion is at least as doubtful as that of Lord Denning. It has since been held in two cases,[8] following *Binions v Evans*, that an irrevocable contractual licence gives rise to a constructive trust under which the licensee has a beneficial interest in the property. Although the later case of *Re Sharpe, Trustee of the Bankrupt v Sharpe*[9] could have been explicable as an example of proprietary estoppel, it is difficult to see on what basis an interest under a trust can be inferred from a mere contractual licence. It should further be noted that the Court of Appeal has subsequently held[10] that the establishment of a beneficial interest in property requires evidence of a common assumption or intention or agreement that a party other than the legal owner should have an interest in the property.[11]

1 [1972] Ch 359, [1972] 2 All ER 70, CA.
2 Snell's *Principles of Equity* (27th edn) p 185.
3 Para 32.24 above.
4 [1972] Ch 359 at 368.
5 [1948] 2 All ER 133, CA.
6 Ch 35 above.
7 Para 35.12 above.
8 *DHN Food Distributors Ltd v Tower Hamlets London Borough* [1976] 3 All ER 462, [1976] 1 WLR 852, CA; *Re Sharpe* [1980] 1 All ER 198, [1980] 1 WLR 219.
9 [1980] 1 All ER 198, [1980] 1 WLR 219.
10 *Bristol and West Building Society v Henning* [1985] 2 All ER 606, [1985] 1 WLR 778, CA; *Annen v Rattee* [1985] 273 Estates Gazette 503, CA.
11 Contrast the definition of a constructive trust given at the beginning of this paragraph.

Conclusions on equitable protection
38.16 One may only conclude that in certain circumstances equity will

intervene to afford protection to those whom the law regards merely as having a revocable licence. The bases for, and implications of, that intervention have not been fully worked out by the courts.[1]

1 See *Re Sharpe* [1980] 1 All ER 198, [1980] 1 WLR 219.

Chapter 39

Covenants

39.1 A covenant is a contractual agreement, usually occurring in a conveyance or a lease, in which one party, the *covenantor*, agrees to do or not to do something for the benefit of another, the *covenantee*. Typical covenants which might be entered into between the parties to a conveyance include covenants preventing building on the land conveyed, or preventing the building of more than one house, or requiring the building of a boundary wall. The parties to a lease may enter covenants requiring the payment of rent and the carrying out of repairs, or preventing sub-letting. All these covenants, being contractual agreements, are enforceable between the original parties according to the ordinary law of contract. However, a covenant may also be a right in land, which is enforceable not only between the original parties to it, but also by and against their successors in title to the property concerned.

The central problem we shall be considering in this chapter is the extent to which the *benefit* of a covenant *runs with the land* of the covenantee, and the extent to which the *burden* of it *runs with the land* of the covenantor.[1] Suppose that P purchases 100 acres of farmland from V and covenants with V that he will use the land for agricultural purposes only. If V then sells the remainder of his land to R, R will wish to know whether he can enforce the covenant entered into by V and P, ie whether the benefit of the covenant has run, with the land, to him. Were P subsequently to sell his land to A, A would wish to know if he was bound by P's covenant, ie whether the burden of the covenant has run with the land to him.

Before considering the rules which govern the enforcement by successors of the original parties of the covenants entered into between freeholders, we first consider the rules which govern the enforcement between successors of the landlord and tenant of covenants in leases. It is most important not to confuse these two sets of rules.

1 See LPA, s80(4).

Covenants in leases
39.2 The rules relating to the enforceability of covenants in leases are essentially two-fold. First, and obviously, all covenants, whether imposing positive or negative obligations, are mutually enforceable between the original parties to the lease. Second, where there has been an assignment of the lease or the reversion, or both, all covenants which 'touch and concern'

the land which is the subject of the lease are mutually enforceable between the persons who are now in the relationship of landlord and tenant, which relationship is known as *privity of estate.*

39.3 Before examining the operation of these two rules, we must first consider what is meant by the phrase 'touch and concern'. It means that the covenant should be reasonably incidental to the relationship of landlord and tenant rather than merely of personal advantage to the particular covenantee. Examples of covenants which have been held to touch and concern the property are a covenant to pay rent, a covenant to repair the property, a covenant not to assign, the landlord's covenant for quiet enjoyment, and a covenant giving the tenant an option to renew the lease. It should be noted that it has been held, anomalously, that to be enforceable against an assignee of the landlord this last covenant must be registered as an estate contract.[1]

Covenants which have been held not to touch and concern the land include a covenant not to open a public house within half a mile of the demised public house, a covenant to pay the tenant £500 unless the lease is renewed, a covenant to pay rates on *other* land, and a covenant giving the tenant an option to purchase the reversion.[2]

1   *Beesly v Hallwood Estates Ltd* [1960] 2 All ER 314, [1960] 1 WLR 549; *Taylor Fashions Ltd v Liverpool Victoria Trustees Co Ltd* [1982] QB 133n, [1981] 1 All ER 897.
2   For these and other examples, see Cheshire *Modern Law of Real Property* (13th edn) pp 431–433.

39.4 We now turn to consider the operation of the two rules relating to leasehold covenants.

We first consider the case where the tenant has assigned his entire leasehold interest:

$$L$$
$$|$$
$$T \rightarrow A$$

T has, usually by selling it, assigned his leasehold interest to A. L and A are now in the relationship of landlord and tenant. Therefore covenants in the lease which touch and concern the land are enforceable by L against A, and by A against L. Thus, for example, A will be bound by a covenant to pay rent, L by the covenant for quiet enjoyment.

If A was in breach of a covenant touching and concerning the land, such as the covenant to pay rent, L could, and normally would, take action against A to remedy the breach.[1] However, it must be remembered that there is still a contract between L and T under which T remains liable on the covenants for the rest of the term. By virtue of the LPA, s79, when originally entering into the relevant covenant, T is deemed to covenant not only that he will perform the covenant but also that his successors in title will do so. This does not of itself make the successors in title liable, but it does mean that, should a successor of the tenant fail to perform a covenant, the original tenant is in breach of his contractual obligation. This means that instead of, or as well as,[2] suing A, L may also sue T in respect of A's breach of covenant. In practice L is only likely to do this where A has failed to pay rent and is insolvent. It is to be noted that T will be liable even where the rent has been increased under a rent review occurring after the assignment.[3] If L does sue T, T may then sue A in an attempt to recover money paid to L, either in quasi-contract[4] or, if the assignment to A was for valuable consideration, for breach of a term implied by statute[5] that A and those deriving title from him will perform the covenant and, if they do not, will indemnify T.

1 Paras 37.14–37.22 above.
2 He may not recover twice in respect of the same loss.
3 *Brayton v Morgan* (1888) 22 QBD 74; *Centrovincial Estates plc v Bulk Storage Ltd* (1983) 46 P & CR 393; *Selous Street Properties Ltd v Oronel Fabrics Ltd* (1984) 270 Estates Gazette 643, 743.
4 Para 16.2 above.
5 LPA, s77(1)(c) and Sch 2.

39.5

$$L \rightarrow R$$
$$|$$
$$T$$

In this case, the landlord has assigned his reversion to R. R and T are now in the relationship of landlord and tenant. Covenants which touch and concern the subject matter of the lease are mutually enforceable between R and T. It is provided by the LPA, s141 that 'rent reserved by a lease, and the benefit of every covenant...therein contained, having reference to the subject matter thereof ... shall go with the reversionary estate in the land'. It has been held that the effect of this is that, once the reversion has been assigned, only R, and not L, can bring an action against T for breach of covenant, whether the breach occurred before or after the assignment.[1] Consequently, after the assignment of the reversion the contract between L and T becomes irrelevant, a situation which contrasts sharply with the position where it is the lease which is assigned.[2] If T owed rent prior to the assignment of the reversion, and L has not taken action to recover it, he loses the right to do so once he assigns his interest to R.

1 *Re King, Robinson v Gray* [1963] Ch 459, [1963] 1 All ER 781, CA; *London and County (A and D) Ltd v Wilfred Sportsman Ltd* [1971] Ch 764, [1970] 2 All ER 600, CA.
2 Para 39.4 above.

39.6

$$L \rightarrow R$$
$$|$$
$$T \rightarrow A$$

Here both landlord and tenant have assigned their interests in the property. All covenants which touch and concern the land are mutually enforceable between R and A, the new landlord and tenant. Furthermore because of the effect of s141, if the assignment T → A took place before the assignment L → R, R could nonetheless sue T for breaches of covenant occurring before R acquired the reversion even though there had never been any contract between the parties and they had never been in the relationship of landlord and tenant.[1] Equally, should A be in breach of a covenant which touches and concerns the land, R (and only R) may take action; if need be, against T.

1 *Arlesford Trading Co Ltd v Servansingh* [1971] 3 All ER 113, [1971] 1 WLR 1080, CA.

39.7 The rules illustrated in the foregoing paragraphs apply equally to covenants in leases (within the LPA, s54(2)[1]) not exceeding three years made in writing,[2] or, presumably, orally, though in the latter case an assignee may have difficulty ascertaining the details of some covenants. Where there is merely an agreement for a lease,[3] all covenants are mutually enforceable between the original parties to the agreement. In such a case, if the 'landlord' assigns his interest in the land, the effect of the LPA, ss141, 142 and 154 is to make the benefit and burden of covenants in the agreement run with the land to the assignee.[4] However, it would seem that, since under the law of contract the 'tenant' may assign only the benefit and not the burden of covenants in the agreement for a lease,[5] an assignee of the 'tenant' will not be bound by any of the obligations contained in the agreement for a lease. This was doubted, obiter, in *Boyer v Warbey*[6] by Denning LJ who considered that both the benefit and burden of covenants in an agreement for a lease could be assigned.

1 Para 33.4 above.
2 *Boyer v Warbey* [1953] 1 QB 234, [1952] 2 All ER 976, CA.
3 Para 33.6 above.
4 *Rickett v Green* [1910] 1 KB 253.
5 Para 39.11 below.
6 [1953] 1 QB 234, [1952] 2 All ER 976, CA.

39.8 Of course, where it has been validly varied,[1] a covenant which runs with an assignment, under the above rules does so in its varied form. In addition, there is authority[2] that the benefit and burden of any promissory estoppel in relation to, or waiver of,[3] an obligation under a covenant runs with an assignment where the estoppel or waiver is final and irrevocable. It follows that, if a landlord promises a tenant that he will never require compliance with a particular covenant, in circumstances giving rise to a promissory estoppel or waiver, an assignee of the lease takes the benefit of the promissory estoppel or waiver and the covenant cannot be enforced against him.

1 Para 6.35 above.
2 *Brikom Investments Ltd v Carr* [1979] QB 467, [1979] 2 All ER 753, CA.
3 Paras 6.16 to 6.18 and 6.36 to 6.37 above.

39.9 To conclude this section we consider the case where the tenant sub-lets:

T has created a sub-lease out of his own lease. In this case while there is a contract between L and T and a contract between T and S, there is no contract between L and S, nor are L and S in a relationship of landlord and tenant. Therefore enforcement between L and S of covenants contained in the head-lease (L-T) depends not on the foregoing rules but on the rules to be described in the next section.

Covenants where no privity of estate

39.10 We are here concerned with the enforcement of covenants between persons who are not, either as original parties or as assignees, in the relationship of landlord and tenant. In other words, we are mainly concerned with the enforcement of covenants between freeholders. In this area, common law and equity have separate rules. Both permit the benefit of a covenant to run with the land. Common law, however, does not allow the burden of a covenant to run, while equity allows the burden of negative covenants, which restrict the use of the land, to run. This means that the burden of positive covenants, which require the covenantor to do something in connection with the land, will not run with the land.

39.11 Clearly, covenants entered into between freeholders, perhaps on the sale of land by one to another, are mutually enforceable between the original parties on the basis of the contract between them. Furthermore, like other contractual rights, the benefit of a covenant may be assigned to a third party who may then enforce the benefit in his own right. It should also be noted that in certain exceptional cases the LPA, s56 allows a person to enforce a covenant relating to property as if he were a party to it, even though he is not named as a party to the covenant, so long as he is in existence at the time of the covenant, identified by it, and the covenant purports to be made *with* him.[1] Such a person is deemed to be a covenantee. Suppose X purchases land, and in the conveyance covenants 'with the vendor and also with his assigns, owners for the time being of land adjoining the land conveyed',[2] the persons who are owners for the time being of adjoining land purchased from the vendor are treated as covenantees along with the vendor. Although not naming them, the covenant identifies them and purports to be made with them. It should be noted that only those who, *at the time the covenant was made*, were owners of adjoining land are deemed to be covenantees by virtue of s56.

1   *White v Bijou Mansions Ltd* [1937] Ch 610, [1937] 3 All ER 269.
2   See *Re Ecclesiastical Comrs' Conveyance* [1936] Ch 430.

The running of the burden

Positive covenants
39.12 In the absence of privity of estate (ie where the parties are not in the relationship of landlord and tenant), the burden of a covenant does not run with the land at common law.[1] Since, as we shall see, equity allows the burden of restrictive (negative) covenants to run with the land of the covenantor, the effect of the common law rule is that the burden of positive covenants will not run with the land. This rule, 'the greatest and clearest deficiency' in the law of covenants,[2] is of considerable practical significance since it means, prima facie, that covenants which import positive obligations, such as to keep premises in repair, to erect boundary walls, and to contribute to the maintenance of roads, cannot be enforced against successors of the original covenantor.

An inability to ensure compliance with positive obligations to repair would clearly be a grave disadvantage in the case of a block of freehold flats. Indeed, the rule has, in the words of the Law Commission,[3] cast a blight on developments of freehold flats, which for example are not considered to be a particularly good security for a mortgage; it is usual practice therefore for flats to be sold leasehold, thus ensuring that positive covenants are enforceable.[4] The inability to enforce positive covenants against successive owners would also appear to present a problem where a contribution towards maintenance of common facilities is required from residents of a housing estate or block of freehold flats.

For these reasons, legal ingenuity has devised a number of methods of achieving the enforcement of positive obligations against successive freehold owners without transgressing the rule preventing the enforcement of positive covenants against successors of the covenantor. The first point to note is that by virtue of the LPA, s79 unless a contrary intention is expressed, a covenantor covenants that both he *and* his successors will abide by the covenant. Should a successor fail to do so, the covenantee may sue the original covenantor for breach of contract. The covenantor (and his successors likewise) should therefore ensure that purchasers from him undertake to indemnify him in the event of his being sued for their non-performance of an obligation. Such a chain of indemnity provides an indirect method of enforcing covenants, but like all chains it is only as strong as its weakest link.[5] Indeed, as the Law Commission has pointed out[6] none of the devices used to achieve enforcement of positive obligations can be said to provide an effective general solution to the problem. Of these devices, we shall briefly consider the right of entry and the estate rentcharge, and the doctrine of benefit and burden. It will be noted that while these devices could be useful in enabling a developer or management company to enforce positive obligations against successive residents of a housing estate or block of flats, they do not enable the residents to enforce such obligations against each other.

1 *Austerberry v Oldham Corpn* (1885) 29 ChD 750, CA. S33 of the Local Government (Miscellaneous Provisions) Act 1982 provides that local authorities may enforce positive covenants made under seal against successors of the covenantor.
2 Law Commission Report on the Law of Positive and Restrictive Covenants; Law Com. No 127.
3 Ibid.
4 On the principles expounded in paras 39.2 to 39.8 above.
5 Law Com No 127.
6 Ibid.

39.13 *Rights of entry* A right of entry may be used to secure compliance with positive covenants even though the covenants themselves are not enforceable as such.[1] A person having a right of entry has the right to enter property should certain conditions occur and take possession of it, thereby ending the interest of the person holding the land. For example, a vendor of property might insert in the conveyance a covenant requiring the purchaser and his successors to keep the property in repair and reserve to himself a right of entry exercisable should the property fall into disrepair. The threat that this right will be exercised will ensure that the purchaser and his successors comply with a positive covenant to repair. However, such a right of entry suffers two disadvantages: first, it is equitable, and in unregistered land depends for its enforceability against subsequent purchasers of the covenantor's land on the doctrine of notice, since it is not registrable in the Land Charges Register.[2] Second, it is subject to the rule against perpetuities, that is, there is a limit to how far in the future the right may be exercised.[3] To overcome these two disadvantages, it should be annexed to, ie incorporated with, an estate rentcharge.

1 *Shiloh Spinners Ltd v Harding* [1973] AC 691, [1973] 1 All ER 90, HL.

2 *Shiloh Spinners Ltd v Harding* [1973] AC 691, [1973] 1 All ER 90, HL. In registered land it should be protected by a notice.
3 Para 36.7 above.

39.14 *Estate rentcharges* A rentcharge is any annual or other periodic sum charged on or issuing out of land, except rent reserved by a lease or tenancy or any sum payable by way of interest.[1] If it is perpetual or for a term of years it is a legal interest.[2] The Rentcharges Act 1977 prohibits the creation of rentcharges for the future, subject to the important exception of the estate rentcharge.

An estate rentcharge may be of two kinds. The first is one created for the purpose of making positive covenants enforceable by the person to whom the rentcharge is paid (the rent owner) against the owner for the time being of the land. Such a rentcharge must not be of more than a nominal amount.[3] This kind of estate rentcharge achieves its object of making positive covenants enforceable against successive landowners by having a right of entry annexed to it. A right of entry annexed to a rentcharge is a legal interest, and thus enforceable in unregistered land against all purchasers of the land affected, and is not subject to the rule against perpetuities.[4] Essentially, annexing a right of entry to this kind of estate rentcharge cures it of the defects which it suffers when not so annexed. Nonetheless, the remedy remains 'clumsy and draconian' and although the device of the estate rentcharge comes closest to providing a solution to the unenforceability of positive covenants, it is undoubtedly artificial and technical in the extreme.[5]

The Rentcharges Act 1977 provides for a second kind of estate rentcharge, defined as one created for the purpose of meeting, or contributing towards, the cost of the performance by the rent owner of covenants for the provision of services, or for the carrying out of maintenance or repairs, or for the effecting of insurance or the making of any payment by him for the benefit of the land affected by the rentcharge. Such a rentcharge must be reasonable in relation to the cost to the rent owner of performing the covenant.[6] Examples of this kind of rentcharge are where the developer of a housing estate reserves to himself a rentcharge from each purchaser to provide him with a fund to maintain the estate roads until adoption by the local authority; or where the management company of a block of flats reserves a rentcharge in respect of each flat to provide a fund for the maintenance of the common parts.

1 Rentcharges Act 1977, s1. A legal rentcharge created out of *registered* land is noted together with the right of entry as an incumbrance in the Charges Register of the landowner's register of title, and the rent owner is substantively registered as the proprietor of a rentcharge and a rentcharge certificate issued to him. LRA, ss2, 19(2) and 49(1); LRR, rr50, 107 and 108.
2 LPA, s1(2).
3 Rentcharges Act 1977, s2.
4 LPA, ss1(2) and 4(3).
5 Law Commission Report on the Law of Positive and Restrictive Covenants; Law Com No 127.
6 Rentcharges Act 1977, s2.

39.15 *Doctrine of benefit and burden* Another possible method of securing the enforcement of positive obligations against successive landowners is the doctrine of benefit and burden elaborated in the case of *Halsall v Brizell*.[1] Under a covenant between the developers of a private housing estate and each purchaser, the purchasers covenanted to contribute towards the cost of maintaining the roads and footpaths of the estate, which were vested in the developer. Upjohn J held that as this covenant was positive it could not be enforced as such against successors of the original purchasers. However, by extending the doctrine that a person who takes the benefit of a deed is bound by any conditions in it, he held that if successors of the original purchasers wished to take advantage of the benefit of the roads and footpaths, which, of course, they had to to, they must also accept the burden of paying for their maintenance. This doctrine is, of course, only of utility where there is a corresponding benefit of which the successors wish to take advantage.

1   [1957] Ch 169, [1957] 1 All ER 371; para 38.14 above.

Restrictive covenants

39.16   The particular contribution of equity, originating in the case of *Tulk v Moxhay*,[1] is to allow the burden of restrictive covenants, those which restrict the uses to which the land may be put, to run with the land. Consequently, although a vendor may not ensure that successors of his purchaser act positively in relation to the land, he may ensure that they refrain from acting in particular ways: he may, for example, restrict building on the land or the carrying on of any trade. Equity will allow the burden of a covenant to run with the land of the covenantor if:

a. it is essentially negative;

b. the covenantee retains land capable of being benefited by the covenant;

c. the parties intend that the covenant should run with the land; and

d. the requirements of registration or of the doctrine of notice are complied with.

Each of these will now be considered in turn.

1   (1848) 18 LJ Ch 83.

39.17   *The covenant must be essentially negative* The essence of the covenant, whether positively or negatively worded, must be negative or restrictive. The case of *Tulk v Moxhay*[1] provides an example. Tulk owned Leicester Square. He sold off the gardens in the centre and retained the surrounding land. The purchaser of the gardens covenanted, inter alia, that he 'his heirs and assigns . . . would . . . at all times . . . keep and maintain the said piece of ground . . . in an open state'. This covenant was held to be binding on a successor of the purchaser. Although the covenant was phrased in terms of a positive obligation, 'keep and maintain in an open state', it was essentially negative, prohibiting building on the land. Conversely, a covenant 'not to let the premises fall into disrepair' is a positive covenant.

There are two reasons for the requirement that the covenant must be essentially negative. The first is that the equitable remedy of an injunction will normally only be ordered to enforce negative obligations. The second is that the equitable remedy of specific peformance (which does enforce positive obligations) will not be ordered where the enforcement of a positive obligation might require constant supervision.[2]

1 (1848) 18 LJ Ch 83.
2 Para 11.26c above.

39.18 *The covenantee must retain land capable of being benefited* In *LCC v Allen*,[1] a developer covenanted with the LCC not to build on a plot which lay across the end of a proposed street. It was held that the LCC could not enforce this covenant against a successor of the developer since at no time did the council have any interest in any land capable of being benefited by the covenant.[2]

It has been held that the reversion on a lease gives the landlord a sufficient interest to enable him to enforce against a sub-tenant a restrictive covenant made by the tenant and contained in the head-lease.[3] Such a covenant may be enforced by the landlord against a sub-tenant having notice of it, despite the absence of a contract or privity of estate between a landlord and sub-tenant. A mortgagee's (lender's) interest has also been held sufficient to enable him to enforce restrictive covenants against successors of the mortgagor/covenantor.[3]

In essence, the requirement that the retained land must be capable of being benefited by the restrictive covenant appears to be the same as the requirement of 'touching and concerning'[4] which, as we shall see, must be shown where it is claimed that the benefit of a covenant has run. The courts will, in fact, readily assume that the retained land is capable of being benefited by the covenant unless the defendant can show that the restriction cannot reasonably be said to be of value to the land.[5] Furthermore, the courts have been prepared to hold that a covenant restraining a purchaser from carrying on a business which competes with that carried on by the vendor on his retained land 'touches and concerns' the vendor's land. Both these points are illustrated in *Newton Abbott Co-operative Society Ltd v Williamson and Treadgold Ltd*,[6] where a covenant imposed by the vendor prohibiting dealing in articles of ironmongery in the property sold was held to touch and concern the vendor's retained ironmonger's shop. Upjohn J stressed the enhanced price the vendor would realise on selling together the land and the business, as a result of the covenant.

1 [1914] 3 KB 642, CA.
2 The Housing Act 1985, s609, now enables local authorities to enforce restrictive covenants despite the absence of dominant land.
3 See *Regent Oil Co Ltd v J. A. Gregory (Hatch End) Ltd* [1966] Ch 402, [1965] 3 All ER 673, CA.
4 Para 39.22 below.
5 *Wrotham Park Estate Co v Parkside Homes Ltd* [1974] 2 All ER 321, [1974] 1 WLR 798. Contrast *Re Ballard's Conveyance* [1937] Ch 473, [1937] 2 All ER 691.
6 [1952] Ch 286, [1952] 1 All ER 279.

39.19 *The parties must intend that the covenant should run* By the LPA, s79, which applies unless a contrary intention is expressed,[1] the parties are deemed to intend that the covenant should run with the land, rather than being merely personal to the parties.

1 See *Re Royal Victoria Pavilion, Ramsgate* [1961] Ch 581, [1961] 3 All ER 83.

39.20 *Registration and notice* In the case of unregistered land, covenants entered into prior to 1926 derive their protection from the doctrine of notice, under which a purchaser of a legal estate for value without notice is not bound, while covenants entered into after 1925 must be registered as a

Class D land charge in the Register of Land Charges, otherwise the covenant will be void against a purchaser of the legal estate for money or money's worth.[1]

In the case of registered land, the covenant must be protected by the entry of a notice in the Charges Register of the burdened land in order to bind the land of the covenantor.[2] The details of the covenant are set out in full on the register and land certificate of the burdened land, or a copy of it is attached to the certificate.

It should be noted that, both in registered and unregistered land, a restrictive covenant entered into between landlord and tenant cannot be registered. Consequently, enforcement of such a covenant by the landlord against a sub-tenant depends on notice in unregistered land; in registered land such a covenant would appear to be overriding within the LRA, s70(1)(g).

1 Paras 33.24 and 33.26 above.
2 LRA, s49; para 34.23 above.

The running of the benefit

39.21 As with the running of the burden, there are certain divergencies between the rules of common law and of equity on this topic. To the extent that equitable rules differ from common law rules, they apply only to restrictive covenants. For our purposes therefore it is appropriate to retain the division of the subject matter into positive and restrictive covenants.

Positive covenants

39.22 At common law the benefit of a covenant will run with the land to a successor of the original covenantee if it is *annexed* to the land, that is, incorporated with it so that on a transfer of the land the benefit automatically passes without the need for any mention being made of it. A covenant will be annexed and the benefit will run where the following conditions are met:

a. *that the covenant touches and concerns land of the covenantee* The covenant must either affect the land as regards mode of occupation or it must be such as in itself, and not merely from collateral circumstances, affects the value of the land.[1] In *Smith and Snipes Hall Farm Ltd v River Douglas Catchment Board*,[2] the Catchment Board covenanted with the owner of the land adjoining a brook that the Board would maintain the banks of the brook. The Court held that the covenant touched and concerned the adjoining land, in that it affected the value of the land per se and converted it from flooded meadows to land suitable for agriculture.

b. *that it was the parties' intention that the benefit should run* In the *River Douglas Catchment Board* case, the Court of Appeal held that it was plain from the language of the covenant, under which the Board undertook to maintain the banks of the brook 'for all time', that it was intended to take effect for the benefit of successive owners of the land. While in this case evidence of intention was sought and found in the language of the document creating the covenant, we shall explain in para 39.24 below, that this may no longer be necessary.

c. *that the land to be benefited should be identifiable from the document creating the covenant (and extrinsic evidence, if necessary)* In the *River Douglas Catchment Board* case, the document creating the covenant referred only to 'certain lands situate between the Leeds and Liverpool Canal and the River Douglas and adjoining the Eller Brook'. This was, however, regarded as sufficient; extrinsic evidence being admissible to prove the precise extent and situation of the relevant land.

d. *that the successor has acquired the original covenantee's legal estate or a term of years absolute derived from it* The common law used to require that the person seeking to enforce the covenant should have the same legal estate as the original covenantee. However, in *Smith and Snipes Hall Farm Ltd v River Douglas Catchment Board*, the Court of Appeal held that the covenant could be enforced against the Board not only by Smith who purchased the freehold from the original covenantee, but also by Snipes Hall Farm Ltd to whom Smith had leased the land. The Court held that the LPA, s78 permits the benefit of a covenant to run to lessees and sub-lessees as well as to successors of the covenantee's legal estate. A further, more radical effect, of s78 is considered in para 39.25, below.

It should be noted that it is not necessary that the covenant should have any connection with the land of the covenantor.

1   *Rogers v Hosegood* [1900] 2 Ch 388 at 395.
2   [1949] 2 KB 500, [1949] 2 All ER 179, CA.

Restrictive covenants

39.23   As with the common law rules, the first requirement of the equitable rules, which apply to restrictive covenants, is that the covenant should *touch and concern* land of the covenantee. A successor in title of the original covenantee must then show that the benefit has passed to him by annexation, *or* by assignment, *or* under a scheme of development.

39.24   *Annexation* It has been explained that at common law annexation requires not only a. that the covenant touches and concerns the land but also b. evidence that it was the parties' intention that the benefit should run, c. that the land should be identifiable, and d. that the successor has acquired the covenantee's legal estate or a term derived from it. As, in general, equity follows the law, it is to be expected that the same rules should also apply in equity (with the exception that equity will allow annexation to any ownership interest in land, legal or equitable). It has, however, been asserted by some writers that the requirements of equity in respect of annexation are more strict than those of the law. A reason put forward for this view is that while it is often clear from the circumstances that positive covenants are intended to benefit particular identifiable land, such an intention is less often clear from the obligations imposed by restrictive covenants. It is therefore said that to annex the benefit of a restrictive covenant in equity an appropriate formula of words *must* be used which clearly indicates the parties' intention and identifies the land;[1] that is, a formula which either demonstrates that the covenant has been entered into for the benefit of identifiable land or that it was made with the covenantee in his capacity as owner of that land.

An adequate formula might simply be to state that the covenant is made 'with the Vendor for the benefit of his property, Oaklands'. Another form

of words, following the classic formula used in *Rogers v Hosegood*,[2] is '...
with intent that the covenant might take effect for the benefit of the
vendors, their heirs and assigns and others claiming under them to all or
any of their lands adjoining or near to the land conveyed'. The covenant is
here expressed to be made with the covenantees in their capacity as owners
of the property to be benefited. The use of this formula would also make it
clear that the covenant is intended to benefit each part of the covenantee's
property[3] and that, as well as the benefit of the covenant passing by
annexation to subsequent owners of the entire benefited land, it will, if the
benefited land is divided up rather than remaining as an entity, pass also to
the owners of the parts.

Certain decisions of the courts[4] have suggested that unless, as in our
example, a form of words is used making it clear that the benefit is annexed
to the whole *and* each and every part of the benefited land, the benefit will
be presumed to be annexed only to the land as a unit. However, the decision
of the Court of Appeal in *Federated Homes Ltd v Mill Lodge Properties
Ltd*[5] is authority that the presumption is to the opposite effect. The Court
held that, if the benefit of a covenant is annexed to the land, it is prima facie
annexed to every part of the land. Consequently, clear words will now be
required if it is desired only that the benefit of the covenant should pass
solely to successors to the whole of the benefited land.

1 It should be noted that other writers have insisted that it is a requirement for annexation
   both at law and in equity that express words of annexation be used.
2 [1900] 2 Ch 388, CA
3 See *Marquess of Zetland v Driver* [1939] Ch 1, [1938] 2 All ER 158, CA.
4 *Russell v Archdale* [1964] Ch 38, [1962] 2 All ER 305; *Re Jeff's Transfer (No 2)*, *Rogers v
   Astley* [1966] 1 All ER 937, [1966] 1 WLR 841.
5 [1980] 1 All ER 371, [1980] 1 WLR 594, CA.

39.25 We think that at present neither at law nor in equity is the use of
express words essential, though it is desirable, to bring about the annexation of the benefit of a covenant. It is arguably a question of construction of
the particular covenant. First, there is authority that annexation can be
implied where, from the document creating the covenant, the land intended
to be benefited and an intention to benefit the land can be clearly
established.[1] As we have explained, these two matters, together with
evidence that the covenant touches and concerns the land, themselves
establish annexation.

Second, and most importantly, it has been decided by the Court of
Appeal in *Federated Homes Ltd v Mill Lodge Properties Ltd*[2] that the LPA,
s78 will cause the benefit of a covenant to be annexed, and hence to run with
the land, where

a. the covenant was entered into after 1925;

b. the covenant touches and concerns the land (a necessary requirement in
all cases, as we have said) and, possibly,

c. the land to be benefited is identified expressly or by necessary implication in the document creating the covenant. Unfortunately, it was not
necessary for the Court of Appeal to decide this last point conclusively as
the wording of the covenant in the particular case sufficiently identified the
land.

Section 78 provides that a covenant relating to any land of the covenantee shall be deemed to be made with the covenantee and his successors in title, including the owners and occupiers for the time being of the land of the covenantee intended to be benefited, and the persons deriving title under him or them, and shall have effect as if such successors and other persons were expressed.

Certainly, the *Federated Homes* case decides that this section will annex the benefit of a covenant where it can be shown to relate to any land of the covenantee ('or, to use the old-fashioned expression, that it touched and concerned the land'[3]) and to sufficiently identify the land. It may decide that it is enough that the covenant simply relates to or touches and concerns the land. If the former, the effect of the decision is to render it unnecessary to show, when seeking to prove annexation, that the covenant evidences an intention to benefit the land. (Where, however, according to its true construction, the covenant makes it clear that there is no such intention and hence no intention to annex then it may be argued that there is no room for s78 to have effect. This would accord with the subsequent decision in *Roake v Chadha*[4] where the covenant provided that it should not take effect for the benefit of successors unless the benefit was expressly assigned to them; it was held that in the face of these clear words, s78 did not cause the benefit to be annexed. There is, however, some difficulty with this result in that s78 does not expressly state that it is subject to a contrary intention in the covenant.)

If, on the other hand, *Federated Homes* decides that the benefit of a covenant runs with the land so long as it touches and concerns the land, it radically simplifies the law. Such a decision would be of benefit both to students learning the law and to those claiming the benefit of covenants but would be disadvantageous in that it would be much more difficult than hitherto for those ostensibly subject to the burden of covenants to know whether the covenant was enforceable against them and if so by whom.[5]

1   *Shropshire County Council v Edwards* (1983) 46 P & CR 270.
2   [1980] 1 All ER 371, [1980] 1 WLR 594, CA.
3   Ibid, at 379.
4   [1983] 3 All ER 503, [1984] 1 WLR 40.
5   A further possibility emerges from the decision at first instance in the *Federated Homes* case. There it was held that a failure expressly to annex the benefit of a covenant is immaterial, not because it is annexed anyway by s78, but because on a conveyance of the land it will, unless expressly excluded, pass by virtue of the LPA, s62 (para 40.23 below), which, inter alia, provides that a conveyance of land passes with it, unless expressly excluded, all rights and advantages whatsoever belonging to the land or, at the time of the conveyance, enjoyed with it. In the light of the Court of Appeal's view of the annexing effect of s78 it was not necessary for it to, nor did it, comment on this approach to s62. In *Roake v Chadha*, doubt was expressed, however, whether the benefit of a covenant not annexed can ever pass under s62.

39.26   *Assignment*   The traditional view of the law that if the benefit of a covenant was not *expressly* annexed to the land by the use of an appropriate formula of words, it was necessary for a successor of the covenantee to show that the benefit of it had been separately expressly *assigned* to him at the same time as the land was transferred to him. However, as we explained in the preceding paragraph, it now appears to be the law that annexation may either be implied or be brought about by the LPA, s78. Thus the circumstances in which it will be necessary to resort to the law of assignment are limited. In particular, where there is no express or, possibly, implied annexation of a pre-1926 covenant, assignment must be considered;

likewise where, as in *Roake v Chadha*,[1] annexation is expressly excluded. On one view of the *Federated Homes* decision, it may also be that assignment must be resorted to where the land to be benefited is not sufficiently identifiable from the document creating the covenant.

The rules as to the assignment of the benefit of a covenant are as follows. The assignment of the benefit of the covenant must be contemporaneous with the assignment of the land; once the covenantee has transferred the land he can no longer enforce the covenant[2] and he thus has no enforceable covenant to assign.[3] To be capable of assignment, a covenant must have been taken for the benefit of ascertainable land which is capable of being benefited by it. The existence and situation of the land to be benefited need not—and, since assignment is being resorted to in the absence of annexation, usually will not—be indicated in the terms of the covenant itself but it is sufficient that, on a broad and reasonable view, it can otherwise be shown with reasonable certainty.[4] In *Newton Abbott Co-operative Society Ltd v Williamson and Treadgold Ltd*,[5] a vendor, in 1923,[6] sold the shop opposite her own ironmonger's shop, imposing a covenant restraining the purchaser from using the shop for the sale of articles of ironmongery. Although the words of the covenant did not indicate an intention to benefit identifiable land, the court held that the attendant circumstances clearly showed that the covenant was taken for the benefit of the retained ironmonger's shop. Therefore, the covenant was assignable on a lease of the shop.

The benefit of an assignable covenant may be assigned separately and at different times with parts of the benefited land.[7]

It was accepted without argument in *Re Pinewood Estate, Farnborough, New Ideal Homesteads Ltd v Levack*,[8] and decided at first instance in the *Federated Homes* case, that the rules as to assignment require a successor of the covenantee, who seeks to enforce a covenant not annexed to the land, to show a 'chain of assignments' from the original covenantee to himself; it is apparently not the law, despite academic opinions to the contrary, that once the benefit of a covenant has been assigned it thereafter and thereby becomes annexed to the land.

1 [1983] 3 All ER 503, [1984] 1 WLR 40; para 39.24 above.
2 *Chambers v Randall* [1923] 1 Ch 149.
3 *Re Union of London and Smith's Bank Ltd's Conveyance, Miles v Easter* [1933] Ch 611, CA.
4 *Marten v Flight Refuelling Ltd* [1962] Ch 115, [1961] 2 All ER 696.
5 [1952] Ch 286, [1952] 1 All ER 229.
6 S78 therefore was not relevant.
7 *Chambers v Randall* [1923] 1 Ch 149.
8 [1958] Ch 280, [1957] 2 All ER 517.

39.27 *Scheme of development* A scheme of development exists where a landowner has disposed of his land in parcels, imposing, on each transfer of a parcel of land, restrictive covenants intended not simply for his advantage as owner of the land but for the advantage of each parcel purchased. Such schemes may be imposed to maintain the character of an area. This scheme of covenants gives rise to what is in effect a local 'planning' law for the area of land disposed of, which is based on reciprocal rights and obligations;[1] in other words, where such a scheme exists the restrictive covenants imposed by the original vendor are enforceable by, and are binding on, all the purchasers and their successors. The use of a scheme of development, then, secures not only the passing of the benefit of the covenants but also the passing of the burden. As soon as the original vendor sells the first parcel of land, the scheme crystallises, and all the land within the area of the scheme (there must be a clearly defined area[1]) is bound, becoming subject to the 'local law'.[2]

Species of scheme of development which may be encountered include the building scheme, designed to provide for and regulate building development, and the letting scheme, under which a common set of restrictions is imposed on leashold interests whether in relation to flats in a particular block or houses on an estate.

1   *Reid v Bickerstaff* [1909] 2 Ch 305 at 319, CA.
2   *Brunner v Greenslade* [1971] Ch 993, [1970] 3 All ER 833.

39.28   In the case of *Elliston v Reacher*,[1] Parker J laid down four requirements of a scheme of development:

a. both plaintiff and defendant in the action to enforce the particular covenant must derive title from the same vendor;

b. this vendor must have laid out his estate, or a defined part of it, for sale in lots, subject to restrictions which were intended to be imposed on all the lots, and which are consistent only with some general scheme of development;

c. these restrictions must have been intended to be, and be, for the benefit of all the lots; and

d. the lots must have been purchased from the common vendor on the basis that the restrictions to which they were subject were to take effect for the benefit of all the other lots. This is an important requirement.

More recent cases have shown that this list does not constitute an inflexible definition. For example, in *Baxter v Four Oaks Properties Ltd*,[2] the estate was not laid out in lots by the original vendor, rather he sold the land in parcels of whatever size the particular purchasers required. Nonetheless the area was held to be the subject of a scheme. In *Re Dolphin's Conveyance, Birmingham Corpn v Boden*,[3] the original owners of an estate, having sold off part in lots, gave the rest to their nephew who continued the process of selling the estate off in lots, imposing the same restrictions. Again, there was held to be a scheme of development, despite the absence of a sole vendor. In these cases the intention to impose a scheme was evident in the conveyancing documents. Where such an intention is not thus evident, it is necessary to consider whether Parker J's four requirements are complied with.

It must be remembered that a scheme of development is a scheme for the reciprocal enforcement of restrictive covenants and that to be enforceable restrictive covenants require protection by registration. Thus, every time a parcel is sold, the common vendor must register the covenants as Class D (ii) land charges against the purchaser,[4] or have the covenants noted on the charges register of the purchaser's register of title,[5] as appropriate. Furthermore, since the nature of the scheme is such that the vendor is impliedly bound by the restrictions (even if he has not expressly covenanted), each purchaser should register the restrictions against the common vendor. Only if this is done can each purchaser enforce the restrictions against subsequent purchasers.

1   [1908] 2 Ch 374.

2 [1965] Ch 816, [1965] 1 All ER 906.
3 [1970] Ch 654, [1970] 2 All ER 664.
4 Para 33.24 above.
5 Para 34.23 above.

Remedies

39.29 We stated earlier[1] that the law of restrictive covenants arose partly from the fact that equitable remedies are only really suitable for enforcing negative obligations. Indeed, equitable remedies are the only remedies available for the enforcement of restrictive covenants against a successor of the original covenantor. Damages, therefore, are not available as of right in the event of a breach by a successor of a restrictive obligation but only at the discretion of the court as an alternative to granting an injunction.[2] A 'good working rule' according to which the court might decide whether to grant damages instead of an injunction was put forward in *Shelfer v City of London Electric Lighting Co.*[3] According to this an injunction will be granted unless

a. the injury to the plaintiff's legal rights is small;

b. it is capable of being estimated in terms of money;

c. it can adequately be compensated for by a small payment, and

d. it would be oppressive to the defendant to grant an injunction.

It should be noted that this is only a good working rule and the court always retains its discretion to refuse an injunction.[4] Nonetheless, in the majority of cases an injunction will be granted. In appropriate cases, a mandatory injunction will be granted; for example requiring the demolition of a building, as in *Wakeham v Wood*[5], where the defendant erected a house blocking the plaintiff's sea view in flagrant disregard of a covenant prohibiting him so doing.

In the event of a breach of a positive covenant, damages at common law will normally be the appropriate remedy, though specific performance may be granted in certain circumstances.[6]

1 Para 39.16 above.
2 Supreme Court Act 1981, s50.
3 [1895] 1 Ch 287, [1891–4] All ER Rep 838.
4 See, for example, *Wrotham Park Estate Co v Parkside Homes Ltd* [1974] 2 All ER 321, [1974] 1 WLR 798.
5 (1981) 43 P & CR 40, CA.
6 See, for example, *Jeune v Queens Cross Properties Ltd* [1974] Ch 97, [1973] 3 All ER 97; para 37.19 above.

Development, planning law and restrictive covenants

39.30 Planning law and restrictive covenants exist side by side as means of controlling development. 'From the individual's point of view, control by private covenant has obvious advantages over planning control, in that it can cover matters of important detail with which a planning authority would not be concerned and the procedure of enforcement is available to a person who is entitled to the benefit of a covenant and is aggrieved by a breach, instead of depending on the planning authority's decision to act'.[1] In the words of a leading textbook on the subject, 'one thing that is abundantly plain is that there is no prospect whatever that restrictive covenants will become unnecessary and that their place will be taken by the planning laws. For planning standards are still too often below the standards imposed by restrictive covenants'.[2] Another point is that, as the Law Commission points out,[3] certain changes of use and certain building operations to which a neighbour might reasonably object do not require planning permission. Furthermore the law of restrictive covenants gives the power of enforcement to the individual affected. It is important to realise that the fact that an individual has planning permission for a particular project in no way permits or excuses the breach of a restrictive covenant burdening his land, though the grant of planning permission may be relevant, but far from decisive, in relation to an application to the Lands Tribunal for the modification or discharge of the covenant.[4]

1   Law Commission, Report on Restrictive Covenants No 11, para 18.
2   Preston and Newsom *Restrictive Covenants Affecting Freehold Land* (7th edn 1982).
3   Report on Positive and Restrictive Covenants, Law Com No 127.
4   Para 39.36 below.

39.31   A purchaser or would-be purchaser of land, discovering that the land is apparently subject to some long-standing restriction preventing intended development, may make an application to the Chancery Division for a declaration as to whether or not the land is, or would in any given event be, affected by the restriction; or as to the nature and extent of the restriction and whether it is enforceable and if so by whom.[1] It should be noted also that it is possible to take out a 'relatively inexpensive'[2] insurance policy against one's plans being thwarted by the enforcement of a restrictive covenant.

1   LPA, s84(2).
2   Law Commission, Report on Positive and Restrictive Covenants, Law Com No 127.

Discharge of restrictive covenants
39.32   Under this heading we discuss ways in which a person claiming the benefit of a restrictive covenant may be prevented from enforcing the covenant. At common law, there are three main possibilities: a. a change in the character of the neighbourhood, b. release of the covenant and c. unity of ownership. Under statute, we consider applications to the Lands Tribunal to discharge or modify the covenant, and (briefly) applications under the Housing Act 1985.

Common law

39.33   *Change in character of neighbourhood* In *Chatsworth Estates Co v Fewell*,[1] Fewell had opened a guest house contrary to a covenant that his house should be used as a private dwelling only. The estate company having the benefit of the covenant sought an injunction against him. Fewell claimed that the covenant was not enforceable on the ground that the character of the neighbourhood had completely changed since the covenant was made because some houses in the area were now used as guest houses, and some schools. Farwell J rejected this argument holding that to succeed on this basis a defendant would have to show so complete a change in the character of the neighbourhood that there was no longer any value left in the covenant at all. This was clearly not so in this case.

1 [1931] 1 Ch 224.

39.34 *Release of the covenant* Release may be express or implied. In *Chatsworth Estates Co v Fewell*, the defendant also argued that the estate company, by allowing others to open guest houses, etc had impliedly released the benefit of the covenants. This, said Farwell J, was a matter of degree, to be decided in this case by reference to the question, 'have the plaintiffs by their acts and omissions represented to the defendant that the covenants are no longer enforceable and that he is therefore entitled to use his house as a guest house?' Again, this was not so in this case.

39.35 *Unity of ownership* If the burdened and benefited land come into the same ownership, any restrictive covenants are extinguished.[1] This follows from the fact that a person cannot have a third party right over his own land. Land subject to a scheme of development, however, forms an exception to this rule. Plots within the area of a scheme, which have fallen into common ownership, remain subject to the scheme and continue to do so if they are later sold off separately.[2] Thus if the common vendor sells, subject to the scheme, a number of lots to a builder, who subsequently sells the lots to separate purchasers, the restrictions are enforceable between those purchasers even though their land had previously been in common ownership.

1 *Re Tiltwood, Sussex, Barrett v Bond* [1978] Ch 269, [1978] 2 All ER 1091.
2 *Texaco Antilles Ltd v Kernochan* [1973] AC 609, [1973] 2 All ER 118, PC; *Brunner v Greenslade* [1971] Ch 993, [1970] 3 All ER 833.

Application to the Lands Tribunal
39.36 Under the LPA, s84(1) the Lands Tribunal[1] has jurisdiction on certain grounds to discharge, wholly or partly, or to modify, restrictive covenants affecting freehold or leasehold land. In the case of leasehold land, the power is limited to where the term is of more than 40 years of which at least 25 years have expired.[2] The majority of applications made to the Tribunal under this section are to modify a covenant; for example, to enable the owner of the land affected to build at a higher density than that permitted in the covenant, or to carry out such projects as the conversion of a house into flats,[3] the building of a house in the garden of an existing house, or the erection of a public house. The fact that an applicant has planning permission for his intended development is in no way decisive of an application under s84, although the Tribunal must take into account the development plan for the area and the pattern of grants and refusals of planning permission in the area.[4]

Provision is made for those having the benefit of the relevant covenant to lodge an objection to the application. If the applicant considers that any objector is not entitled to the benefit of the covenant the Tribunal may make a preliminary determination of that matter,[5] the onus being on the objector to prove his entitlement.[6]

There is no rule preventing the original covenantor making an application under s84, nor preventing modification of a covenant which has only recently been imposed.[7] These are merely factors to be taken into account in the exercise of the Tribunal's discretion.

The Tribunal may in modifying a covenant add other reasonable restrictions which are acceptable to the applicant.[8]

1   Para 2.37 above.
2   LPA, s84(12).
3   See also para 39.39 below.
4   LPA, s84(1B).
5   Ibid, s84(3A); Lands Tribunal Rules 1975, r20.
6   *Re Edis's Application* (1972) 23 P & CR 421.
7   *Ridley v Taylor* [1965] 2 All ER 51, [1965] 1 WLR 611, CA; *Cresswell v Proctor* [1968] 2 All ER 682, [1968] 1 WLR 906, CA; *Jones v Rhys-Jones* (1974) 30 P & CR 451.
8   LPA, s84(1C).

39.37   The Tribunal may exercise its jurisdiction to discharge or modify a covenant on one of four grounds:

a. that the covenant ought to be deemed obsolete by reason of changes in the character of the property or the neighbourhood, or other material circumstances.[1]

In *Re Truman, Hanbury, Buxton & Co Ltd's Application*,[2] the applicant brewers applied on this ground to have a covenant modified to permit the erection of a public-house. The covenant was imposed under a scheme to preserve the character of an estate as a residential area. On appeal from the Lands Tribunal, the Court of Appeal held that only when the original purpose of a covenant can no longer be achieved can it be said to be obsolete. In this case it would be necessary to show that what was intended to be a residential area had become a commercial area, which was not the case. Furthermore, it was clear that the object of the covenant was still capable of fulfilment since the Lands Tribunal had expressly found that the proposed development would injure the objectors.

b. that the persons entitled to the benefit of the restriction have agreed either expressly or by implication, by their acts or omissions, to the discharge or modification.[3]

This ground is rarely relied on by an applicant at the outset, for if there is evidence of agreement to the discharge or modification an application to the Tribunal is probably not worthwhile. However, an individual may amend his application to include this ground once it has become clear that those who are entitled to the benefit of the covenant have failed to object to the application or have withdrawn their objection. The application will then be granted, since the persons entitled to the benefit have shown by their acts or omissions that they agree to the proposals.[4]

c. that the proposed discharge or modification will not injure the persons entitled to the benefit of the restriction.[5]

This ground has been described as a long-stop against frivolous or vexatious objections,[6] being limited to cases where there is no merit in the objections.

d. that the restriction impedes some reasonable use of the land, and either
i does not secure to persons entitled to the benefit of it any practical benefits of substantial value or advantage to them; or
ii is contrary to the public interest;
and that money will be an adequate compensation for the loss or disadvantage (if any) which any such person will suffer from the discharge or modification[7]

The majority of successful applications are made on this ground. The leading case is *Re Bass Ltd's Application*.[8] The company wished to use a site, which was subject to a restriction limiting its use to dwelling-houses, as a loading area for articulated trucks. The site was zoned in the development plan for industrial use and planning permission had been granted. A large number of those having the benefit of the covenant, imposed under a scheme of development, objected. The Tribunal rejected the company's application, giving its decision in the form of answers to questions formulated by counsel:

1   Is the proposed use which is impeded by the restriction reasonable? This question is to be answered leaving aside for the moment the restrictions. Where planning permission has been granted it will be difficult to find the proposed use unreasonable.

2   Does impeding the proposed use secure practical benefits to the objectors?
    The expression 'practical benefits' is very wide: the Tribunal is to consider the adverse effects of the applicant's proposal on a broad basis. Thus, in *Gilbert v Spoor*,[9] the preservation of a pleasant rural view enjoyed not from the benefited land but from a point a short distance away was held to be a practical benefit. The Tribunal in the *Bass* case answered this second question affirmatively, in view of the fact that the proposed development would give rise to increased noise, fumes, vibration, dirt and risk of accidents.

3   If yes, are the benefits of substantial value or advantage?
    The Tribunal has stressed that the benefits are not to be assessed in terms only of financial value. In the *Bass* case the benefits were held to be of substantial advantage, as have been, in other cases, peace and quiet, an unobstructed view[10] and the advantage of not being overlooked.

4   Is impeding the proposed use contrary to the public interest?
    Again, planning permission is relevant, but it must be remembered that planning permission does not necessarily imply that the proposed development is positively in the public interest. In the *Bass* case in view of the noise and amenity problem the development would cause, the economic interest of Bass Ltd could not be equated with the public interest. It is worth noting that the Tribunal has normally interpreted the requirement of public interest strictly and has rejected claims that impeding particular development is contrary to the public interest because, for example, housing land is in short supply or government policy favours high density development.

5   If the answer to 3 is negative, or to 4 affirmative, would money be an adequate compensation?

These questions were clearly not relevant to the *Bass* case. Where the answer to question 3 is negative, the answer to this question would be likely to be affirmative. Where this question is answered affirmatively the Tribunal will go on to consider its order, including whether other restrictions should be added, and to consider the question of compensation.

1   LPA, s84(1)(a).
2   [1956] 1 QB 261, [1955] 3 All ER 559, CA.
3   LPA, s84(1)(b).
4   *Re Dare's and Beck's Application* (1974) 28 P & CR 354.
5   LPA, s84(1)(c).
6   *Ridley v Taylor* [1965] 2 All ER 51 at 58.

7   LPA, s84(1)(aa), (1A).
8   (1973) 26 P & CR 156.
9   [1982] 2 All ER 576, [1982] 3 WLR 183, CA.
10 Ibid.

39.38   The Tribunal may order that the applicant pay to the objectors a sum by way of compensation intended either:

a. to make up for any loss or disadvantage suffered in consequence of the discharge or modification of the restriction; or

b. to make up for any effect of the restriction had, at the time when it was imposed, in reducing the price then received for the land affected by it.[1]

1   LPA, s84(1).

Housing Act 1985, s610
39.39   Application may be made under this section to a county court to vary a restrictive covenant to enable a house to be converted into two or more dwellings. The applicant must either have planning permission for the proposed conversion or prove to the court that (owing to changes in the character of the neighbourhood) the house cannot readily be let as a single dwelling but could if converted. The court must give interested parties an opportunity of being heard, and may vary the covenant (subject to such conditions and on such terms as it thinks just).

Proposals for reform
39.40   The Law Commission has produced a report and draft legislation[1] aimed at comprehensive reform of the law of covenants. The mainspring of their report is the need to deal with the unsatisfactory state of the law concerning positive covenants[2] but they are equally unhappy with the complex and uncertain law relating to restrictive covenants. Their proposal is to introduce for the future a new interest in land, the land obligation.

This interest, which would exist as a legal interest if made by deed for a term equivalent to a fee simple absolute in possession or a term of years absolute, is proposed to take two forms: the neighbour obligation and the development obligation. The former, involving simply a burden imposed on one piece of land for the benefit of another, could take one of three forms: a restrictive obligation, a positive obligation, requiring either the carrying out of works or the provision of services, or a reciprocal payment obligation, requiring the making of a payment towards expenditure incurred by a person complying with a positive obligation.

Development obligations are intended for use where land is divided into separately owned but interdependent units. They are intended to be enforceable either by owners of other parts of the development or by a manager acting on their behalf. Again, such obligations could take the form of restrictive or positive or reciprocal payment obligations; in addition, a development obligation might be imposed to require the servient land to be used in a particular way which benefits the whole or part of the development land, to require payment to a manager of the development in respect of expenditure incurred in pursuance of the development scheme, and possibly for other purposes such as requiring access to be afforded to a manager of the development. Such development obligations would have to be imposed pursuant to a development scheme created by deed, making provision for a system of obligations to be imposed on the separate units within a defined area of development land (which would include a block of flats).

Although it is proposed that land obligations should normally exist as legal interests, it is proposed that they should be registrable and hence be unenforceable if unregistered. In unregistered land, they would be Class C land charges; in registered land, they would need to be protected by entry on the register of the servient land (and of the dominant land in the case of legal neighbour obligations)—they would not constitute overriding interests.

1 The Law of Positive and Restrictive Covenants (1984). Law Com. No 127.
2 Para 39.12 above.

Chapter 40

Easements and profits à prendre

Easements

The nature of an easement

40.1 An easement is a right in respect of another's land, which may be legal or equitable.[1] Some idea of the nature of easements may be gathered from the following dictum of Lord Denning:[2] 'There are two kinds of easements known to the law: positive easements, such as a right of way, which give the owner of land *a right himself to do something* on or to his neighbour's land: and negative easements, such as a right of light, which give him *a right to stop his neighbour doing something* on his (the neighbour's) own land'.

The nature of an easement is best discovered by reference to Cheshire's[3] four essential characteristics of an easement, approved by the Court of Appeal in *Re Ellenborough Park, Re Davies, Powell v Maddison*.[4] In this case, the Court held that the right to use a park or garden adjacent to a group of houses was an easement attaching to those houses. The Court reached its decision by considering whether the right claimed possessed the four characteristics:

a. there must be a dominant and a servient tenement;

b. the easement must 'accommodate' the dominant tenement;

c. the dominant and servient owners must be different persons; and

d. the right must be capable of forming the subject matter of a grant.

Each of these will now be considered.

1 Para 40.16 below.
2 *Phipps v Pears* [1965] 1 QB 76 at 82, [1964] 2 All ER 35 at 37.
3 *Modern Law of Real Property* (13th edn) pp 490–494.
4 [1956] Ch 131, [1955] 3 All ER 667, CA.

There must be a dominant and servient tenement
40.2 This is another way of saying that, as in the case of restrictive covenants,[1] there must be land which enjoys the right (the dominant land (or tenement)) and land which is subject to the right (the servient land or tenement). An easement takes effect for the benefit of *land*; it is annexed to that land and passes automatically with the land on assignment. No one

can possess an easement otherwise than in respect of, and in amplification of, his enjoyment of some estate or interest in a piece of land.[2]

1 Para 39.18 above.
2 *Alfred F Beckett Ltd v Lyons* [1967] Ch 449 at 483, [1967] 1 All ER 833, CA.

The easement must 'accommodate' the dominant tenement

40.3 The easement must, in other words, be of benefit to the dominant land. There must be a clear connection between the enjoyment of the right and the enjoyment of the dominant land. In *Re Ellenborough Park*,[1] the court held that the park became a communal garden for the benefit and enjoyment of those whose houses adjoined it or were in its close proximity; it was the collective garden of the neighbouring houses. The necessary connection between the right and the land was thus shown. In contrast, a right given to the purchaser of a house to attend Lord's Cricket Ground without payment would not constitute an easement, for, although it would confer an advantage on the purchaser and doubtless would increase the value of the property, it would be wholly extraneous to, and independent of, the use of the house as a house.[2]

Similarly, in *Hill v Tupper*,[3] the tenant of premises on the bank of the Basingstoke Canal was given the 'sole and exclusive right' by the owners to put pleasure boats on the canal. He subsequently brought an action against the defendant, who had also started to hire out pleasure boats on the canal, alleging that he was interfering with the plaintiff's easement. The claim failed, the court holding that the plaintiff merely had a licence. As this case was explained in *Re Ellenborough Park*,[4] the plaintiff was trying to set up, under the guise of an easement, a monopoly which had no normal connection with the ordinary use of his land but which was merely an independent business enterprise. So far from the right claimed accommodating the land, the land was but a convenient incident to the exercise of the right. That is not to say that a right which primarily benefits a business carried on on the land may not also be held to accommodate the land. Thus, in *Moody v Steggles*,[5] it was held that the right to affix an inn sign on adjoining property accommodated the plaintiff's public house. The question would seem to depend on whether the court is prepared to find an intimate connection between the land and the business carried on there.[6]

1 [1956] Ch 131, [1955] 3 All ER 667, CA.
2 Ibid, at 173.
3 (1863) 2 H & C 121.
4 [1956] Ch at 175.
5 (1879) 12 Ch D 261.
6 Cf *Clapman v Edwards* [1938] 2 All ER 507.

40.4 It may not be possible to demonstrate the necessary nexus between enjoyment of the right and the dominant land where the dominant and servient properties are at some distance from each other: 'a right of way over land in Northumberland cannot accommodate land in Kent.'[1] On the other hand, it is not necessary that the properties be adjoining. In *Re Ellenborough Park*,[2] a few of the houses having the benefit of the use of the park were some 100 yards from it; nonetheless, the court held that the necessary connection between dominant and servient tenement existed. Again, in *Pugh v Savage*,[3] the owner of field C was held entitled to an easement of way across field A to reach the nearby highway despite the existence of field B, which he had a licence to cross, between the two properties.

1   *Bailey v Stephens* (1862) 12 CBNS 91.
2   [1956] Ch 131, [1955] 3 All ER 667, CA.
3   [1970] 2 QB 373, [1970] 2 All ER 353, CA.

The dominant and servient owners must be different persons
40.5   Clearly, as an easement is a right over another's land, one cannot have an easement over one's own land. However, the freehold owner of two plots may grant an easement over one plot to the tenant of the other, and a tenant may grant an easement to another tenant of the same landlord. Where the owner of two plots of land uses a way across one plot to reach the other, he clearly is not doing so by virtue of an easement, but it is sometimes said that he enjoys a 'quasi-easement'. We consider the relevance of quasi-easements in para 40.21 below.

The right must be capable of forming the subject matter of a grant, ie be capable of being granted
40.6   The meaning of this requirement is not immediately apparent. Essentially the right claimed must be such as could be formulated in a deed of grant by a capable grantor to a capable grantee. For example, a tenant cannot grant an easement in fee simple, nor can an easement be granted to a fluctuating group of persons. Furthermore, the right must be within the general nature of rights recognised as easements. There is no fixed list of easements. In deciding whether a right claimed should be upheld as an easement, the court will take into account three factors recognised as delimiting the nature of an easement.

40.7   The first factor is whether the right claimed is expressed in terms of too wide and vague a character,[1] rendering expression of it in a grant difficult. On this basis the courts have refused to allow as an easement a claim to a general right of light for one's land.[2] A right of light can only exist as an easement in respect of a defined aperture.[3] Similarly, the right to the passage of air generally over one's land cannot exist as an easement,[4] but a right to air to a defined aperture can.[5] The quantum of the right claimed can in that case be expressed with some precision. In *Phipps v Pears*,[6] the Court of Appeal had to decide whether the right to have one's property protected from the weather could exist as an easement. One of two houses, which were very close together but which did not actually support each other, was demolished, thereby exposing to the elements the wall of the other house, which had never been rendered or plastered. Reflecting the policy considerations which must always be present when a claim to a new easement is decided, the Court rejected the claim to an easement on the basis that this was a claim to a *negative* easement,[7] of which the law was said to be chary of creating new examples since they restrict the servient owner in the enjoyment of his own land and hamper legitimate development. We think that the court could instead have based its decision on the fact that the right claimed was of too wide and vague a character, since it could be said that all easements, whether positive or negative, restrict the servient owner in the enjoyment of his land to some degree.

1   *Re Ellenborough Park* [1956] Ch 131, [1955] 3 All ER 667, CA.
2   See *Roberts v Macord* (1832) 1 Mood & R 230.

3 Para 40.39 below.
4 *Webb v Bird* (1861) 10 CBNS 268.
5 *Bryant v Lefever* (1879) 4 CPD 172.
6 [1965] 1 QB 76, [1964] 2 All ER 35, CA.
7 Para 40.1 above.

40.8 A second relevant factor in the decision whether to recognise a claim to an easement is that the claim must not amount to a claim to use and enjoy the servient land jointly with the servient owner. In *Copeland v Greenhalf*,[1] the defendant wheelwright claimed that he was entitled to an easement to store vehicles awaiting and undergoing repair on a strip of land opposite his premises. Upjohn J rejected the claim as being virtually a claim to possession of the servient land, since it involved the defendant and his employees being able to carry out repair work on the land and involved the defendant leaving as many vehicles on the land as he wished, thereby effectively treating the land as his own.[2] It does not follow, however, that an easement to store articles on another's land cannot exist. The possibility was recognised in *A-G of Southern Nigeria v John Holt & Co (Liverpool) Ltd*,[3] and in *Wright v Macadam*[4] it was held, without argument on the point, that the right to store coal in a coal shed was clearly an easement. The question is, no doubt, one of degree. Thus, in *Miller v Emcer Products Ltd*,[5] a case demonstrating that the categories of easements are not closed, the Court of Appeal held that a right to use a neighbour's lavatory could exist as an easement. The Court pointed out that, although at the times when the dominant owner exercised his right the owner of the servient tenement would be excluded, this was a common feature to a greater or lesser extent of many easements, such as a right of way, and in any case this did not amount to so complete an ouster of the servient owner's rights as was held to be incompatible with an easement in *Copeland v Greenhalf*.

1 [1952] Ch 488, [1952] 1 All ER 809.
2 See *Grigsby v Melville* [1973] 1 All ER 385, [1972] 1 WLR 1355.
3 [1915] AC 599, PC.
4 [1949] 2 KB 744, [1949] 2 All ER 565, CA.
5 [1956] Ch 304, [1956] 1 All ER 237, CA.

40.9 A third factor to be considered is that the easement claimed must not involve the servient owner in expenditure. An easement is either a right to do something or a right to prevent something. A right to have something done is not an easement, nor is it an incident of an easement.[1] Thus an agreement by a landlord to supply hot water and heating to the tenants of a block does not give rise to an easement,[2] nor is a right to a water supply paid for by the servient owner capable of being an easement.[3]

There is, furthermore, long established authority that the owner of the servient tenement, though he must not act in such a way as to interfere with the enjoyment of the easement by the dominant owner, is not bound, in the absence of contract, to carry out any repairs necessary to ensure the enjoyment of the easement by the dominant owner; on the other hand, the grant of an easement prima facie confers on the dominant owner the right to enter the servient property to effect necessary repairs.[4] It may now be the case, however, that the servient owner may be liable in negligence or nuisance if he fails to take reasonable steps to repair defects which he is aware or ought to have been aware threaten to interfere with the dominant owner's easement.[5]

An exception to the rule that the right claimed must not involve the servient owner in expenditure is provided by the easement, or 'spurious easement', of fencing. 'The right to have your neighbour keep up the fences is a right in the nature of an easement which is capable of being granted by law'.[6] The cases involve fencing against straying animals, but the principle would not appear to be so limited.

1   *Jones v Price* [1965] 2 QB 618 at 631, [1965] 2 All ER 625 at 628, CA.
2   *Regis Property Co Ltd v Redman* [1956] 2 QB 612, [1956] 2 All ER 335, CA.
3   *Rance v Elvin* (1983) 127 Sol Jo 732.
4   *Jones v Pritchard* [1908] 1 Ch 630; but see *Liverpool City Council v Irwin* [1977] AC 239, [1976] 2 All ER 39, HL (implied contractual obligation to repair and maintain).
5   *Bradburn v Lindsay* [1983] 2 All ER 408; para 40.42 below.
6   *Crow v Wood* [1971] 1 QB 77 at 84–85, [1970] 3 All ER 425 at 429, CA.

Rights similar to easements
40.10   Under this heading we further elaborate the nature of easements by considering rights which are similar to easements and, in each case, what it is which differentiates them from easements.

Restrictive covenants[1]
40.11   A similarity between these two species of rights over another's land can be seen in that both require dominant and servient land. Indeed, restrictive covenants were described by Sir George Jessel MR[2] as being an extension in equity of the doctrine of negative easements, such as the easements of light and of support. Of course, restrictive covenants are equitable only, whereas easements may be legal or equitable. Furthermore, it may be that the content of a restrictive covenant may be of too vague and wide a character to form the subject matter of a grant. So, for example, while the right to a view cannot exist as an easement,[3] the same objective may be achieved by the imposition of a restrictive covenant preventing development which obstructs the view.[4]

1   Ch 39 above.
2   *London and South Western Rly Co v Gomm* (1882) 20 Ch D 562.
3   *Aldred's case* (1610) 9 Co Rep 57b.
4   *Wakeham v Wood* (1981) 43 P & CR 40, CA, para 39.28 above; and see *Gilbert v Spoor* [1983] Ch 27, [1982] 2 All ER 576, CA, para 39.36 above.

Licences[1]
40.12   The right to walk across another's field, for example, may exist either as an easement or a licence. The latter differs from the former in that it depends on permission and, unless supported by some equity, is revocable. Moreover, a licence is a personal right not a proprietary right; it requires no dominant land and, again unless supported by some equity, is in principle not enforceable against a successor of the licensor.[2]

1   Ch 38 above.
2   See, further, para 38.8 above.

Non-derogation from grant[1]
40.13   Where a person conveys or leases land for a particular purpose, he is under an obligation not to use the land retained by him in such a way as to render the land conveyed or leased unfit, or materially less fit, for the particular purpose for which the conveyance or lease was made.[2] *Aldin v*

Latimer Clark, Muirhead & Co[3] illustrates how this principle may confer greater rights than may be conferred as an easement. Land was let to the plaintiff to enable him to carry on the business of a timber merchant. It was held that the landlord could not build on his retained land so as to interrupt the free passage of air to the plaintiff's timber-drying sheds. It will be remembered that a general right to air cannot exist as an easement, only a right to air to a defined aperture.[4]

1   Para 37.3 above.
2   *Browne v Flower* [1911] 1 Ch 219 at 226.
3   [1894] 2 Ch 437.
4   Para 40.7 above.

Public rights

40.14   While there are other public rights such as the rights to fish and navigate in tidal waters, the difference between easements and public rights is best illustrated by considering the difference between easements of way and public rights of way. Clearly the major difference is that an easement must exist in favour of land while a public right of way is vested in the public at large. A public right of way is said to exist over a 'highway', which does not have to be a made-up road, but may be a footpath, bridleway or carriageway. A highway may be created expressly or impliedly, at common law or under statute. At common law, a highway is deemed to be created by implication by the process of 'dedication and acceptance': where long enjoyment as of right is shown the landowner may be deemed to have dedicated the way to the public, and the public deemed to have accepted the right. Under statute,[1] a highway may be created by 20 years' public use as of right. Both at common law and under statute, the landowner may prevent the creation of a highway by physically obstructing the way, commonly for one day per year.

1   Highways Act 1980, s31.

Customary rights

40.15   Customary rights are not public rights, available to the general public at large, but are confined to the inhabitants of a particular locality. They differ from easements in that there is no necessity for dominant land and in that they are not capable of forming the subject matter of a grant, since a fluctuating body of inhabitants is not a capable grantee. A customary right must be ancient, continuous, certain and reasonable.[1] Examples include the right of fishermen of a particular parish to dry their nets on private land[2] and the right of the inhabitants of a village to hold a fair on private land.[3]

1   Para 3.53 above.
2   *Mercer v Denne* [1905] 2 Ch 538, CA.
3   *Wyld v Silver* [1963] Ch 243, [1962] 3 All ER 309, CA.

Acquisition of easements

Legal and equitable easements

40.16   An easement is legal if it is created in fee simple or for a term of years absolute,[1] and is expressly or impliedly made by deed[2] or is presumed by law to have been so made.[3] An easement is equitable if it is created for a lesser interest than a fee simple or term of years, eg for life, or if it is not created by deed.

For an easement expressly created by a proprietor of registered land to be a legal interest, the disposition must be completed by registration, that is by entry of the right in the property register of the dominant land (if it is registered) and by entry of a notice in the charges register of the servient land.[4] Any legal easement appearing on the title at the time of first registration must similarly be entered on the register.[5] A legal easement not required to be entered on the register takes effect as an overriding interest.[6] An equitable easement must be protected by notice or caution on the title of the servient land.[7] It has been held, in *Celsteel Ltd v Alton House Holdings Ltd*,[8] that equitable easements constitute overriding interests, but this is doubtful.[9]

In unregistered land, a legal easement binds all comers without the need for registration; an equitable easement must be protected by registration in the Land Charges Register either as a Class D (iii) land charge or, in theory, where it takes the form of an agreement to create a legal easement, under Class C (iv) as an estate contract.[10]

1 LPA, s1(2).
2 LPA, s52.
3 Para 40.28 below.
4 LRA, ss19(2), 22(2).
5 LRA, s70(2); para 34.19 above.
6 LRA, s70(1).
7 LRA, ss54, 59(2).
8 [1985] 2 All ER 562, [1985] 1 WLR 204.
9 Para 34.19, n1 above.
10 Land Charges Act 1972, s2(4), (5).

Express grant or reservation

40.17 An easement may be *granted* expressly, either on the transfer by a landowner of part of his land or independently of the transfer of land. An easement is *reserved* where the grantor of land reserves to himself a right over the land granted in favour of his retained land. Any ambiguity in the terms of a grant will be resolved in favour of the grantee and against the grantor, but any ambiguity in the terms of a reservation is to be resolved in favour of the person who reserved the right, albeit that it was doubtless he who drew up the reservation.[1]

1 *St Edmundsbury and Ipswich Diocesan Board of Finance v Clark (No 2)* [1975] 1 All ER 772, [1975] 1 WLR 468, CA.

Implied grant or reservation

40.18 This method of creation is applicable only where a landowner is selling or leasing a part of his land and is retaining the remainder (or disposing of the whole in parcels), because only in such a case is there a transaction into which the grant or reservation of an easement can be implied.

The courts will imply the grant *or* reservation of easements of necessity and of intended easements, and will imply the grant (but *not* the reservation) of easements which, being necessary to the reasonable enjoyment of the property, are continuous and apparent, and enjoyed at the time of the grant by the owner of the whole of the land for the benefit of the part granted. We consider each of these in turn.

40.19 *Easements of necessity* Where a vendor sells or retains land which as a result is left without any legally enforceable means of access, ie which is 'landlocked', the law will imply from those circumstances that the parties intended a right of way of necessity to be granted or reserved.[1] It is for the vendor to select the route which must, however, provide convenient access. Such a right of way is limited to what was necessary in the circumstances of the transaction in which the implication that the parties intended a way of necessity is made. Thus, in *London Corpn v Riggs*,[2] the defendant retained a plot of land used for agriculture, which was completely surrounded by land which he had sold to the Corporation. The defendant thereby acquired a right of way of necessity, the conveyance containing no express mention of easements of way. He then put in hand plans to build refreshment rooms open to the public on the retained land. The Corporation successfully sought to restrain him from using the right of way for any purposes other than those connected with the agricultural use of the retained land. Although the law is uncertain, we think that an easement of necessity does not come to an end when the need for it ceases. We consider, in para 40.20 below, another possible example of an easement of necessity.

1 *Nickerson v Barraclough* [1981] Ch 426, [1981] 2 All ER 369, CA.
2 (1880) 13 Ch D 798.

40.20 *Intended easements* The law will readily imply the grant or reservation of such easements as may be necessary to give effect to the common intention of the parties to the grant of real property, with reference to the manner or purposes in and for which the land granted or some land retained by the grantor is to be used, but it is essential for this purpose that the parties should intend that the subject of the grant or the land retained by the grantor should be used in some definite and particular manner.[1] In *Re Webb's Lease, Sandom v Webb*,[2] in which a landlord sought to show that he had the right to use the outside wall of demised premises for displaying advertisements, the court held that the mere fact that the tenant knew of the presence of the advertisements at the time of the lease was insufficient to show an intention common to both parties that the landlord should have reserved the right to maintain the advertisements. A landlord or vendor seeking to show the reservation of an intended easement must show that the facts are not reasonably consistent with anything but a common intention.

The categories of easements of necessity and intended easements overlap. For example, reciprocal easements of support will be implied on the sale by their owner of one of two adjoining properties. This may be regarded as an easement of necessity, although some regard it as an intended easement.[3] Conversely, the case of *Wong v Beaumont Property Trust Ltd*[4] was held to concern an implied easement of necessity, although it could equally well be regarded as concerning an intended easement. Here, cellar premises were let to a tenant who covenanted that he would carry on business as a restaurateur, would not cause any nuisance, and would control and eliminate all smells and odours in conformity with the health regulations. The tenant subsequently assigned to Wong. In order to comply with the health regulations, Wong sought the landlord's permission to affix a ventilation duct to the outside wall of the landlord's premises. The landlord refused but Wong obtained a declaration that he was entitled to affix the duct. The Court of Appeal held that, where a lease is granted which imposes a particular use on the tenant and it is impossible for the tenant so to use the premises legally unless an easement is granted, the law does imply such an easement as of necessity.

1   *Pwllbach Colliery Co Ltd v Woodman* [1915] AC 634, HL.
2   [1951] Ch 808, [1951] 2 All ER 131, CA.
3   *Jones v Pritchard* [1908] 1 Ch 630.
4   [1965] 1 QB 173, [1964] 2 All ER 119, CA.

40.21   *Easements within the rule in Wheeldon v Burrows*   In addition to the two bases of implication just discussed, there has evolved an extension of the doctrine of non-derogation from grant.[1] This is known as the rule in *Wheeldon v Burrows*,[2] whereby the *grant* of easements will be implied into a conveyance or lease of land. The rule states that where a landowner sells or leases part of his land, certain easements will pass, by implication in the conveyance (and also, in practice, by implication in the contract[3]). These are easements which are 'continuous and apparent easements (by which, of course, I mean quasi-easements[4]), or, in other words, all those easements which are necessary to the reasonable enjoyment of the property granted, and which have been and are at the time of the grant used by the owners of the entirety for the benefit of the part granted'.[5] Thus, where prior to the sale or leasing of part of his property, the owner has found that the exercise of some right over the part he is retaining is necessary to the reasonable enjoyment of the part he is selling, that right will pass to the purchaser or lessee as an easement, provided it is continuous and apparent. It is said that, strictly, a 'continuous' easement is one that is enjoyed passively, without the need for action on the part of the dominant owner, such as the right of light.[6] Something is 'apparent' if it is discoverable on a careful inspection by a person ordinarily conversant with the subject.[7] Thus the presence of a window on the dominant tenement receiving light from the adjoining land suggests a continuous and apparent easement. However, the courts have extended the concept of what is 'continuous and apparent' beyond these narrow confines; the phrase is regarded as being 'directed to there being on the servient tenement a feature which would be seen on inspection and which is neither transitory nor intermittent'.[8] Thus, it is well established that a right of way over a made-up road or worn track can pass as an easement under the rule in *Wheeldon v Burrows*, provided it is necessary to the reasonable enjoyment of the property.[9] Similarly, a right to use drains running through the vendor's retained land may also be created as an easement under this rule.[10]

1   Para 40.13 above.
2   (1879) 12 Ch D 31.
3   *Borman v Griffith* [1930] 1 Ch 493; *Sovmots Investments Ltd v Secretary of State for the Environment* [1977] QB 411, [1976] 1 All ER 178.
4   Para 40.5 above.
5   (1879) 12 Ch D 31 at 49.
6   Megarry & Wade, *Law of Real Property* (5th edn) p 863.
7   *Pyer v Carter* (1857) 1 H & N 916 at 922.
8   *Ward v Kirkland* [1967] Ch 194 at 225, [1966] 1 All ER 609 at 616.
9   *Borman v Griffith* [1930] 1 Ch 493.
10   *Ward v Kirkland* [1967] Ch 194, [1966] 1 All ER 609.

Creation of easements by the operation of the LPA, s62
40.22   The creation of easements under the LPA, s62 does not come about by implication in the conveyance, rather the words creating the easement are deemed by virtue of the section, to have been expressed in the

conveyance. However, it is convenient to treat s62 here, because of the interrelation of the section and the rule in *Wheeldon v Burrows*.

40.23 The section provides that a conveyance of land shall be deemed to include and shall by virtue of the Act operate to convey, with the land, all liberties, privileges, easements, rights and advantages, whatsoever, appertaining or reputed to appertain to the land or any part thereof, or, at the time of the conveyance, enjoyed with the land or any part thereof. This provision applies to dispositions of registered land by virtue of the LRA, ss19(3) and 22(3).

Section 62 makes it clear that existing easements enjoyed with the land pass on a conveyance of the land. Furthermore, where part of the land conveyed originally had the benefit of an easement, the section enlarges the right so that, after the conveyance, it takes effect for the benefit of the whole. Thus, in *Graham v Philcox*,[1] where an easement of way was granted to the lessee of the first floor of a converted coach house, the easement passed under s62 on the conveyance of the freehold of the whole, for the benefit of the coach house as a whole. What matters for the purposes of s62 is that the right was enjoyed with the land conveyed or at least part of it.

The section has a further most important effect, namely that it operates to convert mere privileges and advantages into legal easements. In effect s62 states that a conveyance of a piece of land operates to convey with that land all advantages appertaining to, or, at the time of the conveyance, enjoyed with the land, so as to convert such advantages into legally enforceable rights.[2] These rights and privileges must actually be enjoyed at the time of the grant with the land granted or a part of it. Furthermore, they must have been enjoyed by an occupier of the land other than the grantor, over other land of the grantor.[3] It follows that, while the dominant and servient lands must have been in common *ownership* prior to the transaction creating the easement, they must have been in separate *occupation*.

It should be noted that the section does not operate to create easements out of rights not capable of existing as such; thus the right to protection from the weather,[4] or to the provision of hot water and heating,[5] cannot pass under s62.

1 [1984] 2 All ER 643, CA.
2 *Nickerson v Barraclough* [1981] 2 All ER 369 at 381–382.
3 *Sovmots Investments Ltd v Secretary of State for the Environment* [1979] AC 144, [1977] 2 All ER 385, HL; *Long v Gowlett* [1923] 2 Ch 177.
4 *Phipps v Pears* [1965] 1 QB 76, [1964] 2 All ER 35, CA.
5 *Regis Property Co Ltd v Redman* [1956] 2 QB 612, [1956] 2 All ER 335, CA.

40.24 The operation of s62 is illustrated by *International Tea Stores Co v Hobbs*.[1] A tenant, with the landlord's permission, made use of a roadway on the landlord's property. Subsequently, the tenant acquired the freehold and it was held that the right to use the roadway passed to him as an easement under s62. Similarly, in *Wright v Macadam*,[2] a tenant was given permission by the landlord to use a coal shed belonging to the landlord. The Court of Appeal held that on the renewal of the lease the right to use the coal shed passed as an easement, although previously depending on permission. These cases constitute a warning to landlords to revoke all licences granted to a tenant prior to renewing the lease or selling the reversion, or, preferably, to otherwise exclude the operation of s62.[3]

1 [1903] 2 Ch 165.
2 [1949] 2 KB 744, [1949] 2 All ER 565, CA.
3 Para 40.27 below.

40.25 Another warning as to the possible effect of the section appears from *Goldberg v Edwards*.[1] Edwards leased an annexe at the rear of her house to Goldberg. This annexe could be reached by an outside passage at the side of the house. Goldberg was allowed into possession before the lease was executed and was given permission to use a passage through the landlord's house to reach the annexe. The lease was executed some time later. Edwards subsequently let her house to Miller, the second defendant, who barred the door to Goldberg. Goldberg claimed he was entitled to a right of way either under the rule in *Wheeldon v Burrows*[2] or under s62. The Court of Appeal held that the claimed right of way had not passed under *Wheeldon v Burrows* since it was not necessary for the reasonable enjoyment of the annexe, which could conveniently be reached via the outside passage. However, the right did pass as an easement under s62 since, at the time of the conveyance (ie when the lease was finally executed), the privilege of going through the house was enjoyed with the annexe and thus passed as an easement when the lease was executed.

1 [1950] Ch 247, CA.
2 Para 40.21 above.

40.26 The case of *Borman v Griffith*[1] demonstrates that s62 operates only in respect of 'conveyances' and thus will not operate to pass easements in an agreement for a lease of more than three years.[2] Just as *Goldberg v Edwards* illustrates how an easement may pass by virtue of s62 where *Wheeldon v Burrows* is inapplicable, so *Borman v Griffith* shows how easements within the rule in *Wheeldon v Burrows* may pass where s62 is inappropriate. Borman occupied a house in the grounds of Wood Green Park under an agreement for a seven-year lease. He made use of the main drive of the park which ran by the front of his house although the agreement contained no reference to a right of way and although his house could be reached by an unmade track at the rear. Borman claimed a right of way along the main drive in this action against the tenant of the remainder of the park who had prevented Borman's use of the drive. The court rejected the claim based on s62 as Borman had only an agreement for a lease. However, the court in effect held that, just as easements within the rule in *Wheeldon v Burrows* will be implied in a grant, so continuous and apparent easements necessary for the reasonable enjoyment of the property will be implied in an agreement for a grant,[3] and, since the drive was plainly visible and was necessary for the reasonable enjoyment of the property, a right of way over it passed to Borman.

1 [1930] 1 Ch 193.
2 A lease for three years or less (at the best rent without taking a fine) does not require to be made by deed and does constitute a conveyance for this purpose; see para 33.4 above.
3 *Sovmots Investments Ltd v Secretary of State for the Environment* [1977] QB 411, [1976] 1 All ER 178.

40.27 *Contract and conveyance* Section 62 is stated to apply only if and so far as a contrary intention is not expressed in the conveyance. Therefore its effect can be excluded by making it clear in the conveyance that rights which might otherwise pass under the section are not intended to be conveyed. The conveyancing process, as will be seen later,[1] comprises two stages: the contract stage and the conveyance stage, except that in the case of a lease these two stages may admittedly be telescoped into one. Section 62 takes effect in the conveyance, as does the rule in *Wheeldon v Burrows*, but it is important to realise that the purchaser is entitled to have conveyed to him only that which he has contracted to buy; that and no more. It is the contract which governs the content of the conveyance. If, then, s62 operates to convey easements which the parties did not, by their contract, intend to be granted, the conveyance may be rectified so as to accord with the contract, thereby excluding easements under s62.[2] Rectification is a discretionary remedy and may not be ordered, for example, where the vendor has delayed in seeking the remedy or has misled the purchaser.[3] However, if it is granted the conveyance will be rectified to pass only those easements to which the purchaser is entitled expressly or by implication under the contract. Whilst the grant of easements under the rule in *Wheeldon v Burrows* may in fact be implied in the contract and hence such easements would in any event pass on the conveyance, this implication may—and commonly will—be excluded by the express terms of the contract. Where this is done, easements within the rule will not in fact pass on the conveyance.[4]

1 Ch 43 below.
2 *Clark v Barnes* [1929] 2 Ch 368.
3 Para 12.18 above.
4 *Squarey v Harris-Smith* (1981) 42 P&CR 118, CA.

Prescription

40.28 Prescription is the method whereby the law confers legality on long enjoyment of a right, by presuming it had a lawful origin in a grant. An easement acquired by prescription is a legal easement. The law of prescription has been described as unsatisfactory, uncertain and out of date,[1] particularly because there exist side by side three methods by which a claim to have acquired an easement by prescription may be made: at common law, under the doctrine of lost modern grant, and under the Prescription Act 1832. Whichever method is being relied on as the basis of a claim (and it may be advisable to rely on more than one method) it must be shown that there has been continuous enjoyment of the alleged right, in fee simple, as of right. In some cases, a preliminary question may arise as to the precise nature of the enjoyment. For example, in *Davis v Whitby*,[2] a householder had, for 30 years, gained access to the rear of his house across the garden of a neighbouring house. However, for the first 15 years he had used one route, for the second 15 years, another. The court regarded this as enjoyment of a right of way for 30 years, it being treated as a right to pass and re-pass over the neighbouring land rather than a right of way along a particular path.

1 Law Reform Committee, 14th Report, Cmnd 3100 (1966).
2 [1974] Ch 186, [1974] 1 All ER 806, CA.

40.29 *Continuous enjoyment* This requirement does not mean that the right claimed must have been used ceaselessly day and night throughout the prescriptive period. In *Diment v N.H. Foot Ltd*,[1] the use of a path between six and ten times a year was considered sufficient in regularity and extent to constitute continuous enjoyment. The claim to a right of way by prescription was, however, unsuccessful for other reasons.[2]

1 [1974] 2 All ER 785, [1974] 1 WLR 1427.
2 See para 40.31 below.

40.30 *In fee simple* An easement (other than one of light[1]) may only be acquired by prescription by a fee simple owner against a fee simple owner.[2] Where the servient land is held by a tenant under a lease throughout the period of enjoyment on which the dominant owner's claim to have acquired an easement is based, the claim will be unsuccessful. However, as long as the period of enjoyment began at a time when the servient land was held by the freeholder, the fact that subsequently the land became subject to a tenancy will not defeat the claim, unless the servient owner, the freeholder, can show that he had no knowledge that the enjoyment was continuing while the tenant was in possession.[3]

Long enjoyment of a right by a tenant will not enable the tenant to claim an easement by prescription, but his enjoyment of the right accrues to the freeholder; the right is thus acquired by the freeholder. It follows from this, and from the fact that a person cannot have an easement over his own land, that a tenant cannot acquire a prescriptive right against his landlord, nor can a tenant acquire an easement by prescription against another tenant of the same landlord.[4]

1 Para 40.40 below.
2 *Wheaton v Maple & Co* [1893] 3 Ch 48, CA.
3 *Pugh v Savage* [1970] 2 QB 373, [1970] 2 All ER 353, CA.
4 *Kilgour v Gaddes* [1904] 1 KB 457, CA.

40.31 *As of right* A person claiming to have acquired an easement by prescription must show that he has thus far enjoyed the right on the basis that he was entitled to it. This he does by showing that his enjoyment was *nec vi, nec clam, nec precario*, ie not by force, nor secretly, nor by permission.

a. *nec vi* There can be no claim to an easement by prescription where the alleged right has been exercised by force or in the face of opposition from the servient owner.

b. *nec clam* Where the servient owner has no knowledge, or means of knowledge,[1] of the enjoyment, that enjoyment cannot be said to be acquiesced in; it cannot be said to be as of right. Enjoyment 'as of right' cannot be secret but must be of such a character that an ordinary owner of the land, diligent in the protection of his interests, would have, or must be taken to have, a reasonable opportunity of becoming aware of that enjoyment.[2] Consequently, it was not possible to claim by prescription an easement in respect of the support of a dry dock where none of the supporting rods was visible on the alleged servient land.[2] Similarly, the intermittent discharge of borax at night into a sewer could not, even over a long period, ripen into an easement; the servient owner clearly would have no means of knowledge of the use.[3] Where long enjoyment is shown, knowledge on the part of the servient owner will be presumed, and it is for the servient owner to rebut the presumption.[4] The knowledge of a tenant or of the servient owner's agent will not be imputed to the servient owner.[5]

c. *nec precario* To succeed in a claim to have acquired an easement by prescription, the dominant owner must show that the servient owner acquiesced in his enjoyment as if it were an established right. If, in fact, his enjoyment depended on getting the permission of the servient owner, it is clear that the latter did not regard the enjoyment as an established right, since he could have terminated it at any time by withdrawing his permission.

1   *Dalton v Angus & Co* (1881) 6 App Cas 740 at 801, HL.
2   *Union Lighterage Co v London Graving Dock Co* [1902] 2 Ch 557 at 571, CA.
3   *Liverpool Corpn v H. Coghill & Son* [1918] 1 Ch 307.
4   *Pugh v Savage* [1970] 2 QB 373, [1970] 2 All ER 353, CA.
5   *Diment v N.H. Foot Ltd* [1974] 2 All ER 785, [1974] 1 WLR 1427.

The three methods of prescription

40.32   *Common law* Thus far we have said that a claim to have acquired an easement by prescription depends on showing long enjoyment as of right. Strictly, at common law, it is necessary to show enjoyment as of right since a time before 1189, which time, for historical reasons, is regarded as 'time immemorial' or 'a time whereof the memory of men runneth not to the contrary'. Obviously, a need to prove enjoyment since before 1189 would in most cases present insuperable hurdles, thus enjoyment since time immemorial is presumed on proof of enjoyment during living memory or even of 20 years' enjoyment. However, this presumption can be rebutted, and the claim will fail, if it is shown that at some time after 1189 the right did not exist or could not have existed. In many cases this will be easy to show; for example, in the case of a claim to an easement of support, by showing that there was no building on the land in 1189. Because rebutting the presumption is often so easy the doctrine of lost modern grant was developed.

40.33   *Lost modern grant* By this fiction, the court presumes that a comparatively recent grant was made of the easement but has since been lost. In this way a lawful origin to long enjoyment is presumed without the need to show immemorial enjoyment. A lost modern grant will be presumed on evidence of 20 years' continuous use in fee simple as of right. This presumption is a fiction; it cannot be rebutted by evidence that there was in fact no grant but only by evidence showing that a grant could not possibly have been made.[1]

1   *Dalton v Angus & Co* (1881) 6 App Cas 740; *Tehidy Minerals Ltd v Norman* [1971] 2 QB 528, [1971] 2 All ER 475, CA.

40.34   *Prescription Act 1832* 'The Prescription Act 1832 has no friends. It has long been criticised as one of the worst drafted Acts on the Statute Book'.[1] The Act was apparently drafted with the aim of avoiding the pitfalls involved in a claim at common law. In view particularly of its complexity, the Act provides few advantages over the other two methods with which it co-exists. Nonetheless, it may, in fact, be of some utility to those claiming an easement by prescription. The Act provides for a claim to an easement other than light to be based either on 20 years' enjoyment as of right without interruption or on 40 years' such enjoyment; its provisions relating to easements of light will be considered separately in a later paragraph.[2]

1 Law Reform Committee, 14th Report, Cmnd 3100 (1966).
2 Para 40.40 below.

40.35 Where a claim under the Act is based on *20 years' enjoyment* as of right without interruption it cannot be defeated by evidence that enjoyment began later than 1189, although it may be defeated in any other way in which a claim at common law may be defeated.[1] Thus it is still necessary to show that enjoyment was continuous, in fee simple, *nec vi, nec clam, nec precario.*

The period of enjoyment must have immediately preceded a court action relating to the claim.[2] Enjoyment for 20 years simpliciter will not do. There must be some court action to confirm the inchoate right as an easement. This can take the form either of an action by the dominant owner for a declaration that he is entitled to the right or an action by the servient owner to prevent continued enjoyment, in which the dominant owner relies on the Act as a defence. If there has been no enjoyment for some time prior to the court action, then even if there has been 20 years' enjoyment, a claim under the Act cannot, subject to what follows, succeed.

To constitute an interruption of the period of enjoyment an act must be submitted to or acquiesced in for one year after the party interrupted has had notice of both the interruption and the person making it.[2] It follows that, if a landowner has enjoyed a right of way for 20 years over neighbouring land and is then prevented from using the way by the neighbour, he will still be able to claim an easement under the Act if he brings an action to claim the right before one year elapses from the time he became aware that the neighbour was obstructing the way.

Time during which the servient land is held by a person who is a minor, lunatic or tenant for life is to be excluded from the computation of the 20 year period, so that the claimant must show 20 years' enjoyment on top of that time.[3]

1 Prescription Act 1832, s2.
2 Ibid, s4.
3 Ibid, s7.

40.36 A claim to an easement under the Act based on *40 years' enjoyment* as of right without interruption is deemed to be absolute and indefeasible unless it is shown that the enjoyment depended on written consent.[1] Again, the 40-year period must immediately precede some court action. 'Interruption' has the same meaning as in relation to the 20-year period.

Although a claim based on 40 years' enjoyment will only be defeated by proof of written permission, the enjoyment must be 'as of right'. Therefore, enjoyment which depends on regular permission (written *or* oral)—as in *Gardner v Hodgson's Kingston Brewery Co*[2] where an annual payment of fifteen shillings had to be made for the use of a right of way—will not ripen into an easement even if the permission is oral and the enjoyment has continued for 40 years, because the enjoyment is 'precario'. Oral permission given at the outset and not renewed will not defeat a claim based on the 40-year period, though it will defeat a claim based on 20 years' enjoyment.

In computing the 40-year period, any time during which the servient land was held under a lease of more than three years is to be deducted, provided that the claim to the easement is resisted by the servient owner within three years of the ending the lease.[3] Thus, providing the servient owner resists the claim within the time limit, the dominant owner must show that he has enjoyed 40 years' use on top of the period of the lease. If the dominant owner is unable to show this he may be able instead to base his claim on 20 years' enjoyment, for in that case the period of the lease is not deductible. However, the existence of the lease will then be relevant to the question of whether the 20 years' enjoyment was in fee simple.[4]

1 Prescription Act 1832, s2.
2 [1903] AC 229, HL.
3 Prescription Act 1832, s8.
4 See *Palk v Shinner* (1852) 18 QB 568.

Extinguishment of easements
40.37 No provision exists for the modification or discharge of easements, unlike the case of restrictive covenants.[1] Easements may be extinguished by being released, expressly or impliedly, by the dominant owner, or by ownership and possession of the dominant and servient properties falling into the same hands. Implied release is not shown merely by proof that the dominant owner is not using the right. It must be shown that the dominant owner intends to abandon the right, and abandonment of an easement can only be treated as having taken place where the person entitled to it has demonstrated a fixed intention never at any time thereafter to assert the right himself or to attempt to transmit it to anyone else.[2]

1 Paras 39.36 and 39.37 above.
2 *Tehidy Minerals Ltd v Norman* [1971] 2 QB 528 at 553, [1971] 2 All ER 475 at 492, CA.

Particular easements

Right of way
40.38 A right of way may be limited, as to the times it may be used or as to the purposes for which it may be used (eg agricultural purposes only) or as to the modes of enjoyment (eg on foot only), or it may be unlimited.

The question may arise whether the extent to which the dominant owner is making use of the right is greater than his true entitlement. In answering this question, the method of creation of the easement is relevant. Where the easement was expressly granted or reserved, the question turns on the construction of the relevant deed in the light of the circumstances surrounding its making, in particular the nature of the road or track over which the right was granted.[1] Where the extent of the right granted is unclear, ambiguities in the deed are resolved in favour of the person having the benefit of the easement.[2] In the case of easements of way arising by implication, enjoyment is circumscribed by the situation prevailing at the time of the grant.[3] The extent of enjoyment permitted in the case of an easement of way acquired by prescription is determined by the nature of the enjoyment during the prescriptive period, though an increase in the frequency of use is unobjectionable unless it results from a change in the nature of the enjoyment.[4] For example, where a right of way had been acquired by prescription to a site used by a small number of caravans, the servient owner could not object to a considerable increase in the number of caravans using the site.[4]

Enlargement of the dominant tenement is not of itself sufficient to extinguish or affect entitlement to a right of way unless as a consequence the permitted extent of enjoyment would be exceeded.[5]

1 *Cannon v Villars* (1878) 8 Ch D 415.
2 *St Edmundsbury and Ipswich Diocesan Board of Finance v Clark (No 2)* [1975] 1 All ER 772, [1975] 1 WLR 468, CA.
3 *London Corpn v Riggs* (1880) 13 Ch D 798.
4 *British Railways Board v Glass* [1965] Ch 538, [1964] 3 All ER 418, CA.
5 *Graham v Philcox* [1984] QB 747, [1984] 2 All ER 643, CA.

Right of light

40.39 The right to light can exist only as an easement and then only in respect of a defined aperture, usually a window.[1]

1 See *Levet v Gas Light and Coke Co Ltd* [1919] 1 Ch 24.

40.40 *Acquisition by prescription* A right of light acquired by prescription is often referred to as 'ancient lights'. Ancient lights can be acquired by all three methods of prescription, though acquisition by proof of immemorial enjoyment at common law is highly unlikely. Special rules apply, however, under the Prescription Act 1832. Under the Act, a claim to an easement of light based on 20 years' enjoyment (immediately preceding a court action), without interruption, gives rise to an absolute and indefeasible right, unless the light was enjoyed by written consent.[1] There is no requirement that enjoyment be as of right, so the fact that the light was enjoyed by virtue of regular oral permission is no bar to a claim to have acquired a prescriptive right. Furthermore, as it is not necessary to show enjoyment in fee simple, a tenant may acquire an easement of light against his landlord or against another tenant of the landlord.[2]

An act does not constitute an interruption for the purpose of the Act unless submitted to or acquiesced in for one year.[3] Enjoyment of the light could, of course, be interrupted by the erection of a structure blocking the light to the particular window, and traditionally this is done by the erection of a hoarding. However, this method may fall foul of the planning laws, and so, as an alternative, the servient owner may apply under the Rights of Light Act 1959 for registration in the local land charges registry[4] of a notice, which is treated as being equivalent to an actual obstruction of the light. The application for registration must state the size and position of the opaque structure which the notice is intended to represent.[5] Before such a notice can be registered, the Lands Tribunal must certify that all those likely to be affected by the registration have been notified.[6] Registration is effective for one year.

1 Prescription Act 1832, s3.
2 *Morgan v Fear* [1907] AC 425, HL.
3 Prescription Act 1832, s4.
4 Para 43.5 below.
5 Rights of Light Act 1959, s3.
6 Ibid, s2.

40.41 *Extent of right* Generally speaking an owner of ancient lights is entitled to sufficient light 'according to the ordinary notions of mankind' for the comfortable use and enjoyment of his house as a dwelling-house, if it is a dwelling-house, or for the beneficial use and occupation of the building if it is a warehouse, a shop, or other place of business.[1] Where there is a right of light, a dominant owner may only bring an action in respect of a reduction in the amount of light received where the reduction constitutes a nuisance, that is if the light received is reduced below what is sufficient according to the ordinary notions of mankind. In determining this question, the court may take into account the nature of the locality and may have regard to the fact that higher standards may be expected as time goes by.[2] In *Allen v Greenwood*,[3] the plaintiffs, who for at least 20 years had had a greenhouse in their garden, close to the boundary with the neighbouring property, sought an injunction restraining the neighbours from obstructing the light to the greenhouse. The obstruction was caused by a fence the neighbours had erected and by the neighbours' caravan which was parked close to the greenhouse. Albeit that the greenhouse still received enough light to read by, the Court of Appeal held that this was insufficient for the ordinary purposes of mankind for the use and enjoyment of a greenhouse as a greenhouse (which is regarded as a building with apertures). The question of light necessary for ordinary purposes is determined by the nature and use of the building, and thus a high degree of light may be necessary in a particular case. Alternatively, the Court held that it is possible to acquire a prescriptive right to a greater than ordinary amount of light. Just as the extent of enjoyment during the prescriptive period determines the extent of a prescriptive right of way, so it determines the extent of a right of light acquired by prescription. The greenhouse having enjoyed an extraordinary amount of light for 20 years, to the knowledge of the servient owner, a prescriptive right to that amount of light had been acquired.

1   *Colls v Home and Colonial Stores Ltd* [1904] AC 179 at 208.
2   *Ough v King* [1967] 3 All ER 859, [1967] 1 WLR 1547, CA.
3   [1980] Ch 119, [1979] 1 All ER 819, CA.

Right of support
40.42   All landowners automatically have a natural right of support whereby they may bring an action should the support to their *land* be removed. For example, in *Redland Bricks Ltd v Morris*,[1] the plaintiff successfully sought damages and an injunction[2] when part of his market garden slipped into the defendant's land as a result of their digging for clay for their brickworks, and, in *Lotus Ltd v British Soda Co Ltd*,[3] the plaintiff was held to be entitled to damages when the pumping of brine from boreholes on adjacent land resulted in withdrawal of support from and consequent subsidence of the plaintiff's land, with resultant damage to the buildings on it. There is no natural right of support in respect of *buildings*. Such a right of support must be acquired as an easement. However, as *Lotus v British Soda* shows, damages may be claimed in respect of damage to buildings which results from infringement of the natural right of support to the land on which they stand.

An easement of support may be acquired expressly, by implication or by prescription. A servient owner who by an act of his own interferes with a right of support does so at his peril;[4] if he removes the support he must provide an equivalent. There is, however, established authority that he is under no obligation to repair that part of his building which provides support for his neighbour; he can let it fall into decay. On the other hand, the owner of the dominant tenement may enter and take the necessary steps to ensure the support continues by effecting the required repairs.[5] More recently though, it has been held that a servient owner who allows his property to fall into decay in circumstances where he should reasonably have appreciated the risk to his neighbour's right of support may be liable in negligence or nuisance for failing to take reasonable steps to prevent or minimise the risk.[6]

1 [1970] AC 652, [1969] 2 All ER 576, HL.
2 He failed to obtain a mandatory injunction: para 31.17 above.
3 [1972] Ch 123, [1971] 1 All ER 265.
4 *Brace v South East Regional Housing Association Ltd* (1984) 270 Estates Gazette 1286, CA.
5 *Bond v Norman* [1940] Ch 429, [1940] 2 All ER 12, CA.
6 *Bradburn v Lindsay* [1983] 2 All ER 408.

Profits à prendre

40.43   A profit à prendre is a right to take from another's land the natural produce of the land, minerals, or wild animals on the land. Examples of profits are, most importantly, the profit of pasture, whereby grass (a natural product of the land) is taken from the land by being eaten by the profit-owner's animals; the rights to take gravel and minerals from the land; the rights to catch fish and shoot game.

40.44   A profit may be legal or equitable. The rules outlined in para 40.16 above, apply also to profits. In the case of registered land a profit which is not entered on the register is an overriding interest whether it is legal or equitable.

A profit may be several or in common. A several profit is owned by one person to the exclusion of others. A profit in common (or simply 'common') is owned in common with others. A common pasture is perhaps the most important type of profit in common.

A profit may be appurtenant or in gross. If appurtenant, it is, like an easement, annexed to a dominant tenement. If so, the profit is limited to the needs of the dominant land. For example, an appurtenant profit of pasture will be limited to the number of cattle the dominant land is capable of supporting. A profit in gross is owned independently of land and is unconnected with any dominant tenement. Nevertheless, it is still a right in land.

A several profit may be acquired by express grant or reservation, under the LPA, s62, or by any of the three methods of prescription; a profit in common by express grant or, if appurtenant, under the Prescription Act 1832. Under the Prescription Act 1832, the same rules apply as outlined earlier in relation to easements other than light,[1] except that the shorter period is, not 20 years, but 30 years, and the longer period is, not 40 years, but 60 years. However, in computing the longer period, no deduction can be made for leases of more than three years, unlike the case of easements.[2]

1 Paras 40.35 and 40.36 above.

2   Para 40.36 above.

40.45   Under the Commons Registration Act 1965, any common right or common land (ie land subject to common rights) existing before 2 January 1970 must have been registered in the appropriate county council's register of commons before 31 July 1970, otherwise it ceased to be exercisable.

Chapter 41

Mortgages

41.1 A mortgage of land is a transfer of an interest in the land as security for a debt. It enables the creditor, in the event of the debtor being unable or unwilling to pay off the debt, to enforce the debt against the land, for example, by selling it and recouping what he is owed. Mortgages are created most commonly where a building society or other institutional lender lends money towards the purchase of a home. A mortgage may, however, be granted by a landowner to secure (ie as security for) a bank loan, or a loan from a finance company, or to secure a current account, as well as, in the commercial sphere, to secure a loan to finance the purchase of property or the expansion of a business. The creditor, the lender of the money to whom the mortgage is granted, is called the mortgag*ee*, the debtor or borrower is called the mortgag*or*.

41.2 Provisions in mortgages for the repayment of the debt, principal plus interest, vary considerably. In the traditional form of mortgage, in relation to which the law of mortgages developed, the principal is to be repaid in a lump sum, although provisions will normally be made for regular payments of interest in the interim. The endowment mortgage, now common in the case of house purchase, is a variety of this '*standing*' type of mortgage. Under this scheme, the mortgagor makes regular payments of interest to the mortgagee while at the same time paying premiums on an endowment assurance policy[1] which on maturity will provide a lump sum for the repayment of the principal.

Today, more common than the standing mortgage is the *instalment* mortgage under which the principal is repayable in instalments. This may take one of two forms. It may be provided, as in a standing mortgage, that the entire principal be repaid at a fixed (early) date but subject to a proviso that so long as instalments of principal and interest are regularly paid, the provision for repayment of the whole sum will not be enforced. Alternatively, and this is more common, a building society instalment mortgage provides that the principal and interest are to be repaid over a period of years, subject to a proviso that the entire sum due shall become payable in the event of default.

1   The life assurance policy itself is mortgaged by way of assignment to the building society or other mortgagee as further security.

41.3 A mortgage may be legal or equitable. We begin by considering the creation of legal mortgages.

Creation of legal mortgages

Unregistered land
41.4 By virtue of the LPA, ss85(1) and 86(1) legal mortgages of freeholds and leaseholds may be created by one of two methods: the 'demise' method and the 'charge' method. The latter is the usual method; we begin, however, with the demise method.

By demise

41.5 *Freehold* A freeholder may mortgage his interest in the land by granting (demising) to the mortgagee a long term of years subject to a provision for cesser on redemption (that is, a provision that the lease shall come to an end when the mortgage is redeemed by being paid off). The Act lays down no duration for the term of years, but, by analogy with the provision next to be explained, 3,000 years is common.

Prior to the passing of the 1925 Act, the normal way for a freehold to be mortgaged was for the mortgagor to assign his entire interest in the land to the mortgagee. (Such rights as the mortgagor thereafter had in the land were protected by equity, in the form of his 'equity of redemption'.[1]) Should a mortgagor today purport to mortgage his freehold by conveying it to the mortgagee, the transaction is to take effect as a demise of the land for a term of 3,000 years, subject to a provision for cesser on redemption.[2]

A freeholder may wish, providing his land offers sufficient security, to create a second, or third mortgage. A second or subsequent mortgage by demise involves the grant of a term one day longer than the terms vested in the preceding mortgagee.[2]

1 Para 41.13 below.
2 LPA, s85(2).

41.6 *Leasehold* A lessee may create a mortgage by sub-demise, ie by granting a sub-lease of a term at least one day (in practice, ten days) less than his own, again subject to a provision for cesser on redemption. Should the lessee purport to mortgage his interest simply by assigning his term to the mortgagee, the transaction takes effect as a sub-demise for a term ten days less than the leasehold interest being mortgaged. Second or subsequent mortgages take effect as sub-demises for a term one day longer than the term vested in the preceding mortgagee, where possible, and in any event at least one day less than the mortgaged term.[1]

1 LPA, s86.

By charge
41.7 Both freeholds and leaseholds may be mortgaged in the same way by this method, that is, by the mortgagor charging his land, by a deed[1] expressed to be 'by way of legal mortgage', with the payment of the mortgage debt.[2] The LPA, s87(1) states that a mortgage by charge by deed expressed to be by way of legal mortgage confers on the mortgagee 'the same protection, powers and remedies' as if the mortgage had been created by demise.

The charge method is the preferred one, and is particularly favoured by the institutional lenders, as involving a shorter, simpler deed, under which both freehold and leasehold land can be mortgaged together, and which, to the layman, more obviously creates a mortgage than does a document which by its terms leases the land for 3,000 years. A practical advantage in the case of leaseholds is that a mortgage by charge does not constitute an infringement of a covenant, absolute or qualified, against sub-letting.[3]

We might mention here, as an aside, that a mortgagee of a leasehold by sub-demise or by charge may seek relief from forfeiture proceedings instituted by the head landlord in respect of a breach of covenant by the lessee.[4]

1 Para 33.3 above.
2 LPA, s87(1).
3 Para 37.12 above.
4 LPA s146(4); *Grand Junction Co Ltd v Bates* [1954] 2 QB 160, [1954] 2 All ER 385; *Abbey National Building Society v Maybeech Ltd* [1985] Ch 190, [1984] 3 All ER 262; para 37.18 above.

Registered land

41.8 A legal mortgage of registered land, freehold or leasehold, may be made in the same way as a mortgage of unregistered land.[1] However, the registered proprietor's power to mortgage is normally exercised by the creation, by deed, of a charge under the provisions of the LRA, s25. Such a deed need not be expressed to be by way of legal mortgage for, unless it is expressed to take effect by demise or sub-demise, it is deemed to be a charge by way of legal mortgage.[2] It is in fact common for institutional lenders to use the same form of charge by way of legal mortgage for both registered and unregistered land. A charge on registered land created under the LRA, s25 must, of course, be completed by registration.[3] Details of the charge and its proprietor, ie the mortgagee, are entered in the charges register of the mortgagor's register of title; the mortgagor's land certificate must be retained by the registry,[4] and the mortgagee is issued with a charge certificate.[5] Unless and until registered as a registered charge, the mortgage takes effect as a minor interest which, in theory, should be protected by the entry on the mortgagor's register of a notice or caution.[6]

1 LRA, s106(1); LPA, ss85(3) and 86(3).
2 LRA, s27(1) and (2); *Cityland and Property (Holdings) Ltd v Dabrah* [1968] Ch 166, [1967] 2 All ER 639.
3 Ibid, s26.
4 Ibid, s65.
5 Ibid, s63.
6 Ibid, s106(2) and (3).

Creation of equitable mortgages

Unregistered land

41.9 An equitable interest in land, such as life interest under a strict settlement, may only be mortgaged in equity. The major category of equitable mortgage, however, is constituted by informal mortgages.[1]

1 Cf para 33.6 above.

Mortgages of equitable interests

41.10 The owner of an equitable interest[1] may mortgage it by outright assignment, in writing,[2] to the mortgagee, subject to a provision for reconveyance on redemption. Such a mortgage will be overreached on a conveyance of the settled land.[3]

1 Para 35.2 above.
2 LPA, s53(1)(c); para 33.5 above.
3 Para 35.25, above.

Informal mortgages
41.11 A mortgage is constituted in equity:

a. where the parties fail to employ a deed as required at law;[1]

b. where the parties agree to create a legal mortgage, such agreement, in order to be enforceable, being required to be evidenced in writing or accompanied by acts of part performance;[2] or

c. by the mortgagor depositing his title deeds with the mortgagee.

An intended legal mortgage not made with the formality of a deed is regarded, as would be an informal lease,[3] as a contract to create a legal interest. As such, both such an informal mortgage, and an actual agreement to create a legal mortgage, are regarded by equity as specifically enforceable provided they are sufficiently evidenced in writing. Hence they give rise to an immediate equitable interest. This equitable mortgage (unless protected by deposit of title deeds, mentioned below) requires protection by registration in the Land Charges Registry under Class C (iii).[4]

The most common form of equitable mortgage arises where the mortgagor deposits his title deeds with the mortgagee as security for a loan. Such an arrangement is regarded in equity as giving rise to a contract to create a legal mortgage. The deposit of the title deeds is regarded as a sufficient act of part performance to render the agreement enforceable not merely by the mortgagor but also by the mortgagee. This equitable mortgage, being protected by deposit of title deeds, is not registrable in the Land Charges Registry under Class C (iii), nor it would seem, under Class C (iv). This form of mortgage, commonly employed to secure a bank loan or overdraft, is, in fact, usually accompanied by a memorandum of deposit evidencing the terms of the agreement and it is normal for this memorandum to be under seal, as this makes available to the mortgagee the statutory remedy of sale.[5] In such cases this so-called informal mortgage is at least as formal as a legal mortgage. A memorandum showing an intention to deposit title deeds as security constitutes an equitable mortgage even if the deeds are not in fact deposited, in which case, there being no deposit, the agreement should be registered under the Land Charges Act.

1 LPA, ss52 and 87; para 33.3 above.
2 Paras 43.11 to 43.19 below.
3 Para 33.6 above.
4 Para 33.23, above.
5 Para 41.22, below.

Registered land
41.12 Again, according to the LRA, s106, a proprietor of registered land may mortgage the land in any manner which would have been permissible if the land had not been registered. The LRA, s66 confers power on the

proprietor to deposit his land certificate as security for a loan. The mortgage so created may be protected by the mortgagee giving to the Registrar notice of the deposit, which operates as a caution under s54,[1] or by the entry of a notice or caution[2] on the register of title. An equitable mortgage created in any other way should be protected by notice or caution,[3] unless accompanied by deposit of the land certificate, in which case it may be protected by notice of deposit.[4]

1　LRR, r239.
2　Paras 34.23 and 34.24 above.
3　LRA, s106(3).
4　*Re White Rose Cottage* [1965] Ch 940, [1965] 1 All ER 11, CA.

Mortgagor's rights

To redeem
41.13　As we pointed out in para 41.5 above, prior to 1926 a legal mortgage of land was effected by an outright conveyance of the mortgagor's estate to the mortgagee, subject to a provision for reconveyance on payment of the moneys due. The mortgage would provide that redemption should take place on a fixed date. At common law, if the moneys due under the mortgage were not repaid on that date there could be no reconveyance. Further, the mortgagor, having lost the right to have his land reconveyed, remained liable to repay the money he owed. This harsh common law rule was radically altered by equity. In equity, the essence of a mortgage was seen to be the provision of security for a debt and hence the mortgagee would be compelled to reconvey the land on payment of what was owed to him, ie the principal plus interest (and costs), even though the contractual (or legal) date for redemption had passed. Equity, recognising that the mortgagor still had rights in the land despite having conveyed the legal estate to the mortgagee, conferred on the mortgagor an interest in the land, known as his 'equity of redemption' which, in particular, gave him the right to redeem the mortgage.

Once it was established that redemption was possible after the contractual date, that date came to be fixed at an early date, conventionally six months from the date of the mortgage. This clearly did not affect the mortgagor's equitable right to redeem, but enabled him to redeem at that early date if he wished. The contractual provision for redemption was not dispensed with, because—on the passing of the date fixed—the mortgage money was regarded as due and the mortgagee was thenceforward in a position to exercise his remedies for non-payment.

We have shown that today a legal mortgage cannot be effected by an outright conveyance;[1] the mortgagor thus retains the legal estate. He is nonetheless to be regarded as also having an equity of redemption in respect of the land, but essentially all this gives him is his right to redeem the mortgage despite the passing of the contractual date for redemption. In a standing mortgage and in certain instalment mortgages,[2] an early date for redemption is still fixed, commonly at six months from the date of the mortgage. Neither party intends that the mortgage should be redeemed at that date, the provision is inserted simply to bring into play the mortgagee's remedies, as the mortgage money is then due. In those instalment mortgages which do not provide for an early contractual date but provide for payment of principal and interest over a number of years, perhaps 20 or 25, it is usual for the parties to provide that the entire mortgage moneys become due should the mortgagor default in respect of one or two instalments. Where the contractual date for redemption has passed, the mortgagor is entitled, subject to any express provision in the mortgage providing otherwise,[3] to redeem the mortgage by paying the principal plus interest on giving the mortgagee six months' notice or six months' interest in lieu of notice.[4]

It may be briefly noted at this point that where a mortgagor has separately mortgaged a number of properties to the same mortgagee, or those mortgages have been acquired by the same mortgagee, then provided the right has been expressly reserved in at least one of the mortgages, and the mortgage moneys are due in respect of each mortgage, the mortgagee will be entitled to *consolidate* the mortgages, treating them as one. In such a case the mortgagee may refuse to allow redemption of one mortgage unless all are redeemed.[5]

On redemption, the mortgagee should, in the case of unregistered land, endorse on or annex to the mortgage deed a statutory receipt, stating the name of the person who paid the money, which operates as a discharge of the mortgage and puts an end to the mortgagee's interest. However, where the mortgage is redeemed not by the mortgagor but by, for example, a subsequent mortgagee, the effect is not to discharge the mortgage but to transfer it to the person redeeming.[6] An alternative form of statutory receipt may be used by building societies, but it cannot be used to effect a transfer of the mortgage since it does not name the person who paid the money. In the case of a registered charge under the LRA, discharge is effected by cancellation of the entry in the register on receipt of the prescribed form of discharge.[7]

As an alternative to redemption out of court, an action for redemption may be brought in complex cases in the Chancery Division, or, within the financial limits of its jurisdiction, a county court. Where such an action is brought by a second or subsequent mortgagee to redeem a prior mortgage, then not only must the prior mortgagee(s) be a party to the action, but also the mortgagor and any intervening and subsequent mortgagees. The reason is that in such actions the mortgagee seeking to redeem must 'redeem up, foreclose down'. For example, where M has mortgaged his property to A, B, C and D, C, in an action for redemption of A's mortgage, must also redeem B and seek foreclosure[8] in relation to D and M, thus giving each of these the opportunity to 'redeem up' or be foreclosed. The court may as an alternative order sale of the mortgaged property.[9]

1 Paras 41.5 and 41.6 above.
2 Para 41.2 above.
3 But see paras 41.14 ff below.
4 *Browne v Lockhart* (1840) 10 Sim 420; *Cromwell Property Insurance Co Ltd v Western and Toovey* [1934] Ch 322.
5 *Jennings v Jordan* (1881) 6 App Cas 698 at 700.
6 LPA, s115.
7 LRA, s35.
8 Paras 41.33–41.35 below.
9 LPA, s91; para 41.35 below.

Impediments to full redemption

41.14 Equity is assiduous to protect the essential nature of a mortgage as a transaction involving the giving of security for a loan, a proposition reflected in the maxim, 'Once a mortgage, always a mortgage'. In particular, it requires that there should be 'no clogs or fetters on the equity of redemption', that is, that the mortgage should not by its terms impede the ability of the mortgagor to redeem his property free of the conditions of the mortgage. We shall see that the case law in the following paragraphs establishes that the court will declare void a provision in a mortgage which either is inconsistent with the mortgagor's right to redeem his property unfettered by any term of the mortgage or is unfair and unconscionable.

Provisions excluding redemption

41.15 It follows from what we said in the preceding paragraph that a provision in a mortgage excluding redemption is of no effect.[1] Thus where the mortgage deed confers on the mortgagee an option to purchase[2] the mortgaged property, that provision is void[3] because, of course, at the option of the mortgagee, the mortgagor may be prevented from redeeming his property and be forced to sell. However, there is nothing to prevent the parties, by a separate transaction genuinely independent of the mortgage, agreeing that the mortgagee should have an option to purchase the property.[4]

1   *Re Wells, Swinburne-Hanham v Howard* [1933] Ch 29 at 53.
2   Para 33.23 above.
3   *Samuel v Jarrah Timber and Wood Paving Corpn Ltd* [1904] AC 323, HL; *Lewis v Frank Love Ltd* [1961] 1 All ER 446, [1961] 1 WLR 261.
4   *Reeve v Lisle* [1902] AC 461, HL.

Provisions postponing redemption

41.16 Rather than provide for redemption at the conventional six months, the mortgage may provide that it may not be redeemed for some longer period. Such a postponement of the right to redeem is not automatically void, but, first, it must not be such as, for all practical purposes, to render the mortgage irredeemable. In *Fairclough v Swan Brewery Co Ltd,*[1] F mortgaged his seventeen-and-a-half year lease to the brewery, the mortgage containing a clause prohibiting redemption until six weeks before the expiry of the lease. This clause was held to be void. A second requirement is that a postponement of the right to redeem must not be unfair or unconscionable. In *Knightsbridge Estates Trust Ltd v Byrne,*[2] the plaintiff company, wishing to pay off an existing debt, sought a loan of £310,000 from the friendly society of whom the defendants were trustees, at $5\frac{1}{4}$% interest repayable over 40 years. The society agreed and a mortgage was executed providing for repayment in half-yearly instalments over 40 years. Five-and-a-half years later the plaintiff company brought an action claiming to be entitled to redeem the mortgage, on the basis that the postponement of redemption for 40 years was a clog on the right to redeem. The Court of Appeal rejected their claim, holding that equity is concerned to see only *two* things—one that the essential requirements of a mortgage transaction are observed and the other that oppressive or unconscionable terms are not enforced. Equity does not interfere with mortgage transactions merely because they are unreasonable, which, in any event this transaction was not.

Instalment mortgages of the traditional building society repayment variety, although providing for repayment over 20 or 25 years, normally permit redemption at any time.

Under the provisions of the Companies Act 1985, s193, a company may create an irredeemable mortgage.

1 [1912] AC 565, PC.
2 [1939] Ch 441, [1938] 4 All ER 618, CA; affd on other grounds [1940] AC 613, [1940] 2 All ER 401, HL.

Provisions conferring collateral advantages
41.17 The parties may by their agreement confer on the mortgagee some advantage additional to repayment of the principal plus interest plus costs. Where such an additional advantage, such as an option to purchase, renders the mortgage irredeemable, it is clearly void, unless contained in some separate and independent transaction.[1] A similar case is where the advantage conferred fetters the right of full redemption. Thus, while a commercial tie imposed by the mortgage, such as that the mortgagor should only buy, and sell on the premises, beer supplied by the mortgagee,[2] may be valid for the duration of the mortgage, it may be invalid if it purports to continue beyond redemption. In *Noakes & Co Ltd v Rice*,[3] a provision in a mortgage tying the mortgaged leasehold property to the mortgagee brewery not only for the duration of the mortgage but for the duration of the entire lease, was held void, for its effect would have been to permit the mortgagor, who mortgaged a free house, to redeem only a tied house thus fettering his right to redeem.

It may be, in some cases, that the court will be able to construe a provision contained in a mortgage deed which confers some additional advantage on the mortgagee as in fact being a separate transaction, albeit that it is contained in the same deed.[4] In this way the advantage will not be struck down as being inconsistent with, or a clog on, the right to redeem. Thus, in *Kreglinger v New Patagonia Meat and Cold Storage Co Ltd*,[5] the mortgage between the plaintiff woolbroker and the defendant meat packers provided that for a period of five years, whether or not the loan was paid off earlier, the defendants would give the plaintiff the right to buy all sheepskins. The mortgage was redeemed after two years and the defendants disputed the plaintiff's right thereafter to the sheepskins. The House of Lords held that the plaintiff remained entitled to the skins. The grant of the right to purchase sheepskins was in substance independent of the mortgage.

In the *Kreglinger* case, the House of Lords held that, in any event, an advantage collateral to the security will not be held void unless it is:

a. unfair or unconscionable; or

b. in the nature of a penalty clogging the equity of redemption; or

c. inconsistent with or repugnant to the contractual and equitable right to redeem.[6]

The advantage conferred on the mortgagee in the *Kreglinger* case was none of these, being a 'perfectly fair and businesslike transaction'.

1 Para 41.15 above.
2 *Biggs v Hoddinott* [1898] 2 Ch 307, CA.
3 [1902] AC 24, HL.
4 *Kreglinger v New Patagonia Meat and Cold Storage Co Ltd* [1914] AC 25, HL; *Re Petrol*

Filling Station, Vauxhall Bridge Road, London, Rosemex Service Station Ltd v Shell Mex and BP Ltd (1968) P & CR 1.
5 [1914] AC 25, HL.
6 Ibid. at 61.

Validity of other terms

41.18 The principles expounded in the foregoing paragraphs are of general application in regard to all the provisions of a mortgage, namely that the court will strike down any provision which impedes full redemption of the mortgaged property unfettered by the terms of the mortgage or which is unfair, oppressive or unconscionable. This is illustrated by *Multiservice Bookbinding Ltd v Marden,*[1] where the mortgage provided for the repayment by instalments of the capital sum plus interest at 2% above the bank rate (minimum lending rate) payable on the whole sum throughout the term of the loan. Further, each instalment was subject to index-linking in the form of a 'Swiss franc uplift', that is, the amount payable was then to be increased (or, theoretically, decreased) in proportion to the variation in the rate of exchange between the pound and the Swiss franc since September 1966. (Furthermore, the loan could not be called in, nor was the mortgage redeemable, for ten years.) Browne Wilkinson J held that although the mortgage might be unreasonable this is not the relevant test; the question is whether any of the terms of the bargain are unfair and unconscionable, which in the opinion of Browne Wilkinson J requires that the terms have been imposed in a morally reprehensible manner. In this case the parties were business men, who entered the agreement with their eyes open, with the benefit of independent legal advice and without any compelling necessity on the part of the company to accept the loan on these terms. The company was therefore bound to comply with the mortgage.

By way of contrast, in *Cityland and Property (Holdings) Ltd v Dabrah,*[2] the mortgage provided for the repayment by instalments over six years of a sum representing the capital sum advanced together with a premium of 57%. On the mortgagor's default, the court refused to permit the mortgagee to enforce payment of the stated sum, allowing him only the principal plus interest, which was fixed at 7%. In the circumstances, the provision for the payment of a premium was unconscionable, particularly as this was not a bargain between trading concerns but a case of house purchase by a mortgagor of limited means.

1 [1979] Ch 84, [1978] 2 All ER 489.
2 [1968] Ch 166, [1967] 2 All ER 639.

41.19 *Restraint of trade* In *Esso Petroleum Co Ltd v Harper's Garage (Stourport) Ltd*[1] the House of Lords held that the restraint of trade doctrine, which we discuss in paras 14.8 to 14.7 above, applies to provisions in a mortgage. Thus collateral advantages contained in a mortgage, perhaps providing for a commercial tie, may not only be invalidated as preventing full redemption or as being unfair and unconscionable, but also as being in unreasonable restraint of trade.

1 [1968] AC 269, [1967] 1 All ER 699, HL. See, in particular, para 14.15 above.

41.20 *Consumer Credit Act 1974* Under ss137 to 139 of this Act, power is conferred on the county court to 're-open extortionate credit bargains' and to 'do justice between the parties' in consequence. Thus any mortgage where the mortgagor is an individual may be re-opened if it provides for the mortgagor to make 'grossly exorbitant' repayments or if it otherwise grossly contravenes ordinary principles of fair dealing. In determining whether the agreement is extortionate, the court is to take into account, amongst other relevant factors, interest rates prevailing at the time the agreement was made, the age, experience and business capacity of the mortgagor and the extent to which he was under financial pressure. In reopening the agreement, the court may, inter alia, alter its terms or set aside the whole or part of any obligation imposed by it.

The Act further regulates mortgages granted to secure loans not exceeding £15,000, other than loans by building societies, local authorities and certain bodies (including insurance companies and friendly societies) specified in subordinate legislation. Amongst the provisions of the Act relating to such mortgages (which, notably, include second mortgages to finance companies), we would point out that which provides for the prospective mortgagor to be given an opportunity to withdraw from the transaction, those providing for the form and content of the agreement, that which prevents a higher rate of interest being charged on default, and, particularly, (and to be borne in mind in relation to the mortgagee's remedies) that providing that a mortgage regulated by the Act may only be enforced by order of the court.

Mortgagee's remedies

Action on the personal covenant

41.21 As we have intimated, the mortgagor's covenant to repay may take a number of forms. For example, he may covenant to repay the loan at a fixed date, commonly six months from the date of the mortgage, and until repayment of the whole of the loan to pay regular instalments of interest, or he may covenant to repay by instalments of principal and interest over a period of years. Should he default on his obligations, he may be sued for breach of covenant by the mortgagee. Where the mortgage provides for repayment on a fixed contractual date, the mortgagee's right to sue arises in the event of failure to pay on that date. Where the mortgage provides for repayment in instalments, the mortgage may sue for unpaid instalments. It is, however, usual to include a default clause providing that the whole sum becomes due in the event of failure to pay, perhaps, two instalments. Where the mortgage makes the whole sum payable on demand, the right of action accrues at the start of the mortgage unless, as is common, there is provision for notice to be given.[1] However, where a default clause in an instalment mortgage provides for default to result in the mortgage money becoming payable on demand, the demand must first be made before the right to sue accrues.[2] If the mortgage is by deed, no action may be brought after 12 years from the date on which the cause of action accrued.[3] If it is not, when it can only be equitable, the limitation period is six years. As a general rule, not more than six years' arrears of interest may be recovered.[3]

1 *Re Brown's Estate, Brown v Brown* [1893] 2 Ch 300.

2   *Esso Petroleum Co Ltd v Alstonbridge Properties Ltd* [1975] 3 All ER 358, [1975] 1 WLR 1974.
3   Limitation Act 1980, s20.

Sale

41.22   Where the mortgagee brings an action against the defaulting mortgagor for breach of his covenant to repay, he is clearly not relying on the fact that he is a secured creditor. While such action may be worthwhile where the reason for default is the reluctance of the mortgagor to pay, it is scarcely so where the reason is the mortgagor's inability to pay. In such a case particularly the mortgagee will wish to enforce his security, and he will normally do this by exercising his power of sale. While it is possible to provide expressly for a power of sale, it is usual to rely on the statutory power conferred by the LPA, or that power as modified by the terms of the mortgage.

The power of sale
41.23   Where the mortgage is made by deed[1] and contains no expressed contrary intention, the LPA, s101 confers on the mortgagee the power to sell the mortgaged property when the mortgage money has become due. The mortgage money becomes due when the contractual date for redemption has passed, if such a date is fixed, or, in the case of mortgages providing for repayment in instalments of principal and interest, when an instalment is due and unpaid.[2] The contractual date of six months or earlier usually fixed in standing mortgages is incorporated therefore, not with the object that the mortgage should be redeemed at that time, but in order that the remedy of sale and other remedies for enforcing the security should become available at an early opportunity. As to mortgages providing for repayment by instalments of principal and interest, the mortgagee may only exercise his power of sale to enforce his security in respect of instalments in arrear,[2] unless, as is normal, it is provided that failure to pay one or more instalments causes the entire sum to become due. In endowment mortgages it is likewise usual for a default clause to provide that failure to pay instalments of interest makes the entire sum, principal and interest, due.

Although the mortgagee's power to sell *arises* when the mortgage money has become due, he may not, by virtue of the LPA, s103, *exercise* the power, unless and until:

a.   notice (in writing) requiring payment of the mortgage money has been served on the mortgagor, and he has not, within three months thereafter, paid the sums due; or

b.   some interest under the mortgage is in arrear and unpaid for two months after becoming due; or

c.   there has been a breach of some provision contained in the mortgage deed or in the LPA other than the covenant for repayment.

The provisions of the mortgage deed itself may, and commonly do, vary or extend the statutory provisions,[3] for example, by providing that the power of sale should be exercisable as soon as it arises.

1   Ie legal mortgages and equitable mortgages by deposit where the memorandum is under seal; see para 41.27 below.

2   *Payne v Cardiff RDC* [1932] 1 KB 241.
3   LPA, s101(3).

Exercise of the power

41.24   The power of sale is exercised, and the mortgagor's right to redeem thus barred, as soon as the mortgagee enters into a binding contract to sell.[1] The mortgagee may not purport to sell the land to himself.[2] There is, however no hard and fast rule that a mortgagee may not sell to a company in which he is interested. Where he does so, the mortgagee and the company seeking to uphold the transaction must show that the sale was in good faith and that the mortgagee took reasonable precautions to obtain the best price reasonably obtainable at the time.[3]

Although the mortgagee has only a term of years or equivalent charge in respect of the land, he has full power to convey the mortgaged freehold or leasehold together with fixtures attached to the land, the mortgage term or charge and any subsequent terms or charges being merged in the estate conveyed or extinguished, as the case may be.[4]

The purchaser takes the estate subject to rights having priority to the mortgage, but freed from rights to which it is prior. The Act provides that the purchaser's title may not be challenged on the ground that the mortgagee's power was not, in fact, *exercisable*, or due notice was not given, or the power was otherwise improperly or irregularly exercised. The Act further provides that the purchaser is not concerned to inquire as to these matters.[5] It would thus appear that, unless the power of sale has not *arisen* in which case the purported sale takes effect as a transfer of the mortgage, the purchaser takes a valid legal title to the mortgaged land. However, it has been suggested that, if the purchaser becomes aware of any facts showing that the power is not *exercisable*, or that there is some impropriety in the sale, he does not get a good title.[6] In any event a person affected by an improper or irregular exercise of the power of sale has a remedy in damages against the mortgagee.[5]

1   *Property and Bloodstock Ltd v Emerton* [1968] Ch 94, [1967] 3 All ER 321, CA.
2   *Farrar v Farrars Ltd* (1888) 40 Ch D 395 at 409; *Williams v Wellingborough Borough Council* [1975] 3 All ER 462, [1975] 1 WLR 1327, CA.
3   *Tse Kwong Lam v Wong Chit Sen* [1983] 3 All ER 54, [1983] 1 WLR 1349, PC.
4   LPA, ss88 and 89, and see LRA, s34.
5   LPA, s104.
6   *Lord Waring v London and Manchester Assurance Co Ltd* [1935] Ch 310 at 318.

41.25   *Price* In exercising its power of sale, a building society is under a statutory duty to take reasonable care to ensure that the price at which the property is sold is the best price which can reasonably be obtained.[1] In any event it is now established that all mortgagees are under a duty to the mortgagor (and, indeed, to a guarantor of the loan) in the tort of negligence to take reasonable care to obtain 'a proper price' or 'the true market value'.[2] Sale by auction does not necessarily show that reasonable care has been taken to obtain the proper price.[3] The case law suggests that a mortgagee proposing to sell should consult professional advisors such as estate agents as to the method of sale and the way to secure the best price. This is not to say that the mortgagee must exercise his power of sale as a trustee would. On the contrary, he is entitled to exercise it for his own purposes whenever he chooses. It matters not that the moment may be unpropitious and that, by waiting, a higher price could be obtained. However, and by way of example, should the mortgagee or an agent, such as an estate agent, employed by him, in advertising the property for sale, negligently fail to mention that it has the benefit of planning permission, the mortgagee will be liable to account to the mortgagor for the difference between the price obtained and 'a proper price' or 'the true market value'.[2] A purchaser in such a case would appear to be protected by the LPA, s104,[4] unless, perhaps, he was aware of the irregularity.

1 Building Societies Act 1962, s36.
2 *Cuckmere Brick Co Ltd v Mutual Finance Ltd* [1971] Ch 949, [1971] 2 All ER 633, CA.
3 *Tse Kwong Lam v Wong Chit Sen* [1983] 3 All ER 54, [1983] 1 WLR 1349, PC.
4 Para 41.24 above.

41.26 *Proceeds* As to the proceeds of sale, the LPA, s105 provides that, first, any prior mortgages to which the sale was not made subject must be discharged. Then the proceeds are held by the selling mortgagee in trust a. to pay the costs and expenses of the sale; b. to pay off the principal plus interest and costs due under the mortgage; c. to pay the surplus to any subsequent mortgagee of whom he has notice (he should therefore search the Land Charge Register or register of title as appropriate), or, if there is no subsequent mortgagee, to the mortgagor.

41.27 *Equitable mortgages* Unless an equitable mortgage is effected by deed, or a memorandum of deposit is under seal, the mortgagee may not sell, save by order of the court.[1] Where the mortgage is under seal, the statutory power under s101 is available; however, there is some doubt as to whether it enables an equitable mortgagee to sell the legal estate or simply his own equitable interest.[2] Although this latter would seem unlikely, to avoid any doubt it is usual for the memorandum to confer on the mortgagee a power of attorney to vest the legal estate in a purchaser on a sale. Alternatively (or as well) the memorandum may contain a declaration that the mortgagor holds the legal estate on trust for the mortgagee, conferring on the latter the right to appoint himself as trustee in place of the mortgagor and thus enabling the mortgagee to acquire, and vest in a purchaser, the legal estate.

1 LPA, s91(2); para 41.35 below.
2 *Re Hodson and Howes' Contract* (1887) 35 Ch D 668; *Re White Rose Cottage* [1965] Ch 940, [1965] 1 All ER 11, CA.

Possession
41.28 As a matter of legal theory, which has little relation to practical reality,[1] possession of the mortgaged property is not a remedy available to the legal mortgagee, but a right, in the sense that, in the absence of agreement to the contrary, the right of the mortgagee to possession has nothing to do with default on the part of the mortgagor. The mortgagee may go into possession before the ink is dry on the mortgage. He has the right because he has a legal term of years (or its statutory equivalent) in the property.[2] Furthermore, despite dicta to the contrary[3] equity never interferes to prevent the mortgagee from assuming possession save to adjourn the application for possession for a very short time in the unlikely event that there is a reasonable prospect of the mortgagor paying off the

mortgage in full.[4] The rigour of this apparently harsh rule, that the mortgagee may have possession of the property at any time, is in fact mitigated in a number of respects, with the result that possession is almost invariably resorted to only as a remedy in the event of default and then as a preliminary step to an exercise of the power of sale, so that the sale may be made with vacant possession.

A legal mortgagee may take physical possession by peaceably entering on the property[5]. It is usual, however, to seek a possession order requiring the delivery of vacant possession within a specified time, generally, in the case of a dwelling-house, from a county court.[6] It may indeed be the case that possession of a dwelling house can only be obtained by a court order.

The mortgagee is also regarded as taking possession where he serves notice on the tenants of the mortgagor to pay rent to him.[7]

1 Paras 41.30 and 41.31 below.
2 *Four-Maids Ltd v Dudley Marshall (Properties) Ltd* [1957] Ch 317 at 320, [1957] 2 All ER 35 at 36.
3 *Quennell v Maltby* [1979] 1 All ER 568 at 571.
4 *Birmingham Citizens Permanent Building Society v Caunt* [1962] Ch 883, [1962] 1 All ER 163.
5 For regulated credit agreements, see para 41.20 above.
6 Except where the rateable value is above the county court limit or where the property is in Greater London.
7 See *Davies v Law Mutual Building Society* (1971) 219 Estates Gazette 309, DC.

41.29 In contrast to the position of the legal mortgagee, it appears, though the matter is in some doubt, that an equitable mortgagee has no right to possession, in the absence of an expressly reserved right or a court order for possession.[1]

1 *Barclays Bank Ltd v Bird* [1954] Ch 274 at 280, [1954] 1 All ER 449 at 452.

Restrictions on the mortgagee's right to possession
41.30 First, the terms of the mortgage may expressly provide that the mortgagee may only go into possession in the event of default. This is normal in building society and similar mortgages.

Second, although the legal mortgagee's right to possession should not be lightly treated as abrogated or restricted,[1] the court may find that the mortgagee has by implication contracted out of his right to possession. In particular, the court will be ready to find an implied term that the mortgagor may remain in possession until default in an instalment mortgage, but there must be something on which to hang such a conclusion other than the mere fact that it is an instalment mortgage,[2] as where the mortgage speaks of the mortgagee having the power to eject the mortgagor in the event of default.[3]

Third, a mortgagee who goes into possession is liable to account strictly to the mortgagor, that is he must account not only for what income he has received since taking possession, but also for what, without wilful default, he might have received. Thus, where a mortgagee in possession leased[4] the mortgaged premises (a public-house tied to the mortgagee brewery), the mortgagee was held liable to account to the mortgagor not only for the rent received but also for rent which would have been received had the property been let as a free rather than a tied house.[5] For this reason in particular, a mortgagee desirous of receiving the income of the mortgaged property to cover unpaid instalments is better advised to appoint a receiver, a remedy which we consider at para 41.32 below.

1 *Western Bank Ltd v Schindler* [1977] Ch 1 at 9, [1976] 2 All ER 393 at 396.
2 *Esso Petroleum Co Ltd v Alstonbridge Properties Ltd* [1975] 3 All ER 358, [1975] 1 WLR 1974.
3 *Birmingham Citizens Permanent Building Society v Caunt* [1962] Ch 883, [1962] 1 All ER 163.
4 For powers of leasing, see para 41.37 below.
5 *White v City of London Brewery Co* (1889) 42 Ch D 237, CA.

41.31 In relation to mortgages of *dwelling-houses*, what particularly causes the right to possession to be seen solely as a remedy in cases of default, is the power of the court in an action for possession to delay giving the mortgagee possession. By the Administration of Justice Act 1970, s36, in an action for possession brought by a mortgagee of a dwelling-house, the court has power to adjourn the proceedings or to make an order but suspend its operation or to make an order postponing the date for possession, if it appears to the court that the mortgagor is likely within a reasonable period to pay any sums due under the mortgage or to remedy any other default under the mortgage.

A particular problem with this section as it stands concerns the usual provision in instalment mortgages that, in the event of default, the entire sums due under the mortgage become immediately payable. Where there is such default, it is highly unlikely in many cases that the mortgagor will within a reasonable period be able to pay the entire sums due and thus the court will be unable to delay possession.[1] Parliament has sought to fill this gap by the Administration of Justice Act 1973, s8. This provides that in the case of instalment mortgages, or other mortgages providing for deferred payment of the principal, which contain such a default clause, the sums due under the mortgage are to be regarded, for the purposes of s36, as being what would have been required to have been paid had there been no default clause, ie simply the arrears. In such a case the court may exercise its power to delay possession where it appears likely that within a reasonable period the mortgagor will pay the instalments owing and that he will keep up with the instalments. Possession cannot be delayed indefinitely; a definite period must be fixed.[2]

Section 8, which was enacted to remedy deficiencies in the drafting of s36, is itself unhappily worded. In particular, the question has arisen as to the circumstances in which a mortgage can be said to provide for deferred payment and thus enable the court to exercise its power to delay possession. In *Habib Bank Ltd v Tailor*,[3] the mortgage to secure the defendant's overdraft contained a provision in the usual banker's form that the mortgagor would repay the sums owing on demand in writing. The Court of Appeal held that, as the principal was not due until demanded in writing, there was no provision for deferment of payment of the principal since this presupposes that payment is due but deferred. This might suggest that the common endowment mortgage under which payment of the principal is not due until the end of the mortgage term is not within the ambit of s8. In *Bank of Scotland v Grimes*,[4] however, the Court of Appeal held that the section should be given a purposive construction so as to encompass endowment mortgages under which there is no obligation to pay until the end of the term.

An interesting development in relation to the statutory power to delay possession of a dwelling-house is the case of *Western Bank Ltd v Schindler*.[5] In this case the Court of Appeal emphasised that a mortgagee may seek possession not simply as a remedy to enforce the security but also as a right which, despite the duty to account, might be of value to him to protect the security, for example, to enable him to effect repairs or to protect the property against vandalism. The Court went on to hold, by a majority, that the court's power to delay possession of a mortgaged dwelling-house, under the Administration of Justice Act, s36, applies whether or not the mortgagor is in default. If this is so, it follows that in the case of dwelling-houses, an absolute right to possession has in effect become a right exercisable with the permission of the court on good cause being shown.

1   *Halifax Building Society v Clark* [1973] Ch 307, [1973] 2 All ER 33, CA.
2   *Royal Trust Co of Canada v Markham* [1975] 3 All ER 433, [1975] 1 WLR 1416, CA.
3   [1982] 3 All ER 561, [1982] 1 WLR 1218, CA.
4   [1985] 2 All ER 254, [1985] 3 WLR 294, CA.
5   [1977] Ch 1, [1976] 2 All ER 393, CA.

Appointment of a receiver

41.32   In the case of commercial or tenanted properties, the mortgagee may wish to secure payment of any instalment due to him without taking action to realise his security, by appointing a receiver to manage the property and receive its income or rents. The statutory power to appoint a receiver arises and is exercisable on the same conditions as the power of sale,[1] again, subject to any extension or variation in the mortgage deed. The appointment and removal of the receiver must be in writing. A receiver appointed under the statutory power is deemed to be the agent of the mortgagor.[2] The mortgagee will be liable to account to the mortgagor only for what he receives from the receiver, and not for what, without wilful default might have been received.[3] The receiver has power to demand and recover rents due but may not himself grant leases unless he has the sanction of the court[4] or the mortgagee has delegated his power of leasing to him. The receiver is to apply money received by him in the following order:

a. in discharge of all outgoings affecting the mortgaged property;

b. in making payments under prior mortgages;

c. in payment of his own commission of insurance premiums payable under the mortgage, and of the cost of carrying out repairs required by the mortgagee;

d. in payment of interest due under the mortgage;

e. in or towards paying off the principal if required by the mortgagee; and

f. in paying the residue to the mortgagor.[5]

1   LPA, ss101 and 109; para 41.23 above.
2   LPA, s109.
3   See para 41.30 above.
4   *Re Cripps* [1946] Ch 265, CA.
5   LPA, s109.

Foreclosure

41.33 As soon as the mortgage money is due,[1] or in the event of a condition of the mortgage being broken,[2] the mortgagee may apply to the court[3] for foreclosure. A mortgage is foreclosed when a court order of foreclosure is granted to the mortgagee which has the effect of putting an end to the mortgagor's right to redeem and vests the mortgaged property in the mortgagee, subject to any prior mortgages but freed from any subsequent ones.[4] On the face of it, this is, from the point of view of the mortgagor and any subsequent mortgagees, a harsh remedy in that their rights in respect of the property are extinguished. For this reason both the mortgagor and any subsequent mortgages must be made parties to the foreclosure action. Because of the severity of the remedy it is in fact made subject to a number of restrictions which have had the effect that foreclosure is sought somewhat infrequently, mortgagees preferring to enforce their security by seeking vacant possession of, and subsequently selling, the mortgaged property. An application for foreclosure remains of utility in certain cases, particularly where there is no statutory power of sale, for example, in the case of equitable mortgages of a legal estate not made by deed.

1 Para 41.23 above.
2 Eg a covenant to pay instalments of interest: *Twentieth Century Banking Corpn Ltd v Wilkinson* [1977] Ch 99, [1976] 3 All ER 361.
3 A county court, within the financial limits of that court's jurisdiction, otherwise the Chancery Division.
4 LPA, ss88(2) and 89(2); LRA, s34(3).

41.34 On an application for foreclosure, the court will first grant an order *nisi*, to the effect that accounts should be taken of what is due to the mortgagee in respect of principal, interest and costs and that the mortgagor should within (usually) six months thereafter pay the sums due or be foreclosed in default. In the event of non-payment an order absolute for foreclosure may be made. Where there are subsequent mortgagees, they too have the opportunity to redeem but in default will be foreclosed.[1]

The court has a discretion to extend the period given for repayment of the sums due or even to 'open the foreclosure' after an order absolute has been made. Relevant factors in the exercise of this latter discretion include whether the mortgagor made his application within a reasonable time, whether he was prevented from redeeming only by some accident, the value of the mortgaged property as compared to the sums due (for the courts are reluctant to allow the mortgagee a windfall profit), and any special value the property had for the mortgagor.[2] A foreclosure order has even been reopened after the mortgagee had sold the property to a third party, but only where the sale took place immediately after the foreclosure and the third party had notice of the facts which gave rise to the order being reopened.[2]

Furthermore, in cases of instalment (or other deferred payment) mortgages of dwelling-houses, power is conferred on the court by the Administration of Justice Act 1973, s8 to adjourn the proceedings or suspend its order, where it appears likely that the mortgagor will pay the instalments owing and keep up with future instalments.[3]

1 Para 41.13 above.
2 *Campbell v Holyland* (1877) 7 Ch D 166.

3   Para 41.31 above.

41.35   Perhaps more influential than the foregoing in reducing the importance of foreclosure as a remedy is the fact that, under the LPA, s91(2), the
court has power on the application of any interested party to order sale of
the property instead of foreclosure. Clearly, the court will be particularly
willing to exercise this power where it is shown that the value of the
property exceeds the amount due under the mortgage. Sale may be ordered
on such terms as the court thinks fit; for example, it may even require that
the mortgagor pay into court a sum sufficient to protect the mortgagee
against loss. While it may order immediate sale, it may equally provide time
for redemption of the mortgage. Conduct of the sale will usually be given to
the mortgagor since he will be most concerned to realise the highest price
for the property. A reserve price will be fixed, and the purchase money must
be paid into court.
   Given that sale of the mortgaged property is highly likely as a result of an
application for foreclosure, it will be preferable for the mortgagee to
exercise his power of sale to realise his security. However, that power must
have arisen and must be exercisable.[1] In *Twentieth Century Banking Corpn
Ltd v Wilkinson*,[2] the mortgage provided that, for the purposes of the LPA,
the mortgage money was not due until the end of the mortgage term. The
mortgagor defaulted on his obligation in the meantime to pay instalments
of interest and the mortgagee sought an order for sale or foreclosure. The
court held that the power of sale would not arise until the mortgage money
became due, but that the mortgagee was entitled to seek foreclosure since
the mortgagor was in breach of a condition of the mortgage. Since the
mortgagee was entitled to foreclosure the court had a discretion to order
sale instead, which it did.

1   Para 41.23 above.
2   [1977] Ch 99, [1976] 3 All ER 361.

Registered land
41.36   The proprietor of a registered charge has all the powers of a legal
mortgagee. Sale of the mortgaged property and an order of foreclosure
must be completed by registration respectively of the purchaser or mortgagee as proprietor of the land and by cancellation of the charge.[1]

1   LRA, s34.

Leasing
41.37   Both the mortgagor, while in possession, and the mortgagee, if he
has taken possession or has appointed a receiver,[1] are empowered by the
LPA, s99[2] to grant leases in accordance with that section. The leases
authorised by the section are agricultural or occupation leases for a term
not exceeding 50 years, and building leases for a term not exceeding 999
years. Such leases must take effect in possession not later than 12 months
from their date, must reserve the best rent reasonably obtainable, and must
contain a covenant for payment of rent and a condition of re-entry in the
event of breach.[3] The lessee must execute a counterpart of the lease. If in

good faith a lease is granted which does not comply with these requirements, it takes effect in equity as a contract to grant an equivalent lease in
accordance with the statutory power.[4] Save in relation to mortgages of
agricultural land[5] and the grant of new tenancies of business premises under
the Landlord and Tenant Act 1954, Part II,[6] the statutory power applies
only to the extent that it is not excluded by the parties. In fact it is normal
practice to exclude the mortgagor's statutory power of leasing altogether.
In this way the mortgagor is prevented from creating, for example, a
regulated tenancy within the Rent Act,[7] which would devalue the mortgagee's security. Where the mortgage terms exclude the power to create any
tenancy, breach is commonly expressed to give rise to the mortgage money
becoming due, and hence to the mortgagee's remedies becoming available.
Where the mortgagor's power of leasing is so excluded then any purported
tenancy granted by the mortgagor is binding on the parties to it by estoppel[8]
but does not bind the mortgagee,[9] nor is the tenant entitled to the
protection of the Rent Act.[10]

1 To whom the power of leasing may be delegated.
2 See also LRA, s34.
3 Further conditions are imposed in respect of building leases.
4 LPA, s152(1).
5 Agricultural Holdings Act 1948, Sch 7.
6 Para 37.27 above.
7 Para 37.25 above.
8 Para 32.29 above.
9 *Iron Trades Employers Insurance Association Ltd v Union Land and House Investors Ltd*
   [1937] Ch 313, [1937] 1 All ER 481.
10 *Dudley and District Benefit Building Society v Emerson* [1949] Ch 707, [1949] 2 All ER 252,
   CA; and see *Quennell v Maltby* [1979] 1 All ER 568, CA.

Insurance

41.38 The mortgagee is empowered by the LPA, s101 to insure the
mortgaged property against loss or damage by fire up to the amount
specified in the deed or up to two thirds of the amount which would be
required to reinstate the property in the event of total destruction.[1] The
premiums become part of the mortgage debt. It is common expressly to
provide that the mortgagor shall insure the property for a specified sum or
the full value of the property or, particularly in building society mortgages,
that the society will effect the insurance for a specified sum but the
premiums will be payable by the mortgagor.

The mortgagee may require that all moneys received under an insurance
of the mortgaged property effected under the terms of the Act or the
mortgage deed be applied by the mortgagor in making good the loss or
damage or be applied in or towards the discharge of the mortgage money.[1]
Should the mortgagor independently of any obligation in the mortgage
insure the property the mortgagee is not entitled to any money received, but
where the money is payable in the event of fire he can require that it be used
towards reinstatement,[2] and in any event it is common to exclude the
mortgagor's power independently to insure the property.

1 LPA, s108.
2 Fires Prevention (Metropolis) Act 1774, s83.

Priorities

41.39 The issue of priorities between competing mortgagees arises where the value of the mortgaged property is insufficient to provide security for all the mortgages to which the property is subject. The incidence of this problem should be rare in times of rapidly increasing property values, so long as mortgagees act with care. However, should the problem arise and the property be sold to realise the security, the several mortgagees do not share in the proceeds equally or rateably in proportion to the size of their mortgage. Rather the mortgagee having priority is paid in full before any money is passed to the second in priority, and so on. The rules for determining the priorities differ according to whether the mortgaged property is subject to the Land Registration Act or not.

Unregistered land

41.40 As regards legal and equitable mortgages of a *legal estate*, we must distinguish between those protected by deposit of title deeds and those not so protected. The latter category must be registered under the Land Charges Act 1972, as a puisne mortgage (Class C (i))[1] if legal, or as a general equitable charge (Class C (iii))[1] if equitable. As to deposit of title deeds, under the law as it existed prior to 1926 it followed from the fact that a legal mortgage was created by outright conveyance of the legal estate that the mortgagee was entitled to the title deeds of the property. Despite the change in machinery for creating legal mortgages since 1925,[2] the mortgagee's right to the title deeds is preserved.[3] A first legal mortgagee will thus take the title deeds and this confers on him priority over all subsequent mortgagees[4] unless he is by his conduct estopped from asserting his priority, or guilty of fraud or gross negligence in relation to the title deeds, as by for example, releasing them to the mortgagor to enable the latter to grant another mortgage by representing himself as the owner of an unencumbered legal estate.[5] A first equitable mortgagee by deposit will similarly lose priority if guilty of fraud or gross negligence. He will also lose priority where a subsequent legal mortgagee has no notice of the prior equitable mortgage, although this is somewhat unlikely given the absence of the mortgagor's title deeds.

Subsequent mortgages, legal or equitable, must be registered in the Land Charges registry and rank for priority according to date of registration.[6] Failure to register such mortgages renders them void against a purchaser for value of any interest in the land, including subsequent mortgagees, legal or equitable.[7] Failure to register does not affect the enforceability between mortgagor and mortgagee, but postpones the unregistered mortgage to the subsequently created one.

Morgages of *equitable interests*[8] have priority in accordance with the order in which notice in writing of the mortgage is given to the trustees of the settlement or the trustees for sale, as the case may be.[9]

1 Para 33.23 above
2 Para 41.5 above.
3 LPA, ss85(1) and 86(1).
4 LPA, s13.
5 *Walker v Linom* [1907] 2 Ch 104; *Northern Counties of England Fire Insurance Co v Whipp* (1884) 26 Ch D 482; *Perry Herrick v Attwood* (1857) 2 De G & J 21.
6 LPA, s97.

7   Land Charges Act 1972 s4(5).
8   Para 41.10 above.
9   *Dearle v Hall* (1823) 3 Russ 1; affd (1827) 3 Russ 1 at 48; LPA, s137.

Registered land

41.41   Registered charges[1] rank for priority as between themselves in order of registration.[2] Mortgages by deposit of the land certificate[3] take effect subject to overriding interests and entries on the register[4] but otherwise have priority.[5] Mortgages created off the register[6] take effect as minor interests in equity[7] and rank as between themselves in order of creation, but will be overridden by a registered charge or mortgage by deposit unless protected by entry on the register.[8] Mortgages of certain equitable interests, such as a life interest, rank in order of their entry in the little known and little used Minor Interests Index reserved specifically for the purpose.[9]

1   Para 41.8 above.
2   LRA, s29.
2   Para 41.12 above.
4   LRA, s66.
5   See *Re White Rose Cottage* [1965] Ch 940, [1965] 1 All ER 11, CA; *Barclays Bank Ltd v Taylor* [1974] Ch 137, [1973] 1 All ER 752, CA.
6   Para 41.12 above.
7   LRA s106.
8   *Barclays Bank Ltd v Taylor* [1974] Ch 137, [1973] 1 All ER 752, CA.
9   LRA, s102(2); LRR, rr11 and 229.

Tacking of further advances

Unregistered land

41.42   Where a mortgagee makes a further loan, or advance, to the mortgagor, in certain circumstances it may be 'tacked on' to the original mortgage so as to enjoy the priority of that mortgage. Tacking of further advances is particularly important where a person mortgages property to a bank to secure his overdrawn current account. The overdraft at the time of the mortgage represents the original debt for which the mortgage is security: each subsequently honoured cheque represents a further advance. The bank will, of course, wish to ensure that it does not lose priority in respect of these further advances to an intervening mortgage of the property created by the debtor.

The circumstances in which tacking is permitted are:

a. if an arrangement has been made to that effect with the subsequent mortgagees; or

b. if the mortgagee had no notice of such subsequent mortgages when he made the further advances; or

c. where the mortgage imposes an obligation to make further advances, in which case it matters not that the mortgagee had notice of subsequent mortgages.[1]

In one particular type of case, registration of a subsequent mortgage in the Land Charges Register does not constitute notice for the purposes of b. above. This is where the mortgage is expressly made as security both for the original loan and any further advances (as in the case of building society mortgages and mortgages to secure overdrafts). In such a case, the original mortgagee therefore need not search the Land Charges Register before making each further advance.

1 LRA, s94.

Registered land

41.43 Where a registered charge is made for securing further advances, that fact will be noted on the register of title. Any further advances will have the priority of the original charge unless and until the mortgagee receives (or ought in due course of post to have received) a notice from the Registrar of an entry on the register which prejudicially affects the priority of further advances. Further advances made under a registered charge imposing an obligation on the mortgagee have the priority of the original charge, the obligation being noted on the register to warn prospective mortgagees.[1]

1 LRA, s30.

Chapter 42
Adverse possession

Possession
42.1 English law protects possession, a proposition reflected in the well-known maxim, 'possession is nine points of the law'. The right of a person who is in possession of land to that land is enforceable under English law against all-comers, except someone who can show a better legal right to possession.[1] Thus, as between A, the owner of land with the 'paper' title, and B, who takes possession of the land from him, A has the better right to possession. But were B subsequently to be himself dispossessed of the land by C, the latter could not in law say to B, 'you have no more title than I have, my possession is as good as yours', for B's possession constitutes good title against all but A.[1] As between the rival claimants A and B, or B and C, English law in effect regards 'ownership' as meaning 'having the better right to possession'.[2]

1 *Asher v Whitlock* (1865) LR 1 QB 1.
2 Megarry and Wade *The Law of Real Property* (5th edn) p 106.

Adverse possession
42.2 'Adverse possession' means possession of land inconsistent with the title of a person having a better right to possession. It is, in other words, possession as a trespasser[1] or, as it is generally put, possession by a squatter. A person whose land is the subject of squatting is entitled to recover possession of the land;[2] but the law places a limit on the time within which he should take action to recover possession, for it is the policy of the law, first, to protect undisturbed possession and, second, that a person should pursue his lawful claims with diligence. This is the principle of 'limitation of actions'.[3] The effect of adverse possession and of the limitation principle is that a person who has the right to possess land may lose that right if someone else takes possession of the land in a way which is inconsistent with his possession, and remains in adverse possession for the statutory 'limitation period', which is, generally, 12 years.[4] In such a case, the adverse possessor puts an end not only to the original owner's right to take action to recover possession but also, thereby, puts an end to his title to the land.[5]

1 Ch 25 above.

648

2 Should he choose self-help rather than seeking a court order for possession he should take
   care to avoid transgressing the criminal law; see para 25.10 above.
3 Limitation Act 1980.
4 Ibid, s15(1). This period may be extended in cases of fraud, concealment or acknowledgment; paras 11.36 to 11.39 above.
5 Ibid, s17. Note, however, para 42.5 below.

The operation of the Limitation Act

42.3 The Limitation Act 1980 provides[1] that no action may be brought to
recover land after the expiration of 12 years from the date on which the
right of action accrued. The right of action is deemed to accrue on the date
on which the person in possession was dispossessed or discontinued
possession[2] and continues only so long as another person is in adverse
possession of the land.[3]

1 Limitation Act 1980, s15(1).
2 Ibid, Sch 1, para 1; but see paras 11.36–11.39 above.
3 Ibid, Sch 1, para 8; but see paras 11.36–11.39 above.

Unregistered land

42.4 In the case of unregistered land, the title of the person entitled to
bring an action for possession is extinguished on the expiration of the
limitation period.[1] The effect of the Limitation Act 1980 is not to convey
from one to another but to extinguish;[2] hence, the squatter does not acquire
the title or estate of the owner whom he has dispossessed,[3] but acquires a
new title of his own. However, it is important to remember that the only
rights extinguished for the benefit of the squatter are those of persons who
might, during the statutory period, have brought, but did not in fact bring,
an action to recover possession of the land.[4] Thus the squatter has no
answer to the claim of a third party seeking to enforce, for example, an
easement or a restrictive covenant;[5] these rights continue to bind the land in
accordance with normal principles.

1 Limitation Act 1980, s17.
2 *Tichborne v Weir* (1892) 67 LT 735.
3 *Fairweather v St Marylebone Property Co Ltd* [1963] AC 510, [1962] 2 All ER 288, HL.
4 *Re Nisbet and Potts' Contract* [1906] 1 Ch 386 at 409.
5 *Re Nisbet and Potts' Contract* [1906] 1 Ch 386, CA.

Registered Land

42.5 In the case of registered land, the LRA, s75 provides that the
Limitation Act applies to registered land in the same manner and to the
same extent as to unregistered land except that, at the expiration of the
statutory limitation period, the title of the registered proprietor is not
automatically extinguished. Instead, the registered proprietor is deemed to
hold his estate on trust for the squatter. The latter may then apply to be
registered as proprietor of the estate, such registration being treated as first
registration. A provision of this nature is necessary in applying the
Limitation Act to registered land in order to deal with the fact that one only
acquires title to registered land when registered as proprietor. Although s75
purports to apply the Limitation Act to registered land in the same way as
in unregistered land, there is an argument that it goes further so that the
squatter actually acquires title to the estate of the 'paper' owner, rather

than a new estate of his own. The argument is that the 'paper' owner has held on trust for the squatter his estate and it is that estate of which the squatter is subsequently registered as proprietor. Prior to his registration as proprietor, the rights acquired by the squatter constitute an overriding interest, as indeed do rights in the course of being acquired by adverse possession.[1]

1   Land Registration Act 1925, s70(1)(f); para 34.19 above; *Re Chowood's Registered Land* [1933] Ch 574; para 34.28 above.

Leases

42.6   *Unregistered land* Where a person occupies land adversely to a tenant throughout the statutory limitation period, the tenant's title is extinguished.[1] There is, again, no transfer of the tenant's interest to the adverse possessor, ie no statutory assignment of the lease. It follows that the squatter is not bound by covenants in the original lease,[2] but where there is a proviso for re-entry in the event of breach of covenant the threat of forfeiture will secure the squatter's compliance.[3] Although time runs against the tenant, the landlord is not affected; time only begins to run against the landlord when the lease expires.[4] It has, furthermore, been held, by the House of Lords in *Fairweather v St Marylebone Property Co Ltd*,[5] that where a lessee's title is extinguished as a result of twelve years' adverse possession, it is so extinguished as against the squatter but not against the landlord: as between the landlord and the lessee, the lease remains on foot. The effect of this in the instant case was that the lessee whose title had been extinguished was held to be entitled nonetheless to surrender his lease to the landlord before the expiration of the term. This, it was held, brought the lease to an end and enabled the landlord, since only then did time begin to run against him, to take action to recover the land from the squatter. A tenant can thus defeat a successful squatter by surrendering his lease and taking a new tenancy.

1   Limitation Act 1980, s17, subject to Land Registration Act 1925, s75, paras 42.4 and 42.5 above.
2   *Tichborne v Weir* (1892) 67 LT 735.
3   Para 37.15 above. (A right of re-entry in a lease is a legal interest binding on all comers).
4   Limitation Act 1980, Sch 1, para 4.
5   [1963] AC 510, [1962] 2 All ER 288, HL.

42.7   *Registered land* There is an argument that the *Fairweather* case applies equally to registered land. However, if another argument were accepted, namely that the effect of the LRA, s75 is that the proprietor acquires title to the 'paper' owner's estate, it would instead follow that the squatter acquires the lessee's term and hence that the lessee would have nothing to surrender to the landlord. It would equally seem to follow that the squatter would be bound by covenants in the lease. In any event, it has been held, in *Spectrum Investment Co v Holmes*,[1] that, once the squatter is registered as proprietor, the original lessee cannot surrender the term, since the estate can only be disposed of by a registered disposition by a registered proprietor.

1   [1981] 1 All ER 6, [1981] 1 WLR 221.

42.8 *Tenants as squatters* As indicated earlier, time only begins to run in favour of a tenant in respect of the land of which he is tenant on the expiry of the lease.[1] A lessee who takes possession of land belonging to his landlord which adjoins the land of which he is tenant is presumed only to acquire that land by adverse possession as tenant on the same terms and conditions as the original subject matter of the lease.[2]

1 Limitation Act 1980, Sch 1, paras 4 and 5.
2 *Smirk v Lyndale Developments Ltd* [1975] Ch 317, [1974] 2 All ER 8, CA.

The nature of adverse possession
42.9 According to Slade J in *Powell v McFarlane*,[1] a person claiming to have been in adverse possession of land must show not only factual possession but also the necessary intention to possess the land (*animus possidendi*). Whether a person has factual possession depends on the circumstances, particularly the nature of the land and the way in which land of that nature is commonly used or enjoyed. Basically, however, what is required is that the squatter should have been dealing with the land as an occupying owner might have been expected to deal with it and that no one else has done so. The *animus possidendi*, according to Slade J, involves the intention, in one's own name and on one's own behalf, to exclude the world at large, including the owner with the paper title, so far as is reasonably practicable and so far as the processes of the law will allow. The courts are reluctant to attribute possession to someone other than the 'paper' owner and hence, according to *Powell v McFarlane*, require clear evidence that the squatter not only had the requisite intention to possess but made that intention clear to the world. Such evidence is likely in most cases to be a matter of inference from the alleged squatter's acts. Enclosure of the land by the squatter, as by putting up a fence,[2] is strong evidence of the requisite *animus*, but even this may be equivocal. It may, for example, be that it is done to protect an easement enjoyed over the 'paper' owner's land from interference by others, rather than to establish possession.[3] In such a case it can readily be appreciated why establishing an intention to possess requires evidence of an intention to exclude not just the world at large but the 'paper' owner as well. It is not so clear why this should be required in other cases, especially as this would be more than the processes of the law in fact allow the squatter. Nonetheless, in *Powell v McFarlane*, the plaintiff failed to show 12 years' adverse possession since his acts in respect of the land (grazing animals, cutting and taking the hay crop and shooting on the land) were not done with the necessary *animus*. It would not have been evident to the world that he was more than simply a persistent trespasser but was seeking to dispossess the owner. His apparent intention was to continue until stopped; he had no real thought of asserting ownership of the land.

1 (1977) 38 P & CR 452.
2 *Williams v Usherwood* (1981) 45 P & CR 235, CA.
3 *Littledale v Liverpool College* [1900] 1 Ch 19, CA.

42.10 The Limitation Act 1980, Sch 1, para 1 requires that, for the limitation period to begin, the 'paper' owner must either be dispossessed or must discontinue his possession. Dispossession refers to a person coming in and putting another out of possession, while discontinuance refers to the case where the person in possession abandons possession and another takes it.[1] The smallest act by the 'paper' owner will be sufficient to show that there was no discontinuance[2] since the owner with the right to possession will be readily assumed to have the requisite intention to possess.[3] Thus, the acts of the 'paper' owner, in *Leigh v Jack*[4] in repairing a fence on the land, and, in *Williams Bros Direct Supply Ltd v Raftery*[5] in measuring the land for development and depositing rubbish on it, were sufficient to show no discontinuance.

As to dispossession, it would seem that if the squatter takes factual possession of the land with the necessary *animus* the 'paper' owner is dispossessed. There is thus no difference between establishing adverse possession and establishing dispossession of the 'paper' owner.[6] Once again, however, the evidence may be equivocal. Where there is evidence that the 'paper' owner retains his intention to possess, as in *Leigh v Jack*,[7] the question arises whether the acts of the squatter show, not *adverse* possession, inconsistent with that of the 'paper' owner, but only concurrent possession. In such a case, according to *Leigh v Jack*,[8] there must be evidence of acts by the squatter which are 'inconsistent with the owner's enjoyment of the soil for the purposes for which he intended to use it.'

In cases where the 'paper' owner intends to use the land for a particular purpose in future but meanwhile leaves it unoccupied, having no present use for it, the *Leigh v Jack* requirement has proved difficult to satisfy. Thus storage of waste on land intended by the 'paper' owner for future use as a highway,[9] and cultivation of unoccupied land intended by the 'paper' owner for future development,[10] have been held insufficient to amount to dispossession of the 'paper' owner. In one case, *Wallis's Cayton Bay Holiday Camp Ltd v Shell-Mex and BP Ltd*,[11] the Court of Appeal appears to have elevated the principle laid down in *Leigh v Jack* into a requirement whenever the 'paper' owner has future, but no present, plans for the land, even though the evidence of adverse possession was otherwise in no way equivocal. In effect, as implied by the Court of Appeal in the later case of *Treloar v Nute*,[12] this is wrongly to impose on squatters an additional requirement that their acts must inconvenience the 'paper' owner. In the *Wallis's* case also, Lord Denning had held that the law would imply that a squatter's use of land was enjoyed by virtue of a licence from the owner whenever that use was not inconsistent with the owner's plans. That aspect of the decision is now statutorily overruled by a more widely drawn provision of the Limitation Act[13] which states that it is not to be assumed by implication of the law that a squatter's occupation is by permission of the owner merely because that occupation is not inconsistent with the owner's present or future enjoyment. A licence may of course be implied where the facts genuinely support such an implication, and in such a case possession will clearly not be adverse.[14]

---

1 *Powell v McFarlane* (1977) 38 P & CR 452.
2 *Leigh v Jack* (1879) 5 Ex D 264, CA.
3 *Powell v McFarlane* (1977) 38 P & CR 452.
4 (1879) 5 Ex D 264, CA.
5 [1958] 1 QB 159, [1957] 3 All ER 593, CA.
6 *Treloar v Nute* [1977] 1 All ER 230, CA.
7 (1879) 5 Ex D 264, CA.
8 (1879) 5 Ex D 264 at 273.
9 *Leigh v Jack*, above.

10 *Williams Bros Direct Supply Ltd v Raftery* [1958] 1 QB 159, [1957] 3 All ER 593, CA.
11 [1975] QB 94, [1974] 3 All ER 575, CA.
12 [1977] 1 All ER 230, [1976] 1 WLR 1295, CA.
13 Sch 1, para 8(4).
14 Compare *Hyde v Pearce* [1982] 1 All ER 1029, [1982] 1 WLR 560, CA: 14 years' possession by intending purchaser following contract, without transaction having been completed by conveyance, held not to be adverse, but referable to contract, which purchaser had not clearly repudiated.

Chapter 43
Sales of land

43.1 We propose to consider in merest outline in this chapter the steps involved in a typical sale of a freehold interest in land, noting certain important features surrounding the two major steps in the transfer process, the contract and the conveyance (or transfer). The sale of a leasehold interest follows esentially the same path, but we note certain aspects peculiar to the assignment of a leasehold interest towards the end of the chapter.

Pre-contract stage

Initial negotiation
43.2 The typical sale by private treaty, rather than by auction, begins when the parties, introduced probably by an estate agent, discuss and agree on a price for the property. Although at this very early stage it might appear that vendor and purchaser are now parties to a legally enforceable contract, this will rarely be the case. One likely reason for this is that the parties will have entered their agreement 'subject to contract'.[1] The use of this phrase prima facie means that the parties are regarded as remaining in negotiation until a formal contract is concluded, usually by 'exchange of contracts'.[2] There might, however, be a 'strong and exceptional' context which would induce the court not to give the words that meaning in a particular case.[3] If the words 'subject to contract' have been inserted in correspondence or otherwise introduced into the negotiations, their effect carries on all the way through those negotiations unless the parties agree or must be taken to have agreed otherwise.[4] If the parties negotiate subject to contract, then, despite having apparently reached agreement, they are in fact free to back out, and, for example, the vendor is free to increase his price, at any time up to the conclusion of the formal contract. While it is clear that the effect of the use of the phrase 'subject to contract' at the outset is to leave the parties in a pre-contractual state, the use of any other qualifying phrase may not achieve this object.[5] Should the parties fail to use an appropriate phrase to signify the lack of any binding agreement, it may conceivably be that the presumption that the agreement was legally binding may be rebutted by evidence that the parties, although ignorant of the lawyers' hallowed 'subject to contract', nonetheless did not intend any binding agreement to come into effect and intended that each should be free to resile until the conclusion of the formal contract.[6] Finally, even were the parties unable to

654

rebut that presumption, the agreement would remain legally unenforceable without sufficient written evidence of it (which a letter written 'subject to contract' would not be), or acts of part performance, a matter we consider in paras 43.11 to 43.19 below.

In the course of negotiations it is not uncommon for the purchaser to pay, normally to an estate agent, a pre-contract deposit, ie a sum of money paid as an earnest of his intention to go ahead with the transaction. £50 or £100 is a common amount for a pre-contract deposit. Payment of this deposit does not prevent either party from withdrawing from the transaction at the pre-contract stage. In addition, until an enforceable contract is made, a pre-contract deposit is always repayable on demand to the purchaser and the vendor has no right to it if it is in the hands of an estate agent, unless the estate agent is expressly authorised to receive it as agent for the vendor. In the light of these rules there seems to be little point as a matter of law in requiring payment of a pre-contract deposit.[7]

1 Para 5.33 above.
2 *Eccles v Bryant* [1948] Ch 93, [1947] 2 All ER 865, CA.
3 *Alpenstow Ltd v Regalian Properties plc* [1985] 2 All ER 545, [1985] 1 WLR 721.
4 *Sherbrooke v Dipple* (1980) 255 Estates Gazette 1203, CA; *Cohen v Nessdale Ltd* [1982] 2 All ER 97, CA.
5 Para 5.33 above.
6 Para 6.2 above.
7 Cf para 43.9 below.

Enquiries and searches

43.3   At this stage the wise purchaser will usually put matters in the hands of professional advisers: a surveyor to report to the purchaser[1] on the structural state of the property and solicitors to carry out the transaction. The purchaser's solicitor will now institute a search in the local land charges register maintained by the district council[2] under the provisions of the Local Land Charges Act 1975.

1 Where, as is usually the case, the purchaser wishes to finance the purchase by means of a mortgage, a valuation survey will also be carried out, at the purchaser's expense, on behalf of the mortgagee (lender).
2 Or London Borough Council: Local Land Charges Act 1975, s3.

Local land charges

43.4   A search of the local land charges register, whether personal or, as is usual, an official search (by officials of the registry), will reveal such matters as whether there exists in respect of the property any revocation of planning permission or order requiring the discontinuance of an existing use, whether any building on the property is subject to a building preservation notice or is listed as being of special architectural or historical interest, and (a charge of a private rather than a public character) whether a light obstruction notice is registered pursuant to the Rights of Light Act 1959.[1] Registrations of these matters are made against the land in question. By virtue of the Local Land Charges Act 1975, s10 charges of a public character which are not registered are not thereby rendered unenforceable.[2] However, if a personal search fails to turn up the existence of a charge because it was not registered, or an official search fails, for whatever reason, to reveal an existing charge, the purchaser will be entitled to compensation payable by the registering authority for any loss suffered by reason of that failure.[3]

1 Para 40.40 above.
2 Cf land charges, para 33.26 above. The legal basis of the enforceability of certain unregistered local land charges is unclear.
3 Local Land Charges Act 1975, s10.

Supplementary enquiries

43.5 When he requisitions an official search of the local land charges register, the purchaser, or his solicitor, will submit a list of additional enquiries to the district council.[1] While these supplementary enquiries form an essential adjunct to a search of the local land charges register, the procedure has no statutory basis. The district councils merely voluntarily answer the enquiries; nevertheless they may be liable to be sued for negligence in answering them. These enquiries cover such matters as whether the roadways abutting on the property are maintained at the public expense, whether it is proposed to construct any road or flyover close to the property, whether the property is drained to a sewer, whether the property is in a slum clearance area and other matters within the knowledge of the district council.

1 Or London Borough Council.

Enquiries of vendor

43.6 Meanwhile, the vendor or his solicitor will be preparing a draft contract of sale, doubtless using one of the available standard forms containing general conditions of sale, such as the National Conditions of Sale or the Law Society's General Conditions of Sale. At this stage of the transaction it has become common, in the case of registered land, for the vendor to send to the purchaser, along with the draft contract, office copies (obtained from the Land Registry) of his register of title, title plan and any documents referred to on the register which are filed at the Registry; in the case of unregistered land, the abstract of title may be sent along with the draft. Thus, as we explain in paras 43.25 and 43.29 below, the vendor, in practice, may take the first step in fulfilling his contractual obligation to prove his title before the contract is formally entered into. On receipt and perusal of the draft contract the purchaser will despatch his enquiries of the vendor. A set of general enquiries before contract is available in a standard form and includes questions as to the boundaries of the property, as to the fixtures and fittings included in the sale, and as to whether the vendor is aware of any adverse rights or overriding interests affecting the property.[1] It is common to add to the standard form of enquiry of the vendor additional questions; for example, whether any local authority improvement grants have been made in respect of the property or, in the light of cases such as *Williams and Glyn's Bank v Boland*,[2] where there is a sole vendor, as to whether he or she is married, and if so requiring an endorsement on the contract by the spouse releasing his or her rights and undertaking not to prevent the vendor carrying out his contractual obligations.

1 Para 34.19 above.
2 Para 34.20 above.

Sale by auction
43.7 Where sale is conducted by auction there is a legally binding contract as soon as the property is knocked down to the highest bidder. A person wishing to bid for a property may make pre-contract enquiries and searches before the auction; or the vendor may produce the relevant evidence at the auction, or the contract may provide for the searches to be made after the auction, giving the purchaser the right to rescind if the searches produce adverse results.

The contract

Exchange
43.8 It is the almost invariable conveyancing practice for the contract to come into being by 'exchange of contracts'. Each party signs a copy of the contract and these copies are exchanged, at least in theory. 'When you are dealing with contracts for the sale of land, it is of the greatest importance to the vendor that he should have a document signed by the purchaser, and to the purchaser that he should have a document signed by the vendor. It is of the greatest importance that there should be no dispute whether a contract had or had not been made and that there should be no dispute as to the terms of it. This particular procedure of exchange ensures that none of these difficulties will arise'.[1] In fact, it is commonly the case today that exchanges are effected not in person but through the post, and it would therefore seem that the contract is formed not when each party receives the other's copy of the contract, but when the second (vendor's) copy is posted.[2] Since it is often the case as regards the purchase of houses that the parties are part of a chain of transactions—the purchaser needing to sell his property before he can buy the vendor's, the vendor needing to sell in order to buy another property to move to—it is a matter of some importance that there be as near as possible simultaneous exchanges of contract in respect of each of these transactions. One method of achieving this object, sanctioned by the Court of Appeal,[3] is the 'telephonic exchange'. In this case, either each solicitor holds his own client's signed part of the contract or one solicitor holds both parts, and they then, by telephone, deem the contracts to be exchanged, the date of exchange then being entered on each part. Actual physical exchange by post follows.

1 *Eccles v Bryant* [1948] Ch 93 at 99, [1947] 2 All ER 865 at 866, CA.
2 Para 5.22 above.
3 *Domb v Isoz* [1980] 1 All ER 942, [1980] 2 WLR 565, CA.

Deposit
43.9 At exchange of contracts it is usual for the purchaser to pay a deposit. The purpose of this is that, in effect, it gives the vendor a remedy, which is available without bringing a court action, in the event of the purchaser failing to complete. This is because the vendor is normally entitled to retain the deposit should he terminate the contract for breach. The court does, however, have an unqualified discretion to order the repayment of the whole deposit under the LPA, s49(2).[1] Although general conditions of sale fix the amount of the deposit at 10% of the purchase price, it is increasingly common to find, in the case of the sale and purchase

of residential property, that the parties provide for a lesser sum to be paid subject to conditions requiring payment of the full 10% deposit if, for example, completion of the transaction does not take place on the agreed date. The requirement of a deposit is a fundamental term (ie a condition) of the contract, breach of which entitles the vendor to terminate the contract and sue for damages including the amount of the unpaid deposit.[2] Apparently, however, where failure to pay the deposit is the result of mere oversight, the vendor must notify the purchaser that he intends to treat the breach as repudiatory and must give him an opportunity of paying the deposit before proceeding to terminate the contract.[2]

The deposit is normally paid not to the vendor but to his solicitor (or to the auctioneer or, occasionally, to the estate agent) who holds it as agent for the vendor or as stakeholder. An agent for the vendor is obliged to hand over the deposit to the vendor on demand, whereas a stakeholder is personally responsible for its safe keeping until one party or the other becomes entitled to it.

1   *Universal Corpn v Five Ways Properties Ltd* [1979] 1 All ER 552, CA.
2   *Millichamp v Jones* [1983] 1 All ER 267, [1983] 1 WLR 1422.

Terms
43.10   The actual contract itself is most commonly drawn up in accordance with a standard form and is subject to one of a number of standard sets of general conditions of sale, as modified by any special conditions agreed to by the parties. Should the parties not have agreed terms beyond the identity of the parties, the property and the price, then, if the contract is by correspondence, it is subject to the Statutory Conditions of Sale drawn up by the Lord Chancellor under the LPA, s46. The phrase 'contract by correspondence' conveys the notion of an exchange of letters, and not merely an acceptance by letter of an oral offer or an oral acceptance of an offer by letter. It does not, furthermore, include letters confirming an oral contract.[1] Where a contract is 'open' (ie where its terms cover only the identity of the parties, the property and the price) then further terms will be implied by the general law. If the LPA, s46 is inapplicable, common law terms are implied. Important terms implied under an open contract, or wherever the contract is silent on the matter, are: that the vendor must show good title, or (in registered land) absolute title, must give vacant possession and must execute a proper conveyance, and that completion (ie the transfer or conveyance of the property) must take place within a reasonable time. The standard forms of general conditions modify and supplement these terms, for example, by specifying the time for completion; failure to meet that deadline would then be a breach of contract entitling the innocent party to damages,[2] though only entitling him to terminate for breach where time is made of the essence.[3] The general conditions provide that either party may make time of the essence by serving a notice to complete on the other party requiring completion in the time laid down by the conditions.

1   *Stearn v Twitchell* [1985] 1 All ER 631.
2   *Raineri v Miles* [1980] 2 All ER 145, [1980] 2 WLR 847, HL.
3   Paras 8.11 to 8.14 above.

Enforceability

43.11 The LPA, s40(1) provides:

'No action may be brought upon any contract for the sale or other disposition of land or any interest in land, unless the agreement upon which such action is brought, or some memorandum or note thereof is in writing, and signed by the party to be charged or by some other person thereunto by him lawfully authorised.'

The section is comprehensive. It applies to a contract for any disposition of *any interest in land*, whether by sale, mortgage, lease or otherwise. A contract to enter into a formal contract for the disposition of any interest in land is itself a contract for the disposition of any interest in land and must satisfy section 40(1) in order to be enforceable.[1] The expression 'any interest in land' includes sporting rights and other profits,[2] the beneficial interests under a trust for sale[3] and *fructus naturales*[4] unless they are to be severed by the vendor or the contract binds the purchaser to sever them at once.[5]

1　*Daulia Ltd v Four Millbank Nominees Ltd* [1978] Ch 231, [1978] 2 All ER 557, CA.
2　Para 40.43 above.
3　*Cooper v Critchley* [1955] Ch 431, [1955] 1 All ER 520, CA; para 35.36, above.
4　Para 32.7 above.
5　*Smith v Surman* (1829) 9 B & C 561; *Marshall v Green* (1875) 1 CPD 35.

43.12 The effect of non-compliance with the requirements of s40 is not to make the contract void or voidable. It merely makes it unenforceable by action against a party who has not signed a sufficient memorandum or note, unless, and until, he has signed such a memorandum or note. The reason is that the agreement is incapable of proof.[1] A defendant who wishes to rely on the absence of writing must specifically plead non-compliance with s40 in his defence. A plaintiff is caught by the section whenever he has to rely on an oral or insufficiently evidenced contract for the disposition of any interest in land, even though he is not directly claiming damages for its breach.[2]

Admittedly, in depriving a party of his right to enforce the contract by an action, the section deprives him of what is usually his most important right. Nevertheless, since the contract is valid and subsisting, a person who has received money or property in accordance with the terms of the contract obtains a good title to it and the contract can be enforced in any way other than by action. Thus, if the purchaser pays a deposit to the vendor under an oral contract, the vendor can keep that deposit if the purchaser defaults and, if sued for its recovery, can plead the oral contract as a defence.[3]

1　*Maddison v Alderson* (1883) 8 App Cas 467, esp 488, HL.
2　*Delaney v T P Smith Ltd* [1946] KB 393, [1946] 2 All ER 23, CA.
3　*Thomas v Brown* (1876) 1 QBD 714; *Monnickendam v Leanse* (1923) 39 TLR 445.

Formal requirements of the LPA, s40(1)

43.13 The section requires that the agreement, or some memorandum or note thereof, shall be in writing and signed by the party to be charged, ie the defendant, or by some person lawfully authorised by him for that purpose. If the contract is in writing, as in the vast majority of conveyancing transactions it will be, no difficulty arises. However, whether there is written evidence sufficient to constitute a signed memorandum or note (which can come into existence at any time before action is brought to enforce the contract) is a somewhat complex question because, although the section does not specify the form and contents of a signed memorandum or note, the following rules have been laid down by the judges:

Contents of the 'memorandum or note'
43.14 a. The memorandum or note must name the parties to the contract or so describe them that they can be identified with certainty.[1]

b. The memorandum or note must describe the whole subject matter[2] but may sufficiently describe it although it has to be supplemented by extrinsic evidence. In *Plant v Bourne*,[3] for instance, a memorandum, recording the sale of '24 acres of land, freehold, and all appurtenances thereto at Totmonslow, in the parish of Draycott, in the county of Stafford' was held sufficient on proof that the vendor had no other land there.

c. The memorandum or note must accurately set out the material terms of the oral contract other than any implied terms.[4] If it differs as to or omits a material term it will not be a memorandum or note of the contract and the plaintiff will not be able to rely on it.[5] Thus, in *Tweddell v Henderson*,[6] the parties orally contracted for the sale and purchase of a plot of land at a price of £8,700 payable in four instalments. The defendant then wrote to the plaintiff saying he had asked his solicitor 'to get the contract drawn up at the fixed price of £8,700'. The defendant subsequently refused to go through with the transaction. The plaintiff was held to be unable to enforce the contract as there was no sufficient memorandum since the letter did not contain all the material terms, in particular the term requiring payment in instalments. However, if the memorandum or note merely omits a term which is for the *exclusive benefit of the plaintiff* then, but only then,[7] the plaintiff can waive the term and enforce the contract without it.[8] Similarly, if the omitted term is for the *exclusive benefit of the defendant* the plaintiff can enforce the contract provided that he agrees to perform that term.[9] Thus, in *Scott v Bradley*,[10] where the written memorandum failed to state that one of the terms of the contract was that the purchaser would pay half the legal costs of the vendor, it was held that, on submitting to pay half the legal costs, the purchaser (who was the plaintiff in the action) could rely on the memorandum and was entitled to specific performance of the contract of sale.

d. The memorandum or note must state the consideration.[11]

e. There is authority for the proposition that the memorandum or note must not only state the terms of the contract but must also contain an acknowledgement or recognition by the signatory that a contract has been entered into.[12] Although the present requirement has been doubted,[13] it may be justified in that, unless it acknowledges the existence of the agreement, the memorandum is merely a list of the terms alleged to be agreed; it is not evidence of the *agreement*. It was held in *Tiverton Estates Ltd v Wearwell Ltd*[14] that a letter expressly written 'subject to contract' could not constitute a memorandum as it clearly did not recognise the existence of a contract. It follows that even if the parties have concluded a binding oral contract, this will remain unenforceable if, as is invariably the case, their solicitors or estate agents use the phrase 'subject to contract' in any correspondence on which it is sought to rely as written evidence.

1   *Williams v Jordan* (1877) 6 Ch D 517; *Rossiter v Miller* (1878) 3 App Cas 1124, HL.
2   *Burgess v Cox* [1951] Ch 383, [1950] 2 All ER 1212.
3   [1897] 2 Ch 281, CA.
4   *Cook v Taylor* [1942] Ch 349, [1942] 2 All ER 85.
5   *Beckett v Nurse* [1948] 1 KB 535, [1948] 1 All ER 81, CA.
6   [1975] 2 All ER 1096, [1975] 1 WLR 1496.
7   *Hawkins v Price* [1947] Ch 645, [1947] 1 All ER 689.
8   *North v Loomes* [1919] 1 Ch 378.
9   *Martin v Pycroft* (1852) 2 De G & G 285; *Scott v Bradley* [1971] Ch 850, [1971] 1 All ER
    583.
10 [1971] Ch 850, [1971] 1 All ER 583.
11 *Laythoarp v Bryant* (1836) 2 Bing NC 735 at 742.
12 *Tiverton Estates Ltd v Wearwell Ltd* [1975] Ch 146, [1974] 1 All ER 209, CA; *Thirkell v
    Cambi* [1919] 2 KB 590, CA.
13 *Law v Jones* [1974] Ch 112, [1973] 2 All ER 437, CA; *Daulia Ltd v Four Millbank Nominees
    Ltd* [1978] Ch 231, [1978] 2 All ER 557, CA.
14 [1975] Ch 146, [1974] 1 All ER 209, CA.

Signature

43.15   The document must be signed by the party to be charged or by his agent lawfully authorised to sign for him. The extent of an agent's authority is determined by agreement or trade usage, but, for example, an auctioneer has authority to sign a memorandum on behalf of both vendor and purchaser.[1]

The section does not require signature by both parties or their agents, merely signature by the party to be charged, ie the party against whom it is sought to enforce the contract, or his agent.[2] Thus, where there is a contract between A and B, and B alone has signed a memorandum or note of it, A can enforce the contract against B, but B cannot enforce it against A.

The word 'signed' has been liberally interpreted. Provided the name, or even the initials, of the party to be charged appears in some part of the memorandum or note in some form, whether in handwriting, stamp, print or otherwise, there will be a sufficient signature, if that party has shown in some way that he recognises the whole document as a record of the contract.[3] Thus, a memorandum in the handwriting of Crockford, the person to be charged, which began 'I, James Crockford, agree' without any other signature, was held in *Knight v Crockford*[4] to have been sufficiently signed on the ground that, by writing these words, Crockford had shown that he recognised the existence of the contract mentioned in the document. However, unless there is such a recognition the mere fact that a party's name appears in the document does not make it signed by him.[5]

1   *Sims v Landray* [1894] 2 Ch 318 at 320.
2   *Laythoarp v Bryant* (1836) 2 Bing NC 735.
3   *Halley v O'Brien* [1920] 1 IR 330 at 339; *Leeman v Stocks* [1951] Ch 941, [1951] 1 All ER
    1043.
4   (1794) 1 Esp 190.
5   *Hubert v Treherne* (1842) 3 Man & G 743.

Purpose for which document prepared irrelevant

43.16   It is irrelevant that the document was never intended to serve as a note or memorandum but was prepared for some entirely different purpose. The question is not one of intention of the party who signs the document but of evidence against him.[1] In *Cohen v Roche*,[2] for instance, a note in an auctioneer's book was held to be an effective memorandum, and so was a letter to a third party in *Moore v Hart*.[3] Moreover, a written offer signed by the defendant and orally accepted by the plaintiff is a sufficient memorandum, even though the contract does not come into existence until after the offer has been accepted.[4] In addition, a letter repudiating liability under an alleged contract is a sufficient memorandum of the contract if it constitutes an unambiguous recognition of the existence of the contract and of its terms and merely denies liability under it, but not if it denies the contract was made on the terms alleged.[5]

1 *Re Hoyle, Hoyle v Hoyle* [1983] 1 Ch 84 at 99.
2 *Cohen v Roche* [1927] 1 KB 169.
3 *Moore v Hart* (1682) 1 Vern 110 at 201.
4 *Reuss v Picksley* (1866) LR 1 Exch 342.
5 *Thirkell v Cambi* [1919] 2 KB 590, CA; 43.14 above.

Joinder of documents

43.17 A memorandum or note may consist of various documents, each in itself insufficient, so long as there is some internal reference between them. A plaintiff who wishes to rely on a memorandum or note allegedly constituted by more than one document must prove:

a. the existence of a document signed by the defendant (the party to be charged);

b. a reference in the *signed document*, express or implied, to some other document(s) or transaction. Where any such reference can be spelt out of the signed document, then oral evidence can be given to identify the other document(s) referred to, or, as the case may be, to explain the other transaction, and to identify any document relating to it;

c. that a sufficient memorandum or note is constituted when the signed document and the other document(s) which has been revealed are read together.[1] Thus, where the documents relied on as constituting a memorandum were a cheque for the payment of a deposit, signed by the defendant and made payable to the plaintiff's solicitors, and a receipt for the sum of the deposit, which described the property, they were held not to constitute a sufficient memorandum. The document signed by the defendant, the cheque, contained no reference, express or implied, to any other document or transaction, particularly as it was made out, not to the plaintiff, but to his solicitors.[1]

Where two documents are *both signed* then, even though neither expressly or impliedly refers to the other or to another transaction, they can be joined so as to form a memorandum, if, on placing them side by side, it is obvious without the aid of oral evidence that they are connected.[2] In this way a series of correspondence between the parties may be read as constituting a memorandum or note of an oral agreement.

1 *Timmins v Moreland Street Property Co Ltd* [1958] Ch 110 at 120, [1957] 3 All ER 265 at 276, CA; see also *Elias v George Sahely & Co (Barbados) Ltd* [1983] 1 AC 646, [1982] 3 All ER 801, PC.
2 *Studds v Watson* (1884) 28 Ch D 305; cf. *Timmins v Moreland Street Property Co Ltd* [1958] Ch 110, [1957] 3 All ER 265, CA.

Part performance

43.18 Under the equitable doctrine of part performance the courts allow the terms of an oral, or insufficiently evidenced, contract for the disposition of any interest in land to be proved by oral evidence if the party seeking to enforce the contract has done acts in part performance of his obligations under it.[1] If the rules of part performance are satisfied, a contract whose terms have been proved by the oral evidence admitted is enforceable in equity in favour of the party who has partly performed it. Nevertheless, a contract which is enforceable under the doctrine of part performance is not in as good a position as one properly evidenced in writing. A contract merely supported by part performance may be enforced in equity by an order of specific performance[2] if the case is a proper one, but that lies *in the discretion* of the court and no damages can be awarded if specific performance could not, or would not, be awarded. On the other hand, a contract properly evidenced in writing is enforceable at law and the plaintiff is *entitled* to damages, the equitable remedy of specific performance also being available to him at the court's discretion.

1   *Brough v Nettleton* [1921] 2 Ch 25.
2   Paras 11.25–11.27 above.

43.19   Four conditions must be satisfied to bring the doctrine into operation:

a. *The acts in question must, in the light of their surrounding circumstances, be referable to the alleged contract* The acts in question must be such as must be referable to some contract and may be referred to the alleged one: they must be such that they prove the existence of some contract and are consistent with the contract alleged.[1] In other words, the acts of part performance in the circumstances in which they were performed must point to the existence of some contract and not be inconsistent with the contract alleged, the plaintiff having to prove that they do so on the balance of probabilities.[2] It has not yet been conclusively decided whether the acts of part performance need only be referable to *some* contract *whatever its nature*[3] or whether they must be referable to *some* contract *concerning land*.[4] The latter seems the preferable view.

A good example of the operation of the present requirement is provided by *Wakeham v Mackenzie*.[5] B, a widower of 72, who was in poor health, orally agreed with the plaintiff, a widow of 67, that, if she would give up her council flat, move into his house and look after him and the house without wages, and pay her share for food and coal, he would leave his house to her in his will. The plaintiff observed all her obligations under the oral contract but B left her nothing in his will. The plaintiff was awarded specific performance of the oral contract. Her acts of giving up her flat, moving into a new home, looking after B and his house and contributing towards food and fuel were referable to some contract and were not inconsistent with the contract which she alleged. The same decision was reached in *Steadman v Steadman*.[6] After the breakdown of their marriage the parties made an oral contract whereby: the wife was to transfer her interest in the matrimonial home to the husband for £1,500; the wife would agree to the discharge of a magistrates' maintenance order in her favour; the husband would pay her £100 in part discharge of arrears under the order, and the wife would consent to the discharge of the balance. The agreement was revealed to the magistrates, who approved the relevant part of it. The husband then paid the £100 to the wife and his solicitors then prepared and sent a form of transfer of the wife's interest in the house, but she refused to sign it and claimed that, being oral, the contract referred to above was unenforceable under the LPA, s40(1). The House of Lords ordered specific performance of the contract, holding that the payment of the £100, together with the announcement of the agreement to the magistrates and the preparation and sending of the form of transfer, amounted to sufficient acts of part performance by the husband because the acts were such as to indicate that they had been carried out by him in reliance on a contract with the wife and were not inconsistent with the contract alleged.[7]

b. *Fraud on the part of the defendant* The plaintiff must have been induced, or allowed, to alter his position in reliance on the contract, so that it would be a fraud on the part of the defendant to take advantage of the contract not being sufficiently evidenced in writing.[8] In *Rawlinson v Ames*,[9] the defendant agreed to take a lease of a flat from the plaintiff but the agreement was insufficiently evidenced in writing. At the defendant's request the plaintiff carried out alterations to the flat, but the defendant refused to take the lease. It was held that, as the plaintiff had materially changed her position for the worse in carrying out her part of the contract, it would be a fraud in the defendant to take advantage of the contract not being sufficiently evidenced in writing. The other conditions of part performance also being satisfied, the plaintiff was granted a decree of specific performance.

It was formerly thought that a result of the present condition was that the payment of money could never be a sufficient act of part performance by the payer because he could recover his payment if the payee refused to perform the contract, so that there would be no fraud on the part of the payee in setting up the defence of non-compliance with s40. However, the House of Lords decision in *Steadman v Steadman* clearly establishes that there is no general rule that the payment of money cannot be a sufficient act of part performance. Nevertheless, a payment alone will frequently not suffice since it may not, on balance, be referable to any contract, let alone a contract concerning land.[10] On the other hand, as the decision in *Steadman v Steadman* shows, the payment of money together with other acts may be highly indicative of a contract.

c. *Contract must be specifically enforceable* The contract to which the acts of part performance refer must be of a type of which the court can direct specific performance.[11] The availability of specific performance is subject to certain general rules, which we mention in para 11.19 above, and if specific performance is not available under them the doctrine of part performance cannot be relied on.

d. *Proper evidence* There must be proper evidence, whether written or oral, of the existence and terms of the contract, which is let in by the acts of part performance.[12] In other words, acts of part performance having been proved and evidence having been admitted in consequence, that evidence must show that a contract has been concluded and what its terms are: if the evidence does not do so the doctrine of part performance cannot be relied on.

1 *Kingswood Estate Co Ltd v Anderson* [1963] 2 QB 169, [1962] 3 All ER 593, CA; *Wakeham v Mackenzie* [1968] 2 All ER 783, [1968] 1 WLR 1175; *Steadman v Steadman* [1976] AC 536, [1974] 2 All ER 977, HL.
2 *Steadman v Steadman* [1974] 2 All ER 977 at 1000.
3 This was the view taken by Viscount Dilhorne and Lord Reid in *Steadman v Steadman* [1974] 2 All ER 977 at 992 and 981.
4 This was the view taken by Lords Salmon and Morris in *Steadman v Steadman* [1974] 2 All ER 977 at 1005 and 986–7, and by Walton J in *Re Gonin, Gonin v Garmeson* [1979] Ch 16, [1977] 2 All ER 720.
5 [1968] 2 All ER 783, [1968] 1 WLR 1175.
6 [1976] AC 536, [1974] 2 All ER 977, HL.
7 Cf *Re Windle (bankrupt), exp Trustee of Bankrupt v Windle* [1975] 3 All ER 987, [1975] 1 WLR 1628 (preparation of draft transfer and payment of legal fees held to be part performance) and *Sutton v Sutton* [1984] Ch 184, [1984] 1 All ER 168 (consent to divorce petition held to be part performance in the circumstances).
8 *Caton v Caton* (1865) LR 1 Ch App 137 at 148 (affd. (1867) LR 2 HL 127).
9 [1925] Ch 96.
10 Cf *Cohen v Nessdale Ltd* [1981] 3 All ER 118 (court prepared to accept payment of ground rent as part performance in the circumstances).
11 *McManus v Cooke* (1887) 35 Ch D 681 at 697.
12 *Kingswood Estates Co Ltd v Anderson* [1963] 2 QB 169, [1962] 3 All ER 593, CA.

Vendor's liability for defects

43.20 It is said that an underlying rule in contracts for the sale of land is *caveat emptor*, let the buyer beware; in other words, it is for the buyer to discover defects in the property he is buying, and not for the seller to warn him of them. However, this rule is subject to a number of important exceptions. First, the vendor may be liable for misrepresentation, the law as to which we discussed at paras 13.1 to 13.39 above. Second, he may be liable for breach of contract for misdescription of the property in the contract; for example, if he describes his interest in the property or the size of the property as being greater than it is. Where the misdescription is substantial, the vendor cannot enforce the contract unless the purchaser affirms it; where it is not, he may, but subject to a possible abatement of the price. In either case, the purchaser may enforce the contract subject to possible abatement, or may sue for damages. Third, the vendor is under an implied contractual duty to disclose all *latent* defects in his title to the property, ie defects which the purchaser could not discover on a reasonable inspection of the property. Thus, for example, the vendor is obliged to disclose that his title is dependent on adverse possession, or that the property is subject to restrictive covenants. Where there is a duty to disclose, failure to do so constitutes a breach of contract, the effects of which are the same as misdescription. The vendor's liability under each of these three heads is likely to be modified by the terms of the contract. However, as to liability for misrepresentation, the Misrepresentation Act 1967, s3[1] should be borne in mind when drafting any clause restricting or excluding liability. It should be noted that in addition to the foregoing, a vendor may, in appropriate circumstances, be liable to his purchaser in negligence or under the provisions of the Defective Premises Act 1972.[2]

1 Para 13.31 above.
2 Paras 23.27 to 23.30 above.

Remedies
43.21 The contractual remedies of particular relevance to sales of land are of course applicable to contracts in general and little need be said here additional to our earlier discussion of these remedies.

a. *Rescission* It is open to a purchaser to rescind the contract *ab initio* in the face of misrepresentation by the vendor,[1] although it should be remembered that he may be debarred from so doing after completion has taken place in a case where the property is purchased with the aid of a mortgage; for the mortgagee will be a purchaser of an interest in the property for value.[2]

b. *Termination of the contract for repudiatory breach*[3] The injured party may not only accept the repudiatory breach of the defaulting party as terminating the contract but may also sue for damages for loss of the bargain or wasted expenditure and any other loss which is not too remote.[4]

c. *Damages* As in the general case, a breach of the contract for the sale of the land entitles the innocent party to sue for damages for loss of the bargain or for wasted expenditure, at his option, and any other loss which is not too remote. This is subject, however, to the anomalous rule in *Bain v Fothergill*[5] whereby should a vendor, *despite using his best endeavours*, be unable, through no fault of his own,[6] to comply with his contractual obligation to show good title,[7] the purchaser will be entitled to damages for his conveyancing costs and the return of his deposit with interest but to no more than nominal damages for loss of his bargain. Although the vendor must use his best endeavours to obtain a good title, this does not require him to enter litigation with an adverse claimant to perfect his title.[8] In other cases, the date at which damages for loss of bargain are assessed is normally the date of breach though some other date may be chosen where otherwise injustice might be caused.[9]
   Where there has been any misrepresentation by the vendor, the purchaser may choose to sue for damages for misrepresentation, rather than for breach of contract, a matter which we discussed in paras 13.18 to 13.24 above. A vendor who cannot show good title may have represented otherwise in answer to enquiries. Where that misrepresentation is fraudulent, damages are not limited by the rule in *Bain v Fothergill*.[10] Where, however, the vendor is liable under the Misrepresentation Act 1967, damages will be measured in tort, not contract, and hence damages for loss of bargain may not be recoverable.[11]

d. *Specific performance* It will be remembered that the law regards every plot of land as unique, with the result that contracts for the sale or lease of land are always prima facie specifically enforceable by a purchaser and, because of the principle of mutuality, a vendor.[12] This does not mean that the remedy will always be granted, since it is discretionary. Where the court refuses to grant specific performance to either party, it has a discretion to order the repayment of the deposit,[13] wherever this is the fairest course between the parties.[14] Further, the court has a discretion to award damages in addition to, or in substitution for, specific performance. Where the innocent party obtains specific performance, but the order is not complied with by the party in breach, the innocent party, having elected to affirm the contract, cannot then unilaterally terminate for breach. He must return to the court, under whose supervision the performance of the contract now is, to seek enforcement of the order or dissolution of the order and termination of the contract.[15]

1   Para 13.14 above.
2   Para 13.16d above.
3   Para 9.4 above.
4   Paras 11.2 to 11.10 above.
5   (1874) LR 7 HL 158.
6   *Malhotra v Choudhury* [1980] Ch 52, [1979] 1 All ER 186, CA; *Ray v Druce* [1985] 2 All ER 482, [1985] 2 WLR 39.
7   Para 43.25 below.
8   *Sharneyford Supplies Ltd v Edge* [1985] 1 All ER 976.
9   Para 11.11 above.
10 (1874) LR 7HL 158 at 207.
11 *Sharneyford Supplies Ltd v Edge* [1985] 1 All ER 976; cf *Watts v Spence* [1976] Ch 165, [1975] 2 All ER 528.
12 Para 11.26 above.
13 LPA, s49(2).
14 *Universal Corpn v Five Ways Properties Ltd* [1979] 1 All ER 552, CA.
15 *GKN Distributors Ltd v Tyne Tees Fabrication Ltd* (1985) 275 Estates Gazette 53.

Passing of the risk

43.22   On the conclusion of a binding contract, the purchaser becomes entitled to call for it to be specifically performed. Moreover, since equity looks on that as done which ought to be done, the purchaser is regarded as having an equitable interest in the property.

The vendor is regarded as a (constructive) trustee for the purchaser.[1] Although the vendor is under an obligation to manage the property as a trustee, this is not an entirely straightforward trust since the vendor himself retains a beneficial interest in the property until the purchase price is paid and until then is entitled to remain in occupation and receive the income of the property. The purchaser, however, is entitled to any capital appreciation in respect of the property. On the other hand, he must also bear any capital losses, which means that on exchange of contracts the risk passes to him as regards any matter other than a breach of the vendor's duties (including the duty to prove title). The purchaser should therefore on the conclusion of the contract insure the property against fire, flood etc. This is so despite the LPA, s47, which provides that where any money becomes payable under any policy of insurance held by the vendor in respect of damage or destruction to the property, the vendor is to hold it on behalf of the purchaser and pay it over on completion, since a. the vendor may not have insured the property; b. it is common for the contract to make it clear that the vendor is under no obligation to maintain such a policy.

1   Para 38.15 above.

Estate contract

43.23   On the conclusion of the contract, an estate contract (that is, 'a contract to convey or create a legal estate') is created,[1] and the purchaser may register it. In unregistered land registration is in the Land Charges Registry against the vendor's name;[2] in registered land registration is effected by means of a notice, caution or restriction entered on the vendor's title register.³ In this way the purchaser's rights will be protected against third parties. Commonly, such registration does not take place and the purchaser simply relies on completion occurring within a short time and the vendor doing nothing untoward in the meantime.

1 Para 33.23 above.
2 Para 33.27 above.
3 Paras 34.22 to 34.24 above.

Conveyance or transfer stage

43.24 Up to exchange of contracts the procedure for transferring owner-ship of land is broadly the same whether the title to that land is registered or unregistered, and, indeed, to a considerable extent, whether it is freehold or long leasehold. After exchange of contracts, the procedures followed differ depending on whether the title to the land is registered or not. Where the transaction is the occasion for first registration of title, the procedure followed is that for unregistered land; title is then registered after com-pletion.

Registered land

Proving title

43.25 At this stage it is for the vendor to carry out his contractual obligation to prove his title, ie to prove that he is in a position to sell what he has contracted to sell. Under an open contract his obligation is to show absolute title, so that special provision must be made in the contract where he cannot do this. In the usual case the first stage of this process will already have taken place in that the vendor will have furnished the purchaser with office copies of his register of title, etc.¹ These office copies can be relied on to the same extent as the originals² and do not need to be verified against them.

The vendor should also furnish documentary evidence available relating to any overriding interests, such as tenancies to which the property is subject, and, in the case of land registered with possessory or qualified title, such evidence relating to the pre-registration title.³ The purchaser's solicitor will inspect the office copies and any documents required to be furnished to ensure all is well. He may also raise *requisitions on title*, that is, make enquiries of the vendor for further particulars, for example, as to adverse entries on the register, or, more likely, simply point them out and require their removal.⁴ A failure by the vendor to answer a proper requisition on title may lead to the purchaser terminating the contract for breach or may lead to him applying to the court to require an answer under the summary procedure provided by the LPA, s49(1).

At this stage, also, the purchaser's solicitor should draft the transfer of title, using the prescribed form.⁵

The next stage of the procedure is for the vendor to supply the purchaser, or his solicitor, with an authority to inspect the register.⁶ Armed with this, the purchaser or his solicitor will, rather than make a personal search, normally request an official search of the register. This search need only be restricted to entries appearing on the register since the date of the office copy provided by the vendor. The official certificate of search which results confers a priority period of 30 working days from the date of the application for search.[7] (There is provision for extending this period once completion has taken place.) The transaction should be completed and the purchaser apply to be registered as proprietor within this priority period for then the purchaser will not take subject to entries made in the register during that time. Where a person suffers loss as a result of an error in an official search he is entitled to an indemnity.[8] He is still bound by any entry which the search fails to reveal.[9] It may be necessary to raise requisitions as to entries revealed by the official search, for example, to require removal of a notice protecting a spouse's statutory rights of occupation[10] entered since the date of the office copy.

1   Para 43.6 above.
2   LRA, s113.
3   Paras 34.12 and 34.13 above. The pre-registration title is thus dealt with in accordance with *un*registered procedure.
4   See *Re Stone and Saville's Contract* [1963] 1 All ER 353, [1963] 1 WLR 163, CA.
5   Land Registration Rules, r98, Sch, Form 19.
6   LRA, s113.
7   Land Registration (Official Searches) Rules 1981.
8   LRA, s83(3); para 35.28 above.
9   *Parkash v Irani Finance Ltd* [1970] Ch 101, [1969] 1 All ER 930.
10 Para 33.25 above.

Completion

43.26   Completion, the execution of the prescribed deed of transfer, now takes place. This document is in simple form, requiring few of the formalities which are included in a conveyance of unregistered land, but it must be signed, sealed and delivered.[1] On completion, the purchaser is entitled to the land certificate[2] relating to the property. If, however, as is quite likely, the property is subject to a mortgage in the form of a registered charge, the land certificate will already be lodged at the Registry.[3] In this case, assuming the mortgage is to be paid off, the vendor must obtain the charge certificate from the mortgagee together with a discharge of the mortgage. If the purchaser charges the land by registered charge by way of mortgage, the land certificate will remain lodged at the Registry.

1   Para 33.3 above.
2   Para 34.17 above.
3   Para 41.8 above.

Registration

43.27   It will be recalled that the deed of transfer itself does not pass the legal estate to the purchaser. Only registration of the purchaser as proprietor vests in him the legal estate.[1] The purchaser should therefore, within the priority period conferred by the official search,[2] apply to the Registry for registration as proprietor. His application should be accompanied by the land certificate, or where appropriate, the charge certificate; by the deed of transfer stamped with the correct stamp duty; where appropriate, by an application to register the discharge of the vendor's mortgage, and, again where appropriate, by an application to register the charge effecting the purchaser's mortgage.

1   LRA, ss19(1) and 22(1); para 34.6 above.
2   Para 43.25 above.

Unregistered land

43.28 As might be imagined, the procedure to be gone through on a conveyance of unregistered land is slightly more complex than that required for registered land.

Proving title

43.29 *Commencement* Under the terms of an open contract, the vendor is required to show 'good' title. In the case of a freehold, this means that he must show that he is in a position to pass that freehold, unencumbered, to the purchaser. This involves him in tracing the course of dealings with the land, by means of the relevant documents, over the period commencing with a 'good root of title' at least 15 years old[1] and extending up to the time of the transaction.

A good root of title is a document in which the legal and beneficial ownership of the property to be sold is fully set out, the property is sufficiently described that it may be identified, and no doubts are cast on the vendor's title.[2] The prime example of a good root of title is a conveyance on sale of the freehold. A legal mortgage of the property is sometimes accepted as a good root, on the basis that the mortgagee will have satisfied himself as to the title, though it does not fall within the strict definition of a good root. If the purchaser does not investigate the vendor's title commencing with a good root at least 15 years old he is affixed with constructive notice of all those equitable rights dependent on the doctrine of notice which he would have discovered had he fully investigated the title.[3] As it would be quite a coincidence to find a good root of title exactly 15 years old, it is likely to be necessary in order for both vendor and purchaser to fulfil their obligations to go back to a good root more than 15 years old. To accept a shorter title is to risk being affixed with constructive notice. A purchaser who investigates the title going back to a good root at least 15 years old is not affected by constructive notice of any equitable rights which he might have discovered had he investigated the pre-root title. The purchaser remains bound by registered land charges affecting the property which are undiscovered or undiscoverable as being prior to the good root of title, but he is entitled to compensation payable by the Chief Land Registrar for loss suffered as a result.[4] In practice, he is unlikely to need this as pre-root official search certificates should be furnished by the vendor thus providing the names against which to search.

1 LPA, s44(1), as amended by LPA 1969, s23.
2 Williams, *Vendor and Purchaser* (4th edn) p. 124.
3 Para 33.16 above.
4 LPA 1969, s25; para 33.27 above.

43.30 *Abstract of title* In the first instance, the vendor fulfils his obligation to trace the links in the title from the root to the time of the transaction by delivering to the purchaser an abstract of title. Traditionally this took the form of a laboriously prepared summary of the various documents and events relating to the title and of their effect, with important matters being set out in full. Nowadays this traditional form is being replaced by an epitome of title, a list of the relevant documents and events, together with photocopies of the documents, including official certificates of search of the Land Charges Registry. Under an open contract, the abstract must be delivered within a reasonable time of the contract, but, as we have said, it is commonly delivered before exchange of contracts.[1]

1 Para 43.6 above.

43.31 *Requisitions* Just as, in registered land, the purchaser's solicitor peruses the office copies of the register and the official certificate of search and raises requisitions on any defect or apparent defect,[1] so in unregistered land he will do the same with regard to the abstract of title. Examples of such requisitions might be to require that the vendor produce evidence that an abstracted mortgage has been discharged, or to request production of land charges search certificates in respect of estate owners whose names do not appear in the abstracted documents.[2]

At this stage also, the purchaser's solicitor will draft the conveyance in traditional form. This should then be sent to the vendor for approval.

1 Para 43.25 above.
2 Para 33.27 above.

43.32 *Verification of title* Prior to completion the vendor or his solicitor should search, or, more likely, request an official search of, the Land Charges Register.[1] Finally, to ensure further that the vendor's title is unencumbered (with rights enjoyed by others), or is encumbered only to the extent specified in the contract, the purchaser or his solicitor should check the abstract of title against the title deeds themselves. In view of the current practice of replacing the abstract with an epitome together with photocopies of the deeds, this examination is often postponed until just before completion as it is then merely a question of checking the accuracy of the photocopies.

1 Paras 33.29 and 33.30 above.

Completion
43.33 Completion takes place (within the priority period conferred by the official search[1]) when the conveyance is signed, sealed and delivered,[2] the purchase price is paid and the legal estate thereby passes to the purchaser. At this stage also the purchaser becomes entitled to the title deeds relating to the property, whether they have been held by the vendor or his mortgagee. The conveyance must now be stamped with the appropriate duty. The title deeds will then usually be forwarded to the purchaser's mortgagee.[3]

1 Para 33.29 above.
2 Para 33.3 above.
3 Para 41.40 above.

Covenants for title
43.34 Where the vendor is, and is expressed in the conveyance (or, indeed, in registered land, in the transfer) to convey as beneficial owner of the property, then by virtue of the LPA, s76 certain covenants for title are implied in the coveyance, which are intended to afford the purchaser some

recourse against the vendor in the event of some defect in the title becoming apparent. It is implied:

a. that the vendor has full power to convey the subject matter expressed to be conveyed;

b. that the purchaser shall have quiet enjoyment of the property;[1]

c. that the property is free from, or otherwise the vendor indemnifies the purchaser against, incumbrances;

d. that the vendor will do what is necessary to cure any defect.

The benefit of these covenants runs with the land,[2] which means that a purchaser takes the benefit both of his vendor's covenants and of previous vendors' covenants. In registered land, where registration with absolute title is sometimes said to give a 'state guarantee', these covenants are largely superfluous.

1 Para 37.2 above.
2 Para 39.21 above.

Leasehold conveyancing

43.35 The assignment on sale of an existing leasehold interest proceeds in essentially the same manner as the sale of a freehold interest. To a large extent, so also does the grant of a new leasehold interest, though contract and conveyance stages may be telescoped into one, with either a formal lease being granted or an agreement for a lease being entered into. Leases taking effect immediately at a rent for a term not exceeding three years may simply be created orally.[1]

It will be remembered that there are imposed by statute certain restrictions on the purchaser's investigation of the title to the leasehold. In essence, under an open contract, the intending purchaser of an existing leasehold interest is limited to investigating the lease or sub-lease, and where appropriate, assignment thereof, under which the other contracting party holds. He cannot investigate the title to the freehold.[2] However the parties may contract for a fuller investigation of the title.[3] In the case of registered land where the other contracting party is registered with absolute title, the restrictions on investigation of title are of little moment.[4]

Two things with which a purchaser of a leasehold interest must particularly concern himself, for fear of possible forfeiture,[5] are

a. where (as is usual) the lease requires that the lessor's licence be obtained before the lease may be assigned, that that licence is obtained, and

b. that all covenants in the lease (including for payment of rent) have been observed.

As to the former, under an open contract it is for the vendor to use his best endeavours to procure the lessor's permission, the purchaser being obliged to provide such references as may be required. It is usual to provide that the vendor's failure to obtain the necessary licence, while not amounting to a breach, enables the vendor to terminate the contract. As to the observance of covenants, it is provided that, unless he discovers otherwise, the purchaser must assume—on production of the receipt for the last payment due for rent under the lease before completion—that all the covenants and provisions of the lease have been duly performed and observed up to the date of completion.

The purchaser must further assume, again unless he discovers otherwise, that the lease itself is validly granted.[6] If the purchaser does discover a defect in the title, the vendor cannot enforce the contract. The assignor of the lease, then, is under no *contractual* obligation to prove that the lease was validly granted or that the covenants in it have not been broken. However, it is provided by the LPA, s76,[7] that where the vendor is, and expressly conveys the leasehold interest as, beneficial owner, it is further implied in the conveyance (in addition to the covenants for title implied on the coveyance of freehold land) that the vendor covenants a. that the lease is valid, and b. that the rent has been paid and the covenants observed and performed.

Finally, we must mention that a covenant is implied on the part of the purchaser to observe the covenants in the lease and to indemnify the vendor in respect of any breach.[8]

1 LPA, s54(2); para 33.4 above.
2 LPA, s44.
3 See, for example, Law Society's Conditions of Sale, 1980, No 8(2).
4 Paras 34.10 and 34.26 above.
5 Para 37.15 above.
6 LPA, s45.
7 Note also LRA, s24, which, for transfers of registered leasehold interests, omits the covenant that the lease is valid.
8 LPA, s77; LRA, s24; para 39.4 above.

Boundaries

43.36 Finally, we turn, by way of an aside, to the question of boundaries. Clearly it is of importance to a landowner to know the exact boundaries of his land, in order to know precisely what he has bought and can sell, or to prevent neighbours encroaching, or to know how much space is available for building. The situation of the boundary may be marked by some physical object, but the boundary itself is an imaginary line which marks the confines or line of division of two contiguous parcels of land.[1] Although it would appear to be important that the line of the boundary be clearly delineated in the conveyance or transfer of the property and that the question of who owns any boundary features be dealt with, this is frequently not done or the matter is left unclear with the result that the question remains to be settled after the property has been transferred, often as a result of a boundary dispute between neighbours. Obviously any boundary structure exclusively on one side of the boundary belongs to the owner of that side, even though the neighbour may have the right that it be maintained.[2] The problem lies in determining to whom it belongs. In the ordinary case, party walls are regarded as being vertically severed, each side having the right to support from other.[3]

1 Halsbury's *Laws of England* (4th edn) vol 4.
2 See para 40.42, above.
3 LPA, s38.

43.37 Where the title to the land is *registered*, the land to be transferred is generally described in the transfer deed merely as 'the land comprised in Title Number ...' a form of words which thereby incorporates the description of the land in the Property Register of the register of title. However, since this description normally gives only the address and refers to the Filed Plan, and since that plan, though an accurate Ordnance Survey Plan, is usually on a scale of 1:1250 and in any event does not purport to show the exact line of the legal boundary,[1] there remains much scope for uncertainty as to where the boundaries of the property lie.

1   LRR, r278.

43.38   In *unregistered* land, the determination of the boundaries is a matter of construction of the conveyance as a whole. A clear verbal description in the 'parcels clause' of the conveyance will be conclusive (subject to what is said in para 43.43 below, concerning alteration of boundaries). If a verbal description is clear, but is inconsistent with a plan incorporated in the conveyance, the plan will prevail where it is referred to in words to the effect that the property is 'more particularly delineated' in the plan.[1] The verbal description will prevail where the plan is referred to 'for the purpose of identification only'.[2] Where, however, the verbal description is unclear or ambiguous, the court may have regard to a plan, however it is referred to,[3] in order to elucidate and supplement the verbal description, so long as it does not conflict with it.[4]

Any plan incorporated in a conveyance must be adequate to perform its intended function. In particular, if the plan is intended to prevail over any verbal description or is the sole means of identification, it is of the utmost importance that it is drawn to a sufficiently large scale to make it possible to represent the property and its boundaries in precise detail, giving dimensions and any other features which may be necessary to put beyond doubt the subject matter of the conveyance.[5]

The vendor is obliged to convey what he has contracted to sell, no more and no less. Thus in *Spall v Owen*[6] where the conveyance referred to a developer's site plan 'for identification only' and described the property simply as 'known as plot 1', the court had regard to the fact that the same description and plan were used in the contract for sale. It was therefore held that 'plot 1' was as delineated on the plan rather than as fenced on the ground subsequent to the contract being concluded. In *Jackson v Bishop*,[7] a developer, whose conveyance by reference to an inaccurate site plan led to a boundary dispute between neighbouring purchasers, was held liable in the tort of negligence to the purchaser deprived of the land he had thought he was acquiring. It was held that a developer selling plots on his estate by reference to a site plan owes a duty of care to purchasers to ensure that the site plan is accurate and relates to the existing features on the ground and is not misleading.

Where the conveyance as a whole still leaves the matter of the boundaries unclear the court will have regard to extrinsic evidence, such as the contract itself,[8] auction particulars,[9] and any acts of ownership in relation to some boundary feature by one of the parties, such as the erection and maintenance of a boundary fence.

In a number of cases, where other evidence is lacking as to the line of the boundary, the courts resort to certain *rebuttable* presumptions, which we consider in the following paragraphs.

1 *Eastwood v Ashton* [1915] AC 900, HL.
2 *Hopgood v Brown* [1955] 1 All ER 550, [1955] 1 WLR 213, CA.
3 And even if it is only annexed to the conveyance but not referred to in it: *Leachman v L & K Richardson Ltd* [1969] 3 All ER 20, [1969] 1 WLR 1129.
4 *Wigginton and Milner Ltd v Winster Engineering Ltd* [1978] 3 All ER 436, [1978] 1 WLR 1462, CA.
5 *Scarfe v Adams* [1981] 1 All ER 843 at 852.
6 (1981) 44 P & CR 36.
7 (1984) 49 P & CR 57, CA.
8 *Spall v Owen* (1981) 44 P & CR 36.
9 *Scarfe v Adams* [1981] 1 All ER 843, CA.

43.39 *Walls* Where property is described as being bounded by a structure which would usually be the subject of a separate conveyance or transfer, that structure is presumed to be excluded. The outside of any external wall is presumed to be included in a sale or lease of the property, thus in one case[1] it was held to constitute trespass for a landlord to affix advertising hoardings to the outside wall of premises which he had let on the second floor of his property. As to where the legal boundary lies between two floors of a building, which have been separately let, it has been held that the ordinary expectation is that the demise entitles the tenant to occupy all the space between the floor of his flat and the underneath of the floor of the flat above.[2]

1 *Goldfoot v Welch* [1914] 1 Ch 213.
2 *Graystone Property Investments Ltd v Margulies* (1984) 47 P & CR 472, CA.

43.40 *Hedges and ditches* Where a hedge or bank together with a ditch runs along the boundary, the presumption of the law is that the boundary runs along the edge of the ditch further from the hedge or bank. This presumption derives from the quaint notion that the ditch was originally dug by the landowner at the furthest edge of his land and then, to avoid trespass, the resulting earth was thrown behind him onto his own land.[1] This presumption only applies where there is a hedge (or bank) and a ditch together. Where land bounded by a hedge is conveyed expressly by reference to the Ordnance Survey map, it appears that the courts may, in the absence of other evidence, presume that the boundary lies down the middle of the hedge, following what has been the Ordnance Survey practice.[2] It does not follow that this presumption automatically applies to registered land transfers[3] because it is expressly stated that the plan does not purport to fix the legal boundary.[4]

1 *Vowles v Miller* (1810) 3 Taunt 137.
2 *Fisher v Winch* [1939] 1 KB 666; *Davey v Harrow Corpn* [1958] 1 QB 60, [1957] 2 All ER 305, CA.
3 Para 43.37 above.
4 LRR, r278.

43.41 *Highways*[1] It is presumed that, wherever land is expressed in the conveyance to be bounded by a highway, the conveyance passes half of the road, so that the boundary line lies down the middle of the road.[2] This presumption, which applies only where there is no other evidence as to the boundary, is easily rebutted, for example, in the case of a building estate where the developer might intend to retain ownership of the roads for construction purposes and for dedication to the public. We should add the important caveat that where the highway has been adopted by the highway authority,[3] there vests in that authority the surface and so much above and below the surface as is necessary for the carrying out of their duties as highway authority. Thus, where the highway is adopted, we are concerned only with ownership of the subsoil. In the case of registered land, it is not the practice of the Land Registry to show ownership of the subsoil where the highway is adopted.

1 Para 40.14 above.
2 *Central London Rly Co v City of London Land Tax Comrs* [1911] 1 Ch 467 at 474.
3 Highways Act 1980.

43.42 *Rivers, etc* In the case of non-tidal rivers which form a boundary to land, it is presumed that the boundary runs down the middle of the river bed. The rights of fishing and abstraction, described in para 32.10 above, would therefore be divided midstream between opposite riparian owners. In the case of land bounded by a tidal river or by the seashore, the boundary lies at the medium high water mark, the foreshore being vested in the Crown. There appears to be no presumption to assist in determining the boundary where the land of several owners is bounded by a lake.

Alteration
43.43 The line of a boundary may be altered subsequently to the transfer of the property by agreement of the parties, as in *Davey v Harrow Corpn,*[1] where adjoining landowners agreed to the erection of a post and wire fence along the boundary, thereby rebutting any presumption which might otherwise have been relevant in determining the boundary line between the two properties, which were separated by a hedge and a ditch but had been conveyed by reference to the Ordnance Survey map. The line of the boundary may also be changed by the effect of rectification of the title register where the Land Registration Act applies,[2] by the effect of the Limitation Act[3] (as where a landowner moves the boundary fence so as to incorporate some of his neighbour's land and remains in adverse possession for the requisite period), and by the operation of the doctrine of estoppel. An example of this last is provided by *Hopgood v Brown.*[4] The boundary between the plaintiff's land and the defendant's land was unclear from the conveyancing documents. With the assistance of a predecessor of the plaintiff, the defendant had built a garage, the edge of which it was agreed between the parties formed the boundary. The court found that in fact the true line of the boundary was such that the garage encroached on the plaintiff's land. It was held, however, that the plaintiff was estopped, by the words and conduct of his predecessor, from denying that the boundary was other than along the edge of the garage.

1 [1958] 1 QB 60, [1957] 2 All ER 305, CA.
2 Para 34.27 above.
3 Ch 42 above.
4 [1955] 1 All ER 550, [1955] 1 WLR 213, CA.

Index

Index

690

Index